HISTORY

EDITORIAL CONSULTANT **ADAM HART-DAVIS**

HISTORY

FROM THE ANCIENT TO THE MODERN WORLD

 Penguin
Random
House

Senior Art Editors
Ina Stradins, Maxine Lea

Senior Editor
Angeles Gavira Guerrero

Art Editors
Alison Gardner, Mark Lloyd, Francis Wong

Section Editors
Nicola Hodgson, Rob Houston, Constance Novis,
Ruth O'Rourke, Rebecca Warren, Ed Wilson

Designers
Brian Flynn, Kenny Grant, Peter Laws,
Matt Schofield, Rebecca Wright

Editors
Sam Atkinson, Tom Broda, Kim Bryan, Mary
Lindsay, Ferdie McDonald, Sue Nicholson, Paula
Regan, Nigel Ritchie, Carey Scott, Giles Sparrow,
Steve Setford, Alison Sturgeon, Claire
Tennant-Scull, Miezan Van Zyl, Jo Weeks

DTP Designers
John Goldsmid, Laragh Kedwell,
Robert Strachan

Jacket Designers
Lee Ellwood, Duncan Turner

Editorial Assistants
Tamlyn Calitz, Manisha Thakkar

Cartographers
Ed Merritt, John Plumer,
David Roberts,
Advanced Illustration Ltd:
Paul Antonio, Russel Ikin

Indexers
Indexing Specialists (UK) Ltd.

Production
Elizabeth Warman

Picture Researcher
Louise Thomas

Managing Editor
Sarah Larter

Senior Managing Art Editor
Phil Ormerod

Publishing Manager
Liz Wheeler

Art Director
Bryn Walls

Reference Publisher
Jonathan Metcalf

TALL TREE

Art Director
Ed Simkins

Managing Editor
David John

Designer
Ben Ruocco

Project Editor
Rob Colson

2015/2016 EDITIONS
DK UK

Senior Jacket Designer
Mark Cavanagh

Senior Editors
Rob Houston, Helen Fewster

Jacket Design Development Manager
Sophia MTT

Jacket Editor
Claire Gell

Managing Art Editor
Michael Duffy

Managing Editor
Angeles Gavira Guerrero

Art Director
Karen Self

Producers, Pre-production
Luca Frasinetti,
Francesca Wardell

Publisher
Liz Wheeler

Producer
Mary Slater
Naomi Green

Publishing Director
Jonathan Metcalf

Special Sales and Custom Publishing Manager
Michelle Baxter

DK DELHI

Project Art Editor
Parul Gambhir

Editors
Arpita Dasgupta, Sonia Yooshing

Jacket Designer
Suhita Dharamjit

Managing Jackets Editor
Saloni Singh

DTP Designer
Anita Yadav

Senior DTP Designer
Harish Aggarwal

Picture Researcher
Deepak Negi

Managing Editor
Rohan Sinha

Pre-Production Manager
Balwant Singh

Managing Art Editor
Sudakshina Basu

TALL TREE

Designer
Jonathan Vipond

Editors
Rob Colson, Camilla Hallinan,
David John, Kieran Macdonald

First published in 2014
This edition published in 2016 by
Dorling Kindersley Limited
80 Strand, London, WC2R 0RL
Content previously published in History (2007, second edition 2015)

Copyright © 2007, 2014, 2015, 2016 Dorling Kindersley Limited

A Penguin Random House Company

2 4 6 8 10 9 7 5 3 1
001 – 300948 – Sept/2016

A CIP catalogue record for this book
is available from the British Library.

ISBN 978 0 2412 9150 4

Printed in Hong Kong

A WORLD OF IDEAS:
SEE ALL THERE IS TO KNOW

www.dk.com

Editorial Consultant **Adam Hart-Davis**

Main Consultants

Dr Karen Radner

Rulers and Hierarchies

Lecturer in the Ancient Near East, University College London, UK

Professor Richard Lim

Thinkers and Believers

Professor of the history of the Ancient Mediterranean World and Late Antiquity, Smith College, Massachutetts, US

Dr Roger Collins

Warriors, Travellers, and Inventors

Honorary Fellow, School of History and Classics, University of Edinburgh, UK

Dr David Parrott

Renaissance and Reformation

Fellow and lecturer in Modern History, New College, Oxford University, UK

James Freeman

Industry and Revolution

Postgraduate researcher, specializing in 18th and 19th century history, Cambridge University, UK

Professor Richard Overy

Population and Power

Professor of History, University of Exeter, UK

Contributors and Specialist Consultants

Contributors: Simon Adams, Lindsay Allen, Robin Archer, Debbie Brunton, Jack Challoner, Nick McCarty, Thomas Cussans, Erich DeWald, Brian Fagan, Emma Flatt, Abbie Gometz, Reg Grant, Alwyn Harrison, Ian Harrison, James Harrison, Michael Jordan, Ann Kay, Paul Kriwaczek, Keith Laidler, Siobhan Lambert Hurley, Sarah Lynch, Margaret Mulvihill, Liz Mylod, Owen Miller, Sally Regan, Nigel Ritchie, J.A.G. Roberts, Natalie Sirett, Giles Sparrow, Paul Sturtevant, Jenny Vaughan, Philip Wilkinson.
Consultants: Human evolution Dr Fiona Coward, Bournemouth University, UK; **Early Mesoamerica and South America** Dr Jim Aimers, UCL Institute of Archaeology, UK; **India** Professor David Arnold, University of Warwick, UK; **Food and diseases** Professor Kenneth Kiple, Department of History, Bowling Green State University, US; **Latin America** Professor Alan Knight, Department of History, University of Oxford, UK; **Japan and Korea** Dr Angus Lockyer, Department of History SOAS, UK; **How We Know** Dr Iain Morley and Dr Laura Preston, McDonald Institute for Archaeological Research, University of Cambridge UK; **Consulting editor** Philip Parker; **China** J.A.G. Roberts , University of Huddersfield, UK.

CONTENTS

4
RENAISSANCE & REFORMATION
1450–1750

5
INDUSTRY & REVOLUTION
1750–1914

Foreword

The history I learned at school was a mass of seemingly endless lists, formed of dates and the names of kings and queens. As a result, I hated it, and never saw the connections between the various strands of the subject. I now realize that history *is* important and that we can all learn from the triumphs – and mistakes – of our ancestors. Both utterly fascinating and hugely informative, *History* is a reference book that teases out the sparks of wars and revolutions, and uncovers the deep roots of great civilizations. It brings the subject to life, painting broad pictures of history's great sweep, aiming to excite and enthuse the reader by focusing on the most interesting, exciting, and dynamic people, events, and ideas of the past.

The photographs, maps, and graphics throughout *History* are spectacular, compelling you to dip in and discover what each page will reveal. One of the joys of this book is that most subjects, however vast in scale, are presented within self-contained spreads. Some describe hundreds of years of ancient Egyptian civilization, or momentous periods of upheaval like the religious Reformation in 17th-century Europe or the Industrial Revolution of the 19th century. Others take as their theme much shorter periods of history, such as the English Civil War or the Russian Revolution. There are also spreads devoted to "Decisive Moments" – key events that proved to be historical turning points, for example the assassination of Archduke Franz Ferdinand, which triggered World War I, or the 1755 Lisbon earthquake, which shook Europe to its very foundations.

But *History* isn't just about the events that have shaped us. A key strand in the book focuses on the ideas that have changed the world, exploring concepts such as democracy, evolution, and globalization. It also features biographies of some of history's most important and influential individuals from Alexander the Great to Adolf Hitler. And, as an enthusiast of science and technology, I am delighted to see coverage of the crucial innovations, inventions, scientific discoveries, and theories that have had an impact on the human story, from metalworking to the internet, and DNA to global warming.

ADAM HART-DAVIS

RULERS AND HIERARCHIES

3000–700 BCE

When humans started banding together in organized communities, they began to develop greater powers of communication, create complex belief systems, and form cultured urban civilizations, particularly in the Middle East, India, Europe, China, and Central and South America.

Archaeological evidence suggests that prehistoric hunter-gatherers were robust and healthy. Their diets – mainly raw fruits, leaves, and vegetables, with some lean meat and fresh fish – were probably very well attuned to the needs of the human body.

MOVING AROUND

As they were constantly on the move, and not living in large groups, hunter-gatherers probably **suffered rarely from infectious diseases**. Life expectancy was low, but this probably had more to do with physical dangers than disease or want.

FLINT DRILL

MEDICAL INTERVENTION

During the Neolithic period, people began to make sophisticated stone tools and weapons. Some tools were used in **primitive attempts at surgery**. For example, flint-tipped dental drills, found in Pakistan, date back as far as 7000 BCE. Teeth in remains found nearby showed signs of skilful drilling to remove rotten dental tissue.

LIVING TOGETHER

As people began domesticating animals and crops, communities grew larger, and their inhabitants started living more closely together. They lived close to their livestock, too, and this led to a **proliferation of diseases** that had not been a problem before. Waste was another hazard, and water supplies quickly became contaminated.

CHANGING DIETS

Settled, or sedentary, farming first appeared in the **Fertile Crescent** in what is now the Middle East, around 10,000 BCE. An agricultural lifestyle brought with it diets very different from those of hunter-gatherers. There was less variety, and a single crop – often wheat – usually dominated. Repetitive tasks, such as grinding grain to make flour, caused excessive wear to people's joints, leading to arthritis. At the same time **more food was cooked**, a process that can destroy vitamins and introduce toxins, while babies depended less on their mothers' milk. These changes led to populations of smaller stature and with weaker bones, as well as new conditions such as **anaemia and scurvy**.

GRINDING GRAIN

EARLY HEALERS

Other medical interventions were practised besides dentistry (see above). Often, serious bone fractures were successfully reset – remains show signs of regrowth. And in caves at Lascaux, France, archaeologists have found preparations of **medicinal herbs** dating back to 13,000 BCE.

At the beginning of the Bronze Age, around 3000 BCE, the civilizations of Mesopotamia (see pp.14–15), ancient Egypt (see pp.24–31), and the Indus Valley (see pp.18–19) were already well established. Busy, booming cities were surrounded by fertile land given over to agriculture, and farming became so efficient that only a relatively small proportion of the population needed to be involved in producing food. This led to the development of trade, mathematics and astronomy, writing, and a flourishing of cultural activities.

The price of progress

Along with the many benefits of their way of life, however, people in early civilizations suffered from some ill effects. Their diets were generally lower in fibre and higher in fat and salt than their hunter-gatherer predecessors. There is evidence that this led to an increase in conditions such as high blood pressure, heart disease, and cancers – a trend that began with the rise of agriculture several thousand years earlier, and continues today. This pattern was repeated elsewhere. In Central America, for example, early Maya people began relying on maize as a staple in civilizations originating around 1000 BCE. This led to a population explosion, but at the price of a dangerously restricted diet.

As the Bronze Age gave way to the Iron Age in Europe and Asia after about 1000 BCE, many killer diseases arose for the first time in human populations. Smallpox and anthrax are two good examples. In both cases, and in many others, the pathogens (disease-causing organisms) evolved to cross species barriers from livestock, and were able to take hold because people were living so close together in mostly unsanitary conditions. Rats, fleas, and lice thrived, and carried diseases such as the plague and typhoid. In times of flood, drought, or war, these problems were heightened.

Explaining disease

No one in early civilizations could understand disease the way modern medical science does. And so, it was normal to attribute the causes of disease to supernatural forces. People believed that they became unwell as the result of possession by evil spirits – demons – or because of angry gods or sorcery carried out by their enemies.

Just as explanations of disease appealed to the supernatural, so too did most attempts to cure people. In most cultures, priests and sorcerers were at least as important as physicians – and exorcism of demons, sacrifice to the gods, shamanistic rituals, and counter-sorcery were commonplace. The Ebers papyrus, written in Egypt in the 2nd millennium BCE and discovered in the 19th century, contains a long list of "medical" incantations designed to turn away evil spirits.

Herbalism

Healing based on supernatural beliefs is an example of folk medicine. Herbal remedies also fall into this category. Many ancient treatments based on herbs or other plants evolved through trial and error, and are so successful that they are still used today for their analgesic (pain relief), antibiotic, or anti-fungal action. In Mesopotamia, for example (see pp.14–15), a willow bark extract was used to relieve headaches and reduce fevers. That extract is salicylic acid, the basis of aspirin.

Hole in the head
The earliest known surgery, dating back to 40,000 BCE, was trepanning – drilling a hole in the skull. This was probably done to release evil, disease-causing demons. The practice occurred in Central America, Europe, and Asia.

China has the strongest tradition of using herbs and roots in medicine. According to legend, one of its pioneers was the emperor Shen Nong, who is supposed to have lived in the 3rd millennium BCE. The story goes that he tested hundreds of different herbs, searching for ones with medicinal effects. He is also credited with the introduction of tea drinking – for its remedial qualities.

The therapeutic use of plants is found in almost every corner of the world. The Olmec in Central America, for example (see pp.32–33), had areas of their gardens set aside for growing medicinal herbs. Papyri from ancient Egypt list remedies involving plants such as thyme, juniper, frankincense, and garlic – although there were others that used beer and animals' entrails. Herbalism is also central to Ayurvedic medicine, which originated in the Vedic period of India (see p.96) shortly before 1000 BCE. Ayurveda (literally knowledge of life") is a holistic system that uses a combination of religion and science to create physical, mental, and spiritual well being.

Organized approach

The Ayurvedic system is typical of the approach to science and technology that began to emerge – in China and India in particular – during the 1st millennium BCE. People began to think rationally, to organize their thoughts, discuss them with others, and derive theories. This approach led not only to an encyclopaedic knowledge of human anatomy and of a vast range of diseases, but also to well thought-out systems of diagnosis and treatment – the basis of modern medicine.

Sickness and Health

The desire to stay alive and healthy is a basic human instinct. It is no wonder, then, that people in early civilizations attempted to explain the origins of disease – and intervened to soothe pain, encourage healing, and effect cures. Some of these traditional approaches to medicine are still in use today.

Egyptian surgical instruments
In ancient Egypt sharp bronze and copper instruments were used when embalming the dead, as well as for operating on the living.

The god Pazuzu, who as "king of the evil spirits" can ward off disease, looks down from the top of the amulet.

The "heavenly domain" shows the symbols of the highest gods, such as the star of the goddess Ishtar.

Priests dressed in fish skins perform exorcism rituals at the bedside of the patient, probably a mother who has given birth. The lamp on the left indicates that this happens at night.

Pazuzu, who has a dog's head, a scorpion's tail, and bird talons, chases the malevolent Lamashtu back to the netherworld.

Lamashtu, the demonic goddess who preys on pregnant women and babies, has the naked torso of an old woman – with a pig and a dog drinking from her breasts. She carries a poisonous snake in each hand.

Purging demons
The Mesopotamians had a complex belief system of supernatural beings and forces. This Assyrian bronze amulet highlights the importance of these beliefs in explaining and treating disease.

CHASTEBERRY (MENSTRUAL PROBLEMS)

ROSEHIP (SOOTHING TONIC)

GINSENG (STIMULANT)

Medicinal plants
The health-giving or healing properties of many roots, seeds, and leaves have been recognized since ancient times and confirmed by modern medical science.

HOW WE KNOW

SKELETAL HEALTH

Many of the ancient ideas about health and disease can be gleaned from the art, writing, and artefacts of the time. But equally important are human remains, such as bones, teeth, and other tissues. Skeletal remains are the most valuable, because they decay very slowly. They often show physical signs of deformity or malnutrition, and can also provide a physical record of certain medical interventions, including primitive surgery. Further details can be revealed under the microscope and by carrying out tests. Analysis of the chemical isotopes present and examination of the DNA can reveal subtle clues to what a person ate, how old they were, and how they lived and died.

HEALED BONE FRACTURE, ANCIENT EGYPT

AFTER

During the 1st millennium BCE medicine became more systematic, but supernatural explanations and non-scientific folk remedies prevailed until after the scientific revolution of the 18th century.

ACUPUNCTURE
Acupuncture aims to **restore health** and well-being, and to **relieve pain**. Still one of the mainstays of Chinese medicine, it was probably developed in **Han China 82–83 〉〉** around 200 CE – although there is some evidence that it was used earlier. The locations

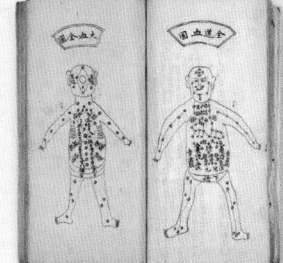

ACUPUNCTURE POINTS

of tattoos on a well-preserved body, nicknamed Ötzi after its discovery, tally very closely with important acupuncture points. Ötzi's body was discovered in 1991, in the Alps between Italy and Austria – he lived about 3350 BCE.

INDIAN PROGRESS
The Ayurveda system flourished across the Indian subcontinent. Its main exponent was **Sushruta**, whose 6th-century BCE work *Sushruta Samhita* describes more than 100 surgical instruments and 300 surgical procedures. Many historians of medicine refer to him as the **"Father of Surgery"**.

ANCIENT GREEK MEDICINE
The **thinkers of ancient Greece 58–59, 84–85 〉〉** were among the first to apply careful observation and **rational thought** to philosophical questions, and this extended to medicine. Medical practice was dominated by the theory of "humours". According to this, the human body was composed of **four humours**: blood, phlegm, black bile, and yellow bile, and illness was the result of an **imbalance between them**. Although much of ancient Greek medicine was derived in isolation, Greek thinkers were influenced by Egyptian medicine, which had many excellent herbal remedies.

GALEN DISSECTING

ROMAN MEDICINE
Doctors in ancient Rome followed Greek medical practices, but while the Greeks had used philosophy to explain disease, the Romans reverted to explanations that depended on the whims of the gods. The greatest Roman physician and anatomist was **Claudius Galenus (Galen)**, who lived in the 2nd century CE. His ideas about **anatomy** were based on **careful observation**, but many were false. Nevertheless, they dominated Western medicine until the 16th century. Ancient Rome is celebrated for its initiatives on **public health**. Their water supplies, sewage and heating systems, and public baths were well ahead of their time.

‹‹ BEFORE

Settled life in Mesopotamia dates back 10,000 years. A rich archaeological record documents the growth of irrigation, agriculture, trade, writing, towns, and complex societies.

EARLY SETTLEMENT

HALAF POTTERY FIGURE

Farming began in c.8000BCE in the case of **Halaf culture** in the north and c.6000BCE in the southern, **Ubaid culture**.

IRRIGATION AND ORGANIZATION

Settlements grew due to **irrigation schemes**. The surplus crops grown were traded, **creating wealth**. The organization and control needed resulted in more complex, **layered societies**.

THE RISE OF URBAN CENTRES

By the 3000s BCE, the first **urban centres** were in place, with the southern **Sumer** region home to a thriving civilization by 3500BCE.

FROM TRADING TO WRITING

The record-keeping needed to control trade used seals featuring symbols and pictures, followed by the development of early writing **22–23 ››**.

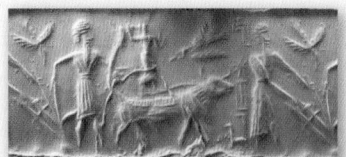

SEAL SHOWING PLOUGHING WITH AN OX

EMPEROR, DIED c.2284 BCE

SARGON OF AKKAD

Seen traditionally as a great warrior-king, Sargon established the Akkadian dynasty and ruled c.2340–2284BCE. He founded his capital city, Akkad, and created a centralized state that oversaw the first real empire in Mesopotamia. Few tales about Sargon can be verified. It has been suggested that he established himself as a successful independent ruler first and then began his expansionist policies. His military prowess could be explained by Akkadian techniques being more efficient than those of rival armies. We know about Sargon's rule from an ancient document called the Sumerian King List.

BRONZE CAST HEAD, 2334–2154 BCE, OF AN AKKADIAN RULER, PROBABLY SARGON

The civilization of Mesopotamia thrived across an area that today includes Iraq, southwest Iran, east Syria, and southeast Turkey. Mesopotamia is Greek for "between rivers" – civilization here rested on a prime position between the rivers Euphrates and Tigris. This dependence on rivers echoes that of three other civilizations: those in contemporary Egypt (see pp.16–17) and the Indus Valley (see pp.18–19), and in China a little later (see pp.20–21).

As in Egypt, Mesopotamian crops relied on rich silts deposited by the river waters, while marshlands provided fish and waterfowl for eating as well as reeds – used for roofing and baskets in Mesopotamia. Irrigation and land-reclamation schemes required well-drilled marshalling of large numbers of people. This laid the foundations for what is thought to be the world's first stratified (layered) society – reaching its height of sophistication slightly ahead of Egypt.

City-states and empires

By around 3000BCE, Mesopotamia was entering an era known as the Early Dynastic, which lasted 700 years. Civilization was focused initially on city-states in the south, an area often called Sumer after the Sumerian language widely spoken there. The pattern of Mesopotamia's history emerged at this stage: cities and city-states (see p.48), often linked by trading and diplomatic ties, would co-operate and compete, rise and fall. Certain city-states and city-based dynasties – Uruk, Kish, Akkad, and Ur – rose to control others for a while before being dominated by yet others. This contrasts with Egypt and its centralized rule, but bears some similarity to the later life of the Greek city-states (see pp.48–49). Great cities of the 3rd millennium included Ur, Lagash, Kish, Eridu, and Uruk Ebla, and

Tomb treasure
The lavish jewels worn by Queen Pu-abi (Ur, c.2500 BCE) feature precious metals and semi-precious stones from Ur's varied trading partners.

One figure is shown larger than everyone else. It is likely that this is the king, glass in hand, at his court, with this top row depicting a banquet scene.

The Cradle of Civilization

Mesopotamia, a fertile land embraced by rivers, was the site of the first complex societies. By 3000BCE, competing city-states of great wealth and sophistication were flourishing here, with advanced irrigation and agricultural schemes, established trade, the first known writing, and grand palaces and temples.

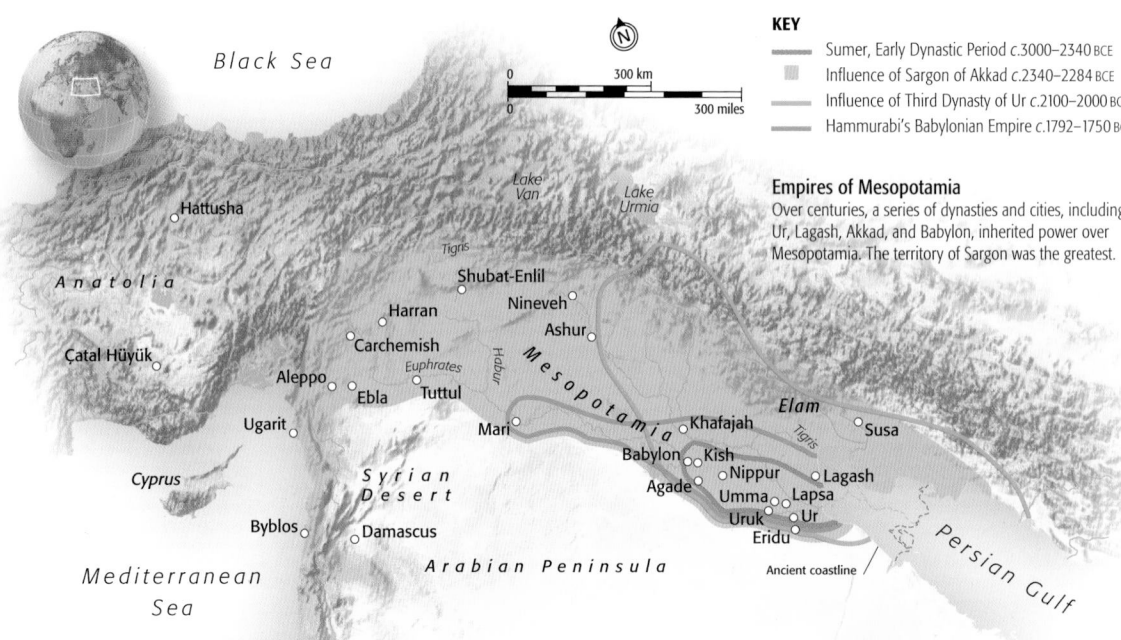

KEY

— Sumer, Early Dynastic Period c.3000–2340 BCE
▪ Influence of Sargon of Akkad c.2340–2284 BCE
— Influence of Third Dynasty of Ur c.2100–2000 BCE
— Hammurabi's Babylonian Empire c.1792–1750 BCE

Empires of Mesopotamia

Over centuries, a series of dynasties and cities, including Ur, Lagash, Akkad, and Babylon, inherited power over Mesopotamia. The territory of Sargon was the greatest.

Black Sea
Lake Van
Lake Urmia
Hattusha
Tigris
Shubat-Enlil
Nineveh
Anatolia
Harran
Ashur
Çatal Hüyük
Carchemish
Euphrates
Aleppo
Ebla
Tuttul
Mesopotamia
Habur
Elam
Ugarit
Mari
Khafajah
Susa
Cyprus
Syrian Desert
Babylon
Kish
Tigris
Agade
Nippur
Lagash
Umma
Lapsa
Byblos
Damascus
Uruk
Ur
Eridu
Mediterranean Sea
Arabian Peninsula
Ancient coastline
Persian Gulf

300 km
300 miles
N

A courtier, one of several celebrating with their ruler, sits on a wooden stool and raises a cup in honour of the great occasion.

A court musician plucks at a lyre, decorated with the bull's head that appears repeatedly on examples of this apparently popular Mesopotamian instrument.

Standard of Ur
This purpose of this object, found in the royal tombs at Ur, is a mystery. With 50cm- (20 in-) wide wooden panels inlaid with shell, red limestone, and lapis lazuli, it reveals much about Mesopotamian life. This panel may show war booty being brought to court.

During the next millennium, a succession of cultures inherited the land between rivers.

AKKADIAN DECLINE
As the Akkadian empire faded, local leaders won regional power in Kish, Uruk, and Lagash. The rule of **Gudea of Lagash** saw his city's last thriving era. Irrigation systems were set up, temples rebuilt, and statues of Gudea were carved.

GUDEA OF LAGASH

THIRD DYNASTY OF UR
After the Akkadian era, the Third Dynasty of Ur (*c.*2100–2000 BCE) fought off competing city-states to found a short-lived empire built on Akkadian achievements. The **kings of Ur** revived central rule to create a **Sumerian renaissance** harking back to the region's former glories.

OLD ASSYRIAN ERA
As the Ur dynasty faded, returning the south to rival city-states, the Assyrian city-state of Assur (*c.*2000 –1800 BCE) **38–39 ≫** emerged as the centre of a vast trade network in the north.

OLD BABYLONIAN ERA
Since *c.*1900 BCE, the city of Babylon, north of Sumer, had been emerging as a dominant power. The Old Babylonian era (*c.*1894–1595 BCE) saw the rule of **Hammurabi** (*c.*1792–1750 BCE) and his famous **law code,** a rich source of information about life in the Babylonian state.

MITTANI AND BEYOND
The Hurrian people of **Mittani 36–37 ≫** dominated the north (*c.*1600–1350 BCE), until control passed to the **Hittites 36–37 ≫** and the **Middle Assyrian kingdom 38–39 ≫**. In the south, the **Kassites 36–37 ≫** controlled middle-era **Babylonia** (*c.*1400–1100 BCE). In *c.*1100 BCE, the Babylonian state collapsed along with other great Bronze Age powers **36–37 ≫**.

Oxen, sheep, and donkeys are apparently being brought in procession to the banqueting court. Perhaps they are being presented as spoils of war.

Heavily laden people in the procession are shown stooping visibly under the weight of sacks filled to the brim with foodstuffs and other valuable merchandise.

Fine detail in this scene gives insight into the clothing of the time. This figure is seen in a fringed skirt, while others sport woollen fleeces.

Mari. By the 24th century BCE, many southern lands were under one king: Lugalzagezi of Umma. Farther west, Akkad became the centre of a dynasty begun by Sargon (see left), whose influence expanded to the Mediterranean and Anatolia, resulting in the Akkadian language being used for official documents and diplomacy for many centuries to come (see pp.22–23, 26–27, 36–37).

A place for everyone
Mesopotamian society had a hierarchy and a centralized structure headed by rulers who were all-powerful but, unlike Egypt's pharaohs, were rarely thought to be divine. Grand royal palaces appeared throughout the region in the Early Dynastic era. We know of the sophistication and wealth of these palace cultures from discoveries such as the lavish, finely wrought

Royal game
This game board of *c.*2500 BCE, inlaid with shell and lapis lazuli, was found in a royal tomb in Ur. This game was popular right across the Middle East, Egypt, and India.

artefacts found in tombs at Ur where either royalty or priestesses (or figures combining both roles) were buried. As in Egypt, specialists were needed to support such a society and its administration – a "professional" layer of experts such as bureaucrats, scribes, and merchants. In this urbanized civilization, many city-dwellers lived in impressive town-houses of locally sourced mud brick, mud plaster, and wooden doors.

A large labour force was needed to cultivate the land and man the great irrigation and building projects. However, there was some social mobility. Some labourers appear to have owned land or received rations linked to their work for central government.

Rule and religion
In common with other civilizations of the time, politics and religion were intertwined. Rulers took a lead in directing religious matters, while priests and priestesses conversely took on "state" functions; some cities were ruled by priests. Each city had a massive central mud-brick temple (such as the famous Ziggurat at Ur, see p.31), which was the home-on-Earth of the city's god and where priests carried out rituals to win the god's favour. Keeping order was made easier by the people's belief that they must do the gods' bidding, to the extent that, when royalty died, palace staff entombed themselves with their king or queen. Around 74 bodies were found in one grave at Ur.

A world player
Poor in natural resources such as metal and stone, the Mesopotamians, like the Egyptians, were forced to forge wide-ranging trade, and so diplomatic,

Precious lyre
Playing lyres seems to have been a part of court or temple life in Mesopotamia. A bull's or cow's head is a recurrent decoration.

links over a region that included modern Iran, Afghanistan, the Persian Gulf, and the Indus Valley. This drove much of the progress and expansion of their culture and gave them a leading profile in world politics. Mesopotamia took the lead in so many fields. Its art included exquisite jewellery, musical instruments, and beautiful stone carving dating back to 4th-millennium Uruk. In science, their numerical system based on the number 60 dates back to the Sumerians of the 3rd millennium BCE. It lives on today in our division of a circle into 360 degrees and in our splitting of the hour and the minute into 60 smaller parts.

BEFORE

The great Egyptian civilization of the Old Kingdom with its god-like pharaohs had its origins in earlier dynasties.

PRE-DYNASTIC EGYPT

The period between early Neolithic settlement and c.3100 BCE is known as the Pre-Dynastic Era. **Egypt existed in two parts – the north (Lower Egypt) and the south (Upper Egypt)**. Evidence discovered in tombs suggests a wealthy society, and that people believed in an afterlife.

NARMER

EARLY DYNASTIC ERA

The Early Dynastic Era (c.3100–2686 BCE) covers the 1st and 2nd dynasties. **Menes, or Horus Aha** who united the kingdoms of Upper and Lower Egypt, is usually thought to be the first pharaoh. However, **Narmer** may have come first, or Narmer may be another name for Menes.

A SENSE OF IDENTITY

The Early Dynastic Era gave Egypt a strong sense of identity. It brought a sudden (as yet unexplained) rise to greatness, with more complex **irrigation schemes**, grander **royal tombs**, a form of **writing**, and a centralized state headed by a **semi-divine king**.

ARCHITECT AND PHYSICIAN

IMHOTEP

Imhotep is credited as the main architect of Djoser's Step Pyramid. Djoser was the second pharaoh of the 3rd dynasty (c.2686–2613 BCE) and Imhotep was his chief adviser and physician, as well as being the leading genius of his day. His Step Pyramid is seen as the building that helped establish the Old Kingdom as an era of remarkable achievement. The oldest surviving building made from cut blocks of stone, it was the first proper Egyptian pyramid. Giza's great tombs adapted Imhotep's design, but filled in the stepped sides to produce what we now think of as the classic pyramid. Imhotep's skills as a physician were such that he was worshipped as a god in later ancient Egypt and Greece.

IMHOTEP

The Divine Pharaohs

Egypt's Old Kingdom (c.2686–2181 BCE) flourished on the flood-enriched banks of the River Nile. It was an era of prosperity, relative stability, and strong centralized rule, during which the great pyramids were built and Egyptian society worshipped their mighty kings, or pharaohs, as "gods on Earth".

Old Kingdom society was tightly controlled by a centralized government headed by a highly powerful ruler, the pharaoh. Central to life, politics, and religion, which were all closely combined, was the idea that the pharaoh was a semi-divine figure who acted as mediator between the gods and his subjects.

As a religious and political leader, the pharaoh not only oversaw elaborate religious rituals that underlined his links with the gods, he also headed a vast, highly organized political and administrative bureaucracy, peopled by an army of advisors and officials, chief of which was an officer called a vizier. The bureaucracy also included local governors, who oversaw regions called *nomes* (former independent regions). Pharaohs are often seen as being despotic. However, although their word was law, the pharaohs did delegate a significant amount to the governors and, as the Old Kingdom progressed (see AFTER), gave them more and more power.

Kingdom of the Sun

The first pharaohs were believed to be earthly representations of the mythical figure Horus, son of the god Osiris, and Isis (see pp.28–29). Horus was strongly linked with Ra (or Re), creator of life and falcon-headed god of the Sun. The Sun cult became very important during the Old Kingdom and Ra emerged as a separate figure to Horus. "Ra" even became incorporated into pharaohs' names.

Through these connections, the pharaoh was the upholder of a justice system that aimed to reflect the cosmic order. He was also, vitally, the figure who worked with the gods to ensure that the Nile brought silt-rich annual floods each year, keeping the Nile valley fertile enough to support the great Egyptian state.

The pharaoh was the ultimate all-seeing, all-knowing figure. He was often depicted dressed in a kind of kilt and false beard, bearing a crook, flail, and sceptre, and with the double crown of Lower and Upper Egypt on his head. A cobra, the "eye" of Ra, was shown rising up off his forehead. He was accompanied by the royal fan-bearer and people fell prostrate before him. Egyptians did seem to realize he was a flesh-and-blood human, but they stood in awe of his sacred power.

"Gift of the Nile"

Ancient Greek historian Herodotus described the Nile's bounty as a "gift". The mighty river cut a huge valley in the northeastern corner of Africa (see pp.24–25). To the north, in Lower Egypt, the Nile's tributaries fanned out to create a wide, fertile delta, home to a high concentration of people. At the delta's south was the "capital city" of Old Kingdom Egypt – Memphis. Further south, in Upper Egypt, the valley snaked away in a narrow strip, with towns clinging to its fertile banks.

The Nile's annual inundation left in its wake the rich black silt on which the Egyptians relied to grow their crops. Vast irrigation schemes were

The pharaoh Khafre
Khafre, also known as Khafra, Chephren, or Khephren, was the fourth king of the 4th dynasty. This statue, showing him wearing a false beard and striped "nemes" headcloth, is from his pyramid-tomb complex at Giza.

Population of builders
This relief of an Egyptian shipyard is from a 5th-dynasty (c.2494–2345 BCE) official's tomb at Saqqara. Ships were vital for travel along the Nile and for trade with some of Egypt's neighbours.

devised to direct the waters to wide areas of agricultural land. Marshlands along the banks provided waterfowl for eating (by wealthy people only) and the papyrus reed, used for making writing materials. The river waters themselves supplied fish and a means of getting from one place to another. The Egyptians, surrounded by vast stretches of arid, inhospitable desert, were only too aware of how dependent they were on this massive floodplain, As a result, "lookouts" were posted along the Nile in southern Egypt to spot early signs of high or low waters that would affect the annual harvest.

Society's pecking order

Society was fairly clearly divided into different levels. At the top was the royal family, presiding over court and administrative officials, such as scribes, and also priests. There was a strict pecking order and showing duty and loyalty were top priorities.

The Great Pyramid of Khufu
The largest and oldest of the three Giza pyramids, this is what many people now think of as the greatest "true" pyramid ever. It probably took about 20 years to build, involving a workforce of thousands.

The Giza pyramid complex
The vast size of these royal tombs reflects the divine status of the 4th-dynasty kings. The most distant tomb is Khufu's "Great" pyramid; in the centre is Khafre's; the smallest pyramid, in the foreground, is that of the pharaoh Menkaure.

Working the land
This fresco shows people harvesting corn. The Egyptians created large areas for cultivation, using complex irrigation schemes fed by the Nile.

It is said that most ordinary people in the Old Kingdom led miserable lives pressed into the pharaoh's service, building vast constructions or growing crops to feed the cities, in return for just enough sustenance to stay alive. However, evidence suggests that there was an independent local life too, including markets where people sold produce and simple crafts. The fact that anyone could, theoretically, gain high office also contradicts the idea of a total dictatorship.

The age of the pyramids
The Old Kingdom is best known for its advances in stone building techniques, which saw fruition in the famous Step Pyramid at Saqqara, (see Imhotep, left) and then in the colossal royal pyramid tombs of the 4th dynasty (c.2613–2494 BCE). Built at Giza, close to Memphis at the edge of the desert, these are among the greatest building achievements in history. The Great Pyramid – the tomb of the pharaoh Khufu – was one of the Seven Wonders of the ancient world, and the only one that survives intact today. Just to the east of the pyramid lies the Great Sphinx, a massive part-lion, part-human statue, thought to have Khufu's features. The Giza pyramids are one of the earliest examples of using quarried stone. Huge blocks of limestone were transported from some distance away, cut with incredible precision, and lifted into place to make a perfectly fitted construction. No one knows exactly how this was achieved. Each pyramid may have been surrounded by a sloping bank, built upwards as the pyramid grew higher. The stone blocks may have been moved up the slope manually by using rollers and levers.

Mallet
Simple, short-shafted wooden mallets like this were used with chisels to cut stone slabs with great precision and to produce fine relief carvings.

2 MILLION
The number of limestone blocks, each weighing 15,000kg (32,000lb), used to construct Khufu's Great Pyramid at Giza.

A Middle Eastern power
Egypt became a major player in Middle Eastern politics during the Old Kingdom period. There is evidence of long-distance contact with many regions, including parts of modern Syria, Libya, Lebanon, and the Sudan. Contact arose because Egypt wanted to keep its borders safe, and to trade for materials, such as wood. Borders cannot be maintained or crossed without negotiation, so Egypt must have started to develop the diplomatic skills for which it became famous.

AFTER

There are countless theories about the Old Kingdom collapse; but no one knows for certain what happened.

NOBLES AND NOMES
By the 6th dynasty (c.2345–2181 BCE), the pharaohs **granted certain powers to nobles and governors** of the *nomes* (regional districts). This may have gradually undermined the pharaoh's authority. It is also suggests that as the pharaoh lost control, others were able to take more power for themselves.

PEPY II

THE OLD KINGDOM COLLAPSES
At the end of the 6th dynasty, especially after the reign of **Pepy II**, the Old Kingdom started to fade and Egypt moved into a more uncertain time called the First Intermediate Period 24–25 ≫. **Royal authority weakened** and Memphis lost some of its importance compared with other towns and cities.

WHAT HAPPENED?
Links have been made with Egypt's dependence on the Nile, saying that **extreme flooding, drought, or both brought great destruction or famine.** This would have been especially disastrous if central authority was weak. Threats to Egypt's borders may also have been a factor in the Old Kingdom's decline.

BEFORE

Indus Valley culture grew largely out of developing farming cultures west of the valley.

EARLY FARMING CULTURES
Most notable was the Neolithic **Mehrgarh** culture, starting *c.*7000 BCE in modern Pakistan.

HARAPPAN PHASES
The "Early Harappan" phase of the Indus Valley culture (*c.*3300–2800 BCE) saw the first examples of the **Indus script**, more **sophisticated agriculture**, and **growing trade links**.

Indus Valley script
Indus valley seals are rich sources of imagery, featuring animal, human, and mythical figures alongside samples of the undeciphered script.

The Indus Valley civilization peaked between about 2600–1900 BCE, in what is often called its "Mature Harappan" period. It flourished across an extensive area of present-day northwest India, Pakistan, and Afghanistan, along the fertile Indus and Ghaggar-Hakra rivers.

At its height, the Indus Valley ranked among the first great early civilizations, in the company of Mesopotamia and Egypt (see pp.100–103). Like them, it depended heavily on farmland nourished by major rivers. Also in common with them, its people developed expert knowledge about how to harness and control the annual flooding patterns of the rivers.

Artistic skills
The refined artefacts produced in the Indus Valley region clearly show this to have been an advanced civilization. They include finely worked jewellery in gold and fired steatite (soapstone); figurines fashioned from bronze, terracotta, and faience; pottery; gold and silver ornaments; and seals. The latter often featured images of animals common to the area, such as elephants and zebu (oxen).

These artefacts seem to tell us that there was not only skill, but also prosperity and an elite class, which hints further at a society with different social and economic levels. There are quite a few different artistic styles, too, perhaps pointing to a diverse ethnic mix within the population.

Some Indus Valley artefacts, most famously the jewellery, have been found at sites elsewhere in the world, indicating widespread trading links. The Indus people relied heavily on trading arrangements and their partners included Mesopotamia (see right), Iran, and Afghanistan. Trading practice was boosted by advances in methods of transport, especially in boats suited to long-distance travel along sea routes. Sets of weights have also been found among excavated artefacts, and the Indus people seem to have been among the first to develop a precise weights

Indus rulers
This famous figure from Mohenjo-Daro is known as "the priest-king", despite no evidence of rule by priests or kings.

Advanced sanitation
Highly developed plumbing included drains (above), some of which were covered, and latrines. To give each dwelling access to clean water, wells were built with high, sealed walls to avoid contamination problems.

Mohenjo-Daro
The city's grid-pattern is visible here. Archaeologists have guessed at its structure by giving certain excavated areas names such as "Citadel Mound", "Lower Town", and "the Great Bath", but these remain contentious issues.

HOW WE KNOW
TRADE WITH MESOPOTAMIA

Maritime trading connections with Mesopotamia were especially important to the Indus Valley civilization. We know that they traded with Mesopotamia as Indus or Indus-influenced artefacts have been excavated there – notably a set of etched carnelian beads, like those below, found at the city of Ur in the tomb of Queen Puabi, *c.*2550–2400 BCE.

CARNELIAN BEADS

Mysteries of the Indus

A fertile cradle of river-fed land, crossing parts of modern India, Pakistan, and Afghanistan, gave birth to the Indus Valley culture. People in its impressive, well-planned cities lived a refined life, but unlocking more about them is tantalizingly out of reach, as their script remains mostly undeciphered.

KEY
▪ Area of Harappan culture
○ Harappan site
● Site of Mehrgahr culture

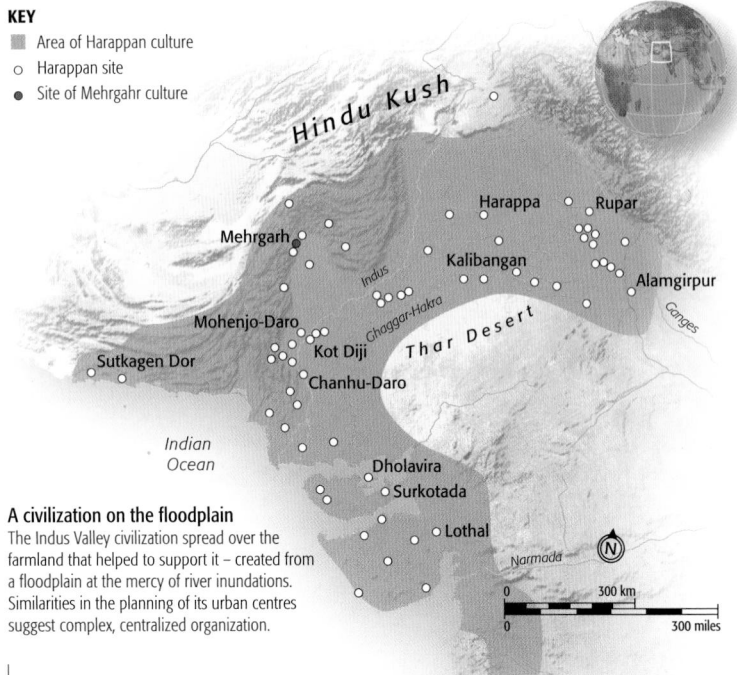

A civilization on the floodplain
The Indus Valley civilization spread over the farmland that helped to support it – created from a floodplain at the mercy of river inundations. Similarities in the planning of its urban centres suggest complex, centralized organization.

and measures system. Behind this system lay the kind of expert knowledge that explains why their city buildings were so impressive.

The world's first town planners?
A large number of settlements are associated with Indus Valley culture. The most spectacular, Mohenjo-Daro and Harappa (in modern Pakistan), were probably the world's first planned cities. Here were broad avenues and narrow side streets lined with spacious townhouses, all set out in a well-defined grid pattern. Remarkably, Indus cities thousands of kilometres apart were laid out in a similar way, suggesting a centralized state and local civic organization. Whether there was such a structure, and other details about government and society, remain largely a mystery, as although many distinct symbols appear on Indus artefacts, they remain undeciphered and their secrets locked away.

AFTER

The Indus Valley civilization went into an unexplained decline, with most of its main cities deserted by *c.*1700 BCE.

MOHENJO-DARO
The city suffered **severe flooding** in the 1700s BCE, and was laid waste by unknown attackers.

LIFE IN THE VALLEY
Part of the river system may have dried up, overstretching the cities' resources, although some southern settlements endured. Later Asian civilizations, such as the **Vedic 78 »** and **Hindu cultures** of the 1st millennium BCE, reveal cultural aspects of the Indus Valley civilization.

Bronze Age China

The Shang dynasty flourished from c.1600 to 1100 BCE and was the first society to produce cast bronze on a large scale. Believed to be semi-divine, the ruling Shang kings performed rituals to please their ancestors and gods. The artefacts that they used reveal a sophisticated society.

A "taotie" – the head of a ferocious animal with horns and bulging eyes – is hidden within the labyrinth-like decoration.

BEFORE

In the Neolithic period (8000–1500 BCE), the Chinese began farming millet and rice, and keeping animals. This required a static population, so people began to build houses, and to live together in villages.

NEOLITHIC HEMUDU

In 1973, a Neolithic (late Stone Age) settlement dating from c.5000 BCE was discovered at Hemudu, in southeast China. The finds included terracotta pottery, wooden and bone articles, and the remains of pigs and buffaloes. There were also some whistles made from the bones of birds, possibly used to attract birds to snares. The most exciting discovery was **evidence that the people of Hemedu cultivated wet rice**.

YANGSHAO CULTURE

The area of Yangshao, in the eastern province of Henan, was first excavated in the 1920s, and yielded some significant finds. In the **village of Banpo**, which was occupied c.4500–3750 BCE, the inhabitants cultivated millet, used polished stone hoes, and knives, and **wore hemp, and possibly silk**. Their village had a residential area with about 100 houses and other buildings. They produced pots made of red clay, some decorated with spiral patterns, and others with human or animal designs painted on them.

YANGSHAO CLAY POT

LONGSHAN CULTURE

Soon after the discoveries at Yangshao, a completely different type of Neolithic pottery was found at Longshan, in Shandong province. It was much finer than Yangshao ware, and was black, decorated with rings and grooves, and often elevated on a circular foot. Some of **the pots may have been turned on a wheel.** Longshan culture, which also produced polished stone axes, spread along the middle and lower Yangzi (the longest river in China). In time, it overtook Yangshao culture, which was already dying out.

BRONZE AGE ERLITOU

The Xia dynasty was long thought to be a mythological one, but in 1959, **palace-like buildings, tombs, and bronze artefacts** dating c.1900–1350 BCE were found at Erlitou, in Henan. The bronze objects found there are the **oldest yet found in China**. Their shapes suggest that they may have derived from Longshan pottery.

The Bronze Age in China produced two major achievements: a developed system of writing, and the discovery of bronze. The highly prized metal, which was produced on a huge scale, was cast for weapons, tools, and vessels used exclusively by the noble classes for religious rituals. Early Bronze Age civilization in China was a rigidly hierarchical society, ruled by a supremely powerful king and his nobles. The people of the Shang – the second of China's ancient dynasties – believed that the king was invested with divine power from his ancestors, whose spirits were able to shape contemporary life if appeased with offerings. Bronze vessels were used for the sacrificial food and wine offered during these rituals, which can be seen as a precursor to the ceremonies of state used by later Chinese emperors (see pp.80–81). Much of what is known of Shang society has been gleaned from the study of the writings found on the "oracle bones" (see right).

The Shang state

In addition to support from aristocratic clans with whom they had family connections, Shang kings ruled their state with the assistance of officials. The Shang were frequently threatened by nomadic tribes from the inner Asian steppes (a vast belt of grassland that stretches from Europe to China), and the state was kept on a war footing. Nobles performed military duties in return for land. Shang kings waged wars against their neighbours, thereby obtaining slave labour and loot. They established new settlements, and cultivated captured land for farming. Despite being a warlike society, Shang civilization was based on agriculture and hunting. The production of bronze, too, resulted in a relatively settled society, as a static community was required to mine and smelt the ores that contain copper and tin, the metals needed for bronze casting.

Shang capitals

The Shang ruled over much of northern China and the centre of the country. The most important capitals were Zhengzhou, the capital in the earlier period of the dynasty, and Anyang, which was occupied c.1300–1050 BCE. At Zhengzhou, a defensive city wall 6.4km (4 miles) long enclosed a large settlement; the wall and the buildings within were constructed of stamped earth. The houses and workshops that have been excavated, and the variety of artefacts found inside them, indicate that Shang society was highly organized and rigidly ordered. Outside the capital of Anyang,

Shang dynasty China

Key Bronze Age sites include the early capital city of Zhengzhou, which later moved to Anyang. Pre-Bronze Age finds have been made at the Paleolithic (c. 100,000–10,000 BCE) site of Zhoukoudian, and Neolithic (8000–1500 BCE) pottery has been discovered at Banpo and Hemudu.

KEY

- ● Palaeolithic site
- ○ Neolithic site
- ■ Bronze Age site
- ▨ Extent of Shang influence

Sea of Japan

Zhoukoudian

Shandong
Anyang
Longshan
Yellow River *Zhengzhou* *Yellow Sea*
Erlitou
Miaodigou
Banpo
Henan
Han River
Sanxingdui
Yangtzi River
Hemudu
East China Sea
Zhejiang
Xin'gan
Jiangxi

0   500 km
0   500 miles

Strong handles were necessary for such a heavy pot to be removed from the fire.

Chariot burials
When an important person died, his chariot, charioteers, and horses were buried with him, as seen in this example found close to Anyang.

at Xiaotun village, the remains have been uncovered of what was the ceremonial and administrative centre of the late Shang state.

Burial customs

At Xibeigang, just north of Xiaotun, 11 huge graves have been found, which may belong to the 11 Shang monarchs who reigned at Anyang. When Shang kings died, they were buried in large cross-shaped graves. Their bodies were placed in wooden coffins surrounded by goods important to the deceased. The bodies of scores of slaughtered horses and human victims – possibly prisoners of war – were laid out on the ramps that led down to the burial chamber.

Bronze industry

The most prized archaeological finds from the Shang period are the bronze objects, made primarily for ceremonial purposes. The production of bronze was controlled by the king, and the quantity of bronze objects found indicates that it was a major industry, employing large numbers of skilled craftsmen. Early bronze technology in the West allowed an object to be cast from a single mould, but early Shang vessels were cast in several moulds, and the parts assembled later. Important finds of bronze vessels were made at the two capitals of Zhengzhou and Anyang. These vessels had ritual functions; some were intended for the preparation of sacrificial meats, others

for the heating of wine. Bronze was also used for musical instruments and for weapons, including swords and halberds, and fittings for chariots (see above).

Writing system

Along with a mastery of bronze, a complete writing system was created by the Shang, which had a huge effect on their organizational capabilities. Although some forms of early symbols appear on Neolithic pots and early Shang bronzes, the oldest inscriptions of complete sentences are found on oracle bones (see below). Over half of the known 2,500 symbols carved into the oracle bones can be read, and many closely resemble the Chinese characters of later times (see AFTER).

Bronze dagger
The highly ornamented handle of this dagger possibly depicts a stylized ram's head. Weapons such as this were probably used for ritual and sacrificial purposes.

Tripod shape is reminiscent of Longshan (Neolithic) pottery (see BEFORE)

Bronze ritual vessel
This highly patterned vessel was probably used by the Shang for the preparation of meat offerings.

AFTER »

Considered a tyrant, the last Shang ruler, Di Xin, was overthrown by the state of Zhou in the 11th century BCE. Many of the achievements of the Shang period however, remain central to Chinese culture.

CHINESE CHARACTERS
The writing system created by the Shang developed over time into the **Chinese characters in use today**. The script was fixed in its present form during the Qin dynasty (221–206 BCE) **80–81 »**, and in 1716 the Kangxi Dictionary was published containing over 47,000 characters. Studies in China have shown that full literacy requires a knowledge of 3,000–4,000 characters.

ANCIENT TEXTS

CALENDAR
The Shang created a lunar/solar calendar based on the zodiac, with ten "heavenly stems" and twelve "earthly branches". When combined together, the stems and branches formed cycles of sixty days or sixty years. The Shang model, although modified, **remains the basis for the traditional Chinese calendar**.

ANCESTOR WORSHIP
The Shang people worshipped many deities, most of whom were royal ancestors, and communicated with them through divination. This **veneration of ancestors** has remained an essential part of Chinese religious practice in modern times.

DIVINATION STICKS

HOW WE KNOW

ORACLE BONES

Sold in the 19th century as "dragon bones", an ingredient of Chinese medicine, "oracle bones" are actually the shoulder blades of cattle. Questions about the future would be scratched on the bones, to which a heated bronze tool was applied, and the resulting cracks were interpreted for an answer. Often, the predictions would be compared with the real event. They provide fascinating evidence not only of events in the Shang period, but also of early Chinese writing.

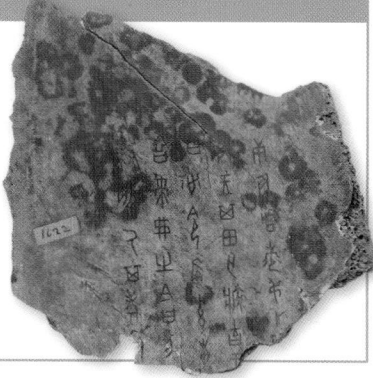

« BEFORE

People used symbols to keep records long before the invention of true writing.

TALLY BONES

Identifying the earliest recording systems is difficult. **Bones** dating back 30,000 years have been found in Europe and Africa bearing engraved "**tally**" marks. Some experts think the marks **recorded lunar months**.

CLAY TOKENS

From 9000–3000 BCE, people in the Middle East used **clay tokens** to record commercial transactions, sealing them into **clay envelopes** called *bullae*. A token's **shape** symbolized either **goods** (animals, grain) or specific **large numbers**. The example to the left is from **Uruk ‹** and is dated to 3700–3200 BCE.

CLAY TOKENS AND A BULLA

STAMP AND CYLINDER SEALS

A **seal ‹‹ 14–15** was a detailed engraved image **identifying the sender** of a message. The seal was pressed on wet clay by stamping, or rolling in the case of cylinder seals. Such seals appeared millennia before the development of writing.

THE ROSETTA STONE

Hieroglyphs were deciphered in 1822–24 by French Egyptologist and linguist Jean François Champollion. He used the Rosetta Stone – a stele of Ptolemy V bearing the same inscription in three scripts: hieroglyphic Egyptian (top), demotic Egyptian (middle), and Greek (bottom). He deciphered the Egyptian scripts by comparing identifiable words, such as names, in all three scripts, allowing him to work out the sound of each Egyptian sign from the Greek.

ROSETTA STONE

A ccording to ancient tradition, writing was either invented by an individual or handed down to humanity by the gods. The Sumerian poem *Enmerkar and the Lord of Aratta* describes how King Enmerkar invented writing instantly to record a message too complicated for his messengers to memorize. We now know, however, that the development of writing was a gradual process, taking centuries, and occurred separately several times, showing its value as a technology. Degradable materials, such as papyrus, bamboo, and parchment, have not survived. In Egypt, the earliest known inscriptions tend to be found on monuments. They take the form of hieroglyphs, far too sophisticated to be the first use of writing in Egypt. In Mesopotamia (see p.14–15), however, people wrote on durable clay tablets that survive in huge numbers, so the progression of their earliest writing can be traced. At early stages, writing was

CUNEIFORM A writing technique widely used in the Middle East between 2500–330 BCE. Writers used symbols consisting of wedge-shaped impressions made in clay or carved into stone. Many languages and civilizations used cuneiform, from Sumerian to Persian.

The **Writing** on the **Wall**

The development of writing – the symbolic representation of spoken language – represents an enormous step forward in the intellectual evolution of humans. Writing developed independently in different areas, including Mesopotamia, Egypt, China, and Mesoamerica.

Message from a temple

This clay tablet was written in a temple of Mesopotamia in 3100–2900 BCE. The script is a kind of proto-cuneiform – an early, pictorial stage in Mesopotamian writing development. The tablet probably describes grain either distributed by or offered to a temple. Thousands of tablets such as this have been unearthed at Uruk in Mesopotamia (see pp.14–15). They recorded transactions and contracts made by the temples.

The barley symbol is very common in ancient Mesopotamian writing. Barley was one of the most important commodities and was used to make bread and beer – the two staples of the Mesopotamian diet.

Drawn symbols were used in proto-cuneiform. Drawing was a messy and time-consuming process compared to impressing standardized wedge signs, as was done later by cuneiform scribes.

A box of symbols represented one transaction or sentence. Writers of proto-cuneiform grouped signs in boxes, not lines or columns.

A seal impression acted as a signature. People involved in contracts authenticated them by pressing their seal into the clay, rather than writing their names. In this case, the seal image represents a hunting dog.

The walking (transport) symbol suggests the items specified elsewhere on the tablet were moved. The absence of verbs makes it impossible to say whether the transport was to or from the temple in which the tablet was found.

A transaction tablet was usually sized to fit into the palm of the scribe's hand, although much larger cuneiform tablets do exist.

Egyptian hieroglyphs
Formal writing in Egypt retained the use of pictorial symbols – hieroglyphs – for more than 3,000 years. This example from a 4th-century-BCE sarcophagus differs little in style from the earliest surviving inscriptions made in c.3200 BCE. When reading hieroglyphs, the reader starts at the top on the side the signs face (in this case, right).

FROM PICTORIAL SYMBOLS TO CUNEIFORM

The earliest cuneiform, or proto-cuneiform, was pictorial and drawn into clay. Later, for unknown reasons, all proto-cuneiform signs were rotated by 90 degrees. True cuneiform appeared when scribes began to form signs from impressed wedge shapes.

Date	3200 BCE	3000 BCE	2400 BCE	1000 BCE
GIN "to walk"				
UD "day"				
MUSEN "bird"				
SE "barley"				

Cuneiform stylus
Cuneiform signs were formed by pressing a stylus into wet clay, each time producing a wedge shape. Cuneiform means "wedge-shaped" in Latin.

Numerals are expressed with these circular impressions. They mirror the shaped clay tokens once used to signify numbers (see BEFORE). They appear next to the sign for the commodity (barley). Before the invention of numerals, scribes had to draw a sign once for each item.

made up of pictures of the things it recorded. Over time, these pictures were simplified and made abstract to make writing quicker and easier. This process resulted in wedge-based cuneiform writing (see above).

Many early scripts were logographic, meaning that each symbol represented an entire word or idea. A logographic system may use thousands of signs. Modern Chinese writing remains logographic, using around 12,000 symbols that allow written communication between the many different dialects of Chinese. Cuneiform and Egyptian hieroglyphic scripts, meanwhile, mixed logograms with symbols representing sounds. Such sound signs were combined to form words, which reduced the total number of signs to around a hundred in scripts such as Akkadian cuneiform. Egyptian and Maya hieroglyphs remained pictorial for decorative use in religious writing and inscriptions on monuments. For everyday use, however, the Egyptians developed a more efficient, abstract system called hieratic. It was written with fragile reed pens, which restricted the shapes the scribe could form. When written on papyrus, hieroglyphs were painted with brushes, allowing the scribe a freer hand.

Chinese writing also diverged, with multiple systems developing for different uses. In most Chinese scripts, the meaning of signs was simplified as well.

The earliest written signs refer only to objects (usually goods) and numbers (quantities of goods and periods of time). These symbols were not grammatically linked, so cannot be read as language, but they aided the memories of people who knew their meaning already. It seems likely that others could have understood it with a little training. Writing was soon taken up by the elites of ancient societies, however, and adapted to reproduce spoken language, allowing them to write literary, religious, and scholarly texts. From this point, special training was needed to read and write.

Spread of the written word

Cultures in the 3rd and 2nd millennia BCE were not really literate societies. Once writing became abstract, rather than pictorial, only a small number of merchants, administrators, and elites would have had enough schooling to read and write. It is thought that only one per cent of Egyptians were literate.

Ancient rulers used writing to manage the information on which their states ran, not to disseminate it. Royal political inscriptions might be combined with imagery, and it seems that the masses would have read only the images, while the writing was aimed at fellow elites and at posterity. Assyrian kings, for instance, buried inscriptions in the foundations of temples, recording their exploits so that future kings rebuilding those temples would read them.

Egyptian scribe
Education of scribes began in childhood, lasting at least 10 years, and included mathematics and accountancy. The scribal profession usually ran in families.

Writing systems became simpler and more sophisticated, but the spread of written communication was slow until printing spread through Europe in the Renaissance.

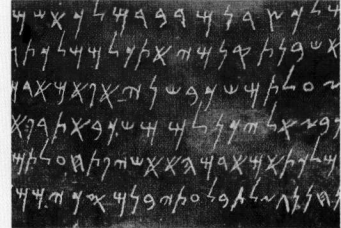

PHOENICIAN ALPHABETIC SCRIPT

ALPHABETIC SYSTEMS

At first, written symbols represented a variety of words, syllables, ideas, or sounds. The concept that every symbol should denote a sound was an innovation in the Middle East and led to the alphabet. The **first alphabetic writing**, with each sign representing a **consonant** but with **no vowels**, appeared in the 2nd millennium BCE, using adapted Egyptian hieroglyphs. The people of **Ugarit** in Syria developed a cuneiform alphabet, but the need for clay prevented its spread. Alphabets became important in 1000–700 BCE, being used for **Hebrew, Aramaic, and Phoenician** writing. The Phoenicians 40–41 ⟫ used separate signs for vowels, **influencing Greek and Latin** writing.

AMERICAN SYSTEMS

Some of the earliest surviving American writing is on 600 BCE **Zapotec** monuments in Mexico, listing the **names of sacrificed captives**. Later inscriptions on **Maya monuments** record conflicts between city-states 92–93 ⟫. The **cultures of the Andes developed quipu 158 ⟫** – a system that recorded numerical information with patterns of knots on webs of colour-coded string.

ZAPOTEC CALENDAR

PRINTING

The spread of written material was hampered by the need to **copy by hand**. In Europe from 1454, with the **Gutenburg printing press 193 ⟫** featuring **movable type**, books were produced quickly and cheaply on a large scale.

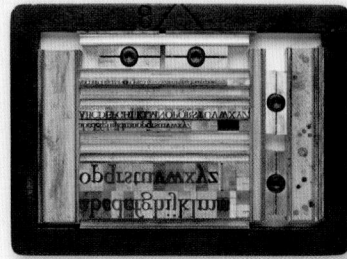

LETTERS OF MOVABLE TYPE READY FOR PRINTING

◀◀ BEFORE

At the collapse of the Egyptian Old Kingdom
◀◀ 16–17 centralized rule broke down
and an unsettled time known as the First
Intermediate Period (c.2180–2040 BCE) began.

FIRST INTERMEDIATE PERIOD

Egypt saw **civil war, drought** and **famine**,
and oppression by local **tyrants**. However, the
greater powers of non-royals at the end of the
Old Kingdom ushered in some broader-minded
thinking, including a **better justice** system for all.

HERAKLEOPOLIS VERSUS THEBES

One of the **competing factions** was a
dynasty of kings based at Herakleopolis,
central Egypt. They were bitter rivals of
the **Theban kings** farther south.

REUNIFICATION

In the 11th Dynasty, Thebes sealed its
rise to prominence when Theban
king, **Nebhepetre Mentuhotep
II** (c.2060–2010 BCE; right),
defeated his rivals from
Herakleopolis. He **reunified
Egypt** and so took it into
the **Middle Kingdom** era.

**NEBHEPETRE
MENTUHOTEP II**

Traditionally, ancient Egyptian
history is seen as periods of
order and prosperity separated
by "intermediate" periods of chaos.
Historians now think this is an
over-exaggerated contrast, but
prosperous eras under strong
centralized rule were certainly
separated by times of division.
Through all of this, however,
ancient Egyptian culture and
ways of life continued with
surprising consistency for
thousands of years – far
longer than those of any
other ancient civilization.

Middle Kingdom

Often said to last from
Dynasty 11 to Dynasty
13, the Middle Kingdom
(c.2040–1730 BCE) saw
Thebes becoming a
major royal centre,
although the seat of
government stayed
near Memphis (see

tombs but also on irrigation systems
(for example at Fayum near Memphis)
that benefited all. The country's
defences were strengthened and new
trade routes sprang up. Nubia, which
came under Egyptian control,
supplied gold and copper as well as
the labour to mine these, and
personnel for Egypt's army.

Disorder and restoration

The Middle Kingdom's stability
dissolved when local governors
pushed for more power. Civil war
brought about another unsettled
era – the Second Intermediate
Period (c.1730–1550 BCE; late
Dynasty 13 to 17). During this
time, a people called the Hyksos
gained control and ruled
Egypt as pharaohs. Egyptian
dynasties continued
to rule Upper Egypt
from Thebes. Theban
rulers triumphed
when the Hyksos
were finally expelled

Keeping order
Powerful figures called viziers, as depicted
by this 12th-dynasty statue, headed the
administration of the Middle Kingdom.
In the New Kingdom, one took control in
Lower Egypt and another in Upper Egypt.

and statues of Rameses II (c.1279–
1213 BCE; see pp.26–27) were erected.
Southern Theban culture prevailed,
with Thebes being rebuilt and great
temples erected to the sun-god,
Amun-Ra. Royalty was now buried in
elaborate underground tombs, centred
on Thebes' Valley of the Kings.
Amenophis IV (1352–1336 BCE) took
sun-worship to extremes, bending his
kingdom to the cult of Aten – worship
of the sun's disk alone – and renaming
himself Akhenaten in honour of his
beliefs (see pp.28–29).

379 The number of diplomatic
letters in the archive of
El-Amarna, Akhenaten's capital, recording
Egypt's role as the world's leading power.

Just as the Old and Middle Kingdoms
had dissolved, so too did the New
Kingdom. It is unclear why outside
threats (see AFTER) again became
impossible to hold back. Rebellion and
internal corruption may have played a
part, but the truth remains a mystery.

Egypt in Order and Chaos

**Over 100 years of uncertainty and lack of centralized control followed the collapse of Old Kingdom
Egypt. However, order and glory weree restored once again with the great Middle Kingdom and New
Kingdom eras, which were themselves separated by another period of some disorder.**

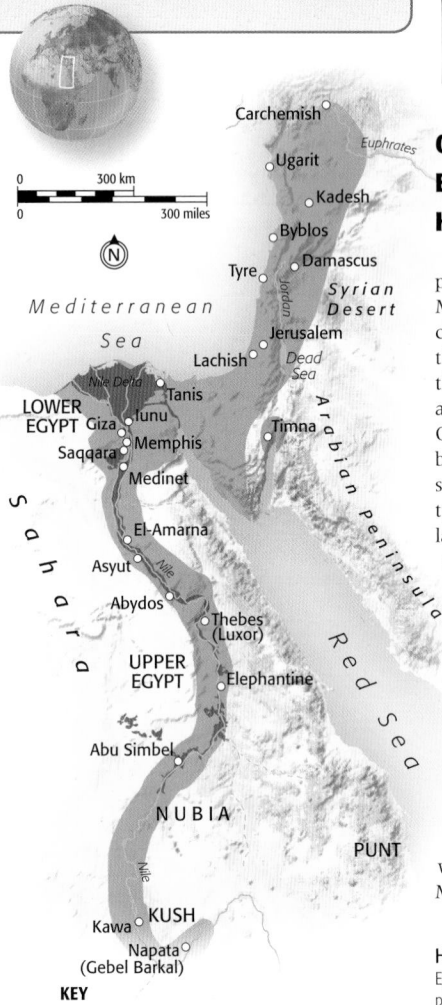

KEY
- ▢ Regions of control under Thutmosis III
- ▪ Fertile land in the Nile valley

pp.16–17) at the new city of Itj-Towy.
Middle Kingdom Egypt had a distinct
character, but it was not as different to
the Old Kingdom as once thought. In
the 12th Dynasty, the royals regained
a strong grip – perhaps as strong as in
Old Kingdom times. The pharaoh took
back some powers from nobles, but
society did not return to a more feudal-
type structure (in which powerless
labourers worked for the pharaoh) –
society was more democratic.

Rise of the bureaucrat

One of society's democratic features
was that posts formerly held by
royals passed to high-ranking "civil
servants". Egypt was now run
more like a corporation than an
extension of the royal family.
Greater rights for ordinary people
included access to mummification
(see pp.28–29), and more interest
was taken in the poor and needy.
Money was spent not only on royal

Height of Egyptian control
Egypt's lands reached their height under New Kingdom
pharaoh Tuthmosis III (c.1479–1425 BCE). Marked here
are major centres of royal, religious, and administrative
control during the Old, Middle, and New Kingdoms.

under pharaoh
Amose I, and the
New Kingdom
(c.1550–1069 BCE;
Dynasties 18 to
20) began. This era
is often seen as a
time of glorious
"empire", with a
militaristic, nationalistic
outlook and new heights of
wealth and power. The king's
role as warrior–defender of his
lands gained a new emphasis.

New kingdom power

During the New Kingdom, trade links
extended and the art of diplomacy
intensified, as seen in the famous
Amarna letters and the treaty of Kadesh
(see pp.26–27, 36–37). Egypt quashed
threats to the throne, thanks greatly to
warfare techniques borrowed from the
Hyksos – especially the use of two-
wheeled, horse-drawn chariots that
were fast and lightweight.

The New Kingdom was an age of
spectacular architecture and art. The
lavish tomb contents of the pharaoh
Tutankhamun (c.1336–1327 BCE) were
interred and the monumental buildings

In-fighting
Private armies abounded during the Intermediate
Periods, gathered by the leaders of regional factions
fighting endlessly for control. This model army of
Nubian archers is from the tomb of a governor of Asyut.

New Kingdom opulence
Queen Ankhesenamun annoints her young king,
Tutankhamun, in a scene taken from a gold-inlaid
throne entombed with the pharaoh in the Valley of
the Kings. Tutankhamun's short reign continued the
New Kingdom's grandeur and returned Egypt to its
traditional religious practices after the Aten-cult
worship of his predecessor, Akhenaten.

QUEEN, ACTIVE *c.*1300s BCE

NEFERTITI

The most famous wife of Akhenaten (see p.24), Nefertiti seems to have taken a prominent role in her husband's rule. Art of the period frequently shows her alongside her king, sharing his worship of the sun's disc. She is even depicted in warrior-like poses suggestive of royal power. Nefertiti may have died in 1338 BCE, when all record of her disappears. Some believe that Smenkhkare, a mysterious figure who seems to have ruled jointly with Akhenaten for some of his reign, was in fact Nefertiti.

AFTER »

Egypt's New Kingdom had become a vast empire, increasingly difficult to police. Late in the 20th dynasty, central authority again gave way to a destabilized spell – the Third Intermediate Period (*c.*1069–664 BCE).

THIRD INTERMEDIATE PERIOD
Spanning Dynasties 21 to 25, this era lasted about **400 years** and saw a complex mixture of **foreign control** and **Egyptian independence**. **Native pharaohs** in Upper Egypt gave way to a period of **Libyan** control. Lower Egypt split into **many separate regions**.

KUSHITE RULE
By the 25th Dynasty, at the end of the Third Intermediate Period, Kushite rulers from **Nubia**, notably Piye (*c.*747–716 BCE) controlled both Lower and Upper Egypt under their rule, so **reunifying Egypt**.

KUSHITE PHARAOH TAHARQA WORSHIPPING THE FALCON-HEADED GOD, HEMEN

ASSYRIAN OCCUPATION
Kushite sovereignty ended with the reigns of Taharqa and Tantamani (*c.*690–656 BCE). Their rule gave way to nearly a **decade of occupation** by **Assyrians 38–39** » at the end of the Third Intermediate Period. Next came a brief Egyptian renaissance – the **Saite Dynasty 72** ».

Rameses II

" All the lands... have fallen prostrate **beneath his sandals** for eternity."

PEACE AGREEMENT WITH THE HITTITES, *C.*1258 BCE

The greatest pharaoh of the New Kingdom (*c.*1550–1069 BCE), Rameses II reigned supreme for almost 70 years and brought a stability and prosperity to Egypt. Like a present-day international statesman, he skilfully used diplomacy, military strategy, and propaganda to promote Egypt and maintain his empire. In doing so he became a major figure in Middle Eastern politics.

The future Rameses II was born just before the 19th dynasty (*c.*1295–1187 BCE), and became its third pharaoh. From his father,

Portrait and cartouche
This impressive statue of Rameses II (left) stood in the temple of Luxor, in Egypt. The oval carving, or cartouche, (right) has symbols representing Rameses as king, and wearing the double crown of Upper and Lower Egypt.

Seti I, Rameses inherited an established empire that stretched from modern-day Syria in the north to Sudan (then Nubia) in the south. Like his father, he had territorial ambitions in Syria, but he had to contend with the threat from the Hittite Empire (see pp.36–37) further north in Anatolia. His most famous confrontation with the Hittites was at the battle of Kadesh (or Qadesh), in Syria in *c.*1275 BCE. Rameses claimed this as a single-handed victory for himself, while others said the Hittites won decisively. The truth is probably somewhere in between, with neither side winning outright or making any major gains.

Rameses the diplomat

Around 1258 BCE, after further skirmishes, the Hittites and Egyptians drew up a groundbreaking agreement, effectively ending hostilities between them (see right). Mindful of his role as a diplomat serving Egypt's wider interests, Rameses later underlined this new accord by making at least one Hittite princess one of his wives.

The new, friendly tone of relations between the two powers is also clear from the letters found in the archives of the Hittite capital, Hattusha. Like the famous "Amarna Letters" from the reigns of Amenophis III and Akhenaten (see pp.24–25), this correspondence is written on clay tablets in Akkadian cuneiform script (the language of

Rameses II as a boy
This limestone fragment from a stele (commemorative pillar), shows Rameses sitting next to hieroglyphs that indicate he is destined to become king of Egypt. He wears the side plait and a heavy ear decoration that were typical of a young Egyptian prince.

diplomacy, see pp.22–23), and features exchanges between a range of Middle Eastern powers and peoples. These lively letters are the earliest significant evidence of international diplomacy, painting a clear picture of long-distance trade, political agreements, and diplomatic and daily affairs. The letters between Egypt and the Hittites, and specifically between Rameses II and the Hittite king, Hattusili III, with whom the 1258 treaty had been made, discuss issues from international politics to medical problems and wedding plans.

Artistic licence

An outstanding feature of Rameses' reign were his buildings. All over Egypt, monuments sprang up or old ones were added to. Giant statues and images of the pharaoh swiftly appeared, and craftsmen wrote inscriptions praising him on every available surface.

He created the new capital city of Per-Rameses in the Nile delta, close to modern-day Cairo. It was beautiful, and convenient for military forays into Asia. He also built the famous temples dedicated to himself and his favourite wife, Nefertari, at Abu Simbel, close to Egypt's modern border with the Sudan. The four massive statues of Rameses at Abu Simbel are among the greatest achievements of Egyptian art. Their style was not subtle, but Rameses' creative lead helped the arts to thrive as they had under his father.

Another major site was Rameses' vast mortuary temple, the Ramesseum. This was built on the west bank of the

Battle of Kadesh
This bas relief from Abu Simbel portrays Rameses II fighting the Hittites single-handedly. He is seen astride a chariot, wielding a bow and arrow, and wearing the "crown of war".

The Ramesseum
A symbol of the pharaoh's power and wealth, this funerary temple was part of a grand complex including a splendid funerary temple, a palace, a smaller temple dedicated to his parents, courts framed with massive statues of Rameses II himself, and grand avenues of sphinxes.

> " What will people say, when it is heard of **you** [his soldiers] **deserting me**."
>
> RAMESES' CLAIM THAT HE FOUGHT THE HITTITES SINGLE-HANDEDLY 1275 BCE

DECISIVE MOMENT

THE FIRST PEACE TREATY

The 1258 BCE peace treaty between Rameses II and Hattusili III was first recorded on a silver tablet (contemporary clay copy shown below). An astonishingly modern document, it is seen as the first real international peace treaty, containing clauses on advanced concepts, such as amnesty issues for refugees and extradition for fugitives. It is thought to be such a milestone in international relations that a copy of it is hanging in the headquarters of the United Nations.

Nile at Thebes, the southern capital where Rameses created many new architectural projects. A palace, religious and political centre, and also a seat of learning, the Ramesseum inspired the English Romantic poet Percy Bysshe Shelley's famous 1817 poem, "Ozymandias".

Keeping control
Rameses II kept a tight grip on his lands and on his people. Government records that survive from his rule build a picture of a highly organized leader with a strong interest in law-making and order. With major centres at Per-Rameses and around Thebes, he ensured strong control over both Lower and Upper Egypt. He appointed

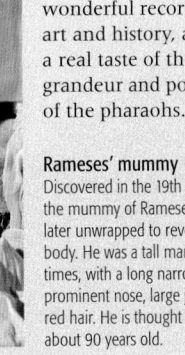

a tight web of able officials including many old friends and many of his own very numerous (over 100) children.

There seems little doubt that Rameses II was a major figure in Middle Eastern history, despite his undoubted skill for self-promotion. His reign was the last great era of imperial glory for ancient Egypt, and he made his presence felt as far away as modern Turkey. He left a wonderful record of art and history, and a real taste of the grandeur and power of the pharaohs.

Rameses' mummy
Discovered in the 19th century, the mummy of Rameses II was later unwrapped to reveal his body. He was a tall man for the times, with a long narrow face, prominent nose, large jaw, and red hair. He is thought to be about 90 years old.

TIMELINE

- **c.1302 BCE** The future Rameses II is born, a son of Seti I, whose family came of non-royal stock, and his wife Tuyu. The crown prince Rameses is made regent while still young, to ensure that he would succeed his father.

- **c.1292 BCE** The young Rameses bears the rank of army captain aged only about 10 (this title was probably honorary); accompanies his father on military campaigns to learn his craft.

- **c.1287 BCE** Rameses is married to Nefertari, who is aged around 13 and younger than her husband. Often said to be his favourite wife, she certainly seems to have been one of his chief wives for around 20 years. He may have had as many as eight wives, but also had a harem.

- **c.1279 BCE** Rameses is inaugurated as pharaoh, probably in his early to mid twenties. He begins his reign by travelling south to officiate at his father's funeral in Thebes.

- **c.1277 BCE** Appears to have defeated some pirates, possibly Shardana people, who have been linked with the mysterious, controversial "Sea People". The defeated pirates appear to have been absorbed into the pharaoh's army.

- **c.1276 BCE** First campaign in Syria.

- **c.1275 BCE** Second foray into Syria culminates with the battle of Kadesh against the Hittites, who had long posed a threat to Egypt. Rameses' opponent was King Muwatalli. The building of the Abu Simbel temples is probably under way.

- **c.1260s BCE** A large number of Hebrew peoples may have been living in Egypt, perhaps forcibly "press-ganged" into the pharaoh's service. There may have been an historically important "Exodus" of these peoples from Egypt into Sinai at some point in the 1260s.

- **c.1258 BCE** After repeating his father's pattern of years of indecisive power struggles with the Hittites, Rameses and the current Hittite king, Hattusili III, draw up a famous peace agreement.

- **c.1259–1255 BCE** It is likely the temples at Abu Simbel were complete.

- **c.1256 or 1255 BCE** Probable date of death of Nefertari. Another wife, Isetnofret, now seems to become Rameses' principal queen.

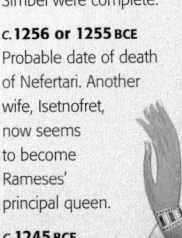

- **c.1245 BCE** Rameses marries the eldest daughter of the Hattusili III. She is called Maathorneferure.

NEFERTARI (MURAL FROM HER TOMB)

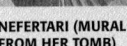

- **c.1230 BCE** Rameses probably marries another Hittite princess.

- **c.1224 BCE** One of Rameses' many sons, Merneptah, is named as his heir.

- **c.1213 BCE** Rameses' reign of about 66 years ends with his death, probably from an infection (possibly a dental abscess).

BEFORE

The ancient Egyptians believed in many gods, and in an afterlife. Various gods rose to prominence and then faded again.

LIFE AFTER DEATH

Items found in graves from pre-dynastic Egypt (before c.3100 BCE) suggest that, even then, Egyptians performed **PRE-DYNASTIC GRAVE GOODS** death-related rituals.

THE ORIGINS OF OSIRIS

Belief in Osiris is thought to have begun in the Nile Delta region and probably developed from the local god of a place called Busiris. Initially, Osiris may have been a **god of agriculture**, linked with fertility and the afterlife. He gained popularity throughout Egypt and by the middle of the Old Kingdom ≪ **16–17**, c.2400 BCE, had become a dominant figure, associated with death and the **resurrection of the ruler.**

RIVALRY WITH RA

Before Osiris, the cult of Ra (or Re), god of the Sun and bringer of life, held centre-stage. Ra is depicted with a falcon's head on which is carried the sun.

RA, THE SUN-GOD

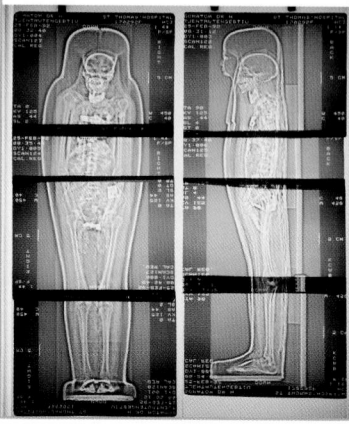

For the ancient Egyptians, the need and desire to please their gods were driving forces that influenced most aspects of their lives. They believed that the god Osiris judged them on the lives they had led and that those who had lived "good lives" would attain a happy eternity alongside the gods. He was thought to preside over their complex burial rituals, including embalming and mummification (see opposite), which they devised to ensure a passage through the underworld to an afterlife.

Osiris's cult continued to develop during the Old Kingdom (c.2686–2181 BCE). People came to believe that the pharaohs – Egypt's leaders – were reborn as Osiris after death. This powerful link to the Egyptians' belief in kings as gods was reflected in the "rebirth" elements of their burial rituals.

Cult of the people

After the collapse of the Old Kingdom (see pp.16–17), the popularity of the Osiris cult was assisted by the shift in government dynamics. With the pharaoh no longer an all-powerful figure, local officials gained in importance. In this slightly more democratic climate, the burial rites and the right to rebirth, once strictly confined to the pharaohs, were increasingly extended to ordinary Egyptians. At the height of Osiris's popularity, even mere mortals were believed to connect with the god at

His grandfather was Ra (see BEFORE) and his brother was Set, god of chaos. Osiris was husband (and brother) of Isis, a protective and magical goddess, and father of Horus, who was god of the sky and protector of the ruler of Egypt. Myth also told that the jealous and vengeful Set trapped Osiris in a coffin-like chest and threw it in the river Nile, then took his brother's position as king. Isis found and hid the body of her beloved husband, only for Set to discover it and tear it apart, scattering the pieces. It was said that Isis lovingly sought out all the remains and buried them where she found them, so aiding the spread of the cult. His body was then reassembled and bound with bandages, and he so became the first mummy. Isis revived Osiris by magic, and he travelled to the underworld to become king of the dead.

A matter of life and death

From these myths it is clear that the Egyptians' burial practices, particularly mummification and embalming, were a reflection of Osiris' own sufferings and the journey his soul made to the afterlife. Ideas about the soul and spirit were central to burial practices, and to beliefs in general. The Egyptians came to believe that each human being consisted not only of a physical body, but also of three spiritual parts. First, the *ka*, was part of a kind of "soul" and the essential life-force – a person's

A jury of 12 gods sits in judgement of the deceased. They pronounce their decision in a chamber often referred to as the "hall of Ma'at".

Osiris figurine
The god was traditionally portrayed partly bandaged, as if being mummified.

The deceased, Any, followed by his wife, walks into the "court", ready for the weighing of his heart and judgement by the jury of gods above.

The Realm of Osiris

The growth of the cult of Osiris, king of the dead, was immensely important to the ancient Egyptians. Osiris gradually became the dominant figure among a cast of potentially vengeful gods. These gods had strong moral codes, so living a good and honest life was vital if you were to gain eternity.

their death (this identification with Osiris was considered essential to reach eternital afterlife). Previously, such an honour was confined to their kings.

Family drama

Despite his growing importance, Osiris remained part of a broad and complex family of divine characters, each with a vital role to play in the Egyptian belief system. Tradition held that Osiris was the son of Geb, god of the earth, and Nut, goddess of the sky, and that he was once king of Upper Egypt.

"double". The *ba* formed another part of the "soul" and, in modern terms, an individual's personality. Finally, the *akh* was the form in which a deceased person existed in the afterlife, when the *ka* and *ba* were reunited.

It was typically believed that the *ka* and *ba* were released from the body at death and needed to find each other again in the afterlife in order to create a happy, eternal *akh*. The released *ka* returned to the dead body, feeding off it to stay alive. If the body was decayed or unrecognizable, the *ka* might not be

> "**Homage to thee, Osiris**, lord of eternity, king of gods, **whose names are manifold.**"
>
> THE EGYPTIAN BOOK OF THE DEAD, 1240 BCE

The bird-goddess Ma'at, keeper of truth and harmony, daughter of Ra and linked with Thoth, perches symbolically atop the scales of justice.

Osiris, the supreme judge of such ceremonies, sits among the jury of gods. He is wearing the crown of Upper Egypt.

Amun-Ra was an amalgamation of the Sun-god Ra and the god of the air Amun. He has a falcon's mask and bears the solar disc on his head.

AFTER

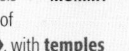

The cult of Osiris survived beyond the ancient Egyptian period, and influenced newly developing belief systems.

CHANGING CULTS

By the Ptolemaic period in Egypt (323–30 BCE) **72–73 »** the cult of Osiris had begun to fade and **the cult of Serapis** was on the rise. This combined the cults of Osiris and the sacred bull Apis. At first Serapis was identified with Osiris, but then became entirely separate. Cults of Osiris and Isis lived on in various provinces of the Roman Empire **64–67 »**, with **temples to Isis** built in Roman London and Pompeii.

ROMAN-ERA MUMMY

THE IMPACT OF OSIRIS

Many scholars believe that the ideas surrounding Osiris and his kingdom of the dead influenced the development of the world's major religions **96–99 »**. The belief in a god's rebirth and the idea that happiness in the next life could be achieved by being good can be reinterpreted as the concepts of **resurrection and salvation**. The performance of rites to connect humans with a divine presence is related to the idea of **sacrament**. These ideas are present in a variety of religions, including **Christianity**.

FREEMASONRY

Osiris lives on today within the "secret society" known as the **Freemasons**. Some of their beliefs and symbolism are connected to the figure of Osiris, partly as a way of evoking a sense of order and mystery **rooted in ancient wisdom**.

Any's heart, depicted with the Egyptian hieroglyph for "heart", lies in one pan of the scales of judgement.

The scales are supervised by the jackal-headed Anubis. Considered to be Osiris's son, Anubis was an underworld guide.

The Feather of Ma'at lies in the other pan. If the heart weighs the same as the feather, eternal afterlife is assured.

Thoth, chief scribe of the gods, notes the results of the weighing of Any's heart.

Ammit, a strange beast that is part lion, crocodile, and hippopotamus, waits to devour any heart that is found wanting.

Osiris sitting in judgement

This papyrus scene, from the *Book of the Dead* of Any (New Kingdom, c.1550–1069 BCE), shows Osiris deciding Any's destiny in a ceremony believed to take place after death. Any's heart is weighed against the feather of Ma'at, goddess of truth and justice. Bearing instructions on dealing with obstacles in the afterlife, a "book of the dead" was commissioned just before the subject's death, and always showed a favourable judgement.

able to feed and survive to reach the afterlife. This is why preservation was so important – to keep the "soul" alive after death.

Preserving the body

Embalmers washed the body, preferably in water from the Nile. They then removed the intestines, stomach, liver, and lungs and placed them in four vessels called canopic jars. The brain was removed through the nostrils, but the heart, considered to be the source of intelligence, was left in place. The body was then stuffed with

Organ storage

The removed organs were placed in canopic jars to prevent decay. The jar second from right represents Anubis, the main god of embalming.

linen (to keep its proper shape and appearance) and made whole again. It was soaked with preservative salts, resins, and oils, and decorated with protective charms, called amulets. Those shaped like a scarab beetle were especially potent as the insect's life cycle reflected the daily "rebirth" of the sun. The body was wrapped in linen bandages, placed in a coffin, and buried along with other amulets or items from everyday life to provide comfort in the hereafter.

IDEAS

THE CULT OF ATEN

During the period of Egypt's New Kingdom (c.1550–1069 BCE), when Osiris worship was at its peak, the 18th-dynasty pharaoh Akhenaten created a breakaway cult of his own. He decided to worship the Sun's disc, in the form of a god called Aten. The cult, which some scholars cite as the first example of the worship of a single god (monotheism), came to an end at the close of Akhenaten's reign, after which the old order returned. This image shows Akhenaten with his chief wife, Nefertiti (see p.25), and one of their daughters (they are known to have had at least six) worshipping the Sun's rays.

« BEFORE

Large-scale architecture was one of the earliest features of civilization.

NEOLITHIC BUILDING
Early Neolithic-period **stone structures** include walls in Jericho, now in Palestine (c.8500 BCE), and a possible stone temple at Gobekli Tepe in Anatolia, now Turkey (c.9000 BCE).

STONE BUILDINGS, GOBEKLI TEPE, TURKEY

TEMPLES IN MESOPOTAMIA
The oldest known structures in Mesopotamia are temples dating from the **Ubaid Period** (5900–4300 BCE). On sites **long-held sacred**, the temples were rebuilt many times.

PITS AND MOUNDS IN EGYPT
Tombs in **pre-dynastic Egypt** (before 3100 BCE) were simple, sand-covered pits. Early royal tombs were elaborations of this model, covering a rock-cut chamber with a **mound of sand**.

FIRST MONUMENTS IN THE AMERICAS
Mud-brick platforms called **huacas** appear along the coast of Peru **32 »** from 4000 BCE. Used as **ritual sites**, they were often built in pairs.

Mortuary temple of Queen Hatshepsut
After the Old Kingdom came to an end, fewer pyramids were built and attention transferred to the mortuary temples. These were often built at the foot of cliffs, which were possibly viewed as natural pyramids.

Almost every form of ancient Egyptian monumental architecture can be interpreted as part of a temple. The pyramids were not isolated structures, but parts of mortuary (memorial) temple complexes. Egyptians believed that their kings became gods when they died, so the tombs were dedicated to their worship.

The first pyramid, the Step Pyramid, was built in c.2667–2648 BCE (see Imhotep, p.16) for pharaoh Djoser of the 3rd dynasty. The design probably evolved from the earlier sand mounds that covered tombs (see BEFORE). True pyramids appeared in the 4th dynasty, the first being built for pharaoh Snefru in c.2580 BCE. Its shape imitated a ramp of solidified sunlight on which the pharaoh ascends in a solar barque – a mythical boat – to join the god Ra (see p.68). This is described in the "Pyramid Texts" – religious inscriptions on the walls of later pyramids.

Egyptian temples were carefully constructed models of the universe. The inner sanctum represented the ordered heart of creation, and the temple's outer walls, the cliffs at the edge of the

Nile Valley, held back the chaos that lay beyond. Colonnades (rows of columns) and hypostyle halls (halls with pillars holding up the roof) represented the riverbanks, with the columns denoting reeds, while the ceilings symbolized the sky, and were decorated with images of stars and the Sun. Since pharoahs were considered divine, palaces were seen as temples and were built along the same

lines. Pharaohs gained such prestige from their building schemes that some even appropriated the projects of their predecessors, erasing their names and claiming them as their own.

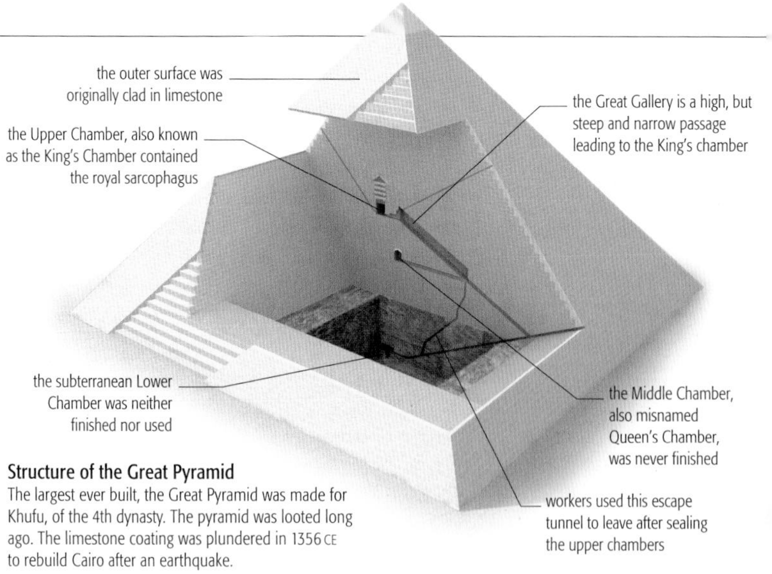

The step towers of Mesopotamia
In Mesopotamia (a region made up of what is now Iraq and parts of Syria, Turkey, and Iran, see pp.14–15), the

the outer surface was originally clad in limestone

the Upper Chamber, also known as the King's Chamber contained the royal sarcophagus

the Great Gallery is a high, but steep and narrow passage leading to the King's chamber

the subterranean Lower Chamber was neither finished nor used

the Middle Chamber, also misnamed Queen's Chamber, was never finished

workers used this escape tunnel to leave after sealing the upper chambers

Structure of the Great Pyramid
The largest ever built, the Great Pyramid was made for Khufu, of the 4th dynasty. The pyramid was looted long ago. The limestone coating was plundered in 1356 CE to rebuild Cairo after an earthquake.

Building for Eternity

The construction of monuments, such as temples, palaces, and tombs, was one of the key features of developing civilizations. Most monuments had religious functions and were intended to legitimize the position of the rulers who built them by connecting them with the gods.

architecture, although its structure was different to that of the Egyptians, also had a religious pupose and shared similar functions. Mesopotamian gods were linked with particular cities, and the temples in those cities were seen as their homes. Divination – the practice of foretelling the future – was a key part of the religion. The people believed that the gods controlled fate, so divination was used to determine the gods' intentions, and rituals were performed in an attempt to negotiate a better future. Astrology was a key part of this tradition, and ziggurats – the tall, stepped towers attached to major temples – were also used as stellar observatories.

In Mesopotamia, the construction of temples was seen as both the king's privilege and duty. Mud bricks did not endure long, so temples were often renovated or rebuilt. Royal palaces also became increasingly important there, especially under the powerful Assyrian Empire (see pp.38–39). They were not only centres for the royal court but also for the civil service. Apart from a few exceptions, Mesopotamian kings were considered earthly governors appointed to rule on behalf of the gods, rather than being gods in their own right.

Symbolic riches

Ancient temples were not simply places of worship, but also important centres of administration. Most were part of large tracts of land that provided considerable income and trading power. Before it was destroyed at the end of the 7th century BCE, the temple of Ashur – the city at Assyria's ancient heart – was the richest in the world.

The demonstration of power

To build monumental buildings required enormous resources, organization, and labour. These buildings acted as a potent demonstration of the ruler's power over his subjects, and periods of

> **CORVÉE** Most ancient societies used corvée labour to provide a regular supply of unskilled labourers. Corvée labourers worked on state building projects for a set amount of time each year instead of (or in addition to) paying taxes in the form of money or produce.

prosperity usually show evidence of new construction. When a kingdom lacked central authority, or access to resources, building stopped.

The Egyptian pyramids also provide evidence of ancient methods of construction. Rather than hundreds of thousands of slave labourers or conscripts working seasonally, as had been previously thought, the pyramids were built by 20–25,000 professional craftsmen and corvée labourers who worked all year round. Snefru's first pyramid was finished in only a few years, so he had first a new palace and then two more pyramids built. The decreasing size of pyramids after the 4th dynasty is probably due to an increase in the number of projects, rather than evidence that the 4th dynasty's grand projects had bankrupted the kingdom.

Great Ziggurat of Ur
Ziggurats, such as this reconstructed example, were in constant use, with astrologers working all night, every night. They provided an unbroken view across the plain of Mesopotamia.

Choga Zanbil
Mud-brick architecture does not preserve well. No one knows exactly how this ziggurat in Elam (southwest Iran) looked when new.

Monumental construction has continued to the present day all around the world.

MESOAMERICAN ARCHITECTURE
Olmecs **32–33 ≫** built pyramid-shaped mounds in Mesoamerica in 1000–500 BCE. Successive cultures in the region built **pyramid temples**. To them, everything possessed a spirit, and mountains were particularly powerful beings, so places of worship were constructed in their image. Pyramid building continued until the **Spanish conquest 170–171 ≫**.

GREAT PYRAMID, CHICHEN ITZA

THE SEVEN WONDERS OF THE WORLD
A list of the **Seven Wonders of the World** – the most breathtaking achievements of human construction – was publicized in the Greek world from the 2nd century BCE. Included were the **Pharos of Alexandria 51, 72 ≫** and the **pyramids of Giza** – the only wonder surviving today. Also on the list were the **Hanging Gardens of Babylon** in Mesopotamia – described as constructed in tiers, like a ziggurat. No trace of the gardens has yet been uncovered.

LATER MONUMENTS
The Greeks **94–95 ≫** and Romans **64–67 ≫** continued the monumental tradition. In Europe, the building of stone monuments was revived by the medieval Christian church **142–143 ≫**.

IDEA

THE TOWER OF BABEL

The Biblical story of Babel may have begun as a reaction of Jewish exiles in 6th-century BCE Babylon to ziggurats. The Babylonians saw ziggurats, with their stepped levels leading progressively upwards, as pathways to the heavens, providing access for astrology. Jewish writers were horrified by the thought of humans climbing to heaven, and wrote that a displeased God disrupted the project by diversifying and confusing the languages of the builders.

« BEFORE

Early civilization in the Americas centred initially on the Andes in South America, and later on Mesoamerica to the north.

EARLY CITIES

One of the **first cities** in the Americas was **Caral**, 200km (125 miles) north of modern Lima, Peru. The city, which was well established by *c.*2500 BCE, included **pyramid structures** built around the same time as those at Giza, Egypt.

CARAL EXCAVATIONS, MAY 2001

MESOAMERICAN CULTURE

By *c.*1500 BCE, **agricultural settlements** had formed in the area archaeologists call Mesoamerica (central Honduras and Costa Rica to northern Mexico). The main crops were maize, beans, squashes, chillies, and cotton. There was **not yet an urban culture** to rival that at Caral.

The years between about 1500 and 900 BCE saw the first real stirrings of more advanced civilization in Mesoamerica. Agricultural skill and productivity improved, pottery became more complex, possibly through contact with Andean cultures in South America, and the temple-pyramid emerged. This was also the period when Mesoamerica's first great civilization sprang to life – the Olmecs.

Life in the lowlands

The Olmecs established themselves in the humid, fertile lowlands of south Mexico, and their culture was flourishing by about 1200 BCE. By around 800 BCE their influence had

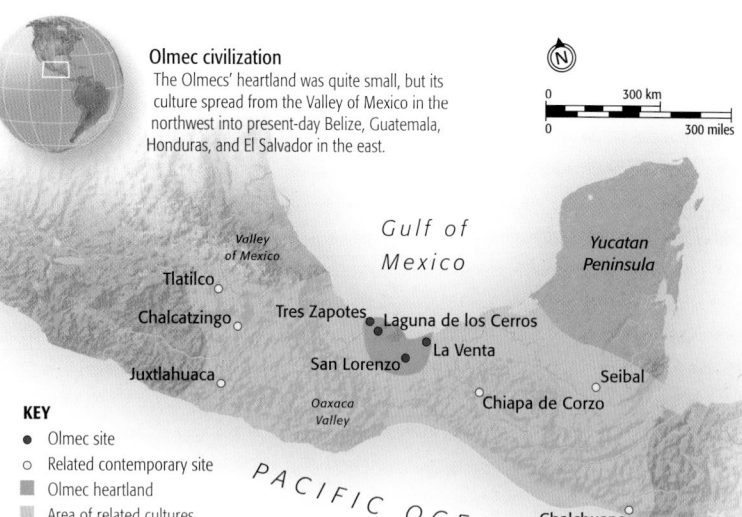

Olmec civilization
The Olmecs' heartland was quite small, but its culture spread from the Valley of Mexico in the northwest into present-day Belize, Guatemala, Honduras, and El Salvador in the east.

KEY
- ● Olmec site
- ○ Related contemporary site
- ▪ Olmec heartland
- ▫ Area of related cultures

People of the Jaguar

The first great civilizations of Mesoamerica and South America rivalled those of Mesopotamia, ancient Egypt, and China. In Mesoamerica, the Olmecs established a blueprint for later cultures in the region. At the heart of Olmec belief was jaguar-worship, which they shared with their South American counterparts.

VOTIVE OBJECT An artefact offered to a deity as a gift of some kind in order to thank or appease them, or enhance the success of prayers. Small "votive axes" carved out of jade were common in Olmec culture.

IDEA

WERE-JAGUAR MYTHOLOGY

The jaguar, found across Mesoamerica and South America, was viewed with reverential fear by the early cultures of these regions. It was often depicted as a "were-jaguar", which combined often infant-like human and jaguar features, typically with a downturned mouth, large lips, and oval eyes. The were-jaguar is especially associated with the Olmecs. It appeared as jade figurines and larger sculptures, and was carved into altars and other surfaces. Were-jaguar babies were common, usually shown held by a seated male figure (right). The were-jaguar's exact significance is unclear, but it may be a "transformation figure" used by shamans to connect with the gods or harness the animal's natural power.

FIGURINE OF SEATED MALE WITH WERE-JAGUAR BABY

spread out over a wider area of Mesoamerica. It seems that Olmec symbolism was adopted by various other groups in Mesoamerica, possibly as a result of trading links.

Olmec farming practices were not particularly advanced, perhaps because they did not need to be, since the staple crop, maize, grew in ready abundance. The Olmecs were hunters rather than pastoralists, because there were no large herd animals in the region that could be domesticated. Animals were not used for transportation and, unlike in Eurasia, there were no wheeled vehicles – which, in any case, would have been of little use in the wet and swampy Olmec heartland.

The rise of San Lorenzo

The first important Olmec centre was San Lorenzo, on a plateau above the Coatzacoalcos River in the southern Mexican state of Veracruz. San Lorenzo was at its height between 1200–900 BCE. It was most likely a chiefdom rather than a city-state, with a hierarchy comprising an elite class, skilled workers, and labourers. The population was possibly only around 1,000.

The buildings at San Lorenzo were esrected on earthen mounds and arranged around open plazas. They included temples and houses made of poles and thatch, and the city seems to have had an advanced drainage system. There were also many stone monuments, such as giant carved heads, altar-like

Giant head sculptures
The Olmecs are famed for their huge stone head sculptures, which were up to several metres tall and about 20 tonnes in weight. With distinctive flattened features, they are probably connected with Olmec gods.

structures, huge sculptures of seated people, and depictions of a variety of animals, most notably the jaguar (see left). Blood-letting and sacrifice may have been part of ritual practice, but this is purely speculation.

Near the San Lorenzo site, 1.6km (1 mile) away at Cascajal, a stone dating from *c.*900 BCE has been found bearing symbols that may be Olmec writing. This could suggest the Olmecs developed one of the first writing systems in Mesoamerica (see pp.22–23).

San Lorenzo seems to come to an end around 900 BCE. Evidence of widespread destruction of monuments has led some

experts to suggest that there was a major uprising or invasion. Others think that environmental factors may have caused San Lorenzo's decline.

La Venta

The other major Olmec centre was the city of La Venta, near the border of modern Tabasco and Veracruz states, which had a much larger population than San Lorenzo. Thriving between about 900–400 BCE, La Venta effectively took over from San Lorenzo as the principal Mesoamerican settlement. As at San Lorenzo, colossal stone heads and jaguar figures and imagery were found at La Venta, as well as temple-ceremonial complexes, including a giant pyramid. The major buildings at the site were all precisely aligned, perhaps linked with ideas about astronomy.

Olmec art was accomplished, especially its stone carving, including many small jade figures. Skilled relief carvings have been found at La Venta, along with other Olmec artefacts, including iron-ore mirrors that were worn around the neck. These may have been used by Olmec leaders as evidence of their "special" powers, as the mirrors could have been used to start fires or even project images.

The Chavín of South America

To the South, the Peruvian Chavín culture began to develop in the Andes region around 1000 BCE, and then spread along a great strip of the Peruvian coast. The major excavated site associated with Chavín culture is that of Chavín de Huántar, high in the Andes, almost 300km (185 miles) north of Lima.

Chavín de Huántar may or may not have been the centre or birthplace of the culture, but it was certainly of great importance. At the heart of this sizeable settlement, which could have been home to around 3,000 people, was a monumental ceremonial complex made of stone blocks and decorated with impressive relief carving.

As in Olmec culture, Chavín art often shows figures combining both human and animal features. At the centre of the Old Temple at Chavín de Huántar is a sculpture showing the great Chavín god, El Lanzon, with a human body, a cat-like head, and serpentine hair. Such depictions may be "transformation" images associated with religious ritual, perhaps signifying that priests could transform themselves into deities.

The buildings and site at Chavín de Huántar reveal the great engineering and architectural expertise of peoples in this part of the world, especially in the face of difficult terrain. Flat terracing had to be created to build the Old Temple, just as the Olmecs had to reshape the plateau at San Lorenzo, and the later Zapotecs would master the ultimate challenge of building Monte Albán (see p.92) on top of an artificially levelled mountain.

Chavín jaguar imagery
Several well-preserved panels depicting jaguars – important in Andean culture as well as Mesoamerican – have been found at Chavín de Huántar. They would have surrounded the impressive main plaza of this ancient site.

Olmec ritual
These small jade figures and upright artefacts are Olmec finds from La Venta. The figures have the part-human, part-feline features of the were-jaguar. The scene probably represents some kind of sacred ritual, with the artefacts being votive objects.

AFTER

Different but often closely related cultures wove themselves into a complex web – rising, fading out, existing simultaneously, or persisting in some places more than others.

FROM OLMECS TO ZAPOTECS
Olmec culture had peaked by 600–400 BCE, but its influence was strongly felt in various regional cultures that persisted afterwards throughout Mesoamerica, specifically the Zapotecs at Monte Albán 94–95 ≫, in the Oaxaca Valley of southeastern Mexico.

THE BIRTH OF MAYA CIVILIZATION
Maya culture 92–93 ≫ arose from Native American settlements in Mexico's Yucatán Peninsula and Central America. Significant early developments were taking place in the 600s or 500s BCE, and the culture had really established itself by around 200 BCE.

SOUTH AMERICAN CULTURES
While Chavín culture was declining by c.200 BCE, other cultures (such as those of the Paracas and Nazca in Peru) were flourishing. Although regional in nature, they often had similar characteristics.

JAGUAR IMAGERY
The jaguar remained important to the Maya culture, and also to the much later Aztecs.

Chavín culture
Stretching from the Andes to the coastal plains of present-day Peru, Chavín culture developed the first coherent, recognizable style of Andean art. The Chavín also improved maize production and weaving techniques.

KEY
▪ Chavín heartland
○ Early Chavín sites, 2000–850 BCE
◉ Chavín sites, 850–200 BCE

33

BEFORE

Small Neolithic villages on Crete gave way to large Minoan settlements, as Crete led Europe into the early Bronze Age.

NEOLITHIC SOCIETY
Dating back to c.6500 BCE, the Neolithic people of Crete probably **originated in Asia Minor**. Their simple life centred around rearing livestock, growing crops, and making basic pottery.

EARLY BRONZE AGE
The earliest evidence of the Minoan civilization is c.3000 BCE. During the 3rd millennium BCE, **trading towns** on the Cretan coast **expanded.** Early trading partners included the people of the Cyclades (islands north of Crete in the south-western Aegean), whose culture emerged at the same time. On the mainland, too, **Europe was entering the Bronze Age**, with bronze reaching most regions in the 2000s BCE. Bronze axe heads were common and were invested with religious significance in addition to practical uses.

EARLY CYCLADIC FIGURINE

BULGARIAN BRONZE AGE AXE HEAD

INVENTION

THE FIRST MOVABLE TYPE?

The Phaistos Disc is an archaeological mystery. Made of clay, both sides of the disc feature symbols arranged in a spiral, and each symbol has been pressed into the clay with a punch. The script is unique and has not yet been deciphered. Discovered in the early 1900s during excavations of the palace at Phaistos on Crete, it has been dated to the period 1850–1350 BCE. Its meaning and usage is not fully understood but, as it features reusable stamps, some archaeologists believe it to be the earliest form of movable printing type, predating anything comparable by 2,000 years.

PHAISTOS DISC

Europe's First Civilization

The first civilization to make its mark in western Europe was the Bronze Age culture of the Minoans, based on the Mediterranean island of Crete. Frescoes in the grand palaces depict a highly sophisticated way of life, and hint at a society where women played an unusually dominant role for the times.

A rchaeologists named the ancient Cretan civilization "Minoan" after Minos, a mythical king of Crete (see pp.56–57). The Minoan civilization flourished between c.3000–1400 BCE, peaking around 1600 BCE, during the late Bronze Age. It is famous for its extensive trading links across the sea, well-planned cities, beautiful palaces and artefacts, goddess worship, and a tradition of "bull-leaping" (see right).

Intriguingly, however, what we know of Minoan culture is scant and based purely on their ruins as experts are unable to fully decode their writing, known simply as "Linear A". The Mycenaeans (see AFTER) modified Linear A to write the early form of Greek that they spoke. But while this Mycenaean script has been decoded using knowledge of Greek, the Minoans unknown, pre-Greek language still remains a mystery, and most of what they wrote down appears to be economic records.

Seafaring traders
An island location meant limited resources, so trade was crucial. As skilled seafarers, the Minoans employed a range of sophisticated vessels. They are often credited with having developed the first "navy", albeit used for trade rather than war. The Minoans' impressive trading network gave them influence across the Aegean Sea in the eastern Mediterranean, and far beyond. Minoan artefacts have been found in Egypt, modern Lebanon, Syria, Israel, and Cyprus. Not only were Minoan goods widely transported, but the Minoans themselves also settled in their trading destinations. Murals excavated at Tell el-Dab'a (ancient Avaris) in Egypt are Minoan in style and feature typical Cretan symbols such as bulls. Minoan-style paintings have also been unearthed at Tel Kabri in Israel.

Palace culture
Minoan life was characterized by highly developed urban settlements dominated by splendid palaces, which were home to Crete's rulers. The major cities on Crete were Knossos, Phaistos, Mallia, and Zakros, of which Knossos was the most opulent. The cities, like those of Mesopotamia (see pp.14–15) and other civilizations of the time, were political, religious, administrative, cultural, and trading centres. Kings played both a political and a religious role and many government officials were likely to have been priests.

Natural inspiration
This jar is from the late Minoan period (c.1450–1400 BCE), when Mycenaean influence was evident. Natural imagery was popular, and octopuses would have been a common sight.

Minoan women
This detail taken from one of the stunning, brightly coloured wall paintings at Knossos, shows a trio of refined Minoan ladies with attractively dressed hair, wearing fashionable clothes that left them exposed to the waist. There is evidence that Minoan women took a significant lead in many aspects of life.

sophisticated, multi-roomed houses. Those that did not follow a craft worked the land, providing for the cities that powered Cretan society; tasks would have included tending the vines and olive trees that produced large quantities of wine and oil.

Mythology and religion

Excavated artefacts give us an insight into Minoan religious practices and beliefs. People appear to have been buried with possessions or offerings, showing a belief in an afterlife. Cretan vases and frescoes are suffused with imagery featuring bulls, axes, snakes, and goddesses. All Minoan gods were female and one of the most popular was the "Snake Goddess", depictions of whom have been found in the ruins of houses and small palace shrines.

The bull image is widespread, being linked to King Minos. According to legend, his failure to sacrifice a bull sent by the sea-god Poseidon caused Minos' wife to give birth to the Minotaur – a creature that was half-man, half-bull. Minos trapped the Minotaur in a labyrinth, and young people were sacrificed to the creature every year.

Cretan frescoes also show young men and women leaping over bulls, which may have been performed for sport or for religious purposes.

Women in Minoan society

Women played an equal role to that of men in Minoan society, and participated in all occupations and trades, including the priesthood. Female "bull-leapers" are depicted alongside the men, and there is even evidence to suggest that Minoan society might have been "matrilineal" (with inheritance passed down the female line).

AFTER »

The rich and highly successful Minoan civilization started to wane around **1500 BCE**, but its complete decline took hundreds of years.

VOLCANIC ERUPTION
The **Thera eruption** in 1600 BCE (see above) may have resulted in the loss of the Cretan fleet, making Crete more vulnerable to outside powers and influence. Trade networks may also have been wiped out, causing "ripple-effect" damage throughout the whole region.

ARRIVAL OF THE MYCENAEANS
By 1500 BCE, the **Mycenaeans**, a late Bronze Age people from mainland Greece, had arrived on Crete. The Minoan and Mycenaean cultures had already influenced each other through trade. However, by 1400 BCE, the Mycenaeans **dominated Crete and the Aegean**. Their takeover may have been aided by an **earthquake** on Crete in the 1400s, which partially destroyed some Minoan cities.

JOINT DECLINE
The Mycenaeans adopted much Minoan culture, and a wonderful fusion of Minoan–Mycenaean styles flourished during this period. However, by 1200 BCE, the Cretan palace-cities were in decline 36–37 », and the **Greek Dorian** people moved in. The increasing use of iron for tools and weapons, and in trade, may also have put the Bronze Age culture at a disadvantage, and have been a factor in the civilization's decline.

Some scholars think that these main cities resembled small city-states (see pp.48–49), each ruling a specific part of the island and with a focus on trade. Minoan palaces themselves were vast sumptuous complexes with well-lit

gold jewellery for which the Minoans were famed. A distinctive feature of Minoan culture was its "Kamáres ware" pottery – including cups, jugs, jars, and enormous urns (*pithoi*), used to store food – with stylized designs often painted in black, white, and red.

Evidence suggests that many ordinary Minoans worked as craftspeople, making items for home use and export. The wealth that this industry created meant that they, too, lived in relatively

1,000 The number of rooms thought to make up the famous frescoed palace at Knossos, "capital city" of the Minoan civilization.

rooms arranged around internal courtyards. The palaces had advanced drainage systems, similar to those in the Indus Valley (see p.18–19), and plumbing that featured interlocking clay pipes and flushing toilets.

A culture of craftspeople

Courtiers and wealthy families living in villas surrounding the palace would have owned exquisite artefacts and

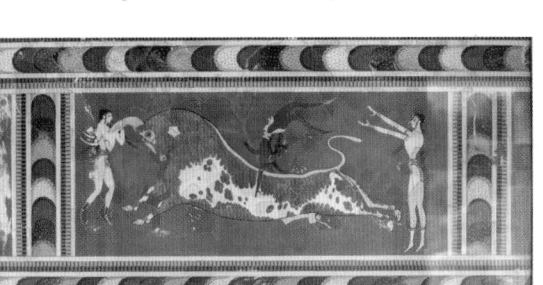

Bull-leaping
A Knossos palace fresco reveals the perilous art of bull-leaping in which young men and women took turns to somersault over a bull's back.

Knossos palace
Around 1700 BCE, the Knossos palace complex was destroyed by an earthquake or an invasion. When rebuilt, the palace was even more splendid, with stone steps linking the different buildings on its hilly site.

Dolphin fresco
This beautiful fresco was discovered in a palace throne room. The Minoans moved from a decorative artistic style in their early days to the naturalistic style of art seen here.

❮❮ BEFORE

The Late Bronze Age began with the rise of several new powers.

THE HITTITES
The Hittite Old Kingdom formed in **Anatolia** (modern Turkey) in the 17th century BCE, but declined due to infighting. The New Kingdom emerged in the 15th century and expanded to challenge first **Mittani** (see below) and then **Egypt**. The state was divided into multiple kingdoms, each with a governor appointed by the great king, who ruled from the capital, **Hattusa**.

OLD-HITTITE GODDESS

KASSITE BAYLONIA
In 1595 BCE the **Hittite king, Mursili II** sacked Babylon, ending the **Old Babylonian period ❮❮ 15**. Babylonia then rose slowly as a power under the **Kassites** – an Indo-Iranian group that had immigrated centuries before. The Kassites were known for *kudurru* ("boundary stone") sculptures, which commemorated land grants.

KASSITE KUDURRU

MYCENAE
The civilization that **dominated Greece** in the Late Bronze Age (1600–1100 BCE), Mycenae **❮❮ 35** controlled much of the **Aegean Sea** and absorbed the **Minoan civilization ❮❮ 34–35**.

MITTANI
The kingdom of Mittani, populated by the **Hurrian people**, formed in **northwest Mesopotamia** in the 16th century BCE. Mittani **conquered Assyria 38–39 ❯❯**, holding it as a dependent state until the 14th century, as well as fighting Egypt for control of southern Syria. The **Mittanian capital, Washshukanni**, has not yet been excavated or even precisely located.

EGYPTIAN NEW KINGDOM
During its **New Kingdom ❮❮ 24–25** (1550–1069 BCE), Egypt became the **world's leading power** and the major force in the Middle East. Expansionist policies created an empire that, in the 15th century BCE, stretched from modern-day **Lebanon to Sudan (ancient Nubia)**.

EGYPTIAN BRONZE AGE WAR CHARIOT

Rameses III battles the Sea Peoples
Pharaoh Rameses III smites his enemies in his battles against the "Sea Peoples" during the 12th century BCE. Long blamed for the Bronze Age collapse, the Sea Peoples may have been opportunists attacking weakened states.

The kingdoms of the Late Bronze Age – Babylonia, Mittani, Elam, Egypt, Mycenae, Alashiya, and the Hittite Empire – were potent powers, whose might was based on the war chariot. Where their frontiers met, they fought, but they made no attempt to conquer each other's core territories, so relative stability was maintained for four centuries from c.1600–1200 BCE.

The flow of bronze

The key to this stability was the need for supplies of copper and tin to make bronze for weapons and tools. Copper was abundant, but the source of tin at the time was in distant Afghanistan. Long-distance trade in metals therefore needed to be maintained, and the states rapidly formed a diplomatic community,

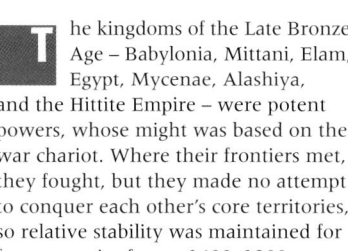

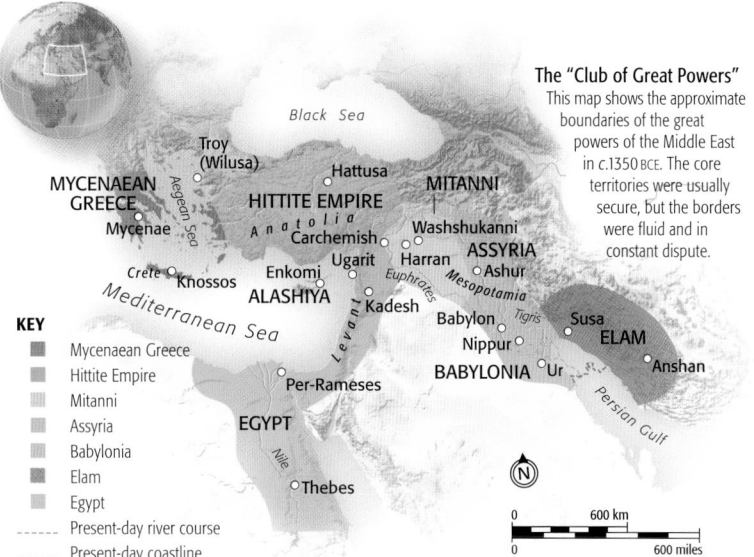

The "Club of Great Powers"
This map shows the approximate boundaries of the great powers of the Middle East in c.1350 BCE. The core territories were usually secure, but the borders were fluid and in constant dispute.

KEY
- Mycenaean Greece
- Hittite Empire
- Mitanni
- Assyria
- Babylonia
- Elam
- Egypt
- ------ Present-day river course
- ------ Present-day coastline

AFTER

New kingdoms, including the Hebrew states of Israel and Judah, were founded in the former territory of the Bronze Age powers.

ARAMAEAN KINGDOMS
Migrations were a key feature of the collapse and the most significant migrants were the Aramaeans. By the 10th century BCE, a patchwork of **small Aramaean kingdoms** covered the Levant and northern Mesopotamia and the **Aramaic language** was on its way to replacing Akkadian **‹‹ 14–15** as the Middle East's *lingua franca*. Aramaic was used in the Assyrian **38–39 ››** and Persian **46–47 ››** empires.

PHILISTINES

These people settled on the coast of the Levant at the end of the 2nd millennium BCE. They may equate to the **Peleset** – one of the "**Sea Peoples**" mentioned by the Egyptians – and are the **origin of the name Palestine**. Their architecture and culture appear Greek, suggesting that they began as displaced Mycenaeans **‹‹ 35**.

PHILISTINE FUNERARY MASK

IRON-AGE ECONOMY
Iron ore was more readily accessible than the ingredients for bronze, but the transition to an iron economy was highly disruptive, so the great powers stuck with bronze. After they fell, **iron came into common use**. By the 10th century BCE, Assyria was making the change, and the emerging new states were already using iron.

Bronze Age Collapse

In the Late Bronze Age of the Middle East, a diplomatic community of empires maintained a thriving international system based on bronze. Between 1200–1050 BCE, the records of these powers hint at tumult and upheaval – then most simply fall eerily silent, signifying a dark age of history.

based on intensive correspondence, dynastic intermarriage, and exchange of gifts. Whatever the current political balance and regardless of who was fighting whom, bronze was delivered.

Diplomacy also allowed the empires to make peace when strategically necessary. For instance, Egypt and Mittani initially fought over southern Syria, but Mittani made peace with Egypt to concentrate on the Hittite threat from the north. The Hittites later came into conflict with the Egyptians, but formed an alliance with them to repel the Assyrians. The Assyrians, formerly vassals of Mittani, were newcomers to the "Club of Great Powers", and it was some time before these upstarts were fully accepted.

Disintegration of kingdoms

The collapse began in c.1200 BCE. The first sign was that Mycenaean citadels in Greece were destroyed (see p.35), most likely by northern invaders. It seems that dispossessed Mycenaeans flooded outwards looking for new lands. This is probably the origin of the story of Troy (see pp.56–57), which equates to a kingdom in Anatolia known to the Hittites as Wilusa.

What follows in the scant records available seems to be a cascade of mass migration, disruption, and destruction. Around 1180 BCE the Hittite Empire abruptly disappeared from history.

Hittite capital
The ruins of Hattusa, destroyed around 1180 BCE, were unearthed at Bogazkoy in central Turkey. The palace was burnt and the whole city abandoned.

Most likely, marauding Mycenaeans drew Hittite forces away from Hattusa, the capital, which was then destroyed by tribes of northern Anatolia, leaving the rest of the empire to fragment.

The Egyptians fought off invasions by groups they called the "Sea Peoples", whom they blamed for the fall of the Hittite Empire, although many of these groups seem to have had connections to former Hittite territories, meaning they were probably displaced by the empire's fall, rather than the cause of it. Egypt's New Kingdom declined and eventually fragmented in 1069 BCE.

Meanwhile, Babylonia's wars with Assyria and Elam resulted in Babylon's Kassite dynasty dissolving in 1154 BCE and Elam again disappearing from the

records a few decades later, when its capital, Susa, was sacked. Assyria also fell silent by 1050 BCE for over a century. The last few records speak of endless border skirmishes, as the kings attempted to hold back mass migrations of "Aramaeans" and "Mushki".

What happened?

This period is one of the most hotly debated subjects in ancient history. The events are known from only a handful of sources, such as the Ugarit letters (see right) and the Egyptian accounts of the Sea Peoples. After 1050, there are simply no records at all and the period 1050–934 BCE is termed a "dark age". The collapse represented only the removal of the top layer of elite culture, however – a dark age is simply a period in which the elite stop producing monuments and written records. The political map was redrawn, but the lives of most people would not have changed.

Although many kingdoms fell, only a few cities were utterly destroyed. Assyria and Elam were the only Bronze Age powers to return, but new kingdoms soon arose. The patterns of the Bronze Age were still deeply ingrained, but the new technology of iron would soon allow states such as Assyria (see pp.38–39) to break free of the old system of diplomacy and bid for world domination on their own.

HOW WE KNOW

THE UGARIT LETTERS

Correspondence survives between the king of Ugarit, a regional ruler of the Hittite Empire, and the king of Alashiya, on Cyprus. The letters talk of hostile marauders plaguing the Ugarit area and are brought to a sudden stop soon after 1200 BCE by the city's destruction. They mention that the Hittites had called the bulk of Ugarit's forces away to fight elsewhere, leaving it defenceless. The marauders are never named but, as many cities around Ugarit were left unscathed, it is possible that they were displaced Mycenaean Greeks looking for a rich port to loot, as with the suspected fate of Troy.

LETTER AND ENVELOPE

« BEFORE

Assyria rose to prominence in northern Mesopotamia « 14–15 in the 14th century BCE, but its foundations were laid by rulers up to 600 years earlier.

OLD ASSYRIAN PERIOD
The Assyrian Empire's roots can be traced to the period c.2000–1800 BCE when **Shamshi-Adad I** created a kingdom including the great trading city of **Ashur**, once an independent **city-state**.

MIDDLE ASSYRIAN PERIOD
By 1400 BCE, the Assyrians were vassals of their neighbour, the **kingdom of Mittani « 36–37**. As Mittani crumbled, Ashur broke free, its rulers proclaiming themselves "**kings of Assyria**". Under **Ashur-uballit I** (1365–1330 BCE), Assyrian lands expanded over all of modern north Iraq, and Assyria came into conflict with Babylonia and the Hittites. Like other Bronze Age powers « 36–37, Assyria declined in the 11th century BCE, but the state survived.

ASSYRIAN SOLDIERS

The Assyrians were Semitic people living in northern Mesopotamia (modern Iraq) and they reached the height of their empire – during the "Neo-Assyrian" era – in the 800s and 700s BCE. The Neo-Assyrian Empire built on the foundations of the Middle Assyrian period (1350–1000 BCE, see BEFORE), during which Assyria commanded much wealth and resources, improving agriculture and irrigation, erecting impressive buildings, and establishing key administrative centres.

Legendary warriors
The Neo-Assyrians were famed as fierce warriors and they showed innovative military prowess, which helped them to expand their territories. Chariot warfare had already become established during the Neo-Assyrian period, when the Middle East was still in the Bronze Age (see pp.36–37). However, military success in the Neo-Assyrian period was aided by the Assyrians' effective adoption of new Iron Age warfare techniques. Their highly disciplined army featured a mix of chariots, infantry, and horseback

Life in an Assyrian military camp
This 9th-century relief from Ashurnasirpal II's palace at Nimrud shows a priest, bottom left, preparing to predict the future by studying a sheep's entrails. Foretelling the future was a prominent aspect of Assyrian life.

population movements were more like resettlements than deportations, because the people were given land and state assistance. This resettlement was the fate of the people known in Biblical tradition as the "Ten Lost Tribes" – of the conquered Hebrew kingdom of Israel. They were moved to the Upper Habur area of northern Mesopotamia and the Zagros mountains of southwest Iran.

> **SEMITIC** A language group that includes Hebrew and Arabic, and a description of people from the Middle East who trace their ancestry to the biblical Noah and his son, Shem. The group includes both Jews and Arabs.

Food, probably a meat stew (perhaps from the divined sheep), is being prepared on a stove.

Rulers of the Iron Age

By the 9th century BCE, a great Assyrian empire dominated the Middle East and stayed in control for two centuries. It is often seen as the first real "world empire", and much of its success can be traced to a stable political system and skilful exploitation of new Iron Age warfare techniques.

ASSYRIAN KING, RULED 721–705 BCE

SARGON II

Coming to the throne in suspicious circumstances, Sargon II probably had a hand in the disposal of his brother and predecessor, Shalmaneser V. Sargon consolidated the gains of his father, Tiglath-pileser III, in Babylonia and the Mediterranean, and further enlarged the empire to Iran and far into Anatolia. With a vast workforce from all over the Middle East at his command and heavy tribute and taxes filling his coffers, Sargon built a new residence city called Sargon's Fortress (modern Khorsabad) in the Assyrian heartland – its palaces and temples bearing lavish stonework.

riders. This was the first army to use cavalry units, which, along with the Assyrians' use of iron weapons, gave them a great advantage over less advanced enemies. The fighting forces mixed a standing army of professional soldiers, including foreign mercenaries, under the control of the king with provincial contingents mustered as part of regional tax obligations.

Creating an empire
Famed too for the barbaric subjugation of their enemies, the Assyrians used impalement, mass execution, and the ruthless mass "deportation" of those who opposed them. But such methods were also used by other powers throughout the Middle East. The Assyrians certainly invented a new way of dealing with conquered people by moving them en masse to other parts of the empire and replacing them with other people from within the empire. However, the

Resettlement was designed to create a uniform population, although it created some hotbeds of dissent. The policy also made central Assyria a cultural melting pot. By the 7th century BCE, the royal entourage included scholars, craftsmen, and singers from Babylonia, Anatolia, Egypt, and Iran.

Stable foundations
Military effectiveness was crucially backed up by a relatively stable political system. Various factors contributed to this. The first was the royal bloodline, which was considered all-important, so that outsiders could not become king. A crown prince and heir apparent was selected as soon as a new king took the throne. There was always a successor, and he played an important role in running the empire. If the king died unexpectedly, the succession arrangement was already in place.

Second was the way in which power was delegated from the king to local officials. Assyria was organized into

An Assyrian priest, recognizable by his hat, joins another man in butchering a sheep so that he can "read" its entrails.

Coded signs written by the gods were believed to be hidden in sheep's entrails.

Regional power
Assyrian governors often enjoyed great wealth. This mural detail is from a governor's residence at Til Barsip, during the reign of Tiglath-pileser III (744–727 BCE).

A servant sets out a bowl of soup, roasted animal ribs, and flat bread.

A fan is used by the servant to protect the meal from flies.

An Assyrian man is sliding food into or out of an oven.

The oven would have been used to bake bread or roast meat.

The Assyrian Empire

The empire is shown here at its height in 705 BCE, but before the incursions into Egypt. Assyria was for 200 years the principal power in the Middle East, before it was crushed by the Medes and Babylonians.

KEY

▨ Assyrian Empire at the death of Sargon II, 705 BCE
------ Present-day river course
------ Present-day coastline

provinces, and newly conquered kingdoms were incorporated as provinces (with each one usually split up into two or more). The governors in charge of the provinces were directly appointed by the king. However, instead of governors being drawn from the local dynasty who had ruled before Assyria took over, or from the ruling family, the Assyrian king relied on eunuchs to represent his interests. As the eunuch governors could not have children, there was no danger that they would try to start their own dynasty.

The strong administration kept close control over the regions. It ensured that the provinces raised taxes and sent troops directly to wherever they were needed. At the top of the hierarchy, the king, the ultimate lawgiver, was aided by a powerful aristocracy from whom leading officials and army commanders were drawn. At the bottom, most of

the population were peasants, paying their local lord with goods or services in return for protection. Village life changed little through successive kings.

Managing the empire

Assyrian rule had all the hallmarks of a strong empire: clever control tactics, good communication links, and varied trading connections. The Assyrians shrewdly sought to dominate areas that they had previously conquered in the Middle Assyrian period, which made it appear that they were reasserting their natural rights to those territories.

Parts of the empire were linked with a system of roads. "Royal roads" had stations for the express delivery of state correspondence using despatch riders. This ambitious road network formed the basis of the later Persian system (see pp.45–45, 46–47). The roads were useful for overland trade too. Strong trading links were developed with the Phoenician city-state of Tyre (see pp.40–41, 86), and Assyria built an impressive trading network across the Mediterranean as well as connections with the Arabs, and an ancient Iranian people called the Medes.

Tribute from Israel

Jehu, king of Israel, prostrates himself before the 9th-century-BCE Assyrian king, Shalmaneser III. The scene is one of several such reliefs on a public monument erected at Nimrud in 825 BCE.

AFTER »

> "The Assyrian came down **like the wolf on the fold**, And his cohorts were gleaming in **purple and gold**."
>
> LORD BYRON, FROM HIS POEM "THE DESTRUCTION OF SENNACHERIB", 1815

The Assyrian Empire, so aggressively built, could not withstand internal division.

KING SENNACHERIB

The Assyrian king **Sennacherib** (704–681 BCE), based at his spectacular capital, Nineveh, **aggressively defended** the empire's borders. His campaigns included sacking **the city of Lachish in Judah** (south of Israel), and **crushing**

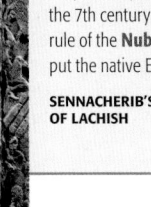

SENNACHERIB'S CAPTURE OF LACHISH

Babylonia by **destroying its capital, Babylon** – although the city was later rebuilt by Sennacherib's son, **Esarhaddon**. Babylonia had once been a major Mesopotamian kingdom in the 2nd millennium BCE **« 15, 36–37**and emerged again from Assyria's shadow at the end of the 7th century BCE **44, 46»**.

CONQUEST OF EGYPT

Assyria conquered **Egypt « 25** in the 7th century BCE and ended the rule of the **Nubian dynasty**. They put the native Egyptian **Saite**

dynasty into power as puppet rulers, but Egypt then regained independence **72–73 »** under the Egyptian pharaoh **Psammetichus I** (664-610 BCE).

BROTHER WAR

The empire was weakened in 652–648 BCE by a war between **Esarhaddon's sons**: Shamash-shumu-ukin, whom he had installed as ruler of Babylon, and **Assurbanipal**, the eventual victor.

BABYLONIANS AND MEDES

On Assurbanipal's death, the empire endured a succession crisis, and when the **Babylonians and Medes** attacked and captured the city of **Ashur** in 614 BCE, the empire quickly disintegrated.

BEFORE

By around 3000 BCE trading centres were developing in the eastern Mediterranean, the Arab peninsula, and Nubia.

MEDITERRANEAN MARITIME CITIES

By c.3000 BCE, the maritime cities that would become the heartland of "Phoenician" (a later Greek label) civilization were developing or well established along the eastern Mediterranean coast. These included the cities of Tyre, Byblos, and Sidon (all in modern Lebanon).

THE ARABS

During the 3rd millennium BCE, states were flourishing in the better watered parts of the Arabian peninsula. The "Magan" area (modern Oman) was an important trade partner for Mesopotamia **‹‹ 14–15**. Magan was valued for its **copper and diorite**, while it received goods such as textiles and wool.

NUBIA

Also during the 3rd millennium BCE, Nubia (modern Sudan) was forging links with Egypt by trading goods, providing a corridor to Africa through which Egypt obtained **ebony, ivory, gold, incense, and exotic animals**.

IVORY COMB, EGYPT'S OLD KINGDOM

HOW WE KNOW

THE INCENSE TRADE

Since ancient times, tales circulated about a "lost city" on the Arabian peninsula. Archaeological discoveries in the 1980s and 1990s, using images taken from space, appear to have found this city and identified it as Ubar (a region, not a city), in modern Oman. Items unearthed there include frankincense burners and it is thought that this was a major Arabian trading post on the incense route, probably thriving by 900 BCE.

Incense was so precious, and its trade so important, because it masked unpleasant smells and was used in religious ceremonies. The trees from which aromatic resins are obtained grow only in Oman. This is why the incense, gold, and myrrh brought to Jesus by the three kings were such special gifts.

INCENSE BURNER

Tyre, Byblos, and Sidon formed the core of a great maritime trading network. These city-states on the east Mediterranean coast, a region known as Canaan in the 2nd millennium BCE and as Phoenicia to the Greeks, prospered between 1200–600 BCE.

The Phoenicians used maritime trade to expand a relatively small land base and keep at bay powers looking to control them. These included Egypt and the Hittites, from whose dominance Phoenicia emerged around 1200 BCE, and the ancient Greeks.

The Phoenicians' extraordinary seafaring prowess made them the control centre for routes crossing the the Mediterranean. Their trading links extended to Mesopotamia and, through the Red Sea, to Arabia and Africa. They were also successful merchants

Conquering Sea and Desert

During the 2nd millennium BCE, a variety of peoples in coastal and desert areas fringing more populated regions established vital trading networks that linked a cross-section of cultures.

and manufacturers, supplying a range of goods – from rich, exotic fabrics and glass to cedar wood – which found a lucrative market in Assyria.

A vast network of trading posts included Carthage in North Africa and Cadiz (Gades) in Spain (Iberia), close to the centres of tin production. Trade made Phoenicia an important force in international cultural exchange and spread the influential writing system that they developed (see pp.22–23).

The "Phoenicians", as the Greeks called them, are the same as the "Canaanites"; while the port of Ugarit (see p.37) was abandoned in the course of the collapse of the Late Bronze Age system most other Canaanite cities survived intact and formed close trading links with the Philistines and other new arrivals.

Arab trade

Important trading networks were also established in the Arab world at this time. By the late 9th century BCE, there were major centres in southern Arabia (modern Yemen), including the Minaean and Sabaean kingdoms, and in the north. The lives of the semi-nomadic Arabs were transformed by the domestication of

the camel, around the 12th century BCE. This made it easier to create settlements in the desert, based around large oases, and to travel across arid regions in search of new resources.

Secrets of the desert

Camel trails marked out routes that became part of an "Incense Road", carrying incense and spices. Only the Arabs knew the secrets of traversing their dangerous desert routes. This knowledge made them powerful and wealthy, and they did their best to shroud their trails and sources in fabulous myth.

The Kingdom of Kush

A valuable nexus of trade routes was also thriving farther west, around the kingdom of Kush, in southern Nubia, bringing precious materials such as ivory and gold to the ancient world. By the 8th century BCE, Kush, and its capital Napata, was enjoying a glorious period as a major trade centre freed from Egyptian domination. The value of Nubia's trade routes was one of the main reasons why Egypt had worked so hard, from about 2000 BCE, to exert control here and the two cultures had a lasting impact on each other.

The earliest archaeological evidence for the Phoenician colony at Carthage dates to the second half of the 8th century BCE. Traditionally, the date of this trading post is given as 814 BCE.

ATLANTIC OCEAN

IBERIA

Gades
Mainaca
Lixus

Balearic Islands

Corsica
Sardinia
ITALY
Rome
Nora
Pithecusa
Hippo Regius
Utica
Panormus
Hadrumetum
Carthage
Sicily
Thenae
Lilybaeum

NUMIDIA

Sabrata
Oea
Leptis

Sahara Desert

This stone slab (stele) from the Amun temple at Kawa shows a Nubian king called Ary, who may be the 8th-century BCE founder of the "kingdom of Kush" (in Egypt and Sudan), worshipping the gods Amun, Mut, and Khonsu.

Kawa

Trade across the desert and sea

All manner of goods, from many different sources, were transported across huge distances by networks that meshed Phoenician-controlled routes with the trade routes of Mediterranean, Middle Eastern, African, and Arabian peoples. For example, the 14th-century BCE ship, found wrecked off Uluburun, (modern Turkey), was carrying goods from Mycenae, Canaan, Egypt, and Assyria. Its "nationality" is uncertain.

Senn

KEY

■ Phoenicia
○ Cities
◖ Phoenician trade centres
▪▪▪ and routes
◖ Incense trade centres
▬ and routes
◖ Gold and ivory trade
▬ centres and routes

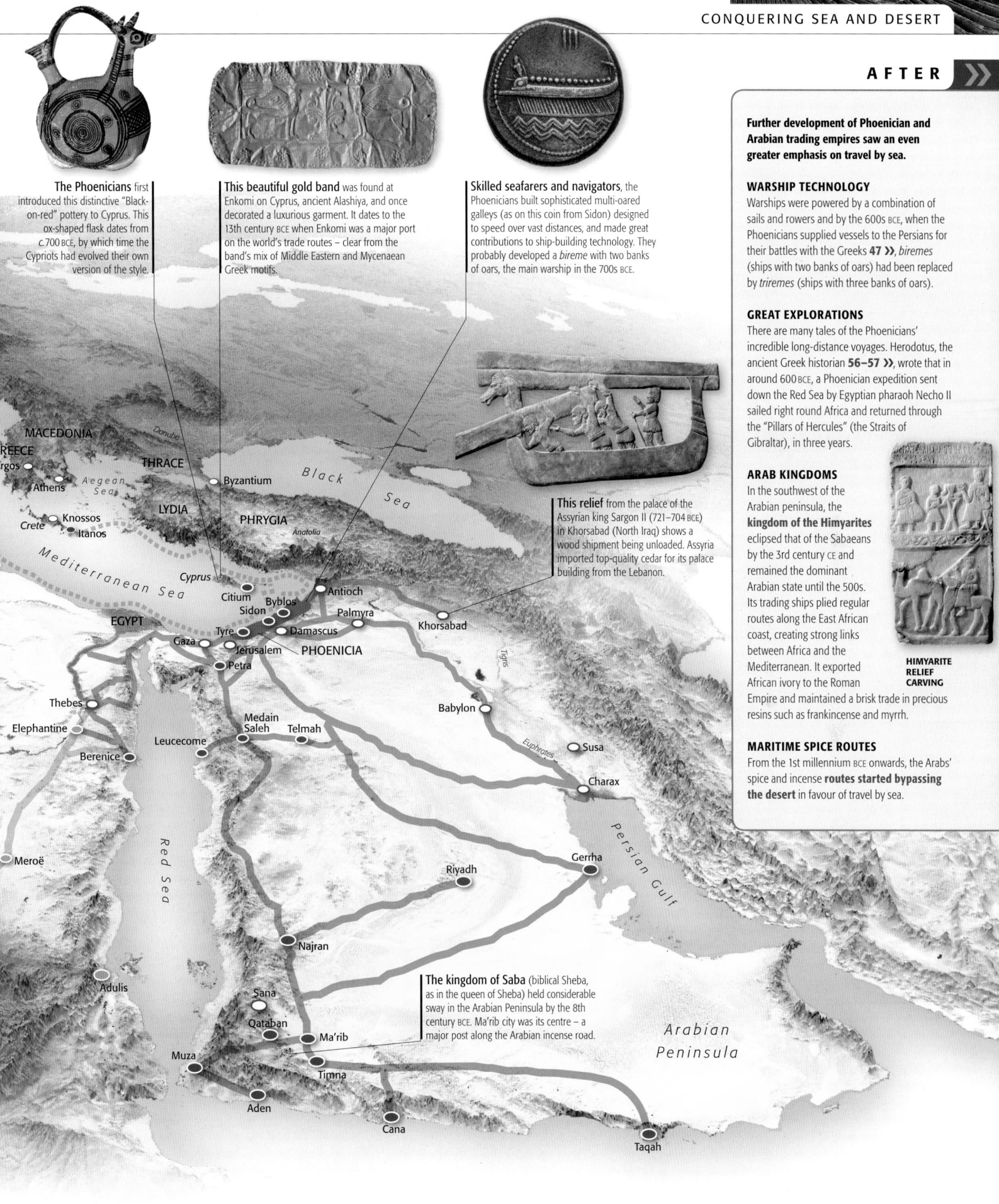

The Phoenicians first introduced this distinctive "Black-on-red" pottery to Cyprus. This ox-shaped flask dates from c.700 BCE, by which time the Cypriots had evolved their own version of the style.

This beautiful gold band was found at Enkomi on Cyprus, ancient Alashiya, and once decorated a luxurious garment. It dates to the 13th century BCE when Enkomi was a major port on the world's trade routes – clear from the band's mix of Middle Eastern and Mycenaean Greek motifs.

Skilled seafarers and navigators, the Phoenicians built sophisticated multi-oared galleys (as on this coin from Sidon) designed to speed over vast distances, and made great contributions to ship-building technology. They probably developed a *bireme* with two banks of oars, the main warship in the 700s BCE.

This relief from the palace of the Assyrian king Sargon II (721–704 BCE) in Khorsabad (North Iraq) shows a wood shipment being unloaded. Assyria imported top-quality cedar for its palace building from the Lebanon.

AFTER

Further development of Phoenician and Arabian trading empires saw an even greater emphasis on travel by sea.

WARSHIP TECHNOLOGY
Warships were powered by a combination of sails and rowers and by the 600s BCE, when the Phoenicians supplied vessels to the Persians for their battles with the Greeks **47 》**, *biremes* (ships with two banks of oars) had been replaced by *triremes* (ships with three banks of oars).

GREAT EXPLORATIONS
There are many tales of the Phoenicians' incredible long-distance voyages. Herodotus, the ancient Greek historian **56–57 》**, wrote that in around 600 BCE, a Phoenician expedition sent down the Red Sea by Egyptian pharaoh Necho II sailed right round Africa and returned through the "Pillars of Hercules" (the Straits of Gibraltar), in three years.

ARAB KINGDOMS
In the southwest of the Arabian peninsula, the **kingdom of the Himyarites** eclipsed that of the Sabaeans by the 3rd century CE and remained the dominant Arabian state until the 500s. Its trading ships plied regular routes along the East African coast, creating strong links between Africa and the Mediterranean. It exported African ivory to the Roman Empire and maintained a brisk trade in precious resins such as frankincense and myrrh.

HIMYARITE RELIEF CARVING

MARITIME SPICE ROUTES
From the 1st millennium BCE onwards, the Arabs' spice and incense **routes started bypassing the desert** in favour of travel by sea.

The kingdom of Saba (biblical Sheba, as in the queen of Sheba) held considerable sway in the Arabian Peninsula by the 8th century BCE. Ma'rib city was its centre – a major post along the Arabian incense road.

2

THINKERS AND BELIEVERS

700 BCE–600 CE

The age of the great classical civilizations, including Greece, Rome, China, and Persia, was a period of remarkable innovation in science, philosophy, art, and politics. Vast empires rose and fell, systems of government that still influence society today were born, and great religions emerged. It is also the period when history was first written down.

Xerxes crossed the Hellespont as part of his Persian campaign to Greece in 480 BCE. The Hellespont was a narrow sea channel that had been both a frontier and pivotal point of empires. A boundary separating Europe and Asia, it was also a conduit of goods and communication between East and West.

Hatra was a rich trading city in territory disputed between Rome and Parthia (see pp.76–77) between 150 BCE–224 CE. At times, it was one of several prominent semi-independent or client states (such as Commagene) between the great Roman and Parthian empires. Hatra's circular layout reflected Parthian city patterns, while the architecture revealed Roman influence.

This Greek depiction of northern nomads, known as the Scythians (see pp.90–91), demonstrates trading contact at the meeting point between settled and nomadic worlds. The Scythians were a group of related tribes sharing a common culture and related languages, who spanned the steppe lands from Siberia to southeast Europe.

BEFORE

The natural geographical zones of Eurasia have shaped the growth of powers, their conflicts, and their contacts. In many ways, Mesopotamia remained the heart of the ancient civilized world.

VALLEYS AND SETTLEMENT

Settled urban life began in the fertile valleys and floodplains of **Egypt « 16–17**, **Mesopotamia** and the **Indus « 18–19**. These valleys became central to growing states during the period 3000–1000 BCE.

EXPANDING POWERS

Between 1550–700 BCE, the rich, ambitious monarchies of **Egypt « 24–25** and **Assyria « 38–39** expanded beyond their valleys into the disputed territory of **the Levant** – the area at the eastern end of the Mediterranean, roughly from modern Turkey south to the Sinai Peninsula. This was a **fertile commercial crossroads** and a gateway to the resources of the Mediterranean.

WORLD DOMINANCE

The Assyrians' heartland lay in the upper part of Mesopotamia, but in c.800 BCE they **dominated their neighbours** more than any state had done before. They fought the mountain tribes to the north and east of their realm, but also developed diplomatic relations with them. The Assyrian Empire at last fell to the Babylonians in c.612 BCE. **Babylon was now at the centre of the world** again.

ISHTAR GATE, BABYLON

DESERTS AND FRONTIERS

In the second half of the 1st millennium BCE, the world's great powers became yet more mobile and ambitious. Peoples with roots as horsemen of the steppes, such as the **Persians 46–47 »**, combined rule of Mesopotamia with expansion from the **Iranian Plateau** to the desert of **Central Asia**. The same heritage of steppe horsemanship brought new military tactics to the **Chinese warring states** in 1000–500 BCE and, later, aided their unification **80–81 »**.

Dura Europos was founded in c.303 BCE during Greek rule of Mesopotamia, on a trade route on the River Euphrates. The city then came under Parthian, Roman, then Persian control. Its cultural diversity is reflected in its religious buildings, which include both the earliest preserved synagogue and this church.

Bisitun was a sacred mountain beside a site used successively as a staging post, garden, and palatial retreat. The mountain towered over the route from Babylon, on the low Mesopotamian plain, to the Iranian Plateau. In c.515 BCE, Persian emperor Darius I (see pp.46–47) carved a monumental relief with an imperial inscription (below) proclaiming his sovereignty over both plateau and plain.

The Indus River was a central link in the route between the Persian Gulf and the interiors of India and Central Asia. The Indus Valley was also a contested frontier between powers including the Achaemenid Persian (see pp.46–47), Seleucid Greek (see pp.52–53), and Mauryan Indian (see pp.78–79) empires.

Kushan statues such as this are relics of a tribal power that in 1–250 CE consolidated a huge land empire between the Hindu Kush mountains and the River Ganges. Known to both Roman and Chinese imperial powers, the Kushans (see pp.90–91) formed a crucial zone of cultural exchange.

AFTER

A series of empires spread across Eurasia in 700 BCE–600 CE, all shaped by their physical environment. The heart of the city-based empires remained in the south, from southern Europe through the Middle East to India and China. The steppe territory to the north continued to support an unsettled, nomadic life, largely uncontrolled by urban states (see pp.90–91). Nevertheless, great changes in the seats of power of both settled and nomadic people took place. Mesopotamia, once the centre of a succession of empires (see BEFORE), became a border region from the 2nd century BCE. Enormous population movements of which we are only dimly aware today seem to have moved frontiers in the European steppe, Central Asia, and northwest China. At the same time, rulers resettled populations as a method of imperial control under the Assyrian, Babylonian, Persian, Roman, and Han Chinese empires.

Limitless ambition

The vast size of these empires was hard for their inhabitants to comprehend, but imperial powers used symbols to reflect the rich diversity of their lands. Assyrian and Persian rulers described the varied resources and people of their territory in inscriptions. Similarly, on unifying the fragmented states of China, the founding emperor of the Qin dynasty, Qin Shi Huang (see pp.80–81) shaped his vast tomb into a microcosm of the lands he ruled.

Views of the frontier

Each dynasty or empire developed its own ideas about the structure of the world. During Assyrian and Babylonian rule from the fertile, low-lying plains of Mesopotamia, mountains were seen as wild, chaotic places threatening danger. On the other hand, the mountainous homeland of the Macedonian Greeks and Persians helped to instill in them a hardy self-image. For these empires, great rivers, such as the Danube and Indus, marked the limits of their realm.

AFTER

The rise and fall of dynasties and empires across Eurasia bequeathed a powerful idea of the inevitable fall of all worldly power. Later states with global ambitions looked back on a series of civilizations whose heirs they presumed themselves to be.

"BABYLON IS FALLEN"

Due to Babylon's dramatic role in the Bible, its fall became the archetypal example of the

"THE FALL OF BABYLON", JOHN MARTIN, 1831

decline of a once-great state. Its **apocalyptic destruction** was often depicted in art in the 19th century. Writers compared it with the **inevitable fate** of contemporary imperial and commercial powers, **Britain and the USA**.

THE FORCES OF CHAOS

To the people of imperial city civilizations, invading nomadic tribes represented the forces of chaos. In Biblical and Islamic tradition, these forces were personified by the legendary "**Gog and Magog**". Waves of migrating people from the north and east, whether Scythians or Huns **138–39, 150–51 »**, were identified by the settled states with the peoples of Gog and Magog – threatening hordes on the borders of civilization.

ISLAMIC IMAGE OF GOG AND MAGOG

Frontiers of Power

From 700 BCE, ambitious powers began bidding for supremacy over all the known world. Each of these imperial movements, from Assyria to Rome, encountered barriers to its empire-building. Chief among them were the terrain and climate of the Eurasian continent, and the resistance of neighbouring powers.

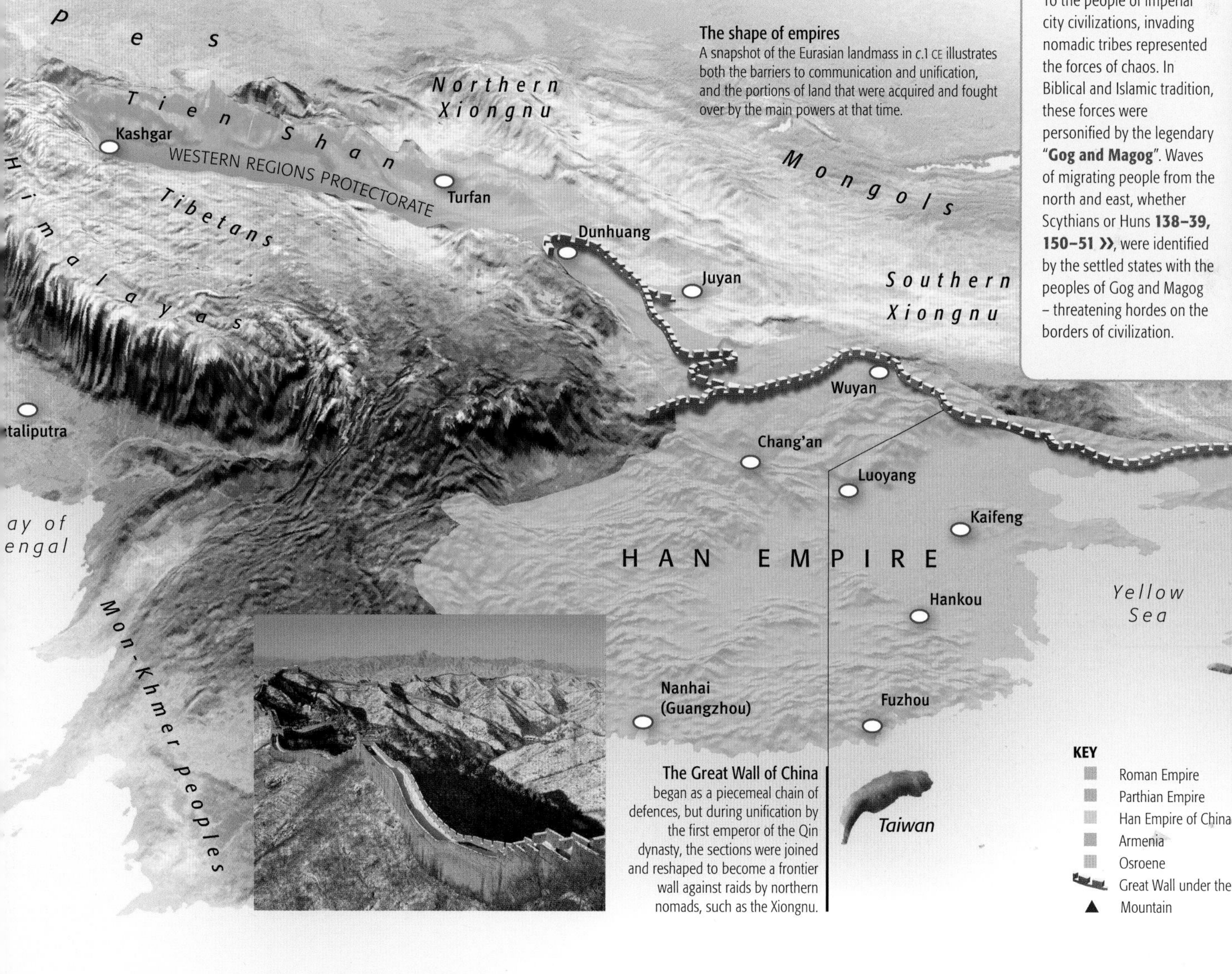

The shape of empires

A snapshot of the Eurasian landmass in c.1 CE illustrates both the barriers to communication and unification, and the portions of land that were acquired and fought over by the main powers at that time.

Persians

Tien Shan

Kashgar

WESTERN REGIONS PROTECTORATE

Northern Xiongnu

Turfan

Himalayas

Tibetans

Dunhuang

Mongols

Juyan

Southern Xiongnu

Wuyan

Chang'an

Luoyang

Kaifeng

Luolang

Pataliputra

Bay of Bengal

HAN EMPIRE

Hankou

Yellow Sea

Korea

Mon-Khmer peoples

Nanhai (Guangzhou)

Fuzhou

Taiwan

The Great Wall of China

began as a piecemeal chain of defences, but during unification by the first emperor of the Qin dynasty, the sections were joined and reshaped to become a frontier wall against raids by northern nomads, such as the Xiongnu.

KEY

- Roman Empire
- Parthian Empire
- Han Empire of China
- Armenia
- Osroene
- Great Wall under the Han
- ▲ Mountain

BEFORE

Earlier great powers of the Middle East set the scene for Persian conquest of the region.

ASSYRIAN EMPIRE
The Assyrian kings **‹‹ 38–39** had ruled lands between the Zagros Mountains of Iran and the Mediterranean. They led campaigns into **Egypt** and into the mountains of **Armenia**. When their **empire fell** in 612 BCE, they left rich cities and trade links open for exploitation by their successors.

DETAIL OF ISHTAR GATE, BABYLON, c.580 BCE

NEW BABYLON
The bulk of Assyrian lands were taken over by a dynasty ruling from the ancient city of **Babylon ‹‹ 15, 37, 44**. These Neo-Babylonian kings rebuilt Babylon into an imperial capital. Although it fell to the Persian army less than a century later, Babylonian techniques of rulership were influential in the next 200 years, inspiring a text of Cyrus (see right) and the redevelopment of cities, such as Susa (see right).

O n the territorial margins of the great powers of Mesopotamia – Assyria and Babylonia (see pp.38–39 and BEFORE) – several small states and tribes resided. Among these were the Medes and Persians. Greek historians, influenced by Persian views, describe how the Medes first developed a luxurious empire to match their Mesopotamian neighbours. Of the Persians who attended their court, one individual, Cyrus, supposedly took over the Medes' empire from within. Archaeological remains do not back up this account, however. Contemporary chronicles unearthed in Babylon instead tell how Cyrus conquered lands surrounding Mesopotamia in the mid-6th century BCE before moving on the capitals of the heartland itself. First to fall was the Lydian kingdom in the west of modern Turkey. This conquest brought Cyrus within sight of Greece. Next to fall to Cyrus was the Babylonian king Nabonidus and his capital. Detailed Babylonian and Mediterranean records also recall the victories of Cyrus's son Cambyses, who invaded Egypt in 524 BCE. Cyrus's conquests of extensive areas in central Asia in the east are less well documented. With Cambyses' annexation of Egypt, the Persians – a small tribal elite from the Iranian plateau – had acquired a world empire within a generation, creating huge pressures on the leaders. When Cambyses died, his brother Bardiya seems to have been recognized as king. But the loudest voice in the following years is that of Darius I, who alleged in a

> " A Persian man has delivered battle **far indeed from Persia**"
>
> TOMB INSCRIPTION OF DARIUS I, 549–486 BCE

The Persian Empire

From provincial beginnings, a dynasty of kings – the Achaemenids – emerged to exert power across the continent of Asia from the Mediterranean to northwest India. The empire of the Persian kings was one of an unprecedented scale.

Persepolis
A griffin head designed to sit at the top of a column watches over Persepolis, the city developed by Darius I and his successors from 519 BCE. The structures included massive columned audience halls (right) and (in the distance) smaller royal palaces built of stone and mud-brick.

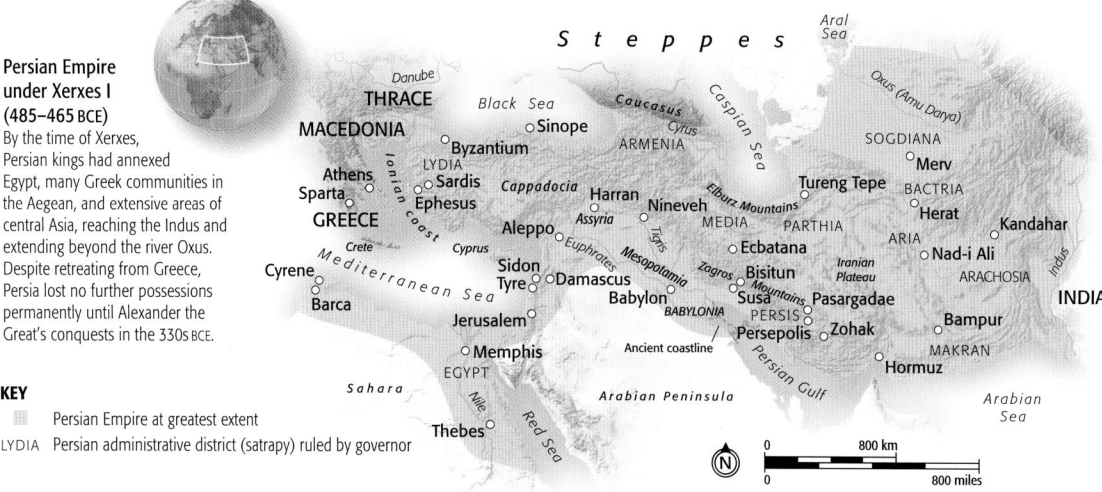

Persian Empire under Xerxes I
(485–465 BCE)
By the time of Xerxes, Persian kings had annexed Egypt, many Greek communities in the Aegean, and extensive areas of central Asia, reaching the Indus and extending beyond the river Oxus. Despite retreating from Greece, Persia lost no further possessions permanently until Alexander the Great's conquests in the 330s BCE.

KEY

▨ Persian Empire at greatest extent

LYDIA Persian administrative district (satrapy) ruled by governor

AFTER

The Persian Wars between Greek city-states and the Persian Empire are seen by many as a period that defined ideas of "East" and "West". Afterwards, the East would be regarded as foreign to the West, and vice versa. The Persian Empire also left more positive lasting legacies.

FALL OF AN EMPIRE
The last king of the Achaemenid dynasty, begun by Cyrus, was **Darius III**, who lost half of his empire to the invasion of **Alexander 50–51 ≫**. He was apparently imprisoned and killed by his own entourage in 330 BCE. Although Alexander cut a swathe through the ruling elite and burned part of Persepolis, the structure and traditions of the Persian empire exerted a huge influence on the rulers and empires who followed **52–53≫**.

AN IMPERIAL LEGACY
Apart from the practical legacy of a functioning empire, over 200 years of Achaemenid Persian rule bequeathed other ideas. **Unifying notions in Greek and Jewish** communities are linked with their experiences in the Persian empire. The Achaemenid period was a catalyst for the development of states and identities across the Middle East. **Sassanid emperors 76–77 ≫** who ruled Persia centuries later, identified themselves as **heirs to the Achaemenids**.

A royal heir
Under Darius, his son Xerxes, and subsequent kings, the image of the monarch carved into the walls of their palaces remained unchanged, emphasizing the continuity of their family line. Here, a royal heir in his court robe resembles the king exactly.

monumental inscription carved into the mountain of Bisitun that Bardiya was an imposter whom Darius had removed. In the wake of this upheaval, Darius tried to create a harmonious image of the empire under his rule. The architecture at his capitals of Persepolis and Susa incorporated peaceful images of all the peoples of the empire. In a foundation document from Susa, Darius claimed that the building materials had come from far-flung corners of his realm, from India to the Ionian coast, and that many subject peoples had brought the splendid structure to completion.

Encounters with Greece
Darius and his successors emphasized harmony and productivity under their rule. Texts on the Persian kings, written by Greeks in small states scattered across the edge of Persian territory, instead concentrate on conflict. They had a complicated relationship with their neighbouring superpower. When Persian-held Greek cities on the Ionian coast revolted in the 490s BCE, Athens and Eretria sent help from mainland Greece. The Persian leaders regarded this as rebellion by an otherwise co-operative people and sent a punitive expedition in 490 BCE, and another led by Darius's son Xerxes in 480 BCE. Although some cities came to terms with the Persians immediately, other Greek states staged valiant resistence. Their acts of defiance became defining moments in Greek consciousness of their independence of rule from the East (see pp.86–87).

A world empire
Despite withdrawal from Greece, Persia continued to wield influence in the Mediterranean, both politically and culturally. The Persian throne did not come under threat until the invasion of Alexander the Great (see pp.50–51) in 334 BCE.

The peoples who offered tribute to the Persian kings reached from Scythians of the steppe to the north, to fortresses on the frontier of Upper Egypt in the south. The range of cultures encompassed by this scope stretched from the historic, settled cities of Babylonia, where an increasingly mixed elite resided, to newly emergent kingdoms on the Caucasus frontier, who sent detachments to the Persian army and copied elements of the Persian court in their architecture and luxury objects. The difficulties of administering such a vast and varied empire were significant – even a journey between two of several royal capitals could take up to three weeks. Official royal routes, supported by regular staging posts and carefully administered travel rations, provided a swift communication network. Across this network, orders, letters, luxury supplies and expert personnel were transported. Armies could be mustered more locally according to need. The ruling Persians spoke their own language (Old Persian), which was recorded only in the limited royal inscriptions appearing on monuments in the cites of the empire. Official communication was in Aramaic, a *lingua franca* (common language) inherited from Assyrian administration, but only a few fragments of such parchment and papyrus documents have survived. Letters from Egypt and records from Afghanistan illustrate how movements of officials and provisions were closely supervised by local administrators, under the authority of "satraps", who were usually Persian governors appointed by and answerable to the king. Such interconnections led to unprecedented transmission of ideas, goods, and people across vast distances.

The Cyrus cylinder
This clay foundation document inscribed in Akkadian (see p.22–23), the traditional literary language of Babylon, gives Cyrus's carefully positive account of his conquest of the city in the 540s BCE, in which he was welcomed by the locals as a better ruler than his predecessor, the Babylonian king Nabonidus.

HOW WE KNOW

THE PALACE OF SUSA

Despite their success, the Persians left no sustained historical account of themselves. The kings did, however, leave monumental statements on their palace walls about how they had wished to be seen. Images and texts found in Darius I's palace at Susa show Darius boasting of massive excavations for a platform for his columned halls. Glazed-brick reliefs on the exterior were inspired by the palaces of Babylon (see BEFORE). They show a Persian guard decked in colourful court robes.

PERSIAN EMPEROR (580–529 BCE)

CYRUS

Folkloric tales of fate and heroism surrounded the early life of Cyrus, the founder of the Persian Empire, and were passed on by Greek writers. In his own words, Cyrus was "King of Anshan", an old city on the Iranian Plateau. He blended architectural styles from the lands he conquered in his garden-filled capital of Pasargadae. Cyrus also adapted local ideas about kingship to cast himself as a desirable ruler in the subject cities of Babylon and Jerusalem. Both Greek and Middle Eastern sources inspired a long tradition of viewing Cyrus as an ideal king.

« **BEFORE**

The period of Greek history leading up to the Archaic period was preceded the rich civilization of Mycenae and a period known as the "Dark Age" of Greece.

EARLY CIVILIZATION

Artefacts from Mycenae, Greece, are evidence of a rich Mediterranean civilization that existed before the rise of the city-states. The Mycenaean culture peaked in the 2nd millennium BCE.

THE "DARK AGE"

Between 1100–750 BCE, ancient Greece was in a "dark age" about which little is known. All of the future city-states were probably clusters of villages at this time.

EARLY ARCHAIC PERIOD

At the start of the Archaic Period (c.750–480 BCE), **increasing Mediterranean populations** fuelled the rise of cities such as Athens, Sparta, Thebes, and Corinth.

THE MAKING OF ATHENS

By the 7th century BCE, **Athens was on the rise as a leading city-state**. Central to its identity was its legal system. Around 621 BCE, Athenian magistrate **Draco** laid down a series of strict laws – probably the city's **first significant legal code**. Later, the Athenian statesman, **Solon** (c.630–560 BCE), brought in laws that helped protect the rights of "ordinary" people.

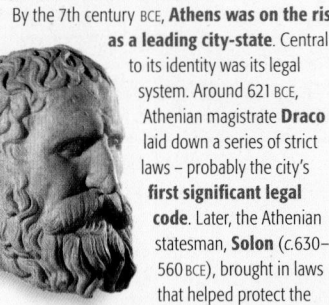

SOLON

INVENTION

GEOMETRY

The period of the city-states saw philosophers and scholars such as Thales of Miletus bringing together mathematical principles from ancient Mesopotamia and Egypt to invent geometry, (*geo* meaning Earth and *metron* measure in Greek). The defining work on geometry was written by Euclid a mathematician from Egypt, born c.300 BCE, author of a treatise on geometry, "The Elements".

11TH CENTURY RELIEF OF EUCLID

The leading centres of civilization in 6th- and 5th-centuries BCE Greece included Athens, Sparta, and Corinth. These communities are now referred to as city-states. Many of the architectural features of these city-states are shared by cities today. Typically, they were walled, with a central citadel or *acropolis* (characteristically a place of refuge housing a temple on raised ground), a main marketplace (*agora*), a sporting and socializing centre

City-states of the Greek model came to be found right across the Aegean and its islands, in western Asia Minor (Ephesus), Sicily (Syracuse), southern Italy (Tarentum), Africa (notably Cyrene, in Libya), and in France (Marseilles).

Athens

A major figure in the story of the city-state was the Athenian magistrate Cleisthenes (c.570–508 BCE) who instituted major reforms in the system

Parthenon treasure
This exquisite sculpture from the Parthenon in Athens is widely believed to have come from the workshop of Phidias, the most famous sculptor in ancient Greece.

The Greek City-states

The rise of the *polis* – city-state – in ancient Greece was a major development in world politics. Great states such as Athens, Sparta, and Corinth provided a variety of models for ruling through a system of law, with Athens in particular paving the way to a ground-breaking idea: democratic government.

(*gymnasium*), and one or more temples. Although termed "cities", population levels were low, and Sparta probably remained principally a cluster of villages. What was important, and central to the city-state concept, was that the inhabitants identified with their state above all else. So, being a "citizen" of Sparta – a Spartan – was more important than being Greek. Beyond this, the city-states often varied greatly in character, each shifting through various types of government at different times. These included monarchy, tyranny (where there was one strong leader, not necessarily an unpopular one as implied by the modern use of the word), oligarchy (rule by a small group of people, typically nobles) and democracy. The eligible male citizens participated to varying degrees in many of these forms. This participation and idea of self-rule became one of the key characteristics of many of the city-states that came later.

CITY-STATE Often translated as *polis* in the context of ancient Greece. These states were independent, self-contained entities bound by the rule of law. They reached their height during the classical period, which lasted from c.480–323 BCE.

of rule. He changed the Athenian tribal system and permanently altered Athens' political structure. He divided citizens into ten "tribes" (*phylae*), named after heroes. Attica (the area around Athens) was divided into three areas – coast, highlands, and city – and the tribes were made up of citizens from each of these areas and subdivided further into *demes*, the smallest voting districts of the polis.

The 5th-century statesman Pericles (c.495–429 BCE) moved Athens further towards a new kind of democracy (see

The acroterion was a decorative feature above the pediment.

The eastern pediment was filled with sculptures depicting Greek mythology.

Theatre at Epidauros
This vast 4th-century theatre was built at Epidaurus, a city-state in the Peloponnese. The best preserved theatre to survive from Ancient Greece, it seated around 12,000 people and has exceptional acoustics. The theatre of the Ancient Greeks influenced both the development of drama and theatre design.

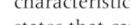

Sanctuary of Athena
This is one of several buildings clustered around the oracle at Delphi, a sacred site close to the Gulf of Corinth.

Temple of Apollo
From about 650–550 BCE, Corinth experienced a golden era. With colonies in the Adriatic and Macedonia, its command of several important harbours made it an important seafaring and trading centre.

GREEK PHILOSOPHER (384–322 BCE)

ARISTOTLE

Born in northern Greece, Aristotle was one of history's greatest philosophers and scientists (see pp.104-5). He wrote on a variety of subjects including government. In his famous work, *Politics*, he analysed many of the Greek city-states in an exploration of what might be the best form of government. In general he had a great respect for the *polis* as a good way to govern and to make the most of people's talents.

pp.54–55). Juried courts were set up, therefore moving judicial power from the city council to its citizens. Its assembly became a democratic council where all male citizens, regardless of background or wealth, had an equal vote. Athens, and the 5th-century city-states have come to be seen as the "birthplace of western democracy".

Athenian city-state life in the 5th and 4th centuries BCE also saw a remarkable flourishing of intellectual and artistic life. Playwrights including Aeschylus, Sophocles, and Euripides explored great philosophical themes that were later tackled by Plato and Aristotle (see left), and the thriving Athens that emerged from the Greek victory against Persia in the 4th century BCE saw its Acropolis rebuilt and the great Parthenon temple (below) completed.

Sparta and Corinth

Athens's great rival, Sparta, had a dual kingship from two royal lines – these kings ruled concurrently. Later, this rule was tempered by a council of aristocrats and an assembly of citizens (the *Homoioi*) – a society of equal male citizens willing to take arms for their state. Sparta also differed from the other Greek states in relying heavily on a serf population known as *helots*. In the 5th century BCE, a small, council-elected body called the *ephorate* came into being. Conceived to oversee government processes, they eventually seized power for themselves and sidelined the monarchy for a time. Sparta was famed for its army and military training.

Another powerful *polis*, Corinth, commanded a strong strategic position geographically on the narrow strip of land connecting mainland Greece.

The struggle for supremacy

The rise of hoplite warfare (see pp.70–71) in the 7th century BCE, was central to the rise of the city-states. As the use of the phalanx formation became widespread (see pp.68–69), citizens who fought for their states expected some political say in return. Rivalry between city-states was constant, particularly between Athens and Sparta. Some events brought the states together, such as the Panhellenic games, which included the Olympic Games, and religious festivals. The city-states combined forces against the Persians in the 5th century (see pp.46–47), in an alliance effectively led by Sparta (although Athens was later dominant). Victory brought confidence and a sense of identity and unity.

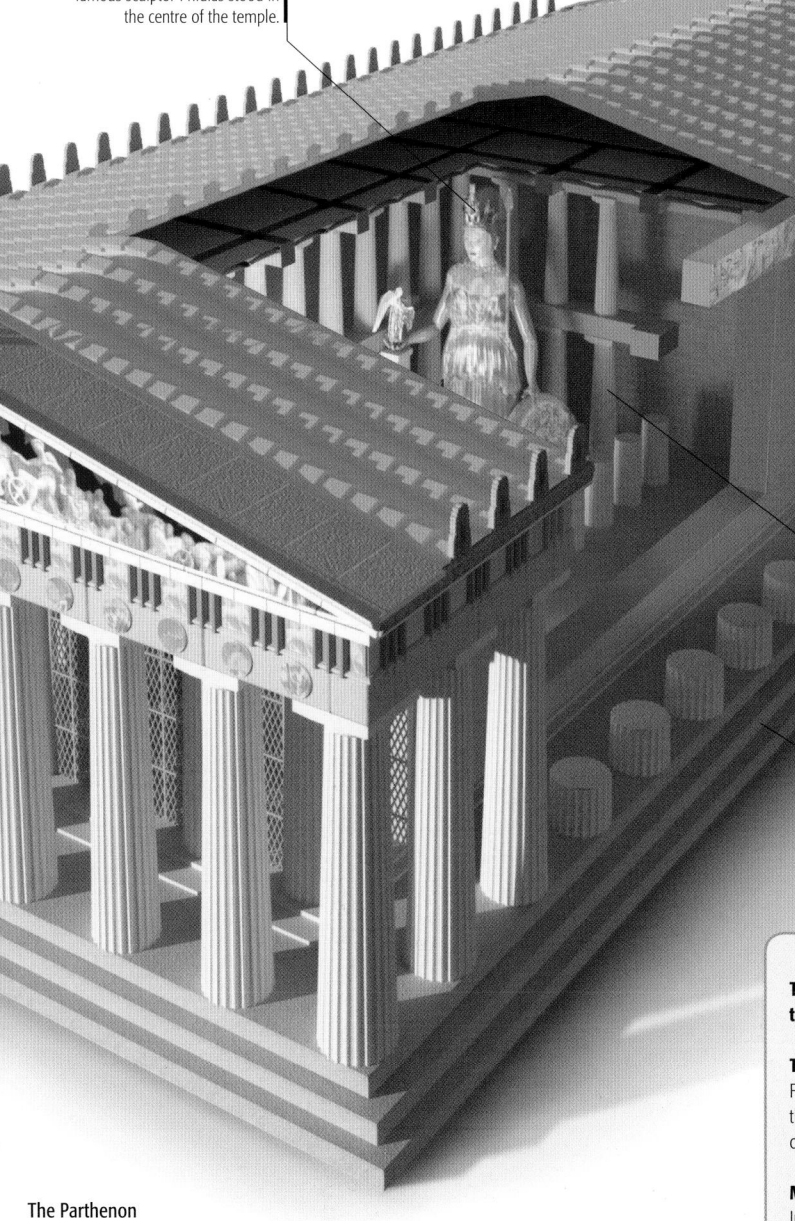

A gold and ivory statue (now lost) of the goddess Athena by the famous sculptor Phidias stood in the centre of the temple.

The many columns were fluted, without bases and with square capitals at the top.

The interior of the temple was divided into three aisles.

Distinctive three-stepped base leading into the temple.

The Parthenon
This breathtaking marble temple was built on Athens' acropolis between 447 and 432 BCE, on a wave of euphoria that engulfed the Athenians after their defeat of Persia. It was dedicated to the city's patron goddess, Athena.

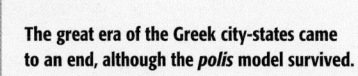

AFTER

The great era of the Greek city-states came to an end, although the *polis* model survived.

THEBAN DOMINANCE
From 371–362 BCE, the city-state of Thebes gained the upper hand. This **chaotic era** brought more city-state conflicts that weakened their power.

MACEDONIAN CONTROL
In 338 BCE, the Macedonian King **Philip II 50–51 »** defeated the Greeks and formed the **League of Corinth** to support his own imperial plans.

THE CITY OF ROME
Rome grew in power **60–61 »** and ruled over an empire using some of the ancient Greek models.

THE MIDDLE AGES AND THE RENAISSANCE
The 11th century CE saw the rise of **Italian city-states** such as Venice and Pisa. By the 13th–15th centuries other examples flourished at Florence, Padua, Hamburg, and Flanders. The Renaissance rediscovery of **classical ideas and learning in western Europe** brought Plato and Aristotle's ideas on government to the fore **190–93 »**.

RULER AND MILITARY LEADER Born 356 BCE Died 323 BCE

Alexander the Great

"There is **nothing impossible** to him **who will try**" ATTRIBUTED TO ALEXANDER THE GREAT

In less than a decade of warfare, Alexander of Macedonia, known as "the Great", created one of the largest land empires the world has ever seen, stretching from Greece to northern India. His career of conquest was built upon that of his father, Philip II, king of Macedonia in Greece. It was Philip who turned Macedonia into a regional power in the Greek world. He created the army of heavy cavalry and pike-wielding infantry that became the instrument for Alexander's empire-building.

From an early age Alexander was marked out among Philip's children as his most likely successor – he acted as regent of Macedonia and keeper of the royal seal while Philip was making an expedition against Byzantium in 340 BCE. At the age of 18 he proved his courage and skill in war, leading a cavalry charge at the battle of Chaeronea in 338 BCE that crushed the Sacred Band – the famed elite Greek infantry from Thebes. Yet his right to the succession was by no means assured, for the throne did not necessarily pass

Alexander in action
This Roman mosaic shows Alexander riding his horse Bucephalus into battle against the Persians at Issus in 333 BCE. Leading his army from the front, Alexander was never defeated in battle, despite fighting armies three times the size of his own.

Birthplace of an icon

The Macedonians originated as hill tribesmen in the mountains of northern Greece, although Alexander was born on the coastal plain, at Pella, where his royal predecessors had established their capital.

> # " A tomb now suffices him for whom the whole world was not sufficient"
>
> SAID OF ALEXANDER AFTER DEATH

to the eldest son and the king had several wives. There were rumours that Alexander's mother, Olympias, tried to have Philip assassinated before a son by another wife could grow old enough to succeed him. Alexander certainly acted ruthlessly to secure the succession once his father was dead, killing anybody at court who threatened his authority.

Heroic ambitions

When, in 334 BCE, Alexander led his army across the Hellespont – the body of water that separates Europe from Asia Minor – to liberate the Greek cities under Persian rule in Asia Minor, he was fulfilling a plan previously announced by his father. But the astounding campaign of conquest that followed was entirely the expression of his own ambition. Alexander claimed descent in his father's line from the Greek hero-god Herakles (Hercules) and through his mother from the legendary hero of the Trojan War, Achilles. One of his first acts on crossing to Asia Minor was to visit the site of Troy as an act of homage to his ancestor. Later, in Egypt, his claims were raised a notch higher when a priest at the desert shrine of Ammon hailed him as the "son of Zeus", the king of the Greek gods, who was believed to be an ancestor of the Macedonian kings. Alexander's self-image as an heroic man of destiny chosen by the gods inspired his relentless drive to conquest.

Military leader

Alexander's army served him as the dedicated followers of a great fighting man. His elite cavalry, the Companions, were a tight-knit group with whom he fought, ate, and drank as the first among equals. On the battlefield Alexander led from the front. He liked to spearhead the cavalry charge and was often the first to storm city walls during a siege. He could be supremely reckless of his own safety, yet he was also thoroughly professional in organizing and motivating his cavalry and infantry in battle. His decisive victories over numerically superior Persian armies at Issus and Gaugamela showed a shrewd eye for the weaknesses of an apparently

Alexandria's lighthouse
Alexander founded Alexandria as a Macedonian capital for Egypt. Its lighthouse was one of the seven wonders of the ancient world.

powerful enemy as well as an instinct for gambling on aggression. It was typical of Alexander's unresting ambition that the conquest of the mighty Persian Empire, achieved by 330 BCE, brought no end to his campaigning. He went on fighting, not just enforcing his claim to rule all the Persian domains, but also pushing further into India.

Persian influence

Alexander saw himself as spreading Greek civilization by the sword. He founded Greek cities, the most famous of which was Alexandria in Egypt, and sought to Hellenize – to make Greek – the Persians whom he conquered. But his adoption of the mantle of the Persian Empire created great strains with his Macedonian followers. The traditions of Persian court ceremony were alien to Macedonians. The Macedonian veterans were also jealous when new Persian followers found favour with Alexander. Discontent came to a head in a series of mutinies that Alexander violently suppressed.

Noble savage

His fame in antiquity was unequalled, yet he left no creative legacy. Alexander was a ruthless man who killed both in anger and in cold blood. After Alexander died at the age of 32, his mummified body was taken to Egypt, where it remained on display for more than 500 years.

LIVING GOD

This silver coin shows Alexander as the semi-divine Herakles, distinguished by his lionskin cap. On other coins he is represented as the horned god Ammon, the supreme Egyptian deity. Alexander's close association with the gods and a suggested direct paternal link to Herakles, rather than Philip, enforced his own sense of destiny. According to one written source, Alexander attended banquets in Persia dressed as gods. The myth of his divinity was widely accepted and shrines were raised in his name.

ALEXANDER AS HERAKLES

- **July 356 BCE** Born in Pella, Macedonia, the son of Macedon's ruler, Philip II, and his fourth wife Olympias.

- **343 BCE** The Greek philosopher Aristotle is brought to Macedon to educate him.

- **338 BCE** Plays a leading role in the defeat of Athens and Thebes at the battle of Chaeronea. His father makes himself leader of all the Greek city states except Sparta.

- **337 BCE** Philip marries a Macedonian woman, Eurydice. She bears him a son who could threaten Alexander's claim to inherit the throne.

- **336 BCE** Philip is assassinated by a bodyguard, Pausanias. Alexander succeeds to the throne and has Attalus, the chief supporter of Eurydice, killed.

- **334 BCE** Crosses the Hellespont at the head of an allied army. He visits the site of Troy and then conquers western Asia Minor, defeating a Persian army at Granicus.

ALEXANDER IDEALIZED

- **November 333 BCE** Defeats Persian King Darius III at Issus in modern Syria, but the Persian ruler escapes.

- **332 BCE** Takes the cities of Tyre (Lebanon) and Gaza (Israel) after sieges. He proceeds to Egypt, and is hailed as pharaoh. He visits the oracle of the god Zeus-Ammon at the Siwa Oasis and founds the city of Alexandria.

- **October 331 BCE** After a long march east from Egypt, he encounters the Persian army at Gaugamela. The Persians are utterly defeated and Darius flees for his life.

- **330 BCE** Darius is murdered by his Bactrian entourage. Alexander establishes himself as successor to the Persian throne. He suppresses a conspiracy in his army; his second-in-command Parmenion is among those put to death.

- **328 BCE** Falling into a rage during a drunken banquet, Alexander kills Clitus the Black, one of his leading Macedonian officers.

- **327 BCE** Marries Roxana (Roxanne), a Sogdian princess. He bloodily suppresses a conspiracy by his royal pages, who oppose his adoption of Persian customs.

- **326 BCE** After invading the Punjab, he defeats King Porus at the battle of the Hydaspes. His beloved horse Bucephalus is killed. Reaching the Hyphasis river his soldiers mutiny and force Alexander to turn back, following the Jhelum, a tributary of the Indus River, to the sea.

- **326 BCE** He leads part of his army back to Persia in a march across the Gedrosian Desert that costs many soldiers their lives.

- **324 BCE** The Macedonians in Alexander's army mutiny as he recruits increasing numbers of Persians. Many Macedonian veterans are discharged. Alexander is plunged in deep grief when his closest friend, and rumoured lover, Hephaestion dies.

- **11 June 323 BCE** Alexander dies of a fever in Babylon, leaving no clear successor.

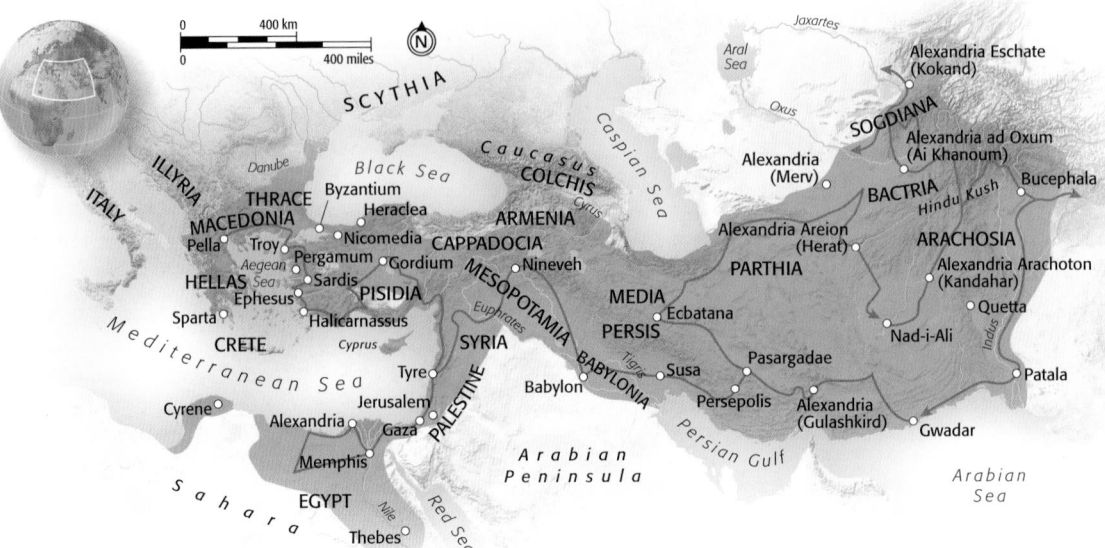

The Greeks in Asia

The Achaemenid Persian Empire had ruled over an area extending from the Mediterranean to the Indus valley. It was all conquered by Alexander the Great in less than ten years, his army bringing with it ideas and tastes from Greek civilization that took root and flourished alongside local traditions.

Alexander's conquests created an empire even larger than the Persian empire at its height. Anybody wishing to rule over it would have to take into account the legacy and traditions of Persia's Achaemenid rulers.

THE ACHAEMENID EMPIRE

The **Achaemenid Empire** << 46–47 reached its greatest extent under Darius I and his son Xerxes I in the 6th century BCE, and lost very little territory before Alexander << 50–51 began his conquest in 334 BCE. Divided into **satrapies** (provinces governed by men appointed by the king), it had several royal capitals. The ceremonial capital of **Persepolis** was largely destroyed by Alexander, but its great stairways, decorated with reliefs of **subject rulers** bringing tribute, survive.

BAS-RELIEF OF SUBJECT RULERS, PERSEPOLIS

Before his death, Alexander had placed the key provinces in the conquered Persian empire under the control of trusted governors. However, he allowed local systems of government, to which the people were accustomed, to continue. Alexander appreciated the role of the Persians as an imperial people and, according to some accounts, tried to create a ruling race through intermarriage between his officers and Persian noblewomen.

The process of changing one mode of rule for another, he knew, was a delicate one and needed patience. He died in Babylon in 322 BCE (see p.51) before he realized his ambition of creating a completely unified empire

The conquests of Alexander the Great

In just ten years Alexander conquered the Persian Empire, the largest empire the world had ever seen. His own empire now stretched from North Africa and the eastern Mediterranean to the Indus valley in northern India. On his death in 323 BCE, his generals fought to decide who could inherit the largest share of the spoils.

KEY

■ Empire and dependent regions of Alexander
— Route of Alexander the Great

The Seleucids were victims of their own initial success. Their sprawling empire was too large and too diverse to hold together.

THE END OF THE SELEUCIDS
In the 2nd century BCE the Seleucids were driven from Persia and Mesopotamia by the **Parthians 76–77 ≫**. By 100 BCE the empire had been reduced to Antioch and a few other Syrian cities. They continued to exist only because powers such as Rome **60–69 ≫** and the **Ptolemaic dynasty 72–75 ≫** in Egypt did not see them as a serious threat. It was the Roman general **Pompey** who finally put an end to the Seleucid Empire, annexing Syria as a Roman province in 64 BCE.

THE PARTHIAN EMPIRE
The end of the Seleucid Empire left the Romans and the Parthians to contest the Middle East. When the Romans tried to invade Mesopotamia in 53 BCE, the Parthians defeated them at **Carrhae**, but the Romans had the better of later clashes, sacking the

Parthian capital of **Ctesiphon** three times in the 2nd century CE. The Parthians, originally a semi-nomadic steppe people, left much of the administrative structure of the Seleucid empire intact – coins with Greek inscriptions were minted as late as the 2nd century CE. All this changed after the Parthians had been ousted by the Persian **Sassanids 76–77 ≫** in 236 CE.

GRAECO-BUDDHIST ART
Aspects of Hellenistic culture also survived further east, in **Bactria** (in Afghanistan) and parts of northern India such as Gandhara. Between the 2nd century BCE and the 4th century CE many sculptures from Bactria and the so-called **Indo-Greek kingdoms 78–79 ≫** display a combination of the artistic styles of India, Persia, and Greece.

GREEK-INFLUENCED BUDDHA; BACTRIA, 3RD CENTURY CE

East meets West in Nemrud Dag, Turkey
In the 1st century BCE, the king of Commagene, Antiochus I, built a mountain-top shrine where the fine statuary depicts both Greek and Persian deities and uses a combination of eastern and western artistic styles.

---

embracing Macedonia, Greece, Egypt, and all the Persian territory he had conquered in Asia.

According to Plutarch's biography of Alexander, written nearly 400 years after the event, his body lay in its coffin for several days without showing any signs of decay, while his generals argued over who should succeed him.

The body, an important talisman for Alexander's potential successors, was embalmed to be taken home, but it was diverted to Alexandria in Egypt, where it was exhibited in a glass case.

Bactrian deities
This plate from Ai Khanoum (in modern Afghanistan) shows the Greek goddess Cybele in a chariot pulled by lions in front of a Persian priest at a fire altar.

Wars of succession
Alexander's wife Roxana had a son in August 332 BCE, but he never grew up to succeed his father – he was killed in 310 by one of the generals competing to take over the empire. Alexander had told his commanders that the succession lay with the "fittest". Bloody conflict to determine who this would be raged almost continuously from 323–279 BCE. By then, three main Hellenistic states had been established. The smallest was the Antigonid kingdom, which ruled in Macedonia and Greece. Constantly involved in wars with the Greek city-states (see pp.48–49), it eventually fell to Rome (see pp.60–69) in 168 BCE. The richest and most secure was the

Ptolemaic kingdom (see pp.72–73), which ruled Egypt and Palestine. It lasted until 30 BCE, when in the reign of Cleopatra VII (see pp.74–75), it was annexed by Rome. The largest of the successor states, however, was the Seleucid Empire, founded in 312 BCE by Seleucus I Nicator, when he secured Babylon and with it control of Persia, Mesopotamia, Syria, and much of Anatolia.

The three empires spread Greek ideas through their political institutions, town planning, and architecture. They were eager to show that they preserved the cultural freedoms of the Hellenic ideal, so the cities they built had all the attributes of a Greek city-state: an *agora*, or place for public debate, temples to all or one God, and spectacular theatres.

Greek culture in Asia
The Seleucid empire established many Greek-style cities to help control their huge territory. Seleucus I had a new capital, Seleucia, built in Mesopotamia, on the Tigris, near Babylon, but the capital was soon moved to Antioch in Syria. The Seleucids had a relaxed attitude to the religions practised in their territories and Greek ideas were accepted alongside old Persian, Jewish, and other local traditions.

In the course of the 3rd century BCE the Seleucids had to abandon their eastern provinces of Bactria and Parthia, but that did not mean the end of Greek influence there. The distant Bactrian kingdom (in present-day Afghanistan) retained a magnificent Greek coinage, and archaeological sites such as Ai Khanoum (thought to be the city of Alexandria on the Oxus) reveal that Bactrian cities continued to follow Greek models with temples and other public buildings fronted by beautiful Corinthian columns.

To the west of the Seleucid sphere of influence, in present-day Turkey, Pergamum, an important new regional

HELLENISTIC The three centuries after Alexander's death in 323 BCE are known as the Hellenistic Age, when post-Classical Greek culture spread far beyond its original homeland. Greek ideas and artistic styles were adopted in Asia, Egypt, and, most importantly, Rome.

power, was emerging. Attalus I Soter, who ruled from 241–197 BCE, took the title of king of Pergamum and made his city into a major centre for literature, philosophy, and the arts. It had its own acropolis, magnificent temples, a theatre seating 10,000 people, and a vast library. Another fascinating Hellenistic state was Commagene in the southeast of present-day Turkey, which broke away from the Seleucids around 162 BCE. It absorbed Persian influences from the east and Greek from the west. Antiochus I, who ruled from 70–38 BCE, built a monument to himself at Nemrud Dag, which is the most extraordinary fusion of Hellenism and Eastern culture.

IDEA
PHILHELLENISM

Admiration for Greek philosophy, poetry, and sculpture survives to this day, although it probably peaked in 18th- and 19th-century Europe. *The Apotheosis of Homer* (right) by Antonio Canova (1757–1822) embodies the spirit of admiration for Classical Greece. Philhellenism (love of Greek culture and the belief that theirs was the perfect way to order society) takes no account of the fact that Greek women had no vote or that Greek society depended on the labour of slaves.

BEFORE

Ancient Greece was not a unified nation but a mosaic of around 150 city-states sharing a common language and religion; the two most important were Athens and Sparta.

A NATION OF CITY-STATES
After the destruction of the Mycenaean civilization (whose stories, including the *Odyssey*, were recorded by Homer), ancient Greece entered a dark age, about which we know little **‹‹ 48**. Cities and their surrounding land became independent units known as city-states (*polis*).

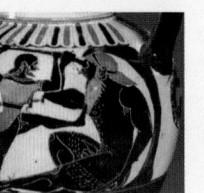

SCENE FROM "THE ODYSSEY"

THE HOPLITE REVOLUTION
The city-states relied on their armies for their protection. Increased trade in the 7th century BCE began a military and political revolution. The new rich could now afford their arms and supplied regiments of hoplites (armoured infantry) alongside the aristocratic cavalry. The need to act collectively in warfare led to a new form of government based on the shared interests of a broader section of society.

A thens' first lawgiver was Draco (*c.*624 BCE). He instigated severe penalties, designed to stop aristocrats from taking the law into their own hands. In 594 BCE military defeat by the city of Megara and growing social tensions led to the appointment of Solon as supreme *archon* (magistrate). Since rural impoverishment had caused an agrarian (farming) and military crisis in Athens, Solon's solution was to abolish slavery brought about by debt, free the peasantry from feudal servitude, and make wealth rather than birth the prerequisite of political office, thus reducing the power of the aristocracy.

To encourage good governance (*eunomia*), he created a council (*boule*) to prepare the weekly business of the lot from each of the 10 tribes, which supplied the smaller 50-member group of council leaders (*Prytaneis*) to administer the daily affairs of government. Its composition was changed on a regular basis so that no one remained in power too long. Jury members for the courts were also chosen by lot to avoid corruption.

The 6,000-strong *ecclesia* convened weekly on the Pnyx, a site near the Acropolis, to vote on matters presented by the *Prytaneis* and elect the 10 generals (*strategoi*). Since Athens' defence could not be left to chance, these powerful officials, who controlled the army and the navy, could be re-elected.

The effect of all these reforms was to reduce the powers of the aristocracy further while creating a united body

Birthplace of democracy
The Acropolis ("high city") of Athens was its spiritual centre. The Parthenon (finished in 431 BCE), the temple at the top of the Acropolis dedicated to the goddess Athena, was built by the Athenian general Pericles following the defeat of the Persians, with money from the Delian League, as a symbol of the city's glory.

> " … a man who takes no **interest in politics**… has no business here at all…"
>
> PERICLES, 495–429 BCE

The **Birth** of **Democracy**

The oldest and most stable democracy in ancient Greece developed in Athens, evolving constitutionally through monarchy, aristocracy, and tyranny before arriving at the principle of equality for all citizens. However, as in other Greek *polis*, women, slaves, and foreigners were excluded from participating.

KLEROTERION

KLEPSHYDRA (WATER CLOCK)

OSTRAKON (VOTING TABLET)

Objects of democracy
The *kleroterion* was used to select jurors. Slots in the device (fragment shown) held volunteers' names and black and white balls were dropped down a tube to select them. Water clocks were used to time the speeches in the assemblies. Citizens inscribed the names of overly ambitious politicians that they wished to ostracize from the city on an *ostrakon*.

citizen's assembly (*ecclesia*), and a popular court of appeal (*heliaia*) for legal redress against abuses of power. Citizens were divided into four classes: aristocrat, "horseman", hoplite, and the poor (*thetes*), each of which elected 100 members to the council. Poor citizens could only vote at this stage.

In 560 BCE, the aristocrat Peisistratus took advantage of incessant internal feuding to seize power in a popular coup, initiating land reforms on behalf of the poor. It was against a backdrop of the increasingly harsh rule of his son that a progressive aristocrat called Cleisthenes overthrew this tyranny in 507 BCE, introducing the revolutionary reforms that would transform Athens into a formidable power and Greece's first true democracy.

DEMOCRACY From the Ancient Greek words "demos", meaning "people", and "kratos", meaning "power".

Athens' democratic evolution
Cleisthenes created a future for Athens' citizens to match their potential. In place of *eunomia*, he promised *isonomia* (equality). To neutralize factional feuding, he tore up the old network of family and regional loyalties, redividing Athens into 139 voting districts (*demes*) arranged into 10 tribes (*phylae*) made up of citizens from each of the three regions – coast, interior, and city – in an elaborate system of checks and balances. Annual membership of an expanded council of 500 was chosen by

of men loyal to Athens above all else. As a further safeguard, ostracism was introduced to banish any "dangerous" leaders from the city for 10 years.

Imperial power
With unity at home, Athens set about raising her profile abroad, investing in a powerful navy after their victory over the Persians at Marathon in 480 BCE, and acknowledging the growing importance of their oarsmen following an impressive naval victory over the Persians at Salamis in 490 BCE. Increasing colonization, dominance of the trade routes, the discovery of silver, and the setting up of the Delian League in 477 BCE – an alliance with other city-states to protect themselves from future Persian invasions – made Athens the dominant power in Greece.

A brilliant orator called Pericles presided over a "Golden Age" of Athenian prosperity (451–429 BCE) and cultural preeminence. He consolidated the democratic "constitution" by compensating the poorer citizens for their time on jury service or attending the *ecclesia*, and limiting citizenship to those with two Athenian parents.

Democracy in Athens was suspended and quickly restored twice during the 5th century BCE. It was finally extinguished during the 2nd century BCE by an expanding Roman Empire.

AFTER

It took a long time for the idea of democracy to become widely adopted, taking until the mid-20th century to become the most common form of government.

ROMAN VOTING

ROMAN DEMOCRACY
Republican government in ancient Rome was based on elected representatives (representative democracy) rather than Athenian-style direct democracy. **Power was shared** between the two Consuls, the Senate (aristocracy), and the Plebs (commoners). Over time, the Plebeian Assembly became the dominant legislature.

AMERICAN GOVERNMENT
The architects of the first modern democracies in the US **232–33 ››** and France **236–37 ››**, modelled them on the Roman Republic with representation limited to the wealthier classes only. The Athenians thought that representative democracy was tilted in favour of wealthier candidates. During the campaign for the 2008 **American presidential election**, the main candidates raised over $25 million each.

THE WORLD'S LARGEST DEMOCRACY
India's democracy governs a population of **over a billion people**.

From Myth to History

As Greece emerged from a "Dark Age" and writing was rediscovered, new ways of passing on knowledge and stories developed. For the first time in the Western world, history was recorded in prose, rather than verse – the poet became historian and artistic licence gave way to the goal of accuracy and explanation.

During excavations at the Palace of Knossos on the island of Crete in 1900, the British archaeologist Arthur Evans found a huge collection of written clay tablets. They had survived a fire that had destroyed the palace some time after 1400 BCE. When the script, known as "Linear B", was deciphered, it turned out to be the first known example of early Greek writing. The art of writing then seems to have been lost to the Greeks during the so-called "Dark Age" (c.1100–c.750 BCE).

The subsequent development of the Greek alphabet and writing led to the recording of history. Before the 6th century BCE, history was recounted in the form of poetry and was mixed with folklore and myth, making it hard to separate fact from fiction.

Ancient Greece's most famous poet, Homer, (see below) is an important

figure in the transmission of history in the Western world, although he probably never wrote down his own poems, and the subjects he used were a mixture of myth, folk memory, and fact. The story of the Trojan War, which may have been an actual event of the 13th century BCE, inspired both his epic poems, the *Iliad* and the *Odyssey*. In the first of these, two intense weeks in the story of the war are told. The *Odyssey* tells the tale of the Greek hero Odysseus's ten-year journey home from the Trojan War. Both stories show a desire to keep alive memory of past glories and hinge on Greek memories of an expedition to Troy in Asia Minor (Turkey). The actual events, if they happened at all, were not recorded in any surviving written accounts. This meant that over the intervening centuries, the facts were mingled with myth and travellers' tales to become the story we know today.

Fantasy and fact

One 19th-century archaeologist, Heinrich Schliemann, became obssessed with the story of the Trojan War and was determined to find evidence that it had actually taken place. Using the text of the *Iliad* as a guide, Schliemann found a vast city complex buried under various layers at Hissalik in northwest Turkey. One layer of the city had been destroyed by fire c.1180 BCE. He was convinced that this was Troy, where the mythical Achilles

had killed the Trojan hero Hector. Schliemann's archaeological practices destroyed a great deal of the value of the site. Later experts were appalled at what he had done and even questioned the authenticity of the many gold artefacts he claimed he had found. Schliemann went on to find more treasures at Mycenae on the Greek mainland, including the mask (see right) that he

Odysseus's voyage
This 3rd century CE Roman mosaic shows Homer's Odysseus on his epic journey. In this part of the story he is lured onto a rocky island by the singing of the sirens.

declared to be one of the leaders of the Greek siege of Troy, saying, "I have gazed into the face of Agamemnon". It is probable that it was in fact part of a royal burial treasure from a period before the Trojan War.

First written history

An early Greek writer to break away from this mix of myth and reality was Hecataeus of Miletus (c.550–490 BCE), who is considered by some to be the first history writer. In one of his works he set down in writing stories that had been passed down orally from generation to generation as well as recording family genealogies. Another writer, Simonides (c.556–469 BCE), referred to events of the Persian invasion of 480 BCE in his poems.

It is a later writer, however, who is known today as the "father of history". Herodotus (484–425 BCE) wrote *The Histories*, which focused on the origins of the war between Greece and Persia that took place at the beginning of the 5th century BCE. He was interested in studying human nature and the world around him and recorded what he saw as he travelled the length and breadth of the ancient world. Although he came from Halicarnassus (modern Bodrum in Turkey), he also lived in Athens for a time. His travels allegedly took him to Egypt, Italy, Sicily, and Babylon, and his writing is full of entertaining detail about the customs and habits of the countries he visited.

>  **HISTORY** The word was first used by the Greek writer, Herodotus. In ancient Greek the word meant "rational enquiry".

Herodotus is remembered today because he was the first to write about events of his own time in prose rather than verse, and to organize his material systematically. He inspired later historians to break with the old epic tradition and write in this style, recounting real events rather than the mythical exploits of heroes and gods.

The work of Herodotus cannot, however, be relied upon as fact. His writing still depended, to some extent, upon oral history and was coloured by folklore and tradition. He claimed to have authenticated his information, but critics in antiquity argued that it was not wholly accurate. The later Greek historian and biographer Plutarch (c.46–119 CE) had a very low opinion

---

BEFORE

Epic narratives often lie between myth and history. Such poetry was born out of an oral tradition and was common in many ancient cultures before written history.

URUK

The epic (long narrative poem) of **Gilgamesh** is the story of a semi-divine king of Uruk that was told by storytellers in the 3rd millenium BCE. Some parts of the story are **fantastical** and others may be based on **real events**.

ANCIENT BABYLON

Scribes in Babylon **« 15, 37, 44** recorded events relating to the **history of their city** from the 2nd millennium BCE. The records contained references to earlier semi-legendary times and were a mixture of fact and fiction.

SCENE FROM THE EPIC OF GILGAMESH

GREEK POET (c.8TH CENTURY BCE)

HOMER

There is no firm evidence about the life of the most famous Greek epic poet. He is believed to have lived in Greece in the 8th or 7th century BCE, but we do not know what he looked like or where he originally came from. Traditionally, he is said to have been blind and to have told his stories as he travelled around Greece. His two great works, the *Iliad* and the *Odyssey*, began life as epic poetry, recited aloud to audiences. Only later were they written down. Homer is still considered one of the most influential writers of the Western world.

"The Mask of Agamemnon"

This astonishing burial mask was found at Mycenae in Greece by the archaeologist Heinrich Schliemann in 1876. He named the mask after the leader of the Greek troops during the Trojan War. It is part of a collection of royal treasure dating from c.1600 BCE.

Over the centuries, written histories, like the folk tales that preceded them, have been shaped by the values of the times in which they have been recorded.

THE EPIC TRADITION

Old stories told in traditional ways **connect powerfully** with the listeners, as they are rooted in local landscape, history, and folklore. *Beowulf* is an English epic poem of the 10th century CE. The story concerns the struggle between forces of **good and evil**. In Cyprus, shepherds still tell stories about one-eyed giants, horned gods, and Bacchanalian feasts in nearby river beds.

BEOWULF MANUSCRIPT

MODERN MYTH AND HISTORY

Kathakali stories of Hindu myth, using dance and masks, costumes and music to accompany oral texts, are still **performed today**. The *Mahabharata* and the *Ramayana*, tales about the various Hindu divinities **97 》**, are told to people who may be **unable to read**, in the same way that the stories of Homer were told in ancient Greece.

KATHAKALI DANCER

of the accuracy of *The Histories* and called Herodotus "a father of lies".

Expressing a viewpoint

The Athenian writer Thucydides (c.460–c.400 BCE) also took a new approach to recording history. His famous *History of the Peloponnesian War*, written in 41 books, tells the story of the war between Athens and Sparta (see p.143). As well as recounting the events, Thucydides examined the long-term causes of the war and the moral issues it raised. A striking characteristic of his writing is the use of long speeches, not reproduced word for word, but rewritten to express Thucydides's personal opinion. One famous example is the speech made by Pericles (see p.54), in which the city of Athens and all its achievements are praised in a funeral oration for those who had died in the war.

Despite their shortcomings – the inaccuracies of Herodotus and the poetic embellishments of Thucydides – the two Greeks are rightly acknowledged as the first true historians in the West. The era of recounting heroic deeds in epic poetry was over and a new method of recording the past had begun.

" To preserve the memory of the past by **putting on record** [our own] astonishing achievements…"

ONE OF THE AIMS OF HERODOTUS, SET OUT AT THE BEGINNING OF "THE HISTORIES", c.440 BCE

HOW WE KNOW

VIEW OF THE WORLD

This map, from a woodcut made in 1867, shows Herodotus's view of the world, based on the descriptions found in his writings, with Asia Minor and the Middle East at its centre. Although he did not venture far in modern terms – he was unaware of northern Europe, for example – he included an extraordinary amount of detail about the places he did visit, (Egypt, Africa, Italy, Sicily, and other parts of the Mediterranean) including the length of rivers and size of continents. Much of this was previously unknown.

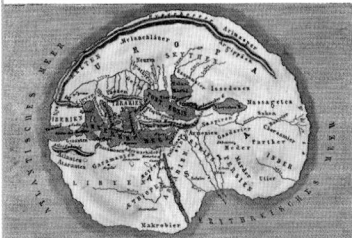

Linear B script

This tablet is inscribed with early Greek writing known as "Linear B". It is thought to be a Bronze Age form of Greek used to record lists and inventories at Knossos.

For the first few hundred years of classical Greek civilization, scientific thought was not unlike that of earlier periods. Just as in Mesopotamia and Egypt, practical knowledge was used to help make life easier. Some individuals acquired skills in mathematics and astronomical observation, but they were used for practical purposes. Mathematics, therefore, was used in commerce and construction, and knowledge of astronomy in timekeeping.

When it came to accounting for natural phenomena, however, ancient civilizations tended to be far less practical. They relied unquestioningly upon fanciful mythological explanations for everyday events. Myths involving supernatural gods were not tested – or even questioned.

After about 600 BCE, however, some began to question these ideas and wonder about the world around them.

Natural philosophers

These thinkers, or "natural philosophers", employed logic and reason to question the accepted myths. Thales of Miletus (c.624–c.526 BCE) is often referred to as the "father of science". Like many of the Greek scientific thinkers, Thales pondered the nature of matter. He suggested that all solids, liquids, and gases are ultimately made of water. This makes some sense – water is one of

Praising the gods
This clay tablet was left at a temple, and was dedicated to god of healing, Asclepius, from someone who believed their foot to have been healed through traditional rather than scientific medicine.

(born c.480 BCE) and his student Democritus (born c.460 BCE) suggested that matter is made up of tiny, indivisible particles separated by empty space. Their ideas are similar to modern atomic theory.

All of these early thinkers grappled with philosophical concepts, such as change, infinity, and existence versus non-existence (see pp.84–85). It is not important whether the theories were

mathematics in formulating their theories. Mathematics can be divided into geometry – the study of the relative position and size of objects including the Earth – and arithmetic – the study of numbers. Geometry had been used to help astronomers and architects, while arithmetic formed the basis of commerce. The natural philosophers used mathematics as a way of seeking truth.

Triumphs of Greek Science

Science is an attempt to understand and explain the world around us. The modern scientific method – a combination of observation, hypothesis, experiment, and theory – was established in the 17th century. But its roots lie with the ancient Greeks who were among the first to think scientifically and search for plausible answers to life's mysteries through logic and observation.

BEFORE

Some of the scientific ideas of the Greeks had been considered by earlier civilizations.

RATIONAL THOUGHT
In ancient India and China philosophers thought about the world rationally, explaining causes of events by "laws", rather than myth.

EGYPTIAN ASTRONOMY
In Mesopotamia, the Babylonians and Egyptians had writing systems and calendars, and managed **impressive construction projects** that required **exact measurements**.

EGYPTIAN CONSTELLATIONS

the few substances that we can observe directly changing between these three states. Another philosopher, Anaximenes (585–525 BCE), suggested that air was the "fundamental" substance, while Heraclitus (535–475 BCE) thought fire might fit the role. Inevitably, a more sophisticated and believable theory emerged, drawing on those that had gone before – the theory of the four elements, put forward by Empedocles (490–430 BCE). This theory explained many common phenomena in terms of the movement and interaction of air, earth, fire, and water.

Towards the end of the 5th century BCE, a new approach emerged. Leucippus

Euclid's theories
Euclid of Alexandria, a Greek mathematician (c.325–c.265 BCE) living in Egypt, wrote a geometry book called *The Elements* (a folio of which is shown here). His ideas on geometry and number theory remain key to mathematics today.

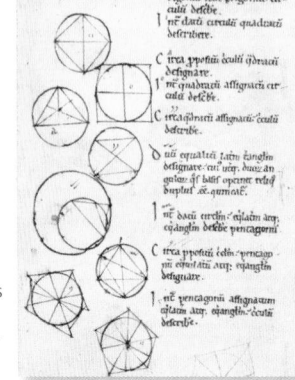

right or wrong, or even plausible, but that the people who constructed them were thinking rationally and philosophically, and were making observations to satisfy human curiosity. That can be seen as the true essence of science, and it had been missing from almost all earlier civilizations.

Philosophers in the ancient civilizations of India and China also employed reason and observation in their attempts to understand the world. They, too, formulated convincing theories similar to the theory of the four elements and atomic theory. In many cases, they made key discoveries before the Greeks. But the lineage of Western scientific thinking leads directly back to ancient Greece.

Science counts
Thales, and many of the other natural philosophers, importantly used

Some philosophers derived elegant mathematical proofs that provided insight into the nature of the world. One of them, Pythagoras (see above), went one step further, suggesting that numbers not only describe reality, but that the world is literally made of numbers. Pythagoras was fascinated by the mathematical relationships between everything, including musical notes. The connection between mathematics and reality is still a central theme in science today.

Mathematics was also crucial to the scientific ideas of Plato (c.427–c.347 BCE), better known for his writings on ethics and politics. He suggested that each element is made of atoms with a particular idealized geometric shape. Plato supposed that the real world was an imperfect reflection of an ideal, "theoretical" and mathematically perfect world.

The Greek philosopher who had the greatest influence on the history of science was

Many of the advances and ideas put forward by the ancient Greeks were lost in the centuries that followed. In many cases, it was not until relatively modern times that they were considered again.

ROMAN SCIENCE

Greek scientific knowledge was used by the Romans, although much was later lost and they tended not to be great theoretical thinkers.

ARAB SCIENTISTS

The ideas of the Greek natural philosophers passed to Arab scholars. In particular, the **Arabs translated the works of Aristotle into Arabic**. Great Arabic philosophers, such as Avicenna and Averroes, who extended classical Greek thinking and added their own ideas and observations **122–25** ».

MAPPA MUNDI

THE CATHOLIC CHURCH

Aristotle's flawed theories were **accepted as fact** by the Catholic Church in Europe, which dramatically set back scientific progress.

MEDIEVAL SCHOLARS

Geographical knowledge was revived with maps of the world (*Mappa Mundi*). This 11th-century example is from Winchester.

SCIENTIFIC REVOLUTION

In the 17th and 18th centuries, many **new thinkers** revived the spirit of scientific approach **206–07** ».

NEW NATURAL PHILOSOPHY

Today, ancient Greek ways of thinking about matter and energy are still relevant; scientists of physics and chemistry ask much the same questions as Thales, Plato, and Aristotle.

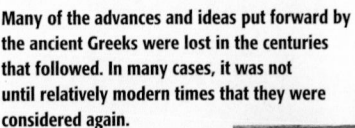

Aristotle (384–322 BCE), a pupil of Plato. Aristotle reversed his teacher's idea about the role of mathematics. He maintained that truth was to be found only in reality – an idea known as empiricism. The theories of both remain important in scientific thinking today.

Using logic and observation, Plato and Aristotle deduced many previously unknown scientific facts. For example, they proved that the Earth is round, and not flat. Aristotle was perhaps the most prolific of the Greek natural philosophers. He wrote texts on a range of subjects, including botany, zoology, astronomy, anatomy, and physics. Aristotle's theories were plausible and well thought-out, but were based on common sense, rather than rigorous logic and careful observation. Unfortunately many were later discovered to be seriously flawed.

Later developments

During the final phase of the ancient Greek period in the 3rd and 2nd centuries BCE, great thinkers began to come full circle, applying the tools of Greek natural philosophy – mathematics and logic – to practical and technical challenges. For example, Archimedes (*c*.287–*c*.212 BCE) was a brilliant theoretical mathematician, but also a great engineer and inventor. Further developments were made at institutions such as the Museum and Library at Alexandria. Competition between centres of learning led to further innovations and the development of science.

MATHEMATIKA The ancient Greek word for "mathematics" is derived from a more general Greek word "mathema", which means "learning" or "study".

The weight of the world

Legend has it that the Greek god Atlas was made by Zeus to hold up the universe as a punishment. This was the sort of idea that the Greek thinkers began to question, with their rational, scientific investigations and theories.

INVENTION

HIPPOCRATIC OATH

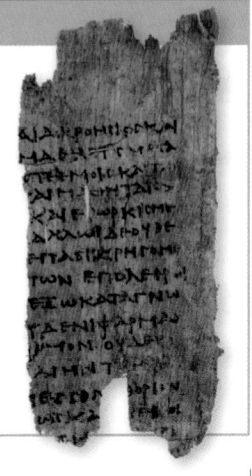

The ancient Greeks' scientific way of thinking extended to the study of medicine. More than anyone, the physician Hippocrates (*c*.460–*c*.370 BCE), promoted a rational, scientific approach to medicine, giving it a firm footing as a professional endeavour. He placed importance on the careful observation of symptoms, and rejected traditional temple medicine theories about illnesses and their cures.

Even today, the ethical "contract" between doctors and patients is known as the Hippocratic Oath. We do not know whether Hippocrates was the author of the original, with promises to work "for the good of my patients according to my ability and my judgement and never do harm to anyone". It is preserved on papyri of later periods, such as this 3rd-century example discovered in Egypt.

‹‹ BEFORE

Before the rise of Rome, Italy was inhabited by several cultural groups. One of these was a Latin-speaking people who settled in villages, including Rome, in the hills above the River Tiber in about 1000 BCE.

EARLY DAYS
In the 8th century BCE, the highly developed **Etruscan civilization** flourished and spread across much of Italy; the Greeks established city-states in southern Italy and Sicily ‹‹ **48–49**; the Latin communities became more complex and Rome began to take shape as an important city.

ETRUSCAN RIDERS

THE BIRTH OF ROME
The date 753 BCE is traditionally given for the founding of the city of Rome. In legend, **Romulus and Remus**, twin brothers who were suckled by a she-wolf as babies founded Rome. Romulus was also the name of the city's first king.

ROMULUS AND REMUS

The **Rise** of **Rome**

Ancient Roman civilization arose from multicultural beginnings, while Rome itself began life as a group of villages on the hills above the River Tiber. From these foundations the powerful Roman Republic was born, whose influence and territories spread across the world, with the great city of Rome at its heart.

INVENTION

THE ARCH

The Romans did not invent the arch, but they took its structural possibilities to entirely new levels. They became adept at working with the form and related structures such as the vault and dome, to help support monumental temples, amphitheatres, walls, aqueducts, viaducts, tunnels, lighthouses, and watermills. The Pons Aemilius (below) is the oldest stone bridge across the River Tiber in Rome, and dates from the 2nd century BCE.

B y 600 BCE, Rome had become a sophisticated city-state ruled by kings. It boasted specialized crafts, a rich aristocracy, monumental buildings, and organized social systems. The king ruled alongside a Senate and an Assembly. The Senate was a council of elders composed of the heads of various clans. It had the power to approve or veto the appointment of the king. The Assembly consisted of all male citizens of Rome; citizenship was granted only to those whose parents were native Romans. The Assembly's main function was to grant absolute power to the monarch once the clan leaders approved the candidate for king.

Rome stood at the crossroads of major trade routes connecting Europe with Asia and North Africa. Trade not only generated great commercial wealth for Rome, it also brought the Romans into regular contact with several different cultures, such as the Greeks, from whom the Romans absorbed diverse influences. The Romans' Etruscan neighbours also had a profound effect on Rome, so much so that from the middle of the 6th century BCE the Roman monarchs were Etruscan. The Etruscans gave the Romans the toga, art, certain religious practices, forms of stone arch (see left), sewage systems, and chariot racing. The Greek influence, often passed on via the Etruscans, was strong in art and architecture (see pp.70–71), philosophy, and science and technology (see pp.58–59). The Etruscans also passed the Greek alphabet to the Romans, who developed it to create the basis for many modern western languages.

Roman engineering
The ancient Romans made considerable advances in building and civil engineering, mainly by clever development of principles obtained from other civilizations they came into contact with. While using fired bricks, tiles, and stone to great effect, they also perfected concrete, developing a form capable of hardening under water. From the 3rd century BCE , Roman builders became the first to use

CARTHAGINIAN GENERAL (247–182 BCE)

HANNIBAL BARCA

Hannibal fought with great valour against the Roman Republic in the Second Punic War (218–201 BCE). He captured the city of Saguntum in Spain, allied to Rome, then advanced on Italy. With Rome blocking the sea routes, Hannibal took 37 elephants and 35,000 men over the Pyrenees and Alps, as shown in this fresco. Despite heavy losses, he won many victories but was defeated at Zama in North Africa. Carthage was destroyed by the Romans and Hannibal fled to Syria where he later committed suicide.

Mixing business and ritual
This relief of the 1st century BCE shows animals being sacrificed to mark a census of citizens, which was done every few years. The figure in the toga (right of altar) is probably the censor (the magistrate taking the census).

The Romans' treatment of conquered peoples varied greatly. To those who seemed to them "civilized" enough and close in kinship, they granted similar rights to those of Roman citizens. Those who actively resisted them received much harsher treatment. Both these approaches were seen as effective ways of enforcing power and influence.

> **REPUBLIC** A society not ruled by a monarch in which power is shared between the aristocracy and the common people. The modern term is taken from the Latin *res publica*: "the public thing".

Mounting problems
Despite its extensive lands, by the 2nd century BCE, Rome was in a state of perpetual war, flux, and social discontent. Farms fell into disrepair while their owners were away fighting, and debts were mounting. While the city of Rome was at the heart of a growing empire, tensions arose because the republic's existing social and political institutions struggled to address new problems. The tensions reached a peak in 137 BCE when the Gracchi brothers, Tiberius and Gaius, (tribunes of the Plebeians, or officials who represented Plebeian interests) pitted themselves against the Patrician Senate by proposing revolutionary social reform that included redistributing public land to the landless poorer classes. Armed struggle broke out and both brothers ended up dead. It was an episode that signalled the beginning of the Roman Republic's decline.

Senators
Members of the Senate were men of considerable personal wealth and standing and wore a toga with a broad stripe (*tunica laticlavia*).

Equestrians
These were upper/middle class men of wealth, often described as "knights". They wore a toga with a narrow stripe (*tunica angusticlavia*).

Plebeians
The common "class" included every freeborn male citizen not a senator or equestrian. It varied from the unskilled poor to wealthy merchants.

Latins
Latins were freeborn citizens from parts of Italy outside Rome. They had certain legal rights and were granted a form of Roman citizenship.

Foreigners
Freeborn inhabitants of Roman territory outside Italy were considered foreigners. They were granted a form of citizenship in the 3rd century CE.

Freedmen
The slaves who had been liberated in a specific ceremony by their masters. They had rights, but their status changed over time.

Slaves
The non-free who had no rights and were bought and sold by their owners. Slaves were considered personal property under Roman law.

Roman social order
Roman society had strict class divisions. These were influenced by family background, wealth, citizenship, and freedom. The system frequently sparked controversy and dissent. Women had virtually no rights and belonged to the same class as their father or husband.

concrete extensively, constructing many large-scale engineering and building projects.

The coming of the Republic
Rome was ruled by seven kings before the last one, the Etruscan, Tarquinius, was overthrown in 509 BCE in a coup staged by Roman aristocrats. Rather than install a new monarch, the Romans dismantled the institution and Rome became a republic.

The early republic had two consuls (to counter over-reliance on one individual), who were elected annually. While the Senate was originally put in place to prevent despotism, it became the true decision-making authority. The law was upheld by magistrates, who also came from the Senate. These public figures were expected to show loyalty to the republic, self-sacrifice for the general good, and lead blameless lives as an example to others.

Citizens and slaves
Roman republican society was divided into the free and non-free (slaves). The most significant free people were citizens, who were able to elect the consuls. Citizens were further divided into Patricians (an elite landowning class), and Plebeians (all other citizens). The Senate drew its members from the Patrician class, therefore the Republic in its early form

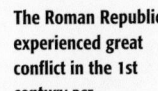

Young boy and boar
Figurine of a young Roman boy in a tunic leading a sacrificial boar. This boy was probably a slave or attendant.

was largely a transfer of power from the king to the wealthiest classes in Rome. Rising Plebeian resentment at this often led to violence in a class conflict that became known as the "struggle of the orders".

The Patricians relied on the Plebeians, as not only did they produce the food and supply the labour that drove the Roman economy, they also formed the ranks in the Roman army (see pp.68–69). This reliance led the ruling classes to bring about social reforms. These included the "Twelve Tables" laws (most of the evidence of these laws is now lost to us), the election of the first Plebeian Council in 366 BCE, and the passing of a ruling in 287 BCE that the Plebeian Council's decisions would henceforth be binding for all citizens, including the Patricians. Rome's unfree people were slaves. From the 3rd century BCE the Romans used slave labour on a large scale for building projects.

Military success
Roman armies won extensive lands for the Republic in wars that gradually took place further afield and with increasing scale. By 264 BCE, Rome emerged from clashes with surrounding communities to dominate Italy, and by 146 BCE Rome had crushed the Carthaginians (see left) in the Punic Wars, which broke out several times in the 3rd and 2nd centuries BCE, to dominate the entire western Mediterranean.

AFTER

THE DEATH OF SPARTACUS

The Roman Republic experienced great conflict in the 1st century BCE.

TIME OF TURMOIL
The 1st century BCE saw a mix of new gains and intensifying civil strife. Some of Rome's former allies, having fought for the republic, became frustrated by Rome's domination over them and failure to grant them Roman citizenship.

SULLA'S DICTATORSHIP
The years 82–80 BCE brought the self-proclaimed **dictatorship of Sulla**. His struggles with rival Marius had already weakened the republic and his rule increased patrician (upper class) power. During his dictatorship there were heightened levels of corruption within the Senate.

THE SLAVE REVOLT
Between 72–71 BCE, Spartacus, a former auxiliary in the Roman army turned slave-gladiator, became **leader of a group of disaffected slaves** and rebels (see above) that swelled to around 120,000; they fought the Romans and dominated much of southern Italy. The Romans were ultimately victorious and **Spartacus was killed** in around 70 BCE. However, the uprising showed the dangers of employing slave labour on a massive scale.

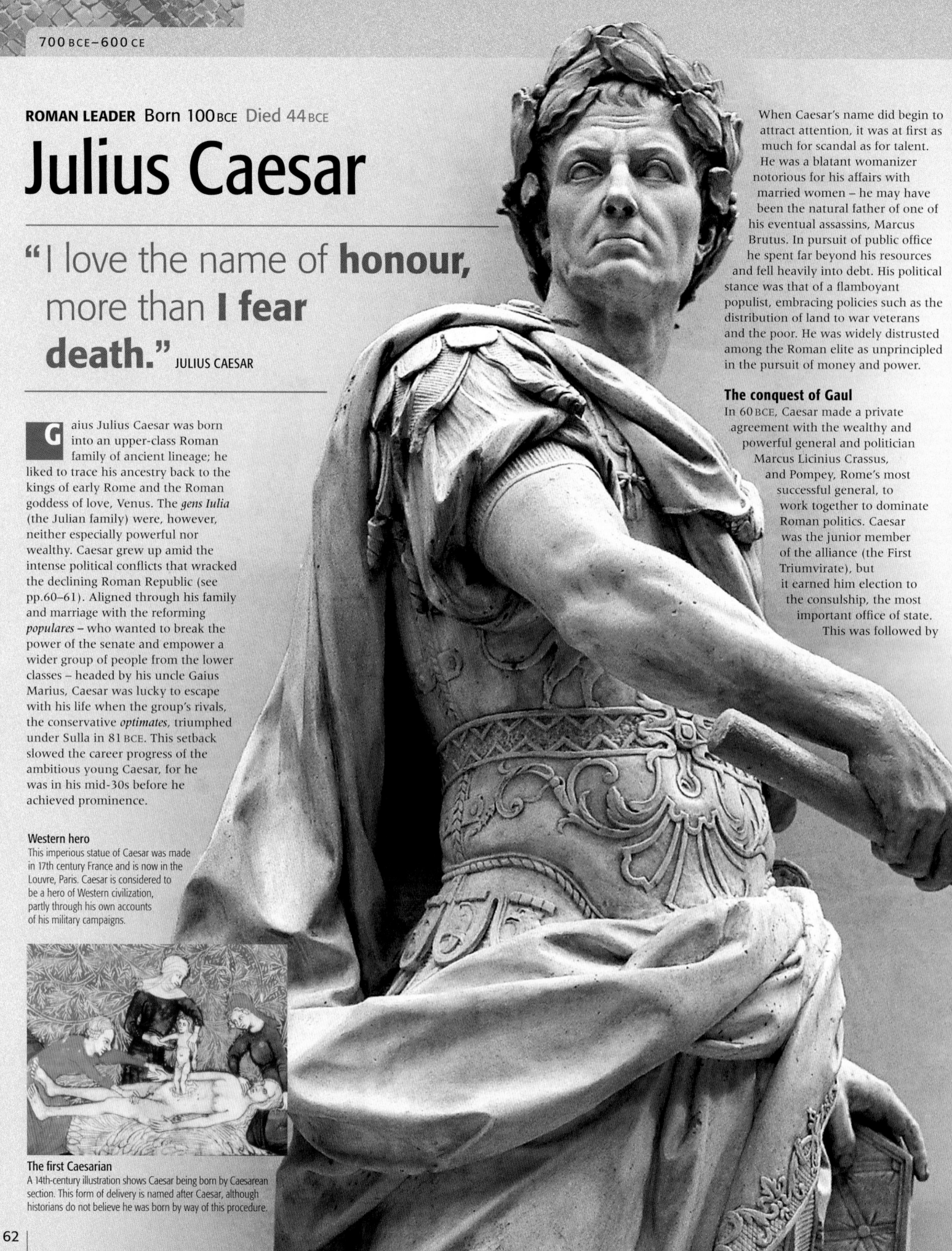

ROMAN LEADER Born 100 BCE Died 44 BCE

Julius Caesar

"I love the name of **honour,** more than **I fear death.**" JULIUS CAESAR

Gaius Julius Caesar was born into an upper-class Roman family of ancient lineage; he liked to trace his ancestry back to the kings of early Rome and the Roman goddess of love, Venus. The *gens Iulia* (the Julian family) were, however, neither especially powerful nor wealthy. Caesar grew up amid the intense political conflicts that wracked the declining Roman Republic (see pp.60–61). Aligned through his family and marriage with the reforming *populares* – who wanted to break the power of the senate and empower a wider group of people from the lower classes – headed by his uncle Gaius Marius, Caesar was lucky to escape with his life when the group's rivals, the conservative *optimates*, triumphed under Sulla in 81 BCE. This setback slowed the career progress of the ambitious young Caesar, for he was in his mid-30s before he achieved prominence.

Western hero
This imperious statue of Caesar was made in 17th century France and is now in the Louvre, Paris. Caesar is considered to be a hero of Western civilization, partly through his own accounts of his military campaigns.

The first Caesarian
A 14th-century illustration shows Caesar being born by Caesarean section. This form of delivery is named after Caesar, although historians do not believe he was born by way of this procedure.

When Caesar's name did begin to attract attention, it was at first as much for scandal as for talent. He was a blatant womanizer notorious for his affairs with married women – he may have been the natural father of one of his eventual assassins, Marcus Brutus. In pursuit of public office he spent far beyond his resources and fell heavily into debt. His political stance was that of a flamboyant populist, embracing policies such as the distribution of land to war veterans and the poor. He was widely distrusted among the Roman elite as unprincipled in the pursuit of money and power.

The conquest of Gaul
In 60 BCE, Caesar made a private agreement with the wealthy and powerful general and politician Marcus Licinius Crassus, and Pompey, Rome's most successful general, to work together to dominate Roman politics. Caesar was the junior member of the alliance (the First Triumvirate), but it earned him election to the consulship, the most important office of state. This was followed by

JULIAN CALENDAR

Based on a lunar calendar, the Roman year was only 355 days long, and was adjusted by the occasional extra month. Caesar introduced a 12-month year of 365 days, with a 366-day leap year once every four years. To align Rome with the solar cycle, 46 BCE was made into a 445-day year. The Julian calendar then came into force in 45 BCE. It was in general use in Europe until the Gregorian calendar was introduced in 1582 CE, and is still used by the Greek Orthodox Church.

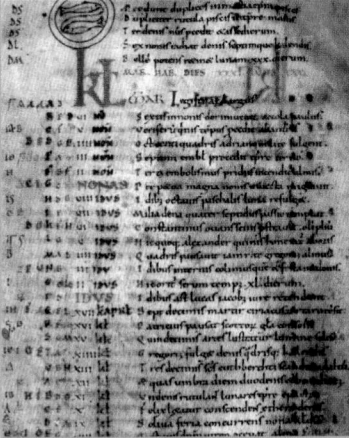

> "I came, I saw, **I conquered.**"

JULIUS CAESAR, BATTLE OF ZELA, 47 BCE

the appointment to command in the Roman provinces of Gaul (modern France). There he showed outstanding energy and ruthlessness in years of campaigning against the Celtic and Germanic tribes of the region. Caesar went beyond the borders of his provincial command, making forays across the Rhine in Germany and north as far as the River Thames in Britain. Victories brought him both wealth and renown. They also gave him an instrument for attaining power: he shared the hardships and dangers of his legions on the march and in battle, praised and rewarded them, and in return they were loyal to him rather than to the Republic.

Rome's civil war

In late 50 BCE the Senate, under the control of Pompey, called on Caesar to disband his army after his ten-year command in Gaul had come to a successful conclusion. Instead, Caesar led his legions across the Rubicon, the

stream separating Cisalpine Gaul (the region of Gaul to the south of the Alps) from Italy proper. Easily occupying Rome, he took on Pompey in an armed struggle for control of the Roman world. After two years of fighting, the battle of Pharsalus in August 48 BCE proved decisive for Caesar. Pompey escaped from the scene of his defeat, only to be murdered a month later in Egypt. Although Pompey's sons, Sextus and Gnaeus, continued the civil war until 45 BCE, Caesar's outstanding military skills had won him the supreme power he sought.

Reform and power

During his brief reign, Caesar revealed a zeal for innovation and reform. He halved the number of Roman citizens dependent on handouts of bread from the state by resettling the destitute in colonies in Italy and abroad, and reformed the calendar, see above. Yet he also exhibited great arrogance. For example, the Republic had in the past appointed a temporary "dictator", a leader with exceptional power to cope with an emergency, but

Caesar's death
Brutus steps forward to stab Caesar in this painting by 19th century artist Vincenzo Camaccini. According to Latin author Suetonius, Caesar said: "You too, my child?", indicating that Brutus may have been his son.

Caesar's column
This column marks the place in Rimini, Italy, where Caesar crossed the Rubicon in 49 BCE.

The heart of the republic
The Forum, the heart of Rome, is where Caesar's supporter, Mark Antony, delivered a funeral oration over his body. A temple to Caesar was later erected on the spot where he was cremated.

Caesar permanently assumed the role, and advertised the fact on coins.

Brutal assassination

In March 44 BCE Caesar planned to lead an army against the Parthians in the Middle East (see pp.76-77). A group of senators led by Gaius Cassius Longinus and Marcus Junius Brutus, inspired by an idealistic attachment to the Republic, and the desire to defend their own privileges, conspired to kill him before he left Rome. They stabbed him in the assembly hall, where he had come to address the Senate. His death caused riots and, ironically, brought about the end of the Republic his assassins were trying to restore. Two years after his death the Senate made him a god. He is remembered today as a skilled orator, author, and military leader.

- **12 or 13 July 100 BCE** Gaius Julius Caesar is born into a wealthy family in Rome.
- **87 BCE** Caesar's uncle by marriage, the famous general Gaius Marius, seizes power in Rome.
- **83 BCE** Caesar marries Cornelia, the daughter of powerful politician, Cinna; he becomes high priest of Jupiter.
- **81 BCE** Sulla, the enemy of Marius and Cinna, becomes dictator of Rome; dismissed from his priesthood, Caesar is forced into hiding.
- **80 BCE** Takes refuge in Bithynia in Asia Minor, where it is alleged he becomes the lover of the Bithynian king, Nicomedes IV.
- **78 BCE** After Sulla's death, Caesar returns to Rome.
- **75 BCE** Kidnapped by pirates, Caesar is ransomed. He later crucifies his kidnappers.
- **69 BCE** After the death of his first wife, Caesar marries Pompeia, granddaughter of Sulla.
- **65 BCE** Appointed *curule aedile* (a public office of the Republic responsible for among other things, the regulation of public festivals), Caesar courts popularity by organizing lavish festivities.
- **63 BCE** Elected *pontifex maximus*, chief priest of the Roman state religion; Cicero, the statesman, accuses him of involvement in the Catiline conspiracy, and of aiming to take over the Republic.
- **62 BCE** Caesar divorces Pompeia.
- **60 BCE** Returning from a spell as governor of Further Spain, Caesar makes a deal to share power in Rome with Pompey and Crassus, forming the First Triumvirate.

COIN BEARING CAESAR'S HEAD

- **59 BCE** Caesar's daughter Julia marries Pompey. Caesar marries his third wife, Calpurnia. He is granted a five-year governorship of Cisalpine Gaul and Illyricum (in modern Albania); Transalpine Gaul is soon added to his command.
- **58 BCE** Caesar begins his conquest of Gaul by defeating the Helvetii and Ariovistus.
- **55–54 BCE** Twice invades Britain and twice bridges the Rhine; his command in Gaul is extended for another five years.
- **10 January 49 BCE** Defying a call from the Senate to disband his army, Caesar crosses the Rubicon river into Italy, precipitating civil war.
- **23 June 47 BCE** The Ptolemaic Queen, Cleopatra, gives birth to Caesarion, probably Caesar's son.
- **August 47 BCE** Caesar defeats Pharnaces, king of Pontus and the Bosporus, at the battle of Zela.
- **March 45 BCE** Caesar defeats the last of Pompey's army, ending the civil war.
- **15 February 44 BCE** Appointed dictator for life.
- **15 March 44 BCE** Assassinated by a group of conspirators set on restoring the Republic.

« BEFORE

The end of the Roman Republic was a long process, marked by the death of Julius Caesar in 44 BCE and Octavian's rise to power in 30 BCE.

POMPEY'S CONQUESTS
From 67–60 BCE, the great Roman general, Pompey, defeated pirates across the

POMPEY

Mediterranean, gained lands for Rome in the Middle East, and formed the First Triumvirate alliance with Marcus Licinius Crassus and Julius Caesar.

THE RISE OF JULIUS CAESAR
By 51 BCE, Caesar was a major political figure « 62–63. The Roman Senate and Julius Caesar's former ally, Pompey, felt increasingly threatened by his growing power. In 49 BCE, Caesar took Rome and war broke out between his and the Senate's forces, now led by Pompey. **Pompey was murdered** by

allies of Caesar who in 45 BCE became dictator for life – Rome's most powerful leader to date.

BLOODY TENSIONS
In 44 BCE, **Caesar was murdered** by a group of senators. His successors, the Roman general, Mark Antony, and Octavian (Caesar's adopted son), became unable to work together, and divided Rome's empire into west (Octavian), and east (Antony). Friction between the two sparked **civil war**, further weakening the republic.

FADING OF THE REPUBLIC
Octavian defeated Mark Antony and Cleopatra **74–75 »** at the **Battle of Actium**, in 31 BCE. A year later, Octavian took over Egypt and became supreme in the Roman state.

PORTRAIT OF MARK ANTONY

The Roman World
The Roman Empire reached its greatest extent in 117 CE, at the start of the reign of emperor Hadrian (ruled 117–138 CE), as shown by this map. The great structures for which Rome has become famed – from walls and aqueducts to amphitheatres and temples – appeared all over the empire and many still survive today.

Emperor Hadrian supervised the building of this wall which takes his name. Built on the northern border of the empire, Hadrian's Wall stretched for almost 120 km (75 miles), coast to coast across northern Britain.

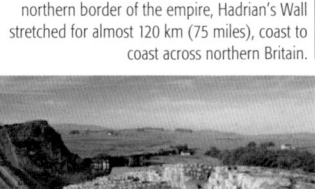

Mosaics, buildings, and streets have survived at the site of the Roman city of Italica, close to modern Seville.

North Sea

BRITANNIA 43 CE
Londinium 78 CE

ATLANTIC OCEAN

GERMANIA INFERIOR
GERMANIA SUPERIOR 83 CE
GERMANIA
Colonia Agrippina
BELGICA
Durocortorum
Mogontiacum
Augusta Vindelicorum
LUGDUNENSIS
GALLIA
RAETIA 58 CE
NORICUM 15 BCE
Virunum
PANNONIA SUPERIOR 9 CE
Carnuntum
Aquineum
PANNONIA INFERIOR 9 CE
MOE INFE
DACIA 106 CE
Sarmizegetusa
Singidunum
MOESIA SUPERIOR 29 BCE
Oescus
THRAC 46 CE

AQUITANIA 58–51 BCE
Burdigala
Octodurum
ALPES GRAIAE ET POENINAE
Lugdunum
Segusio
Cemenelum
ALPES COTTIAE
ALPES MARITIMAE
ILLYRICUM
DALMATIA
Salonae 33 BCE

NARBONENSIS 121 BCE
Nemausus Ucetia
Narbo
27 BCE
Pyrenees
ITALIA
Rome
Ostia
Pompeii

TARRACONENSIS 197 BCE
Tarraco
HISPANIA
LUSITANIA 27 BCE
Emerita Augusta 181 BCE
BAETICA
Italica Corduba
197 BCE

SARDINIA ET CORSICA 238 BCE
Carales

MACEDONIA 146 CE
Thessal
EPIRUS 140 BCE
Nicopolis
Corinth
ACHAEA 146 BCE

SICILIA
Syracuse

Mediterranean Se

Tingis

Caesarea
MAURETANIA CAESARIENSIS
MAURETANIA TINGITANA 44 CE
44 CE
Carthage
Sbeitla
AFRICA (PROCONSULARIS) 146 BCE
NUMIDIA 48 BCE

Cyrene 74 BCE
CYRENA
CR

Leptis Magna
AFRICA 107 BCE

The Colosseum, Rome, is a massive amphitheatre that was originally called the Flavian amphitheatre as it was built by the Flavian emperors. The site of countless gladiatorial combats, its formal opening in 80 CE was marked by 100 days of gladiatorial games.

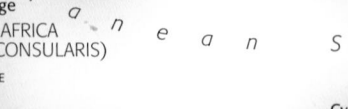

The Pont du Gard aqueduct (an artificial waterway) was built c. 19 BCE to carry water from Ucetia (Uzés) to Nemausus (Nîmes), in France. With three tiers of arches and a height of nearly 50m (165ft) it was the highest aqueduct built by the Romans.

Mount Vesuvius erupted in 79 CE, burying Pompeii in ash (see p.112). It preserved a typical Roman town, complete with villas decorated with wall paintings, such as this example depicting a Roman girl.

The temple of Jupiter near Sbeitla, Tunisia is one part of the impressive remains of the ancient Roman city of Sufetula which probably originated as a fort during campaigns against Numidian rebels.

The remains of a colonnaded street (*cardo maximus*) at Apamea in Syria are 145m (475 feet) long. The street would have been lined along both sides with buildings for public use.

By 27 BCE Octavian was, in effect, the empire's first "Emperor", taking the title Augustus (see p.67). The Romans themselves did not consider that the republic ended with Caesar's death, and when Augustus came to power he did not paint himself as an all-powerful emperor figure. Instead, he claimed to have restored the republic and to have returned power to the Senate and the people. Augustus represented himself as "first among equals" with his fellow senators, although, in reality, he held supreme power.

The empire of Augustus started out with republican pretensions (rule by the Senate and Roman people), but while Augustus retained parts of the existing system he grafted his own autocracy onto it. The republic's system of rule, based on competition among aristocratic families, was replaced by an imperial one in which a single aristocratic family dominated.

A worldwide empire

By the late 1st century CE, and the time of the emperor Trajan (ruled 98–117 CE), Rome headed an empire

praetors, who ruled in the emperor's name. By the 3rd century CE, separate leaders often attended to military matters. Within these provinces, cities looked much like Roman ones and were run according to a Roman-style system of law. One key feature of the 2nd-century empire was the rising status of these provinces and their great cities – for example Ephesus in Asia Minor and Leptis Magna in North Africa (see map, left).

The urban centres of imperial Rome were linked by an impressive transport and communication network made

From **Republic** to **Empire**

As the structures of the republican system gave way to the empire, Rome found itself in command of vast, worldwide territories. The empire encompassed a diverse mix of peoples, and its politics, way of life, artistic achievements, and spectacular feats of engineering, have had a lasting impact.

Black Sea

ARMENIA
114–117 CE

PARTHIAN EMPIRE

BITHYNIA ET PONTUS

nedia
zantium
64 BCE
Ancyra
CAPPADOCIA
Caesarea
18 CE

ASSYRIA
116–117 CE

MESOPOTAMIA
115–117 CE

SIA
33 BCE
GALATIA
25 BCE
CILICIA
Tarsus
115 CE
SYRIA
64 BCE
sus
LYCIA ET
PAMPHYLIA
101 BCE
Antioch
74 CE
CYPRUS
58 BCE
Apamea
Myra
74 CE
Paphus

Caesarea Maritima
Bostra
JUDAEA
6 CE

Alexandria
ARABIA
106 CE

CE

AEGYPTUS
30 BCE

Red Sea

The Library of Celsus at Ephesus (Turkey) was built in the 2nd century CE as a monument to a Roman senator and governor. It stored thousands of manuscripts in scrolls. The front of the building has been faithfully restored.

KEY

DACIA	Province in reign of Hadrian
107 CE	Date of conquest or annexation by Rome
——	Boundary of Roman Empire
——	Province boundary
○	Provincial capital

N
400 km
400 miles

of great wealth, which stretched across a vast area that took in all of the Mediterranean, the Middle East, and a large chunk of northern and central Europe. In the first two centuries of imperial rule, there were probably around 50 million people living in Roman lands.

The bulk of these lands were conquered during the days of the republic. The empire consolidated these areas and added a few new provinces, although these new acquisitions were also the first to be given up later on. Britain, Dacia (modern Romania), Assyria, and Mesopotamia (Iraq) were short-lived gains compared to other territories. Roman rulers were quick to crush any rebellion or threat (from outside or from within), often brutally. This is one reason why the empire was relatively stable during this time.

The expansion that was achieved was greatly helped by the work of emperors such as Trajan and Claudius. Another major factor in maintaining these lands was the Romans' legendary military might. Crucially, the empire had a standing army, unlike during much of the republic. Its soldiers were a professional, highly organized, and skilled machine, and loyal to the emperor (see pp.68–69).

An urban civilization

Ancient Roman civilization was highly urbanized, with a vast network of prosperous cities, filled with beautiful buildings that usually mirrored the city of Rome itself, such as temples and a public forum. The empire's extensive territories were divided into provinces ruled by governors called proconsuls or

possible by the Romans' unique talent for engineering – new roads, bridges, viaducts, harbours, and aqueducts were built throughout the empire.

"Warehouse of the world"

Good communication links also aided the empire's trade, although the road system often proved slow and Roman trade came into its own much more through the use of maritime transport. Rome's huge empire meant that it had at its command a

»

THE ROAD SYSTEM

The empire was connected by thousands of kilometres of expertly made roads, typically consisting of stone slabs laid over rubble. Vital for allowing soldiers to move around as fast as possible – which is why Roman roads are often straight – they helped to control the vast territories. Much of the network in Italy centred on Rome, hence the proverb "All roads lead to Rome". Many Roman roads survive today, some in good condition – such as the Appian Way in Rome (below) which linked Rome with southeastern Italy.

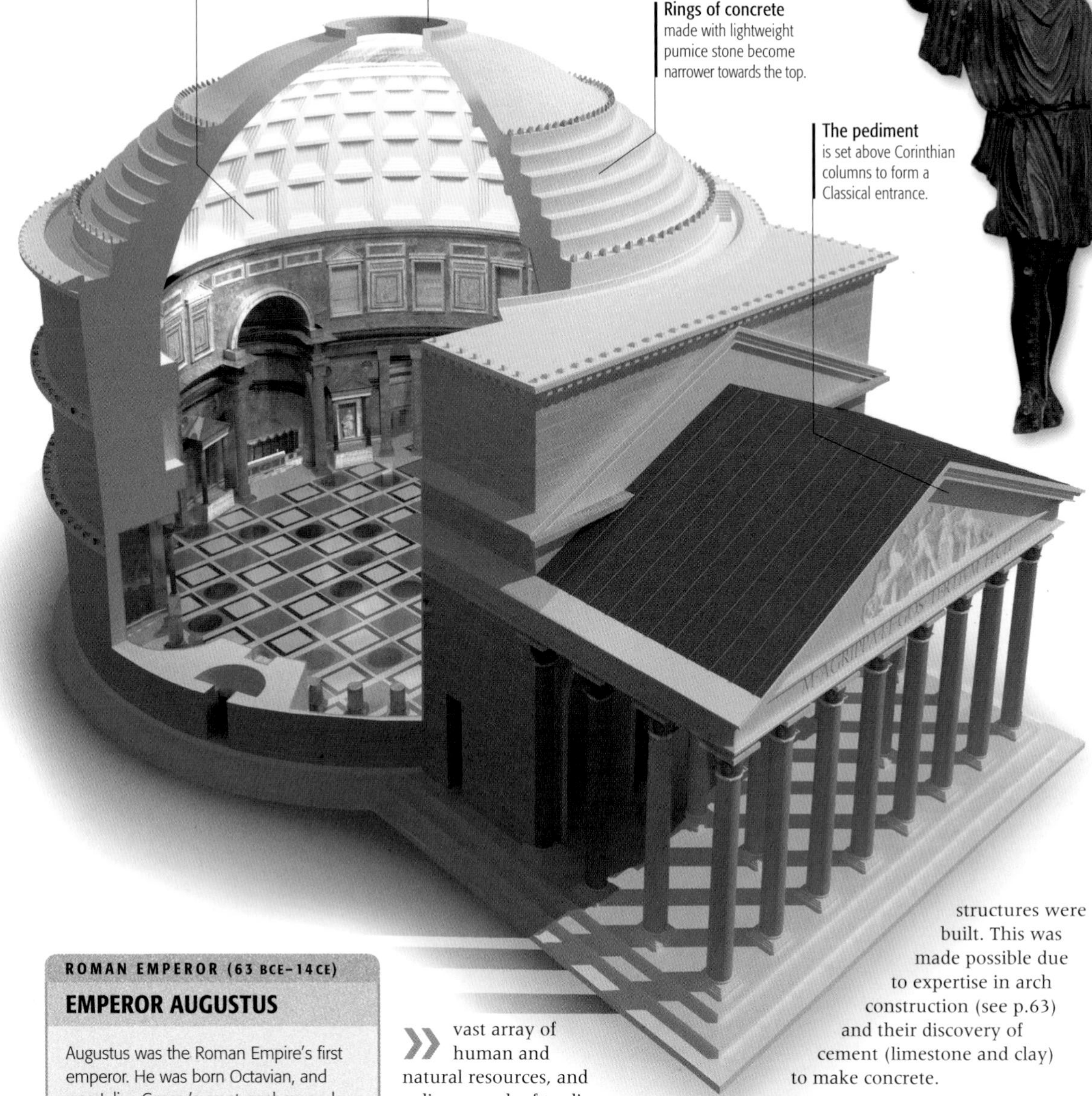

Ceiling coffers or panels diminish in size as they rise, adding to the sense of height.

The oculus ("eye") is open to the elements – rainwater drains away through the floor.

Rings of concrete made with lightweight pumice stone become narrower towards the top.

The pediment is set above Corinthian columns to form a Classical entrance.

Bronze household god
The Romans worshipped a variety of ancestral gods (*lares* and *penates*) as guardians of their homes. This bronze statuette holds a drinking horn, a typical attribute of a household god.

of Augustus (the city's principal public meeting place); Trajan's Column completed in 113 CE, with reliefs celebrating two victories over the Dacians; and Constantine's Arch, finished in 315 CE, to mark the military might of Emperor Constantine I. The triumphal arch is a form that the Roman Empire made its own, and which has been copied up to the present day.

Life in the Roman Empire
Everyday life continued in many ways as it had done during the republic. Male citizens had varying freedoms, while women were mainly confined to the domestic arena. Slaves, with no

The Pantheon
Created as a temple in the 2nd century CE, the Pantheon in Rome is famed for its dome, the largest until modern times. Over 21m (70ft) high, with a diameter of over 43m (140ft), cement mixed with pumice near the top of the dome helps support the structure.

POMPEII

In August 79 CE, a massive eruption from Mount Vesuvius buried the nearby Roman city of Campania (now called Pompeii) in southern Italy under 6m (20ft) of ash and debris. Buildings were buried and people smothered. Neighbouring cities, such as Herculaneum, were similarly affected. Excavation has revealed a perfectly preserved example of a sophisticated Greco-Roman city of around 20,000 people, with buildings such as a forum, amphitheatre, and lavish villas. Even the remains of loaves in bakers' ovens were preserved. Many human bodies left their shapes in the ash, from which plaster casts have since been made (below), showing Pompeii's people as they fell.

EMPEROR AUGUSTUS

Augustus was the Roman Empire's first emperor. He was born Octavian, and was Julius Caesar's great nephew and adopted son. After Caesar's death he assumed the title Augustus, a name that had religious implications, and Princeps, meaning "first citizen". He brought an end to civil war, and appeared to be restoring the republic to its glory days, but in reality ruled as an autocrat. He held power for 41 years of relative peace, heralding the start of the empire that was to last for over four centuries.

» vast array of human and natural resources, and a diverse web of trading connections. Its provinces traded all kinds of basic and luxury goods with each other, ranging from salt to mass-produced statues – which is why ancient Rome is often called the "warehouse of the world".

Throughout its many provincial cities and towns, the empire brought into being some of the really great works of ancient Roman architecture, engineering, and art. Imperial-era buildings and monuments took the Romans' love of impressive grandeur to a peak, proclaiming their wealth and power to the world.

Augustus oversaw the transformation of Rome, saying he "found [it] a city of bricks and left it a city of marble". Many magnificent

50,000 The number of spectators that could fit into the Colosseum in Rome. It was built between c.72–82 CE to stage a variety of "entertainments", including battle reconstructions, gladiatorial combat, dramas, and executions.

The concrete revolution
The Romans had already made great inroads with the use of concrete (see pp.60–61), and by the time of the empire were using it very skilfully on a large scale. The immense load-bearing capacities of concrete, along with further advances in the application of architectural elements like the arch, meant that they could produce massive structures such as Rome's Colosseum, the enormous dome of the Pantheon (above), long aqueducts, and viaducts (bridges), and harbours such as Caesarea Maritima in Judea in the Middle East. Other monumental imperial structures include three famous sights in Rome – the Forum

structures were built. This was made possible due to expertise in arch construction (see p.63) and their discovery of cement (limestone and clay) to make concrete.

Port of Ostia
This great trading seaport lay at the mouth of the Tiber, close to Rome. Large merchant vessels unloaded goods onto barges to continue their journey into the city itself.

Hypocaust remains
These remains in a bathhouse reveal the Roman underfloor heating system (*hypocaust*). The floor, now gone, was raised by short pillars around which furnace-heated air circulated.

Mosaic
Wealthy Romans enjoyed fine interiors in their homes, such as this late 3rd-century mosaic from a villa in Sicily.

freedoms at all, were essential for keeping the wheels of Roman life running smoothly. In the country, up to a third of the population were slaves carrying out agricultural work to supply the towns and cities.

Housing took many different forms. The wealthy lived in magnificent villas with toilets, running water, and central heating. Often centred on a cool inner courtyard, these were filled with statues and artefacts (see pp.70–71) and decorated with beautiful mosaic floors and wall-paintings showing skill in the art of perspective – famous examples survive at Pompeii and in Rome itself, such as the House of Livia. These great houses were often designed and decorated by Greek artists living in these Roman cities. Such villas were the sites of lavish dinner parties. Food and drink was consumed on an excessive scale that has become legendary, and was accompanied by music and dancing.

Many poorer townspeople lived in crowded basic apartment blocks known as *insulae*. Remains of these buildings show similarities to modern blocks of flats, with uniform entrances and windows. The inhabitants of the *insulae* shared public toilet facilities.

Business, pleasure, and worship
Gathering for business or pleasure was a central part of Roman life. Meeting places such as markets, public "forum" areas, bath houses, and even communal toilets were popular spots, with private squalor offset by public grandeur. Meetings were often conducted outside, in open places, to discourage the secret plotting that characterized Roman rule.

Entertainment was also enjoyed in public arenas and theatres. This took the form of athletic games, gladiatorial combat, animal hunts, chariot races, plays and public execution of criminals. In the early centuries, the Romans of the empire believed in a range of gods and goddesses (see pp.94–95), both state and "household", to whom they built temples. For a long time these beliefs existed alongside the growing tide of Christianity (see pp.96–97).

Laws of the land
Augustus made some legal reforms but the basic tenets of Roman law remained. Augustus had final say in determining if a law should be passed. Citizens charged with crimes often had patrons to defend them, and criminal law was administered by Roman magistrates. Punishments were harsh. By the first half of the 2nd century CE, Roman citizens pleading a miscarriage of justice were entitled to appeal to a higher court based in the city of Rome.

AFTER

A variety of factors has been blamed for triggering the gradual demise of the empire.

ANTONINE PLAGUE
Around 165 CE, a plague (possibly smallpox), broke out in the empire and lasted for around 15 years. Huge numbers lost their lives – including two emperors. One consequence was a weakening of the social fabric of the empire.

5 MILLION The number of people estimated to have died of plague in the 2nd century CE.

476 Year the Roman Empire ended in the West.

THIRD-CENTURY CRISIS
The years from 235–284 were a chaotic time with a **rapid succession of emperors** murdered one after the other. A variety of problems beset certain parts of the empire, including starvation, plague, inflation, high taxation, and "barbarian" attacks. Some regions, such as Gaul (France) and Britain, started to assert their own interests and threaten imperial authority. Such chaos made it easier for others to seize control, such as **Queen Zenobia** of Palmyra (modern Syria) in 272–73 CE.

DIOCLETIAN EDICT

FOUR EMPERORS
In 284 CE, the period of crisis in the 3rd century ended when Roman general **Diocletian** made himself emperor. He created the first imperial college of **four emperors** (the Tetrarchy) to oversee four sections of the empire. Diocletian issued an edict in 301 to attempt to stabilize the empire's economy. The second Tetrarchy broke down and partly prefigures the empires' later permanent split into east and west in 395 CE.

A SECOND ROME
In the early part of the 4th century CE, Roman Emperor, Constantine (280–337 CE), established a "second Rome" at Byzantium (modern Istanbul), renaming it Constantinople – a possible further cause of the empire's demise.

MOSAIC FROM CONSTANTINOPLE

Grooming kit
Wealthy Romans were well-groomed. This is a pocket set of tweezers, nail cleaner, and ear-scoop.

Gold coins
These coins left in Kent, England, after the Roman invasion, represent over four years' pay for a Roman legionary. The owner may have intended to collect them in more settled times.

Silver ladle and spoon
Roman silverware came in various styles and showed great technical mastery.

Samian ware bowl
Bright red "Samian" pottery, known for its distinctive red colouring, was used widely during the early imperial period.

Gold bracelet
Snake-shaped bracelets were popular. This one dates from 1st-century CE Pompeii.

The Roman army was not a static organization but evolved over the centuries to meet diverse challenges and overcome new enemies. In its early days it resembled the ancient Greek hoplite army, which was primarily made up of men who volunteered to fight to protect their city. In Rome changes began as soon as the empire expanded. By the time of Julius Caesar (see pp.62–63) in the 1st century the army had become a well organized, mobile fighting force. The "classic" Roman army that we know most about today is that which Caesar (pp.62–63) began and Augustus (see p.66) honed. By the reign of Trajan (98–117 CE), this is the army that seemed unbeatable to its enemies.

A developing force

In the days of the early Republic (see pp.158–59) the army was staffed by volunteers from the aristocratic families. They provided their own weapons and uniform and trained for five or six years. Small units of men (centuries) worked as a team. They worked and lived together and fought with iron discipline, just as the Greek hoplites had done before them. As Roman power expanded, however, a professional army became vital. The general, Marius (157–85 BCE) made many reforms, including opening the army to all. The practice of giving a piece of land to retired soldiers is also attributed to Marius. Caesar (100–44 BCE) oversaw a professional and well-led military force that Augustus (63 BCE–14 CE) maintained, with a stable number of legions to make up the army that would safeguard the empire. Length of service was standardized to 20 years. Every legion had an eagle standard (aquila).

Housesteads fort
This is the most complete Roman fort in Britain and was built c.122 CE on Hadrian's Wall on the northern border of the empire.

a noble family, gained supremacy as a result of his outstanding military career.

All aspects of life were controlled by the army. Soldiers were not allowed to marry formally. If, however, they did take up with a local woman while stationed in a far-flung part of the empire, and they were together when

earning them the nickname "Marius's Mules". Modern studies have estimated the weight based on rations for 16 days and a full set of equipment. At the end of a day spent on the march they often had to set up a fortified military camp for the night, digging boundary ditches and setting up tents. Skilled engineers within the ranks also built bridges and roads, if necessary, in order to reach their destination. Training in physical fitness involved running, swimming,

BEFORE

The Roman army was shaped by confronting enemies with successful armies of their own.

GREEK HOPLITE FORMATIONS
The ancient **Greek hoplites (infantry)** fought in organized formations. The hoplite "phalanx", in which they stood closely together with their shields locked together, allowed them to form **a united front** against the enemy – something that the Roman army used during the republic.

ANCIENT GREEK HOPLITE SOLDIERS

SPARTAN POWER
From birth to death life in Sparta **48–49 »** was tied to the army. Young boys were trained as soldiers and the aim of the state was to produce a perfect and invincible hoplite army. Some of these values were echoed in the self-sacrifice demanded of Roman soldiers.

ALEXANDER'S ARMY
Alexander the Great's army of 30,000 infantry and 4,000 cavalry marched an average of over 32km (20 miles) a day **50–51 »**.

The Roman Army

Perhaps nowhere can the formidable organization and ruthlessness of the Roman world be better seen than in its army. The professional standing army of several hundred thousand men at the height of the empire, was a disciplined and well trained fighting machine.

The aquilifer (who carried the standard) was a coveted position. From this time, soldiers swore their allegiance to the emperor, which was key in ensuring their loyalty and in defending and protecting the empire's borders over the next two centuries.

TRIBUNE A junior officer.

CENTURION A soldier in control of each century of 80 men.

PRIMUS PILUS The chief centurion.

CUSTOS ARMORUM The soldier in charge of weapons and equipment.

LEGATUS LEGIONIS The commander of the legion.

PRAEFECTUS CASTRORUM The camp prefect, responsible for training and equipment.

IMMUNES Those who were excused from regular duties, including medical staff, surveyors, and armourers.

Life in the army

Although the life of a Roman soldier was dangerous and brutal, for many it was an escape from a life of poverty. It was also a way for those without money to gain political power and influence. Young men were expected to do military service as part of their education. Those from wealthier backgrounds saw the army as a step on the ladder to public office. One striking example of the positive effect a successful military career could have is Julius Caesar, who, although born into

he retired, she was given Roman citizenship in her own right.

Although the army was feared by many, it was scrupulously disciplined and generally dealt fairly with local people they came into contact with. Supplies were paid for, rather than taken, and a good general would not allow his troops to loot and pillage at random.

Fitness and training

New recruits had to be physically fit. They would be expected to march up to 30km (20 miles) a day, carrying all their equipment, which may have weighed 30kg (60lb) or more –

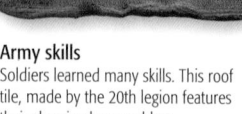

Army skills
Soldiers learned many skills. This roof tile, made by the 20th legion features their charging boar emblem.

wrestling, and throwing games. Exercises designed to build stamina might last for two days without rest. The men also practised military drills and training, as in battle every soldier would be expected to follow commands and fight in formation. One of the most famous of these was the "tortoise" (testudo), in which rectangular blocs of soldiers stood together with their shields facing outwards and upwards towards the enemy.

The life of a Roman soldier was tough, but the discipline, effective leadership, and organization were key to its success for so long.

HOW WE KNOW

VINDOLANDA TABLET

These scraps of wood were found in a waterlogged rubbish heap near a Roman fort in northern England. They provide a detailed snapshot of life on the frontier of the empire from 97–103 CE. As well as personal letters from women and servants – including a birthday invitation – the tablets reveal details about the army. Work rotas, accounts, and reports give us an idea of everyday life as a Roman soldier.

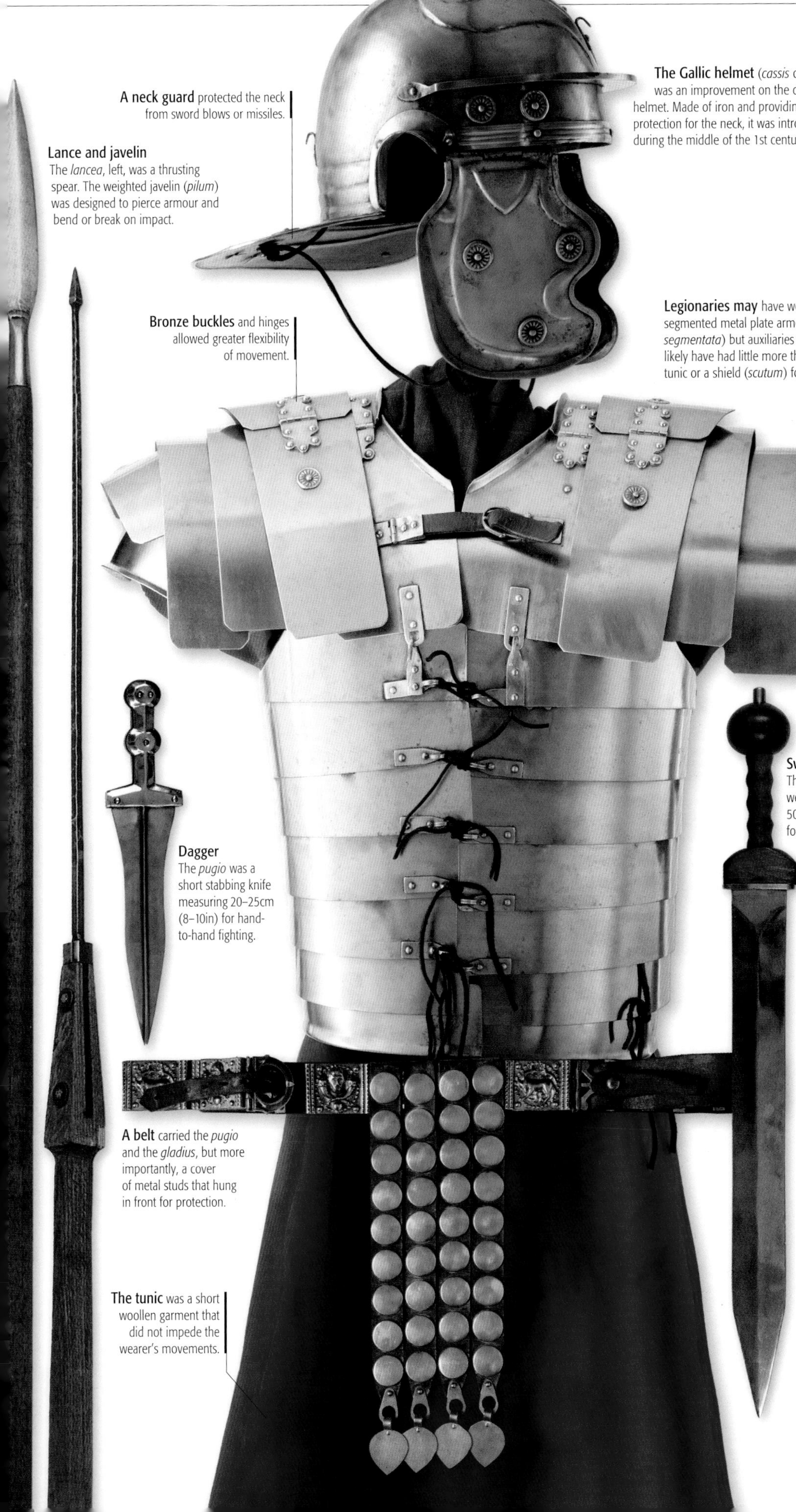

A neck guard protected the neck from sword blows or missiles.

Lance and javelin
The *lancea*, left, was a thrusting spear. The weighted javelin (*pilum*) was designed to pierce armour and bend or break on impact.

The Gallic helmet (*cassis* or *galea*) was an improvement on the older bronze helmet. Made of iron and providing extra protection for the neck, it was introduced during the middle of the 1st century CE.

Bronze buckles and hinges allowed greater flexibility of movement.

Legionaries may have worn segmented metal plate armour (*lorica segmentata*) but auxiliaries would more likely have had little more than a leather tunic or a shield (*scutum*) for protection.

AFTER »

The Roman army changed over time as enemies threatened the empire. The skills and legacy of the Roman army have influenced and inspired later fighting forces.

BARBARIANS AT THE GATE
After the middle of the 3rd century CE the army was forced to evolve to deal with **new challenges at the frontiers**. The ability to adapt to changing conditions helped keep the empire together in difficult times **102–03 »**.

COMMUNICATION NETWORK
Much of the **road network**, built as the most direct route for the marching army, is still in use.

MODERN TANK WARFARE
The tank has taken the place of the tortoise as a **mobile fighting machine** and an armoured unit to hold places of strategic importance.

Dagger
The *pugio* was a short stabbing knife measuring 20–25cm (8–10in) for hand-to-hand fighting.

Sword
The *gladius* was a short weapon measuring about 50cm (20in) long, used for stabbing.

A belt carried the *pugio* and the *gladius*, but more importantly, a cover of metal studs that hung in front for protection.

The tunic was a short woollen garment that did not impede the wearer's movements.

ROMAN ARMY
146,720 MEN
28 LEGIONS

1 LEGION
5,240 MEN
10 COHORTS + 120 HORSEMEN

1 COHORT
480 MEN
6 CENTURIES

1 CENTURY
80 MEN
10 CONTUBERNIA

1 CONTUBERNIUM
8 MEN

Army organization
These figures are for the "classic" army of the 1st century CE. The total number including auxiliaries such as engineers, armourers, and doctors, may have been twice this size.

Sandals
Roman soldiers, who often marched 30km (20 miles) a day wore leather footwear with steel studs.

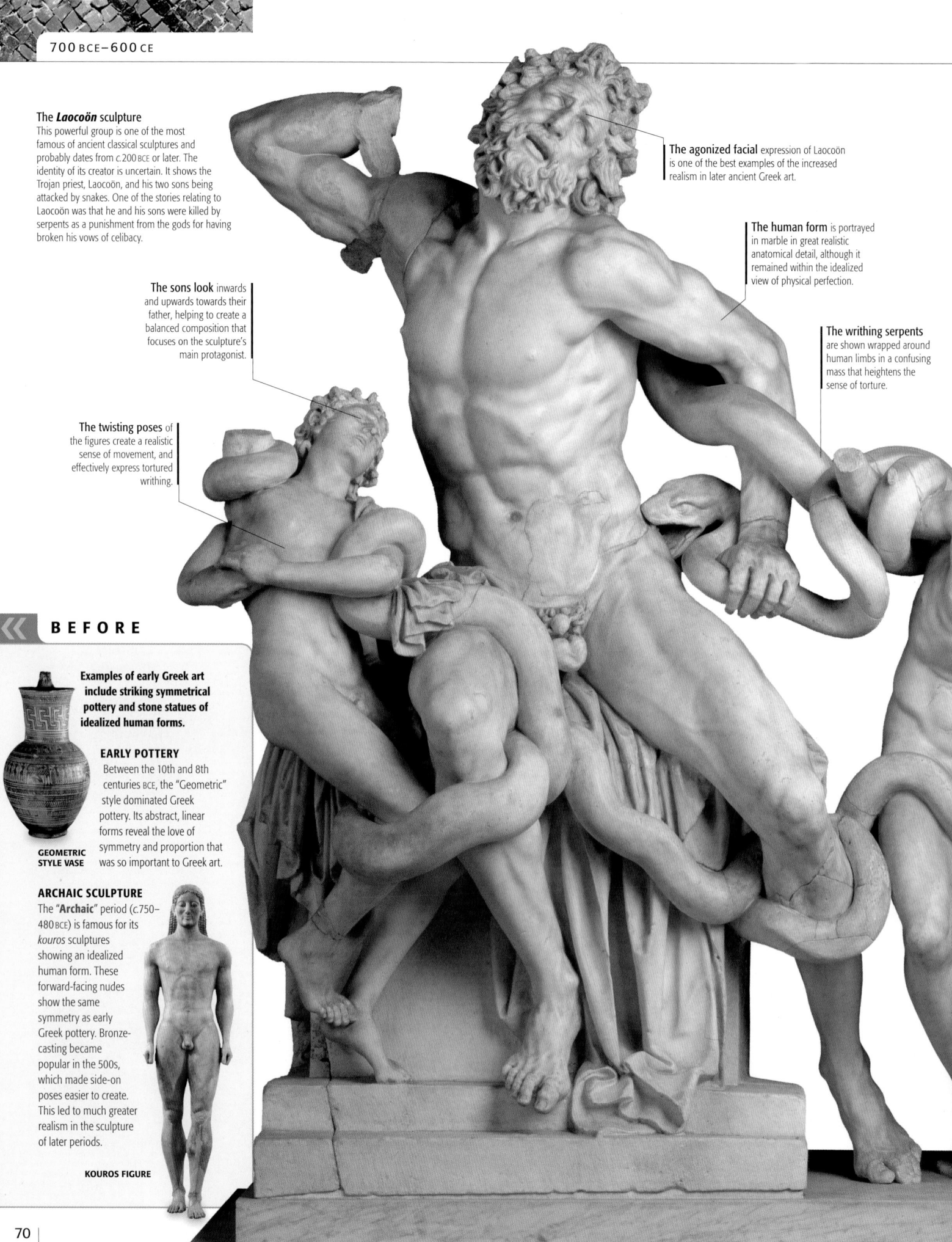

The *Laocoön* sculpture

This powerful group is one of the most famous of ancient classical sculptures and probably dates from c.200 BCE or later. The identity of its creator is uncertain. It shows the Trojan priest, Laocoön, and his two sons being attacked by snakes. One of the stories relating to Laocoön was that he and his sons were killed by serpents as a punishment from the gods for having broken his vows of celibacy.

The agonized facial expression of Laocoön is one of the best examples of the increased realism in later ancient Greek art.

The human form is portrayed in marble in great realistic anatomical detail, although it remained within the idealized view of physical perfection.

The sons look inwards and upwards towards their father, helping to create a balanced composition that focuses on the sculpture's main protagonist.

The writhing serpents are shown wrapped around human limbs in a confusing mass that heightens the sense of torture.

The twisting poses of the figures create a realistic sense of movement, and effectively express tortured writhing.

BEFORE

Examples of early Greek art include striking symmetrical pottery and stone statues of idealized human forms.

EARLY POTTERY

Between the 10th and 8th centuries BCE, the "Geometric" style dominated Greek pottery. Its abstract, linear forms reveal the love of symmetry and proportion that was so important to Greek art.

GEOMETRIC STYLE VASE

ARCHAIC SCULPTURE

The "**Archaic**" period (c.750–480 BCE) is famous for its *kouros* sculptures showing an idealized human form. These forward-facing nudes show the same symmetry as early Greek pottery. Bronze-casting became popular in the 500s, which made side-on poses easier to create. This led to much greater realism in the sculpture of later periods.

KOUROS FIGURE

The art of the classical world took the form of statuary, painted pottery, wall paintings and mosaics, and architecture. In general, Roman art took the ideas of both the Greeks and the Etruscans (a people who dominated northern Italy by the 6th century BCE see p.60) and developed it in new ways. While the Greeks loved idealized beauty, symmetry, and perfect proportion, the Romans showed a practical genius – clear in engineering feats such as the Colosseum (see pp.64–65). The Romans were influenced by Greek art through trading contacts and the changing fortunes of the Greek and Roman Empires: while the Greeks dominated parts of Italy in the Archaic era (see BEFORE), by 146 BCE, the

statue renders fabric with great realism. Polyclitus' *Doryphorus* (Spear Bearer) reveals a more realistic pose and musculature – informed by the Greeks' study of the human body, aided by observing naked athletes. It also displays a mathematically calculated ideal of beauty with perfectly proportioned limbs and body.

Realism

Classical styles continued into the Hellenistic period, but, while sculptures such as the famous *Venus de Milo* retain an ideal of female beauty, works were

Classical black figure vase
Greek vases often had dark figures against a red clay background, as in this example, or red figures on black. The painters were highly skilled and the style evolved over time.

has been lost (except for vase painting), but many Roman wall paintings survive which give an idea of the lost art. Those found in Pompeii (see p.66) and Herculaneum illustrate a particular talent for creating three-dimensional illusions of scenes such as mythological dramas on a flat surface, and for expertly rendering shading, highlights, and perspective.

The art of ancient Greece and Rome has influenced many later cultures.

BYZANTINE ART
Domed buildings, perfected by the Romans, became a distinctive feature of the eastern Byzantine empire. The 6th-century CE church of Hagia Sophia, in the former Byzantine capital, Constantinople, is one example.

HAGIA SOPHIA, ISTANBUL

THE RENAISSANCE AND BEYOND
15th-century CE Europe rediscovered the art and architecture of Classical Greece and Rome 190–91 ››. Sculptors and painters, such as Raphael in Italy, gained a classical understanding of human anatomy and architects created buildings informed by ancient Greek temples.

16TH-CENTURY PAINTING BY RAPHAEL

Classical Art

The art of ancient Greece and Rome – often known collectively as Classical Art – brought into being a wide range of different styles and approaches. These have had an enormous impact on Western art for many centuries, right up to the present day.

Romans controlled all of Greece. Generally speaking, art became more realistic over time, moving from the idealized form of the early period to the realism of the later Hellenistic period (c.323–146 BCE).

Classical Greece

The Classical era of Greek history (c.480–323 BCE) saw the flowering of "high Classical" art in an imperial Athens (see pp.54–55). The magnificent Parthenon temple (see pp.48–49) was built on the city's acropolis, adorned with sculptures created under the supervision of sculptor, Phidias.

During the Classical period, sculpture began to show greater realism than the idealized style of earlier periods. Myron's *Discobolus* (Discus Thrower) is a masterly attempt to freeze realistic movement, and the unattributed Apollo Belvedere

appearing filled with great emotion, dynamism, and expression – such as the Samothrace *Nike* (or *Winged Victory*), the *Laocoön* group (see left), and the *Dying Gaul* (see p.88).

Idealization and beauty now started to seem less important. Images appeared depicting characters from everyday life, such as a woman at a market or a boy strangling a goose.

Workshops in the ancient world at this time produced statues of all styles, in clay, marble, and bronze. These sold all over the world, to a rising number of private patrons. Before the Hellenistic era there had been little sense of "art" as a separate creative entity – statues were made to mark a grave, glorify a temple, or commemorate a war; vases often had practical uses. However, wealthy buyers who had seen statues of famous figures now wanted a portrait of themselves, or figures to decorate their villas. Seeing different styles gave rise to the first sense of a "history of art".

The art of Rome

Many of the Greek statues that survive today are actually Roman copies. In many ways the Romans simply copied the art of the Greeks, although they later went on to create their own artistic identity. Ancient Greek painting

The art of floor mosaics, using tiny pieces of coloured stone (*tesserae*), was invented by the Greeks, but is the Romans who are famous for their mosaic work. Imperial Rome saw mosaic pavements and walls featuring ambitious schemes and imagery.

The Romans created monumental architecture and statues that celebrated the glories and wealth of their rule – Trajan's column and the Arch of Constantine, for example. Trajan's column was designed by a Greek architect, Apollodorus of Damascus, showing a continuing connection between Greek and Roman art. The Romans also used the Greek temple form, often placing it on a platform to make it more impressive and filling its panels with sculptures plundered from Greece. Their grand villas overflowed with statues, while Roman leaders used the power of art as propaganda. Without the Roman use of Greek art much of its style and influence may have been lost to us.

> **"Beauty** consists in the proportions…**"**
> GALEN, GREEK PHYSICIAN, 129–C.200 CE

Corinthian column
The Greeks created several different "orders" (styles) of column for their buildings, which the Romans later adapted. This column is in the Greek Corinthian style, which was especially popular in Rome.

ZEUXIS (5th century BCE) was one of ancient Greece's most famous painters. Ancient writers told a famous tale about Zeuxis painting an image of grapes that was so realistic that birds tried to peck it. Sadly, none of his work survives today.

« BEFORE

After the New Kingdom « 110–11, Egypt suffered a series of invasions, until Alexander claimed it for himself.

BRIEF RENAISSANCE

The Assyrians « 25, 38–39 were ousted, and native Egyptian pharaohs presided over **a renaissance** of their culture – the Saite era, c.664–525 BCE.

LATE PERIOD

Achaemenid Persians « 46–47 dominated in the years 525–400 BCE. Egyptians then ruled until 343 BCE, when the Persians returned to defeat **Nectanebo II**, the last native Egyptian pharaoh.

LATE-PERIOD EGYPTIAN GRAVE STATUE

ALEXANDER'S CONQUEST

In 332 BCE, **Alexander « 50–51** seized Egypt from **Darius III** (the last Achaemenid king) when he conquered the Persian empire.

p.33) there had been a Greek presence in Egypt (see pp.70–71) and the Ptolemies – educated, like Alexander, as Greeks – created a distinctly Greek court and system of administration.

Cultural co-existence

The Ptolemies did not impose their culture on the Egyptians. While the ruling class enjoyed a Greek lifestyle, in all other layers of society, Egyptian culture continued much as before. Furthermore, the Greek rulers styled themselves as native monarchs, taking the title of pharaoh. They even built Egyptian-style temples, and worshipped native gods. The parallel Greek–Egyptian culture is illustrated by the Rosetta Stone, with its Greek, hieroglyphic, and demotic scripts (see p.22).

Ptolemaic rule

If the Ptolemies' co-operative policy was a shrewd political strategy, it paid off, because their rule brought stability to Egypt. Reforms were made to land

location opened Egypt up to the trade and cultures of the Mediterranean. With its library of legendary fame, it became the world's centre of Greek learning.

The Romans

By the middle of the 1st century BCE, the Ptolemaic dynasty was weakened by leadership rivalries. Rome had been increasing its role in Egyptian affairs and was now effectively overseeing the country. Independence was completely lost in 30 BCE, when Cleopatra VII (see pp.74–75) the last Ptolemaic ruler, allied herself with the losing side in the power struggles in the Roman Republic (see pp.64–67). Octavian, the victorious Roman leader, incorporated Egypt as his own personal domain.

Alexandria continued to flourish and became a meeting point for Roman trade routes. It also remained a centre for Greek culture, visited by scholars from across the Greek-speaking world. In the early days of Roman rule, the Egyptian government kept its strong

HOW WE KNOW

ALEXANDRIA HARBOUR

In the 3rd-century BCE, during Ptolemaic times, a great lighthouse was completed on Pharos island, in the harbour of Egypt's cosmopolitan capital, Alexandria. This towering structure – destroyed by an earthquake during the medieval period – was one of the Seven Wonders of the ancient world. During the 1990s, archaeologists made some incredible finds underwater, including possible masonry from the lighthouse, and the remains of some impressive ancient statues. This image shows the recovery of a massive statue that may be one of the Ptolemaic kings.

Life on the Nile
The River Nile remained a vital artery for the Egyptians in Ptolemaic and Roman times. This mosaic from c.100 BCE shows life along the river's banks.

Greek and Roman Egypt

Ancient Egypt's later history is one of fascinating change and diversity. Absorbed into the empire of the Macedonian, Alexander the Great, Egypt joined the Hellenistic (Greek) world under the Ptolemies, before becoming a province first of Rome, and then of the Byzantine Empire.

When Alexander, the Greek-educated king of Macedonia, died in 323 BCE, Egypt was part of his vast empire, and its control passed to one of Alexander's trusted generals, Ptolemy Lagus, who had been his governor there. By 304 BCE, Ptolemy was king of Egypt, and his descendants would rule for 300 years. The "Ptolemaic" period of Greek rule in Egypt came at a time when Greek culture had a wide influence across the Middle East and Mediterranean – a movement known as Hellenism (see p.53). Ever since Mycenaean times (see

ownership, and methods of agriculture improved. Regional administration was organized using the existing Egyptian "nome" system of administrative districts. With an energetic flair for

107 m (350 ft) – the reputed height of the Pharos lighthouse at Alexandria – second only to the pyramids

business, the Ptolemies also began to replace the Egyptian barter system with an early form of monetary banking, created royal monopolies on certain goods, and zealously explored trade opportunities. Ptolemy I moved Egypt's capital from Memphis to Alexandria – the new port-city founded by Alexander – where it was to remain for 900 years. Alexandria became the prosperous symbol of Ptolemaic rule. Its north-coast

Greek culture, but the title of pharaoh became identified with the far-off emperor in Rome. Increasingly, however, Roman influences took hold. The Romans probably retained much of the Ptolemaic system of administration, but they slowly introduced many of their own practices in agriculture and everyday life. As Rome's power faded from the 4th century CE, Egypt came under the influence of the Christian Eastern Roman Empire based in Constantinople (once Byzantium, now Istanbul) and became a melting pot of different religious ideas.

Coptic Christianity

During the 1st century CE, Christianity spread to Egypt. By the later 4th century, it was the Roman Empire's official religion, and by the 6th, Egypt was strongly Christian. A devout Coptic church developed, which later became the principal Christian church in mainly Muslim Egypt. Copts held the "monophysite" belief that Christ was solely divine, and not both human and divine. In 451 CE the Eastern Roman Empire rejected the "monophysite" doctrine at the Council of Chalcedon (in modern Turkey), but the Egyptian Copts continued to adhere to it.

AFTER »

KHOSROW OF PERSIA ATTACKS THE BYZANTINES

Alexandria lost its status as the pre-eminent city of eastern Christianity to Constantinople (Byzantium 144–45 »). The Arabs' arrival in 642 CE dramatically changed Egypt again.

STRUGGLES OF PERSIA AND BYZANTIUM

Persian king **Khosrow II**, wrested control of Egypt from the **Byzantine emperor, Heraclius**, and ruled briefly (616–28 CE) before Byzantium won control back, between 629–641 CE.

ARRIVAL OF THE ARABS

Egypt then passed to the **Arabs 124–25 »**. Caliph 'Amr ibn al-'As founded an encampment near Memphis that would later become Cairo, and introduced **Islam**, which dominates today.

Alexandria
This is a 6th-century Byzantine mosaic of the city, which was a leading centre of Christianity by the 2nd century CE.

ΑΛΕΞΑΝΔΡΙΑ

THE LAST PHARAOH OF EGYPT Born c.68 BCE Died 30 BCE

Cleopatra

"I will not be exhibited in his triumph."

CLEOPATRA REMARKING ON OCTAVIAN'S VICTORY PARADE, 30 BCE

A s a daughter of Ptolemy XII of Egypt, Cleopatra VII belonged to the Ptolemaic Dynasty (see pp.170–71) set up by the first Ptolemy, one of the generals of Alexander the Great (see pp.50–51). In theory, Egypt was independent, but in practice it was controlled by Rome. The Romans supported the Ptolemaic monarchs in return for financial favours. Cleopatra's father put up enormous sums to secure Roman backing, but this did not prevent Cleopatra's older sisters Tryphaena and Berenice from plotting against him.

When her father died in 51 BCE, Cleopatra, as eldest surviving daughter, ascended the throne with a younger brother. According to tradition, the king and queen were brother and sister as well as husband and wife, so she was expected to marry her brother, Ptolemy XIII. However, he and his chief minister Pothinus had other ideas – Ptolemy wished to be sole ruler, and by 49 BCE Cleopatra had been deprived of power and exiled. In 48 BCE, when the Roman political and military leader Julius Caesar (see pp.62–63) led a military campaign to Egypt, Cleopatra feared for her life. In becoming Caesar's lover, she was fighting for survival.

Caesar and Caesarion

With the help of reinforcements from Rome, Julius Caesar defeated an Egyptian army led by yet another of Cleopatra's sisters, Arsinoë IV. During the same campaign, Ptolemy XIII drowned – pulled into the Nile by the weight of his golden armour. Cleopatra was now free to rule Egypt with her youngest brother, Ptolemy XIV. Caesar had returned to Rome when she had their baby, whom she named Ptolemy Caesar, or Caesarion

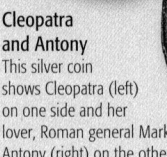

Cleopatra and Antony
This silver coin shows Cleopatra (left) on one side and her lover, Roman general Mark Antony (right) on the other.

Cleopatra as pharaoh
In this relief from a temple at Dendra, Cleopatra is depicted in the style of a pharaoh, wearing the crown of Hathor and a vulture headdress. She holds a staff and an ankh – the sign of life.

A legendary beauty
This 19th-century image depicts the glamorous Cleopatra of myth and legend. In reality, her success as a leader and a lover owed more to her intelligence and charm than her looks.

("little Caesar"). Shortly after, on the official pretext of negotiating a treaty, Cleopatra visited Rome. At the time, it was common practice to display captives in triumphs (victory parades), so during Caesar's triumph, Cleopatra may have witnessed the exhibition of her sister Arsinoë.

After Caesar's assassination, Cleopatra returned to Egypt. It is likely that she organized the assassination of her co-ruler, Ptolemy XIV, replacing him with her son, Caesarion (Ptolemy XV). For the next three years, Cleopatra was careful to avoid the power struggle that broke out after Caesar's death. Instead, she restored order and prosperity to her own kingdom where she was a popular and efficient ruler.

By 42 BCE the Roman general Mark Antony and Octavian (the future emperor Augustus, see p.66) were in control of the Roman world. They split power between them, Antony taking charge of the eastern Mediterranean. He summoned Cleopatra to Tarsus (in modern Turkey). and once again, she set out to conquer a conqueror, dazzling the Romans with her style and guile.

Antony and Cleopatra

At Tarsus Cleopatra and Antony became lovers, but passion had yet to overrule politics. Before long Antony had rejoined his Roman wife, Fulvia, in Greece, where she had fled after a failed rebellion against Octavian in Italy. By 40 BCE Fulvia was dead, which enabled Antony to seal another peace deal with Octavian by marrying his sister Octavia. In the

> ## "Plato admits four sorts of flattery, but she had a thousand."
>
> PLUTARCH, IN HIS BIOGRAPHY
> OF MARK ANTONY, c.75 CE

Cleopatra and Isis
This limestone stele shows Cleopatra (left) breastfeeding her son while making an offering to the goddess Isis. She later claimed to be the reincarnation of Isis.

meantime, Cleopatra had given birth to twins: a boy named Alexander Helios (sun) and a girl named Cleopatra Selene (moon). In 37 BCE, Antony came back to Egypt, and, while still wedded to Octavia, married Cleopatra. By the time he set off on an unsuccessful military campaign against the Parthians (see pp.76–77), she was expecting the baby she would name Ptolemy Philadelphus. Antony's next campaign, in Armenia, was victorious. His return to Egypt as a hero was followed by an event known as the "Donations of Alexandria". Seated on

Cleopatra's decree
This papyrus document is a decree exempting a Roman citizen, Publius Candidus, from paying tax. Written in Egyptian demotic script at the royal chancellery in Alexandria, it has a note by Cleopatra stating: "Thus it shall happen". The Ptolemies, of whom Cleopatra was the last, were Greek-speaking. She was the first and only Ptolemy to learn Egyptian, the language of her subjects.

golden thrones, Cleopatra and Antony proclaimed themselves as living gods – she Isis (see below) and he Dionysus/Osiris – and their children as the rulers of lands currently dominated by Rome.

After this, Octavian had no difficulty in persuading the Roman Senate to provide the means for an all-out war against Cleopatra, who was clearly determined to set herself up as a rival power. After her defeat by the Romans at the Battle of Actium, fought off the coast of Greece, she fled to Egypt with 60 treasure-laden ships, followed by Antony. Besieged at Alexandria, Antony killed himself, and Cleopatra, perhaps aware of her likely fate as the star of Octavian's triumph, also took her own life, supposedly with a poisonous snake hidden in a basket of figs.

Octavian honoured Clewopatra's final request to be buried with Antony. She was 39. Her eldest son, Caesarion, was executed, but it is thought that the other children's lives were spared.

IDEA

THE CULT OF ISIS

Daughter of the earth and sky, and sister-wife of the god Osiris, Isis was the principal goddess of ancient Egypt. When Osiris was murdered by the god Set, Isis found his body and performed rites that would return him to eternal life. Then she retired to raise her son Horus, magically conceived from her husband's corpse, until he was old enough to avenge his father. While the myth of Isis may have arisen as a representation of the flooding of the rich plains (Isis) by the Nile (Osiris) – the cult of the sorrowing wife and loving mother spread far beyond its place of origin. Isis was adopted as a patron divinity of travellers, and had particular appeal to women.

THE GODDESS ISIS

TIMELINE

- **c.68 BCE** Birth of Cleopatra, third daughter of Ptolemy XII of Egypt.

- **55 BCE** Cleopatra's sisters Berenice and Tryphaena are killed for deposing Ptolemy XII.

- **51 BCE** Ptolemy XII dies; Cleopatra VII becomes queen of Egypt with her brother, Ptolemy XIII.

- **49 BCE** Cleopatra is banished by Pothinus, chief adviser of Ptolemy XIII.

- **48 BCE** Julius Caesar arrives in Egypt and defeats the forces of Cleopatra's sister Arsinoë and Ptolemy XIII; Cleopatra is restored to power with another younger brother, Ptolemy XIV.

- **c.47 BCE** Gives birth to a son, nicknamed Caesarion by the people of Alexandria in acknowledgement of his supposed father.

- **46 BCE** Back in Rome, Caesar celebrates with four triumphs (victory parades), the most splendid of which celebrates his victory in Egypt and features Cleopatra's captured sister Arsinoë in chains.

- **44 BCE** Cleopatra leaves Rome for Egypt after the assassination of Julius Caesar. Ptolemy XIV is assassinated, possibly by Cleopatra, and replaced by her son Caesarion (Ptolemy XV).

  OCTAVIAN

- **42 BCE** Octavian (right) and Mark Antony win the Battle of Philippi. Antony and Cleopatra meet in Tarsus and become lovers.

- **40 BCE** Cleopatra bears twins, Alexander Helios and Cleopatra Selene. The father is Mark Antony.

- **37 BCE** Antony returns to the Middle East and Cleopatra funds his military expeditions.

- **36 BCE** Cleopatra has another baby by Antony, Ptolemy Philadelphus.

- **35 BCE** Cleopatra delivers funds and much needed supplies for Antony's defeated army in Syria; Cleopatra and Antony return to Alexandria in Egypt together.

- **34 BCE** Antony returns from a successful military campaign in Armenia and celebrates his triumph in Alexandria. Vast territories and exalted titles are assigned to Cleopatra and her children in a ceremony known as the "Donations of Alexandria", which alarms Rome.

- **33 BCE** In Greece, Cleopatra and Antony organize land and naval forces in anticipation of war with Rome.

- **31 BCE** Cleopatra and Antony lose the Battle of Actium, but manage to return to Alexandria.

- **30 BCE** Rather than be taken to Rome by Octavian as a prisoner of war, Cleopatra kills herself, allegedly by poisonous snake bite.

RENAISSANCE VIEW OF THE DEATH OF CLEOPATRA

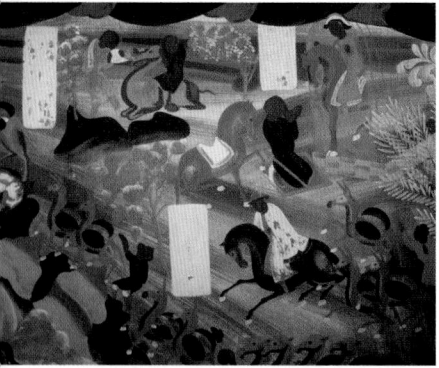

Trade links between Persia and China
This cave fresco in Dunhuang, China, from c.600 CE shows Sogdian merchants (from eastern Persia) on the Silk Road between the Sassanid Empire and China.

Parthian coins of King Gotarzes II
The Parthians retained the use of Greek on their coins – these were minted in 49–51 BCE – despite a fading knowledge of Greek during their empire.

The Greek–Macedonian empire of the Seleucids (see pp.52–53 and BEFORE) incorporated most of the Asian conquests of Alexander (see pp.50–51), including all of Persia and Mesopotamia. This empire was almost as vast as its predecessor – the first Persian empire of the Achaemenids (see pp.46–47) – but by the 3rd century BCE it had started to crumble as its many subjects asserted their autonomy.

Emergence of the Parthians
In the ruins of the empire, a people called the Parthians saw an opening. Once nomads, who had settled in the northeast of the old Persian Empire, the Parthians had gained independence from Seleucid rule by 238 BCE. With

spread west from India along Parthian trade routes. These contacts denied Roman traders access to routes to China and India, leading to battles with the Roman armies. Parthia's most famous victory was the battle of Carrhae (or Harran, southeast Turkey) in 53 BCE when the Roman army was utterly destroyed. Constant fighting with the Romans and nomads may have weakened the Parthians. They left little written record, so historians rely on their art and architecture, and foreign texts to paint a picture of the period.

> **THE PARTHIAN SHOT** A trick used by the Parthians that involved feigning a rapid retreat, only to turn round in the saddle to fire arrows at their pursuers.

Sassanid fortified settlement
Built high above the fertile Iranian plateau, Takht-e-Soleyman, or Solomon's Throne, was one of the holiest sites of the Sassanid Persians. It housed a Zoroastrian fire temple with an eternally burning flame.

fire altars were erected to Ormazd, or Ahura Mazda, god of light, truth, and life. Most Sassanid rulers, however, were tolerant of religions other than their own, and large populations of Jews and Christians inhabited the empire, especially in Mesopotamia.

In the early 7th century the Sassanids suffered a serious military defeat at the hands of the Byzantine Emperor Heraclius. From this point, the weakened empire lay at the mercy of Islamic forces invading from the south.

The Revival of Persia

Persia emerged from Greek rule under the control of the Parthian people. Parthian expansion coincided with that of the Roman Empire, and the two powers spent three centuries at loggerheads with each other. The Persians themselves regained control in 226 CE, founding the rich and opulent Sassanid dynasty.

« BEFORE

The first Persian Empire, based in southwest Iran, was ruled by the Achaemenid dynasty from c.520 BCE « 46–47. When Alexander the Great « 50–51 swept the empire away in 334–323 BCE, the lands were not ruled by Persians for another 500 years.

THE SELEUCID DYNASTY
Alexander's conquests were partitioned after his death. Mesopotamia, Persia, and the east fell to a dynasty of **Greek-Macedonian rulers** founded by **Seleucus I** « 52–53, who had marched with Alexander's conquering army into Asia. Seleucus set up a new capital, **Seleucia**, on the Tigris river.

A GREEK–PERSIAN MIX
Greek and Persian cultures mixed « 52–53 in the territory ruled by Seleucus I and his **Persian wife,**

SELEUCID BRONZE **Apama.** Alexander had dreamed of a Greek–Macedonian–Persian empire with its component cultures taking strength from one another. He had encouraged **intermarriage** between his soldiers and locals.

AN EMPIRE LOST
The Seleucid empire weakened as the remote, **Central Asian Greek city states** « 52–53 of **Bactria** (in modern Afghanistan) and other states further west won independence. The empire retreated from India and Bactria in c.250 BCE.

expansion east, they took control of the silk routes from China and began strangling what was left of the Seleucid Empire itself. Under their king Mithridates I, Parthians overpowered Mesopotamia to control all lands from India to the river Tigris. Mithridates recognized the value of the Greek–Persian culture he was inheriting, so allowed the defeated cities to retain their administrative systems, trading ties, and languages, while placing Parthian governors to oversee them.

Between Rome and China
The Romans defeated and annexed the Seleucid kingdom, thus becoming neighbours to the Parthians. So began an uneasy relationship that cast Parthia as the enemy of Rome for the next 300 years.

Parthians were well suited to frequent border skirmishes. In the north their frontiers were under constant threat from Steppe nomads (see pp.90–91), who they held at bay with a tactic of lightning cavalry strikes.

The Parthians had indirect contact with the Han Chinese, whose envoy Zhang Qian (see p.83) travelled to the west and returned with accounts of their empire. Buddhist ideas, meanwhile,

What is certain is that the Persians re-emerged under Ardashir I of the Sassanid dynasty, who defeated the Parthians in 226 CE, restoring Persian rule until 640 CE.

The Persians back in power
From the Parthians, the Sassanids inherited control of land trade routes to the east. They also faced the Parthians' perennial problems of repelling nomads from the north and east and the Romans from the west. Ardashir's son, Shapur I, won a famous victory over the Romans at Edessa in 259 CE, capturing the Roman Emperor Valerian. Despite this initial success, war with the Romans and their successors, the Byzantines (see pp.144–45), continued through four centuries of Sassanid rule.

The Sassanids built a rich civilization based largely on agriculture and trade. Government was far more centralized than under Parthian rule, with local officials appointed by the king responsible for the building of roads and cities, which was paid for by central government.

Zoroastrianism, the traditional faith of the Persians, was elevated to the status of official state religion, and many new

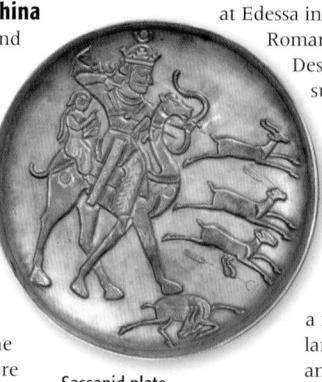

Sassanid plate
This gold plate, typical of Persian artistic refinement, shows the king hunting on a camel – an image found on many Sassanid artefacts.

AFTER »

Persia was rapidly annexed by the Islamic conquerors, but Persian culture lived on in its art and literature.

DEFEAT BY THE ARABS
Arab Muslim armies 122–23 » routed the Sassanids at the **Battle of Qadisiyya** in 637 CE, and Muslims took over the institutions of power.

SEAT OF LEARNING
By 762 CE the **Abbasid caliphate 123 »**, having moved its capital to Baghdad, near Babylon, had become the world's greatest **centre of scholarship**. Scholars of all religions made contributions to law, medicine, astronomy, maths, and philosophy.

PERSIAN HERITAGE
Persia's imperial past was not forgotten. Miniatures were painted and **epic stories** **PERSIAN QUR'AN** collected about the glories of the Achaemenid, Parthian, and Sassanid empires. Ferdowsi's **Shahnameh**, or **"Epic of Kings"** (c.1000 CE), is a key work from this time.

MONGOL CONQUEST
In 1258, the **Mongols 114–15 »** destroyed the art and learning of centuries, although their Islamic successors sought to repair the damage.

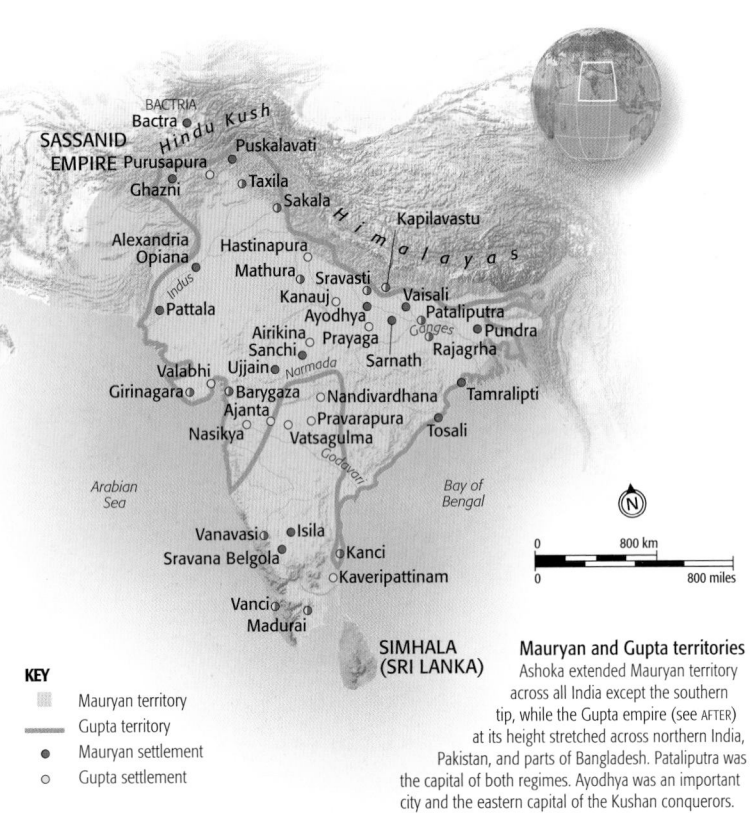

Mauryan and Gupta territories
Ashoka extended Mauryan territory across all India except the southern tip, while the Gupta empire (see AFTER) at its height stretched across northern India, Pakistan, and parts of Bangladesh. Pataliputra was the capital of both regimes. Ayodhya was an important city and the eastern capital of the Kushan conquerors.

KEY
- ▨ Mauryan territory
- — Gupta territory
- ● Mauryan settlement
- ○ Gupta settlement

« **BEFORE**

The Vedic period (c.1500–500 BCE) is named after the Vedas – ancient Indo–Aryan texts that were produced during this time and that are central to the Hindu faith.

EARLY VEDIC PERIOD
Many local dynasties came into being, and by the 8th century BCE, India was divided into many small, competing kingdoms.

LATE VEDIC PERIOD
Around the 8th century BCE large urban states known as *mahajanapadas* started to take shape in northern India. The northeastern **Magadha** area came to dominate the various warring regional powers. Its strategic position in the Ganges valley aided trade and linked it with flourishing ports in the Ganges river delta.

NANDA DYNASTY
In the 5th century BCE, just a few states, including Magadha, dominated India. By the 4th century, after countless wars, Magadha had emerged as the most powerful. Ruled by the prosperous **Nanda dynasty**, it set up complex irrigation projects and an efficient administration system, built a strong army, and established a royal centre at the city of **Pataliputra** (modern Patna).

RISING RELIGIONS
Jainism and **Buddhism 96–99 »** were well established by the 4th century BCE, gaining ground against Vedic traditions – the origin of Hinduism.

India's First Empire

From their northeastern heartland, the Mauryans came to dominate India's massive subcontinent with what became its first real empire. This reached its greatest extent and enjoyed its greatest cultural flowering under the rule of Ashoka, who also played a major part in the rise of the Buddhist religion.

A round 321 BCE, the Nanda dynasty (see BEFORE) was toppled by Chandragupta Maurya, founder of the Mauryan dynasty and what would become the great Mauryan empire (c.321–185 BCE). The emperor Chandragupta won a great deal of new territory, combining smaller kingdoms and uniting – often rather loosely – vast regions of India under one ruler for the first time. The empire embraced much of the Indian subcontinent and part of Afghanistan.

The lands into which Chandragupta expanded included parts of the Macedonian empire won by Alexander (see pp.50–53) and by his successors the Seleucids. The Seleucids' attempts to repeat Alexander's success brought them headlong into the path of the advancing Mauryans, but Seleucus I Nicator ceded his claims to lands around the Indus in a pact with Chandragupta in 305 BCE.

Hellenistic (Greek) culture continued to have an influence in northern India, while Chandragupta based his administration partly on the Persian Achaemenid model (see pp.46–47). His highly efficient and impressive centralized system also owed much to his minister, Chanakya, who produced one of the greatest treatises on politics, administration, and economics ever written – *Arthashastra*.

Chandragupta's legacy

At the core of Chandragupta's newly won empire was its glittering capital at Pataliputra. Under his sure hand, backed by strong military resources and an effective secret service, agriculture and trade flourished. He died around 297 BCE, having fasted to death. As a convert to Jainism, he spent his final days in ascetic repentance for a terrible famine that struck his people and that he was grief-stricken at being unable to hold back.

The second emperor was Chandragupta's son, Bindusara (c.297–265 BCE). Little is known of his reign, but it seems

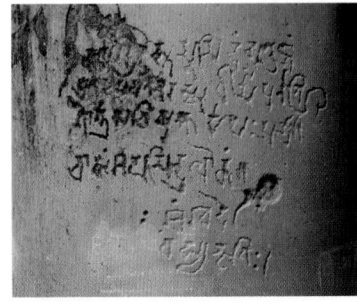

Ashoka pillar
This is one of Ashoka's famous polished sandstone pillars bearing edicts inscribed in Brahmi script to help spread his ideas among his people. They are among the oldest deciphered original Indian texts.

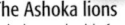

The Ashoka lions
Ashoka made this four-lion motif his symbol of imperial authority and it is now used as India's official emblem.

Sanchi gate

Four magnificent gateways lead to the Great Stupa at Sanchi. Dating from the first century BCE, these "torans" are decorated with intricate carvings that are one of the greatest artistic achievements of ancient Indian art. They show scenes from the life of Buddha and feature motifs such as Ashoka's famous four lions.

500 The number of war elephants presented by Chandragupta to Seleucus I Nicator in 305 BCE, in return for giving up his claims to Indian lands. He used the elephants in battles fought between Alexander's "successors", notably in the defeat of Antigonus at Ipsus in 301 BCE.

Great Stupa of Sanchi

Sanchi, central India, is home to one of the most impressive examples of Ashoka's stupa-building programme in the 3rd century BCE. It was added to over subsequent centuries.

The 1st–3rd centuries CE saw the Kushans from the steppes of Central Asia ruling in the north while small dynasties came and went elsewhere. As these crumbled, the way was paved for the great empire of the Guptas.

DETAIL FROM AJANTA CAVE PAINTINGS

THE GUPTA EMPIRE

Around 320 CE, the region of Magadha gave birth to another great dynasty and empire, the **Guptas**, who dominated northern India until c.540 CE. The Gupta dynasty's real empire-builders were its two first kings: **Chandra Gupta I** (c.320–330) and his son, Samudra Gupta (c.330–380). Great artistic achievements of this well-administrated, prosperous empire include the **Ajanta cave paintings** in western India. Some of these show episodes from the life of Buddha.

ART, RELIGION, AND SCIENCE

The Gupta era is often seen as the "classical" period of Indian culture, especially of **Hindu and Buddhist art**. The Guptas had a strong Hindu leaning, but Jainism and Buddhism also flourished. The classic image of **Buddha** developed, with a peaceful, reflective expression and curls flat against his head. Jain and Buddhist monks also created wonderful sculpted friezes at the **Udayagiri caves** (below). Wealthy patrons also encouraged architecture, dance, drama, and Sanskrit epics, while great advances were made in mathematics, astronomy, philosophy, logic, and medicine.

GUPTA-ERA BUDDHA

DEMISE OF THE GUPTAS

Under the fourth Guptan ruler, Kumara Gupta (c.415–455), cracks began to appear in the empire as it faced incursions by **Hephthalite** nomads (or "White Huns") from the north. By the 6th century, the Guptas had pulled back to their original heartland, and India was again a patchwork of small kingdoms **126 ≫**.

UDAYAGIRI CAVES

---

that he successfully expanded Mauryan territories south into the Deccan, so that only the southern tip of India, plus the Kalinga area in the east (now in Orissa state), were not incorporated in the empire.

Bindusara's son, Ashoka, the third emperor (c.265–232 BCE) was the last major ruler of the Mauryan dynasty and one of the great figures of ancient history. It was Ashoka who brought the empire to its greatest extent, gaining the Kalinga region after a particularly bloody battle. It was said that the waters of the Daya River, next to the battlefield, ran red with the blood of the many thousands fallen.

Ashoka is seen as presiding over a golden age. As his empire prospered, he promoted the arts and sciences and instigated a vast building programme. This included a great many stupas (mound-shaped shrines), built to house supposed relics of Buddha.

At some point in his reign Ashoka converted to the fast-growing religion of Buddhism. According to a story that mirrors the tale of his grandfather's repentance, he converted in remorse at the waste and bloodshed of the Kalinga War, turning his back on violence and embracing the peaceful Buddhist way of life. He sent missionaries to spread the word far and wide throughout Asia, including Sri Lanka, and in so doing played a major role in the development of Buddhism. He also spread the word through his edicts – sayings inscribed on stone pillars and rocks across India, Nepal, Pakistan, and Afghanistan. These set out his principles of peace, morality, respect, and humane rule, and of being the father who guides his people's spiritual welfare.

> "All men are **my children**. What I desire for my own children… I desire for **all men**."
>
> ASHOKA IN ONE OF HIS ROCK EDICTS, c.240 BCE

End of an era

The peace and prosperity of Ashoka's reign did not continue long after his death. Subsequent rulers lost territories and prestige, and there were squabbles over the succession. The last Mauryan emperor, Brihadratha, was assassinated c.185 BCE by his chief aide, Pusyamitra, founder of the Sunga dynasty, which ruled central India until c.73 BCE. India was now revisiting its chaotic, divided pre-Mauryan history. Small kingdoms arose in northern India, among them those of the so-called "Indo–Greek" rulers. The most famous of these was Menander (155–130 BCE), who may have battled with the Sungas.

DECIMAL NUMBER SYSTEMS

Indian mathematics advanced greatly under the Mauryans and Guptas (see AFTER). By the 4th century BCE, scholars were developing the idea of using combinations of units of different sizes. By the 1st century CE, they had devised a decimal-like system using the symbols shown here and refined the concept of zero as a "placeholder" to add and multiply numbers. The concept spread from India to the Islamic world and finally to the West, where it underlies the modern number system.

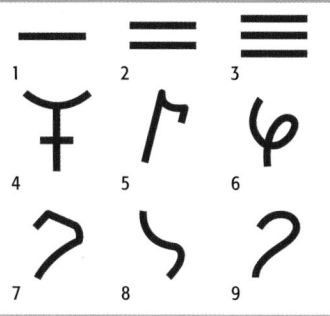

The Unification of China

The rise of the dynamic Qin state, which conquered the Warring States to create the Chinese empire, brought a period of stability and prosperity to China. Under the short-lived but ambitious rule of the First Emperor (221–206 BCE), the laws and infrastructure of imperial China first took shape.

BEFORE

As China moved out of the Bronze Age, the Shang were defeated by the Zhou, the last of the pre-imperial dynasties.

THE ZHOU DYNASTY
The Zhou dynasty (1027–256 BCE) lasted **longer than any other in Chinese history**. During the Zhou period bronze was widely used, and

ZHOU BRONZE

iron technology was introduced in China. The Zhou dynasty saw the **birth of the major indigenous Chinese philosophies**, including Confucianism **85 »**, and a system of government that had many **similarities to the European feudalism of the Middle Ages 134–37 »**.

THE WARRING STATES PERIOD
The Zhou rapidly **disintegrated into a number of independent states**, and from 481 BCE, the start of the era known as the Warring States Period, **regional warlords** were conquering smaller states around them to consolidate their rule.

The terracotta army
The First Emperor's mausoleum was constructed near Xi'an by 700,000 conscripts. In 1974 a chance find led to the uncovering of four pits containing over 7,500 life-size and lifelike terracotta soldiers, horses, and chariots (left). The scale of the mausoleum is a testament to the power of the First Emperor. Today, the terracotta army is visited by two million people every year.

One of the territories to survive the Warring States period was the state of Qin. The people of Qin were situated to the west of Zhou territory along the Yellow River valley – so far west that people said they shared the customs of the Rong and Di, non-Chinese groups regarded as uncivilized. In 316 BCE Qin began a series of campaigns against the other warring states, and in 221 BCE the king of Qin defeated the last remaining state and declared himself Qin Shi Huang (see below), the First Emperor of Qin.

Qin Legalism
In 356 BCE, before the Qin had even begun to conquer the surrounding states, Lord Shang, an exponent of Legalist ideas, became chief minister of Qin. The Legalists opposed the Confucian ideals of filial piety and kingly benevolence (see p.85). Instead, they argued that the interests of the state came before those of individuals, that rulers should apply strict laws and punishments, and that the use of war as an instrument of state policy was acceptable. Lord Shang began a programme of Legalist reform in the state of Qin, where all adult males were registered for military service. Perhaps unsurprisingly, considering its emphasis on the infallibility of the head of state, the First Emperor was a keen advocate of Legalism. During his reign, Li Si, the chief minister, put Legalist principles into practice and introduced measures which are still in effect throughout China today. Among these measures were the abolition of the feudal fiefs (see BEFORE), the standardization of the written script, the application of a strict legal code,

the establishment of official measures for weights and lengths, the issue of a unified currency, and even the regulation of the width of roads.

The Qin Empire
Though the Chinese empire had already been created by the conquest of the Warring States, Qin expansion continued southwards. Expeditions were sent to modern Guangdong, on the south coast of China, and Chinese colonies were established there.

After campaigning against the steppe peoples in the north, the emperor ordered his general Meng Tian to construct a great wall to establish

> **QIN** Pronounced "Chin" – a Chinese dynasty and a likely origin of the English word for China.

control over the Ordos region of Inner Mongolia, in order to help repel further incursions from the steppes. This was the first phase of the Great Wall of China, which was later rebuilt during the Ming dynasty (see pp.114–15). Meng Tian also constructed the Straight Road, which ran 800km (500 miles) north from the capital Xianyang to the Ordos region to facilitate the movement of military troops.

As well as constructing works that enhanced China's defences, Qin Shi Huang also commissioned many grand public building projects – including palaces, bridges, and canals – to strengthen imperial rule in China.

An immortal tomb
As he grew old, the emperor became increasingly obsessed with finding the secret of immortality. This obsession led to the most ambitious building project commissioned by Qin Shi Huang – the construction of his own mausoleum – which began in 212 BCE. According to the description recorded a century later by the Grand Historian, Sima Qian, the tomb contained a model of the empire, which had rivers of quicksilver and a mechanism for operating the tides, and was guarded by traps that would shoot any intruders after the tomb was closed. Not far from this burial chamber, which has yet to be excavated, stood the terracotta army (see left), a legion of life-size pottery soldiers that were constructed to defend the First Emperor in death.

Qin-dynasty coins
Round coins with a square hole, similar to those used in China until the late 19th century, first appeared during the Qin dynasty.

Qin Shi Huang died in 210 BCE on an expedition to the east of China in search of the island of Penglai, where immortals were believed to reside.

Fall of the Qin
After the death of the First Emperor his son took power, but he was never as effective a ruler as his father, and he was forced to commit suicide by his chief minister two years later. China crumbled into civil unrest and much of Qin Shi Huang's work was lost. Palace archives were burnt, destroying evidence of the period. Revolts and uprisings led to the demise of the dynasty less than 20 years after it had begun.

AFTER

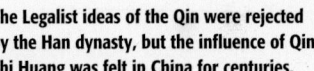

The Legalist ideas of the Qin were rejected by the Han dynasty, but the influence of Qin Shi Huang was felt in China for centuries.

CHINA AS ONE
Following the short-lived Qin dynasty, the expectation that China should be **a unified state** remained strong up to modern times.

A NEW EMPIRE
The Han empire **82–83 »**, which followed the Qin dynasty was to last for 400 years. The Han dynasty **rejected Legalist principles in favour of Confucianism**, and the influence of this philosophy in state affairs is still felt today.

LEGACY OF THE FIRST EMPEROR
Historically, **the rule of the First Emperor was seen in a negative light** by scholars, and his cruelty and obsession with immortality were highlighted. In more recent years modern

MAO ZEDONG

China has come to reevaluate Qin Shi Huang's aims and achievements in political and social terms. Mao Zedong **346–47 »** praised the **First Emperor for his achievements** and endorsed his attack on Confucianism.

FIRST QIN EMPEROR (260–210 BCE)
QIN SHI HUANG

Later Confucian historians have painted a picture of Qin Shi Huang as a ruthless megalomaniac, a reputation that can be traced to two notorious acts committed during his reign. The first of these was the burning of many classical texts that were being used by officials to argue against his decisions, and the second was the alleged burying alive of 460 scholars for disagreeing with him. Yet whatever his failings as an ideal ruler, the achievements of the man who unified China for the first time cannot be underestimated.

« BEFORE

The autocratic actions of China's First Emperor, Qin Shi Huang, alienated the population and his successors were unable to the quell the widespread rebellion that broke out against them.

QIN DYNASTY

Qin Shi Huang's son, the **Second Emperor**, fell under the influence of the eunuch Zhao Gao, who persuaded him to execute Li Si, his father's first minister, by having him cut in two in the market place at Xianyang. The Second Emperor was forced to commit suicide in 207 BCE and was succeeded by his son. By then rebellion had spread and the **Qin dynasty ‹‹ 80–81**, which was to have lasted "ten thousand generations", ended.

THE FIRST HAN EMPEROR

Liu Bang, who came from a poor peasant family, rose to prominence as the leader of a rebel band. At first he supported Xiang Yu, an aristocrat who hoped to revive the feudal states. In 206 BCE Liu Bang captured **Xianyang**, the Qin capital, negotiated the surrender of the last Qin ruler and announced the repeal of the severe **Qin penal code**. His treatment of the inhabitants earned him a reputation for fairness. When Xiang Yu arrived, the city was looted and the royal family killed. The rebel leaders quarrelled and for the next four years they campaigned against each other. Although Liu Bang's forces suffered defeats, he continued to gather allies and in 202 BCE he won a decisive victory at Gaixia in modern Anhui.

HOW WE KNOW

COUNTESS OF DAI'S TOMB

In 1972 the tomb of the Countess of Dai, dated c.168 BCE, was found at Mawangdui in present-day Hunan province. The grave offerings included silk garments, lacquer bowls for wine and food, and wooden figurines of her servants. The beautiful painted banner draped over her inner coffin is one of the earliest surviving examples of Chinese painting on silk. It depicts the route her soul would take on its quest for immortality – to the magic island of Penglai and then to the gates of paradise. The tomb also contained silk manuscripts and a divination board, with markings similar to those found on bronze mirrors of the period.

PAINTED SILK BANNER

The **Centralized State**

The Han dynasty, founded by Liu Bang in 202 BCE, created a powerful centralized state with a highly efficient civil service that would serve as a model for future Chinese emperors over the next two millennia.

Liu Bang (see BEFORE) assumed the style of *huangdi* or sovereign emperor (see p.81), and used Han as the title of the new dynasty. He is usually known as Emperor Gaozu. During his reign, which lasted until 195 BCE, many of the features of the Chinese imperial system took shape.

Gaozu himself was the embodiment of the principle that a man of peasant origins but of outstanding virtue could become emperor. He began his reign by announcing an amnesty and measures to restore peace. In the west and in the area around the new capital that he established at Chang'an, he continued Qin practices, applying direct rule in the form of commanderies (districts ruled by a centrally appointed governor). But in the east and south he initially accepted the existence of ten kingdoms, whose rulers professed allegiance to him, although he later replaced them with members of his own family. In the commanderies he rewarded senior officials, military leaders, and leaders of non-Chinese groups who had submitted to the Han, by conferring on them the rank of marquis. This title allowed them to raise taxes for the state, retaining part of the money for themselves.

Promotion on merit

Gaozu formalized the system of bureaucratic government introduced under the Qin. The emperor was assisted by three senior officials, who were in turn supported by nine ministers, each with a defined area of responsibility.

Gaozu was contemptuous of scholars, but he recognized the importance of the Confucian ideals (see p.85) of

Writing brushes
The ink brush was invented before the Han period, but came into its own under the Han for keeping detailed records – first on silk and then on paper (see right).

education and public service. In 196 BCE he issued an edict on the recruitment of able persons to the imperial government. The sixth Han emperor, Wudi, took this process even further.

Age of scholarship
Hsien Ti, the last of the Han emperors, who reigned c.189–220 CE, is shown in discussion with scholars who have been busy translating Confucian classical texts.

In 124 BCE he established an imperial academy where 50 students studied the classics in preparation for an examination. Those who passed became eligible for official appointments. The same year saw the most celebrated example of social mobility in Chinese history when Gongsun Hong, a former swineherd, was appointed chancellor.

Expansion of the empire
During Wudi's long reign (141–87 BCE) China made extensive territorial gains.

of the modern provinces of Guangdong and Guangxi and north Vietnam. All these military campaigns naturally cost money, so Wudi decided to augment tax revenues by imposing a state monopoly on salt and iron. This provoked a complicated debate over the degree to which the government should interfere in the economy.

Decline and usurpation
Wudi's successful reign came to a sad end, as the emperor in his later years became obsessed with his search for immortality, enlisting the help of the leading alchemists of the day. After his death the dynasty went into a period of decline, marked by weak emperors

> ## "To **learn without thinking** is fruitless; To think without learning is dangerous."
> CONFUCIUS, 551–479 BCE

The emperor's first concern, however, was to secure his northern frontier against invasion by the Xiongnu, a confederacy of nomadic steppe peoples originating in Mongolia (see p.91). In 166 BCE they had penetrated to within 160km (100 miles) of Chang'an. In 138 BCE Wudi sent an envoy, Zhang Qian, to contact the Yuezhi, the traditional enemies of the Xiongnu, in the hope of forming an alliance. Zhang Qian failed to obtain their assistance, but his epic journey extended Chinese influence for the first time into the Western Regions (modern Xinjiang), helping establish trading links with Persia and opening up the Silk Road (see pp.130–31).

Wudi's greatest conquests were to the northeast and the south of the existing empire. In 128 BCE he sent an expedition to Korea and 20 years later a longer campaign led to the establishment of four commanderies in the north of the peninsula. In 111 BCE he sent an expedition south to Guangzhou and subsequently commanderies were established to administer the territory

and the excessive influence of the court eunuchs. One of the eunuchs' main duties was the care of the numerous imperial concubines, any one of whose sons could be named to succeed the emperor. This led to palace intrigues in which the eunuchs played an increasingly significant role. The economy, meanwhile, suffered from financial mismanagement, and there was widespread tax evasion. A further blow came in the early years of the 1st century CE with serious flooding of the Yellow River, which led to its changing to its southern course in 11 CE.

In 9 CE Wang Mang, who had been acting as regent for a succession of child emperors, usurped the throne. He ordered large private estates to be broken up, but was killed in 23 CE.

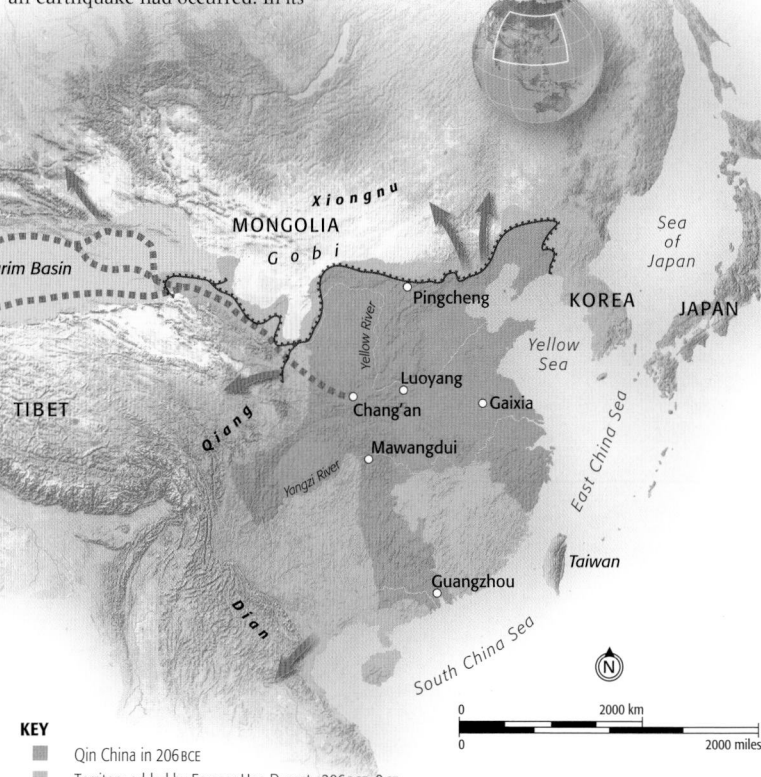
The Later Han
In 25 CE Guang Wudi re-established the Han dynasty, transferring the capital to Luoyang, which became the most populous city in the world. This was an age of scientific and technological progress; major inventions included paper (see below) and an instrument that indicated the direction in which an earthquake had occurred. In its

later years the Han court was weakened by factionalism, and China was menaced by the Xianbei, a new confederation of steppe nomads. Rebellions broke out, and Han generals, the most famous of whom was Cao Cao, contended for power. In 220 Cao Cao died and the dynasty collapsed.

PAPER

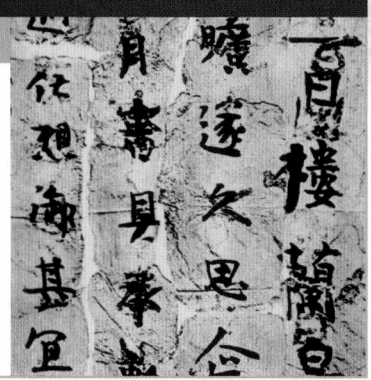

The invention of paper is traditionally credited to Cai Lun, a court eunuch who lived c.50–121 CE. He soaked the bark of a mulberry tree and bamboo in water, pounded the mixture with a wooden tool, and then drained it through cloth, leaving only the fibres. This produced a type of paper that was light, cheap, and easy to make. His invention was adopted rapidly for documents and books and subsequently spread to the Islamic world and the West.

KEY
- Qin China in 206 BCE
- Territory added by Former Han Dynasty 206 BCE–9 CE
- Territory added by Later Han Dynasty 25–220 CE
- ·········· Great Wall under the Han
- ▪▪▪▪▪ Silk Road
- ➤ Main Han military expeditions

0 — 2000 km
0 — 2000 miles

Han dynasty China
Under Wudi, the Han extended their control over south China. The Great Wall of China was originally constructed during the Han Dynasty and rebuilt in later periods.

Xiongnu · MONGOLIA · *Gobi* · Tarim Basin · *Pamirs* · TIBET · *Qiang* · Pingcheng · KOREA · JAPAN · Sea of Japan · Yellow Sea · Luoyang · Chang'an · Gaixia · Mawangdui · *Yangzi River* · East China Sea · Taiwan · Guangzhou · *Dian* · South China Sea

BEFORE

By Socrates' time (see right), Greek thinkers had begun to seek rational explanations, instead of adhering to traditional beliefs.

HESIOD

GREEK MYTHOLOGY

Homer's epics ‹‹ 56–57 of the 8th century BCE, retelling legends from Greek prehistory, underpinned all later classical education. **Hesiod's** poem *Theogony*, ("birth of the gods") *c.*700 BCE, gives the first systematic account of Greek mythology, whose many gods were consulted through divination and oracles, such as the famous oracle at the Temple of Apollo in Delphi. Pre-Socratic philosophers questioned these traditional beliefs. **Xenophanes** (*c.*570 BCE) wrote: "Homer and Hesiod have attributed to the gods everything that is shameful and blameworthy among men."

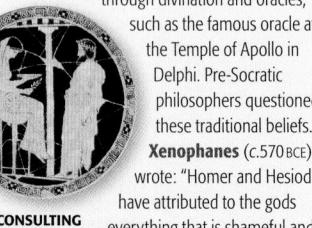

CONSULTING THE DELPHIC ORACLE

TRADING WISDOM

From about the middle of the 7th century BCE the Greek world was transformed ‹‹ 48–49, when a commercial economy developed, with the market place, the **agora**, as the centre of social life in every city. Exposure to new ideas through trade inspired thinkers to challenge traditional wisdom. Greeks exchanged social, political, and philosophical ideas and dared to imagine novel ways of governing society and of understanding the world. **Anaximenes** (*c.*585 BCE) thought the origin of everything was air; **Heraclitus** (*c.*534 BCE) thought it was fire 58–59 ››.

THE FOUNDERS

The Greeks recognized **seven sages** as founders of their intellectual tradition. The names varied but always included **Solon of Athens** (*c.*630 BCE) ‹‹ 54–55, whose maxim was "nothing in excess", and **Thales of Miletus** (*c.*640 BCE) ‹‹ 58–59, the first true philosopher. According to Plato, the other five were **Bias** of Priene, **Chilon** of Sparta, **Cleobulus** of Lindos, **Myson** of Chenae, and **Pittacus** of Mytilene.

> " …the unexamined life is **not worth living**…"
>
> SOCRATES, SPEAKING AT HIS TRIAL, 399 BCE

The School of Athens
This painting by Raphael – painted in 1509 for Pope Julius II – is proof of the enduring influence of Plato and Aristotle (walking in the centre) and Socrates (leaving the picture on the left) on Western philosophy.

Classical Thought

During the 5th century BCE, under the brilliant leadership of Pericles, the city-state of Athens rose to become the political and cultural focus of the Greek world. The thinkers who lived and taught there prepared the ground for much of Western philosophy for the next 2000 years.

Philosophy is a method of rational enquiry used to attempt to understand the world and phenomena around us; it is also the study of the process of philosophical enquiry itself. Three philosophers who taught in Athens are credited with laying the foundations of all classical thought – Socrates, Plato, and Aristotle.

Socrates

Socrates was born around 470 BCE, and became famous for challenging conventional ideas that most people thought they understood. He did this by questioning what was meant by concepts such as "good", "evil", "courage", and "justice", to show people that their understanding of such terms lacked truth. He wrote nothing down, but his logical style of argument is portrayed in the works of his followers, particularly Plato and the soldier and historian Xenophon. His greatest concern was ethics, or how to live a good life. At the age of 70 his constant questioning was thought to threaten the Athenian state. He was condemned to death, and was forced to poison himself.

Plato

A follower of Socrates, Plato was born in c.428 BCE and developed his mentor's ideas. Many of his writings, such as *Symposium* and the *Republic*, were composed as dialogues on subjects such as ethics and justice, the nature of reality, and the immortality of the soul. He also tried to devise a perfect political system. He set up a school, called the Academy, on the outskirts of Athens, which continued to teach philosophy until the 6th century CE.

Aristotle

Plato's student Aristotle (see p.49) taught a different kind of philosophy from that of his master – more practical than theoretical – and insisted on the importance of observing facts (see pp.58–59). He spent three years as

ZENO THE STOIC
Zeno is said to have strangled himself at the age of 69, in accordance with the Stoic belief that a man has the right to determine his own death.

tutor to Alexander the Great (see pp.50–53), whose conquests spread Greek ideas widely in Asia and North Africa. Aristotle founded his own school outside Athens called the Lyceum. His books, compiled from lecture notes, covered subjects ranging from poetry, drama, ethics, and politics to mathematics, physics, logic, zoology, and anatomy. They remained the basis of Western and Islamic science and philosophy until the 17th century.

Many philosophical movements emerged from the work of Socrates, Plato, and Aristotle. Among the most important were Scepticism, Cynicism, Epicureanism, and Stoicism – the last two had the most enduring influence.

SCEPTICISM A philosophical movement that denied the possibility of knowing the real truth with certainty.

CYNICISM A philosophy that taught that virtue and asceticism, rather than pleasure and indulgence, led to happiness.

Epicureanism and Stoicism

Epicurus (born 341 BCE) taught that good and bad should be measured by the pleasure and pain they bring, and that the point of justice is to increase human happiness. He believed that the gods, if they exist at all, had no interest in human affairs and that there was no life after death. He thought that

events in the world were the result of the motion of atoms in empty space – an idea he possibly borrowed from Democritus (born 460 BCE). The Latin poet Lucretius brought Epicurus's ideas to the Roman world, where they strongly influenced writers like Virgil.

Stoicism was founded by Zeno of Citium (born 335 BCE). He divided philosophy into three elements: logic, physics, and ethics. He believed that underlying all matter was energy, which he called divine fire. Zeno claimed that universal human fellowship was more important than narrow loyalty and that man's duty was to accept what fate brings and to behave in accordance with nature.

Stoicism was an inspiration to the Romans who took over the Greek world from the 2nd century BCE (see pp.60–61). Roman thinkers such as Seneca the Younger, Cicero, and Cato the Younger adapted Stoic ideas to the new realities of the Roman Empire. The Roman values of bravery in battle, fortitude in the face of hardship, and the universal brotherhood of Roman citizenship owe their origins to the teachings of the Stoics.

Remembering mortality
Epicureans used the skull as a *memento mori* (which means "remember that you are mortal") to remind them of the importance of enjoying life while it is still possible.

AFTER

Greek philosophical ideas became the common heritage of intellectuals in the Mediterranean world and beyond, well into the Roman period.

THE ROMAN ARISTOTLE
The Romans elaborated on Greek ideas. **Pliny the Elder** (born 24 CE) added to Aristotle's natural history and **Claudius Ptolemy** (born c.90 CE) gave Aristotle's astronomy mathematical treatment. The poet **Horace** (born 65 BCE) was known as the Roman Aristotle for his analysis of literature and drama.

NEOPLATONISM
Plato's teachings on the nature of reality became a renewed doctrine – **Neoplatonism** – with **Plotinus** (born c.205 CE). This had a **profound influence on Christian theology**, particularly through **St Augustine** (born 354 CE), whose Neoplatonist ideas survived his conversion to Christianity.

MARCUS AURELIUS
Stoicism found a welcome in Rome where it became the most popular philosophy among the

MARCUS AURELIUS

elite, idealizing self-control and detachment from emotion. The Emperor **Marcus Aurelius** (born 121 CE) gave expression to Roman Stoicism in his book *Meditations*.

LATER EPICUREANISM
In the US Declaration of Independence (1776) **232–33》**, the right to **"life, liberty, and the pursuit of happiness"** is an Epicurean ideal.

ST AUGUSTINE AT THE SCHOOL OF ROME

« BEFORE

Even before the Greeks began pursuing geographical knowledge from 600 BCE, some people's experience of travel, trade, and communication was extensive.

BABYLONIAN VIEW OF THE WORLD

MYTHICAL GEOGRAPHY

Early concepts of the shape of the world owe much to **myths « 56–57**. People had seemingly fantastical concepts of far-off lands. This schematic diagram of the world (left) dating to 1000–500 BCE describes mythical beings inhabiting the corners of the world. The perspective is **centred on the city of** Babylon in Mesopotamia (modern Iraq), and real locations, labelled with their names, surround it in rough correlation to reality. The tablet is a visual concept of the world rather than a guide to it.

DISTANT CONNECTIONS

Although some people travelled far in the ancient world, the knowledge of geography they acquired only gradually came to be expressed as maps or texts. Instead, the powerful showed off their connections with monuments in the landscape, or by displaying possessions from distant lands.

THE WEALTH OF TRADE CITIES

Since **Phoenician times « 40–41**, cities that could control trade had become wealthy. Some city-states and kingdoms were built on their monopoly on goods such as **incense** or **silk**.

A Wider World

Links across the ancient world were forged by merchants, rulers, and migrants. Through increasing cultural exchange, societies gained knowledge of distant lands, and as awareness of the world grew, the far-flung connections of worldly and wealthy people were admired as marks of status.

A s empires united vast, multicultural regions (see pp.45–46), enterprising explorers and traders found new routes and access to valuable goods. The most luxurious or prestigious commodities were often those that had traveled the greatest distance. Silk that found its way from China to Rome changed hands many times en route, with each middleman taking his mark-up.

Ideas, stories, religions, languages, all traveled along the trade routes between the various lands. During the Hellenistic Period (see pp.52–53), Greek was a common language from Greece to India, and Greek gods, such as Zeus, made appearances as far afield as Bactria (modern Afghanistan). The Greek mythical hero Herakles (Hercules), also recorded in Bactria, appears as a statue over a major trade and military route through the Zagros Mountains of Persia (in present-day Iran, see pp.46–47). But here, his identity is blended with the hero Verethraghna of Persian tradition.

Later, as the spheres of influence of Rome, China, and Parthia expanded and overlapped, cultural interchange began to occur across the whole of Eurasia, and Buddhism spread from India to China via Parthian travellers on the Silk Road. It was a Parthian nobleman called An Shi Kao who, in 148 BCE, was the first to translate Buddhist texts into Chinese.

Traces of trade

The gradual spread of ideas and culture through trade and migration, although little documented, has left many archaeological traces. Artefacts unearthed far from home, such as African ivory in Assyria (see above), a hoard of Roman coins in India, or a Persian carpet in Siberia, provide clear evidence of long-distance trade. The occasional shipwreck can represent a detailed time capsule of information. Ancient writings also build the picture of trails taken by travelers. Documents

Ivory from Africa
Unearthed in Nineveh, the capital of Assyria in 700 BCE, this carving is of elephant ivory, a material the Assyrians would have had access to through contacts with the Phoenicians. Such an exotic commodity from far-off lands would have conveyed status on its owner.

from the Persian capital Persepolis, for instance, note the rations given to official travellers, and the official stops they made across the empire from Sardis (today in western Turkey) in the west to India in the east. In the commercial world, itineraries were drawn up as guides for merchants. One surviving example, written by a Romanized author from Alexandria in Egypt in the 1st century CE, describes the Red Sea and Indian Ocean. It relates the ports and the goods, such as iron, gold, silver, myrrh, and slaves, available for import and export in each, and extends its account to the Ganges River and beyond, to China. Such knowledge was consolidated into an accurate geographical picture of the world by Greek and Roman map-makers. In the 2nd century CE, Ptolemy of Alexandria compiled *Geographia* –

Greek in Central Asia
Common languages spread across vast, multicultural territories. Here, Greek is used on a 150-BCE coin of Afghanistan, unearthed in Turkey.

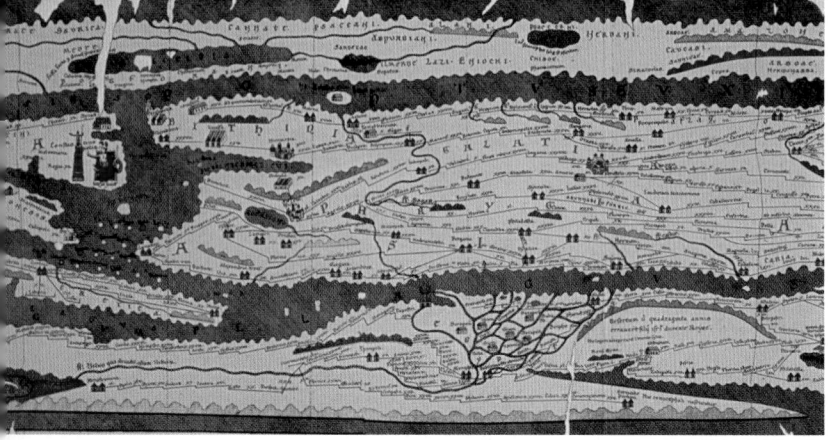

Roman road atlas
This view of the world, known as the Peutinger Table, is a medieval copy of a Roman original. It records journeys made across the Roman world and beyond before the 4th century CE. Distances are distorted unrecognizably to preserve the order of places and routes in a clear itinerary.

a world atlas that laid out instructions on charting the world with lines of latitude and longitude. It featured North Africa, India, Taprobane (Sri Lanka), and Sinae (China), including its capital, Chang'an.

Physical links

The transport networks of the ancient world were not so much constructed as evolved as common routes over millennia. In places, however, roads were cut deliberately by mobilizing forced labor. More often, a route was marked less by a physical road than by a maintained string of stages or settlements. States that expanded over wide areas needed to maintain regular communication by supporting these networks as a crucial aspect of their

Wealth of a caravan city
Petra was the capital of the Nabataean Arabs, who controlled the supply of luxury goods between Arabia and Mediterranean markets. The wealth of such a trade hub is evident in the surviving colonnades, temples, and tombs.

control. Roman skill in road-building grew as they gained control of Italy (see pp.60–61). Likewise, to send letters across their vast empire, the Persians developed a swift messenger system whose reputation for speed spread well beyond their empire. Xenophon, the Greek historian of the 4th century BCE, described relays of horses at stations spaced at one-day intervals and manned by officials. Whenever a letter arrived, the officials immediately sent it on with fresh riders and fresh horses.

Imagining new worlds

The imagination was important in forming ideas of the world. Old tales of exploration were remembered by the next wave of adventurers. When Alexander's army (see pp.50–53)

reached the edge of their known world, they imagined mythical heroes, such as Herakles, had explored the new horizon before them. The Greek historian Herodotus (see pp.56–57) wrote that the gold emerging from east of Persia was mined with the help of giant ants.

After 400 CE, expansion of the world's horizons slowed until geographical knowledge was revived first by medieval Arab and Chinese explorers, then by Renaissance Europeans 250–53 ≫.

ARAB EXPLORATION

New impetus for exploration, trade, and the communication of ideas was provided by the contacts created between the Atlantic and the Far East by the Arab conquests 174–77 ≫.

CLASSICAL WORLD VIEWS

Scholars relied on Classical views of the world for centuries after they were first produced. Both the **Peutinger Table** and **Ptolemy's world map** 320 ≫ continued to be recopied by scribes into the medieval period. Columbus 224–25 ≫

used Ptolemy's inaccurate calculation of Earth's circumference in attempting to sail west to India.

ARAB CARTOGRAPHY

The Muslim cartographer **Al-Idrisi** created a map for his patron, Roger II of Sicily, in the 12th century. Sicily was a contact zone between Muslims and Christians at the time. Al-Idrisi's map is oriented with south at the top, reflecting the outlook from Sicily toward the lands of Islamic rule. This map was one of the triggers for the pioneering Renaissance voyages that were to introduce the Old World to the New.

AL-IDRISI'S MAP

Nexus of trade

By c.1 CE, the world's trade routes had extended, through many intermediaries, from western Europe to China. China was largely self-sufficient, but imported desirable goods, such as spices from Southeast Asia and cavalry horses from Central Asia. Rome, in contrast, was a hub of commerce, dependent on trade. The empire imported food, slaves, animals, spices, silk, incense, and cotton.

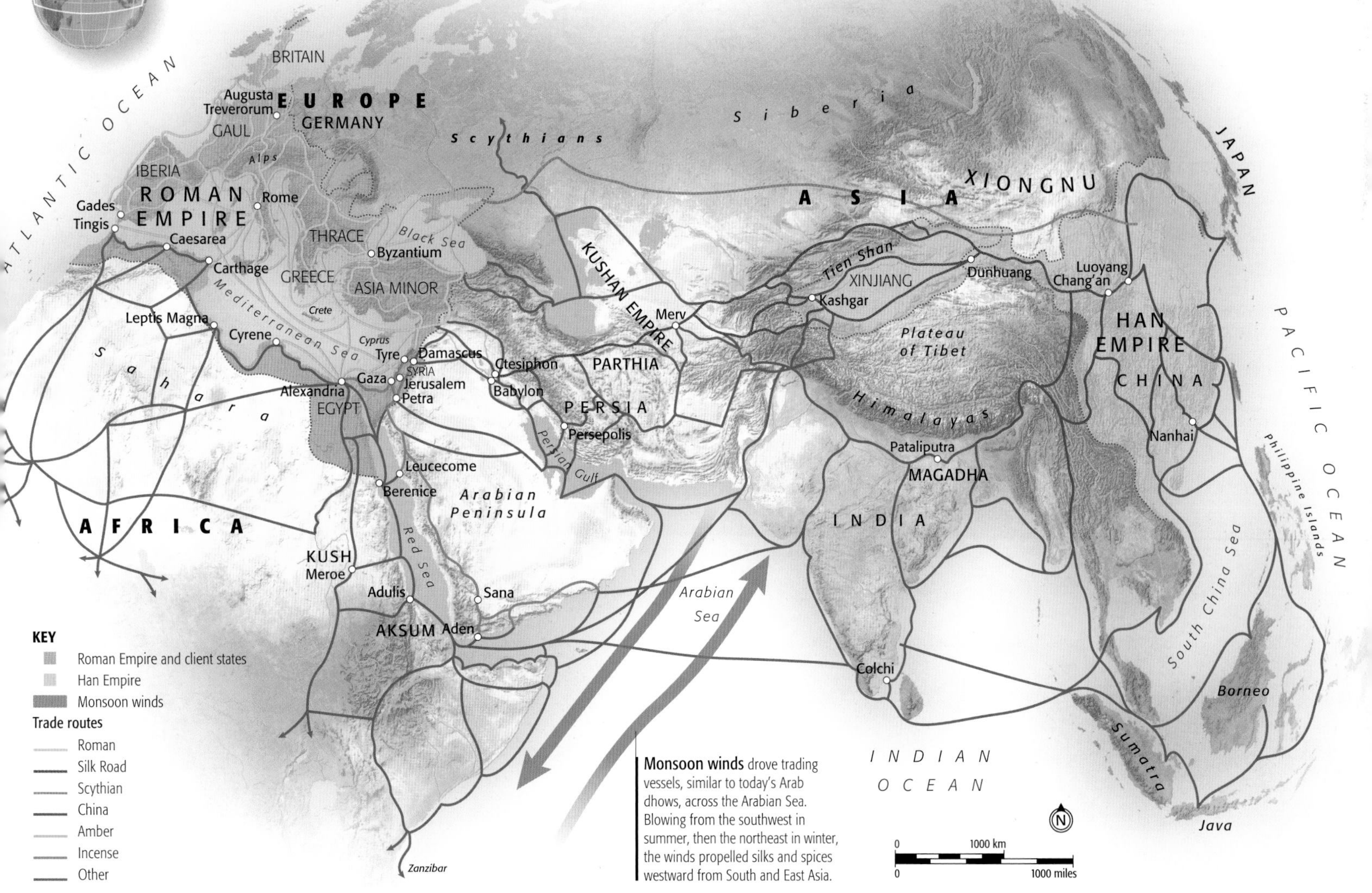

Monsoon winds drove trading vessels, similar to today's Arab dhows, across the Arabian Sea. Blowing from the southwest in summer, then the northeast in winter, the winds propelled silks and spices westward from South and East Asia.

KEY

- ▪ Roman Empire and client states
- ▪ Han Empire
- ▪ Monsoon winds

Trade routes
- — Roman
- — Silk Road
- — Scythian
- — China
- — Amber
- — Incense
- — Other

Map labels: ATLANTIC OCEAN · BRITAIN · EUROPE · Augusta Treverorum · GAUL · GERMANY · Scythians · Siberia · JAPAN · IBERIA · Gades · Tingis · ROMAN EMPIRE · Rome · Alps · THRACE · Black Sea · Byzantium · GREECE · ASIA MINOR · Crete · ASIA · XIONGNU · Tien Shan · Dunhuang · Luoyang · Chang'an · KUSHAN EMPIRE · Merv · XINJIANG · Kashgar · Caesarea · Carthage · Leptis Magna · Cyrene · Mediterranean Sea · Cyprus · Tyre · Damascus · SYRIA · Ctesiphon · PARTHIA · Plateau of Tibet · HAN EMPIRE · CHINA · Sahara · Alexandria · Gaza · Jerusalem · Petra · EGYPT · Babylon · PERSIA · Persepolis · Himalayas · Nanhai · PACIFIC OCEAN · Persian Gulf · Leucecome · Pataliputra · MAGADHA · Berenice · Arabian Peninsula · INDIA · Philippine Islands · AFRICA · KUSH · Meroe · Red Sea · Adulis · Sana · Arabian Sea · South China Sea · AKSUM · Aden · Borneo · Colchi · INDIAN OCEAN · Sumatra · Zanzibar · Java

0 1000 km
0 1000 miles

BEFORE

Some historians have linked Celtic origins with the Urnfield culture (so named because urns containing the ashes of the dead were placed in fields), which dates from around 1200 BCE and was based in France and Germany. It is also thought that Celtic ancestry may be rooted in the Eurasian steppes.

HALLSTATT CULTURE

Archaeological finds place the first Celts in **Hallstatt** (Austria) in around 700 BCE – the early Iron Age. The Hallstatt Celts seem to have been one of Europe's **first Iron Age cultures** and appear to have been wealthy and powerful. Their chieftans' graves contained valuable items such as bronze buckets and jewellery, suggesting trade with Greece and domination of several major European trading routes.

HALLSTATT BRONZE WAGON

CELTIC ADVANCE

By around 500 BCE, the Celts had settled in pockets of France, Germany, and what is now the western part of the Czech Republic. About 100 years later, a significant spread of Celtic tribes into many parts of Europe began, notably into northern Italy. They settled in the Po valley before sacking Rome (c.390 BCE). The extent of the Celtic "invasion" is a matter of debate.

CELTIC QUEEN (DIED 60 CE)

BOUDICCA

Queen of the Celtic Iceni people of eastern England, Boudicca (or Boadicea) led a bloody uprising against occupying Roman forces after the Romans ignored the will of her dead husband, King Prasutagus. The king had left his estate jointly to his daughters and to Rome, but Romans seized his entire kingdom and mistreated his family. Boudicca sacked Colchester and Londinium but was finally defeated, and is thought to have killed herself to avoid capture.

The word "Celt" refers to many groups of Europeans who spoke related Indo-European languages and migrated across Europe from the 5th century BCE. They are sometimes called "the first masters of Europe". Although the Celts were not one cohesive people, and were composed of numerous and fairly diverse groups, they displayed a common culture. This culture was typified by organization into tribes or clans, a nomadic or village life existence, and a strong warrior tradition.

"The Dying Gaul"
This copy of a Greek statue commemorates a Greek victory against invading "Gauls" (Celts) in the 220s BCE. The torc around the Gaul's neck is a sign of Celtic identity.

part of Celtic culture. Stories would also have been about Celtic beliefs and deities. Celtic mythology featured a strong belief in an afterlife – an "otherworld" realm less like a heaven and more of a parallel with the real world, much like the ancient Egyptian afterlife (see pp.28–29). The Celtic otherworld was peopled by gods and supernatural beings, such as Cernunnos, horned god of virility, nature, and plenty. The Celts believed that people journeyed to the otherworld after death, and great feasts were held as preparation for chiefs' burials. Woodland spirits were believed to inhabit the otherworld, and

Celtic Warriors

Fierce warriors and skilled ironworkers with a love of feasting, the Celts swept across much of Europe during the 1st millennium BCE. Their advance brought them into contact with many of the cultures that shaped history, including the Greeks and Romans. Later, they played a part in the rise of Christianity.

By the 200s BCE, Celts and their culture were prevalent across a large swathe of Western and Central Europe. In the 4th century BCE, they had already sacked (plundered) Rome. The next few centuries saw them reach the British Isles and move across Italy, France, Spain, Greece, Macedonia, and modern Turkey, sending delegations to Alexander the Great (see pp.50–51) in the 300s BCE and sacking Delphi, Greece, in 279 BCE. They met with varying fortunes, sometimes victorious and sometimes defeated. Where they did triumph, there was a significant exchange of cultures between the Celts and those they had conquered.

Tribal structure

Celtic society was an agricultural one of fortified villages, and was organized into many inter-fighting tribes or clans. The tribe was more important than the individual. Tribal structure was hierarchical, with a king or chief at the head; followed by noble-warriors and priests (druids); commoners, many of whom were farmers; and slaves. Druids had a very special status in Celtic society. They came from leading families and were exempted from paying taxes or taking part in fighting. The different tribes had cultural, rather than political, common ground. This lack of political cohesion was ultimately a weakness (see AFTER).

Beliefs and mythology

The Celts were illiterate, even at their height, but had a powerful oral tradition of storytelling and poetry. Epic poems of war exploits and glories are an especially important

A godlike figure appears to dip a man into, or remove him from, a cauldron, perhaps as an "Otherworld" rebirth or initiation ritual.

Noble horsemen may be riding away after rebirth in the cauldron. Their helmets have symbolic decoration such as crescent shapes, boars, or birds.

elements of the natural world were central to Celtic beliefs. Oak trees and mistletoe were thought to be sacred. The rituals performed by druids often took place outside, especially in woods.

Celtic art and crafts

Motifs from the natural world are important in Celtic art, too. The Celts were skilled metalworkers and they

Gundestrup cauldron
This Celtic silver vessel was found in a Danish peat-bog in 1891. It dates from about the 1st century BCE, and it may have had a ritual purpose.

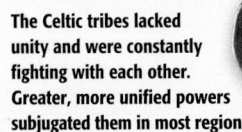

The Celtic tribes lacked unity and were constantly fighting with each other. Greater, more unified powers subjugated them in most regions.

CARTHAGINIAN COIN, IBERIA

ROMAN RULE
By the 1st century CE, the spread of Roman power had ended Celtic domination in Italy, Gaul (after the Gallic uprising by **Vercingetorix** had been put down), and in England. In northern Italy, Celts had been incorporated as Roman citizens under Caesar **« 62–63**, who had even raised two legions from this area for his conquest of Gaul. The Romans fought for control of Iberia (Spain), with the **Carthaginians « 40–41** and native Celts, although the area remained **"Celtiberian"**, despite Carthaginian and Roman rule.

GERMANIC VICTORY
Germanic tribes fought against both the Romans and the Celts, and successfully pushed the Celts out of the Rhine Valley.

ON THE MARGINS
Subdued by Roman and Germanic forces, Celtic strongholds were increasingly pushed into the margins of their former lands. Ultimately, they lingered on for longer in **Ireland** and other pockets where Celtic culture persists today, such as **Cornwall**, **Wales**, and the **Scottish Highlands**. It is likely that, during the 4th–6th centuries CE, the Anglo-Saxons further supplanted the Celts in England.

IRISH BROOCH

RISE OF CHRISTIANITY
Christianity reached the non-Roman-ruled Celtic people around the 4th century CE. **Celtic churches** played an important role in the early **spread of the Christian religion** in northern Europe.

> " The whole Celtic race is **obsessed with war**."
>
> STRABO, ANCIENT GREEK HISTORIAN AND GEOGRAPHER, 1ST CENTURY BCE

spread their knowledge, especially of ironworking techniques, wherever they migrated. Gold and bronze were popular for luxury items – the Celts are famed for wearing gold torcs (neck bands with sculpted ends), as well as bracelets and impressive brooches. They were affected by foreign cultures, too. Some of the geometric and curvilinear shapes in Celtic art were influenced by the various peoples the Celts came into contact with, from the Greeks and Etruscans to steppe people such as the Scythians (see pp.90–91).

Weaponry, war, and dominance
Because a talent for warfare and horsemanship was central to Celtic culture, great artistic skill was poured into weaponry, armour, harnesses, and chariots. Some particularly fine weapons were borne principally as badges of honour and rank, or used for ceremonial purposes rather than in active service. These great warrior-people used shields, swords, and spears as weapons. Some Roman tools of war – such as the *scutum* (a type of shield) – reveal Celtic influences. Chariots were used widely in earlier times and skilled horsemanship was greatly prized. Some Celtic tribes painted or tattooed themselves with plant dyes to look more alarming to their enemies.

The Celtic La Tène culture (named after an archaeological site in Switzerland) followed on from Hallstatt culture (see BEFORE) and grew in influence, becoming dominant between 450–15 BCE. Although it subsequently dwindled, Celtic culture persists today and Celtic languages are still spoken in Brittany (the Breton language), Wales, Scotland, Ireland, and the Isle of Man.

Warriors on foot with shields and spears, marching towards the left, may be dead soldiers approaching a ritual rebirth in the cauldron.

Musicians blow on long Celtic trumpets. This style of trumpet (*carnyx*) was held vertically and had a mouth shaped like a boar's head. It was played in battle.

Gundestrup detail
This is one of the panels on the Gundestrup cauldron, decorated with a scene of gods and men. Celtic mythology linked cauldrons with feasting and regeneration, and this particular panel, and the cauldron itself, may echo those beliefs.

BEFORE

The steppes and prairies covering much of the Eurasian interior, especially in the west, were suited to varying degrees of farming and grazing.

BRONZE AGE STEPPE CULTURE

By the Bronze Age **≪ 43** the Eurasian steppe peoples were living a mainly **agricultural life**. They kept horses and domesticated animals. Earthen burial mounds called **kurgans** were a major cultural feature from central Europe to Siberia.

KURGANS ON THE STEPPES

MASS MIGRATION

By c.2000 BCE a **major movement of steppe peoples** into adjacent lands seems to have begun, linked to **altered agricultural practices** and a search for **better farming conditions**.

In geographical terms, the Eurasian steppe can be divided into western and eastern regions. The western area begins in Hungary and stretches north of the Black Sea to the Altai Mountains in the east. The eastern portion, which is mostly at a higher altitude, runs east from the Altai range across Mongolia to Manchuria in China.

The western steppe, such as the fertile lands around the Danube, is wetter and greener. As you move east, summers become hotter, winters colder, and rain more scarce. Tribes of the eastern steppe often migrated west or south to areas of higher rainfall and fresh grazing pasture.

Scythian horseman
The Scythians are famed for creating beautiful artefacts, especially in gold, and for being formidable horsemen. This item, found at Kul Oba, in the Crimea, combines both aspects. It dates from the 4th century BCE.

skills were supplemented by a talent for fighting. Steppe society was organized into "kinship" groups (effectively extended families) and tribes. On occasion, tribes might assemble to create a larger body. Such gatherings were usually temporary, formed for a specific purpose, such as defence or attack. The rulers of steppe tribes were often thought to be divine.

Riding to victory

The early history of the horse's domestication is unclear, but by c.700 BCE, horses were extremely important on the steppes, and were bred in large numbers. They were

Nomads of the Steppes

The steppes – grasslands stretching from Eastern Europe to China – have been home to nomadic and semi-nomadic groups for millennia. The history of the steppe people has been influenced by geography, while their territorial ambitions brought clashes with a range of powers that changed the world map.

HOW WE KNOW

THE PAZYRYK TOMBS

Pazyryk is a valley burial site in the Altai Mountains, in modern Kazakstan, dating from the 5th to 3rd centuries BCE. Much of what we know about the Scythians comes from grave goods discovered in royal kurgans at Pazyryk. These goods included horses, burial chariots, and some of the earliest known textiles – felt and wool items such as appliquéd saddle-covers and colourful carpets (below).

Such migrations reinforced the nomadic lifestyle. It also brought various groups into contact with each other, which is why there are many cultural similarities between the different steppe peoples.

Life on the steppes

Relatively little is known about steppe life before the 11th century CE. We do know that the steppe tribes spoke Indo-European languages, and that

they kept domesticated animals, such as cattle and sheep. They often used animal caravans and rivers to transport goods, and their superb horsemanship

Mongolian herdsman
Nomadic pastoralism involves moving herds of domesticated animals over large distances. In some steppe regions it has changed little in thousands of years.

ideal animals for people who had to move over vast distances to find suitable pasture for their livestock, because they not only provided transportation but also meat and even milk.

By this time, the steppe people could fight very effectively on horseback, possibly having copied the techniques of the Assyrians (see pp.38–39). Crucial to the development of their fighting prowess were the composite

»

IDEAS

STEPPE BELIEFS

Steppe peoples were heavily influenced by the expansive skies of the open steppelands, which, as a major navigational guide, played a huge role in their lives. Some peoples certainly believed in a sky deity, a "heaven", and an afterlife, and shamanistic practices may also have been widespread. Shamans are people thought to have the power to cure sickness and communicate with the spirit world. Mirrors, a traditional shamanic tool, are believed to reflect secret truths and ward off evil spirits.

MONGOLIAN SHAMAN'S MIRROR

bow and stirrups. The composite bow is a short bow that is easy to fire from a horse, yet very powerful. The stirrup, which probably originated on the steppes around the 2nd century BCE, made it easier to ride well in full armour.

Steppe armies were skilled at springing sudden mounted attacks – usually raids rather than attempts at territorial conquest – and overran rival settlements with ease. Although some campaigns, such as the Cimmerian attack on Asia Minor c.690 BCE, were large-scale onslaughts, many

raids were small affairs. The popular idea of invading hordes is misleading – a few fierce horsemen riding at speed would seem overwhelming to an agricultural village.

Scythian and Kushans

The Scythians were a group of steppe peoples who had migrated from Central Asia to southern Russia by the 7th century BCE. Their warriors fought with bows and arrows, and axes. They wore felt caps and, except for some members of the aristocracy, no armour.

The Scythians possessed sizeable territories at different periods, including a large area of the Middle East. One group, the "Royal Scythes", controlled an area around southern Russia, where stunning grave finds of gold artefacts point to a well-developed Scythian culture. By the 2nd century CE, the Scythians had been quashed by the Sarmatians, who were in turn defeated by the Huns (see pp.102–03).

THE AMAZONS, the famous female warriors of Greco-Roman legend, may have been based on Eurasian steppe women, who some believe took an active role in raiding and fighting.

Kushan head
This sculpture shows the mix of Greco-Roman and Indian influences that infused much of Kushan art.

Steppe nomads often integrated with people living in areas they invaded. In the 1st–3rd centuries CE, for example, the Kushans migrated from the fringes of Mongolia to the western steppe, into lands that once formed part of the Achaemenid Persian Empire (see pp.46–47) and the empire of Alexander the Great (see pp.50–52). Like the Parthians (see pp.76–77), the Kushans developed a settled, sophisticated culture that readily incorporated Greek, Persian, and Indian influences.

The Xiongnu

The Xiongnu (or Hsiung-nu) is a term for a loose grouping of different steppe peoples (including some Scythians) whose warriors were raiding China by the 3rd century BCE. Some aspects of their culture seem to have been adopted from the Chinese regimes they attacked. The Xiongnu were a dominant force in Central Asia for five centuries.

Steppe peoples continued to make their mark on groups across Eurasia, from displaced Germanic tribes to rising Islamic powers.

THE HUNS

Between the 4th and 5th centuries CE, pastoral steppe nomads known as Huns **controlled huge swathes of Europe and Asia,** conquering other tribes they encountered, including the Germanic Ostrogoths. In the mid-5th century, some of those peoples **fought back** successfully against the Huns, and the **Eastern Roman Empire** also closed its borders. The Huns were soon a **spent force.**

HUN DINARS

TURKIC TRIBES

By c.500 CE, the Turkic people (originally nomads in the Altai Mountains) **dominated much of the Asian steppe.** By c.700 CE, their power hadbeen weakened, and various Turkic tribes scattered westward following **wars with the Tang Chinese 108–09 »**. However, they remained a major presence, playing a key role in Middle Eastern history and the rise of Islam.

RISE OF THE MONGOLS

The Mongols managed to conquer and create a confederate of all the nomads on the Mongolian steppes in the early 13th century **112–13 »**.

Paracas textile
The Paracas people of Peru made beautiful textiles. Many feature a god-like creature known as the "oculate being", depicted here wearing a gold diadem and holding a snake.

A dvanced American societies in this era had much in common: quarrying stone, creating beautiful artefacts, and worshipping multiple gods usually linked to nature (for example, the jaguar, the Sun, and the Moon). South American cultures were more advanced in their use of metals, but it was a Mesoamerican culture – the Maya – that left the most powerful and enigmatic monuments.

The Maya

The "Classic" period of Maya culture is normally dated from c.300–900 CE. It flourished over a wide swathe of Central America, especially the Yucatán and Guatemala's steamy lowlands. At its heart stood a large number of important cities. Originally ritual centres, many grew into populous city-states.

The Maya built huge, often pyramidal stone temples, such as those at Tikal in Guatemala, and showed a great talent plotting the positions of the Sun and Moon and predicting solar eclipses. Their calendar had two main cycles: a 260-day sacred year (13 cycles of 20 days) and a 365-day solar year (18 months of 20 days each, plus an "unlucky" 5-day period which the Maya spent appeasing the gods).

Monte Albán and Teotihuacán

While Maya civilization was thriving, the Zapotec people of southern Mexico were creating their major centre at Monte Albán (see BEFORE). The ruins of the city's sacred and political centre, dating mainly from c.300 CE onwards, show that this was another highly sophisticated society. A great central plaza is surrounded by monumental platforms, pyramids, staircases, and terraces. Other buildings include a ball game court and an observatory. The architecture at Monte Albán shows influences from another significant

Early American Civilizations

Various advanced cultures flourished simultaneously in the Americas between the 1st century BCE and c.400–600 CE – a period that includes part of the great Mesoamerican "Classic" eras. Perhaps the best known of these cultures was that of the Maya people, who with their stunning temples and scientific knowledge created one of the most extraordinary early American civilizations.

« BEFORE

The advanced societies of Meso- and South America in the 1st centuries CE built on the legacy of earlier cultures, the Olmecs in Mexico, and the Chavín in Peru.

OLMECS AND ZAPOTECS

Maya **writing**, their calendar, and understanding of astronomy all owe a debt to the **Olmec culture** **« 32–33** that flourished c.1200–400 BCE near the coast of the Gulf of Mexico. The **Zapotec** city of Monte Albán in the valley of Oaxaca, which first appeared at the time of the later Olmecs, remained an important centre until c.600 CE.

BALL COURT AT MONTE ALBÁN

CHAVÍN CULTURE

Chavín culture **« 32–33**, widely diffused across Peru c.1000–200 BCE, gave way to smaller coastal societies such as the Moche and the Nazca.

for carved stone reliefs, with some especially fine examples at Palenque in Mexico. Cities also featured palaces, open plazas, terraces, and courts where a sacred ball game was played. This seems to have been a strenuous affair in which the participants used their heads, hips, and shoulders to direct a rubber ball at its target.

Religious ritual played a major part in Maya life. They practised forms of "auto-sacrifice" (self-mutilation involving the piercing of body parts), but more extreme scenarios involving torture and human sacrifice seem to be highly inaccurate and sensationalized.

Writing and the calendar

While the Olmecs developed a form of writing, some consider that the Maya should be credited with the first "real" Mesoamerican writing because theirs was more closely connected with actual speech. Their system comprised at least 800 glyphs (symbols).

The Maya also had a sophisticated calendar – probably using earlier Olmec concepts. This incorporated advanced astronomical knowledge that included

Moche stirrup-spouted jar
The Moche often combined different animals in their artefacts – this jar has the head of a deer, feline fangs, and a snake's body.

cultural centre, that at Teotihuacán (see right), a huge city northeast of present-day Mexico City that flourished c.300–600 CE and had cultural links across Mesoamerica.

Peruvian societies

In South America, various Peruvian cultures flourished up to about 400–600 CE. The people of southern Peru's Paracas peninsula were a mainly agricultural people, but were also extraordinarily talented weavers and embroiderers. Their art is preserved in the beautiful cloaks that the Paracas wrapped around mummified bodies.

The Nazca people lived on Peru's southern coast, with an important centre at Cahuachi in the Nazca Valley. They created irrigation systems to support intensive grain production as well as puzzling "lines" in the desert that remain a mystery today.

On Peru's northern coast, the Moche built a great administrative and religious complex at Sipán. Formidable warriors and inventive artists, they also created advanced valley irrigation techniques.

AFTER »

Meso- and South America continued to give rise to a variety of new cultures, while Maya civilization underwent a major shift.

SOUTH AMERICA

From around 600 CE, the **Tiahuanaco** and **Huari** cultures emerged in the highlands of Bolivia and Peru respectively. The **TIAHUANACO GOD**

Chimú of coastal Peru created a large state that fell to the **Incas 158–59 »** in the 15th century.

THE LATE MAYA PERIOD

From the 9th century CE, a number of southern Maya centres were abandoned – due to a range of factors, including **depleted resources** resulting from **intense cultivation** – while northern ones such as **Chichén Itzá 156–59 »** were still thriving and expanding. The Maya culture lived on and today there are around 6 million Maya in Mexico, Guatemala, and Belize.

Maya ritual
This carving shows a bloodletting "auto-sacrifice". Lady K'ab'al Xook pulls a thorny rope through her tongue as her husband, the king of Yaxchilán, holds a torch over her.

«

BEFORE

In earliest times, much religion seems to have been related to fertility or the seasons. As people's social organization changed, so too did their conception of their gods.

EARLIEST SUPERNATURAL BELIEFS

Remains of Stone Age ritual burials suggest that belief in the **afterlife** and the **spirit world** is at least as old as 60,000 years. Neolithic monuments and traces of ritual life suggest a spiritual outlook reflecting the **cycle of seasons** and the **motion of the heavens**.

PREHISTORIC RELIGIOUS SYMBOLS

Religious artefacts from prehistoric societies reveal more about beliefs, despite the lack of written evidence. Male and female figurines with exaggerated features may be related to a desire for **fertility and prosperity**. Ritual sites that contain animals, either their physical remains, or images, suggest the worshippers were preoccupied with the supply of **animals for food and materials**.

HIERARCHY OF GODS

Early religion often involved **polytheism – the worship of many deities**. With the emergence of more complex societies in the first towns, the new social order was mirrored in religion: the gods were organized, like society, into a **hierarchy**, with the ruling god at the apex.

IDEA

HUMANS BECOMING GODS

Individuals with power over others were sometimes given the status of a god. The deified ruler may have been seen as the earthly embodiment of a certain god, or may have been worshipped as a god in their own right, giving his or her subjects protection in return. Rulers deified in their lifetime or after their deaths became more common in the Mediterranean world after the 4th century BCE. Below, the Roman emperor Claudius is being deified straight after his death in 54 CE.

Greek gods
Found in the Mannella region of southeast Italy, this Greek clay sculpture from the first half of the 5th century BCE, features the Greek goddess and daughter of Zeus Persephone and the god of the underworld, Hades.

Gods and Goddesses

Gods and goddesses were believed to be responsible for many aspects of the human experience in the ancient world. The importance of a god was determined by their place in a hierarchical order. The worship of certain gods spread to far-removed places with the expansion of the ancient empires.

AFTER »

From 300 BCE–700 CE, the religious landscape was changed by the spread of the "world religions" – Hinduism, Buddhism, Judaism, Christianity, and Islam.

MONOTHEISM
Within pantheons of gods, lesser deities may diminish and disappear. If only one god remains, people's beliefs become **monotheistic 96»**. Both **Judaism** and the **Zoroastrianism** of Persia have roots in earlier, polytheistic religions.

ENDURING EASTERN BELIEFS
The period 700 BCE–100 CE gave rise to most of today's established belief systems. In the East, **Taoism, Shintoism, and Confucianism « 87** all follow teachings more than 2,000 years old.

UNIVERSAL RELIGION
In antiquity, it was common for people to regard gods as the figureheads of their culture. Their religion was part of their ethnic identity, so it was **not encouraged in foreigners**. In multicultural kingdoms, tolerance of many beliefs was a fact of life. Some new religions, notably **Christianity 96–99 »** and **Islam 122–25 »** changed these ideas by proposing that, in theory, all humanity could and should share a single set of religious beliefs and practices.

B
efore the spread of some notable "world religions" (see pp.96–97), most people practised polytheism (see BEFORE). While some of their many gods held sway over a large area, others were gods of a single city or feature in the landscape, such as a river. The deities, who were often depicted with human features, influenced almost every aspect of life. Even the weather was believed to be the result of the current mood of an individual god or goddess.

Social or political changes could influence the way in which godliness was perceived. In times of war and territorial expansion, mortal leaders, such as Roman emperors (see left) were sometimes worshipped as if they were gods, which served to focus loyalty to that leader. As societies became more complex, the relationships between the gods became more elaborate and many cultures

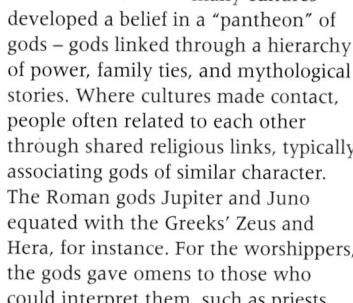

Gods and symbols
This Babylonian is paying his repects to the gods Marduk (symbolized by a triangular-headed spade) and Sin (a crescent moon).

developed a belief in a "pantheon" of gods – gods linked through a hierarchy of power, family ties, and mythological stories. Where cultures made contact, people often related to each other through shared religious links, typically associating gods of similar character. The Roman gods Jupiter and Juno equated with the Greeks' Zeus and Hera, for instance. For the worshippers, the gods gave omens to those who could interpret them, such as priests,

King of the Persian gods
The two sphinxes on this seal are supporting the winged Ahuramazda, patron god of the Persian monarchy (see pp.92–93). His appearance mirors that of the king below. Seals transmitted religious images across great distances.

diviners, and oracles. In return the worshippers offered the gods gifts, sacrifice, or ritual tributes to secure their good will.

Supreme gods
In the same way that human societies have leaders, each pantheon also had a "supreme god". A god was recognized as supreme either by being given prominence by a ruler or city, or by being identified with key symbols in human life, such as a parent, or natural phenomena, such as the Sun, sky, ocean, or storms. Gods became supreme gods when people came to think of them as "father" of a family of gods. One such god was Zeus, who was part-father, part-monarch of a quarrelling cohort of Greek deities. A god could also be promoted to supreme deity if their city or people became dominant. Bel Marduk, for example, was the patron god of the city of Babylon from about 2000 BCE. When Babylon began

> **"Men create gods after their own image..."**
> ARISTOTLE, GREEK PHILOSPHER, 384–322 BCE

to dominate southern Mesopotamia from 1780 BCE, Marduk's status was elevated and he acquired family ties with the gods of local regions and cities, eventually becoming supreme.

Gods in the landscape
A wide world of gods was imbued in the landscape itself, although physical evidence of their worship is hard to find, as it can be nothing more than a cluster of plaques by a spring. An ancient description of Persian religion revealed the practice of open-air rituals, and many Persian tablets record gods related to nature. Fertile places were revered across Asia and were the sites of gardens and Buddhist temples. Mountain sanctuaries could be the

> **MYSTERY RELIGION** One of many diverse religious cults involving a belief in death and regeneration or resurrection, which often required personal secret initiation. Early Christianity included many elements of a mystery cult.

focus of cults, such as that devoted to an ancient "Mother of the Gods" on Mounts Sipylos and Dindymene in Anatolia. Mountains were sometimes used as billboards to promote a belief. The towering Buddhas in the cliff-face at Bamiyan in Afghanistan were sited strategically to overlook a major road to the East from Rome through Persia.

Migrant gods
Ever-wider cultural interconnections during the 1st millennium CE (see pp.86–87) enabled divine entities, such as the Buddha (see pp.96–99) to spread like never before. Gods could migrate with travellers, soldiers, and merchants across the entire Roman Empire. In London, temples to a rich variety of immigrant gods have been

uncovered. The gods included Serapis, who was first popular with the Greeks of Egypt (see pp.72–73), then hitched a ride with Roman settlement across Europe. Mithras, also worshipped in London, may have begun as the Persian Mithra. Such gods with "exotic", or Eastern origins, often the focus of "Mystery" cults requiring initiation, were popular with the shifting populations of the Roman world.

Exotic god
Dressed in a Phrygian cap and Persian clothing, and slaying a bull in Italy, the exotic origins of Mithras are highlighted in this Roman statue of the 2nd century CE.

Zeus' temple
The 5th century BCE temple of Zeus at Olympia in Greece contains a huge gold- and ivory-covered statue of the supreme god.

BEFORE

Faith in a spiritual dimension to human existence probably evolved separately in many parts of the world among bands of Paleolithic hunter-gatherers.

ANIMISM

The earliest belief of the hunter-gatherers is known as animism. In animism all of **physical nature has a spiritual counterpart** and everything becomes part of a chain. Each object, living or inanimate, is a link, but the links

GREEK GOD ZEUS

are fluid so that a man can become a bird, an animal can be disguised as a rock, and a bird can transform into a cloud. The power for these changes stems from a world of vaguely defined guardian spirits.

MANY GODS

As tribes became settled into farming communities, pantheons of more **clearly identifiable gods** emerged. Each god was responsible for overseeing

a part of the temporal world, and still acting as the guardian of his or her domain – such as Zeus, the Greek god of thunder and lightning and also the ruler of Mount Olympus. This is **polytheism** (meaning "many gods") **‹‹ 94–95**, which early Christians dubbed "paganism", a derogatory term from the Latin *pagani* meaning "peasants".

THE NEXT WORLD

The belief in an afterlife may extend back even further in time than animism, because **Neanderthal** burial

sites sometimes included medicinal herbs and other items, which could suggest that they thought the deceased was embarking on a **journey to another place**.

PANTHEISM A doctrine or belief presenting the natural world, including humankind, as being part of the divine. It is the predominant belief in Hinduism, but is rejected by beliefs that hold that God is transcendent – a being above the created world – such as Christianity and Islam.

hough many different religious sects and movements have flourished briefly throughout history, five great faiths have emerged and spread sufficiently to become major world religions.

Hinduism

The oldest of these five religious faiths is Hinduism, which has a range of very diverse traditions but no formal system of beliefs. The origin of the religion can be traced to about 1500 BCE, when it is believed that Aryan horsemen from Central Asia invaded the Indus Valley in northern India (see pp.18–19), accompanied by a creator god Indra and a pantheon of lesser deities (see p.95). These were the Vedic gods, who feature in the *Vedas*, the

3,000-year-old sacred texts that are central to the development of Hinduism. The religion evolved to focus on three main gods: a senior, somewhat remote deity called Brahma; Vishnu the creator; and Shiva the destroyer, along with their various consorts or *shaktis*.

From the 6th century BCE Brahmanism became the dominant form of Hinduism and triggered the composition of the Brahmanic, Epic,

> "There is probably no subject in the world about which **opinions differ** so much as the nature of religion."
>
> JAMES FRAZER, FROM "THE GOLDEN BOUGH", 1922

no fixed abode", later known as Hebrews, came together under Moses and settled in Palestine. In 587 BCE Jerusalem, the city that the legendary King David had made the capital of Israel, was destroyed by the Neo-Babylonians (see p.46) and the Israelite elite deported to Babylon. Cyrus the Great (see p.47) allowed the exiles home in 539 BCE to form a religious state based on the Hebrew book of law (the Torah) and the Jewish

MONOTHEISM

The religious faith of the Israelites rested in a universal god, a unique, unchanging, and physically unseen revelation that contrasted starkly with the polytheism of neighbouring cultures in the ancient Middle East. Tradition has it that this omnipotent deity, also the God of Islam and Christianity, was first recognized by Abraham – one of the patriarchal ancestors of the Israelites.

Spreading the Faith

In the first millennium BCE the scope of religions, supported not just by local traditions, but by sacred writings, widened immensely. Hinduism and Buddhism spread across Southeast Asia, while the Middle East saw the expanding influence of Judaism, followed by its monotheistic offshoots, Christianity and Islam.

Holiest of holy sites
Christianity, Islam, and Judaism view this site in Jerusalem as holy. In the foreground people can be seen praying at the Western Wall, and behind it is the Dome of the Rock mosque.

and Puranic literature, including the great texts of the *Mahabharata* and *Ramayana*. Hinduism remains polytheistic (see BEFORE).

Buddhism

Buddhism emerged not as a belief in a god, but as an ascetic way of life. Its teachings involve the belief that death marks the transition to a new earthly life – reincarnation. The only way to escape this painful cycle of death and rebirth, known as *samsara*, is to achieve perfection, which is accompanied by an extinction of passions, or *nirvana*.

Buddhism evolved in part as a reaction against polytheistic Hinduism and attracted a body of disciples willing to practise asceticism (abstention from earthly comforts). The historical Buddha (distinguished from earlier wholly mythical characters) was born into the royal Shakya clan in northeast India (modern Nepal) in about 563 BCE. After his death in about 483 BCE his original companions established the *Theravada* ("doctrine of the elders") school that would become the basis of more conservative Buddhist teaching.

The first monotheistic faith

Judaism, the monotheistic (see above right) religion of the Jews, evolved from the older, ritualistic, temple-based cult attributed to Moses. The ancestors of the Jews, the wandering Israelite tribes or *habiru*, literally "people of

religion flourished, first under Persian control then the rule of Alexander the Great (see pp.50–51). When one of Alexander's successors, Antiochus Epiphanes, tried to introduce aspects of Greek cults, the resulting uprising led to a dynasty of priest-kings, the Hasmoneans. In 63 BCE Greater Judea was incorporated into the Roman order and hard times followed, culminating in 70 CE when much of the population of Jerusalem was scattered (see p.98).

Followers of Jesus Christ

The second major monotheistic religion, Christianity, arose from Judaism. There is no evidence that Jesus envisaged

founding a religious movement. It was only through his death on the cross, during which Christians believe he atoned for humanity's sins, that the early Church emerged. The first Christians met in private houses and had no formal dogma; only after several decades did formal places of worship appear. The new religion endured spates of often bloody persecution from orthodox Jews and also from Roman emperors, notably Nero in 64 CE and Domitian at the end of the 1st century CE. Rather than destroying the religion, however, persecution had the effect of reinforcing the convictions of its devotees. »

JESUS

Jesus of Nazareth was the inspiration for the religious movement of Christianity, which derives from Greek *christos*, synonymous with Hebrew *messiah*, meaning "a chosen one". Jesus probably saw himself as a social reformer, but to some Jews under Roman occupation he became the deliverer predicted in Jewish scripture. In the Christian gospels he is described as the son of God. For much of his life Jesus moved around the Sea of Galilee accompanied by a local band of disciples and followers. Only after journeying to Jerusalem and his death by crucifixion did his following grow and his messianic fame spread.

HINDU AUM SYMBOL

BUDDHIST WHEEL OF THE LAW

JEWISH STAR OF DAVID

CHRISTIAN CROSS

Religious symbols
The Aum symbol represents the sacred Hindu syllable for God. The wheel of the law represents both the teachings of the Buddha and the cycle of death and rebirth. The six-pointed hexagram or Star of David is widely accepted as the symbol of Judaism, although it has only been adopted as such over the last 200 years. The cross in Christianity is symbolic of the death, and resurrection, of Jesus Christ.

The emergence of Islam
Islam emerged in the 7th century CE. It recognizes the transcendental god of Judaism and Christianity, but by the name of Allah. The Prophet Muhammad promoted a doctrine based on personal divine revelation, which was incorporated into the holy book of Islam, the Qur'an.

Travelling faiths
From their Asian beginnings Hinduism, Buddhism, Judaism, Christianity, and Islam all spread out across the globe, carried in some cases by conquering armies, in others by migrants, traders, and missionaries.

Spread of Hinduism
Hinduism was firmly established on the Indian subcontinent by 700 BCE. From around 600 BCE belief in reincarnation was established and Hinduism spread on a wave of popular fervour from India into Sri Lanka, Cambodia, and Malaysia. It reached Indonesia and the Philippines in about the 1st century CE. Hinduism also evolved into a wide range of branches and sects, each

devoting itself to a particular deity or aspects of a deity. The largest and most universal of these were the *Vaishnava* and *Shaivite* movements, worshipping the two main creator deities, Vishnu and Shiva. Much of the burgeoning popularity of Hinduism also stemmed from the set of religious texts known as the *Puranas*, committed to writing in 450–1000 CE, but known in oral tradition from much earlier. Despite a multitude of different facets, Hinduism became a powerful cohesive force among people who were disparate in language, culture, and social position.

Paths of Buddhism
In the centuries after the death of Gautama Buddha (c.483 BCE), members of the Indian *sanghas* (communities of monks) elaborated his teachings and paved the way for the development of a host of schools. One of the principal branches, *Hinayana* Buddhism, following the ancient "way of the elders" or *Theravada*, arose in the 4th century BCE and spread mainly south and east from India into Sri Lanka, Myanmar, Cambodia, Laos, and Thailand. The other main branch, *Mahayana* (the "Great Vehicle") Buddhism developed later, in the 1st–3rd centuries CE, and became the dominant element in 300–500 CE, spreading mainly north and east. Among *Mahayana's* splinter sects is the influential *Vajrayana* school, also sometimes called tantric Buddhism. Other more austere *Mahayana* schools were carried by itinerant monks through China and thence to Japan, where further adaptation resulted in Zen Buddhism. The faith has been described as the "Vagrant Lotus" because its history has been one of migration from one culture to another. As a result the Buddhism of India stands in sharp contrast with that found in Japan and Korea.

Jewish diaspora
The spread of faith often went hand in glove with politics, and Judaism was no exception. Dispersal began with the forcible deportation of the Jewish elite to Babylon in 587 BCE, thus triggering the *diaspora* – the scattering of Jewish communities outside the Land of Israel.

The process intensified when the Roman general Titus sacked Jerusalem in 70 CE, causing many inhabitants to flee. By the end of the 1st century the local population had largely recovered, rebuilding its faith through observance of the Torah. Although the Romans protected the right of Jews to practise their religion throughout most of the history of the empire, they targeted Judaism after several revolts in the 2nd century CE. The emperor Septimius Severus (193–235 CE) instituted a tax on self-identified Jews and forbade conversion to Judaism. From 527 CE the Byzantine emperor Justinian subordinated the Jews to orthodox Christians. Jews continued to use the trade networks of the empire, however, establishing themselves wherever trade took place. By 600 CE they had founded settlements as far as Cordoba in Iberia, Cologne in Germany, Oxyrhynchus in Egypt, and Charax at the mouth of the Persian Gulf. Jewish populations became particularly concentrated in Asia Minor and in Mesopotamia.

Footsteps of Christianity
The Roman Empire was also largely responsible for the spread of Christianity. Although successive emperors suppressed its fledgling communities, St Paul was able to move freely across Europe and establish Christian cells in Corinth, Thessalonica, Ephesus, Galatia, and elsewhere. When Emperor Constantine the Great converted to Christianity early in the 4th century CE (see pp.100–01), expansion truly gained pace.

Even before the reign of Constantine, Christianity had extended rapidly into Syria and northwest into Asia Minor and Greece. In the 2nd century a thriving community of Greek-speaking Christians was established in the Rhone valley in France, and by 200 CE the Church was also well established

in North Africa, centred on Carthage. To the northeast, beyond the imperial frontier, a language barrier slowed progress, although by the 3rd century a church was founded at Edessa in modern Turkey. However, most missionary work was focused on Western Europe – in Italy, France, and Spain. Britain probably felt little influence until the mid-3rd century, but by 400 CE it was largely Christian.

MONK (c.563–c.483 BCE)
GAUTAMA BUDDHA

Also known as Shakyamuni and Siddhartha he lived in northern India during the 6th and 5th centuries BCE. One of the many ascetic philosophers of his day, he achieved enlightenment – an awakening to the ultimate truth – at Bodhgaya and subsequently wandered for the rest of his life teaching Buddhist philosophy and gathering a community of disciples or *sangha*. He taught the Eightfold Path to enlightenment, which includes disciplined guidance on all aspects of morality, wisdom, and meditation.

PROPHET (c.570–632 CE)
MUHAMMAD

Born in Mecca, Muhammad succeeded in ridding southern Arabia of polytheism and replacing it with the worship of a single God, Allah. In Islamic doctrine he is the "end of a line" of prophets, the ultimate deliverer of divine revelation. From about 610 CE he witnessed a series of angelic visitations that became the foundation of Islamic theology. In 622 CE, in a journey known as the Hegira, he fled Mecca to escape persecution and settled in Medina with a growing band of supporters. In 631 CE he returned to Mecca on a final pilgrimage accompanied, it is said, by 120,000 devotees. He died in Medina aged 63.

Spreading the Christian faith
St Paul (Paul of Tarsus) received a rabbinical education in Jerusalem. Originally an opponent of the early Christians, he was converted in c.33 CE and became the leading Christian apostle, or missionary, especially among the non-Jewish communities. Upon arrest by the Roman authorities, he appealed to the emperor but was executed in Rome circa 62 CE.

The basilica of St Peter's in the Vatican City, Rome, is the focus of devotion for millions of Catholics worldwide. The original was destroyed in the early 16th century. Its replacement, which is topped by a magnificent dome designed by Michelangelo, took over a century to build.

Faiths spread throughout the world, and regional changes occurred where some religions were adopted by new cultures.

UNIVERSAL TEACHINGS

The guru – a revered teacher of spiritual matters – became central to Hinduism. New Hindu schools have arisen, aiming to make its thought more universal. A celebrated modernist, Sri Ramakrishna (1836–86) taught the **essential unity of all religions** and the Ramakrishna Mission spread far beyond India.

DISPERSION

The Jewish diaspora continued and by the middle ages France and Spain had become two of its most important centres. During the 19th century an exodus of Jews took place from Russia and Poland, and in the Nazi holocaust **322–23 »** many of the old European communities were **virtually annihilated**. In 1947 the **modern state of Israel 336–37 »** was born, annexed from the indigenous population of Palestinians. Today, the main focus of diaspora Judaism is America.

REGIONAL DIFFERENCES

Buddhism evolved into **various regional forms** as its influence extended through Central and Southeast Asia, China, Japan, and most recently, the West.

GREAT CHANGES

By the 11th century Christianity had split into two, the western Church under the papacy in Rome and the eastern Orthodox Church. In the 16th century it split again when **challenges to papal authority** resulted in the Reformation **196–99 »**.

The Hagia Sofia in Istanbul, Turkey, is a magnificent example of Byzantine architecture. It was dedicated as a church by the Roman emperor Justinian I in 537 CE, then in 1453 CE was converted into a mosque. In 1935 it was turned into the Ayasofya Museum.

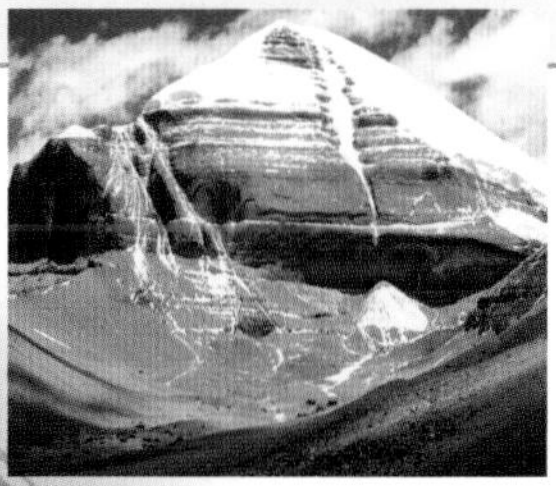

Mount Kailas, on the border between Tibet and Nepal, is a holy place for Buddhists and Hindus alike. Pilgrims trek up the Humla valley to walk around the mountain, but no one has ever climbed its slopes.

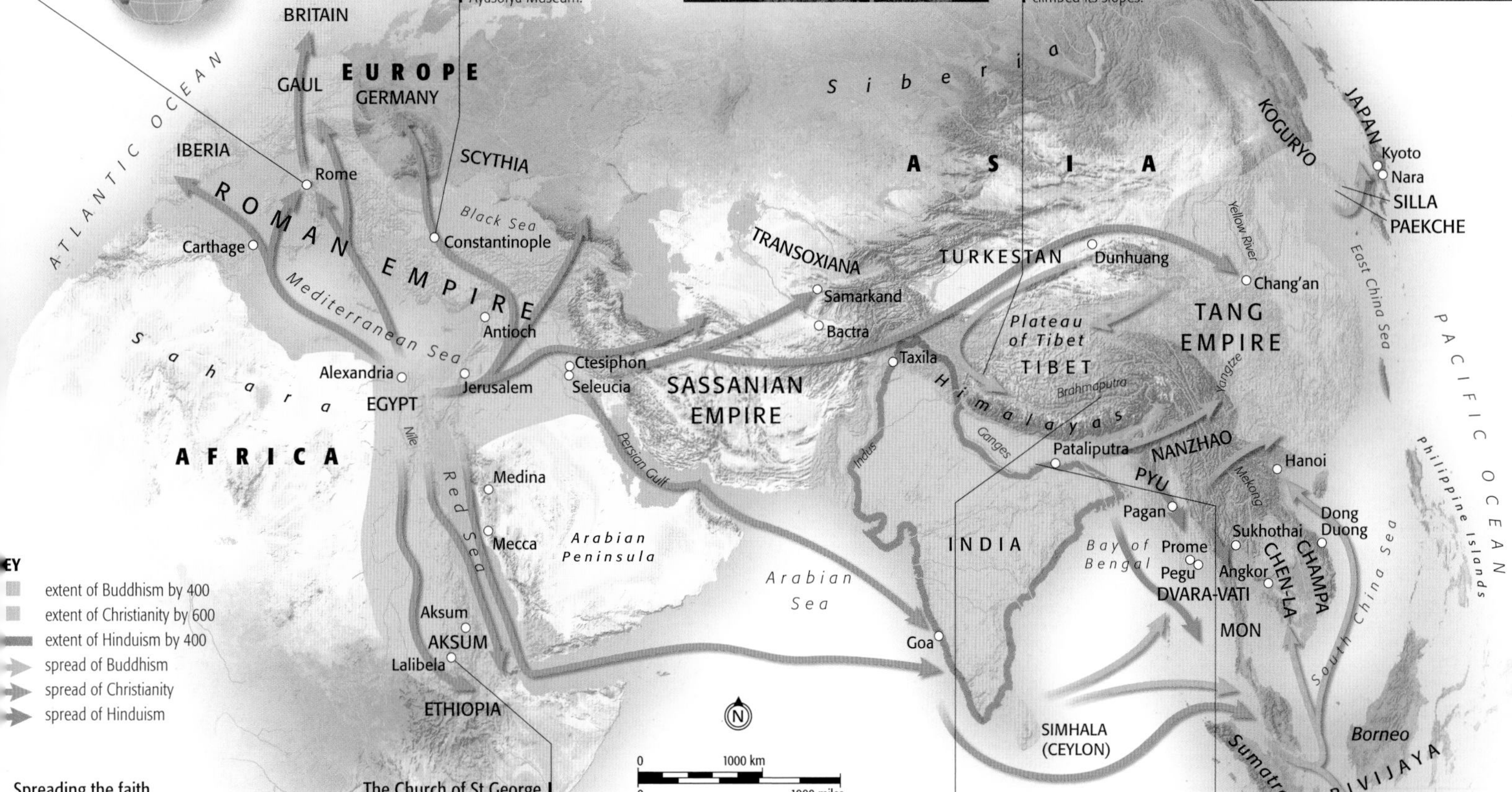

Map labels

BRITAIN
GAUL
EUROPE
GERMANY
IBERIA
SCYTHIA
Rome
Carthage
ROMAN EMPIRE
Constantinople
Black Sea
ATLANTIC OCEAN
Mediterranean Sea
Antioch
Sahara
Alexandria
Ctesiphon
Seleucia
Jerusalem
EGYPT
AFRICA
Nile
Medina
Red Sea
Mecca
Arabian Peninsula
Aksum
AKSUM
Lalibela
ETHIOPIA
Siberia
ASIA
TRANSOXIANA
Samarkand
Bactra
TURKESTAN
Dunhuang
Chang'an
KOGURYO
JAPAN
Kyoto
Nara
SILLA
PAEKCHE
East China Sea
Yellow River
TANG EMPIRE
Plateau of Tibet
TIBET
Taxila
Himalayas
Brahmaputra
Ganges
Indus
Pataliputra
NANZHAO
Hanoi
PYU
Pagan
Mekong
Yangtze
INDIA
Bay of Bengal
Prome
Pegu
Sukhothai
Dong Duong
Angkor
CHEN-LA
CHAMPA
DVARA-VATI
MON
Arabian Sea
Persian Gulf
SASSANIAN EMPIRE
Goa
SIMHALA (CEYLON)
PACIFIC OCEAN
Philippine Islands
South China Sea
Sumatra
Borneo
SRIVIJAYA
Palembang
Java
Borobudur

KEY

- extent of Buddhism by 400
- extent of Christianity by 600
- extent of Hinduism by 400
- spread of Buddhism
- spread of Christianity
- spread of Hinduism

0   1000 km
0   1000 miles

N

Spreading the faith

This map charts the principal routes along which the faiths of Hinduism, Buddhism, and Christianity expanded during their early development, including smaller branches on which more isolated outposts arose. In most instances the newly introduced religion was not the only faith practised in the region, but in many areas it became the dominant one.

The Church of St George at Lalibela is one of eleven churches carved from volcanic rock high in Ethiopia's Amhara Mountains. The 13th-century church is a place of Christian pilgrimage and has been declared a world heritage site.

The vast Potala Palace that towers above Lhasa, Tibet, dates from 1645. Once the seat of the Tibetan government, it houses the tombs of past Dalai Lamas, the spiritual leaders of Tibetan Buddhists, and is a major pilgrimage destination.

The city of Varanasi in the Indian state of Uttar Pradesh is one of the holiest pilgrimage sites for Hindus, who come to bathe in the sacred waters of the Ganges and to cremate the dead.

The great Buddhist shrine at Borobudur, Java, is topped with bell-shaped stupas containing images of Buddha. The temple complex was built in the 8th century.

C·VAL·AVREL·CONSTANTINI
IMP·VICTORIA·QVA·SVBMERSO
MAXENTIO·CRISTIANORVM
OPES·FIRMATAE·SVNT

Battle of Milvian Bridge

In 312 CE, bitter rivals Constantine the Great and Maxentius met in battle outside Rome. Much was at stake, but foremost was the struggle for leadership of the western Roman Empire. Constantine went into the fray inspired by his Christian beliefs, while Maxentius put faith in pagan gods. The outcome was a turning point in the rise of Christianity.

In October 312 CE, Maxentius was making preparations behind Rome's walls to withstand a siege by Constantine. Previously, the two had separately been proclaimed emperor. Maxentius, being in Rome and having senate backing, perhaps had more legitimacy, but Constantine planned to take the city and claim the western empire as his alone.

Despite capturing some Maxentian strongholds as he crossed Italy that summer, Constantine must have felt some misgivings heading south from Gaul (France). He had a much smaller army than Maxentius, and its strength lay in a mobile cavalry that performed best in the open. However, before the battle, he apparently experienced a religious "conversion", which he may have felt put the Christian God on his side. Accounts include visions of a flaming cross in the sky and orders to place Christian symbols on his soldiers' shields.

As the battle began, Maxentius, fighting in the name of Mars, the Roman god of war, emerged into the open, giving Constantine the advantage. Maxentius had already dismantled Milvian Bridge to halt his opponent, so he and his troops had to cross the River Tiber using a bridge made from boats. In the ensuing battle, Constantine's cavalry disrupted enemy ranks with expert charges. Maxentius's troops had nowhere to go but into the Tiber, where many, including their leader, drowned. The next day, a triumphant procession, led by Constantine, marched through Rome with Maxentius's head on a spear.

Some view Constantine's "conversion" with cynicism, but he may have seen his victory at Milvian Bridge as a symbol of the power of Christianity. The influence of the faith had been gathering pace for three centuries, assisted by imperial edicts of religious tolerance. A few months after the battle, Constantine issued the Edict of Milan, which returned confiscated property to Christians and increased their status and political standing. His Christian leanings and massive church-building programme helped the religion gain a hold in the west, shaping Byzantine culture (see pp.144–45), the Eastern Orthodox church, and medieval Christian society.

Fighting for Empire
This 16th-century fresco from the Vatican depicts the events at Milvian Bridge. In the centre, the brightly lit Constantine can be seen pushing Maxentius and his troops into the River Tiber. Imperial standards bear crosses and, in the sky above, angels join in the battle.

" …he saw… **a cross of light**… bearing the inscription, **'conquer by this'**."

EUSEBIUS OF NICOMEDIA, BISHOP, 4TH CENTURY CE

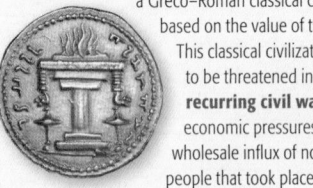

The date of 476 CE is often given as the end of the Roman Empire. This was the year Romulus Augustulus was deposed as emperor. He was, however, a "puppet" child king with a tenuous claim to leadership, and was emperor of only the western empire of Rome. He was removed by Germanic chief, Odoacer, who, though often portrayed as a barbarian warlord, was actually a former Roman commander in Italy.

Collapse would not occur for some time, and it is important to note that while the western empire declined, progress often pushed such groups into other lands – sometimes Roman territory – where they became allies of the empire and helped defend the Romans against Huns and other tribes.

Co-operation and conflict
In fact, it was not unusual for Germanic groups to become official Roman allies, or "federated" people gaining certain Roman-style rights. The situation was far more complex than a simple "barbarians versus Romans" scenario where one side rose and the other fell. Within the imperial system there were commanders and statesmen of Germanic blood. At different times, barbarians either sided with or fought against the Romans, as well as other barbarian groups. For example, the Goths defeated Emperor Valens in 378, at the Battle of Adrianople (Turkey), crushing the imperial army so severely that the Danube borders were left open

The last emperor
Romulus Augustulus is seen as the last emperor of Rome's western empire.

Decline and Fall?

The 5th century CE saw a massive shift in the world's map as the western Roman Empire faded, and a patchwork of new "barbarian" kingdoms dominated Europe. The eastern Roman Empire flourished as the Byzantine culture evolved there. It has been viewed alternately as a time of decline or one of transition.

the eastern Roman Empire, established in the early 4th century CE by Emperor Constantine (see pp.67, 101), thrived. Greco–Roman culture prospered there initially, although it evolved into a highly influential Christian Byzantine civilization that would last for another thousand years (see pp.144–45).

The time can be seen in a positive light and in some ways as one of continuity, rather than bleakly as the end of refined "civilization" when Europe was plunged into chaos. "Decline and fall", was the phrase famously coined by 18th-century English historian, Edward Gibbon, to describe the end of the Roman Empire, but the period could also be viewed as one of transition.

The great migrations
By the 4th and 5th centuries CE, a variety of peoples – many from Eurasia's northern steppe lands – had gained a strong foothold in European and Middle Eastern territories once dominated by the Romans. Germanic kingdoms and tribes spread far and wide during these centuries. For example, the Visigoths in parts of France (a kingdom was founded at Toulouse in 418 CE), Spain, Greece, and Italy; Franks in France; the Vandals in North Africa (their kingdom was founded there in 429 CE); and the Sueves in Spain. The Romans officially withdrew from Britain in 410 CE where the Celts prevailed before Angles and Saxons arrived on British shores.

In the later 4th century CE, westward migrating Hunnic people defeated and forced semi-sedentary people living around the Black Sea area to flee. Their

Showing Roman soldiers striking heroic poses and in command of the situation, this is a powerful piece of imperial propaganda.

Distinctive beards, hairstyles, and clothing mark out the barbarians, who are all shown in agonized submission.

THE DECLINE OF ROME
The 5th and 6th centuries saw incursions from Goths, Visigoths, and Vandals among other groups, contributing to the pressures on the Western Roman Empire.

383 **Emperor Theodisius** signs a peace treaty with the Goths, giving them land and autonomy in exchange for military service.

411 Iberian peninsula divided up between Germanic groups.

439 The Vandals **sack Carthage** and use it as a strategic base to control the Mediterranean.

455 Emperor Valentinian III is assassinated by rivals. Rome is sacked by the Vandals.

476 Warlord Odoacer takes throne from **Romulus Augustulus**, the last western emperor, and becomes first non-Roman "king" of Italy. The Western Roman Empire ends.

c.542 Justinianic plague starts to ravage the empire and continues for 200 years.

378 Goths, with **Alaric** as leader, enter Italy from the Balkans. **Emperor Valens** is captured and killed.

410 Visigoths, led by Alaric, **sack Rome**.

300 CE   **350**   **400**   **450**   **500**

297 Rome defeats the **Persian Empire**.

337 Death of Constantine the Great, the first Christian Emperor.

368 A long series of campaigns against the **Alemanni** (a Germanic tribe) on the Rhine frontier ends in Roman victory.

406 Germanic tribes cross Rhine to enter Roman Empire (Roman legions elsewhere, busy defending Italy against Alaric).

408 Goths, under Alaric, enter Italy again. Death of imperial general **Stilicho**, who had kept Germanic tribes at bay.

489 Theoderic the Ostrogoth takes Italy from Odoacer and becomes effective ruler until his death, though subordinate to the emperor.

535–53 The Eastern empire defeats Ostrogoths, retaking control of Italy and external territories.

This figure on horseback has been identified as Hostilian, who was a Roman general and a short-lived emperor before his death from the plague in 251 CE.

All the Romans in the relief are shown in armour, with clean-shaven faces wearing expressions of calm superiority.

This fine carving includes an incredibly detailed rendering of *lorica hamata* – a kind of metal-link armour worn by certain Roman soldiers.

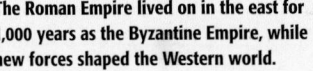

Frankish axe
Lightweight throwing axes, were popular weapons of the Franks in the 5th century CE.

for many years; Romans and Germanic people united to defeat Attila the Hun (see left) at the Battle of Châlons (France) in 451; the Visigoths had been Roman allies while also having a Gallic kingdom, but were then pushed south into Spain by Franks.

On some occasions the Romans tolerated, or were forced to accept, the settlement of barbarian groups on their lands. By 382 CE the Goths had assumed partial autonomy from the Romans and by 418 CE they were granted lands in Gaul (France). Where barbarians took over former Roman territories, they sometimes sought to supplant the old Roman aristocracy (as with the Vandals in North Africa), but in other places coexisted peacefully with them. There was much cultural cross-fertilization between the Romans and barbarians.

Weakening grip?

Another factor in the gradual fading of Roman power was the spread of plague and disease from the east. This led to severe shortages in the army and fewer people in general to support society. Various bouts of plague had spread through the empire in the 3rd century. Then the Justinianic plague broke out. Named after eastern Emperor Justinian who retook the western empire in the mid-sixth century, it began in 542 CE and raged for 200 years. The effect on the population of the eastern Empire was devastating.

Other factors include a general decline in population, inflation, civil war, self-serving Roman corruption, and imperial overcultivation leading to loss of good agricultural land. These have variously been seen as reducing prosperity and resources, hastening the fading of the great urban centres of "classical" civilization and learning.

RELIGIOUS CHANGE

The rise of Christianity also played a major role in the new order. The "Arian" Christianity held by most

Germanic peoples was at odds with the more orthodox Christianity traditionally held by Roman peoples. Furthermore, the increasing power of the Christian church may have eroded some imperial authority (see AFTER).

AFTER

The Roman Empire lived on in the east for 1,000 years as the Byzantine Empire, while new forces shaped the Western world.

BYZANTINE EMPIRE
After damaging wars with the Persians, the Byzantine or East Roman Empire **144–45 »** was too weak to face the challenges posed by Arab Muslim armies.

ARAB ADVANCE
Arab power, **united under the banner of Islam,** grew in the 7th and early 8th centuries with the capture of the Byzantine Levant, much of North Africa and Egypt, and attempts to take Constantinople **122–23 »**.

LATIN CHRISTENDOM
The pope shifted his loyalty from Constantinople's Roman emperor to Frankish king, Charlemagne (747–814), **104–41 »**, crowning him Emperor of the Romans.

LATE ANTIQUITY
Distinctive communities that combined Germanic traditions, Latin Christianity, and aspects of Roman culture began to emerge in the post-Roman west, such as in Anglo-Saxon England.

ANGLO-SAXON BELT BUCKLE

Romans battling barbarians
The famous Ludovisi Battle Sarcophagus, an imperial Roman marble sarcophagus, depicts Romans battling against Ostrogoth barbarians during the 3rd century CE. It has been dated to around 250–60 CE.

Writhing figures struggling closely together convey the chaos and drama of hand-to-hand battle.

3

WARRIORS, TRAVELLERS, AND INVENTORS

600–1450

Contact between East and West increased in the medieval period, as trade routes expanded, leading to the spread of goods and ideas. Warrior tribes founded great empires in China and the Middle East, and in Europe the feudal system took hold, dominated by the might of the Christian church. In the Americas, Africa, and Asia great civilizations flourished.

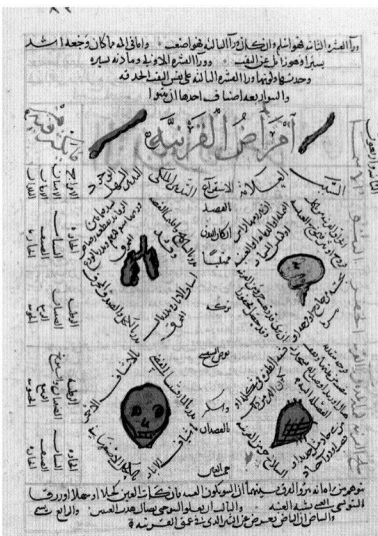

Avicenna's medical encyclopedia
Known as the "Prince of Physicians", the 11th-century Persian scholar Avicenna was a hugely influential figure in both the Middle East and Europe, where his work *The Canon of Medicine* continued to be used as a standard medical text until the 16th century.

≪ BEFORE

As the study of the Bible came to dominate intellectual activity in the West, knowledge of classical Greek learning declined.

CLASSICAL SCHOLARSHIP
Greek and Roman education included the teaching of **grammar**, **logic**, and **rhetoric** (the *trivium*) before moving on to **astronomy**, **arithmetic**, **music**, and **geometry** (the *quadrivium*). At Aristotle's Lyceum and Plato's Academy, students listened to their lecturers discuss philosophy and science.

ROMAN TEACHER AND PUPILS

DECAY OF CLASSICAL KNOWLEDGE
The classical approach continued into the early medieval period, but by now knowledge of the Greek language had largely died out in the West. **Christianity** was dominant, and education focused on **the Bible**. Some fragments of classical knowledge were preserved in texts such as the 6th century philosopher Boethius' *Consolation of Philosophy*. But by the 8th century, education in western Europe was structured almost entirely around the Bible, and scholarship had become largely cut off from Greek science and philosophy.

"**Books** have led some to **learning** and others to **madness**."

FRANCESCO PETRARCH, "REMEDIES FOR FORTUNE FAIR AND FOUL", 1365

Diffusion of Knowledge

Knowledge of classical Greek and Roman culture declined in Western Europe in the early medieval period, but survived in the East. Muslim scholars preserved the works of classical Greek philosophers and, as this knowledge spread west, laid the foundations for the European intellectual revival.

During the late 8th and 9th centuries, something of a literary awakening occurred at the court of the Frankish emperor Charlemagne (see pp.134–35). Before Charlemagne, society lacked many of the basic educational skills – most priests were barely literate and the royal court had difficulty finding educated men to act as scribes and copy out manuscripts. To fix these problems, Charlemagne created schools and assembled the greatest scholars of the age at his court. A Northumbrian scholar, Alcuin of York, was recruited as head of the palace school. A standard curriculum was introduced, and the classical study of the *trivium* and *quadrivium* was re-established (see BEFORE). Latin once again became the formal language of communication across Europe.

The Arab inheritance
Charlemagne's reforms were primarily concerned with creating an educated clergy capable of reforming the Frankish church. Works of classical Greek science and philosophy remained essentially unavailable in the Christian Europe. In Arab Spain, North Africa, and the Middle East, however, the situation

Astrolabe manual
Muslim scholars are shown using the astrolabe, an instrument for locating and predicting the position of the Sun, Moon, and stars. The astrolabe was introduced into Christian Europe via Muslim Spain in the 11th century.

was very different. The Arab societies inhabiting these regions had inherited many aspects of classical Greek culture. Until the 12th century, for example, virtually all that Christian Europe knew of Aristotle came via Boethius (see BEFORE). To Islamic scholars, Aristotle was "the Philosopher" and his works were standard texts. In the 9th–10th centuries, numerous classical Greek works were translated into Arabic, and a flurry of commentaries was composed.

Two individuals stand out during this period. The Persian scholar Avicenna produced a huge range of material covering almost every area of knowledge, from metaphysics to medicine. His *Book of Healing* is the largest encyclopedia of knowledge composed by one person in the period. Averroes (see below), a renowned philosopher, scientist, and lawyer, composed a series of commentaries on Aristotle that for centuries formed the key source for Aristotle's philosophy in the West.

The 12th century renaissance
The diffusion of knowledge from East to West accelerated during the 12th century. In Spain, the Christian reconquest of lands previously held by Muslim rulers encouraged the spread of Islamic learning. In the 13th century, the Spanish king Alfonso X established a programme of translation of Greek and Arab texts in Toledo, previously capital of the Muslim caliphate of Cordoba.

Other important hubs for the exchange of ideas included the Christian crusader kingdoms that were established in the Middle East in the 12th–13th centuries (see pp.146–47) and the Greek empire of Byzantium (see pp.144–45), which fell into the hands of the crusaders in 1204. By the 13th century, Latin translations of the most important classical texts were available to European scholars.

Scholasticism
The rediscovery of ancient philosophical works combined with the ongoing development of Christian theology led to the scholastic movement of the later Medieval period. Scholasticism was not a philosophy in itself, but rather a tool for learning that placed emphasis on logic and reasoning. The works of Plato

ARAB PHILOSOPHER AND SCIENTIST (1126–98)

AVERROES

Born into a learned and cultured family in the city of Cordoba (then part of Muslim Spain) Averroes was an expert in Islamic law and theology, as well as Arabic grammar and poetry. In 1153, he was invited to the court of the Almohad caliphs in Morocco where he worked as a judge and physician, and wrote important works on medicine, philosophy, and law. He later fell out of favour and was exiled. Averroes' writings had a huge influence on European scholarship, but his greatest contribution was a series of commentaries on Aristotle that introduced medieval scholars to the works of the great Greek philosopher.

RHETORIC Derived from the Greek word for "orator", rhetoric is the art of persuasion through spoken or written language. It was an important art in classical Greece, where public speaking was central to political life.

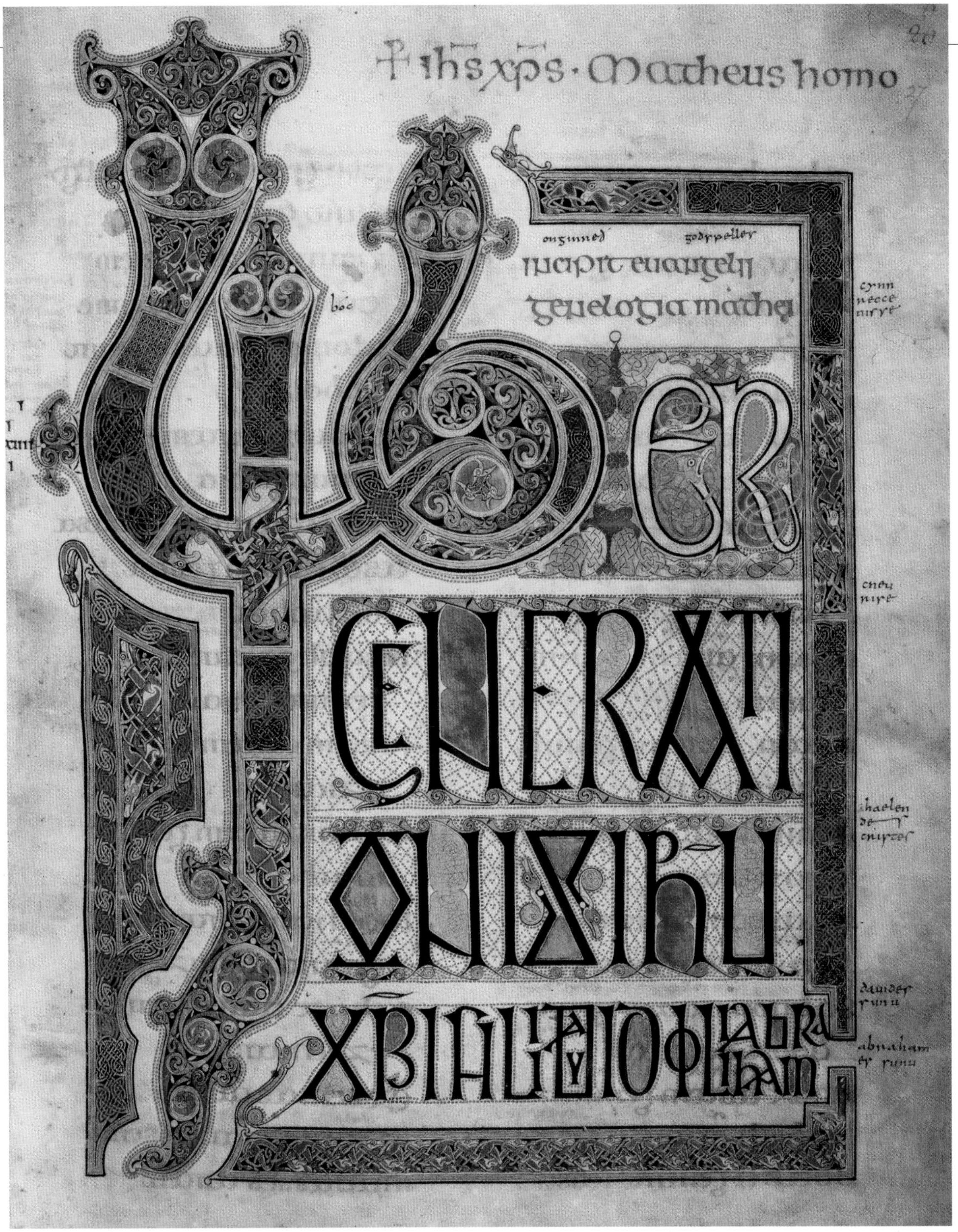

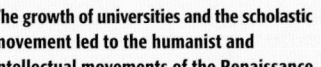

The growth of universities and the scholastic movement led to the humanist and intellectual movements of the Renaissance.

THE RENAISSANCE

The rediscovery of ancient Greek and Latin texts during the later medieval period stimulated interest in classical learning and led to the great **artistic and cultural flowering** of the 15th- and 16th-century **Renaissance 190–91 ».**

PICO DELLA MIRANDOLA

HUMANISM

The key intellectual movement of the Renaissance, humanism emphasized **human reason and dignity** rather than the Christian humility and obedience to authority that had been the focus of the medieval Church. The Italian writer **Pico della Mirandola** captured the new spirit in 1489 with his *Oration on the Dignity of Man*, a preface to 900 theses on religion and philosophy. Renaissance humanists, schooled in Greek and Latin from an early age and often learning Hebrew and Arabic as well, studied the poetry, grammar, rhetoric, and ethics of the classical authors in their original languages.

The Lindisfarne Gospel
Created by the monks of Lindisfarne in Northern England in the 8th century, this illuminated Latin text is a striking example of early-medieval religious art and scholarship. An Old English translation was added in the 10th century – the oldest surviving version of the Gospels in English.

themselves. In Paris, where the main subject was theology, the Church controlled the payment of staff. It took six years to earn a bachelor of arts degree, and a further 12 years for a master's degree and doctorate.

By the 14th century, universities had become central to intellectual life. Theology remained the most prestigious area of study and all students were at least in minor orders (the lower ranks of the clergy). However, the first six years of study now focused on the seven liberal arts: arithmetic, geometry, astronomy, music, grammar, logic, and rhetoric – the classical *trivium* and *quadrivium*. In this way, the universities signalled a move away from an intellectual world entirely dominated by the Church.

Monastic scribe
Before paper became common, scribes used parchment or vellum for their work. Vellum was created by scraping down calf or sheep skins and smoothing the surface with a pumice stone or chalk.

Toledo translation school
Alfonso X "the Wise" of Castile in Spain was patron of a flourishing court of scholars who translated Arabic works on subjects ranging from astronomy to chess.

these authorities to the problems of Christian theology. Thomas Aquinas's *Summa Theologica*, for example, is a masterful synthesis of Aristotle's philosophy and Christian tradition (see p.141).

The universities

A better understanding of the classical art of debate, combined with a growing demand for education, led to the

and Aristotle were important for the followers of the movement, as they provided the basic tools for constructing arguments. But so too were Christian authorities such as St Augustine and above all, the Bible. The scholastic method sought to apply the learning of

foundation of the first universities in the 12th–13th centuries. Medieval universities evolved from earlier cathedral schools and monasteries, and were created to study theology, law, medicine, and the arts.

Most universities did not have a central campus – classes were taught at masters' homes or in churches. In a university such as Bologna in Northern Italy, where law was the most popular subject, students hired and paid the lecturers

‹‹ BEFORE

After the fall of the Han dynasty, the Chinese empire divided into several kingdoms.

ARRIVAL OF BUDDHISM

Buddhism **‹‹ 96–97** had been brought to China from the Indian subcontinent by the 2nd century CE. During the **period of division** that followed the fall of the Han dynasty **‹‹ 82–83**, Buddhism **spread quickly**, despite attempts to suppress the religion by Confucian officials. However, it was not until the Tang dynasty that **Buddhism was at the height of its influence** in China.

SUI DYNASTY

China was reunited in 589 CE under the **Sui dynasty**. The first Sui emperor, **Wendi**, built Chang'an (modern Xi'an), a **new capital city**, and enforced a **clear legal code**. His son, **Yangdi**, carried out a **costly programme of canal building** and launched **ill-fated attacks on Korea**. The Sui dynasty fell to the Tang in 618 CE.

SUI DYNASTY FIGURINE

THE GRAND CANAL

The Sui emperor Yangdi commissioned a **Grand Canal** to run from Hangzhou to Beijing. The total length of the canal was 2,400km (1,490 miles), and it remains **the longest canal in the world**.

CHINESE EMPRESS (625–705 CE)

WU ZETIAN

China's only empress to rule in her own right, Wu Zetian usurped the throne from her son the Ruizong emperor in 690 CE. Although judged to be a shrewd and ruthless ruler, she gave extravagant support to Buddhism and other foreign religions, and engaged in costly frontier campaigns. From 697 CE, she became enamoured with the Zhang brothers. In 705 CE, her senior ministers had the brothers killed, and forced the empress to abdicate. She died later that year.

The reign of the Tang dynasty in China is widely regarded as a golden age of Chinese imperial power and culture. The dynasty itself was founded by Li Yuan, a frontier general, who in 617 rebelled against the Sui dynasty (see BEFORE). He took the capital Chang'an the following year, though it would be a further six years before the whole of China fell under his control. Under the title of Emperor Gaozu, Li Yuan inaugurated a new dynasty, which ruled over China for the next three centuries.

Taizong's reign

Gaozu's successor, the Emperor Taizong, was an intelligent and hard-working, ruler, and his own reign (626–649 CE) became synonymous with a period of prosperity. Taizong improved the system of government which his father had established and reformed the administrative system. State schools and colleges were set up, and government examinations were designed to ensure that the most talented individuals were placed in the highest official positions. For Taizong, this not only had the advantage of

> " Have I not heard that **pure wine** makes a **sage**, And even **muddy wine** Can make a man **wise**? "
>
> FROM "DRINKING ALONE IN THE MOONLIGHT" BY LI BAI, C.701–62 CE

monk, perhaps curious to hear Xuan Zang's impressions of foreign countries. Buddhism continued to have a great influence on Chinese society until its suppression in the late Tang period.

Expansion of the empire

The Tang dynasty saw a remarkable period of Chinese expansion. In 657 Taizong's armies defeated the Turks at the battle of Issyk Kul in modern-day Kyrgyzstan, and advanced China's influence as far west as the borders of Persia. Taizong also launched expeditions against the kingdom of Koguryo in north Korea, though he died before he had established Chinese control over the area. At its greatest extent, in around the year 750 CE, Tang China claimed more land than the preceeding Han dynasty, its borders reaching even further west, south, and east than those of modern-day China.

Xuanzong's golden age

Following the reign of the ruthless Wu Zetian (see left) and several other short-lived rulers, the succession fell to the Emperor Xuanzong in 712 CE.

The Giant Buddha at Leshan
At 71m (233ft) tall, this stone Buddha in the Sichuan region of China is the world's tallest. Its construction began in 713 CE.

China's Golden Age

The peak of the Tang dynasty (618–907 CE) saw the flowering of Chinese art, architecture, and poetry. Silk Road caravans brought exotic goods from distant lands, and Chinese culture became the most cosmopolitan in the world.

delivering an efficient civil service, but also strengthened his own security. Unlike those drawn from China's rival aristocratic families, career officials had no power base of their own with which to threaten the Tang dynasty.

The rise of Buddhism

Though he promoted Confucianism and Daoism (see p.81) within the bureaucracy, Taizong personally embraced the Buddhist religion imported from India (see BEFORE). In 629 CE, the monk Xuan Zang journeyed to India to collect Buddhist texts. His travels were the inspiration for the famous Chinese novel *Record of a Journey to the West*, better known in the West as *Monkey*. When he returned to China in 645 CE, Taizong received the

Xuanzong was a clever and diligent ruler, and in the first part of his reign the fortunes of the Tang dynasty were revived. Sweeping reforms were made to the bureaucracy; large granaries were constructed to stockpile rice; military campaigns were fought against the Turkish, Tibetan, and Khitan peoples; a new network of frontier defences was introduced, with permanent forces of professional soldiers; and contact was made with ambassadors from as far west as the Middle East. All of these measures led to a rich, powerful, and cosmopolitan state; China had reached a golden age.

As China's territory expanded, so did its cultural influence. Thousands of merchants, artisans, and diplomats from distant lands took up residence in the capital, Chang'an, which became

Little Goose Pagoda, Xi'an
Still standing today, this 15-storey pagoda was built between 707 CE and 709 CE to house scriptures of the Buddhist faith.

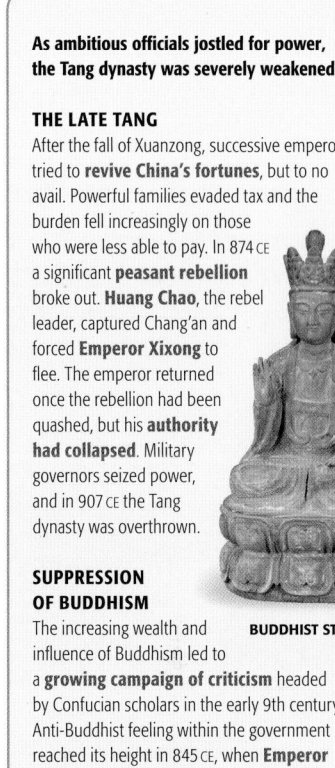

As ambitious officials jostled for power, the Tang dynasty was severely weakened.

THE LATE TANG

After the fall of Xuanzong, successive emperors tried to **revive China's fortunes**, but to no avail. Powerful families evaded tax and the burden fell increasingly on those who were less able to pay. In 874 CE a significant **peasant rebellion** broke out. **Huang Chao**, the rebel leader, captured Chang'an and forced **Emperor Xixong** to flee. The emperor returned once the rebellion had been quashed, but his **authority had collapsed**. Military governors seized power, and in 907 CE the Tang dynasty was overthrown.

SUPPRESSION OF BUDDHISM

BUDDHIST STATUE

The increasing wealth and influence of Buddhism led to a **growing campaign of criticism** headed by Confucian scholars in the early 9th century. Anti-Buddhist feeling within the government reached its height in 845 CE, when **Emperor Wuzong** ordered the **destruction** of 4,600 **Buddhist monasteries** and the surrender of their lands to the state; 250,000 monks were secularized and thrown back into society, and Buddhism never regained its influence in China.

---

the world's largest city. Covering more than 77km² (30 square miles), more than one million people lived inside its walls, and another million beyond them. Linked by a network of roads and canals to the rest of the empire, Chang'an was the terminus of the Silk Road (see pp.130–31), and traders from across Asia came to its great markets. Horses, essential for fighting against the nomadic tribes to the north and east, were imported from the Tarim Basin, and glass goblets came from Byzantium (see pp.144–45). Silk, ceramics, brick tea, and papers were traded in exchange. Foreign cultures were welcomed, and within the city walls were Daoist temples, Buddhist monasteries, Zoroastrian shrines, and Islamic mosques.

Flowering of the arts

Xuanzong was a great patron of the arts, and during his reign Chinese painting and literature reached new levels of sophistication. Two of China's greatest poets flourished in this period: Li Bai and Du Fu, known respectively as the Poet Immortal and the Sage Poet. Li Bai cultivated a reputation for eccentricity; many of his poems celebrate the joys of wine and women. The poems of Du Fu, by contrast, dealt with more serious moral and historical issues. Landscape painting evolved under the poet artist Wang Wei, who painted evocative winter scenes, and Wu Daozi developed a Chinese style of Buddhist sculpture. The court painter Han Gan was best known for his depictions of horses, a subject that continued to inspire artists in later periods.

Three-glaze figurine
Developed in the 7th century, *sancai* (three-colour) glaze, was widely used on vessels and figurines and is typical of the Tang dynasty. Its colours were green, amber, and cream.

The decline of the Tang

In the 730s CE Xuanzong's control over his government began to slip. A number of aristocrats began to displace the career officials. The most notorious of these was Li Linfu, who by 752 CE had made himself virtually a dictator. The emperor, who was 72 years old by this time, had ceased to play an active role in government. He

had become infatuated with Yang Guifei, who was his son's concubine and a famous beauty. After Xuanzong made her imperial consort, she persuaded him to promote her cousin Yang Guozhang to a senior position at court; when Li Linfu died, Yang took his place.

Among the professional soldiers who had been given commands along the frontier was an officer named An Lushan. He became a favourite (and possibly a lover) of Yang Guifei. The rivalry between An Lushan and Yang Guozhang at court led the former to raise a rebellion in 755 CE. The emperor was forced to flee from Chang'an. His military escort demanded the execution of Yang Guifei, blaming her for the emperor's misfortunes, and Xuanzong had no option but to accept. Though An Lushan was eventually defeated and the rebellion brought to an end, the Tang dynasty never recovered its former strength and glory.

INVENTION

PRINTING

The *Diamond Sutra*, the oldest surviving example of a printed book, was found in a walled-up chapel at Dunhuang on the Silk Road. With an inscription dated 868 CE, it predates the earliest European book, the Gutenberg Bible (see pp.196–97), by over 500 years. Seven strips of yellow-stained paper printed from carved wooden blocks are pasted together to form a scroll over 4m (13ft) long. It is one of the most important works of the Buddhist faith. It was called the *Diamond Sutra* because "its teaching will cut like a diamond blade through worldly illusion."

The Song Dynasty

The Song dynasty, established in 960 CE, reunited northern and southern China. Its extraordinary achievements in the arts and sciences outstripped developments in Europe at the time. However, aggression from the Jurchen people to the north gradually led to the surrender of northern China. The dynasty continued to rule in the south as the Southern Song, but were finally ousted by the Mongols in 1279.

« BEFORE

After the fall of the Tang in 907 CE, the empire disintegrated.

CHINA DIVIDED
Between the rule of the Tang and the Song dynasties, the **Qidan Liao** (see below) controlled the northeast of China, while the south fragmented into the

FIVE DYNASTIES SCULPTURE

Ten Kingdoms. Northern China came under the rule of a short succession of **Five Dynasties** until the reunification of north and south was achieved by the first emperor of the Song dynasty in 960 CE.

ALIEN RULE AND SINICIZATION
In 907 CE, the **nomadic Qidan people** founded the **Liao** dynasty. From 947 CE the Qidan Liao ruled over part of northern China. In the south of their territory, they **recruited Chinese officials and modelled their institutions on the Tang**.

Zhao Kuangyin was a general under the Later Zhou, the last of the Five Dynasties (see BEFORE). In 960 CE he usurped the throne and founded the Song dynasty, taking the imperial name Taizu. With a mixture of guile and persuasion he reunified the disparate states of China, apart from the territory held by the Qidan Liao (see BEFORE). Establishing his capital at Kaifeng, Taizu revived the successful administrative system of the Tang government (see pp.114–15), albeit in a modified form.

Some of the magnificence of the Tang era returned to Chinese culture during the Song dynasty. There was a renewed interest in literature and the decorative arts. Artists experimented with brush effects, and landscape, animal, and bird paintings were particularly prized. Song dynasty architecture was also renowned, particularly for its tall structures and pagodas, palaces, and temple roofs.

An economic revolution?
The administrative and technological advances made by the early Song led to economic prosperity. Instead of carrying around large sums of copper coinage, Sichuan merchants began to trade in bills of exchange. These notes proved so successful that the govenment issued its first paper currency in 1024.

The country's infrastructure was also greatly improved during the Song period. The construction of an integrated system of internal waterways extended both the communications and trade networks. Large junks with four or six masts were developed, the magnetic compass was first used for navigation, and seafaring skills were improved. This led to an increase in maritime trade with the rest of East Asia, as well as with India and the east coast of Africa.

The innovations of the Song period affected China's population and urban growth. New methods of rice farming increased food output and led the population to double. Towns and cities grew along the main waterways and

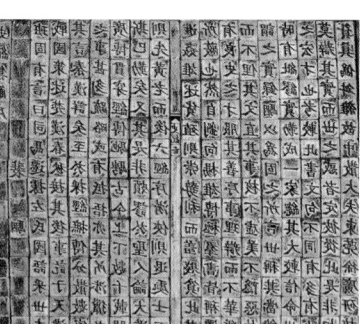

Moveable type
Between 1041 and 1048, Bi Sheng of Kaifeng invented the first printing system of its kind using clay characters held in wax within an iron frame.

along the southern coast, attracting at least ten per cent of the population. Kaifeng became the greatest city in the world; in the 12th century its levels of trade were nearly 50 per cent more than that of London at the turn of the 18th century.

Examinations and officials
Under the Song, the examination system established by the Han dynasty (see pp.82–83) was revived and expanded. Quotas were fixed for the number of candidates who could pass, and steps were taken to guard against cheating and to ensure the anonymity of candidates. Over 140 candidates a year were awarded the *"jinshi"*, the highest degree. In 1002, 14,500 men came to Kaifeng to take the imperial

The Zhang Zeduan silk scroll
The Spring Festival Along the River, by the Northern Song artist Zhang Zeduan, depicts bustling scenes of city life in Kaifeng, the Northern Song capital. Note the upward curve of the roofs, typical of the period.

examinations. The system attempted to ensure that talent, not birth or wealth, enabled a candidate to pass. More than 60 per cent of successful candidates for the *jinshi* degree came from families that had not gained an appointment for an official in the bureaucracy for three generations. However, poor families were still unlikely to foster a successful candidate, as applicants needed to be wealthy or literate to enable them to prepare for the examinations.

From early on in the Song period, scholars and officials were constantly proposing ideas for reforms to rectify the problems of the day. In 1068, Emperor Shenzong entrusted Wang Anshi, China's most famous reformer, with tackling the nation's problems. He identified the main cause of the state's weakness to be a shortage of funds, and raised money by imposing a government monopoly on tea, challenging wealthy families who were evading taxes, and offering interest-free loans to peasants

burdened with debt. To reduce the cost of the standing army, he required every household to supply men for a local militia. These reforms caused an outcry, Wang Anshi was dismissed, and the controversy that his acts had aroused permanently weakened the dynasty.

The Southern Song
The dynasty also had to deal with the challenge of non-Chinese regimes to the north. Part of northern China was already ruled by the Qidan Liao dynasty. In 1115 the Jurchen, a semi-nomadic people from Manchuria, established the Jin dynasty. In 1125 they overran the Qidan Liao, and two years later they captured Kaifeng. The Song court was forced to flee south, bringing an end to the retrospectively named Northern Song. The Southern Song emperors went on to fix their capital at Hangzhou. Although militarily weak, the Southern Song was also a period of continuing economic growth and social change.

Under the Southern Song, new philosophical ideas developed. Neo-Confucianists borrowed concepts from Daoism and Buddhism, and their ideas were synthesized by the scholar Zhu Xi. He emphasized the Dao, or "the Way", a philosophical path that individuals could follow through self-cultivation and the study of Confucian classics (see p.85).

Neo-Confucian values were partly responsible for a deterioration in the rights of women during the Southern Song period. The remarriage of widows was discouraged, and women's property rights were curtailed. Footbinding – the practice of permanently disfiguring a young girl's feet to produce a supposedly attractive shape in later life – became well established during the Song period.

Song porcelain
The Song period is often regarded as the high point in ceramic production in China. Chinese porcelain was first manufactured in the 7th century, a thousand years before the secret of its production was discovered in Europe. True porcelain is made from kaolin, or China clay, the name deriving from Gaoling in Jingdezhen. Song porcelain was the most refined ever produced, and was characterized by the simple elegance of its shape, and its purity of colour. The most famous Northern Song wares were created near Dingzhou in northeast China. After the fall of the Northern Song, manufacture was transferred to Hangzhou. In the south, Jingdezhen in Jiangxi was designated a centre for the manufacture of imperial porcelain in 1004. It has continued as a major porcelain centre to this day.

AFTER

The Mongols took control of China from the Song, ruling as the Yuan dynasty (1279–1368).

THE MONGOLS TAKE CONTROL
The Mongols **destroyed the Jurchen Jin dynasty** in 1234, gaining control of north China. After more than 50 years of attacks by the Mongols, the Song fell in 1279 to **Kublai Khan**, the grandson of Genghis Khan **112–13 》**.

MONGOL LAW
Kublai Khan **divided the population** into

KUBLAI KHAN

four classes: on top were the Mongols, then came peoples from Central Asia, then came the northern Chinese – who had been subjugated first by the Mongols – and lastly came the newly conquered Chinese of the Southern Song.

THE SILK ROAD
After the Mongol conquests it was again safe for **merchants** and **missionaries** to use the Silk Road **130–31 》**. The first European to record his journey was the Franciscan monk **John of Plano Carpini**, who reached Mongolia in 1246.

INVENTION

GUNPOWDER

A 9th century Daoist text warned that mixing charcoal, saltpetre, and sulphur formed a dangerous combination; some who had done so had caused explosions and burned down buildings. By 919 CE gunpowder was being used in a flame-thrower, and by the end of the 10th century simple bombs and grenades had begun to appear. In 1044, the formula for gunpowder was first published, 200 years before it appeared in Europe.

MONGOLIAN WARLORD Born c.1162 Died 1227

Genghis Khan

> "A man of great **ability, eloquence, and valour**."
>
> MARCO POLO, "THE TRAVELS OF MARCO POLO", 1298

B efore he became known as Genghis Khan – a title he took in 1206 to proclaim his leadership of the Mongol tribes – the future warlord and conqueror was known simply as Temüjin. Born around 1162 to a minor chieftain in the mountains of eastern Mongolia, there was little in Temüjin's early life to indicate he would one day be ruler of the world's largest unbroken empire. When he was just five years old, his father was murdered and his family disinherited by their clan. For much of his childhood, Temüjin was forced to scrape a precarious nomadic existence with his siblings and their indomitable mother, Hoelun.

These early years must have done much to forge the great warrior and leader that Temüjin was to become. As the eldest male, Temüjin was the head of his family and he quickly learned to make useful alliances. Having proved himself as a warrior by retrieving some stolen horses, Temüjin claimed a wife, Börte, from a neighbouring tribe. He is said to have used her dowry of precious sable furs to win the favour of Toghrul

Engraving
According to a contemporary Persian chronicle, the Mongol emperor was a tall, long-bearded man with red hair and green eyes. This is how a 20th-century French artist depicted him.

Homage to a chief
Genghis Khan receives the homage of his vassals in this 14th-century Persian miniature. The white horse tails flying from his tent signify peace and diplomacy. Black horse tails meant war.

Battle scene
This Chinese painting depicts the Mongol cavalry in action on a mountain pass. Genghis Khan's highly disciplined army comprised battalions, or *tumens*, of 10,000 warriors, in turn divided into 1,000-man regiments.

Mongolian Empire
This Italian map shows the empire of the Great Khan. *Chataio* (Cathay in English) was the name used by the Venetian traveller Marco Polo to describe northern China when he journeyed through the empire in the reign of Kublai Khan, Ghenghis Khan's grandson.

In 1227, while on campaign in Xi Xia, Genghis Khan fell from his horse, became feverish, and died. The vast empire he left to his sons stretched from Iran and Kazakhstan in the west, across central Asia and northern China to the Sea of Japan.

TIMELINE

- **c.1162** Birth of Temüjin.

- **c.1170** Disinherited after the murder of his father, a minor chieftain. This meant that Temüjin, his siblings, and his mother had to hunt, fish, and gather wild berries for their survival.

- **c.1180** Marries Börte, to whom he was betrothed as a young boy.

- **c.1182** Captured and held captive by a rival tribe, but escapes.

- **c.1184** Temüjin's wife, Börte, is abducted by a rival clan. Temüjin rescues her with the help of his patron Toghrul and ally Jamuka.

- **c.1185** Börte gives birth to a baby boy, named Jochi. Although Temüjin acknowledges him as his son, his paternity is questioned by other members of his family.

- **1190** Unites the Mongol clans, and sets up the humane *Yassa* law code.

- **1201** Defeats his former ally Jamuka.

- **1202** After a victorious campaign against the Tartars, Temüjin is made Toghrul's heir-apparent.

- **1203** Campaigns against former patron Toghrul and his supporters; accidental death of Toghrul.

- **1206** Is proclaimed Genghis Khan.

- **1209** Tangut kingdom of Xi Xia (northeast China) acknowledges Genghis Khan as overlord.

- **1215** Siege and fall of Zhongdu (Beijing), capital of the Jin empire.

- **1215** Birth of Kublai, son of Genghis Khan's youngest son Tolui and of Jamuka's daughter Sorghaghtani Beki, later Kublai Khan.

- **1218** Defeats Kuchlug to annex the Kara-Khitan Khanate of central Asia.

- **1218** Two of Genghis Khan's generals raid southern Russia, Georgia, and the Ukraine.

- **1218** Commercial caravan and a delegation of envoys from Genghis Khan is massacred by a provincial governor of the state of Khwarezm.

- **1219–25** Unleashes a campaign of conquest and ferocious reprisal against the Khwarezmid empire, which comprised parts of present-day Iran and Afghanistan. In the process, the Silk Road cities of Samarkand, Bukhara, and Nishapur are utterly devastated.

- **1220** Karakorum becomes Genghis Khan's headquarters, or capital.

- **1227** Defeats rebellious vassal kingdom, the Tangut kingdom of Xi Xia.

- **1227** Dies from a fever contracted after a fall from his horse on campaign in Xi Xia. In keeping with his request for a secret burial place, his supporters slaughter every living creature that crosses the path of the funeral procession. Each of Genghis Khan's surviving sons inherits their own khanates, which they rule under his third son, Ögedei, the new Great Khan.

(also known as Ong Khan or "Prince King"), an old ally of his father's and leader of the Turkish-speaking Kerait people. When Börte was kidnapped, Temüjin called on Toghrul for help in rescuing her. Soon afterwards Börte had a baby, Jochi, who was acknowledged as Temüjin's son and heir – despite the possibility that he had been conceived while Börte was in captivity.

Campaigns and conquests

Having reclaimed his family's status and secured Toghrul's patronage, Temüjin began to earn his military reputation. Together with Toghrul, he harassed the Chinese empire north and west of the Great Wall. Sometimes he joined forces against other nomadic tribes, notably the neighbouring Tatars, at the behest of the northern Chinese Jin dynasty. Another crucial ally at this time was his "sworn brother" Jamuka, of the Tangut tribe based in Xi Xia in northeast China.

Through a series of brilliant military campaigns and diplomatic manoeuvres, which included the elimination of his

Mongol quiver
This ornate quiver was designed to hold the arrows that mounted Mongol horsemen were capable of aiming and firing when at a full gallop. Mongol boys received intensive training in both horsemanship and archery.

former allies Toghrul and Jamuka, Temüjin made himself lord of all the Mongol tribes. In 1206, at a mass rally, or *kurultai*, Temüjin was proclaimed as Genghis Khan or "universal ruler".

For more than three decades Genghis Khan led the Mongol confederation in a string of victories and in campaigns that ravaged large areas of Asia and subjugated many millions of people.

Warrior and statesman

In conquering this huge empire, Genghis Khan frequently resorted to psychological warfare, using spies, propaganda, and terror as much as military force. Even today, the ruthless warlord who massacred the inhabitants of vanquished cities is hard to reconcile with the tolerant ruler, genuinely interested in the various belief-systems of his empire: Buddhism, Islam, Nestorian Christianity, Confucianism, and Taoism. Genghis Khan introduced a humane law code, the *Yassa*, across his empire, and outlawed the custom of kidnapping women. Moreover, in bringing order to the Eurasian landmass, he brought stability to the Silk Road (see pp.130–31), facilitating the renewal of East–West trade and cultural contact.

> ## "In military exercises **I am always in front** and in time of battle **I am never behind.**"
>

FOUNDER OF YUAN DYNASTY IN CHINA (1216–94)

KUBLAI KHAN

Genghis Khan was grandfather of another famous Mongolian emperor, Kublai Khan. While on his deathbed, the old warrior laid a hand on the young Kublai's head, a gesture interpreted as a sign of future greatness.

The Mongolian empire reached its greatest extent under Kublai Khan. Having inherited Mongolia and northern China, Kublai Khan added southern China to his dominion. He is celebrated as a unifier of China and the founder of the Yuan imperial dynasty. He is also the "Great Khan" of Marco Polo's travels, who entertained the Venetians and gave them passports for their journey.

GENGHIS KHAN'S COFFIN

The **Ming Dynasty**

The Ming, the last native Chinese dynasty, replaced the Mongol Yuan dynasty in 1368. During their rule a new capital city was created at Beijing, and the Forbidden City was built within its walls. The Ming period also saw China construct a defensive barrier against the outside world – the Great Wall.

<< BEFORE

The Mongol Yuan dynasty was destroyed by economic turmoil and peasant rebellions.

YUAN DRAMA
The **earliest Chinese plays**, which were sung, spoken, acted, and mimed, were written by Chinese scholars in the Yuan period. Allegedly the plays contained **protests against the Mongol presence**, and the popular response to them was said to have contributed to the collapse of the Yuan dynasty.

SUPPRESSION OF THE HAN
According to **Mongol law**, the indigenous people of China, the Han Chinese, were the lowest class within Chinese society. In the 1340s a disastrous flood of the Yellow River and **the conscription of thousands of Han peasants for forced labour** led to widespread rebellion, and the Yuan dynasty was finally overthrown in 1368.

ORIGINS OF THE GREAT WALL
Though the Great Wall that survives today was constructed during the Ming dynasty, its foundations were first laid by **Qin Shi Huang << 80–81** in 214 BCE, when he connected the fortifications of the small kingdoms of the **Warring States** era to form a barrier that would **defend the empire** against barbarians.

China under the Ming enjoyed relative stability and saw the development of a sophisticated bureaucracy, but also witnessed a period of imperial tyranny. In contrast to some Western nations of the time, where royal authority was challenged, imperial power under the Ming grew unchecked.

Hongwu, the first Ming emperor, began life as a poor peasant. During his reign he reorganized the army and attempted to reform the land and tax system. In 1380, Hongwu abolished the

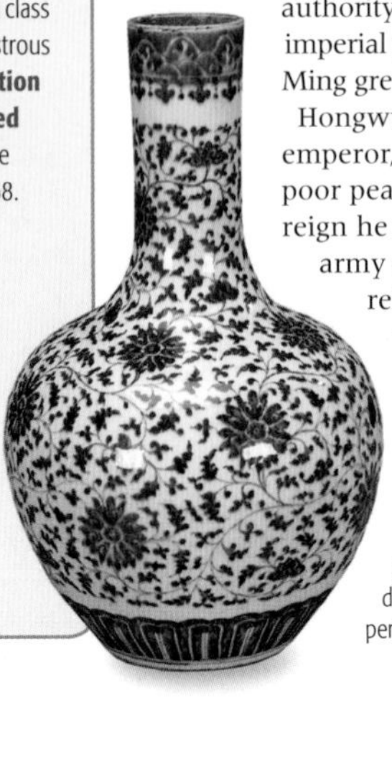

Typical Ming vase
The distinctive cobalt blue glaze of Chinese porcelain, developed by the Yuan, was perfected under the Ming.

post of chief minister, revised the legal code, and ensured that imperial power could not be challenged in court. This was supported by a surveillance system operated by spies, secret agents, and the "Brocade Guards", who carried out major purges of corrupt officials.

Urban growth under Yongle
Hongwu's son usurped the throne in 1403 and reigned as Emperor Yongle. He transferred the capital to Beijing, and began building a magnificent walled palace complex there, the Forbidden City (see right), which nobody was allowed to enter without permission.

Beijing became the main bureaucratic and military centre, but other cities and towns also grew apace. Suzhou and Nanjing became famous for their sophisticated social life and lavish festivals. Jingdezhen turned out blue-and-white porcelain and Hangzhou produced silk. Many of these cities

were connected by the Grand Canal (see p.108); Linqing, one of the main ports on the canal, handled 1.6 million shiploads of freight annually.

A vigorous urban culture accompanied the growth of Ming cities. The spread of printing and the demands of a more literate public led to a publishing boom. Classic novels such as *The Romance of the Three Kingdoms*, *Water Margin*, and *Journey to the West* (otherwise known as *Monkey*) came out for the first time in print, and books with coloured wood-block illustrations were published.

Frontier strategy
After Yongle's death, the Ming dynasty was threatened by a new group of ethnic outsiders – the Mongol-speaking Oirat peoples – who began a massive invasion into Chinese territory in 1449. Emperor Zhengtong rashly counterattacked, but his forces were ambushed at Tumu and he himself was taken hostage. The

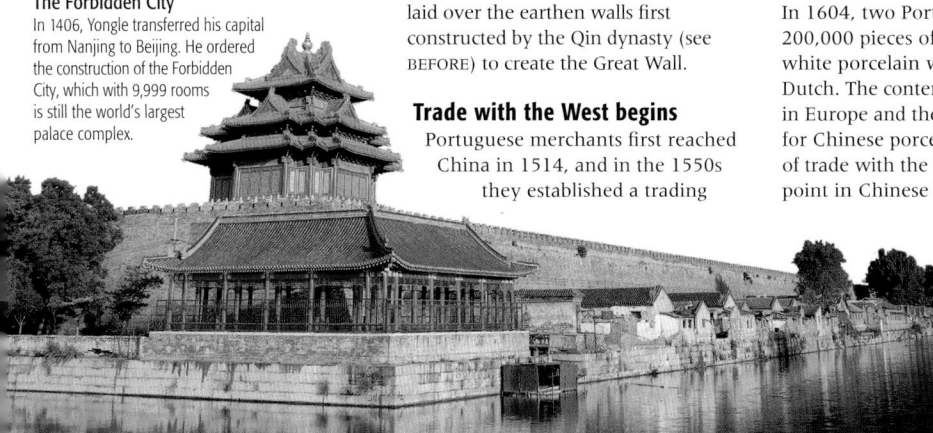

The Great Wall

In 1474, construction began on the brickwork Great Wall that we know today. More than 2,414km (1,500 miles) long, the wall stretched from the Jiayu Pass in the west to the Yalu River in the east. The wall was strengthened and maintained throughout the Ming period.

Oirat failed to take this opportunity to capture Beijing, and Zhengtong was eventually released. Nevertheless, the Tumu incident heralded the end of the expansionist policies of the Ming dynasty; from that point on, frontier strategy became much more defensive. Lacking the military resources to control the steppe regions that had been the source of the Oirat incursions, a barrier was built to contain the

The Forbidden City

In 1406, Yongle transferred his capital from Nanjing to Beijing. He ordered the construction of the Forbidden City, which with 9,999 rooms is still the world's largest palace complex.

CHINESE EXPLORER (1371–1433)

ZHENG HE

Ming rule saw the creation of a vast imperial navy. Between 1405–33, the Muslim eunuch Zheng He commanded seven ambitious maritime expeditions. The first comprised 317 ships and 27,870 men, and put in at several Indian ports. On subsequent voyages, he reached Hormuz on the Gulf of Oman, and ships from his fleet put in at Jidda in Saudi Arabia. Zheng He's voyages took him to 37 countries, and resulted not only in increased trade for China, but also in the capture of pirates that had plagued Chinese waters. An account of Zheng He's voyages was written by the Muslim scholar Ma Yuan.

Mongol threat. Brick and stone were laid over the earthen walls first constructed by the Qin dynasty (see BEFORE) to create the Great Wall.

Trade with the West begins

Portuguese merchants first reached China in 1514, and in the 1550s they established a trading station at Macao on the southeast coast. In 1604, two Portuguese ships carrying 200,000 pieces of Chinese blue-and-white porcelain were captured by the Dutch. The contents were put up for sale in Europe and the auction set off a craze for Chinese porcelain. The beginnings of trade with the West marked a turning point in Chinese history; for the next 300 years, China's fortunes would be inextricably linked to its mercantile relationship with Western powers.

The decline of Ming power and authority was a protracted affair. The Manchu Qing dynasty finally wrested control in 1644.

MING BUREAUCRACY

The Ming had the most **effective central bureaucracy** in the world at the time, but by the end of the Ming period the heavy hand of imperial control, court **intrigues**, and **factional fighting** between groups of officials had made a significant contribution to the fall of the dynasty.

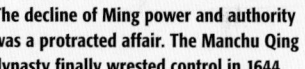

ADMINISTRATIVE SEAL

DECLINE AND FALL

By the late 16th century the Ming dynasty was in decline. Weak emperors were **dominated by their advisors**, who increasingly influenced political decisions. In the north, **a new threat from the nomadic Jurchen** had arisen, as Nurhaci organized the tribes into the Manchu nation **180–81** ». **Economic problems prompted peasant rebellions**, and in 1644 rebel forces under **Li Zicheng** took Beijing. Li was ousted in turn by the invading Manchus.

◀◀ BEFORE

The Asian mainland was the origin of Japan's first settlers and the source of later cultural and technological developments.

THE FIRST JAPANESE
The first inhabitants of Japan arrived from the Asian mainland around 30,000 BCE. By 10,000 BCE they were producing distinctive **Jomon (rope-patterned) pots** for cooking. These early Japanese were hunter-gatherers, but they did not need to travel far to find food.

JOMON POT

ASIAN INFLUENCES
Around 300 BCE, the arrival of rice from East Asia revolutionized Japanese society. **Rice cultivation** required a peasant workforce living in settled communities. Large landowners became **regional rulers** who fought for access to water and fertile land. In the 6th–7th centuries CE, contact with Asia brought the Buddhist religion and with it **Chinese high culture** ◀◀ **108–09**, including writing in the form of Chinese characters.

FUJIWARA JAPAN
Japan's line of **sacred emperors** is historically attested after the 3rd century CE. During the **Heian Period** (794–1185 CE), power devolved from the emperor to the **Fujiwara clan**, which controlled the imperial court and **dominated Japan** until the rise of the samurai.

BUSHIDO A code of conduct and a way of life practised by the samurai. Bushido sought to unite learning and military prowess, and emphasized frugality, loyalty, mastery of martial arts and, above all, honour.

Twelfth-century Japan was a country with an elaborate, subtle, artistic culture that was developed at the imperial court in the capital, Kyoto. But in many areas outside the capital, life was lawless and unruly. In many provinces clans (extended families) of samurai warriors ruled by force. Among the most powerful of them were two long-established families of high standing, the Minamoto and Taira. Their ancestors had been imperial princes who, in the 9th century, were dispatched from Kyoto to uphold the emperor's authority in distant provinces. There, fighting men flocked to serve them and the two families became leaders of powerful warrior clans. From their provincial bases, in the 12th century the Minamoto and Taira returned to compete for supreme power in the capital, Kyoto.

Gempeii Wars
As the dominant family at the imperial court, the Taira at first had the upper hand. But, between 1180–85 a series of fierce conflicts, known as the Gempei Wars, ended with the Minamoto family triumphant. At two decisive battles, in 1184 and 1185, the Taira were slaughtered in combat, driven to mass suicide, or captured and executed.

> "It is not the **way of the warrior** to be shamed and avoid death."
>
> SAMURAI TORII MOTOTADA, 1600

Minamoto Yoritomo (see right), the head of the Minamoto clan, was established as the country's first military dictator, or "shogun", with his court at Kamakura, far to the east of Kyoto. The emperor was left in the old capital as a powerless figurehead.

Shogun rule
The rule of the shoguns, which was to continue until the mid-19th century, established the samurai as the dominant military and social elite. Originally rough fighting men at odds with the effete culture of the court, the samurai evolved into a striking mixture of the savage and the refined. The ideal warrior was as capable of dashing off a poem as he was of slicing off an enemy's head with his two-handed sword. In theory he subscribed to an

Fujiwara fan
Decorating fans was a typical activity of the refined court ladies.

austere code of honour and, rather than face defeat, would commit ritual suicide (*seppuku*) by cutting open the stomach (*hara kiri*). Warfare between samurai followed brutal but elaborate rules – for example, it was customary to cut off the head of a warrior you killed in battle and return it to his family stuck on a spiked board.

Fighting men
The dominant social position of men who were devoted to war as a way of life inevitably spawned violence in a country that had no external enemies. The sole foreign threat in the medieval period came from China. In 1274 and again in 1281, China's Mongol ruler, Kublai Khan (see p.113) attempted to invade Japan by sea from Korea. The samurai united to repel these invasions,

The **Rise** of the **Samurai**

The samurai, an elite class of armoured warriors, dominated Japan from the 12th century. Their fighting prowess and tradition of loyal service to the death – enshrined in the chivalric code of *bushido* – are the stuff of legend. But in reality, samurai ascendancy brought instability, violence, and civil war.

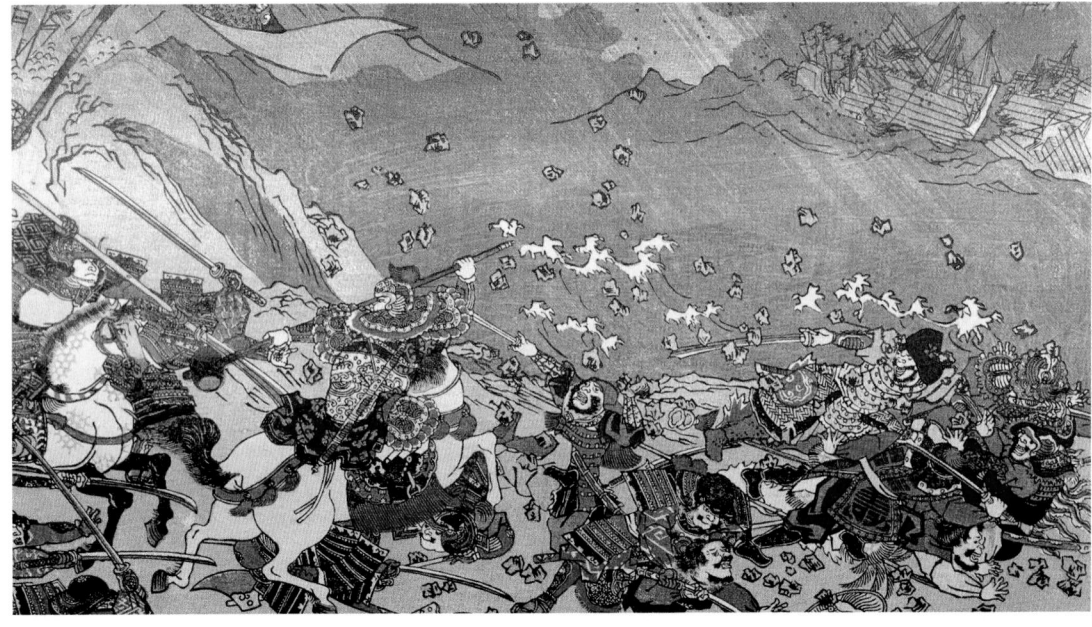

The Tale of Genji
Murasaki Shikibu's long novel *The Tale of Genji* was based on the author's experiences as lady-in-waiting at the imperial court in the early 11th century. It paints a vivid picture of Kyoto courtiers devoted to amorous intrigues and the delicate expression of emotions in verse.

Divine wind
The second attempt by the Mongols to invade Japan met with disaster. The Mongol fleet was scattered by a typhoon, remembered by the Japanese as the *kamikaze* ("divine wind").

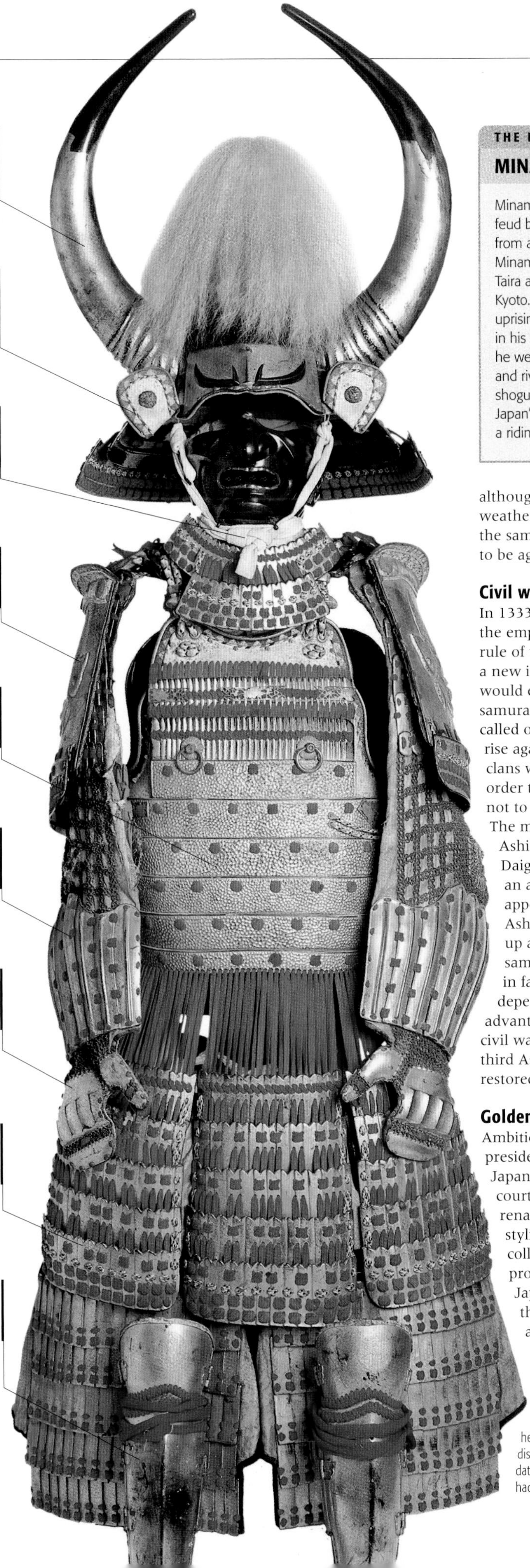

The buffalo horns decorating the helmet are made of carved, gilded wood.

The helmet, or *kabuto*, has a leather-covered sweepback to protect the neck.

The throat defence is attached to the mask, or *mempo*, that covers the lower face.

The shoulder guard, or *sode*, is suspended above the arm defence.

The breastplate is decorated with plates of gold lacquer tied with red silk knots.

The arm guard, or *kote*, combines metal plates with chainmail.

Gloves, or *tekko*, are made of small metal plates bound with string.

The skirts, or *kusazuri*, of the armour are split for ease of movement.

The greaves, or *suneate*, protect the samurai's lower legs.

Warrior's armour
Samurai fought without shields, depending on armour for protection. The magnificent helmets and body armour were intended for display as well as defence. This fine example dates from the 19th century, when the samurai had mostly ceased actual fighting.

THE FIRST SHOGUN (1147–99)

MINAMOTO YORITOMO

Minamoto Yoritomo was involved in the feud between the Minamoto and Taira clans from an early age. In 1160 his father, Minamoto Yoshitomo, was executed by the Taira and he was exiled from the capital, Kyoto. Twenty years later he led a Minamoto uprising against the Taira. Although defeated in his first battle at Ishibashiyama in 1180, he went on to triumph both over the Taira and rivals within his own clan. He became shogun in 1192, marking the beginning of Japan's long feudal age. Yoritomo died in a riding accident.

although they were helped by bad weather. For the rest of the time, if the samurai were going to fight it had to be against one another.

Civil war

In 1333, a major civil war began when the emperor Go Daigo challenged the rule of the shoguns. Aiming to found a new imperial age, in which emperors would exercise real power, with the samurai as their servants, Go Daigo called on warriors across Japan to rise against the shogunate. Many clans were willing to do this, but in order to seize power for themselves, not to restore control to the emperor. The most ruthless of the samurai, Ashikaga Takauji, expelled Go Daigo from Kyoto and enthroned an alternative emperor, who duly appointed Takauji as the first Ashikaga shogun. Go Daigo set up a rival court at Yoshino and samurai across Japan took up arms in favour of one or other emperor, depending where their personal advantage seemed to lie. The resulting civil war lasted 60 years, before the third Ashikaga shogun, Yoshimitsu, restored peace to Japan in 1392.

Golden age

Ambitious and forceful, Yoshimitsu presided over a golden age of Japanese culture. He made his court at Kyoto the site of a cultural renaissance, patronizing the refined, stylized "Noh" drama (see p.183), collecting ink splash paintings, and promoting Zen, a distinctively Japanese variant on Buddhism that profoundly influenced the arts. Yoshimitsu spent lavishly,

building a pavilion coated in gold and surrounded by splendid gardens. In 1402 he negotiated formal trade links with the emperor of China, enabling him to import Chinese artefacts for his cultured capital.

Violence erupts again

Yoshimitsu, and his equally cultured successor, Yoshimasa, presided over an unstable society. The *daimyo*, powerful and brutal warlords who had little allegiance to the shogunate, controlled vast areas in the provinces. While Kyoto practised refinement, from 1467 Japan descended into permanent civil war between the private armies of rival *daimyo*.

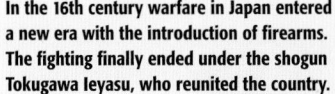

AFTER

In the 16th century warfare in Japan entered a new era with the introduction of firearms. The fighting finally ended under the shogun Tokugawa Ieyasu, who reunited the country.

CHRISTIANITY

The arrival of Europeans in Japan from 1543 brought both guns and Christianity. A mission established by St Francis Xavier flourished until the 17th century, when **Christianity was banned** and converts were persecuted.

ST FRANCIS XAVIER

UNIFYING JAPAN

In the 16th century, ambitious *daimyo* sought to end Japan's endemic civil strife by unifying the country under a single strong ruler. **Odu Nobunaga** and his successor **Toyotomi Hideyoshi** took control of much of Japan between the 1560s–1590s. The unification of the country was completed by **Tokugawa Ieyasu 182–83 »**, who became shogun in 1603, founding a dynasty that was to rule for 250 years.

China was an important influence on the successive rulers of the Korean peninsula.

CHINESE INFLUENCE
In 668 CE, the Korean peninsula was unified by the Silla kingdom, who imported and adapted institutions, ideas, and technology from neighbouring China. **Buddhism** became central to spiritual and political life during this period. During the **Koryo dynasty** (932–1392 CE), Buddhist art and scholarship flourished under state sponsorship. Among the ruling elite of scholar-officials an intellectual import from Song-dynasty China **≪ 110–11** began to gain ground: **Neo-Confucianism**.

A NEW DYNASTY
In 1392, a Koryo general called Yi Songgye seized power, declaring himself the first king of the new **Choson dynasty**. This provided the opportunity for the Neo-Confucians to sweep aside the economic power and "corrupting" political and moral influences of Buddhism.

78 MILLION The number of Korean language speakers around the world who still use the letters of the phonetic *han'gul* script originally devised by King Sejong.

Korea in the Middle Ages

The Choson kingdom dominated Korea from 1392–1910, making it one of history's most enduring royal dynasties. King Sejong is credited with laying the foundations of this longevity during his 32-year reign (1418–50). His greatest legacy is the invention of *han'gul* – an alphabet for the Korean language.

At the heart of Sejong's project was the implementation of the Neo-Confucian view of the world, which had been established as the official ideology of the dynasty by Sejong's grandfather Yi Songgye (see BEFORE). For the Neo-Confucians, human society was an integral part of a universe that included the natural world and the heavens and was governed by a pattern called *li* or "principle". Although it appeared to be abstract, Neo-Confucianism was an intensely pragmatic philosophy that defined the way in which humans should relate to one another socially and the way that society, and the king in particular, should interact with the wider natural world. The role of the ideal Neo-Confucian sage-king was to bring order to heaven and earth according to the requirements of li, and most importantly, to harmonize all aspects of human behaviour with the

underlying universal order. This was an ideal that Sejong ambitiously sought to realize in a way that no other Korean king before or since has done.

At the start of the Choson period the aristocracy, which had grown powerful under the previous Koryo dynasty (see BEFORE), was forced to seek power through a revitalized civil service examination system, based on similar Chinese schemes (see pp.82–83). This new ruling class, which combined features of a hereditary aristocracy and a scholarly bureaucracy, came to be called the *yangban* and remained the most powerful class in Choson society until the beginning of the 20th century.

In addition to maintaining his own ruling dynasty and strengthening the bureaucratic state, Sejong placed much importance on ensuring the wellbeing of his people through innovations that improved their lives.

Sounds for the people
It is easy to identify King Sejong's most important innovation – the invention of the phonetic alphabet for the Korean language, called *han'gul*. As far as contemporary Koreans are concerned, it is a central aspect of everyday life and a source of national pride, but when the king first introduced the alphabet in the mid-15th century, the new writing system seemed to the intellectual elite of the time to be a vulgarization of written language. Writing in Korea had hitherto been limited to complex Chinese characters and was the exclusive property of the *yangban*. Many *yangban* resented these simple and relatively easy-to-learn new characters which for a long time were used mainly by women.

The king explained his motivation for creating the script in his preface to a work illustrating the new writing system,

The introduction of *han'gul*
The new Korean alphabet, today called *han'gul*, is thought to have been largely the work of King Sejong himself and is based on a careful analysis of the Korean language. It was first revealed in 1443 and then formally introduced by the king in 1446 in a ceremony depicted here in a modern Korean painting.

But *han'gul* was more than just a project to bring literacy to the lower levels of society. Like much that Sejong did, it was also an attempt to reflect the order of Neo-Confucianism. It divides the sounds of the Korean language into the two components of the universal principle – yin (dark, female, passive) and yang (light, male, active).

Alongside the new alphabet, King Sejong encouraged the advancement of sciences, particularly astronomy and meteorology, which sought to understand the function of the heavens (see left). His attention also extended into the reform of court music, the encouragement of refined painting that depicted the natural world, and the spread of new agricultural techniques to the country's farmers.

A society of unequals
The foundations of the Choson dynasty rested upon more than just the will of a determined, farsighted king. The Neo-Confucianism that dominated the thinking of Sejong and his officials reflected the reality of Choson's unequal society and actually helped to reinforce its rigid class structures.

The great majority of the population were peasants engaged in agriculture, paying taxes to the state and rent to landlords, and often finding themselves at the mercy of the floods and droughts that beset the Korean peninsula's fragile ecology, bringing with them famine and disease. Beneath the farmers on the social scale were various lowborn groups, including those involved in so-called "dirty occupations" such as butchery and leather working. There was also a large hereditary

> " I have... designed **28 letters**, which I wish to have **everyone** practise at their ease. "
>
> KING SEJONG, PREFACE TO "CORRECT SOUNDS", 1446

published in 1446: "The sounds of our country's language are different from those of China and are not easily conveyed in Chinese writing. Among the ignorant people there have been a great many who... have been unable to express their feelings".

Chongmyo ritual
At Chongmyo shrine in Seoul, the Choson kings frequently held elaborate Confucian rites as a way of honouring their royal ancestors.

Despite the many achievements of the 15th century, problems in the political system of the Choson dynasty began to appear.

INVASION FROM THE EAST
The 16th century saw the rise of a vicious rivalry among the scholar-officials who vied for position in the state bureaucracy and at court. The emphasis that Choson placed on literary scholarship and its favouritism towards a civil rather than military bureaucracy had serious consequences. When **Japan invaded** in the 1590s the country was unprepared. After two invasions in six years brought devastation for the country and its people, the invaders were finally repelled with military aid from Ming China **« 112–13** and a series of naval victories courtesy of the famous admiral, Yi Sunsin.

RECOVERY AND RENOVATION
Choson recovered during the 17th century, but the **fall of China's Ming dynasty** to Manchu "barbarians" in 1644 was a profound shock. The rulers of Choson then saw themselves as the true defenders of civilization and Neo-Confucian orthodoxy. Two kings, Yongjo and Chongjo, ruled for much of the 18th century and the country prospered. A move away from Neo-Confucianism towards solving practical problems and an interest in new ideas from China and Europe followed.

slave class that is thought to have comprised in the region of 30 per cent of the total population and remained a notable feature of Choson society until the 19th century.

In accordance with his ideology, Sejong sought to encourage appropriate relationships between the different classes and cultivate decorum in personal relations. In 1432, he ordered the publication of a didactic text on Neo-Confucian ethics called the *Illustrated Guide to the Three Bonds*, which was reprinted later that century with a *han'gul* text so that a general readership could benefit from its instructions. The three bonds of the title were those that occur between parents and children, between ruler and official, and between husband and wife. Each example of bond was illustrated with a series of short biographies and woodcuts depicting the stories of devoted sons and daughters, loyal officials, and faithful wives.

But the less lofty lives of the common people found an expression in the arts of this period, in particular through *punch'ong* ceramics. These developed from the refined celadon ceramics – crackle-glazed porcelain in a range of jade-like colours – favoured by the Koryo court in previous centuries. The freedom of their incised and stamped designs has often been cited as a key feature of the Korean artistic style, and this apparently artless but graceful form of pottery had a deep influence on Japanese ceramics. Korea's impact on the art in Japan saw a dramatic increase after potters were taken from Korea back to Japan by invading armies in the late 16th century.

Punch'ong ware
Freely decorated ceramics, such as this elegant vase, characterized the earthy aesthetics of the period.

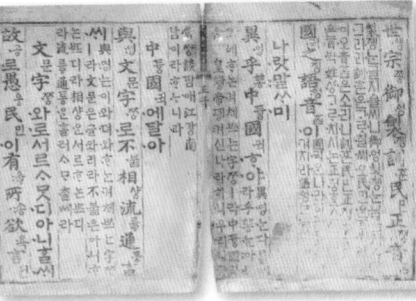

The *Hunmin Chong'um* manuscript
The opening pages of *Correct Sounds for the Instruction of the People* contain Sejong's explanation of the new script in both Chinese characters and *han'gul*. The book was first printed in 1446 at the time of the introduction of the new phonetic script for the Korean language.

KOREAN KING (1397–1450)

KING SEJONG

The fourth king of a relatively young dynasty, Sejong came to the throne of Choson (Korea) in 1418 at the age of 22. He was the grandson of the dynastic founder Yi Songgye and became the first king to be extensively schooled from an early age in Neo-Confucian philosophy and ethics. Today, Sejong the Great is a national icon symbolizing Korea's first "golden age" and is seen by many millions of Koreans every day on the back of the 10,000 won note.

« BEFORE

The Dong Son culture flourished in Southeast Asia during the 1st millennium BCE.

THE DONG SON

Remains of the Dong Son culture that created this drum (1st–2nd century BCE) were first **discovered near Hanoi in Vietnam** in the 1930s. Dong Son culture was centred on **northern Vietnam**, but remnants have been found **across Southeast Asia** as far away as **Java** and **Sumatra**. Dongsonians had an organized society that later cultures in the region would draw upon.

DONG SON DRUM

HOW WE KNOW

BOROBUDUR TEMPLE

The Buddhist monument of Borobudur in Central Java remained largely hidden by jungle until its rediscovery in 1814. Careful study of carvings and inscriptions around the site suggest that it was constructed under the influence of the Srivjaya Empire in the 8th–9th centuries. Almost 2,000m² (21,500ft²) of narrative sculptures provide important information about Buddhist worship and daily life in Java in the period.

Lost Empires

Long seen as a waystation for merchants and missionaries, Southeast Asia has also been home to peoples and empires whose commercial, spiritual, and artistic wealth were rivalled by none. This wealth depended on the movement of people, goods, and ideas across the vast waterways and fertile plains of the region.

Among the great numbers of people that migrated along the waterways of Southeast Asia, many moved from the islands of Java and Sumatra to the coasts of today's Vietnam and Cambodia. These people set up maritime trading centres that traded spices, woods, metals, and animal products from inland for merchandise from elsewhere in Southeast Asia, India, Persia, and Arabia. Many areas grew wealthy as a result of this trade, and the Champa kingdom in southern Vietnam became a great empire, its power and influence lasting from the 7th century CE until its defeat by the Vietnamese emperor 1471.

> **"Rice** is easily had ... and **trade** is easily carried on."
>
> ZHOU DAGUAN, CHINESE DIPLOMAT, DESCRIBING KHMER CAMBODIA, c.1290

Rivers and floodplains

The fertile rivers of the Southeast Asian interior were another source of wealth. Communities around the river basins of the Mekong, Red River, Chao Phraya, and Irrawaddy grew prosperous from rice and livestock. But the rivers were also a source of conflict as the region's empires fought each other for control the most productive arable areas. As early as the 7th century CE, the rulers of the Khmer people, in modern Cambodia,

had fought the declining Funan empire and the Champa city-states for control of the fertile Mekong River delta. While the power of Funan passed, the Champa and Khmer continued to quarrel over the floodplain. After 939, the Champa also had to contend with the northern Vietnamese state of Dai Viet, which was desperate to find territories south of the crowded Red River valley. The Champa preoccupation with the Dai Viet let the Khmer Empire strengthen its grip on the rice lands of the Mekong.

At the same time, to the west of the Khmer Empire in Burma (Myanmar), the Irrawaddy River sustained the growth of a powerful kingdom around the city of Pagan. By the mid-12th century, the Pagan and Khmer empires controlled much of mainland Southeast Asia. As the Khmer began to decline in the 13th century, Thai-speaking peoples migrated down the Irrawaddy and Chao Phraya rivers from further north and took control of many former

Borobudur relief
The Buddhist monument at Borobudur features 2,672 carved reliefs showing both the Buddhist afterlife and the daily existence of the Javanese people.

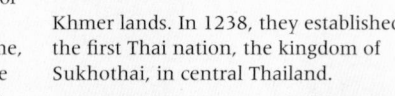

Khmer lands. In 1238, they established the first Thai nation, the kingdom of Sukhothai, in central Thailand.

Island kingdoms

The peoples that remained on Sumatra and Java set up prosperous trading communities rivalling the coastal states of the mainland. By the 8th century, the Srivijaya Empire controlled most of the Sumatra

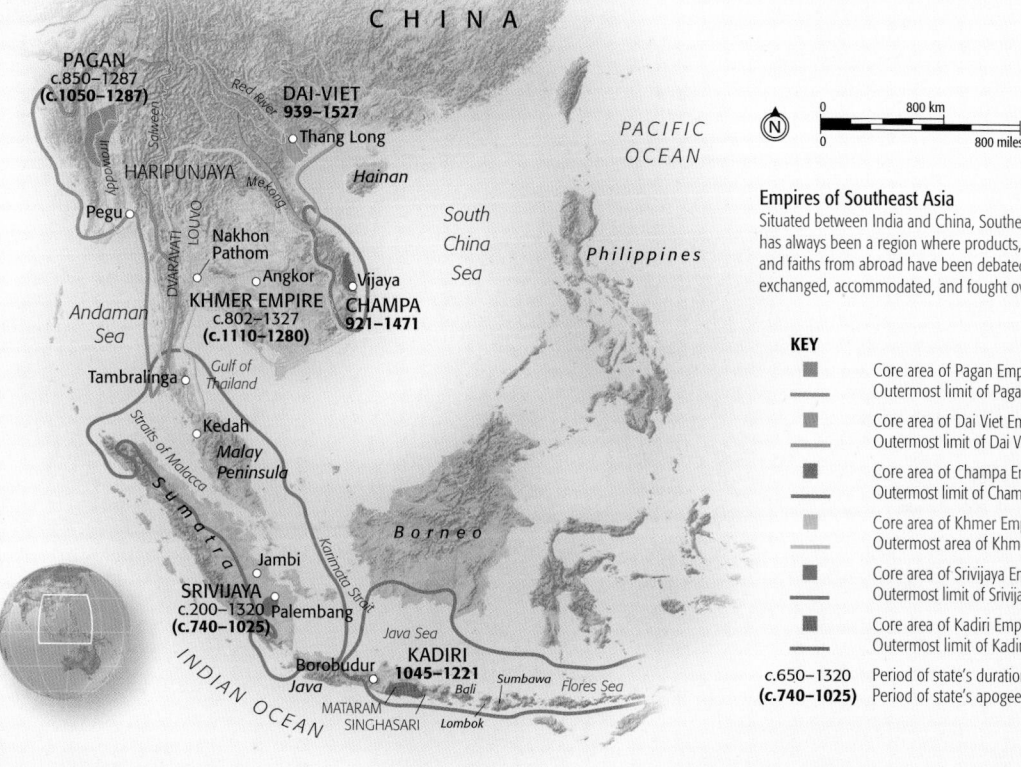

C H I N A

PAGAN
c.850–1287
(c.1050–1287)

DAI-VIET
939–1527

Thang Long

Red River

Salween

Irrawaddy

HARIPUNJAYA

Mekong

Hainan

PACIFIC
OCEAN

Pegu

Nakhon
Pathom

DVARAVATI

LOUVO

Angkor

Vijaya

South
China
Sea

Philippines

*Andaman
Sea*

KHMER EMPIRE
c.802–1327
(c.1110–1280)

CHAMPA
921–1471

*Gulf of
Thailand*

Tambralinga

Straits of Malacca

Kedah

*Malay
Peninsula*

S u m a t r a

B o r n e o

Karimata Strait

Jambi

SRIVIJAYA
c.200–1320
(c.740–1025)

Palembang

Java Sea

Borobudur

Java

KADIRI
1045–1221

Bali

Sumbawa

Flores Sea

MATARAM
SINGHASARI

Lombok

INDIAN OCEAN

N

0 — 800 km
0 — 800 miles

Empires of Southeast Asia

Situated between India and China, Southeast Asia
has always been a region where products, ideas,
and faiths from abroad have been debated,
exchanged, accommodated, and fought over.

KEY

- Core area of Pagan Empire
  Outermost limit of Pagan Empire
- Core area of Dai Viet Empire
  Outermost limit of Dai Viet Empire
- Core area of Champa Empire
  Outermost limit of Champa Empire
- Core area of Khmer Empire
  Outermost area of Khmer Empire
- Core area of Srivijaya Empire
  Outermost limit of Srivijaya Empire
- Core area of Kadiri Empire
  Outermost limit of Kadiri Empire

c.650–1320   Period of state's duration
(c.740–1025)   Period of state's apogee

**Both Christianity and Islam were exported
to Southeast Asia by merchants and traders.**

THE SPREAD OF ISLAM

Islam arrived in Southeast Asia with **Arab
and Indian traders** from the east coast of India.
By the **15th century**, Islam was the most popular
religion in Java and Sumatra, transforming
statecraft among the sultans and **religious
custom** among the peoples of the islands.

EUROPEAN EMPIRE BUILDERS

After the Portuguese seized Malacca on the
south of the Malay Peninsula in 1511 **European
merchants and missionaries** began to
emerge as major players in the commerce and
statecraft of Southeast Asia **164–65 »**.
They sought to channel trade through ports
which they could control and **convert to
Christianity**. Initially limited to the coastal
cities, European influence spread across
mainland Southeast Asia as **missionaries**
travelled inland to
convert people to
Christianity and
engage in
commerce.

**PORTUGUESE
GALLEON**

and the Malay Peninsula, dominating
the shipping routes through the Straits of
Malacca and imposing tolls on the highly
profitable spice trade. Other maritime
kingdoms, such as the Hindu Kadiri
empire grew in influence as the Srivijaya
empire weakened in the 11th century.

The spread of religion

Merchants from India, China,
and Sri Lanka brought
religion as well as trade to
Southeast Asia.

Hinduism first spread among the people
of the islands and the mainland much as
Mahayana Buddhism (see pp.96–99)
later did in the 7th century – on
the boats of traders. In
Vietnam, Confucianism (see
p.81) from China was also
integrated into the daily
workings of government
and society.
The wealth from trade
and agriculture financed
the building of huge
temples and monuments
to the gods. Buddhist
monuments such as

Borobudur in Java (see left) and the
great Hindu temples of Angkor in the
Khmer Empire testify to the impact
these faiths had on the lives of
the people. They also provide
evidence of the Southeast
Asian belief in the power of
the gods to make or break
the prosperity granted by
the land, rivers, and sea.

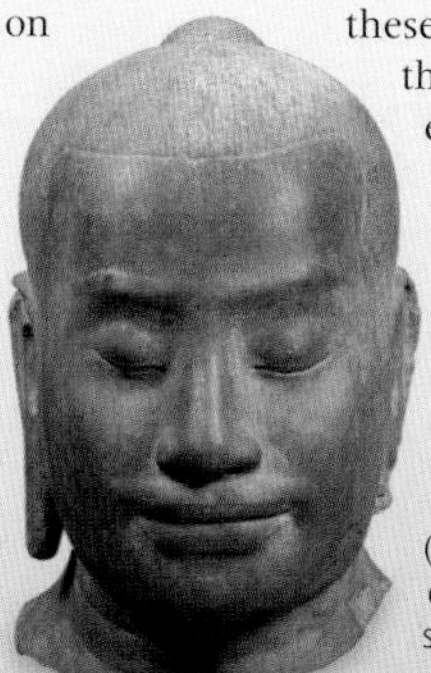

Jayavarman II

The great Khmer ruler Jayavarman VII
(c.1125–1215) built vast temples and
defeated the Champa, but his excessive
spending also impoverished the empire.

Angkor Wat

Constructed in the 12th century during the reign of the
Khmer ruler Suryavarman II and dedicated to the Hindu
god of Vishnu, Angkor is the largest religious complex in
the world. Measuring nearly 260 hectares in area, its outer
wall encircles a temple rising to 65m (21ft) in height and
comprises over 800m (2,600ft) of carved stone.

BEFORE

Prior to the rise of Islam, the Arabian Peninsula consisted of loosely organized federations of peoples and towns.

BEFORE ISLAM

The Arabian Peninsula has always been dominated by sparsely populated, arid desert. Its early inhabitants were mainly nomads such as the **Bedouin**, although there were some farmers around the oases. The few towns were trading centres for goods such as spices. Frankincense, a fragrant tree resin, was one of the most important products. The proximity of the **Silk Road 130–31 »** made it relatively easy for Arabian merchants to trade their goods.

FRANKINCENSE

PRE-ISLAMIC RELIGION

Pre-Islamic Arabs spoke a number of languages and followed a variety of religions, most of which were polytheistic, worshipping several different gods **« 96–97**. **Mecca**, later the most important religious site of Islam, was already a centre of worship.

MUHAMMAD THE PROPHET

Muhammad was a merchant based at Mecca when he had his first revelation from God. Although some people accepted his teachings, the hostility of others forced him into **exile in Medina**. There, he gathered more followers, uniting the local tribes and raiding caravans until he managed to conquer Mecca itself. By Muhammad's death in 632 CE, the whole of the Arabian Peninsula was united under the new Islamic religion. The followers of Muhammad – Muslims – then **expanded** further **towards Syria**, which brought them into contact with the two great empires of Persia and Byzantium.

The spread of Islam
The followers of Muhammad spread out from their Arabian homeland with startling speed in the century or so after the prophet's death. By the mid-8th century, they had reached as far as Spain, stretching the extent of the caliphate to breaking point.

KEY

Muslim lands by 634
Muslim lands by 656
Muslim lands by 756
Byzantine Empire c.610
Sassanian Empire c.610
Frankish Kingdoms c.610

The Ascent of Islam

In 622 CE, Muhammad was forced into exile in Medina from Mecca for his beliefs. By 750, these beliefs had become the basis of a religion whose adherents governed an area stretching continuously from the borders of China to Spain. By 1450 Muslims were ruling in areas as far to the east as Indonesia.

Following the death of Muhammad in 632 CE, his successors, who were known as caliphs, carried Islam far beyond the confines of the Arabian Peninsula. Shortly after the death of the second caliph 'Umar ibn 'Abd al-Khattab in 644, the Muslims conquered the entire Persian Empire (see pp.76–77), as well as taking Syria and Egypt from the Byzantine Empire (see pp.144–45). The new rulers were tolerant towards the religions they found in their conquered territories, and did not force conversion. The constantly expanding area of the Islamic Empire was controlled by governors based in armed camps, each taking their instructions from Medina.

Despite their military successes, the Muslims were soon split by factional differences. The most remote

Kaaba
This 16th-century Turkish tile depicts the Kaaba at Mecca. Originally a site of pre-Islamic polytheistic worship, this square building is the holiest site in Islam, and all Muslims pray towards it.

governors were constantly trying to become independent, and there was tension between the "true" followers of Muhammad and those they believed were simply hungry for power. Things came to a head with the murder in 656 of the third caliph, 'Uthman ibn 'Affan, which led to outright civil war between 'Ali ibn abi Talib, a relative of Muhammad himself, and Mu'awiya ibn Abi Sufyan, a relative of the murdered 'Uthman. When 'Ali was

assassinated in 661, Mu'awiya took power, becoming the first caliph of the Umayyad dynasty.

Although this turbulent period saw a great deal of conflict, it also witnessed the collation and standardization of the Qur'an, the Muslim holy book. The second caliph even introduced a new Islamic "Hijri" calendar, which kept time by following the cycles of the Moon, and dated its years from the time of Muhammad's flight to Medina.

The Umayyad dynasty

The Umayyads took their name from the clan to which the first Umayyad caliph, Mu'awiya ibn Abi Sufyan, belonged.

Dome of the Rock

The Dome of the Rock mosque in Jerusalem is the oldest surviving monument from the early period of Islam. First built in the 7th century, it has been restored and redecorated several times since. The site is sacred not only to Muslims, but also to Jews and Christians, and has been a lasting source of conflict.

While early caliphs had been chosen by community leaders, under the Umayyads the position became hereditary. To improve the government of their expanding empire, the Umayyads moved their capital to the more central Damascus, and borrowed institutions from the Byzantine and Persian rulers of the area, simply changing the administrative language to Arabic.

The Umayyads continued the conquests of previous caliphs, consolidating power over the former Persian Empire and extending the rule of Islam across North Africa. They built monumental shrines and places of worship to emphasize Islamic power, including the Dome of the Rock, on the site in Jerusalem where Muhammad is believed to have ascended to heaven, and great mosques at Damascus, Aleppo, and Medina. Although conversion was still by choice, special taxes on non-Muslims and religious restrictions on senior government positions encouraged the population to become increasingly Muslim and to adopt Arab customs, particularly in the east of the empire, in what are now Iraq and Iran.

Despite all this, factionalism remained rife, with several groups trying to seize power from the Umayyads. One major group still believed that only the descendants of 'Ali, who had lost in the civil war that brought the Umayyads to power, should rule. When one of 'Ali's sons was killed, they proclaimed him a martyr. The resulting dispute triggered one of the biggest splits in Islam and 'Ali's followers ultimately became the Shia branch of Islam.

In 750, several anti-Umayyad factions joined together to overthrow their rulers. The leader of the revolt was descended from another relative of Muhammad, named 'Abbas.

The Abbasid dynasty

The family of 'Abbas was largely based in the old Persian Empire – modern-day Iran, Iraq, and Afghanistan. They moved the capital east to the new city of Baghdad, which was nearer their centre of power, located on major trade routes,

Arab astrolabe

The astrolabe was an astronomical device developed in the Islamic world that used the position of the sun and stars for navigation, and as a tool to locate Mecca.

and closer to fertile farming areas. The new rulers ruthlessly wiped out anyone they perceived as a threat, and replaced the old Umayyad officials with those loyal to them. The Abbasids used a system of intelligence to spy on officials in far-off countries, to make sure they did not get too powerful. They used the words of the Qur'an and Islamic law to justify their claims to power and to further secure their position. They also introduced a more formal system of taxation to pay for their armies and bureaucrats.

The Abbasid period is generally considered a golden age of Islamic art, science, and architecture. Arabic became increasingly important as both a religious and a political language. Large encyclopedias and collections of lore were commissioned, and translations made of Greek and Persian scientific treatises, philosophical works, and literary texts. (see pp.106–07). Without these Arabic copies, the modern world would probably know very little about Greek and Persian literature, and the technological advances of the scientific revolution (see pp.206–07) and after might have been much delayed.

Despite their best efforts, the Abbasids were unable to prevent further revolts and uprisings among their subjects. In the mid-10th century, the Buyids, a group of professional soldiers employed by the Abbasids, staged a coup and took over the caliphate. Content to operate out of sight, they allowed the Abbasids to retain their title, and the Abbasid caliphate survived in name until the arrival of the Mongols in the 13th century.

CALIPH Muhammad's successors as leaders of Islam were known as caliphs (from the Arabic *Khalifat ar-Rasul Allah*, "the successor, representative of the Prophet of God"), and the area over which they ruled was known as the caliphate.

DECISIVE MOMENT

BATTLE OF BADR

The Battle of Badr was crucial to the foundation of Islam. Taking place on 17 March 624, it is one of the few battles mentioned in the Qur'an. The Quraishi rulers of Mecca, frustrated by early Muslim ambushes on caravans in the area, launched a concerted attempt to stop them, but despite overwhelming odds in their favour they were soundly defeated. This illustration of the pursuit of the defeated army comes from a later account of the battle. Victory consolidated the political position of Muhammad and forced the surrounding areas to take him seriously.

"**[The] Arabs... will stand in awe of us forever.**"

AMR IBN HISHAM, ISLAMIC COMMANDER AT BADR, 624 CE

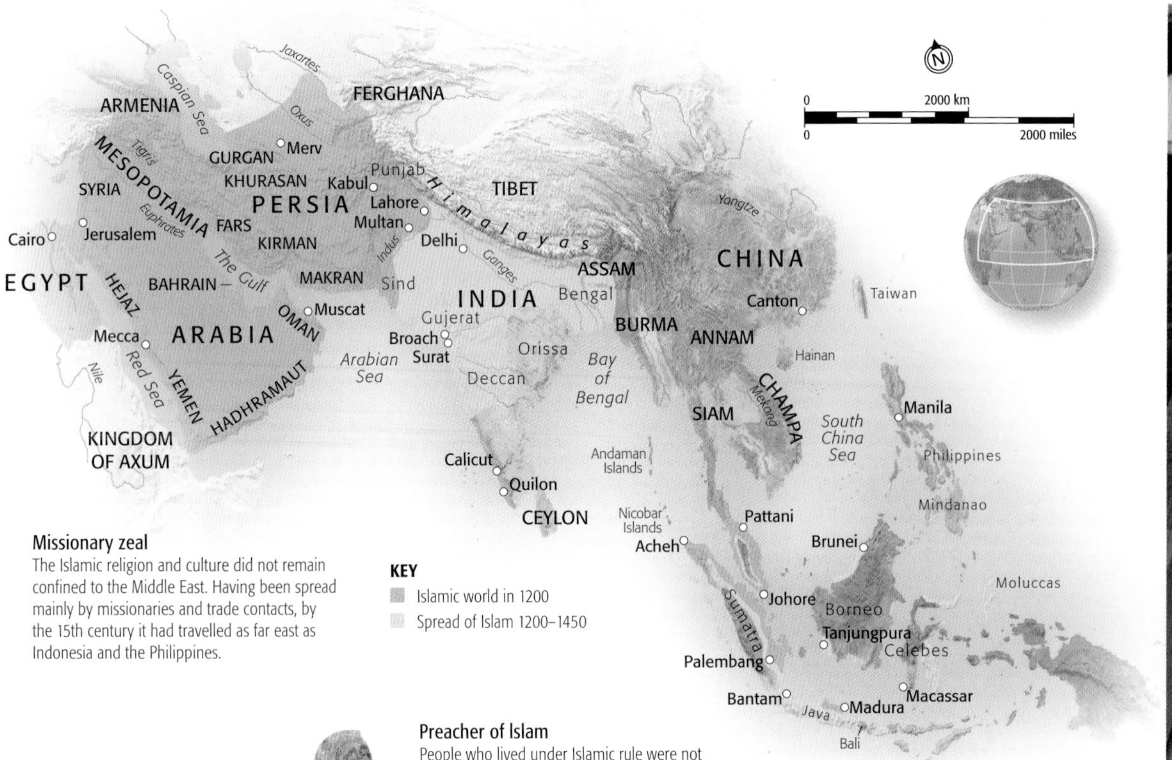

Missionary zeal
The Islamic religion and culture did not remain confined to the Middle East. Having been spread mainly by missionaries and trade contacts, by the 15th century it had travelled as far east as Indonesia and the Philippines.

KEY
- Islamic world in 1200
- Spread of Islam 1200–1450

Preacher of Islam
People who lived under Islamic rule were not forced to convert. Many were converted by travelling preachers such as the one depicted in this 13th-century manuscript.

pilgrims travelled in large groups for protection

preacher

Alhambra palace
The Alhambra was built in the 14th century at Granada in southern Spain. The palace buildings are covered in tiles and plasterwork bearing Islamic geometric designs and inscriptions.

AL- The Arabic word for "the" forms the prefix of many scientific words that were adopted by medieval Europe along with the scientific knowledge of the Islamic world, for example alkali, algebra, alchemy, algorithm, and almanac.

daughter Fatima, emerged from Tunisia to take over North Africa and claim the title of caliph. 'Ubaydallah's "Fatimid" descendants conquered Egypt in 969, and founded the city of Cairo. From there they went on to conquer Syria and Palestine, reaching as far as Aleppo and Damascus. The Fatimid caliph ordered the destruction of the Church of the Holy Sepulchre in Jerusalem, causing uproar in Europe and helping trigger the Crusades (see pp.146–47).

Cairo, meanwhile, became the centre for a trade network that extended throughout the Mediterranean, the Red Sea, and the Indian Ocean. Goods such as porcelain from China and spices from Southeast Asia were brought in by ship to the Egyptian Red Sea ports. Gold and slaves, meanwhile, were brought down the Nile from Ethiopia and the Sudan, to be traded in Cairo.

Most of the merchants were Muslim, although some Europeans from Venice and Genoa were also involved.

As well as being an important trading centre, Cairo was also a site of religious learning. Al-Azhar University, founded by the Fatimids in the 10th century, is one of the oldest universities in existence. It attracted scholars from

Although the Islamic world was united by culture and trade throughout the whole medieval period, it did not always have one government. As the Abbasid dynasty concentrated its power in the east, the areas furthest from the new caliphate began to break away. First was Spain, which in 756 became an independent emirate, or principality, ruled by a branch of the exiled Umayyad dynasty. Shortly after this, independent governors also arose in Morocco, western and eastern Algeria, Tunisia, and Egypt.

By the 10th century Islam had developed into three separate caliphates – the title "caliph" was by now taken by the self-appointed head of any major Islamic community who felt the right to take it. In addition to the Abbasids in Baghdad, there was a Fatimid caliphate in Egypt, and an Umayyad caliphate in Spain.

The Isma'ili Fatimids
The Fatimid dynasty was founded in the early 10th century by an Isma'ili Shia Muslim named 'Ubaydallah. The Isma'ili Shia branch of Islam probably started as a secret movement in Iraq, though its missionary activity soon took its members all across the Islamic world. In 910 'Ubaydallah, who claimed descent from Muhammad's

---

ABBASID CALIPH (763–809)

HARUN AL-RASHID

Harun al-Rashid was the fifth Abbasid caliph, ruling in Baghdad from 786–809. He is famous as a protagonist in many of the stories of *The Book of One Thousand and One Nights* (the "Arabian Nights"), but was also a significant historical figure.

Harun was the first caliph to appoint a vizier (from the Arabic *wazir*, meaning "helper") with many administrative powers – although his own vizier was removed from power in 803. He was also an important patron of the arts, presiding over part of the "Golden Age" which saw the emergence of classical Islamic culture.

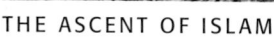

Niujie mosque
One of the oldest mosques in China, Niujie was originally built in the 10th century CE. While Islamic empires never extended their influence to China, strong trade links between the two cultures ensured that Islam gained a foothold in the Far East.

Hassan tower
The huge 12th-century tower at Rabat in Morocco was designed as a minaret for an enormous mosque that was never completed.

Qutb Minar minaret
The Qutb Minar in Delhi, India, is the world's tallest brick minaret. The tower and mosque complex were built in the early 13th century by the founder of the Delhi sultanate.

Great Mosque of Djenné
Although the current mosque at Djenné in Mali is just over a century old, it stands on the site of a mosque first built in 1240. Following its construction, Djenné became West Africa's most important seat of Islamic learning.

Syria, Ethiopia, and the Maghreb, and is still considered the most prestigious site of Islamic learning in the world.

The Fatimid dynasty continued to rule Egypt until their conquest by the Kurdish warrior Saladin in 1171. Saladin used his Egyptian base to retake the Holy Land from the crusader settlers, but his Ayyubid dynasty fell within a century, overthrown by the Mamluks, originally Turkish slave soldiers, who had risen to become commanders of the Egyptian army.

The Umayyads in Spain
The emirate of Cordoba was founded in 756 by the exiled Umayyads, who ruled almost all of Spain. The title of caliph was taken by 'Abd al-Rahman III al-Nasir in 929, possibly as a reaction to the claims of the Fatimids.

The blending of Islamic ideas with Christian and Spanish influences produced a unique cultural fusion across the areas ruled by the Umayyad and the Almoravids, their Moroccan successors. The visual arts of Islamic Spain are expressed most fully at the Alhambra (see above), a palace built for the rulers of the kingdom of Granada. Spain became the wellspring from which Islamic and pre-Islamic knowledge flowed back into medieval Europe, and the influence of highly civilized "Moorish" Spain extended into

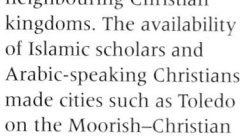

neighbouring Christian kingdoms. The availability of Islamic scholars and Arabic-speaking Christians made cities such as Toledo on the Moorish–Christian frontier a centre for the translation of Arabic texts into Latin.

Other Muslim lands
As traders carried their religion across the ocean with their goods, Islamic belief moved east. The 13th century saw the establishment of an Islamic sultanate in Delhi (see pp.126–27). From here Islam spread into Southeast Asia and the Indonesian archipelago. Muslim traders and missionaries also settled in western and eastern Africa, around Ghana, Senegal, and the Sudan (see pp.128–29).

Hajj certificate
The *hajj*, or pilgrimage to Mecca, is one of the key duties of all Muslims. This certificate, dating from 1207 and depicting the Kaaba shrine, was proof that its owner had completed the pilgrimage.

AFTER

Islam has continued to play an influential role in world history until the present.

FATE OF THE CALIPHATES
The Mongols **112–13** who invaded the Abbasid caliphate in the 13th century assimilated the local culture to become the Ilkhanid dynasty. The Mamluks halted the Mongol advance around 1260, and survived to be conquered in the 16th century by the **Ottomans 152–53**. After 1031, the Spanish caliphate dissolved into smaller states that were slowly conquered by Spanish Christians, the last falling in 1492.

FUNDAMENTALISM
The late 20th century saw the rise of a politicized Islam, advocating **strict adherence to the Qur'an** and revolt against secular governments – as seen in the Iranian Revolution led by Ayatollah Khomeini **364–65**.

AYATOLLAH KHOMEINI

BEFORE «

BEFORE

Kingdoms and empires rose and fell in India in the centuries before the Sultanate.

THE GUPTAS

The Gupta Empire (320–540 CE) **« 78–79** was a **period of stability and prosperity.** It ran from present-day Bangladesh to eastern Pakistan.

HARSHA

In 606 CE **Emperor Harsha** established a **powerful empire** across much of northern India. After his death the empire **fragmented into small kingdoms.**

CHOLA BRONZE

THE CHOLAS

The **Chola Dynasty** (850–1200 CE) ruled all of south India. The empire was a crucial staging post for **Chinese and Arabic merchant ships.**

ISLAM BEFORE THE DELHI SULTANATE

Arab traders had introduced Islam to the region by the 8th century and there were incursions by Muslim armies from **Persia** and **Ghazni** (modern Iran and Afghanistan) in the 8th–11th centuries. Islam's impact at this stage was still very limited.

The Delhi Sultanate

Although Islam was present in parts of South Asia from the 8th century, the establishment of the Delhi Sultanate (1206–1526) marked a new era. Immigrants from Central Asia and Persia brought concepts of kingship, built cities, and founded empires. India was incorporated into the cultural scope of Islam.

In 1175, the nomadic Muslim chieftain Muhammad of Ghur (in present-day Afghanistan) advanced into India. Although the Indian armies were bigger and richer, the nomads had the advantages of horses and a centralized army. Sweeping eastwards over modern-day Turkestan, Pakistan, and northern India, Muhammad's armies sacked Delhi in 1193.

After Muhammad of Ghur's death in 1206, one of his generals, the ex-slave Qutb-ud-din Aibek, gained control of his territories in India and established the Delhi Sultanate (kingdom). To celebrate this and to symbolize the assimilation of new territory into the wider Muslim world (see pp.122–23), he began to build what would become the tallest minaret in the world – the Qutb Minar. This 72.5-m (238-ft) tower came to symbolize the sultanate. As the empire expanded, successive sultans sought to demonstrate their power by building grand monuments around it.

> ### DECISIVE MOMENT
> #### DECCAN REBELLION
>
> In 1345, the governors of the south Indian Deccan provinces revolted against Delhi. The sultan's army defeated the rebels, but some managed to escape and regroup. When the sultan left to quash a rebellion in Gujarat, the Deccan rebels seized their chance and defeated the imperial army. Their leader was declared Sultan Alauddin Bahman Shah at Daulatabad Fort (right) in 1347, establishing the Bahmani kingdom. This was the end of the Delhi Sultanate's expansion, and the start of its long decline.

Sultans and slaves

The early sultans ruled over a fragile kingdom, and their authority was concentrated in a series of fortified towns. The nomadic tribes who made up the nobility did not have a strong tradition of hereditary kingship. Military slaves frequently became sultans, such as Iltutmish in 1211 or Balban in 1266. Women, too, could become sultans if they could muster the support of the nobility, as Razia Sultana did in 1236.

Succession to the throne at Delhi was often secured through violence; during the Slave Dynasty (1206–90) – the first dynasty of the Sultanate – at least five

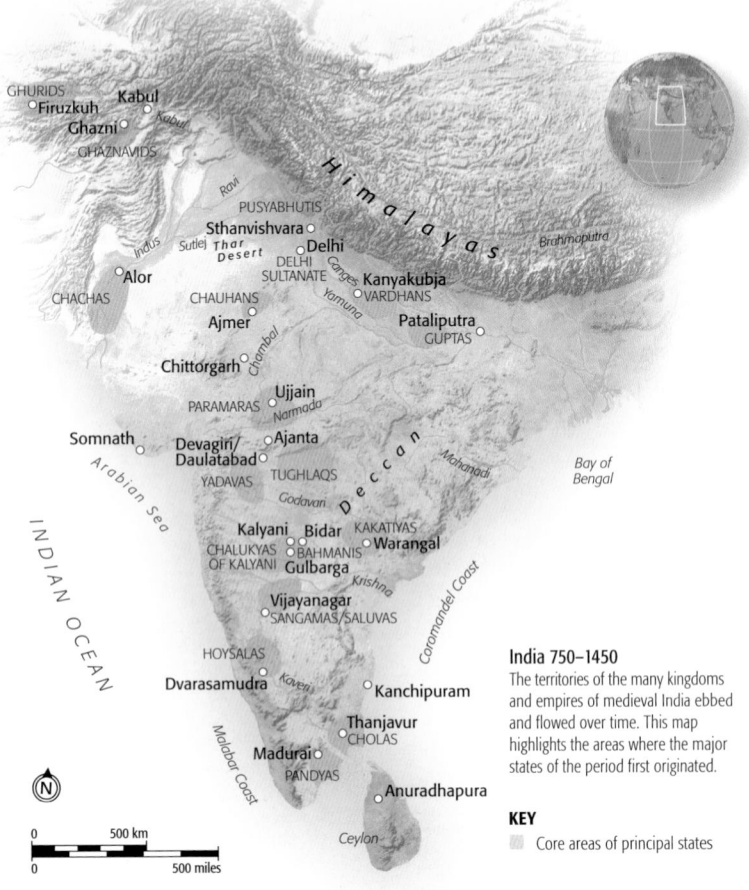

India 750–1450
The territories of the many kingdoms and empires of medieval India ebbed and flowed over time. This map highlights the areas where the major states of the period first originated.

KEY
▨ Core areas of principal states

Sufi poetry

Amir Khusrau was court poet for several of the Delhi sultans and a follower of the Sufi (Islamic mystic) saint Nizammudin. His poetry, an example of which is shown here, is sung today in the devotional music called *Qawwali*.

of the 11 sultans were assassinated. In 1258, refugees fleeing the destruction of Baghdad by the nomadic Mongols (see pp.110–13) came to India, bringing with them new ideas of the divine right of kings and the rituals of the Persian courts of the Sassanids (see pp.76–77). Imperial authority grew stronger as a result, although tribal loyalties and intrigues remained divisive.

Throughout the period of the Delhi Sultanate, the sultans based their policies on pragmatism, rather than the *Sharia* (Islamic) law. Some Hindu temples in zones of military conflict were destroyed, but this had been a military tactic in India before the arrival of the Muslims and there does

not seem to have been a policy of temple destruction. In settled areas, temple building and renovation was sanctioned by the state. Subjects were permitted to practise their own faiths and the *Jizya* tax, which non-Muslims are supposed to pay in an Islamic state, was only enforced sporadically.

Expansion to the south

Between 1299–1305, sultan Alauddin Khilji launched a series of successful military expeditions against the various rich kingdoms south of Delhi, including the Yadava capital of Devagiri, the Somnath temple in Gujarat, Chittorgarh in Rajasthan, and Mandu in central India. In 1311, Alauddin sent his favourite slave, Malik Kafur, on a series of raids into the Deccan (the vast plateau region that covers much of southern India) in search of plunder. The Yadavas of Devagiri, the Kakatiyas of

> **1,600** The number of years that the inscribed iron pillar in the courtyard of the Qutb Minar complex has survived in the open air without any sign of rust. The great pillar dates back to the pre-Islamic empire of the Guptas.

Lodi Tomb

The Lodi Dynasty, the last dynasty of the Sultanate, ruled from 1451–1526. Several octagonal Lodi tombs still stand in Delhi.

Warangal, and the Pandyas of Madurai were all defeated. Their kings were reinstated, but had to acknowledge the sultan's overlordship and send him an annual tribute. After Alauddin's death in 1305, the southern kingdoms stopped paying tribute, and so in 1321 Sultan Ghiyasuddin Tughlaq sent his son Muhammad to annex them. The kings were replaced with governors.

The emperor's new capital

After he became sultan, Muhammad bin Tughlaq (reigned 1324–51) moved the capital 1,100km (700 miles) south to Devagiri, now renamed Daulatabad. In 1327–28 he forced the elite to relocate to Daulatabad, but within two years the inadequate water supply compelled him to reinstate Delhi as the capital. Meanwhile, the empire began to fragment. New kingdoms and political elites, both Hindu and Muslim, came to power in the Deccan region of south India. Telugu-speaking warriors established the Vijayanagar Empire to the south of the Delhi Sultanate in the 1330s, and in 1345 the governors of the Deccan rebelled against Delhi and founded the Bahmani kingdom (see left).

By 1398, when the Mongol warrior Timur sacked and

AFTER

Competing empires to the south weakened the sultanate, but it was a fresh invasion from Central Asia that finally supplanted it.

THE DECCANI SULTANATES
By the end of the 15th century, the **Bahmani** kingdom had fragmented into **five rival sultanates**, constantly at war with each other. In 1565 the **Vijayanagar Empire** was defeated by a rare combination of these five provinces.

THE MUGHALS
In 1525, **Babur** – a descendent of both Timur and Genghis Khan **‹‹ 112–13**– marched from Kabul to India. He defeated the last of the Delhi Sultans at the **Battle of Panipat** in 1526 and established the **Mughal Dynasty 184–85 ››**. The Mughals ruled, until the British removed the last king in 1858 at the start of the **British Raj 282–83 ››**.

destroyed Delhi, the sultanate was no longer a major power. It continued until 1526 when the last of the sultans Ibrahim Lodi was defeated at Panipat, but was by then just one of many states contending for power in northern India.

Qutb Minar Complex

The Quwwat-ul-Islam ("Might of Islam") mosque in Delhi was constructed by Qutb-ud-din Aibek, founder of the Delhi Sultanate, as a symbol of his power. The sandstone base of the Qutb Minar is visible in the background.

BEFORE

Growth in trade across the Sahara led to the formation of more centralized states south of the Sahara desert, such as the Ghana Empire.

MUSLIM TRADERS
Islam spread across North Africa from Arabia in the 7th century CE **《 122–23**. The **introduction of camels** to Africa by Muslim Arabs made travel possible through the desert, enabling Arabs and North African Berbers to open the first regular trade routes between North Africa and regions south of the Sahara desert. Muslim traders created **trading networks** throughout the sub-Saharan regions of East and West Africa.

TRADERS WITH CAMELS CROSS THE DESERT

THE EMPIRE OF GHANA
In the 8th–11th centuries, the Ghana Empire of West Africa grew powerful on the **trans-Saharan gold trade**. Its rulers became **Muslim** in the 11th century, but then it declined in influence and was supplanted in the 13th century by the Mali Empire.

> " ... stones of **marvellous size**... with **no mortar** joining them..."
>
> VICENTE PEGADO, CAPTAIN OF THE PORTUGUESE GARRISON AT SOFALA, 1531

Freestanding masonry
The wall of the Great Enclosure has a marble core, and is bounded on each side by horizontal, free-standing masonry. The wall contains 900,000 large granite blocks, and is decorated with a chevron pattern along the top.

South of the Sahara

Buoyed by trading links with Asia and Islamic North Africa, a number of prosperous empires and commercial centres formed in Africa to the south of the Sahara desert, including the Mali and Songhay empires in West Africa and Great Zimbabwe in south-central Africa.

The cosmopolitan trading towns along the Swahili east coast of Africa were the first to benefit from the commercial activity, their coastal position helping them to monopolize the maritime trade with India, Persia, and Arabia. By the 13th century, Muslim trading cities such as Kilwa, in present-day Tanzania, were at the centre of a highly profitable mercantile network, importing textiles, spices, and ceramics from Asia and exchanging these for African gold, iron, ivory, and slaves.

Great Zimbabwe
The Swahili ports did not produce these goods themselves, but traded in turn with states from within the African interior. At one end of the supply chain lay the settlement of Great Zimbabwe, an important source of gold, and the hub of a prosperous trading empire that thrived in southern Africa during the 11th–15th centuries. In the language of the Shona people of the region, the word *Zimbabwe* meant "houses of stone", a term applied to the hundreds of stone-walled enclosures found throughout the Zimbabwe plateau. Great Zimbabwe is the largest of these, located on the southern edge of the plateau. The spectacular stone ruins today cover nearly 7km² (1,800 acres) and are divided into hilltop and valley complexes.

Built at the head of the Sabi River valley, Great Zimbabwe was well placed to control the passage between the gold fields in the west and the trading cities along the Swahili coast. Local natural resources supported the

Soapstone bird
Likely to represent the bateleur eagle, these bird carvings stood on walls and monoliths in Great Zimbabwe, and have become the national symbol of modern Zimbabwe.

region's economy: seasonal grazing was available for cattle and the soil was fertile enough to support the core cereal crops of sorghum and millet. Timber and ivory were in plentiful supply. In the 12th–13th centuries, Great Zimbabwe also profited from taxes on the trading caravans that passed through the area.

City of stone
In the 13th–14th centuries, the people living in and around Great Zimbabwe probably numbered between 11,000 and 18,000, most of whom would have lived in huts, situated closely together. The ruling elite led a more privileged and comfortable existence, supported by the wealth provided by their control over the export of gold and ivory to the coast. Local granite was used to enclose the hilltop at Great Zimbabwe with stone walls, perhaps as a fortification.

The Great Enclosure
The outer wall of the Great Enclosure at Great Zimbabwe is 250m (820ft) in circumference, and as high as 25m (80ft). An inner wall runs along the outer wall, and forms a narrow passage that leads to the conical tower.

The Hill Complex
The buildings above the Great Enclosure may have been built as fortifications, although the walls offer no access to the top from which to repel attackers. Another theory is that it was created to show the power of the ruler.

Conical tower
The mysterious conical tower at Great Zimbabwe is 10m (33ft) high and 5m (16ft) in diameter. Its purpose is unknown, although it has been suggested that it was a symbolic grain bin.

Set in the valley below the hill, the drystone walls of the Great Enclosure probably served as a palace.

As well as local pottery and ornaments made from copper, bronze, and gold, archaeologists have found many objects of Asian origin, indicating the settlement's prosperity and extensive trade links. These include 13th-century glazed Persian earthenware, 14th-century Chinese dishes, and fragments of painted glass from the Middle East.

In the mid-15th century, however, Great Zimbabwe was abandoned. The end of Great Zimbabwe coincides with the vast conquest by the king of the Karanga, Mutota, who sought to extend his rule over the whole plateau between the Zambezi and Limpopo rivers, including the main gold-bearing areas. But Great Zimbabwe's decline was probably not a result of Mutota's expansion policy. More likely the land could no longer support the concentration of population, forcing many inhabitants to find new areas of woodland where plots could be cleared.

The Mali Empire

In West Africa, the first great empire to be established after the decline of Ghana in the 12th century (see BEFORE) was the Mali. The Mali Empire, like that of Ghana, was based in the Sahel, the savanna region running along the southern border of the Sahara. From the Sahel, it was possible for Mali, like Ghana before it, to exploit the trade across the Sahara to North Africa and control the exchange of gold for salt mined in the desert. The first capital of the Mali

West African terracotta head
The artists of Ile-Ife, near Benin in what is now Nigeria, were renowned for naturalistic sculptures of human heads, created to honour rulers they believed were divine.

empire, Niani, was sited by the Bure goldfields on the Niger river where much of the wealth of the empire originated. Other trade goods included slaves and kola nuts, as well as glass beads and cowrie shells for currency.

Mansa Musa and Timbuktu

The Mali state was founded in 1235 by Sundiata Keita when he united the 12 Mandinke clans of Mali. But it was in the 14th century that the empire reached its peak under Sundiata Keita's grand-nephew Mansa Musa (see below).

A devout Muslim, Musa is renowned for his spectacular "Pilgrimage of Gold" to the holy city of Mecca. Musa also extended the boundaries of the Mali Empire, uniting much of the Western Sudan (the huge West African savanna region to the south of the Sahel) under his rule. The Moroccan traveller Ibn Battuta, journeying through Mali in the 1350s, could write that he had enjoyed "complete and general safety" in the area.

During Mansa Musa's reign the city of Timbuktu on the trans-Saharan trade route to North Africa became a wealthy commercial hub and a great centre for scholarship (see right). Musa had the great Jingereber mosque in Timbuktu built, which still stands in the city today. North African and Egyptian scholars visited Musa's court and he exchanged ambassadors with Egypt, Morocco, and Arabia.

The Songhay

By the early 15th-century the Mali Empire was in decline. Subject states began to break away, including the Songhay kingdom, based around the city of Gao about 400km (250 miles) down river from Timbuktu. During the 1460s, the Songhay king Sunni Ali took control of much of the Mali Empire, including the city of Timbuktu and the crucial trade routes.

Like the Mali, the Songhay Empire depended for its great wealth on the goldfields on the Niger River and the trans-Saharan trade in salt and slaves. At it's height in the 16th century, the Songhay Empire would exceed even that of the Mali in size and wealth.

500 slaves dressed in gold and carrying golden staffs as well as 80 camel-loads of gold accompanied Mansa Musa on his great pilgrimage to Mecca, according to the contemporary Arab historian al-Umari.

TIMBUKTU LIBRARY

The Sankore Mosque in Timbuktu was one of the most important centres of learning in Africa. Manuscripts preserved at Sankore (such as the one below) document the scholarship and the cultural sophistication of medieval Mali. As one West African proverb states: "Salt comes from the north, gold from the south ... but the treasures of wisdom come from Timbuktu."

AFTER »

From the 15th century, Portuguese and other European traders and colonists became ever more involved in African trade and politics.

BENIN

The empire of **Benin** grew to prominence in West Africa during the 15th century. Benin was well known for **hand-cast bronzes**, which could only be made with royal consent. The first **Portuguese** traders arrived in about 1485, and a strong political and mercantile alliance was formed. They traded in ivory, palm oil, pepper, and, perhaps most significantly, in **slaves 218–19 »**.

BENIN BRONZE PLATE

THE MUTAPA KINGDOM

Many of the people of Great Zimbabwe settled on the northeastern edge of the Zimbabwean plateau, where they formed the **Mutapa kingdom**. In 1628, the Portuguese replaced the king with a puppet ruler, who later signed a treaty giving the Portuguese free rein to **mine minerals**. This was the first instance of the **Afro–European concession treaties** that would later become widespread **290–91 »**.

MANSA MUSA

Mansa Musa was the best known of the Islamic emperors of Mali, largely because of his hajj (pilgrimage) to Cairo and Mecca in 1324–25. He was said to have taken 60,000 porters and hundreds of servants decked in gold. During the trip, Mansa gave away or spent so much gold that it apparently took the economy of North Africa a decade to recover. Musa established sound economic and cultural relations with the countries he travelled through. He brought back with him an Arabic library, religious scholars, and the Muslim architect al-Sahili, who built the great mosques at Gao and Timbuktu.

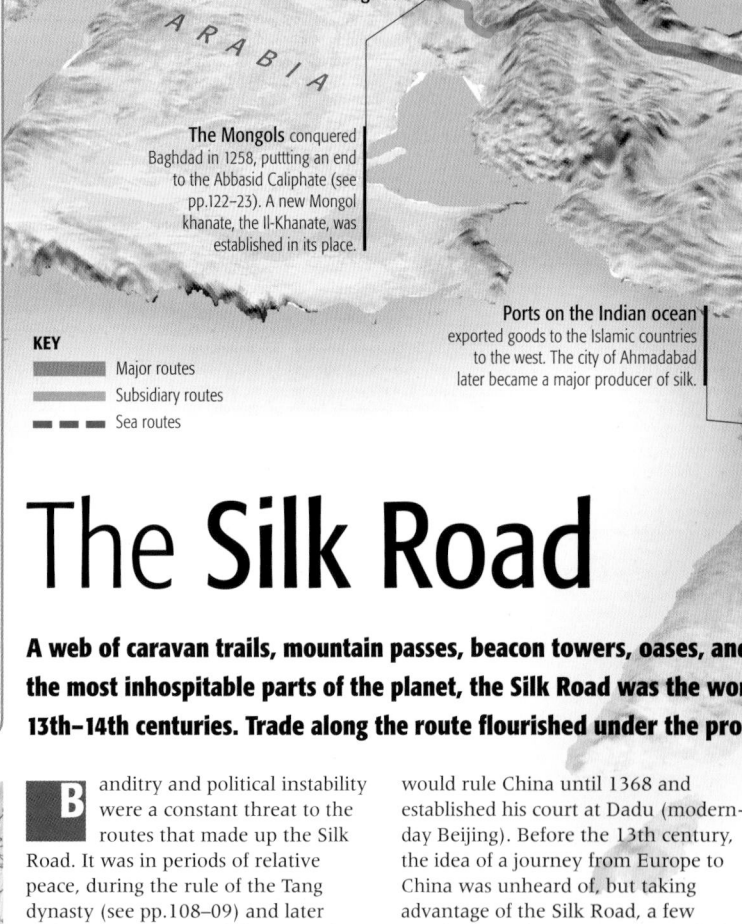

BEFORE

Long-distance trade across Eurasia was stimulated by the demand for luxury goods – precious metals, spices, and silks – by the wealthy inhabitants of powerful empires.

EARLY TRADING LINKS

In Europe and Central Asia, the empires of Persia ‹‹ 46–47, Greece ‹‹ 48–49, and Rome ‹‹ 64–69 opened up **communication and trade** as far east as the kingdoms of India. In the east, the **Qin and the Han dynasties** ‹‹ 80–83 unified China. In 138 BCE the Han emperor Wudi sent Zhang Qian to seek allies to fight their enemies to the northwest of China. The knowledge he brought back of kingdoms to the west led to the opening of **new trade routes**. A network of trading links soon developed between East and West. Silk reached Rome from Han China through a series of intermediaries, principally the Parthians ‹‹ 76–77.

TRADING IN IDEAS

Flourishing in India from the 3rd century BCE, **Buddhism travelled** north to Central Asia and then east along the Silk Road to China, where it was firmly established by the 4th century CE.

ALTERNATIVE TRADE ROUTES

Following the rise of Islam ‹‹ 76–77 Arab traders used the seasonal **monsoon winds** to build up an extensive seaborne trading network around the Indian Ocean. In the 8th century CE they even found a **sea route to China** and traded directly with the **Tang ‹‹ 108–09**. It must have been on the ships of Arab traders that Chinese goods from this era were transported to the east coast of Africa.

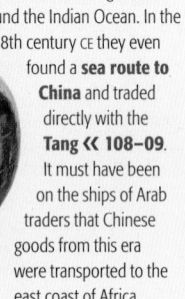

CHINESE VASE FOUND IN AFRICA

Constantinople was a major entry point to Europe for silk and spices, which were shipped to the west by Genoese or Venetian traders.

A subsidiary trade route ran north of the Caspian to Astrakhan in the Mongol Khanate of the Golden Horde, then on to ports on the Black Sea.

To the west of the desert and the Himalayas lies the important oasis town of Bukhara. Its citadel dates back to the 7th century CE.

The Mongols conquered Baghdad in 1258, putting an end to the Abbasid Caliphate (see pp.122–23). A new Mongol khanate, the Il-Khanate, was established in its place.

Ports on the Indian ocean exported goods to the Islamic countries to the west. The city of Ahmadabad later became a major producer of silk.

Delhi, capital of the Islamic Sultanate of Delhi (see pp.126–27) was a major centre for the exchange of goods and ideas.

KEY

 Major routes
— Subsidiary routes
– – – Sea routes

The Silk Road

A web of caravan trails, mountain passes, beacon towers, oases, and garrison forts fringing some of the most inhospitable parts of the planet, the Silk Road was the world's greatest thoroughfare in the 13th–14th centuries. Trade along the route flourished under the protection of the vast Mongol empire.

New world view

Narratives of 13th- and 14th-century travellers transformed European maps of Asia. This image of the Silk Road from the *Catalan Atlas* (1375) possibly shows Marco Polo travelling in a caravan.

B anditry and political instability were a constant threat to the routes that made up the Silk Road. It was in periods of relative peace, during the rule of the Tang dynasty (see pp.108–09) and later under the protection of the Mongols (see pp.112–13), that trade along the Silk Road truly thrived.

The empire of the Mongols

By 1250, Genghis Khan (see pp.112–13) and his successors had conquered an area that stretched from the Yellow Sea to the Black Sea. Under Mongol protection the Silk Road flourished as a 6,400-km (4,000-mile) trade route, along which travellers and traders were able to move in unprecented safety.

Kublai Khan (see p.113), who became Great Khan of the Mongols in 1260, later declared himself emperor of China. He founded the Yuan dynasty that

would rule China until 1368 and established his court at Dadu (modern-day Beijing). Before the 13th century, the idea of a journey from Europe to China was unheard of, but taking advantage of the Silk Road, a few merchants and missionaries travelled all the way to Kublai Khan's capital. They included the Venetian merchants Niccolo and Maffeo Polo who reached Dadu in 1266. There were apparently well received by the Great Khan, who wanted to learn about Christianity and Western science. Five years on, Niccolo and Maffeo's nephew, Marco Polo (see right), reached Kublai's court. Also in the 13th century Rabban Sauma, a Chinese Christian, made a pilgrimage in the opposite direction, from Dadu to Jerusalem, and then on into Western Europe. The accounts of both journeys provide a fascinating glimpse into life along the Silk Road in medieval Asia.

Traffic of treasure

Silk was not the only valuable commodity traded along the Silk Road: there were spices, medicines, ivory, rare plants, exotic animals including leopards, and precious stones such as amber and lapiz lazuli. Commodities from the west included textiles, gold, and silver. From China, caravans carried silk, paper, weapons, lacquer, and even rhubarb. Goods were sold or exchanged for other commodities en route in staging-post bazaars.

The products were carried on camels, horses, bullocks, and yaks, depending on the location. The two-humped Bactrian camel was Central Asia's hardiest beast of burden. It could withstand the searing heat and biting cold and survive without water between oasis towns. Great caravans plied the Silk Road and camel trains of 400 animals were not uncommon.

The **Id Kah Mosque**, in Kashgar, was built in 1422, but includes older structures dating back to the 8th century, and began as a mosque in 996. Kashgar is situated at the meeting point of the northern and southern Silk Roads, and was the gateway to the West. Set up as a garrison town at the foot of the Pamirs by 76 CE, it gave access to the mountain passes into Central Asia, India, and Persia.

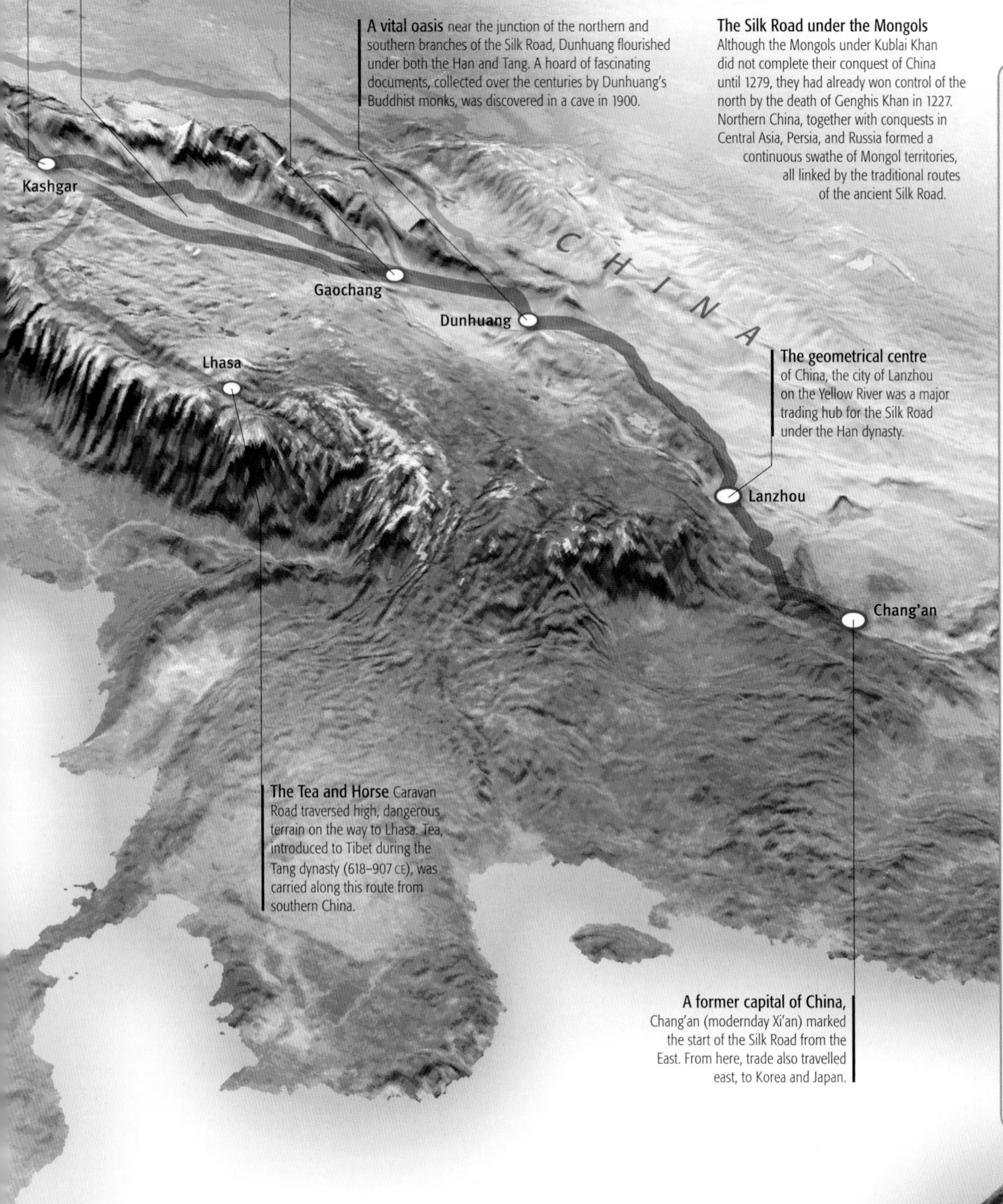

The Taklimakan desert was a major obstacle between China and lands to the west. The Silk Road split into two routes that skirted the desert – one to the north and one to the south.

Built in the 1st century BCE as a garrison town, Gaochang became an important religious centre, where Buddhism was firmly established.

A vital oasis near the junction of the northern and southern branches of the Silk Road, Dunhuang flourished under both the Han and Tang. A hoard of fascinating documents, collected over the centuries by Dunhuang's Buddhist monks, was discovered in a cave in 1900.

VENETIAN MERCHANT AND ADVENTURER (1254–1324)

MARCO POLO

As a teenager, Venetian Marco Polo accompanied his father and uncle on their second expedition to China, where they reached the fabled court of Kublai Khan. Marco learned the Mongol language and the Great Khan employed him as roving envoy and governor for three years in eastern China. He returned to Venice in 1295, but the following year was captured in a naval battle against the Genoese. In captivity, he dictated an account of his travels to a fellow inmate. Marco Polo's *Travels* was the most detailed account of East Asia available to European readers. It was printed in 1483 and influenced the thinking of many later would-be explorers.

"I have not told half of what I saw"

MARCO POLO, 1324

The Silk Road under the Mongols
Although the Mongols under Kublai Khan did not complete their conquest of China until 1279, they had already won control of the north by the death of Genghis Khan in 1227. Northern China, together with conquests in Central Asia, Persia, and Russia formed a continuous swathe of Mongol territories, all linked by the traditional routes of the ancient Silk Road.

The geometrical centre of China, the city of Lanzhou on the Yellow River was a major trading hub for the Silk Road under the Han dynasty.

The Tea and Horse Caravan Road traversed high, dangerous terrain on the way to Lhasa. Tea, introduced to Tibet during the Tang dynasty (618–907 CE), was carried along this route from southern China.

A former capital of China, Chang'an (modernday Xi'an) marked the start of the Silk Road from the East. From here, trade also travelled east, to Korea and Japan.

Kashgar
Gaochang
Dunhuang
Lhasa
Lanzhou
Chang'an
CHINA

AFTER

A number of factors contributed to the decline of the Silk Road, which did not survive into the 15th century.

THE BLACK DEATH
Outbreaks of bubonic plague started in China in the 1330s, and the Silk Road was probably the principal means of transmission of the **Black Death 132–33 »** across Central Asia to Europe.

COLLAPSE OF MONGOL CHINA
Having secured the route since the mid-13th century, the Mongols lost control of China to the **Ming dynasty « 114–15** in 1368.

TRADE UNDER THE MING
In the early 15th century the Chinese joined Arab, Persian, and Indian merchants trading in the Indian Ocean. The **treasure fleets** commanded by **Zheng He « 115** shipped goods such as blue-and-white porcelain to the Middle East and even to Africa.

NEW ROUTE
Trade between Europe and East Asia became possible via the **sea route to India 164–65 »** pioneered by Vasco da Gama in 1498.

ARCHAEOLOGY
The Silk Road was **rediscovered** by European explorers in the 19th century. It was given its name by a German geographer, Ferdinand von Richthofen. A number of **ancient cities** in the Taklimakan region were excavated, including Dunhuang and Gaochang.

GAOCHANG

A NEW SILK ROAD
In 1998, representatives from more than 30 countries met to discuss the possibility of developing a modern **Europe–Caucasus–Asia** equivalent of the ancient routes.

« BEFORE

Infectious diseases have a long history and the first accounts date back to ancient times.

SMALLPOX IN EGYPT
The first known records of infectious diseases include the mummified remains of Egyptian pharaoh **Rameses V** dating back to c.1140 BCE. His head appears to show skin lesions similar to those caused by **smallpox**.

EARLY VACCINATION
In ancient China it has been claimed that a lucky day was chosen on which to blow crusts from the skin of a **smallpox** sufferer into a healthy person's nose through a tube or quill. If the Chinese did inhale a powdered material from the sores of smallpox victims this would be the **first recorded form of vaccination**.

PESTILENCE IN GREECE
The ancient Greek historian **Thucydides** (c.460–401 BCE) recorded in painstaking detail the symptoms of the **great pestilence** of 430–429 BCE, which devastated Athens, "so that it may be recognized by medical men if it recurs". Despite catching the disease

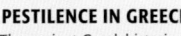

THUCYDIDES himself, Thucydides survived to leave **a harrowing account of the death and despair** that the disease caused, accounting as it did for some 60,000 lives – a quarter of the population of Athens at that time.

FIRST EUROPEAN BUBONIC PLAGUE
From c.542 CE a bubonic plague had reached Egypt and the Roman Empire, from Arabia: it became known as the **Plague of Justinian** (after the emperor Justinian I). Thus the Black Death was not the first such plague in Europe.

60 PER CENT of Europe's population died from the plague in the 14th century according to some of the higher estimates, with densely populated urban areas being the worst affected.

HOW WE KNOW

YERSINIA PESTIS BACTERIUM

Medical researchers have extracted genetic evidence of the sausage-shaped *Yersinia pestis* bacterium (right) from several plague burial sites in England and France from the period 1348–1590. The experts have been surprised to find that the DNA code they extracted matches that of the *Yersinia pestis* responsible for small plague outbreaks today – it was no more virulent. They suggest that local transmission was airborne, rather than via fleas. This may account for the rapid spread and huge death toll.

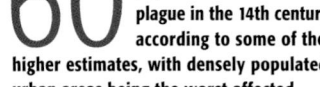

The bubonic plague that came to be known as the Black Death spread to Europe from Central Asia, where it had already left a trail of devastation. It may have first reached Europe in the autumn of 1346, when an army of Muslim Tartars laid siege to the flourishing Christian enclave of Caffa (the modern-day Crimean port of Feodosiya) on the Silk Road (see pp.130–31) and plague struck the besieging troops. Stories of infected corpses being catapulted over the walls into Caffa to spread the plague are probably unreliable. What is not disputed is that the beseiged Christian merchants took the bubonic plague with them, possibly in infected rodent fleas, when they fled by boat back to the Mediterranean via

KEY
- 1347
- Mid-1348
- Early 1349
- Late 1349
- 1350
- 1351
- After 1351
- Minor outbreak

Plague migration
Seaborne transportation carried the plague over vast distances. This map shows the spread of the plague through Europe, from 1347. Iceland remained unscathed, since no ships from Europe landed there in 1349.

The Black Death

Towns and villages of medieval Europe became littered with corpses, and death carts carried so many bodies they could only be buried in deep pits. The medieval world had very little protection against a plague that was to wipe out vast swathes of the population.

Constantinople in 1347, and so the disease arrived in the ports of Europe. Thus the most virulent pandemic then known to, and still ever recorded by man, spread rapidly – and fatally – through much of the Western world.

Diverse strains
Plague is caused by a bacterium called *Yersinia pestis* (see below), which is carried by fleas on wild rodents. Transfer of bacterial infection occurs when the fleas feed on human blood.

There were three variants of the plague: bubonic, in which the patient develops buboes, or swellings, of the neck, groin, or armpit glands and from which this variant got its name; pneumonic, or blood-coughing, in which the lungs are infected because

the disease is carried in the air and inhaled; and septicaemic, or blood-poisoning, in which the bacteria attack the blood system itself.

The bubonic variant was described by contemporaries such as the Italian writer Giovanni Boccaccio who wrote of "certain swellings in the groin or the armpits… some as large as a common apple". It took 3–5 days to incubate, and in 80 per cent of victims, caused death within a further three days.

The pneumonic form, with or without the buboes, was 90–95 per cent lethal within just a few days (today, with treatment, that percentage would probably survive) and could be transmitted directly by sneezing for example. This, some researchers say, explains the great number of deaths. The septicaemic variant, though the least common, led rapidly to death. This most virulent form also caused a victim's skin to turn dark purple, almost black, and may account for the plague's epithet "black" – though this term was not used at the time.

Trail of death
How many perished under its macabre shadow is not known, but it is estimated that in Europe more than 25 million died from this plague pandemic. Other estimates veer up to 50 million out of a population of 80 million in the 1300s. The plague returned repeatedly over subsequent generations, but never again with such devastating loss of life.

AFTER »

The plague's impact on medieval society was immense, but it was not the last pandemic and others may occur in the future.

AFTER-EFFECTS
The traumatic decline in population led to a shortage of labour and a sudden rise in prices, as well as **irreversible social changes**. The European population did not recover until the 16th century. Over the next four centuries another **nine major plague pandemics** hit Europe.

MODERN PLAGUES
Precautionary measures now help to control the spread of disease. In Hong Kong in 2003, for example, tissue-paper masks were used to avoid

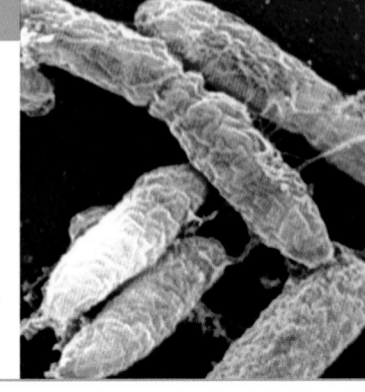

SARS: MODERN PLAGUE

contact with **SARS (Severe Acute Respiratory Syndrome)** – a variety of pneumonic plague. Scientists predict that drug-resistant infections may cause devastating pandemics in the future.

Dance of death
The Black Death touched every level of medieval society, lords and ladies, clergy, and the poor alike. This *Danse Macabre* – a reminder of the universality of death – was a recurrent moral and artistic theme in post-plague Europe.

Der Tod. | Der Tod zum Pabst. | Der Tod zum Kaiser. | Der Tod zu Kaiserin. | Der Tod zum König.

Der Tod zur Herzogin. | Der Tod zum Grafen. | Der Tod zum Abt. | Der Tod zum Ritter. | Der Tod zum Juristen.

Der Tod zur Edelfrau. | Der Tod zum Kaufmann. | Der Tod zur Aebtissin. | Der Tod zum Krüppel. | Der Tod zum Waldbruder.

Der Tod zum Heróld | Der Tod zum Schultheiss. | Der Tod zum Blutvogt. | Der Tod zum Narren. | Der Tod zum Krämer.

Medieval Europe

After the fall of the Roman Empire, Europe fragmented into many small states in which local leaders took power and in some cases, carved out empires for themselves. The Frankish ruler Charlemagne and the Saxon Otto I both held territory that approached the size and power of the Western Roman Empire.

The most successful of the new states to emerge in the period after the end of the Western Roman Empire was the kingdom of the Franks. The Franks were a confederacy of Germanic tribes from the area around modern-day Belgium and Holland. Under their leader Clovis (c.481–511 CE), the Franks conquered most of the old Roman province of Gaul and laid the foundations of an empire that would dominate Western Europe for centuries. Significantly for the future of Europe, Clovis also

Charlemagne reliquary
This silver container, made in the shape of a bust of the emperor, was reputed to have contained parts of his skull.

converted to Catholic Christianity while most of his rivals were Arians, regarded as heretics by the Roman population. In doing so, Clovis ensured that Catholicism, rather than the Arian form of Christianity, would eventually prevail through Western Europe. On his death, Clovis's kingdom was divided among his sons, and it continued to expand in the 6th century under his descendants, known as the Merovingians.

The Carolingians
The power of the Frankish kings declined in the late 7th century. Several died young and rival aristocratic factions vied for power. One of these families, later known as the Carolingians, emerged as dominant as a result of the alliances with other noble houses made by its head, Pippin II. From 719–741 CE his illegitimate son Charles Martel ("the Hammer") controlled the kingdom, ruling in the name of a succession of Merovingian kings. Charles Martel defeated Arab raids from Spain and reimposed Frankish rule east of the Rhine. Anglo-Saxon missionaries such as St Boniface were encouraged to set up monasteries and promote conversion in the conquered territories. In 751, Charles Martel's son Pippin III obtained the pope's approval to depose the last Merovingian king, and became the first ruler of the new Carolingian dynasty.

Charlemagne
Pippin's son, Charles the Great or Charlemagne, reigned for almost half a century from 768. He faced few internal challenges to his authority and was able to initiate a series of aggressive campaigns against the neighbouring

> **4,500** pagan Saxon prisoners were beheaded during a single day in 782 CE, according to one contemporary chronicle, after the emperor Charlemagne ordered them to choose between Christian baptism and execution.

peoples. The king met with the leading lay and ecclesiastical nobles in an annual assembly each spring, in which new laws were agreed and plans made for campaigning later in the year. Frankish society was organized for almost continuous warfare, and the nobles depended on conquest for a continuing supply of treasure and new territories with which to support and expand their own followings.

Under Charlemagne, the Franks undertook 30 years of warfare against the pagan Saxon tribes to the east of the Frankish lands, forcefully converting them to Christianity. In 773, invited by Pope Hadrian I to save Rome from conquest by the Lombard (north Italian) king Desiderius, Charlemagne invaded northern Italy. Following the capture of the capital, Pavia, he proclaimed himself King of the Lombards. An expedition to the Ebro Valley in Spain in 778 was less successful, but Charlemagne's greatest triumph came in 796 with the collapse of the Avar Empire, centred in modern Hungary, as a result of Frankish attacks. He acquired the enormous treasure they had built up over the preceding three centuries, which he used to pay for new churches and monasteries, as well as building a new capital at Aachen in western Germany.

The Carolingian renaissance
Contacts with Italy and the Anglo-Saxon kingdoms enabled Charlemagne to attract scholars to his court, such as Alcuin of York, the Visigothic poet Theodulf, and the Lombard historian Paul the Deacon. Not only did the Frankish court become a centre of learning to which the leading aristocratic

> " A chief in whose shadow the Christian people **repose in peace** and who **strikes terror** into the pagan nations. "
>
> ALCUIN OF YORK, LETTER DESCRIBING CHARLEMAGNE, c.796 CE

families sent their sons, these and other advisors also helped Charlemagne to carry out a programme of reform of the Frankish church. This involved importing model texts from Italy, including works of liturgy, church law, monastic rule, and biblical scholarship. Higher levels of literacy were imposed on the clergy, and new laws were issued throughout the reign to counter errors and abuses in the Frankish church. A reformed and more legible script known as Caroline replaced that used in the Merovingian period, and continued in use throughout Western Europe until the 12th century.

In 802 CE, following the failure of two rebellions against him, Charlemagne imposed oaths of loyalty on all free men over the age of 12. His subjects swore loyalty to "my lord Charles, most

« **BEFORE**

As the power of the Roman Empire came to an end, other leaders took control of the areas that had been controlled by Rome.

WANING OF THE ROMAN EMPIRE
Over the course of the 5th century CE, **military and economic problems** led to the western Roman emperors being unable to exercise direct rule over their provinces **« 102–03**. Instead, power was delegated to a series of commanders from beyond the frontiers who established themselves with their followers. Rome lost control of **Britain** in around 410, **Southern and Western Spain** in 413, **Southwest France** in 418, **North France and the rest of Spain** after 451, and most of the **rest of France** in 473. **Romulus Augustus**, the last Roman emperor, was deposed in 476 by **Odoacer**, leader of a federation of East Germanic tribes, who was crowned King of Italy.

POWER IN THE EAST AND WEST
Barbarians filled the power vacuum left by the end of the Western Empire in the 5th–6th centuries: **Visigoths** in Spain, **Ostragoths** in Italy, **Vandals** in North Africa, **Anglo-Saxons** in England, and **Franks** in Gaul (France). The Eastern Roman Empire survived and became known as the Byzantine Empire **144–45 »**, although further provinces were lost to Slavs in the Balkans and the Arabs in the Near East and Africa in the 6th–7th centuries.

Charlemagne's coronation

Pope Leo III crowned Charlemagne emperor on Christmas Day 800 CE. Charlemagne said he did not want to be crowned by Leo, perhaps because by "giving" the emperor the crown, Leo appeared the more powerful of the two.

adoption of the title was justified by the fact that the throne of the Eastern Roman Empire in Constantinople (see BEFORE) was held by a woman, the Empress Irene, so theoretically vacant. Charlemagne's seal included the Latin tag *renovatio Romani imperii* ("renovation of the Roman Empire") and he is portrayed on coins, in deliberate imitation of the Roman emperors, wearing a military cloak and laurel crown.

Charlemagne himself had doubts about a title that tied him so closely to Rome, and in 813 he held a purely Frankish ceremony for the coronation of his son, Louis the Pious.

After Charlemagne

Louis the Pious was an intelligent and well-educated man, but he lacked his father's leadership abilities. When he died in 840, the empire was divided between his three sons, who quarrelled and in turn had multiple heirs, so the great Carolingian empire was further split. In addition, the security of Europe was threatened by invasions from several directions – Scandinavian Vikings from the north (see pp.148–49), Arabs from the south, and Magyars who had moved into modern-day Hungary from further east. Over the course of the late 9th and early 10th centuries, Western Europe fragmented into many small states, governed by local rulers and Carolingian heirs.

In 911, the last of the eastern Carolingian rulers, Louis the Child, died, and a group of German dukes banded together to choose a king for their lands. The resulting line of rulers, most

Battle of Lechfeld

In 955 CE Otto I decisively defeated the Magyars at Lechfeld, near Augsburg, in Germany. The battle ended the threat from the Magyars, who had taken advantage of divisions in Western Europe to mount their invasion.

of whom were from Saxony in eastern Germany, grew steadily more powerful. The most successful of them all was Otto I (reigned 936–73 CE). Otto benefited from a discovery of silver in the Harz Mountains in Saxony in 938, which gave him the wealth to pay for a huge army and build a string of fortified towns. He pushed the boundaries of his German empire eastwards, inflicting a major defeat on the Magyars at the Battle of Lechfeld in 955 (see above).

Like Charlemagne before him, Otto cultivated the church, encouraging the conversion of non-Christians in his realm and founding new bishoprics. He appointed his own nominees as abbots and bishops and sought to strengthen the authority of the church at the expense of the secular nobility.

»

pious emperor". This use of oaths to create a direct relationship between ruler and subjects reflects the lack of more complex administrative structures, such as had existed in the Roman Empire. Charlemagne made many administrative reforms and created a more efficient bureaucracy than had existed under his predecessors, but he continued to depend on a handful of officials drawn from the local aristocracy. Military action, in

particular, required a large degree of consensus among the nobility.

Imperial authority

Charlemagne also sought to develop the imperial dimension of his rule, borrowing from the authority of the Roman emperors. In 800 he went to Rome to reinstate Pope Leo III and, on Christmas day, he was crowned "Emperor of the Romans". This

> " [Charlemagne] energetically **promoted the liberal arts** and praised and honoured those who taught them. "
>
> EINHARD, HISTORIAN AND COURTIER, FROM "LIFE OF CHARLEMAGNE", C.827 CE

ANGLO-SAXON KING (C.849–899CE)

KING ALFRED

Alfred the Great inherited the throne of Wessex (southern England) in 871 CE. At the Battle of Edington in 878, he defeated the Danes, who had already occupied north and eastern England and were attacking Wessex. Basing his style of rule on that of Charlemagne, he strengthened his kingdom against further attacks, building fortified towns and establishing a navy. Alfred, like Charlemagne, also promoted education and the arts. He left his kingdom much stronger than he found it, and he laid the foundations for his successors to unite England under a single ruler.

In 961 CE, Otto invaded northern Italy and was crowned emperor by the pope, John XII, cementing the relationship between the papacy and the emperor of what would later become known as the Holy Roman Empire.

Feudalism in Europe

The term feudalism is used to describe the system of relationships between kings and nobles in northern Europe during much of the medieval period. In many ways it was the same system used by the Carolingian emperors, who appointed noblemen to administer areas of their empire in return for a certain amount of power and land, sealing the relationship with an oath of loyalty.

The feudal system that evolved in England and France worked in a similar way to the Carolingian example. The king assigned a parcel of land (known as a fief) to a nobleman; in return for the land, the nobleman swore to be loyal to the king and promised to perform various duties. First and foremost, he had to devote a set number of days each year to military service for the king. He was obliged to attend the king's court, where he would give his advice on matters of policy and justice. He would also be asked to contribute payments for certain royal expenses, for example, when the king was building a new castle or when a royal wedding was taking place.

A nobleman who entered into this kind of feudal relationship with the king was termed the king's vassal, and he referred to the king as his lord. Many noblemen apportioned part of their land to sub-tenants, who performed duties and swore allegiance in turn. This meant that the feudal system developed into a hierarchy of lords and vassals. The social networks that were involved could become very complicated, because it was possible for a vassal to accept lands from several lords. This kind of arrangement could lead to conflicting loyalties, especially if two lords were on different sides in a war. So vassals identified one of their superiors as their liege lord, the lord who took precedence over others.

France and England

The feudal system was most highly developed in France and England. Feudalism was already well established in France by the 10th century, when a

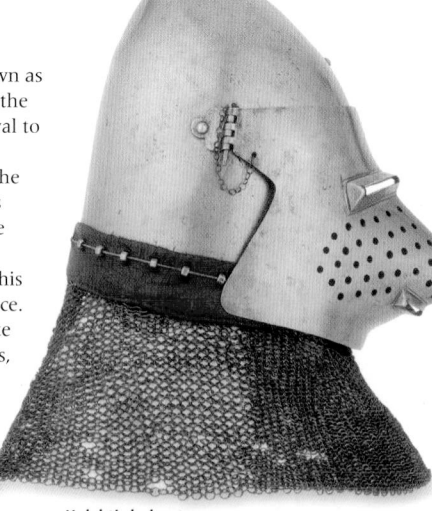

Knight's helmet
This 14th-century helmet was designed for full head protection. The wearer looks out through a narrow slit and there are tiny holes for ventilation.

Dover castle

England's first Norman king, William I, built a castle at Dover following his conquest in 1066, but the massive stone tower and inner walls were the work of Henry II, who upgraded the building in the 1180s. The stronghold was designed to guard the country against invaders arriving by ship across the English Channel, and its thick walls made it one of the strongest castles of its time.

Narrow slits allow archers to shoot out at attackers. Small windows prevent attackers from climbing in.

Battlements protect defending archers and provide a safe refuge.

The main floors of the great tower contain a ceremonial hall for the king and smaller private rooms.

The walls of the great tower are up to 6.4m (21ft) thick to protect the royal apartments from attack.

The forebuilding and entrance were guarded, acting as a barrier between the lord of the castle and intruders.

The king's gateway gives access to small walled area called the North Barbican, where attackers could be trapped.

Spiral staircase in corner tower leads to storage areas below the castle.

In the field

In return for protection and the right to work their lands, peasants worked for the lord of the manor for an agreed number of days per year, as well as giving him a share of their produce.

Viking leader called Rollo agreed to give up raiding the coasts of France in return for the right to settle with his followers in the northern part of the country (see pp.148–49). Rollo became the vassal of the Carolingian ruler, Charles the Simple, and his people became known as the Normans. In 1066, Duke William of Normandy invaded England (see pp.138–39), became its king, and granted lands to many of his Norman followers in return for their fulfillment of feudal obligations. From this time onwards, feudalism was firmly implanted in England.

Much of the rest of northern Europe was made up of a patchwork of smaller states, particularly those that formed part of the mainly Germanic Holy Roman Empire. Here the overlapping rights and responsibilities of emperor, dukes, and other secular and ecclesiastical princes made the political system more complex.

Knighthood and chivalry

The medieval knight fitted broadly into this system of feudal obligation. Having evolved initially from the heavy cavalry who had accompanied rulers such as Charlemagne, by the 11th century the knights had come to represent a distinct caste of professional fighting men. Their status was confirmed and enhanced through symbols and public ceremonies such as the "accolade" – a girding with a sword or hand on the shoulder. In return for this special status, the knight was expected to fight for his lord and to defend those groups, such as the clergy and the poor, who relied on his protection. The 12th-century writer John of Salisbury defined the knight's duties as being "to guard the church, to fight unbelievers, to venerate the priesthood, to protect the poor from injuries, to pour out their blood for their brothers."

Inevitably, the reality of knightly conduct did not always match up to this chivalric code. Towards the latter part of this period, in particular, feudal obligations were superceded by monetary arrangements. By the 14th century, knights would expect to be paid for their service and could themselves often pay a shield tax in lieu of service. Nonetheless, throughout this period knights remained a social and military elite.

The castle

Castles were the headquarters of the medieval feudal system. A castle was a multi-purpose building. It was the home of a lord, his family, and his servants. It was where business was done, the lord met his vassals, and where courts of justice met. It was also a military base and a fortified building from which a whole region could be defended.

Some castles were royal residences. In a period when communications were poor, the best way for a monarch to exercise power in the kingdom was to travel continuously, so rulers usually had castles around the kingdom. Other strongholds were held by vassals on the king's behalf, who ruled as a part of their feudal duties. A castle usually had a courtyard (bailey), surrounded by a strong, fortified wall. Inside the bailey was the main accommodation – a grand hall and private rooms for the lord or king, heated by open fires and decorated with tapestries. In the towers or outer buildings were less luxurious rooms for the stables, garrison, and service buildings.

The inner bailey walls or courtyard housed the hall and other buildings to provide accomdation for the king's houshold, guests, and armed garrison.

> "The **faithful vassal** should ... counsel and aid his lord."

FULBERT OF CHARTRES, LETTER TO DUKE WILLIAM OF AQUITAINE, 1020 CE

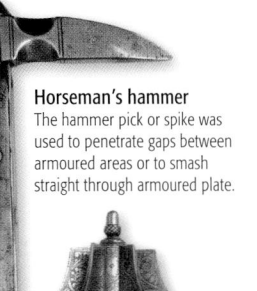

Halberd

The halberd was carried by foot soldiers, who inflicted serious injuries with its sharp point. They also used the weapon to trip or maim a horse or to pull a knight off his mount.

Horseman's hammer

The hammer pick or spike was used to penetrate gaps between armoured areas or to smash straight through armoured plate.

Mace

With its pointed blades, or flanges, a mace like this was a powerful weapon, even piercing plate armour if swung with enough force.

ENGLISH KING (1027–87 CE)

WILLIAM THE CONQUEROR

William, Duke of Normandy, invaded England in 1066, defeated his English rival, Harold, in battle at Hastings, and became William I. He introduced feudal government to England and appointed many French noblemen as his vassals, meaning that the ruling class of England was mainly Norman for many years. William and his nobles built many castles, and he commissioned a famous survey, the *Domesday Book*, detailing the lands and wealth of his kingdom.

AFTER »

The feudal system gradually died out as traders and merchants grew more powerful, and printing led to greater exchange of ideas.

CHANGES IN FEUDAL SERVICE

During the 14th and 15th centuries social changes made **feudal relations decline in importance**. Increasingly, vassals paid feudal dues in money rather than by military service. At the same time, the **middle classes**, who made their living by buying and selling goods, became more powerful.

RENAISSANCE

Writers and artists began to look back to ancient Greece and Rome for inspiration. This cultural rebirth, or **Renaissance 190–95 »**, resulted in a new realism in painting, changes in architectural styles, and translations of classic texts.

SPREAD OF PRINTING

In *c.*1438 a German metalworker called Johannes Gutenberg invented a method of making metal printing type. This enabled books to be printed and the **rapid circulation of ideas** in Europe.

Battle of Hastings

The Battle of Hastings was fought in southern England between an Anglo-Saxon army under Harold of Wessex and a force of invading Normans led by William of Normandy. The Normans were victorious and their leader became William I of England, known ever since as William the Conqueror.

In 11th-century England, several contenders vied to become king, largely because of the actions of Edward the Confessor (1003–66). In 1051, Edward told William of Normandy that he would be king after Edward's death, but when a Viking invasion looked likely in the early 1060s, Edward made a pledge to the Danish Svein Estrithsson too. Harald Hardraada of Norway had also been promised the throne by an earlier English king. However, English nobles wanted a native ruler, and Edward made yet another oath, this time to Harold of Wessex.

In January 1066, Edward died and Harold took the throne. But he soon faced a challenge – Harald Hardraada invaded northern England. Harold marched north to face his rival in battle and emerged the victor. At the same time, William of Normandy set sail across the English Channel with an invasion force, and landed on the south coast. As soon as he heard the news, Harold marched south, hoping to take the invaders by surprise.

William's scouts were watching for Harold's army and soon after his arrival the Normans attacked. The two armies were well matched in numbers, with around 8,000 men each. At first, the English seemed invincible. Their foot soldiers fought in close, efficient formations and their axe-men dealt fearsome blows. When a rumour spread that William had been killed, the Norman soldiers started to break up in disarray. But William held up his helmet to show that he was still alive. From then on, the Norman archers and mounted knights dominated the English, who were exhausted after their long march south. Finally Harold was wounded and then, after being set upon by Norman knights, he was killed. William claimed victory.

On 25th December 1066, William was crowned king of England. He quickly strengthened his position by granting lands to his nobles, thereby ensuring the spread of Norman power across the country. For many generations to come, England was ruled by kings from Normandy or other parts of France. The ruling class of England was Norman, the language of government and the court was French, and many senior churchmen were from Norman families.

The Bayeux Tapestry
This unique historical record is a 70-metre (230-ft) long embroidered panel that tells the story of events leading up to the Battle of Hastings and the battle itself. Although it is thought to have been created in England, it tells the story from a Norman perspective.

> "They are a **race inured to war**, and can hardly live without it."

WILLIAM OF MALMESBURY, FROM "DEEDS OF THE KINGS OF THE ENGLISH", DESCRIBING THE NORMANS, 12TH CENTURY

« BEFORE

Christianity survived the fall of Rome and prospered. Christian Europe expanded, and Church and State became intertwined.

SURVIVAL OF THE LATIN CHURCH

The decline of the Western Roman Empire and the **influx of barbarian peoples** in the 4th–6th centuries CE did not spell the end for Christianity in Western Europe. Many of the Germanic tribes were **Arian Christians**, a variant of Christianity at odds with Roman doctrine. Others, such as the Franks, entered as **pagans** but were **converted to Christianity**. Throughout the lands of the Roman Empire in Western Europe, Latin Christianity survived and, by the 6th–7th centuries, had **triumphed over Arianism**.

From the late 6th century under Pope Gregory the Great, and throughout the 7th–10th centuries, **Christian missionaries** began to spread Latin Christianity into the remaining pagan areas of Europe such as Anglo-Saxon England, Denmark, and the Slavic territories of Central Europe.

THE EAST–WEST SCHISM

Long after the collapse of the Western Empire, the **Roman Empire in the east** continued to thrive **144–45 »**. The Eastern Church under the **Patriarch of Constantinople**, became gradually more estranged from the Latin Church, culminating in the **Great Schism of 1054**.

THE IMPERIAL CHURCH

Under the emperor **Charlemagne « 134–35** church and state enjoyed a **close relationship**. Charlemagne made the church central to his government, using clerics as teachers and administrators, and used the spiritual authority of the church to **enhance his own authority** as emperor and defender of Christianity. In 800 he was **crowned by the pope** in Rome. This policy was adopted by other secular rulers such as the German emperor **Otto I 141–42 »** who used his influence over the appointment of clerics to strengthen his own authority at the expense of the nobility.

THE FIRST CRUSADE

By 1095, Christian Europe felt confident enough to mount a **military campaign** outside Europe in order to recapture the **Holy Lands** of the Middle East from the Muslims **146–47 »**.

A CRUSADER

The **Power** and the **Glory**

Medieval Western Europe was dominated by a common religious culture. Under a series of strong-willed, reform-minded popes, the Church became more centralized, powerful, and assertive. But over time, the Church also grew increasingly intolerant and politically divided.

A t the start of the 11th century, Western Europe was emerging from a long period of raids by tribes outside its borders, including Vikings from the north (see pp.148–49), Muslims from the south (see pp.122–23), and pagan Magyars from the Eurasian steppes. By 1000 CE the worst of the raids were over and Latin Christendom ceased to feel on the defensive. Freed from the threat of pagan and Muslim aggressors, the Church grew more prosperous, self-confident, and assertive.

The church reform movement

With this increasing confidence came a desire for reform. This impulse was felt first in the monasteries, which had served as an important repository for Christian learning and observance during the previous centuries. Prior to the 11th century, individual monasteries spread across Europe tended to follow their own interpretations of the monastic rule, often under the control of secular lords and benefactors. The reform movement, centred on the Burgundian

The monk in the white habit may represent Bernard of Clairvaux, abbot of the reformed Cistercian order.

An unidentified bishop wears a pallium, a yoke-shaped band of white wool, embroidered with crosses.

A senior cardinal (Niccolo Albertini di Prato) stands at the right hand of the pope in his broad-brimmed, cardinal's hat.

Pope Benedict XI dominates the piece – as pope he is God's representative on earth and the supreme spiritual authority.

Several nuns wear the black and white habit of the Dominicans; others wear Franciscan and Carmelite habits.

Priests and monks from the Augustinian, Benedictine, Carmelite, Dominican, and Franciscan orders are shown engaged in prayers and debate.

The sheep symbolize the pope's human flock and are guarded by black and white dogs that represent the Dominican order – a play on the phrase *Domini canes*, Latin for "Lord's hounds".

monastery of Cluny and on Gorze in the Rhineland, sought to impose a more consistent interpretation of the original monastic "Rule" of St Benedict. Under the influence of Cluny, Europe's monasteries merged into more uniform "orders" with a renewed commitment to discipline, prayer, and study.

Other new monastic orders emerged in the period following the Clunaic reforms. In 1098 an abbey was founded at Cîteaux in France that gave its name to one of the most significant of these movements, the Cistercians. Under the influence of the charismatic preacher Bernard of Clairvaux, the Cistercians rejected Cluny's wealth to focus on manual labour, strict discipline, and austerity. Cistercian monks played a vital role in the settlement and cultivation of inhospitable and dangerous lands along the borders of medieval Europe.

Papal reform

This reforming impulse also drove the agendas of several influential popes of the late 11th century, who wished to see a Church in which the sacred was more clearly differentiated from the worldly. Popes such as Leo IX (1049–54) sought to limit practices such as clerical marriage and the purchase of church positions (simony). He also attempted to extend papal authority by making ceremonial journeys and summoning bishops to synods (church councils) held at major towns. In his campaign Leo was ably assisted by a group of

THOMAS AQUINAS

The Italian Dominican friar Thomas Aquinas was the medieval Church's greatest thinker. His key contribution to theology was to reconcile the newly rediscovered work of the ancient Greek philosopher Aristotle with Christianity. His most important work, *Summa Theologica,* provided a systematic synthesis of Aristotle's theory and Christian tradition – the result provided the intellectual foundation of the medieval Church and still forms the basis of Catholic doctrine today. A fat and amiable man, the "angelic doctor" was well liked even by his intellectual adversaries. Thomas Aquinas was canonized in 1323.

reformers one of whom, a Clunaic monk named Hildebrand, later became Pope Gregory VII – a key figure in the increasingly powerful papacy.

The investiture controversy

Gregory VII was determined to promote the authority of the papacy in both spiritual and temporal spheres – even if this meant clashing with the authority of the secular kings and princes. In 1075, shortly after he was elected, he composed a detailed statement outlining his status as the spiritual head of Christendom. In it Gregory claimed that, since the pope owed his position to God, he was superior in authority to all earthly rulers.

A major area of dispute between the resurgent papacy and secular rulers was over the appointment (investiture of bishops and other senior church officials. Since the time of Charlemagne, (see pp.140–41) secular rulers had used their right to be involved in this process to ensure a compliant and sympathetic church. Gregory was determined that control over investiture should lie with the Church and, ultimately, with himself.

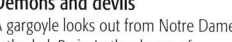

Demons and devils
A gargoyle looks out from Notre Dame cathedral, Paris. In the drama of medieval Christendom, demons and devils battled angels and saints.

Matters came to a head in 1076 when Gregory opposed the appointment of the archbishop of Milan by the German emperor Henry IV. A clash between the uncompromising pope and the formidable emperor seemed inevitable.

Henry persuaded the bishops of the German empire to declare the pope deposed; Gregory retaliated by excommunicating (excluding from the Church) Henry. When the German princes rebelled and elected an alternative emperor, Henry decided that he had no option but to do public penance and appeal to the pope to lift his excommunication. After four days of penance, Henry was granted absolution, but conflict between papacy and empire rumbled on. In 1122 a compromise was reached at the Concordat of Worms – but by then the controversy had divided Europe and caused almost half a century of civil war inside Germany.

Popes and antipopes

All over Christendom, the stage was set for a series of clashes between Church and State. In 12th-century England Henry II clashed with Thomas Becket, Archbishop of Canterbury, about whether clergy should be subject to common law rather than that of the Church. »

The Holy Roman Emperor
Charles IV holds the orb, symbolizing the emperor's special responsibility for the security of the Church.

King Charles V of France stands to the left of the emperor, representing the other secular rulers of Latin Christendom.

An unidentified noble occupies the final seat, his sword a reminder of his role as a defender of the Church.

The Church in society
This 14th-century fresco, *The Church Militant and Triumphant* by Andrea da Firenze, presents an idealized view of the medieval social order. Enthroned in the centre, the pope presides over the representatives of the Church to his right, and State to his left.

The laity fill the right-hand side of the picture, with representatives of various secular occupations. The man in white wears a golden garter showing he is a knight and a member of the English Order of the Garter.

Four pilgrims carry the symbols of the major medieval pilgrimage sites: a seashell for Santiago de Compostela, a veil for Rome, and a palm for the Holy Land.

Gothic stone angel
Serene figures such as this one from Reims Cathedral, France, were symbolic of the joys of heaven as well as a consolation for the sufferings of the faithful on earth.

Burning of heretics
Watched by the French King Philip II Augustus, a group of Amauricien heretics are burned outside Paris in 1210. Philip II's reign also saw the launch of the Albigensian Crusade against Cathar heretics in southern France.

personal property and were not attached to richly endowed abbeys. The friars were a part of the new urban culture, building churches and schools in the middle of towns and preaching in public squares. To support themselves, they depended on charity, putting them more closely in touch with ordinary people. The Franciscan friars, in particular, sought a return to the simplicity and poverty of the early Church, living among the people, caring for the poor or needy and preaching repentance.

Heretics and the Inquisition

Wearing black and white habits, the Dominicans were dedicated to teaching and preaching, and emphasized religious orthodoxy and obedience to the papacy. The Dominican order had its roots in the campaign against the Albigensians, or Cathars, a heretical (holding beliefs contrary to the established teachings of the Church) movement in southern France. The Albigensians believed that the existence of evil contradicted the notion of one benign God.

As the papacy came to define Christian doctrine with a new exactitude during the 13–14th centuries, there was a corresponding intolerance of unorthodoxy and of deviants such as the Albigensians. By the Synod of Toulouse in 1229, the ecclesiastical tribunals known as inquisitions had developed into a more formal institution charged with the suppression of heresy.

Staffed by Dominicans, the medieval Inquisition operated mainly in France and Italy. The systematic persecution of heretics – and, increasingly, the persecution of any views that diverged from strict Roman Catholic orthodoxy – was the dark side of the highly organized and efficient medieval Church.

Large stained glass windows
let light and colour flood in to the building, a feature typical of Gothic churches and cathedrals.

>> Becket's murder by a group of Henry's knights made him a martyr to the cause of church independence. The shrine containing his relics at Canterbury became a centre of pilgrimage for people all over Europe.

By the late 14th century, the Church and the papacy itself were divided. Pope Urban VI, elected in 1378, alienated his supporters in the papal court, and the cardinals responded by electing a rival pope. This "antipope" Clement VII, established his papal court at Avignon in France. A European crisis developed as the German emperor recognized the Roman claimant, the French king supported his rival, and other states and kingdoms took one side or the other. The resulting split, or "Great Schism", between a succession of popes and antipopes undermined the prestige and authority of the papacy; for several years there were three rival claimants. The schism was eventually resolved in 1414 at the Council of Constance, with the pope in Rome recognized as legitimate.

New devotions
For all its power, the established Church was increasingly cut off from the spiritual life of the growing urban classes. Merchants, craftsmen, and their families could now read and write, ending the clergy's monopoly on the transmission of ideas. These people were often better educated than the clergy, and more open to new forms of religious devotion.

The growing impulse for a more personal, informal relationship with God is expressed in spiritual works such as Thomas à Kempis' *The Imitation of Christ*, published around 1418. These ideals also permeated poetry and art, which began to focus more on "Our Lady", the Virgin Mary. Mary was held to be more approachable and sympathetic than other saints, and the relic of her tunic

at Chartres cathedral was a major attraction for pilgrims from all over Europe. Such holy relics were considered miraculous, capable of inducing cures for all manner of physical and spiritual ills. For the well-to-do, a pilgrimage to a shrine was also a relatively pleasant way of doing penance and, hopefully, earning remission from time in purgatory.

Early in the 13th century, two new religious orders were founded. The Franciscan and Dominican friars were known as mendicants, from the Latin word for "beggars", for they renounced

Medieval pilgrimage
A group of pilgrims leave Canterbury, site of the shrine of Thomas Becket and a major place of pilgrimage, in a version of the prologue to Geoffrey Chaucer's *The Canterbury Tales*.

FOUNDER OF THE FRANCISCANS (c.1180–1226)

ST FRANCIS OF ASSISI

The son of a wealthy merchant in the Italian town of Assisi, Francis led a carefree youth. In 1209, he was inspired by a sermon to give away all his possessions. He began to live like a beggar, travelling barefoot, preaching repentance, and aiding the poor. In time he was joined by two companions, and they determined to live by the rule of poverty and simplicity that Christ had given to his apostles. In 1210, Francis gained the blessing of Pope Innocent III for his new order, the Franciscans. By his death in 1226, his followers, inspired by St Francis' humble and compassionate example, numbered many thousands.

3,000 **SQUARE METRES** of stained glass were used in the windows at Chartres cathedral. **152 out of 186 original stained glass windows at Chartres still survive today.**

Ribbed vaulting helps to support the weight of the high, wide nave ceiling, the highest in France at the time it was built.

High pointed spires are made possible by pointed arches and flying buttresses, making Gothic buildings such as Chartres taller and lighter than any previous structures.

Chartres Cathedral
The great cathedral at Chartres is a striking example of the "Gothic" style of architecture that emerged in 12th-century France and flourished throughout the late medieval period. Gothic buildings, with their pointed arches, large windows, clustered columns, and soaring spires were intended to invoke the majesty and splendour of God. The main Gothic portion of Chartres was built between 1194–1220.

Flying buttresses surround and support the high walls and spires. Typically for a Gothic building, the buttresses at Chartres cathedral are turned into a decorative feature.

The west rose window depicts the Last Judgement. There are three rose windows in total, bathing the interior in a warm and golden light.

The royal portal features intricate carvings of religious scenes including Christ sitting in judgement. Statues of kings and queens symbolize the religious authority of the French monarchs.

The spacious nave is the widest in France and permits an unbroken view along the entire length of the cathedral.

Allegations of corruption and excess in the Church, as well as new ideas and forms of religious belief spread by new technology undermined the unity of the Church.

THE REFORMATION
In the 16th century, the movement known as **the Reformation 196–99 »** ended the religious unity of Western Europe and resulted in the establishment of **Protestant churches** that owed no allegiance to the pope. The catalyst for the Reformation came in 1517, when a priest named **Martin Luther** nailed a list of propositions to the door of the Castle church in Wittenberg, Germany. He intended to start a debate and, thanks to the new technology of the **printing press**, his ideas for reform of the Christian Church were being read and discussed throughout Germany within two weeks and throughout Europe within a month.

By 1600, **Lutheran** churches were established in Germany and Scandinavia, **Calvinist** churches in Scotland, Switzerland, and the Netherlands, and **Anglican** churches in England and Wales.

THE GREAT BIBLE

VERNACULAR BIBLES
For **Luther**, as for other Protestant reformers such as **Calvin** and **Zwingli**, the authority to oppose the Church came from **Holy Scripture**, the **direct word of God**. To make holy writ readily available to ordinary men and women it had to be translated from **Latin** – the language of the clerical elite – into the **vernacular**, the spoken languages of everyday life. Luther lost no time in **translating the Bible** into German. This Bible facilitated the spread of Lutheranism from Germany to Scandinavia, Poland, and Hungary. Elsewhere, the momentum for the production of **printed Bibles in the vernacular** was equally unstoppable. The **first authorized edition of the scriptures in English**, the Great Bible, was produced by Miles Coverdale and published in 1538.

> "Where there is **charity and wisdom**, there is neither **fear nor ignorance**."
>
> ST FRANCIS OF ASSISI, "ADMONITIONS", *c.*1220

BEFORE

The Byzantine Empire grew out of the eastern Roman Empire, gradually acquiring a distinctive new Greek Christian culture that replaced the traditions of ancient Rome.

ANCIENT BYZANTIUM
According to legend, the Megaran king, **Byzas**, founded the Greek city of Byzantium in 667 BCE on the advice of the oracle at Delphi **《 48**.

FIRST DIVISION OF THE EMPIRE
In 293 CE the emperor **Diocletian** split the Roman Empire **《 64–67**, with two emperors (*Augusti*), one ruling in the east, the other in the west, assisted by two younger co-emperors (*Caesares*).

A NEW CAPITAL
When **Constantine 《 100–01** defeated his last rival to become sole emperor in 324 CE, he decided to build a new capital, Nova Roma (New Rome), at Byzantium. Completed in 330 CE, it became known as **Constantinople** after his death.

FINAL DIVISION
In 395 CE the Roman Empire was definitively split into eastern and western divisions by Emperor **Theodosius**, the eastern empire being ruled from Constantinople. The last western emperor was deposed in 476 CE, but by then the true rulers in the west were the Goths, Vandals, Franks, and other Germanic peoples **《 134–35**.

The term "Byzantine Empire" suggests a separate entity from the Roman Empire. The Byzantines, however, called themselves Romans and their realm Romania. Constantinople had been the capital of the Roman Empire since the reign of Constantine (306–37 CE), and the centre of gravity of Mediterranean civilization had shifted to its eastern shores long before the final collapse

Hagia Sophia
Built by Justinian I in five years (532–37), the Hagia Sophia church (meaning "holy wisdom") was converted into a mosque in 1453 by the Ottomans. Despite later additions, it remains one of the finest examples of Byzantine church architecture.

The **Byzantine Empire**

A great metropolis when the capitals of Western Europe were little more than villages, Constantinople stood for more than a millennium at the heart of its empire, a centre of religion and culture, and a military power forming a protective barrier that allowed Europe to emerge from the ruins of the Roman Empire.

of Rome. The city stood at a strategic position that controlled the trade routes between Asia and Europe, as well as the passage from the Black Sea to the Mediterranean.

When the German Odoacer deposed the last western emperor, Romulus Augustus, in 476 CE, the Byzantine emperor Zeno became sole heir to the Roman Empire. One of his most significant acts was to persuade the Ostrogothic leader Theodoric, who was threatening to do in the east what other barbarian tribes had done in the west, to conquer Italy rather than to take part of the eastern empire.

Conquests and losses
The first emperor to attempt to regain lost territories in the west was Justinian, who reigned from 527–65. His armies won back North Africa from the Vandals and also reconquered much of Italy. In addition to these conquests, Justinian left a substantial cultural legacy in the form of magnificent churches and a thorough codification of Roman law.

In the east, however, things did not run so smoothly. The Persian Sassanids (see pp.76–77) broke a treaty made

Rare Byzantine relic
A survivor of the sack of Constantinople in 1204, this gilt enamel reliquary is said to contain a fragment of the cross on which Jesus Christ was crucified.

with Justinian and entered imperial territory in 540, seizing the city of Antioch. There followed an exhausting series of military clashes until the emperor Heraclius won a decisive victory over the Persians in 628. No sooner had he won control of the east, however, than the Muslim Arabs (see pp.122–23) invaded, and the empire lost its eastern provinces to Islam. Constantinople was besieged for four years in 674–78. It survived thanks to the secret weapon Greek fire, a flammable liquid used as a flamethrower, whose composition remains a mystery to this day.

The empire faced many enemies besides the Arabs, including the Lombards in Italy and the Bulgars in the Balkan peninsula, but somehow Byzantium survived. Heraclius introduced a system of government, in which the empire was divided into military provinces, called "themes", each governed by an independent *strategos* or general.

Orthodoxy
Despite the chronic instability of its empire and periodic outbreaks of plague, the city of Constantinople

The Mosaic of the Donors
Located above the imperial bodyguard's Vestibule of the Warriors, which today serves as the exit, the Mosaic of the Donors illustrates the consecration of the Hagia Sophia, its dedication to Christ, and Constantinople's status as capital of a Christian empire.

The emperor Justinian
offers the Church of Holy Wisdom (the Hagia Sophia) to the Virgin Mary and the baby Jesus.

BYZANTINE EMPRESS (500–48 CE)

THEODORA

Daughter of a circus bear-keeper, Theodora was a comic actress and, some claim, a prostitute, before marrying Justinian in 523. When he became emperor of Byzantium in 527, Theodora proved herself a talented ruler in her own right. Her advice quelled the Nika riots of 532, probably saving the empire. She is regarded as an advocate for women's rights who used her position to help her society's oppressed, and she is venerated as a saint in the Orthodox church.

BYZANTINE The word was not used regularly to indicate the eastern Roman Empire until after its fall in 1453. It is also applied to the empire's style of architecture, notable for its domes and mosaics, and is a derogatory term for complex, obscure political processes.

was the largest in the world. Part of its strength lay in its importance as a centre of Christianity. The Byzantine church was the "Orthodox" church – in contrast to the various other forms of eastern Christianity that it considered heretical. The fact that the emperor was held to be God's representative on Earth gave him great authority, but could also cause serious problems. Leo III, who ruled from 717–41, banned religious icons because he said they were being worshipped as idols. This became known as the Iconoclast controversy. The empire erupted in protest, and the icons were restored, to be "venerated" but not worshipped. Controversies of this kind added to the growing distance between the churches of the east and west.

Revival and collapse

The empire's fortunes revived under the "Macedonian" emperors of the late 9th–early 11th centuries. It regained control of the Adriatic Sea, southern Italy, and all of Bulgaria. Cities grew and prospered, trade increased, and artistic and intellectual life flourished.

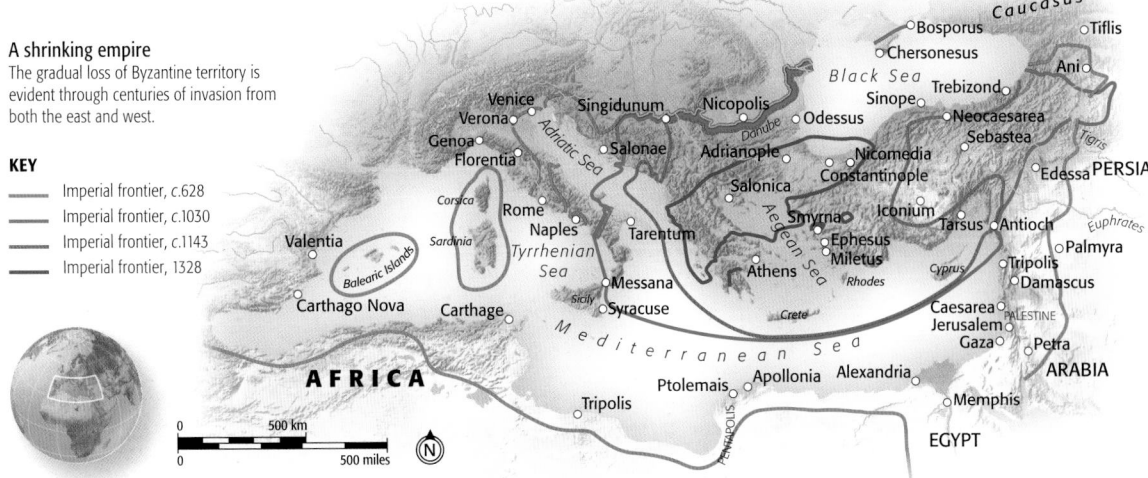

A shrinking empire
The gradual loss of Byzantine territory is evident through centuries of invasion from both the east and west.

KEY
Imperial frontier, c.628
Imperial frontier, c.1030
Imperial frontier, c.1143
Imperial frontier, 1328

However, after 1025 Byzantium fell into difficulties again. A string of weak rulers after Basil II (928–1025) allowed the once-formidable armed forces to fall apart. At the same time, the empire was faced with new, ambitious enemies, such as the Normans, who had taken southern Italy by 1071. But the greatest danger came from the Seljuk Turks in Asia Minor (present-day Turkey). By 1080, most of Asia Minor had been lost and Byzantium's fatal decline had begun. Desperate, Emperor Alexius sent embassies to Western Europe asking for help. The result was the series of military expeditions known as the Crusades (see pp.146–47). However, instead of helping their eastern brothers, the crusaders mostly pursued their own interests. Intended to bring support to Constantinople, the so-called Fourth Crusade was the single most catastrophic event in Byzantine history. In 1204 a crusader army that was supposedly on its way to defend the Holy Land, brutally sacked the city of Constantinople and dismantled the empire.

Bronze horses stolen from Constantinople
These horses once adorned the Hippodrome erected by Constantine in Constantinople. Looted by the Venetians in 1204, they were installed in St Mark's basilica, Venice.

The Virgin Mary and Jesus are depicted in the highly stylized form of Byzantine icons.

Constantine I, the first Christian emperor and founder of Constantinople, offers the city itself to Mary and Jesus.

AFTER

In 1204 much of the Byzantine Empire was divided up between its crusader conquerors, but it survived and limped on until the fall of Constantinople to the Ottomans in 1453.

CONSEQUENCES OF THE SACKING
After the Fourth Crusade Constantinople was left underpopulated and in ruins. The city never really recovered. Chief beneficiary was the **Venetian Republic** which took over much of the Byzantines' trade as well as shipping fabulous quantities of loot back to Venice.

CONSTANTINOPLE BECOMES ISTANBUL
On 29 May, 1453, the **Ottoman Turks 152–53 ≫** took Constantinople, renaming it **Istanbul**, and making it the capital of the Ottoman Empire **186–87 ≫**.

STOPPING THE OTTOMANS
Once Byzantium had fallen, the Ottomans completed their conquest of the Balkans with ease. Their progress was finally stopped by the Habsburg victory at Vienna in 1683.

« BEFORE

The Crusades

For more than two centuries, the Middle East became a battleground in which Christian armies from Europe, inspired by an ideology of legitimate religious warfare, fought Muslims for control of the Holy Land (Palestine).

The spread of Islam on the borders of Europe coincided with the growth of a pious and aggressive warrior society in Western Europe.

ANGEL GABRIEL

THE SPREAD OF ISLAM
In 610 CE, following a visitation from the Angel Gabriel, **the prophet Muhammad** proclaimed the religion of **Allah** (God) among the tribes of the Arab Peninsula. **Islam took root** over much of Asia, North Africa, and parts of Europe **‹‹122–23**.

THE EUROPEAN SITUATION
By the 11th century, as opportunities for territorial expansion within Western Europe declined, an aggressive warrior society began to turn its attention to the lands outside Europe's borders. The Christian **Byzantine empire ‹‹144–45** had long acted as a buffer between Western Europe and Asia, but in 1071 the Byzantine army was destroyed by the Muslim **Seljuk Turks** at Manzikert.

I n 1095 CE, in a small field outside the cathedral at Claremont in France, Pope Urban II made an impassioned appeal. He called for a military expedition to liberate the holy city of Jerusalem and free Christians from the yoke of Muslim rule. In exchange, Urban stated that any soldiers who died fighting the enemy would earn remission from all sins. The crowd erupted with cries of "God wills it!". Over the next two years alone, thousands of crusaders, as these soldiers became known, took the cross and joined this pilgrimage to the Holy Land.

Foundations of the crusade
Urban's sermon may have been the catalyst, but the roots of the crusades stretch further back.

KEY
- ■ Muslim lands
- ■ Greek Christian (Orthodox)
- □ Roman Church (Papal authority)

11th-century religion
Three faiths dominated Europe, North Africa, and the Middle East: Catholicism, Islam, and the Greek Orthodox Church of the Byzantine empire.

Scandinavia
Canterbury
Paris
RUSSIA
EUROPE
Kiev
Seville
BYZANTIUM
Rome
Steppes
ASIA
Constantinople
Asia Minor
Manzikert
Bukhara
Samarkand
Antioch
Edessa
Aleppo
PERSIA
Lahore
Acre
Damietta
Jerusalem
Isfahan
AFRICA
EGYPT
INDIA
Medina
ARABIA
Mecca

0   1000 km
0   1000 miles

The crusades to the east
There were several major expeditions from Europe to the Middle East and Egypt in the period 1095–1272 CE.

Crusader sword
This type of broad-bladed sword, with simple cross-guard and pommel, became popular during the Crusades. It would have been devastating against lightly armoured opponents.

Most obviously, Urban was responding to the political situation in the east: following the defeat of the Byzantine armies at Manzikert in 1071, the emperor had sent an appeal to the pope for military assistance. Urban saw the proposed expedition east as a chance to flex papal power and check the expansion of Islam, as well as an opportunity to conquer what he perceived as pagan areas.

The huge popular response to his appeal, although unexpected, was the product of a number of factors, including the growth of a fervent lay piety over the preceding centuries and the need of a land-hungry warrior class to find an outlet for their martial energies. The crusades united these impulses by legitimizing the concept of religious warfare.

The First Crusade
The first of the armies to enter Anatolia, in modern-day Turkey, met with disaster. The "people's crusade" was a ragged and disordered movement of peasants, knights, and religious zealots led by a charismatic preacher, Peter the Hermit. Lacking military discipline and blinded by religious fervour, the band was massacred soon after entering Seljuk Turk territory.

The army that followed was a far more professional body: a largely Frankish (northern French) force made up of several princely armies. Trekking overland through inhospitable country, they captured the heavily fortified town of Antioch in Syria in 1098. A year later the crusaders arrived

The Church of the Holy Sepulchre had been destroyed by the caliph in 1009. It was rebuilt after the crusaders conquered Jerusalem in 1099.

The Patriarch of Jerusalem was the spiritual leader of the kingdom and representative of the pope in Rome.

Mounted and heavily armoured knights formed the heavy shock troops of the crusader armies.

The defence of Jerusalem
Crusader knights guard the Church of the Holy Sepulchre in Jerusalem. As the traditional site of Jesus's crucifixion and burial, this was the physical destination for pilgrims and crusaders alike.

1189–1192 The Third Crusade is led by the kings of France and England and the German emperor. English king, Richard I, makes a truce with Saladin.

1198 The Fourth Crusade never reaches the Holy Land. Crusader armies are diverted to fight the Christian Byzantine empire at Constantinople.

1291 Following the **fall of the port of Acre** the remaining Crusader states in the Holy Land are evacuated.

1095 Pope Urban II preaches the crusade at the **Council of Clermont**. The response exceeds all expectations.

1145–49 The Second Crusade fails to recapture Edessa, lost 1144.

1217–21 The Fifth Crusade captures Damietta in Egypt but surrenders before reaching Cairo.

1248–54 The Seventh Crusade ends with the capture of Louis IX of France, who is ransomed for 50,000 gold bezants.

1050	1100	1150	1200	1250

1071 Seljuk Turks destroy the Byzantine army at the **Battle of Manzikert**. The Byzantine emperor appeals to the Pope for assistance.

1099 The First Crusade ends with the **capture of Jerusalem** and the formation of Christian Crusader states in the Holy Land.

1187 After unifying the Muslims in the east, Saladin destroys the Christian armies at **the Battle of Hattin**. By the end of 1187, Saladin **recaptures Acre and Jerusalem**.

1228–29 The Sixth Crusade ends when Frederick II negotiates the return of Jerusalem and a 10-year truce with the Ayyubid sultan of Egypt.

1244 Jerusalem is retaken from the Christians by the Ayyubids.

1270 Louis IX of France is diverted to Tunis in North Africa during **the Eighth Crusade**. He dies before he can set sail for the Holy Land.

The fleur-de-lis was the emblem of the king of France. Most of the leaders of the First Crusade were Frankish.

The imperial eagle was the emblem of the Holy Roman Empire. German emperors led armies to the east in 1145, 1189, and 1228.

SALADIN

Founder of the Ayyubid dynasty and unifier of Muslim states in the Middle East against the crusaders, Saladin was also renowned throughout Christendom as an honourable and chivalrous leader. Contemporary accounts abound with stories of his gallantry.

In 1187 Saladin annihilated the crusader armies at Hattin. When Jerusalem fell three months later he allowed neither massacre nor looting. Although he failed to expel the crusaders from the Holy Land, and was defeated at Arsuf in 1191 by Richard I of England, Saladin paved the way for the later elimination of the Crusader states.

1,000 The number of beds in the pilgrim hospital run by the Order of St John of Jerusalem, also known as the Knights Hospitallers. During the 12th century the knights adopted a military role.

members took vows of poverty and chastity to dedicate their lives to the defence of the Holy Land. These warrior monks were the closest thing the crusaders had to a standing, professional army. They often pursued their own interests at the expense of their fellow Christians, but they built a fearsome reputation – after the battle of Hattin in 1187, the sultan Saladin (see above) allowed the ransom of all prisoners except for the Templars and Hospitallers, whom he had executed.

The later crusades

Never again would the Muslim states of the Holy Land be so unprepared as they had been at the time of the First Crusade. A second crusade was organized in 1145, following the fall of Edessa, but failed to retake the city from Nureddin, a Muslim ruler who had united much of Syria against the crusaders. By the 1180s, most of the Muslim inhabitants of Syria and Palestine were united under Nureddin's successor, the sultan Saladin. In 1187 Saladin destroyed the armies of the crusader kingdoms at Hattin and seized Jerusalem, gallantly sparing the lives of the Christians in the city.

Subsequent crusades to Egypt and the Holy Land enjoyed some success but many setbacks. The Fourth Crusade, in 1198, never made it to the Holy Land, instead seizing the Christian city of Constantinople from Byzantium (see pp.144–45). Major expeditions from Europe were sporadic, and the fortunes of the crusader states altered with the balance of power in the east.

After the fall of the port of Acre in 1291 defence of the mainland territories became impossible. The remaining Christian cities were abandoned and the crusaders expelled from the Holy Land.

Siege machine
Long sieges, such as Antioch and Jerusalem in 1097–99, were common during the crusades. Siege machines such as this trebuchet were used by both sides to bombard opposing soldiers, fortifications, and siege towers.

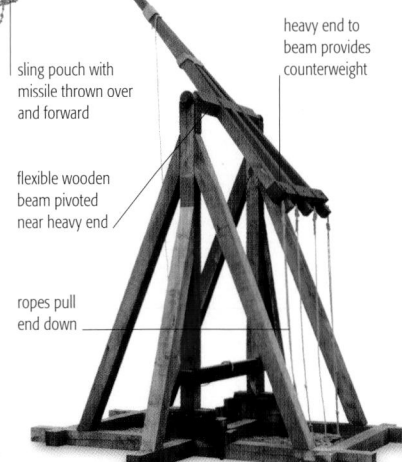

heavy end to beam provides counterweight

sling pouch with missile thrown over and forward

flexible wooden beam pivoted near heavy end

ropes pull end down

AFTER »

Greed and political expediency gradually came to undermine the ideals of the early crusades.

CRUSADES IN EUROPE
The crusading ideal of war against the enemies of Christianity in the Holy Land soon lost focus. As early as 1193 Pope **Celestine III** proclaimed a crusade against **pagans in northern Europe**. In 1209, **Innocent III** announced a crusade against **heretics** within France – the **Albigensian Crusade**. By the 1230s popes were using crusades as a political weapon against rivals.

END OF THE KNIGHTS TEMPLAR
Military orders such as the Templars grew immensely **rich and powerful**, attracting much criticism. In 1307, intending to seize their assets, **Philip IV** of France charged the Templars with **heresy**. Pope **Clement V** disbanded the order.

at Jerusalem. After a lengthy siege the city fell. The crusaders slaughtered all Muslims and Jews in the city – a bloody climax that set the tone for much that was to follow.

Outremer

The crusaders now held a thin strip of coast in Palestine along which they established various crusader states, including the Kingdom of Jerusalem, the Counties of Edessa and Tripoli, and the Principality of Antioch. These territories

Templar seal
United in the service of Christ, two knights are shown sharing one horse.

were known collectively as *Outremer*, meaning "the land overseas".

In time, the crusaders built huge fortresses to defend these outposts, such as Crac de Chevalier. Despite this, their grip on the territories was never strong: they were often threatened by resurgent Muslim forces, and relied on further crusades from Europe to come to their aid. The period also saw the formation of the military orders, the Templars and the Hospitallers, whose

BEFORE

Long before the Vikings spread across the continent, Europe had experienced raids by outsiders and established trade links with the east.

FLOCKING TO AN EMPIRE
During 5th century many different peoples moved from further east to trade, and often to settle in the relative **safety and prosperity** of the Roman Empire **《 64–67**

PEOPLE PRESSURE
During the 4th and 5th centuries BCE immigrants arrived in such numbers that they destabilized a Roman world already in crisis **《 102–03**.

BREAKING UP THE EMPIRE
ROMULUS AUGUSTUS The Roman empire in Western Europe ended when the boy-emperor, Romulus Augustus, was deposed by his own general, Odoacer, in 476 **《 102–03**. Without Rome's protection, many **small kingdoms, principalities, and lordships** were more vulnerable to raiders.

There is a great deal of debate about why warriors from Denmark, Norway, and Sweden left their homelands and began to raid places in Western Europe in the 8th century CE. Most historians believe there was rapid population growth in Scandinavia during the 7th and 8th centuries, and, because of the harsh climate and rough terrain, there was limited land suitable for farming. This competition for land meant that not only was food in short supply, but local rulers began to fight among each other in order to expand their control over resources. One alternative, especially to a warrior society such as that of Scandinavia, was raiding. To the south

northeast coast of England, was pillaged by a Viking raid in 793 CE. Many of its monks were left dead. In 795 CE, monastic communities on the Scottish island of Iona, and Rathlin Island, off the northern coast of Ireland, suffered a similar fate. The situation was so bad that monks prayed for stormy weather so the "Northmen" would be unable to set sail.

The Vikings' focus on monasteries meant that contemporary writers, all of whom were monks themselves, often portrayed them as enemies of God. They recorded the calamities that befell their brothers with genuine anguish and horror. But while the Viking attacks were vicious and

highly skilled. The ships were light, with shallow bottoms, and could be sailed far inland on rivers and lakes, taken out of the water, and dragged across land to another river.

Planning to stay
The nature of Viking involvement outside Scandinavia began to change during the 9th century. At first, they began to overwinter on islands in the Seine and at the mouth of the Loire River in France. Then, in 850 CE, Charles II of France gave a group of Vikings land to settle on in exchange for aid in a conflict against his brother, Emperor Lothar. Events like this gave the Vikings influence over local power

Raiders and Traders

From the 8th to 10th centuries CE, Scandinavians were both the terror of Europe and its most active traders and explorers. These people swept through the treasure houses of monasteries, founded towns and cities, and even became rulers in England and France. They were called the Vikings.

lay the Carolingian empire (see pp.134–35), Anglo-Saxon England, and Ireland; all were lands divided or weakened by internal power struggles.

Lightning attacks
The first Viking raids were carried out against soft targets, such as villages and monasteries, on the coast of Frisia (Netherlands) and eastern England. Monasteries were particularly attractive to the Vikings because they were rarely fortified, and were filled with spectacular treasures donated by local Christians. The monks were unable to defend themselves, and the Vikings, who were not Christian, had no qualms about sacking the monasteries and making off with gold and silver chalices, crosses, and book covers. The monastery at Lindisfarne, on the

ruthless, they were not deliberately anti-Christian, as some of the records suggest.

Vikings also threatened the relatively powerful Carolingian empire in the last years of Charlemagne's reign. His death marked a decline in central power and a rise in political instability. The Vikings exploited this power vacuum and expanded their attacks. By the 830s CE, they were able to raid the important town of Dorestad on the river Rhine three times.

Element of surprise
Early Viking raids were so effective because they struck unexpectedly. By the time locals could organize their defence, the Vikings were gone. They fought using the same basic weapons as their opponents, such as swords, spears, and axes. However, Viking long ships were superior in design and their sailors

Viking sword
Viking swords were often buried with their owners to accompany them on their journey to the hall of the dead warriors, Valhalla.

struggles, and encouraged them travel to settle outside Scandinavia. From this point on, even though they were often involved in raids, the Vikings became much more interested in acquiring land and establishing trade. Many kingdoms paid them off with huge amounts of silver and land in order to stop attacks. Between c.991–c.1014, for example, the English paid 68,000kg (150,000lb) of silver as tribute to Scandinavian kings, a payment known as Danegeld. A band of Vikings established the Duchy of Normandy in France when a chieftain named Rollo was given Rouen and the surrounding

Viking war helmet
Viking helmets were similar to those used by other cultures at this time. The myth that their helmets had horns attached to them probably came about because Vikings were often compared to demons and devils.

HOW WE KNOW
ARABIC DIRHAMS

The Vikings raided and traded across an enormous geographical area. We know this through the types of coins found at Viking sites, in graves, and connected to towns. This 9th century hoard of Arabic dirhams was found at a Viking site in Scotland, and provides proof that Scandinavians sailed from the Baltic and along the rivers of Russia to reach the economic spheres of both Byzantium (see pp.144–45) and the Islamic caliphate (see pp.122–23). Arabic coins of a similar date have also been found at Viking trading centres at Birka in Sweden and Hedeby, Denmark.

Viking war spear
This spearhead was attached to a long pole, and thrown at the enemy, much the same way a modern javelin is thrown.

Viking war axe
The axe is the weapon that Vikings are most identified with. It could be wielded as a hand weapon or used for throwing.

Iron trading weights
These brass-covered weights were found in Hemingby, Sweden. Each has been stamped with a different number of circles corresponding to its weight.

Crystal necklace
This crystal necklace of Viking origin with Eastern elements demonstrates how Scandinavian craftsmen adopted the styles and techniques of the various cultures they came into contact with.

Gold bridle
Viking metalwork was complex and often consisted of intertwining animal shapes.

Viking longship
This ship was excavated from a royal burial site at Oseberg, Norway, and probably dates from 815–20 CE. While it is very similar to the type of ship used for everyday travel, it was almost certainly ceremonial in nature, as it is heavy and highly decorated.

longship was built of fine oak

a square sail was attached to this mast

Viking brooch
Brooches are frequently found in Viking graves, and were used to fasten cloaks.

Viking longship at sail
A viking longship was usually about 21m (70ft) long and 5m (16ft) wide. The prow was carved with interlaced decorations, and a square sail was rigged to the mast.

15 oar ports were located on each side of the longship

"Behold the church of St Cuthbert **spattered with the blood of the priests of God.**"
ALCUIN OF YORK, 793

AFTER

The Viking Age came to an end during the 11th century. The kingdoms of Norway, Sweden, and Denmark evolved into more centralized states, as was happening elsewhere in Europe.

END OF THE VIKING AGE
Launching a lightning raid on a centralized state did not have the same effect as it did in the 9th and 10th centuries because, by 1500, these states had developed **organized armies and navies**. This meant that communities were able to defend themselves against attacks of the kind that the Vikings carried out.

ATLANTIC SLAVE TRADE
Raids later became central to the establishment of the Atlantic slave trade **280–81 »** in the 16th, 17th, and 18th centuries, where communities in western Africa bore the brunt of such attacks.

CARIBBEAN RAIDERS
Raid tactics similar to those of the Vikings' were used during the same period in the Caribbean, where European navies, privateers, and pirates **sacked trading posts** and **preyed on shipping routes**.

THE HANSEATIC LEAGUE
Trading in the later medieval period (1100–1500) could be dangerous. In the 12th century, merchants from cities in northern Germany and the Baltic formed an alliance called the **Hanseatic League 276–77 »**. They traded between the Baltic, the Netherlands, and England, and carried goods from Arabia and beyond across the Russian steppes. Kiev and Novgorod, founded by Vikings, became gateways to the East. At its height **merchants from over 60 cities** had joined, but by the end of the 15th century the league was in decline.

area by Charles the Simple in c.911 CE. Rollo's great-great-great grandson became William the Conqueror (see pp.138–39). Between 1016–1035, a Dane, Cnut the Great, ruled both Denmark and England.

The Vikings also became great traders, sailing from Iceland to Russia and the Islamic empire. As early as 841 CE a permanent Viking settlement was founded at Dublin and the ancient English city of York. Vikings are even credited with being the founders of the Grand Duchy of Kiev, the forerunner of the kingdom of Muscovy and, later, Russia.

Battle of 'Ayn Jalut

United by Genghis Khan in 1206, the Mongols formed a group of tribes that embarked on a series of raids across Asia. By 1260, they had conquered an area stretching from the Pacific Ocean to the Mediterranean Sea, and were considered invincible. On 3 September 1260, the Mongols reached 'Ayn Jalut in Palestine where they were met by the Mamluk Sultans.

The children and grandchildren of the Mongol leader Genghis Khan (see pp.112–13) took control of the Mongol tribes on his death in 1227. One of these grandchildren, Hülegü Khan, was given power over part of the Mongol army. He took this army into northwest Persia in 1255, raiding and looting as he went. In 1258 he defeated the Abbasid Caliphate (see pp.122–23), capturing and destroying the city of Baghdad, and massacring the inhabitants. The Mongols now controlled Iraq and Persia. From here the Mongols pushed westwards towards the Mediterranean. They overran Palestine and Syria, capturing the main city, Damascus, in 1259.

With Palestine and Syria conquered, Hülegü turned his attention to Egypt, the next major power to the west. He sent a message to its rulers, the Mamluks, asking them to surrender without a fight. Originally slaves taken from Turkish tribes and formed into an army by the previous rulers of Egypt, the Mamluks had overthrown the old government and taken power for themselves. Their new government was based on military principles making it ideally suited for waging war and unlikely to give in to threats. The Mamluk response was to kill Hülegü's envoys, and march toward the Mongol army in Palestine.

At the same time, Hülegü was informed that his brother, the Mongol Emperor (or "Great Khan") was dying. With ambitions to gain control of the Mongol Empire for himself, Hülegü took most of the army with him and headed back to his brother.

Meanwhile, the Mamluks entered Palestine with an army equal in size to the Mongol force Hülegü had left behind. At 'Ayn Jalut – also known as Goliath's Spring – they defeated the Mongols, using their heavy cavalry to great effect. The Mamluks took control over Syria and Palestine, expelling the remaining Crusaders (see pp.146–47) in 1291.

The Mongols had never been so emphatically defeated before, and this halted their conquests to the west. The internal fighting that followed split the Mongol tribes into different sections. In Iraq and Persia, they became the Illkhanid dynasty and gradually took on the customs, religion, and language of the people they had conquered.

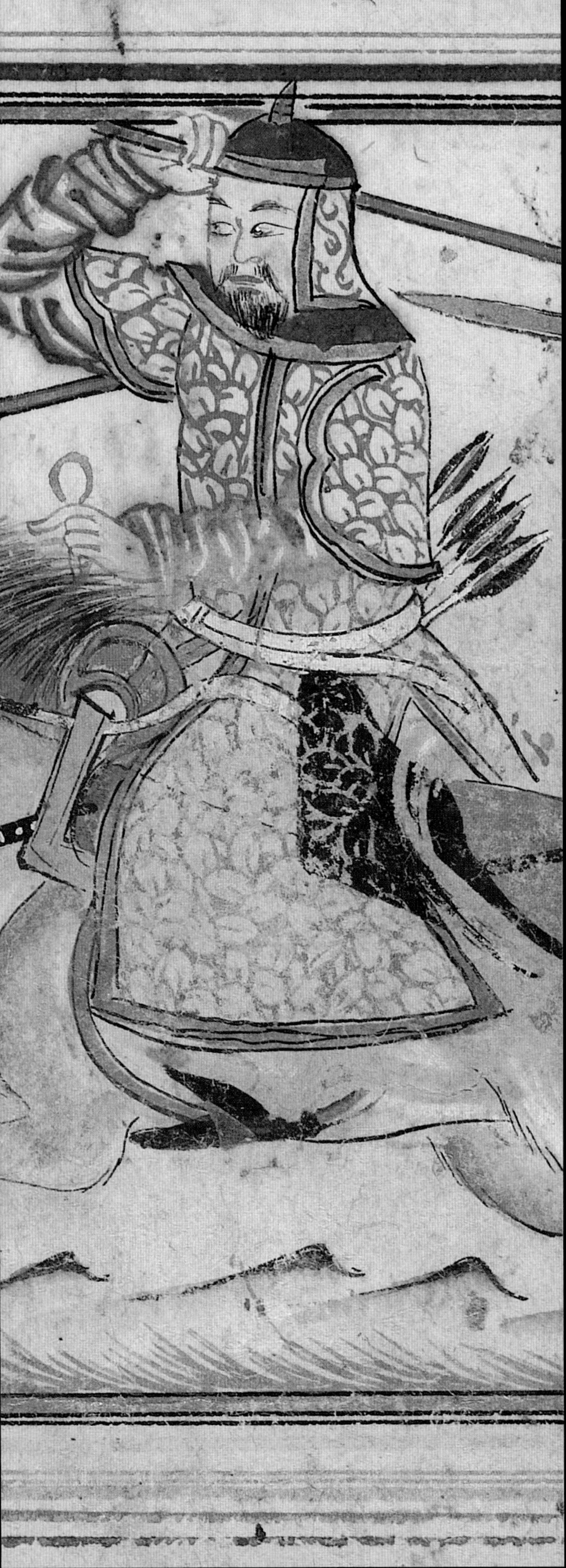

Mongol soldiers
This 13th-century Persian picture depicts Mongol soldiers in battle. The Mongol Empire was founded by Genghis Khan in 1206 and was one of the largest empires in history with an estimated population of 100 million people. At its height it included territories from East Asia to central Europe.

> **"**It is for you to fly and **for us to pursue**… Fortresses will not detain us.**"**
>
> A MESSAGE FROM HÜLEGÜ TO THE MAMLUKS DEMANDING THEIR SURRENDER, 1260.

BEFORE

The Turkish tribes that founded the Ottoman Empire were originally semi-nomadic farmers who inhabited the steppes of Central Asia.

THE TURKS

Turkish tribes made early contact with the Islamic world through trade, warfare, and missionaries. They were also used as **slave warriors** by the **Abbasid caliphate ‹‹ 122–23** – the Islamic empire based in Baghdad – which led to the conversion of the Turks to Islam. The Ottoman lands in Anatolia bordered wealthy non-Muslim areas, which brought opportunities for expansion.

ANATOLIA

Before the influx of the Muslim Turkish tribes, Anatolia was ruled by the **Byzantine Empire ‹‹ 144–45.** It was inhabited mainly with small communities of settled Greek Christian farmers, interspersed with larger towns such as Nicaea (now the city of Iznik in Turkey).

Seljuk soldiers
This 13th-century stone relief depicts the armoured warriors who were used to maintain Seljuk power. The Seljuks were a Sunni Muslim dynasty that ruled parts of Central Asia and the Middle East from 11th–14th century.

The Rise of Ottoman Power

The Ottoman Empire was founded by a small group of nomadic Turkish warriors in Anatolia (modern-day Turkey). It lasted for 700 years, becoming a vast empire whose power and influence spanned the globe.

In the 10th century, the caliphate based in Baghdad (see pp.122–25) began to fragment into separate political entities, until it controlled only the provinces immediately around it. At the end of the 10th century, the remains of the caliphate were conquered by Turkish tribes from Central Asia. The Seljuk family who led the tribes took power as *sultans* (from the Turkish word for "authority"), restoring political authority to the caliphate, while exercising real power themselves through the figurehead caliphs. Although the Seljuks took over the existing system of government, their power was inherently unstable as it relied heavily on their nomadic warriors, who frequently clashed with settled peoples.

In 1071, the Seljuks defeated the Byzantine emperor in eastern Anatolia, and Byzantine rule was replaced by that of the Rum Seljuks, who were a branch of the Seljuk dynasty. This, and the fact Anatolia was well suited to the way of life practised by the Turks, led to an influx of semi-nomadic tribes.

Disintegration

Another group of nomadic peoples from Central Asia were the Mongols (pp.204–05), who invaded most of Asia and parts of Europe. By 1258, the invading Mongol army had conquered most of Anatolia, Iran, and Iraq, replacing the Seljuks with the Ilkhanid dynasty (from the Mongol word for leader, *khan*). The Turks in Anatolia were forced to move westwards into areas previously ruled by the Byzantines.

The Ilkhanid hold over Anatolia was never strong, and the peninsula soon began to disintegrate into multiple tribes and principalities. One of these small groups was led by Osman, son of Ertughrul, after whom the Ottoman Empire was named. This group was located in a strategically important area controlling the approach to Constantinople from the east. From here, the Ottomans managed to take over many Byzantine cities in Anatolia, which brought them more wealth and resources. The Ottomans then annexed land along the Dardanelles, which allowed them to control the crossing to Europe.

Ottoman war helmet
This battle helmet dates from c.1500. Technological advances in warfare gave the Ottomans an edge in battle.

Finding a barrier
blocking the route to the estuary on one side of Constantinople, the Ottomans dragged their ships overland to surround the city.

The creation of an empire

In the mid-14th century, the Ottomans aided the Byzantine emperor John VI Kantakouzenos in a civil war, and were rewarded with their first lands in Europe, on the Gallipoli peninsula. At the same time, the Ottomans expanded their lands in central and western Anatolia. After this, they spread into Europe, moving through eastern Thrace and across the Balkans. It was then that they probably encountered artillery for the first time.

KEY

- ■ Nucleus of Ottoman Empire c.1300
- ■ Conquests of Osman I, c.1300–26
- ■ Conquests of Orkhan I, c.1326–62
- ■ Conquests of Murad I, c.1362–89
- ■ Conquests of Bayezid I, c.1389–1402
- ■ Further Ottoman conquest by 1481
- ■ Vassal of Ottoman Empire by 1481
- ■ Under Venetian control c.1450
- ● Siege

Ottoman Empire

The Ottoman Empire was very extensive until the end of the 15th century. At the centre was Constantinople, whose fall to the Ottomans in 1453 is shown opposite. Its central location made its capture essential if the Ottomans were to rule in both Asia and Europe successfully.

High towers aided the defenders. The Ottomans used siege towers to try to get the attackers to the same height, but these were also repelled.

Constantine XI Palaeologus, the last reigning Byzantine emperor, personally led the final defence of the city and died in the final attack.

The city walls withstood numerous assaults before being breached. The Ottomans tried to mine under the walls, but were thwarted each time.

The Siege of Constantinople
This 16th-century fresco shows the 1453 siege of Constantinople. The Ottomans had besieged Constantinople twice before, but had failed each time. Three days of looting followed its fall on 29 May 1453, and Sultan Mehmed II, who led the attack, spent much of the rest of his reign restoring and repopulating the city.

Ottoman artillery was far superior to Byzantine artillery. Huge cannons eventually breached the city walls allowing them to enter.

Hagia Sophia Church in Constantinople was converted into a mosque immediately after the capture of the city.

The waters of the Bosphorus protect Constantinople. Mehmet II fortified castles on either side of the Bosphorus to prevent reinforcements arriving by sea.

AFTER

OTTOMAN SULTAN (1432–81)

MEHMED II

Mehmed II was sultan of the Ottoman Empire from 1451–81. This 15th-century watercolour shows him in a peaceful pose. The reality was very different. One of Mehmed's first acts as sultan was to have his infant brother strangled to prevent further civil wars. His reign was one of ceaseless campaigning, which extended the empire to include most of the Balkans and Greece, Anatolia, the upper Euphrates valley, and sections of the Black Sea coast.

Later wars with Hungary, which was threatened by Ottoman expansion, led to the adoption of artillery-based military tactics. It was this development that made the Ottoman conquest of Constantinople possible.

Attacks by a neighbouring principality in Anatolia in 1397 forced the Ottomans to take action, resulting in the conquest of most of eastern Anatolia. This bordered on the territory of the Mongol warlord Timur, whose empire stretched across Central Asia, southern Russia, Iran, and Azerbaijan. In 1402, Timur invaded Anatolia, capturing Bayezid, the Ottoman leader, and plundered Anatolia for a year. The remaining small portion of Anatolian territory, and Ottoman lands in Europe, were split between the sons of Bayezid. Civil war ensued for two

Fritware pottery
Produced in the Middle East in the 13th century, Fritware combined ground glass with clay to produce white ceramics.

generations. The eventual winner, Murad II, spent most of his life fighting to restore the lands the Ottomans had lost to Timur and securing his borders. He abdicated in 1444 in favour of his 12-year old son, but was recalled by his viziers (ministers) when the king of Hungary attacked the empire. At Murad's death in 1451, the Ottoman Empire dominated western and northern Anatolia and a large part of the Balkans.

Murad was succeeded by one of the Ottoman Empire's most able leaders, Mehmed II (see left). After securing his borders, he laid siege to the city of Constantinople in 1453. Just 50 years after the near destruction of the Ottomans, despite civil war and in-fighting, they captured a wealthy imperial city, and brought down the remains of the Byzantine Empire.

The Ottoman Empire continued to be a pre-eminent cultural and military power until the 17th century and beyond.

IZNIK POTTERY
Iznik pottery became popular in the 16th century. Under sultans such as Suleyman the Magnificent (1520–66) the Ottomans enjoyed a golden age of cultural development **186–87 ≫**.

IZNIK POTTERY

THE JANISSARIES
Originally the sultan's household infantry, the Ottoman Empire used the janissaries in all its **major campaigns** of the 16th–17th centuries **186–87 ≫**. By the 18th century the janissaries even dominated government. After revolting in 1826, they were abolished. **JANISSARY**

BEFORE «

After the end of the Roman Empire, Europe's cities and trading networks fell into decline.

THE ROMAN EMPIRE

Under the Romans « **60–69**, a wide network of cities and roads was established throughout Western Europe and **trade flourished**. Large towns were built even near the frontiers of the empire, such as at Trier in Germany. After 476 CE, when the last emperor was deposed in the West, **roads fell into disrepair** and some **towns were abandoned**. Political insecurity meant people hoarded their money rather than using it for trade and the economy became reliant on **bartering**.

ROMAN GATE AT TRIER

Throughout the early part of this period, urban populations remained low. Some old Roman towns developed into religious centres, with bishops becoming the most powerful of the local lords. Other towns were used mainly as places for defence. Trading continued, but widespread unrest disrupted travel across Europe. With fewer coins being minted – a result of shortages of silver and political instablity – people had to rely on exchanging one good for another, or bartering.

From the 11th century onwards, Western Europe began to stabilize. The supply of silver increased when deposits were found in the German province of Saxony. This meant that more coins could be produced and trade could be carried out more easily. However, it was the towns of the Italian peninsula that were first to benefit from these developments. Italy was ideally situated in the centre of the

bankers, lending money to rulers across Europe. The Riccardi family of Lucca effectively financed the reign and costly wars of Edward I of England (1271–1307), for example, although they would later go bankrupt when subsequent English kings refused to pay back the loans. Pisa, Genoa, and Venice all became great ports. Venice

Wealthy Flemish couple
This oil painting by Matsys depicts a Flemish money-changer and his wife. The clothes, books, and glasswear indicate the prosperity of the new merchant class.

Cities and Trade

Between 600 CE and 1450, the cities and towns of medieval Europe began to expand from simple defensive settlements into cosmopolitan centres of trade, power, and art. In Italy, cities became independent states, some building empires. In Northern Europe, the towns of Flanders became centres of manufacturing.

> "He who is not a **citizen** [city-dweller] is not fully a **man**."
>
> REMIGIO DE GIROLAMI, DOMINICAN FRIAR, 14TH-CENTURY FLORENCE

Bridging Britain and the Continent
This map from 1572 shows all the principal towns in Flanders, including Bruges and Antwerp. These towns were major manufacturing centres and, in the medieval period, specialized in processing English wool.

Mediterranean and was the natural crossroads for goods coming from east and west. Most importantly, many of its towns were effectively independent of overlords and emperors. The German Holy Roman Emperors Frederick Barbarossa and Frederick II were unsuccessful in their attempts to intervene in Italian affairs in the 12th–13th century (see right). This left the Italian cities free to run their own affairs and concentrate on trade.

Italian city-states

Textile production, banking, and shipping made enormous fortunes for the Italian cities and the families involved in these occupations. Tuscany, especially the cities of Florence and Siena, produced fine woollen cloth that was exported across Europe. Silk was produced around Milan and Pavia in the north. The Italians were also accomplished

Milanese gold ducat
This 15th-century gold coin could be transported more easily than the equivalent value in silver.

also managed to build an empire in the Balkans and Greece, making the city the principal maritime power in Europe.

The great success of Italy, however, was Florence, whose fortune was built on textile production and banking, and on its central position on the Italian peninsula. Florence was an oligarchy, a society ruled by the wealthiest merchants. During frequent struggles between the Germanic Holy Roman Empire and the Papacy in the 11th–12th centuries, it always backed the popes and gained privileged access to the lucrative Roman market as a result. The city aggressively guarded its position within Tuscany and eventually came to dominate the other banking cities of Siena and Lucca, and the port of Pisa. In time, one family, the Medicis, came to dominate the city.

The Italian city-states made many important economic advances. They issued gold coins, which made it easier to deal in goods of a high value than

BATTLE OF LEGNANO

The Battle of Legnano, on 29 May 1176, marked the point at which the city-states of Northern Italy gained autonomy from the Holy Roman Emperor, Frederick Barbarossa. A group of these towns, called the Lombard League, objected to the emperor's interference in their internal affairs and, supported by Pope Alexander III, rebelled. The emperor looked sure to triumph when he laid waste the city of Milan. However, the Lombard League defeated his armies at Legnano, northwest of Milan, and he was forced to make peace.

when using silver coins. They also invented the modern financial practices of accounting and insurance to keep track of complicated transactions and prepare for losses due to shipwrecks.

Great trading networks

In northern Europe, the county of Flanders grew rich and powerful during the 13th century. Like Italy, its geographical location was key to its development. It straddled an area of modern Belgium and the Netherlands that meant it was ideally positioned to benefit from trade with France, England, and the Holy Roman Empire.

Flanders was ruled by the counts of Flanders and Hainault, who encouraged trade by giving generous privileges to manufacturers. Huge annual fairs took place in the Flemish towns of Lille and Antwerp and further south in the Champagne region of France. Here, Flemish merchants could sell the cloth that Flanders was famous for producing.

The three main cities of Flanders were Ghent, Bruges, and Ypres. Known simply as "The Three Cities", they housed the workshops where wool was processed into cloth and the homes of the great merchants and guilds. The woolworker and merchant guilds became very powerful and came to dominate politics in the trading cities.

30,000 The number of workers involved in Florence's cloth industry in the 1330s, according to the Florentine chronicler Villani, out of an estimated population of just 100,000.

Bruges: canals for pleasure and trade
Trade transformed small towns, making merchants and artisans wealthy; this image from about 1520 shows Bruges at the height of its wealth and power. Bruges' North Sea port and canals formed vital arteries for trade, linking the town to England, Genoa, and other trading cities.

Flanders imported most of its raw materials, including wool to make cloth, from England. Flanders itself grew corn and rye, which it exported, and plants to make dye for the cloth manufacturers. However, trade was often damaged by regulations brought in by English kings, who sought to encourage home-grown cloth production. From 1277, Flanders began to look elswhere and started to trade more extensively with Genoa and other Italian cities.

Towers of San Gimignano
These towers in Tuscany were not built to protect the town from outsiders, but to defend rival family factions within the town from each other.

AFTER

The great centres of trade shifted away from Flanders and Italy during the 16th century.

ITALIAN CITY-STATES
A dispute between the French and Spanish over the **Duchy of Milan** turned Italy into a battlefield, damaging Italian trade. By 1527, the Holy Roman Emperor Charles V captured Rome and the city was sacked by his mercenaries, the Landsknechts.

After the **discovery of America**, the focus of trade shifted from the Mediterranean to the Atlantic. Countries such as England, Portugal, and Spain benefited, while Italian trade declined.

NORTHERN EUROPE
Flemish trade suffered as **English manufacturers** began to process their own wool, helped by Flemish immigrants. The **Hanseatic League**, a trading alliance of northern European towns, began to operate through the Baltic as far as England, providing a great stimulus for the northern economies.

LANDSKNECHT

BEFORE

The Maya, Aztecs, and Incas had the most advanced cultures of all the peoples living in America before the arrival of the Spanish.

THE MAYA

The **Maya ‹‹ 92–93** had lived in parts of Mexico, Guatemala, Belize, and Honduras for more than 1,000 years before the first great flowering of their culture c.300 CE.

THE AZTECS

The **Aztecs** are thought to have arrived in **central Mexico** in the 13th century, either from northern Mexico or from the southwest United States, but their exact origins are unclear.

THE INCAS

Beginning as a tribe in Cuzco in the 12th century, the Incas **spread** throughout **the Andes** regions of modern-day Peru, Ecuador, and Chile.

MISSISSIPPIAN CULTURE

Mississippian culture of the **southeast United States** had much in common with Mesoamerican cultures: **agriculture** based on **maize**, towns with wide plazas, and giant ceremonial mounds.

Pre-Columbian Americas

Characterized by their advances in astronomy and the arts, the Maya, Aztecs, and Incas had the richest and most complex societies in pre-Columbian America. Although distinct cultures, they shared similar traditions, including ritualized religious worship and a belief in the value of education and spirituality.

Whereas the Aztecs and Incas subjugated neighbouring peoples to create powerful empires, the Maya never formed an empire, nor did they have a single ruler or dominant capital city. They were a loose federation of city-states bound together by a common language, culture, and religion. The priest-rulers, who maintained power through their superior education and contacts with the gods, led the Maya to extraordinary achievements in mathematics, astronomy, architecture, fine arts, engineering, and writing.

Religious practices

Along with the Aztecs and Incas, the Maya had a pantheon of gods and their religious practices were based on their interpretation of the cycles of nature. These gods were rarely discrete entities but instead combined a wide variety of forms and ideas. They could be both young and old, take both human and animal forms, and often had a counterpart of the opposite sex.

The supreme deity of the Maya was Itzam Ná, who was represented iconically as an old man; he was the inventor of writing and patron of learning and sciences. His wife, IxChel, was goddess of the old Moon, as well as of weaving, medicine, and childbirth.

Religious rituals were performed to satisfy the gods and ensure order in the world. Ceremonies usually began with fasting and abstinence, followed by offerings of food,

Quetzalcoatl mask

This mask is thought to represent the Aztec god Quetzalcoatl, who is often depicted as a feathered serpent. It is made of cedar wood, and covered in turquoise mosaic, and the teeth are made of shell.

ornaments, dancing, and an occasional human sacrifice, although not on the scale of the Aztecs (see right). During the ceremonies the priests might impersonate the gods, or use hallucinogens to enhance their powers of divination. Finally, there would be feasting and drunkenness.

Later Maya civilization

Around 800 CE, some lowland Maya city-states went into decline, and by 900 CE had all but collapsed. Many explanations have been proposed for this, ranging from natural causes, such as disease or climate change, to soil exhaustion, war, or loss of control by the priest-aristocracy, but no theory can be proven absolutely.

After c.900 all the main Maya centres were in the northern part of the Yucatán. One, Chichén Itzá, was founded in the second half of the 8th century by a confederation of groups drawn from the Maya lowlands and the Itzá people, whose origins are unknown. The city, which appears to have experimented with new rituals and forms of shared government, was a thriving community in the 9th and 10th centuries, but collapsed after 1050.

The architecture of Chichén Itzá (see pp.158–59) is strikingly similar to that of Tula, the capital of the Toltecs 65km (40 miles) to the north of Mexico City, which flourished at around the same time. It is not exactly clear which of these cities influenced the other, but there must have been extensive cultural and trade links across central and southern parts of Mexico at this time.

The Aztec Empire

The Aztecs, or Mexica as they called themselves, were the most powerful people in the Valley of Mexico during the 15th and 16th centuries. Their capital, Tenochtitlán (now Mexico City), was founded in the 14th century on an island in Lake Texcoco. The marshes that surrounded the city might seem an unpromising environment, but the Aztecs were expert managers of water. They not only built dams to trap the fresh water from the rivers that flowed into the lake, they also grew a wide variety of crops on *chinampas*, fertile artificial islands created in the shallow lake.

Aztec society was class-based, with nobility at the top and slaves at the bottom. Education seems to have

> "We beheld… **cities** and towns **on the water**… it was like the things of **enchantment**."
>
> BERNAL DIAZ DE CASTILLO, ON ENTERING THE AZTEC CAPITAL TENOCHTITLÁN, 1519

Carving on stone lintel at Yaxchilan
This carving shows the accession rituals of the ruler Bird Jaguar. His wife Balam-Ix, sitting opposite, performs a blood sacrifice by drawing a rope through her tongue.

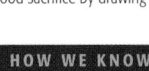

HOW WE KNOW

MAYA ASTRONOMY

The pyramid of Kukulcán at Chichén Itzá is a solar calendar, built on top of an earlier lunar calendar. The pyramid is full of symbolism: the four stairways leading to the central platform at the top each have 91 steps, totalling 364 – added to the central platform this makes 365, which is the number of days in the solar year. On either side of each stairway are nine terraces, which makes 18 on each face: a number that equals the number of months in the Maya solar calendar. The facing of each terrace contains 52 panels, representing the 52-year cycle during which the solar and religious calendars become realigned.

Stone sacrificial altar
The *cuauhxicalli*, which translates as "eagle gourd vessel", was used by Aztecs to make their most sacred offerings – human hearts.

been universal with schooling provided for both boys and girls. A boy's education included training to fight in wars because the Aztecs were a culture with a proud warrior tradition. By 1520 they had an empire that stretched right across Mexico from the Gulf of Mexico to the Pacific.

Like the Maya, the Aztecs had a large number of gods, related to the creation of the cosmos, to the Sun, and to fertility, death, and war. The two main temples on the pyramid in Tenochtitlán were dedicated to Huitzilopochtli, the god of war and Tlaloc, the god of rain and water. Another important god was

Quetzalcoatl, the feathered serpent god of wind, creativity, and fertility. Although the Aztecs had a rich culture that showed particular respect for poetry and song, they are remembered more for their human sacrifices. They believed that if they did not satisfy the gods with sacrifices, the Sun would not continue its journey across the sky.

Their rites took many different forms, some more brutal than others. One performed for the fire god, Huehueteotl, involved captives being anaesthetized and thrown into a fire. Before they died, priests retrieved them using hooks and removed their hearts. »

Civilizations of America *c.*1520

The Incas occupied the Andes mountains of South America. The Aztecs were centred on Tenochtitlán, now Mexico City, while the Maya inhabited the Yucatán Peninsula.

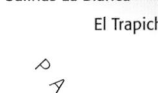

KEY
■ Aztec Empire
■ Inca Empire
■ Maya cultural region

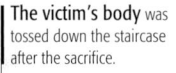

The beating heart was lifted into the air by the priest, who pronounced it "precious eagle cactus fruit" as an offering to the Sun god.

The priest drove a flint or obsidian knife into the breast of the victim, killing him almost instantaneously, then slit the arteries round the heart in order to pull it from the body.

The fire in which the heart was burnt was contained in a special vessel carved to represent an eagle.

Aztec sacrifice
In this depiction of an Aztec sacrifice, the pyramid temple represents the Sacred Snake Mountain, where, according to Aztec mythology, Huitzilopochtli, god of war and the Sun, dismembered his sister the Moon goddess Coyolxauqui.

The sacrificial victim was stretched out on his back over a stone by a number of assistants, usually four.

The victim's body was tossed down the staircase after the sacrifice.

In contrast, the method of honouring Tezcatlipoca consisted of choosing the most handsome and brave prisoner of war to be an incarnation of this complex god, who is often considered to be the rival of Quetzalcoatl. After a year of being pampered, the prisoner's last month was spent in the company of four "goddesses" who met his every desire. He would then be sacrificed.

The Incas

In South America, the Incas used both conquest and peaceful assimilation to expand their empire, until it was the largest in pre-Columbian America. Expansion was remarkably rapid, only starting in earnest in the reign of Pachacuti ("transformer of the earth"), which began around 1438. He and his son, Tupac Inca, created a huge federal system consisting of four provinces, each overseen by an Inca governor. Following each new conquest, magnificent roads, many of them paved, were built to link it to the capital Cuzco

Lost city of the Incas
Machu Picchu is the best preserved of the known Inca settlements. Abandoned in the 16th century, it is a fine example of Inca architecture and planning. High-quality building work and numerous shrines suggest that the site had religious importance.

and the rest of the empire. The Incas had no horses, nor had they discovered the wheel; messages were carried by relays of runners, while llamas served as pack animals. Their superior organization enabled them to absorb many existing states, the largest being Chimor on the coast of northern Peru, home to the influential Chimú culture. By Tupac Inca's death in 1493, Inca rule reached north to Quito in Ecuador.

Like other American cultures, the Incas built temples devoted to their gods, of whom there were many – the Sun god, Inti, being most important. Their worship included divination, and animal and human sacrifice. Although fairly rare, human sacrifice normally involved children taken from villages around the empire.

QUIPU

The Incas used collections of knotted coloured threads, called *quipu*, to record information. Spun from llama and alpaca hair, there might be just a few threads in a *quipu*, or hundreds or even thousands. Like decimalization, the system is based on the number 10. *Quipucamayocs* – accountants in Inca society – would use the *quipu* to perform simple mathematics, calculate taxes, and keep records of labour or livestock, for example. They were also used for censuses and for tax accounting, and to track events and time. Inca historians used them to tell the Spanish conquistadors their history, although it is unknown whether the strings simply recorded important numbers or contained the history itself.

Culture and architecture

Elaborate architecture is one of the most important legacies of Inca civilization. The complex stone temples built by the Incas used a mortarless construction process that had been developed between 300 BCE and 300 CE by the Pucara peoples in lands to the south of Cuzco, around Lake Titicaca. Each stone was carved to slot exactly into the one below it. Final adjustments were made by lowering the rock onto the one below, raising it again, and chipping away any sections on the lower rock where marks in the dust indicated that the fit was not perfect. This attention to detail meant that buildings constructed by this method were extremely stable.

Machu Picchu

Apart from Cuzco itself, much of which was damaged by the Spanish conquistadors (see AFTER), the most complete remaining example of the Incas' careful planning and building techniques is Machu Picchu. Situated 70km (40 miles) northwest of Cuzco, it is

Chimú pottery
The Chimú, one of the many peoples whose lands fell to the Incas in the 15th century, produced strikingly sculpted pottery figures. Their civilization owed much to the earlier Moche (see p.92).

Temple of Kukulcán
Dominating the centre of Chichén Itzá is the Temple of Kukulcán (Quetzalcoatl, the plumed serpent of the Aztecs and Toltecs). At the spring and autumn equinox the Sun creates undulating patterns of triangles of light on the temple stairway. These link up with the massive carvings of snakes' heads at the foot of the stairs, suggesting a giant serpent zigzagging down the face of the pyramid.

thought that Machu Picchu is a relatively recent construction, dating perhaps from the mid-15th century. The quality of the stonework, the high altitude of its position, and the many shrines that have been identified among its ruins seem to indicate that this settlement was much more important than a mere rural village. It has been suggested that Machu Picchu was one of a number of royal estates built by Pachacuti. According to Spanish chroniclers, these settlements were used as country estates when the Inca ruler travelled out of Cuzco.

Mississippian culture

Although not geographically close to the Mesoamerican civilizations of the Maya and the Aztecs, the Mississippians had many things in common with their cultures, most notably the construction of monumental pyramids. The arrival of the Spanish also spelled the end of their civilization but for different reasons (see AFTER).

The Mississippian culture developed from *c*.800 CE in the

valley of the Mississippi River and spread to much of midwestern, eastern, and southeastern North America. The Mississippian peoples lived in a highly structured society with close ties to the land: they relied on maize for their food. Key settlements were created at Spiro Mounds in eastern Oklahoma, Moundville in Alabama, and Etowah Mounds in northern Georgia; the most elaborate centre was based at Cahokia Mounds in Collinsville, Illinois.

Cahokia was inhabited from the 7th to the 14th centuries and at its peak, had around 30,000 inhabitants. The inhabitants made flat-topped mounds on which they built houses, burial buildings, and temples. Over 120 mounds were built and many were enlarged several times.

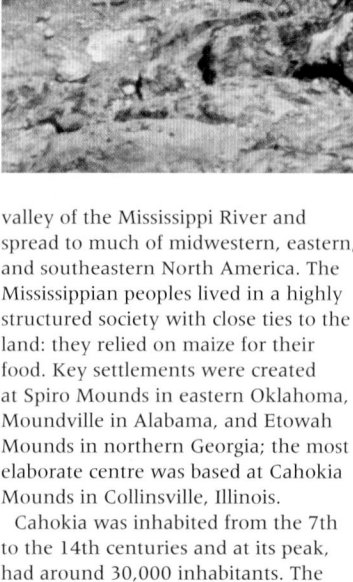

It is thought that Cahokia went into a gradual decline beginning around 1200, and was completely abandoned by 1400. The inhabitants left no written records, and the city's original name is unknown – "Cahokia" refers to a nearby Illiniwek clan that was present in the area when French settlers arrived in the 17th century.

The Mississippians were accomplished craftsmen, and archaeological excavations have revealed a range of ceramic vessels, some of them sculpted to look like trophy heads taken in warfare. Intricately carved pipes and ceremonial axes have also been found. Excavations carried out at the Spiro Mound have produced shell gorgets (decorative discs worn round the neck) with representations of warriors and snakes.

Monks Mound, Cahokia
Large Mississippian settlements were dominated by massive pyramidal mounds of earth that served as bases for temples – where the people could observe celestial events such as the summer and winter solstices – or the residences of the more powerful individuals.

AFTER »

The arrival of the Spanish conquistadors (conquerors) had far-reaching effects on the peoples of Mesoamerica and much of South America, devastating traditions and ways of life that had existed for hundreds of years.

THE CONQUISTADORS
Arriving in Mexico in 1519, **Hernán Cortés 170–71 »** heard about the wealthy Aztec city Tenochtitlán. With a group of Spanish soldiers and some local enemies of the Aztecs, he took control of the city in 1521. Most of the city was destroyed, but was rebuilt by the Spanish as Mexico City, capital of the Viceroyalty of New Spain.

The **Spanish** reached the **Yucatán** in about 1524. Although individual independent centres did fall to the conquistadors, the Maya often put up a fierce fight. The last stronghold submitted in 1697.

In 1532, **Francisco Pizarro 171 »** obtained permission from Spain to overcome the Inca, who had already been weakened by a civil war and smallpox. They finally fell to the Spanish in 1572.

THE FATE OF THE MISSISSIPPIANS
The decline of the Mississippian culture began before the arrival of the Spanish and French as a result of inter-tribal warfare and malnutrition, compounded by the spread of European diseases.

« BEFORE

Today's "Polynesians" are linked by language and DNA evidence to two prehistoric peoples.

POLYNESIAN ORIGINS
Polynesians today are descended from a southeast Asian group (probably from modern-day Taiwan), and a group indigenous to Melanesia (near Papua New Guinea). These two peoples gave rise to the **Melanesian "Lapita" culture**, whose pottery dates back as far as 1600 BCE. In the early centuries CE, these people split into many tribes and explored the South Pacific.

HOW WE KNOW

MOA BIRD

The enormous moa was one of many victims of the Polynesian expansion. These giant, wingless birds, up to 3.6m (12ft) tall, were hunted to extinction by Maori settlers of New Zealand. Later European expeditions collected remains for study by scientists such as Richard Owen (1804–92), below.

Polynesian Expansion

By approximately 700 CE, the Polynesians had reached all corners of the South Pacific, spreading across the uninhabited islands of Micronesia and reaching the extreme limits of their exploration and settlement at New Zealand and Easter Island, leading to a diverse range of cultures.

Archaeological evidence for the presence of Polynesian settlers from around 700 CE has been found in places as far flung as Samoa, Hawaii, and New Zealand. The islands, however, never formed a single empire of the type found elsewhere in the world – each group of settlers lived mostly in isolation, occupying territories that ranged in size from a small portion of an island, to a whole group of small islands. For this reason an incredible range of diverse cultures developed across Polynesia, each with its own way of life, customs, and tools. Some built huge stone cities, while others lived in villages on the beach. Contact with other groups among the isolated islanders was rare, while among groups sharing an island, war was frequent.

Across the ocean
The Polynesians were great shipbuilders, navigators, and sailors, and probably reached America more than a hundred years before the Vikings. They sailed on long voyages,

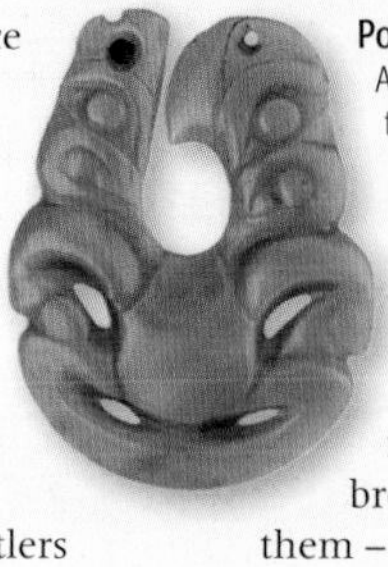

Polynesian pendant
Although the Polynesians did not use metal, they were able to create intricate tools and jewellery, such as this greenstone pendant.

into the unknown and often against the prevailing winds, to reach and populate far-flung islands. Often they brought their whole world with them – an entire family travelling together, their boats laden with all the possessions, tools, animals, and plants they would need in order to make a distant island a new home.

Some have argued that the colonization was largely accidental – without even a compass to aid their navigation, the Polynesians surely did not achieve this intentionally – they must have been blown off course. However, recent studies have shown

Double-hulled canoe
The Polynesians explored the ocean more extensively than anyone before in vessels like this. Supplies could be stored in the double hull.

that ancient Polynesian methods of navigation using the stars, birds, winds, currents, and tides, would have been surprisingly reliable when crossing even the widest gulf of ocean. Some recent explorers have even repeated these epic journeys in replica boats. Although Polynesian islanders are often depicted as living at one with nature, in reality they altered

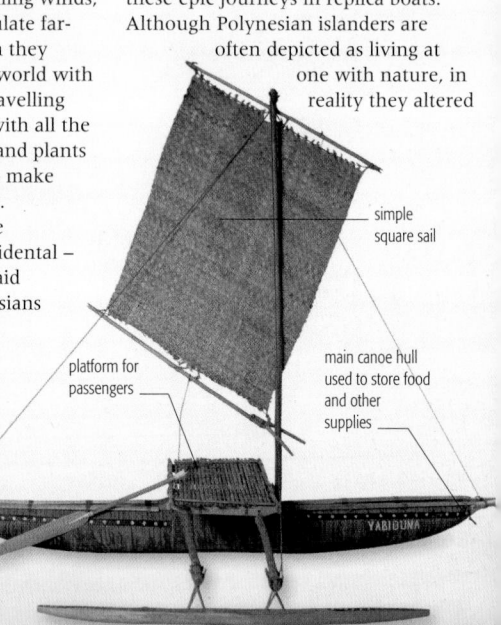

simple square sail

main canoe hull used to store food and other supplies

platform for passengers

887 The number of *Moai* statues found across Easter Island. Nearly 400 lie in the quarries where they were carved, but 288 were moved and erected successfully. The remainder were abandoned on roads.

INVENTION

STICK CHART

This stick chart from the Marshall Islands, in the Pacific Ocean, demonstrates one of the many unique methods the Polynesians used to navigate the seas. Made of sticks and shells, and bearing little resemblance to a normal map, it is a representation of local tides and currents. Rather than taking the chart on voyages, Polynesian navigators memorized them prior to departure, often with the aid of chants.

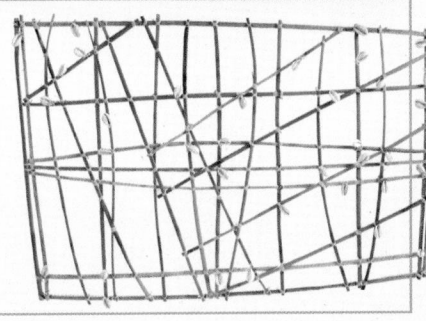

when the Polynesians arrived; some claim it was as early as 300 CE, while recent studies claim a late date of about 1200 CE.

Archaeologists do know that around 1000–1200 CE, the trees of Rapa Nui began to disappear. Climate change

16 MILLION The number of palm trees thought to have stood on Rapa Nui before the arrival of humans.

and the arrival of seed-eating rats may have increased the speed of the decline, but it seems to have largely been triggered by the colonists' obsessive construction of giant stone heads called *Moai*. These were carved in one piece from compressed volcanic ash and required wooden frameworks during the carving process, and wooden rollers for transport from the quarries to ceremonial sites along the coast.

No one knows for certain why the *Moai* were built, or what they represent; and as they were built over a long period of time, the tradition may have been influenced by a variety of changing

With the arrival of western ships, Polynesian isolation came to an end.

EUROPEAN CONTACTS

From 1567, European ships began to explore the islands of the South Pacific **164–65 »**. Colonists soon followed, crushing **indigenous cultures** with weapons, gods, and diseases. Some went down fighting – this spear is from the New Zealand Wars (1845–72), fought between the Maori and the British.

MAORI SPEAR

their environment just as much as any other group of settlers. Polynesians arriving on new islands brought with them domesticated animals, such as dogs, chickens, and pigs, and they (along with the rats which stowed away) were highly destructive. The Polynesians also brought new plants for farming, and chopped down trees to make boats, tools, and fire. In fact, one reliable method for dating the Polynesian expansion across the Pacific is to look for archaeological evidence of large flora and fauna extinctions.

Because of this, each of the Pacific islands today has its own unique ecosystem, consisting of the different plants and animals that

happened to survive the arrival of the Polynesians, mingled with whatever invading species that were introduced to the island with the colonists.

Mysteries of Rapa Nui

Rapa Nui (also known as Easter Island) is one of the most isolated islands in Polynesia. It lies 2,000km (1,290 miles) from the nearest island and is believed to have been named Easter Island because the first European visitor arrived on Easter Sunday, 1722. Historians still do not agree on

factors. However, as the heads replaced the trees, environmental disaster struck, and Rapa Nui's ecosystem collapsed. Birds had nowhere safe to nest, so they became extinct. The loose soil washed into the sea, leaving a lifeless landscape. The inhabitants could not even build boats for fishing – they resorted to cannibalism to stay alive, and began to tear down and deface the heads that had affected their environment so much.

Moai heads

Those *Moai* that made it to their final destination were erected along the coast of Rapa Nui, facing inland. According to one theory, they represent great chiefs from the island's history.

4

RENAISSANCE AND REFORMATION

1450–1750

Within 30 years of Columbus's first Atlantic crossing in 1492, a Spanish expedition had circumnavigated the globe. As European explorers set sail in search of new lands to conquer and colonize, commerce and trade expanded internationally. It was also an age in which established beliefs were questioned, leading to conflict and change.

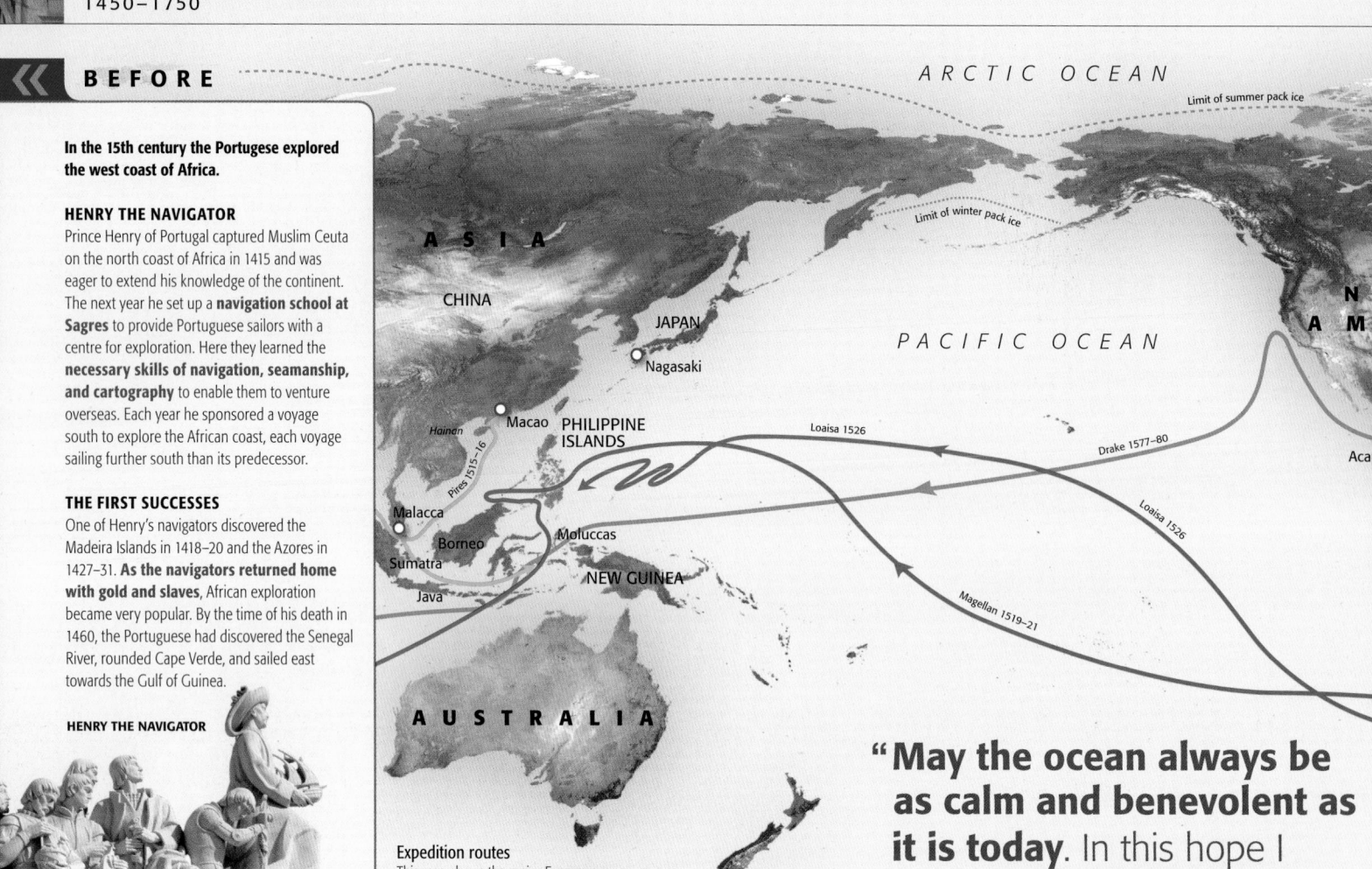

« BEFORE

In the 15th century the Portugese explored the west coast of Africa.

HENRY THE NAVIGATOR

Prince Henry of Portugal captured Muslim Ceuta on the north coast of Africa in 1415 and was eager to extend his knowledge of the continent. The next year he set up a **navigation school at Sagres** to provide Portuguese sailors with a centre for exploration. Here they learned the **necessary skills of navigation, seamanship, and cartography** to enable them to venture overseas. Each year he sponsored a voyage south to explore the African coast, each voyage sailing further south than its predecessor.

THE FIRST SUCCESSES

One of Henry's navigators discovered the Madeira Islands in 1418–20 and the Azores in 1427–31. **As the navigators returned home with gold and slaves**, African exploration became very popular. By the time of his death in 1460, the Portuguese had discovered the Senegal River, rounded Cape Verde, and sailed east towards the Gulf of Guinea.

HENRY THE NAVIGATOR

Expedition routes

This map shows the major European ocean voyages of the 15th and 16th centuries. Each colour corresponds to the country of the explorer, whose name and expedition date appears above the line. Arrows indicate the direction of travel and major ports or stopovers are indicated with white dots.

> "**May the ocean always be as calm and benevolent as it is today**. In this hope I name it the **Pacific Ocean**."
>
> FERDINAND MAGELLAN ON FIRST ENTERING THE PACIFIC OCEAN, 27 NOVEMBER 1520

Voyages of Discovery

In little over a century, European navigators left their continent and sailed the world, opening up new sea routes to India and the east. They discovered a continent previously unknown to them, and began a process that eventually resulted in the total European colonial and economic domination of the world.

PORTUGUESE EXPLORER (1480–1521)

FERDINAND MAGELLAN

Magellan was a Portuguese soldier and adventurer who had taken part in four expeditions to India and Malaya. He fell out with the Portuguese king, Manuel I and left the country in 1514 to enter the service of Spain. In 1519 he proposed a voyage west to the Spice Islands, which promised great wealth to Spain if successful. Magellan set out in 1519 with five ships and about 260 men. He sailed south across the Atlantic, and in November 1520 through the straits that now bear his name and into the Pacific. He then crossed the ocean, the first European to do so, reaching the Philippines in April 1521, where he was killed in a local war. His deputy, Juan Sebastian del Cano, took charge, eventually returning to Spain in September 1522 with only one ship and 17 members of the crew.

A t the start of the 15th century, European knowledge of the world was surprisingly limited. Sailors used world maps based on the cartography of Ptolemy, a Greek geographer who had died 13 centuries earlier in 168CE. Europe, the Mediterranean, and western Asia were reasonably well mapped, but Africa was vague in shape as no one knew how far south it stretched, while the Americas were missing altogether. Poor ship design that restricted ocean-going voyages and primitive navigation instruments kept ships close to the coast. At best, navigators used dead reckoning – intelligent guesswork based on speed through the water, winds, and currents – to assess their location.

The development of the ocean-going caravel (see right) by the Portuguese and new navigation instruments transformed this situation. The magnetic compass, the astrolabe, which measured the height of the Sun at noon, and the cross-staff and quadrant, which measured the height of a star, all helped navigators determine their latitude, or how far north or south they were. Lack of accurate marine chronometers (see p.220) meant that longitude – distance east or west – was not accurately calculated until the mid-18th century.

New technology, new worlds

Armed with this new maritime technology, the Portuguese tentatively explored the coast of Africa. Diogo Cão sailed round the Gulf of Guinea and then headed south, exploring the Congo River before making his final landfall at Cape Cross in what is now Namibia in 1486. Two years later Bartolomeu Dias rounded the Cape of Good Hope and sailed into the Indian Ocean, while in 1498 Vasco da Gama crossed the Indian Ocean to Calicut in southern India. These expeditions

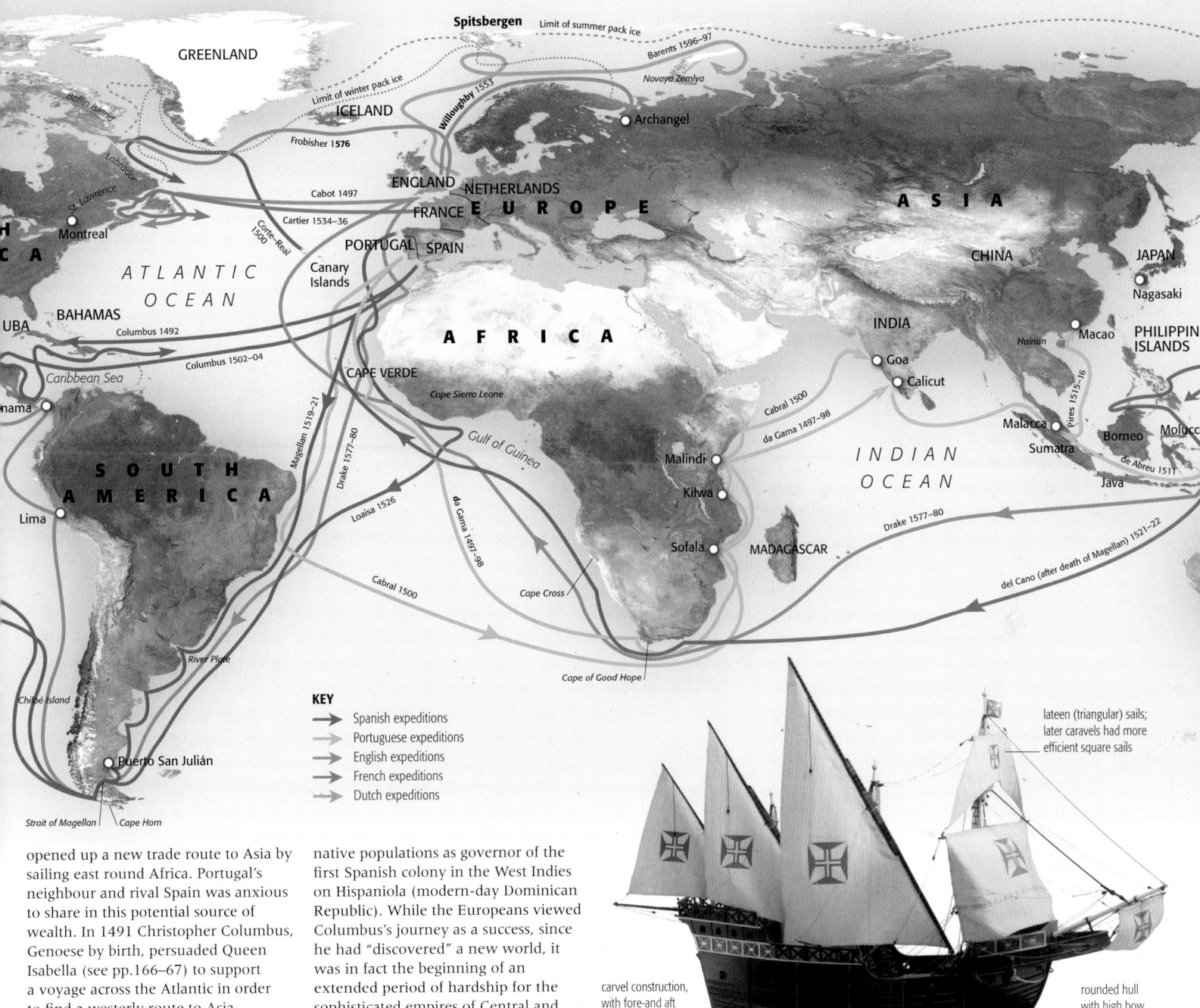

GREENLAND

Baffin Island

Spitsbergen — Limit of summer pack ice

Barents 1596–97

Novaya Zemlya

Willoughby 1553

Limit of winter pack ice

ICELAND

Frobisher **1576**

Archangel

Labrador

St. Lawrence

Corte-Real 1500

Cabot 1497

ENGLAND NETHERLANDS

Cartier 1534–36

FRANCE E U R O P E

Montreal

A T L A N T I C
O C E A N

PORTUGAL SPAIN

Canary Islands

A S I A

CHINA

JAPAN

Nagasaki

UBA

BAHAMAS

Columbus 1492

A F R I C A

INDIA

Hainan

Macao

PHILIPPINE
ISLANDS

Columbus 1502–04

CAPE VERDE

Goa

Calicut

Cabral 1500

Pires 1515–16

Caribbean Sea

Cape Sierra Leone

da Gama 1497–98

Malacca

Borneo

Moluccas

nama

Magellan 1519–21

Gulf of Guinea

Sumatra

de Abreu 1511

Java

I N D I A N
O C E A N

S O U T H
A M E R I C A

Drake 1577–80

Loaisa 1526

da Gama 1497–98

Malindi

Lima

Cabral 1500

Kilwa

del Cano (after death of Magellan) 1521–22

Cape Cross

Sofala

MADAGASCAR

MADAGASCAR

River Plate

Chiloé Island

Cape of Good Hope

KEY

→ Spanish expeditions
→ Portuguese expeditions
→ English expeditions
→ French expeditions
→ Dutch expeditions

Puerto San Julián

Strait of Magellan | Cape Horn

opened up a new trade route to Asia by sailing east round Africa. Portugal's neighbour and rival Spain was anxious to share in this potential source of wealth. In 1491 Christopher Columbus, Genoese by birth, persuaded Queen Isabella (see pp.166–67) to support a voyage across the Atlantic in order to find a westerly route to Asia.

He set sail in 1492 with three ships, using dead reckoning to calculate his position. Like other navigators of his day, he knew that the world was round – it is a myth to think that the common belief of the time was that the world was flat – but accepted Ptolemy's incorrect calculation of its size. Thus when he stumbled upon the islands of the Caribbean (see pp.168–69) he assumed these were outlying islands of Asia. Three further voyages, in 1493–96, 1498–1500, and 1502–04, failed to convince him that he had found not Asia but a previously unknown continent – the Americas.

Columbus in context

Columbus has been much criticized in recent years both for his geographical ignorance and for his treatment of the

native populations as governor of the first Spanish colony in the West Indies on Hispaniola (modern-day Dominican Republic). While the Europeans viewed Columbus's journey as a success, since he had "discovered" a new world, it was in fact the beginning of an extended period of hardship for the sophisticated empires of Central and South America and the other peoples of the continent. However, had Columbus not made this first landing, another navigator would have done so within a few years. But he was first, and as a pioneer, he opened up the prospect of European expansion overseas.

Round the world

The desire to seek new trade routes to Asia continued to preoccupy European sailors and merchants. The Spanish explored a route to the west. In 1519 Ferdinand Magellan (see left) set out to sail to the rich Spice Islands (the Moluccas in Indonesia). In so doing he started a voyage that, after his death in 1521, was completed by his deputy who, with the 17 surviving members of the crew, became the first Europeans to sail around the world.

lateen (triangular) sails; later caravels had more efficient square sails

carvel construction, with fore-and-aft planks flush to each other

rounded hull with high bow and stern

The caravel

The Portuguese voyages of the 15th century were made possible by the development of the caravel, so named because of its flush-planked carvel construction. The caravel was lighter than its predecessors and more seaworthy, enabling it to venture far from land. A small ship, only 20m (60ft) long, it carried a crew of about 25.

Both routes to Asia were arduous. French and English navigators explored the coast of Canada hoping to find a northwest passage to Asia, a feat not achieved until the Norwegian Roald Amundsen completed the voyage in 1906 (see pp.250–51). English and Dutch navigators also looked for a northeast passage around Siberia, again a feat not achieved until Finn Nils Nordenskjöld made the voyage in 1879.

AFTER ≫

Competing Spanish and Portuguese discoveries in the Americas and Asia created a clash between these two maritime nations.

TREATY OF TORDESILLAS
In 1494 Pope Alexander VI negotiated a treaty that **divided the world along a line** drawn south across the Atlantic Ocean: west of the line was Spanish, east was Portuguese. The treaty was useful when the Portuguese began to colonize Brazil, but problems arose in the Spice Islands of Southeast Asia. The treaty was vague about what happened on the other side of the world.

QUEEN OF SPAIN Born 1451 Died 1504

Isabella of Castile

"I... am ready to **pawn my jewels** to defray the expenses of it..."

ISABELLA TO COLUMBUS, SPEAKING ABOUT HIS PROPOSED VOYAGE TO ASIA, 1492

According to a contemporary chronicler, Isabella I of Spain was a neglected child: "The Queen, Our Lady, from childhood was without a father and we can even say a mother… She had work and cares, and an extreme lack of necessary things." Isabella's father, John II of Castile (a Spanish kingdom), died when she was three, at which point her depressed mother shut herself away. Her young brother died of a plague-like illness in 1468, and her older half-brother, the mentally unstable Henry IV, perceived her as a threat. However, Isabella emerged from this Cinderella-like childhood an extremely strong-willed and intelligent young woman.

As a leading contender for the throne of Castile, Isabella attracted many suitors – including the king of Portugal and brothers of the kings of England and France – but she herself decided to marry Ferdinand of Aragon: "It has to be he and absolutely no other." In marrying the young prince of Aragon – whom she had yet to meet – 17-year-old Isabella

risked the wrath of Henry, who had not given his consent. But Isabella knew that this was the marriage most likely to bring her power. In 1469 they were married in the Spanish city of Valladolid, and for much of the next 10 years they fought for recognition of their right to become joint rulers of the unruly kingdom of Castile.

Love and war

In 1474 Henry died and civil war broke out. However, within a few years it was clear that Isabella and Ferdinand were winning on every front. By 1476 they had set up the *hermandad* ("brotherhood"), a network of local

Catholic New World
This 17th-century altarpiece from Guatemala reveals the impact of Spanish culture in the Americas. Isabella regarded it as her sacred duty to bring Christianity to her subjects in the New World.

Isabella the Catholic
Isabella's strong will helped bring about fundamental changes to Spain. Her reign led to the permanent unification of Spain (which had previously been a collection of kingdoms) and her decision to sponsor Christopher Columbus's journey to find a new route to Asia laid the groundwork for an era of global commerce and trade.

Fall of Granada
Isabella's greatest achievement was the conquest of Granada, the last Moorish kingdom in Spain. She and her husband are pictured (left) accepting the submission of their new Muslim subjects, but in practice promises of religious toleration were not kept.

Having achieved so much for "God's cause", Isabella had time for other activities. She and Ferdinand agreed to sponsor the "enterprise of the Indies", the first transatlantic voyage of Christopher Columbus (see pp.168–69), which led to the development of a global Spanish empire (see pp.174–75).

Isabella's final years

In her final years, Isabella was distressed by a succession of family tragedies. She had five children: Isabella, John, Joanna, Maria, and Catherine. Both Isabella and Maria married into the Portuguese royal family, while John and Joanna married the daughter and son of the Habsburg Emperor Maximilian I. The first husband of Catherine was Arthur, Prince of Wales; the second, Henry VIII of England.

But Isabella's son and heir, John, died soon after his wedding, and this loss was followed by the death in childbirth of Isabella's eldest daughter, Isabella. Then, before he was two, her grandson Michael died in her arms. Since it was clear that the unhappy Joanna "la loca" (the mad) had lost her reason, all hope for the future of the dynasty rested with Isabella and Ferdinand's Habsburg grandson, the future Holy Roman Emperor Charles V. It is thought that these events contributed to a decline in Isabella's health, and her death in 1504.

militias that formed a basic police force, and eventually became the basis of a national Spanish army.

In 1477 Isabella and Ferdinand entered the city of Toledo in triumph – they were the unchallenged monarchs of Castile. Their partnership was carefully worked out. In keeping with their motto "*Tanto monta, monta tanto, Isabel como Fernando*" ("It's the same thing, Isabella is the same as Ferdinand"), they issued joint decrees and approved coins and stamps. Although Ferdinand's name preceded Isabella's on state documents, her coat of arms came first. They were a united front, fully supporting each other's decisions.

The Catholic Monarchs

Isabella may have viewed the turmoil of her childhood as a sign of God's displeasure with the weak rule of her half-brother Henry. Her sense of duty and passion for order and unity led to the establishment of the Spanish Inquisition in 1478. This was a court run by the Catholic Church with the aim of ensuring royal subjects remained faithful Christians. Within Isabella's own lifetime, this institution – whose first victims were Jews and conversos (Christians of Jewish ethnicity) – became a byword for cruelty and terror. By 1492, the year of the fall of Granada, those who died because of its denunciations may have exceeded ten thousand in number.

In 1480 Isabella and Ferdinand announced their intention to go to war against Granada, the last Moorish (Muslim) kingdom in Spain (see pp.122–23). In 1492, after being besieged for a year and a half, Granada surrendered. For this victory, Isabella and Ferdinand were congratulated by

Family portrait
This painting in a Dominican monastery in Avila shows Isabella, Ferdinand, and their children John and Joanna at prayer before the image of the Madonna and Child.

the monarchs of Europe, and awarded the title of the "Catholic Monarchs" by the pope. In addition to forming the final episode in the centuries-long battle by the Christian church to reclaim the Iberian peninsula, Granada's conquest was widely seen as compensation for the loss of Constantinople to Muslim Ottoman Turks in 1453 (see pp.152–53).

New-found wealth
This 15th-century gold coin was minted in Seville with the images of both monarchs. Spain had access to vast amounts of silver and gold in the Americas.

KING OF SPAIN (1452–1516)

FERDINAND OF ARAGON

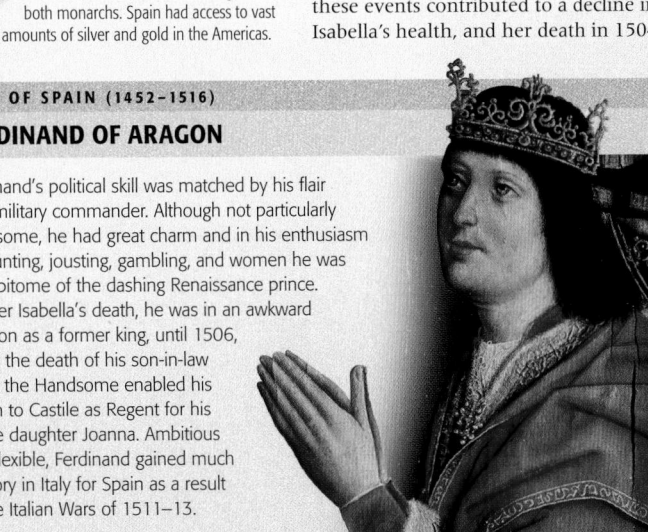

Ferdinand's political skill was matched by his flair as a military commander. Although not particularly handsome, he had great charm and in his enthusiasm for hunting, jousting, gambling, and women he was the epitome of the dashing Renaissance prince.

After Isabella's death, he was in an awkward position as a former king, until 1506, when the death of his son-in-law Philip the Handsome enabled his return to Castile as Regent for his fragile daughter Joanna. Ambitious and flexible, Ferdinand gained much territory in Italy for Spain as a result of the Italian Wars of 1511–13.

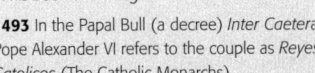

THE BOOK OF PRIVILEGES

Columbus lands in the Caribbean

The arrival of a small, Spanish-sponsored fleet on the Caribbean island of San Salvador was to have dramatic effects on both sides of the Atlantic Ocean. European explorers would be galvanized by the discovery of what eventually proved to be two whole new continents, while the native populations were about to enter a period of prolonged suffering and repression.

Christopher Columbus was born in Genoa around 1451, going to sea at an early age. For eight years he sought sponsors for a plan to sail west from Europe to eastern Asia and the island kingdom of Cipangu (Japan). By finding a direct sea route to Asia, he hoped to open the wealth of the region for European trade. He finally won backing from Isabella of Castille (see pp.166–67) in 1491.

Columbus set off from the Spanish port of Palos on 3 August 1492. His fleet consisted of a three-masted cargo ship, the *Santa Maria*, carrying 40 men, the smaller *Pinta*, with 26 men, and the four-masted *Niña*, with 24 aboard. The fleet dropped anchor in the Canary Islands, southwest of Spain, for repairs, but on 6 September it finally resumed its journey across the Atlantic.

On the evening of 11 October 1492, Columbus, aboard the *Santa Maria*, thought he saw "a light to the west. It looked like a little wax candle bobbing up and down." Two hours after midnight, Rodrigo de Triana,

lookout on the *Pinta*, sighted land. Columbus had crossed the Atlantic.

He claimed the island he had found for Spain, naming it San Salvador, and traded with the Arawak natives (calling them "Indians" in the belief that he was off the coast of Asia). The island's true location is unclear – for years, it was assumed to be present-day San Salvador in the Bahamas, but in 1986 a team from the US National Geographical Society judged it must have been Samana Cay, 125km (78 miles) southeast, and a later study concluded it was probably Grand Turk, 320km (200 miles) further southeast.

On 14 October, Columbus set off in search of gold. He explored three small islands before sailing to Cuba, and then to Hispaniola (Dominican Republic and Haiti), where he established the first European transatlantic settlement since the Vikings (see pp.148–49), 500 years earlier. On 16 January 1493 he set off back to Spain, quite convinced he had sailed to Asia and back.

Columbus makes landfall
Columbus was captivated by the island he named San Salvador (meaning "Saint Saviour"). "Everything is green and the vegetation is like that in Andalusia in April." He did not, however, discover the gold he sought, nor did he realize that this was not an outlying island of Asia, but part of a new continent – the Americas.

... in honour of **God** who guided us and **saved us from many perils**."

COLUMBUS' WORDS AFTER CLAIMING SAN SALVADOR FOR SPAIN, 12 OCTOBER 1492

BEFORE

On the eve of European conquest, three highly advanced civilizations occupied much of Central and South America.

MAYANS

The Mayan states **92–93 »** clustered around the Yucatán peninsula of what is now southeast Mexico. All **16 states were independent**, and in 1480 there was a major war for regional supremacy. The lack of a single ruler made these states more difficult to conquer.

AZTECS

The Aztec Empire **« 156–59** was based around the city of Tenochtitlán (on the site of present-day Mexico City). Under **Itzcóatl** (reigned 1428–40) and his successors, the empire expanded rapidly, so that by the reign of **Moctezuma II** (1502–20), **over 10 million people** were subject to Aztec rule, which stretched from the Caribbean across the valley of Mexico. Central to their belief system was the need to provide human sacrifices for their Sun god **Huitzilopochtli**.

15th CENTURY MAP OF TENOCHTITLÁN

INCAS

During the reigns of **Pachacuti** (1438–71) and his son **Tupac Yupanqui** (1471–93), the Inca empire, established around 1230 in the South American Andes, grew rapidly **« 156–59**. By 1525, the empire was at its greatest extent, stretching from modern-day Ecuador in the north to Chile in the south. The empire was **rich in gold** and had a 20,000-km (12,500-mile) network of roads.

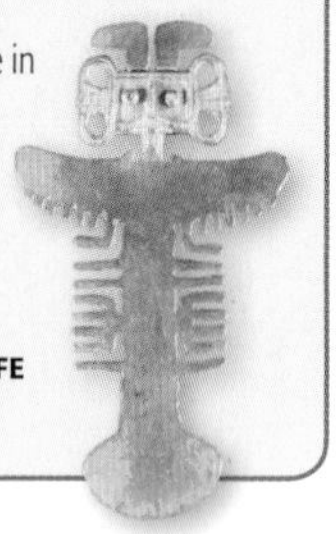

GOLD INCA KNIFE

> **"**Shipmates and friends. There lies **the hard way**, leading to Peru and wealth.**"**
>
> FRANCISCO PIZARRO, ON GORGONA ISLAND OFF THE PACIFIC COAST OF COLOMBIA, 1526

Contact Americas

Forty years after Columbus first set foot in the Americas, the Spanish had built a vast empire in North, Central, and South America. With remarkable ingenuity and treachery, and considerable bravery, two small bands of soldiers felled two mighty empires and initiated three centuries of Spanish rule.

CONQVISTA DE MEXÍCO POR CORTES. 7

The Spanish came to the Americas for a variety of reasons. They sought wealth in the form of gold, spices, and other goods. They came to claim land for their king, and saw the locals as inferiors to be subdued and exploited. They came to convert, for in their eyes this was a godless continent. And they came for adventure – Vasco de Balboa was an unsuccessful pig breeder, Hernan Cortés a failed law student – but the Americas gave men such as these the chance of gold and glory. Initial conquest and settlement was confined to the Caribbean islands. The first permanent mainland settlements were founded from 1510 and included Vasco de Balboa, soon to become the first European to see the Pacific, and Francisco Pizarro. Balboa found gold, and learned of a rich land across the Pacific called Birú (Peru). By now, the Spanish were realizing that this new world was rich, but its wealth was not to be taken easily. In 1518 the Spanish governor of Cuba sent 11 ships under the command of Cortés to explore the coast of the Yucatán peninsula for gold. Cortés learned of a great empire inland, and on 16 August 1519 set out from the Mexican coast with 15 horsemen, 400 soldiers, and a few hundred porters. Using local guides and interpreters, he arrived at Tlaxacala, an independent city and enemy of the Aztec empire. With the Tlaxacalan army as willing allies, he approached the Aztec capital, Tenochtitlán, in November 1519.

▷ **Spanish stronghold**
The Spanish fort of San Lorenzo del Chagres was built on the Caribbean coast of Panama and guarded the route across the isthmus to the Pacific Ocean.

The Aztec emperor Moctezuma was fearful of the Spanish, aware of their military reputation and capacity for ruthlessness. He placated them with gifts and housed them in a palace in his island capital. The Spanish were also wary, as they were now effectively prisoners of the Aztecs. Cortés launched the desperate scheme of taking Moctezuma prisoner, although this simply encouraged their captors to chose another leader, as they were hostile to the Spanish presence.

Tenochtitlán began its descent into chaos when Cortés's soldiers massacred a large number of young Aztec nobles who were taking part in a festival of feasting and dancing. As the city rebelled, Moctezuma proved powerless to calm the Aztecs; he was stoned by his own people and later died of his wounds.

Cortés fought his way out of the city, losing three-quarters of his men in the disastrous "Night of Sorrows". However, the Aztecs failed to deliver the fatal death blow to Cortés's bedraggled survivors. Boosted with large numbers of new soldiers attracted by rumours of huge wealth, and by a vast auxiliary army of native peoples anxious to throw off the yoke of Aztec dominance, Cortés undertook a second, and this time definitive, siege of Tenochtitlán, forcing the Aztecs into a final surrender after a desperate struggle in August 1521.

◁ **The capture of Tenochtitlán**
The destruction of the Aztec capital by Cortés in 1521 is shown in this somewhat fanciful late 18th-century painting by an unknown Spanish artist. The splendour of the city on its island in Lake Texoco is clear, though not perhaps the brutality of the conquest.

▽ **Inca storehouses**
The Incas were great stonemasons, building depots to store their harvested crops, and roadside hostels for royal messengers and other travellers.

Inca Gold Armlets
Gold jewellery in the Inca empire was a sign of wealth and power. Gold was used also used for ceremonial items.

While Cortés set about organizing his new territory, others were exploring to the south. Birú excited the Spanish, who sent an expedition along the Pacific coast in 1522 that found no gold but confirmed reports of a rich empire inland. Further expeditions continued to map the coast, and two of these were led by Francisco Pizarro, an illiterate but brave 51-year-old soldier.

In 1527 Pizarro landed at Tumbes, an Inca outpost (see pp.210–13), trading goods for gold, silver, jewels, and cloth. With this treasure, he returned via Panama to Spain and sought permission to mount an armed expedition.

By 1531 he was back with three ships and 180 men. Reaching Tumbes, he found it ruined by a civil war between Atahuallpa (see right) and his brother Huáscar for control of the Inca empire. Learning that Atahuallpa and his army were across the mountains at Cajamarca, Pizarro, with his 106 footsoldiers and 62 horsemen, set out on a trek to meet Atahuallpa. They were received by an imperial envoy bearing gifts from the emperor, who was camped with his army outside the city. Pizarro lured Atahuallpa into Cajamarca, took him hostage, and was offered an enormous ransom. With the treasure amassed by July 1533, and panicked at rumours of an Inca counterattack to liberate Atahuallpa, Pizarro and his officers executed the emperor. The Spanish then marched on the capital, Cuzco, and seized control of the entire Inca empire.

An uneven struggle

Both Aztec and Inca empires fell to remarkably small Spanish armies. But the Spanish had guns, horses, and armour, and ruthlessly exploited their opponents' weakest points – the repressive rule of the Aztecs over their subjects, and the Inca civil war. From a strategic point of view, they

recognized that both empires were highly centralized states ruled over by all-powerful emperors. Capture the emperor and the state was paralysed.

Following the conquest, the Spanish exploited the religion of the Aztecs, using their desire for captured enemies to sacrifice to turn them into allies on the battlefield. Pizarro was also helped by the superb Inca road network that enabled his troops to cross otherwise inaccessible terrain.

Perhaps most importantly, though, the Spanish brought with them diseases to which the Americans had no resistance. Diseases decimated local populations as the Spanish took control of their lands. In everything but numbers, the Spanish had the advantage and the luck.

AFTER »

The arrival of Europeans in force on the American mainland had lasting consequences on all sides.

CONTINUED RESISTANCE
Spanish conquest of Central and South America did not end with the fall of the two main empires. The **last Inca stronghold** fell to the Spanish in 1572, and the Inca hinterland was largely untouched until the early 1800s. Conquest of the Aztecs and Central America was more complete, but the Maya were a greater challenge, as their states had to be conquered one by one.

NEW FOOD
Other than gold and silver **174–75 »** the Spanish discovered and subsequently exported many new plants, such as tobacco, and foodstuffs. In return, the Europeans introduced a variety of crops, livestock, and diseases **176–77 »**.

TOBACCO

BEFORE

LLAMAS IN PERU

Until the end of the 15th century, the New World and Old World had entirely separate agricultures, and most of the serious diseases of Europe and Asia had not crossed the Atlantic.

DOMESTICATED CROPS

New World domesticated crops – those whose growth was controlled by farmers – included **corn, tobacco, cocoa, and cotton**. The Old World was equally productive, but apart from cotton it shared few crop types with the Americas. Amongst its most important crops were **wheat, rice, and tea**.

DOMESTIC ANIMALS

Europe and Asia had an abundance of domesticated animals – such as **horses, cattle, goats, sheep, chickens, and pigs** – in the pre-Columbian Americas the only equivalents were **turkeys, guinea pigs, dogs, alpacas, and llamas**. The Americas, however, had an incredible range of wild animals, hence much meat in the diet was obtained through hunting and fishing.

DISEASE

Before Columbus, the Americas had enjoyed a long period of population growth. Nevertheless, **mortality rates remained high** from diseases such as tuberculosis and health was plagued with water-borne parasites. The Europeans suffered similarly, but **they went on to export some of their deadly diseases**.

Columbus's (see pp.168–69) very first voyage in 1492 introduced new species to the Americas – it contained 28 horses, three mules, and an assortment of sheep, goats, cattle, chickens, dogs, and cats. Apart from the dogs, these were all unfamiliar creatures to the indigenous Americans, but Spanish colonization in the 16th century quickly expanded stock holdings. The numbers of domesticated animals imported by Europeans grew at different rates depending on the species, and brought different social effects. Sheep, goats, pigs, and chickens bred rapidly (the Europeans found excellent grazing land), and became useful not only as sustenance for the colonists, but also as foods to trade with American Indians for fruits and vegetables. Geographically, grazing animals also spread quickly – by 1519 sheep flocks could be found from northern South America up to the southwestern corner of what is today the United States.

Horses and cattle

Horse and cattle numbers grew more slowly because of the animals' longer breeding cycles and smaller numbers of offspring. Nevertheless, during the 16th century they spread through Peru and Chile and reached northwards through New Spain, which covered Central America and much of southern North America. Horses were central to the early Spanish military conquests – many American Indians were at first terrified of horses, believing them to be divine creatures – but they also introduced effective transportation, providing the future means for a wider

The Great Exchange

Columbus's arrival in the Americas in 1492 began one of the greatest revolutions in global food habits ever seen. Plants and animals previously separated by some 5,000–6,000km (3,000–4,000 miles) of ocean would now be exchanged.

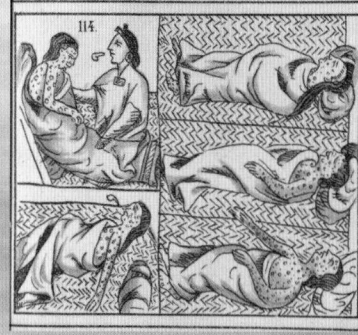

Deadly trade
An early colonial artwork shows the lethal effect of smallpox on the American Indians. The first major smallpox outbreak in the Americas occurred between 1520–24, but epidemics returned regularly until the late 1800s.

European colonization of North America. American Indians later fuelled the growth of cattle herds with a newly acquired love of beef and leather.

Transatlantic foods

The "exchange" of animal foods between the Old and New Worlds was mainly one sided, with Europe importing its domesticated animals into the Americas. The exchange of plant life, by contrast, ran both ways. The European colonists attempted to grow all the traditional Old World Crops in the Americas, with sugar cane, bananas, and lemons, for example, all doing well in the tropical climate. Grain crops such as wheat grew better in mountainous regions and later found perfect growing conditions in the temperate plains of North America. By the end of the 16th century, sugar cane was growing in huge amounts in the Caribbean, Peru, Brazil, and Mexico, with entire forests being cleared for its growth. Exported in the opposite direction were crops that changed the diets of much of Europe

Potatoes and wheat
Wheat, an Old World crop, grows alongside potatoes in a hilly region of South America. Wheat needs cooler temperatures to grow, and the first attempts to grow the plants in the American tropics largely failed.

and Asia, including maize, beans, potatoes, and tobacco. Potatoes were introduced across Europe between 1570–1600, and two centuries later they would be one of the most important crops of the Old World, alongside corn. Cocoa (a base ingredient of chocolate) transformed European confectionery, while tobacco introduced a whole new pastime. Tomatoes became staples of Mediterranean cooking, while chili peppers introduced new spices to Old World palates.

Destruction and disease

This great exchange steadily transformed the world's diets, but also had dramatic human consequences. Along with food, the Europeans also brought diseases that devastated indigenous populations, principally smallpox, measles, bubonic plague,

typhoid, scarlet fever, cholera, whooping cough, diphtheria, mumps, and (from Africa) malaria and yellow fever. The only major disease that possibly traveled in the opposite direction was syphilis, although many experts dispute its origins.

Compounding the horrors of disease were the social effects of Old World agriculture in a New World setting. Local communities were displaced to make room for grazing cattle, or were forced to labour on farms and plantations. New types of weed choked native plants. Serious overgrazing problems occurred in places such as New Spain, with large areas turned practically to desert, having been stripped of vegetation and suffering from soil erosion. For better or worse, the New World had imported much more than just plants and animals.

New cuisine
This Italian cookery book from 1622 was an effort to teach Italians how to cook the exotic foods arriving from the Americas, such as tomatoes.

The Great Exchange had far-reaching implications across the world, irrevocably changing the global ecosystem.

EXPORT OF TEA
Tea was first imported to the Dutch settlement of New Amsterdam in North America in 1650, and during the second half of the 17th century its popularity spread along the eastern seaboard. By the 19th century, **tea clippers were making regular tea runs from Europe** to Boston, New York, and Philadelphia.

TEA CLIPPER

CHANGED LIVES
In the late 1400s the native population of North and South America numbered around 40 million, but by the late 1700s that **figure had fallen by 70–90 per cent**, mainly because of European-introduced diseases. The consequent collapse of the local workforce in the Americas contributed to the creation of the **transatlantic slave trade**, in which millions of Africans were forcibly shipped to the Americas to live and work on plantations 218–19 »

Plains horses
The introduction of horses had a profound effect on the history of the Americas. Horses had existed on these continents previously, but were hunted to extinction by 7000 BCE. Once American Indian tribes of the plains (stretching from the Rocky Mountains to the Mississippi River in the US) mastered the use of the horse, it transformed their way of life. They were now able to travel faster and further than ever before, and their hunting efficiency increased exponentially.

Spanish Silver

From the 1540s onward, the Spanish New World was shaped by the discovery, exploitation, and trading of silver around the world. The steady stream of silver into the empire's coffers allowed Spain to become the superpower of its day.

<<

BEFORE

By the late 15th century, silver was in desperately short supply across Europe.

EARLY SILVER

Silver is documented as being used as far back as the 3rd millennium BCE in the Middle East. It became the **most common coinage metal in Europe** from the 5th century BCE onwards. Ironically, although the pre-Columbian civilizations of the Americas **<< 156–59** had silver, it was cocoa beans and spiny oysters shells that were used as payment. Silver was mainly used to make jewellery.

PLUNDERING THE NEW WORLD

Imports from America included pearls, sugar, dyestuffs, and cowhide, but gold and silver were most highly prized. It was the **quest for gold and silver** that drove the Conquistadors and the early colonial ventures **<< 170–71**. Gold and silver were plundered during the conquest. At first soldiers seized or bartered objects belonging to the American Indians. When these supplies were exhausted, gold was prospected by natives washing out surface gold from stream beds. Silver, however, required mining.

The discovery of silver at Potosí (present-day Bolivia) in April 1545 was not the first time the Spanish colonialists had encountered this precious metal. It was already being mined in the arid hills of New Spain (present-day Mexico), and in Peruvian mountain sites previously exploited by the Incas. In 1540, Spaniards began mining silver at Porco, located like Potosí to the southeast of Lake Titicaca. But five years later, the discovery of an entire mountain of silver ore – the biggest single concentration of this precious metal ever found – changed everything. Potosí quickly sprawled into a shanty village, growing in the next century to become the largest city in the New World with a population between 100,000 – 160,000. A royal mint, established there in 1585, still stands today.

Real exploitation of the Potosí mines took off around 1560 when a new and more productive method of refining silver came into use. The new process required mercury, for which the main source was the Almadén mines in Spain, but it yielded more silver than traditional smelting, and made it worthwhile to extract lower grade, less concentrated seams of ore. The mercury was imported in leather bags from Spain and became an important trade in itself. Silver mining also boosted the demand for supplies of

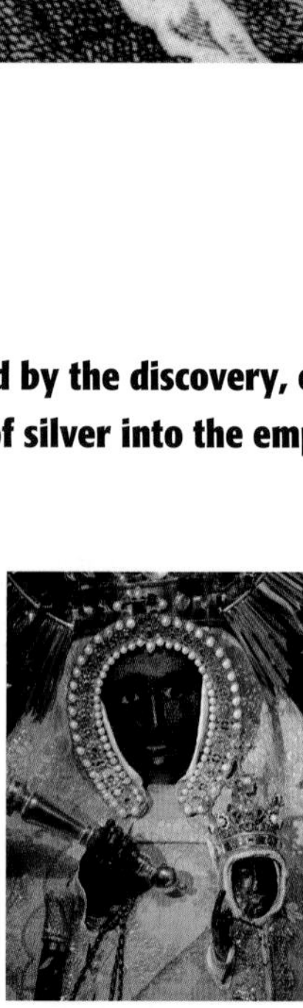

Mestizo madonna
Catholic veneration of the Virgin Mary, adopted by Spanish American mestizo society (of mixed native American and European descent), produced this icon.

beef, leather, and tallow candles. Mules were used to carry supplies to the mines and bring back silver, so ranching and mining grew together.

Hard labour was soon in great demand, driving the import of African slaves (see pp.218–19). As both Mexico and Peru became wealthy from their mineral resources, the numbers of slaves increased – imported for the mining industry, and to work as servants. Many native Americans

economy was relatively light and the *flota* continued to ensure the regular supply of silver and the royal share, the *quinto real* (the royal fifth). From the 1580s Philip II could expect two to three million ducats a year from the treasure fleets, and this flow of coins gave him the freedom to make his audacious attacks on other European powers (see pp.212–13).

The accountants take over

It was not just the sailors who ensured the silver took a secure route, but also the civil servants. They ran an extensive and accountable system of bureaucratic government that was set up to replace the violent, quarrelsome, and independent-minded Conquistadors (see pp.170–71). The Council of the Indies, established in Spain from 1522, was charged with

Silver mining
The conical mountain of Cerro Potosí became the chief source of the Spanish Empire's dazzling wealth after the discovery of silver there in 1545. The huge outcrop of silver ore was soon honeycombed with mine workings, as shown in this engraving from the 18th century.

were used as forced labour, but others were paid as skilled craftsmen to produce fabulous silverware.

The first transatlantic convoys

From 1503 to 1660 some 16,000 tonnes of silver were shipped to Seville (compared with 185 tonnes of gold), tripling the existing silver resources of Europe. Seville was the "mistress" port, enjoying a monopoly of all these precious cargoes until 1680. Each *flota* (a convoy escorted by armed galleons) sailed from Vera Cruz, Cartagena, and Nombre de Dios to Seville over two months. The system worked – there were only two occasions when whole convoys were intercepted and defeated; once in 1628 by Dutchman Piet Heyn and once by the English Admiral Robert Blake in 1657. Individual galleons, so large and laden with bullion and guns, were often wrecked by poor navigation, preyed on by privateers, or swept under in storms, but the impact on the Spanish

The mistress port
Seville was already a thriving trading port when, in 1503, it was given the exclusive monopoly on silver brought back by the fleets from Mexico and Peru. Between 1516 and 1525, 499 ships left Seville port for the Indies.

the business of the new imperial territories, presenting reports and policy documents to the king, and acting as the link between Spain and the administrators in the Americas. In order to maintain crown control of the new colonies, all the major posts in the colonial administration, from the Viceroys (king's deputies) of New Spain (Mexico) and Peru, from judges to senior churchmen, were either fixed-term appointments or always chosen from the Spanish elites – never from those already in the New World. For the next 200 years, government relied on continuous contact between Madrid, which became Spain's permanent capital in 1561, and the great centres of the Atlantic Empire. It could be slow and cumbersome, and the imposition of a Spanish-born ruling class was deeply resented by the "Creole" population of Spaniards born and bred in the New World. But it achieved the aims of the Spanish Crown, preventing the colonies slipping towards independence, and maintaining a high level of control over the resources of the New World, including of course silver production.

Bullion and coins passed from silver merchants on the Seville waterfront to European royal mints, bankers such as the Fugger family and the Genoese,

holes release scented smoke

incense rests on hot coals

Silver censer
An elaborate silver church censer from about 1630, was suspended by chains and used for burning incense in Catholic ceremonies, shows the direct link between the prosperity of Spanish–American society and silver production.

chain to swing censer back and forth

Philip II
Spain's King Philip II was a bureaucratic ruler, issuing decrees, laws, and rules from his fortress-monastery El Escorial. He relied greatly on advisers and officials to run both his government and his armies.

and the newly created stock exchanges in Antwerp and Bruges (see pp.214–15). In exchange came weapons, powder, and troops. Even Elizabeth I (see pp.200–01) and the merchants of England sought to ensure their share of the treasure through loans. The silver trail stretched east via Italy to the Eastern Mediterranean, and across Persia and India into East Asia, where it was the one commodity in steady and undiminishing demand from Europe in exchange for spices, silks, and Chinese porcelain. Silver, in effect, became the foundation of a global economy.

> **AFTER**

> "The last load of silver… arrived **just in time to pay the German infantry** and cavalry we are recruiting."
>
> LETTER FROM FRANCISCO DE ERASO, FINANCIAL ADVISOR OF EMPEROR CHARLES V, 1558

The influx of Europeans had a lasting effect on the American continents. It was over 300 years before the emigrants shook off their colonial shackles.

REVOLUTIONARY TIMES
Spanish and Portuguese rule in South America began to crumble during the Napoleonic Wars of the early 1800s **240–07 ≫**. Napoleon's invasion of the Iberian peninsula **238–39 ≫** undermined Spain's power and inspired

independence movements and revolutionaries. This led to the Spanish–American Wars of Independence **248–49 ≫** and the **Mexican Revolution**.

HYBRID CULTURE
Modern festivals such as the **Dia de los Muertos** or "Day of the Dead" are a living reminder of how Spanish Catholicism was bolted onto earlier native traditions to create a vibrant and unique celebration.

DAY OF THE DEAD ARTWORK

The **Pilgrim Fathers**

The arrival of 102 settlers in Plymouth, Massachusetts on 11 December 1620 is one of the legendary stories of US history. These men, women, and children are lauded as the Pilgrim Fathers, the founders of what became the United States. Yet they were by no means the first Europeans to settle in the country.

<< BEFORE

The first Europeans to visit America were adventurers rather than settlers.

FRENCH CANADA
Frenchman **Jacques Cartier** explored the St Lawrence River from 1535 to 1542, and renamed Hochelaga, Mont Réal (Montreal). Fishermen and fur traders followed.

HOCHELAGA

Permanent French settlers arrived much later – after the foundation of Québec in 1608.

ALGONQUIN INDIANS

SURVIVAL TECHNIQUES
To survive in this **new and hostile environment**, the French formed alliances with local tribes, notably the Algonquin Indians. The Iroquois tribe later became allies of the British.

In the century after Columbus arrived in the Americas (see pp.168–69), European contact with North America was remarkably limited. The Spanish, obsessed with gold and conquest, concentrated on exploiting the wealthy empires of Central and South America. To the north, the French explored the rich fishing and fur-trapping regions of the St Lawrence River. Those European navigators who did visit America were more concerned with finding a route around it to Asia than exploring the continent itself.

While the Spanish established bases to protect their bullion fleets, such as St Augustine in Florida, and the French traded in Canada to the north, it was the English who first attempted colonization of the eastern seaboard. In 1584 the English adventurer Sir Walter Raleigh established a settlement on Roanoke Island, but lacked the resources to sustain it. The settlement is believed to have been overrun by the local Croatoan tribe in 1590. By then the defeat of the Spanish Armada in 1588 (see pp. 200–01) gave the English the incentive to attempt to intervene in the relatively undefended and undercolonized continent of North America. In 1607 the Virginia Company of London took advantage of this, and set up a colony in Jamestown, Virginia.

The Pilgrims

The men and women who settled Jamestown came to acquire land and hopefully wealth. Those that landed at New Plymouth in 1620 came to escape religious persecution in Europe. Often described as Puritans, they were more accurately religious dissenters who had left England for the Netherlands in 1608, but then decided to build their own society in a new land. Armed with a Virginia Company land grant, they set sail in the *Mayflower*. After a two month voyage, they arrived in the New

1630, Catholics in Maryland in 1634, religious free thinkers in Rhode Island in 1636, and Quakers in Pennsylvania in 1682. Other colonies, notably the Carolinas, were given by the English king to supportive noblemen.

Dutch and Swedish trading companies also joined the colonial scramble. The Dutch West India Company, started in 1621, established Fort Orange (present-day Albany) on the Hudson River in 1623. It then purchased Manhattan from the native Canarsees for 40 guilders in 1626. Further south, the Swedish West Indian Company set up New Sweden on the Delaware in 1638. The Dutch ended Swedish rule in 1655, but were then conquered by the British in 1664. English rule thus stretched the length of the east coast, from New England in the north to the Carolinas and, in 1724, Georgia in the south.

Labour and work

The English saw their colonies as "transplantations" of English society to a "New World" – the word "plantation" was used to describe both Jamestown and Plymouth – and made no attempt to meet their neighbours. The English colonists preferred to create closed, self-sufficient communities. When their efforts failed, as they often did, the settlers seldom conciliated the natives, but instead tried to defeat, destroy, or drive them away. To the English, the Native American was an obstacle to be overcome, not a valuable resource to be exploited.

This proved a problem as the colonies grew in strength. Those in the north became successful merchant communities, where farming was for food, not export, and so had little need for local labour. Those in the south, however, required workers. The growing of tobacco and other export crops led to the development of large farming estates. These were worked first by white indentured servants from England, but then increasingly by African slaves (see pp.218–19), the first 20 of whom arrived on a Dutch ship in Jamestown in 1619.

The Mayflower
This painting shows the 12-year-old *Mayflower* in Delft harbour at the start of its voyage to the Americas. It was a merchant ship with a crew of 25–30, and was previously used to transport wine.

Plymouth area. A year later, the settlers celebrated their first successful harvest with a dinner, an event still celebrated every November as Thanksgiving.

The settlers, who called themselves "Saints" or "Strangers" depending on their religious beliefs – the name Pilgrims was applied later – received help initially from two American Indians, Samoset and Tisquantum (Squanto), who spoke English as well as their native language Algonquin. Indeed, Squanto had been taken to England in 1605 by an English seafarer and stayed for nine years. The Pilgrims were not the first Europeans to live in the area, as the seaboard was well known to English fishermen from the early 1500s, many of them wintering on its sheltered coast and gathering stocks of food for the journey home.

Religion and trade
Many English colonies on the eastern seaboard were religious in origin: Puritans settled in Massachusetts in

Colonial Northern America
This map from 1721 shows the extent of the British rule (shown in yellow) along the Atlantic coast. Spain (blue) ruled what is now Florida, while France (pink) controlled much of Canada. The blue area in the north of Canada had both French and British settlements.

hilt made of horn; decorated with cartridge butts

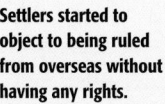 steel blade

 animal skin sheath decorated with porcupine quillwork

Native trapping
Colonists traded blades, often imported from Sheffield, England, with American Indian nations in return for furs from animals trapped and killed by the Indians.

AFTER

Settlers started to object to being ruled from overseas without having any rights.

COLONIAL RULE
By 1750 most of the **13 colonies** were governed in much the same way. Each had a local assembly – Rhode Island's met in

COLONY ASSEMBLY MEETING HOUSE

the Meeting House in Newport (above right) – and a governor appointed or approved by the monarch. Each colony made its own laws and was **internally self-governing**. They were therefore relatively independent, with political and social institutions that differed quite markedly from those in Britain.

IMPERIAL RULE
Colonies were **subject to the British parliament and government**, which regulated their trade and currency to prevent them from competing with British industries. When in 1765 the British government began to levy direct taxes on the colonies to pay for its recent colonial wars, the colonists strongly objected to paying without having proper representation in the British Parliament. This was one of the **major causes of the American Revolution 232-33 ≫**.

Pilgrim housing
This reconstruction of the Plymouth settlement shows how the settlers built their homes: a simple wooden frame covered with wood slats and roofed with thatch kept out the worst of the elements.

Inside a Pilgrim house
The furniture was made from local wood, the curtains and bedding spun from home-grown flax or wool. There were no luxuries – anything that the settlers could not make, they did without.

Spain, Portugal, and France were nations under the rule of autocratic monarchs and their courtiers. Any overseas trade was firmly tied to royal finances.

The Portuguese established the pattern for empire-building: within 15 years of their arrival in the Indian Ocean in the 1480s, they had destroyed Arab naval power. Portugal had limited population and natural resources, but a wealth of nautical and navigational expertise. By forging an empire it could tap into the lucrative Asian spice trade, giving it greater financial security. Bases at Malacca, Ormuz, and Goa in the Indian Ocean, established by Portuguese navy general Afonso da Albuquerque, ensured control of the Persian Gulf and major spice trade routes to the east. Macau, in Southern China, followed in 1517, and by the 1560s, Portugal

> " Let it be known that if you are **strong in ships** the commerce of **the Indies is yours**."
>
> FRANCISCO DE ALMEIDA, FIRST PORTUGUESE VICEROY OF INDIA, c. 1507

imported 50 per cent of Europe's spice supply and 75 per cent of its pepper. At the same time, the Portuguese were importing the first African slaves to Brazil (see pp.218–19), ensuring the colony became the world's largest sugar producer.

Between 1580–1640, Portugal and Spain operated their empires in parallel under the king of Spain. Spain's trade bureaucracy ensured that the monarch received 20 per cent of all precious metals mined in the New World, in exchange for protective convoys. New colonies in the Philippines ensured a transit point between America and China, while Portugal helped Spain dominate East Asian trade, carrying gold and silver to China and bringing back silk via the Pacific and Atlantic oceans.

It was the mercantile commercial philosophy of the French Richelieu and later Colbert that drove France's

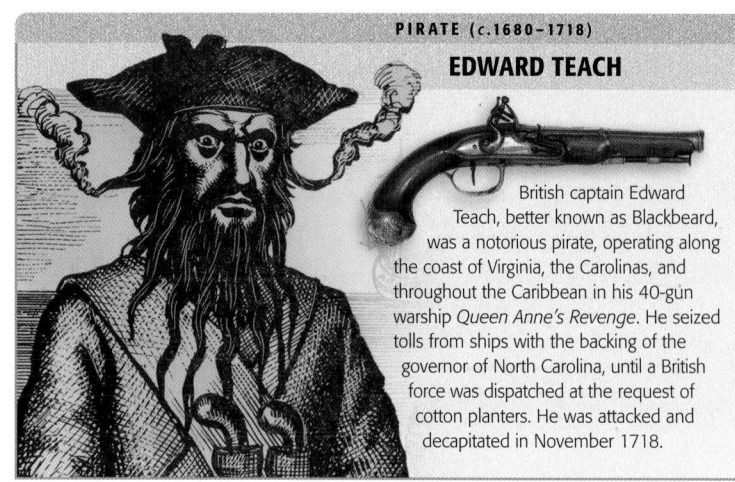

colonial ambitions under Louis XIV (see pp.216–17). France's empire was a state creation, and at first excited little enthusiasm among the French merchant classes. One notable exception was the fur trade created in New France (Canada), along the trading network around the Great Lakes.

Trade for France's rulers, as for Spain's, meant reaping the benefits of colonial resources in order to

safeguard a position in Europe. In both countries, the interests of merchants themselves came a poor second.

Empires of merchants

Traders and adventurers were at the forefront of England and Holland's "private-enterprise" empires. Both

Wampum fur trade belt
Belts of small seashells, called wampums, were made by Iroquois natives along the New England coast. Dutch traders used wampum beads as currency in the fur trade with the Iroquois from the early 1600s.

Trade and Empire

Between the late 15th and 18th centuries many European nations developed large trading empires stretching to Africa, Asia, and the Americas. Imperial growth tended to follow one of two patterns – centralized, bureaucratic, and monarchical, or mercantile and occasionally chaotic.

BEFORE

Advances in navigation opened new doors.

EXIT THE DRAGON
Between 1405–33 seven major Chinese naval expeditions explored and traded across the oceans as far west as Africa. Chinese trade and empire could have been carried further, but the project was abandoned – largely due to imperial mistrust of foreigners.

MARINER'S MIRROUR 1588

NAVIGATION AIDS
From the 15th century onward, improvements to maps and navigation manuals allowed European sailors to venture across the world's oceans. *Mariner's Mirrour* was the first book to show standardized symbols for buoys, channels, safe anchorages, and submerged rocks.

were helped by the establishment of banks, bourses, and joint-stock companies (see pp.214–15), and particularly the East India Companies. Shareholders accepted the need for private defence forces, navies, and fortifications to safeguard their commercial interests, but they were not interested in ruling subject peoples.

With the focus on commerce rather than empire, the Dutch built up the most extensive trade network of any European power, including a toehold in Japan. Ships of the Dutch West India Company spurred the Caribbean sugar plantations, and carried the first slaves to the tobacco plantations of Virginia (see pp.218–19).

England was another latecomer to empire-building, content to harass and plunder Spanish convoys, but somewhat overshadowed by the Dutch. England's East India Company was founded two years before the Dutch, but its less sophisticated financial system and preoccupation with internal affairs gave the Dutch a better start. This changed around the end of the 17th century. New Navigation Acts set out a framework for colonial trade and monopolies, the Hudson's Bay Company traded out of Canada, and the 1715 Treaty of Utrecht gave England a monopoly on supplying slaves to the Spanish American empire. As a result, English foreign trade doubled by 1780.

CLOVES

Lloyd's LIST. N° 996

current rates of annuities for sale

Lloyd's list

Lloyd's List was started by Edward Lloyd, in London (see pp.214–15). It was first published as a source of information for the merchants and insurance underwriters who regularly met at Lloyd's coffeehouse. In 1764 the *Lloyd's Register* was launched. It listed all merchant ships over 100 tonnes. Merchants used it to check on the progress of shipments arriving from around the world, including the Spice Islands.

stock prices over three days on the London stock exchange

CINNAMON

NUTMEG

AFTER ⟩⟩

The expansion of European influence around the world had lasting effects.

EXOTIC TASTES

Western society's taste for drugs of many kinds originated in the period of global seaborne empires. Tea and coffee, tobacco, opium, sugar, and chocolate, all became **highly prized commodities** traded back and forth between imperial powers and their colonies. Where conflicts arose, the great empires were ruthless in enforcing their commercial interests – most notably in the **Opium Wars** of the mid-19th century 284–85 ⟩⟩.

COMMERCE AND INDUSTRY

The increased availability of foreign raw materials helped to fuel the Industrial Revolution 292–95 ⟩⟩, while products manufactured in the West were frequently re-exported back to the very regions that supplied the raw materials. As trade in commodities became more complex, so the **monetary and financial institutions** established in the era of the trading empires developed into the increasingly involved financial world of today. The growing importance of the market influenced many thinkers, leading to the development of free market capitalism 226–29 ⟩⟩ and the application of its principles to other areas of thought such as economics, politics, and philosophy.

Building Batavia

Located on the northwest coast of Java, Batavia (now Jakarta, capital of Indonesia) was seized by Jan Pieterzoon Coen on 30 May 1619 and became the trading hub of the Dutch East Indies. The new city resembled a typical Dutch town, complete with canals.

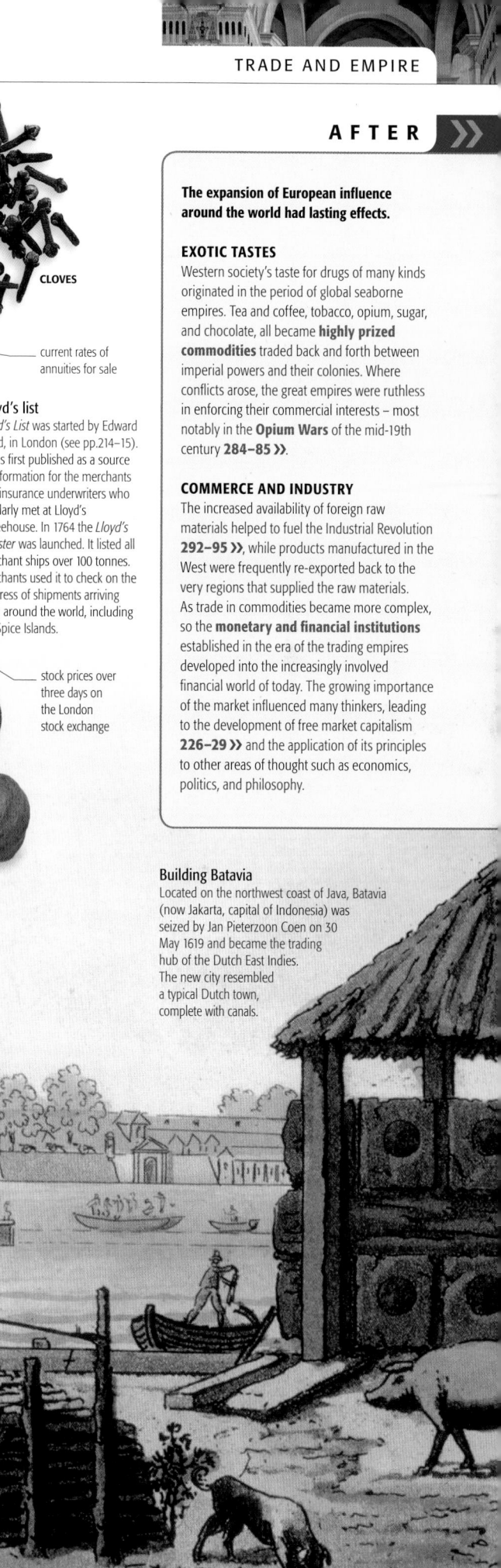

BEFORE

While the last few emperors of the Ming dynasty were distracted by internal rebellion, a new power was gathering in the north.

THE JURCHEN BANNERS
The Jurchen people were descended from the founders of the **Jin dynasty ‹‹ 111**. By the 16th century the Jurchen were living near Jilin in modern-day northeast China, where they hunted, farmed, and traded extensively with the Chinese. In 1616, the Jurchen leader **Nurhaci** founded the Later Jin dynasty and began to organize his people, as well as the Mongols and Chinese who had submitted to Jurchen rule. The entire population were enrolled into **four military units** called banners, each being identified by the colour of their standards.

300 Jurchen families were formed into one *niru*, or company.

25 *niru*, or 7,500 families, were organized under one banner.

FROM JURCHEN TO MANCHU
Nurhaci's successor, **Huang Taiji**, introduced Chinese-style institutions among the Jurchen. In 1636 he changed the name of his people to Manchu (a word of unknown origin) and in 1637 renamed the Later Jin dynasty, adopting the dynastic name **Qing**, meaning "clear". The banner system was expanded by the conquests of Huang Taiji to include eight Manchu, eight Mongol, and eight Chinese banners by 1644.

By the early 17th century, the Ming dynasty (see pp.114–15) was beset by internal popular rebellions and the threat of a Manchu invasion. In April 1644, the rebel leader Li Zicheng took Beijing, and the Ming emperor committed suicide. Li tried to persuade Wu Sangui, the most powerful commander on the frontier, to join him. Instead Wu negotiated with the Manchus, allowing them to pass freely through the Great Wall. The Manchus took control of Beijing in June and Li Zicheng fled. Fulin, the six-year-old son of Huang Taiji (see BEFORE), became the Shunzhi emperor, thus inaugurating the Qing dynasty (1644–1911).

Imperial Poetry
Emperor Kangxi was an accomplished poet as well as a sponsor of the arts. The poetry in this album is attributed to him.

The Manchus continued their advance south, crushing any resistance from Ming loyalists. They also ordered all male Chinese to show that they submitted to Qing rule by shaving their foreheads and adopting the *queue*, a long, braided ponytail, which was compulsory in China throughout the Qing period.

Having gained control over China, the Qing instituted a bureaucracy that relied on features retained from the Ming administration, which included the system of government examinations. Few Manchu could speak Chinese, and even fewer had any experience of office, so all senior posts within the bureaucracy were assigned to both a Manchu and a Chinese official, a policy that went some small way to easing the resentment felt by the Chinese at being ruled over by alien invaders.

The Prosperous Age
Shunzhi showed great promise as a ruler, but he died of smallpox at an early age. It was his three successors who were responsible for consolidating Qing power in China.

Shunzhi's son, the Kangxi emperor, was the longest-reigning emperor in Chinese history. Though born a Manchu, Kangxi became the epitome of a Chinese emperor. He read and commented on

The **Three Emperors**

The reigns of the Three Emperors, Kangxi (1661–1722), Yongzheng (1722–35), and Qianlong (1736–95), are known collectively as the "Prosperous Age", a period when the Chinese empire expanded to its greatest extent and its population doubled.

more than 50 memorials every day, and travelled extensively. He was a patron of the arts and encouraged scholarship. During his reign he crushed a major internal rebellion and led successful campaigns against the Zunghar people of Mongolia.

Emperor Yongzheng, who may have usurped the throne, succeeded Kangxi. Yongzheng insisted on the use of the Manchu language at court and raised the salaries of officials to discourage corruption. To ensure ideological conformity he ordered that the Sacred Edict, which exhorted subjects to revere the emperor, be read out twice a month at Confucian temples.

The reign of the fourth Qing emperor, Qianlong (see right), saw the boundaries of China reach their farthest extent (see left). The addition of territory led to an expansion of the economy, as well as a significant population increase.

Missionaries
The first Christian Jesuit mission in Beijing had been established in 1598. When the Manchus came to power, they continued the Ming practice of

Map

RUSSIAN EMPIRE
Nerchinsk
Amur River
Ussuri
Zunghar
Outer Mongolia
1757
1696
Manchuria
Xinjiang
Inner Mongolia
Rehe
Beijing
Sea of Japan
1757
KOREA
JAPAN
Yellow River
Yellow Sea
TIBET
1717, 1750
Xi'an
Shanghai
Lhasa
Chengdu
Nanjing
NEPAL
Yangtze River
East China Sea
BHUTAN
INDIA
ASSAM
Changsha
BURMA
Guangzhou
Taiwan
Macao
Bay of Bengal
ANNAM
South China Sea
LAOS
HAINAN

KEY
under Manchu control by 1644
under Manchu control by 1660
Qing acquisitions by 1770
→ Main Qing campaigns

0   2000 km
0   2000 miles

Qing territory
The Treaty of Nerchinsk, 1689, defined the border between China and Russia. In 1750, Qianlong declared Tibet a Chinese protectorate. In 1757 a Zunghar rebellion was mercilessly crushed, and their territory was incorporated into the empire.

The sails of a junk could be moved inward, allowing it to sail into the wind much like today's windsurfers and catamarans.

Bamboo battens stiffened the sail and made it easier to roll up in high winds. They also prevented the sail from tearing too easily.

EMBROIDERED SILK ROBE

CARVED JADE

PORCELAIN VASE

GREEN TEA

GINGER ROOT

The rowing boat was hung from the very high poop deck at the stern of Chinese junks, rather than from the sides of the ship as on Western models.

Rudders affixed to the stern were used on junks centuries before their adoption by the West.

Model of a traditional Chinese junk
Introduced in the Han dynasty (see pp.128–29), these ocean-going vessels were in use throughout Chinese history. Qing dynasty trading junks carried a variety of products, from tea and spices to silk and jade.

MANCHU EMPEROR (1711–99)

QIANLONG

Qianlong projected an image of himself as a model Chinese ruler, attending to affairs of state in the morning and painting and writing poems in the afternoon. Though not particularly gifted, he was a prolific poet; more than 40,000 poems have been ascribed to him. The later years of his reign were marred by the growing power of his favourite, Heshen (see AFTER).

AFTER

The last few decades of Qianlong's rule saw the "Prosperous Age" come to an end.

QING CORRUPTION
In 1775, the imperial bodyguard **Heshen** became a favourite of Qianlong, and he began to build a network of corrupt patronage. Qianlong gave him control of the imperial revenues, and allowed him to appoint his henchmen to senior official posts. Heshen is considered to have begun a trend of corruption that continued through the 19th century, gradually undermining the status of the Qing dynasty.

THE OPIUM TRADE
Opium, grown in India, was smuggled into China by British firms. Until 1821 imports of opium averaged 4,500 chests a year. Then the price was lowered and by 1830 the trade had soared to 18,956 chests. Opium smuggling surged again to more than 40,000 chests a year in 1834, costing 34 million silver dollars and causing a significant drain on imperial revenues. Chinese attempts to curb the trade led to the Opium Wars **284–85 »**.

OPIUM PIPE

300 **MILLION** The population of China in 1762, according to government estimates.

employing Jesuits for various official tasks. Kangxi gave Father Adam Schall responsibility for preparing the imperial calendar, for example. When a mistake was detected, Schall was accused of treason and narrowly escaped death. Other Jesuit priests were engaged as diplomats, architects, artists, and mathematicians. In 1692, after Jesuit missionaries had cured the emperor of malaria, Kangxi issued an "edict of toleration", which permitted the teaching of Christianity. However, when the pope forbade all Chinese Christians from performing the rites of ancestor worship, the preaching of Christianity in China was forbidden.

The tea trade
China had long-standing commercial links by land with Central Asia and by sea with Southeast Asia. From the late Ming period, China also had dealings with the European powers. By the 18th century, Britain had become China's major Western trading partner. Interest in Chinese ceramics and silk was still strong, but tea quickly became China's leading export. However, the Chinese would only accept silver in exchange for tea, and it was British attempts to create a demand for a substitute that led to the trade in opium (see AFTER). Under the Qing, foreign trade was regulated closely and from 1760 it was confined to the city of Guangzhou. Complaints over trade restrictions led the British government to send the Macartney embassy to China in 1792 (see p.284).

Japan's Great Peace

In the 17th century Japan shut the door to the outside world. Anybody venturing abroad and daring to return would be executed. For the next 250 years a newly unified Japan was steered along a path of *sakoku*, or national seclusion, and developed its economy and a unique cultural identity.

Imagine a 17th-century city of towering stone walls, long wooden parapets, huge gatehouses, and massive moats, all sprawling out from the largest castle in the world. This bustling town-port with artisans, traders, and labourers is Edo (present-day Tokyo), a city twice the size of the largest cities in Europe at the time, such as London and Paris. Its busy thoroughfares were filled with people from different classes, all of whom were beneficiaries of a new period known as the "Great Peace" or Edo Period. Early-modern Japan was experiencing a period of previously unknown calm that was to last over 250 years.

Shogun authority
Under the newly installed shogun (see pp.116–17) ruler Tokugawa Ieyasu, Edo became the military capital of Japan. The emperor and his court – though revered – were consigned to ceremonial stature at Kyoto, which was Japan's capital at that time. The Imperial court, powerless but prestigious, conferred the title shogun and Ieyasu manipulated this "support" to best advantage. But the key players in the pacification of Japan were the *daimyo* (see pp.116–17), regional leaders who controlled the provinces. The shogun, while exercising control from Edo, had to work with these local magnates, in order to maintain power in distant provinces that were difficult to reach. It was an uneasy alliance veering between accommodation and manipulation: the *daimyo* had to obey the shogun on important policies, and their wives and children had to live in Edo periodically to act as collateral, but they exercised a good deal of freedom and control in their local areas. They were allowed to demand physical labour and duties from local villagers, including taxes and rent.

> " [Edo] is on most days **more crowded than** a public street in any of the most populous towns of **Europe**."
>
> DUTCH TRADER ENGELBERT KASMPFERER, 1621

The great change
Under the shogunate, Japanese society was put through a largely successful experiment of "social engineering". The population was labelled as to whether they were samurai, farmers, craftsmen, or merchants. At the apex of the system were the warrior class, the samurai, who were the only individuals allowed to carry weapons. As a class, samurai were controlled by the military leaders and worked as government officials, guards, policemen, or for local authorities, serving either the shogun or one of the local *daimyo*.

The great change in Japanese society was the elevation of farmers – who made up 80 per cent of the population, and whose labour was critical to the economy – to the second rank of society. Although at the mercy of the *daimyo* and samurai, the peasant farmers enjoyed a high degree of village autonomy. They elected leaders and formed collective assemblies that decided on local issues. They paid taxes (in rice) as a village unit and were granted individual rights to cultivate the land registered to them. In return they had to

BEFORE

Before the Edo period, Japan was a politically divided and unstable country.

CIVIL WAR
From the 12th to the end of 16th century Japan experienced intermittent civil war **≪ 116–17**.

THE COMING OF PEACE
The battle of **Sekigahara** was the last great field battle between two Japanese armies. The victor, Tokugawa Ieyasu, the son of a *daimyo* (warlord) took the title of **shogun** (military dictator).

Edo, largest town
This print by the Japanese artist Ando Hiroshige reveals an 18th-century view of Edo, which was the one of the largest cities in the world throughout the 18th century. Today the Japanese view Edo, upon which Tokyo grew, as the home of their traditional culture, and people born in Tokyo are still known as *Edo-ko*, or children of Edo.

Construction of a Noh mask
Noh masks must be light, as they are worn throughout an entire performance. Traditionally, each mask is carved out of a single piece of cypress wood.

Surface of the mask is painted with layers of gesso (primer) mixed with glue and then sanded down to give the mask its final shape

Black ink is used to outline the eyes and trace hair

Eyes have been gilded

Tea ceremony
A coloured woodcut of a classic Edo era scene: geishas at a formal tea ceremony. *Cha-no-yu*, as it is called, was – and still is – considered a traditional art in Japan.

ensure they did not neglect their farms, which meant they were forbidden to move away from the villages they occupied.

Below the farmers in terms of rights and restrictions were the artisans and craftsmen; merchants and shopkeepers were considered the lowest rank in this strict class structure. Commerce, however, developed in the expanding urban centres of Edo, Osaka, and Kyoto, and the merchant class made money trading and broking, coming to enjoy a certain amount of financial power, which offset their "low class" status in this society.

Despite the oppressively rigid classification of society and the strict codes of behaviour governing every aspect of life from clothing to social etiquette and even tea drinking, Japan also experienced a cultural renaissance in the 17th century.

Edo culture
The Edo Period produced much of what we recognize today as traditional Japanese culture. *Haiku*, the 17-syllable poem still in use today, was born; zen gardens, flower arranging, and the tea ceremony all came into their own; and *Noh* theatre was transformed. *Noh* had its roots in the 11th century in the

provinces. It originally consisted of acrobatic and juggling displays, but the addition of operatic dance and recital transformed it into a highly stylized and symbolic drama. As with all other forms of cultural life in the Edo period, *Noh* theatre was strictly governed and the lower classes were forbidden to learn the techniques of the art form. *Kabuki, ukiyo-e*, porcelain, and lacquer-ware all developed and thrived during this period. *Ukiyo-e*, or "pictures of the floating world", was an art form that proved highly popular for its depictions of sensual courtesans, erotic prostitutes, and flashy kabuki actors. The *Ukiyo-e* style broadened from screen prints into wood block prints to show scenes of Edo and landscapes, as typified by Hiroshige (see left). The genre also later proved influential to Western artists such as Vincent Van Gogh, Claude Monet, Edgar Degas, and Gustav Klimt.

AFTER

The 18th and early 19th century in Japan were marked by severe famines, increasing social tensions, and repeated but unsuccessful attempts at political reform.

DECLINE OF THE SHOGUNATE
By the beginning of the 19th century, a growing number of Japanese saw the **shogunate system as inflexible and unresponsive** to new challenges **286–87 »**.

JAPAN'S MODERNIZATION
Japan was **forced to open** its borders by the US in 1854 and its **Westernization** began **286–87 »**. The Bank of Japan (including a modern mint) was established in 1882.

JAPANESE COINS

Noh and Kabuki
There are four main categories of *Noh* masks, each representing a different *Noh* genre: god, demon, warrior, woman. *Noh* plays deal with a universal truth, displayed on stage in a kind of visual metaphor. The masks used in *Noh* theatre use neutral expressions, which means that the actors have to use great skill to bring the characters "to life". Pictured to the right are a 14th-century warrior mask and two Edo-period masks.

While *Noh* theatre's restraint and elegance appealed to upper class Japanese society, *Kabuki* theatre, which was garish and bawdy, was embraced by the merchant class.

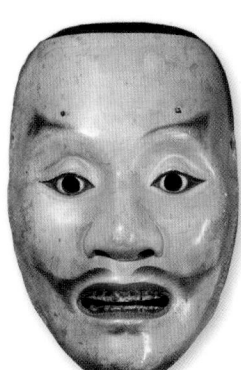

NOH WARRIOR

NOH DEMON

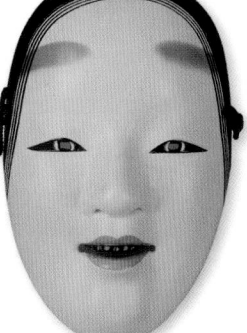

NOH WOMAN

THE MUGHAL DYNASTY
After an initial period of expansion and consolidation, the Mughal Empire remained a stable and vibrant entity for over 170 years (1556–1719). A long, slow decline ended with the empire's dissolution in 1857.

1527 Babur leads his army to victory in an important battle against a confederacy of Rajput kings at Kanua.

1540 Humayun becomes a royal exile, leaving **Sher Shah Sur** as undisputed ruler of northern India.

1579 Akbar **abolishes the residence tax** on non-Muslims in an important symbolic act that implied Muslims and non-Muslims were no longer unequal within the empire.

1605 Akbar dies and **Jahangir** accedes to the throne.

1628 Shah Jahan accedes to the throne.

1658 Shah Jahan dies and **Aurangzeb** accedes to the throne.

THE MUGHAL DYNASTY
After an initial period of expansion and consolidation, the Mughal Empire remained a stable and vibrant entity for over 170 years (1556–1719). A long, slow decline ended with the empire's dissolution in 1857.

| 1500 | 1550 | 1600 | 1650 | 1700 | 1750 | 1800 | 1850 |

1530 Babur dies; **Humayun** accedes to the throne.

1627 Jahangir dies.

1654 The **Taj Mahal** is completed at Agra.

1707 Aurangzeb dies.

1739 Nadir Shah **sacks Delhi** and seizes the Mughal treasury.

1838 Accession of the last Mughal emperor, **Bahadur Shah II**.

1555–56 Humayun restores Mughal rule. Dies 1556. **Akbar** accedes to the throne with Bairam Khan as regent.

1585 Akbar transfers the capital from Fatehpur Sikri to **Lahore**.

1571 Akbar moves the empire's capital from Agra to a newly built city at **Fatehpur Sikri**.

1648 Shah Jahan takes up residence in his new capital, **Delhi**.

1857 The Indian Mutiny leads to the **dissolution of the Mughal Empire** and rule over India by the British crown.

The Great Mughals

One of the most powerful states of the 17th century, the Mughal Empire had a complex administrative system that enabled it to rule over more than 100 million people across most of the Indian subcontinent. The splendour and sophistication of its court was world famous.

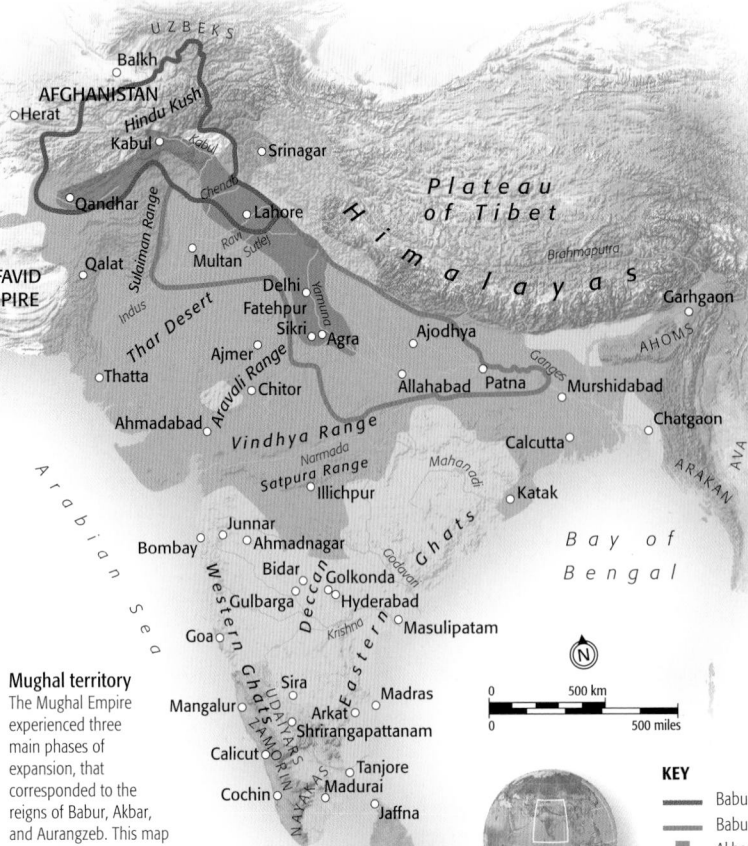

The first Mughal emperor
Babur, founder of the Mughal Empire, is shown here capturing sheep from the Hazara tribe. Babur is remembered as much for his literary prowess as for his military achievements. This picture is from his memoir, the *Baburnama*, which provides a frank insight into his life.

The decisive battles in Babur's (see left) conquest of north India were his defeat of the Afghan Sultan of Delhi, Ibrahim Lodi, at Panipat in 1526 and his success over a confederacy of Rajput kings at Kanua the following year. Using firearms and an experienced and efficient cavalry, he had consolidated Mughal (Persian for Mongol) rule over the rich cities and productive lands of northern India from his capital at Agra by his death in 1530.

His son, Humayun, met with less success. By 1540, he had lost his father's kingdom to the Afghan ruler, Sher Shah Sur, and had been forced into exile at the Safavid court in Persia. In mid-1555, with Persian support, he restored Mughal rule by defeating Sher Shah's weaker descendants, thus duplicating his father's conquests. However, he died just seven months later, leaving the empire to his 12-year-old son, Akbar, with an influential noble, Bairam Khan, as his regent.

Together, they extended Mughal control over northern India, in the region bounded by the Indus and Ganges rivers, to form an imperial heartland that, in time, was framed by palace fortresses at Agra, Allahabad, Ajmer, and Lahore. After he came of age in 1560, Akbar achieved a further series of military successes; by his death in 1605, his empire reached from Kashmir in the north and Afghanistan in the northwest, to Bengal in the east and the Deccan plateau in the south.

Structure and tolerance

To consolidate his position, Akbar established a centralized system of government. This was administered by warrior-aristocrats (*mansabdars*) of various ranks who could be appointed to bureaucratic or military positions and were accompanied by their own households or troops. The most senior *mansabdars* were paid with land grants (*jagirs*). They had the right to collect taxes from this land, but could not own, govern, or occupy it.

Akbar had a policy of religious tolerance, which was evident in his own marriages to women of different faiths, whom he did not force to convert to Islam. This was a shrewd

BEFORE «

On the eve of its conquest by the Muslim Mughals, India was very fragmented.

MUSLIM AND HINDU INDIA
Muslim rule over India's predominantly Hindu population began in the north with the **Delhi Sultanate** (1206–1526) **«** 126–27. The south was dominated by the Hindu **Vijayanagar Empire**. The centre consisted mainly of Muslim sultanates, while the **Hindu Rajputs** and **Lodi Afghans** quarrelled over the north.

BABUR IN AFGHANISTAN
To the northwest, in Central Asia, **Babur**, a descendant of Genghis Khan **«** 112–13, had been exiled from his home in Ferghana by the Uzbek Shaibani Khan. He seized Kabul, capital of Afghanistan in 1504, then moved on to India.

Mughal territory
The Mughal Empire experienced three main phases of expansion, that corresponded to the reigns of Babur, Akbar, and Aurangzeb. This map shows the extent of empire at the end of each of their reigns.

KEY
— Babur's domains, 1525
— Babur's acquisitions prior to Mughal expulsions, 1539
■ Akbar's domains, 1556
▨ Areas held by Mughals at Akbar's death 1605
▢ Additional areas acquired up to the death of Aurangzeb, 1707

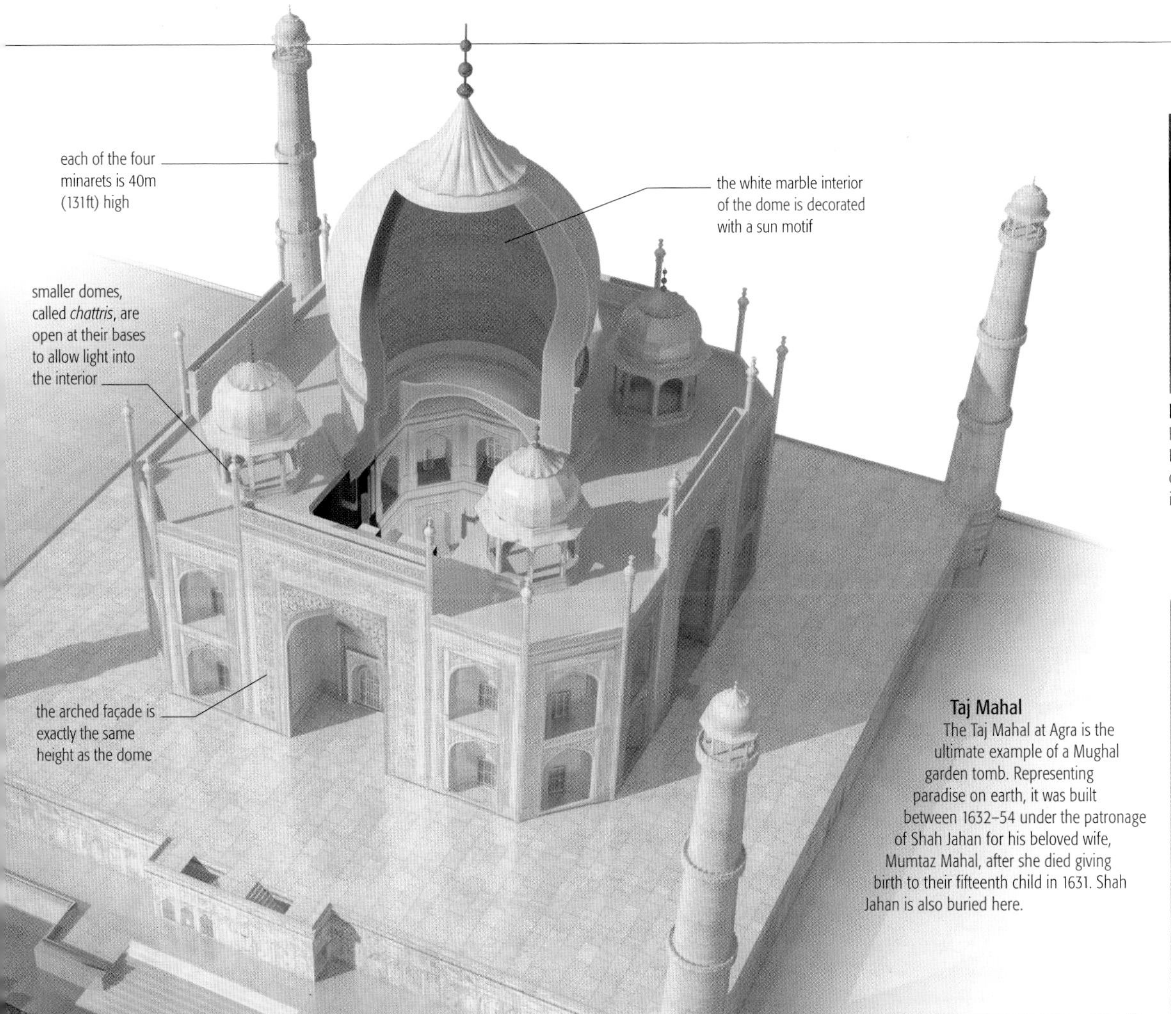

each of the four minarets is 40m (131ft) high

the white marble interior of the dome is decorated with a sun motif

smaller domes, called *chattris*, are open at their bases to allow light into the interior

the arched façade is exactly the same height as the dome

Red Fort
Repeating scalloped arches of red sandstone in the Red Fort at Delhi. The Red Fort, or Lal Quila, was at the heart of Shah Jahan's new city. From 1648 it functioned as his imperial palace and the Mughal administrative centre.

AFTER

In the 18th century Mughal sovereignty became limited to Delhi and its hinterland.

END OF MUGHAL RULE
The emperor retained some authority within India as a whole as the *shahanshah*, or "king of kings". His court patronized religious and cultural developments.

BAHADUR SHAR II

EAST INDIA COMPANY
During the early 19th century, any remaining authority was eroded systematically by the expanding **East India Company 282 ≫**. A final attempt to restore Mughal rule was connected to the Indian Mutiny of 1857. This led to the dissolution of the Mughal Empire and the establishment of British crown rule in India **282–83 ≫**. **The last Mughal emperor**, Bahadur Shah II, died in exile in Burma in 1862.

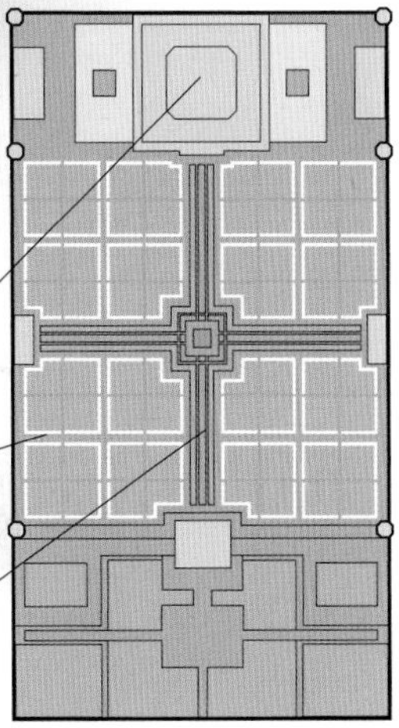

Taj Mahal
The Taj Mahal at Agra is the ultimate example of a Mughal garden tomb. Representing paradise on earth, it was built between 1632–54 under the patronage of Shah Jahan for his beloved wife, Mumtaz Mahal, after she died giving birth to their fifteenth child in 1631. Shah Jahan is also buried here.

the tomb is placed at one end, not at the centre. This is unique among garden tombs

geometric brick-lined flowerbeds

streams are thought to represent the four rivers in the Islamic depiction of paradise

The paradise garden
The Taj Mahal garden is thought to represent paradise – the word "paradise" is from the ancient Persian for "walled garden". Mughal formal gardens, *charbaghs* (four gardens), were based on those of the Persians, who saw great significance in the number four. The design was brought to India by Babur. The plan of the Taj Mahal garden (left) shows the use of units of four.

political move that would help to unite the many faiths of his empire. He also allowed the Hindu Rajputs to negotiate entry into his nobility if they offered their daughters in marriage. Eventually, he relied more on Rajputs and Persians than on his own Central Asian nobles.

Reform and the arts
During his reign, Akbar also reduced the influence of Muslim scholars (*'ulama*), abolished taxes on Hindu pilgrims and non-Muslim residents (*jizya*), and introduced the Bengali calendar, a solar calendar to replace the Muslim lunar cycle. At his new palace at Fatehpur Sikri near Agra, he held

religious debates in a purpose-built *ibadat-khana*, or "house of worship", that gave representation to different faith groups. These policies were highly pragmatic in a country that was predominantly non-Muslim, but they were also a reflection of his eclectic spirituality, further revealed in his establishment of a cult based on the worship of light and sun (*din-i-ilahi*).

Music and art also interested Akbar. He induced the famed singer and musician, Tansen, to join his court, and began patronizing what became known as north Indian classical music. At Fatehpur Sikri, he established a school of Mughal painting, combining Persian

and Indian influences in a style that was to reach its peak during the reign of his son, Jahangir (1605–27).

Peak and decline
Jahangir's son, Shah Jahan (1628–58) contributed more artistic treasures, such as the Taj Mahal at Agra and a majestic new capital at Delhi, which included the Red Fort and the Jama Masjid. These huge projects were also symbols of Mughal wealth, dependent on flourishing agriculture and trade. From his accession in 1658, the last "great" Mughal, Aurangzeb oversaw the expansion of the empire to its largest extent. Yet his reign also

signified the beginning of the end. He was often away from his capital on military campaigns, and he depleted the treasury attempting to defeat the Marathas in the south who were trying to establish their own empire. Some scholars also believe his strict interpretation of Islam offended his Rajput collaborators and Hindu subjects.

The empire was further weakened by a rapid succession of rulers following Aurangzeb's death in 1707. In 1739, Nadir Shah, the Safavids' successor, sacked Delhi and seized the Mughal treasury. The empire was all but dead. In 1857, the British deposed Babadur Shah II, the last Mughal emperor.

The Ottoman Empire

For over 600 years the Ottoman Empire dominated the political and religious life of the Middle East, viewed with awe by the Christian West, and a byword for wealth, power, unimaginable opulence, and – in its latter years – widespread corruption.

The harem of the Topkapi Palace
This 18th-century miniature by Fazil Enderuni shows concubines bathing in the Topkapi Palace harem. All concubines were non-Muslim captives taken in war or bought from slavers.

≪ BEFORE

The Ottoman Empire was forged in a bloody furnace of continual intrigue and conflict.

THE CREATION OF THE EMPIRE

In the 13th century a band of **Turkish warriors** led by **Ertughrul** and his son **Osman ≪ 152–53** came to Anatolia from the Central Asian Plains. Ertughrul came to the aid of the Seljuk Sultan Kaihusrev II and was rewarded with land, which grew to become the *Osman-li*, the Ottoman Empire.

JANISSARIES

Osman's son, **Orhan**, formed the "akinci"

SIPAHI WARRIOR (standing cavalry formations) and the celebrated "Janissaries" (highly trained infantry). With this formidable army, Orhan and his son **Murad I** seized most of the Balkans, and achieved the Ottoman goal of conquering Anatolia. The **Sipahis** were mounted warriors in the army recruited from land-owning Turks. They considered themselves an elite force.

EMPIRE ACHIEVED

After defeat by the Mongols at Ankara in 1402, the reigns of **Murad II** and **Mehmed II ≪ 153** finally saw the Ottoman empire restored.

The emergence of the Ottomans as a world power began with the rule of Mehmed II in 1451. Mehmed led his army west to attack Christian Constantinople, capital of the once great Byzantine Empire (see pp.144–45). Using the world's largest cannon to pound the allegedly "impregnable" walls, and with more than 160,000 men against the defenders' 7,000, he swiftly crushed all resistance. On 29 May 1453 Constantinople fell. Mehmed pushed on into Europe, seizing territory, until his failure to take Belgrade in 1456 brought the conquest to a halt and left the Ottoman Empire's border with Western Europe static for the next 60 years.

Meanwhile, the Ottoman eastern borders were threatened by the rise of the Persian Safavids. It was not until the Battle of Chaldiran in 1514 that Selim I humbled the rival dynasty. A great expansion followed. Selim led his troops east and south, taking Jerusalem's holy sites and conquering Cairo in 1517. Selim's son, Suleyman, known as "The Magnificent" in Europe for his wealth and power, proved no less a conqueror than his father. Despite his success, Suleyman's personal life ended in tragedy.

Suleyman's two favourite sons, Mustafa and Bayazid, were accused of conspiring against him. To save his throne, Suleyman was forced to have them both executed. He never

Dagger and scabbard
Ottoman weaponry was renowned for its beauty and functionality. This dagger and scabbard, richly encrusted with semiprecious stones, were probably the possession of an Ottoman noble.

recovered from this loss and, a sad and broken figure, became a virtual recluse in the Topkapi Palace, leaving his Grand Vizier (chief minister) to run the empire. While both Mustafa and Bayazid had been trained to rule, the grieving Suleyman had left Selim, his untutored surviving son, in the febrile atmosphere of the harem (the women's area of the palace). This neglect had disastrous consequences for Ottoman rule.

Ottoman decline

Many historians date the beginnings of decline from the accession of Selim, known as "The Drunkard". With no political or military training, Selim's formative experiences were food, drink, and women. On his accession Selim handed over control of the empire to his Vizier. This set the pattern for the next century of Ottoman rule, with catastrophic results.

Without a strong ruler, government corruption flourished, and the indifference of the bureaucracy to predatory local officials eroded public support for the regime. Lacking the controlling hand of the Sultan the

---

RULER OF OTTOMAN EMPIRE (1520–66)

SULEYMAN

This king is known as "Suleyman the Magnificent" in the Western world and in the Islamic world as *Kanuni*, "The Lawgiver" – a tribute to the prosperity his reign brought to the Ottoman Empire. Suleyman believed himself to be the spiritual heir to both Alexander (see pp.50–51) and Caesar (see pp.62–63), and claimed title to all the lands they had ruled over. Within a year of his accession his armies had taken Belgrade, and by the time of his death the Ottomans controlled large parts of southeast Europe, the North African coast, and the Middle East. His rule saw a cultural renaissance of Islamic civilization. His support of the arts and the rule of law that he implemented remain his legacy.

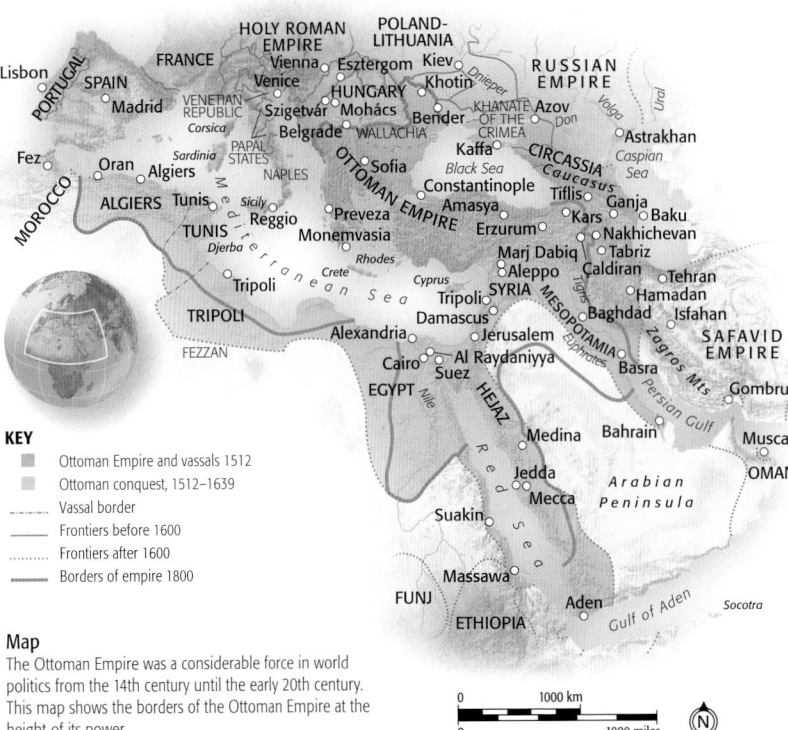

Map

The Ottoman Empire was a considerable force in world politics from the 14th century until the early 20th century. This map shows the borders of the Ottoman Empire at the height of its power.

KEY

- Ottoman Empire and vassals 1512
- Ottoman conquest, 1512–1639
- Vassal border
- Frontiers before 1600
- Frontiers after 1600
- Borders of empire 1800

various elements of government – the Diwan (supreme Court), Grand Vizier, and Janisseries (elite army units) – all vied for power. The Sublime Porte (Ottoman Government) presented a united face to its enemies, but a century of nepotism and greed slowly ate it from within.

Although there had been a few attempts to stem the tide of misgovernment, it was only in the 1650s with Mehmet Kopprulu, Grand Vizier to Mehmet IV, that a systematic and enduring effort to root out corruption began. He also planned a resumption of Ottoman conquest, but died before his plans came to fruition. His brother-in-law, Kara Mustafa, continued Mehmet's expansionist policies, marching on Vienna, the capital of the mighty Habsburg Empire, in 1683. However, a combination of innovative cavalry tactics and superior artillery resulted in Mustafa's defeat.

With this defeat a steady European encroachment on Ottoman lands began, and for most of the 18th century they were at war with one or more European powers. Mahmud I brought respite to the weary empire, capturing Belgrade, and holding it under the Treaty of Belgrade of 1739. But given the ongoing corruption within government, further losses seemed inevitable.

The Blue Mosque

Built for Sultan Ahmed I between 1609–16 by master architect Sedefhar Mehmet Aga, the Sultan Ahmed mosque in Istanbul is lined with more than 20,000 handmade ceramic tiles.

Calligraphy

This is the exquisite *tugra* – a form of calligraphic monogram or seal – of Sultan Murat III and dates from 1575. Initially *tugras* were used only on official documents such as *fermans* (orders of the Sultan), but later they began to appear as a symbol of sovereignty on stamps, coins, and flags. *Tugras* even appeared on ships, mosques, and palaces.

AFTER

After 1750 the Ottoman Empire's story is one of slow, continuous decline.

LOSING GROUND

In the early 1800s reforms were introduced to stabilize the Ottoman Empire, but its **slow dismemberment** continued. The Greeks seized independence in 1829, and the Russo–Turkish War of 1828–29 led to further losses **260–63 »**. Bosnia-Herzegovina rebelled in 1875, and in another war with Russia between 1877–78 the Empire ceded Romania, Serbia, and Montenegro. What was left of the Ottoman Empire became known as "the Sick Man of Europe".

END OF EMPIRE

Two more **Balkan Wars** (1912–13) saw the empire lose most of its remaining European territory. By the end of **World War I 296–97 »** in 1918 the empire effectively ceased to exist, the Treaty of Sèvres of 1920 formally confirming its dissolution.

OTTOMAN COAT OF ARMS

Battle of Lepanto

The largest battle fought by galley fleets in the Mediterranean, the Battle of Lepanto was a clash between the Ottoman Turks and the Holy League of Spain, the Papacy, Venice, and Genoa. The aim of the Europeans was to save the island of Cyprus from the westward advance of the Ottomans, who already occupied most of Hungary and threatened Vienna and the Austrian lands. The result was a huge defeat for the Ottoman forces.

The Ottomans, from northwestern Turkey (see pp.186–87), had taken territory from the Byzantine Empire (see pp.144–45). In 1453 they conquered the empire's capital Constantinople (modern Istanbul) and in the next few years took over most of its lands, from Serbia and Bosnia in the west to Anatolia in the east. By the early 16th century they were expanding again, destroying the power of Hungary at the Battle of Mohacs in 1526, and laying siege to Vienna in 1529 – although they had to pull back from the city when they ran out of supplies and winter came.

In 1570, the Ottomans invaded the island of Cyprus. By moving into the Mediterranean, they threatened the freedom of wealthy cities such as Genoa and Venice to continue to travel and trade freely in the region (see pp.154–55). The Habsburg rulers of the Holy Roman Empire (see pp.188–89) were concerned they would be attacked again, and the Catholic Church also felt threatened by the Muslim Ottomans. As a result Venice, Genoa, Spain (ruled by Philip II), and the Papacy formed an alliance, called the Holy League, in order to defend the Mediterranean against the Ottomans. The League assembled a huge fleet of some 210 ships commanded by Don John of Austria, illegitimate son of the Habsburg emperor, Charles V. In 1571, Don John spotted the Turkish fleet, rather bigger than his own, off Lepanto (now Navpatkos), on the western coast of Greece. Both fleets were made up mainly of galleys, large warships powered by oarsmen. Don John also had six galleasses, powerful hybrid vessels with sails as well as oars, and with heavy cannons mounted along their flanks.

The ships of the League attacked quickly. The Turks preferred to fight by ramming their enemy's ships, but Don John deployed the formidable firepower he carried. The tactics were a resounding success. The Ottoman commander, Ali Pasha, was killed, as were thousands of his men.

The Holy League destroyed the Turkish navy, but they did not destroy the Turks. The Ottomans built a new fleet, which was afloat within a year. The Turks kept control of Cyprus and the rest of their empire. But they did not expand further westward, as they might have done if they had won.

Don John of Austria goes to war
This painting by 16th-century Italian artist Andrea Micheli depicts the Battle of Lepanto, which was the last battle fought by galleys. The Holy League sank or captured around 200 of the Ottoman ships, losing only 15 of their own.

" Strong gongs groaning as the guns boom far... "
G K CHESTERTON, BRITISH AUTHOR, FROM THE POEM *LEPANTO*, 1915

The Renaissance

During the 15th and 16th centuries, art and learning flourished in cities and at royal courts in many parts of Europe, but most especially in Italy. The works of the exceptional individuals who made this "renaissance" are among the marvels of the world.

The Renaissance was part of an ongoing process that changed the shape of European culture over many centuries. The term "Renaissance" refers to a "rebirth" of interest in the legacy of ancient Greece and Rome, but the texts of pre-Christian writers had in fact been copied and read in Christian Europe at least from the time of Charlemagne (747–814 CE; see pp.134–35). The paintings of artists such as Giotto, and the writings of Dante, Petrarch, and Boccaccio in the 14th century are among many works that prefigured the Renaissance. The period of the Renaissance is, however, conventionally dated to around 1450–1550, as a time of exceptional curiosity and inventiveness in European art, architecture, ideas, and technology.

IL LIBRO DEL CORTEGIANO DEL CONTE BALDESAR CASTIGLIONE.

Early book
Baldassare Castiglione's *Book of the Courtier* (1528), was a guide to behaviour at a Renaissance court.

Wealth and culture
Economic prosperity was the basis for the Renaissance. Art and learning were luxuries that could be afforded through the increasing wealth of a social elite. The major centres of Renaissance cultural activity were the thriving city-states of Italy, such as Florence, Milan, and Venice, prosperous cities in Germany, and the Flemish Netherlands (see pp.154–55, 214–15). Grown rich on the proceeds of banking, trade, and manufacture, cities spent freely on cultural luxuries out of civic pride or to enhance the prestige of local rulers such as the Medici family in Florence or the Sforzas in Milan. Wealthy kings such as Matthias Corvinus in Hungary and Francis I in France also patronized artists and intellectuals as a way of advertising their own power and status. Renaissance popes such as Alexander VI (pope from 1492–1503) and Julius II (1503–13) made Rome another focus of excellence, lavishing money raised from their Christian flock on extravagant artistic and architectural projects such as St Peter's Basilica.

The Classical world
The Renaissance was still far from the modern world of science and reason – astrology and alchemy (see p.206) were major fields of study, and one

Dante standing before Florence
Domenico di Michelino painted this image of the poet Dante alongside his native city, Florence. Florence was home to many artists, including architect Brunelleschi, who designed the famous cathedral dome, visible on Dante's left.

Michaelangelo's David
This massive marble statue was made by Michelangelo for the city of Florence in 1504. Its celebration of the nude male form reflects the influence of classical antiquity, but its subject is the biblical hero David.

Humanist group
Painted by Domenico Ghirlandaio around 1490, this detail from a fresco in the church of Santa Maria Novella in Florence shows a group of humanist scholars including Marsilio Ficino, head of the Platonic Academy.

of the period's most famous books was *Malleus Maleficarum* (1486), a treatise on hunting witches. Renaissance intellectuals and artists were in a sense backward-looking; self-consciously seeking to learn from and emulate the achievements of the ancient world and to reconcile the best of the wisdom of ancient Greece and Rome with their Christian faith. But they were also inspired by a confident belief in progress through free enquiry and fresh inventions.

Humanism
The loose international network of scholars who spearheaded the Renaissance are known as "humanists", reflecting the degree to which they placed humankind, rather than God, at the centre of their world-view. A typical treatise published by humanist Pico della Mirandola in 1486 was entitled "On the Dignity of Man". These scholars studied ancient texts more critically than had been done before, reading in Greek as well as in Latin, which had long been the

« **BEFORE**

In medieval times, some artists and thinkers were already breaking with tradition.

THE FIRST RENAISSANCE
Historians have identified an early "renaissance" in 12th century Europe. **Contact with the Muslim world and the Byzantine Empire** gave access to the works of Islamic and ancient Greek philosophers and scientists **« 106–07**.

GIOTTO
Florentine artist **Giotto di Bondone** (c.1267–1337) initiated a **revolution in European painting** a century before the Renaissance proper. His religious frescoes broke with the conventions of Christian art, showing realistic figures engaged in dramatic scenes.

DIVINE COMEDY
In his epic *Divine Comedy*, describing a journey through Hell and Purgatory to Paradise, Florentine poet **Dante Alighieri** (1265–1321) combined the classical past with a medieval Christian view of the universe.

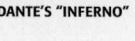

DANTE'S "INFERNO"

language of the educated in Europe. They also strove to establish an accurate text for the Bible – renowned humanist Erasmus regarded his Greek version of the New Testament as his major achievement. Humanists were often employed as tutors for the children of the rich and powerful, and they devised influential systems of education, focusing on subjects such as Latin, history, grammar, and rhetoric.

Feats in architecture

Architecture was an area in which the emulation of antiquity was most fruitful. One of the first great achievements of the Renaissance was the dome built for the cathedral in Florence by Filippo Brunelleschi. Brunelleschi had studied the ancient ruins in Rome, including the domed Pantheon (see pp.64–67), before embarking on the work. Completed in 1436, it was the largest dome ever built, a nearly miraculous feat of engineering as well as an aesthetic masterpiece. Domes were established as a crowning feature of the most ambitious Renaissance buildings, including St Peter's Basilica in Rome,

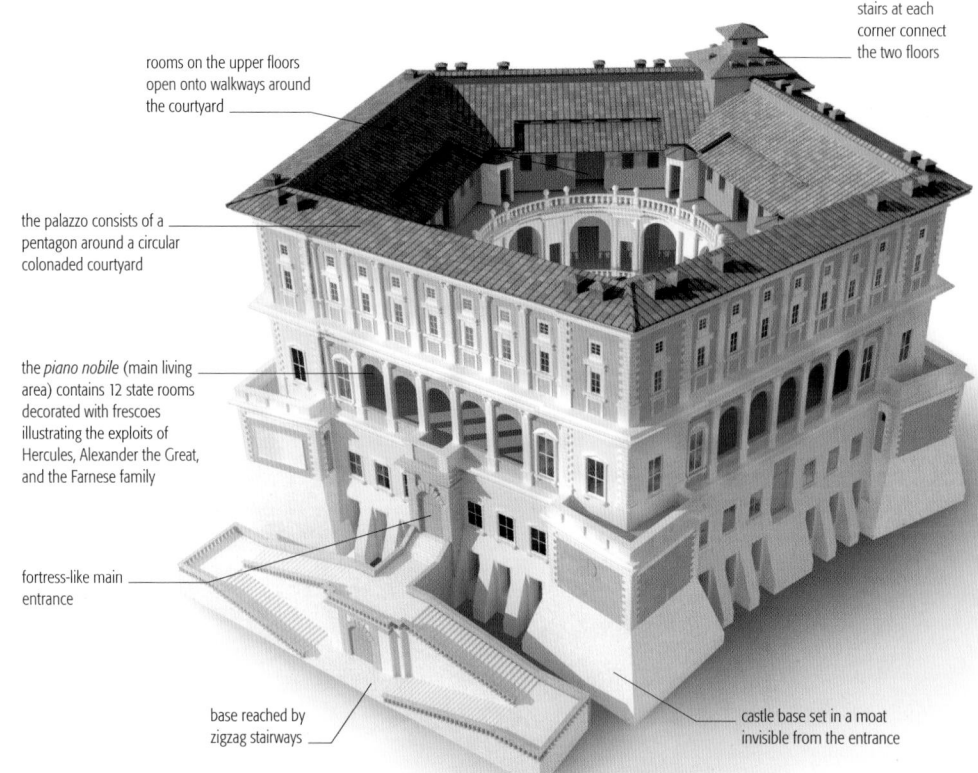

stairs at each corner connect the two floors

rooms on the upper floors open onto walkways around the courtyard

the palazzo consists of a pentagon around a circular colonaded courtyard

the *piano nobile* (main living area) contains 12 state rooms decorated with frescoes illustrating the exploits of Hercules, Alexander the Great, and the Farnese family

fortress-like main entrance

base reached by zigzag stairways

castle base set in a moat invisible from the entrance

while antique-style columns, arches, and statues (see pp.70–71) abounded in palaces, villas, and in churches.

Artists and art

In painting and sculpture the influence of ancient Greece and Rome was evident, for example, in the interest in an ideal version of the naked human body, seen especially in the painting and sculpture of Michelangelo Buonarroti. Artists also added classical pagan mythology to their subject matter (see pp.94–95), although usually for the private enjoyment of wealthy connoisseurs. Christian and biblical themes predominated in art for public display. As well as a desire to match the art of antiquity, however, there was a novel drive to represent the visual world with illusionistic precision. Flemish artists such as Jan van Eyck led the way with oil paintings that represented human features and the surfaces of objects with astounding accuracy of detail. In the second half of the 15th-century, Italian artists such as Piero della Francesca and Andrea Mantegna pioneered the use of linear perspective, intended to create a perfect illusion of three-dimensional space on a flat

Villa Farnese
Commissioned by the wealthy Farnese family, the Villa Farnese is considered a masterpiece of late Renaissance architecture. Architect Giacomo Barozzi de Vignola worked on the building from 1559–73.

The Birth of Venus
Produced around 1483, Sandro Botticelli's famous painting is unusual in having an overtly pagan (non-Christian) theme drawn from classical mythology. This was possible because it was destined for Lorenzo de Medici's private villa, not for public display.

Sistine ceiling
Commissioned by Pope Julius II in 1508, the ceiling of the Sistine Chapel in the Vatican is one of the masterworks of Florentine genius Michelangelo Buonarroti. Depicting scenes from the Old Testament, the frescoes took four years to complete.

CLASSICAL SCHOLAR (1466–1536)
ERASMUS

Dutch humanist Gerhard Gerhards, better known by his pen-name Erasmus, was ordained as a priest but lived as an independent scholar. In works such as *In Praise of Folly* (1509), he criticized the corruption of the Church, advocating a life governed by firm moral and religious principles. Erasmus's writings were among the first printed books to achieve a wide readership and they helped prepare the way for the Protestant Reformation (see pp.196–97).

"Our century, like a **golden age** has restored... the liberal arts."

MARSILIO FICINO, FLORENTINE PHILOSPHER, 1492

surface. Associated with geometry and optics, painting was part of the mainstream of intellectual development in the Renaissance.

Overtaking the Ancients

Striving for an exact depiction of the world in art was related to a wider trend towards the close observation of nature, rather than reliance on received wisdom. This produced clear advances on the knowledge inherited from the Ancients. For instance, the dissection of corpses by the Brussels-born anatomist Andreas Vesalius at the University of Padua allowed the long-accepted views of Galen, the revered medical authority of antiquity, to be superseded. The geographical notions of the ancient Greek Ptolemy were corrected thanks to the efforts of European explorers and mapmakers. Nicolaus Copernicus challenged the current Christian view of the Universe by asserting that the Sun, not the Earth, was at the centre of the Solar System (see p.206).

Craftsmanship

Underpinning the achievements of the celebrated geniuses of the Renaissance was a widespread culture of practical ingenuity and skilled craftsmanship. Fine craft objects, such as the elaborate suits of armour made by the metalworkers of Nuremberg and Augsburg, or the products of Venetian or Florentine goldsmiths, were collected as avidly as any painting or sculpture. More practically, it was during this time that gunpowder weapons came into general use in European warfare

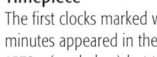

Timepiece
The first clocks marked with minutes appeared in the 1570s, (see below) but truly accurate timekeeping was not possible until pendulum clocks were introduced in the 17th century.

A dagger carries an abbreviated Latin inscription, AET. SVAE 29. This gives the age of the subject, France's ambassador to England Jean de Dinteville, as 29.

Jean de Dinteville is depicted with his friend, French envoy Georges de Selve. The objects between them suggest their wealth and learning.

The celestial globe, showing the constellations, was the latest model, made by German astronomer Johannes Schöner. Its presence echoes the terrestrial globe below.

The scientific instruments are devices for navigation and time measurement. They are resting on a valuable Turkish rug, imported from the Ottoman Empire.

The Ambassadors
Painted by German artist Hans Holbein at the court of English King Henry VIII in 1533, this painting shows the Renaissance's fascination with scientific instruments as well as its taste for hidden meanings and visual tricks.

In the foreground is a a distorted representation of a skull, an obvious symbol of mortality. The skull appears correctly if viewed from a precise low point to the side of the painting.

The open book is a Lutheran hymnal, open at the hymns "Come Holy Ghost" and "Man Whilt Thou Live Blessedly". It probably hints at the religious conflicts of the Reformation.

(see pp.212–13). Mechanical clocks, which had first started to appear in the towers of Italian cities in the 14th century, became more widespread. Navigational instruments such as magnetic compasses were essential tools of expanding seaborne trade.

The printed word

By far the most influential product of European enterprise, however, was the printing press. Fresh thinking became readily available through the relative speed with which new printed books could be produced and distributed. Literature in the vernacular – everyday languages such as English, Italian, and French, rather than scholarly Latin – received an enormous boost. Humanist scholars were able to circulate accurate, standardized versions of major texts. The most important of these was the Bible. Providing people with direct access to what was regarded as the word of God was a prime cause of the great religious upheaval of the Reformation (see pp.196–97).

Political turmoil

The cultural developments of the Renaissance took place within a context of acute political and religious conflicts. The Italian city-states that were such dynamos of creativity were also the site of vicious power struggles. In Florence the dominant Medici family were twice driven into exile by popular uprisings, in 1494 and 1527, and twice restored to power. Civil conflicts were complicated by the intervention of the armies of the kings of France and the Habsburg emperors,

who fought one another in Italy in a series of wars from the 1490s to the 1550s. Rome was laid waste by an imperial army in 1527. Observing these conflicts at close hand inspired Florentine Niccolo Machiavelli to write his cynical political handbook *The Prince* in 1513 (published in 1532), advising the wise ruler to use any methods, however immoral, to stay in power. Whether or not this was good advice, it certainly described the normal practice of Renaissance political leaders. Machiavelli's model for *The Prince* was the ruthless Cesare Borgia (1476–1507), the illegitimate son of Pope Alexander VI, who was suspected of many murders, including that of his elder brother.

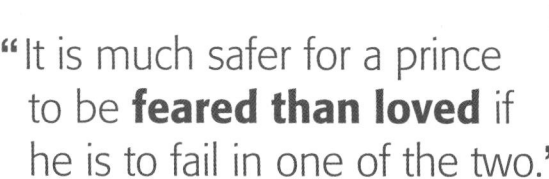

Niccolo Machiavelli
Author of *The Prince*, Machiavelli based his pragmatic political philosophy upon his experiences as a diplomat in the service of Florence.

Challenge to the Church
Religious disputes grew out of a discontent with the state of the Church that was simmering throughout the

15th century. Much of the thrust of Renaissance humanism, especially in the works of Erasmus, consisted in an attack on the ignorance and corruption of the clergy, including successive popes, and calls for a return to a purer form of faith. On the other hand, Renaissance artists, as purveyors of luxury goods sometimes with pagan connotations, found their works under attack from religious reformers.

Religious revival
Between 1494–98 a radical monk, Girolamo Savonarola, won control of Florence and led an orgy of book-burning and destruction of works of art in his campaign against wealth and corruption. One of the main provocations for the Reformation that challenged papal authority from 1517 was outrage at the money being spent on commissioning men such as Raphael and Michelangelo to beautify Rome. The atmosphere

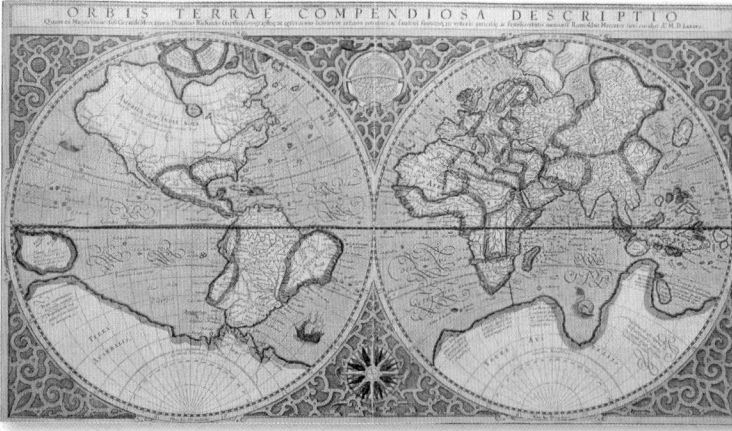

Mercator map
Representing the latest knowledge of geography, this map was created by Flemish cartographer Gerardus Mercator in 1587. Mercator's projection, his famous method for representing the globe on a flat surface, was still in widespread use four centuries later.

of religious revival in the Reformation and the Counter-Reformation (see pp.198–99) was broadly hostile to the spirit of free inquiry and invention that animated the Renaissance. In the second half of the 16th century both zealous Protestants and Catholics cracked down on the "free-thinking" that undermined their religious orthodoxies. But in the longer term, there was to be no turning back from the development of scientific and philosophical enquiry, the dissemination of knowledge and culture in printed books, and innovation in the arts.

Renaissance clock
The introduction of spring-powered timepieces at the start of the 16th century allowed smaller portable clocks such as this to be made for domestic use.

> "It is much safer for a prince to be **feared than loved** if he is to fail in one of the two."
>
> NICCOLO MACHIAVELLI, FROM "THE PRINCE", 1532

AFTER »

Renaissance thinkers came into conflict with the Church, but their achievements lived on.

RELIGIOUS REACTION
In 1542 the Catholic Church established the Congregation for the Doctrine of the Faith in Rome as a body to **suppress ideas contrary to the Church's teaching.** In 1564 Pope Pius IV established an **Index of Proscribed (banned) Books,** which included the works of Erasmus and Copernicus. Giordano Bruno, a wide-ranging thinker in the Renaissance tradition, was **burnt at the stake** in Rome after the Congregation found him guilty of heresy in 1600.

ART AND ARCHITECTURE
Through the 16th century European painting, sculpture, and architecture developed in a less naturalistic direction, **valuing expression above harmony and true proportion.** This more artificial style has been labelled "Mannerism" by art historians. Mannerism evolved into the exuberant Baroque style dominant in the 17th century.

GALILEO
Working in Italian cities including Pisa, Padua, and Florence, Galileo Galilei (1564–1642) built on the **Renaissance spirit of enquiry and observation** to lay the foundations of the Scientific Revolution 206–07 »

LATE RENAISSANCE
In some countries the Renaissance is generally agreed to have flowered at a later date. In both England and Spain, the height of the Renaissance did not occur until the second half of the 16th century and early 17th century, when writers, musicians and artists, such as Thomas Tallis, Edmund Spenser, William Shakespeare, El Greco, and Miguel Cervantes all flourished.

INVENTION

THE PRINTING PRESS

The first effective press for printing books using moveable metal type and oil-based ink first emerged in 15th century Europe. Its invention is attributed to Johannes Gutenberg, a German artisan and entrepreneur. The Bible that he published in 1455 was the first book printed in this way. The new technique spread, with presses established in Paris in 1470 and London in 1476. The most prestigious early printer, Aldus Manutius, set up the Aldine Press in Venice in 1494. By 1500 some 35,000 different books were in print. Much cheaper than handwritten works, printed books revolutionized the diffusion of knowledge.

heavy platen or printing plate

bar to lower platen

tympan

leather ink ball, stuffed with horsehair

sliding coffin

sturdy wooden frame

> "**A spring of truth** shall flow from it…"
>
> GUTENBERG, 15TH CENTURY

ARTIST AND INVENTOR Born 1452 Died 1519

Leonardo da Vinci

"All our **knowledge** has its origins in our perceptions."

LEONARDO DA VINCI

One of the great geniuses of the Italian Renaissance (see pp.190–93), Leonardo was the illegitimate son of a peasant woman; his father married a Florentine heiress eight months after his birth. Raised in the countryside outside Florence, he received little formal education, and only learned Latin, the basic accomplishment of an educated man of his day, in adulthood. Instead, he studied the animals and landscapes around him. It was characteristic of Leonardo that, at a time when artists and philosophers were fixated upon learning from the classical past, he concentrated on direct observation of the human and natural world.

It is possible to present Leonardo's career as that of an ambitious artisan and entrepreneur, a poor boy making good use of opportunities for profit and advancement. He had the good fortune to be born near Florence, home to the finest concentration of painters, sculptors, and architects in 15th century Europe. Aged about 14, he was apprenticed to Andrea del Verrocchio, a leading sculptor whose studio had recently branched out into painting. Leonardo's outstanding talent, especially in the relatively new medium of oil painting, was unmistakable, and in his mid-20s he was able to set up a studio of his own.

Leonardo's paintings are now his most famous achievement, but in the 15th century, even with his own studio, an artist was only a craftsman touting for commissions. The next step up was to be taken on by a prince as a member of his household. Thus, in about 1482, Leonardo proposed his services to Ludovico Sforza, the ruler of Milan. Judging that the warlike Milanese ruler

Ducal commission
This document from Cesare Borgia, lord of the Romagna, dates to 1502, commissioned "architect and engineer" Leonardo to survey palaces and fortresses.

Self-portrait
Leonardo drew this haunting self-portrait when he was in his mid-60s, three or four years before his death. The long hair and beard give him the air of a traditional sage or wwir.

Florence Cathedral
During his apprenticeship in Florence, Leonardo helped place the orb and cross on top of the city's famous cathedral dome.

INVENTION

FLYING MACHINE

From an early age Leonardo was obsessed by the idea of flight. He studied birds on the wing, commenting that "a bird is a machine operating according to mathematical laws". This model is a full-size realization of his design for an ornithopter – a machine powered by flapping artificial wings. It could never work because human muscles are not strong enough in proportion to the weight of a human body. Indeed, none of Leonardo's flying machines were practical – they were simply flights of imagination.

AN ORNITHOPTER

might have more need of a military engineer than of an artist, Leonardo listed at length the "infinite variety of machines for attack and defence" that he could create, including armoured cars, portable bridges, and cannons, before mentioning as an afterthought his skills at painting and sculpture.

A man of talent

Leonardo's all-round skills, including his ingenuity at designing machines, were exactly what Renaissance princes were looking for and he rarely lacked employment for the rest of his life. Even at the end of his career, he was engaged by the French monarchy as firstly "engineer" and then "painter and architect". Leonardo's boundless imagination and experimentation led to many failures and disappointments. For Ludovico Sforza he designed one of the largest equestrian statues ever conceived, but it is unlikely that it could have been cast and only a clay model was built. His *Last Supper*, reckoned one of the ultimate masterpieces of Western art, was painted using an innovative technique that meant it started decaying almost as soon as it was finished. In the service of the ruler of Florence from 1503, he produced a

Anatomical drawing
Leonardo's sketch of a cross section of a human skull showed impressive anatomical details, which are due to the autopsies he performed.

grandiose project for a canal linking the city to the sea, which was never built, and he also undertook to paint the Anghiari fresco for the Palazzo Vecchio, which was never completed. The machines he dreamed of were ingenious and forward-thinking but mostly impractical.

In fact, much of Leonardo's most remarkable work consisted of writings and sketches in his private notebooks, material that remained unpublished until long after his death. It was in these notebooks that Leonardo's fertile, enquiring, adventurous mind and eye found full expression. The pages are packed with an astonishing number of ideas, observations, projects, and

experiments. They include studies of the movement of water and speculations on the nature of the cosmos, as well as reflections on fossils, and on the principles of flight. They also include the record of one of his greatest achievements, the systematic exploration of human anatomy. Leonardo obtained about 30 corpses for dissection from which he produced the most refined, accurate, and annotated sketches.

A modern thinker

Leonardo's idiosyncratic personality and free-ranging mind could easily have brought him into conflict with the authorities. His homosexuality was both a sin and a crime in the society he inhabited, even if it was not generally disapproved of in sophisticated circles. Dissecting corpses was of dubious legality and almost got him into trouble in Rome in about 1515. He seems to have had no fixed religious beliefs and certainly did not allow Christian doctrine to set limits to his thinking. In his declining years, Leonardo was respected, even revered. Around 1515 he appears to have suffered a stroke. Unable to undertake major works, he found a sympathetic patron in the French King Francis I, who appreciated the prestige of having such a renowned figure in his employ. It is reported that Francis said he could never believe there was another man born in this world who knew as much as Leonardo. Few of Leonardo's paintings have survived, but their scarcity has if anything enhanced his legendary status.

> " Art is **never finished**, only abandoned."
>
> LEONARDO DA VINCI

The Last Supper
Leonardo painted *The Last Supper* in the refectory of the church of Saint Maria delle Grazie in Milan, using a mix of tempora and oil, rather than a traditional fresco technique. As a result, the paint soon began to flake off.

TIMELINE

- **15 April 1452** Born near Vinci, a small town outside Florence, the illegitimate son of a peasant woman and a local lawyer.
- **1466** Apprenticed to Andrea del Verrochio.
- **April 1476** Accused of homosexual activity, an offence that could carry the death penalty.
- **1477** Sets up his own studio in Florence.
- **1481** Commissioned to paint the *Adoration of the Magi* for the monastery of San Donato.
- **1482** Enters the service of Ludovico Sforza, known as Ludovico il Moro, the ruler of Milan.
- **25 April 1483** Commissioned to paint an altarpiece for the church of San Francesco in Milan, now known as the *Virgin of the Rocks*.
- **1487** Starts to write a notebook, which he fills with sketches and his imaginative thoughts.
- **1490** Engages Giacomo Caprotti, known as Salai, as a young assistant who almost certainly becomes his long-term lover.
- **1491** Paints a portrait of Ludovico's mistress, now known as *The Lady with the Ermine*.
- **1492** Produces the famous drawing of the Vitruvian Man, showing the idealized proportions of the human body.
- **1498** Completes fresco of *The Last Supper*.
- **1502** Enters the service of the lord of the Romagna, Cesare Borgia, as a military architect and engineer.

LA GIOCONDA

- **1503–04** Returns to Florence and paints the *Mona Lisa*, probably a portrait of the wife of silk merchant Francesco del Giocondo. Works on a failed project for a canal to give Florence direct access to the sea.
- **1504** Starts work on a fresco, the *Battle of Anghiari*, for the Council Hall in the Palazzo Vecchio, Florence. It is never completed.
- **July 1504** His father dies. Family intrigue denies Leonardo a share of the inheritance.
- **1506** Returns to Milan and enters the pay of Louis XII of France.
- **1508** Produces obsessive images in his notebooks of whirlwinds and swirling rainstorms.
- **1509** The mathematician Pacioli's *De Divina Proportione* is published with geometrical illustrations by Leonardo.
- **1510** Completes *The Virgin and Child with St Anne*.
- **1513** Moves to Rome, entering the service of Guiliano de' Medici; settles in the Villa Belvedere, lent to him by Guiliano's brother, Pope Leo X.
- **1515** Suffers an illness, possibly a stroke which leaves him paralysed down one side.
- **1516** Appointed Premier Engineer, Painter, and Architect to Francis I of France. Lives in Clos Luce near the royal chateau at Amboise.
- **2 May 1519** Dies at Amboise.

« BEFORE

The Catholic Church dominated Europe throughout the medieval period and into the 16th century.

EARLY REFORMERS

The Lollards from England in the 14th century and the

HUSSITES

Hussites from Bohemia in the early 15th century both proposed reforms of the Catholic Church **to end corruption** and purify church doctrine.

THE GREAT SCHISM

Pope Clement V moved the papacy to Avignon in France in 1309 to avoid **internal feuding in Rome**. An attempt to return the papacy to Rome in 1379 led to the election of two rival popes, causing a **schism « 140–41**. A Church meeting in Germany in 1417 elected a third pope to replace the two rivals.

RENAISSANCE EXCESS

The building of a vast new basilica in Rome was funded by the **sale of indulgences**, or pardons for sins, which typified the **extravagance** of the Catholic Church in the 15th century.

ST PETER'S BASILICA, ROME

120 The number of years it took to build St Peter's Basilica in Rome. Pope Leo X financed construction partly through the sale of indulgences and used the leading artists of the Renaissance (see pp.190–91) to design and decorate it.

The Reformation

A simple but effective protest against corruption in the Catholic Church in 1517 soon turned into a major force for religious change known as the Reformation. It transformed the political, social, and economic face of Europe over the next few centuries and its legacy can still be seen around the world today.

M artin Luther's (see below) challenge against the Catholic Church in Wittenberg, Saxony, came after the arrival in the area of German preacher Johann Tetzel, who was selling indulgences (see BEFORE) to raise money for Pope Leo X. Indulgences had long been criticized by Catholic theologians (scholars of religion) but their financial success ensured the practice was too lucrative to end. Luther's response, on 23 October 1517, was to post a document bearing 95 theses (statements) onto the door of the town church. Luther's theses were not radical, but they attracted a wide audience and due to recent advances in printing methods (see p.253) they were widely distributed and read. Luther's initial criticism of the church focused on the sale of indulgences, but he went on to attack the core Catholic teachings of transubstantiation (the belief that bread and wine change into the body and blood of Christ when received during communion), clerical celibacy, and papal supremacy. He also called for a reform of religious orders such as monasteries, and a return to the simplicity of the earlier church.

The Lutheran church

Luther's challenge to the established church won him many followers, but he initially wished only to reform the existing church rather than set up an entirely new system. Several attempts were made to reconcile Luther with the religious authorities, until, in 1521, he

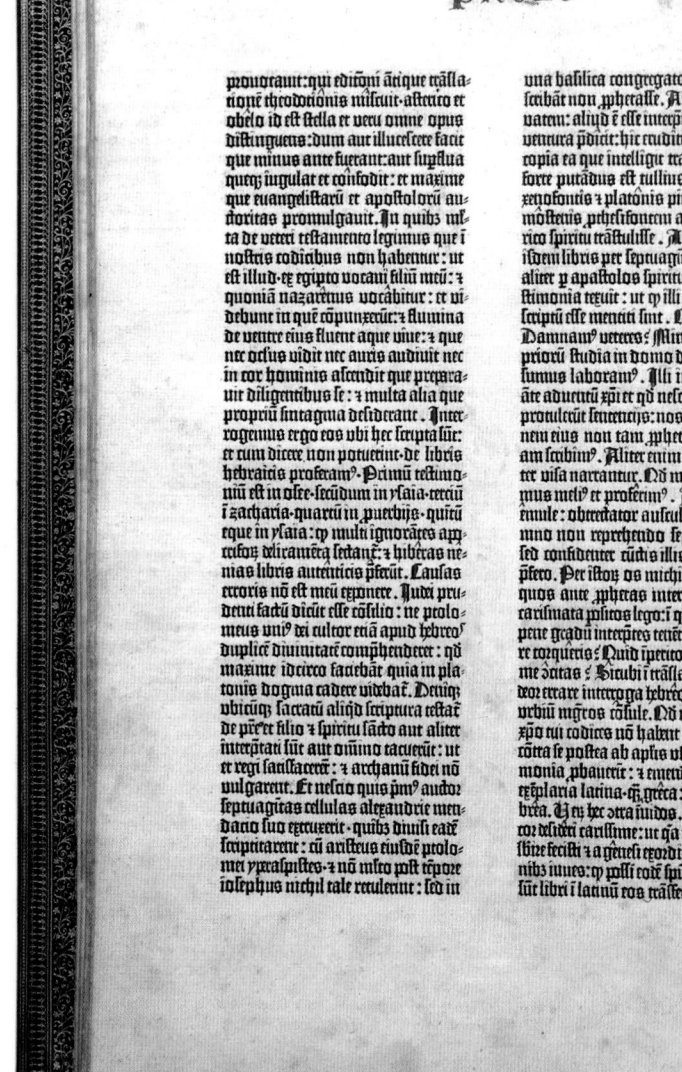

Leather bindings enclose parchment pages. About 170 copies of the Bible were printed, its 1,200 pages appearing in two separate volumes.

The Gutenberg Bible
The world's first printed Bible was produced, in Latin, by the German printer Johannes Gutenberg in 1455. Bibles in the vernacular, or common language, first appeared during the Reformation.

RELIGIOUS REFORMER (1483–1546)

MARTIN LUTHER

A university-educated priest and friar, Martin Luther became a professor of theology (the study of religion) at Wittenberg University in 1512. His disagreements with the Catholic Church hierarchy over its conduct led to a revolt against the institution in 1517 that soon spread across Europe. Luther was a reluctant revolutionary, preferring at first to reform the Church from within, but once excluded from the Church in 1521, he proved to be an energetic and skilled leader, making good use of the new printing technology to write and distribute pamphlets publicizing his views. His belief in order, and his conservative political views, put him at odds with many who wished to develop more radical religious doctrines.

" Here I stand. I can do no other. **God help me**. Amen."

MARTIN LUTHER, ADDRESSING THE DIET OF WORMS, 18 APRIL 1521

Decorative margins and headings were inscribed by hand before the printed sheets were bound together.

Gothic printed type modelled on German handwritten script.

"… the **only supreme head** on Earth of the Church in England."

DESCRIPTION OF HENRY VIII OF ENGLAND IN THE ACT OF SUPREMACY, 1534

was summoned to present his views at an imperial Diet (parliament) at Worms in front of Holy Roman Emperor Charles V, who ruled over much of Europe. Luther refused to retract his views and, having already been excommunicated (expelled from the church) by the pope, was now outlawed by the emperor. His response was to set up his own independent church. He also set to work translating the Bible into German; previous editions of the Bible had been transcribed in Latin – Luther's edition would allow people to read the Bible in their native language for the first time.

Part of the power of Luther's teachings lay in their appeal to German identity. Germany at this point was made up of many independent states, nominally controlled by Emperor Charles V. German princes wishing to exert their power against the dominance of Charles V saw Luther's teachings as a way of breaking both imperial and church control over Germany. What began as a religious debate soon became a political revolt. In 1524 the Peasants' War broke out in southwest Germany as a result of economic hardship in the region. A league of German princes, supported by Luther, crushed the revolt in 1526 with great loss of life. The revolt horrified Luther as much as it did the secular leaders it was aimed at. One by one, the north German states of Saxony, Hesse, Brandenburg, Brunswick, and others adopted Lutheranism. Each state took control of the church, strengthening the hold of the ruler over his people.

Worldwide appeal

The appeal of Lutheranism was not restricted to Germany. In 1527 Gustavus Vasa, the ruler of Sweden, which had only gained independence from Denmark–Norway in 1523, seized church lands to provide funds for his new state. He then reformed the new state church along Lutheran lines. A similar process saw the adoption of Lutheranism in Denmark–Norway in 1536. In England, a break with the church in Rome came about after the pope refused Henry VIII a divorce from his wife, Catherine of Aragon. Henry replaced the Pope as head of the English church.

Political fallout

The political response to the Lutheran reformation was led by Emperor Charles V. However, his vast territorial domains in Europe brought him into conflict with, among others, France. War between these two sides, as well as between Charles and the growing might of the Muslim Ottoman

The Renaissance papacy
Pope Leo X became a cardinal while still a child. He promoted the sale of indulgences to pay for the rebuilding of St Peter's Basilica, prompting Luther's protest against this practice in 1517.

empire in the Mediterranean and Balkans (see pp. 186–87), meant he could not devote all of his resources to crushing the Lutherans in Germany. Charles defeated the Lutherans in battle at Mühlberg in 1547, but he could not crush them politically. A religious and political compromise was finally reached by the Peace of Augsburg in 1555, by which the emperor allowed each prince within the empire to choose between Catholicism and Lutheranism and impose that belief upon his subjects.

»

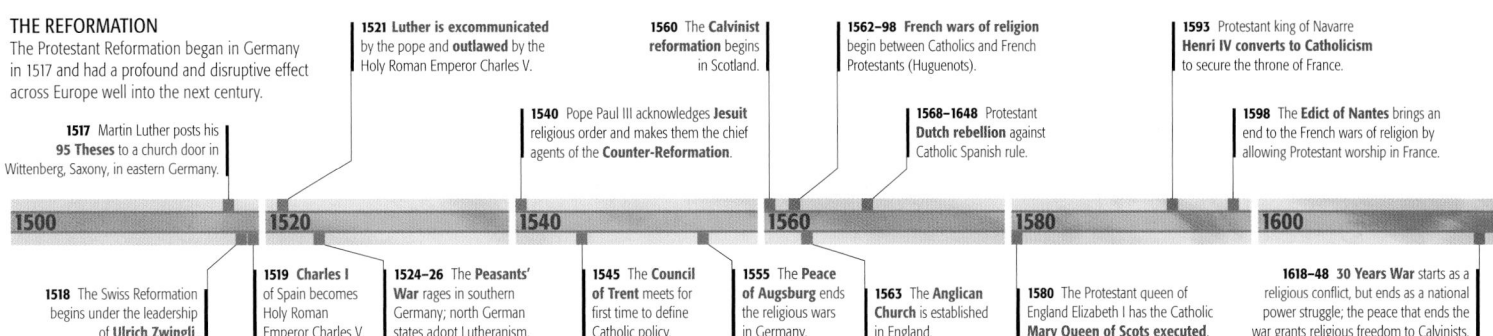

THE REFORMATION

The Protestant Reformation began in Germany in 1517 and had a profound and disruptive effect across Europe well into the next century.

1517 Martin Luther posts his **95 Theses** to a church door in Wittenberg, Saxony, in eastern Germany.

1518 The Swiss Reformation begins under the leadership of **Ulrich Zwingli**.

1519 Charles I of Spain becomes Holy Roman Emperor Charles V.

1521 Luther is excommunicated by the pope and **outlawed** by the Holy Roman Emperor Charles V.

1524–26 The **Peasants' War** rages in southern Germany; north German states adopt Lutheranism.

1540 Pope Paul III acknowledges **Jesuit** religious order and makes them the chief agents of the **Counter-Reformation**.

1545 The **Council of Trent** meets for first time to define Catholic policy.

1560 The **Calvinist reformation** begins in Scotland.

1555 The **Peace of Augsburg** ends the religious wars in Germany.

1562–98 French wars of religion begin between Catholics and French Protestants (Huguenots).

1563 The **Anglican Church** is established in England.

1568–1648 Protestant **Dutch rebellion** against Catholic Spanish rule.

1580 The Protestant queen of England Elizabeth I has the Catholic **Mary Queen of Scots executed**.

1593 Protestant king of Navarre **Henri IV converts to Catholicism** to secure the throne of France.

1598 The **Edict of Nantes** brings an end to the French wars of religion by allowing Protestant worship in France.

1618–48 30 Years War starts as a religious conflict, but ends as a national power struggle; the peace that ends the war grants religious freedom to Calvinists.

1500 | 1520 | 1540 | 1560 | 1580 | 1600

» Luther himself was conservative in theology and in his respect for order, but many of those who followed him were far more radical.

Zwingli and Calvin

In Zurich, Switzerland, Ulrich Zwingli (1484–1531) converted the city along Lutheran lines: his 67 theses of 1523 were adopted by the city council as official doctrine. However, he disagreed with Luther about the nature of the Eucharist (the bread and wine received during communion) and began to lead the Swiss Church in a more radical, anti-hierarchical direction. His death in 1531 while defending Zurich against the Catholic cantons (provinces) of Switzerland slowed the momentum of the reformation in Switzerland. Calvin (see below), who was starting to create a new religious centre in the city of Geneva, subsequently emerged as the key figure associated with protestant reform in Switzerland.

Calvin had converted to the new reformed faith in 1533 and settled in Geneva in 1536. There he developed a more austere form of Protestantism, based on his own reading of scriptures and his rigorous academic training, stressing predestination – God's control of all human actions. Though Calvin himself did not develop any practical theory of resistance to "ungodly authority", such as the Catholic Church or Catholic rulers, many of his successors were prepared to justify violent resistance through his teachings. Like Luther, he stressed both an individual's direct relationship with God without a papal or priestly intermediary and the primacy of the Bible – now widely distributed in modern languages

---

RELIGIOUS REFORMER (1509–64)

JOHN CALVIN

Born in France, John Calvin prepared for a church career in Paris, but in 1533 experienced a "sudden conversion" to the reformed faith. He wrote the *Institutes of the Christian Religion* (1534), rejecting papal authority in favour of justification by faith alone. He settled in Geneva in 1536, where he sought to create a society in which the demands of "godly behaviour" were strictly enforced by a combination of church and civil authorities. The duty of the citizen was to interpret the Bible and create a godly society.

Warhaffte Abbildung des Heil: Concily oder Kirchen-Versamlung zu Trient, so Anno 1545. vnd gerndet 1563. wie solche Herr oberster Melchior Lussy Ritter vnd Lo... Als gewester Abgesanther van den 7. Lobl. Lhat. Cantonen in seinem Wahnhaus Abmahlen Lassen: Disere Tafel hat Herr Haubtman Felix Leonti Reyser... aman zu Ehren vnd gedächtnus Hochermelten Herren Lussis als seines gewe... Herren Copieren, vnd in das Capuciner-Convent vbersetzen Lassen...

A Ist das orth wo Herr Lussy in dem Concilio den sütz gehabt, der Keüserliche portugössiche, vnd venetianische Abgesandte hate den Vor Rang, Wie B. ... aber nach ihme, der spanische Aber sasse bey Dem Herren Secretario g...

Council of Trent
The Counter-Reformation was conceived in the Italian Alpine town of Trent, then under Austrian Habsburg rule. Here, in the cathedral, the Church Council met in 1545–47, 1551–52, and finally in 1562–63, to reform the doctrines and practices of the church to meet the threat posed by the Protestant Reformation.

Pope Paul III convened
the first session of the Council of Trent in 1545; the second and third sessions were convened by Julius III and Pius IV.

Catholic cardinals
and bishops and leading Catholic theologians attended the council; no Protestants attended.

IDEAS

COUNTER-REFORMATION

The Counter (or Catholic) Reformation set out to challenge the appeal of the new Protestant churches by reforming and remodelling the Catholic Church, drawing on a great mass of reformist sentiment and enthusiasm within the church that had been building up since the late 15th century. It strengthened the spiritual institution of the papacy, reformed old and formed new religious orders, most notably the Jesuits, who set up schools and missions to preach Catholic virtues, and clarified church doctrines. Congregations were lured back into church through increased use of ornament and spectacle, best personified by the glorious new churches in the Baroque style in Austria and Italy – the spectacular ceiling of St Ignatius Church in Rome (right), dating from around 1707, shows the missionary work of the Jesuits.

and not the Latin of the church – as the foundation of all preaching and teaching. Unlike Luther, however, who believed in the political subordination of the church to the state, Calvin preached that church and state should act together to create a "godly society"

in which religious beliefs and strict codes of conduct should shape every aspect of daily life. Calvinism took hold in Scotland, the Netherlands, and in large parts of France, where followers were known as Huguenots, and in areas across the German states, Bohemia, and Transylvania. Calvinism also inspired the Puritan movement in England and, later, North America, whose members wished to purify the Anglican church of its remaining Catholic elements, notably the authority of bishops and the "popish" adornment of church vestments, ornaments, and music.

The Catholic response

The initial Catholic response to the Reformation was to excommunicate (exclude from the sacraments of the church) those who rebelled against it. As it became clear that it could not crush the Reformation, the Catholic

Church began to reform itself, drawing on a groundswell of internal calls for church reform that long predated the emergence of Luther.

Meeting in three sessions at Trent in the Italian Alps from 1545–63, the Catholic Church initiated a Counter-Reformation (see above). The Catholic Counter-Reformation succeeded in its aims, strengthening Catholicism both theologically and politically, although a more authoritarian orthodoxy was instituted. Poland, Austria, and Bavaria now became solidly Catholic. But while Germany remained largely at peace, the strong Calvinist (Huguenot) presence in France prompted a lengthy religious war that was only ended with the granting of religious toleration in the Edict of Nantes in 1598. By the end of the century, perhaps 40 per cent of Europe's population followed one or other of the reformed beliefs.

St Bartholomew's Day Massacre
The French wars of religion reached a bloody climax on St Bartholomew's Day (24 August) 1572 when the French regent, Catherine de Medici, authorized the massacre of about 200 Huguenot leaders meeting in Paris for her daughter's wedding. Catholic mobs then went on the rampage, killing thousands more Huguenots.

Reformation in Europe
By 1600 the religious map of Europe was largely settled. Lutheran churches were well established in Germany and Scandinavia, and Calvinist churches in Switzerland, the Netherlands, and Scotland. The Anglican religion was established in England and Wales. France, Spain, Portugal, Italy, southern Germany, and Poland were largely Catholic, although Calvinist beliefs were strong in south and west France, while Austria was evenly split.

AFTER

The impact of the Reformation continued to be felt well into the 17th century.

WARS OF RELIGION
Religious fervour continued to inflame European politics. The **30 Years War 262–63 »** of 1618–49 began as a religious conflict between Catholic Austria and Protestant Bohemia (in the present-day Czech Republic), although in its later stages it became a political struggle for supremacy between France and the equally Catholic nations of Spain and Austria. The **Wars of the Three Kingdoms** in the British Isles (including the English Civil War **264–65 »**), which developed after 1639, were largely caused by Charles I's emphasis on an Anglican church, which stressed ritual and the importance of the sacraments, actions that were regarded as "popish" by the Calvinist Scots and Charles' enemies among the puritan English. Not until the signing of the **Treaty of Westphalia** ending the 30 Years War in 1648 did **religion become secondary to the state** in European politics.

KEY
- Catholic
- Protestant
- Frontiers 1590

Map labels
SCOTLAND, Edinburgh, IRELAND, Dublin, York, ENGLAND, London, Canterbury, Paris, Nantes, Troyes, FRANCE, Cognac, Bordeaux, Lyon, Geneva, SAVOY, Avignon, Genoa, Venice, Milan, NAVARRE, BÉARN, Lisbon, Madrid, SPAIN, Barcelona, Seville, PORTUGAL, Balearic Islands, North Sea, ATLANTIC OCEAN, DENMARK-NORWAY, SWEDEN, Stockholm, Copenhagen, Hamburg, Riga, COURLAND, Baltic Sea, NETHERLANDS, SMALL GERMAN STATES, Berlin, BRANDEN, PRUSSIA, Prague, Warsaw, POLAND–LITHUANIA, Cracow, BAVARIA, AUSTRIAN HABSBURG POSSESSIONS, HUNGARY, Buda, Debrecen, TRANSYLVANIA, VENETIAN REPUBLIC, REPUBLIC OF GENOA, Florence, PAPAL STATES, Rome, NAPLES, Naples, Adriatic Sea, WALLACHIA, Belgrade, OTTOMAN EMPIRE, Salonica, Adrianople, Aegean Sea, SARDINIA, Mediterranean Sea

0   500 km
0   500 miles

QUEEN OF ENGLAND Born 1533 Died 1603

Elizabeth I

"**I** have the body but of a **weak and feeble woman**, but... the **heart... of a king**" ELIZABETH I AT TILBURY, 1588

From her earliest years, England's future Queen Elizabeth I was surrounded by danger and intrigue. Her birth was a disappointment to her father, Henry VIII, who was desperate for a male heir. He had declared himself head of the English Church so he could divorce and marry again, in an effort to produce a son with his new wife. Elizabeth was two and a half when her mother, Henry's second wife Anne Boleyn, was executed on his orders, accused of adultery. Declared illegitimate, Elizabeth was relegated to court life, finding safety in discretion. After Henry's death in 1547 she was taken under the protection of his widow and sixth wife, Catherine Parr, and educated together with her half-brother, the future Edward VI.

Her elder half-sister Mary's accession to the throne in 1553, placed Elizabeth in a perilous situation. The Catholic Mary

Gloriana
Elizabeth I's style of dress expressed both her love of finery and her desire to present an image of power and magnificence.

The Tudor Rose
The symbol of the Tudor dynasty, of which Elizabeth was the fourth monarch, was created by Henry VII.

Henry VIII
Elizabeth I's father was a true Renaissance man. He was highly educated, fluent in several languages, and was adept at sports such as tennis. He was also a keen huntsman. One of Henry's lasting legacies is the establishment of the Church of England.

The Spanish Armada
The sea was described as "groaning under the weight" of the Spanish fleet sent to attack England in 1588. The decisive defeat of the armada was Elizabeth's finest hour.

had every reason to distrust a sister who could be put forward as a Protestant candidate for the throne. Elizabeth survived by steering clear of plots against Mary and maintaining a facade of loyalty. The worst she suffered was a brief imprisonment in the Tower of London, in 1554.

The Golden Age

The early deaths of her siblings brought Elizabeth to the throne at the age of 25. From the start of her reign she chose her advisers well, especially her chief secretary of state, William Cecil. The goal she set them was the survival of her person and her state – a goal dictating caution, suspicion, and ruthlessness

when required. Elizabeth refused to endorse Protestant extremism, insisting on royal control over the Church but trying to avoid complex issues of doctrine. Plots and rebellions by English and Irish Catholics plagued her reign and she had her cousin, Mary Queen of Scots, imprisoned and eventually executed as a dangerous Catholic claimant to the throne. Elizabeth similarly attempted to avoid involvement in the religious wars racking Europe, but was reluctantly drawn into backing the Protestant Dutch against Catholic Spain.

The Virgin Queen

Elizabeth's role in the cultural flowering that occurred in England during her reign and the feats of English mariners is hard to assess. She supported the arts financially, although her taste in theatre was more for clowning than for refined wit. Adventurers such as Sir Francis Drake enjoyed her fitful support, backed when their schemes served her purposes. For the last two decades of her reign, England was at war with Spain. Elizabeth's advisers tried to

WRITER AND POET (1564–1616)

WILLIAM SHAKESPEARE

William Shakespeare, son of a Stratford-upon-Avon wool dealer, was one of the actors and dramatists financially supported by Elizabeth I. He is considered to be the greatest writer of the English language, and is believed to have written at least 37 plays and 154 sonnets. He excelled at both comedy and tragedy, and his works explored the universal human experience. *Twelfth Night* was written specifically to be performed at court for Elizabeth I.

seek national security through an advantageous marriage between the queen and a foreign prince. Although Elizabeth toyed with proposals, she accepted none. Her aversion to marriage was simple. Unmarried she ruled; once married, she inevitably would have had to cede part or all of her power to her consort, as were the conventions of the day.

In Elizabeth's later years the deaths of favourites and counsellors left her an isolated figure. Yet she never lost her popularity with her people. In her final speech to parliament before her death, she deftly balanced her arrogant sense of an untramelled "divine right" to rule with her aspiration to lead by popular consent: "Though God hath raised me high," she stated, "yet this I count the glory of my crown, that I have reigned with your loves."

Drake knighted
Elizabeth I knighted Francis Drake on board his ship, the *Golden Hinde*, after his round-the-world voyage. The knighthood was a calculated political gesture, effectively giving royal backing to his plunder of the lands of the Spanish empire.

Royal offering
These gold-embroidered textile gloves were presented to Elizabeth I on a visit to Oxford University in 1566.

TIMELINE

- **7 September 1533** Anne Boleyn gives birth to the future Elizabeth I in Greenwich Palace; she is recognized as heir presumptive to the throne ahead of her half-sister Mary, daughter of Henry's first wife Catherine of Aragon.

- **19 May 1536** Anne Boleyn is executed; Elizabeth is declared illegitimate and loses her right of succession to the throne.

- **June 1543** An act of parliament restores Elizabeth to the line of succession, after her brother Edward VI and sister Mary.

- **28 January 1547** Henry VIII dies; Elizabeth becomes a ward of his widow, Catherine Parr. He is succeeded by his son, Edward VI.

- **20 March 1549** Catherine Parr's fourth husband, Thomas Seymour, with whom Elizabeth has been closely associated, is executed for treason.

- **19 July 1553** Elizabeth's Catholic sister Mary accedes to the throne.

- **18 March 1554** Elizabeth is imprisoned in the Tower of London for alleged complicity in a rebellion against Mary led by Sir Thomas Wyatt; she is released on 19 May.

- **25 July 1554** Mary marries Philip II of Spain in Winchester Cathedral; Roman Catholicism is restored as the primary religion in England.

- **17 November 1558** Elizabeth accedes to the throne on the death of Mary; she is crowned in Westminster Abbey on 15 January 1559.

- **8 May 1559** The Act of Supremacy asserts the Queen as head of the Church of England, restoring the Anglican Church in place of Mary's Catholicism.

- **1564** Elizabeth makes her favourite Robert Dudley the Earl of Leicester.

- **9 November 1569** The Catholic Earls of Northumberland and Westmoreland lead the Northern Rebellion against Elizabeth.

- **20 February 1570** The Northern Rebellion is defeated.

- **4 April 1581** Elizabeth knights Francis Drake after he completes a voyage around the world.

- **1585** Anglo–Spanish War begins: Elizabeth supports the Netherlands, in revolt against Spanish rule.

- **July 1588** The Spanish Armada, an attempt by Philip II of Spain to invade England, fails.

- **1590–96** Edmund Spenser's epic poem *The Faerie Queene*, in praise of Elizabeth (or Gloriana in the poem), is published.

- **4 August 1598** William Cecil (later known as Baron Burghley), Elizabeth's chief adviser since the start of her reign, dies.

- **30 November 1601** Elizabeth makes her last address to Parliament.

- **24 March 1603** Elizabeth dies in Richmond Palace, Surrey.

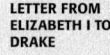

LETTER FROM ELIZABETH I TO DRAKE

"Germany… is a place of dead men's skulls… and **a field of blood.**"

EDWARD CALAMY, ENGLISH PREACHER, 1641

Defenestration of Prague
Protestants assembled in Prague's Hradschin Castle where they threw two Catholic regents out of a window in protest for violating guarantees of religious freedom.

Battle of White Mountain, 1620
This was the first major military encounter of the 30 Years War. The Catholic League and imperial forces had a numerical advantage over the Protestant troops, routing them in just two hours.

The 30 Years War

The Habsburg-controlled Holy Roman Empire sought to re-establish its imperial authority against an array of disparate enemies from 1618–48. Initially a civil war between rival religious factions in Germany, the 30 Years War became a battle for European supremacy.

BEFORE

Religious divisions, dynastic ambition, and the impact of the Reformation ‹‹ 196–97 all had a role in sowing the seeds of the 30 Years War.

HELMET OF CHARLES V, HOLY ROMAN EMPEROR

HOLY ROMAN EMPIRE
Frankish king, Charlemagne (742–814), was the empire's first ruler ‹‹ 134–35. By the end of the 16th century **the empire included much of Germany**, part of the Netherlands, Bohemia (Czech Republic), and many states in Italy.

THE STRUCTURE OF GERMANY
During the Reformation, Holy Roman Emperor Charles V allowed the princes of each state within his realm to choose their state's religion ‹‹ 196–99. **Many German states adopted Protestantism**, causing tension within the Holy Roman Empire.

Throughout the 16th century, the Catholic Church was the only continent-wide institution in Western Europe, remaining part of the daily routine of millions of its inhabitants. But the words of Martin Luther, John Calvin, and the Reformation (see pp.196–99) had challenged the previously unquestioned authority of the pope. The result was the agreement in 1555 of the Peace of Augsburg. The Holy Roman Emperor, Charles V, along with the Imperial Diet (legislative assembly) headed by the empire's great princes, agreed each ruler in the empire should be able to choose between Catholicism or Lutheranism as their realm's religion. This gave Lutherans equal rights under the imperial constitution.

Tension still existed between Catholics and Protestants however. In 1607 a riot between the two sides broke out in the south German city of Donauwörth. The emperor authorized Catholic Duke of Bavaria, Maximilian I, to restore order. When the duke imposed a rigorous Catholic settlement on the city, German protestants formed a defensive Protestant Union led by Frederick V, ruler of the Rhineland Palatinate. This was swiftly followed by the formation of the Catholic League led by Maximilian I. The Imperial Diet tried to resolve the ill-feeling, but the more radical Protestants walked out and the Diet did not meet again until 1640.

The real flashpoint came in 1617. A Habsburg duke, the devoutly Catholic Ferdinand of Styria, was named

Plug bayonet
Musketeers during the 30 Years War used their muskets as clubs when too close to fire, relying on pikemen to defend them. Later the plug bayonet, fitted into the gun's muzzle, was a better close-quarters weapon.

Crown Prince and Emperor Matthias's successor as King of Bohemia, a primarily Protestant realm. As a result of his push for a Catholic Reformation in Bohemia, Protestant nobles rebelled in 1618 with the "Defenestration of Prague" (see above). Regents representing

ENDEMIC WAR
The 30 Years War was a series of conflicts spurred by religious bigotry and imperial paranoia that divided Europe from 1618–48. For the people living in central Europe, this period was one of continuous warring.

1620 Ferdinand crushes Bohemian revolt in the **Battle of White Mountain**.

1619 Death of Habsburg Emperor Matthias; Ferdinand becomes Holy Roman Emperor.

1629 Treaty of Lübeck marks the Danish defeat and end to involvement in the 30 Years War.

1632 Swedish king **Gustavus Adolphus** is killed at the battle of Lützen, Saxony, Germany.

1634 Battle of Nördlingen; Swedes are crushed by Holy Roman Empire.

1635 France intervenes, preventing pro-Habsburg peace.

1643 Battle of Rocroi, Northeast of Rheims, France. Spanish army crosses into France, stops to besiege Rocroi.

1648 Treaty of **Westphalia** ends 30 Years War.

1645 France defeats Bavarian army at **Alerheim**.

1618

1628

1638

1648

1618 Members of **Bohemian aristocracy revolt** after Ferdinand becomes King of Bohemia in 1617 and pushes Catholic reform.

1626 Danish **King Christian IV** intervenes to help German Protestants against Holy Roman Empire.

1631 First **Battle of Breitenfeld**, outside Leipzig, Germany. Swedish–Saxon Alliance is formed against Ferdinand. An imperial army invades Saxony in an attempt to break the alliance.

1637 Death of Emperor Ferdinand II.

1642 Second **Battle of Breitenfeld**. Swedish general Torstensson ravages Habsburg lands in Austria.

1647 Truce of Ulm is signed by Bavaria, Cologne, France, and Sweden.

The site of the battle was a small, low hillside, just outside Prague where 27,000 Austrian imperial and Catholic forces faced about 15,000 Protestants of the Bohemian Estates' army and the Czech nobility under Frederick V, king of Bohemia.

Imperial forces outnumber the Estates forces, though the latter had well-trained mercenaries and the advantage of being on higher ground.

The Estates army formed two echelons of foot-soldiers, about 5,000 cavalry, and reserves. The right wing flanked a garden, the left backed against a hillock.

Blocks of troops were typical of this period: being less spread out they were easier to command. However, any accurate artillery shell or side-on cavalry charge on such a formation spelt disaster, as the target was that much larger.

AFTER

By the end of the 30 Years War there had been a shift in power among the states involved and a framework for a modern Europe of sovereign states was established.

EMERGENCE OF SOVEREIGN STATES
The Peace of Westphalia paved the way for the concept of the sovereign state. **Fixed geographical boundaries** for the many countries involved were established and states of the Holy Roman Empire were **granted full sovereignty**. It was recognized that citizens were bound to the laws of their own government rather than those of neighbouring powers, whether religious or secular.

THE RISE OF FRANCE
The end of the war left Germany decentralized and divided into many territories. Both Portugal and the Dutch Republic declared independence from a politically weakened Spain. France continued to war with Spain until 1659, when it emerged as the **dominant Western power**.

RELIGIOUS TOLERANCE
Calvinism, Lutheranism, and Catholicism were all recognized as **legitimate faiths**. While religious conflicts still occurred, there were no further great religious wars in mainland Europe.

DECLINE OF THE MERCENARY
The hiring of mercenaries had been commonplace in realms that lacked standing armies. However, the size of these armies had grown massively making them **very costly to maintain**. They also caused great destruction as the soldiers attempted to live off the land, often taking from civilians. These limitations gave rise to the idea of the national "professional" army.

7 MILLION The estimated number of dead in the 30 Years War. It was the most costly war in terms of human life to be fought on European soil until the two world wars of the 20th century.

Ferdinand were publicly slung out of Hradschin Castle windows onto the moat some 15m (50ft) below, although they were unharmed.

On Matthias's death in 1619, the election of Ferdinand as King of Bohemia and Holy Roman Emperor, the Habsburg's religious issues became imperial. The Bohemian rebels appointed Frederick V as King of Bohemia, who took the throne and called for support from the Protestant Union in his revolt. Spain lent Ferdinand financial aid, as well as troops, which, together with the newly mustered Catholic League army led by Count Tilly, marched into Bohemia to crush the German Protestant rebellion.

After the battle of White Mountain on 8 November 1620 (see above), Bohemia lost its independence, and Protestantism in the region was exterminated.

Murky motives
Various countries supported the cause of the Protestants for their own ends, political or territorial, entering into war with the Habsburgs at different times. Cardinal Richelieu of Catholic France supported the rights of the German princes against the Catholic Habsburgs, led by state politics and trading interests rather than any shared cause.

Self interest of the sovereign state was also behind the intervention of the Dutch Republic and Sweden in the war rather than any anti-Catholic solidarity with the German protestants. The Dutch had trading rights to protect across Europe and the rest of the world.

Sweden was a small country of peasant farmers and a pre-eminent gun foundries industry. Under the decisive leadership of Gustavus Adolphus II (see p.212) Sweden became a key power on the Baltic coast. Having crushed Count Tilly at the Battle of Breitenfeld in 1631,

Gustavus was killed at the ensuing Battle of Lützen in 1632. The desire for peace, and resentment against marauding armies looting their land, was now overwhelming in Germany, and the Peace of Prague was forged in 1635 between the Holy Roman Empire and most Protestant states.

Reconciliation between Catholics and Protestants in Germany was imminent, but Richelieu, displeased to see the Habsburgs retain power, entered into the war against them that year, with Swedish support.

The theatre of war now spread to most of Europe, with fighting between the Dutch Republic and France against Spain. With the Treaty of Westphalia in 1648, Habsburg power in Europe was fatally checked.

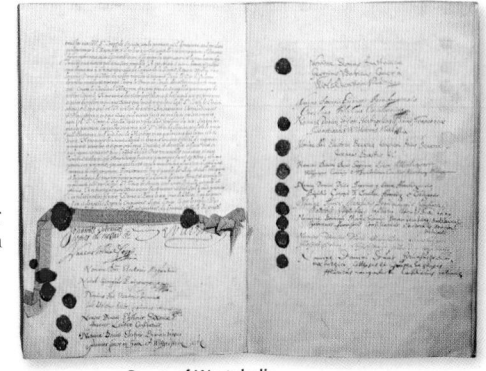

Peace of Westphalia
Signed on 24 October 1648, this document ended the 30 Years War, establishing that more than one religion could coexist in Habsburg Europe.

The English Civil War

The conflict between monarchy and Parliament had its origins in Charles I's belief in the Divine Right of Kings. The English Civil War was really three wars fought between Parliamentarians and royalists from 1642–46, 1648–49, and 1649–51.

> **"God** has brought us to where we are…**"**
>
> OLIVER CROMWELL, ADDRESSING THE ARMY COUNCIL, 1654

On 22 August 1642, Charles I raised his battle standard at Nottingham, signalling the start of a civil war that split England down the middle, pitting brother against brother and father against son. By the time it was over, around 10 per cent of Britain's population were dead.

This war was not just the product of a quarrel between Parliament and the king. Religion also played a key role, as for many Parliamentarians, Catholicism and tyranny were inseparable. In 1640 Charles had recalled Parliament in order to raise money to quell a revolt in Calvinist (see pp.198–99) Scotland against his clumsy attempts to impose "popish" reforms, such as the Anglican prayer-book, upon them. However, instead of granting him cash, they countered with their own catalogue of recriminations, fuelled by 11 years of grievances. He was forced to dismantle the institutions of absolute rule

Statue of Charles I
The reign of Charles I was characterized by religious conflict. Combining charm with stubborness, his absolutist tendencies, (see p.217) put him on a collision course with Parliament.

and lost his right to dissolve Parliament. Rumours of his complicity in an Irish rebellion against Protestant English rule increased the tension. When news reached Charles that Parliament intended to impeach (charge with improper conduct) his Catholic queen, Henrietta Maria, he took drastic action. In January 1642, he entered the House of Commons with an armed force, intending to arrest five leading radical MPs for high treason. Forewarned, they took refuge in the City of London, which considered Charles's actions an outrage. Fearing for his safety, Charles went north to raise an army, while his queen went abroad to raise funds to pay for it.

The years of conflict

While the king commanded the loyalty of Wales, the west, and the north, Parliament controlled London, the east, and the south. The initial battles were inconclusive – a draw at Edgehill was followed by victories for the royalists, or Cavaliers, at Landsdown and Adwalton Moor in 1643, and for the Parliamentarians, or Roundheads, at Turnham Green and Newbury. Numerical supremacy and Scottish involvement led to Roundhead victories at Marston Moor in 1644, and at Naseby

« BEFORE

Since the 13th century, the English monarch had needed Parliament's approval to raise taxes; its increasing interference infuriated the Stuart kings.

THE TUDOR REFORMATION
When the pope refused **Henry VIII** a divorce from his first wife, Henry rejected the pope's authority and declared himself head of the Church of England in 1534. **The Reformation « 196–99** that followed was consolidated during **Elizabeth I's « 200–01** reign by legislation making **Protestantism** England's national religion. Since she was childless, she was succeeded in 1603 by her Stuart cousin, **James VI of Scotland**.

KING JAMES I
James's belief in the **Divine Right of Kings** (that the king was god's representative on Earth with unlimited authority) antagonized Parliament. He quarrelled with them over taxes and religious laws.

KING CHARLES I
Relations between James's son **Charles I** and Parliament disintegrated further, exacerbated by his anti-Puritan **199 »** policies. By 1629, he had dismissed Parliament three times, governing alone during the "Eleven Years Tyranny" (1629–40). He enforced royal authority through the Courts instead and raised money by selling titles.

The conspirators meet and Lady d'Aubigny (left) shows them Charles's Commission of Array (a royal commission summoning his officers to war) – to be proclaimed once Charles sends word of his advance.

The conspirators intend to seize the Tower of London and secure the forts, while Royalist forces from Oxford meet up with the advancing Cornish forces under Sir Ralph Hopton.

The Guildhall is the planned storehouse for the conspirators' magazine (arms and gunpowder).

With suspicions aroused, the Commons order the detention of the King's emissary Alexander Hampden on 22 May. On 31 May, they order the arrest of the suspected conspirators on the evidence of a spy.

Parliamentarian uniform
The New Model Army, formed in 1645 by Parliament, was England's first professional army. The foot regiments, comprised of pikemen and musketeers, were provided with the distinctive red tunic shown here.

red coat was the only uniform item officially issued to the New Model Army

soldiers were often issued swords, also called tucks

woollen breeches

Foiled royalist plot
This propaganda print was probably intended for popular consumption. It is a graphic account of the "Malignants' plot" against Parliament that was unearthed on 31 May 1643.

coloured bow, which was used to fasten breeches

The plan is to arrest the leading parliamentarians, including their (Puritan) leader John Pym, along with two members of the House of Lords.

The conspirators are hanged at the Tyburn gallows. Responding to the Covenant, the King issues a proclamation making all who support it guilty of treason. The die is cast.

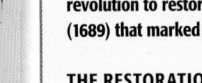

In response to John Pym's report on the royal plot, the Commons accepts the imposition of a vow of support for Parliament known as "the Covenant", which is sent around the country as a test of loyalty. On 15 June the City of London observe a day of Thanksgiving to celebrate the prevention of this "wicked plot".

and Langport in 1645. After the fall of Oxford in 1646, Charles's surrender to the Scots at Newark marked the end of the first civil war.

Parliament's supporters now split into those who wanted to share power with the king, and a more radical group, supported by the army generals, that wanted a republic. Despite his confinement, Charles continued to bargain with various parties, finally making a deal with the Scots to adopt Presbyterianism (their system of church government) in England in return for their support. The royalists rose again in July 1648 and the Scots invaded England. The New Model Army (see caption, left) easily suppressed these uprisings before crushing the Scots at Preston. They then marched on Parliament and dismissed most of its members. The 58 who remained – known as the Rump Parliament – were ordered to set up a High Court to try the king for treason. Charles I was found guilty and beheaded on 30 January 1649. This was truly revolutionary – monarchs had been deposed or killed before, but never legally executed. Parliament now abolished the monarchy and the House of Lords, declaring England a republic or "Commonwealth".

The Lord Protector
Before the civil war, Oliver Cromwell was a landowner and Puritan Member of Parliament. By the war's end, he was Parliament's most powerful military leader. He spent the next two years campaigning in

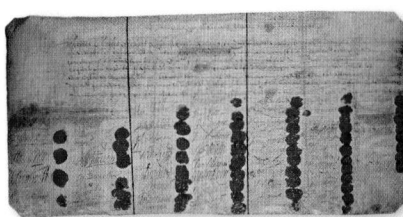

Charles I's death warrant
On 29 January 1649, Charles I was found guilty of being a traitor. His death warrant, shown here, is endorsed by many signatures, including that of Oliver Cromwell.

Scotland and Ireland, crushing local uprisings and bringing them firmly under English control. His defeat of a Scottish army loyal to Charles I's son (later Charles II) at Worcester in 1651 finally brought an end to the civil war.

In 1653, Cromwell dismissed the Rump Parliament, unhappy at its failure to pass any reforms. After being appointed Lord Protector for life – a role that effectively made him a military dictator – he divided England and Wales into 10 districts ruled by army generals. His rule, based on strict Puritan principles, included the banning of most public entertainments.

In September 1658, Cromwell died and was succeeded by his son Richard. With no powerbase, he was helpless against the army generals and resigned after less than a year.

Statue of Cromwell
A devout military leader and shrewd politician, Oliver Cromwell became king in all but name.

AFTER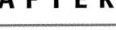

In 1660 the monarchy was reinstated to restore national unity. A second revolution to restore Protestantism was followed by a Bill of Rights (1689) that marked the start of a more limited, constitutional monarchy.

THE RESTORATION
After Cromwell's death, **the throne was offered to Charles II** on condition that he supported religious toleration and pardoned those who had fought his father. Puritan rules were swiftly dropped – theatres and music halls reopened, and public festivals, such as Christmas, were restored. Nell Gwyn, a former orange-seller turned actress, became one of the king's most popular mistresses.

NELL GWYN

THOMAS HOBBES
Hobbes, one of England's most influential political thinkers, lived through the bloodshed of the civil war. His book *Leviathan*, published in 1651, **advocates strong government** at the expense of personal freedom, arguing that mankind's natural state is one of unending conflict.

THE "GLORIOUS REVOLUTION"
The openly Catholic **James II**, who succeeded Charles II in 1685, alienated his subjects by placing religion above politics. His advisers secretly invited the Dutch Protestant prince, **William of Orange** to take over the throne in 1688.

BEFORE

«

Throughout the late medieval period, physicians and "natural philosophers" began to develop what was later known as the "scientific method".

CUTAWAY OF A MAN

ANATOMISTS

Taboos surrounding the desecration of corpses prevented physicians of the 2nd–14th centuries from studying human anatomy in any detail. As a result, the work of classical writers such as **Galen** and **Hippocrates « 58–59** went unchallenged for centuries. It was only with the arrival of **the Black Death « 132–33** in the late 1340s that the restrictions on dissection were eased. It took the genius of **Leonardo da Vinci « 194–95** to turn anatomy into a truly **scientific discipline**.

ALCHEMISTS

A mix of **proto-science and superstition**, alchemy was the forerunner of chemistry which developed from the 11th century into the Renaissance (1300–1650CE) **« 190–93**. Practitioners used methods we would recognize today in pursuit of a mythical "philosopher's stone" attributed with a variety of powers, such as the ability to give everlasting life or to make gold.

ALCHEMISTS AT WORK

For almost 1,500 years (from about 200 CE), European thought was overshadowed by the legacy of the classical world. Just as the Catholic Church reigned supreme in religious affairs, so too in matters of "natural philosophy" (the general term for science before the 19th century) nearly all thinkers deferred to ancient authorities such as Plato, Hippocrates, and Aristotle (see pp.84–85).

Despite this, the new way of thinking had a long gestation. Arab scholars took many Greek ideas and developed them further (see pp.122–25). As their works began to filter back into European libraries, they helped to inspire a growing recognition that not everything the Greeks said was accurate. During the 18th century, failings were exposed in a number of areas, and a new method of philosophy, in which observation and experiment took precedence over authority, began to establish itself.

The knowledge explosion

The scientific revolution could not have taken place without the printing press (see p.193), and the rapid spread of information that printed books brought with them. Suddenly, ideas could be transmitted accurately and rapidly across the entire European continent. At the same time, the onset of trade with remote parts of the world and the discovery of a whole new continent – the Americas – meant that there was far more to investigate (see pp.170–71). Collectors, such as the Dane Ole Worm, created "cabinets of curiosities" – early

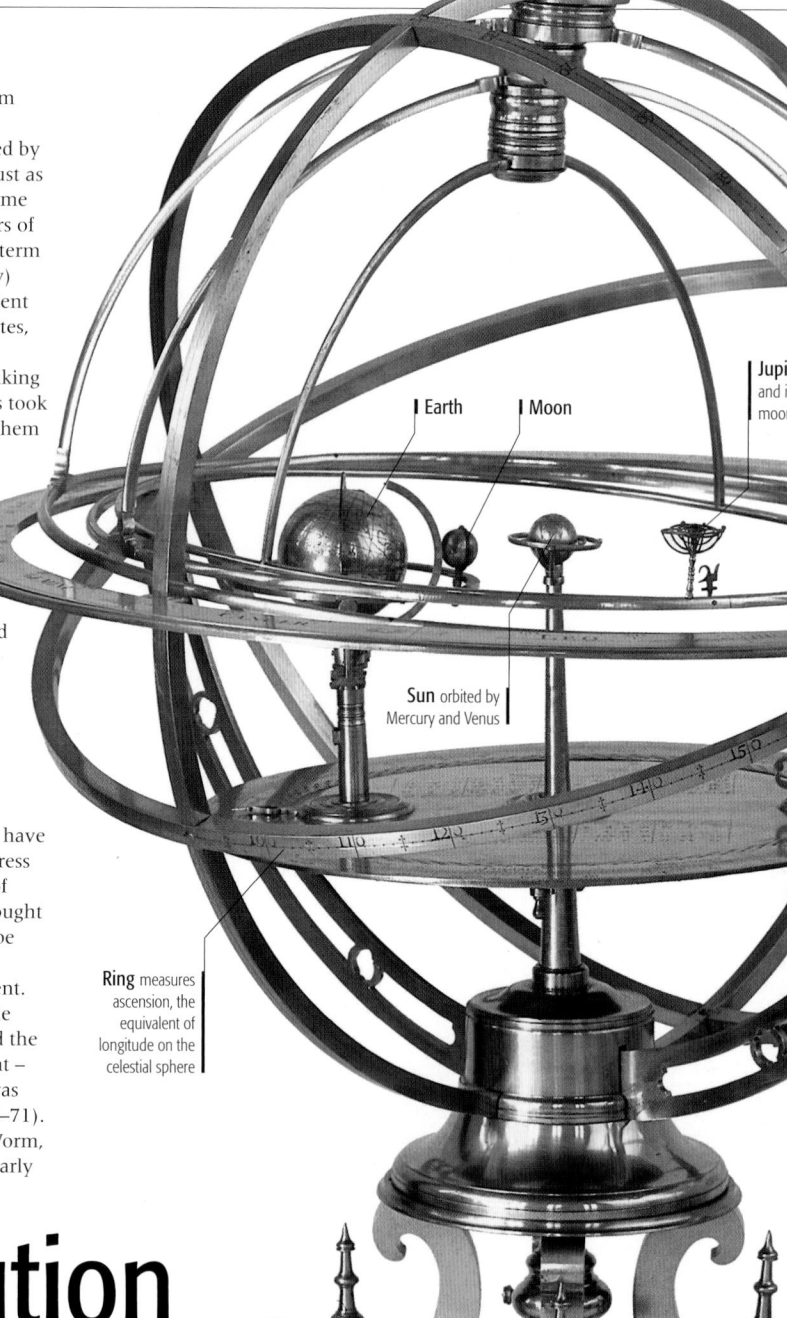

| Earth | Moon

Jupiter and its four moons

Sun orbited by Mercury and Venus

Ring measures ascension, the equivalent of longitude on the celestial sphere

Scientific Revolution

The 16th and 17th centuries saw a metamorphosis in European thinking about the natural world. The Renaissance had transformed art, and the Reformation loosened the ties of religious dogma. A third revolution produced a new view of the Universe.

THE HELIOCENTRIC UNIVERSE

The idea that the Universe orbited the Earth is an ancient one. Celestial objects were thought to be mounted on spheres. However, there were problems – Mercury and Venus never strayed far from the Sun, and Mars occasionally reversed its motion. In 1543, Polish priest and astronomer Nicolaus Copernicus published the first widely read proposal for a new system with the Sun at its centre (pictured right), and the Earth the third of six planets orbiting around it.

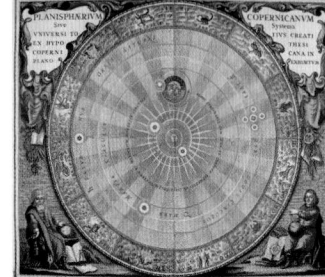

Celestial sphere *c.* 1700

This armillary sphere is an astronomical teaching device, developed by Greek and Arab astronomers. It is a skeletal representation of the "celestial sphere" used for measuring astronomical co-ordinates. From the early 17th century onward, the Sun was placed at the centre of the sphere, as shown here.

Ring measures declination, the equivalent of latitude

Plane of the Solar System

Timekeepers

Improvements in time measurement aided both astronomy and navigation. The weight-driven brass lantern clock was one step forward, although this Japanese version from the mid-17th century still does not have a minute hand. The pendulum clock invented by Christiaan Huygens in 1656 marked a further advance in precision.

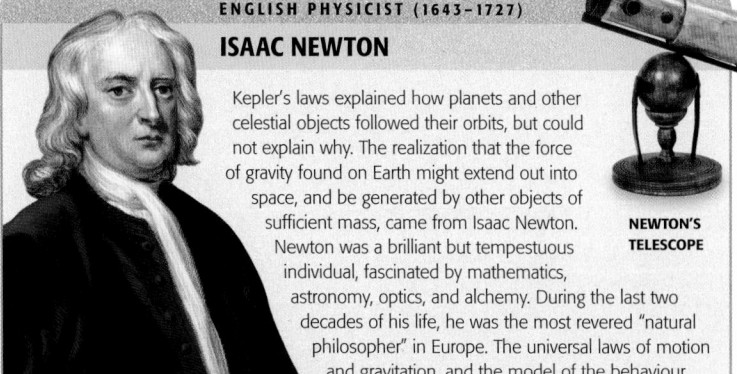

ENGLISH PHYSICIST (1643–1727)
ISAAC NEWTON

Kepler's laws explained how planets and other celestial objects followed their orbits, but could not explain why. The realization that the force of gravity found on Earth might extend out into space, and be generated by other objects of sufficient mass, came from Isaac Newton. Newton was a brilliant but tempestuous individual, fascinated by mathematics, astronomy, optics, and alchemy. During the last two decades of his life, he was the most revered "natural philosopher" in Europe. The universal laws of motion and gravitation, and the model of the behaviour of light that he discovered, remained the foundations of physics for two centuries.

NEWTON'S TELESCOPE

equivalents of today's natural history museums. Exotic plant species brought back from around the world were cultivated in botanical gardens, and the collection of new specimens became an increasingly important part of exploratory and trading missions overseas.

The growing interest in novelty undermined the reliance on the ancients, as it became clear that they had not after all known everything. The classical geographers had nothing to say about the new lands now being discovered, and since the authorities were also silent about the many new species of plant and animal, the scholars of the time had no choice but to investigate for themselves, and start to draw their own conclusions.

Written in the stars

Improved technology was also undermining other long-held theories. The most celebrated casualty of the entire revolution was the ancient, Earth-centred model of the Universe. Italian physicist and astronomer Galileo Galilei is often credited with discovering that the Earth and planets orbit the Sun, using one of the first telescopes. However, the idea had been in the air for several decades (see left). Galileo's discovery in 1610 of the four moons orbiting Jupiter showed that the Earth was not the centre of all motion in the Universe, and his observation of the Moon-like phases of Venus showed that it must be orbiting the Sun. The most persuasive evidence for this theory came from the observations of Danish

astronomer Tycho Brahe. He used another refined form of technology – a precise measuring device known as a mural quadrant, developed from Arabic astrolabes (see p.123).

However, these observations alone could not have created a new theory – they merely disproved the old one. The crucial leap was made by Brahe's one-time student, German astronomer Johannes Kepler. Careful study of Brahe's measurements allowed him to develop a set of laws, published in 1609, that showed how the planets follow elliptical, rather than circular, orbits around the Sun. The acceptance of Kepler's laws involved a brutal divorce from classical ideas of circular perfection, and was not helped by the lack of a model to explain what force kept the planets on their elliptical courses – that had to wait until the century's end, and the breakthroughs of Isaac Newton (see above).

Advances in biology

While astronomy and physics were undergoing their revolution, medicine and anatomy were also in a period of rapid change. The discovery of a lost text by Galen in the early

Life through a lens
The first book of microscope observations was Robert Hooke's *Micrographia* of 1664, which described and illustrated Hooke's observations of insects, plants, and living cells. This illustration of an ant shows more detailed anatomy than was previously possible.

16th century intrigued the Flemish anatomist Andreas Vesalius, who discovered that Galen had clearly never dissected a human body. Vesalius' great atlas of anatomy, *De Humani Corporis Fabrica* (1543), inspired a new generation to continue the study of anatomy without undue deference to authorities from the past.

One great battleground between traditionalism and the new approach was the nature of the circulatory system. Galen taught that the blood did not circulate through the body, but rose and fell in "tides", along with the body's other "humours" (phlegm, and black and yellow bile). Imbalances in the humours supposedly caused a variety of ailments, and much of medieval medicine focused on how best to regulate them.

Only when Galen's description of the heart was proved wrong did physicians begin to question this theory. In 1603, Italian anatomist Hieronymus Fabricius discovered valves within certain blood vessels, but it was not until 1628 that William Harvey, personal physician to Charles I of England, announced his discovery that the valves only worked in one direction. Blood vessels must therefore form two distinct groups – arteries taking blood away from the heart, and veins carrying blood back towards it.

Harvey's discovery met with fierce resistance, not only because it undermined Galen, but also because, with no visible connection between

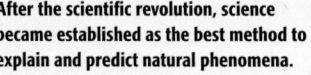

Mountains on the Moon
Using a telescope Galileo discovered the varying terrain of the Moon (shown here), and spots on the Sun.

arteries and veins, it relied on tiny "capillaries", too small to be seen, to complete the system. By stating the evidence rather than attacking rival ideas, Harvey formed a template for later scientific publications. In 1661, improvements to the recently invented microscope finally allowed direct observation of the capillaries, vindicating Harvey and confirming the supremacy of the new method of observation, experiment, and deduction.

AFTER

After the scientific revolution, science became established as the best method to explain and predict natural phenomena.

SCIENCE AND SOCIETY
The 17th century saw the foundation of many scientific societies across Europe. Establishment of true **scientific method** inspired thinkers in many other fields, giving rise to economic, social, and political sciences among others.

THE RATIONAL UNIVERSE
Newton's "clockwork" model of the Universe following immutable physical laws inspired Enlightenment philosophers **210–11 »**, yet left many in fear of an essentially meaningless Universe. **Darwin's theory of evolution 270–71 »** had a similar traumatic effect.

TECHNOLOGY AND EMPIRE
The rise of science led to rapid technological advance in Western Europe, culminating in the **Industrial Revolution 226–27 »**. The growing supremacy of Western technology ensured longevity of the nascent European empires.

Lisbon Earthquake

The Lisbon earthquake was the one of the worst natural disasters in European history. Up to 100,000 people perished in the earthquake itself and in the tsunami and fire that followed. The physical shockwaves were felt across the world; but the event also caused people to question established beliefs.

In the 18th century, Lisbon, situated on the southwest coast of Portugal, at the mouth of the River Tagus, was a grand, affluent city that formed the hub of a vast global empire. But by 10am on 1 November 1755 an earthquake measuring an estimated 9 on the Richter Scale (the highest number on the scale being 10) had reduced Lisbon to a scene of utter devastation. Cracks as wide as 5m (16ft) appeared in the ground, swallowing buildings and people.

In panic, many inhabitants had fled towards the port at the mouth of the river, clambering aboard the ships moored there in the belief that they would be in a safer place. But the earthquake was followed by a massive tsunami, a huge wall of water some 6m (20ft) high, that crashed into the city and roared up the river, causing further death and destruction. All along the coast of Portugal towns were inundated by catastrophic floods. Agadir, in North Africa was flooded, leaving thousands dead, and the wave travelled as far as northern Europe and across the Atlantic as far as Barbados. Once the ground had

stopped shaking and the waters had receded, the third disaster, fire, struck Lisbon. The flames continued to burn for six days. These three catastrophes resulted in the destruction of three-quarters of Lisbon's buildings, including the city's vast royal library, which held priceless works of art and historical records detailing Portuguese expeditions to Southeast Asia.

The earthquake had struck on All Saints Day, one of the holiest days in the Christian calendar. Priests saw the timing as an indication that God was punishing people. The earthquake caused others to question the very existence of a higher being. The event became a key topic of discussion for thinkers of the Enlightenment (see pp.210–11), who began to look for the causes of such disasters in the natural world, rather than blaming the wrath of God. The French writer and philosopher Voltaire used the earthquake to attack blind faith in God; while the German philosopher Immanuel Kant argued that the causes of the disaster should be examined scientifically, and that it is the responsibility of humanity to prepare itself for such events.

Disaster strikes
As the earthquake struck, Lisbon's buildings waved backwards and forwards. Ships were torn from their anchorages and buildings collapsed, killing most of the people inside.

"I assure you this **once opulent city** is nothing but **ruins**..."
REVEREND CHARLES DAVY, AN EYEWITNESS, 1755

The **Enlightenment**

This detailed scene from a pastrycook's kitchen shows the various tasks involved in pastry making. The *Encyclopédie* paid particular attention to everyday professions, keen to preserve artisan skills and techniques for posterity.

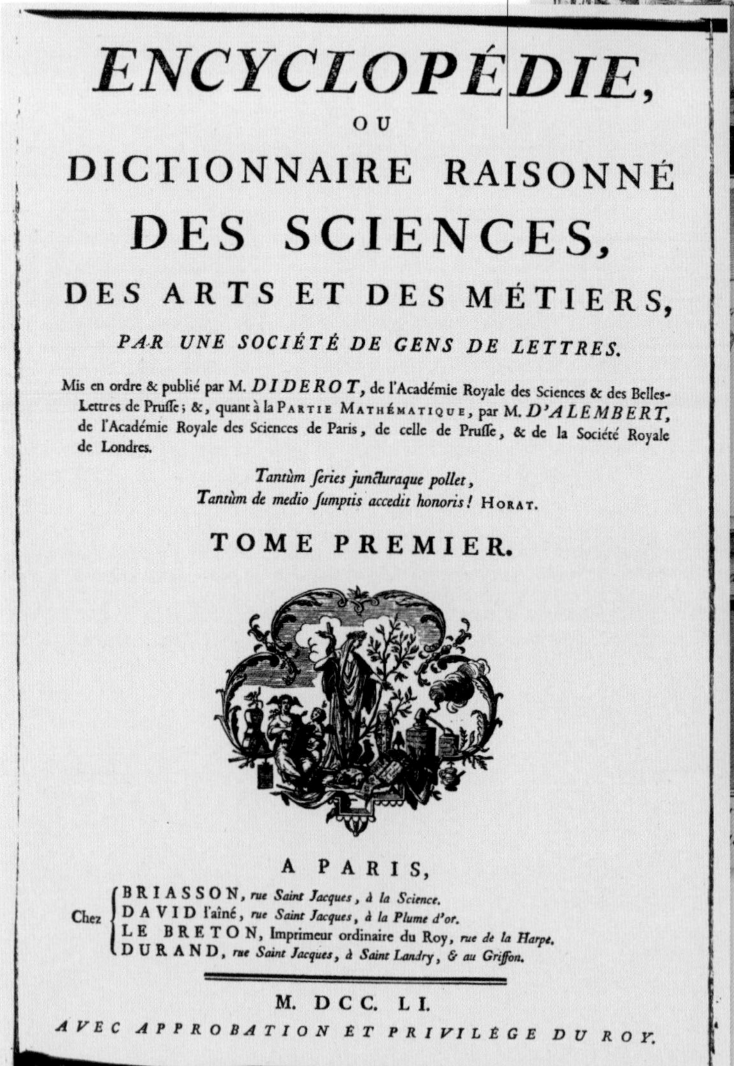

The German philosopher Immanuel Kant described the Enlightenment as "… man's release from his self-inflicted immaturity", meaning that people should use their reason without taking direction. His motto, *Sapere aude*! ("Dare to know!") encouraged readers to challenge outdated traditions.

The Enlightenment was an intellectual "current" that flowed across Europe and beyond during the 18th century thanks to an explosion in printing and the widespread use of the French language. The thinkers, known as *philosophes,* applied ideas from advances in science (see pp.206–07) to change the way that people thought about government and society, seeking to replace superstition, tyranny, and injustice, with reason, tolerance, and legal equality.

From 1750, a "republic of letters" emerged in Paris, aided by the existence of literary salons and the *Encyclopédie* (see right). "What does it mean to be free?" asked François-Marie Arouet – better known as Voltaire – probably the most famous *philosophe* of them all. "To reason correctly and know the rights of man. When they are well known, they are well defended."

Questioning received wisdom led the *philosophes* to attack many things: general ignorance and intolerance;

Madame de Pompadour
A woman renowned for her beauty and wit, Jeanne Poisson (1721–64) was installed in Versailles Palace as Louis XV's mistress. She was a keen patron of artistic and intellectual projects.

outdated privilege among nobles and clergy; absolutism or tyranny in all its forms, such as the royal *lettres de cachet* that allowed anyone to be locked up without evidence; and the Church (for encouraging superstition and persecution).

The Swiss thinker Jean-Jacques Rousseau railed against moral decadence and inequality in his essays on *The Arts and Sciences* (1749) and on *Equality* (1755), which challenged basic Enlightenment beliefs by arguing that social progress had helped to corrupt human nature. His bestselling novels *La Nouvelle Heloise* (1761) and *Emile* (1762) tapped into a rich vein of "sentimentalism" and made him the darling of the chattering classes. But he soon found himself an isolated figure, in conflict with other *philosophes.*

Spreading ideas

The most influential tool for spreading Enlightenment values was the 28-volume *Encyclopédie,* which boasted an impressive array of contributors, including Jacques Turgot, Voltaire,

The Encyclopédie (1751–72)
Diderot and d'Alembert edited this 28-volume magnum opus over 20 years. Its 17 volumes of text and 11 volumes of engravings contained 72,000 articles and over 2,500 plates.

Frontispiece for the first volume of the *Encyclopédie* or "Reasoned Dictionary of the Sciences, Arts and Trades".

and Rousseau under the editorial guidance of Denis Diderot and Jean d'Alembert. Its aim was to assemble and disseminate all existing knowledge in clear, accessible prose and to educate public opinion by "changing accepted habits of thought". Banned twice for its anti-Catholic tone, its survival relied on the support of the state censor.

A more effective way of spreading similar ideas was through satire. The

political theorist Montesquieu started this trend with *Lettres Persanes* (1721), which depicted French and European customs through the eyes of Persian visitors, poking fun at the Church, Court, and French society. Voltaire perfected it in *Candide* (1759), an account of a naïve young man's adventures, by exposing the hypocrisies of the institutions and attitudes that he encountered.

« BEFORE

MONTAIGNE'S "ESSAYS"

The roots of the Enlightenment lay in the Renaissance and English political and intellectual culture.

HUMANISM
A cultural movement of the Renaissance **« 190–93**, humanism **laid the foundations** for the Enlightenment by emphasizing the dignity and reason of man. Humanists such as the French moralist **Michel de Montaigne** wrote essays questioning anything and everything.

POLITICAL REFORMS
In 1688, the English king James II was overthrown and replaced by William III. **Subsequent political reforms** inspired French writers, such

as **Voltaire.** He promoted the English legal system, religious toleration, and its constitutional monarchy as alternatives to French absolutism in his *Lettres Philosophiques* (1734); it was immediately banned.

ENGLISH ROOTS
Enlightenment thinkers adopted **three English philosophers** as their "patron saints": Francis Bacon (1561–1626) for his development of scientific method based on experiment and observation; John Locke (1632–1704) for his political theory and empiricism (acceptance of knowledge based only on direct experience); and Isaac Newton (1643–1727) for his unifying scientific laws and discoveries.

FRANCIS BACON'S "THE ADVANCEMENT OF LEARNING"

[Encyclopédie title page reads:]

ENCYCLOPÉDIE,
OU
DICTIONNAIRE RAISONNÉ
DES SCIENCES,
DES ARTS ET DES MÉTIERS,
PAR UNE SOCIÉTÉ DE GENS DE LETTRES.

Mis en ordre & publié par M. *DIDEROT*, de l'Académie Royale des Sciences & des Belles-Lettres de Prusse; &, quant à la Partie Mathématique, par M. *D'ALEMBERT*, de l'Académie Royale des Sciences de Paris, de celle de Prusse, & de la Société Royale de Londres.

Tantùm series juncturaque pollet,
Tantùm de medio sumptis accedit honoris! Horat.

TOME PREMIER.

A PARIS,
Chez { BRIASSON, rue Saint Jacques, à la Science.
DAVID l'aîné, rue Saint Jacques, à la Plume d'or.
LE BRETON, Imprimeur ordinaire du Roy, rue de la Harpe.
DURAND, rue Saint Jacques, à Saint Landry, & au Griffon.

M. DCC. LI.
AVEC APPROBATION ET PRIVILÈGE DU ROY.

Detailed legends precede each set of labelled plates, which are grouped by themes, such as artisans and musical instruments.

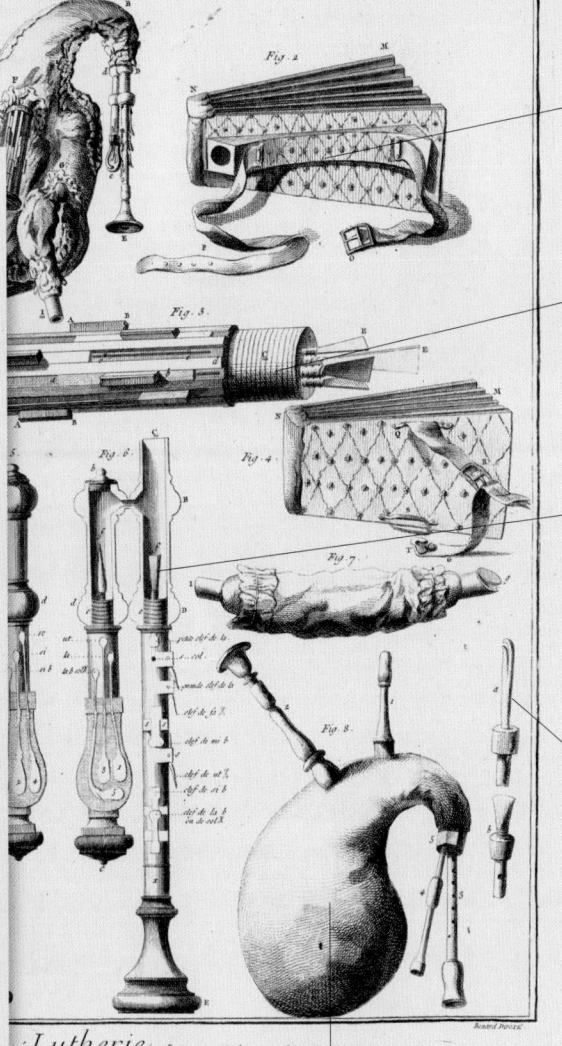

The soufflet was a type of bellows to which a sound-producing object such as a chanter (see below) could be attached.

The four-reed drone fitted onto the *musette de cour* shown above it; a type of bellows-blown bagpipe. Finger-holes were uncovered by moving sliders.

The chanter fitted onto the end of the *musette*. With three keys and seven finger-holes it gave the range of one octave; annotation relates each finger-hole to its note.

Other mouthpieces for the bagpipes are illustrated – the editors intended the engravings to be as comprehensive as possible.

Lutherie, Instruments 'a vent: Musette Cornemuse.

The tools of the trade of a pastrycook (*patissier*) are shown here, including bowls of varying sizes, a baking tray, a pestle and mortar, and a rolling pin.

A fully inflated cornemuse (a type of bagpipes) shows the positioning of the mouthpiece, fingering tubes, and venting tube.

The Enlightenment provoked both radical change and growing criticism of its ideas.

REVOLUTIONS

Increasing demands for political representation helped pave the way for the **American and French Revolutions**. The Founding Fathers incorporated many of Montesquieu's political ideas, including the **separation of powers**, into the US constitution **232–33 »**. However, in France, a combination of revolutionary wars and the "Terror" **236–37 »** served to **dissolve Enlightenment optimism** in a sea of blood.

ROMANTIC BACKLASH

Enlightenment ideas were so widespread by the second half of the 18th century that few failed to share confidence in the "Cult of Reason". But the 19th-century Romantic movement **268–69 »** emphasized emotion, imagination, and a love of nature over reason and industrial progress.

ENLIGHTENED MODERNITY

After the horrors of World War II **314–325 »**, the United Nations (UN) was founded in 1949 to resolve international relations based on the Enlightenment idea of **universal citizenship**. In practice, the self-interest of modern nation states often comes first.

UNITED NATIONS

> "The consent of **the people** is the **sole basis** of a government's authority."
>
> JEAN-JACQUES ROUSSEAU, "THE SOCIAL CONTRACT", 1762

One of the most popular targets of the *philosophes* was the Church, which some saw as one of the main obstacles to reform. They argued that for states to be progressive, politics and religion should be kept apart. Yet many also believed that religion was necessary for upholding the social order, creating an insoluble conflict. Anticlerical sentiments, spread by satirical prints and novels, were fuelled by anger at the Church's corruption and abuse of power. Freemasons lodges sprung up across Europe as secular spaces for disciples of the "Cult of Reason" to gather and exchange ideas.

The other main target was royal absolutism. The French king and his ministers were often in dispute with the *parlements* – French law courts dominated by the aristocracy. Montesquieu transformed the political debate by proposing, in his bestselling treatise *Spirit of the Laws* (1748), a limited monarchy based on a three-way division of powers between the executive (king), the legislature (parliament), and the judiciary.

This was a time when thinkers believed that a rational, scientific approach could be applied to almost any subject. Scotsman Adam Smith's analysis of capitalism, in his book *Wealth of Nations* (1776), invented the new science of economics, while Kant's *Critique of Pure Reason* (1781) presented a more scientific approach to philosophy and knowledge.

IDEA

ENLIGHTENED DESPOTISM

Enlightenment ideas on the state, attacking outdated traditions, filtered down to some of Europe's rulers, including Empress Maria Theresa of Austria, Catherine II "the Great" of Russia, and Frederick II "the Great" (left) of Prussia, who briefly employed Voltaire as his advisor. Frederick tried to govern his subjects as the "first servant of the state". His "revolution from above" created an enlightened welfare state with a modern bureaucracy and law system, transforming Prussia into a semi-constitutional state. Prince Karl Frederick of Baden went one step further, abolishing serfdom outright.

BEFORE «

Decades of war in Europe resulted in advances in military tactics and techniques, although the development of improved weaponry was slow to follow.

BATTLE-READY

The 30 Years War (1618-48) **«202–03** put **Europe on an all-out war footing**. Innovative tactics were employed by field commanders, and training manuals, maps, and field glasses began to be more widely used. But the idea of a permanent or **"standing" professional army** as a fixed piece of machinery of state (just like the non-military civil service) was still in its infancy.

TECHNOLOGY OF WAR

Despite the fact that gunpowder had been developed 400 years before **«110–11**, it remained highly volatile and liable to explode at any time. The **copper and bronze weaponry** made to fire it was slow in development and far from uniform in design or ammunition. Cannons varied in size and were classified by ball weight, the largest being referred to as the "90 pounder". **Giant cannons** known as bombards could weigh 5 tonnes (4,500 kg) and throw an iron ball nearly 1km (0.6 mile). These cannons were useful for demolishing fortifications.

Battle with pikes
As military tactics became more sophisticated, full-on cavalry charges and standardized artillery became integral to more sustained and offensive tactics than the older pike-style warfare, shown above.

Stalemate
The Four Days' Battle was fought from 11–14th June 1666 as part of the Second Anglo–Dutch War, (1665–67). It was fought at close quarters between an English fleet of 56 ships under the Duke of Albermarle and a larger Dutch fleet commanded by their great admiral Michiel de Ruyter.

D uring the 17th century Europe became an almost permanent theatre of war, witnessing more battles than in any other place or time. If there was a dispute to settle then war was the way to do it – diplomacy came when treaties were made.

From the late 17th century, trade – not religion or dynasty – became the dominant cause of conflict between Europeans. The nascent nation-states were increasingly concerned about their freedoms to trade, and thereby to profit and to protect monopolies both on the high seas and in overseas possessions. This became the dominant factor in state formation.

Quarrels about trade around the world were now a concern of European states-in-the-making. For example, from 1652–74 two former republican allies – England and the Dutch Republic – embarked on three Anglo–Dutch Wars centred around trade, colonial possessions, and shipping rights. France and Denmark also entered the conflicts periodically.

The initial cause was an act passed by the English parliament that forbade any foreign ship to carry, and therefore trade, English goods. The Dutch carried massive quantities of English goods in their ships, which made them huge profits that they were prepared to fight to protect. The Treaty of Breda (1667), which ended the second Anglo–Dutch War, was the first multi-nation peace settlement, concerned as much about Europe's overseas interests as its European boundaries. Significantly, the wide-ranging Peace of Westphalia that had ended the 30 Years War

Masters of War

By the 17th century, Europe had emerged from a series of violent wars fought over religion. Such conflicts were quickly replaced with battles over trade rights in both Europe and the ever-increasing number of European colonies abroad. The increasing sophistication of military tactics across the continent outpaced advances in artillery design and production.

KING OF SWEDEN (1594–1632)

GUSTAVUS ADOLPHUS II

Gustavus Adolphus II came to the throne of Sweden in 1611 and is considered the father of modern military tactics. He promoted a more standardized and much lighter artillery, more compact supply trains, offensive tactics (a quick offensive campaign gave the enemy little time to prepare its defence), and provisioning troops by negotiation not looting. To achieve this he needed well trained and disciplined troops, and Gustavus ensured that his men were regularly paid. His military innovations in troop formations and combinations led to a permanent increase in the size of European armies. Sweden was a major power in Europe by the time of his death.

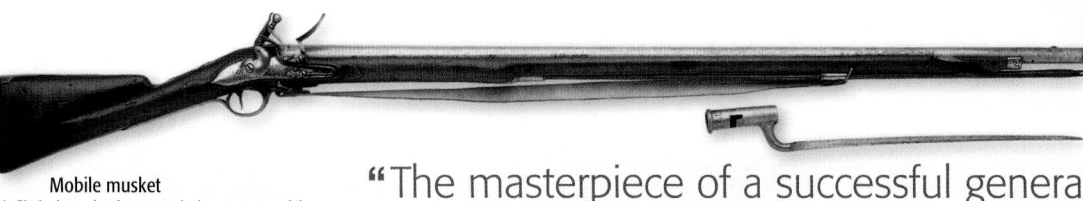

Mobile musket
This flintlock musket from 1741 is the precursor of the rifle. More portable and accurate than earlier guns, it also had a fixed ring bayonet.

> "The masterpiece of a successful general is to **starve his enemy**."
>
> FREDERICK II OF PRUSSIA, ATTRIBUTED

only 19 years earlier (see pp.202–03) contained almost nothing about non-European matters in its collection of treaties, which demonstrates how rapidly Europe's overseas possessions had grown in importance.

On a war footing
One knock-on effect of frequent wars was that large and properly equipped armies and navies had to be maintained, and this required centralized and bureaucratic states to run them. Countries now developed national armed forces as they became an integral element of nation-building. The Dutch were a typical example of how a government's administration and finance were now geared to the ability to mobilize for war and buttress the state's power.

With Europe's political geography much more stable at home, the "standing army" of well-drilled, better provisioned, and uniformed troops that

did not "stand down" (disband) every winter slowly became the norm. The days of the mercenary captains raising private armies for a fee were numbered. Militarism, the central aim of which was the financing and organizing of professional armies, was increasing so that by the 1690s France, fighting a European coalition, could mobilize upwards of 340,000 troops. Even at peace the French standing army numbered 150,000 troops, compared

with 55,000 in the 1660s. Prussian mobilization in the 18th century could raise an army of 185,000 from a population of only five million. Warfare came of age with key developments in the study of strategy, siege tactics, topography, and ballistics. Weapons and ammunition were also refined, and logistics became more of a science as soldiers were now part of the state's permanent expenses. The emphasis switched to defence from aggression.

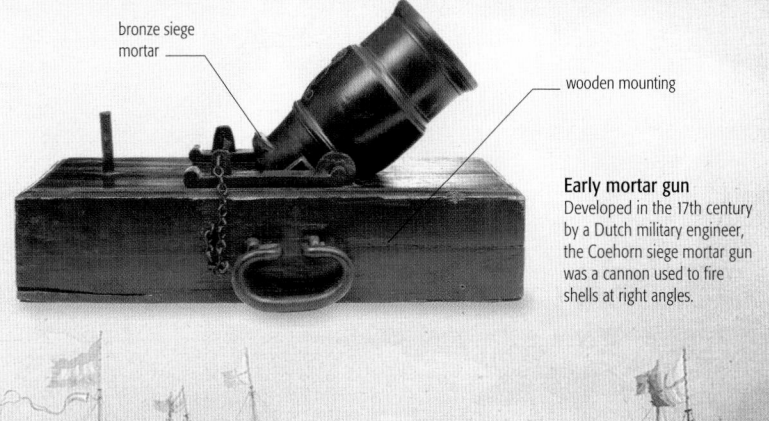

bronze siege mortar

wooden mounting

Early mortar gun
Developed in the 17th century by a Dutch military engineer, the Coehorn siege mortar gun was a cannon used to fire shells at right angles.

Europe's military power grew in sophistication and scope, soon to be "exported" to the rest of the world.

NAPOLEONIC WARFARE
Warfare went through another modernization during the Napoleonic period **240–41 »** with the **formation of military training schools**. During the Napoleonic Wars (1799–1815) Napoleon Bonaparte introduced the method of deploying massed artillery at a specific point in a battle thereby giving him sensational victories.

EUROPE'S FIRST PROFESSIONAL ARMY
Russia had the first European army in which **all the men wore uniforms** and private soldiers were decorated for bravery – almost unknown in the rest of Europe. Troops were directly recruited and financed by the state – **peasant conscripts served for life** until 1793.

THE SEVEN YEARS WAR
The Seven Years War **230–31 »** involved both Europe and colonies in the Americas for the first time. It is considered to be the first truly global conflict in history.

The **Rise** of **Capitalism**

From the 15th century, capitalism – investing and trading goods for profit – became a key force in European economies, politics, culture, and even warfare. The establishment of overseas empires and the creation of trading centres to finance them, spurred this new wave of global commerce.

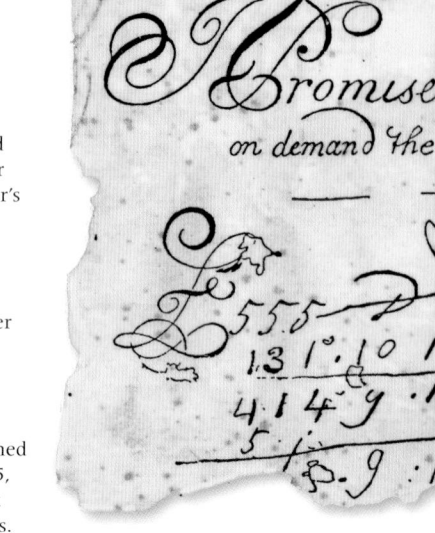

The discovery of the Americas (see pp.168–69) and the development in the 15th century of ocean-going ships capable of sailing vast distances (see pp.164–65), kick-started the modern era of capitalism. The enterprise of investing money to make money now had a global reach with potentially massive profits, simply because of the scarcity of the precious commodities – from silver to silk, porcelain to pepper – and the large distances involved. The value of goods from the East was so huge in Europe that it paid for the costs of such voyages many times over.

The return on investment might be high but so were the risks. Ships often succumbed to storms, reefs, and pirates, with the result that all of the goods accrued over many months would be lost in an instant. Investment in ships, rigging, guns, and crew, as well as refurbishing and filling the ships with outgoing stock was also huge. Such undertakings tied up large sums of money for long periods, sometimes years, before any profit could be realized. In Europe, a glut of a certain commodity could depress prices. So, a large number of speculators needed to be persuaded to share the risk.

Merchant capitalism

The need to secure the required investment saw the creation of joint stock companies. Investors bought into the companies – even if they had no personal links to its trading activities – by buying stocks in them on the open market. They could sell their stocks,

Edward Lloyd's coffee shop
Ship owners meet at Lloyd's coffeehouse to discuss future voyages with underwriters – men who insure things against loss for a premium. This gathering developed into insurance giant Lloyd's.

but crucially, could not withdraw their capital. An investor's share in the company's stock could also be sold at whatever price the buyer and seller agreed upon. The Muscovy Company was the first joint-stock enterprise established in England in 1555, but the Dutch East India Company was the most famous. It was chartered by the States General in 1602 and consisted of a grouping of six provincial chambers each with its own capital and share distribution of total profits. They appointed 17 general directors, the Heeren XVII, who became the central management. The Heeren XVII controlled the administration of factories and territory in the East Indies, the marketing of imported goods to Amsterdam, and how ships were to be freighted and employed.

Even the Bank of England, when it was founded by royal charter in 1694, was organized at first on joint-stock lines to raise money for what were effectively trade-based wars against France. No other joint-stock banks were permitted in Britain until 1826.

Other company enterprises included the United Company of Merchants of England (1600), Companhia Geral do Comércio do Brasil (1649), Compagnie de Chine (1698), the French East India Company (1723), Compagnie de Sénégal (1673), the Royal African Company (1672), the Dutch West India Company, the Hudson's Bay Company (1670), and the South Sea Company (1711) – the name of each often giving away the nature of the enterprise.

The lynchpin of capitalism

A vital innovation, the joint-stock company enjoyed a much more long-term and independent existence than other companies, as it built up its capital and a buoyant market for its shares over time. In return for being given a commercial monopoly abroad and the authority to negotiate with Asian and Indian rulers, these companies provided protection on the ocean and employed their own armed ships and troops

Dutch trader's manual
A Dutch trader's manual from the 1500s with pictures of coins, which was used to conduct business.

◀◀ **BEFORE**

In the medieval period the attitude of the Catholic Church to usury (moneylending with interest charged) prevented capitalism from developing. The papal ban on levying interest was not repealed until the 15th century.

EUROPE'S FIRST BANKERS

In the 12th century, the Italian cities of Genoa and Venice saw the rise of **Europe's first bankers ◀◀ 154–55**, with the earliest forms of bills of exchange and double-entry book-keeping, which is the basis of modern banking and accounting systems. The Genoese had helped finance the Crusades ◀◀ **146–47** and profited from lucrative trading rights and shipping contracts in the Middle East. They had also unwittingly brought **the Black Death** back to Europe ◀◀ **132–33**.

> " ... freedom of trade is based on **a primitive right** of Nations..."
>
> HUGO GROTIUS, FROM "CONCERNING THE LAW OF PRIZE", 1604

Royal exchange
As a London cloth merchant who supplied the tapestries for Henry VIII's Hampton Court, Richard Gresham had visited Antwerp's trading centre. He recognized its vital trade link, and urged the establishment of a similar centre in London. In 1565 his son Thomas established the Royal Exchange of London, shown here.

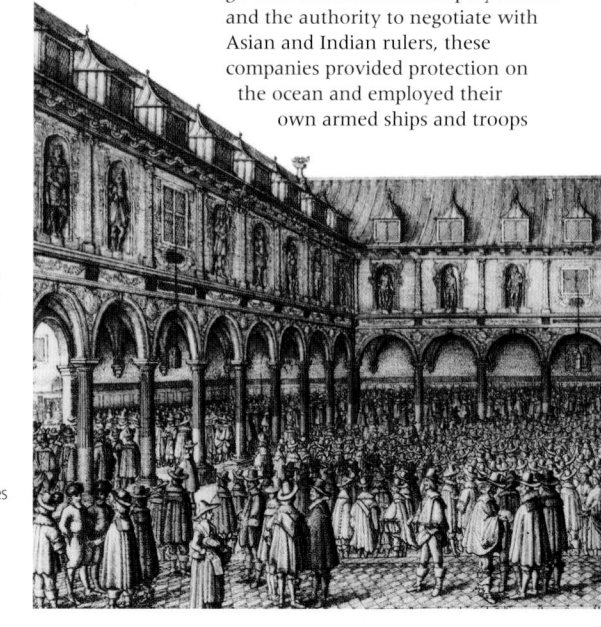

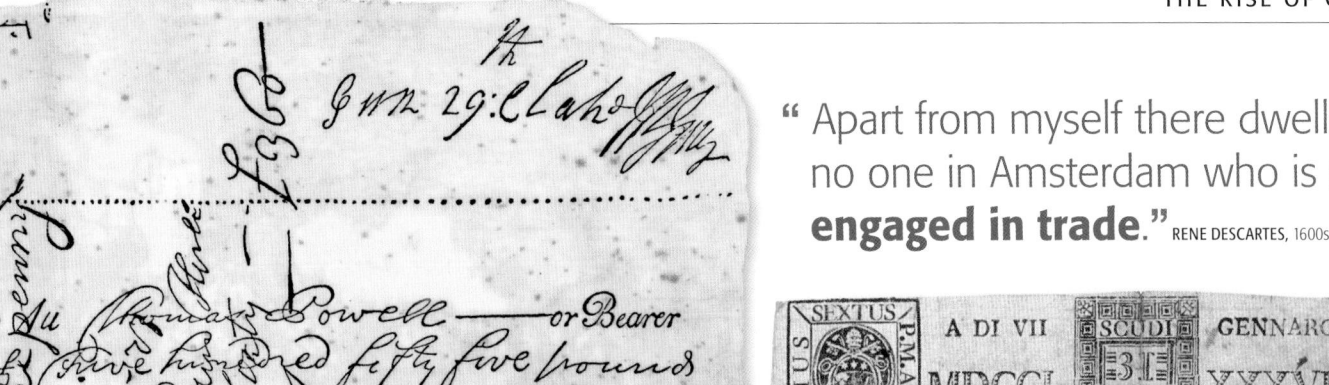

" Apart from myself there dwells no one in Amsterdam who is not **engaged in trade**." RENE DESCARTES, 1600s

Paper money in the UK
The first British bank notes, issued by the Bank of England from the mid 1690s, showed the image of Britannia. From 1727 Scottish bank notes featured the monarch's head.

New banking services
A handwritten cheque for £70 dates to 1725. Its function is much like a modern cheque. A large range of financial services offered by banks were provided by legal clerks, merchants, and goldsmiths in the 18th century.

Papal paper money
The Bank of the Holy Spirit at Rome was Europe's first national bank, established in 1605 by Pope Paul V. This note (above) was issued for circulation in the Papal States under Pope Pius VI in 1786.

to protect their coastal factories and trade. In effect, they made local war and peace.

Specialist traders now emerged willing to arrange deals between buyers and sellers of stocks and shares (in an enterprise or commodity with which they had no direct connection) in return for a cut on each transaction. They were called brokers. In London the brokers gathered at first in coffeehouses, and a system of stockbroking

gradually became established. The first coffeehouse in London opened in 1652 (coffee itself being a valuable commodity and newly fashionable refreshment). At Edward Lloyd's coffeehouse, merchants, brokers, ship owners, and sea captains met to discuss investment and insurance for new voyages. At Jonathan's coffeehouse in Change Alley brokers negotiated with investors to buy and sell shares in joint-stock companies and trading ventures.

In 1698 stock dealers were expelled from the Royal Exchange (see left) for rowdiness and began their dealings in the streets and coffeehouses nearby, in particular in Jonathan's Coffeehouse. It was in these coffeehouses that brokers also came up with the idea of producing lists of share prices and shipping departure data.

In the same year, John Castaing began publishing a twice weekly newsletter of share and commodity prices, called *The Course of the Exchange and other things* which he sold at Jonathan's. It is the earliest written evidence of organized trading in stocks in London and the precursor of the famous insurance

exchange Lloyd's of London and the Lloyd's Register of Shipping (see pp.178–79).

A "bourse" is born
From the early 16th century in Antwerp, merchants had a base within which to trade – a Bourse. It was purpose-built and regulated as a market for the sale and purchase of trading companies' shares and stocks. The Bourse – the continental term for a stock exchange – became the symbol of capitalism and an expanding economy, in which ships were chartered, cargo insured, and stocks and shares bought and sold. After the siege of Antwerp in 1585, trading moved to Amsterdam.

The Dutch formalized the idea of a stock exchange building to market shares: in 1609 the *Amsterdamsche Wisselbank* (Amsterdam Exchange Bank) was founded, which made Amsterdam the financial centre of the world until the Industrial Revolution (see pp.226–29). As with marine insurance, double-entry book-keeping, and other business techniques, the bank was copied from Italian models.

AFTER »

As a global economy began to emerge, financial institutions became privatized and monarchs and state governments began to lose their dominion over the economy.

CAPTAINS OF INDUSTRY
Adam Smith's *Inquiry into the Nature and Causes of the Wealth of Nations* (1776) supported the massive growth in the banking industry. The **Industrial Revolution 226–29 »** spurred a new system of ownership and investment, and moneyholders were able to reduce state intervention in economic affairs. The captains of industry had arrived.

LLOYD'S OF LONDON
Within the vast atrium of the Lloyd's of London building stands the Lutine Bell. It was rescued from HMS *Lutine* which sank in 1799 with its crew and cargo of gold and bullion. Now mainly reserved for ceremonial purposes, it was traditionally rung once for the loss or delay of a ship and twice for its safe arrival.

THE LUTINE BELL INSIDE LLOYD'S OF LONDON

KING OF FRANCE Born 1638 Died 1715

Louis XIV

"L'Etat, c'est moi." (I am, myself, **the state**) LOUIS XIV, KING OF FRANCE

Louis XIV was only four years old in 1643, when he succeeded his father, Louis XIII, as king of France. During the regency of his mother, Anne of Austria, the effective ruler of France was her chief minister, Cardinal Mazarin. When Mazarin died in 1661, the 23-year-old King Louis XIV was expected to appoint a chief minister of similar calibre. Instead, he announced his intention of being his own first minister, and ruling as an absolute monarch (see right).

Expensive wars

For the first 20 years of his personal reign (1661–81), Louis was constantly waging war. He began with an attack on the Spanish Netherlands in 1667 to gain land, but his territorial ambitions there were thwarted by an alliance between Holland, England, and Sweden. In 1672, having detached England from that alliance, he invaded Holland, but under William of Orange the Dutch managed to stand firm against him. Although this campaign led to the formation of another European alliance against France, Louis did make some territorial gains along France's frontiers.

In 1688 he was at war again, against a "Grand Alliance" that included Holland and England, both now ruled by William of Orange. A factor in this alliance for the Protestant member states, was Louis' revocation of the Edict of Nantes in 1685 (see pp.198–99), which meant that Huguenots (French Protestants) no longer had the right to practice their faith in France. The War of the Grand Alliance lasted until 1697. There were a few years of peace until 1700, when the death of the king of Spain led to the War of the Spanish Succession (see right).

To fund his constant military campaigns, Louis XIV relied on his director of finances, Jean-Baptiste Colbert. Colbert improved the tax collection system, brought

The Sun King portrait
This magnificent portrait by Hyacinthe Rigaud of the "Sun King" fits contemporary descriptions of Louis XIV. By all accounts, Louis was attractive, with a strong nose, piercing eyes, and a healthy complexion.

Royal family tree
Louis XIV was a member of one of the most powerful and widely distributed royal dynasties in Europe, the Bourbons. His mother, Anne of Austria, was a member of another great dynasty of the period – the Habsburgs.

Theatre
Madeleine Béjart was the leading lady of the theatrical company managed by Molière, the genius of French comedy whose plays entertained Louis and his court.

Palace of Versailles
Once established at Versailles, Louis' court become a magnet for all the talent in France, and a monument to French cultural and political prestige.

1648 Treaty of Westphalia brings to an end the Thirty Years War (see pp.202–03).

industry under state control, and did what he could to boost French naval power. He was also in charge of the royal household's finances, a responsibility that included the cost of Versailles.

The court of the Sun King

Versailles began as a modest hunting lodge near Paris, where the young Louis XIV entertained his intimate friends. In the late 1660s Louis started to devote more attention to the project of reconstructing and extending the old hunting lodge into a royal palace. There was method behind Louis' extravagant plan to build a great royal palace. By making Versailles the permanent base of the royal court and the seat of government from 1682, Louis created a hugely attractive nexus of power and influence, which the nobility found irresistible, and which persuaded them to trade provincial power for influence and rewards at Court, under the direct auspices of the king. Above all, the Court was a centre of conspicuous consumption and magnificence, principally intended to glorify the "Sun King", as Louis was

Sun motif
This gilded sun emblem made of carved wood is found on the walls of the palace of Versailles. Sun motifs served as logos for Louis XIV's golden reign.

styled by artists paid to glorify him. And, like the sun-god Apollo, Louis wished to appear a great patron of the arts, provided that the artists obeyed the various controls imposed by the royal academies. At the heart of the royal palace, which at its height was the size of a small town containing upwards of 10,000 people, were the apartments of Louis, his Spanish Queen, Marie Thérèse, and the royal mistress. It was usual for the current royal mistress to enjoy court honours, and the children resulting from the relationships were acknowledged by the king.

The Sun King died at the age of 77, in the 56th year of his personal rule. His final years were clouded by bereavement, military defeat, and a catastrophic country-wide collapse in the French economy. The sudden deaths of his son, the dauphin (heir apparent), his grandson, and his elder great-grandson – all within a matter of months – meant that his kingdom passed to his five-year-old great grandson, Louis XV.

ABSOLUTE MONARCHY

From the moment of his coronation (pictured, right) Louis XIV demonstrated his belief that he had a "divine right" – God-given duty – to rule France as an absolute monarch, without consulting parliaments, ministers, or senior nobles. Blessed with stamina, confidence, and a passion for order, he was an extraordinarily capable ruler. Even when he was at war, he insisted on daily progress reports about the construction of Versailles. Other monarchs envied his power and his palace; the scale of the palace of Versailles was mimicked all over Europe.

TIMELINE

- **1638** Birth of Louis, long awaited first-born child of Anne of Austria and Louis XIII of France.

- **1643** Death of Louis XIII; Anne of Austria and chief minister Cardinal Mazarin effectively rule France.

- **1648–53** The period of internal troubles and civil war in France known as the Fronde.

- **1648** Treaty of Westphalia brings to an end the Thirty Years War (see pp.202–03).

- **1659** Treaty of Pyrenees brings peace with Spain, cemented by a proposed marriage alliance between Louis XIV and the Spanish princess, Marie Thérèse.

- **9 June 1660** Marriage to Marie Thérèse of Spain.

LOUIS XIV'S MARRIAGE

- **1661** Death of Cardinal Mazarin; Louise de la Vallière becomes the official royal mistress; Louis begins his personal rule; birth of Louis' eldest son, the dauphin Louis.

- **1666** Death of Anne of Austria.

- **1667** Louis XIV establishes the French Academy of Science.

- **1668** Treaty of Aix-La-Chapelle marks France's successful annexation of part of the Spanish Netherlands.

- **1672–78** France goes to war against the Dutch.

- **1682** The full court moves to the new palace of Versailles, 19km (12 miles) west of Paris; birth of Louis' first grandson, the Duc de Bourgogne.

- **1683** After the death of his wife, Louis XIV marries his long-term companion Madame de Maintenon in a secret ceremony.

- **1685** Louis XIV revokes the Edict of Nantes, ending the freedom to worship of French Protestants (Huguenots), hundreds of thousands of whom leave France; the indignation of Europe's Protestant powers, Holland, England, and Sweden contributes to the formation of the Grand Alliance against France.

- **1689** William of Orange, now also king of England, leads the Grand Alliance against France.

- **1700** Charles II of Spain (half-brother of Louis' queen, Marie Thérèse) dies without heirs. His will bequeaths the throne in the first instance to Louis XIV's' grandson, the Duc d'Anjou, who becomes Philip V of Spain.

- **1701–13** War of the Spanish Succession is triggered by counter-claims to the Spanish throne by Holy Roman Emperor Leopold I and Louis' expansionist policies. The war ends in 1713 at the Treaty of Utrecht, with Philip V left on the Spanish throne, but the Spanish Empire partitioned.

- **1711–12** Deaths of Louis XIV's eldest son (the dauphin), grandson (the Duc de Bourgogne), and elder great-grandson.

- **1715** Louis XIV dies at Versailles; he is succeeded by his only surviving legitimate descendant, his great-grandson who becomes Louis XV.

« BEFORE

The Afro-European slave trade began in around 1440, when Portuguese traders began to ship captured Africans to work on plantations, to feed Europe's growing demand for sugar.

SUGAR PLANTATIONS

The first sugar plantation was established by the **Portuguese in Madeira**, an island off the northwest coast of Africa, in 1452. At first, **Africans were kidnapped** and forced into slavery to work on plantations, but in 1458 a deal was brokered with African rulers to **purchase slaves**. Up to the mid-17th century, 90 per cent of the 140,000 slaves imported from Africa were bought by the sugar planters of the West African islands (the Canaries, Madeira, São Tomé, and Cape Verde). The rest

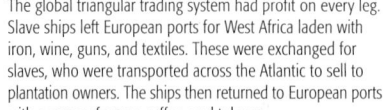

SUGAR CANE were shipped to the Americas.

The Slave Trade

The brutal trade in African slaves began in the mid-15th century and reached its height in the 18th century. Altogether, around 10 million Africans were captured, shackled, and shipped to the Americas to work on sugar, cotton, and tobacco plantations.

A lthough African slave labour was used in the production of other commodities, such as minerals, coffee, cocoa, indigo, cotton, and tobacco, it was Europe's craving for sugar that brought European traders to Africa to buy and barter slaves. The Swedes, Danes, French, British, Dutch, and Portuguese established over 30 slave forts along the West African "Gold Coast", and a series of ports for exporting slaves stretched over 3,200km (2,000 miles) from the Senegal River south to Angola in Senegambia, Dahomey (Benin), and Ouidah.

Slaves in Africa

Slavery was already part of Africa's tribal economy and society – more so than land ownership – before the arrival of the European traders. For example, women and children whose menfolk had been killed in battle were usually enslaved, becoming part of a tribal ruler's extended family. The East Africa slave trade was also well-established, with captured slaves transported north across the Saharan desert and east into Arabia, the Middle East, and India by Arab and Ottoman slave traders.

African chiefs were complicit in providing the European seafarers with slaves. However, they did not want the Europeans to settle inland. (In any case, the Europeans themselves were deterred by the difficulties of travel in Africa's interior, and the threat of disease.) As a result, African chiefs leased out land along the coast so the Europeans could establish trading forts. African slaves captured in raids or after battle were transported to the forts by their African captors, then sold to the European traders. Some African rulers were especially accommodating. For

example, in 1726 the King of Dahomey suggested that the Europeans should establish plantations in his kingdom – he would supply the slaves.

Money without morals

With only a toehold on the African coast, Europeans were unable to monopolize the slave trade. Slaves

Slave ship

This horrific image shows how many slaves could be packed into the hold of the slave ship, *Brookes*, to maximize profit. In 1789, anti-slavery campaigners published 700 posters of the drawing, sparking the beginning of the end of the slave trade in Britain.

The triangular trade

The global triangular trading system had profit on every leg. Slave ships left European ports for West Africa laden with iron, wine, guns, and textiles. These were exchanged for slaves, who were transported across the Atlantic to sell to plantation owners. The ships then returned to European ports with a cargo of sugar, coffee, and tobacco.

KEY

Slave routes
→ European slave traders
→ Arab slave traders
→ Ottoman slave traders
● African slaving centres

Goods routes
→ Tobacco, sugar, cotton
→ Metals, tobacco, sugar, coffee
→ Iron, cloth, shells, guns

NECK RING

Instruments of torture

Slaves were seen as chattels, or goods, not as human beings, demonstrated by the assortment of heavy iron shackles that they had to endure. Male slaves were chained up in gruesome ankle and neck chains.

FOOT SHACKLES

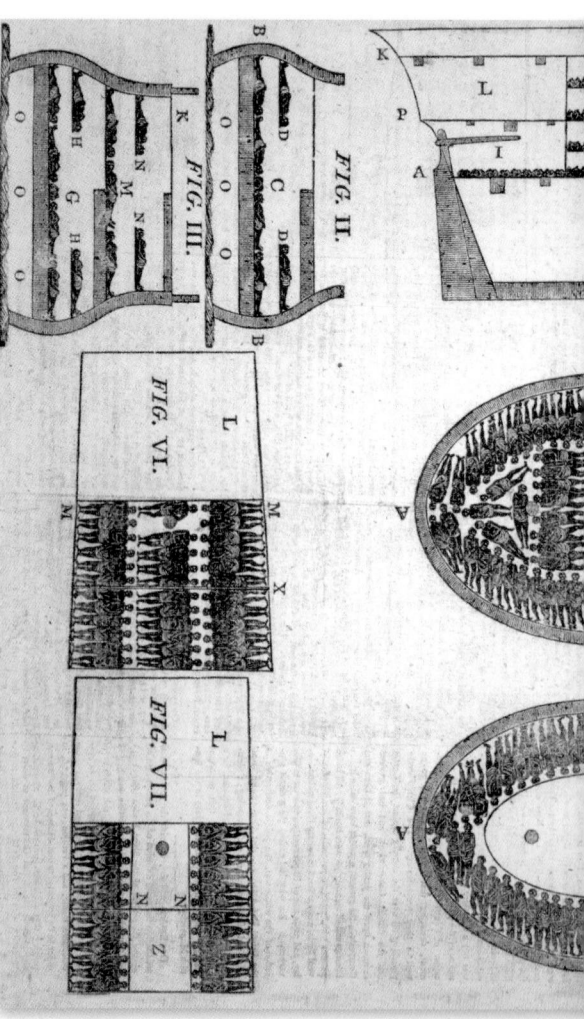

"There was nothing to be heard but the **rattling of chains**, smacking of whips and groans and **cries** of our... men.**"**

OTTOBAH CUGOANO, FREED SLAVE, 1787

were either collected directly from leased forts in exchange for goods, such as guns or alcohol, or ships plied the Gold Coast hoping to pick up a cargo of slaves from private dealers.

For the mercantile companies, shareholders, captains, and other traders involved, there appeared to be no moral qualms at all: slaves simply oiled the wheels of a well-organized and highly lucrative business. For example, by the 1780s the plantations of the French colony Saint-Domingue (Haiti) accounted for 60 per cent of France's overseas wealth, supplying

Slaves were shackled in rows
between the hold and the deck, lying on their back or sides. Each slave had only around 30cm (12in) space around them.

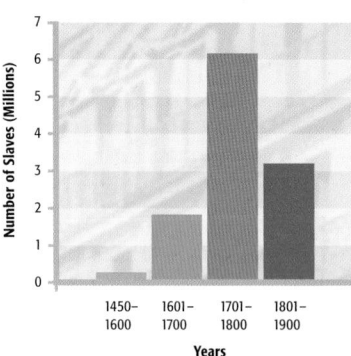

Branding iron
When they were bought, all male slaves were forcibly branded with a hot iron as proof of ownership.

40 per cent of all the sugar and 60 per cent of all the coffee consumed in Europe.

The middle passage
Slaves from the African coastal forts were packed on ships bound for South, Central, and North America – a journey called the "middle passage".

This diagram shows how 482 slaves
could be packed on board. This ship had previously carried as many as 609 slaves (351 men, 127 women, and 113 children).

From the 16th–19th centuries, some 54,000 trade voyages were recorded. This peaked in the 1780s at 78,000 slaves a year, with half of them carried on British ships.

A typical middle passage journey took around 10 weeks. Each ship carried 140 – 600 slaves in appalling, cramped conditions. Men were chained together in a suffocatingly small space between the deck and the hold. Women were usually left unchained and were allowed on deck to help with the cooking. However, they risked constant sexual harrassment and rape by the European crew.

Hygiene on board ship was crude. Few ships were equipped to deal with bodily functions and, as they were shackled together, it was hard for the men particularly to avoid catching dysentery and smallpox – the two biggest on-board killers. After a month at sea, a slave ship stank of sweat, urine, faeces, and vomit. It was said that a slave ship could be smelled two days before it actually arrived in a port.

Each morning, the slaves were dragged up onto deck and their shackles were inspected. Any slave who had died during the night was unchained and thrown overboard. Rations included boiled mash of horse beans and yams, biscuits, rice, plantain, and occasionally meat. One food bucket was usually shared among many, resulting in quarrels – and infection.

Captains and crew succumbed to disease and death as much as their cargo. In 1787, of the slave-ship crews that embarked from Liverpool in England, less than half returned alive.

Auctioned
Arriving in Brazil or the Caribbean islands, the slaves were sold at auction then delivered to their new owners. This was often followed by a period of "seasoning" – about a year in which the slave either succumbed to disease or survived to live a life of human bondage and misery.

Number of slaves exported from Africa
Records suggest that between 1450–1700, 2 million Africans were enslaved, rising to 6 million in 1701–1800. Accounting for those dying in transit to forts and on slave ships, the figure is probably closer to 12 million.

AFTER »

The slave trade was finally abolished in England in 1807, after years of campaigning by anti-slavery groups.

ANTI-SLAVERY CAMPAIGN
Thomas Clarkson, a leading anti-slavery protestor in England, gathered evidence such as shackles and the oral accounts of former slave captains to publicize the horrors of the trade.

The fight gained momentum when it was taken up in parliament by MP William Wilberforce. The Abolition of the Slave Trade Act was passed in England in 1807, followed by the **Emancipation Act of 1833**, which made owning slaves illegal. A string of legislation followed, with slavery abolished in the US in 1865, Cuba in 1886, Brazil in 1888, ending with Sierra Leone in 1927 and the Gold Coast in 1928.

ANTI-SLAVERY POSTER, BOSTON, 1851

SLAVERY TODAY
Modern-day human rights campaigners point out that the fight against slavery is far from over. It is estimated that there are **over 27 million slaves** in the world today, including people in forced labour, women and girls trafficked for work in the sex industry, and children kidnapped and forced to fight as soldiers.

FIG. I.

Men were chained together
at the front of the boat; women were held in a separate area. Most transported slaves were between 16–45 years old.

Food and water were stored
in the hold below the slaves. Both food and water were rationed so there was enough to last the voyage. Any slave refusing to eat out of misery or rebellion was whipped.

Destination and number of slaves exported from Africa (in millions)
Most slaves bought by European traders were shipped to the Caribbean or Brazil, altering the population dynamics: by 1800, half of Brazil's population was of African origin.

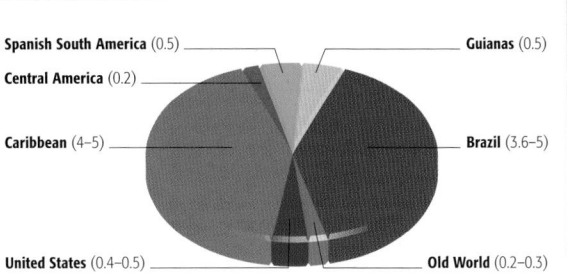

Spanish South America (0.5)
Guianas (0.5)
Central America (0.2)
Caribbean (4–5)
Brazil (3.6–5)
United States (0.4–0.5)
Old World (0.2–0.3)

CHAINED SLAVES IN ZANZIBAR

‹‹ BEFORE

Some Pacific lands were settled many millennia before they were charted by Europeans in the late 18th century.

AUSTRALIA AND NEW ZEALAND
The **Maori**, from Polynesia, settled New Zealand by about 1400 **‹‹ 160–61**. But arid Australia remained uninviting except to the **Aborigines** who landed there 40,000 years earlier.

UNCHARTED TERRITORY
To Europeans, *Terra Australis Incognita* (Unknown Southern Continent) was a hypothetical landmass somewhere in the Pacific Ocean **250–51 ››**.

INVENTION

HARRISON'S CHRONOMETER

The problem of determining longitude on an endless horizon was one of the greatest challenges for sailors navigating the Pacific Ocean in the 18th century. John Harrison (1693–1776) had no formal training in clock-making but built five marine timekeepers, the best of which could keep time at sea to within about one second per day – a staggering positioning accuracy of about 500m (1600ft) – solving the navigational problem. This huge clock was his first prototype, called H1. It measures about 1m x 1m (3ft x 3ft) and weighs 33kg (72lb). It performed admirably at sea.

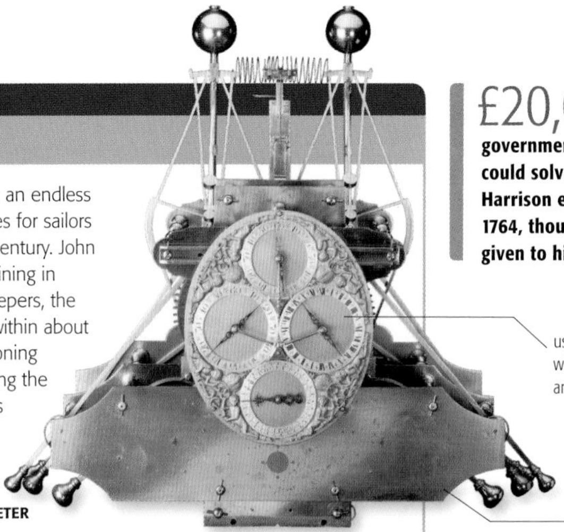

NAUTICAL CHRONOMETER

uses 24 hour dial; runs without pendulum or any lubrication

two 2kg (5lb) weights counteract the movement of a rolling ship

£20,000 The prize offered by the British government in 1714 to the person who could solve the longitude problem. John Harrison eventually won the prize in 1764, though the full amount was not given to him until 1773.

Exploring the Pacific

Less than 250 years ago the Pacific Ocean remained the last great unknown area on Earth, at least to European explorers and traders. European superpowers were rapidly exploring the rest of the world from the 15th century onwards, yet the Pacific Ocean remained a mystery for another 400 years.

By the middle of the 18th century, Europeans had mapped the coastlines of North and South America, Asia, and Africa, and vast empires were well underway in these areas. So it may seem odd that the Europeans did not attempt to colonize the islands of the Pacific Ocean until the late 18th century.

The problem of the Pacific
Simply put, there was nothing to lure the Europeans to the Pacific – no tales of El Dorado, no indigenous empires to conquer and convert, and no lucrative trade to exploit. There were also geographical, technological, and logistical barriers: the Pacific covers an area larger than all the continents'

landmass combined, and the prevailing winds also narrowed the sea routes available. Earlier Polynesian voyagers – the Maori who had sailed to New Zealand and the discoverers of the Hawaiian Islands (see pp.160–61) – had steered their canoes by means of the Sun and the stars, and patterns in the ocean's currents and waves. European sailors had effective sextants, compasses, and other navigational aids, but they still could not determine longitude. This is the measurement of the position of a point east or west of the Prime Meridian (where longitude is 0°). It can be calculated by comparing the time at any point to the time at the Prime Meridian, but to know the time at Greenwich (the British meridian) after

a voyage to the other side of the world required an extremely accurate clock. The ability to determine longitude was vital – it would allow sailors to chart their precise location and that of the islands they visited. The Solomon Islands, for example, were sighted and reported in 1568 but were not

Maori war canoe
The Maoris had giant war canoes (*waka taua*), which carried between 70–140 armed warriors. Led by a Maori chief (*rangatira*), a war canoe had a hull carved out of a single tree trunk and an intricately carved prow.

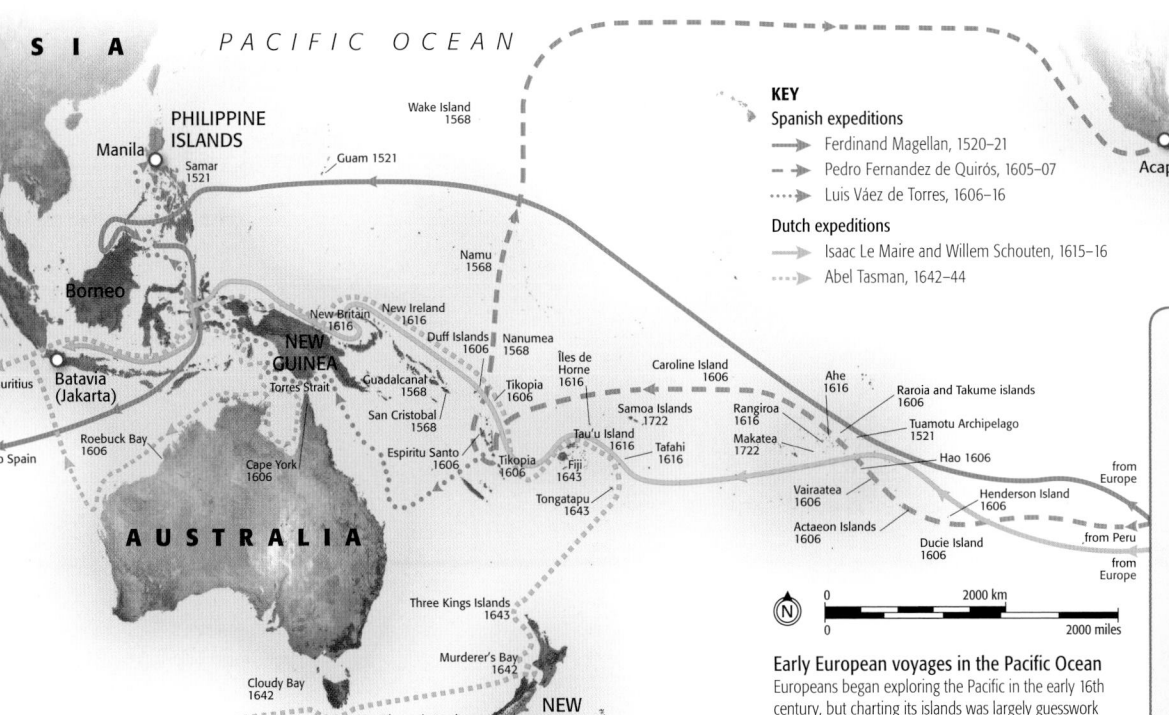

KEY

Spanish expeditions
- Ferdinand Magellan, 1520–21
- Pedro Fernandez de Quirós, 1605–07
- Luis Váez de Torres, 1606–16

Dutch expeditions
- Isaac Le Maire and Willem Schouten, 1615–16
- Abel Tasman, 1642–44

Early European voyages in the Pacific Ocean
Europeans began exploring the Pacific in the early 16th century, but charting its islands was largely guesswork until Cook's voyages of 1768–79 (see pp.250–51).

AFTER

As European settlers arrived, some under duress, the Pacific region began to develop whaling and agricultural industries.

PENAL COLONIES
In January 1788 **the first fleet of convicts** and settlers arrived from England to set up the penal colony of New South Wales, which began the European settlement of Australia **250–51 ».**

WHALING
Whaling was a lure in the Pacific for Europeans and Americans from 1789 onwards. Whaling ships called in to refuel all over the Pacific. They impacted on the islands' native communities as well as stimulating further **maritime expansion**.

SHEEP FARMING
British settlers in Australia and New Zealand introduced sheep to temperate regions of the continent. Today, Australia is the **biggest fine-wool producer in the world**.

MERINO SHEEP GRAZING IN AUSTRALIA

properly charted until 1793. Accurate chronometers (see left) were a huge boon as they allowed sailors to measure exact longitude for the first time. Other obstacles to colonization included malaria, settlers' reliance on imported livestock, the poor quality of land for farming, and tropical storms.

Spanish monopoly
The biggest disincentive to exploring the Pacific region was reflected in a Dutch East India Company report on Abel Tasman's voyages to Tasmania and New Zealand: "No riches or things of profit, but only the said lands."

Maori eel trap
A Maori eel trap (*hinaki*) was finely woven from vines and allowed eels to swim in, but not out. It was placed in lakes or waterholes.

The Spanish Empire claimed the exclusive right of navigation in Pacific waters. They used the Pacific primarily to ship South American silver to the Philippines to trade with China and the East Indies. Spain's greatest rival, the Dutch East India Company, concentrated on its possessions in the Indonesian archipelago, discouraging its captains from long, fruitless, and costly ocean voyages in the region. Breakthrough voyages, such as Luis Vaez de Torres' 1606 sailing between New Guinea and Australia that proved the former to be an island,

received no publicity. The Spanish did not want Dutch and English ships passing through the Java Sea to the Pacific and on to South America.

The race for land begins
When British Captain James Cook (see pp.250–51) set out for Tahiti on the *Endeavour* in 1768, his orders were to observe the Transit of Venus, a rare astronomical event when the planet passes across the face of the Sun. But, the British also wanted to forestall any French ambitions of gaining land in the area. The second, secret purpose of Cook's voyage was to survey the vast Pacific Ocean to see if Tahiti was the possible gateway to the landmass of a southern continent, Australia.

5

INDUSTRY AND REVOLUTION

1750–1914

From the middle of the 18th century, the world experienced radical change. Political revolutions challenged established governments, aiming to throw off the shackles of oppression and privilege. New methods of mechanization and transport resulted in an age of industry and manufacture that gave birth to new cities and consolidated empires.

« BEFORE

Despite advances in farming practices and knowledge, pre-18th century food production was inefficient and reliant on manual labour.

ENCLOSURE

The enclosure system was first developed in England in the 12th century, and saw the division of large, commonly-owned fields into small, privately-owned plots. Labourers were forced from the fields by land owners thanks to a series of Enclosure Acts. This practice spread through Europe during the 19th century.

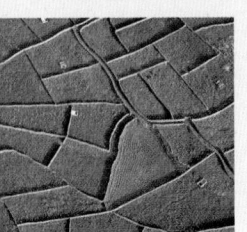

ENCLOSURE SYSTEM

NEW METHODS

By the mid-17th century many farmers began to treat **farming as a science**. They adopted new winter feeding methods, which made fresh meat available all year round. Improved seeds in Holland and later in England yielded new varieties of fruit and vegetables, and numerous new horse-drawn threshers, cultivators, grain, and grass cutters were used.

POPULATION GROWTH

In 1750 the world population began to boom. Although this had happened before, each time the population had ceased to grow because agriculture could not feed the extra people. However, by 1750 the onset of agricultural technology allowed this population growth to be sustained.

The mid-18th century witnessed a dramatic increase in world population. The British economist Thomas Malthus (see right) believed that this rise would eventually be halted by a shortage of food. He had not accounted, however, for vast improvements in agricultural practice.

In 1701, Jethro Tull had developed the horse-drawn seed-drill, a machine for efficiently planting seeds, while a four-year system of crop rotation dispensed with the need to replenish fields by leaving them unfarmed for a season. These changes would have been impossible under the old common-field system, but a spate of Enclosure Acts (see BEFORE) during the 19th century allowed landowners to evict peasants from the land, and experiment with new farming techniques without the consent

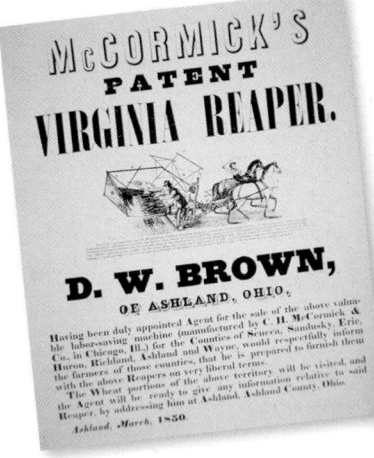

Mechanical reaping
Cyrus McCormick's mechanical reaper of 1831 was a boon to wheat farmers in the American Mid-West. It could do the work of three men, and was soon exported around the world.

Changing practices
Rural scenes like this one in Norfolk, England in 1887 had remained relatively unchanged for centuries. Eventually, with the introduction of steam power, horse ploughs became redundant.

The Food Revolution

The Agricultural Revolution that began in the mid-18th century saw a massive increase in food production. The dramatic increase in efficiency fed a rising population, allowing it to expand further. Workers moved away from the fields and into the factories, providing labour to help drive the Industrial Revolution.

THOMAS MALTHUS

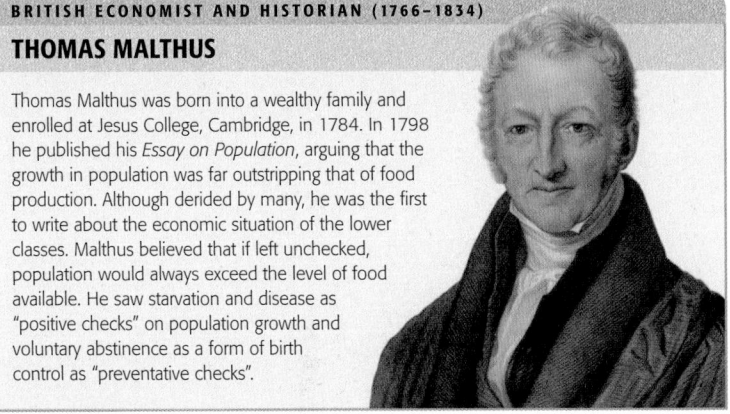

Thomas Malthus was born into a wealthy family and enrolled at Jesus College, Cambridge, in 1784. In 1798 he published his *Essay on Population*, arguing that the growth in population was far outstripping that of food production. Although derided by many, he was the first to write about the economic situation of the lower classes. Malthus believed that if left unchecked, population would always exceed the level of food available. He saw starvation and disease as "positive checks" on population growth and voluntary abstinence as a form of birth control as "preventative checks".

Agricultural labour
The technological innovations of the 19th century changed the way the labour force was deployed. As food production increased, workers moved away from agriculture, into industry.

The involvement of technology in food production continues in the 21st century, though not without controversy.

FAST-FREEZING
Clarence Birdseye developed advanced techniques for freezing food in the 1920s. The popularity of frozen food increased during World War II **314–27 》**, as it used less packaging than canning.

ADDITIVES

As more people moved to cities, food had to be transported and stay fresh for longer. This was made possible by the introduction of additives to prevent food decay.

FOOD MOUNTAIN

FAMINE VERSUS PLENTY
The 20th century witnessed increasing concern about commercial and intensive agriculture **386–87 》**, which led to **large food surpluses** in developed countries, while many other parts of the world suffered from devastating **famines**.

GM FOODS
Since James Watson and Francis Crick broke the genetic code in 1953, the **engineering of genes** has been possible. Genetically modified food first appeared in the shops in the 1990s, but the industry is controversial: GM crops are banned in some countries due to concerns about safety and their environmental impact **464–65 》**.

of other farmers. In America, the mechanical reaper, invented by Cyrus Hall McCormick in 1831, further reduced the need for farm labour. Steam power invaded the countryside with the introduction of the Fowler steam plough in the 1850s.

In the second half of the 18th century better livestock was introduced with selective breeding, by British agriculturalists Robert Bakewell and Thomas Coke. This increased profit and food supplies. In the mid-19th century, the British scientists Joseph Gilbert and John Lawes demonstrated that plants required nitrogen and other nutrients, improving techniques for farming crops.

Food preservation
These food cans date from the Boer War (1899–1902). During wars, demand for canned food increased. At home, it was a status symbol among the middle classes.

Around the world
As Europeans explored the globe, they carried with them their farming methods and crops (see pp.172–73).

In 1788, the first European settlers arrived in Australia, and influenced early practices in wool production. In America thousands had moved west in the 1850s to escape poverty and overcrowding in east coast cities such as Boston and New York. But lack of wooden fences meant farmers could not keep cattle off their crops. The invention of barbed wire (made commercially successful by Joseph Glidden in 1874) solved this problem and transformed farming in the Mid-West in the process. Prairie grassland was hard to cultivate, but the development of farm machinery, such as John Deer's sod buster plough, changed this situation. High-yield crops from the Americas, such as peanuts, started making their way to China and the Far East, where, after their introduction, significant increases in population took place. These crops from the Americas triggered an agricultural revolution in Africa. Maize and sweet potatoes reached the western shores of Africa with slave traders, who introduced them into that continent to provide food for their human cargoes.

Preservation and transport
Equally important to this improvement was that crops could be preserved and distributed efficiently and safely. Although drying and salting had been used for millennia, new preservation techniques were invented during the 18th and 19th centuries. In 1795, French chef Nicolas Appert developed a process for preserving food in airtight bottles after sterilization. This process was patented in England by Peter Durand in 1810, including the provision of using "tin canisters". The rights to this were bought by engineers Donkin, Hall & Gamble who set up the world's first canning factory in 1813 in London. Modern refrigeration began in the 1850s when the French inventor Ferdinand Carré pioneered the vapour compression system.

Preserved food made its way around the world on steam railways and steamships (see pp.226–27). This also enabled agriculture to pursue price and profit globally, rather than focus on a small, local economy, allowing farmers to import specialist seeds, foods, and livestock that suited their terrain.

At last, the population could expand without risk of starvation. A period of high productivity and low food prices meant people did not spend all their money on food. Amid this wealth, however, was the Irish potato famine (see right), which ravaged the Irish population.

THE IRISH POTATO FAMINE

In 1846, blight – a fungus that damages plants – ruined the potato crop in Europe, leading to starvation for many people in Ireland, where potatoes were a staple food. There was another blight in 1847, accompanied by an outbreak of typhoid. All attempts to deal with the problem failed and Ireland's population was decimated, in this, the last peacetime famine in Western Europe. By 1851, the population of Ireland had fallen from 8.5 million to 6.5 million. Many people had died, while others had emigrated, principally to the US.

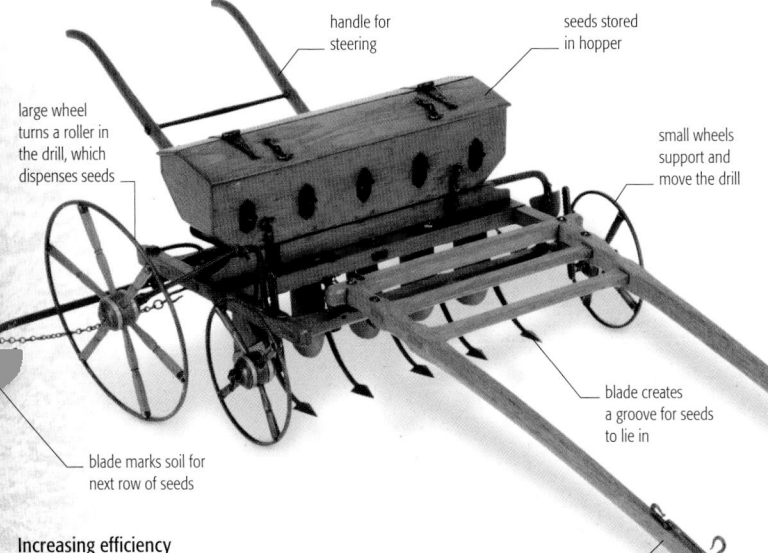

Increasing efficiency
This Morton seed drill of 1828 shows how seeds were passed from a hopper by grooved rollers. This gave a more precise coverage of seed than spreading by hand, ensuring more seeds fell on fertile soil.

- handle for steering
- seeds stored in hopper
- large wheel turns a roller in the drill, which dispenses seeds
- small wheels support and move the drill
- blade creates a groove for seeds to lie in
- blade marks soil for next row of seeds
- attachment for horse harness

« **BEFORE**

Abundant raw materials and significant technological advances created the conditions for industrialization in Britain, which then spread to Europe and America.

BRITAIN FIRST

Access to cheap imports, such as cotton, silk, and wool, from its colonies, gave Britain an advantage in being able to industrialize faster than the rest of Europe.

RAW MATERIALS

IRON MASTERS

Two key innovations made by British ironworks owners contributed to industrialization. Firstly, in 1709, Abraham Darby's use of **coke** (processed coal that burns at **much higher temperatures**) instead of charcoal reduced the cost of ironmaking, due to coke's relative abundance. Secondly, Henry Cort's "puddling" and "rolling" processes of the 1780s produced a **purer form of iron** that was **malleable** and more useful to industrial processes than the brittle "pig", or "cast iron".

TRANSPORT NETWORK

Transport was another vital element during industrialization. Raw materials had to be moved to the point of manufacture and finished goods went to cities and ports for distribution. Britain had a network of navigable rivers, which it enhanced by building canals. The Bridgewater Canal, Manchester, cut in 1761, was followed by other canals that were connected to major rivers.

BRIDGEWATER CANAL

6,800 **KILOMETRES** **(4,250 miles) of inland waterways were built in England between 1760–1800.**

FOLLOWING THE SEAM

The **rich belt of coal** that runs through the industrial north of England also runs through Silesia, the Ruhr Valley, and across the Atlantic to Pennsylvania, which would also become **heavily industrialized** when that coal was exploited.

FREEDOM TO TRADE

An empire, unhindered by continental Europe's **internal frontiers** and **trade barriers**, gave Britain a trading advantage. Slave plantations in America and the West Indies « 218–19 had given Britain a supply of cheap cotton, and when slavery was abolished in 1807, trade with the colonies continued. Even after the American War of Independence 232–33 » the United States was still an important market.

The **Industrial Revolution**

The world we live in today owes much to the industrialization that took place first in Britain, in the late 18th century, and swept across Europe and North America during the 19th. It transformed the western world from a rural society to an urban one, and set the foundations for modern capitalist society.

T he term "Industrial Revolution" implies a sudden and universal change, but it was not a single event, rather a series of technological innovations, social developments, and economic growth spurts that fed into each other. Britain was fortunate in having the conditions it needed to be the industrial pioneer. Firstly, there was a natural abundance of the raw materials: water, iron, and coal. Secondly, there was available capital: interest rates were low, and members of an increasingly wealthy middle class, looking for ways to invest their money, were keen to support new inventions and technology. Finally, Britain had an unusually large market for its manufactured goods, with an expanding empire, and a dominance of the seas, along with a strong merchant navy to trade and transport goods around the world.

The steam engine powered the revolution. Invented by Thomas Newcomen in 1712, the improvements

> **" I sell here Sir,** what the world desires to have – **power."**
>
> MATTHEW BOULTON, BRITISH ENGINEER, 1776

Child labour
Child labour was cheap, and in demand, as small hands could reach into machines. These children spinning cotton in South Carolina, in 1903, have bare feet, because nails on their shoes might produce a spark, causing a fire.

made by James Watt, (see below) have remained an essential element of steam engines ever since. When, in the 1770s, Watt went into business with Matthew Boulton, an entrepeneur and factory owner, they manufactured steam engines to Watt's patented design. These went on to power all stages of industrial production – pumping the mines; powering machinery in the factories and mills; and driving the steamships and railway locomotives.

The "iron horse"

The huge demand for steam resulted in an increased need for coal. Improvements in both the mining of coal and its distribution via canals, and later, railways, dramatically cut its cost. The use of refined coal (coke) to smelt iron (see BEFORE) further fuelled industrialization by enabling engineers to build better tools and machines. Iron was also used as a building material for

and became increasingly concentrated in towns. Textile production rapidly mechanized – by 1835 there were more than 120,000 power looms in textile mills. "Domestic" or "cottage" work (where home-workers were paid per item produced), ran alongside factory work, where workers operated machines that carried out just one task in a production line.

Reaction to progress

The Industrial Revolution undoubtedly improved productivity, and drove technological and economic progress, but it also became synonymous with appalling living and working conditions. Men, women, and children flocked to the cities, but with so many seeking

TRADE UNION An organization devoted to protecting the interests of its members, who are drawn from a specific profession or trade.

employment, the value of their labour was reduced, and they worked long hours for low pay. Many formed trade unions, but workers' conditions improved only slowly: legislation passed by parliament was limited in scope, and frequently ignored by factory owners.

Opposition to industrialization also came from skilled workers, who had been made redundant by mechanization, and unemployed factory workers. Rioting, and the wrecking of

Forging a revolution
These men working in a Minnesota metalworks formed part of a large, but unprotected workforce. By the late 19th century, Minnesota was one of the largest producers of iron ore in the US.

Steam powered
Trains, like this British one from 1908, were both the product and driving force of the Industrial Revolution. They were enabled by the growth of coal mining, and transported raw materials and goods at high speed.

bridges, ships, and railways. By 1850, about 2 million tons of iron had been used for railway tracks and there were 10,000km (6,214 miles) of railway tracks around Britain. Known as "iron horses", locomotives could pull huge loads and reach speeds of up to 65kph (40mph). The speed and efficiency of the railways made the growth of the great manufacturing cities possible, and by the 1840s, it had cut the cost of moving goods by up to 50 per cent. Railway timetables changed timekeeping, with the standardized use of Greenwich Mean Time (GMT) replacing local time across Britain.

Dark satanic mills

With the harnessing of steam power, factories and mills no longer needed to be sited near natural resources such as rivers,

INVENTION

THE STEAM ENGINE

In 1712 Thomas Newcomen built an "atmospheric engine" in which a vacuum produced by condensing steam caused atmospheric pressure to pull down a beam. This device was useful for pumping water out of coal mines. Sixty years later James Watt improved its efficiency, and added modifications for driving machinery. In 1804 Richard Trevithick put a high-pressure steam engine on wheels to make the first steam locomotive, and in 1830 the *Rocket* pulled the first passenger train on George Stephenson's Liverpool–Manchester railway.

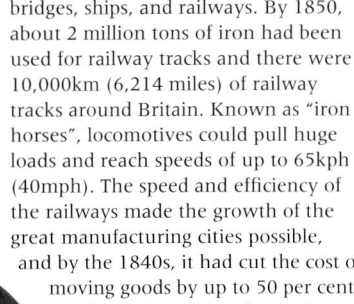

>> machinery, was carried out by gangs known as "Luddites". The British government sent troops to control them, and at a mass trial in 1813, more than 50 people were sentenced to death or penal transportation to Australia (see pp.280–81), where they would be forced into unpaid labour.

Continental challenge

The first phase of the Industrial Revolution took place largely in Britain, but not exclusively so: Britain's

American colonies had ship-building and iron-production industries; and some German states began to industrialize their metal-working. At the start of the period, France's total industrial output was close to Britain's, but progress was stalled by the French Revolution (see pp.234–35). The first continental nation to industrialize was Belgium, from 1820 onwards.

A second wave, sometimes called the Second Industrial Revolution, took place in Germany, Switzerland, and the US after the development of their

railways between 1840–70. German industrialization accelerated massively after unification in 1871 (see p.263), and by the turn of the century, both Germany and the US had overtaken Britain's industrial output.

European industrialization was made possible not just by technology, but also by the availability of a workforce recently freed from serfdom – those

◁ **Eiffel Tower**
Finished in 1889, Gustave Eiffel's tower, made from 18,038 separate pieces of iron, was a sign of France's industrialization. The tower was the world's tallest structure for 41 years.

> "**Avarice**, the spur of industry."
>
> DAVID HUME, SCOTTISH PHILOSOPHER, "OF CIVIL LIBERTY", 1742

△ **French railway construction**
As with industrialization itself, railway building in France suffered a false start. France's first railway opened as early as 1832, but subsequent development was hindered by political and financial problems.

▷ **Trading fuel**
London's Coal Exchange (1849) was symbolic of the Industrial Revolution in two ways – the existence of the exchange was evidence of the increased value of coal, while the building itself, with its 22m- (72ft-) iron and glass dome, would not previously have been possible.

SPREAD OF THE INDUSTRIAL REVOLUTION

From Britain, industrialization with its mechanization, market economy, and profound social change swept in waves across Europe, the United States of America, and Japan.

1802 First **Factory Act** passed in Britain. Modest regulations imposed on working conditions.

1837 Term "Industrial Revolution" coined by Louis-Auguste Blanqui to describe the changes in Britain during the preceding 50 years.

1828 First modern **blast furnace** goes into operation, in Silesia.

1849 The first continental use of coke in iron-making occurs on the Ruhr.

1850 Britain owns half the world's ocean-going ships, contains half the world's railways, and produces more than half of Europe's steam horsepower (but produces less horsepower than the US).

1855 Bessemer process developed in England.

1900–14 Industrialization in **Japan**, **Austrian** part of **Habsburg Empire** and, to a lesser degree, **Spain** and **Hungary**.

1895 Huge acceleration of industrialization in **France**.

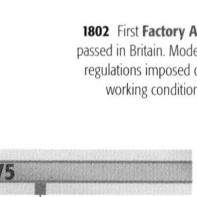

| 1750 | 1775 | 1800 | 1825 | 1850 | 1875 | 1900 |

1771 Richard Arkwright develops the first water-powered mill in Derbyshire, England.

1781 The **condenser** steam engine is first used in Europe.

1830–70 Railway networks completed in **Britain**, **Belgium**, and **Germany**, accelerating industrialization in those countries. French coal and iron output had doubled by the early 1850s.

1870s onwards "2nd industrial revolution": Massive acceleration in industrialization, particularly in **Germany** and **USA**, which began to challenge Britain's supremacy.

1890s Russia and **Sweden** begin massive programme of railway building and industrialization.

1905 Italy's industrialization, based on chemicals and textiles.

▽ Forth Rail Bridge, Edinburgh
Completed in 1890, this was the world's first steel cantilever bridge. It cost the lives of 57 of its 4,000 construction workers.

△ British coal miners lead pit ponies
Coal fuelled the industrial revolution, and in Britain output increased almost sixfold in fifty years, from 11 million tons in 1800 to 65 million tons in 1854.

△ Trade and transport
National and international transport networks were vital to the continued momentum of the Industrial Revolution. London's Albert Dock was opened in 1880 as the second of the Royal Group of Docks.

Until the advent of the steam locomotive, the fastest form of transport on Earth was a galloping horse. Industrialization changed everything: the dominance of agriculture was over, cities now ruled, and the consumer society was born.

THE THIRD WAVE
After the first phase of the industrial revolution in Britain, and the second in Belgium, Germany, and the US, economic growth was slowed by a **worldwide depression**. Recovery was triggered by a **third wave of industrialization** from the 1890s onwards in countries including Russia, Sweden, France, Italy, and Japan. Where the first wave had centred on textiles and iron production, and the second on heavy engineering and steel, the third wave saw the application of industrial processes to **chemical and electrical engineering**,

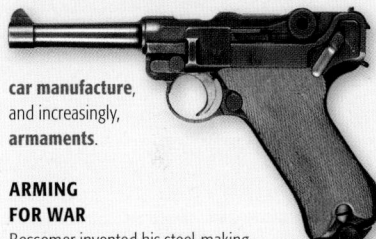

car manufacture, and increasingly, **armaments**.

LUGER PISTOL

ARMING FOR WAR
Bessemer invented his steel-making process (see below) after the French complained that a **new artillery shell** he had invented for use in the Crimean War was **too powerful** for their cast-iron cannons. The advent of steel sparked an **arms race** which changed the face of warfare forever with the introduction of mass-produced guns, heavy artillery, and tanks.

OMINOUS SIGNS
German dominance in industrial production and weaponry towards the end of the 19th century led its increasingly nervous neighbours to accelerate industrialization. Russia, France, and Italy all **invested in arms manufacturing**, and Russia improved its railway network specifically for transporting troops to defend its borders.

---

tied for life to work their landowner's land – which was abolished in France during the 1790s, in Germany between 1811–1848, and in Russia and Poland in the 1860s. In the US, immigrants moving to America from Europe brought new skills and labour.

17
The number of men employed by German steel manufacturer Krupp in 1826 – this number rose to 122 in 1846 and 70,000 in 1910.

The age of steam and steel
The second wave of industrialization was founded on new industrial enterprises: chemicals, engineering, and steel production, aided by the Bessemer process (see right).

Railways provided the momentum for continued industrialization. In addition to transporting raw materials and finished products, they also affected the economies of industrializing nations. Not only did they connect previously disparate economic regions, but financing railways required new approaches to investment, such as a shift from private to joint-stock banking (see pp.214–15), which provided greater access to capital for industry in general.

Similarly, the progression from sail to steamships had an impact on global trade. Foodstuffs and raw materials could be bought from the cheapest supplier, and the market for finished products increased. Improved communications, such as the invention of the telegraph and telephone (see pp.274–75), enabled businesses to respond relatively quickly to changes in the marketplace. They were also able to establish links with the furthest parts of the world which, thanks to the developments of the Industrial Revolution, had become intimately linked with their own.

INVENTION

BESSEMER PROCESS

Steel-making was one of the key characteristics of the second phase of the Industrial Revolution. Previously, engineers had used cast iron (strong when compressed) or wrought iron (strong under tension). On 17 October 1855, building on previous investigations in this field, English metallurgist Henry Bessemer filed a patent for a means of producing mild steel by blasting cold air into molten iron in a "Bessmer Converter". This reduced the amount of carbon in the iron, making a stronger, more versatile product used for railway lines, shipbuilding, and armaments.

« BEFORE

The war of 1756–63 followed an eight-year conflict that had involved many of the same powers, although they did not consistently fight on the same sides.

SCHÖNBRUNN PALACE

WAR OF THE AUSTRIAN SUCCESSION
The death of the Austrian Habsburg emperor **Charles VI** in 1740, prompted war in Europe. France and Prussia attempted to prevent his heir, **Maria Theresa**, acceding to the Austrian throne – the summer seat of which was the Schönbrunn Palace, in Vienna – and her husband, **Francis of Lorraine,** becoming Holy Roman Emperor. The Aix-la-Chapelle peace treaty of 1748 confirmed both Maria Theresa and her husband on their respective thrones, but left **Austria weakened** against the growing power of **Frederick II's** Prussia, which had snatched the rich province of Silesia from Austria during the war. Although the treaty formally brought peace to Europe, it also left many **issues dangerously unresolved**.

PRUSSIA EMERGES
Prussia's annexing of Silesia saw it emerge as a significant figure on the European stage, leading to diplomatic overtures from Britain and France.

COLONIAL CONFLICT
Alongside the war in Europe, Britain and France continued their **colonial rivalry** overseas. Britain captured Louisbourg on Cape Breton Island in Canada from the French in 1745, only to lose Madras in India to France the next year, although the British Royal Navy won a **number of notable victories**. The **Treaty of Aix-la-Chapelle** returned both gains to their original owners, but the conflict remained intense.

The War of the Austrian Succession ended in 1748 without proper resolution (see BEFORE). Tensions over colonial possessions continued between Britain and France, while Austria plotted to regain the province of Silesia, after Frederick II of Prussia (see right) had siezed it in 1740.

A state of uneasy peace lasted until 1756, when Frederick signed a treaty with Britain to protect Hanover, in northwestern Germany. This powerful new alliance gave Maria Theresa of Austria an excuse for a "diplomatic revolution", when she allied with her former enemy, France, and strengthened ties with Empress Elizabeth of Russia, to safeguard against a British and Prussian alliance. In a pre-emptive strike, Frederick II marched 70,000 of his troops into Saxony, which was sandwiched between Prussia and Austria. Fighting broke out almost immediately.

Far-flung hostilities
This new conflict soon spread beyond Europe, as Austria and Prussia's allies, France and Britain, had already been battling in the Americas and the Far East. Fighting between the colonial rivals had erupted the previous year, over control of the Ohio River Valley.

In India, war broke out in 1756, when an ally of the French, the Nawab of Bengal, captured the British trading base at Calcutta, and held 145 prisoners overnight in a small cell in Fort William: subsequent British exaggeration of the numbers held, the number of deaths, and the size of the cell, turned the incident known as "the Black Hole of Calcutta" into an imperial myth.

A turning point
In Europe, Frederick had failed to achieve a decisive victory in Saxony, and found himself surrounded by hostile nations. But in June 1757 the statesman William Pitt the Elder took charge of the British war effort. Frederick won a great victory at Rossbach, in Saxony, over the French, another over the Austrians in Silesia in December, and defeated the

The First Global Conflict

For seven years, the major nations of Europe waged war not just on the European continent itself, but also, for Britain and France, in their colonial possessions overseas in the Americas and Asia. The Seven Years War was the first approximation to a world war, and gave birth to a new, truly global empire.

KING OF PRUSSIA (1712–86)

FREDERICK II

Frederick II, king of Prussia from 1740, is perhaps the archetypal 18th-century enlightened despot (see p.211). He believed in absolute power, but generally used it for the good of his subjects, establishing religious toleration, abolishing torture as an instrument of state power, and freeing the slaves on his own estates. An able and cultured man – he corresponded with the French philosopher Voltaire, and wrote music for the flute, which he played well – he was also a ruthless figure on the European stage and a brilliant military commander, raising Prussia to the first rank of European powers.

> "In the end God will have pity on us and **crush this monster**."
>
> AUSTRIAN EMPRESS MARIA THERESA SPEAKING OF FREDERICK II, 1757

Russians at Zorndorf, Prussia, in August 1758. In India, British general Robert Clive (see pp.282–83) defeated the Nawab of Bengal at Plassey in June 1757, while the British navy routed the French off the Indian coast in 1758–59.

The turning point of the war came in 1759, the British "year of victories". The first years of the war in America had seen French success, but James Wolfe turned the tide for the British, by capturing Louisbourg in 1758, and then by defeating general Montcalm in Quebec, the capital of French North America, in 1759. In Europe, an Anglo–German army defeated the French in Hanover, while the French navy was crushed off the coast of Brittany.

The seizure of French Montreal in 1760, and Pondicherry, in India, in 1761 effectively marked the end of the war, despite the entry of Spain on the French side in 1761. With the succession in 1762 of the pro-Prussian Peter III in Russia, all nations were ready for peace. The 1763 Treaty of Paris saw Britain take French North America, and all French lands east of the Mississippi, as well as parts of the Caribbean, and every French fort in India. Spain gave Britain Florida, but received French lands west of the Mississippi in return. With the French excluded from North America and India, Britain now controlled a massive colonial and trading empire.

The Battle of Zorndorf

Frederick II of Prussia followed up his decisive defeats of the French and Austrians in 1757 with an equally impressive victory over the Russians at Zorndorf in western Poland on 25 August 1758.

The end of the war saw Britain victorious, but also vulnerable.

AMERICAN WAR OF INDEPENDENCE
French revenge on Britain was swift. France helped America in their war of independence against Britain after 1777 **232–33 »**.

THE BIRTH OF THE BRITISH RAJ
The end of French power in India left Britain without a rival in her **conquest of the entire subcontinent**. By the 1830s, Britain had gained Bengal and Bihar in the east, and ruled over much of the south and centre **282–83 »**.

BRITISH RULE IN INDIA

POLAND
A bi-product of the war was the **end of Poland** as an independent nation. Squashed between Prussia, Austria, and Russia, Poland was divided by the three powers after 1772. In 1795, it was absorbed piecemeal by Russia, Prussia, and Austria, and did not reappear until 1918.

BEFORE «

In the 18th century settlers in Britain's American colonies became increasingly intolerant of European rule and paying taxes from which they did not benefit.

COST OF WAR

Britain was ceded French territory in North America during the Anglo-French wars (1754–63) but the cost was high, and the British felt the colonials had failed to pay their share.

PROTEST

Until the 18th century British **North America was subject to English Law**. Settlers thought the new laws passed after 1763 to raise money

BOSTON TEA PARTY

for the British extremely irksome. The Stamp Act, a direct tax on paper, caused riots. In 1773 a group of Bostonians disguised as native Americans threw a cargo of highly taxed EIC tea into Boston harbour. The American slogan was **"no taxation without representation."**

INTOLERABLE ACTS

The British response to this episode was rapid. In 1774, laws were passed in reprisal that the Americans dubbed "Intolerable Acts". Intended to restore order, instead they **united the colonies in further protest**. Fiery leaders began to emerge – they cried out that the actions of the British government were illegal and stirred the colonists to take further action.

The war between the North American colonies and Britain in 1775 was the predictable climax to years of bitter quarrels between the two sides (see BEFORE).

The first shots were fired in a minor skirmish. On 19 April 1775 General Thomas Gage, Commander of the British forces in North America, despatched troops to seize an arms cache in Concord, a town just outside Boston. At Lexington, Massachusetts, the British encountered a small force of American militia (armed civilians). It is unclear which side fired the first shot, but later it was referred to as "the shot heard around the world". When the British made it back to Boston they were besieged by militias, and had to wait there for reinforcements. With

On 15 June 1775 George Washington became commander of the new Continental army. He immediately began turning the militias into a more professional fighting force. Washington failed in his attempt to invade Canada in 1775. His men also suffered a major blow in the summer of 1776 when the British captured New York. However, news of the revolts had spread, and the colonists' cause was rapidly gaining momentum.

Independence

The American colonists made their decisive break with Britain on 4 July 1776 when their leaders agreed to the Declaration of Independence. The declaration stated that "life, liberty and the pursuit of happiness" were the

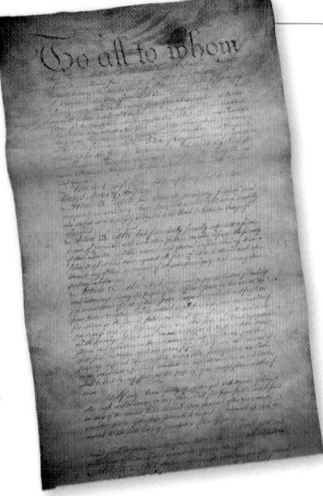

The Articles of Confederation
Adopted by Congress – the formal assembly of government representatives – in 1777. This was the first governing document, or constitution, of the USA, and was ratified by all thirteen states in 1781.

American Declaration of Independence

Until the end of the 18th century, Europe and its colonies were dominated by monarchies. The American Declaration of Independence undermined the old order and proclaimed a new republic in which people would be free to govern themselves.

their arrival on 26 May Gage decided to capture hill positions that overlooked Boston. The resulting Battle of Bunker Hill in June 1775 was a disaster. Although they captured the hill positions, half the British troops were wounded or killed, and they failed to break the American siege on Boston.

"unalienable rights of all men", and when a government attempted to destroy these rights it was "the Right of the People to alter or abolish it, and to institute new government". The Declaration of Independence was a momentous event, and made a peaceful settlement with the British much less likely. It was largely the work of Thomas Jefferson (see left).

Washington had won important battles in what is now New Jersey – at Trenton on 26 December 1776 and Princeton on 3 January 1777 – which reinforced his reputation. On 2 March 1776 with a force of over 17,000 men and a build-up of artillery stocks, the Americans began bombarding the blockaded British troops in Boston. They were forced to depart for Halifax, Nova Scotia. Although the British went on to capture New York, an American victory at nearby Saratoga in October 1777 stirred French interest in an alliance with the colonies. On 6 February 1778 France and America signed treaties of alliance. It was a major turning point – the Americans were no longer fighting alone.

All hope of a British victory ended on 19 October 1781. Lord Cornwallis was forced to surrender at Yorktown, in Virginia, after an 18-day siege.

AMERICAN PRESIDENT (1743–1826)

THOMAS JEFFERSON

Thomas Jefferson was the third president of the USA. An intellectually outstanding figure of the period, Jefferson was chosen as the principal drafter of the Declaration of Independence at the age of 33. He served as governor of Virginia during the War of Independence and afterwards became the USA's first Secretary of State.

Jefferson's vision of the newly created USA – as a loose union of self-governing states with central government having limited powers – gave birth to the Democratic Republican Party. Jefferson founded the University of Virginia and died on the 50th anniversary of the Declaration of Independence.

"Oh God! It's all over."

PRIME MINISTER, LORD NORTH, UPON HEARING OF THE SURRENDER OF THE BRITISH TROOPS TO THE AMERICANS, 1781

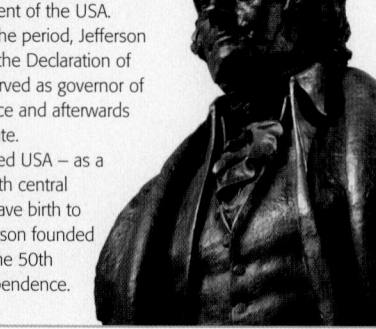

Declaration of Independence
This painting by John Trumbull depicts the committee of five who drafted the Declaration of Independence, presenting it to the Continental Congress on 4 July 1776.

The British Prime Minister at the time, Lord North, broke down and sobbed when he heard the news.

Birth of a nation

After the British withdrew, Loyalists were allowed to remain, but about 2 per cent opted to emigrate to Canada and the Caribbean.

The British government gave the Americans their independence in return for a trade agreement that would benefit both sides. The Treaty of Paris, signed in 1783, gave the Americans a western border on the Mississippi, and control of the Old North West – an area extending from the Ohio and Mississippi rivers to the Great Lakes.

Conflicts over the issue of slavery threatened to divide the nation, but the new republic had great political hopes which they set out in the 1781 Articles of Confederation, and later the Constitution of 21 June 1788. George Washington was elected as the first president in 1789, giving the federal

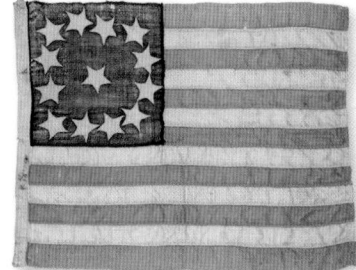

Stars and Stripes
Dating from about 1830, this hand-sewn flag has 13 stars and 13 stripes, to commemorate the 13 original colonies that rebelled against the British.

(central) government exclusive power in the conduct of diplomacy, commerce, and war. Congress was to consist of two chambers, the Senate and the House of Representatives. In addition, a Supreme Court was set up to interpret laws and safeguard the Constitution, which stated that all men were born equal, and had an equal voice in government.

French territories were incorporated into the USA, but the growing north–south divide eventually led to Civil War.

FURTHER EXPANSION

The **new nation quickly expanded** to the south and west. Ohio became a state in 1803, Indiana in 1816, Illinois in 1818, and Alabama in 1819. In 1803 President Jefferson purchased the Louisiana territory from France **242 》**.

WAR OF 1812

Fought under the motto **"free trade and sailor's rights"**, the War of 1812 against Britain was a result of British maritime policies during the Anglo–French wars when American sailors were seized and forced into the British navy. President James Madison saw the war as a way to **strengthen republicanism**, and believed it could secure possession of Canada as a bargaining chip against Great Britain. Although three attempts were made to invade Canada, all of them ended in failure. The war

was, however, the first step in establishing the USA as a serious, and permanent, presence in **international politics**.

CIVIL WAR

The USA was divided on **the issue of slavery**. For years slaves were used in southern plantations, but in the north slave labour was forbidden. Eventually seven southern states split from the Union when Abraham Lincoln **246–47 》**

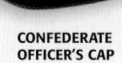

CONFEDERATE OFFICER'S CAP

was elected president and, in 1861, formed the **Confederate States of America 244–45 》**. They were later joined by four other states. Civil war broke out, as the North tried to save the Union. The war ended in 1865 with victory for the Union, but it led to economic disruption. **Slavery was abolished,** but Abraham Lincoln was assassinated in the month the war ended.

Storming of the Bastille

In the summer of 1789 a revolution broke out in France against the despotic government of Louis XVI. Many different factors caused this revolution, but the one event that symbolized the collapse of royal power in the face of widespread popular dissent was the storming of the Bastille prison on 14 July 1789.

Built between 1370 and 1383 as part of the walled defences of Paris, the Bastille first became a prison for high-ranking state prisoners during the early 17th century. It also served as an arsenal, storing large quantities of gunpowder and arms. In 1789 the prison was defended by 18 cannon and 12 smaller artillery pieces manned by a regular garrison of 82 *invalides* – veteran soldiers no longer fit for active service – and reinforced by 32 grenadiers from a Swiss mercenary regiment summoned to Paris by the king some days before.

On 14 July, rumours spread through Paris that troops were marching on the city to crush dissent against the king. Responding to this threat, a crowd of between 600 and 1,000 strong, armed with weapons seized from the Hôtel des Invalides, a military hospital, assembled in front of the Bastille to acquire its arsenal and defend their city from attack.

At around 10.30am the first of two delegations met the governor of the Bastille, Bernard-René de Launay, asking him to distribute its weapons to the crowd. Both delegations were unsuccessful. By 1.30pm, the crowd had lost patience, and surged into the undefended outer courtyard. Gunfire rang out, although it is unclear which side first opened fire. At around 3pm, a detachment of 62 mutinous Gardes Françaises arrived at the prison armed with two cannon, which they placed in front of the gates leading to the inner courtyard. As fighting intensified, de Launay threatened to blow up the fortress; but the soldiers within the garrison surrendered, forcing him to open the gates.

At 5.30 pm, the crowd stormed the prison. The governor was led away to the *Hôtel de Ville*, the town hall, where he was stabbed to death, along with at least two defenders. One defender and 98 attackers died in the actual fighting, with another 73 attackers wounded.

The news of the fall of the Bastille spread quickly across France, prompting uprisings in many cities. In reality, the prison was an almost empty symbol of royal tyranny – it held a mere seven prisoners – but the storming did signify that power had now passed from those who discussed political change to those who took direct action to achieve it.

First blood
One of the first victims of the storming of the Bastille was its governor, Bernard–René de Launay, shown here, surrounded by soldiers. He was seized by the mob, stabbed to death, and then decapitated. His head was fixed to a spike and paraded through the streets of Paris.

"It was the best of times, it was the worst of times."

CHARLES DICKENS, "A TALE OF TWO CITIES", 1859

« BEFORE

In the 1780s, France faced a mounting crisis. A century of foreign wars had left the country with huge debts and threatened bankruptcy.

IMMEDIATE CAUSES

France's humiliation by England in the **Seven Years War** (1756–63) **«230–31**, losing her North American colonies, motivated heavy French expenditure on the **American War of Independence** (1775–83) **«232–33**. Its effect was to put financial reform at the top of the political agenda. Under the *ancien régime* (pre-revolutionary "old order"), French society was divided into three estates: clergy, nobility, and commoners. Nearly 40 per cent of the land was owned by the nobles and clergy who made up less than 3 per cent of the population and were exempt from taxes, placing the tax burden on the bourgeoisie (middle class) and peasantry. Enlightenment ideas **«210–11** against tyranny led the growing professional classes to demand a greater role in the running of the country. Bad harvests (1788–89) almost doubled the price of bread, worsening social tensions.

THE TENNIS COURT OATH

Louis XVI's attempts at economic reform were blocked

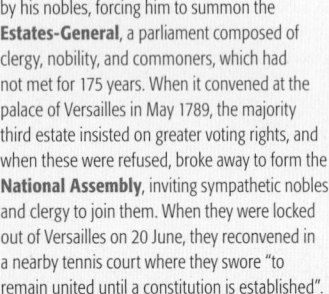

TAKING THE OATH

by his nobles, forcing him to summon the **Estates-General**, a parliament composed of clergy, nobility, and commoners, which had not met for 175 years. When it convened at the palace of Versailles in May 1789, the majority third estate insisted on greater voting rights, and when these were refused, broke away to form the **National Assembly**, inviting sympathetic nobles and clergy to join them. When they were locked out of Versailles on 20 June, they reconvened in a nearby tennis court where they swore "to remain united until a constitution is established".

Revolution in France

A violent upheaval shook France at the end of the 18th century as several causes of disaffection came together at one explosive moment: national bankruptcy, the burgeoning ambitions of the bourgeoisie, the king's lack of authority, and growing social discontent caused by high taxes and rising bread prices.

The formation of the National Assembly on 17 June 1789 (see BEFORE) was the first step towards revolutionary change. Louis XVI's dismissal of Jacques Necker, the popular finance minister on 11 July, along with the concentration of troops outside Paris, provoked agitation in Paris for arms amid wild rumours of a royal clampdown. Several days of rioting ended with the 14 July capture of the Bastille prison (see pp.234–35), symbolizing an important blow against the oppressive forces of the *ancien régime*, while placing Paris and mob violence at the centre of events.

The revolt spread to the countryside where wild rumours resulted in the "Great Fear", in which peasants attacked their landlords, burning their châteaux. On 4 August, National Assembly deputies voted to abolish feudal privileges (see pp.136–37), sweeping away an entire system of property ownership in one stroke. On 5 October, Parisian women, frustrated by bread shortages and the king's indecision, marched to Versailles to force his move to Paris, where he could be more closely monitored.

Between 1789–91, the National Assembly passed a series of reforms that further undermined the *ancien régime*. These included publishing the "Declaration of the Rights of Man",

reforming the army, dividing France into 83 *départements*, selling off the Church's land, and forcing the clergy to take a civic oath to the state. This last measure split the Church, alienating the conservative peasantry and sowing the seeds of future counter-revolution.

A new constitution showed the National Assembly's distrust of the masses by dividing the population into active (higher income voting) and passive (non-voting) citizens.

This period also saw the growth of political clubs – such as the Cordeliers and Jacobins – that tried to exert pressure on the Assembly. The Jacobins were the first real political "party", with clubs dotted throughout France.

In June 1791, the king attempted to flee abroad, but was captured at Varennes, east of Paris, by a postmaster. This marked a key turning point, for it lost the king his people's trust.

Threatened on all sides

In April 1792, a new Assembly declared war on Austria and Prussia, hoping to distract attention from

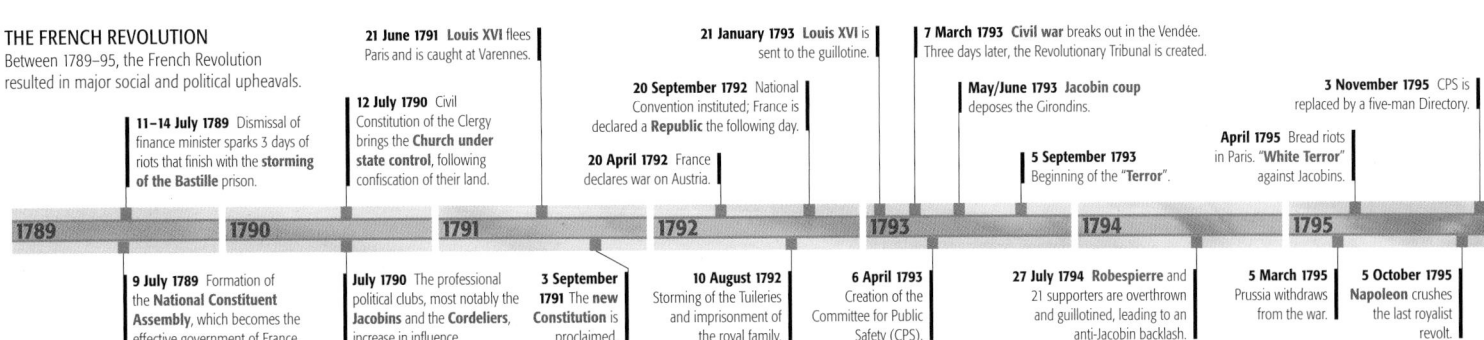

11–14 July 1789 Dismissal of finance minister sparks 3 days of riots that finish with the **storming of the Bastille** prison.

21 June 1791 Louis XVI flees Paris and is caught at Varennes.

12 July 1790 Civil Constitution of the Clergy brings the **Church under state control**, following confiscation of their land.

21 January 1793 Louis XVI is sent to the guillotine.

20 September 1792 National Convention instituted; France is declared a **Republic** the following day.

20 April 1792 France declares war on Austria.

7 March 1793 Civil war breaks out in the Vendée. Three days later, the Revolutionary Tribunal is created.

May/June 1793 Jacobin coup deposes the Girondins.

5 September 1793 Beginning of the "**Terror**".

3 November 1795 CPS is replaced by a five-man Directory.

April 1795 Bread riots in Paris. "White Terror" against Jacobins.

1789	1790	1791	1792	1793	1794	1795

9 July 1789 Formation of the **National Constituent Assembly**, which becomes the effective government of France.

July 1790 The professional political clubs, most notably the **Jacobins** and the **Cordeliers**, increase in influence.

3 September 1791 The **new Constitution** is proclaimed.

10 August 1792 Storming of the Tuileries and imprisonment of the royal family.

6 April 1793 Creation of the Committee for Public Safety (CPS).

27 July 1794 Robespierre and 21 supporters are overthrown and guillotined, leading to an anti-Jacobin backlash.

5 March 1795 Prussia withdraws from the war.

5 October 1795 Napoleon crushes the last royalist revolt.

domestic problems. While saluting the revolution with one hand, the king plotted with the other, hoping that French defeat would restore his fortunes.

A series of military defeats brought panic to Paris. A Prussian manifesto that threatened the French people if any harm came to Louis inflamed the Parisian radicals, who stormed the Tuileries on 20 August, deposing the king. At the same time, a revolutionary Commune took control of the city and encouraged the massacre of 1,200 "counter-revolutionary" prisoners, provoking international horror. A third more radical Assembly (the Convention) was elected and a crucial victory at the battle of Valmy on 20 September helped to restore national confidence.

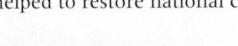

"The Incorruptible"
Maximilien Robespierre, a radical politician, was the effective leader of France during the Reign of Terror.

The next day, the Convention declared France a Republic. In January 1793, the king was found guilty of "the crime of being a king" and guillotined, sending shockwaves through Europe. Foreign invasion once more threatened the nation and France became more militarized. It relied on conscription and revolutionary zeal for its citizen armies fighting a series of revolutionary wars that were bankrolled by loot from newly "liberated" countries. At the same time, a major counter-revolution, provoked by mass conscription, broke out in Brittany and the Vendée (western France). Atrocities became commonplace on both sides.

Execution of Marie Antoinette
When Queen Marie Antoinette was guillotined on 16 October 1793, few mourned. Deeply unpopular, she was found guilty of treason by the Revolutionary Tribunal.

IDEA
HUMAN RIGHTS

The French Revolution's most lasting legacy was its *Declaration of the Rights of Man and Citizen*, published on 26 August 1789. Inspired by the political writings of John Locke and Jean-Jacques Rousseau, this bold document stated that all "men are born and remain free and with equal rights", and that the duty of government was to preserve these "natural and inviolate rights… liberty, property, security and resistance to oppression" through a constitution, rooted in the rule of law. Although originally neglecting women's rights, its universal appeal made it the basis for the constitutions of many countries as well as the UN's *Universal Declaration of Human Rights*, published in 1948.

LA DÉCLARATION

> ## "Virtue without which terror is deadly; terror without which virtue is impotent."

MAXIMILIEN ROBESPIERRE, 5 FEBRUARY 1794

Faced by mounting military and economic problems, the government founded the Revolutionary Tribunal, to provide instant justice, and the Committee for Public Safety (CPS), to centralize power. Meanwhile, increasing conflict within the Convention culminated with the expulsion of a faction known as the Girondins on 2 June, and the rise to power of the Jacobins.

The Jacobins and the "Terror"
Under Robespierre's leadership, the Jacobins aimed to create a new "Republic of Virtue". "Citizen" became the common form of address, a new revolutionary calendar was introduced, towns were renamed, and the education system reformed.

On 5 September 1793, "terror" was made "the order of the day" and "war" declared on those suspected of counter-revolutionary sympathies, creating an oppressive climate of informers and instant justice. In 10 months, 20,000 "enemies of the revolution" were executed across France. A decisive military victory over Austria in June 1794 eased the pressure, but there was no let-up in the daily flow of victims to the guillotine. Robespierre and his supporters were finally toppled by fearful fellow deputies and this was followed by an anti-Jacobin backlash (the "White Terror") and a return to more moderate policies. In 1795, the CPS was replaced by a five-man Directory. Royalist–radical tensions pulled France in both directions and two elections were annulled. In 1799, a coup d'état installed Napoleon Bonaparte (see pp.238–39) as leader – five years later, he became emperor of France.

AFTER

The success of the French Revolution, and its spirit of "liberty, equality, fraternity", helped to inspire wars of independence far beyond Europe.

IMPACT OVERSEAS
In 1791, **Toussaint l'Ouverture** led a successful **slave revolt** in the French colony of Sainte Domingue (Haiti). From 1808, **revolutionary nationalism** inspired the wars of independence against Spain in Latin America **248–49 ≫**

LEGACY IN FRANCE
While the revolution failed in some ways, the legacy of popular insurrection established a radical tradition in Paris that continues today. **Charles X**'s attempts to return to the past provoked one revolt in 1830, while his successor Louis-Phillipe's misjudgement of the mood for reform in 1848 provoked another **260 ≫**, which spread across Europe. In 1871, there was a short-lived and bloody **Paris Commune** based on the one from 1792. In 1968, Paris students almost toppled de Gaulle's government. Today, the French still protest to show their discontent.

PARIS RIOTS 1968

A REVOLUTIONARY TEMPLATE
Vladimir Lenin **301 ≫** studied the French Revolution as a **model for change**. During the **Russian Revolution** **300–01 ≫**, he adopted the need for revolutionary terror along with a citizens' army to defend against invasion and civil war. **Rebuilding society from scratch** found echoes in the Chinese Cultural Revolution **346–47 ≫** and in Cambodia's attempt to relocate the towns to the countryside (1975–79).

EMPEROR OF FRANCE Born 1769 Died 1821

Napoleon Bonaparte

"**Death is nothing**, but to live defeated and inglorious is to die daily." NAPOLEON BONAPARTE

The future French Emperor Napoleon Bonaparte was born Napoleone Buonaparte, a member of a poor Corsican noble family of Italian origin. A wild island of bandits and vendettas, Corsica became a part of France in 1768, the year before Napoleon's birth. When he was nine years old Napoleon learned French at school so he could attend the military school at Brienne-le-Château in France but he always spoke with a strong Italian accent. His family was poor enough to have his school fees paid by the state.

That he was an able man was evident at an early stage and, after graduating in 1784, he went on to complete a two-year course at the Royal Military School in Paris in 12 months, proving notably strong in maths, geography, and science. He was commissioned as a sub-lieutenant of artillery at the age of just 16.

Revolutionary opportunities
On the death of his father in 1785, Napoleon was elected head of his family, despite not being the eldest son. Corsica remained the focus of his life for some years, to the neglect of his army career. It was only after his family left the island in 1793 because of their pro-French views that Napoleon shifted his ambitions to France. A superb opportunist, he seized the chances for rapid advancement opened up by the French Revolution (see pp.236–37). Appointed a brigadier-general by the Jacobins, a prominent political club of

Portrait of Napoleon
Napoleon carefully controlled his public image, employing only the finest portrait artists of the day to present his desired view of himself to the people. This picture of Napoleon was painted c.1807 by Hippolyte (Paul) Delaroche.

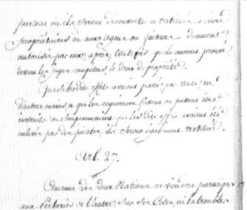
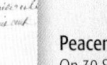

Peacemaker
On 30 September 1800, Napoleon signed the Treaty of Mortefontaine, ending a smouldering naval conflict between France and the US, brought about by US reaction to the French Revolution.

Carve up
Drawn in 1805, this caricature by the cartoonist James Gillray demonstrates the greed of great powers. The British Prime Minister, William Pitt the younger (1759–1806), and Napoleon are carving up the world – the Frenchman seizing a slice of Europe while Britain takes most of the rest.

NAPOLEONIC CODE

The Civil Code, drawn up on Napoleon's orders between 1800–04, is often regarded as his most enduring legacy. His personal influence upon the code favoured patriarchal authority and "family values". At Napoleon's insistence, the code states: "The wife owes obedience to her husband". Men under 25 could not marry without their parents' consent. Although divorce was permitted, it was difficult to obtain. Napoleon's code broadly upheld the rights and freedom of conscience established by the French Revolution.

COPY OF NAPOLEONIC CODE

Imperial insignia
In his imperial crest, Napoleon alludes to Emperor Charlemange, his 9th century predecessor (ivory hand of justice) and the Roman Empire (eagle).

Retreat from Moscow
As the French withdrew from Russia in 1812, Marshall Ney (centre) inspired the rearguard of the Grande Armée to resist the Russian cossacks.

"Bonaparte's whole life, civil, political and military, **was a fraud**."

DUKE OF WELLINGTON, 1835

the Revolution, at the age of 24, he survived their fall and relaunched his career by providing artillery to defend their successors, the Directorate, against an uprising in October 1795 (see right). France fought all the major European powers, either individually or in coalitions, between 1793–1815 (see pp.240–41). Once Napoleon was made head of the Army of Italy in March 1796, there was no looking back. Reviving a moribund force, he had a spectacular series of victories, including defeat of the Papal army, that made him a French hero.

Supreme power
Napoleon was not content with being recognized as a superb general. Only supreme political power could satisfy the scope of his grandiose ambition to create an empire. Brought in as the military muscle to back a political conspiracy against the Directorate in 1799, he effortlessly shifted into the leading role in government as First Consul, and from there to absolute imperial power in 1804. Napoleon was a hard-working, intelligent head of government who supervised the creation of a new legal, administrative, and educational system in France. He was, however, also a man inspired by a sense of destiny, who believed in his

carefully nurtured public image as saviour of France and successor to the Holy Roman Empire of Charlemagne (see pp.134–35).

Military genius
Napoleon genuinely desired peace – on his own terms – but spent almost the entirety of his years in power at war. He demonstrated his military genius time and again, manoeuvring large-scale armies at speed to engage the enemy in decisive battle with maximum application of force. It was a style of warfare that often required his men to sustain heavy casualties in the pursuit of victory. Nevertheless, he was popular with the soldiers and

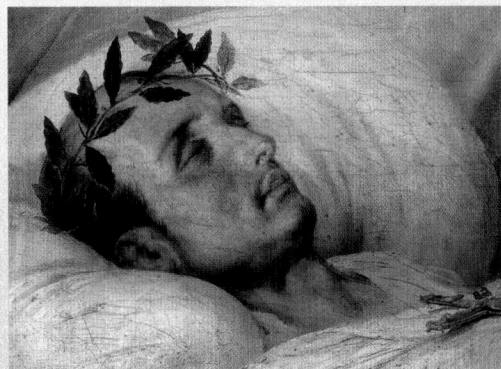

Deathbed scene
Horace Vernet depicted the dead Napoleon crowned with laurel leaves, as a Roman emperor would have been, and with Christ-like features. Napoleon's admirers believed he was poisoned by the British, but he probably died of stomach cancer.

his presence on the battlefield always heartened them. He knew how to use titles and decorations – including the *Légion d'honneur*, which he instituted – to reward and inspire effort.

Downfall
Napoleon's character undoubtedly had defects. He was often dishonest, lying in battlefield dispatches to aggrandize his own role. By the time he invaded Russia in 1812, his grasp of the realities of power had begun to waver. Overreaching was always likely to be his downfall. He was finally defeated at Waterloo in 1815 and imprisoned on St Helena, an island in the Atlantic. To the last he devoted himself to the service of his self-image, writing his memoirs in captivity. He left a legend, but not the imperial dynasty that he had hoped to found.

- **15 August 1769** Born in Ajaccio, Corsica.
- **1779–84** Attends military school.
- **September 1785** Commissioned as a sub-lieutenant in the artillery after a year at the Royal Military School in Paris.
- **1791–93** Elected a lieutenant-colonel in the Corsican National guard.
- **June 1793** Flees from Corsica with his family.
- **10 August 1794** Briefly arrested because of his links with the Jacobins, a radical political group.
- **5 October 1795** Supresses an attempted royalist coup in Paris. The Directorate give him command of the Army of the Interior.
- **9 March 1796** Marries Josephine de Beauharnais.
- **March 1796–April 1797** As commander of the Army of Italy, claims a series of victories over Austria, and Piedmont in Italy.
- **May 1798–August 1799** Leads Army of the Orient to invade Egypt and Palestine.
- **9 November 1799** Back in France, he takes part in a coup that establishes a new government – the Consulate; the following month he becomes its leader (First Consul).
- **14 June 1800** Defeats the Austrians at Marengo in Italy.
- **24 December 1800** Survives an assasination attempt by royalists.
- **2 August 1802** Declared Consul for life.
- **2 December 1804** Crowns himself Emperor of France in Notre Dame Cathedral, Paris.
- **2 December 1805** Defeats the Austrian and Russian armies at Austerlitz.

FRENCH CURRENCY BEARING NAPOLEON'S IMAGE

- **14 October 1806** Defeats Prussia at the twin battles of Jena and Auerstadt.
- **15 July 1809** Marriage to Josephine annulled; marries the Austrian Archduchess Marie Louise in March the following year.
- **20 March 1811** His son is born, styled by Napoleon as the King of Rome.
- **June 1812** Invades Russia, but retreats in October.
- **16–19 October 1813** Defeated at Leipzig by the forces of Prussia, Sweden, and Austria.
- **6 April 1814** Abdicates after Paris is occupied by the Allies (Prussia, Russia, and Austria); he is exiled to the Mediterranean island of Elba.
- **20 March 1815** Escapes from Elba and enters Paris.
- **18 June 1815** Defeated at Waterloo in Belgium by the British and Prussian armies.
- **15 July 1815** Surrenders to the British.
- **5 May 1821** Dies a prisoner on the island of St Helena.

BEFORE

In 1792 France was declared a Republic **<< 236–37**. The change in government occurred during a series of wars in Europe and beyond.

REVOLUTIONARY WARS

The French Revolutionary Wars (1792–1802) were initially fought to protect French borders from other European

NAPOLEON'S SABRE powers. However, they brought in their wake **a citizen's army** inspired by revolutionary principles, an aggressive foreign policy, and a war economy dependent on forced enlistment, conquest, and loot, all of which facilitated **Napoleon Bonaparte**'s rise to power **<< 238–39**.

RISE OF NAPOLEON

Having been tainted by association with the Jacobins after Robespierre's fall, Napoleon redeemed himself in October 1795 by crushing the last popular revolt in Paris, and then by conducting a **brilliant military campaign** in Italy – he was welcomed as a hero on his return to Paris in 1797. Following a highly popular but less successful campaign into Egypt, he returned to Paris in 1799 to seize power through a **military coup**.

Once in power, Napoleon behaved like an enlightened despot (see pp.210–11). He banned democracy, and set up a network of police spies responsible for censorship, and for arresting his political opponents.

Following an assassination attempt in 1800, Napoleon was able to harness widespread support for his own dynastic ambitions, to fend off any attempt to restore the Bourbons – the royal family that had ruled France between 1589 and 1792 – and to establish himself as the French leader. In 1804 Napoleon crowned himself "first Emperor of the French", in a ceremony overseen by the Pope, thereby sanctifying his position.

The building of an empire

Between 1805 and 1815, Napoleon's armies took on seven different coalition armies made up of various European powers. He won his most notable victories in 1805 at Austerlitz in the modern Czech Republic against the Austrians and Russians; in 1806 at Jena in Germany against the Prussians; and in 1807 at Friedland against the Russians, in their own country, forcing them to sue for peace. In 1812, at the height of his power, France's rule comprised 130 administrative regions.

Napoleon's ambitions outside Europe were more low-key. In 1803, he abandoned France's claims to the Americas by selling Louisiana to the US for $15 million (see pp.242–43). In the French West Indies, the sugar plantations were disrupted by slave revolts and foreign invasion, although San Domingo (now Haiti) was the only one to gain its independence in 1804.

Napoleon's empire grew in two stages: 1800–07 and 1807–12. During the first stage, he incorporated the Low Countries (The Netherlands and Belgium), northern Italy (Piedmont), and western Germany under his rule, emulating Charlemagne's achievements of 1,000 years earlier (see pp.134–35). In 1806, the Confederation of the Rhine unified the small German states, such as Bavaria and Saxony, into kingdoms allied to France. French legislation, such as the Napoleonic Code, took root in this "Inner Empire".

After 1807, his conquests included southern Italy, Spain, northern Germany, Illyria (the southern Balkans), and the Duchy of Warsaw (Poland). Charles Talleyrand, Napoleon's scheming foreign advisor, warned against extra expansion during this period, and these

The Battle of Trafalgar
On 21 October 1805, the English Admiral Horatio Nelson sank 22 French and Spanish ships in the pivotal sea battle of the Napoleonic wars, sealing Britain's naval supremacy for the next 100 years.

The Napoleonic Wars

Between 1805 and 1815 Napoleon's armies conquered most of western Europe in a series of notable victories, creating an empire with 44 million French subjects. However, his plans to invade England were thwarted with naval defeat at Trafalgar, and his obsession with conquest led to a disastrous campaign in Russia. Napoleon was finally brought down at Waterloo in 1815.

regions often rejected France's influence. Napoleon, however, was obsessed with restoring the Roman Empire by mastering Italy and conquering Britain. However, his dynastic aspirations reflected an increasingly dictatorial character prone to errors of judgement, such as overthrowing the Bourbon dynasty in Spain and replacing it with his own dynastic

successor, his brother Joseph, thus provoking the Peninsular War – a long and disastrous campaign that raged between 1808 and 1813 and which became known as "the Spanish ulcer".

Defeat and downfall
The destruction of two French fleets by English admiral Horatio Nelson at Aboukir Bay, Egypt, in 1798, and Trafalgar off the coast of Spain in 1805 scuppered Napoleon's plans for invading

Napoleonic Empire
In 1812, at the height of France's conquests, more than 44 million subjects lived within the empire, some ruled directly from Paris, some by proxy rulers.

KEY
▮ French territory ruled directly from Paris
▮ Dependent state

Britain. However, he insisted on crippling England economically, by maintaining a maritime blockade, and it was this that eventually led to his downfall. It caused unnecessary wars against Portugal (1808–13) and Russia (1812), creating two simultaneous fronts and provoking his most disastrous defeats. These were epitomized by the humiliating retreat from a burnt-out Moscow in October 1812, when he lost over half a million men in total. These campaigns left him vulnerable to a legacy of European resentments and military exhaustion following his defeat at Leipzig (the Battle of the Nations) in 1813. He was finally defeated at Waterloo in 1815, by Prussia, and the Duke of Wellington's Allied army of British, Dutch, Belgians, and Germans.

IDEA
MASS CONSCRIPTION

Between 1792 and 1815, mass conscription supplied the 4 million men that fought in Napoleon's campaigns, including his first major success in Italy against the Austrians (1796–97, pictured below). In 1805 and 1812 he raised two vast armies, known as "*grand armées*", from across his empire to fight in his Austrian and Russian campaigns. The first had 200,000 men and the second more than 600,000. Napoleon owed much of his success to these armies. It is estimated that around a million soldiers died in creating Napoleon's empire.

"**History is a set of lies**... people have agreed upon."
NAPOLEON, FROM HIS MEMOIRS, 1823

AFTER ≫

Following Napoleon's resignation in 1814, Europe's rulers met at the Congress of Vienna to carve out a new balance of power.

POST-NAPOLEONIC EUROPE
Most of the hereditary monarchies overthrown by Napoleon were restored, allowing 30 more years of reactionary rule. Indeed, both Napoleon's son and nephew (right) went on to rule France.

NAPOLEON III

REPUBLICAN MOVEMENTS
Nationalist republican movements were quick to break out – first in Serbia, Greece, and Belgium; then, in 1848, in a wave of urban revolts that ultimately lead to Italian (1861) and German (1871) unification **260–61 ≫**. Napoleon's fall also paved the way for Britain to become the world's leading imperial power.

NAPOLEON'S DREAM
The **unification of Europe**, started by his legacy of a new legal code and metric system of weights and measures, was realized in 1957 in the shape of the EEC (now the EU) **374–75 ≫**.

BEFORE

During the 18th and early 19th centuries, Britain, Spain, France, and Russia all laid claim to parts of North America, often without consideration for the American Indian tribes who already lived there.

REVOLUTION

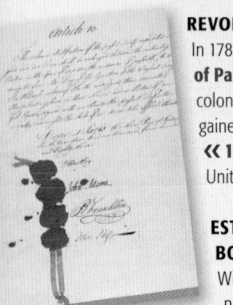

In 1783, under the **Treaty of Paris**, 13 North American colonies under British rule gained independence **<< 168–69** and formed the United States of America.

TREATY OF PARIS

ESTABLISHING BOUNDARIES

With the Treaty of Paris, the northern border with British Canada through the Great Lakes was agreed. In 1783 **Britain returned Florida to Spain**, which also controlled the Louisiana Territory. Spain ceded the Louisiana Territory back to France in 1800.

NEW STATES

The **1787 Northwest Ordinance** allowed the formation of up to five new states to the northwest of the USA on land ceded by various states to the US government. This increased the conflict between settlers and the local tribes. In 1795, 12 American Indian tribes were persuaded to sign the **Treaty of Greenville** giving land to the USA. They were then moved to vacant land in the west.

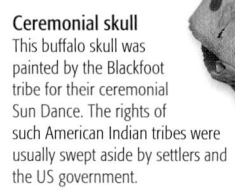

Ceremonial skull
This buffalo skull was painted by the Blackfoot tribe for their ceremonial Sun Dance. The rights of such American Indian tribes were usually swept aside by settlers and the US government.

Pioneer spirit
Settlers, such as this family, travelled west across the Great Plains, often in large convoys for safety. The wagons carried all their worldly goods, plus tools for farming and building.

From its beginnings, squashed between the Atlantic Ocean in the east and the Appalachian Mountains in the west, the United States quickly expanded westwards to the Mississippi River and beyond. The land between the Appalachians and the Mississippi was ceded by the British at independence. Expansion across the Mississippi began after the Louisiana Purchase in 1803 whereby the French sold the entire Louisiana Territory (see BEFORE) to the US. In May 1804, US President Jefferson sent Meriwether Lewis, his secretary, and William Clark to explore this practically unknown area. The pair set off from St Louis and sailed up the Missouri River.

DECISIVE MOMENT

FIRST TRANSCONTINENTAL RAILROAD

On 10 May 1869 at Promontory Point, Utah, a grand ceremony marked the opening of the first railroad to cross America. The 1,738km (1,086 miles) of eastern Union Pacific track and the 1,100km (690 miles) of the western Central Pacific track were linked. Leland Stanford, president of the Central Pacific Railroad, swung a silver hammer at a golden spike – a bolt made of gold – to symbolically join the tracks. Envoys from the Union Pacific Railroad also had a turn at hammering it home. America now had its first transcontinental railroad.

Expanding the Frontier

The independent United States of America that emerged in 1783 was, in reality, the United East Coast. The land to its west appeared to be limitless. In the century that followed independence, the frontier was pushed west across the continent until American dominion stretched from ocean to ocean.

With the help of Shoshone guides, they crossed over the Rocky Mountains, and in December 1805 reached the Pacific coast. The route was hard, but they met friendly tribes and returned with details of the new frontier.

Division of the land

An agreement with Britain in 1818 straightened out the northern border with Canada along the 49th parallel line of latitude. Another agreement in 1842 confirmed the northeast border in Maine. To the south, Florida was acquired from Spain between 1813–19. This led to conflict with the Seminole tribe. To deal with hostilities, the government passed the Indian Removal Act in 1830, giving the US president power to move tribes west across the Mississippi to the "Indian Territory" (now Oklahoma). The Cherokees were the first to arrive, having been displaced by the discovery of gold in their home in Georgia. In 1838, the so-called "Trail of Tears" involved the enforced removal of about 17,000 Cherokees; 4,000 died, often from disease contracted while they were in the transportation camps.

Californian gold rush

The discovery of gold in the Lower Sacramento Valley in December 1848 lured prospectors west to California. They arrived by land and sea to seek their fortune, often carrying few possessions apart from a tin bowl to pan for gold.

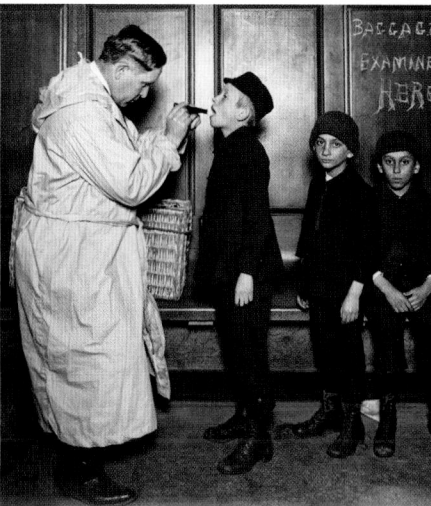

American immigrants
From 1892 to 1954, 12 million people passed through the main immigration centre of Ellis Island, New York. Like these children, all were given a health check before being allowed to enter.

America continued to expand into the 20th century. There were many opportunities to purchase or otherwise take control of land beyond its shores.

FIRST CATCHES
Alaska was bought from Russia in 1867 and **Hawaii, Midway Island, and Wake Island** were annexed in 1898.

BATTLESHIP MAINE

FURTHER AFIELD
A war with Spain, precipitated, among other disagreements, by the **sinking of the battleship USS Maine** off the coast of Cuba in 1898, brought **Puerto Rico, Guam,** and the **Philippines** under American control. The following year, the USA acquired **Samoa** as a naval base and refuelling station for ships trading with Asia. In 1917, the **Virgin Islands** were purchased from Denmark to protect Caribbean sea routes.

RELINQUISHING CONTROL
The US has given up some of its empire. The **Philippines gained independence in 1946**, while three former Japanese island groups in the western Pacific held since 1945 became independent in 1994–96. The **Panama Canal Zone**, American since 1903, was returned to Panama in 1999.

|45 The number of states in the Union in 1900.

> "It is our **manifest destiny to overspread the continent** allotted by Providence for the free development of our yearly multiplying millions."

JOHN L O'SULLIVAN, "NEW YORK MORNING NEWS", 27 DECEMBER 1845

In 1846, Oregon Country was split with the British, again along the 49th parallel, providing a Pacific frontier.

Further expansion came quickly. In 1836, Texas had become independent from Mexico. Its annexation by the USA in 1845 led to war with Mexico, bringing California, Nevada, Utah, Arizona, and New Mexico into the nation in 1848. The Gadsden Purchase from Mexico in 1853 provided the land for the Southern Pacific Railroad to California and so confirmed the southern border. With the purchase of Alaska from Russia in 1867, the USA completed its continental growth.

Land of opportunity

As politics and war settled the frontiers, countless intrepid migrants settled the land. Families travelled west from the Mississippi along designated trails.

The numbers were impressive. Three years after the opening of the Oregon Trail through the Rockies in 1841, 5,000 settlers a year were making the challenging journey.

Through the 1862 Homestead Act the government offered farmers ownership of 160 acres of public land after they had farmed it for five years. Nebraska had been described by an army expedition in 1820, as "wholly unfit for farming", yet 72,000 people flocked there in four years to build houses of earth, and live from the soil. Land was not the only draw; the discovery of gold in California in 1848

Alaskan cheque
In 1867, the year before this cheque was issued, the US agreed the puchase of Alaska with the Russian imperial government.

attracted 80,000 prospectors within a year. Others went west to start up new businesses or seek adventure.

The completion of a transcontinental railroad in 1869 (see left), and three more by 1883, further opened up the west. The railroads brought new settlers west and also helped farmers already there, as cattle and grain could be transported easily to cities back in the east.

The massacre of the Sioux ghost dancers at Wounded Knee on 29 December 1890 ended the wars with the American Indians. America had overcome the obstacles to its occupation of the continent.

The Civil War was the result of years of conflict between the north and south.

NEW MEMBERS OF THE UNION
In the years following independence ❮❮ 232–33, more territories joined the original 13 colonies of the United States (known as the Union).

SLAVERY
The Constitutional Convention of 1787 allowed **individual states to permit slavery**; northern states abolished it, while southern states kept it.

THE NORTH–SOUTH DIVIDE
The issue of slavery itself revolved around **state versus federal** (central) rights, and whether a slave was a person's property, the right to which was guaranteed by the US Constitution. Admitting new free states (a state where slavery was outlawed) to the Union would be problematic, as it would upset the balance between slave and free states and possibly provoke a **federal move to abolish slavery**.

THE MISSOURI COMPROMISE
This 1820 amendment to the Missouri statehood bill balanced admission of slave and free states, but in 1857 the Supreme Court ruled it unconstitutional, in favour of slave-owning states. With increasing numbers of free territories wishing to gain Union status, and an armed raid in 1859 by anti-slavery militant John Brown to free slaves at Harpers Ferry, Virginia, the **southern states began to feel threatened**.

JOHN BROWN

> "The war is over – the **rebels** are our countrymen again."
>
> ULYSSES S GRANT, 1865

The American Civil War

In 1861 the United States split apart over the issue of slavery. It fought a lengthy, bloody civil war that lasted until 1865. Thousands were killed, and while the issue that caused the war was resolved, its divisive legacy lasted for years.

The catalyst for war was the election in November 1860 of the first Republican Party president, Abraham Lincoln (see pp.246–47), against a divided Democrat opposition. Lincoln opposed slavery in territories wishing to achieve Union membership, and won the votes of every free state (see BEFORE) but one. The southern states voted for a pro-slavery Democrat, John Breckenridge. The impact of the result was immediate.

On 20 December 1860, South Carolina voted to leave the Union. By June 1861, 10 more states had joined these rebels, known as the Confederacy, but not every slave state joined: Kentucky remained neutral, while Delaware, Maryland, and Missouri were loyal to the Union. Virginia joined the Confederacy, causing West Virginia to separate, and become a Union state.

The first shots were fired by Confederate cannons on 12 April 1861; their target was the Union-held Fort Sumter in Charleston harbour, South Carolina. Three days later, Lincoln issued a call for loyal state governors to send 75,000 militia troops to protect Washington DC. The war had begun.

A country divided

The two sides were not well matched; the Union had the larger population (22 million compared to 9 million in the south, of whom 3.5 million were slaves it would not arm) and greater resources. The Confederacy, however, had the better generals. Its simple strategy was to defend itself from attack and win recognition as an independent state. The Union government had no option but to attack the Confederacy by blockading its coastline and seizing its capital of Richmond, Virginia.

Both sides required troops and issued regular calls for volunteers. When numbers were insufficient, conscription was introduced, by the Confederacy in 1862, and the Union the next year. By the war's end, 50 per cent of the eligible population in the Union had been mobilized, as were 75 per cent of the Confederacy. Both armies were mainly white; initially Congress would not allow free African-Americans or escaped slaves – totalling about 500,000 – to join the Union army, but changed the law after emancipation (the freedom of the slaves) in 1863. Almost 200,000 joined up, although they were paid less than white troops and could not become officers. In the Union, many women joined the Sanitary Commission, which ran kitchens and hospitals, and raised funds.

AMERICAN GENERAL (1822–85)

ULYSSES S GRANT

Ulysses S Grant trained at West Point military academy but failed to make a success of army life and then saw his Missouri farm fail during the 1857 depression. His military training won him the rank of colonel when war broke out, and early successes and aggressive tactics – notably at Shiloh in 1862 – earned him promotion. In March 1864 Grant was appointed as overall commander of the Union troops. In July 1866 he took control of the US army, until becoming Republican president in 1869. His tenure was marred by scandal, but he held office until 1877.

Battle of Gettysburg
Total casualties for both sides at Gettysburg are estimated to have exceeded 46,000, with the dead left on the battlefield. This was the first conflict to be extensively documented by war photographers.

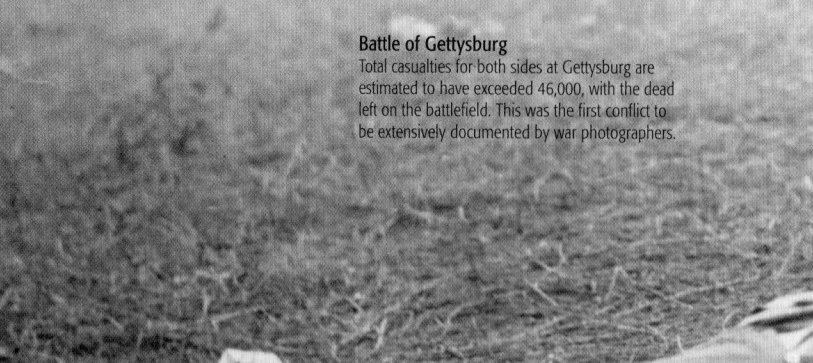

Standard issue
Both armies used versions of this .58 calibre rifle-musket. In the north it was known as the Springfield, after the Massachusetts' armoury in which it was made.

Victories and defeats
Superior Confederate leadership led to early success, notably with "Stonewall" Jackson's victory at Bull Run, Virginia in July 1861, reprised in August 1862, when Union forces failed to push the Confederates away from Washington. The turning point was Confederate

84th Regiment
This flag belonged to the 84th Regiment, United States Coloured Troops, and is inscribed with some of the battles in which they participated, alongside a larger force of Union army volunteers.

general Robert E Lee's attempt to invade the Union, and his defeat at Gettysburg, Pennsylvania in a three-day battle in July 1863.

In the west, Union general Ulysses S Grant (see left) held Shiloh, Tennessee in April 1862, and then took Vicksburg on the Mississippi in July 1863, cutting Arkansas, Louisiana, and Texas off from the rest of the Confederacy. In the autumn of 1864 Union general William Sherman began to advance through Georgia to the sea, before moving north through the Carolinas. In Virginia, Grant's victories against Lee reduced the

Confederate flag, Snodgrass Hill
The 2nd Battalion Hilliard's Alabama Legion attacked Snodgrass Hill during the Battle of Chickamauga, Georgia, September 1863. Their flag was pierced 83 times by Union troops.

Confederate army to barely 60,000 troops. The fall of the Confederate capital on 3 April 1865 led to Lee's surrender to Grant at Appomattox Court House on 9 April. The Union had won.

The reckoning
This was the first modern technological war. Railroads transported men and supplies to the front, messages were telegraphed, iron-clad warships fought for the first time, and photographers and journalists brought the war to people every day via newspapers. The human toll was immense: 360,000 Union dead and 275,000 wounded, 258,000 Confederate dead and 100,000 wounded. Economically, the south was ruined.

The main outcome of the war was emancipation. Lincoln had initially fought to preserve the Union, not free the slaves, but abolitionists in the north, and the effect of escaped slaves fighting in the Union army, changed his mind. On 1 January 1863 Lincoln's Emancipation Proclamation had freed the slaves in the Confederacy, though he did not have the constitutional authority to abolish slavery, nor the power in the south to do so. Lincoln himself did not live to see the effects of this action: he was shot at a theatre in Washington on 14 April 1865, and died the next day.

Although the end of the war led to the reunification of the country, it took years for the new laws to be accepted.

EMANCIPATION
The Emancipation Proclamation of 1863 became the 13th amendment to the US Constitution in 1865. The 14th amendment, passed in 1868, gave the **former slaves US citizenship** (American Indians had to wait until 1924), and the 15th amendment of 1870 guaranteed their **right to vote**. In many cases, however, these were paper rights, as racial discrimination lasted for the next century.

EMANCIPATION PROCLAMATION

RECONSTRUCTION
After the war, the south was occupied by federal troops. From 1866–77 Congress attempted **"Reconstruction" in the south**. Former Confederate officials were prohibited from holding public office, veterans were required to pledge allegiance to the Union, and newly freed slaves stood in state elections. Confederate states were re-admitted to the Union only after they had accepted the 14th amendment. However, the founding of the white supremacist Ku Klux Klan in Tennessee in 1865 showed the reluctance of some southerners to accept emancipation.

16TH PRESIDENT OF THE UNITED STATES Born 1809 Died 1865

Abraham Lincoln

"Government **of the people, by the people, for the people,** shall not perish from the Earth." ABRAHAM LINCOLN, GETTYSBURG ADDRESS, 19 NOVEMBER 1863

A braham Lincoln grew up in Kentucky, in what was then America's wild western frontier. His father Thomas Lincoln was a farmer and carpenter who set his son to hard manual labour from an early age. Abraham disliked his father and his limited world of subsistence farming. He became a lifelong believer in technological progress and financial economy as escape routes from the backwardness into which he had been born.

Lincoln had little schooling, but was encouraged in self-education by his stepmother Sarah. Eloquent and ambitious, by the time he was 30 he was a lawyer and, as a member of the liberal progressive Whig Party, held a seat in the Illinois House of Representatives. In higher social circles his backwoods manners were seen as rough and gauche, yet he was successful enough to persuade a plantation-owner's daughter, Mary Todd,

Wartime president
This photo-portrait of Lincoln was taken by Alexander Gardner in November 1863. It shows the president's stubborn resolve, but also reveals the sadness and strain that afflicted him as a wartime leader.

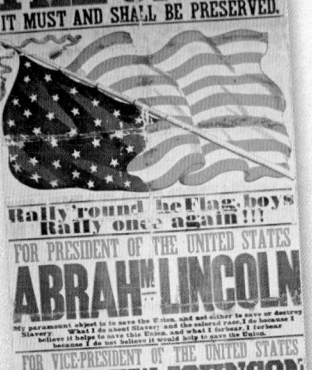

On the campaign trail
In 1858 Lincoln's public debates during the Illinois contest for the Senate attracted nationwide attention. Lincoln was at this time clean-shaven, adopting a beard in 1860 to improve his electoral chances.

CAMPAIGN BADGE, 1864

A united front
In the presidential election of 1864, Lincoln stood with the Democrat, Andrew Johnson, as his vice-presidential running mate. With war-weariness widespread, Lincoln's re-election was far from a foregone conclusion.

to marry him in 1842. Mary actively promoted her husband's political career, but was violently jealous and given to bouts of wild extravagance. As a couple, they did not find happiness; the death of two sons in childhood preyed upon Mary's mind, while Lincoln himself was prone to fits of depression.

Elected to the US Congress in 1846, Lincoln's first foray to the US capital, Washington D.C., was not a success, so he returned to Illinois to dedicate himself to the law and making money. It was the eruption of the slavery issue through the Kansas–Nebraska Act of 1854 that propelled him back into politics. Lincoln participated in the formation of the Republican Party to resist the spread of slavery in the expanding United States. His attitude to slavery had been formed as a child, since his family attended anti-slavery Baptist churches. But it was above all his personal experience of self-advancement that determined his views. Lincoln felt that his rise from humble origins showed that any free

Man of letters
Lincoln wrote this letter to his Secretary of War, Simon Cameron, in May 1861, recommending that his friend, Alexander Sympson, be given a contract to supply the army with horses. In other letters, Lincoln constantly urged his generals to prosecute the war with greater energy and resolution.

A Presidential visit
Lincoln visits the Union army camp at Antietam in October 1862. He is flanked by intelligence chief Allan Pinkerton (left) and General John A McClernand, one of the Union army's many lamentably unsuccessful military commanders.

> "Let us strive on to finish the work we are in; to **bind up the nation's wounds.**" ABRAHAM LINCOLN, INAUGURAL ADDRESS, 4 MARCH 1865

man could make something of himself. Slavery denied an individual the chance of self-betterment.

The reluctant abolitionist
Although he denounced slavery as morally wrong, Lincoln did not adopt an abolitionist stance, accepting that slavery would persist in the southern states. Even so, his anti-slavery position during public debates with Illinois Democrat Stephen A Douglas in 1858 made him a figure of hate for southerners. His statement that the United States government "could not endure permanently half-slave and half-free" was seen as an invitation to civil war.

As an inelegant, awkward westerner with limited political experience, Lincoln was not the obvious choice for Republican presidential candidate in 1860, but he slipped through as a compromise between conflicting factions. With the Democrats divided, he won the presidency with less than 40 per cent of the popular vote. Diehard southerners had made it clear his election would provoke secession (withdrawal) from the Union. So bitter was the atmosphere that Lincoln had to sneak into Washington in disguise to take up his office because of the threat of assassination.

Lincoln at first fatally underestimated the strength of secessionist sentiment and the force that would be required to overcome it. However, with the outbreak of civil war in 1861 between the northern states (the Union) and southern states (the Confederacy), Lincoln showed an unflinching will for victory. His position as president was precarious. He was despised by the political elite, opposed by factions on both wings of his own party, and threatened by discontented generals. He had to manoeuvre and compromise to maintain the support for the war. Yet with almost no

military experience, he showed a better grasp of the principles of warfare than most of his generals. It was not until 1864 that he found in Ulysses S Grant a commander-in-chief whose implacable will matched his own.

Lincoln's legacy
Even in the thick of the war, Lincoln found a chance to advance the material progress in which he so firmly believed. He oversaw the creation of a National Bank, laid the foundations for the building of the Pacific Railroad, and prepared the way for the carving up of the prairies into small farms with the Homestead Act. On slavery, it was only after his re-election in 1864 that he was able to press for a constitutional amendment to abolish the practise and to advocate full citizenship and voting rights for black Americans.

Lincoln's unequalled rhetoric, both in his Gettysburg Address of 1863 and his second inaugural speech of 1865, gave the war a dignity it would otherwise have lacked. His assassination by fanatic John Wilkes Booth at the moment of victory for the Union army was a national tragedy.

THE GUN THAT SHOT LINCOLN

Assassination at Ford's theatre
Watching the play *Our American Cousin*, alongside his wife Mary, Lincoln was shot in the head by John Wilkes Booth. He was carried to a boarding house opposite the theatre, where he died early the following morning.

Mexican revolutionaries
A Mexican rebel group, c.1911, shoots from a boulder overlooking a desert valley filled with factories. Thousands of labourers and landless peasants fought to reclaim lost lands.

« BEFORE

When the Spanish and Portuguese arrived, native Latin American cultures were to be subdued under colonial rule for 300 years.

CONQUISTADORS

The Spanish *conquistadors* (conquerors), bold and brutal adventurers, established **Spain's claim to the New World**. In 1513, Vasco Núñez de Balboa was the first European to see the Pacific. Eight years later, Hernán Cortés's Spanish expedition **conquered the Aztec Empire** of Moctezuma II in Mexico, and in 1532 the Spanish brought down the **Inca** Kingdom of Peru « 170–71. Mexico and Peru had rich silver and gold mines, and Mexico City became the capital of New Spain.

MOCTEZUMA HEADDRESS

SPANISH AND PORTUGUESE SETTLEMENT

In the 16th century Spanish colonists advanced north into what is now Florida and California, and south to today's Venezuela and Argentina. In the 18th century **precious metals** and stones were discovered, and coffee cultivation began in Brazil. The Portuguese **explored Amazonia**, and formalized their claim to it in 1750.

Latin America Liberated

The people of Latin America span the entire continent of South America, Central America, Mexico, and the islands of the Caribbean. They share a history of conquest and colonization, by the Spaniards and Portuguese, a struggle for liberty, and centuries of political instability.

When Napoleon turned on his Spanish allies in 1808 during the Peninsular War (see pp.238–41), events took a disastrous turn for Spain. With the Spanish king and his son Ferdinand taken hostage by Napoleon, leaders jostled for power across Spanish America and juntas filled the void. Not many lasted long, but by 1810, the process towards independence was underway.

The independence movements in South America rose from opposite ends of the continent. From the south came José de San Martín. In 1817, San Martín, a former Spanish military officer, directed 5,000 troops across the Andes from Argentina and struck at a point in Chile where loyalist forces had not been expecting an invasion. San Martín then freed the Spanish stronghold of Peru.

From the north, came Simón Bolívar (see RIGHT). Bolívar's forces invaded Venezuela in 1813, waging a ferocious campaign, but the rebels achieved only short-lived victories. In 1817 a larger and revitalized movement for independence emerged, and won the struggle in the north. Bolívar was named president of Gran Colombia in 1819, a union of Venezuela, Colombia, Panama, and Ecuador. The tide had

turned in favour of independence, and by 1821 further military campaigns had liberated New Granada and Venezuela. In the central Andes, the southern and northern armies attacked in a pincer movement to crush the remaining loyalist strength, and in 1824 Peru gained its independence.

In Mexico, a unique movement emerged in 1810, led by a radical priest, Miguel Hidalgo y Costilla.

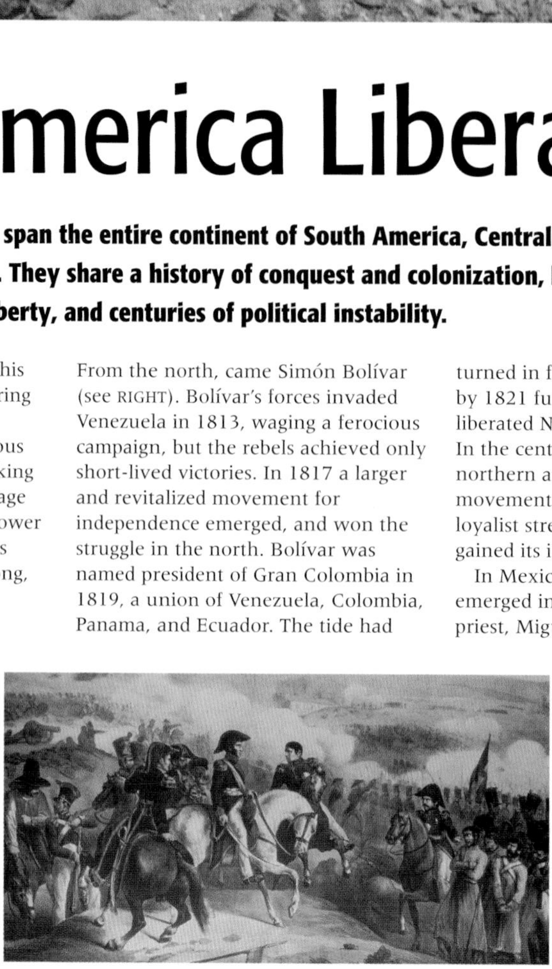

Battle of Maipú
José de San Martín led his rebel troops over the heights of the Andes to fight Spanish royalists. The Battle of Maipú, in 1818, gained Chile liberty from Spanish domination. The Spanish army was so demoralized – 2,000 died and 3,000 were captured – that San Martin was also able to liberate Peru.

Revolutionary poster
Urging peasants to unite under the name of Zapata, the commander of the Liberation Army of the South, this poster says, "The land should belong to those who work it". Large landed estates were forcing peasants from the land.

Plundered resources
Coffee was a non-native crop introduced by the Europeans. Before 1800 it was mainly produced by slaves on plantations controlled by colonists.

Hidalgo appealed to the indigenous Mexicans to eject from the village of Dolores the wealthy classes of Spanish descent. This became known as the *Grito de Dolores* ("Cry of Dolores"). Hidalgo's untrained army grew to number 80,000 as it conquered towns and larger cities, and threatened Mexico City itself. After a dramatic defeat, Hidalgo was captured in 1811 and executed. But by then Mexican independence was on its way to being realized, and was achieved in 1822.

Brazilian independence
In Brazil, the discovery of a conspiracy against Portuguese rule in 1789–98 showed that some groups there had

already been contemplating the idea of independence in the late 18th century. The reliance of the Brazilian upper classes on African slavery, (see pp.218–19) however, favoured their continued ties to Portugal. The key step in the relatively bloodless end of colonial rule was the flight of the Portuguese court from Lisbon to Rio de Janeiro in 1808, to escape Napoleon's invading troops. After 13 years, King John returned to Portugal leaving his son Pedro as regent. Dom Pedro I proclaimed Brazil independent in 1822, with himself as emperor. In 1831, however, he abdicated, leaving his five year old son, Dom Pedro II, as regent, until 1840, when he was made emperor. He reigned until 1889, when he was deposed, and a republic was proclaimed.

Building new nations
The former Spanish America split into more than a dozen separate countries. Adapting models from northern Europe and the US, republics were set up across the region. The earliest were in Venezuela, Chile, and New Granada between 1811–12. Factional fighting caused the first constitutional governments to fail, however, and the unrest led to more centralized regimes by the mid-19th century. Governments changed rapidly in most regions, and the use of force became common. Military men, "caudillos", rose to positions of dominance and consolidated their power through strategic alliances.

In many countries, difficult financial circumstances contributed to political instability. But by the 1860s and 1870s, manufacturers from England, the US, and other nations were welcomed, and there was a surge in demand for sugar, coffee, wheat, and beef. Traditional exports such as silver recovered, and exceeded previous production levels.

When domestic funding was scarce, European investment helped to provide money for improved infrastructure. Foreign firms, from countries such as

> **JUNTA** A Spanish word for a governing group, often used to refer to military officers who seize power and establish an authoritarian government.

Britain, constructed railways, streetcar systems, and electricity networks. Latin America underwent a thorough integration into the world economy. While urban populations flourished, however, rural life remained poor.

The Mexican Revolution
In 1876 General Porfirio Díaz forcibly seized power in Mexico and set up a dictatorship. He opened up the country to foreign investment and allowed the owners of foreign estates to take more of the Indian peasants' lands. Resentment of these policies exploded in the revolution of 1910. Díaz was overthrown in 1911, but fighting broke out between rival factions. Díaz's successor, Francisco Madero, failed to carry out promised agrarian reforms and was overthrown in 1913. President Álvaro Obregón (1920–24) finally implemented them and fighting ceased.

AFTER »

After centuries of colonial rule, industrialization and democracy came to Latin America only slowly.

NEW CONSTITUTION FOR MEXICO
In 1917, President Venustiano Carranza, began to create the **modern Mexican state** with **land reforms** and more limits on the Church's power.

CARRANZA

NEW INDUSTRY
Shortages of goods caused by the two World Wars were an **incentive to industrialization**. The Great Depression of the 1930s **306–07** », however, hit Latin America hard. Heavy industry was not established until the 1950s. Brazil, Mexico, and Argentina became Latin America's leading producers of iron, steel, and machinery.

THE DAWN OF MASS POLITICS
Latin America has often been politically unstable. Many countries have swung between **extremes of left and right**, but most countries are now democracies **344–45, 360–61** ».

SOUTH AMERICAN REVOLUTIONARY LEADER (1783–1830)
SIMÓN BOLÍVAR
Simón Bolívar was a South American patriot, and hero of the struggle for independence from Spain. Born an aristocrat, Bolívar began his revolutionary career in Venezuela in 1813, after visits to Europe and the US, where he had absorbed anti-colonial ideas. He was called "El Libertador" ("The Liberator"). Bolívar spent his remaining years unsuccessfully trying to forge a union of the newly independent states.

> " ... **experience** comes from bad judgement."
> SIMÓN BOLÍVAR, ATTRIBUTED

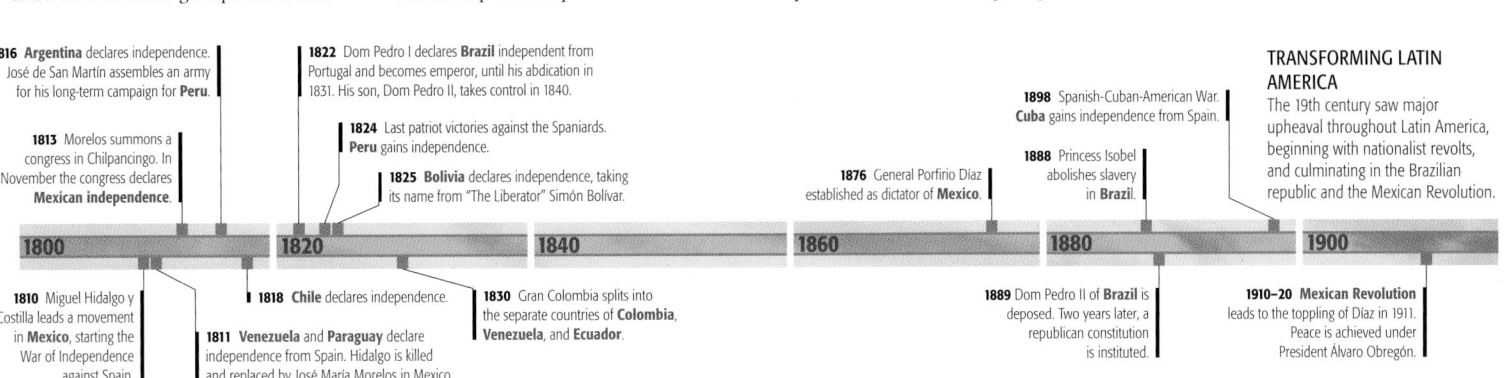

1816 Argentina declares independence. José de San Martín assembles an army for his long-term campaign for **Peru**.

1813 Morelos summons a congress in Chilpancingo. In November the congress declares **Mexican independence**.

1822 Dom Pedro I declares **Brazil** independent from Portugal and becomes emperor, until his abdication in 1831. His son, Dom Pedro II, takes control in 1840.

1824 Last patriot victories against the Spaniards. **Peru** gains independence.

1825 Bolivia declares independence, taking its name from "The Liberator" Simón Bolívar.

1898 Spanish-Cuban-American War. **Cuba** gains independence from Spain.

1888 Princess Isobel abolishes slavery in **Brazil**.

1876 General Porfirio Díaz established as dictator of **Mexico**.

1810 Miguel Hidalgo y Costilla leads a movement in **Mexico**, starting the War of Independence against Spain.

1818 Chile declares independence.

1811 Venezuela and **Paraguay** declare independence from Spain. Hidalgo is killed and replaced by José María Morelos in Mexico.

1830 Gran Colombia splits into the separate countries of **Colombia**, **Venezuela**, and **Ecuador**.

1889 Dom Pedro II of **Brazil** is deposed. Two years later, a republican constitution is instituted.

1910–20 Mexican Revolution leads to the toppling of Díaz in 1911. Peace is achieved under President Álvaro Obregón.

1800   1820   1840   1860   1880   1900

TRANSFORMING LATIN AMERICA
The 19th century saw major upheaval throughout Latin America, beginning with nationalist revolts, and culminating in the Brazilian republic and the Mexican Revolution.

BEFORE ◀◀

A great age of world exploration began in the 1400s, and lasted for over 400 years.

EARLY MAPPING

At the beginning of the 15th century, European sailors used maps based on the writings of ancient Greek geographer **Ptolemy,** showing Europe, the Mediterranean, and western Asia. The voyages of explorers such as **Christopher Columbus** ◀◀ **168–69** and **Ferdinand Magellan** ◀◀ **164–65** were instrumental in helping cartographers more accurately map the globe. However, European knowledge of the southern hemisphere was still sketchy. A Dutch map from the late 1500s shows

1486 ENGRAVING OF PTOLEMY MAP

an area labelled **Terra Australis Nondum Cognita** ("not yet known southern land"): it was thought Earth's land was equal in size north and south of the equator.

BRITISH EXPLORER (1728–79)

CAPTAIN JAMES COOK

One of five children, James Cook was born in Yorkshire, northern England, the son of a farm-hand. Apprenticed into the Merchant Navy, Cook studied astronomy and navigation and, after joining the British Royal Navy in 1755, made a name charting parts of Canada during the Seven Years War (see pp.230–31). He led three voyages to the Pacific, and was greatly respected by his crew, believing in good diet and hygiene. Despite mainly successful efforts to forge friendly relations with the Polynesians he visited, Cook was killed in Hawaii.

Completing the Map

Led by the desire to discover new land and lay claim to its riches, to open trade routes, or simply in a spirit of adventure, explorers of the 18th and 19th centuries mapped the continents of Australia, Africa, and North America, and set out to conquer the poles.

The continuing belief in the mid-18th century was that some vast southern continent must exist south of the equator to balance the Asian landmass in the north (see BEFORE). In 1768, Captain James Cook's reputation as a cartographer earned him the leadership of a British expedition to the Pacific. With instructions to chart coastlines and annex trading posts in the name of the British Crown, Cook's first Pacific voyage (1768–71) took him around New Zealand and along the coast of eastern Australia.

Matthew Flinders later

Cook's chronometer, K1, 1769
Invented by John Harrison, the chronometer (see p.222) enabled the measurement of longitude. Cook was one of the first to know his exact position while sailing uncharted waters.

circumnavigated Australia (1801–03), proving it was one large island. The west coast Swan River colony, founded in 1829, confirmed British claims to the whole continent, but few ventured deep into the interior until 1860, when Robert Burke and John Wills left Melbourne and headed north. By the following year they had crossed Australia.

Into Africa

Africa posed a great challenge to explorers as there were still many blank spaces in European maps of the continent. The British, Portuguese, French, and Germans were all eager to lay claim to its lands, with various religious, commercial, political, and colonial agendas. Major exploration of Africa's interior began when a Scot, Mungo Park, travelled in the Niger valley (1796–1805). Later in the 19th century several explorers, including Richard Burton,

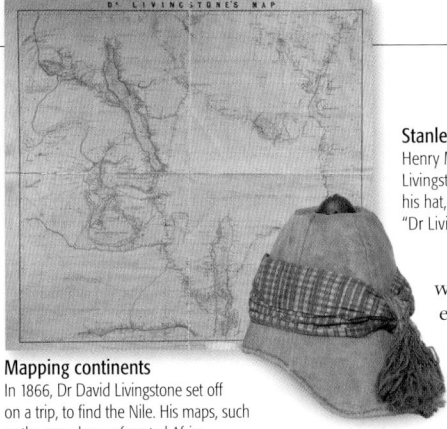

Mapping continents
In 1866, Dr David Livingstone set off on a trip, to find the Nile. His maps, such as the one above of central Africa, changed mapping of Africa.

John Hanning Speke, and Verney Cameron, endured great hardships to continue their explorations. The Scottish missionary David Livingstone, attempted to open up trade routes favourable to Britain. He navigated lakes and rivers, including the River Zambezi and Victoria Falls, crossing Africa from east to west. Livingstone and Henry Morton Stanley (the man who was sent to find Livingstone when he went missing in 1866–71) were important in mapping this enormous continent. The last gaps in Africa's map were not filled in until the 1920s.

The Americas
The first European to make the long trek across North America

Stanley's pith helmet
Henry Morton Stanley was sent to Africa to find Livingstone. On finding him, in 1871, he doffed his hat, and uttered the now famous words; "Dr Livingstone, I presume".

was the Scottish-Canadian explorer Alexander Mackenzie in 1793, as he searched for the Northwest Passage – a water route to the Pacific Ocean. In 1804, with settlements becoming overcrowded and people migrating west, US President Thomas Jefferson sent Meriwether Lewis and William Clark to explore Louisiana and the mountains and plains beyond it. They crossed the US from east to west by canoe, horse, and foot, reaching the Pacific Ocean in 1805.

A test of endurance
The North (Arctic) and South (Antarctic) poles were so inhospitable they offered little chance for exploitation, but there was prestige in being the first nation to conquer them. In 1893, Norwegian Fridtjof Nansen had failed to reach the North Pole. Competition to be the first to reach the pole intensified. A pair of Americans, Frederick Cook in 1908 and Robert Peary in 1909, both made claims to have reached the North Pole – claims that remain disputed to this day.

While navigators of many nations had charted the coastline of Antarctica in the extreme south it took an American expedition led by Lieutenant Charles

Wilkes (1840) to confirm that it is a continent. In 1911, two expeditions landed separately on the Ross Ice Shelf, about 1,450km (900 miles) from the South Pole. Both the Norwegian Roald Amundsen and an Englishman Robert Falcon Scott sought to demonstrate their technological prowess and endurance. With husky-drawn sledges, Amundsen reached the pole on 14 December 1911. Halfway there, Scott sent his ponies back and dragged the sledges by hand. He reached the South Pole a month after Roald Amudsen, but died of starvation on the return journey.

Through such feats of human endeavour, geographers were able to draw the first accurate outline of the world. By the turn of the 20th century, all seven continents – Europe, Asia, Africa, North and South America, Australia, and Antarctica – were on the map.

> **"So we arrived,** and planted our flag at the geographical South Pole. **Thanks be to God!"**
> ROALD AMUNDSEN, NORWEGIAN EXPLORER, 1912

AFTER ➤➤

In the 21st century, little uncharted territory remains on Earth. However, human endurance and scientific curiosity have kept polar and space exploration alive.

POLAR EXPLORATION
The **first crossing of Antarctica** was accomplished by the British **Vivian Fuchs** and the New Zealander **Edmund Hillary** in 1957–58. American **Ralph Plaisted** became the first to reach the **North Pole using surface transport** in 1968.

SPACE HIGHLIGHTS
In April 1961, the Russian cosmonaut **Yuri Gagarin** became the first person in space. In July 1969, the US made history when Apollo 11 successfully landed on the Moon **382–85 ➤➤**.

1969 MOON LANDING

Le Petit Journal

Polar dispute
This 1909 French cartoon depicts Peary and Cook, who both claimed to be the first to reach the North Pole. The fray that followed discredited both men.

Cook in New South Wales
On 22 August 1770, Captain James Cook (centre, raising hat) declared the southeastern coast of Australia British and named it New South Wales. Eighteen years later, to ease prison overcrowding, the British government sent the first fleet of around 750 convicts to settle at Sydney Cove.

BEFORE

From the advent of agriculture, people have lived in communities. The city has evolved as a centre of commerce and power.

ANCIENT CITIES
Towns and cities emerged in Asia and Egypt in the 4th millennium BCE. Larger towns grew into **densely populated walled cities**, with streets running at right-angles to each other, to form a grid pattern. Ancient Greek **‹‹48–49** and Roman cities **‹‹64–67**, like Herculaneum, became centres of intellectual, religious, and commercial life.

HERCULANEUM, ITALY

THE MEDIEVAL PERIOD
After the fall of the Roman Empire **‹‹102–03** western European cities declined. In the medieval period towns began to expand again, often around a castle or monastery **‹‹134–35**.

REVIVAL OF CITY LIFE
Town planning was revived during the Renaissance **‹‹190–93**, and the grid pattern was popularized in 17th-century America.

The cause of the phenomenal growth of cities from the 19th century onwards is fairly straightforward – the ascendancy of industry over agriculture – but the effects of this change in lifestyle were far more complex. The mechanization of agriculture (see pp.224–25) and the abolition of serfdom in Europe left an excess of labour in rural areas, and that labour force flooded into the cities when the Industrial Revolution (see pp.226–29) provided a new form of employment in the shape of factories and workshops.

Many centres of industry developed in cities that had existed for centuries. Others expanded from small villages, or developed as new cities where raw materials were available, or main roads or rail routes converged. Industrial buildings and railway marshalling yards tended to be close to the city centre, with the workers – who had no means of transport – living in cheap housing within walking distance of the factories. In many heavily industrialized cities a "factory culture" arose, whereby the population of whole streets and even neighbourhoods were connected by their employment at one particular local mill or factory.

Urban transportation
The need for mass transport capable of dealing with steep hills led to the development of San Francisco's cable car system in 1873. The cable car's popularity resulted from it replacing horse-drawn transport.

Flocking to the cities
This urban expansion was apparent throughout the industrialized world. In 1850, London, Paris, Constantinople (now Istanbul), and St Petersburg were the only European cities with more

City Living

Humans have lived together in cities since ancient times, but in 1800 urban areas were home to just 3 per cent of the world's population. The massive explosion of urbanization that accompanied the Industrial Revolution saw that figure rise 15 per cent in the space of 100 years.

than 500,000 residents – just 50 years later 23 European cities had passed that landmark, nine of which had more than a million inhabitants: London, Paris, Berlin, Vienna, St Petersburg, Manchester, Birmingham, Moscow, and Glasgow. However, despite this massive increase in city living, at the turn of the 20th century the majority of people – even in industrialized nations – still lived in the country.

Squalor, space, and sanitation

For those who were forced to move to the cities life was often squalid and miserable. In the first half of the 19th century the influx of people to the cities outstripped the facilities available, which meant that in some poor urban areas food supply and sanitation were so bad that the high mortality rate (both from malnutrition and from diseases caused by overcrowding, such as cholera and typhoid) kept urban growth relatively slow. Indeed, not all cities experienced continuous growth –

1.7 MILLION
The number of people living in Chicago in 1900. The population more than tripled in the 50 year period from 1850–1900.

some even declined. Water was polluted with human filth, the air with industrial pollution, and rats and insects quickly spread disease. Not surprisingly, the situation was worst in the world's most populous cities such as London, Paris, Constantinople, and particularly Peking (now Beijing), which in 1800 was the only city with more than a million inhabitants.

The appalling conditions in the working class slums close to his father's cotton mill in Manchester, in the north of England, inspired German philosopher Friederich Engels to write *The Condition of the English Working Class in 1844*. It impressed the political philosopher Karl Marx (see pp.264–65), and provided valuable information for the socialist movement (see pp.266–67). It also added to the demands for improved health and sanitation in city slums. Such developments meant that urban populations began to expand naturally, rather than as a result of rural immigration, prompting the expansion that took place between 1850 and World War I.

Urban planners also came to realize that space was as important to health as sanitation. One result of this was the provision of "green lungs" – city parks

aimed at improving people's health and comfort – and another was the emergence of model towns. While industrialists are often characterized as exploiting the masses, many were philanthropists. In 1786, Scottish cotton magnate David Dale built the model town of New Lanark (see pp.266–67) for his workers, and his example was followed by several other industrialists during the 19th century, including his son-in-law, Robert Owen. In 1898,

Sir Ebenezer Howard published *Tomorrow: the Peaceful Path to Real Reform*, in which he outlined his vision of the "Garden City", an idealized town incorporating extensive green spaces. This was a great influence on 20th-century urban planning.

»

Manhattan, New York City
Elevated railways, such as this one in Manhattan, photographed in 1895, allowed expanding cities to accommodate multiple modes of transport.

INVENTION

UNDERGROUND RAILWAYS

In many of the world's cities, underground railways are referred to as the "Metro" after the world's first example: the Metropolitan Railway in London (now part of the Metropolitan Line), which opened with steam traction on 10 January 1863. Putting the railway underground by cutting or boring a tunnel was a means of providing rapid, frequent, and cheap transport around a crowded city. Continental Europe's first underground railway was the Tünel, opened in Istanbul in 1875, though it only covered 573m (1,880ft). The first "subway" in the US opened in Boston in 1897.

WILLIAM LE BARON JENNEY

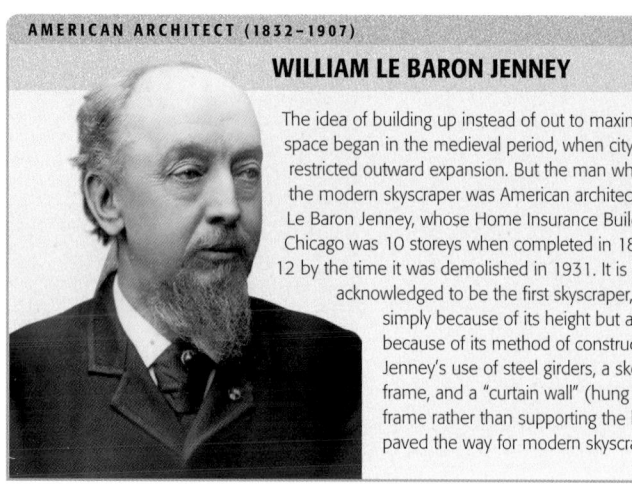

The idea of building up instead of out to maximize living space began in the medieval period, when city walls restricted outward expansion. But the man who inspired the modern skyscraper was American architect William Le Baron Jenney, whose Home Insurance Building in Chicago was 10 storeys when completed in 1885 and 12 by the time it was demolished in 1931. It is generally acknowledged to be the first skyscraper, not simply because of its height but also because of its method of construction. Jenney's use of steel girders, a skeleton frame, and a "curtain wall" (hung from the frame rather than supporting the building) paved the way for modern skyscrapers.

The first such town was Letchworth, in Hertfordshire, England, in 1903. Harvey's idea was adopted by the American architecht Walter Burley Griffin in his work on Canberra, the capital of Australia.

The spread of urbanization

As cities expanded, so did their infrastructures. Urban transport networks improved, with innovations such as urban trams in 1832 in New York City, underground railways in London in 1863 (see p.253), and the elevated railway, in 1867, again in New York City. The improvements in transport led to more middle-class workers moving away from the city centres, giving rise to the concept of suburban living and the commuter belt – residential areas on the periphery of a city. This in turn led to the expansion of the suburbs, which in some cases meant cities absorbing entire towns and villages into their urban sprawl and filling the spaces that once separated them with new housing and facilities. In some countries this resulted in legislation limiting the extent of expansion and the creation of "green belts" around cities.

City living was not simply about the buildings in which people lived and worked; it also affected their habits and ways of thinking. City-dwellers had greater anonymity than rural villagers, which gave them greater licence in many aspects of their lives. This included sexual practices – infidelity and prostitution were higher in the cities – and religion: atheism was markedly higher in urban areas, which led to an increase in church-building and to the establishment of institutions like the Salvation Army, to bring people back to religion.

Leisure and pleasure

By the end of the 19th century two new social phenomena had emerged: the leisure industry and consumerism. These arose from a combination of

"Hell is a city much like London…"

PERCY BYSSHE SHELLEY, ENGLISH POET, 1819

▽ **Moscow, Russia**
This wide, shop-lined street, photographed in 1890, is typical of the ambitious building programme that occurred in Moscow in the late 19th century.

▽ **Glasgow, Scotland**
Glasgow's population increased twentyfold from 1780 to 1900, by which time it was known as "The Second City of the Empire". This picture, from 1860, shows the cramped conditions resulting from a population boom.

◁ **Piccadilly Circus, London**
Despite being built in the early 19th century, by the time of this photograph, taken in 1910, the roads of London's Piccadilly Circus were having to accommodate early motor cars (see pp.344–45), as well as more traditional horse and carts.

◁◁ **Manchester, England**
By the end of the 19th century, Manchester was a thriving industrial city. Market Street (shown here) is one of the city's main thoroughfares.

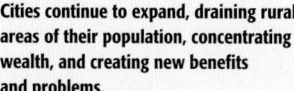

△ Chicago, USA
By 1900, thanks to industry and railways, Chicago was America's second largest city. Good transport links encouraged trade, such as markets, like this one on South Water Street.

△ Paris, France
Paris expanded rapidly from the 1840s due to the arrival of the railways. During the 1850s Napoleon III ordered a massive remodelling by Georges Haussmann, who replaced entire medieval districts of narrow, cramped streets with the wide boulevards, such as this one, for which the city is now famous.

World's biggest cities
These graphs show the extraordinary population growth in the world's top five cities. The list of top cities changes between 1800 and 1900 from mainly Asian cities to European and American ones.

factors: the spread of mass production, which reduced costs and thus lowered retail prices; the availability of the technology for mass entertainment such as cinema (see pp.274–75); the concentration of people in the cities to consume products and entertainment; and the fact that by 1900, for the first time, standards of living in the industrial West had risen so significantly that most people had some disposable income.

Not only were people earning more money, but the focus of their lives was undergoing a gradual shift away from the workplace – average working hours were shorter, leading to a division between work and leisure time. Rising income enabled people to decide what they did with that spare time. By the early 20th century a wide range of diversions were available, including popular theatre, music hall, motion pictures, and professional sports. Much of this entertainment directly or indirectly used the technologies whose development had led to urban growth: directly, in developments such as cinema, and indirectly in that railways and transport systems improved people's access to these leisure facilities.

3 PER CENT The proportion of the global population living in towns of over 200,000 people in 1800.

15 PER CENT by 1900.

30 PER CENT by 1950.

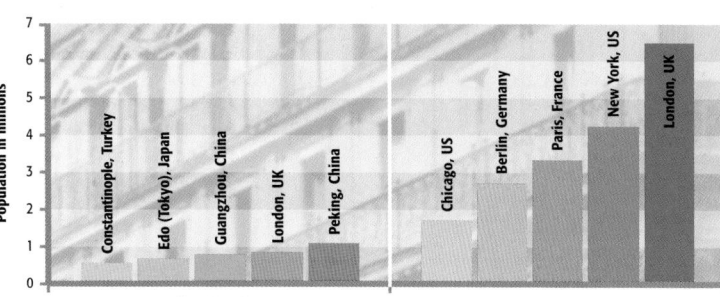

Population in millions

Top five cities in 1800
Constantinople, Turkey · Edo (Tokyo), Japan · Guangzhou, China · London, UK · Peking, China

Top five cities in 1900
Chicago, US · Berlin, Germany · Paris, France · New York, US · London, UK

Cities continue to expand, draining rural areas of their population, concentrating wealth, and creating new benefits and problems.

CONTINUED GROWTH
The number of people worldwide living in cities has **continued to rise** since the medieval period.

6.2 MILLION The average size of the world's 100 largest cities in 2000.

SLUMS AND SHANTIES
As urbanization continued to accelerate during the 20th century, the new phenomenon of the shanty town appeared on the **fringes of cities** in Africa, Asia, and South America, where there is a **wide gap between rich and poor**. Shanty towns are haphazard collections of unlicensed **makeshift houses** which are built from any available waste materials. The rural poor are drawn to shanty towns in the hopes that living **close to the city** might bring them employment, housing, health services, education, and utilities, but for the vast majority it is a false hope. Conditions are far worse than those they have left behind in the country, with hunger and poverty made worse by crime and disease. According to the United Nations, more than half the world's population now lives in cities, almost one third of that number in slum areas or shanty towns.

SHANTY TOWN LIFE

LIGHT POLLUTION
In urban areas, problems are caused by an **excess of artificial light**. These include adverse effects on human health and disruption of ecosystems governed by sunlight.

INNER CITY CONGESTION
During the 20th century the problems of overcrowding in cities changed from those encountered during the 19th century. Problems of food supply and sanitation were replaced by those of **pollution and traffic congestion**, together with the perennial problem of overcrowding. For a long time a feature of third-world cities, bicycles are now commonly seen on the roads of developed first world cities as people attempt to reduce pollution and find a quick route through the congestion **400–01 »**.

A CITY CYCLIST

12 MPH The average speed of traffic in London in the year 1900 and in the year 2000.

« BEFORE

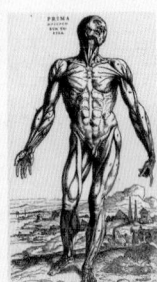

The theories of ancient Greece ‹‹ 58–59 dominated medical thinking for 2,000 years.

GREEK MEDICAL THEORY

In ancient Greece (*c*.500 BCE), it was believed that health depended on the body **maintaining a balance** of four fluids, or **"humours"** – blood, yellow bile, black bile, and phlegm. Each humour had its own characteristic qualities, combinations of hot, cold, wet, and dry. Blood, for example, was hot and wet. Disease was thought to arise when there was an imbalance of humours.

TEMPERAMENT

An **excess** of a particular humour was thought to give people their character, or **"temperament"**. A sanguine temperament was believed to produce an excess of blood, which made the person cheerful, even-tempered, and optimistic, though feverish.

SKETCH FROM VESALIUS'S WORK

THE TRAVELS OF GREEK MEDICINE

These ideas spread from ancient Greece across the globe and dominated medicine for 2,000 years. They travelled across Europe during the Roman Empire, then spread to the Middle East, and to European colonies. While the core theories remained constant, doctors added to the Greek understanding of anatomy. In the 16th century, the Belgian physician **Andreas Vesalius**'s groundbreaking *On the Workings of the Human Body* contained detailed anatomical sketches.

In the 18th century, doctors researching human anatomy realized that some diseases, such as cancer, produced swellings in the solid parts of the body or changes to the appearance of organs such as the lungs and liver. The idea that disease was located in the solid parts of the body, not the fluids (see BEFORE), was firmly established by Parisian research into pathology in the early 19th century. In the city's huge hospitals, doctors carefully recorded the progress of many of the diseases suffered by hundreds of patients they treated. Those who died were dissected, to discover how their illness had affected the organs in their body. Using this approach, doctors were able to monitor the progress of many diseases, and to make precise distinctions between diseases of the heart and of the lungs, for example.

During the rest of the century, doctors explored the structure of the human body in finer detail. They described the various tissues which made up the organs and, using improved microscopes, began to explore the cells that formed the tissues. While some researchers studied the minute structures of the human body, others began to research into the functions of the organs. By experimenting on animals, their patients, and sometimes themselves, doctors began to understand

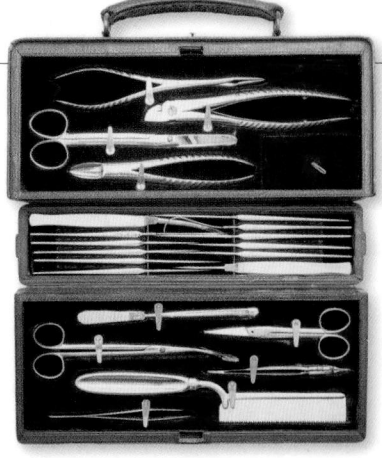

19th-century surgeon's kit
Although antisepsis is often associated with the British surgeon Joseph Lister and the use of carbolic acid, safe surgery owed much to simple ideas – like making surgical instruments from steel, which were sterilized after every operation.

Germ Warfare

In the 19th century, a number of significant developments in medical science greatly increased doctors' knowledge of anatomy and disease. Coupled with the transformation of hospitals into specialized treatment centres came a crucial understanding of the spread of infection and how to halt it.

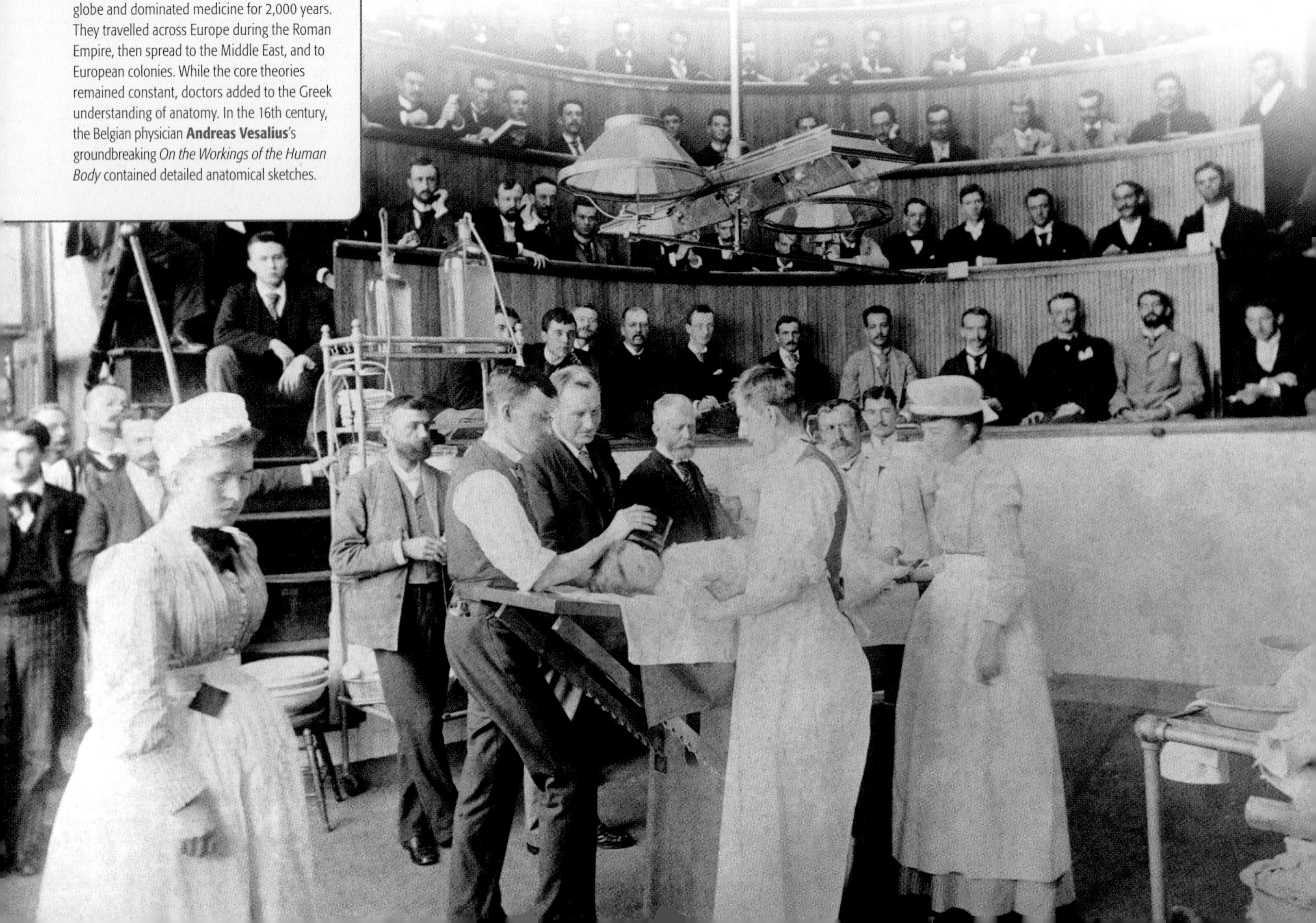

"A **hospital**... should do the **sick no harm**."

FLORENCE NIGHTINGALE, BRITISH
NURSE AND PHILANTHROPIST, 1859

the role of the liver and pancreas in the digestive system and the function of the kidneys. This in turn gave them new ways of diagnosing illnesses, such as identifying kidney disease by analysing the chemicals found in a patient's urine.

Surgery

Once doctors began to think of disease affecting the solid organs of the body, they realized they might be able to cure patients by cutting out the diseased part. However, in the 18th century, surgical operations were used only as a last resort, because of the pain involved in cutting into the patient's body, and the high probability of wound infection.

From the beginning of the 19th century, surgery began to change with the introduction of anaesthetics – the British surgeon Robert Liston's use of ether during an amputation had an impact throughout Europe. Now surgeons could work more slowly, reducing blood loss by tying up blood vessels, and carefully cutting out damaged or diseased tissue. Around the same time, they tackled the problem of wound infection: first by keeping their instruments and the wound clean, and later by using antiseptics to kill the germs that caused infection. At the end of the 19th century, modern aseptic techniques were introduced to eliminate contamination from the operating theatre: staff wore gowns, masks, and rubber gloves, and every instrument was sterilized. This allowed surgeons to operate safely, and to devise a range of operations to cure diseases.

Therapy

Although the practise of bloodletting – draining a patient of blood in the hope it would cure their illness – was stil used in the 19th century, by 1900

Early operating theatre

This 1898 photograph of an operating theatre reveals that the idea of asepsis (the reduction of contamination) spread very slowly. The surgeon wears an apron, but no mask, and the room is filled with observers wearing ordinary clothes.

INVENTIONS

SCOPES AND X-RAYS

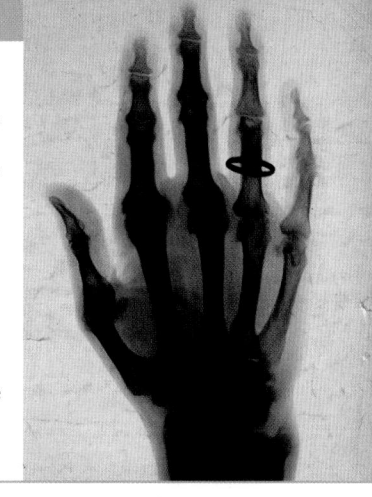

The idea that disease was located in the body's organs led to a string of inventions helping doctors to "see" inside their patients while still alive. In 1816 René Laennec created the first crude stethoscope when he rolled up some papers into a tube, and discovered he could hear sounds made by the lungs and heart. The 19th century saw the invention of a number of "scopes" for seeing into the ear, eye, and the throat. The ability to see inside the living body became a reality in 1895 when Wilhelm Röntgen discovered that X-rays passed through flesh but not bone. X-ray images, such as this one from 1895, became an invaluable tool in helping doctors to repair damaged limbs.

---

doctors had abandoned most of the old "humoural" therapies (see BEFORE). However, there were still few effective remedies. Opium was used to relieve pain, but as an addictive substance it was not without risk. Doctors could treat serious injuries and broken limbs with the aid of anaesthetics and improved surgical methods. Quinine (made from the bark of the cinchona tree) was used to treat malaria, and digitalis (made from foxgloves) was an effective treatment for heart conditions. In 1897, aspirin (based on a chemical found in willow bark) was launched. Salvarsan, the first synthetic drug, was introduced in 1910, and was prescribed in cases of syphilis. However, many remedies did not cure disease, but only soothed the symptoms, for example cough syrup eased coughing, and poultices reduced

30 SECONDS was said to be all it took for the 19th-century surgeon Robert Liston to amputate a human leg – without administering an anaesthetic.

---

swellings. Bed rest, nutritious food, and careful nursing were still the basis of medical care for most forms of illness.

Caring for the sick

Hospitals were crucial to the development of new medical ideas and practices, and in turn these medical innovations completely transformed the nature of the hospital. In the medieval period, hospitals across Europe were originally linked to monasteries and abbeys and were created to offer food and shelter – literally, hospitality (see pp.146–47).

They cared for the poor, the sick, and religious pilgrims. In the 18th century, hospitals were still charities caring for the sick and poor. In the 19th century, they became centres for treatment, open to all who could afford to pay. Operating theatres – so called because they enabled students to view surgery – were built, with specialized lights and equipment, lined with glass and tiles that could be easily cleaned. Some teaching hospitals invested in new equipment such as the first X-ray machines (see above). They also began to offer specialist treatments for complaints of the ear and eye, or conditions affecting children. As a result, hospitals treated a greater number of seriously ill patients, and the amount of staff, especially nurses,

Microscope

From 1830, the microscope played a crucial role in understanding the structure of the body. Doctors diagnosed cancer by examining tissues under the microscope, and confirmed infection by identifying disease-causing bacteria.

objective lens

stage for specimen slide

primary lens to focus light source

AFTER »

In late-19th and 20th century, the greatest medical developments came in the form of new treatments.

VACCINES

Smallpox vaccination had been developed in the 1790s, based on the **chance observation** that milkmaids who caught cowpox (a mild disease) did not catch smallpox. Other forms of immunization were developed as doctors began to understand how the body resisted disease. In the 1880s, the French scientist Louis Pasteur developed a vaccine against rabies based on a **weakened form of the virus**. This was

followed by vaccines against tetanus and diphtheria in the 1890s. **Mass immunization** against common childhood diseases came in the 20th century – with a vaccine against polio in 1957 and against measles and mumps in the 1960s.

LOUIS PASTEUR

NEW DRUGS

The first drugs that treated infections were produced in the 1930s, but they were replaced by the **discovery of penicillin**, which became available in the 1940s **388–89 »**. Before then, most drugs were derived from plants, but since the 1950s, **synthetic drugs** have predominated.

grew enormously to provide round the clock care. Nurses, who were almost always women, played a crucial role in the new hospitals. They kept the wards scrupulously clean and tidy to limit the possibility of infection, monitored patients' symptoms, and administered medicines. However, even experienced and skilled nurses were expected to follow the doctors' directions at all times.

While the relatively well-equipped hospitals were able to treat a wider range of conditions, many people, particularly the poor, continued to die of infectious diseases transmitted by bacteria and viruses. Cholera, typhoid fever, tuberculosis, and influenza killed thousands. Children were particularly vulnerable, and many died from measles, mumps, diphtheria, and scarlet fever. Doctors could do little to cure these diseases, but they could control their spread. Increased supplies of clean water, and improved sanitation helped to clean up cities (see pp.252–53) and stop the spread of water-borne infections. Patients suffering from infectious diseases were isolated in special hospitals, or in their homes. Quarantine was used, so those travelling from areas where disease was present were forced to stay away from towns until it was certain that they were not carrying infection.

Our Country

In the late 18th century nationalism emerged in Europe and the American colonies as a force for liberty, equality, and fraternity. But during the 19th century nationalism revealed its uglier side, proving to be an equally strong force for militarism, oppression, and racism.

« **BEFORE**

Until the 18th century the idea of the nation-state was linked to the monarchy and, in smaller states, people were unified by shared language and culture.

KING AND COUNTRY

Europe comprised a small number of powerful kingdoms – Britain and France were the oldest, with the Netherlands, Portugal, Spain, and Sweden emerging between the 15th and 17th centuries. Only in politically independent kingdoms was there any sense of nationhood. This was reinforced by **loyalty to the crown**, the flag, and, later, by patron saints.

FRENCH MONARCH'S CROWN

CULTURAL NATIONALISM

In smaller states and principalities – territories ruled by a prince – political loyalties were localized, but a sense of unity was provided by **common language and culture**. Around 1765 German historian Friedrich Meinecke observed a single national spirit even "where 20 principalities could be seen during a day's journey".

The term nationalism describes a loyalty to one's nation, pride in its history and culture, a belief that its interests are of primary importance, and a patriotic desire to achieve or maintain its independence.

Nationalism emerged as a political force in the late 18th century and since then the idea that nations have the right to form their own political states has shaped the map of the world as we know it today. This ideal, known as national self-determination, inspired major upheavals, such as the American Revolution (see pp.232–33), provided the impetus for smaller nations to seek independence from large empires, and encouraged nations divided into a collection of small states, or principalities, such as Germany and Italy, to seek unification.

Nations or nationalism?

Although the word "nation" is commonly used to describe a state or country, it is technically a group of people united by ethnicity, culture, language, and/or religion. A state is

defined as a geographical territory with its own independent government. These are not always the same thing – for example, the Kurdish people are a nation with no defined state, while South Africa under apartheid (see pp.376–77) was a state whose nations were forcibly divided (hence its new self-image as a multi-cultural "Rainbow Nation"). A country whose

"Liberty Leading the People"
This painting of the July Revolution of 1830 that made Louis-Philippe the French king is both a depiction of and an act of nationalism. The artist Eugene Delacroix wrote: "if I haven't fought for my country at least I'll paint for her".

> ## "Our country… may she always be in the right; but our country, right or wrong."
>
> STEPHEN DECATUR, US NAVAL OFFICER, 1816

FRENCH SOLDIER (1790–UNKNOWN)

NICOLAS CHAUVIN

Chauvin was an idealistic young soldier whose fierce patriotism remained undiminished even though he was wounded numerous times while serving in Napoleon's Grand Army (see pp.304–07). Napoleon decorated Chauvin with the Sabre of Honour but when his brand of unquestioning nationalism fell out of fashion he found himself satirized in several French plays. As a result of his unfortunate fame, the name "chauvinist" is now applied disparagingly to those who display excessive belief in the superiority of their country or of any other cause they embrace.

state boundaries correspond to those of a particular nation is described as a nation-state.

The precise origins of nationalism are unclear. One idea, called primordialism, is that nations are simply the outward, territorial expression of the divisions between people of different ethnicity or culture. This idea of "cultural nationalism" was first expressed by the 18th-century German philosopher Johann Gottfried von Herder. He believed that nature had separated nations by "languages, inclinations, and characters". Opposition to this idea states that the concept of nationalism came first, followed by the artificial creation of nations, for political or economic reasons. In the 20th century, Czech-born British social philosopher Ernest Gellner said: "Nationalism is not the awakening of nations… it invents nations where they do not exist". More recently, it has been proposed that national identities evolve by merging with new ethnic and cultural influences.

Today the idea of the nation-state is well established, but that was not always the case. Until the medieval period most people's loyalties were specific: to their tribe, religious leader, or feudal landlord. As people developed a sense of nationhood (see BEFORE) they began to demand the right to self-government. In America and France the liberal ideals of freedom, equality, and brotherhood (fraternity) led to nation-states that granted their citizens unchallengeable rights and were governed in the name of the people.

Consequences of nationalism

Once nation-statehood had been achieved, some less savoury aspects of nationalism emerged. Napoleon tried to impose the French identity on much of Europe (see pp.238–39), and the belief that the United States had a "manifest destiny" (see pp.242–43) to take over North America came at the expense of the native population. The idea that the nation-state should cherish itself above all others could lead to racism, religious intolerance, and imperialism. The British politician Cecil Rhodes said "if there is a God, then He would like to see me… colour as much of the map of Africa British red as possible." Britain's imperialism went on to encourage nationalist movements within the territories of its empire.

AFTER

Throughout the 20th century nationalism showed its two faces, freeing some while subjugating others.

FANATICISM AND FASCISM
In 1815 French foreign minister **Charles-Maurice de Talleyrand-Périgord** wrote of German nationalists: "The unity of the German Fatherland is their slogan, their faith and their religion, they are **ardent to the point of fanaticism**… Who can say where a movement of that kind might stop?" The fanaticism described by Talleyrand-Périgord turned to fascism as **Adolf Hitler 312–13 »** took advantage of extreme nationalist sentiment to seize power, culminating in World War II **314–27 »**.

NAZI PROPAGANDA

FREEDOM
Nationalist movements brought independence to former European colonies throughout Africa and Asia, such as Egypt, Indonesia, and Algeria **334–35 »**.

REACHING EXTREMES
Nationalism was also the the root of civil war and genocide in, for example, the former Yugoslavia **372–73 »**, and the terrorist activities of **nationalist groups** such as the IRA in Northern Ireland **358–59 »** and ETA in Spain.

Europe Redefined

Nationalism was one of the 19th century's most potent political ideologies. Over the course of the century, popular and state-led movements inspired by emerging concepts of national identity radically redefined the borders of Europe, replacing traditional monarchies with modern nation states.

During 1814–15, statesmen from the powers that had brought down Napoleonic France (see pp.238–41) gathered at Vienna to decide how to redraw the borders of Europe (see BEFORE). The resulting settlement was essentially conservative – an attempt to contain the seeds of nationalism that had shattered the old order of Europe. Most of the monarchies that had been overthrown by Napoleon's armies were restored. In Spain, King Ferdinand VII was given back his father's throne; Italy was divided once again into scores of principalities; the 39-state German Confederation was formed; Austria was given back most of the territories it had lost in Italy; Norway and Sweden were joined under a single ruler; and Russia was handed Finland and given effective control over the new kingdom of Poland.

But the forces to which the age of revolution gave birth were not so easily contained. Traditional loyalties to the old dynasties of Europe had declined; in their place came new loyalties to national groups and demands for nation-states. Over the following century, the old order of Europe would be fundamentally transformed.

National independence

Nationalist movements took two main forms in the 19th century: the political form of advocating independence from an alien rule; and the introduction of nationalist ideology to unite divided

Giuseppe Garibaldi
The Italian soldier and statesman Giuseppe Garibaldi became the hero of the Italian nationalist movement known as the *Risorgimento* ("resurgence").

against a foreign oppressor. In 1830, revolution also broke out in Belgium (part of the Kingdom of the Netherlands) and an independent Belgian state was formed in 1831.

A wave of radical agitation swept across Europe in 1848. In Paris the Bourbon monarchy, restored to the French throne in 1814, was overthrown, and replaced by a republic. On hearing of events in France, the people of Vienna, Budapest, and Prague rose up against the Habsburg rulers of the Austrian Empire. For a time this empire – which covered much of central and southeastern Europe – showed signs of collapse, but the revolutions of 1848 failed within the Habsburg territories.

National unification

The national impulse that led to the division of the Ottoman Empire into independent nation-states could also act as a force for unification. In 1814,

1859. With the help of France, Piedmont repelled Austria, leaving the way open for Cavour to take control of most of northern and central Italy.

The following year the charismatic Italian patriot Giuseppe Garibaldi invaded southern Italy with an army of a thousand volunteer "Red Shirts" and conquered Sicily and Naples. By 1871, the unification of Italy was essentially complete.

»

IRELAN

ATLANTIC OCEAN

Bay of Biscay

Oporto

PORTUGAL
Lisbon

Madrid

SPAIN

GIBRALTAR
to Britain

BEFORE

In the 18th century a number of national revivals made the concept of national identity a significant force in European politics.

MAGYAR RENAISSANCE
When **Joseph II**, the energetic ruler of the Habsburg Empire from 1780–90, decreed that German replace Latin as the empire's official language, the Hungarians (Magyars) in his empire reacted by insisting on the right to use their own tongue. This sparked a **renaissance** of Magyar Hungarian **language** and **culture**.

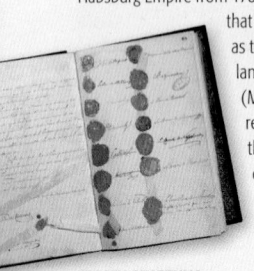
TREATY OF VIENNA

NATIONAL REVIVALS
The Magyar national reawakening subsequently triggered national revivals among the **Slovak**, **Romanian**, **Serbian**, and **Croatian** minorities within Hungary. In 1789, a **revolt** broke out in the **Austrian Netherlands** in reaction to the emperor's centralized policies, and in **Ireland** a swell of nationalism and a mass rebellion for **democratic rights** erupted against British rule in 1798. These revivals later blossomed into the nationalist movements of the 19th–20th centuries.

TREATY OF VIENNA
The French Revolution **«« 234–37** and the conquests of **Napoleon Bonaparte «« 238–41** shattered the old order of Europe and undermined many of the old certainties. The 1815 **Treaty of Vienna** was an attempt to redraw the borders of Europe and secure peace and stability.

> ## "Let him who **loves his country** ... follow me."
> GIUSEPPE GARIBALDI, 1882

groups within a state. Large, ethnically diverse states such as the Ottoman Empire (see pp.186–87) were particularly vulnerable to the first type of nationalist movement. During the first part of the 19th century, there was a series of uprisings by Greeks, Serbs, Romanians, and other ethnic groups within the Ottoman Empire. Serbia was semi-independent by 1817, and Greece declared its independence from the Ottomans in 1829. The Greek War of Independence, in particular, caught the imagination of writers and artists such as the poet Byron (see pp.268–69) and the painter Delacroix, helping stimulate a romantic ideal of national struggle

the Congress of Vienna had divided the Italian peninsula into a patchwork of independent states. In spite of this, the idea of a single Italian nation had potent popular appeal. A revolutionary society known as the *Carbonari* (coal-burners) agitated for national unification and organized insurrections, and in 1831 the Italian patriot and author Giuseppe Mazzini formed the political movement known as "Young Italy", which called for one Italian nation – "independent, free, and Republican". Italian statesmen were quick to grasp the opportunities. Cavour, the Prime Minister of Piedmont in northern Italy, provoked a war against Austria in

The sick man of Europe
This cartoon depicts Abdul Hamid II, the last Ottoman emperor (ruled 1876–1909), having his empire whipped out from underneath him by Bulgaria and Austria. Bulgaria became independent from the Ottomans in 1908.

NORWAY

FINLAND

SCOTLAND

Christiania

SWEDEN

Helsingfors

St. Petersburg

Edinburgh

Stockholm

North Sea

Moscow

GREAT
BRITAIN

Dublin

ENGLAND

WALES

London

Amsterdam

DENMARK

Copenhagen

Baltic Sea

Riga

RUSSIAN
EMPIRE

MECKLENBURG

Hamburg

HANOVER

Hanover

Danzig

POMERANIA

WEST
PRUSSIA

EAST
PRUSSIA

Brussels

NETHERLANDS

PRUSSIA

Berlin

BRANDENBURG

Rhine

Cologne

Elbe

POSEN

Posen

Vistula

Warsaw

Brest-Litovsk

POLAND

Kiev

Seine

Paris

THURINGIAN
STATES

SAXONY

PRUSSIA

SILESIA

Cracow

Dnieper

FRANCE

BAVARIA

Loire

BAVARIA

Stuttgart

Prague

BOHEMIA

GALICIA

Dniester

WÜRTTEMBERG

HOHENZOLLERN

PR. OF
NEUCHÂTEL

BADEN

Munich

Vienna

AUSTRIAN EMPIRE

Odessa

Bordeaux

NAVARRA

Geneva

Lyon

SWITZERLAND

AUSTRIA

Buda

Pest

MOLDAVIA

SARDINIA

Milan

LOMBARDY-
VENETIA

Venice

HUNGARY

TRANSYLVANIA

ANDORRA

PARMA

MONACO

MODENA

ILLYRIAN KINGDOM

MILITARY FRONTIER

Bucharest

WALLACHIA

Sebastopol

Marseille

MASSA AND
CARRARA

SAN
MARINO

Belgrade

Danube

Black Sea

LUCCA

TUSCANY

PAPAL
STATES

Barcelona

Corsica

MONTENEGRO

Rome

SARDINIA

Naples

OTTOMAN EMPIRE

THRACE

Constantinople

Balearic
Islands

SARDINIA

KINGDOM OF THE
TWO SICILIES

Corfu
to Britain

Salonica

ANATOLIA

Mediterranean Sea

Palermo

Ionian
Islands
to Britain

Athens

Smyrna

Changing European boundaries, 1815–1914
Independence and unification during the 19th century altered Europe's borders dramatically. The lines on this map show the borders as they were in 1815, while the areas of colour document the territorial changes that had happened by 1914.

Malta
to Britain

Cyprus

Crete

KEY

Great Britain	Spain
Norway	France
Denmark	Belgium
Sweden	Netherlands
Russian Empire	Luxembourg
Portugal	German Empire

Switzerland	Romania
Italy	Bulgaria
Austro-Hungarian Empire	Greece
Montenegro	Ottoman Empire
Albania	German Confederation, 1815
Serbia	Frontiers, 1815

N

0   250 km
0   250 miles

A show of strength
Prussian troops parade in the Champs Elysées in Paris in January 1871 after their takeover of the city during the Franco–Prussian War. Such displays showed off military strength, and helped build nationalistic pride.

National identity
National symbols and rituals such as the flag and Pledge of Allegiance, shown in this US school (c. 1900), could help to forge the identity of a young nation such as the US, which was largely made of immigrants.

AFTER »

Another politician who understood the power of the desire for national unity was the Prussian statesman Otto von Bismarck (see below). At the time of the 1848 revolutions, Germany was a loose confederation of states, of which the most powerful was Prussia. Bismarck's primary objective was to secure the supremacy of Prussia in Central Europe – but by encouraging the other German states to unify under Prussia, he was also the architect of the German nation.

The process began in 1864, when Prussia joined forces with Austria to annex the duchies of Schleswig and Holstein from Denmark. Two years later Bismarck was ready to deal with Austria, Prussia's chief rival for dominance in Germany. Allied with Italy and several smaller German states, Prussia defeated Austria – who counted the German states of Saxony and Bavaria among their allies – at the Battle of Königgrätz. Final unity came when the southern principalities of Germany joined Prussia in its war against France in 1870. A German victory led to the proclamation of a unified German Empire in 1871. Bismarck was appointed Chancellor.

National identities
The principle that nations share a unique, common identity based on a common culture and history was well established by the late 19th century.

National languages became paramount, often at the expense of regional dialects. During the struggle to unify Italy, for example, the Italian dialect spoken in Tuscany was chosen, and energetically promoted by writers such as Alessandro Manzoni, who revised and republished his great patriotic novel, *The Betrothed,* in this new national language. Symbols of national identity, such as music and literature, flourished. Sport was a focus of national pride. Military campaigns cemented a growing patriotic fervour with symbolic state emblems and flags. National Days were created, education systems enforced a standard curriculum, and fanfares, marches, and national anthems became prolific across Europe.

In some areas, a particular national identity was enforced by the state in an attempt to suppress or maintain control over other ethnic groups. In Hungary, where the ethnic Hungarians (Magyars) were outnumbered by non-Magyar minorities, the government enforced Magyar as the only legitimate language of administration – a policy known as

"Magyarization". Anyone who opposed this policy was liable to be charged with "incitement to national hatred". In 1900, the Russian Tsar proclaimed Russian the state language of Finland in an attempt to supress Finnish national identity – the "Russification of Finland".

Militarism
As liberal nationalism, which had focused on civil rights and a constitution, gave way to imperialist nationalism, based on national pride and expansion, a strong army became essential. Until Napoleon, armies were essentially professional forces whose manpower was drawn from the less socially and economically useful elements of the population. The old idea of loyalty to the king was replaced in the Napoleonic armies (see p.241) with loyalty based upon national patriotism fired by the idea of social revolution. This made it possible for Napoleon to raise the type of mass armies that came to characterize the national armies of the 19th and 20th centuries. The entire population was expected to contribute to the war and conscription was gradually introduced across Europe. Consequently, armies began to expand to record size.

Mass armies required large supplies of arms. The Industrial Revolution (see pp.226–29) enabled mass production, and advances in technology changed warfare. The Russo–Turkish War of 1877–78 was the first war in which modern repeating rifles were uniformly used, increasing the accuracy of fire, and breech-loading cannon, which loaded from the rear for safety and efficiency, replaced front-loading cannon. By the outbreak of the Russo–Japanese War (1904–05) the use of indirect heavy artillery fire was standard practice. The result was that the armies of the early 20th century had an unprecedented killing capacity.

AFTER »

Nationalism and a desire for independence dominated events in Europe in the years leading up to World War I.

EUROPEAN NATION-STATES
In the years preceding World War I, nationalism in many countries had turned **intolerant, imperialist, and expansionist**. Colonial acquisitions were greeted with enthusiasm and there was a growing sense that nations were in competition with each other. Italians, Serbs, Romanians, Greeks, and Bulgarians dreamt of extending their national borders to include their people who were living outside of their nation-state. This **expansionist nationalism** pitted the nation-states against each other. In 1912, a coalition of Bulgaria, Serbia, Montenegro, and Greece invaded, occupied, and partitioned the Ottoman Empire's European provinces. Disagreement over the spoils led to the **Second Balkan War** (1913) in which Greece and Serbia gained large territories.

INDEPENDENCE
The Russification of Finland in the late 19th century caused such resentment among the Finns that on the outbreak of the Russian Revolution **300–01 »** **Finland declared itself independent**. A war of independence and civil war was fought in 1918, and Finland officially became a republic in 1919.

FINNISH DECLARATION OF INDEPENDENCE

Poland had disappeared from the map in 1785, partitioned between Russia, Prussia, and Austria. In 1915, the Germans expelled the Russians from Poland and promised Poland independence. However, the Poles joined the Allies in World War I and their pleas for **freedom** were finally answered in **Versailles** in 1919 when an independent republic was recognized **299 »**.

Similarly, Ireland had also been fighting to shake off alien rule. In 1916, the Easter Rising was crushed by the British **358 »**. In 1921, however, the British signed a treaty with the Irish majority party Sinn Féin to bring about Irish Independence, except for the six northern counties, and in 1922 the Irish Free State came into being.

WORLD WAR I
By the early 20th century, **nation-states** replaced small principalities in Europe. In Africa and the East, Europeans were continuing to annex territories for reasons of national pride and **economic advantage 280–81 »**. These were also joined by a new generation of powers, whose interests were largely economic. Foremost among them were the US and Japan. But nationalism had within it the seeds of destruction. Rivalries between the powers intensified and their ambitions came into conflict. The result was to be **World War I 372–75 »**.

THE REPUBLIC OF IRELAND'S FLAG

CHANCELLOR OF GERMANY (1815–98)
OTTO VON BISMARCK

Otto von Bismarck became Prime Minister of Prussia in 1862. His ambition was to unite Germany under Prussian leadership – a result he believed could only be achieved by force. Victory in the Franco–Prussian War (1870–71) persuaded the other German states to join together to form an empire. He became the first chancellor of the unified Germany. Although conservative, Bismarck introduced some social reforms in an attempt to reduce the appeal of socialism.

"It is **not by means of speeches** and majority resolutions that the great issues of the day will be decided – that was the great mistake of 1848 and 1849 – **but by blood and iron**."

OTTO VON BISMARCK, 30 SEPTEMBER 1862

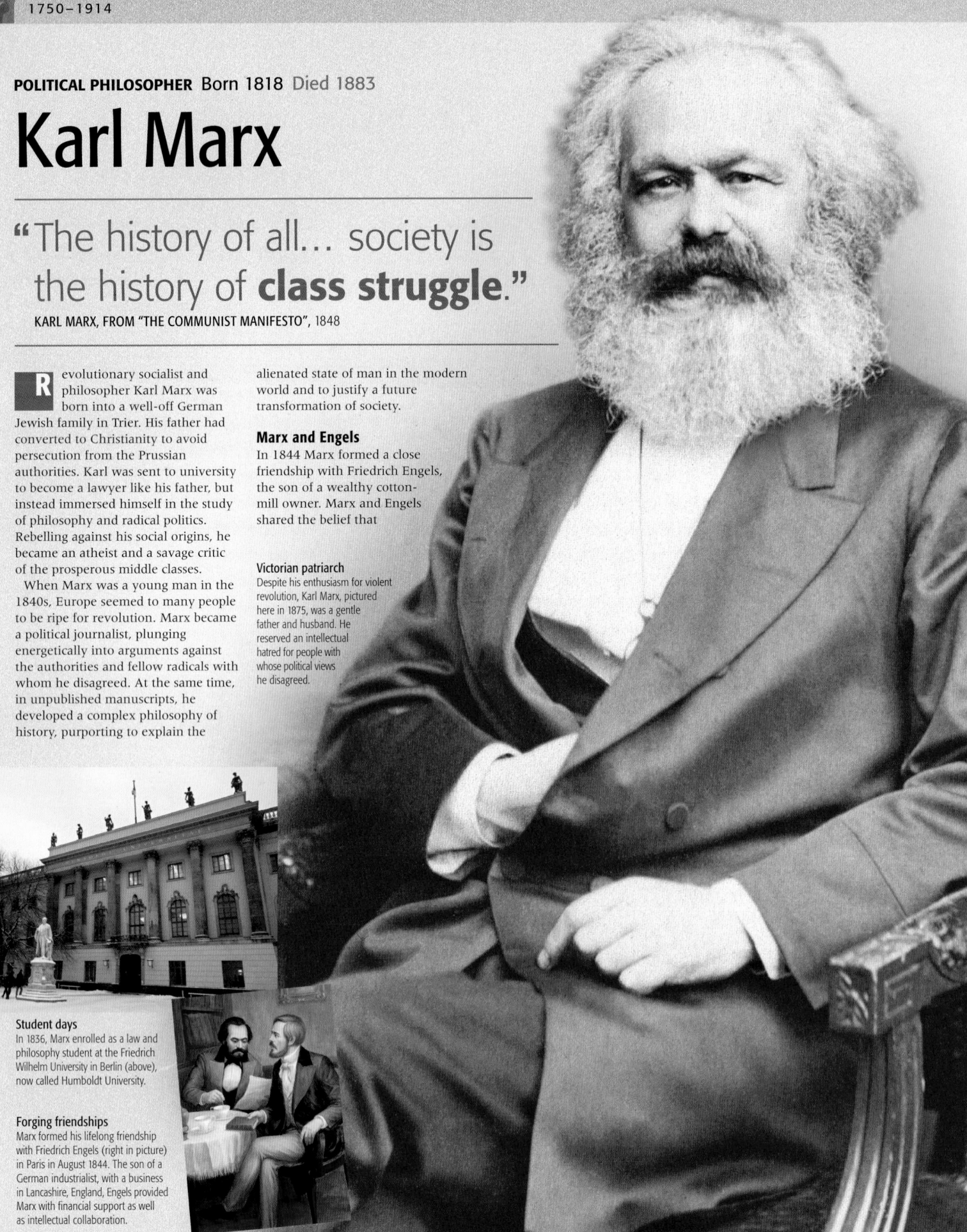

POLITICAL PHILOSOPHER Born 1818 Died 1883

Karl Marx

"The history of all... society is the history of **class struggle**."

KARL MARX, FROM "THE COMMUNIST MANIFESTO", 1848

Revolutionary socialist and philosopher Karl Marx was born into a well-off German Jewish family in Trier. His father had converted to Christianity to avoid persecution from the Prussian authorities. Karl was sent to university to become a lawyer like his father, but instead immersed himself in the study of philosophy and radical politics. Rebelling against his social origins, he became an atheist and a savage critic of the prosperous middle classes.

When Marx was a young man in the 1840s, Europe seemed to many people to be ripe for revolution. Marx became a political journalist, plunging energetically into arguments against the authorities and fellow radicals with whom he disagreed. At the same time, in unpublished manuscripts, he developed a complex philosophy of history, purporting to explain the alienated state of man in the modern world and to justify a future transformation of society.

Marx and Engels
In 1844 Marx formed a close friendship with Friedrich Engels, the son of a wealthy cotton-mill owner. Marx and Engels shared the belief that

Victorian patriarch
Despite his enthusiasm for violent revolution, Karl Marx, pictured here in 1875, was a gentle father and husband. He reserved an intellectual hatred for people with whose political views he disagreed.

Student days
In 1836, Marx enrolled as a law and philosophy student at the Friedrich Wilhelm University in Berlin (above), now called Humboldt University.

Forging friendships
Marx formed his lifelong friendship with Friedrich Engels (right in picture) in Paris in August 1844. The son of a German industrialist, with a business in Lancashire, England, Engels provided Marx with financial support as well as intellectual collaboration.

Cartoon of Paris Commune, 1871
In 1871 a revolutionary government, the Commune, briefly seized power in Paris. Marx had no influence on the uprising, but hailed it as "the glorious harbinger of a new society".

Radical journalism
Marx (left) and Engels (centre) collaborate on the *Neue Rheinische Zeitung*, a radical newspaper that they edited in 1848–49, a time of revolutionary upheaval in Europe. Marx was an excellent journalist, writing with humour and style as well as insightful political analysis.

industrial workers, inspired to rise up against the capitalists who exploited their labour, could be the vehicle for revolutionary change. In 1847, Marx and Engels both joined a small subversive organization known as the League of the Just, soon renamed the Communist League. For this they wrote *The Communist Manifesto*, a powerful appeal for the overthrow of society by a worldwide workers' revolution. It was a timely document, for in 1848 there were revolts in many cities across Europe, including Paris, Berlin, and Vienna. Marx contributed to the agitation with his writings, though neither he nor the Communist League had any significant impact on events. After the suppression of the uprisings in 1849, life for radicals such as Marx became impossible in continental Europe. He moved to Britain, a relatively liberal country that was tolerant of the activities of political refugees.

Theorizing revolution

In the 1850s the prospect of a triumph for the workers' revolution seemed remote, and the Communist League withered away. Marx instead devoted himself to an immense theoretical effort, intended to place the revolutionary critique of capitalist society on a secure scientific and philosophical basis. Although he earned some money from journalism, Marx did not work to support himself and his growing family, depending mostly on hand-outs from Engels. Thus he was free to write full-time, becoming a familiar presence in the British Museum Reading Room in London. The major result of his labours was the first volume of his analysis of capitalism, *Das Kapital,* in 1867.

By then Marx had resumed practical political activity. In 1864 he joined the International Working Men's

The Communist Manifesto
The *Manifesto* of 1848 is the most succinct statement of Marx's and Engels' ideas.

Association, an attempt to co-ordinate the efforts of assorted left-wing groups. Marx immediately established himself as a dominant force in the group, but his inability to tolerate the views of those who did not share his own ideas led to conflicts. When a revolutionary Commune briefly took control of Paris in 1871 (an uprising provoked by France's defeat in war with Prussia) the International played only the most marginal role in events. Yet after Marx wrote a pamphlet in praise of the uprising, the International received much of the blame (or credit) for it, giving Marx unprecedented notoriety.

Still, there was no reason in the last decade of Marx's life to suppose that he would become one of the most

> ## "The **workers** have nothing to **lose**… but their **chains**."
>
> KARL MARX, FROM "THE COMMUNIST MANIFESTO", 1848

influential figures in history. His writings, combining German philosophy and economic analysis, were often dauntingly intellectual. Yet a conviction spread that Marx had proved the inevitability of the fall of capitalism and of a workers' revolution. After his death, Marxism was adopted as a belief system by revolutionary groups, and became the official ideology of states such as the Soviet Union and Communist China. What Marx himself would have thought of the actions carried out in his name we cannot know, although Engels claimed that Marx once declared: "I am not a Marxist".

COMMUNISM

Marx saw history as a struggle between social classes. In 19th-century Europe, the bourgeoisie, or middle class, owned the means of production – factories and machinery. By paying the working class (proletariat) less than their labour was worth, the bourgeoisie accumulated capital. Laws and government were arranged to defend their power. According to communist ideals, it was the historic role of the working class to carry out a revolution, establishing a "dictatorship of the proletariat" and creating a classless society free of exploitation or want.

BEFORE «

Throughout history different economic systems governed the production and distribution of goods and services in society.

FEUDALISM

Feudalism was the system of land ownership that predominated in Western Europe during the medieval period **«134–35**. Land was held by a **vassal** on behalf of a lord or a king, in return for loyalty and military service. **Serfs**, mostly unfree peasants, laboured for the vassals in a state of virtual slavery in return for the right to farm some of the land for themselves.

MERCANTILISM

During the 17th and 18th centuries a trading system called mercantilism, operated in Europe, particularly England, France, and the Netherlands. It aimed to amass national wealth, especially in the form of gold bullion.

GOLD BULLION

CAPITALISM

Modern capitalism has existed in a recognizable form since the 16th century **«214–15**. Under the system the **means of production are privately owned** and goods are produced for a profit. Capitalism promotes a free market that is regulated by supply and demand.

HUMANISM

Humanism, a belief in the dignity and value of people, emerged during the Renaissance **«190–93** in Europe. Humanist values run counter to the harsh treatment of working people during the Industrial Revolution **«292–93**, and they made an important contribution to the development of socialist thinking.

Consequences of industrialization
The drive by 19th-century industrialists to maximize profits resulted in dirty and dangerous conditions for most working people – both in factories like these Pittsburgh steel mills and in overcrowded, inadequate homes. Disease was rife, and made worse by air and water pollution. These appalling conditions were the subject of numerous campaigns by social reformers.

"From each according to his ability, to each according to his need."

KARL MARX, FROM "CRITIQUE OF THE GOTHA PROGRAMME", 1875

Workers Unite!

While factory owners enjoyed huge profits during the Industrial Revolution, the new working class was impoverished. This inequality gave rise to political ideas that aimed to organize and inspire the workers, so that they could share the wealth they had created.

The hope of making the world a fairer place had existed for centuries. However, it was largely in response to the Industrial Revolution (see pp.226–29) that this idea developed into a political philosophy called socialism. Socialism seeks to share wealth by putting it in the hands of its creators – the working class. However, a central issue of socialist debate was whether this could be achieved gradually or whether through a revolution in which the working class seized power.

Socialism in practice

Early 19th-century socialists included Robert Owen, a Welsh industrialist, who came to believe, along with other "Utopian Socialists", in the construction of societies in which property was owned collectively. After establishing an experimental model community around his cotton mill at New Lanark in Scotland (see below), he continued to attempt to found co-operative communities, most significantly at New Harmony, in Idaho, US, though this was not a success. One of the more radical beliefs for the age held by Utopian socialists was that men and women should have equal rights.

In France Henri Saint-Simon, often called the "father of French Socialism", looked for a society in which there would be equal opportunities for all, while his followers proposed an end to private property. Among the many other radical ideas to emerge in the early 19th century, particularly in continental Europe, was anarchism, which held that the state itself could be replaced by a system of voluntary co-operation between workers.

From the 1840s, the German-born philosopher and economist Karl Marx (see pp.264–65) brought together several strands of revolutionary thought to produce a coherent political theory, which he named "scientific socialism". Marx viewed history as a series of class struggles that would

ultimately lead to the end of capitalism and the arrival of an ideal, classless society without private property, and free from exploitation and want – a theory he called communism. He published his beliefs in the *Communist Manifesto* (1848), which he wrote with Friedrich Engels. Marx believed that such change could only be reached through a process of violent revolution.

The rise of Marxism

It is highly unlikely that many working class people read the work of Marx or other socialist figures, but their discontent was evident. In 1848 Europe was shaken by a series of revolutions, which erupted as a result of various factors, including high unemployment. Although all the revolutions were quashed, labour movements emerged strong. Many of these were greatly influenced by the theories of Marx.

Marx played a more direct role in one of these movements in 1864, when a group of workers and intellectuals formed the International Working Men's Association, or First International. Marx dominated the movement with his revolutionary theories. However, an alternative version of socialism, known as "Social Democracy", was beginning to gain momentum in Germany and spreading to other European nations. Inspired by the work of the German philosopher, Ferdinand Lasalle, Social Democrats asserted that it was possible

French newspaper report
Karl Marx featured on the front page of the newspaper *L'Illustration* in November 1871. Nine months earlier Parisian workers had set up the Commune, a short-lived government that was hailed as the first example of "the dictatorship of the proletariat" – or communism.

for a fair government to free workers from want and exploitation. This form of socialism is still prevalent in European politics today.

For Marx, such a compromise was unacceptable. In his eyes capitalism and the growth of socialism were steps towards revolution and communism. The revolution Marx sought eventually took place in Russia, though he had envisaged it happening in more industrialized societies, like Britain. In 1917, under the leadership of Vladimir Ilyich Lenin, Russian socialists overthrew the prevailing government and created the Union of Soviet Socialist Republics (see pp.300–01).

New Lanark
In 1800 Robert Owen set up a model community at this mill in Scotland. New Lanark provided decent conditions for the workers and education for their children and still succeeded in making a profit.

Differing interpretations of socialism were adopted in the 20th century.

SOCIALISM IN ONE COUNTRY

While Karl Marx saw socialism as an international movement, Lenin's successor, **Joseph Stalin 302–03 ≫**, concluded that socialism must be built in one country – the Soviet Union. He **isolated** the nation from the rest of the world, and its economy, and those of other European countries modelled on the same system, was almost **entirely state-run** until the collapse of the Soviet Union in 1991 **368–69 ≫**. Similarly in China **346–47 ≫**, after the Communist Party came to power in 1949, the economy was largely state-run.

TRADE UNIONS IN BRITAIN

From the early 19th century British workers organized themselves into associations called **trade unions** to protect their common interests. The **Labour Party** grew out of the trade union movement and was formed in 1906 by socialist politician **James Keir Hardie**.

JAMES KEIR HARDIE

SOCIAL DEMOCRACY

Political parties espousing social democracy have held power for long periods during the 20th century – particularly in the Scandinavian countries, Germany, and France. They created societies in which wealth was – at least partially – redistributed among all their citizens.

May Day poster
This Italian Workers' Party poster is advertising a rally on *Primo Maggio*, which means "first of May". Many countries celebrate May Day in honour of the achievements of workers' movements.

Membership card
The holder of this card was a member of *Parti Ouvrier Français*, or the French Workers' Party. It was founded in 1882, as a result of a split within France's first socialist party, the *Fédération des Travailleurs Socialistes de France* (Federation of French Socialist Workers).

The Romantic Movement

The art movement known as Romanticism revolutionized art and philosophy in the late 18th century and the period that followed. Elevating the importance of self-expression, intuition, emotion, and the imagination over reason, Romanticism saw the beginning of the distinction between art and science.

BEFORE

Before Romanticism, Enlightenment thinkers sought answers to profound questions in science and reason. Romanticism challenged this.

CLASSICISM

The Classical art movement of the Renaissance **《 190–93** imitated that of the ancient Greeks and Romans **《 70–71**, which was characterized by **precision, elegance, and simplicity**. Classicists followed the formal rules of art set down by ancient cultures.

THE ENLIGHTENMENT

The Enlightenment **《 210–11** spread a spirit of enquiry across Europe and its colonies during the 18th century. **Valuing reason, science, and progress**, its ethos was summmarized by the English poet **Alexander Pope**: "Nature, and Nature's laws lay hid in night: God said, Let Newton be! and all was light". Inspired by **Isaac Newton's 《 207** scientific enquiry into the world, Enlightenment thinkers had a thirst for knowledge that coincided with **a period of great scientific discovery and exploration**.

CHALLENGING IDEAS

French philosopher **René Descartes** advocated **doubting everything** until rational grounds had been established for believing it, which led enlightened thinkers to **challenge previously accepted truths**. Among them were Scottish economist **Adam Smith** (left), whose *Inquiry into the Nature and Causes of the Wealth of Nations* revolutionized economics and social thinking, and the French philosopher **Jean-Jacques Rousseau**, whose works were an inspiration for the French Revolution **《 236–37**.

ADAM SMITH

THE ROLE OF ART

Until Romanticism the word "art" was synonymous with "craftsmanship", and the word "artist" was used interchangeably with "artisan". Craftsworker-painters were connected to the courtly, religious, and corporate institutions in society, and the nature of their art was guided by the patron, who funded and commissioned the work, rather than the artists themselves.

"The Little Girl Lost"
This illustrated poem is part of *Songs of Experience*, a poetic collection written and illustrated by the English Romantic poet and engraver William Blake. Its celebration of emotion and imagination is typical of Romantic poetry.

R omanticism emerged as a reaction to the 18th-century Enlightenment ideals of rational thought and order (see BEFORE). It was the French philosopher Jean-Jacques Rousseau (see p.210) who first voiced the need for a counterpoint to the "Age of Reason". He was concerned that emotion and imagination were being overwhelmed by the importance placed on rational thought. Romanticism found its first expression not in France but among German writers, as a form of "cultural nationalism" (see p.256); the ideals of

Romanticism gave Germans a sense of national unity at a time when "Germany" was little more than a fragmented group of states. Led by Johann Wolfgang von Goethe (see below) with his novel *The Sorrows of Young Werther*, German writers and poets advocated *sturm und drang* ("storm and stress"), flouting convention by rebelling against their rational educations and emphasizing emotion in their work.

The German pioneers also established other motifs that would become characteristic of the movement. These included a respect for traditional folk art and customs, a sense of wonder at the marvels of nature, and an enthusiasm for ancient mystical and pagan beliefs. Above all, emotion was considered

> ## "**Romanticism** is… neither in choice of subject nor exact truth, but in a way of **feeling**."
> CHARLES BAUDELAIRE, FRENCH POET, "THE SALON OF 1846", 1846

superior to reason. This led to the cult of the artist as hero, capable of expressing thoughts and feelings beyond the realms of ordinary people.

Art for art's sake

The Romantic ideal was that art should be a form of self-expression rather than a commodity, and that artists should not be treated as hired hands. Painters began to distance themselves from their craft-based heritage and increasingly art became an imaginative product rather than merely a possession of the artist's patron. This reinforced the Romantic idea of the artist as a gifted individual, intrinsically different from "ordinary" people – a status indulged to its fullest by the English poet Lord Byron, and the German composers Ludwig van Beethoven and Richard Wagner.

Many painters abandoned the strict rules of classicism and instead brought personal significance to their work. Epitomized by the work of William

GERMAN WRITER AND THINKER (1749–1832)

JOHANN WOLFGANG VON GOETHE

Goethe was a major inspiration for the Romantic movement, of which he eventually came to disapprove. In 1773 he wrote the archetypal Romantic drama *Götz von Berlichingen*, about a young genius rebelling against the conventions of society. He went on to create more misunderstood heroes, but Goethe's masterpiece was the classically-influenced *Faust*, a reworking of the tale of a disillusioned scholar who sells his soul to Satan.

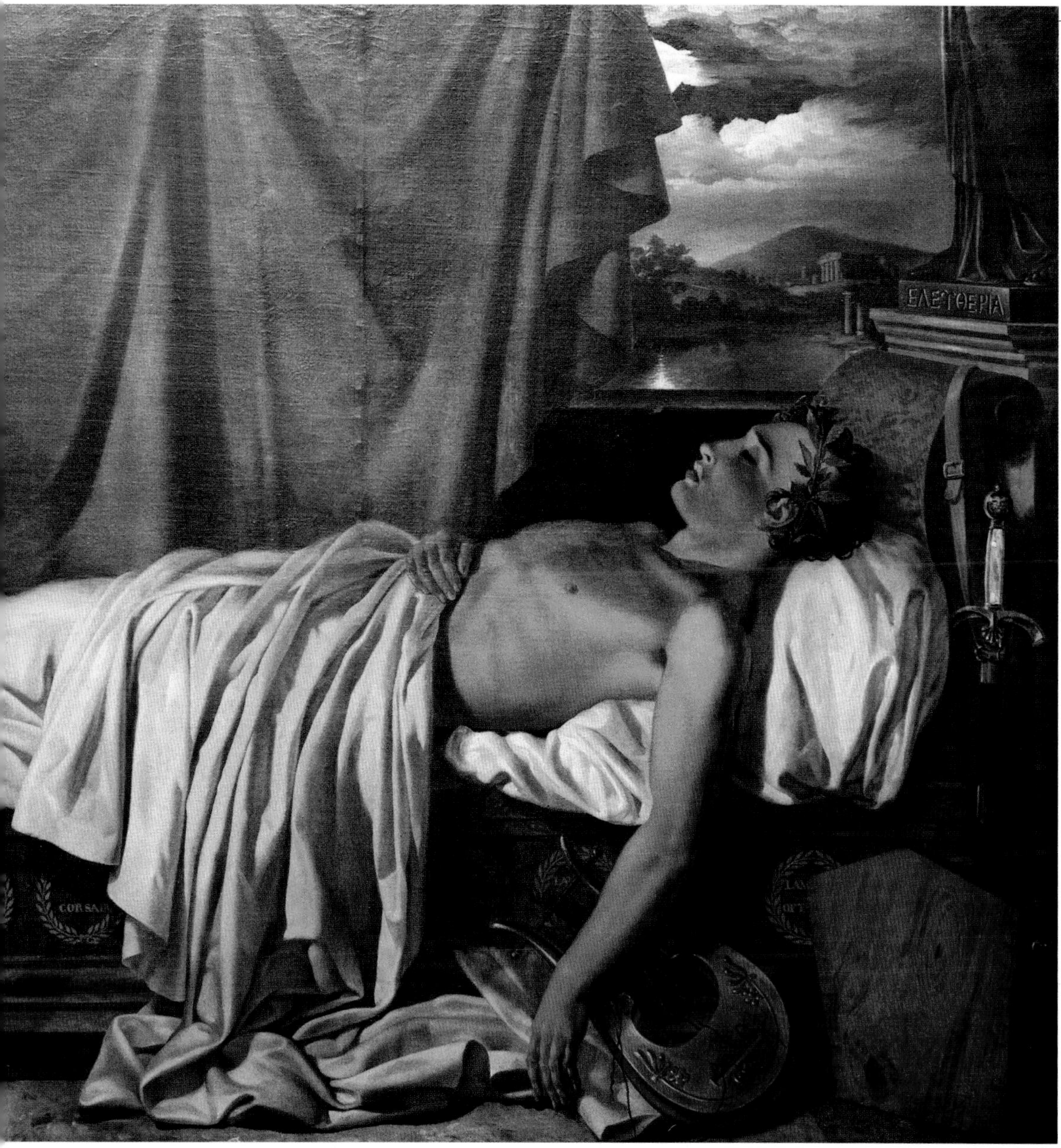

Gothic revival
Romanticism celebrated the medieval Gothic style in art, literature, and architecture. Above is Keble College, Oxford, England, controversial for its use of Gothic-style red brick rather than traditional stone.

"universal nightmare" for all other composers, because no one would ever be capable of bettering it.

The cult of the individual

Romanticism fundamentally changed the way society views art and the artist, reintroducing the classical idea that the creative act sets the artist apart. This contributed to a separation of arts and sciences and to the notion of the *avant garde* – of artists ahead of their time, pioneering new ways of thinking. Part of this was the cult of the individual, encapsulated in William Blake's comment: "I must create a system or be enslaved by another man's; I will not reason or compare: my business is to create".

The Death of Byron
Lord Byron is depicted lying on his deathbed by the Flemish Romantic painter Joseph-Denis Odevaere. Byron, who tried to help liberate Greece from Ottoman rule, is presented as a classical Greek hero.

Blake and JMW Turner in England, Théodore Géricault and Eugene Delacroix in France, and Caspar David Friedrich in Germany, Romantic painters explored the subjects of nature, individual consciousness, and the cultural history of their nations. Similarly, poets explored themes of childhood, subjective experience, and the mysteries of the natural world,

often using traditional poetic forms. Lord Byron became the embodiment of the Romantic ideal. He presented himself as a restless hero, in perpetual search of a deeper understanding through his work.

Perhaps the best expression of Romanticism is found in classical music. From the powerful symphonies of Ludwig van Beethoven, the Romantic songs of the Austrian Franz Schubert, and the epic operas of Richard Wagner, 19th-century composers produced many masterpieces that are still popular today. On hearing Beethoven's Ninth Symphony, the French composer Claude Debussy declared that it was a

Art song
This is Franz Schubert's 1814 handwritten score of *Gretchen am Spinnrade*, a selection of text from Goethe's *Faust*. It is a typical example of a *lied*, or "art song" – a musical rendering of a literary text.

AFTER

Artistic movements continued to spring from reactions to what was going on in society, as well as influencing social change themselves.

PRE-RAPHAELITES
In 1848 a growing reaction against materialism and industrialization in Britain contributed to the foundation of the Pre-Raphaelite Brotherhood by British artists **John Everett Millais, Dante Gabriel Rossetti,** and **William Holman Hunt**. They sought refuge in **legendary worlds** and yearned for a return to the spirituality of the medieval period and Renaissance **‹‹ 190–93**. They had links to the literary world, and Rossetti and his sister Christina were both notable poets.

REALISM
As art became more of a commodity for the middle classes to acquire, its subject matter became tied to their values. Realism was a reaction against idealization in art and a rejection of literary or exotic subjects. French painter **Gustave Courbet** embodied its ideals, believing that an artist should only paint **scenes of everyday life**.

NATIONALISM
The German Romanticism that valued the folk tales and legends of German literature and music became corrupted into an extreme form of nationalism **258–59 ››**.

"PROSERPINE" BY ROSSETTI

« BEFORE

In Judaeo-Christian cultures, the Biblical story of the Creation was so fundamental to the way people viewed the world that challenges to it were almost unthinkable.

ADAM AND EVE

CREATIONISM

Creationism is the belief that the universe and everything in it was created by a god. Jewish and Christian creationists believe that the world was created exactly as stated in the Bible. Based on a **literal reading** of this, the Church believed that the **world was created between 6000 and 4000BCE**, and that the Earth and its species of plants and animals, including humans, are unchanging. The young Charles Darwin was influenced by theologians such as **William Paley**, who argued that the natural world was too complex not to have had a creator.

CHALLENGES TO CREATIONISM

In 1785 Scottish geologist **James Hutton** proposed that the Earth is being **continuously reshaped by steady change**, not by Biblical events such as the Creation and the Flood. This "steady state" view was later added to by British geologist Sir Charles Lyell, in his *Principles of Geology* (1830). Other challenges came from Darwin's grandfather, **Erasmus Darwin**, who in 1794 noted a **progressional change** in animals. French naturalist **Jean-Baptiste de Lamarck** also proposed a **theory of progressive development** in his *Philosophie Zoologique* published in 1809.

Scientific specimens
Darwin collected these specimens – two fish and an eel – during his five years on HMS *Beagle*, between 1831–36.

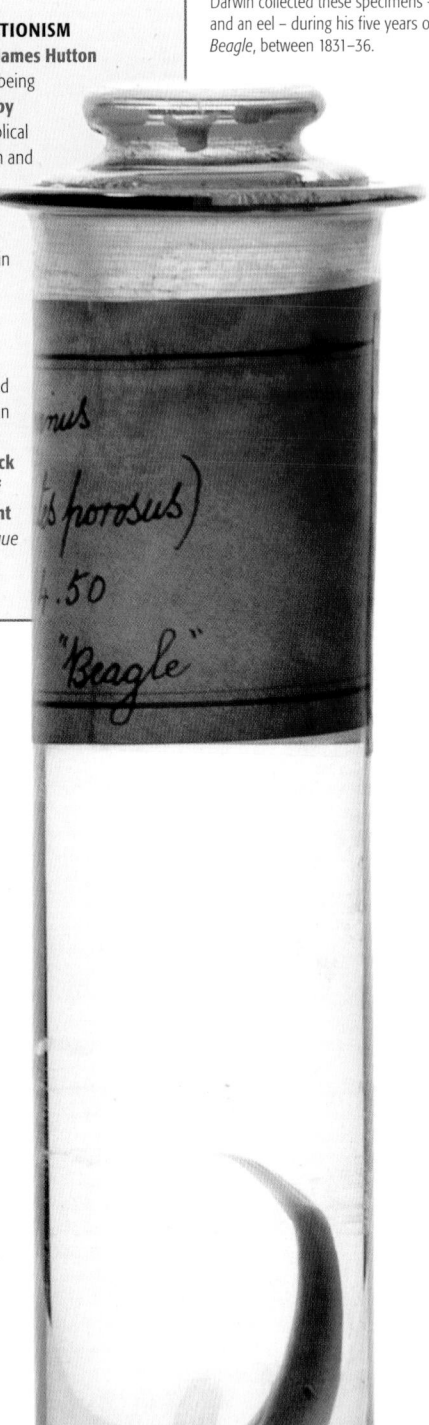

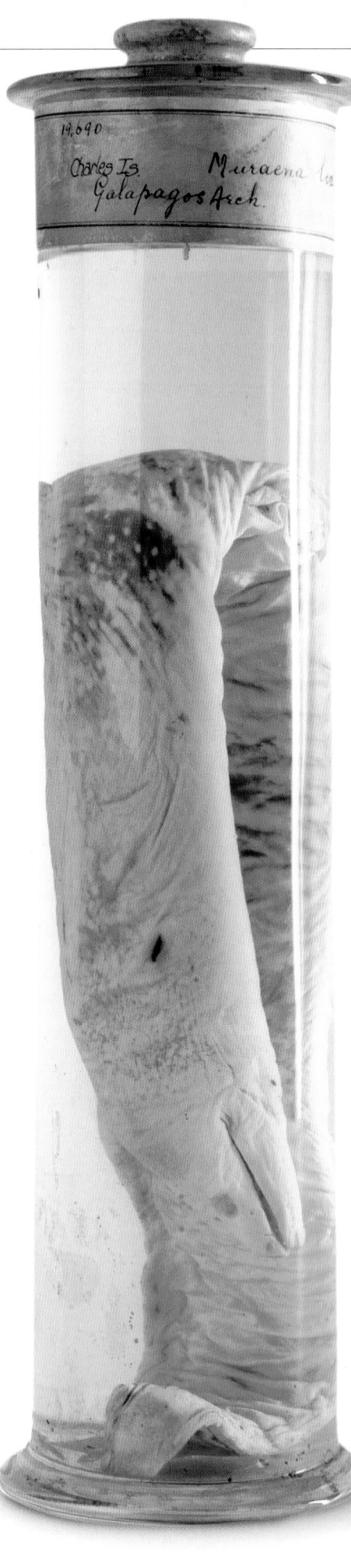

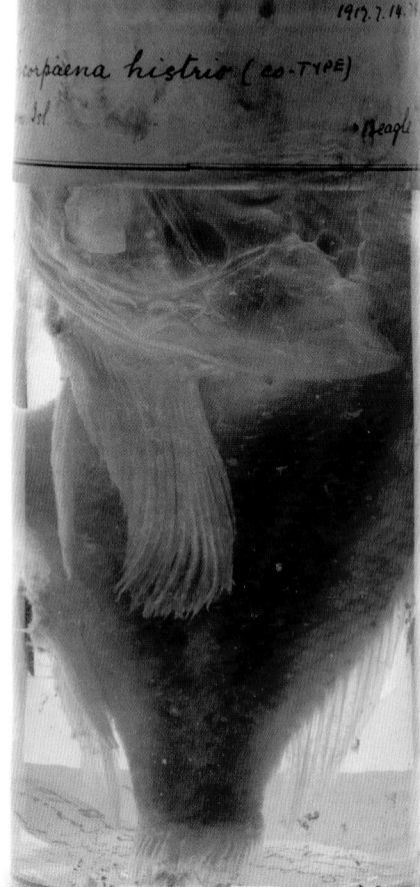

"Man with all his noble qualities… still bears in his bodily frame **the indelible stamp of his lowly origin.**"

CHARLES DARWIN, FROM "THE DESCENT OF MAN", 1871

Origin of Species

The theory of evolution is often called "Darwinism", after the British naturalist, Charles Darwin. In 1859 Darwin published the results of his research in the first evolutionary theory based on scientific evidence. His controversial work known as *On the Origin of Species* changed our view of the world.

BRITISH NATURALIST (1809–82)

CHARLES DARWIN

Charles Darwin showed little application at school, causing his father to comment: "you will be a disgrace to yourself and your family". Darwin studied medicine and law, but dropped out of both, before finally completing a degree in Divinity and later embarking upon a career as a naturalist on HMS *Beagle*'s scientific expedition around the coast of South America. After the voyage he gained wide respect for the papers he published describing his findings and then, plagued by illness, he painstakingly prepared the publication that was to change the course of scientific history. Darwin was respected by his scientific peers, including the biologist TH Huxley. Upon his death, Darwin was buried in London's Westminster Abbey alongside the physicist Isaac Newton.

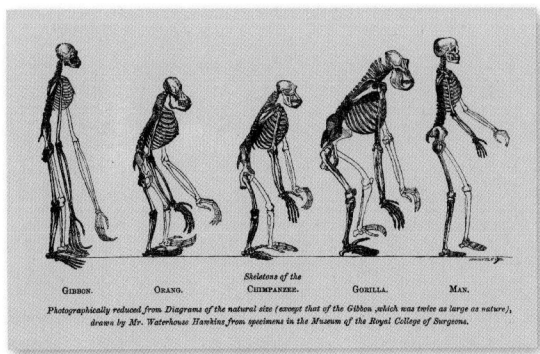

Evolving forms
TH Huxley (see pp.342–43) was the foremost exponent of Darwin's theories. This frontispiece to his *Evidence as to Man's Place in Nature*, 1863, reveals the similarities in the skeletons of (from left to right) a gibbon, orang-utan, chimpanzee, gorilla, and human.

Although the uproar caused by *On the Origin of Species by Means of Natural Selection* might suggest otherwise, the idea that humankind and animals had evolved from more primitive creatures was nothing new, even in Darwin's day. The first theory that all living creatures are descended from shellfish was proposed as early as the 6th century BCE. Some 2,500 years later, in 1844, Scottish encyclopedist Robert Chambers scandalized Victorian society by anonymously publishing *Vestiges of the Natural History of Creation*. Chambers argued that fossil evidence suggested that animal species had changed over time, contradicting the Biblical notion that they had been unchanged since their creation by God. Chambers' ideas were unscientific and unsubstantiated, but the very idea of evolution was enough to ensure that the book sold in huge numbers.

Natural selection

From 1831–36 Darwin travelled as a naturalist aboard HMS *Beagle*, on a scientific survey of South American waters. During the voyage he found evidence to support the geologist Charles Lyell's idea that the world had evolved through gradual processes (see BEFORE), but it was not until several years later that Darwin began to forge his own theory. In the meantime he read Thomas Malthus's 1798 "Essay on the Principle of Population" (see p.225), which argued that the size of an animal population is limited by its food supply. When Darwin's friend, the ornithologist John Gould, realized that the species of finches that Darwin had brought back from his voyage shared common ancestors, Darwin wondered why. He concluded that those animals most suited to acquiring food would survive and pass on their characteristics to their offspring, while the unsuited would die out – a concept which Darwin called "natural selection", but which British philosopher Herbert Spencer later called "the survival of the fittest".

Darwin began to work on what he called his theory of "transmutation" in 1842. By 1844 he had written 230 pages, but set it aside, partly because of ill health, but also because he was troubled by his conclusions. Darwin finally published when it emerged that zoogeographer Alfred Wallace was working on a similar theory. Charles Lyell persuaded Darwin to submit a paper to London's Linnean Society (a biological society), which was read on 1 July 1858, the same night as Wallace's essay. Darwin's *On the Origin of Species* was published in 1859.

> **5,500** **The number of biological and anatomical specimens Charles Darwin collected during the voyage of the *Beagle*, the details of which were put in 12 catalogues.**

The Descent of Man

The novel element in Darwin's theory was natural selection. His version, that individuals compete with each other for resources, differed from Wallace's idea that they competed against the environment. Humanity's descent from the apes was a minor part of *On the Origin of Species*, but his 1871 book, *The Descent of Man*, argued that it was walking on two legs that led humankind to evolve differently. This was controversial, gaining both support and criticism from scientific and religious figures. Zoologist Ernst Mayr (1904–2005) said that it "demanded the rejection of some of the most widely held and most cherished beliefs of western man" (see pp.272–73).

Darwin's finches
Darwin's illustrations of some of the species of finch he discovered in the Galapagos Islands. The realization that the separate species were all derived from common ancestors influenced Darwin's theory of natural selection.

AFTER ≫

> Although Darwin's theory has been highly influential, and is widely taught, debate over the origin of life on Earth continues.

EVOLUTIONARY SYNTHESIS

As Darwin completed his book, Austrian botanist **Gregor Mendel** was researching **heredity in plants**. In the 20th century, after years of neglect, Mendel's work led to the new science of **genetics**, which explains how the mutations necessary for natural selection occur and are passed on. Scientists have since formed Darwin and Mendel's work into the modern theory of "**neodarwinism**".

INTELLIGENT DESIGN

Many people still doubt that complex living things such as human beings could have been created by entirely natural processes. They prefer an alternative theory of "intelligent design". In this theory, God created a universe that would run itself: one analogy is of God as **cosmic watchmaker.** Popular in the 19th century, the idea was revived in the late 20th century.

BEFORE

Before the 17th century, religion was practically unchallenged as a framework for understanding the world, but the scientific revolution offered alternative explanations for our existence.

GALILEO AND THE INQUISITION

In 1632, Italian scientist Galileo Galilei asserted his belief that the Earth revolved around the Sun – a theory first put forward a century earlier – in his book *Dialogues on the Two Chief World Systems*. The Catholic Church banned it and the Inquisition (a religious tribunal) **<< 142** forced

GALILEO FACES THE INQUISITION

Galileo (above) to denounce his own work as heretical. He was placed under house arrest but during his confinement he wrote *Discourses Upon Two New Sciences*, which later inspired Isaac Newton **<< 209** to scientific discoveries that further challenged Biblical doctrine.

SOCIETIES AND ACADEMIES

During the 17th century the emergence of **scientific societies** such as the Royal Society in Britain and the Académie des Sciences in France provided forums for debate and encouraged the **formalization of the scientific method**. The societies also gave science respectability, though it continued to face opposition from the Church.

NEWTON'S GOD

Isaac Newton's scientific discoveries were criticized because it was thought that they had **demystified the world,** but Newton was

MECHANICAL MODEL OF THE SOLAR SYSTEM

devoutly religious: he did not present **science as an alternative to God**, and nothing in his work intentionally excluded God from the universe he described. Newton believed that God was the force behind the natural systems his science had sought to explain, with the Universe as a clockwork machine (above) created by God.

THE ENLIGHTENMENT

Newton's discoveries caused a **revolution in physics** and inspired a new intellectual and philosophical movement known as the Enlightenment **<< 210–11**, whose thinkers based their work on **reason and evidence**, rather than superstition and accepted beliefs.

> "Was it through his grandfather or his grandmother that he claimed his **descent from a monkey**?"

BISHOP WILBERFORCE, ADDRESSING THOMAS HUXLEY AT A MEETING OF THE BRITISH ASSOCIATION FOR THE ADVANCEMENT OF SCIENCE, 1860

On 30 June 1860 science clashed with religion on a stage at Oxford University's Museum Library. Weighing in on one side of the debate were Bishop Samuel Wilberforce and the Anglican Church; on the other was English biologist TH Huxley, armed with a copy of *On the Origin of Species*, published by Charles Darwin, the British naturalist, the year before (see p.271). Darwin's book, which advanced the theory that all creatures had evolved through natural selection, critically undermined the literal interpretation of the Bible, which held that God created the world, including humans, during a period of six days around 6,000 years ago. But religion was more than ready to defend

Heated debate
Cartoons from the magazine *Vanity Fair* show Bishop Samuel Wilberforce (left) and TH Huxley. Their debate became known as "the moment that science clashed with religion".

Science v. God

In 1859 Charles Darwin published *On The Origin of Species by Means of Natural Selection*, in which the naturalist put forward his theory of evolution. This sparked a public debate over the roles of religion and science in providing the means by which humans understood the world around them.

its position. Bishop Wilberforce attacked Huxley over a perceived lack of evidence, while Huxley quipped that he would rather be descended from a monkey than a bishop.

Hard evidence

This challenge to previously accepted ideas was not a deliberate attack on religion by science, but came simply from the fact that discoveries were being made that were at odds with Christian doctrine. As a Christian himself, Darwin found the situation very difficult and was reluctant to publish his theory for fear of the public's reaction, ruefully referring to himself as "the Devil's Chaplain". Philosophers had been challenging the literal interpretation of the Bible since the Enlightenment (see pp.210–11), but in the late 18th and early 19th

centuries scientific evidence added a new dimension to the debate. From 1785 to 1835 four scientists – James Hutton, Georges Cuvier, William Smith, and Sir Charles Lyell – provided

The Creation of Adam
Michelangelo's depiction of God creating Man adorns the ceiling of the Sistine Chapel in Rome. It is part of a series of panels depicting stories from the book of Genesis, the first book of the Bible.

metaphorical, with the six days of creation being interpreted as epochs, or geological time periods. The idea that humans themselves were descended from apes – derided as the "monkey theory" – was much harder to accept. Some found a way to reconcile the information with their religious beliefs. The novelist and theologian Charles Kingsley wrote: "I have gradually learnt to see that it is just as noble a conception of the Deity to believe that He created primal forms capable of self-development as to believe that He required a fresh intervention to fill the [voids] which He himself had made."

THE PERIODIC TABLE

In 1869 Dmitri Mendeleev, a Russian chemist, wrote the name of each chemical element on a card with its chemical properties and atomic weight. Having noticed repeating (or "periodic") patterns in them, he arranged the cards in a grid according to property (by row) and weight (by column) — the modern Periodic Table has reversed this system. His grid also allowed him to predict the existence and properties of unknown elements, which were not discovered until later.

"Irrationally held truths
may be more harmful than
reasoned errors."

T H HUXLEY, "THE COMING OF AGE OF 'THE ORIGIN OF SPECIES'", 1880

The march of science

During the 19th century, the elevation of science from a hobby of the eccentric to a respected and even admired discipline was marked by the use of a new word: its practitioners became known as "scientists", where previously they had been called "natural philosophers".

Science gained credibility alongside religion, rather than instead of it, and Christianity proved resilient to change. The reduction of the Church's influence by the state following the French Revolution in 1789 (see pp.236–37) resulted in greater religious freedom throughout Europe, with a move away from state religions towards more numerous denominations. Competition between them resulted in the strengthening of religious loyalties, while a rise in atheism in urban areas

led to increased church building in many European cities.

Scientific progress continued, with people experiencing its effects through technology and medical advances. Governments began to address the need for scientific education: research-based university departments were established, as were scientific and technical institutions. As scientific knowledge filtered through society it became more accessible. Despite the fears of the Church, society was not faced with a stark choice between science or God. Instead, these advances led in many cases to the acceptance of both science and belief.

rock and fossil evidence that suggested the Earth was much older than had been thought, casting doubt on Biblical chronology and the story of creation, though 19th-century geology was not sufficiently developed to make accurate estimates of the Earth's age

The Church was able to cope with these new theories relatively easily. Many Christians were willing to consider Biblical chronology as

Geological evidence
The discovery of fossilized ancient creatures such as these ammonites (prehistoric molluscs) seriously undermined the teachings of the Bible regarding the age of the Earth and the way it was created.

AFTER »

Science has continued its attempts to explain the universe, while the isssue of Creationism still causes debate today.

"Science without religion is **lame**, religion without science is **blind**."

ALBERT EINSTEIN, PAPER FOR CONFERENCE ON SCIENCE, 1940

BIG BANG

In 1927 Georges Lemaître, a Belgian scientist and Catholic priest, proposed that the universe was created by the explosion of a "quantum singularity", or "big bang" – a state of nothingness, existing outside space and time, containing the potential for everything there is, has been, or will be.

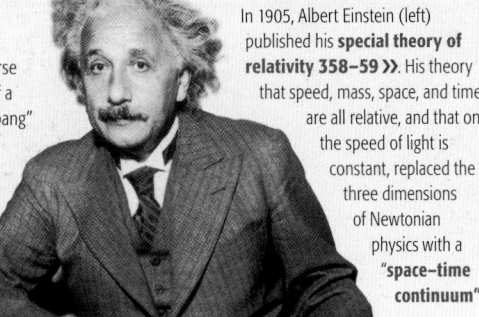

ALBERT EINSTEIN

EINSTEIN'S THEORY

In 1905, Albert Einstein (left) published his **special theory of relativity 358–59 »**. His theory that speed, mass, space, and time are all relative, and that only the speed of light is constant, replaced the three dimensions of Newtonian physics with a "**space-time continuum**".

CREATIONISM The belief that the universe was created by a god, rather than being formed by a process of evolution.

CREATIONISM

In mainstream Western thinking scientific theories have largely replaced Creationism. However, there is still a vociferous creationist minority, and in modern usage Creationism usually refers to Christian fundamentalists who oppose the teaching of scientific theories such as evolution and the Big Bang.

BEFORE

From the advances of the 17th century, scientific progress gathered momentum, leading to many 19th-century innovations.

SCIENTIFIC REVOLUTION
During the 17th century drastic changes took place as European science was revolutionized by the ideas of people like Galileo Galilei and Isaac Newton **‹‹ 208–09**. By the late 17th century **dramatic advances** had been made in mathematics, astronomy, and biology.

INDUSTRIAL REVOLUTION
In the late 18th century Western Europe began to industrialize rapidly **‹‹ 226–29**. Coal was used to power steam engines that drained mines and eventually drove machinery.

ADA LOVELACE

MECHANICAL CALCULATION
In the 1840s **Charles Babbage**, an English mathematician, worked on the development of an **Analytical Engine** which, had it been completed, would have been capable of performing calculations similar to the early computers of the 1940s. **Ada Lovelace**, a woman fascinated by mathematics, saw the possibilities of the machine. In 1843 she published the **first known computer program.**

Ingenious Inventions

The four essentials of technological advances are the right idea, the method to execute it, the perfect moment in time, and the availability of the right materials. The 19th century saw these elements merge in an explosion of technology, which introduced mass production and fed mass consumption.

The Industrial Revolution (see pp.226–27) had brought with it an increase in population and urbanization as well as an emerging "middle class", which profited from industrial growth. Factories were filled with a labour force as agricultural manual work gave way to mechanization. Manufacturing produced cheaper goods for a mass market, encouraged by the rise in wages and standards of living. The traditional work place, and the home, was being rapidly transformed.

Few men had a greater impact on life in the 19th century than Michael Faraday. Faraday discovered that an electric current was produced in a coil of wire when a magnet was moved through the coil.

His experiments with electricity in the 1830s led to dramatic developments in the sphere of communications. In 1837, British scientists William Cook and Charles Wheatstone patented the electric telegraph, a method of sending messages through wires to a remote receiver. Telegraphy expanded across the world. By 1876 the inventor Alexander Graham Bell, a Briton living in America who had spent much of his professional career working with the deaf, developed the telephone. This innovation went on to eclipse the telegraph.

Another electrical discovery in 1887 further revolutionized communications, when a German scientist called Heinrich Hertz proved the existence of radio waves. An Italian entrepreneur, Guglielmo Marconi, was convinced that Hertz's work could lead to messages being sent over long distances without the use of cables and was soon transmitting "wireless" signals. In 1906 Marconi achieved his final goal by transmitting speech over the airwaves using radio transmissions.

Other inventions were rapidly changing the world. By the turn of the 20th century wars were being fought with more advanced weapons, food was preserved in new tin cans (see pp.224–25), and domestic refrigeration was evolving. Cars emerged on the roads, shipbuilding was prolific, railways spun their way across continents, and the first plane was about to take off. In the US Wilbur and Orville Wright progressed by way of gliders to a fabric-covered wooden biplane. On 17 December 1903 they made a flight in the world's first powered plane; by the early 1930s the modern airplane was beginning to take shape (see pp.382–85). Domestic life was being slowly transformed by sewing machines, washing machines, electric cookers, electric heaters, and vacuum cleaners. Families had clearly defined "leisure time". They listened to gramophones, which played flat discs, and, in March 1895, people thrilled to the sight of flickering pictures when a film of workers leaving the Lumière factory during their lunch hour was shown. The cinema was born.

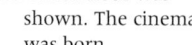

Gatling gun
Richard Gatling's mechanical gun of the 1860s consisted of six barrels mounted in a revolving frame. It was easy to use, reliable, and effective.

Can-opener
While early tin cans were opened with a hammer and chisel, lighter steel cans made the can-opener possible. "Bull's head" pierce-and-prise openers, like this one, appeared in the 1860s.

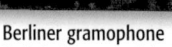

Berliner gramophone
Emile Berliner created the forerunner of modern records and record players. This 1890s model plays grooved flat discs, which were cheaply produced.

Tin can
A discovery in 1810 that food could be preserved by heating it and sealing it in jars led to two British men, Bryan Donkin and John Hall, developing tin cans.

Bell "Box" telephone
Alexander Graham Bell had transmitted speech along a wire by 1876. This early Bell telephone has a combined trumpet-like mouthpiece and earpiece.

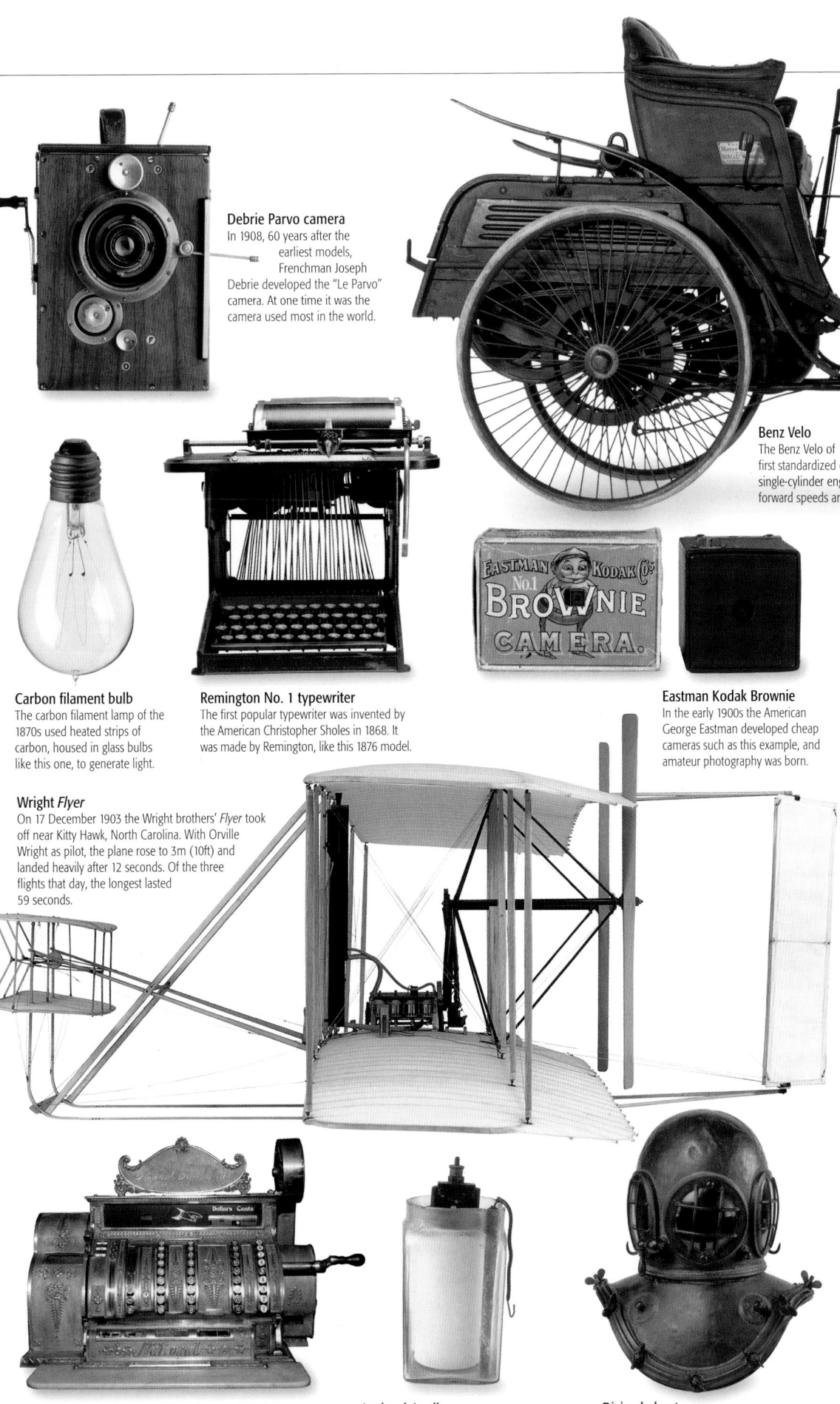

Debrie Parvo camera
In 1908, 60 years after the earliest models, Frenchman Joseph Debrie developed the "Le Parvo" camera. At one time it was the camera used most in the world.

Benz Velo
The Benz Velo of 1895 was the world's first standardized car. Powered by a single-cylinder engine, there were two forward speeds and no reverse gear.

Carbon filament bulb
The carbon filament lamp of the 1870s used heated strips of carbon, housed in glass bulbs like this one, to generate light.

Remington No. 1 typewriter
The first popular typewriter was invented by the American Christopher Sholes in 1868. It was made by Remington, like this 1876 model.

Eastman Kodak Brownie
In the early 1900s the American George Eastman developed cheap cameras such as this example, and amateur photography was born.

Wright *Flyer*
On 17 December 1903 the Wright brothers' *Flyer* took off near Kitty Hawk, North Carolina. With Orville Wright as pilot, the plane rose to 3m (10ft) and landed heavily after 12 seconds. Of the three flights that day, the longest lasted 59 seconds.

AMERICAN INVENTOR (1847–1931)
THOMAS EDISON

Edison was a self-taught inventor. At the age of seven he set up his first chemistry laboratory at home. Attending school for only three months, from the age of 12 he began devoting all of his spare time to scientific experimentation. Edison's large-scale research laboratories were the first of their kind in the world, issuing 1,093 devices patented in his name, including an improved telephone, a successful electric lamp, and the first cinema projector.

Cash register
The American James Ritty invented the cash register in 1879 to stop theft by cashiers. The keys operated gears that added together the money paid in.

Leclanché cell
This late 19th-century Leclanché cell is an early example of a battery. Most batteries today are Leclanché cells encased in metal.

Diving helmet
This helmet is part of a watertight diving suit from 1839, which allowed the diver to operate in depths of up to 100m (328ft).

AFTER »

Science continued to progress in the 20th century, making technology accessible, and breaking down barriers to communication.

THE DAWN OF TELEVISION
In 1926 the Scottish engineer John Logie Baird **transmitted pictures and words** using radio waves **382–85** ».

PLASTICS
Domestic products were increasingly made of plastic **460–63** ». The **first versatile domestic plastic** was Bakelite, invented in 1909.

COMPUTER REVOLUTION
The first electronic computers were developed in secret in Britain and the United States during World War II. The **miniaturization** of computers by the use of silicon chips in the 1960s changed communication and industry **406–09** ».

◀◀ **BEFORE**

Growing populations in Europe in the 16th–17th centuries led to the search for new lands.

CONQUISTADORS

The Americas were the greatest attraction for European settlers. Within 50 years of its discovery in 1492 ◀◀ **168–69**, Spanish Conquistadors (conquerors) had occupied more than 2.6 million km² (1 million square miles) of the new continent and named it "New Spain" ◀◀ **170–71**.

EXPLORERS OF AFRICA

In 1652 the Dutch founded a **settlement** at Cape Town, southern Africa, to provision their ships. Mungo Park, a Scot, then **explored** the Niger Valley in 1796–1805. Others, such as David Livingstone, soon followed ◀◀ **250–51**.

PIONEERS IN NORTH AMERICA

Spain founded a colony in Florida in 1565, but after their defeat by Britain in 1586 ◀◀ **200–01**, Britain became the **dominant power**. By the end of the 18th century the British had driven the Dutch and the Swedes from North America, and the French from Canada ◀◀ **230–31**. Migration to America gathered pace after the American War of Independence ◀◀ **232–33**.

The world in 1900
European influence stretched across the world. Britain, Russia, and France were the pre-eminent powers, but Portugal, Germany, and Denmark all controlled parts of Africa, Southeast Asia, and South America.

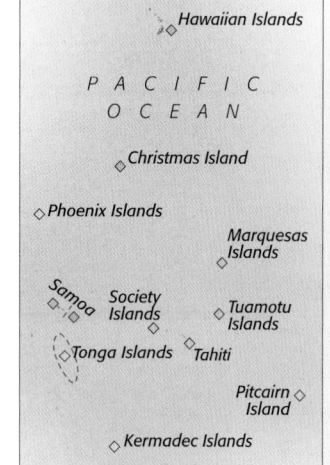

KEY

■ Ottoman Empire	■◇ Netherlands and possessions
■◇● Britain and possessions	■◇● German Empire and possessions
■◇● France and possessions	■○ Russian Empire and possessions
■◇ Denmark and possessions	■ Japan and possessions
■◇● Spain and possessions	■ Italy and possessions
■◇● Portugal and possessions	■◇ US and possessions

The Imperial World

In the space of 400 years Europeans transported the civilization of their continent into every corner of the world. Imperialism – empire building – expanded so rapidly that by 1900 extensive areas of the inhabited world were governed by Europeans.

M any factors drove imperial expansion. The newly discovered continents of the world offered huge wealth, for example, but once this was realized, traders preferred to do business under their own administration. When Britain seized South Africa it was because they wanted to deal with the British, rather than native Africans or the Dutch Afrikaner settlers, called Boers.

These new worlds provided exotic luxuries, such as spice from the Indies, tobacco and silks, and with the onset of the Industrial Revolution (see pp.228–29), a steady supply of raw materials such as cotton. It also became apparent that they were an abundant source of cheap labour.

Another factor in imperial growth was the political rivalries of the major European powers. French imperial ambitions were designed to restore France's reputation after the crushing defeat in the Franco–Prussian War (see pp.240–41). For Germany, the colonies

were a symbol of prestige. In some cases, colonization was simply a matter of claiming a nation before another power could get there. This was particularly so in the "Scramble for Africa" (see pp.290–91).

There were also strong ideological motives. Many felt it their duty to spread Christianity, believing it was, in the poet Rudyard Kipling's words, the "white man's burden" to "civilize" the native population.

European success

Europeans had the men, money, ships, and guns to succeed in their ambitions, and military superiority helped invading nations to subdue local resistance.

The colonial nations found Australasia and North America sparsely inhabited. But elsewhere, such as India, they

discovered populous nations with sophisticated systems of government already in place. This necessitated a different approach to colonization. Communities of merchants were established, with garrisons to protect them, and only rarely did the colonists take formal control. In India, British control of the country (see pp.282–83) by the British East India Company only occurred after a long period of trading.

Empire and migration

New lands beckoned European settlers. Population pressure at home, combined with improved overseas transport,

19th century spice box
Throughout history the country that has controlled the spice trade has been the richest. In the 19th century Britain's maritime prowess established it as the leading colonial power.

led to large-scale migration. In the 19th century, as the frontier of the USA moved west (see pp.242–43), millions arrived from across the Atlantic Ocean. The miseries of the Industrial Revolution led many to emigrate. In Victoria, Australia, the discovery of gold in the 1850s triggered a rise in the population from 76,000 to 540,000 in just ten years. Colonists exported their dress, language, and religions around the globe. Western hairstyles, fashion, and

RUSSIAN EMPIRE
Siberia

ICELAND
NORWAY
SWEDEN
FINLAND
○ St. Petersburg
○ Moscow

DENMARK
BRITAIN
NETH. GERMAN Berlin
○ London BELGIUM EMPIRE POLAND AUSTRO-HUNGARIAN
Paris Vienna EMPIRE
FRANCE SWITZ. Budapest
ROMANIA
SERBIA
PORTUGAL SPAIN BOSNIA- BULGARIA
HERZEGOVINA Rome ITALY ○ Istanbul
○ Lisbon ○ Madrid MONTENEGRO
GIBRALTAR GREECE ○ Athens CYPRUS
Ceuta Malta *British occupied*
Melilla

Gobi

QING
EMPIRE

KOREA JAPAN
○ Beijing ○ Port Arthur
○ Weihaiwei
○ Jiaozhou ○ Tokyo

Nanjing ○ Shanghai

MOROCCO
IFNI

ALGERIA
OTTOMAN EMPIRE
TUNIS
Sahara

Tehran
PERSIA
AFGHANISTAN
Himalayas
NEPAL BHUTAN

Delhi
KUWAIT
BAHRAIN
Gwadar
to Oman
TRUCIAL
OMAN
INDIA
Chandernagore

PACIFIC
OCEAN

Taiwan
Hong Kong
Macao
Guangzhouwan

Cairo
EGYPT
Ottoman
dominions
under
British control

Beduins

*Arabian
Peninsula*

BURMA

DE ORO
FRENCH
WEST AFRICA
*France in terms of 1899
Franco-British agreement.
French control in part notional*

ANGLO-
EGYPTIAN
SUDAN

ERITREA

HADHRAMAUT

Diu
Damão
Bombay

SIAM

Manila

Goa
Madras
Pondicherry
Karikal

Aden
Socotra

FRENCH
INDO-CHINA
Saigon

PHILIPPINE
ISLANDS

Bangkok

PORTUGUESE
GUINEA
Sahel
NIGERIA

FRENCH SOMALILAND
Addis
Ababa
ABYSSINIA
BRITISH
SOMALILAND
ITALIAN
SOMALILAND

Mahé

CEYLON

BRITISH
NORTH BORNEO
BRUNEI
MALAYA SARAWAK

RA LEONE
GOLD
COAST

LIBERIA

TOGO
Fernando
Po
SAO TOME
AND
PRINCIPE
RIO
MUNI

KAMERUN
FRENCH
CONGO

Maldive Islands

INDIAN OCEAN

SUMATRA

Singapore
BORNEO
DUTCH EAST INDIES
Batavia
JAVA

○ Ascension

CONGO
FREE STATE
*nominally
independent
under Belgian control*

GERMAN
EAST
AFRICA

Zanzibar

Seychelles

Amirante Islands

Chagos Islands

*Christmas
Island*

PORTUGUESE
TIMOR

○ St. Helena

ANGOLA
BAROTSELAND-
NORTHWESTERN
RHODESIA

NORTHEASTERN
RHODESIA

BRITISH
CENTRAL
AFRICA

Comoro Islands

Cocos Islands

AUSTRALIAN
COLONIES

GERMAN
SOUTHWEST
AFRICA
WALVIS BAY–
*to Cape
Colony*
BECHUANA-
LAND
SOUTHERN
RHODESIA
PORTUGUESE
EAST
AFRICA
MADAGASCAR

Mauritius

Réunion

Mariana
Islands
Marshall
Islands
Guam
Caroline
Islands
Gilbert
Islands
KAISER WILHELM'S
LAND
BISMARCK
ARCHIPELAGO
NEW
GUINEA
Solomon
Islands
Ellice
Islands
PAPUA
Santa Cruz
Islands
PACIFIC
OCEAN
New
Caledonia
Fiji

SOUTH AFRICAN
REPUBLIC
ORANGE FREE STATE
Orange Riv.
NATAL
CAPE
COLONY
BASUTOLAND
Cape Town ○

Lord Howe
Island
Sydney ○

NEW
ZEALAND

AFTER »

Deportation
By the mid-19th century the French government reduced prison costs by sending "undesirables" to their far off colonies. This woodcut depicts the deportation of prisoners from Toulon to Cayenne on the steamboat *Ceres*.

administration were all emulated, and Japan was able to modernize rapidly by adopting European ideas (see pp.286–87). However, despite being of European descent, the Boers of South Africa moved into the Natal, Orange Free State, and Transvaal regions of the country, so eager were they to escape British rule (see p.291). By 1900, much of the inhabited world was governed, directly or indirectly, by Europeans, or those of European descent.

After World War II, most colonies were granted, or won their independence. Today, only a few remnants of the great colonial powers survive.

THE END OF COLONIALISM
Portuguese possessions were some of the last colonies to become independent 334–35 ». In North and South America, and Australia, **European rule left a permanent stamp.** In China, it left scarcely a trace.

AFRICA
Africans increasingly gained independence after World War II 314–327 », but economic difficulties often caused **political instability** in the new nations. This often led to dictatorships – by 1976, 21 African countries had military governments.

AFRICAN IMMIGRATION TO EUROPE
Economic and political development failures in Africa, and new immigration and refugee policies in Europe, saw **mass migration** by African

peoples. Between 1960–89 an estimated 70,000–100,000 highly skilled African workers went to Europe, but they often faced discrimination.

INDIGENOUS PEOPLES
Indigenous peoples such as the forest people of the Amazon, the tribal people of India, and the Inuit of the Arctic **lost their land** during colonization. There is still a threat of territorial invasion, and the plundering of resources, in these places.

BRITISH QUEEN Born 1819 Died 1901

Queen Victoria

"We are not **interested** in the possibilities of **defeat**."

QUEEN VICTORIA, TO ARTHUR BALFOUR, M.P., 1899

Queen Victoria, the longest reigning monarch in British history, was the only child of the Duke of Kent, the fourth son of George III, and his German wife, Princess Victoria of Saxe-Coburg-Saalfield. Fair-haired and blue-eyed, she spent most of her childhood in the seclusion of London's Kensington Palace, and had little contact with her uncle, William IV. She was 11 when she found out her royal destiny, at which point she famously declared: "I will be good."

On the death of William IV in 1837, the 18-year-old Princess Victoria acceded to the throne. Until then, she had slept in her mother's room and one of her first decisions, on moving into Buckingham Palace, was to insist on a bedroom of her own. In political matters,

Victoria's first prime minister, the fatherly Lord Melbourne, was her early mentor, but within a couple of years he was replaced by the love of her life, Albert of Saxe-Coburg-Gotha.

A royal courtship

As one of Victoria's German cousins, Albert was considered an appropriate husband. He was just three months younger than Victoria – in fact the same midwife had assisted at both of their births – but he was mature for his age. He was an

A picture of royalty
A photographic portrait of the "great white queen". Photography, an invention of her reign, made Victoria an international icon, spreading her image around the world.

Prince Albert
Albert was married to Victoria for 21 years. After his death, Victoria reputedly made decisions based on what she thought he would have done.

The Victorian family
As a loving couple with a happy home life, the queen and her consort, seen here with some of their nine children, exemplified respectable "Victorian" family values.

intelligent, deeply serious young man, fluent in several languages and acutely conscious of his duties as the unofficial king of England. But it was his looks as much as his character, and his recommendation by Victoria's uncle, Leopold I of Belgium, that persuaded her to propose to this "perfect being". She was drawn to his appearance, adoring his "exquisite nose" and "beautiful figure", which she described as "broad in the shoulders".

Exhibiting the world
Victoria arrives for the opening of the Great Exhibition "of the works of industry of all nations" at the Crystal Palace in London's Hyde Park.

First Boer War
This jug, bearing Victoria's image, commemorates the First Boer War, 1880–81, in which Transvaal Boers resisted British efforts to annex South Africa, winning self-governance under nominal British oversight.

Love and marriage

Victoria and Albert presented the public with the novel spectacle of a young and serenely happy royal family. In the space of 17 years they had nine children, four sons, and five daughters. The birth of the Princess Royal ("Vicky") in 1840 was followed, a year later, by the birth of a son and heir, the future Edward VII. For the birth of her eighth baby, Prince Leopold, Victoria had pain relief in the shape of newly available chloroform. She found it "soothing, quieting and delightful beyond measure", and this royal endorsement made it easier for other women to opt for pain relief in childbirth.

To reach their new homes at Balmoral in Scotland and Osborne on the Isle of Wight, the royal family took advantage of the railways, another recent invention. For Victoria, Balmoral Castle, with its specially designed turrets and tartans, was a

Victoria Cross
This military decoration for conspicuous bravery was created by Queen Victoria in 1856.

"dear paradise" and "… Albert's own creation, own work, own building, own laying-out". Her beloved husband's interest in art and design culminated in the Great Exhibition of 1851, for which 112,000 items from across the world were displayed in the Crystal Palace, a glass and iron exhibition hall in Hyde Park, London, of roughly 85,000m² (21 acres).

The widow of Windsor

Albert's sudden death from typhoid in 1861 was a shock from which Victoria never fully recovered. As the "widow of Windsor", she withdrew from public life and lost some of her early popularity. But time was on her side. Partly as a result of Albert's steadying influence, she had removed herself from direct involvement in political conflicts, so that the Crown eventually came to be seen as above party politics, a neutral guarantee of constitutional stability. Even so, Victoria had strong personal opinions on the major issues and

personalities of the day. She disliked the great Liberal leader, William Ewart Gladstone, because he spoke to her as if she were "a public meeting". She had a much better relationship with his rival, Benjamin Disraeli, who coaxed and flattered the widowed queen into renewing her interest and participation in public life. It was Disraeli who had Victoria proclaimed Empress of India, a title and a role in which she took great interest and pride.

By 1887, the year in which she celebrated her Golden Jubilee, the 50th anniversary of her reign, Victoria had regained her early popularity. Ten years later, on the occasion of the Diamond Jubilee of 1897, the queen-empress commanded global esteem and affection. The spectacular celebrations in London were attended by representatives of her 387 million subjects around the world. Soon afterwards, her health began to fail and she was 81 when she died in January 1901. By that time, she was related to so many royal families that she was popularly known as the "grandmother of Europe".

End of an era
The funeral procession of Queen Victoria, February 1901. She was laid to rest in the Frogmore mausoleum at Windsor Castle, alongside Albert.

"We are **not** amused."

QUEEN VICTORIA, ATTRIBUTED, 1900

‹‹ BEFORE

From 1511, the Portuguese, Dutch, Spanish, English, and French bargained and fought for control of Southeast Asia and Australasia.

EUROPEAN PROFITS

The Portuguese captured the Malaysian peninsula in 1511, moved on to the Spice Islands (the Moluccas) in 1513, and then China, Japan, and Indonesia. The Spanish arrived next, setting up **plantations** in the Philippines in 1565. Two

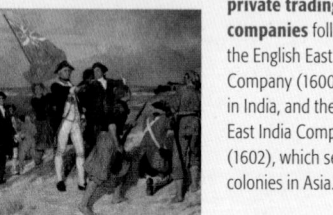

private trading companies followed – the English East India Company (1600), based in India, and the Dutch East India Company (1602), which set up colonies in Asia.

COOK IN BOTANY BAY

CLAIMS ON AUSTRALIA

In 1770, James Cook **‹‹ 250–251** explored Australia's fertile east coast, and claimed New South Wales for Britain. In 1829, Britain claimed the whole of Australia, and in 1840, annexed New Zealand too. In both cases, this action pre-empted French colonization.

The European colonization of Australia began in 1788 with the establishment of a British penal colony in Botany Bay (modern Sydney), New South Wales. Until then, Britain had transported convicts to North America, but the American War of Independence (see pp.232–33) made this impossible. The use of Britain's new Australian colony for this purpose had been proposed in 1779, by English botanist Sir Joseph Banks. The natives seemed more peaceful than the Maoris of New Zealand – and this was to prove

and armed resistance proved ineffectual. Foreign diseases, to which the Aboriginal population had little resistance, also caused widespread mortality. A smallpox epidemic broke out in 1789, followed by influenza, typhus, chicken pox, whooping cough, tuberculosis, and syphilis.

A stolen generation

The prevalent view of Aborigines is of a desert people, but this is only because they were driven into arid areas that were of no interest to British settlers: in

Waitangi with the Maoris in 1840. The chiefs ceded sovereignty in return for protection and guarantees against further encroachment on their lands.

However, the treaty was not upheld, and the settlers' continuing demands for land led to the New Zealand (or Maori) Wars, fought between 1843–47 and 1860–72. The Maoris were equipped with firearms acquired through decades of trading, and fought back staunchly. The first outbreak of war was contained relatively quickly, but the second became a protracted

Colonial Resistance

Resistance to the European colonization of Australia, New Zealand, and Southeast Asia brought very different outcomes for the indigenous populations. In Australia and New Zealand, it led to the subjugation of the Aborigines and Maoris; in Southeast Asia, to eventual independence.

Dene-Harding revolver
The explosive power of European firearms such as this Dene-Harding revolver ensured that the colonizing powers swiftly overcame indigenous populations.

their downfall. When James Cook landed in 1770 (see BEFORE), there were 300,000– 350,000 Aborigines in Australia. Over the next 150 years, this figure declined by 80 per cent. Initially, relations between native inhabitants and settlers were amicable, but as the colony expanded, the Aborigines resisted. Their arrows and spears were no match for British guns however,

1788 the Aborigine population was concentrated in the same fertile areas as the most populous parts of modern Australia. British governors were instructed to protect the Aborigines, but they often imposed British values and, in the late 19th century, even removed native children (the "Stolen Generation") from their families, and moved them into state institutions.

Maori wars

Maori resistance to European settlers in New Zealand was more fierce. Both Dutch explorer Abel Tasman and Cook received violent receptions, but Cook noted that tribal differences made united resistance unlikely. By the early 19th century, European and US seal and whale hunters were trading with the Maoris. As disputes among tribes and between Maoris and settlers were common (and to pre-empt French and American interests), Britain negotiated the Treaty of

guerilla campaign that cost the lives of around 1,000 Europeans and some 2,000 Maoris.

> **3 MILLION** acres of Maori land was confiscated in the 19th century, and most Maoris were confined to New Zealand's less fertile North Island

> **75 PER CENT** of the Maori population still lived there at the end of the 20th century

The Dutch East Indies

During the 17th and 18th centuries, the Dutch monopolized trade with the Spice Islands (so named because prized spices, such as nutmeg, originated there), and took control of most of what is now Indonesia. In the 1790s, the Dutch East India Company (see BEFORE) collapsed and the Dutch government took over. From 1830 it forced Indonesian peasants to grow export crops, such as indigo and coffee, at set prices and, from 1870, allowed Dutch investors to lease land and establish plantations. This led to an outbreak of nationalist resistance and the Dutch fought a series of wars between 1821 and 1901. Ultimately,

Ticket of leave
After being transported to Australia in chains, some convicts who had served a proportion of their sentence with good behaviour were granted a Ticket of Leave (TOL) passport and allowed restricted travel.

Conflict in Burma
From 1823–87, the British fought three wars to gain control of Burma (now Myanmar), and in 1886 the country was proclaimed a province of British India.

political organization brought success, with Dr Sukarno's Indonesian National Party finally forcing independence in 1949.

French Indochina
The first Europeans in Indochina (Vietnam, Laos, and Cambodia) had been French missionaries, who took Roman Catholicism to Vietnam during the 17th century. The murder of French Christians there provided the pretext for Emperor Napoleon III to invade in 1858, but resistance was strong, both from the Chinese, who claimed sovereignty over Vietnam, and from the indigenous population. In 1863, France took control of southern Vietnam and established a protectorate in Cambodia. Between 1874–1884, the

"The loss of America what can repay? New colonies seek for at Botany Bay."

JOHN FREETH, ENGLISH POET, c.1731–1808

Maori *wahaika*
Weapons such as this *wahaika* – a short club made from wood, whale-bone, or stone – were used for close fighting. By the time of the Maori Wars, the Maoris had also acquired firearms.

French set up more protectorates in northern and central Vietnam. In 1887, these were incorporated, along with Cambodia, in the Union of French Indochina. What is now Laos and was then ruled by Siam (present-day Thailand), became a protectorate in 1893. The French tried to impose French culture on the Union. However, along with communism, it was Gallic education that inspired the Indochinese to seek the French ideals of *liberté, egalité,* and *fraternité* (see pp.236–37).

British Malaya
Britain first established a presence in Malaya in 1786, and in 1826 formed a colony called the Straits Settlements, which included Malacca and Singapore. During the 19th and early 20th century Britain set up protectorates over a number of Malay states including part of Brunei and North Borneo. By 1914, Britain had colonial control of British Malaya (now known as Malaysia).

The British established highly profitable tin mines and rubber plantations in Malaya. However, rather than exploiting the indigenous population, they imported Chinese labour for the mines, and Indian workers for the plantations, while encouraging the Malays to farm for a living. The result was a more peaceful co-existence than in many other European colonies in Southeast Asia.

AFTER

World War II irreversibly altered the balance of world power, and led to the dismantling of the European empires.

ASIA AFTER IMPERIALISM
Britain granted commonwealth status to Australia in 1901, and New Zealand in 1907, recognizing their self-government within the empire. British Southeast Asian colonies were made independent between 1957–84. Indonesia became independent from the Dutch in 1949, and in 1954 the French lost Indochina, leading to the division of Vietnam **334–35 》**.

MIXED FORTUNES
After European withdrawal, the Philippines, Indonesia, and Vietnam all experienced civil unrest or war

while Japan and, later, Malaysia, Singapore, and Indonesia went on to achieve such rapid economic growth that they were dubbed the **"Tiger economies" 380–81 》**.

AUSTRALIA'S ABORIGINES
While Southeast Asian independence meant self-representation for indigenous people, the same was not true in Australia. The **Aboriginal population declined** to 60,000 in 1921 and the inter-war period saw **renewed confiscation** of land. In 1938, on the 150th anniversary of European colonization, Aborigines declared Australia Day, the national holiday, to be a day of mourning.

DR SUKARNO, FIRST INDONESIAN PRESIDENT

« BEFORE

BEFORE

A rich supply of lucrative resources led to competition between European powers for a stake in India. As the Mughal Empire's controlling grip on the area weakened, British influence increased.

RICHES OF THE EAST

Europe's craze for spices made India very alluring. The **lucrative** spice trade had tempted **the Portuguese** to India since the mid-15th century. By the 16th century, India was visited by **Italians, English, French, and Dutch** all keen to trade, seek adventure, or to spread Christianity in the area.

EAST INDIA COMPANY (EIC)

To rival Portugal, **the EICs were formed by England (1600) and the Netherlands (1602)** « **214–15**. These

companies acted as trade organizations, and later provided a military presence in the region.

ENGLISH EAST INDIA COMPANY COAT OF ARMS

MUGHAL EMPIRE

The English EIC prospered, and worked with the ruling Mughal emperors « **184–85** well into the 19th century. However, as the **British fortunes rose, the fragile Mughal Empire went into decline**.

BRITISH INVOLVEMENT

Short reigns, protracted war, and peasant revolts undermined the Mughals. Indian provinces became more independent of central rule, paving the way for **British interference**.

The British Raj

The desire for power and wealth has led nations to expand their influence far beyond their frontiers. India became the jewel in the British Empire's crown and the British Raj (Hindi for rule) – which ran from 1858 to 1947 – was the culmination of decades of British involvement and domination in the Indian subcontinent.

A t the turn of the 18th century, the long-established East India Company (see BEFORE) enabled Britain to enjoy unprecedented privileges in India, with footholds in economic, political, and military life. To protect this situation, the EIC had increased the number of troops deemed necessary to defend its establishments. Rivalry with other trading companies, especially the French, was fierce and led to the Seven Years War (see pp.230–31), a slow, stuttering campaign for British expansion and control. In 1756, under Robert Clive, a soldier and statesman described as "the conqueror of India", the British claimed the richest Mughal province, Bengal, in the northeast of the country. This became the foundation of British rule in India. The recapture of Calcutta by Clive in late 1756, the storming of nearby French Chandernagore in early 1757, and Clive's success at Plassey in June of that year were milestones in the British domination of India. Finally, in 1763, the Mughal Emperor Shah Alam II formally inducted the EIC, and Clive, into the Mughal hierarchy. As *Diwan* (chancellor) for Bengal, the EIC received a title that amounted to

Viceroy Curzon at the Maharajah's Palace
Nathaniel George Curzon (fourth right) was Viceroy of India from 1898 to 1905, and ruled in place of the monarch. Devestating famines, and a dispute with Lord Kitchener, chief of the Indian army, led to his resignation.

sovereignty over the province. The British gained administrative powers throughout India and became more of a government than a trading concern.

British influence knew no bounds, from the building of roads, an extensive railway network, and schools, to an administrative system of officials that emerged as a model for the British civil service. There was an agreement to allow Christian missions to operate in India, aided by influential figures in London such as the anti-slavery campaigner William Wilberforce (see pp.308–09). Hinduism was seen as something from which the people were to be emancipated. This evangelical zeal led to the eventual erosion of British tolerance and support of Indian faiths.

Indian locomotive
The *Fairy Queen*, built in Britain in 1855 for the East Indian Railways, still survives and is the world's oldest working engine.

subject to increased supervision from the British government. When its royal charter – sovereign permission to operate as a corporation – was renewed in 1813, the EIC had to surrender its monopoly of trade in India, allowing other corporations to operate in the region.

The Indian mutiny

Under the EIC, there was some rebellious behaviour among Indian soldiers (sepoys) serving in the British army, who were aggrieved at their treatment. These sepoys bore the brunt of the First British–Afghan war (1838–42) and were shipped to China to fight in the Opium Wars (see pp.284–85).

By the late 1770s the East India Company was burdened with massive military expenditure and was in dire financial straits. India was of huge national importance to Britain, and so the British government decided to overhaul the EIC. The Regulating Act of 1773 resulted in the EIC becoming

The Siege of Lucknow
The British Garrison in Lucknow, in northern India, was besieged by Indian rebels on 1 July 1857. Despite the large numbers of mutineers, the siege was finally ended by Sir Colin Campbell's relief force in November 1857.

"The **key** of **India** is **London**."

BENJAMIN DISRAELI, ADDRESSING THE HOUSE OF LORDS, MARCH 1881

impose tariffs or subsidies on imports and exports. Instead they invested in the country's infrastructure, especially trains, which assisted economic development, and irrigation works. On the tea estates which proliferated from the 1850s, indentured labour was widely employed. Most Indians lived in abject poverty, a state not helped by severe famines in the second half of the 19th century. Conditions for migrants were miserable and mortality rates high. Their plight, and the continued deployment of Indian troops on imperial service in other countries, stirred nationalist feelings, resulting in an awakening Indian political consciousness.

> **INDENTURED LABOUR** A type of labour that binds apprentice to master. The employer offers little pay, but provides food and lodgings.

In December 1885, the Indian National Congress, or Congress Party, met for the first time in Bombay (now Mumbai). As the main nationalist political party, it was initially moderate and widely representative. By the beginning of the 20th century, however, a younger, more politically militant generation of Indians emerged, calling for independence from British rule (see pp.330–33).

AFTER

Rule Britannia

Initially, after the Indian Mutiny and the decline of the EIC, many policies remained unchanged, yet British attitudes towards Indians shifted from openness to insularity. As more British families arrived with their servants, private clubs were set up that became symbols of wealth and snobbery. Facilitated by new railways, exports such as cotton, wheat, and tea enriched the British, yet profits rarely reached native pockets. Despite the fledgling nature of industries such as textiles, and their potential for collapse, the British insisted on an economic policy of *laissez-faire*, or free trade, refusing to

The flash-point was reached in 1857, in Meerut, northern India, when rumour spread that the British had introduced a new rifle and cartridge into the Indian Army. The cartridges, which soldiers had to bite open, were lubricated with a grease containing pig and cow fat, offending both Hindu and Muslim soldiers. The revolt spread across the country, and was finally quelled in 1859 after much bloodshed. In 1858 a royal decree stated that all EIC rights were to be handed over to the British Crown. Victoria assumed the role of Queen of India and Britain. The reign of the EIC was over, and the British Raj had begun.

Christian miniature
Indian artists often painted Christian subjects in order to appeal to the increasing Christian population of the country and patrons of the British Raj.

In the 20th century, demands for Indian independence grew. Indian sovereignty was accompanied by the division of the country.

THE FREEDOM STRUGGLE
At the end of the 19th century, calls for Indian independence were growing. In 1905, Lord Curzon **partitioned Bengal**, dividing it into two states. This led to a nationwide protest.

RELIGIOUS DIVIDE
Bengal's population was mainly **Hindu in the west** and **Muslim in the east**. Partition was reversed in 1911 after great political unrest.

PARTITION OF INDIA
The move for **Indian independence** was galvanized by the arrival of **Mahatma Gandhi 330–31 》》**. Committed to ridding his motherland

FLAG OF PAKISTAN

of foreign rule, his charismatic personality helped to unite the country in the struggle. After arduous constitutional negotiations, the British agreed to transfer power on **15 August 1947**. As they left India, the **largest mass migration in history** took place. Freedom led to partitioning, with the creation of the independent nations of **the Dominion of Pakistan and the Union of India 332–33 》》**.

SRI LANKA
Sri Lanka (**Ceylon** before 1972) lies 31km (19 miles) off the coast of India. Parts of Sri Lanka were colonized by the Portuguese and Dutch in the 16th and 17th centuries. The whole country was **ceded to the British Empire in 1815**. A nationalist movement arose in the early 20th century and independence was granted in 1948.

« BEFORE

The Opium Wars of the mid-19th century were the culmination of more than 50 years of strained Anglo–Chinese relations.

THE "LADY HUGHES"

In 1784 a British merchant ship, the *Lady Hughes*, fired a cannon salute and **accidentally killed two Chinese officials**. Chinese law required that whoever was responsible should be surrendered to the authorities. The gunner was reluctantly handed over, and he was immediately strangled. Thereafter, Westerners **refused to submit to Chinese law**.

THE MACARTNEY EMBASSY

In 1792, **Lord Macartney** led a large British delegation to the summer palace of **Emperor Qianlong** at Rehe to request the accreditation of a British minister at court, the opening of more ports, and the provision of an island base. He was granted an audience but **refused to perform the kotow**, the respectful ceremonial three prostrations and nine head knockings. Qianlong accepted Macartney's gifts but **rejected all the envoy's requests**.

The Opium Wars

By 1838, use of opium, a highly addictive drug, was spiralling out of control in China. Increasingly concerned by the British trafficking of the narcotic, the Chinese government took prohibitive action, leading to a series of conflicts between the two countries.

Opium smoking
Opium imports were sanctioned under the 1858 Treaty of Tianjin and, in consequence, opium growing and addiction to the drug spread throughout China. In 1906, opium cultivation was finally banned and opium dens were forced to close. The apparatus for opium smoking was confiscated and burnt in public bonfires.

In an attempt to curb the opium problem, the Chinese government appointed a leading official, Lin Zexu, to suppress trade in Guangzhou, a port city in the south of the country. On his arrival, Lin confiscated all opium stocks, and forced foreign residents to sign a bond agreeing to stop trading in the drug. The British government, having learnt that its citizens had been imprisoned, sent an expeditionary force to China.

This force blockaded Guangzhou and, moving north, threatened the capital Beijing. Negotiations followed that left neither side satisfied. In 1842, a larger expeditionary force brought about a Chinese surrender, ending the First Opium War. China was compelled to negotiate the Treaty of Nanjing (see right), which ceded Hong Kong to Britain, admitted missionaries, controlled external tariffs, opened five treaty ports, and removed Westerners from Chinese jurisdiction. However, the relationship between Britain and

Sword used in Opium Wars
The outcome of the conflict between Britain and China was largely determined by weaponry. Chinese swords – like this example, captured by a British naval officer in 1842 – were no match for British firearms.

China remained uneasy, and war flared up again in 1856. In this Second Opium War (also known as the Arrow War), the British were joined by the French. By 1860 China had been defeated, and was forced to grant further privileges to Britain, which were later extended to other Western powers.

The Taiping Rebellion

China in the mid-19th century was not only under attack from foreign powers, it was also under threat from a series of internal rebellions, the largest of which was the Taiping Rebellion.

In 1836, a Christian teacher, Hong Xiuquan, had a series of dreams that led him to believe he had a mission to restore China to Christianity. He made converts among peasants and miners in Guangxi, south China, and in January 1851 declared the establishment of the *Taiping Tianguo*, the Heavenly Kingdom of Great Peace. In 1853, Taiping rebels

The Chinese Army 1880
China's first modern army, the Anhui Army, which was raised by statesman Li Hongzhang to campaign against a series of mid-19th-century rebellions, adopted Western-style drills and Western-style weapons.

agreement that envoys of both sovereigns will sign the treaty, in English

signatures of the three Chinese ambassadors, Qiying, Yilibu, and Niu Jian

The Nanjing Treaty
The Treaty of Nanjing, 1842, was the first of the "unequal treaties", which gave benefits to Western powers without offering reciprocal advantages to the Chinese state.

agreement that envoys of both sovereigns will sign the treaty, in Chinese

signature of Henry Pottinger, the British ambassador to China

captured Nanjing, and established a state in which gambling and opium smoking were both banned, Taiping Christianity was the only religion, land was to be shared out equally, and women were given equal rights.

In 1860, a Taiping assault on Shanghai was defeated by the Western-trained "Ever-Victorious Army". In 1864, the Hunan army – organized on a network of personal loyalty and financed by a new tax on internal trade – recaptured Nanjing. Hong Xiuquan committed suicide and the rebellion came to an end, though pockets of Taiping resistance continued until 1868.

Missionaries

Christian missionaries gained the right to preach, travel, and own property in China under the unequal treaties (see above). After 1860, the number of Protestant and Catholic missionaries operating in China rose sharply. Missionaries initially concentrated on converting the population, but later ran schools and hospitals. Their presence

threatened the position of the Chinese scholar-officials, and anti-missionary incidents occurred; the most notorious being the massacre of French Sisters of Charity at Tianjin in 1870.

Self-strengthening

After the Opium Wars, the scholar Wei Yuan suggested "building ships, making weapons, and learning the superior techniques of the barbarians". The first "self-strengthening" projects began in the 1860s. In 1866 Wojen, a Mongol Grand Secretary, complained that self-strengthening ideas were not compatible with traditional Confucian government. Nevertheless, in 1872 the statesman Li Hongzhang started a steamship company to compete with foreign shipping on the Yangzi, and later established coal mines that led to the building of China's first railway.

However, Japan's dramatic defeat of China's army and navy in the Sino–Japanese War (see below) seemed to indicate that attempts at self-strengthening were a failure.

DECISIVE MOMENT

SINO–JAPANESE WAR

The origins of this conflict lay in a struggle between China and Japan over influence in Korea. Despite expectations of a Chinese victory, the contest was one-sided. First the Huai army was defeated at Pyongyang in present-day North Korea. Then, in September 1894, the Chinese Beiyang fleet engaged the Japanese fleet off the mouth of the Yalu River, at the border of North Korea and China. Four Chinese ships were destroyed; the rest took refuge at Weihaiwei. China was forced to sign the Treaty of Shimonoseki, recognizing Korean independence, and ceding Taiwan to Japan.

AFTER

In the wake of the Opium Wars, China experienced a period of unrest, both domestically and internationally.

SCRAMBLE FOR CHINA
China's defeat in the Sino–Japanese War precipitated a **scramble for territory**: Russia obtained an agreement to extend the Trans–Siberian railway across Manchuria in northeast China; Germany seized Qingdao in the north; France obtained commercial concessions in the southwest; and Britain gained a 99-year lease on the "New Territories", opposite Hong Kong Island.

THE EMPRESS DOWAGER
In 1856, a concubine named **Yehonola** gave birth to the future Tongzhi emperor. As Empress Dowager Cixi **she dominated the court until 1908**. She has been accused of having murdered her daughter-in-law, of misappropriating naval funds, and of supporting the Boxer Uprising (see below).

EMPRESS DOWAGER CIXI

THE BOXER UPRISING
The Boxers United in Righteousness – so called because of the ritual "invincibility" boxing they practised – attacked Beijing in May 1900 in a backlash **against Christian missionaries**. Britain sent 2,000 troops to stop them, but the Empress Dowager ordered the Imperial army to turn them away. Westerners were executed and thousands of **Chinese Christians were killed**. In the aftermath of the siege, Chinese officials were executed and compensation was paid to the West.

« BEFORE

Japan's history reveals it rarely to have been at peace. For centuries, the Imperial court and the warrior classes wrestled for control.

REUNIFICATION OF JAPAN

From the mid-15th to late -16th century, Japan was riven by **civil wars,** and by 1560 a handful of **warring families** vied for supremacy **« 116–17**. The emperor remained as a **figurehead**, without power, and three outstanding leaders:

TOKUGAWA IEYASU

Oda Nobunaga, Toyotomi Hideyoshi, and **Tokugawa Ieyasu** displayed **superior military tactics** and **shocking acts of brutality** to unify Japan. Ieyasu was made a shogun in 1603, and was recognized as the greatest power in the land.

TOKUGAWA RULE

With Japan reunified, Ieyasu's aim was to maintain control. **All foreign influences were discouraged**, and from 1635 Japanese subjects were unable to leave Japan – those Japanese who were overseas at the time were refused re-entry on pain of death. Christianity was banned, and foreign merchants and missionaries expelled. With its **borders closed,** contact with outsiders could be strictly regulated by the shogun **« 182–83**.

A CLOSED COUNTRY

For two centuries descendents of the Tokugawa shoguns kept the peace, and the population prospered. But from the early 19th century environmental and political troubles caused the **shoguns' grip on power to slip**. Famine and earthquakes caused thousands of deaths, trade within Japan widened the gap between rich and poor, and foreigners sailed into Japanese waters.

Rising Sun

The "Land of the Rising Sun", as it is known to most Japanese, has had a turbulent history. For centuries it was a society ruled by fierce warlords, and for over 200 years was closed to the rest of the world. Ambitious and industrious Japan quickly caught up with the West, but success came at a heavy price.

Japan's development from a land of feudal lords into a world power began in the 19th century. During the reunification of Japan (see BEFORE), the country was closed to foreign visitors and trade, but in 1853 the American government sent Commodore Matthew Perry to Edo (Tokyo) in command of four warships. Perry demanded the opening of Japanese ports for trade, making it clear he would return. Resistance seemed futile in the face of superior naval power. In 1854, Perry returned with an even larger fleet, and the shogunate (military rulers) signed the Treaty of Kanagawa. Japan was forced to open its borders.

Westernizing society

Similar treaties with Britain, France, Russia, and The Netherlands followed. They too were successful in demanding rights to trade, and Japan gradually lost control over its own customs duties. The Japanese people viewed these unequal treaties as humiliating, and a series of rebellions brought nearly 700 years of shogunate rule to an end. Following the Meiji Restoration (see right), the

Tokyo–Yokohama railway
This poster, dating from 1875, celebrates the Tokyo terminus of the railway, built in 1872 with the aid of foreign engineers. The image was issued only seven years after the Meiji Restoration opened Japan to foreign ideas.

new regime thought that Western ideas might make Japan stronger, more able to compete. A popular slogan of the day was *"oitsuke, oikose"* ("catch up, overtake"). The old feudal class system was restructured from "samurai warrior–farmer–artisan–merchant" to "nobles–samurai descendants–commoners". In 1873, conscription was introduced so that all men, not just those from the noble class, as previously, could join the military. In 1877, in a further move towards Westernization, Tokyo University was established, and employed several foreign

teachers. A modern mint was set up, and in 1882 The Bank of Japan opened with a standardized decimal currency based on the yen.

Population shift
Perhaps the greatest symbol of Japan's modernization was the railway. The first was opened in October 1872, and within 15 years 1,600km (1,000 miles) of track had been laid. It had a profound effect on the country and its economy. Suburbs grew as people now lived away from their place of work, and the age of commuting had begun.

> **SHOGUN** Prior to 1868, shoguns ruled Japan. They were hereditary leaders who commanded armies that included a warrior class known as the samurai.

Japan at war
After years of turmoil, there was a revived sense of national identity and pride in Japan. The cry was not only *"oitsuke, oikose"* but also *"fukoku kyohei"* ("rich nation, strong army"). Japan was not to be toyed with. In the spring of 1894, Korea called for military aid from China to put down a rebellion. China obliged, and so did Japan. The rebellion was swiftly dealt with, but both sides had interests in Korea and stayed on. The Japanese were determined to fight, and officially declared war on 1 August.

The Sino–Japanese War had begun. In the battles that followed, Japan proved superior, especially at sea. The naval base of Port Arthur in Manchuria, on the northeast coast of China, was seized in November, and the Chinese fleet destroyed at Weihai in the eastern province of Shandong in February 1895. The Treaty of Shimonoseki in April 1895 saw China abandon its interests in Korea and cede territory to Japan, including Taiwan. Japan also gained rights in Manchuria, which had rich natural resources of timber, iron, oil, gold, and uranium.

This was the first major step in Japan's empire-building in Asia. Russia reacted by persuading the French and German governments that Japan should give up its stronghold in Manchuria because it caused instability. Japan bowed to pressure and reluctantly agreed. When Russia refused to withdraw its troops from China, following an uprising against foreign influences known as the Boxer Rebellion (see pp.284–85), the increasing tension with Russia eventually erupted into war in 1904.

Japan was by now an impressive military force, while Russia was severely disadvantaged by the 1905 Revolution (see pp.300–01). Japan was triumphant. The ensuing Portsmouth Treaty, signed in September 1905, recognized Japan's interests in Korea and granted them occupation of the Liaodong Peninsula in Manchuria. Japan quickly established control over Korea. It disbanded the army and annexed the nation in 1910 with no international opposition.

Japan had succeeded in its aims – it was now taken seriously by Western powers. The unequal treaties, which had caused so much bitterness, were revised and full tariff (customs) control restored in 1911. In a mere half century, Japan had gone from being virtually dismissed as a backward country to a major world power.

"Enrich the country, strengthen the military."
JAPAN'S NATIONAL SLOGAN DURING THE MEIJI ERA, 1868–1912

As Japan entered the 20th century, it seemed stable. This soon changed. Economic depression and dissatisfaction with Japan's role in world affairs eventually led to war.

DISCONTENT
During World War I **296–97 ≫** industrial production grew five-fold and exports more than trebled in Japan. After the war **prices collapsed and economic recession** set in. Rural incomes fell sharply and the gap between rich and poor, city and countryside widened. Both the military and public became increasingly angry, and many **blamed the influence of Western ideas**.

AN UNEASY ALLIANCE
Japan maintained an **uneasy relationship** with foreign powers. Japan attended the Versailles Peace Conference in 1919 **298–99 ≫** where the victors of World War I met to negotiate peace treaties with the defeated Germany. But **Japan did not always feel a true equal**. In 1920, Japan was one of the founding members of **the League of Nations 298–99 ≫**, which was set up to work towards disarmament and diplomacy, but it was upset that its proposal for a racial equality clause in the league's charter was rejected. To compound matters, the Washington Arms Limitation Treaty of 1922 limited Japan to three warships, compared with five American and five British.

NATIONALISM
After years of trying to gain respect abroad without success, **Japanese frustration** towards Westerners **turned to contempt**. Fiercely ambitious, Japan was set on a path of confrontation with Western powers **324–25 ≫**.

EMPEROR HIROHITO OF JAPAN (1901–89)

Modern power
A Japanese naval squadron is shown here steaming in to bombard Port Arthur, Manchuria, and attack Russian ships. During the Russo–Japanese war Japan proved militarily superior, especially at sea.

DECISIVE MOMENT

THE MEIJI RESTORATION

After the demands of the US naval officer Matthew Perry in 1854, the shoguns seemed incapable of dealing with the foreign threat. A group of leading samurai (warriors) formed an alliance, believing that only the restoration of the emperor could save Japan. In 1868 a short civil war brought nearly 700-year shogunate rule to an end. Emperor Mutsuhito was restored and a new era began. The period of modernization that followed was called the Meiji (1868–1912), but not all were content. In 1877 there was a major rebellion in Kyushu. Traditional forces, including samurai infuriated at no longer being allowed to carry swords, were defeated by the new conscript army. The emperor promised a national assembly, and in 1889 the first ever formal constitution adopted outside North America and Europe was proclaimed. In this woodcut, Meiji officers in Western-style uniforms are shown accepting the surrender of the samurai rebels.

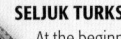

‹‹ BEFORE

Since the 8th century, interaction between the Islamic world and the West has been marked with conflict and unease.

MUSLIM EXPANSION

The Prophet Muhammad was both a political and a spiritual leader. By the time of his death in 632 CE, all of Arabia was **united under Islam**. His first successor, **Abu-Bekr**, proclaimed a Holy War against Byzantium and Persia. Palestine was captured and Egypt seized. In 711 CE a force of 7,000 Arabs invaded southern Spain **‹‹ 122–23**.

SELJUK TURKS

At the beginning of the 11th century a great wave of Seljuk Turks **‹‹ 125, 152**, led by **Tughril Beg**, conquered Iran. His successor, **Alp Arslan**, led the Seljuks to conquer Georgia, Armenia, and much of Asia Minor. They overran Syria and in 1071 defeated the Byzantine emperor **Romanus IV** in eastern Turkey **‹‹ 145**. This gave the Seljuk Turks a reputation as defenders of Islam and was a major factor in starting the Crusades **‹‹ 146–47**.

SELJUK BOWL

OTTOMAN EMPIRE

A number of Islamic states emerged during the 16th century. The largest was the Ottoman Empire **‹‹ 186–87**, which grew from its original base as a Turkish warrior state in western Anatolia. Ottoman forces took Constantinople in 1453 **‹‹ 153** and Syria and Egypt in 1516–17. In South Asia, **Babur** founded the Mughal Empire **‹‹ 184–85**. **Islamic teachings** were carried round the world by missionaries and merchants.

MILITARY LEADER (1881–1922)

ENVER PASHA

Enver Pasha was born in the Black Sea town of Apana in 1881. Enrolling with the military, he was posted to Greece, where he joined a secret group hoping for modernization of the Ottoman Empire. In 1908 Pasha was one of the leaders of the Young Turks that rebelled against the rule of the Sultan Abdul Hamid. During World War I, as minister of war, he aligned Turkey with Germany and Austria–Hungary. On defeat in 1918, Pasha fled to Turkistan, where he was killed in 1922.

Modernizing the empire
Constantinople, at the heart of the Ottoman Empire, was modernized from the 1870s onwards with constructions such as the Galata Bridge (pictured), electric lights, a water system, streetcars, and telephones.

The Young Turks Revolt

Five times a day millions of Muslims face Mecca to pray. Peace is the avowed aim but the spread of Islam has not been without its conflicts. During its history Muslim societies, such as the Young Turks and the Ottoman Empire, have struggled to define themselves in the modern world.

From the 11th century onwards Islam, under the leadership of the Turks (see BEFORE), had consolidated its hold on the Middle East and made further gains in India, the Far East, and Europe. However, by the 18th century Europeans came to dominate much of the Muslim world from north Africa to Southeast Asia, and this Western imperialism prompted a religious and political crisis.

Some believed that Islam could be restricted to private life and that public life might embrace modern, European ideas about technology, education, and law. One prominent modernist was Jamal Al-Din Al-Afghani (1838–97). Al-Afghani was a major catalyst for Islamic reform. He travelled all over the Muslim world strengthening communities in the hope of driving out the Western powers, but he was convinced that science and technology could be successfully adopted by Islamic countries without compromise to their religion or culture. In the late 19th century other modernists, such as the Indian Syed Ahmad Khan (1817–98), recommended the reformation of Islamic society along similar lines. He was responsible for founding the Muhhamedan Anglo–Oriental College at Aligarh, northern India, in 1875, where Muslims could study Western ideas without alienating themselves from their religion.

Rejecting the West

Conservative Muslim leaders were convinced that Muslim impotence in the face of Christian imperialism was a result of divergence from Islam and deviation from their traditions. Many called for a total rejection of Western ideas. Some concluded that where Muslims no longer lived under Islamic rule in an Islamic territory, they were now in a state of warfare requiring armed struggle, known as *jihad*. A series of *jihad* revivalist movements led to the emergence of Islamist states in Nigeria, Libya, and the Sudan.

During the 19th century, European expansion became an increasingly important force in Muslim societies, and the major states that remained independent responded by undertaking a wide range of reforms. In the Ottoman Empire (see BEFORE) reforms began with attempts by Selim III, who reigned between 1789–1807, to institute a *Nizam-i cedid*, or "New System" of military and bureaucratic organization. His successor, Mahmud II, went on to restore the power and authority to the central government that had been usurped by powerful local lords. Mahmud II's successor, Abdülmecid I, who reigned from 1839–61, embarked on a programme of reform that would become known as the *Tanzimat* ("reorganization"). As the empire sought to modernize, it gained the support of the British, and the Crimean War (1853–56) found Britain and the Ottomans allied against Russia. In 1876 Abd al-Hamid II came to the throne and Russia declared war

> **ISLAMISM An ideology that considers Islam to be both a religion and a system of government. Islamist states are guided by *sharia* – Islamic religious law.**

on the Ottoman Empire in 1877, in an attempt to liberate the Balkan Peninsula from Ottoman rule. In a swift campaign, the Russians drove the Ottomans back and forced them to sign the disastrous Treaty of San Stefano in 1878. This treaty deprived them of most of their European territories, including Bulgaria. Further territorial losses included the loss of Tunisia to the French in 1881 and Egypt to the British in 1882. In order to maintain greater control over the remaining empire, Abd al-Hamid continued the reform process. Great changes were made in education, military affairs,

> **"Turkey is a Muslim country, and Muslim ideas and influence must preponderate."**
> YOUNG TURKS (COMMITTEE OF UNION AND PROGRESS), 1910

The victorious Young Turks
This illustration from *Le Petit Journal* shows the Young Turks' successful revolution of 1908. After they marched on Constantinople, the sultan surrendered himself as a prisoner in his palace, the Yildiz Kiosk.

joined by Macedonian rebels as well as large numbers of Young Turks. This group called itself the Committee of Union and Progress (CUP). Abd al-Hamid was forced to give in to the revolutionaries' demands. A constitution was adopted and a parliament created and the Young Turks of the CUP, led by a triumvirate – a group of three people who share power – of whom Enver Pasha (see left) would become the best known, were in command of the empire.

The Young Turks continued the Ottoman reform process, opening schools to women and overseeing legislative progress in women's rights. However, they made a disastrous foreign policy decision. An appraisal of Germany's military capability led them to break neutrality and enter World War I in 1914 on the side of Germany and Austria–Hungary (see pp.296–99).

Revolutionizing the army
Enver Pasha (centre) holds a *chibouk*, a traditional smoking pipe. Pasha had trained in Germany and wanted to improve the efficiency of the Ottoman Armed Forces along German lines.

LA RÉVOLUTION EN TURQUIE
Sanglant combat autour d'Yildiz-Kiosk. -:- Victoire des Jeunes-Turcs

and bureaucracy, but he was intolerant of opposition to his rule from groups who thought his reforms were too mild.

In 1902 a meeting in Paris brought together the leadership of the "Young Turks" – a coalition group composed of fervent nationalists wishing to save Turkey from decay and ruin. In the early 1900s, Bulgarian and Macedonian terrorists started bombing Ottoman government buildings, demanding total independence. The two rebellions eventually joined in 1908 when an army regiment stationed in Macedonia rebelled and fled into the hills. It was

AFTER

The 20th century witnessed continued polarization between some aspects of the Islamic world and the West.

END OF THE OTTOMAN EMPIRE
At the end of World War I **296–99 》** the Allied Powers began the dismemberment of the Ottoman Empire. This led to parts of Turkey

MUSTAFA KEMAL DURING THE TURKISH WAR OF INDEPENDENCE

being distributed to Greece. Mustafa Kemal – a Turkish soldier and statesman, widely known as **Atatürk** – led a successful resistance against this during the Turkish War of Independence (1918–23).

ISLAMIST RESURGENCE
The late 1960s signalled a turning point and the dawn of a new phase in Islam. The Arab–Israeli War in

1967 and the loss of Jerusalem to Israel **336–37 》** was a blow to Muslim pride, provoking a call for a return to Islam. The Arab oil embargo of 1973 was a catalyst for resurgence, as was the Iranian revolution of 1978–79 **364–65 》**.

FUNDAMENTALISM
The attack on the World Trade Centre on 11 September 2001 marked a new era in Islam's continuing internal and external struggle to deal with the challenge of the West **390–91 》**.

« **BEFORE**

Europeans began colonizing the African continent as early as the 15th century.

PORTUGUESE EXPLORATION
Portuguese explorers began charting the coast of Africa in 1419. In 1575, the Portuguese built their first colony in what is now **Angola**.

CAPE COLONY
In 1652, the Dutch East India Company « **214** founded **Cape Town** as a colony where Dutch ships could stock up on provisions for their onward voyages east.

OTTOMAN INFLUENCE
Between the 16th and late 19th century, northern Africa was loosely under the control of the Ottoman Empire « **186–87**. Consequently, many aspects of Turkish culture took root in the region. The most profound example of these was **Sufism**, a mystical tradition within Islam.

SLAVE SHACKLES

SLAVERY
Between 1500–1880 Europeans shipped an estimated **15 million African slaves** to the Americas, where they worked on plantations or in domestic service « **218–19**.

ZULU WARRIOR KING (c.1787–1828)

SHAKA ZULU

In 1816, Shaka became king of the Zulus of southeastern Africa. He revolutionized the Zulu army by introducing strict and arduous training regimes, new battle formations, and new weapons, such as the long-bladed *assegais* (a spear). Shaka led the Zulus in raids on neighbouring Nguni villages, which they razed to the ground. In this way he systematically expanded his territory and created a powerful kingdom that covered vast areas of the southern coastal and interior regions of Africa, which are known today as KwaZulu-Natal. Shaka was assassinated by his half-brother Dingane.

The Scramble for Africa

Motivated by accounts by explorers and missionaries of vast untapped resources in the heart of the African continent, rival European countries raced to gain possession of African territory during the late 19th century. The race became known as the "Scramble for Africa".

A lthough several European trading nations had secured coastal settlements around Africa by 1600, by the early 19th century the interior of the continent remained largely uncharted by Europeans, partly because many explorers feared contracting malaria in the vast tropical expanses. In 1820, the development of quinine, an effective treatment for the disease, enabled the exploration of the tropics. By 1835, Europeans had mapped most of northwestern Africa. From the 1840s the Scottish missionary David Livingstone journeyed extensively in central and southern Africa. Expeditions in the 1850s and 1860s by Richard Burton, John Speke, and James Grant located the great central lakes and the source of the Nile. By the end of the

Privileged few
Like this British official, government staff based in Africa in the early 20th century enjoyed many privileges, including servants who tended to their every need.

century, Europeans had charted the courses of the Nile, Niger, Congo, and Zambezi rivers, and the world now knew about the vast resources of Africa. In 1869, the opening of the Suez Canal, a direct trade route from Europe to Asia, focused European attention on the continent's economic and strategic importance. This interest was intensified by the Industrial Revolution (see pp.226–29) and the urgent need for raw materials and new markets, and so it was not long before European countries began to scramble for African territory.

In 1875, on the eve of this territorial carve-up, the European colonial presence was still fragmented. There was the former Ottoman territory of Algeria, whose conquest by France had begun in the 1830s; a few Spanish settlements; Angola, which was held by Portugal, along with trading posts on the west coast; and British and French trading stations in west Africa. The Cape Colony was administered by the United Kingdom, and just north of Cape Colony there was the Orange Free State and the Transvaal. These two states were established by Boers (Afrikaners of Dutch origin), after the Great Trek of 1835–36. This was a mass migration of 12,000 Boers, known as the "pioneers", who left Cape Colony in a search for new pastureland and to escape unwelcome British rule.

The African continent at this time was in turmoil. Much of the southern interior had been depopulated in the first quarter of the century by the territory-hungry Zulus under Shaka's leadership (see above). States such as Egypt were expanding. There were Islamic holy wars, called *Jihads*, taking place in the west. Cultural groups were being torn apart by the continuing slave trade, and new states were

emerging in East, Central, and West Africa. The Europeans capitalized on these disruptions, conquering territory with reasonable ease. In some cases, such as the Anglo–Zulu wars in 1879, they used military force; in others, African and European leaders agreed joint control over territory.

Divided continent
The competition between the Europeans often resulted in violent conflict. In southern Africa the first of two wars between the Boers and the British took place from late 1880 to early 1881 (see right), while North Africa became a theatre for Anglo–French rivalry. Between 15 November 1884 and 26 February 1885, the Berlin Conference was convened by German Chancellor Otto von Bismarck (see p.263) in an attempt to settle rival claims. At the conference it was agreed that imperial powers could only claim colonies if they had agreed treaties with chiefs, and had administrative powers in the region.

By the close of the century virtually all the continent was under European control. Portugal expanded its empire to include Mozambique; Belgium took over the enormous Congo region;

"If I could, I would **annex other planets**."

CECIL RHODES, POLITICIAN, AND COLONIZER OF RHODESIA

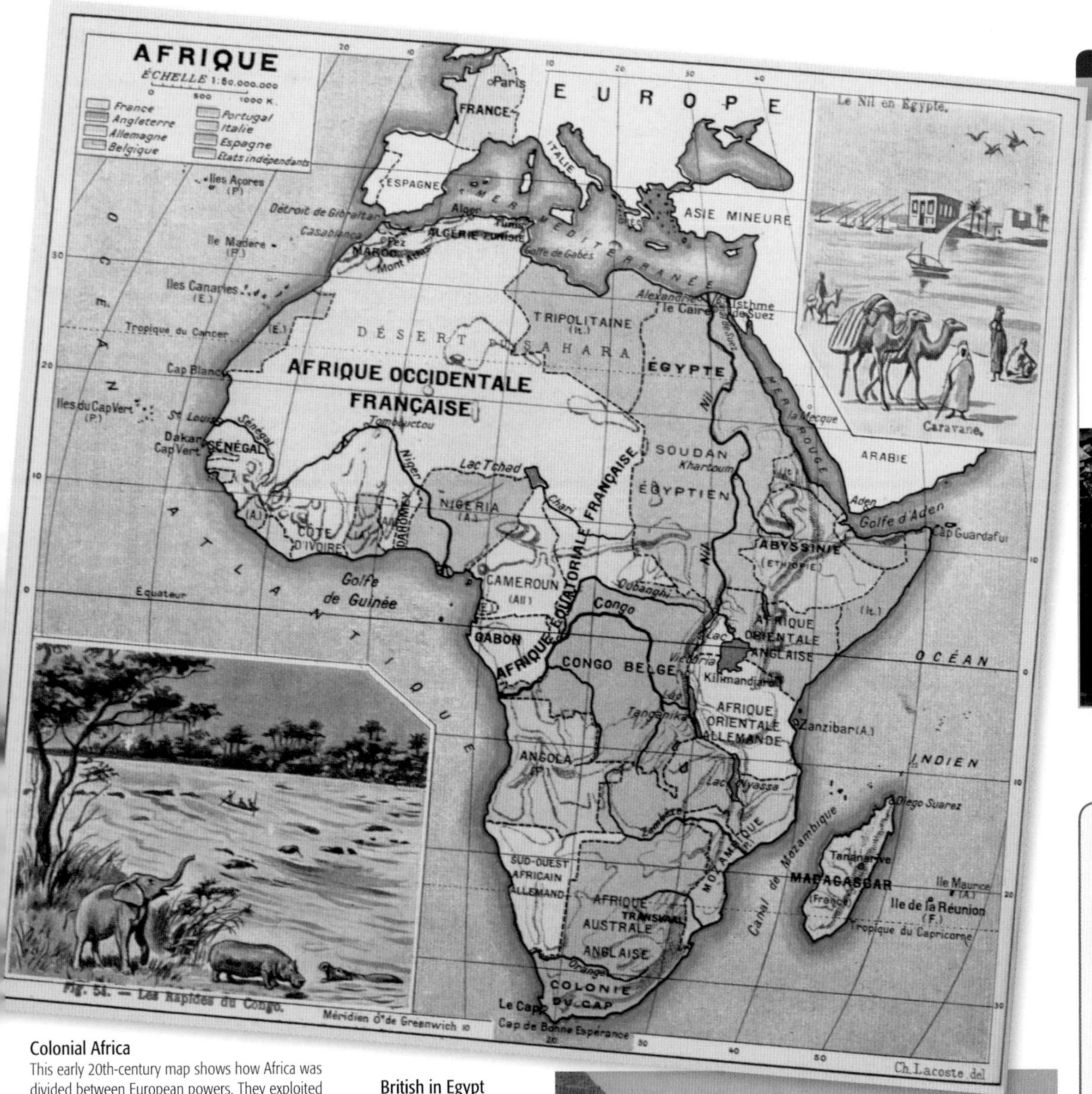

Colonial Africa

This early 20th-century map shows how Africa was divided between European powers. They exploited the continent's resources to benefit industry and commerce in their own countries.

British in Egypt

These Scottish soldiers are pictured in front of the Sphinx at Giza in the summer of 1882, just after their victory at the Battle of Tel-el-Kebir, a dispute between the British and the Egyptians over the control of the Suez Canal.

and Germany gained new colonies in southern Africa. France and Britain acquired new territory in West Africa, and Britain also built a network of colonies in East Africa running from South Africa to Egypt. By 1914, the French had occupied Morocco and the Italians had conquered Tripoli. Only Ethiopia remained fully free, having beaten an Italian force at the Battle of Adowa in 1896.

Africa under foreign rule

Although the styles of rule adopted by the colonial powers varied, in general the Europeans made no attempt to develop their colonies, exploiting them as sources of raw materials and markets for their manufactured goods. Africans were excluded from decisions that affected their lives, and European settlers established themselves in relatively temperate areas of Africa where the land was fertile, often banishing Africans from the best land. The Europeans also brought changes to the African way of life. They imposed property taxes, and to pay these taxes Africans were forced to undertake waged labour, working on railroads, plantations, and mining operations. By forcing Africans into these jobs, Europeans caused resentment. This grew into violent anti-colonial resistance, which spread across the continent in the early 20th century.

In 1904–05, the Herero of central Namibia rose up against their German rulers. In 1905, the Maji-Maji rebellion erupted in German East Africa.

In 1912, Zulus united to form the South African National Congress, which became the African National Congress, or ANC (see pp.376–77), to further the rights of native peoples. This marked the beginning of an organized movement for self-rule in Africa.

DECISIVE MOMENT

BOER WARS

In retaliation for the British annexation of the Transvaal in 1877, Transvaal Boers (below) launched the first Anglo–Boer war in December 1880. In March 1881 the British admitted defeat and granted the Transvaal self-rule. A second Anglo–Boer war was fought between October 1889 and May 1902. After a long, hard-fought struggle the British, aided by Canadian troops, won and absorbed the Boer republics of the Orange Free State and Transvaal into the British Empire.

AFTER

After World War II Africa's colonial rulers faced demands for self-rule. By 1978, most countries were independent. White minority rule in southern Africa lasted longer.

AFRICAN NATIONALISM

Almost two million Africans served in the armies of their colonizers during World War II. When the soldiers returned home, they yet again faced the exploitation and indignities of colonial rule. Discontent grew and many men joined the **independence movements**, which had been increasing in strength since before the war. Most African countries gained independence between 1956 and 1968 **334–35 »**, and by 1978 European rule had almost disappeared.

MAJORITY RULE

There were long and protracted struggles for **black majority rule** in Zimbabwe and South Africa. Majority rule was achieved in Zimbabwe in 1980 when **Robert Mugabe**, leader of Zanu PF, was voted into power. The **ANC** and the

INKATHA FREEDOM PARTY ELECTION POSTER

Inkatha Freedom Party (IFP) fought for majority rule in South Africa until 1994 when, led by **Nelson Mandela**, the ANC won the country's first multi-racial elections **376–77 »**.

6

POPULATION AND POWER

1914–present

The modern age has seen the two bloodiest and costliest wars in human history, conflicts that spanned the globe. It has been a period of opposing political beliefs and ruthless dictators, of rapidly expanding populations and diminishing resources. But it has also been one of startling technological innovation and unprecedented prosperity.

The **Assassination** at **Sarajevo**

The spark that caused the European tinderbox to ignite into World War I was lit in the Bosnian capital of Sarajevo. The assassination of Archduke Franz Ferdinand, heir to the Austro–Hungarian throne, triggered a series of reactions that would lead to a full-scale European war within five weeks, a war that soon spread around the world.

The archduke and his wife Sofia were making an official visit to Sarajevo to inspect military manoeuvres. Austria–Hungary had occupied the Turkish province of Bosnia–Herzegovina since 1878 and fully annexed it in 1908. Neighbouring Serbia resented this, as the province was mainly populated by Serbs, so relations between the two states were tense.

As the royal couple drove to an official reception at the town hall, a bomb was thrown into their car. It bounced off the rear canopy and exploded under the car behind, injuring two royal aides and 18 others. After the reception, the archduke changed his route out of the town but on the way, his driver took a wrong turning and halted. By chance, a group of conspirators involved in the earlier incident but not detained by the police were loitering there. One of them, Gavrilo Princip, a 19-year-old student, leapt on to the car's running board and shot the royal couple at point-blank range, hitting the archduke in the neck and his wife in the abdomen. They both died within a few minutes.

It was clear that Princip had not acted alone. He and his five fellow assassins were members of the Black Hand, a secret nationalist society led by Colonel Dragutin Dimitrijevic, head of Serbia's military intelligence. Austria–Hungary then accused the Serbian government of complicity in the assassination. It also asked its ally, Germany, for support against Serbia. When this was confirmed, Austria–Hungary issued an ultimatum on 23 July that would have effectively ended Serbian independence. Serbia's reply was received in the Austrian capital just two minutes short of the 48-hour deadline. It had agreed to almost all of Austria's demands, but also appealed to Russia for help and offered to refer the dispute to the International Court. The reply was rejected. The next day, 26 July, Austria–Hungary mobilized its forces, declaring war on Serbia on 28 July. The countdown to war had begun.

Arrest
Soldiers arrest 19-year-old Gavrilo Princip after the assassination of Archduke Franz Ferdinand and his wife, Sofia, in Sarajevo.

" The lamps are going out all over Europe. We shall not see them lit again in our lifetime."

SIR EDWARD GREY, BRITISH FOREIGN SECRETARY, 3 AUGUST 1914

« BEFORE

The origins of the world war lie in European rivalries stretching back more than 40 years.

TRIPLE ENTENTE

German unification in 1871, **« 260–63** and its rise to military and industrial power, combined with its commercial and imperial ambitions in Europe, the Middle East, and Africa alarmed its neighbours. The German defeat of France in 1871 had made the two countries bitter enemies. Germany constructed **defensive alliances** with first Austria–Hungary and then Italy, while France looked to Russia and Britain. A naval **arms race** between Britain and Germany added to the growing military tension.

SCHLIEFFEN PLAN

RUSSIAN THREAT Fearing war on two fronts, against France and Russia, in 1905, the German Chief of the General Staff, General von Schlieffen drew up a plan for Germany to deliver a **knock-out blow against France**, before turning to face the huge, but slow to mobilize, Russian army.

The beginning of the twentieth century saw Europe divided into two armed camps. Germany had formed an alliance with Austria–Hungary in 1879 (see BEFORE) as it felt threatened by the hostile nations at its borders and needed to protect its interests in Central Europe and the Balkans. France, Russia, and later Britain formed their own alliance, in part to protect themselves against possible German aggression.

The road to war

The spark that caused the war was the assassination of Archduke Ferdinand, heir to the Austro–Hungarian throne, by a Serb fanatic in Sarajevo, capital of Austrian Bosnia (see pp.294–95).

Austria accused Serbia of complicity in the murder, and gained German support. Austria refused a compromise with Serbia and, on 28 July declared war. Continental war was unavoidable as both sides honoured commitments to their allies. Russia mobilized its troops in support of Serbia, and when German demands for it to stop were refused, Germany declared war on Russia on 1 August. Knowing that France would support Russia, Germany then declared war on France on 3 August and implemented the Schlieffen Plan (see BEFORE) sending its army through Belgium in an attempt to knock France out of the war, before turning its attention on Russia. Britain initially held back, but honoured its

guarantee of Belgian independence, agreed by treaty in 1839, and declared war against Germany on 4 August.

Deadlock

The initial German advance was halted in early September 80 km (50 miles) east of Paris, by a combined French and British army. Both sides then raced north towards the English Channel in an attempt to break through round the side of their enemy's lines. When this failed, the two sides dug in along the length of the Western Front. Stalemate lasted there until almost the end of the war, as the defensive capabilities of the machine gun prevented any significant advance by either side. Allied attempts to break the deadlock at Neuve

The Great War

In July 1914 a war broke out in the Balkans that within days spread to the rest of Europe. That war was expected to be over by Christmas but it dragged on for more than four years. At the time it was known as the Great War. We know it now as World War I.

Going over the top
The order to climb out of the relative safety of the trench and advance – assaulted by gunfire and weighed down by weapons and heavy equipment – across the mud of no-man's-land toward the enemy was often met with terror.

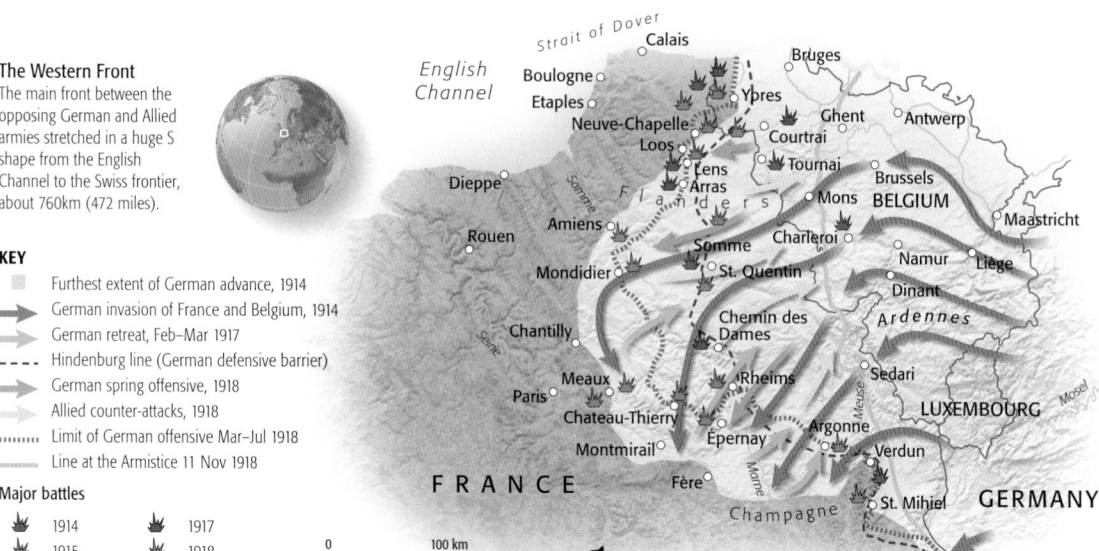

The Western Front

The main front between the opposing German and Allied armies stretched in a huge S shape from the English Channel to the Swiss frontier, about 760km (472 miles).

KEY

- ■ Furthest extent of German advance, 1914
- → German invasion of France and Belgium, 1914
- → German retreat, Feb–Mar 1917
- --- Hindenburg line (German defensive barrier)
- → German spring offensive, 1918
- → Allied counter-attacks, 1918
- ······· Limit of German offensive Mar–Jul 1918
- — Line at the Armistice 11 Nov 1918

Major battles

⚜	1914	⚜	1917
⚜	1915	⚜	1918
⚜	1916		

Map labels: Strait of Dover, English Channel, Calais, Bruges, Boulogne, Ypres, Ghent, Antwerp, Etaples, Neuve-Chapelle, Courtrai, Loos, Tournai, Lens, Arras, Mons, BELGIUM, Brussels, Maastricht, Dieppe, Amiens, Somme, Charleroi, Namur, Liège, Rouen, Mondidier, St. Quentin, Dinant, Chantilly, Chemin des Dames, Ardennes, Meaux, Rheims, Sedari, Paris, Chateau-Thierry, Epernay, Argonne, LUXEMBOURG, Montmirail, Verdun, Fère, St. Mihiel, GERMANY, Champagne, FRANCE, Flanders, Mosel

0   100 km
0   100 miles

Trench life

Infantrymen wait in a trench near the front line for the order to go over the top. Conditions in the trenches were appalling – muddy, waterlogged, and infested with rats.

Chapelle, Ypres, and Loos in 1915, and the Somme in 1916, were hugely costly – 57,470 British troops were killed or injured on the first day of battle on the Somme – and failed to break German lines. German attacks on the French city of Verdun throughout 1916 were intended to make France "bleed to death". By the time the battle ended in stalemate, there were more than 750,000 French and German casualties.

The other fronts

The Eastern Front was far more fluid. A Russian advance into German East Prussia was halted at Tannenberg in August and the Masurian Lakes in September. German and Austrian advances into Russia in 1915 were countered by a major Russian offensive into Austria in 1916.

In the Balkans, Serbia repelled an Austrian invasion, but the entry into the war on Germany's side by the Ottoman Empire in November 1914 and Bulgaria in September 1915, tipped the scales. By January, Serbia and its ally Montenegro were overrun, while Romania was defeated the following year. An Allied attempt to force the Ottomans out of the war by invading the Gallipoli peninsula in Turkey failed miserably in 1915. Italy, once a German ally, joined the war in April 1915 on the Allied side, lured by potential territorial gains, but soon became bogged down in battles with Austrian troops on the Isonzo River in the far northeast of the country.

All the main protagonists except Austria had extensive overseas empires (see pp.276–77). British and French imperial troops occupied German colonies in Africa and the Pacific, the Japanese seizing German colonies in the western Pacific and China. British and Indian troops also invaded Ottoman Mesopotamia (now Iraq), while in 1916 the British incited the Arabs to revolt against Ottoman rule.

At sea, the expected clash between the naval fleets of Britain and Germany never really happened. There were battles in the South Atlantic and at Jutland in the North Sea, but although German U-boats did substantial damage to Allied shipping, the British navy was the stronger force. »

"What a bloodbath… Hell cannot be this **dreadful**."

ALBERT JOUBAIRE, A FRENCH SOLDIER AT VERDUN, 1916

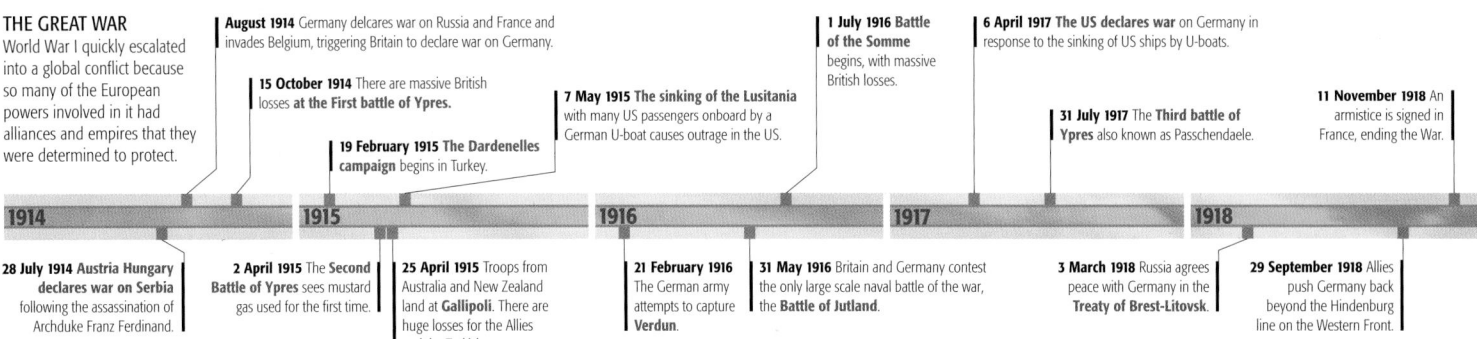

THE GREAT WAR
World War I quickly escalated into a global conflict because so many of the European powers involved in it had alliances and empires that they were determined to protect.

August 1914 Germany delcares war on Russia and France and invades Belgium, triggering Britain to declare war on Germany.

15 October 1914 There are massive British losses **at the First battle of Ypres.**

19 February 1915 The Dardenelles campaign begins in Turkey.

7 May 1915 The sinking of the Lusitania with many US passengers onboard by a German U-boat causes outrage in the US.

1 July 1916 Battle of the Somme begins, with massive British losses.

6 April 1917 The US declares war on Germany in response to the sinking of US ships by U-boats.

31 July 1917 The Third battle of Ypres also known as Passchendaele.

11 November 1918 An armistice is signed in France, ending the War.

1914 **1915** **1916** **1917** **1918**

28 July 1914 Austria Hungary declares war on Serbia following the assassination of Archduke Franz Ferdinand.

2 April 1915 The Second Battle of Ypres sees mustard gas used for the first time.

25 April 1915 Troops from Australia and New Zealand land at **Gallipoli**. There are huge losses for the Allies and the Turkish army.

21 February 1916 The German army attempts to capture **Verdun**.

31 May 1916 Britain and Germany contest the only large scale naval battle of the war, the **Battle of Jutland**.

3 March 1918 Russia agrees peace with Germany in the **Treaty of Brest-Litovsk**.

29 September 1918 Allies push Germany back beyond the Hindenburg line on the Western Front.

1917 was a difficult year for all sides. The Allied naval blockade of Germany and the German U-boat campaign against Allied merchant shipping led to severe food shortages: Germany ran out of wheat flour during the winter, while Britain had run out of sugar by April, and had only enough wheat to last six weeks.

Mutiny and revolution
The French army mutinied in April as a result of the losses it had endured. Riots in Russia in March led to the abdication of the tsar, and when the Bolsheviks (see pp.300–01) siezed power in November, they agreed a ceasefire with Germany. The Italians had weakened the Austro–Hungarians, but when the Germans attacked in November, only the swift deployment of British and French troops saved Italy.

The Allies launched a new attack on the Western Front at Arras in April, and in July at Ypres. Both failed: with 250,000 casualties at Ypres.

US joins the war
Two events were to break the stalemate. In February 1917, Germany announced it would attack all foreign ships, in order to starve Britain out of the war. The threat to US shipping was clear, but Germany tried to divert American attention by encouraging Mexico to

Women at work
With men away fighting at the front, women were required to work in industry, services, and on the land. By the end of the war, one million British women worked in munitions (as pictured left) and engineering works.

attack the US. Publication of a telegram sent by the German foreign minister to Mexico outraged Americans and in April the US declared war.

The second event was the mass use of tanks by the British at the Battle of Cambrai in November 1917. Tanks were one of the few developments in military technology during the war, along with airships and planes for reconnaissance, or bombardment.

The final nine months
In March 1918 Germany and Russia signed a peace treaty at Brest-Litovsk. Germany now shifted all its troops to the Western Front, and attacked on 21 March before US troops arrived. But the Germans outran their supplies and the attack was halted on 18 July. A mass tank advance by the British at Amiens on 8 August and French–US attacks to the south then forced the Germans back into Belgium.

Germany's Bulgarian allies sued for peace at the end of September, while the Italians won a massive victory against the Austro–Hungarians in October. The Austro–Hungarian and Ottoman empires then both agreed an armistice with the Allies. In Germany, food and fuel shortages led to the country collapsing from within. After the naval fleet mutinied at Kiel, Kaiser Wilhelm II abdicated and the new government agreed armistice terms. At 11 am on the morning of 11 November 1918, the war came to an end.

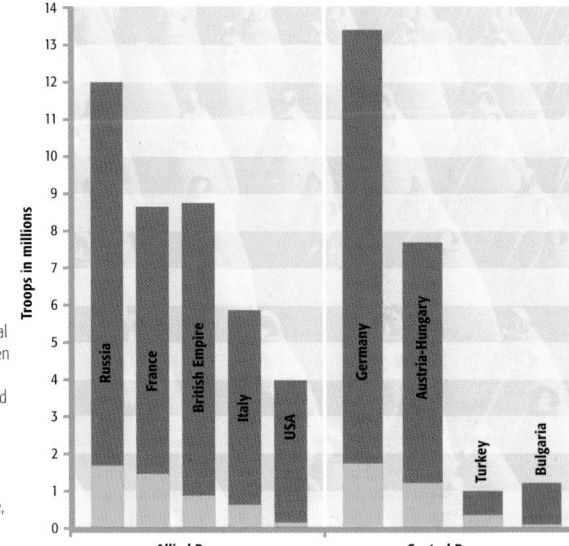

Land Army
Women worked the land. It was vital both in the US and Europe, where U-boat attacks and an economic blockade reduced food supplies.

KEY
- Mobilized military
- Military dead

War casualties
The human cost of the war was immense: a total of around 65 million men fought during the war, of whom 8.5 million died and 21.2 million were seriously injured. An estimated 6.6 million civilians also died from the fighting, or blockade, and disease.

Troops in millions

Russia
France
British Empire
Italy
USA
Germany
Austria-Hungary
Turkey
Bulgaria

Allied Powers **Central Powers**

AFTER

The war had short-term political effects in redrawing the map of Europe, but had longer-lasting social and economic consequences.

POST-WAR PEACE TREATIES
Under the **Versailles Treaty** signed in June 1919, Germany reluctantly accepted guilt for causing the war and agreed to pay **reparations** (war damages). It lost its colonies to the Allies as "mandates" – territories under the supervision of the League of Nations, an international organization founded to promote peace through diplomacy – and gave up territory to France, Belgium, Denmark, and Poland. Germany's armed forces were limited in size; the Rhineland was **demilitarized** and the industrial Saar region became a League of Nations mandate.

THE MAP OF EUROPE REDRAWN
The treaties of **St Germain** with Austria (September 1919), **Neuilly** with Bulgaria (November 1919), and **Trianon** with Hungary (June 1920) **redrew the map** of Central and Eastern Europe, with defeated nations paying war reparations. *Anschluss* **314 》**, union between Austria and Germany, was forbidden. The **Treaty of Sèvres** with the Ottoman Empire was agreed in August 1920 but later rewritten at Lausanne in July 1923.

WOMEN AND WORK
The **mobilization of women** into war industries and agriculture temporarily raised their economic status, although most returned to work in the home at the end of the war. As a result of their war work, **women gained the vote** in Britain in 1918 and in America in 1920 **356–57 》**.

REMEMBRANCE
The profusion of red **Flanders poppies** growing along the Western Front after the war inspired the British Legion to sell paper poppies to raise money for injured soldiers. On, or near **11 November** each year, commemorations are held across Europe to remember those who were killed or injured.

POPPY APPEAL

TOTAL WARFARE
World War I has been identified as the first "total war" in history, as the entire national economy, industry, and population were directed towards winning the war. British success in this **total mobilization** was one of the main reasons it, and the Allies, overcame Germany.

" No more slaughter, no more **mud and blood**... "

LIEUTENANT RG DIXON, BRITISH SOLDIER, 11 NOVEMBER 1918

« BEFORE

When Nicholas II acceded to the throne as Tsar (Emperor) in 1894, Russia was dangerously divided between the wealthy aristocracy and the discontented poor.

NICHOLAS II

Nicholas was an **autocrat** – believing that only he had the authority to rule Russia; however he lacked the strength of will to fulfil this role. To remain a dominant European force, Russia desperately needed to industrialize, but with modernization came inevitable **demands for civil rights** from impoverished Russian workers. There were few freedoms for the predominantly peasant population. Nicholas, a natural conservative, repeatedly failed to work with moderate forces and reform society, losing the opportunity to transform Russia into a modern nation.

BOLSHEVIKS AND MENSHEVIKS

The **Russian Social Democratic Labour Party** (RSDLP) was formed in 1898, and was heavily influenced by the theories of Karl Marx **« 264–65**. In 1902, the party divided into two strands; the **Bolsheviks**, led by Lenin (see right) who advocated change through violent revolution, and the more moderate **Mensheviks**, who believed in a more gradual process of change.

JAPANESE WAR FLAG

RUSSO–JAPANESE WAR

In 1904 Russia became involved in a **war with the Japanese**, over competing ambitions in Korea and Manchuria (a province in northeast China) **« 286–87**. Weakened by successive defeats, Russia signed the **Treaty of Portsmouth** in 1905, ending the conflict.

1905 REVOLUTION

As Russia suffered defeats abroad, violence erupted at home. Petrograd (St Petersburg) experienced **a brutal massacre** when 200,000 disaffected workers and their families **marched on the Winter Palace** (the residence of the Tsar) to demand better pay and working conditions. The protesters were met by Cossack cavalry who, sabres drawn, charged the crowd, killing many. Across Russia, the **population rose up** against the Tsar. Discipline broke down among troops and at Odessa, **sailors mutinied** against the appalling conditions on the battleship *Potemkin* (the subject of a 1925 film by Sergei Eisenstein).

POSTER FOR "BATTLESHIP POTEMKIN"

The **Russian Revolution**

Described by US journalist John Reed, a first-hand observer of the event, as "Ten Days That Shook the World", the October Revolution of 1917 saw the Bolshevik Party seize power in Russia, after decades of discontent. The Bolsheviks went on to create the world's first Communist state.

In the wake of the 1905 revolution (see BEFORE), Nicholas II agreed to instigate a new constitution for Russia, which included the formation of an elected parliament, or Duma. However, the Tsar retained the ability to disband the Duma at will, which he did when the assembly met in 1906 and 1907. Two subsequent Dumas met from 1907–1912, and 1912–17, although they were in almost constant conflict with Nicholas, who struggled to remain in control of the worsening political situation. The outbreak of World War I in August 1914 briefly united Russians against a common German enemy.

The war did not go well for Russia. By 1917, having sustained enormous losses on the battlefield and with the war effort creating high prices and food shortages, resentment towards the Tsar increased. Industrial workers across Russia began a crippling general strike. With violence erupting on the streets of Petrograd and Moscow, Nicholas was finally forced to abdicate. The Duma handed over power to the Provisional Government, which aimed to establish a liberal democracy. But discontent was still in the air, as the government refused to withdraw from the war. The power was increasingly contested by the Petrograd Soviet of Workers and Soldiers, one of many workers' councils (soviets) springing up all over the country. The Petrograd Soviet had the crucial support of troops garrisoned in the capital. It denounced the new government as "bourgeois" (middle class), and claimed to be the only true representative of the Russian people.

Peace, land, and bread

In April 1917, Lenin (see right), a key member of the revolutionary Russian Bolshevik Party returned to Petrograd from exile in Western Europe. Lenin was convinced that collapse of world capitalism, as predicted by Karl Marx, was imminent. His aim was to supervise a proletarian (workers') revolution, with the rallying cry of "peace, land, and bread, [and] all power to the Soviets". In April the Bolshevik newspaper *Pravda* ("*The Truth*") published Lenin's demands for the overthrow of the government and withdrawal from the "imperialist" war.

Lenin's anti-war stance gained mass support in July, when a Russian offensive ended with huge casualties. For three days, soldiers and workers rioted in Petrograd in an uprising so damaging that the prime minister, Prince Lvov, resigned. He was replaced by Alexander Kerensky, who branded Lenin a German spy. Lenin fled to Finland and the prospect of revolution seemed to recede.

However, Lenin's followers soon received assistance from an unlikely source. General Lavr Kornilov, the Russian army's commander-in-chief, believed that the country would descend into anarchy if the Bolsheviks were to gain ground, and in August

" History will not forgive us if we do not **assume power** now.**"**

LENIN, 1917

May Day protest
On 1 May 1917, a massive labour demonstration took place in Petrograd. Every Soviet (workers' council) in Russia was represented at the march. Many carried banners bearing political slogans.

Street fighting
Supporters of Lenin flee the gunfire of Provisional Government forces in Petrograd, July 1917.

In the aftermath of the Russian Revolution, the Bolsheviks faced both internal and international opposition. They acted ruthlessly to tighten their grip on power.

THE ROMANOV FAMILY

EXECUTION OF THE ROMANOVS

After his abdication Nicholas II and his family were kept under **house arrest**, moving in the spring of 1918 to Ekaterinburg in the Urals. On 17 July, as anti-Bolshevik forces were advancing, Nicholas, his wife, their five children and servants were taken into the cellar of the house and shot. There is no evidence of a direct command from Lenin: the **death sentence** was passed by the local regional Soviet. The family's execution removed one of many threats to the Bolsheviks' rule.

CIVIL WAR

RED ARMY BADGE

In 1918 the anti-Bolshevik **White Army** launched attacks against the new regime. They received military support from many countries including Britain, France, and the USA. During the next three years the **Bolshevik Red Army** fought invasions in the Baltic, the Caucusus, Siberia, and the Ukraine.

BIRTH OF THE SOVIET UNION

By the end of 1920 the counter-revolutionaries were defeated and absolute Bolshevik military and political power was established. Russia was re-named the **Union of Soviet Socialist Republics (USSR)** or **Soviet Union** in 1922.

NEW ECONOMIC POLICY

During the civil war, the Soviet economy teetered on the **brink of collapse**, and money became virtually worthless. With the urban population and the army close to starvation, the state seized surplus food from peasant farmers without payment. In 1921 Lenin's "**New Economic Policy**" replaced these seizures with a regulated tax and as trade increased, the economy revived.

COMINTERN

Also known as the "Third International", Comintern was founded to promote **worldwide revolution**. Stalin **302–03 ≫** dissolved the association as a gesture of goodwill to the Allies in **World War II 304–05, 314–327 ≫**.

COMINTERN MEMBERSHIP CARD

BOLSHEVIK Founded by Lenin in 1912 the Bolshevik Party was committed to a workers' (proletarian) revolution and the overthrow of the imperial regime.

1917 he ordered troops into Petrograd to protect the government. Fearing that Kornilov intended to seize power for himself, Kerensky asked the Bolsheviks for assistance, which they duly provided, in the form of a mass of workers, who persuaded the troops to turn around.

The Kornilov affair seriously weakened the Provisional Government, and in October Lenin secretly returned to Petrograd. He announced to the Bolshevik Party's Central Committee that the time for revolution had arrived, entrusting the military organization of the revolution to Leon Trotsky (see pp.304–05).

October Revolution

On October 25th – according to the old Russian (Julian) calendar, November 7th in the modern (Gregorian) one – Trotsky's men executed an almost bloodless coup in Petrograd. Armed squads of pro-Bolshevik revolutionaries occupied key positions such as railway stations, banks, post offices, and telephone exchanges. The battleship *Aurora*, flying the Bolshevik Red Flag from its mast, dropped anchor in the river Neva with its guns trained on the Winter Palace, where Kerensky's government was in session. After firing just a single blank shell from the ship and two more shells from another gun position, the government surrendered.

That night, Lenin issued a powerful address to the Russian people, entitled "To All Soldiers, Workers, and Peasants", in which he promised to transfer the lands of the aristocracy, the church, and crown to peasant committees and to establish the workers' control over Russia's industries. The people of Russia would at last become their own masters. The Bolsheviks moved quickly to secure supremacy over other political groups, ensuring that soviets took over control across Russia, and ensuring that they alone would form the new government.

Lenin's immediate concern was to make peace with Germany and end an exhausting and costly war. Firmly believing that revolution would soon spread across the capitalist world, he accepted Germany's peace terms, failing to anticipate the furious international reaction against his new Russia that was about to be unleashed.

VLADIMIR ILYICH LENIN

Lenin became politicized after his elder brother was hanged for his part in a plot to kill Tsar Alexander III. In 1895 he was exiled to Siberia for revolutionary activities. On his release, Lenin spent several years in Europe, where he studied Marxist theory. His 1902 essay "What is to be done?" argued for a workers' revolution, under the leadership of a strong government. Lenin came to power in the October Revolution, but died less than seven years later. However, his politics provided the inspiration for further Marxist revolutions in many countries.

LEADER OF THE SOVIET UNION Born 1878 Died 1953

Joseph Stalin

"I believe in one thing only, **the power of human will.**"

JOSEPH STALIN

The future dictator of the Soviet Union was born in 1878 in Georgia, in the southeastern Russian Empire. Joseph Dzugashvili (not yet Stalin, the "Man of Steel") attended a theological college in the Georgian capital, Tblisi, where he became involved in radical politics. He joined the Marxist Social Democratic Labour Party (SDLP), and with Lenin sided with the Bolshevik faction (see p.301) when the SDLP split in 1904.

Many Russian Marxists, including Lenin (see pp.300–01) were forced to live in exile, devoting themselves to complex theoretical debates. In Russia Stalin engaged in practical subversive activities, ranging from armed robbery to distributing illegal pamphlets. His efforts attracted the attention of both the Bolshevik leadership and the police. After several arrests, Stalin was facing exile in Siberia when he was unexpectedly freed after the overthrow of the Tsar in March 1917 (see pp.300–01).

Father of the people
Stalin's official portrait of 1940 is intended to suggest his far-sighted wisdom. The photograph shows no sign of the smallpox scars that disfigured him from childhood.

Information card
Stalin was arrested several times before 1917. This is a police record of one of his crimes. The future dictator was photographed and his fingerprints were recorded.

Rise to power
Stalin proved himself a tough enforcer of Lenin's policies during the upheavals that brought the Bolsheviks to power in 1917 and the Civil War that followed. Hard-working and devious, once the Soviet Union was established he became one of the most powerful men in the country. In 1922 Stalin was appointed General Secretary to the Central Committee of the Communist Party. He exploited this post to fill Party positions with his appointees and expel his enemies. Lenin belatedly turned against Stalin, calling for someone "more tolerant… more polite". But by then, Stalin's hold was too strong. Stalin's manoeuvring after Lenin's death in January 1924 was a masterly exercise in political

manipulation. He pitted his rivals for power against one another, then used his control of the Party to ensure that it expelled or demoted them. By the time Leon Trotsky – once fellow Bolshevik and now bitter rival – was exiled from the Soviet Union in 1929, Stalin had established himself as the country's undisputed leader.

In an early example of his taste for rewriting the past, Stalin celebrated his 50th birthday that year, discreetly adjusting his birth date to 1879. The celebrations initiated the personality cult that was to continue for the rest of

his life. Hailed by his propagandists as "the Universal Genius" and the "Man of Steel", factories, towns, and even mountains were named after him across the Soviet Union, and every reference to him was couched in terms of grovelling flattery (see pp.304–05).

Socialism in one country
In 1924, Stalin proposed the slogan "Socialism in One Country". In practice, this meant building up the power of the Soviet Union, the one country where Marxist revolution had succeeded. Stalin was acutely

conscious of Russia's economic and cultural backwardness, and he despised the peasant majority. His successor, Nikita Khruschev, wrote: "for Stalin, the peasants were scum." From 1928–29, Stalin aimed to transform the Soviet Union into a major international power, and the process of the collectivization of agriculture and industrialization (see pp.304–05) reflected his belief in the use of terror to achieve radical change. During the 1930s, millions of Soviet citizens were killed by the state, used as slave labour in prison camps, or died in famines to

STATE CENSORSHIP

Stalin's censors distorted the past to preserve the myth of his infallibility. Individuals who had fallen out of favour were eliminated from the historical record. Retouching photographs was a striking aspect of this enforced amnesia. In charge of the secret police in 1936–38, Nikolai Yezhov, known as the "Poisoned Dwarf", was responsible for the worst of the Stalinist purges. When he was also executed on Stalin's orders in 1940, all traces of his association with the "Great Leader" were eradicated. Thus Yezhov's image was removed from this photo taken at the Moscow–Volga canal.

ORIGINAL PHOTOGRAPH

RETOUCHED VERSION

> "**The death of one man** is a tragedy. **The death of millions** is a statistic."
>
> JOSEPH STALIN, ATTRIBUTED

which Stalin's policies contributed. His aims were achieved, but at an astounding human cost.

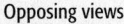

Opposing views
This German cartoon satirizes the Stalinist state by showing it as fighting against itself. In sharp contrast, this statue depicts Stalin as a regal leader.

Behind closed doors

The situation in the country was mirrored at Stalin's "court" in the Kremlin, Moscow, where his entourage lived in constant fear of arrest, torture, or execution. The assassination of Sergei Kirov, a member of Stalin's inner circle, in 1934 precipitated a wave of arrests and executions – although it is possible that Stalin himself had Kirov killed. Between 1936 and 1938, Stalin unleashed the secret police upon the Communist Party leadership and army officers. Thousands were executed after grotesque "show trials" in which they confessed to absurd crimes.

Wartime leader

World War II showed Stalin at his best and worst. Shrewd and cunning, he entered an alliance with Nazi Germany in 1939 that arguably gave him time to strengthen his military position before the German invasion of the Soviet Union in June 1941. Yet he showed poor judgement in refusing to believe evidence of the imminent German attack. His military policy of "no retreat, no surrender" vastly inflated Soviet losses in the early battles of the war, yet he later bowed to his generals' judgement. His reign of terror over the Soviet people was unrelenting, but he sensibly encouraged patriotism and even allowed a revival of religion to

boost morale. He handled the wartime alliance with the United States and Britain in masterly fashion, winning the trust of US President Roosevelt, and the grudging respect of British Prime Minister, Winston Churchill.

Postwar and death

Victory over Nazi Germany in May 1945 took Stalin to the pinnacle of power, but he became increasingly paranoid as ever more bizarre plots against him were allegedly uncovered by his secret police. Stalin's suspicion of the Western powers made the ideological struggle between the communist nations and the capitalist West – the Cold War – seem inevitable (see pp.328–29). By the time he died in

1953, Stalin was responsible for the deaths of at least five million Soviet citizens, yet throughout the country people wept at the news of his death. The horrors of his rule were denounced only three years later by his successor, Khrushchev. Stalin seems destined to be remembered, like Ivan the Terrible or Peter the Great, as one of the monster-heroes of Russian history.

(see pp.328–29)

World leader

The Soviet Union played a vital role on the side of the Allies in World War II. Stalin used his military advantage to bargain for greater Soviet influence in Eastern Europe. He is pictured here with Churchill (left) and Roosevelt (centre) at the Yalta Conference where the leaders planned the future of post-war Europe.

- **18 December 1878** Born Joseph Vissarionovich Dzugashvili in Gori, Georgia, son of a cobbler.
- **1901** Joins the Marxist Russian Social Democratic Labour Party.
- **1912** Joins the Bolshevik Party Central Committee and becomes editor of *Pravda*.
- **1913** After several arrests, Stalin is sentenced to exile for life in Siberia.
- **13 March 1917** Freed from exile.
- **9 October 1917** Joins the Bolshevik Committee to make an armed seizure of power.
- **March 1919** Joins the Politburo, the most powerful body of the Bolshevik regime.
- **3 April 1922** Appointed General Secretary to the Communist Party's Central Committee.
- **December 1922** In his "last testament", Lenin calls for Stalin to be removed from his post.
- **21 January 1924** Lenin dies. Stalin, Zinoviev, and Kamenev exclude Trotsky from power.
- **19 October 1926** Trotsky, Zinoviev, and Kamenev expelled from the Politburo.
- **1928** The collectivization of agriculture and rapid industrialization is begun.
- **February 1929** Trotsky is exiled from the USSR.
- **1932–34** Around four million die in Ukranian famine caused by Stalin's policy of collectivization and requisition of grain.
- **December 1934** Arrests and executions within the Communist Party follow Sergei Kirov's assassination.
- **1936–38** Around 690,000 executed in "The Great Terror".
- **August 1939** Stalin makes a neutrality pact with the Nazis, secretly agreeing the partition of Poland between Germany and the Soviet Union.

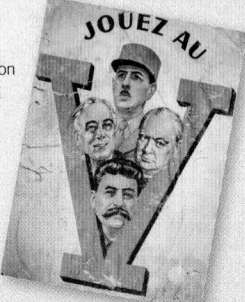

JOUEZ AU V

ALLIED PROPAGANDA

- **21 August 1940** Trotsky murdered in Mexico by an agent of Stalin.
- **3 July 1941** Calls for Soviet resistance to the German invasion.
- **28 July 1942** Decrees the death penalty for unauthorized retreat by the army.
- **November–December 1943** Stalin meets US President Roosevelt and British Prime Minister Churchill at Tehran; and again at Yalta in 1945.
- **March 1948** Coup in Czechoslovakia completes the Stalinist takeover of Eastern Europe
- **July 1948–May 1949** USSR blockades Berlin, trying to evict the US, British, and French forces.
- **25 June 1950** With Stalin's backing, North Korea invades South Korea, starting the Korean War.
- **1952** Allegations of a plot by Jewish doctors to assassinate Stalin and other Soviet leaders
- **5 March 1953** Stalin dies at his dacha in mysterious circumstances (see p.305).

BEFORE

In the 19th and early 20th centuries, Russia's rocky path led her from despotic Tsarist rule through revolution, civil war, and the creation of a new state. In 1920 the Union of Soviet Socialist Republics was formed.

SIBERIAN WORK CAMPS
During the 19th century, political activists and criminals were sent to work in forced labour camps in Siberia (northeast Russia). Stalin vastly extended the use of these work camps.

PRISONERS IN SIBERIA, 1897

SOVIET DEMOCRACY
Lenin held Marxist ≪ 264–65 beliefs and strove to achieve a "dictatorship of the proletariat". After seizing power for the workers, the Communist Party's role was to guide them. In theory, workers held political power through locally elected councils, or "soviets", but there was heavy state control and power was centralized in the Party.

When Lenin came to power after the Russian Revolution (see pp.302–03), he quickly established a highly centralized system of government. He banned all rival political parties, and empowered the Communist Party's dominant Central Committee to expel anyone who failed to follow the party line. Disagreements with Trotsky (see right) and other members soon led to Lenin favouring Joseph Stalin, a rising star in the party. Stalin was already a member of the Politburo, the most powerful body of the regime, which made decisions on foreign relations, war, economics, and domestic policy, and the Orgburo, which was responsible for the Party's internal affairs. In 1922 he was appointed General Secretary of the Central Committee. After Lenin's death in January 1924, Stalin plotted to discredit and expel Central Committee

members who opposed his leadership, most notably Leon Trotsky (see opposite). All his rivals would eventually meet with violent deaths.

Stalinism
Over the course of Stalin's rule, Lenin's version of communism mutated into what became known as Stalinism. Between 1928–37, Stalin instituted the first and second Five Year Plans, huge and ambitious schemes that aimed to transform the Soviet Union into an industrialized society. While the rest of the developed world was suffering economic depression, Stalin achieved extraordinary growth (see pp.306–07).

"Death solves all problems –
no man, no problem." JOSEPH STALIN

Agriculture in the Soviet Union was also transformed. Frustrated by his dependence on a rebellious peasantry to provide grain for the exports needed to finance his industrial plans, Stalin enforced a policy of "collectivization". Land belonging to peasants and kulaks (prosperous rural farmers) was confiscated and turned into vast farms that were collectively run and worked by cooperatives. It was initially

30 MILLION The number of Russians who moved into cities and industrialized regions between 1928 and 1937, the time of Stalin's Five Year Plans.

The Hammer and Sickle

In 1921, with revolution achieved, and civil war at an end, the Soviet Union entered a 20-year period of relative peace. Lenin and the Bolshevik Party could turn their attention to the task of transforming the former Russian Empire, putting Karl Marx's vision of communism into practice.

Soviet farm tractor
In the 1930s, the first Soviet tractors were produced. They were kept at district stations and could only be used with party permission, thus keeping the farms under tight political control.

disastrous, producing reduced grain yields, violence, and famine. But over time, agriculture adjusted and living standards slowly began to rise.

The "Great Terror"

Such rapid growth and change came at a price. Throughout his rule, while Stalin cultivated a propaganda image of himself as father of his people – benign, even God-like – the Soviet people suffered appalling hardships. Living standards were often sub-human, work was compulsory, and absenteeism a crime. Criticism of the communist system could lead to a sentence in those same forced labour camps created by the Tsars to crush dissent (see left). A network of new prison camps was erected west of Moscow to house the thousands who fell foul of Stalin's demands. The period 1936 to 1938, known as the "Great Terror", saw the secret police launching witch-hunts against the party elite and the army. Political opponents were forced to confess to plotting against Stalin and summarily executed. In two years, some 690,000 people were executed and many thousands more imprisoned or exiled.

Symbol of socialism
These figures raise the hammer, symbol of the industrial worker, and the sickle, symbol of the peasantry. "Socialist Realism" was the only art style permitted under Stalin.

The official truth
Pravda, meaning "truth", was the official newspaper of the Soviet Union between 1918 and 1991. Often used to parrot the views of the Communist Party, many regarded the paper as telling everything but the truth.

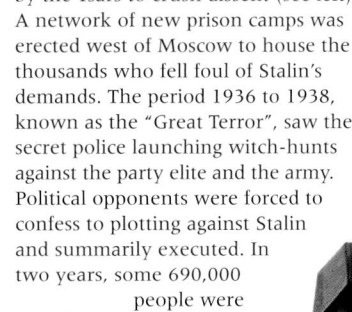

Ideal peasants
Without mechanized equipment, a Soviet women's brigade uses crude rakes to gather up the hay harvest on a collective farm, in this 1941 photograph. Images such as this one tried to show that the peasants were happily carrying out Stalin's severe agricultural policies; the reality was often very different.

Heroic images
This poster links Stalin with the revered Lenin, and typifies the heroic images Stalin used to promote himself.

The Soviet Bloc

The German invasion of the Soviet Union in 1941 caught Stalin by surprise, but after a bitterly fought war, his nation was ultimately victorious. At the 1945 conferences of Yalta and Potsdam, intended to secure lasting peace in the post-war world, Stalin secured the territories of eastern Poland and the Baltic States for Russia. New communist regimes emerged in Bulgaria, Romania, Hungary, Czechoslovakia, and East Germany. These became known as the Soviet Eastern Bloc, and were organized under Moscow's control, replicating Soviet policies and institutions. The Soviet Union had become the only world power to rival the United States. Relationships with her western allies quickly soured after the war. Russia and the Eastern Bloc became engaged in what would be termed the Cold War with the capitalist West (see pp.328–29).

AFTER

Despite the hardships that the Soviet people had suffered during Stalin's rule, there was genuine grief on his death in 1953. However, his legacy was a difficult one for the leadership of the Soviet Union.

DEATH OF STALIN

Stalin died in **mysterious circumstances** after eating dinner with close political colleagues, including **Lavrenty Beria**, former head of his secret police, and Stalin's successor Nikita Khrushchev. It has been suggested that he had swallowed warfarin, a type of rat poison. His body was embalmed, and displayed in the Lenin Mausoleum in Red Square. After Stalin's crimes were exposed, his **remains were removed** in 1961, and reburied in the Kremlin wall.

DE-STALINIZATION

Khrushchev swiftly began a process known as **De-Stalinization**, introducing basic legal rights, **allowing writers and artists greater freedoms**, and releasing huge numbers of political prisoners. Khrushchev also **encouraged foreign visitors** to the Soviet Union, but travel

KHRUSHCHEV

abroad for citizens remained strictly controlled. In 1956, Khrushchev denounced Stalin's regime of "suspicion, fear, and terror" in a secret speech to the inner circle of the Communist Party and a report was issued to the public pointing to some of Stalin's mistakes. The dominance of Stalinism finally began to diminish and a lesser cult of Lenin returned. That year, riots broke out in Poland, and the Hungarian people rebelled against Soviet rule. The **Hungarian uprising 370–71 »** was brutally repressed by the Soviet Red Army.

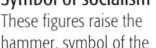

« BEFORE

BEFORE

After World War I the world economy slid into a recession that resulted in mass unemployment. Much of Europe experienced high rates of inflation.

NORTH AMERICA AFTER THE WAR
The post-war recession was reasonably short-lived in North America. Factories that produced goods for the war effort soon adapted to producing consumer goods, such as radios and cars, and from 1922 until 1927 the North American economies showed consistent growth.

EUROPE AFTER THE WAR
European agriculture and industries failed to adjust to the reduced demand of peacetime trade, so when millions of soldiers returned home, many could not find jobs. Germany, which had machinery confiscated by the victors, struggled to make **war reparation payments « 298–99** to the Allies, who in turn had trouble paying off war debts, and **recovery loans** provided by the US.

HYPERINFLATION IN GERMANY
As the Germans thought they would win the war and intended to force the losers to pay for their costs, they chose not to finance it through taxation. Instead the government ordered the *Reichsbank*, or central bank, to print more and more money to cover its ever-increasing war expenses. The *Reichsbank* continued to print money until 1923, when the purchasing power of the money in circulation plummeted as the price of everything in Germany inflated rapidly (hyperinflation). At the peak of hyperinflation the exchange rate was **one trillion marks to the US dollar**. Paper money was worth so little that people burned it to heat their houses.

WORTHLESS MARKS

BREAD **In 1918 in Germany a loaf of bread cost 0.63 marks. During the hyperinflation crisis the price rose to 201,000,000,000 marks in November 1923.**

The Great Depression

The US stock market collapsed in October 1929, triggering worldwide economic recession. Authoritarian regimes rose to power as people lost faith in democratic governments.

During the early 1920s the American economy flourished, but by 1927 the country was overproducing goods for which it did not have a market. Agricultural and factory production soon slowed down, leading to the loss of millions of jobs. Despite the downturn in demand for goods and rising unemployment, financiers and bankers continued to speculate recklessly on New York's Wall Street stock exchange, relying on borrowed money and false optimism.

The Wall Street Crash
In October 1929 stock prices began to decline and investors lost confidence in their shares, opting to sell them all. The first day of real panic, 24 October, is known as "Black Thursday". The panic began again on "Black Monday", and on "Black Tuesday", 29 October, 16 million shares were sold, and prices on the stock market collapsed completely in what became known as

In the news
The Crash affected all Americans, even making the headlines in this entertainment newspaper.

173 MILLION shares sold on US stock exchange in 1921.

451 MILLION shares sold in 1926.

1.1 MILLION shares sold in frantic trading in 1929.

the Wall Street Crash. Fortunes were lost and companies failed overnight. Wages for those still fortunate enough to have work fell dramatically. Many banks had made loans to businesses and people who could no longer repay them. Some banks also lost money in the Crash – when people hit by the economic depression needed to withdraw their savings, the banks often did not have the money to give them. This caused other bank customers to panic and demand their cash, so many banks were ruined. As people lost their jobs and savings, mortgages on many homes and farms were foreclosed and the properties were repossessed. Many people were forced to take shelter in shantytowns, which were nicknamed "Hoovervilles" out of resentment for President Herbert Hoover, who refused to provide aid to the unemployed.

Government intervention
As a result of the Crash the US investors withdrew many foreign loans, causing the collapse of the system of international loans set up to handle war reparations (see BEFORE). European countries, including Germany, needed these loans to pay for their imports, and were unable to do so once the funds were taken away. This affected trade between Europe and North America directly. Other parts of the world were also badly hit as much of their trade relied on selling food and raw materials to Europe and North America. The price of commodities, or traded goods, dropped drastically,

---

EFFECTS OF DEPRESSION
The economic slump that gripped the US spread across the globe. Ill-conceived government measures exacerbated the hardships suffered in many countries.

1929 US loans to and investments in Europe end, causing a worldwide **slump in productivity** and prices.

1929–33 Stalin collectivizes Soviet agriculture.

May 1931 Austria's largest bank collapses, which in its turn sets a series of **banking collapses** all over central Europe.

Winter 1931–33 Britain introduces protective import tariffs, but in the **Ottawa Agreements** gives preferential rates for its overseas territories.

9 March–15 June 1933 The American Congress passes Roosevelt's **New Deal** programme.

1929	1930	1931	1932	1933

24–29 October 1929 The Wall Street Crash follows panic selling of stocks and shares.

28 October 1929 The London stock exchange collapses.

17 June 1930 The Smoot-Hawley Tariff, the highest tax on imports to the US in history, is signed into law by the American Congress.

20 June 1931 President Hoover halts war reparations by Germany as part of an effort to limit the financial fall-out of the banking collapse.

30 January 1933 Hitler becomes German chancellor, winning the post by exploiting popular resentment of the depressed economic and social conditions.

On the road
Evicted from their farm in Missouri, this family travelled to California in search of work on the farms there.

In an effort to avoid the economic problems that arose after World War I, delegates from 44 Allied nations met in 1944 to plan for the end of World War II.

INTERNATIONAL MONETARY FUND
New **rules for financial and commercial transactions** between states in the developed world were agreed and the **International Monetary Fund** (IMF) was established to implement international monetary rules.

WORLD BANK
The World Bank was established to provide **finance and advice** for the economies of developing countries. World Bank activities focus on the development of heath, education, rural development, and legal institutions.

became dictatorships (countries ruled by one person with no recognized opposition). Some states set about building empires to secure supplies of raw materials. In October 1935 Italy's fascist leader, Benito Mussolini (see pp.308–09), ordered the invasion of Abyssinia in East Africa. Hitler (see pp.390–91) began a programme of active expansion, annexing Austria in March 1938. In response Britain and France began to rearm, and World War II (see pp.312–327) erupted in 1939. The renewed war in Europe created new jobs in armament factories, revitalizing the world economy and ending the economic depression.

" I pledge you, I pledge myself, to a **new deal** for the **American people**."

FRANKLIN D ROOSEVELT, DEMOCRATIC PRESIDENTIAL NOMINATION ACCEPTANCE SPEECH, 1932

falling to 45 per cent of 1929 values in 1932. Nations sought to protect their own industries. President Hoover introduced the Smoot-Hawley Tariff in 1930, imposing a 42–50 per cent tax on imports, and European governments responded with similar protectionist measures. This made matters worse, as it crippled international trade.

Hoover was criticized heavily for the way he handled the Depression and he was voted out of office in 1932 when Franklin D Roosevelt won a landslide victory on the promise of a "New Deal", a series of relief programmes devised to restart the economy and provide new jobs (see right). Roosevelt extended US government responsibilites into new economic areas and created social welfare assistance on a national level. Ultimately this large-scale government intervention worked and was adopted by other liberal democracies.

Rise of the far-right

Mass unemployment and poverty caused great anger, leading to civil unrest in some countries. Many people turned to right-wing leaders who promised to restore national prosperity by force if necessary (see pp.308–09). Between 1929–39, 25 countries

IDEA

NEW DEAL

Roosevelt's New Deal was a series of programmes that aimed to tackle economic depression and rescue millions of Americans living in need. The scheme vastly increased the scope of the federal government's activities. Business practices were reformed and welfare policies were introduced. Huge public projects were set up, creating millions of new jobs. One successful project turned the Colorado river basin into a vast wealth-producing area by building more than 20 dams and hydroelectric stations.

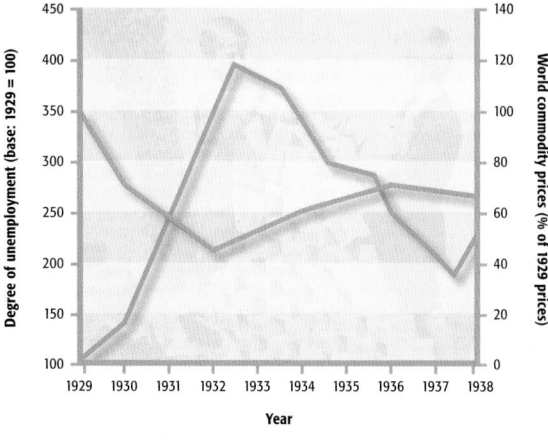

Commodities
There was a direct relationship between world commodity prices and employment between 1929–32. When commodity prices fell to their lowest value in 1932 unemployment peaked. In the same year commodity prices began to recover and unemployment began to decline in response.

KEY

Unemployment

World commodity prices

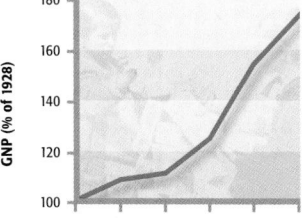

Soviet growth
Soviet economics followed a different path to those countries affected by the Great Depression. GNP rose as Five Year Plans for industrial growth and the state collectivization (see pp.304–05) of agriculture transformed the way the economy was run. The Soviet Union moved from being a rural and traditional economy to an urbanized, industrial base and emerged from this period of growth as a world power.

« BEFORE

After the atrocities and humiliations of World War I nationalist, right-wing ideals took hold in many European countries.

ACTION FRANÇAISE

Founded in France in 1898, *Action Française* was an extreme, **right-wing movement** led by Charles Maurras, his political vision included the re-establishment of the French monarchy. The group distributed a daily bulletin of the same name.

CHARLES MAURRAS

THE GERMAN IDEAL

In the 19th century the concept of an eternal, ideal German *Volk* (people) and *Volksgeist* (spirit of the nation) began to emerge. The philosopher **George Hegel** spoke of the German spirit as the **"spirit of the new world"** and Friedrich Nietzsche envisioned a "master morality" in which strength triumphs over weakness, unrestricted by the "tyranny" of virtue. These concepts appealed to Hitler, who twisted them to suit his own purposes.

THE PAN-GERMAN PARTY

Georg Schönerer founded the Pan-German Party in the 1880s in Austria. Its aim was to **unite all German-speaking peoples** under German rule. The Party had a presence in the Austrian Parliament but Schönerer's violent racism, which had led to his imprisonment for assaults on Jews, was too extreme for the politics of the day.

ITALIAN NATIONALISTS SEIZE FIUME

In 1919 Italian patriots, led by the poet **Gabriele D'Annunzio**, occupied the Italian-speaking port of Fiume on the Croatian coast. This action, which had popular support in Italy, was born of fury at gaining a mere 9,000 square miles in post-World War I peace settlements.

Fascism

World War I left Europe exhausted. Unemployment was rife as economies struggled to adapt to peacetime conditions. Disillusioned in their existing forms of government, many people were drawn to a new brand of nationalism known as fascism.

National Socialist Party poster
The Nazi Party promised to bring stability and order to Germany after the economic and social upheaval of the 1920s. It appealed to the people's basic demands, as this election poster from 1932 shows, with its promise of "Work, Freedom, and Bread".

The emergence of fascism and Nazism in Europe was made possible by a range of conditions. Economic hardship after World War I was a primary factor. In addition, the period 1918–20 was marked by political instability. Violence and lawlessness erupted across much of Eastern Europe, Germany, Italy, and Spain, between communists (see p.265) and their political opponents. Political thinking on the left was fractured, with communist, socialist, and trade union groups often in conflict with each other. On the right of the political spectrum the nationalist philosophies of fascism began to gain ground. Fascists loathed communism's internationalist thinking and had no faith in democratic government. Many, including Hitler and Mussolini, were veterans of World War I (see pp.296–99) and resented the old ruling elites who had led them into

a disastrous war. With no attachment to church or monarchy, fascists put all their faith in love of their nation, favouring a strong, ordered state.

The massive human and economic costs of the World War I left Italy's government undermined. In 1920 bands of "Blackshirts" – adopting the Roman symbol of the *fasces* (see right), which represented their belief in collective strength and authority over individual freedom – began to take the law into their own hands, attacking

> **FASCISM A radical nationalist ideology. Fascists believe in strong, authoritarian leadership and a collective, classless society bound by racial allegiance.**

socialists and striking trade unions. In the absence of government authority, the Fascists were widely seen as the protectors of law and order. In October

Italian coin
"Fascist" comes from the Roman *fasces* – a bundle of sticks (weak on their own but collectively strong) surrounding an axe – a symbol of authority.

1922, Fascist leader, Benito Mussolini, ordered his Blackshirts to march on Rome and seize power. King Victor Emmanuel III refused to back his Prime Minister's request for military support and invited Mussolini to form a new government. In 1926 Mussolini assumed absolute power, dissolving all other political parties and brutally silencing political opponents. Known to his people as "*Il Duce*", or "the Leader", Mussolini cultivated an image of himself as Italy's one true leader, the choice of the masses. In reality, Italy was a police state.

The right-wing governments of Germany and Italy backed the nationalists in the Spanish Civil War. Fascist parties continue to draw support to the present day.

SPANISH CIVIL WAR

GENERAL FRANCO

In 1936 fighting began in Spain between the socialist and republican left and nationalists led by **General Franco 310–11 >>**. A bitter civil war ensued which lasted until the nationalist victory in 1939. **Hitler 312–13>>** and Mussolini both sent military aid to support Franco while **Stalin 302–03 >>** supported his opponents.

NEO-FASCISM

Political groups of the far right have continued to emerge since World War II. Some, termed Neo-Nazis, believe in reviving Hitler's national socialism. Neo-fascist groups share elements of Nazi beliefs and tend to concentrate on a nationalistic, anti-immigration stance. These groups have included *Alternativa Sociale* in Italy, led by Mussolini's granddaughter Alessandra; the French *Front National*, founded by Jean-Marie Le Pen; and Jörg Haider's Austrian Freedom Party.

Nuremberg Rally
In the 1930s the Nazis held annual rallies for the party faithful at Nuremberg, as in the picture above. Thousands of soldiers stand listening to Hitler speak.

March on Rome
Mussolini's Blackshirts, shown above, were ordered to march on the Italian capital, Rome, in 1922. The Blackshirts, also called *"squadristi"* or squadrons, acted as paramilitary forces for the Fascist Party.

In 1918 the government of Germany's new Weimar Republic also faced huge problems. Germans were scarred by defeat in World War I and resentful of the peace settlements under which territory had been lost (see p.299). Economic troubles were made worse by war reparation payments imposed on Germany by her victorious enemies. In 1919, an Austrian-born soldier, Adolf Hitler, joined a small Munich-based political group: The German Worker's Party. Hitler had ambitions for power. His tirades against capitalists, communists, and Jews (at whose door he laid blame for all Germany's ills), would soon catch the public ear. His party was re-named the National Socialist German Workers Party (the NSDAP or Nazi Party, see pp.312–13).

Although the Nazi Party had much in common with Mussolini's Fascists, it also had a quasi-religious element, with its all-powerful Führer who demanded submission and a zealous belief in the superiority of the German race. Taking up Hegel's idealist concept of nation (see BEFORE) Nazism's goal was to unite all German-speaking people in a great German *Reich*, or empire (see p.315), that would last for a millennium. The Nazis believed races such as the Slavs and Jews were racially inferior to Aryans (white Caucasian people, the purest having blue eyes and blonde hair) and as such they would be banished from the *Reich* to preserve Aryan racial purity. Later, the Jews were to be wiped out in the "Final Solution" (see pp.322–23).

Mass movements with fascist ideologies arose in many countries during the 1920s and 1930s. The Austrian government had fascist leanings well before the country was annexed by Germany (see pp.314–15). In Britain, the politician Oswald Mosley formed the British Union of Fascists. Mosley's "Blackshirts" acted as guards at political rallies and fought with left-wing and Jewish groups.

> ## "The truth is that men are **tired of liberty.**"
>
> BENITO MUSSOLINI, 7 APRIL 1923

ITALIAN LEADER (1883–1945)

BENITO MUSSOLINI

Mussolini rose to political prominence before World War I in the Italian Socialist Party. In 1915 he broke with the socialists over intervention in World War I and became a radical nationalist. In 1919 he founded the Blackshirts and the Italian Fasicist Party in 1921. He became Prime Minister of Italy in 1922. Italy fought alongside Nazi Germany in World War II and when the Allies invaded Italy in 1943, Mussolini was stripped of his powers, though he led a Social Republic in the north of the country until he was shot in April 1945.

« BEFORE

BEFORE

When Spain lost control of its American colonies, it began to lose its political stability.

REIGN OF ALFONSO XIII
Defeat in the 1898 Spanish–American War **« 248–49** damaged Spain's monarchy. **Republican movements** pressed for greater democracy, and support for anarchism took root. In response to violent strikes, King Alfonso XIII became increasingly dictatorial and authoritatrian. In 1921 Spain was defeated in a **rebellion by tribes in its Moroccan colony**, which aggravated the economic crisis, and domestic violence escalated. In September 1923 **General Miguel Primo de Rivera** led a *coup d'état* and became military dictator until he lost the army's support and resigned in 1930. In 1931 Alfonso agreed to

ALFONSO XIII

municipal elections. The result was overwhelming majorities for those who were in favour of a republic, and Alfonso was forced into exile. He died in 1941.

SECOND REPUBLIC
The left-wing Second Republic alienated many groups with its reforms. In 1933, a **right-wing election victory** led to a general strike on 4 October 1934 and an armed rising in Asturias, northern Spain. When the left-wing **Popular Front** won the 1936 general election, their radical rhetoric alarmed conservatives. Tension mounted as street battles between rival groups and widespread strikes paralysed the nation.

ANARCHISM is a political belief that society should have no police, government laws, or other authority.

Spanish Civil War

The Spanish Civil War is regarded as the first ideological conflict between international fascism and international communism. Some of the military tactics that were employed during the fighting foreshadowed those later used in World War II.

On 21 February 1936 Spain's new left-wing Popular Front government promised liberty, prosperity, and justice, but some people considered their policies to be too progressive. On 17 and 18 July Spanish military forces based in Morocco revolted against the elected government. They expected little opposition, but supporters of the Second Republic and its government resisted, and Spain found itself in the grip of civil war. The Republicans received weapons and volunteers from the Soviet Union and Mexico, and aid from supporters of liberal democracy, communism, and the anarchist movement. Left-wing parties, such as the Socialists and the Anti-Stalinist Marxist Party, which was formed in 1935, also supported the government. The insurgents, who became known as the Nationalists, had the backing of monarchists, Catholics, and the Falange

Fallen soldier
This photograph shows a Republican militiaman being shot at Cerro Muriano on the Cordoba front on 5 September 1936. It was taken by Hungarian photographer Robert Capa.

> "Better to **die on one's feet** than to **live on one's knees**."
>
> DOLORES IBARRURI, SPANISH WRITER AND POLITICIAN, 18 JULY 1936

War of words
US writer and journalist Ernest Hemingway observes a member of General Lister's Loyalist Vth Army Corps on the east bank of the Ebro River on 5 November 1937. A new kind of war journalism emerged during the Spanish Civil War, with eyewitness accounts of the brutality of war reported in the first person.

Call to arms
During the Spanish Civil War, recruiting posters were an important means of communication as many people were illiterate. The Nationalist poster c.1936 on the left and Anti-Fascist forces poster on the right are designed to carry a clear message without needing to be read.

to Spain to protect the Popular Front government. Their ranks included anyone who was opposed to fascism, and Spain became the *cause célèbre* for left-leaning intellectuals across the Western world. The British government, which proclaimed itself neutral, warned that Britons who enlisted on either side would be liable to two years in prison, and urged other states to prevent the dispatch of volunteers. Despite this deterrent, thousands of foreign idealists made their way to Spain, many of them to defend the capital city, Madrid.

Battle for Madrid

At the outbreak of war, Madrid was controlled by the Popular Front government. Franco was anxious to capture the capital, and bombing raids began on 28 August 1936. On 30 September, he captured Toledo, which is only 65km (40 miles) from Madrid. Toledo had been in Republican hands since the beginning, despite the onslaught from thousands of Nationalist soldiers. Its capture was a huge morale boost for the Nationalists and did much to enhance Franco's reputation. By 1 November, 25,000 Nationalist troops under General José Varela had reached the western and southern suburbs of Madrid. Five days later Varela's men were joined by the German Legion Kondor (a unit from the *Luftwaffe*, see p.314) and the siege of Madrid began. It was to last for nearly three years.

Fascist victory

In December 1936, Benito Mussolini (see p.309), Italy's fascist ruler, began to supply the Nationalists with men and equipment. After failing to take Madrid in a full frontal assault in 1937, Franco's forces launched la campaign to conquer the Basque Provinces, Asturias, and the industrial areas of northern Spain. During this offensive the first large-scale aerial bombing of civilians took place, including the infamous German raid that destroyed

the Basque town of Guernica, an event foreshadowing episodes that occurred in World War II.

Franco was under pressure from both Hitler (see pp.312–13) and Mussolini to obtain a quick victory by taking Madrid, so he blockaded the road that linked the city to the rest of Republican Spain, and his troops attacked Guadalajara 65km (40 miles) east of the capital on 8 March 1937. The Republican Army counterattacked making use of Soviet tanks, and many lives were lost.

Infighting

Meanwhile there was serious infighting among Republicans in Barcelona. On 6 May 1937 death squads assassinated a number of prominent anarchists, and rioting followed. These events severely damaged the Popular Front and led to a new government being formed under the leadership of Juan Negrín. Negrín was a Communist sympathizer, and this enabled Joseph Stalin (see pp.302–03) to influence the Spanish government.

In April 1938, the Nationalist Army broke through the Republican defences in the north, and Franco moved his troops towards Valencia with the aim of encircling Madrid. Negrín, keen to show that the Republican government was still viable, insisted on a policy of attack, rather than defence. However, at the Battle of Ebro (25 July–16 November 1938), the Republicans were all but destroyed as an effective fighting force. On 26 January 1939 Barcelona fell to the Nationalist Army. It was a stunning victory. With further victories in Catalonia, Vinaroz, and other towns along the eastern coast,

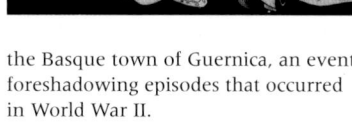

Nazi medal
The Spanish Cross, or Kondor Legion Cross, was a campaign medal instituted on 14 April 1939 to recognize those Germans who served in the Spanish Civil War on the side of General Franco.

Franco believed the war was over and in radio broadcasts urged the Republicans to surrender. On 27 January 1939, British Prime Minister, Neville Chamberlain, recognized the Nationalist government headed by Franco. The Nationalist Army entered Madrid virtually unopposed on 27 March 1939. Four days later, Franco declared the end of the war.

> **ARMY OF AFRICA** A highly professional army formed from Spanish troops, members of the Spanish Foreign Legion (modelled on the French Foreign Legion), and Moroccans from Spanish Morocco, known as *Regulares*.

(a Spanish fascist party). The fascist Italian and German governments also became involved, supplying troops and weapons, which gave the civil war a dramatic international character.

On 19 July 1936, General Franco (see below), a leader of the insurgent forces, assumed command of the Army of Africa based in Morocco and took it to Spain. This army played a key part in gaining Nationalist control of southwestern Spain. At the outbreak of the war, the Republican Army was about one-third larger than the Nationalist Army. However, by the time the Army of Africa arrived in Spain, the figures were close to equal.

International Brigades

Socialists and communists from all over Europe formed groups of volunteers called International Brigades and went

59 THOUSAND **foreign volunteers joined in the fight.**

500 THOUSAND **people lost their lives during the conflict.**

25 THOUSAND **people died from malnutrition.**

Guernica
Spanish artist Pablo Picasso painted this mural for the Spanish pavilion at the Paris World's Fair (an exhibition). It expresses his feelings about the destruction of the Basque town of Guernica by German air raids in 1937.

Adolf Hitler

"When starting and waging a war, it is **not right** that matters, **but victory**."

ADOLF HITLER, 22 AUGUST 1939

World War I was the pivotal event in the life of German dictator Adolf Hitler. Before the war, this son of a minor official in the Austro-Hungarian Empire was a failed artist, nursing fantasies of greatness but in reality living an aimless, embittered existence on the margins of society. Four years serving on the Western Front put Hitler in touch with the shared experience of millions of Germans: the participation in modern warfare at its most destructive and of a defeat so painful that it had to be met with denial.

Like many other ex-servicemen, Hitler found it impossible to demobilize mentally, regarding himself as a frontline soldier (*"Frontkämpfer"*) for the rest of his life.

Speaker and politician

Hitler had no particular interest in politics before or during World War I, nor had he expressed any particular dislike of Jews. But amid the political and social chaos of post-war Germany, he adopted views by which many Germans explained away the collapse of their country: that the war had been lost through a "stab in the back" by socialists and Jews, and that Germany

The "Führer"
Nazi propaganda photos depicted Hitler as the towering leader – *führer* – of his people. He was totally convinced by his personal myth, seeing himself as a "man of destiny", leading the German people to greatness.

Hitler the soldier
This image shows Hitler as a corporal in the German Army in April 1915. As a "runner" carrying messages to the frontline trenches, he was wounded three times. In 1918, he was awarded the Iron Cross (right) for bravery under fire.

"Mein Kampf"
Hitler wrote his autobiographical political statement *Mein Kampf* (*My Struggle*) while in prison for nine months for his part in the Munich Putsch of 1923 (see right). Published in 1925, the book expressed his hatred of Judaism and Communism and his ambition to establish a German empire in the east.

NATIONAL SOCIALISM

Much of the "national" element of the ideology behind Hitler's National Socialist German Workers' Party (Nazi Party) appealed to the masses because it was in line with a long tradition of German nationalism; for example, belief in the creation of a self-sufficient "Greater Germany", incorporating all ethnic Germans within its borders. The term "socialism" was associated with ethnic exclusivity rather than equality. Hitler strongly opposed Marxist socialism (see pp.264–65) and purged from the party all those who wanted socialism in the sense of workers' power or the overthrow of capitalism. The core of National Socialism was not class war, but race war. Hitler intended to create a military state along racial lines. While the supposed evil power of the Jews would be crushed and "inferior" races would be used as slave labour, the privileged German *Volk* ("people") would unite behind the heroic leadership of their *Führer*.

TIMELINE

- **20 April 1889** Born in Braunau, Austria, the son of a customs official.
- **1907** Fails the entrance exam for the Viennese Academy of Fine Arts.
- **May 1913** Moves from Vienna to Munich to evade military service in Austria.
- **August 1914** Joins the German Army as a volunteer at the outbreak of World War I.
- **August 1918** Awarded the Iron Cross, First Class, after four years' service as a dispatch runner on the Western Front.
- **1919** Comes into contact with the German Workers' Party (DAP) in Munich.
- **July 1921** Becomes leader of renamed National Socialist German Workers' Party (Nazi Party).
- **9 November 1923** Attempts to overthrow the German government in Munich Putsch.
- **December 1924** Released from prison after serving nine months for treason.
- **March 1932** Belatedly takes German nationality and contests presidential elections, narrowly losing to Paul von Hindenburg.
- **30 January 1933** Appointed chancellor through a backstairs deal with conservative German politicians and forms government.
- **23 March 1933** Exploits crisis caused by a fire at the Reichstag (House of Representatives) on the 27 February; pushes through the Enabling Act to gain exceptional powers for four years.
- **30 June 1934** Purges the SA (Stormtroopers), the Nazi Party's paramilitary wing, in the "Night of the Long Knives" – more than 80 people are murdered.
- **19 August 1934** Becomes dictator of Germany after the death of Paul von Hindenburg.
- **7 March 1936** Sends German forces into the demilitarized Rhineland in defiance of the Versailles peace treaty.
- **12–13 March 1938** Germany annexes Austria in the Anschluss.
- **29–30 September 1938** Wins British and French backing for the German takeover of the Sudetenland area of Czechoslovakia at the Munich Conference.
- **1 September 1939** Orders invasion of Poland, triggering World War II.
- **30 March 1941** Addresses his generals about the planned invasion of the Soviet Union and calls for "a war of annihilation"; the invasion is launched on 22nd June.
- **11 December 1941** Declares war on the United States after the Japanese attack on Pearl Harbor.
- **19 December 1941** Takes personal command of the German armed forces.
- **20 July 1944** Survives an assassination attempt at his headquarters at Rastenburg.
- **30 April 1945** Shoots himself in his bunker in Berlin as the city falls to the Soviet Red Army.

AUSTRIAN STAMP 1945

" Who says I am not under the special protection of God?" ADOLF HITLER, 23 MARCH 1933

Hitler off duty
Hitler relaxes with Eva Braun, the woman who was his companion from 1932. Hitler married her in his Berlin bunker on 29 April 1945; they both committed suicide the following day.

was the victim of an international Jewish conspiracy. It was while mixing in political extremist circles in Munich that Hitler chanced upon an exceptional talent. When he addressed political meetings in beerhalls, his speeches stirred the crowd in a way no other agitator could achieve. His hypnotic ability to dominate and sway his listeners' emotions treated him to the first intoxicating experience of power. By the mid-1920s, through the failed Munich Putsch, a coup in which Hitler tried to overthrow the government; his subsequent nationally publicized trial; and the publication of *Mein Kampf*, Hitler had re-invented himself as the messianic leader of a German national revival. His image was manufactured and dramatized by the propagandists of the Nazi Party (see above), but it depended upon a steely self-belief.

Rise to power
Hitler was an opportunist who exploited a democratic system he despised to obtain absolute power, never wavering from his long-term goals – establishing a dictatorship; overturning the Versailles peace treaty that had marked the end of World War I; defeating "world Jewry"; and creating a German empire to the east in the Slav lands

taken from Germany in 1919. In the political manoeuvres and campaigns from 1929 to 1935 that brought him to absolute power in Germany, he showed a ruthless instinct for his opponents' weaknesses, alternating savage rhetoric and physical intimidation with gestures of moderation. Inherently given to fits of rage, he learned to manipulate this side of his personality for effect, raging one moment, soothing the next. Those who thought they could control him – the military, politicians, businessmen – underestimated his power, to which they all eventually submitted.

Once in control, Hitler took little interest in the day-to-day business of government. While his subordinates worked to fulfil what they guessed to be "the *Führer*'s will", the *Führer* himself dabbled in grandiose architectural projects, such as the huge Königsplatz in Munich, or enjoyed the Alpine views at his Berchtesgaden retreat. Hitler was a teetotal vegetarian, obsessed with cleanliness – he had no taste for

Final days
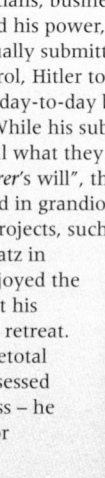
On 20 April 1945, looking tired and haggard and facing imminent defeat, Hitler appeared in the Reichs Chancellery garden in Berlin with some of his officers. Ten days later, he committed suicide.

luxurious self-indulgence. His only intimate relationship was with Eva Braun, and little is known about it.

Leaving domestic administration to his aides, Hitler turned his obsession to the pursuit of power in foreign and military affairs. He used the same tactics to get his way on the world stage as he had in Germany – alternating threats of violence with offers of peace, and taking outrageous risks to achieve his aims.

War and downfall
In September 1939, Hitler invaded Poland and finally tipped Europe into war. The startling success of German arms fatally confirmed Hitler's view of himself as an infallible leader. By the end of 1941 he had gone to war with both the Soviet Union and USA, and taken direct control of the German armed forces. When the tide of war turned against Germany, Hitler's mental and physical state deteriorated and his grasp on reality weakened. Yet he never lost his savage desire for power. Obsessed with his own historical greatness, Hitler was quite prepared to see Germany destroyed to create a grandiose funeral pyre for his ego. Eventually, holed up in his Berlin bunker, Hitler realized he had been defeated. As the Soviet army advanced into the city, he committed suicide.

‹‹ BEFORE

Scarred by World War I, Britain and France sought to avoid war with Nazi Germany but were thwarted by Hitler's ambitions.

MUNICH PACT
The Munich Pact was agreed between Britain, Germany, Italy, and France in 1938. It ordered the surrender of German-speaking areas of Czechoslovakia to Germany. Anglo–French **appeasement** of Hitler's wishes is criticized, but in 1938 neither nation could challenge Germany.

HITLER'S QUEST FOR *LEBENSRAUM*
The need for *Lebensraum*, or "living space", informed Hitler's plans for war. He believed that for the "superior" **Aryan race ‹‹ 308–09** to dominate, Germany needed more land. He targeted neighbouring territories with ethnic German populations. In 1938 Hitler entered Austria. *Anschluss* (the union with Austria) was followed by occupation of the Czech provinces, Bohemia and Moravia, in violation of the Munich Pact.

ANSCHLUSS

The Blitz
After defeat in the Battle of Britain (see right), Hitler launched 57 consecutive nightly bombing attacks on London, known as "The Blitz". In this image a German Heinkel 111 bomber flies over the River Thames in London during a bombing raid.

Pushing the war effort
This poster was issued by the British Ministry of Home Security to encourage citizens to join the Fire Guard. Fire Guards, known as "The Midnight Watch", were volunteer patrols who extinguished fires after German air raids. The poster's tone is typical of the propaganda produced by the wartime government to promote the war effort.

Blitzkrieg

On 1 September 1939 Nazi Germany invaded neighbouring Poland. France and Britain declared war two days later. Well-equipped German forces then pushed into Scandinavia and the Netherlands, crushing all opposition. Within a year, a seemingly invincible German army had conquered vast tracts of Europe.

G ermany's assault on Poland began with the airforce (*Luftwaffe*) blanket-bombing roads, railways, towns, and villages, sending terrified local populations fleeing ahead of the German advance. The chaos of refugees on the roads disrupted Polish counter-attacks and the German land invasion swept across the country at astonishing speed. This was *Blitzkrieg*. The response of the British and French (the Allies) to German progress was hesitant. In the next two weeks they did little more than survey the situation, while the German armed forces, or *Wehrmacht*, soon had the Polish capital, Warsaw,

surrounded. Poland capitulated when the Soviet Union, who had agreed a pact of non-aggression with Hitler, invaded from the east. There then followed several months of little military action, known as the "Phoney War", in which the Allies built up weapon stocks and dropped leaflets to persuade the German people of the evils of their Nazi leaders.

On 9 April 1940 Hitler invaded Denmark and Norway in a pre-emptive strike against the British, who had threatened to occupy Scandanavia. The Phoney War was over. On 10 May Hitler pushed westwards towards France, conquering the Netherlands,

Belgium, and Luxembourg in just two days, to arrive at the French border. Both British and French commanders believed that the *Wehrmacht* would be held at the Maginot Line, fortifications

BLITZKRIEG The tactic used by the German army to invade Poland. Meaning "lightning war", it involved swift, intense attacks that aimed to destroy the enemy quickly. It often included bombing raids.

constructed along the German border, and by the Belgian forests of the Ardennes, which they considered impassable for tanks. However, the Nazis swiftly broke through and

Air power
RAF Fighter Command had a numerical advantage over the German fighter force for most of the Battle of Britain. The British built 1,900 fighter planes, such as this Spitfire, the Germans built only 775.

SPITFIRE MK V

Evacuating Dunkirk
A total of 693 ships rescued 340,000 British and French troops, such as those stranded on the beach above, from the northern French port of Dunkirk. The British people sailed their own fishing boats across the English Channel to support the Royal Navy's fleet. Churchill described the event as a "miracle of deliverance".

advanced to Abbeville, on the north French coast, trapping British and French forces. The French begged the British for more military support, but the British Prime Minister, Winston Churchill, persuaded that France was lost, kept forces in reserve to protect Britain from German attack. From 27 May to 4 June Allied troops were evacuated from Dunkirk.

On 22 June 1940, it seemed that Germany had all but won. In an act of revenge, Hitler forced France to sign an armistice (peace agreement) in the same railway carriage where the terms of Germany's defeat were agreed at the end of World War I (see pp.296–99). Hitler's popularity in Germany reached new heights. Each German offensive

had achieved victory, and for many German citizens, untouched by war in their homeland, the process was easy.

Turning points
The Battle of Britain was waged from August to October 1940, and proved to be a turning point in Hitler's fortunes. The battle, fought by air, was intended as a prelude to German invasion. The *Luftwaffe* targeted airfields and ports along the English Channel but the Royal Air Force's (RAF) early warning systems gave Britain the advantage. Hitler abandoned "Operation Sealion", his invasion plan and began to target British cities instead (see left).

Perhaps if Hitler had consolidated his gains in Western Europe, Germany might have been victorious. But, he chose to invade Russia. Stalin's demand that Romania return Bessarabia to Russia and his annexing of the Baltic

The Axis in Europe
The alliance between Nazi Germany, Fascist Italy, and later, Japan was known as the Axis. It was formalized in the Tripartite Treaty signed in 1940. Other minor powers became Axis satellites, supporting Germany's war aims.

States in 1940, infuriated Hitler. By 1941 Germany and her allies had overrun Yugoslavia and Greece, and with Romania, Hungary, and Slovakia in support, Hitler was confident of a broad front for the attack. In June 1941, Germany invaded Russia. Initially, the campaign, "Operation Barbarossa", made rapid advances, but the Soviet Red Army and a bitter Russian winter put paid to *Blitzkrieg* tactics. Long battles ensued, some lasting many months, with enormous suffering and loss of life on both sides. In August 1942 a fierce battle began at Stalingrad (see p.316), which resulted in a German defeat. The tide of war had begun to turn.

BRITISH PRIME MINISTER (1874–1965)

WINSTON CHURCHILL

Born into the British aristocracy, Winston Churchill joined the army in his youth and served with the 4th Queen's Own Hussars, which gave him valuable first-hand knowledge of war. He entered parliament in 1899, holding many posts, including Secretary of State for War during World War I. As British Prime Minister (1940–45 and again in 1951–55) he resisted calls to settle a peace with Hitler, insisting that Britain should go down fighting. He is famous for his pugnacious war leadership and brilliant oratory. He was a prolific writer and was awarded the Nobel Prize for Literature for his book *The Second World War*.

AFTER

In France, the government collaborated with the Nazis, but here, as throughout occupied Europe, resistance movements formed.

VICHY FRANCE
After France's defeat **Marshal Pétain** took control of the French Government and agreed to the division of France into an **occupied zone** and a **non-occupied Vichy zone**. Vichy France was administered by the French Government under Petain, on condition of full collaboration with the Germans. Petain sympathized with Nazi ideology. He replaced France's motto of "Liberty, Equality, Fraternity" with "Work, Family, Fatherland", and formed a militia who sent French Jews to die in Nazi concentration camps.

FIGHTING BACK
Resistance movements rose up against the Nazis all over occupied Europe. The *"Maquis"*, a French organization, attacked German installations and helped stranded British airmen. In Poland, partisans blew up bridges to stop German supplies reaching battle zones. In Yugoslavia, **communist partisans** were led by **Josip Tito 372 »**, who narrowly escaped capture to go on and lead the country after the war.

TITO'S PARTISANS

KEY
- Frontiers, 1937
- Frontiers, Nov 1942
- Greater German Reich
- German occupation
- Italian territory
- Axis satellite
- Finnish territory
- Neutral
- Allied territory
- Allied occupation, 1941

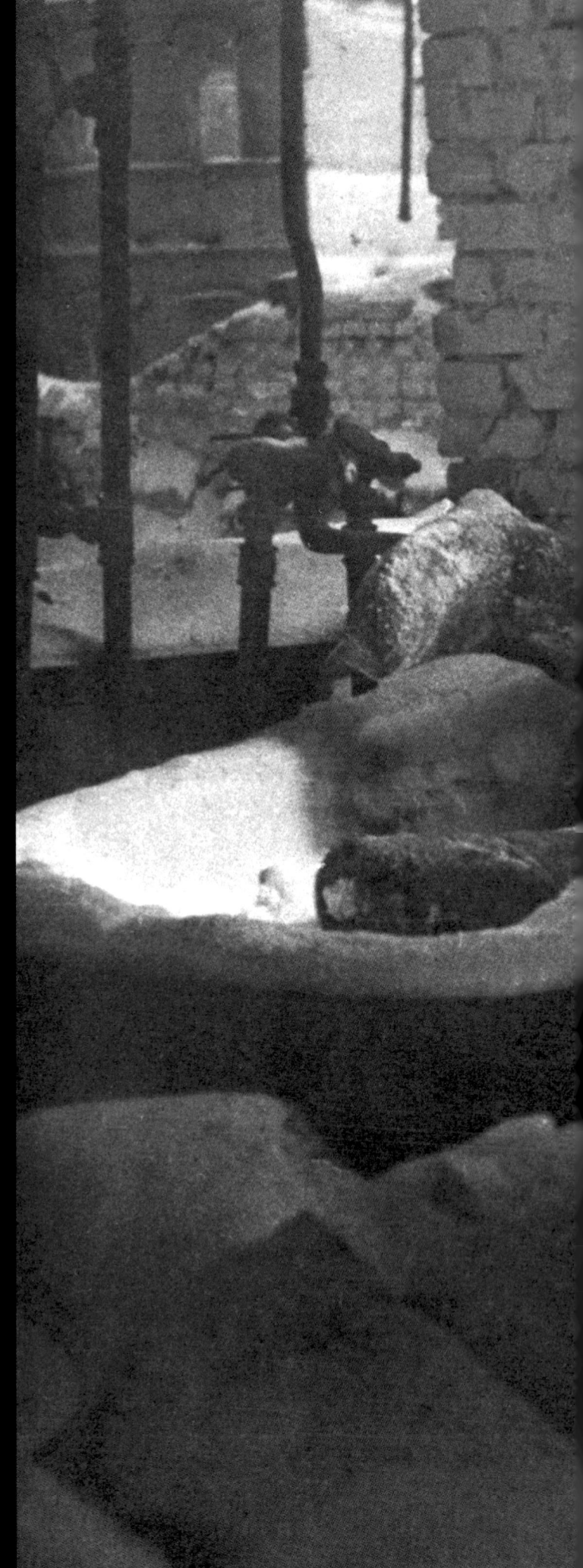

Stalingrad

In the early hours of 2 February 1943, the last German general still fighting in the Russian city of Stalingrad surrendered to the Soviet Red Army. At midday a German Luftwaffe reconnaissance aircraft circled over the city. The pilot radioed back to base: "No more sign of fighting in Stalingrad." The most decisive battle on the eastern front during World War II was over.

The industrial city of Stalingrad stood on the west bank of the River Volga in southern Russia. It controlled the vital river and rail connections that carried oil supplies to the armament factories of central Russia and to the Soviet Red Army itself. The city was not the original target for the Germans. Operation Blue, the German offensive that began on 28 June 1942, aimed to capture the Caucasus oilfields to the southwest and establish a secure position on the Volga. The Soviets responded to the German advance by concentrating their forces in Stalingrad, threatening the northern flank of the German army. On 23 July, Hitler ordered General Paulus and his Sixth Army to capture Stalingrad at all costs.

The assault began on 23 August with sustained air attacks. The same afternoon, German troops reached the Volga, north of the city. By 3 September, Stalingrad was surrounded, with the only means of escape east across the river. The battle became intense. Stalin, the Soviet leader, had ordered "Not One Step Backwards", for this city bore his name and could never be surrendered. Hitler was equally determined. German air and artillery shelling reduced buildings to rubble, but the Soviet troops held fast. As the Germans advanced into the city, the Russians fought them house by house. The two sides were often so close they fought each other from different storeys of the same building.

On 19 November, with the Russians now occupying a narrow strip along the river bank, the Red Army launched Operation Uranus, an audacious attack on German positions from the rear. Four days later, the Germans were surrounded.

A German attempt to rescue their trapped army failed in December. The battle raged into the New Year and, worn out by constant Soviet attacks, cold, and hunger, the remnants of the German army finally surrendered on 2 February. The cost to both sides was immense: since November, the Red Army had lost 479,000 men but crucially German losses were also high, with 147,000 deaths and 91,000 troops captured. The myth of German invincibility was shattered. The Red Army could now go on the offensive against Nazi Germany.

Fighting for each floor

A Soviet soldier perches in a bathtub as he takes aim from a ruined building. The best marksmen would become snipers; using rifles equipped with telescopic sights, they could pick off German troops one by one from secure positions. They won the title of "noble sniper" if they killed more than 40.

The **God of War** has gone over to the other side."

ALFRED JODL, GERMAN MILITARY OFFICER, FEBRUARY 1943

« BEFORE

From the start of World War II governments sought ways to unite people in the war effort. When the US entered the war in 1941 the Allied cause was bolstered.

PROPAGANDA

Governments at war mobilized their citizens by using **propaganda**; posters were a favoured

means of communicating **war aims**. All sides invested heavily in propaganda to encourage people in the **war effort** and **boost morale.**

US POSTER

THE ANGLO–AMERICAN ALLIANCE

The Alliance was signed in December 1941 as the US entered the war. It agreed joint military command for all Anglo–American operations. The pact was born of the close understanding between the British leader, **Winston Churchill « 314–15**, and US President, **Franklin D. Roosevelt « 306–07**. This period of close co-operation helped Britain in the war.

nnovations in military technology played a key role in determining the outcome of World War II. One of the greatest battles of the war was fought at sea. The German navy began to target US merchant ships carrying weapons, raw materials, food, and eventually troops across the Atlantic Ocean to Britain. German submarines, or U-boats, sank three million tonnes of Allied shipping over the course of the war. Churchill later admitted that the threat to the lifeline of US supplies was the one thing that really terrified him; without it Britain might have been starved into submission. The Battle of the Atlantic, as this theatre of war became known,

was won partly by the development of longer range aircraft that could reach U-boats. Support from the Canadian and US navies played a major role, as did better intelligence, and the development of centimetric radar to find submerged U-boats.

Desert warfare

Tanks and aircraft played a decisive role in the campaigns in North Africa, where mobility was crucial for crossing the deserts. Mussolini (see p.309) had wanted to extend the Italian empire by invading Egypt in 1940. Desperate to protect British interests in Africa, troops from Britain and Commonwealth countries (former British colonies, see

pp.276–77) were sent in to stop him. Initially the British drove the Italians back to Libya, despite Italy having superior numbers of troops and equipment. To aid its weaker ally,

1240
The number of days Australian troops held out under siege at Tobruk against Rommel's forces before being relieved by Allied troops.

Germany sent in the Afrika Korps under Field Marshal Rommel. By May 1941 he had won back all the territory lost by Italy. It was not until October 1942 and the British victory under

Total War

As the war in Europe raged on, the Atlantic Ocean and the deserts of North Africa became backdrops for fierce battles. Securing vital supply lines from the US enabled Britain and her allies to drive back the German and Italian troops. With the Red Army advancing from the east, Nazi Germany was surrounded.

Depth charge
Coastguards stand on the deck of the US Cutter *Spencer* watching the explosion of a depth charge blast a Nazi U-boat out of the water. The U-boat's target was the large convoy of merchant and troop ships seen on the horizon. Allied support and the advances in radar technology ensured Britain's Atlantic lifeline to the US and Canada stayed open.

Storming of Bardia 1942
The Allies captured territory held by the Italians with relative ease early on in the North African Campaign. Here, Australian troops storm the town of Bardia in Libya. German Field Marshal Rommel's Afrika Korps came to Italy's assistance and fighting continued in Egypt, Algeria, Morocco, and Tunisia.

General Montgomery, at El Alamein, that Rommel's advance was checked. The next month, the "Torch Landings" in Morocco and Algeria brought Allied reinforcements with US tanks and fresh troops. Within six months, after fierce fighting in Tunisia, the Axis powers (see p.315) were defeated in Africa.

The Axis surrender in North Africa was followed by the successful Allied invasion of Sicily, after which Hitler's key ally, Italy, secretly surrendered. In 1944, while the Red Army drove Axis forces out of the Soviet Union, Allied troops invaded Normandy, France (see pp.320–21). After the liberation of France, Germany made one last stand at the Battle of the Bulge in the Ardennes, Belgium, where more than 80,000 US troops and a similar number of

Germans were lost. Once Belgium and The Netherlands were liberated, the Allies entered Germany from the west and Russia invaded from the east. The Red Army's arrival in Berlin in April 1945 was followed by Hitler's suicide and unconditional German surrender. Victory in Europe was declared on 8 May 1945.

The Road to Berlin

By 1943, after Germany's defeat at Stalingrad (see p.316) and victories for British and US forces in Africa, the Allies held the advantage. British and US forces landed in Italy, while Soviet troops swept across Eastern Europe. With the D-Day landings (see p.321) in 1944, and Allied bombings, the Nazis faced attack on all fronts.

Relief at the end of war in Europe was tempered by grief at the immense loss of life and a resolve to achieve world peace.

ENDING THE WAR

After the Red Army took Berlin the end of the war in Europe (VE Day) was officially declared on 8 May 1945. Huge celebrations took place, particularly in London. **War with Japan** continued until VJ Day on 15 August 324–25 ≫

SOVIET TROOPS RAISE THE FLAG IN BERLIN

COSTS OF WAR

The costs of World War II were immense. In terms of loss of human life the statistics are appalling. The financial costs have been estimated at over US$2 billion.

DEAD **25 million Russians, 6 million Poles, 5 million Germans, 400 thousand French, 300 thousand Britons – almost 60 million died worldwide.**

YALTA AND POTSDAM CONFERENCES

In 1945 leaders from Britain, the Soviet Union, and the US met at conferences at Yalta (in Ukraine) and Potsdam (Germany) to deal with the **political and economic issues** raised by the war. Among the measures decided on were the creation of a new world peace-keeping organization, **the United Nations**, and the division of Germany into four zones of control each administered by an Allied power.

KEY

- ▬▬ Greater German Reich, 1942
- ➤ Allied offensives
- ● city severely bombed
- ⚔ major battle
- ● partisan resistance
- ─── frontiers 1942

Map labels: Murmansk · Norwegian Sea · ATLANTIC OCEAN · Shetland Is. · Orkney Is. · NORWAY · SWEDEN · FINLAND · USSR · Oslo · Stockholm · Helsinki · Glasgow · North Sea · GREAT BRITAIN · IRELAND · Baltic Sea · ESTONIA · LATVIA · Moscow · Liverpool · Birmingham · HOLLAND · Bremen · Copenhagen · Hanover · Königsberg · E. LITH. · Minsk · London · Essen · Hamburg · PRUSSIA · GERMANY · D-day landings 1944 · St. Lô · Berlin · 1945 · Warsaw · Kursk · Caen · BELG. · Cologne · Düsseldorf · Dresden 1945 · Prague · POLAND · Kiev · Red army advance 1944 · Stalingrad · Paris · Frankfurt · Mannheim · UKRAINE · FRANCE · Bay of Biscay · Stuttgart · Munich · SLOV. · VICHY FRANCE · SWITZ. · AUSTRIA · HUNGARY · ROMANIA · Turin · Milan · CROATIA · Ploești · Crimea · Genoa · SERBIA · Black Sea · Marseille · Corsica · ITALY · Bucharest · SPAIN · PORTUGAL · Balearic Is. · Sardinia · Anzio · Cassino · MONT. · BULGARIA · Mediterranean Sea · Aegean Sea · TURKEY · ALBANIA · Sicily · 1943 · GREECE · Leros · North African landings 1942 · Kos · Rhodes · MOROCCO · ALGERIA · Malta · Crete · Cyprus · TUNISIA · LIBYA · El Alamein · EGYPT

0 — 500 km
0 — 500 miles

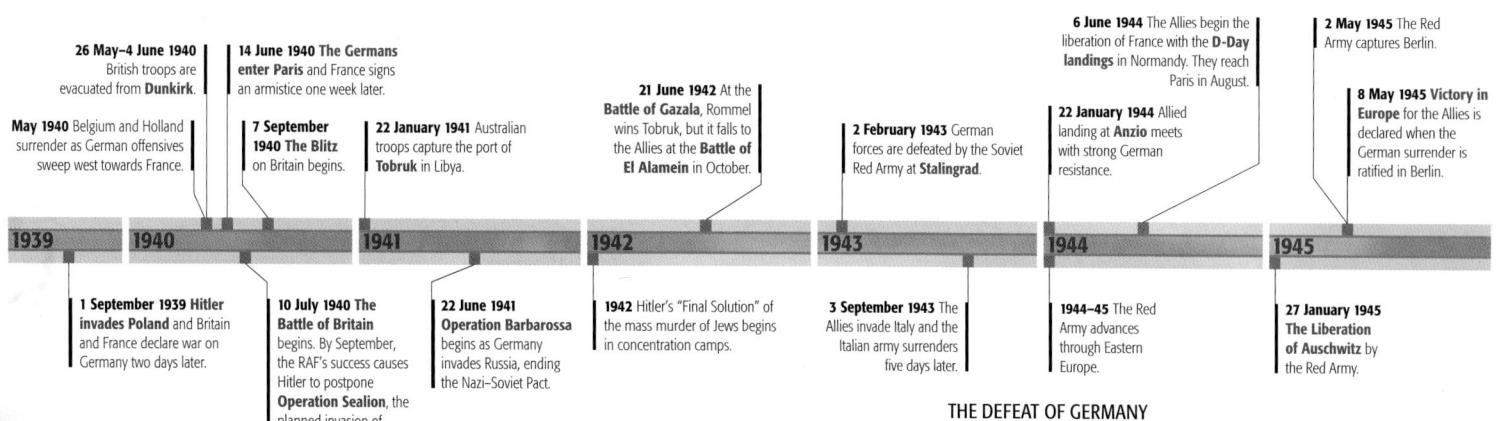

26 May–4 June 1940 British troops are evacuated from **Dunkirk**.

14 June 1940 The Germans enter Paris and France signs an armistice one week later.

May 1940 Belgium and Holland surrender as German offensives sweep west towards France.

7 September 1940 The Blitz on Britain begins.

22 January 1941 Australian troops capture the port of **Tobruk** in Libya.

21 June 1942 At the **Battle of Gazala**, Rommel wins Tobruk, but it falls to the Allies at the **Battle of El Alamein** in October.

2 February 1943 German forces are defeated by the Soviet Red Army at **Stalingrad**.

6 June 1944 The Allies begin the liberation of France with the **D-Day landings** in Normandy. They reach Paris in August.

2 May 1945 The Red Army captures Berlin.

22 January 1944 Allied landing at **Anzio** meets with strong German resistance.

8 May 1945 Victory in Europe for the Allies is declared when the German surrender is ratified in Berlin.

| 1939 | 1940 | 1941 | 1942 | 1943 | 1944 | 1945 |

1 September 1939 Hitler invades Poland and Britain and France declare war on Germany two days later.

10 July 1940 The Battle of Britain begins. By September, the RAF's success causes Hitler to postpone **Operation Sealion**, the planned invasion of Britain, indefinitely.

22 June 1941 Operation Barbarossa begins as Germany invades Russia, ending the Nazi–Soviet Pact.

1942 Hitler's "Final Solution" of the mass murder of Jews begins in concentration camps.

3 September 1943 The Allies invade Italy and the Italian army surrenders five days later.

1944–45 The Red Army advances through Eastern Europe.

27 January 1945 The Liberation of Auschwitz by the Red Army.

THE DEFEAT OF GERMANY

From 1939–41, Nazi Germany blazed across Europe annihilating any opposition in neighbouring territories. With troops fighting in North Africa and facing the Soviet Red Army outside Moscow, German forces had conquered vast territories by the winter of 1941. Yet in April 1945 the Allies were swiftly advancing on the German capital, Berlin.

D-Day

After almost four years of planning, a combined American, British, Canadian, and Free French force launched "Operation Overlord", aiming to wrest control of Europe from Nazi Germany. Beginning on D-Day with a five-pronged attack on the coast of northern France, the operation was to prove a crucial turning point in World War II.

The largest of the five assault areas was at Colleville-sur-Mer, codenamed Omaha Beach. Heavy Allied air and naval bombardment, effective at the other landing points, had made little impact on the well-prepared German defences at Omaha, where the US 29th Infantry Division – untested in combat – attacked alongside the US 1st Infantry Division. Horrendous weather had forced General Dwight D Eisenhower, Supreme Commander of the Allied forces, to delay the attack for 24 hours. The mission launched with little improvement in conditions, but further delay would have set the operation back by several weeks.

The adverse weather wrought havoc with the Allied landing craft: some sank in the rough seas, while German mines ripped through others. Of 29 amphibious tanks launched at Omaha Beach, 27 sank with their crews still trapped inside them. Many of the soldiers emerging from the landing craft were swept off their feet by heavy surf and drowned as they attempted to wade ashore, while others proved easy targets for German fire, picked off from the clifftops as they struggled up the beach, weighed down by wet kit and heavy sand. The average age of the dead was just 22. By early afternoon, the Americans had managed to secure a small strip of beach, 9.7km (6 miles) wide, and around 3.2km (2 miles) deep. This patch of land came at a cost of 3,000 casualties.

Encountering less resistance at beaches codenamed Utah, Gold, Juno, and Sword, the Allies landed 150,000 troops by nightfall. Six days later they had linked the five beachheads into a continuous front and begun using artificial "Mulberry Harbours" to land armoured vehicles, heavy artillery, and more troops with which to further the advance. On 27 June, after two weeks of intense fighting, the Americans captured Cherbourg; on 9 July the British and Canadians overcame two Panzer divisions to take Caen; and on 25 July the tanks of the US 7th Army advanced south through St Lô, breaching the German defences. This was the vital breakthrough that led to the liberation of Paris on 25 August and, in early September, the crossing of the Siegfried Line into Germany.

Omaha beach
The first wave of troops to land at Omaha Beach arrived just before dawn. Photographer Robert Capa landed with them. Waist-deep in the icy sea with bullets tearing into the water around him, he captured the intense struggle as they fought their way onto the beach.

"We will accept nothing less than **full victory**."
GENERAL DWIGHT D EISENHOWER, D-DAY ORDER SPEECH, 1944

« **BEFORE**

Genocide – the murder of a group of people, for their religion or race, for example – has long been part of human life. The Holocaust is the result of such a policy, but it was not the first genocide of the 20th century.

ANTI-SEMITISM IN EUROPE AND RUSSIA

Anti-Semitism has its roots in the Roman Empire when **early Christians attacked Jews**, blaming them for the death of Jesus Christ. During the Crusades of the 11th century « 146–47, Jews were expelled from many western European nations « 167. Numerous Jews died in **pogroms** (organized massacres) in Russia in the late 19th century.

ANTI-SEMITISM Discrimination, hostility, or prejudice directed at Jews as a religious, racial, or ethnic group, expressed in actions that can range from individual hatred to state-prosecuted persecution and violence.

ARMENIAN MASSACRE

In April 1915, the government of the Turkish Ottoman Empire accused the 1.75 million Armenians under its control of collaborating with the enemy, Russia. Over seven months, **600,000 Armenians were killed**. In addition **500,000 were deported** to what is now Iraq. Of these only 90,000 survived. A further **400,000 Armenians lost their lives** when the Turks invaded the Russian Caucasus in 1918. The **massacres continued until 1922**, when the remaining Armenians were driven from Turkey.

POSTER FOR ARMENIAN RELIEF

A central feature of the world view of the German dictator Adolf Hitler (see pp.312–13) was an alleged struggle between Germany, as the only state capable of rescuing European civilization, and an international Jewish conspiracy to subvert and dominate the world. He picked up these views from the popular anti-Semitism of the time which saw Jews both as parasitical capitalists and as revolutionary Bolsheviks (see p.300). Either way, Hitler saw the Jews as an evil, implacable enemy of Germany, who should be driven from the *Reich*.

The Nazis in power

Hitler took power in January 1933 and began a slow process of reducing the civil rights and economic position of the country's half million Jews. They were sacked from state office and from many of the professions in 1933–4 and their shops and businesses boycotted. Thousands took refuge in exile abroad, and by 1939 fewer than half of Germany's Jews remained. In September 1935 the notorious Nuremberg Laws stripped Jews of their German citizenship and prohibited marriage or sexual relations between German Jews and ethnic Germans, or "Aryans" (see p.309). In 1936 a programme was set in motion to strip Jews of their assets and by the outbreak of war most Jewish wealth had been taken by the state or bought at knock-down prices, to be sold on to "Aryan" owners. It was not until November 1938 that the Jews were threatened with widespread violence. A pogrom, known as the *Kristallnacht* ("Night of Broken Glass") led to the destruction of 7,500 businesses and the

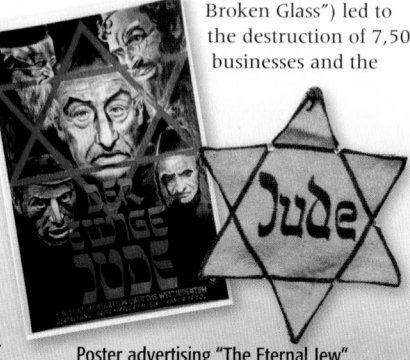

Poster advertising "The Eternal Jew"
In the film made by Joseph Goebbels, Hitler's Minister of Propaganda, scenes of Polish Jews living in Warsaw were intercut with images of rats. The Star of David had to be worn by all Jews under Nazi control from 1941.

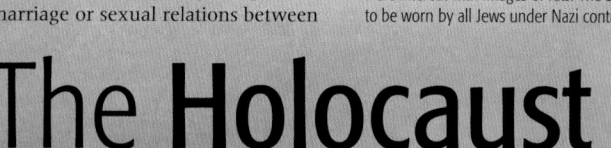

"Kristallnacht"
The shattered glass of the many Jewish properties that were attacked on 9–10 November 1938 gave the night its name.

death of 91 Jews. After this 8,000 Jews were expelled from Berlin and around 25,000 Jewish men sent for a short spell in German concentration camps where they were subjected to a brutal regime of punishment and labour.

Jewish isolation

Initially, Hitler's object was to exclude the Jews from Germany. The Nazis reached an agreement with the Zionist movement to speed up emigration to Palestine (see pp.336–37). But by 1939, as thousands more Jews came under German control in Austria and areas of Czechoslovakia, it proved difficult to get other countries to accept Jewish immigrants. At the Evian Conference

5-6 MILLION Jews were killed, including 3 million Polish Jews.

212 THOUSAND Roma and Sinti gypsies were also exterminated.

70 THOUSAND disabled people in Germany were killed.

The Holocaust

The word "Holocaust" comes from two Greek words: *holo*, "whole", and *kaustos*, "to burn". The term is most closely associated with the deliberate attempt to annihilate the Jewish race in Europe from 1941 to 1945, probably the most shocking and far-reaching act of the age.

Death factory
At Auschwitz–Birkenau, train tracks lead to the main guardhouse, which prisoners called the "gate of death". From 1940, three labour and death camps were built here; more than 1 million Jews died here from 1941 to 1945, when the Soviet Red Army liberated the camps.

in France in July 1938 on the refugee question, only 2 out of 32 countries present agreed to accept higher quotas of Jews. Britain restricted Jewish access to Palestine due to the growing civil war there between the Arab population and Jewish settlers. The last emigrants left Germany in 1941.

Ghettoization and murder

The German invasion first of western Poland in September 1939, and then of the USSR in June 1941, radically and tragically transformed Germany's anti-Semitic policies. With 3.1 million Jews in Poland and 2.7 million in the western

"… Europe will be **combed through** from west to east [of all Jews]."

MINUTES OF THE WANNSEE CONFERENCE, 20 JANUARY 1942

USSR – as well as more than a million in occupied France, the Low Countries, the Balkans, and Scandinavia, the Nazi authorities' reliance on emigration and small-scale attacks to "clear" Jews was no longer feasible. In Poland, the *"Einsatzgruppen"* (action groups made up from the SS – the elite core of the Nazi Party, whose leaders controlled the police and security) herded Jews into restricted areas of towns known as ghettos. Thousands more were sent to labour camps, where they worked for

the German war effort. As German troops swept into the USSR, the SS shot, or gassed in mobile vans as many Jews as they could find. In Kiev, 33,771 Jews were marched out to the Babi Yar ravine and shot on 29–30 September 1941, one of many such incidents.

The "Final Solution"

Although a written order from Hitler has never been found, historians now date a decision on the "Final Solution of the Jewish Question" to late 1941. On 20 January 1942 Reinhard Heydrich, head of the Gestapo, summoned senior bureaucrats to a villa at Lake Wannsee in Berlin to ensure their support for his plans. Jews were now to be transported to camps in Eastern Europe, where they would be worked to death, or killed on the spot. Death was caused by mass gassing in sealed chambers, and the disposal of the bodies took place in huge crematoria staffed by Jews themselves. The death camps – Auschwitz, Belzec, Chelmno, Majdanek, Sobibór, and Treblinka – were supplied with trainloads of Jews from occupied and Axis Europe, except for Bulgaria whose king refused to co-operate.

The killing was on a vast scale. Reports filtered out to the Allies, and the Auschwitz camp was photographed by a US reconnaissance plane in August 1944, but photo-interpreters were more concerned with a nearby chemical factory. Only when the Soviet Red Army advanced westwards in 1944–45 did the camps cease work and the Holocaust end, with the total defeat of Nazi Germany in May 1945.

Ghetto round-up
Across Poland and occupied Russia, Jews were herded into walled or fenced ghettos in poor urban areas, where they had little or no food.

Death train
Jews across Europe were rounded up and sent to the five main death camps in Poland. Many thought they were being sent to work in factories.

Mass murder
After death, Jews were stripped of everything, even their hair and the gold in their teeth. These shoes come from one day of gassing at Auschwitz.

The Holocaust ended in 1945, but its legacy is still with us. Jews now have a homeland, but it is not without problems, and large-scale massacres of people, solely due to their race or beliefs have continued to occur.

STATE OF ISRAEL

International repulsion at the Holocaust led the United Nations to create a **Jewish state of Israel** inside a partitioned Palestine in May 1948 **336–37 ≫**. The **Law of Return** (1950) made **Israel home** not only for its inhabitants, but **for all Jews**, wherever they might live.

"ETHNIC CLEANSING"

Genocide did not begin or end with the Holocaust. Anti-Jewish pogroms broke out in Poland in 1947, resulting in the deaths of some Jews who had survived Auschwitz, while 2 million Cambodians were killed by their revolutionary government in the **"killing fields"** of Year Zero in 1975–79. More recently, **750,000 Tutsis** were massacred by the majority Hutu tribe in Rwanda in 1994; while

RWANDAN REFUGEES

Serbs systematically killed thousands of Muslims in Bosnia in 1992–95 **372–73 ≫**.

YAD VASHEM

The Jewish national **Holocaust memorial** at Yad Vashem, Israel, remembers those who died, and focuses on the resistance of Jews to Nazi terror. Memorials now exist in many European cities, notably Berlin, and a **National Holocaust Day** is commemorated in many countries on 27 January, the anniversary of the liberation of Auschwitz. Yet **"holocaust denial"** has gained ground in recent years, as some historians and politicians have tried to rewrite, or even obliterate, historical events for their own ends.

« BEFORE

Japan's desire to build an empire in Asia and the Pacific drew her into conflict with China and met with condemnation from the US.

JAPANESE EXPANSION IN ASIA

In 1931 the **Japanese took control of Manchuria 346–47 »** a vast region now in northeast China, and established the state of **Manchukuo** there. China was the first target in Japan's plan to create an empire in Asia and the Pacific, and it soon began to stage incursions into Chinese territory. In July 1937 a minor incident, surrounding a missing Japanese soldier, caused Japanese and Chinese forces to open fire on each other at the Marco Polo Bridge near Beijing. The conflict quickly escalated, leading to the **second Sino–Japanese war** and ultimately to both countries' involvement in World War II. Although European colonial interests were affected, they were absorbed by growing problems in Europe and resisted involvement.

US FREEZES DEPOSITS

German victories at the beginning of World War II encouraged Japan to start **empire building** in earnest. She signed the **Three-Power Pact** with Germany and Italy in 1940 and occupied French Indochina (Vietnam). The US responded by freezing Japanese deposits in the US and embargoed exports of crucial materials, such as aviation fuel, to Japan.

War in the Pacific

In 1941 Japan attacked the US navy base at Pearl Harbor, throwing down the gauntlet to all Western powers seeking to restrict the expansion of the Japanese Empire. The US and Britain immediately declared war on Japan. World War II had arrived in Asia and the Pacific and was now truly global.

US President Franklin Roosevelt had transferred his navy's battleship force to Pearl Harbor, Hawaii in April 1940, to deter Japanese aggression. The combined effects of war with China and foreign trade embargoes left Japan desperate for oil and other raw materials available in European colonies in the Southeast Asia and the East Indies. The Japanese raid on Pearl Harbor destroyed many US battleships and killed around 3,000 US personnel, reducing the threat to Japan's southward expansion.

Having gained an advantage, Japanese leaders put their plans into action. Their aim was to construct an imperial perimeter around Southeast Asia and the central Pacific. Pearl Harbor was followed by the Japanese invasion of most of their target territories including Burma, British and Dutch Borneo, Hong Kong, and the Dutch East Indies. Between March and June of 1942 the Japanese survived fierce confrontations with Allied forces to conquer Singapore, Guam, and the Philippines, and established control in Indonesia, Malaya, and Burma. Having ousted the old colonial regimes, Japan made attempts to win over the mass of Asian peoples so that they would support them in the war. A degree of independence was granted to a few

Burma river patrol
Forces were sent into Burma to protect British colonial interests in the country. In the picture above, British troops patrol villages along a river as they search for Japanese soldiers.

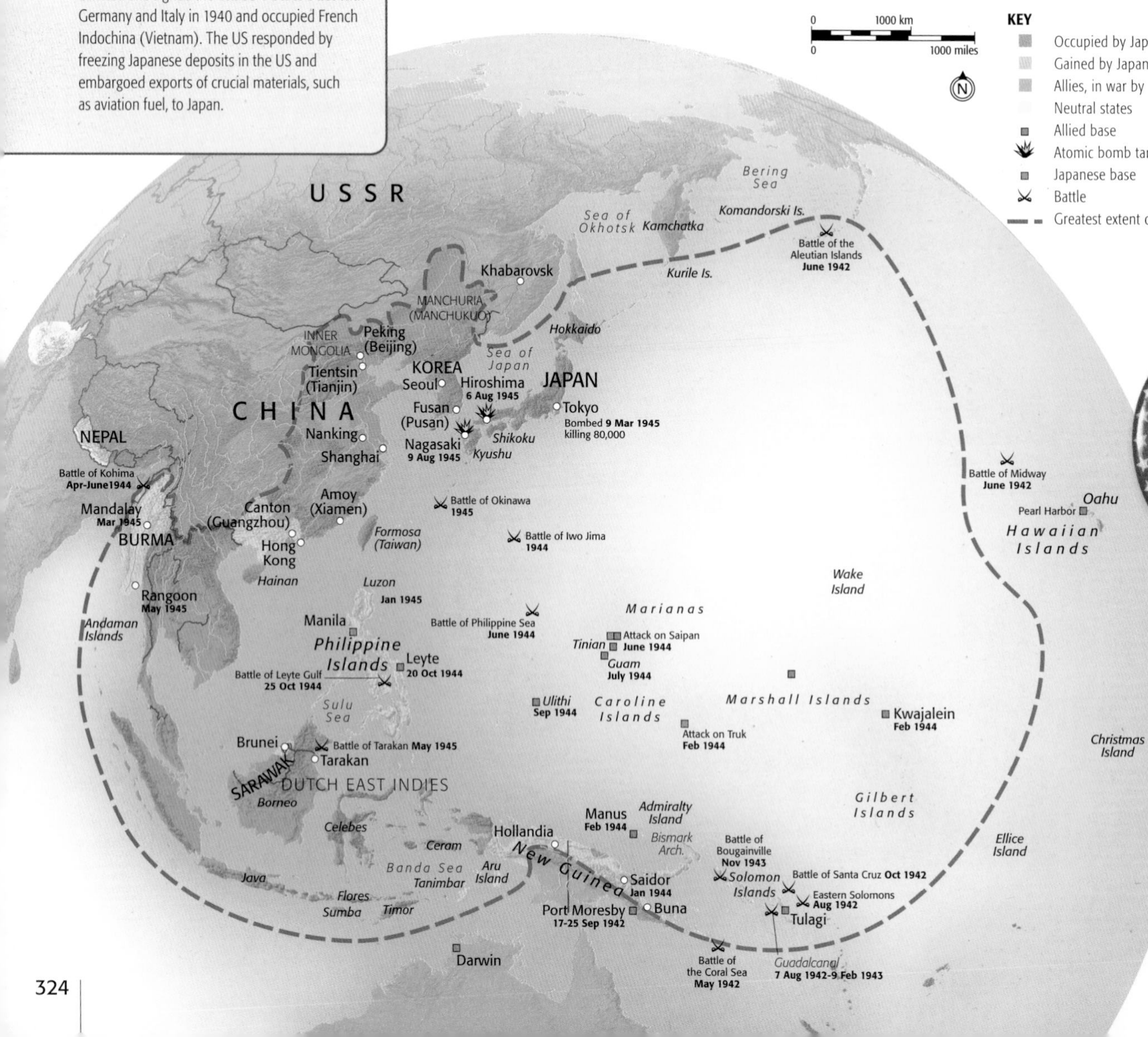

KEY

▪	Occupied by Japan, and held until end of war
▪	Gained by Japan and lost to Allies before end of war
▪	Allies, in war by 1944 (exclusive of Japanese occupied areas)
	Neutral states
▪	Allied base
☀	Atomic bomb target
▪	Japanese base
✕	Battle
– – –	Greatest extent of Japanese perimeter

US Badge
This badge commemorates those who died in the Japanese attack on the US base at Pearl Harbor in 1941.

Pacific empire
The Japanese aimed to build an empire in the Pacific and by 1942 they had seized vast swathes of the region. After huge Japanese losses at the Battle of Midway, at the eastern edge of Japan's territorial perimeter, the Allies went on the offensive. Land was won back island by island, until US forces stood poised to invade the Japanese mainland in 1945.

Map labels: USSR · Sea of Okhotsk · Kamchatka · Bering Sea · Komandorski Is. · Khabarovsk · Kurile Is. · Battle of the Aleutian Islands June 1942 · MANCHURIA (MANCHUKUO) · Hokkaido · INNER MONGOLIA · Peking (Beijing) · Tientsin (Tianjin) · KOREA · Seoul · Sea of Japan · Hiroshima 6 Aug 1945 · JAPAN · Tokyo Bombed 9 Mar 1945 killing 80,000 · CHINA · Nanking · Fusan (Pusan) · Shikoku · Nagasaki 9 Aug 1945 · Kyushu · NEPAL · Shanghai · Battle of Kohima Apr–June 1944 · Mandalay Mar 1945 · Amoy (Xiamen) · Battle of Okinawa 1945 · Battle of Midway June 1942 · Oahu · Pearl Harbor · Hawaiian Islands · BURMA · Canton (Guangzhou) · Hong Kong · Formosa (Taiwan) · Battle of Iwo Jima 1944 · Hainan · Luzon Jan 1945 · Wake Island · Rangoon May 1945 · Manila · Marianas · Andaman Islands · Philippine Islands · Battle of Philippine Sea June 1944 · Tinian · Attack on Saipan June 1944 · Leyte 20 Oct 1944 · Guam July 1944 · Battle of Leyte Gulf 25 Oct 1944 · Sulu Sea · Ulithi Sep 1944 · Caroline Islands · Marshall Islands · Kwajalein Feb 1944 · Brunei · Battle of Tarakan May 1945 · Tarakan · Attack on Truk Feb 1944 · Christmas Island · SARAWAK · DUTCH EAST INDIES · Borneo · Celebes · Manus Feb 1944 · Admiralty Island · Gilbert Islands · Ceram · Hollandia · Bismarck Arch. · Battle of Bougainville Nov 1943 · Ellice Island · Banda Sea · Aru Island · New Guinea · Saidor Jan 1944 · Solomon Islands · Battle of Santa Cruz Oct 1942 · Java · Tanimbar · Eastern Solomons Aug 1942 · Flores · Sumba · Timor · Port Moresby 17–25 Sep 1942 · Buna · Tulagi · Darwin · Battle of the Coral Sea May 1942 · Guadalcanal 7 Aug 1942–9 Feb 1943

Scale: 0 1000 km / 0 1000 miles · N

After the war, communists won power in China, causing nationalists to flee. The US presence in Japan lead to political change.

COMMUNISTS SEIZE POWER IN CHINA

During World War II Chinese political factions had united against the Japanese, but open civil war reignited in 1946. In 1949, the **communist People's Liberation Army** won emphatic victories against forces of the Guomindang Nationalist Party at Huai-Hai and Nanjing, forcing the nationalists to retreat. **Mao Zedong**, leader of the Chinese Communist Party, declared the **People's Republic of China 346–47 >>**.

CHINESE REGIME IN TAIWAN

After his defeat, the nationalist leader **Chiang Kai-shek** fled China with 600,000 troops and two million refugees. Chiang refused to acknowledge Mao's government and established his alternative government in Taipei on the former Japanese colony of Taiwan.

US OCCUPATION OF JAPAN

Japan was occupied by the Allies until 1952. Her war machine was destroyed and war-crimes trials held. In 1947 a new constitution introduced universal suffrage (the right to vote) and banned Japan from having an army. In the 1950s, a memorial park was built in the centre of Hiroshima in remembrance of the nuclear attack.

HIROSHIMA PEACE PARK

territories, including Indonesia and Burma, in return for guaranteed loyalty to Japan. The Japanese were often guilty of barbarism. Atrocities were committed against Chinese citizens and in Japan's notorious prison camps, where medical experiments were conducted on prisoners of war.

Turning points

The Japanese advance was checked in May 1942 when a naval force heading for southern New Guinea was defeated in the Coral Sea. A far more significant defeat came at the Battle of Midway in early June. The Japanese Admiral Yamomoto assembled a powerful force of aircraft carriers, battleships, submarines, and destroyers with the intention of surprising the US fleet at the American-held Midway Islands. However, US intelligence had cracked the Japanese code and the US Navy was well-prepared for their arrival. In the ensuing battle Japan lost her main fleet of aircraft carriers and hundreds of pilots.

The Allied counteroffensive

As was the case in Europe, the tide of war in the Pacific turned in favour of the Allied Powers during 1943. This change was in many ways due to the

Kamikaze
A Japanese volunteer *"Kamikaze'"* pilot flies his explosive-laden plane into a US battleship. Japan introduced this desperate tactic in 1944. By the end of the war over 2,000 such suicide attacks had been launched.

extraordinary military and industrial resources of the US. Once the US war effort was mobilized, Japan began to struggle to match her enemies, and Allied troops began to recapture occupied territories. In early 1945 British troops invaded Burma, under Admiral Lord Louis Mountbatten and Field Marshal Sir William Slim, liberating the country in May.

During 1944 and 1945, US power at sea and in the air began to have a decisive effect. A sea blockade of Japan cut off all imports, strangling the Japanese war economy. Another decisive US naval victory at the Battle of Leyte Gulf in October 1944 opened the way for America to regain the Philippines. In February 1945 the US invaded the island of Iwo Jima, gaining a base for fighter escorts to support

Pearl Harbor
Japan carried out a surprise bombing raid on the American fleet at Pearl Harbor, Hawaii, on 7 December 1941. Thousands of American lives were lost, as well as many battleships, as seen engulfed in flames above.

US bombing raids on mainland Japan. Around 80,000 people died in the US fire-bombing of Tokyo. Victory in the Pacific was in sight for the Allies, but still Japan refused to surrender.

On 6 August 1945 the Allies dropped an atomic bomb on the Japanese city of Hiroshima (see p.327), and three days later on the city of Nagasaki. As news of the devastation sank in, the Soviet Union broke a neutrality pact with Japan by declaring war and invading Japanese-occupied Manchuria. These events persuaded the Japanese to sign an unconditional surrender on 2 September 1945.

US GENERAL (1880–1964)

GENERAL MACARTHUR

US General Douglas MacArthur was the Supreme Allied Commander in the Pacific. He was born into a military family and began his distinguished military career in World War I. He rose to the rank of Army Chief of Staff in the inter-war years. At the end of World War II he became Supreme Allied Commander in Japan and oversaw the drafting of a new Japanese constitution. In 1950–51 he led UN forces in Korea (see pp.328–29).

Hiroshima

Around 7.15am, Japanese radar detected three American aircraft flying south at high altitude. Because it was thought the planes were on reconnaissance, the air raid alert was lifted. At 8.16am, the unchallenged leading B-29 bomber, named *Enola Gay*, dropped "Little Boy" over the city of Hiroshima. A nuclear weapon had been exploded in warfare for the first time.

The decision to bomb Hiroshima, and Nagasaki three days later, was taken by US president Harry Truman. The war against Nazi Germany had ended in May, but Germany's ally, Japan, refused to surrender. Any invasion of Japan would result in a huge loss of both military and civilian life, as well as massive physical destruction. Truman therefore decided to use atomic bombs to force Japan to surrender. Hiroshima was chosen because of its industrial and military significance. The Hiroshima bomb exploded 600 metres (1,950ft) above the city with a blast equivalent to 13 kilotons of TNT. An estimated 90,000 people were killed instantly; another 50,000 died by the end of the year. About 90 per cent of Hiroshima's buildings were damaged or destroyed.

The physics that made this bomb possible grew out of the realization that the atom was not stable and indivisible but had the potential to release immense amounts of energy. In 1938, German scientists Otto Hahn and Fritz Strassmann split uranium atoms by bombarding them with neutrons. The process used, known as nuclear fission, had obvious military uses and scientists in the UK and US grew concerned that Germany might use it to make bombs. On 2 August 1939, Albert Einstein and the Hungarian physicist Leó Szilárd wrote to President Roosevelt urging him to take action. He set up the Uranium Committee to pursue research. After the US entered the war in December 1941, the "Manhattan Project", under the direction of J Robert Oppenheimer, developed a nuclear bomb.

Three devices resulted from this work: the "Trinity" test of a plutonium bomb detonated at Alamogordo in New Mexico, US, the enriched-uranium bomb detonated over Hiroshima, and the plutonium bomb dropped on Nagasaki. In 1949 the USSR exploded its first atomic bomb. Britain, France, and China soon followed. Today, Israel, India, Pakistan, and North Korea have joined the nuclear club. The threat of nuclear war might have acted as a deterrent and kept the peace between the main nuclear powers. The ability to destroy the world, however, has made our planet an infinitely more dangerous place.

Atomic cloud
The devastating force of the explosion threw a huge mushroom cloud thousands of metres into the sky. The searing heat of the bomb was so intense it vaporized people, and caused a firestorm that destroyed the city.

"My God, what have we done?"

ROBERT LEWIS, CO-PILOT OF "ENOLA GAY", 1945

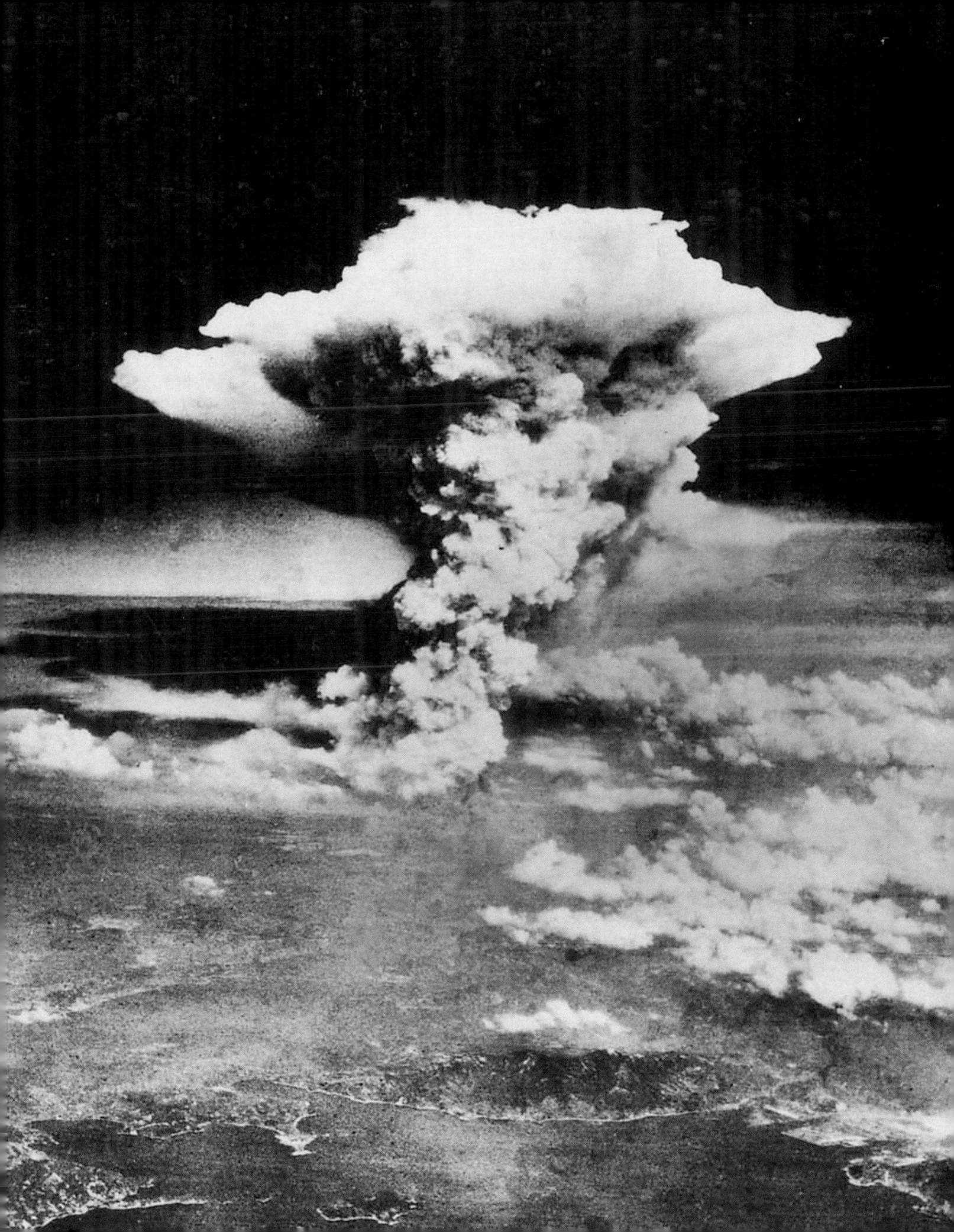

BEFORE

Historic distrust and ideological differences between the Soviet Union and the United States led to tension between the two.

US IN SIBERIA
Antagonism between the Soviet Union and the US began in the **Russian Civil War ‹‹ 301** when the US intervened in Siberia (northeast Russia). Between 1918–20 US troops fought on the side of the White Army against the Bolsheviks. Although the US later sent aid to the fledgling Soviet state, diplomatic relations were not in place until 1933.

US TROOPS IN SIBERIA

CLASH OF IDEALS
Even as their wartime alliance defeated **Nazi Germany 314–19 ››**, relations cooled between the Soviet Union and the Western powers. In the US there was unease about the rise of European communism **‹‹ 265**, an ideology that advocated worldwide revolution and the end of capitalism. The West, led by the US, was equally mistrusted by the Soviet Union.

COMMUNIST POSTER

The Cold War

After World War II global politics became polarized as countries around the world allied themselves with either the United States or the Soviet Union. The East–West divide between communism and capitalism dominated world events for the next 40 years.

When the Allied powers met at Yalta and Potsdam to shape post-war Europe (see p.319), Stalin's insistence that Soviet borders be extended to cover Eastern Poland and the Baltic States raised anxieties about his expansionist ambitions. Between 1945–47, the Soviets gained in influence as communist governments were founded in other Eastern European states (jointly known as the Eastern Bloc). With Britain's status as a world power damaged by six years of war, it became clear that the only Western power with comparable strength to the Soviet Union was the United States. In 1947 the British prime minister, Winston Churchill, had to request US support in Greece where a civil war was raging between the royalist government and communist partisans. The request prompted US President Truman to pledge assistance to all states trying to defend democracy against external threat. This became known as "The Truman Doctrine". Truman argued that the spread of communist regimes must be combated or America's national security would be at risk. This marked a new phase in US foreign policy called "containment". Over the next few years through measures such as the Marshall Plan (see p.374), the US poured millions of dollars in financial and military aid into non-communist European states, bolstering their economic recoveries. The Soviet Union saw US containment measures as imperialist and aggressive. It reacted by strengthening its own power base. In 1947 Andrei Zhdanov, a senior Soviet official, stated that the world was split into two camps: Western imperialists and socialist anti-imperialists. He set up the Cominform, an organization that supervised the strict ideological conformity of Eastern Bloc regimes with Moscow's party line. The first confrontation of the Cold War occurred in Berlin.

Korean War propaganda
The Korean communists produced anti-capitalist propaganda, such as this poster. It aims to demoralize US troops, stating they will die for capitalist greed.

Berlin Airlift
Berlin's children greet one of the British and American transport planes that flew a total of 2.3 million tonnes of food, medicines, and fuel into their beleaguered city between 1948–49.

TWO CAMPS ON THE BRINK

At several points throughout the Cold War tensions almost reached boiling point, but direct conflict or "hot" war between the US and the Soviet Union was avoided.

1961 The building of the **Berlin Wall** is ordered by Walter Ulbricht, leader of East Germany, to stop the flow of refugees across the border from East to West Berlin.

1961 The US funds and organizes Cuban exiles in a bungled attempt to invade Cuba at the **Bay of Pigs** and depose the communist leader Fidel Castro.

1964–73 The US enters the **Vietnam War** to back the South Vietnamese army against North Vietnamese communists, the Vietcong. By the time a ceasefire is signed 58,000 US lives and many more Vietnamese are lost.

1970 The **Nuclear Non-proliferation Treaty** agreed between the US and the Soviet Union, to build an effective system of controls to prevent the spread of nuclear weapons comes into effect.

1983 US President Reagan announces the **Star Wars** programme, which gives the US space-based protection against attack from the Soviet Union, which he calls the **Evil Empire**.

1987 The **Intermediate-Range Nuclear Forces Treaty** is signed by presidents Reagan and Gorbachev ending the arms race.

1950 | **1955** | **1960** | **1965** | **1970** | **1975** | **1980** | **1985**

1950–53 US and South Korean forces fight against North Korean and Chinese troops in the **Korean War.**

1955 The Soviet Union and the Eastern Bloc formalize their military and political alliance in the **Warsaw Pact.**

1962 The discovery of Soviet missiles in Cuba leads the US to threaten the Soviet Union with attack unless installations are dismantled. For 14 days war seems imminent until Khrushchev agrees to US President Kennedy's demands.

1970–75 The **Cambodian War** breaks out between the communist Khmer Rouge and Cambodia's republican government. The republicans are backed by the US but the Khmer Rouge triumphs.

1979 Soviet troops enter Afghanistan to prop up the failing communist regime.

1985 Gorbachev comes to power in the Soviet Union. He reforms the country's failing institutions and opens up talks on nuclear disarmament.

1989 On 9 November the East German government opens gates along the Berlin Wall. Citizens set about dismantling it.

After World War II, Germany was divided into four zones, each separately administered by the US, France, Britain, and the Soviet Union. The German capital, Berlin, was situated deep in the Soviet zone and was split into four allied sectors. In 1948 the Western allies planned a separate West German state, uniting the US, French, and British zones. The Soviets tried to stop this by cutting off land routes into the Western sectors of Berlin, leaving only air access. For the next year, as diplomatic battles raged, the Berlin Airlift (see below) brought supplies to besieged Berliners. By 1949 division of Germany appeared to be inevitable. The German Democratic Republic was created in East Germany and the Federal Republic of Germany in the west. Berlin remained a divided city. In 1961 the barbed wire partitions were replaced by the Berlin Wall (see p.348).

The Cold War hots up

The superpowers' possession of weapons of mass destruction generated much of the fear and paranoia that characterizes the Cold War era. Initially the US was the only nation in possession of nuclear weapons but once the Soviets tested their own nuclear bomb in August 1949, any future conflict carried the threat of global destruction. In 1953 the Soviet leader, Nikita Khrushchev, promoted a policy of "peaceful co-existence" with the West and periodic attempts were made on both sides to create a thaw in relations. However, there were many flash points that refuelled tensions and suspicions, bringing the world to the brink of catastrophe. In 1962, crisis was narrowly averted after a tense stand-off when Soviet missile installations were discovered in communist Cuba. The superpowers continued to stockpile nuclear arms, reasoning that nuclear war could only be prevented if each side had an equal capacity to destroy the other. A range of arms agreements were negotiated during the Cold War, but disarmament was not considered to be a possibility.

Cuban missile crisis
Nuclear weapons were mobilized in Havana (above) as the US and the Soviet Union threatened each other with nuclear attack in an escalating argument over the building of Soviet nuclear installations on Cuba.

DECISIVE MOMENT

SIGNING THE NATO TREATY

On 4 April 1949 the North Atlantic Treaty Organization (NATO) was founded by the leaders of the United States, Canada, Britain, France, and several other European countries. NATO was, first and foremost, a military alliance that guaranteed assistance between member states and, crucially, allowed the US to maintain military bases in Europe. In 1953, Greece and Turkey entered NATO but a Soviet request for membership was rejected.

AFTER »

The reforming political leader Mikhail Gorbachev unintentionally set off a chain of events that would break up the Soviet Union.

COLLAPSE OF COMMUNISM

In 1985 **Gorbachev** started to campaign for economic and political reforms known as *glasnost* and *perestroika* **368–69 »**. Two years later he became president and modernized the Soviet system, encouraging the creation of a private sector and openness with the West. He aimed to keep a one-party political system but his social reforms sparked a chain reaction that led to the collapse of the Communist Party as Russians demanded choice in their leaders.

DISSOLUTION OF THE SOVIET UNION

In the Baltic States, Kazakhstan, and other parts of the Soviet Union nationalists rose up to demand independence from Moscow. Gorbachev tried to hold the Soviet Union together, imposing sanctions and sending troops into Georgia and Azerbaijan. In 1990 **Boris Yeltsin** resigned from the Communist Party and began to campaign for its dissolution. In 1991 he emerged as the new Russian leader. He banned the Communist Party and disbanded the Soviet Union.

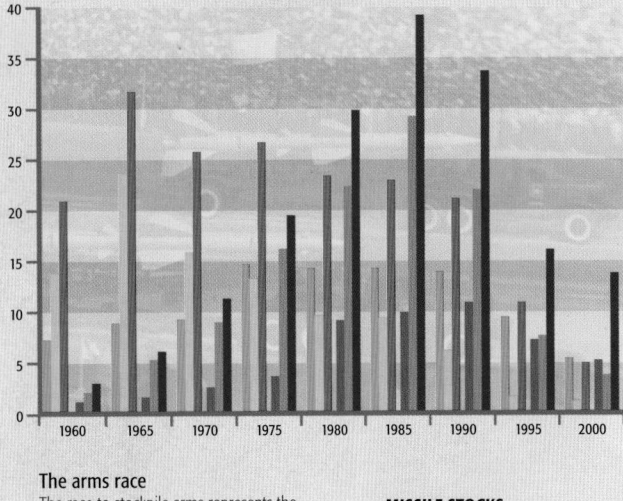

The arms race
The race to stockpile arms represents the superpowers' Cold War conflict in graphic terms. Each side rapidly developed the capacity to destroy the world many times over, but both continued to manufacture weapons at huge expense, competing to develop missiles that were ever more efficient.

(Graph y-axis: Warheads x 1,000; x-axis years: 1960, 1965, 1970, 1975, 1980, 1985, 1990, 1995, 2000)

MISSILE STOCKS

US	USSR/RUSSIA
Strategic	Strategic
Tactical	Tactical
Stockpile	Stockpile

POLITICAL AND SPIRITUAL LEADER Born 1869 Died 1948

Mahatma Gandhi

"**Silent suffering**... speaks with an **unrivalled eloquence.**" GANDHI, 1923

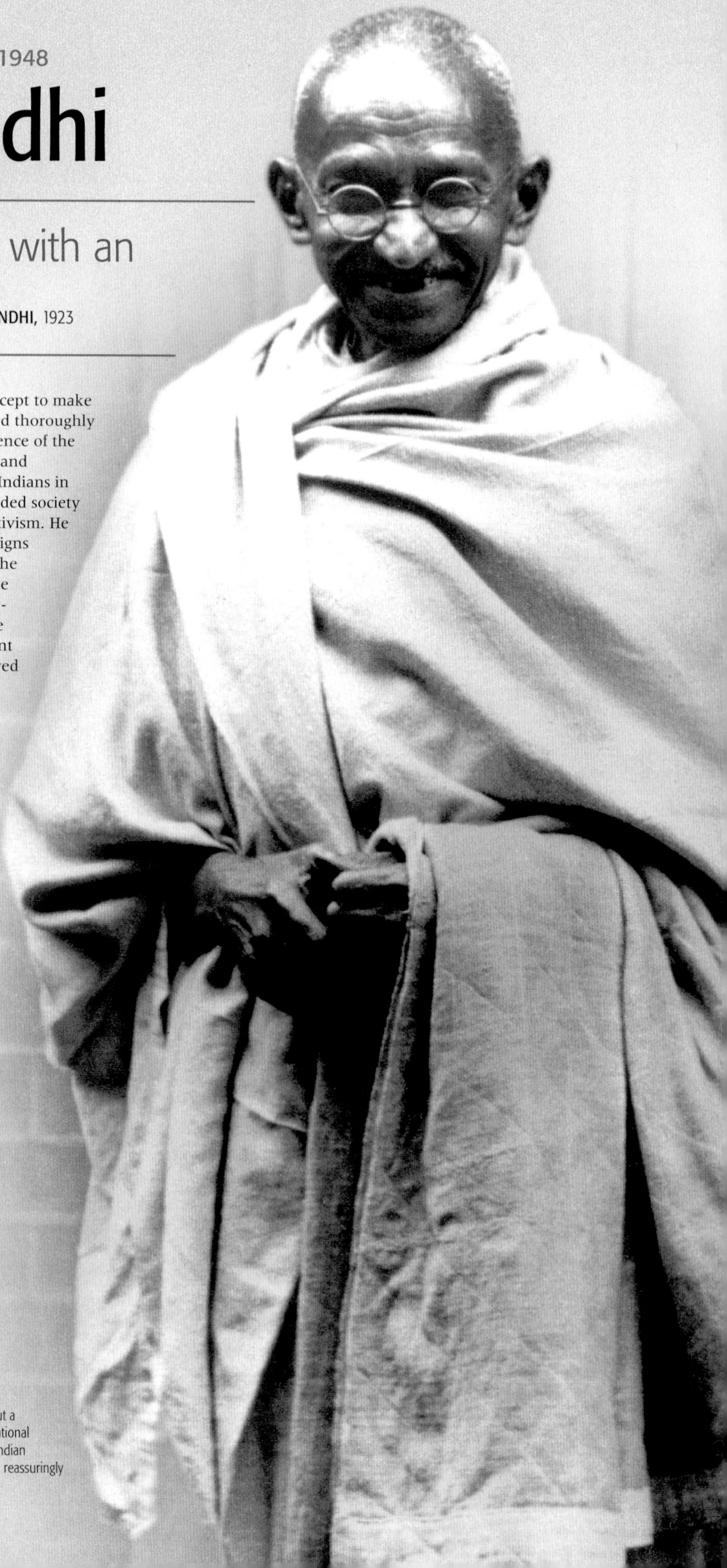

Mohandas Karamchand Gandhi, known as Mahatma ("Grand Soul"), was born into the *vaisya* caste of Hindu society, traditionally devoted to trade. His father was prime minister of the tiny princedom of Porbandar, part of British-ruled northwestern India. Typical of privileged sectors of Indian society at that time, his life was shaped both by old Indian customs, such as an arranged marriage at an early age, and by the influence of European attitudes and ideas.

The young Gandhi was sceptical about his family's Hindu practices, however, including the avoidance of meat, and leapt at the chance of studying law in Britain. Ironically, it was as a student it was in London that he first encountered the *Bhagavad Gita*, a sacred Hindu text that was to influence him profoundly, and he became a committed vegetarian.

When Gandhi went to South Africa as a 23-year-old lawyer in 1893, he had no clear purpose in life except to make money, at which he proved thoroughly successful. But the experience of the discrimination, prejudice, and mistreatment suffered by Indians in South Africa's racially divided society drew him into political activism. He led a series of mass campaigns during which he devised the method of political struggle he called *satyagraha* ("love-force" or "truth-force", see right). This was non-violent civil disobedience, conceived by Gandhi as a moral and spiritual effort, seeking to bring about a change in the hearts and minds of the oppressors by

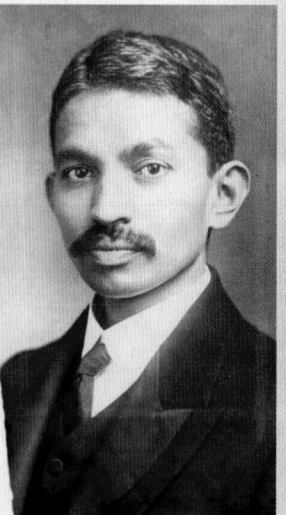

Gandhi the lawyer
As a young London-educated lawyer, Gandhi looked the epitome of a Westernized Asian. He did not adopt traditional Indian dress until 1913.

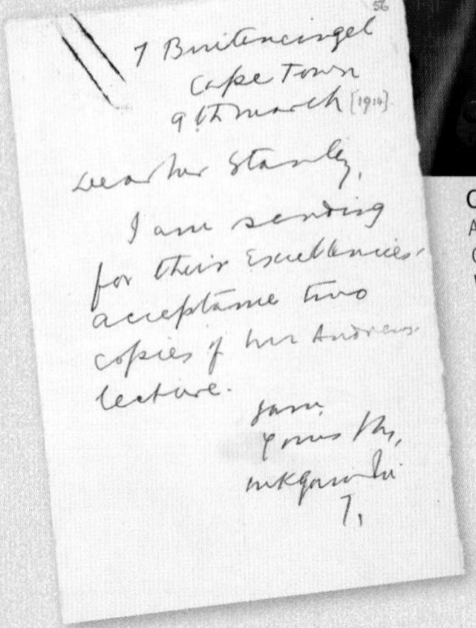

56

7 Buitencingel
Cape Town
9th march [1914].

Dear Mr Stanley,

I am sending for their Excellencies' acceptance two copies of Mrs Andrews' lecture.

I am,
Yours faithfully,
M K Gandhi

Handwritten letter
This letter was written in 1914, the year in which Gandhi definitively quit South Africa after two decades of campaigning for the Indians' rights.

Father of the nation
In his white "dhoti" Gandhi cut a strikingly odd figure at international political conferences. To the Indian masses, though, he seemed a reassuringly familiar type of holy man.

Young companions
The ageing Gandhi is seen here with his "walking sticks" – his great-nieces Manu and Ava – at Birla House in New Delhi.

adherence to the truth and by the readiness to suffer. Gandhi certainly suffered himself, undergoing imprisonment and coming close to being lynched by a racist mob.

Adopting the simple life

When Gandhi returned to live in India in 1915, he was not only a seasoned leader of political protest but also a man with a distinctive set of attitudes based on the rejection of modern industrial civilization. As he was influenced by Russian author Leo Tolstoy and English social critic John Ruskin, he embraced the simple life, believing in the virtue of small artisan communities. He had made a vow of chastity (announced to his wife in 1906), seeking spiritual fulfilment through the renunciation of the passions. He also rejected modern medicine in favour of alternative remedies and a focus on diet.

Gandhi established a community, or *ashram*, at Ahmedabad, northwestern India, where he could live according to his principles, but he soon resumed campaigning. India was entering a period of great upheaval, shaped both by the British government's

commitment in 1917 to progress towards a degree of Indian self-rule, and simultaneous oppression by the British authorities in the Raj, notably the massacre of 379 demonstrators at Amritsar in April 1919. In a very short time Gandhi swept to the forefront of Indian political life, launching a campaign of total non-cooperation with the British, and a boycott of British goods, which attracted mass support. After taking over leadership of the Indian National Congress, he made it into a vital nationwide organization.

Spiritual values

Gandhi never had a politician's attitude, however. His goal was not the attainment of power but the spiritual and moral transformation of Indian society. His advocacy of non-violence ran into difficulty as early as 1922 when a nationalist mob killed 22 policemen at Chauri Chaura, northern India. Gandhi responded by calling off his first non-cooperation campaign, but critics pointed out in following years

Meeting the viceroy
Lord Mountbatten, the last British viceroy (governor) of India, and his wife were on close terms with Gandhi during the run-up to Indian independence in 1947.

that when he stirred up political dissent, in practice, it always led to violence. For much of the 1920s and 1930s Gandhi focused on breaking down communal barriers between Hindus and Muslims, and overthrowing the Hindu caste system – a system of inherited social classes. He also campaigned against industrialization, himself learning to use a hand spinning wheel as a symbol of his great belief in village crafts.

An undisputed leader

Despite these challenges, Gandhi remained both nationally and internationally the most renowned leader of the Indian independence movement. No other Indian leader could have led such an effective protest as the famous "Salt March" of 1930, a symbolic defiance of the British tax on salt. No other leader talked so effectively to the British ruling class, who were fascinated by his exotic dress and manner. And his moral authority in India was immense.

In 1942, reluctantly, he launched the "Quit India" movement, provoking brutal repression from the British authorities. The drift of events saddened his final years. The British decided to grant India independence after World War II, but the rise of Muslim separatism led to partition between India and Pakistan (see pp.332–33), which Gandhi loathed. Even worse was the violence that the subcontinent was plunged into. Fasting and pleading with Hindus and Muslims, Gandhi occasionally managed to halt the slaughter in one place, only for it to break out in another. His conciliatory attitude towards Muslims enraged Hindu extremists. On 20 January 1948 he was shot dead in Delhi by Hindu fanatic Nathuram Godse.

"Truth never damages a cause that is just."

GANDHI, FROM "NON-VIOLENCE IN PEACE AND WAR", 1948

(see pp.332–33)

IDEA

SATYAGRAHA

Gandhi's principle of *satyagraha*, a non-violent political struggle, was influential after his death. It became, for example, a point of reference for Martin Luther King as leader of the American civil rights movement (see pp.432–33), for the founders of the Campaign for Nuclear Disarmament (CND), and for some within the anti-Vietnam War protest movement (see pp.430–31). For Gandhi, *satyagraha* was much more than simply a way of achieving political objectives through civil disobedience. He saw it as a path to spiritual improvement through truth, love, and suffering.

TIMELINE

- **2 October, 1869** Gandhi is born in Porbandar, Gujarat.

- **May 1883** Is married, aged 13, to 10-year-old Kasturba Makhanji.

- **1888–91** Studies law at University College, London, and returns to India as a barrister.

- **April 1893** Travels to Durban, South Africa, to join an Indian law firm.

- **1894** Begins 20 years of campaigning against discrimination and exploitation of Indians in South Africa.

- **1899–1902** During the Boer War Gandhi forms an Indian Ambulance Corps.

- **11 September 1906** Calls for resistance to the registration of Indians in Transvaal, initiating his first campaign of *satyagraha*.

GANDHI AT HIS LAW OFFICES

- **May 1915** Returning to India, he founds the Satyagraha Ashram at Ahmedabad.

- **December 1921** Elected leader of the Indian National Congress.

- **February 1922** Halts the non-cooperation campaign in shock at mob violence.

- **March 1922** Arrested and tried for sedition. Gandhi is sentenced to six years and serves two.

- **December 1928** Congress launches a campaign for dominion status for India.

- **26 January 1930** Millions of Indians take Gandhi's pledge to pursue "purna swaraj" – complete independence.

- **12 March–6 April 1930** Leads the "Salt March" from Ahmedabad to Dandi; he is arrested on 4 May.

- **14 February–5 March 1931** Released from prison. Gandhi negotiates a pact with British viceroy Lord Irwin to end civil disobedience.

- **September–December 1931** Gandhi represents Congress at a Round Table Conference on Indian constitutional reform in London; on his return to India he is arrested.

- **24 October 1934** Disillusioned with politics he resigns from Congress.

- **9 August 1942** Gandhi and Congress leaders are arrested after the launch of the "Quit India" movement for independence from Britain; Gandhi is held in the Aga Khan Palace near Poona.

- **November 1946** Begins a solitary campaign to halt massacres and seek conciliation between Hindus and Muslims.

- **30 January 1948** Gandhi is assassinated at Birla House, New Delhi.

NEWSPAPER REPORT OF GANDHI'S DEATH

BEFORE

Denied civil and political rights, Indians became increasingly disenchanted with British rule in the late 19th century. By the 1920s there was a mass anti-colonial movement demanding home rule for India.

GOVERNMENT OF INDIA ACT

The **British Raj << 282–83** made some limited concessions to Indian civil rights. In 1909 the **Government of India Act** allowed a very small number of Indians to sit on legislative councils, but their responsibilities were minimal.

INDIAN RIGHTS

The **Indian National Congress (INC)** was founded in 1885 by Western-educated Indians campaigning for Indian rights. Although the Congress represented all Indians, its members were mainly Hindu. In 1906 some Muslims broke away from the INC to form the **Muslim League**.

CIVIL DISOBEDIENCE

During the 1920s, under the leadership of **Mahatma Gandhi << 330–31**, the INC demanded Indian independence. In a long campaign of civil disobedience, known as *satyagraha*, Gandhi encouraged the boycotting of British goods, the non-payment of taxes, and passive, or **non-violent resistance**.

VIOLENT RESISTANCE

Not all Indians used peaceful means to resist British rule. When World War II **<< 314–327** broke out, many Indians supported Britain's enemies. The Bengali leader, **Subhash Chandra Bose**, formed the 20,000-strong Indian National Army, which fought alongside Japanese forces.

INDIAN NATIONAL ARMY

The **Partition** of India

British rule in India ended in 1947 and the subcontinent was partitioned along religious lines to form the Hindu-majority state of India and the Muslim-majority state of Pakistan. Many millions of Muslims and Hindus caught on the wrong side of the border were forced to flee their homes.

After World War I (see pp.296–99), Britain promised India a major role in governing itself, in return for Indian support during the war. In 1919 a further Government of India Act (see BEFORE) was passed. It created an Indian parliament to which Indian ministers could be elected to hold positions of responsibility in departments such as health, education, and agriculture. However, only the wealthiest Indians, who formed a tiny ercentage of the population, were allowed to vote for the parliament, and the British still held the real power, controlling all the other departments. Another act in 1935 allowed more Indians to vote, and the British kept only the most crucial departments – revenue, defence, and foreign affairs. These concessions did not go far enough for independence campaigners (see BEFORE). At the end of World War II, in 1945, the British agreed to hand over full power.

Direct action

As independence drew closer, the leader of the Muslim League, Muhammad Ali Jinnah, started to demand a separate Muslim state. The idea was resisted by Hindus, including Gandhi, who believed that India should remain united. In response, Jinnah declared 16 August 1946 "Direct Action Day". On that day Muslims protested all over India to voice their demand for a separate homeland. Tragically, the protest in Calcutta escalated into violent fighting between religious groups, and thousands of people died.

Drawing the line

Lord Mountbatten, the last Viceroy of India, saw that the only way for the British to withdraw was to partition India and to transfer power to two governments. Among the major Indian leaders, only Gandhi refused to agree to partition. He even urged Mountbatten to offer Jinnah the premiership of a united India rather than a separate

Constitutional Assembly crowd

A crowd of people gathered outside the Constitutional Assembly in Karachi as the ceremony to symbolize the transfer of power from Britain to Pakistan took place. During the ceremony Lord Mountbatten read a message from George VI pledging the support of the British Commonwealth (nations that were formerly part of the British Empire) to Pakistan.

ETHNIC TENSIONS
Ethnic and religious rivalries caused the partition of India. Territorial disputes arising from the partition have led to a series of conflicts between neighbouring states.

1940 — **1950** — **1960** — **1970** — **1980**

1947–49 India and Pakistan go to war when Pakistan supports a Muslim insurgency in the independent province of **Kashmir**.

1958–60 Disputes arise between Pakistan and India over the rights to water in the Pakistani **Punjab** region.

1966 The Tashkent agreement commits the countries to resolve differences through peaceful means and non-inteference in each other's foreign affairs.

1971 Civil war breaks out between West and East Pakistan. After the war ends, East Pakistan becomes **Bangladesh**.

1989 Pakistan begins its "moral and diplomatic support" of Muslim militant groups operating in the Kashmir valley. India accuses Pakistan of supporting terrorism.

1946 Jinnah calls for **"direct action"**. Riots erupt and thousands of people are killed.

1947 Partition of the Indian subcontinent leads to a **mass migration** of people and the deaths of one million.

1965 Pakistan launches an offensive in the Indian-held parts of **Jammu and Kashmir**. India invades **Lahore** in retaliation.

1972 The Simla Treaty between the two countries paves the way for the diplomatic recognition of an independent Bangladesh by Pakistan.

1999 War briefly breaks out between India and Pakistan near the Indian Kashmiri town of Kargil.

Muslim nation. Congress president Jawaharlal Nehru, however, would not agree to this plan, nor would his most powerful Congress deputy, Vallabhbhai Patel. Neither felt they could work with Jinnah and were eager to push ahead with running an independent India.

In July 1947 Britain's Parliament passed the Indian Independence Act, ordering the demarcation of the dominions of India and Pakistan and dividing the assets of the world's largest empire. Under the partition plan, Pakistan had two wings – East and West Pakistan. These were located thousands of kilometres apart, in the mainly Muslim east and northwest of the region respectively. India was formed from the remaining area, with the exception of the northern province of Kashmir, which was free to accede to India or Pakistan.

Nehru releases a dove
The Indian prime minister, Nehru, launched a dove of peace at his 65th birthday celebrations in 1954. Nehru held office from 1947–64.

On 14 August 1947 Pakistan gained independence and Jinnah became its first governor-general. At midnight the next day, the independent state of India emerged with Nehru as its first prime minister. As soon as the new borders were announced, more than 12 million Hindus, Muslims, and Sikhs fled from their homes on one side of the borders to what they believed was refuge on the other side. They travelled on foot, in bullock carts, and on trains. The massive exchange of population left a trail of death and destruction. Within two months about one million people were slaughtered in fierce religious riots. The Sikh population, who were caught on the Pakistani side of the new border, suffered the highest percentage of casualties. Most Sikhs eventually settled in India's much-reduced border province of Punjab.

Partition riots
Violent gangs roamed the streets of Calcutta (Kolkata) during riots, which erupted as soon as partition was declared. The sectarian attacks claimed the lives of 4,000 people.

Territorial and ethnic issues continue to cause conflict in the Indian subcontinent.

CONFLICT OVER KASHMIR
India and Pakistan have contested possession of the Muslim-majority state of **Kashmir** since 1947, when the Hindu ruler, **Maharajah Hari Singh**, gave the province to India. Wars were fought over the territory in 1947–48 and 1965. Since 1989 an independence movement has evolved in Indian-administered Kashmir. India blamed pro-Kashmiri militants from Pakistan for attacks on Parliament in 2001 and on Mumbai hotels in 2008, and the countries continue to clash in border skirmishes.

SIKH SEPARATISTS
No provision was made for Sikhs when India was partitioned between Muslims and Hindus. From the early 1980s Sikhs began to demand their own state, which they hope to call **Sikh Khalistan**, meaning "Land of the Pure".

NUCLEAR STANDOFF
India and Pakistan conducted nuclear bomb tests in 1998, provoking international concern. The UN Security Council urged the two countries to stop all nuclear weapons programmes. Tensions were reduced in February 1999 after Pakistan and India signed the **Lahore Declaration**, pledging to intensify efforts to resolve the issues between them. However, the threat of nuclear conflict between the two countries still remains.

End of the Colonial Era

The decline of Europe's empires gathered momentum after World War II as domination of poorer nations by colonial powers came to be considered unacceptable. The transition from empire led to the creation of self-governing nation states in much of the world, but this created many new conflicts.

In 1945, the old justification for empire – that "inferior" races needed the guidance of "superior" Western civilization – came into question. In the aftermath of war there was a real desire to build a new and better world (see p.319). Many colonies had remained deeply impoverished and underdeveloped to suit the economic needs of empire. However, European powers were now forced to admit that this could no longer be accepted and some countries reluctantly began to prepare for a withdrawal from imperial territories.

End of empire
Unfortunately this new recognition of the rights of "Third World" countries to self-govern coincided with the advent of the Cold War (see pp.328–29). The transition to independent status of some former colonies was complicated by the superpowers – the US and the Soviet Union – who competed for influence over the people's choice of government. In the colonies themselves there was conflict between different social, political, and ethnic factions over who should govern. In many cases European powers caused resentment by trying to hold on to their interests in resources, such as oil and gemstones, even after independence had been granted. As a result transitions to independence were often marked by civil wars and intervention from foreign powers.

Withdrawal from colonies
In Indonesia, resentment of their Dutch imperial masters was so intense that Japanese invaders were initially welcomed during World War II. The Dutch were unwilling to surrender their interests in Indonesian oil and rubber. They invaded in 1945 to re-establish control, but conceded Indonesian independence in 1949, although they continued to occupy Western New Guinea. A full Indonesian Republic was not created until 1960. During World War II the German-backed Vichy regime in French Indochina, which incorporated Vietnam, Laos, and Cambodia, also collaborated with Japan. In 1945 the

BEFORE

By the early 20th century the spread of nationalist ideas led to the growth of independence movements in the colonies.

COLONIES AND EMPIRES
Before World War II European powers still **dominated much of the world** – Africa was largely divided between the British, French, Belgian, and Portuguese ❮❮ **290–91**; much of Asia and the Caribbean also remained under imperial rule. In the Middle East, mandates granted by the League of Nations gave Britain and France administrative powers over the region.

COLONIAL ECONOMIES
Colonial territories tended to be under-industrialized, and in many the standard of living was very low. They supplied raw materials to power European industry, but the **development of their own national economies** was not seen as a priority.

RISE OF NATIONALISM
Increasingly, **citizens demanded the right to self-govern**. The imperial powers began to make some concessions towards power-sharing but remained determined to hold on to economic control of the natural resources of their colonies.

PRESIDENT OF EGYPT (1918–1970)

GAMAL ABDEL NASSER

From an early age, Nasser was interested in the fight for Egyptian independence. During World War II, he was involved in plans for a military coup to oust British forces from Egypt. These plans never reached fruition, but in 1952 Nasser spearheaded the Egyptian Revolution, becoming president (1956–70). Nasser's victory in the Suez Crisis of 1956 (see right) established him as a figurehead for Arab nationalism.

Vietnamese nationalist Ho Chi Minh took advantage of the Japanese surrender to declare an Independent Democratic Vietnamese Republic. French troops invaded the new republic and by 1946 had taken control of the south of the country, while Minh's army (Viet Minh) held the north. The French Indochina War lasted from 1946–54, when massive French losses at the Battle of Dien Bien Phu finally precipitated a settlement. The country was divided into North and South Vietnam. Tensions between the two nations later escalated into the Vietnam War (see pp.352–53).

In the British colony of Malaya an initially peaceful transition to self-government developed into conflict in 1948. Hostility towards Britain's intention to maintain business interests in Malay rubber and tin combined with political and ethnic divisions in the population to create civil unrest. An armed insurrection by the communist minority resulted in the death of three European plantation managers in June

Ships scuppered in the Suez Canal
Ships, sunk by Egyptian forces, block the entrance to the Suez Canal. On the extreme right of the picture a British naval salvage vessel attempts to clear the channel.

Dutch leave Indonesia
As Indonesia gains independence in 1949, servants carry 300 portraits of former Dutch governors out of the colonial residence, marking the end of over 340 years of imperial rule.

1948, which led to armed confrontation. British troops defeated the Chinese guerrillas in 1952 and withdrew from Malaya in 1957 once the Federation of Malaya had been established.

The Suez crisis

The most significant crisis of British and French withdrawal from empire came in 1956 when President Nasser (see left) nationalized the Suez Canal. The canal, which links the Mediterranean and Red Sea through Egyptian territory, had been under British and French control since its construction in 1869. It represented a key route for the transport of raw materials to Europe. Anglo–French forces attacked Egypt to wrest the canal back from Egyptian control, but the United Nations, US,

and Soviet Union all refused to support the imperialist invasion. Humiliated, Britain and France withdrew. The crisis ended in a victory for Arab nationalism and signalled the decline of the old powers of Europe.

African conflicts

France's determination to maintain control of Algeria in northern Africa led to guerrilla fighting between the Algerian *Front de Libération Nationale* (FLN) and French security forces from 1954. By 1960, the violence had escalated and the independence issue was bitterly dividing the French nation. French army generals in Algeria then attempted a coup d'état. Independence was agreed in 1962. The struggle left deep scars on both French and Algerian national consciousness.

The dismantling of colonies in Africa spawned many territorial wars between African Nations. This was due in part to

the fact that European governments had divided the continent along arbitrary borders that paid no attention to tribal boundaries (see pp.290–91).

150,000 The estimated death toll in the French–Algerian conflict.

As imperial powers withdrew, many nations also descended into civil war.

When the Belgian government abruptly granted independence to the Congo in 1960, violence erupted as different Congolese factions struggled to gain control of the nation's remarkable natural wealth. The Congo's nominally democratic government, installed at independence, failed in 1965 when Lieutenant General Mobutu seized power in a military coup.

After independence

Through the 1960–70s, transitions to independence were generally peaceful, and it was established across most of the world. However, independent government in the Third World has not equalized the distribution of global wealth and power. While former colonies such as Hong Kong and Singapore (see pp.380–81) have flourished post-empire, many others are among the world's poorest nations.

Paris riots
Growing opposition in France to French suppression of the Nationalist Movement in Algeria exploded into riots on the streets of Paris as French protestors clashed with the French Army and the notorious CRS riot squad in 1961. A ceasefire was agreed in Algeria in 1962. Later that year the Algerian people voted for independence.

AFTER

In many cases democracies established post-empire failed to survive, and military or one-party rule was established.

MILITARY REGIMES

In some countries power was seized in military coups, such as that led by **Idi Amin** in Uganda in 1971. **Ethnic violence and political repression** were rife under the military regimes.

DEMOCRACY

With a few exceptions, such as the independent Republic of Ghana, democracies established post-empire have failed in much of Africa. Elected national parliaments have often been **unable to establish unity** in countries, such as Sudan, that are divided along tribal lines.

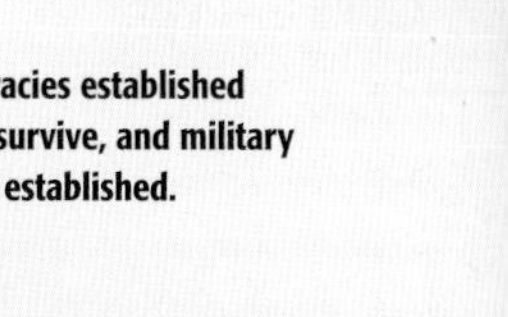

INDEPENDENCE ANNIVERSARY, GHANA

‹‹ BEFORE

In the 1880s many Jews began to emigrate to Palestine to avoid religious persecution in Europe. In the 1890s the Zionist movement demanded a sovereign state in their ancient homeland, and in 1917 the British agreed to the creation of a Jewish state in Palestine.

ZIONISM

Zionism became an organized political movement in 1897 when its founder, Theodor Herzl, convened the First Zionist Congress. The congress called for a Jewish state in Palestine.

EARLY ZIONISTS

SYKES–PICOT AGREEMENT

When the Ottoman Empire **‹‹ 186–87** collapsed during World War I **‹‹ 296–99**, France and Britain signed the 1916 Sykes–Picot agreement, dividing the Empire's Middle Eastern territories between them. France gained the mandate for Syria and Lebanon, and Britain was granted the mandate for Iraq and Palestine.

❙ MANDATE An Ottoman or German territory that was handed to another country to run after World War I.

THE BALFOUR DECLARATION

The 1917 Balfour Declaration was a policy drawn up by the British government that accepted the need for a Jewish homeland in Palestine.

The Promised Land

According to the Bible the land of Palestine was promised by God to the Jewish people. In 1948 the modern Jewish state of Israel was established in the region, causing fury among Palestinian Arabs and in the wider Arab world. It has proved one of the most contentious political acts of modern times.

The period of British rule in Palestine, which formally began in 1919 when the British Mandate (see BEFORE) was granted, was marked by controversy and violence. The majority Arab population strongly contested the Jewish settlers' claim on their country, and some Arabs resorted to aggressive attacks against Jews, their homes, and their businesses. The Jews, feeling that the British authorities were giving them insufficient protection, began to form local defence groups, known collectively as the Hagannah, to protect their communities. During the 1930s the Hagannah turned into a paramilitary organization, developing military training programmes and sourcing arms from Europe.

Jewish refugee
Like many of the Jews who emigrated to Israel in the 1950s, this Yemeni girl stayed at the Shaar reception centre in Haifa when she first arrived in the Jewish state.

The British withdraw

Guerrilla violence between Arab groups and the Hagannah became increasingly difficult for the British to police, so in 1939 they called together Arab and Jewish delegations to the St James Conference, also known as the Round Table Conference, to find a solution for the ongoing tensions.

UN Partition plan

Under the plan the Jews would receive the northern coastal plain, eastern Galilee, and the Negev. The Arabs would get a section of desert bordering Egypt (the Gaza Strip), the Samarian and Judean highlands, and the southern coast.

No agreement was reached at the conference, so the British formed their own policy, which was stated in the McDonald White Paper of 1939. In it the British made concessions to the Arabs on a wide range of issues, the most important of which was a restriction on the free settlement in Palestine of Jewish refugees. This seemed like a death sentence for those Jews trying to flee Nazi Europe (see pp.322–23) to Palestine. Supporters of the Arab and Jewish sides held international conferences during 1946, but the year ended without any workable solutions to the problem. Caught between Arab and Jewish demands, a cash-strapped British government declared its mandate in Palestine "unworkable" in February 1947 and referred the matter to the United Nations. The UN proposed a partition plan, which allocated about 44 per cent of the area for an Arab

state and 56 per cent for a Jewish state, with Jerusalem under international administration. On 29 November 1947 the UN General Assembly voted 33 to 13, with 10 abstentions, in favour of the Partition Plan. The Jews agreed with their decision but the Arabs did not, arguing that the plan ignored the rights of the majority of people living in Palestine. Despite this, Britain

> **"In Israel, in order to be a realist you must believe in miracles."**
> DAVID BEN-GURION, OLORA MANIFESTO, 1948

Wreck of *Altalena*

In June 1948 crowds gathered on the Tel Aviv beachfront to see the wreckage of the burnt out *Altalena*. It had sailed from France to Israel carrying arms for the Irgun (a splinter group of the Hagannah) and about 900 immigrants. Ben-Gurion refused to let it land in respect of a truce with the Arabs, and ordered warning shots to be fired. One hit the vessel and it burned.

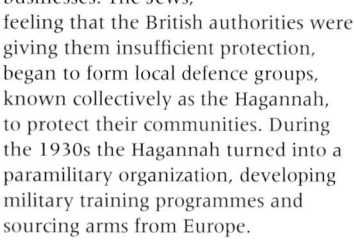

Beirut
LEBANON
Tyre
Haifa
Sea of Galilee
Golan Heights
Damascus
SYRIA
Qunaytirah
Mediterranean Sea
Nablus
SAMARIA
Tel-Aviv
Jaffa
Jerusalem
Amman
Gaza
Gaza Strip
West Bank
JUDEA
Jericho
Dead Sea
Hebron
Rafah
Beersheba
El Arish
TRANSJORDAN
ISRAEL
Negev
Sinai Peninsula
Eilat
Aqaba
Gulf of Aqaba

KEY
- ▮ Proposed Arab state
- ▮ Proposed Jewish state
- ▯ Proposed international zone
- — Border of British mandate 1923

0   100 km
0   100 miles

ISRAELI STATESMAN (1886–1973)

DAVID BEN-GURION

David Ben-Gurion was born in Poland. He moved to Palestine in 1906 and became a prominent member of the Zionist movement, leading the struggle to establish a state of Israel. Ben-Gurion became Israel's first prime minister in 1949. Until his retirement in 1970, he played a major role in Israeli life, developing the state's policies and institutions, and guiding Israel through years of conflict.

withdrew and on 14 May 1948 the Jewish state of Israel was established. It was recognized by the US, the Soviet Union, and other UN members, but not by its neighbouring Arab countries, which refused to accept Israel as a legitimate state.

Evacuation of Jerusalem
This man was among thousands of Jews who were evacuated from Jerusalem by British troops in 1948. The city had come under siege from Arab militias who, in reaction to the Partition Plan, tried to dispossess the 100,000 Jewish people living in the city.

Troubles in the homeland

One of the first tasks for Israel's new leader, David Ben-Gurion, was to create the Israeli Defense Force from the Hagannah and other Jewish paramilitary organizations. Israel had a real and immediate need to defend itself as, once it was established, the country was invaded by Egypt, Syria, Transjordan (later Jordan), Lebanon, and Iraq, beginning the Arab–Israeli War of 1947–49, the first in a series of conflicts between Israel and the Arab world (see AFTER). A further threat to security was the Palestine Liberation Organization (PLO). Formed in 1964 when various Arab guerrilla groups and political factions joined together, the PLO's stated aim was the destruction of Israel through armed struggle. The PLO sponsored innumerable guerrilla raids on Israeli civilian and military targets, giving the organization a worldwide reputation as a terrorist group. In the 1980s, Yasser Arafat, chairman of the PLO since 1969, took on the role of statesman and used diplomacy to achieve the group's ends; he eventually succeeded in reaching an agreement that gave Palestine a measure of self-government.

Entry visa
Dated January 1939, this visa allowed the German Jewish holder to emigrate to the British Protectorate of Palestine. By November in the same year restrictions had been placed on the numbers of Jews allowed to settle in the region.

Despite intervention by the international community, tensions between Middle Eastern Arabs and Jews erupted into conflict periodically after Israel was established.

SECOND ARAB–ISRAELI WAR

In 1956 **Egypt nationalized the Suez Canal Company** « **334–35**, taking the waterway out of French and British control. Since tensions were also growing between Israel and Egypt over the Egyptian-held Gaza Strip, which Israel believed was a base for guerrilla activity, **Israel, Britain, and France joined forces** to invade Egypt.

SIX-DAY WAR

Responding to the massing of Arab forces on its borders, in June 1967 **Israel launched a pre-emptive strike** against Egypt, Jordan, and Syria. After six days, a ceasefire agreement gave Israel control of the Gaza Strip, a large part of the Sinai Peninsula, the West Bank, and the Golan Heights – collectively known as **"occupied territories"**.

YOM KIPPUR WAR

In 1973 **Egypt and Syria** attacked Israel on Yom Kippur, the Jewish Day of Atonement, knowing that the Israeli military would be participating in religious celebrations. The Arabs advanced significantly before Israel rallied and pushed the invaders back beyond the 1967 ceasefire lines.

MOVES TOWARDS PEACE

In 1978 President **Anwar Sadat** of Egypt, Prime Minister **Menachem Begin** of Israel, and President **Jimmy Carter** of the US signed the Camp David Accords. The accords established a **"Framework for Peace"** in the Middle East, leading to the Israel–Egypt Peace Treaty in 1979.

ISRAELI OCCUPATION OF LEBANON

In attempts to curtail attacks by the PLO from Lebanon, Israel invaded in 1978 and in 1982, and kept an occupying force there until 2000. The killing of three soldiers and capture of two others by **Hezbollah**, a Lebanese Islamic paramilitary group, prompted Israel to invade again in 2006.

OSLO ACCORDS

The Intifada (a Palestinian uprising against Israeli rule from 1987–1991) persuaded Israel to join talks. Under the Oslo Accords – signed in 1993 by Israel's President Rabin and Yasser Arafat at the White House in the presence of President Clinton – Israel agreed to withdraw from parts of **the West Bank and Gaza Strip**, and allow an interim Palestinian government in those areas. Subsequent peace efforts failed and opinion on both sides hardened. Islamist groups such as Hamas and Islamic Jihad gained ground in areas ruled by Palestine, while Israeli hardliners pushed through a policy of isolating them by building a "peace wall".

RABIN, CLINTON, AND ARAFAT

SCIENTIST Born 1879 Died 1955

Albert Einstein

"The most **beautiful** experience we can have is the **mysterious.** It is the source of all true **art and science.**" ALBERT EINSTEIN, 1930

German-born physicist Albert Einstein had a largely uninspiring school career, although he displayed a natural talent for mathematics and a love of learning. After graduating from a technical university with a teaching certificate, Einstein found a job at a patent office in Bern, Switzerland, in 1903. Two years later, while still working there, Einstein submitted his doctoral thesis and published four scientific papers. Three of these were to be profoundly important in the history of science.

The first of Einstein's 1905 papers concerned the puzzling phenomenon known as the photoelectric effect, in which electrons are ejected from atoms of metal when light shines onto them.

Instead of the ejection rate gradually building with the intensity of light shining onto the metal surface, the effect suddenly "switches on" when the frequency of light rises past a certain threshold. In order to explain this effect, Einstein showed that light energy must be delivered in discrete packets, or "quanta".

German physicist Max Planck (1858–1947) had used quantization as a mathematical trick in 1900, but had

Einstein the icon
Albert Einstein contributed hugely to our understanding of the Universe – from atoms to stars and galaxies – and became an iconic figure.

Young Einstein
Around the time of this photograph, Einstein – here with sister Maja – received a magnetic compass from his father. He later said that he had found inspiration wondering why compass needles turn.

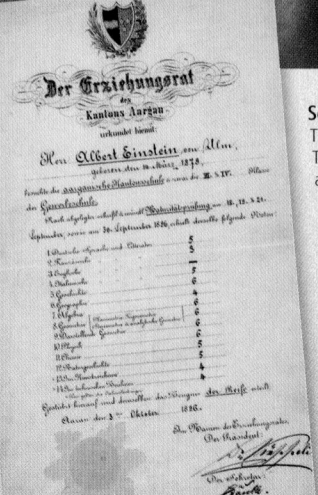

School certificate
There is a myth that Einstein struggled at school. This certificate tells a different story – in physics and maths he scored a maximum six.

never supposed it to be literally true. Einstein's paper was the beginning of quantum theory – a field of physics that provides insight into the behaviour of light, atoms, and subatomic particles. Einstein remained at the heart of its development for the rest of his life.

Einstein's second landmark paper of 1905, entitled *On the Electrodynamics of Moving Bodies*, outlined his Special

Theory of Relativity. The starting point in this paper was the fact that the speed of light is always the same, however fast an observer is moving relative to a light source. He used this to prove that time does not run at a single, "universal" rate – clocks moving relative to each other tick away seconds at different rates (though the effect is only noticeable at very high relative speeds).

Einstein's last publication of 1905 was a bold extension of Special Relativity. Working from the fact that the speed of light could not be exceeded, Einstein

THEORIES OF RELATIVITY

The principle of relativity dates back to the scientific revolution of the 17th century (see pp.266–67). First identified by Italian physicist Galileo Galilei, it states that physical laws should behave in the same way in all isolated frames of reference unless they are being affected by external forces – in other words, natural laws are the same whether one is in motion or not. This is because all motion is relative – there is no universal, fixed reference point.

Einstein's Special Theory of Relativity (1905) reconciles this principle with the fact that light always travels at the same speed relative to an observer no matter how fast they travel relative to its source. In order to do this, Einstein explained how time and

distance measurements become distorted at high relative speeds. The bizarre results of special relativity are used routinely by experimental physicists.

In 1915, Einstein extended Special Relativity to create his General Theory of Relativity. This theory explains gravity as a distortion of spacetime, the four-dimensional "fabric" of the Universe.

The two theories of relativity have been tested countless times and have never yet failed. One effect of general relativity (illustrated by this Hubble Space Telescope image) is a phenomenon called gravitational lensing, in which light from distant stars and galaxies is deflected and warped as it passes close to nearby stars and galaxies.

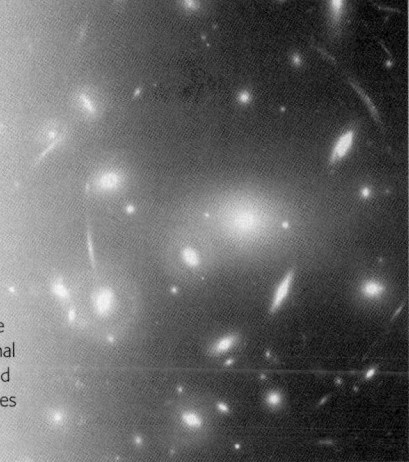

> "Do not worry about your difficulties with **mathematics**. I can assure you mine are **still greater.**" ALBERT EINSTEIN

proved that mass and energy, too, are relative quantities, just as time and space are. Furthermore, he showed that mass and energy are two aspects of the same thing, mass-energy. It was in this paper that he derived his most famous equation, relating mass (m) and energy (E), via the square of the speed of light (c^2): $E = mc^2$. This relationship is the basis of nuclear power: inside a reactor, atomic nuclei are broken apart and lose mass, producing large amounts of energy in agreement with Einstein's theory. This famous equation is also the source of the devastating energy of nuclear weapons.

Recognition

In 1907 Hermann Minkowski, one of Einstein's teachers, showed that time is equivalent to the three dimensions of space, and is intertwined with them. He visualized "spacetime" as a four-dimensional "fabric" of the Universe.

However, few other physicists paid attention to this work at the time. Einstein, meanwhile, set about generalizing his Special Theory of Relativity to include gravity. He realized that time slows down in intense gravitational fields – and one result of this is that light bends as it passes close to very massive objects, such as the Sun. Einstein was able to explain gravity as a

Einstein and politics
Einstein's Zionism brought him into contact with Israel's first prime minister, David Ben-Gurion (above). By 1946, Einstein was already proclaiming the need for nuclear disarmament (right).

distortion of spacetime, and published his ideas in 1915, as the General Theory of Relativity.

A total solar eclipse in 1919 provided a chance to test Einstein's new theory. A team of physicists photographed the area of the sky surrounding the Sun during the eclipse. Stars in the dark sky around the obscured Sun appeared slightly out of place – a result of their light bending as it passed close to the Sun. The shift was inexplicable

using the traditional "Newtonian" (see p.269) idea of gravity, but it matched Einstein's theory exactly.

Einstein became a worldwide celebrity. He won the 1921 Nobel Prize for Physics – the first of many honours – and stayed at the forefront of discovery during a period when physicists were beginning to unravel the Universe's fundamental mysteries. He was celebrated beyond the academic life of science, becoming a cultural icon, and one of the few scientists known by nearly everyone.

Political life

One consequence of Einstein's fame was that people sought his opinions on a wide range of topics. He was acquainted with many world leaders, wrote widely in newspapers, books, and magazines, and became involved with many political causes. In his later years, he lobbied against racism in the US and against nuclear weapons. He was a pacifist and vegetarian.

A German-born Jew, Einstein had Zionist (see p.414) aspirations, and was in favour of establishing a Jewish homeland in the Middle East. Having seen the rise of Nazism in Germany at first hand, it was inevitable that he would become involved in the formation of the state of Israel (see pp.414–15). He was even asked if he would become its president.

Although Einstein's theories are only truly understood by physicists, most people recognize that his work radically changed our understanding of the world, and appreciate that this brilliant man was one of the most enduring characters of the 20th century.

14 March 1879 Albert Einstein is born in a small town called Ulm, Germany. The Einsteins move to Munich the following year.

1892 Aged 13, Einstein begins his studies at the Lutipold Gymnasium (Munich).

1896 In order to avoid military service, he renounces his German citizenship, and begins studying mathematics in Zurich, Switzerland.

1901 Einstein graduates from the ETH, a technical institute in Zurich, with a teaching certificate. He is awarded Swiss citizenship.

1903 Marries his first wife, Mileva Maric, whom he met at college. He begins work at the patent office in Bern.

1905 In Einstein's "Wonderful Year", he writes four ground breaking scientific papers, which are published in the German physics journal, *Annalen der Physik*. He also gains his doctorate from the University of Zurich.

1911 Accepts a professorship at Charles University, Prague. From here, he publishes the first element of his General Theory of Relativity: the idea of gravitational redshift.

1912 Returns to Switzerland, becoming a professor at the ETH in Zurich.

1914 Einstein becomes director of the Kaiser Wilhelm Institute in Berlin and professor of theoretical physics at the University of Berlin.

1915 Publishes his General Theory of Relativity.

1917 Einstein publishes an important paper in which he proposes a "cosmological constant", which would help to explain the expansion of the Universe. He also publishes a paper in which he suggests "stimulated emission" could be possible – this is the principle behind the laser, which was not invented until the 1950s.

1919 A total eclipse of the Sun on 29 May provides crucial proof for Einstein's General Theory of Relativity. Einstein's divorce is finalized, and he marries for the second time, to his cousin Elsa Löwenthal.

1922 Awarded the 1921 Nobel Prize for Physics "for his services to Theoretical Physics, and especially for his discovery of the law of the photoelectric effect".

1933 Einstein and his wife move to Princeton, New Jersey. Einstein takes up a position at the Princeton Institute for Advanced Study.

1939 Writes to the US President Franklin D Roosevelt, warning him that Nazi Germany may be building a nuclear weapon.

LECTURING IN THE US

1940 Einstein becomes a US Citizen.

18 April 1955 Dies of heart failure. He is cremated, but beforehand, his brain is removed and preserved.

The American Dream

From the end of World War II in 1945 to the early 1960s, America's dream of "life, liberty, and the pursuit of happiness", as stated in the 1776 Declaration of Independence, was lived out by the majority. It was a time of wealth, peace, and unity, though not without its downsides.

« BEFORE

During World War II many marginalized sectors were thrust into central roles, only to be sidelined again when the war ended.

WOMEN AND THE WAR
Women played a crucial role in the US victory in **World War II « 314–27**. They served in the auxiliary army and navy services, and also the airforce, flying new aircraft from factories to military bases or repairing those damaged in conflict.

ROSIE THE RIVETER

Many women moved from low-paid administrative or catering jobs into better-paid munitions or engineering work, but were rarely paid equal wages to men. Most women in industry lost their jobs when men returned from the war in 1945.

SEGREGATION
Segregation remained legal in America until well after World War II, despite the US having fought against the Nazis, who held an explicitly racist ideology. **President Truman** desegregated the armed services in 1948, prohibited segregation on interstate travel, and outlawed discrimination by employers and unions. However, the reality for **African-Americans** was still a life as a second-class citizen **354–57 »**.

America emerged from World War II as the richest and most powerful nation on Earth. The only one of the wartime Allies not to be occupied or bombed, its industry – supplying its own military needs as well as some of those of Britain and the USSR – had provided full employment to its workforce and ended the Great Depression (see pp.306–07) of the 1930s. This economic boom continued in peacetime. National output doubled between 1946–56, doubling again by 1970. Most personal incomes nearly tripled between 1940–55.

The new middle class
This buoyant economy created a new middle class that made up 60 per cent of families, who spent their money on consumer goods. Some 83 per cent of American homes had a television by 1958, and two-car families doubled from 1951–58. America had 6 per cent of the world's population (150 million in 1950), consumed one-third of the world's goods and services, and made two-thirds of manufactured goods.

Compared to the starch-rich and relatively expensive diet of their forebears in 1900, food was affordable and varied. The average American in the 1950s had a choice of green vegetables, frozen goods, fresh meat, and fast food. Consumption of hot dogs increased from 750 million in 1950 to 2 billion a decade later. As a result of an improved diet, children were on

Consumer Society
After World War II, American consumption was viewed as a patriotic activity that helped aid economic recovery. The most sought-after items included fridges, cars, televisions, washing machines, toasters, and vacuum cleaners – all items that would modernize their lives.

average two or three inches taller in 1950 than they were in 1900, women could expect to live to 71 instead of 51, and men to 65 rather than 48.

The flight to the suburbs
One urgent need for this new class was decent housing. Inaugurated for the second time as president in 1937, Franklin Roosevelt saw "one-third of a nation ill-housed, ill-clad, ill-nourished." The postwar economy provided food and clothes, but good housing was still in short supply. A rising birthrate was met with a falling number of new house builds. Millions of Americans lived in cramped or inadequate housing.

One answer came from pioneer Bill Levitt, who won a contract in 1941 to build 1,600 terraced houses for shipyard workers in Norfolk, Virginia. Frustrated by union rules and having to organize numerous skilled workers to build and equip a single house, he divided the building process into 27 separate steps, training 27 teams of workers to carry out each one. The fastest workers earned the most pay. It was the principle of the production line. After the war, Levitt applied the same

Pontiac Chieftan
The American dream and the open road came together in stylish automobiles like the soft-top Pontiac Chieftain. Petrol was cheap and young people had diners, shopping malls, and drive-in movies at their disposal. Cars such as the Pontiac and the Cadillac became status symbols of the new wealth and freedom that Americans enjoyed during the 1950s.

"Private **affluence** amid public **squalor**."

J K GALBRAITH, US ECONOMIST, ON THE DISCREPANCIES IN AMERICAN SOCIETY IN "THE AFFLUENT SOCIETY", 1958

Eating out
With increased disposable income, young couples could spend money on recreation, drinking after work, or eating out regularly at the local diner. Such facilities were, however, still segregated in many southern states.

principles to his first development of 2,000 two-bedroomed houses for war veterans on Long Island. Each house cost $6,900, with no down payment for veterans and a mortgage guaranteed by a federal housing bill. Levittown, as it became known, grew in four years to 17,447 houses and a population of 82,000 people. There were some rules: no fences, no laundry lines, no shrubs more than 1.2m (4ft) high along the boundary, and, controversially, no African-Americans, although that exclusion ended in 1949. The houses were all identical, but their inhabitants soon personalized them, adding porches and patios and building extra rooms. Some 13 million new homes were built from 1948–58, almost all of them in new suburbs. This turned many American cities into social doughnuts, with a rich commercial and business centre surrounded by a poor, largely African-American-inhabited inner ring of social housing, surrounded in turn by largely white suburbs.

Teen culture

As America grew richer, it also got younger: 40 million Americans were born from 1950–60. By 1964, 40 per cent of the population was under 20. The idea of the "teenager" emerged as young people developed their own culture.

Popular music had been divided according to race and, partly, class. Crooners dominated white popular music with movie and musical hits. Country and western was popular among the white working class, while African-Americans had blues, gospel, and, in the late 1940s, rhythm and blues. A new hybrid music – merging African-American rhythm and blues and white country and western – by white singers Bill Haley in 1954, and Elvis Presley in 1956, gave young people their own music. Rock and roll was the music of rebellion and teenage angst, echoed in the films of James Dean and Marlon Brando. It fed the emerging counter-culture. Jazz, the Beat poets, novelists like Jack Kerouac, abstract expressionists Jackson Pollock and Mark Rothko, and folk and protest songs of Woody Guthrie and, later, Bob Dylan, defined American culture as much as rock and roll or movies.

> **MCCARTHYISM** The practice, named after Senator Joe McCarthy, of accusing individuals of belonging to the Communist Party or communist organizations despite little supporting evidence. It raised fears of a "red menace" against American society in the Cold War.

Suburbia

The mass production of housing resulted in streets with row after row of identical houses. Singer Malvina Reynolds critiqued the 1950s blandness with her song "Little Boxes", released in 1962, in which she derides the monotony of suburbia and the bourgeois values that it came to embody.

The flipside

The American dream was not enjoyed by everyone. The 1950s was a conservative decade, based on white, middle-class family values where men went to work and wives stayed at home – only 36 per cent of women worked in 1955. Women shared the dream, but relied on men to create it. African-Americans had no such dream. Segregation in jobs, housing, education, and democratic rights was rife, most notably in southern states. The country was also in the grip of the Cold War (see pp. 328–29) giving rise to internal troubles such as the McCarthy witch-hunts (see below).

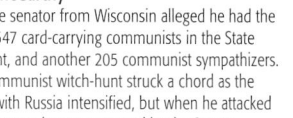

Senator McCarthy
In 1950, the senator from Wisconsin alleged he had the names of 547 card-carrying communists in the State Department, and another 205 communist sympathizers. His anti-communist witch-hunt struck a chord as the Cold War with Russia intensified, but when he attacked the army in 1954 he was censored by the Senate.

Jazz Music
After the artistic excesses of Charlie Parker and bop music in the 1940s, 1950s jazz cooled down to find a new audience, with musicians like trumpeter Miles Davis (above) and college circuit favourite, pianist Dave Brubeck.

AFTER »

In the 1960s and 1970s the reality of the "dream" was laid bare.

VIETNAM
The 1950s American dream became a nightmare in the 1960s, as arguments about **civil rights 356–57 »** and increasing opposition to the **Vietnam War 352–53 »** led to race riots and mass demonstrations in many cities. What appeared to be a cohesive, affluent society was revealed as divisive and fractured along lines of race and class.

IMMIGRANTS
The idea of the American dream is still powerful for many Hispanic immigrants. However, the reality is often harsh. Many immigrants work in seasonal jobs with low pay and few prospects.

LATINO (HISPANIC) WORKERS

DECISIVE MOMENT 22 November 1963 12:30pm

The Death of Kennedy

On Friday 22 November, President John F Kennedy and his wife Jacqueline visited Dallas, Texas, to drum up support for the 1964 US presidential election. As the motorcade drove through Dealey Plaza, at least three gunshots rang out, killing the president instantly. The American people had lost a president they loved, and they had been robbed of their future.

Three days after John F Kennedy's assassination, the world stopped again, united in grief. The funeral of the 35th president of the United States was watched by a million people lining the procession route, and millions more on television. During his brief time in office, the charismatic young president had come to epitomize the hopes of his nation – belief in a better future and the energetic pursuit of progress. With his murder the mood of bright optimism was shattered.

The assassination became the subject of huge controversy. A lone gunman, Lee Harvey Oswald, was arrested shortly after the shooting and charged with murder. He never came to trial; two days later he was shot dead while in police custody by Jack Ruby, a gangster who later gave contradictory reasons for the killing.

Kennedy's successor, Vice President Lyndon Johnson, quickly established an official investigation into the assassination headed by Earl Warren, Chief Justice of the United States. After a ten-month investigation, the commission concluded that Oswald had acted alone, as had Ruby, and

that there was no conspiracy to kill the president. Many people have refused to accept these conclusions, but no firm evidence has ever come to light to suggest otherwise.

After the assassination, the body of the president was flown back to Washington. It first lay in repose in the East Room of the White House and on Sunday afternoon was taken to lie in state in the Capital Rotunda. A brief memorial service was held. Over the following 18 hours, 250,000 people queued up in near-freezing temperatures to pay their respects.

On Monday the funeral procession returned to the White House and then moved on to St Matthew's Roman Catholic Cathedral. Heads of state and representatives from 92 countries attended the service. It was at the height of the Cold War (see pp.328–29), yet even the USSR sent a representative. The Archbishop of Boston led the mass, at which Kennedy's writings and speeches were read. The coffin was taken to Arlington National Cemetery, where Mrs Kennedy lit an eternal flame over the grave. America now faced an uncertain future without JFK.

A son salutes
Moments after his father's casket was carried down the steps of St Matthew's Cathedral, John F. Kennedy Jr, whose third birthday it was that day, saluted his father. His uncle Bobby Kennedy, who stands behind him, was himself assassinated just five years later.

"The **greatest leader of our time** has been struck down by the foulest deed of our time."

LYNDON B. JOHNSON, US PRESIDENT, 27 NOVEMBER 1963

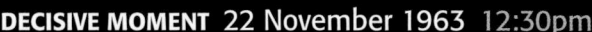

343

Viva la Revolución

After World War I, Latin America entered a period of social unrest and political change that was created in part by the impact of economic crisis. Populist movements, some authoritarian, others revolutionary, swept new regimes to power. In some countries, governments were imposed on the population by the military.

The Perons
Juan Peron and his wife Eva address an economic planning meeting in Buenos Aires. Although Eva Peron was not elected, she was influential in her husband's government. They enjoyed cult status in Argentina, and Eva's death in 1952 resulted in scenes of mass mourning.

BEFORE

300 years of colonial rule by the Spanish and Portuguese came to an end in Latin America at the beginning of the 19th century.

INDEPENDENCE FROM COLONIAL RULE
The transition from colonial rule to self-government in Latin America **≪248–49** was generally smooth in terms of economic stability. In the early years of the 20th century, many Latin American countries had **flourishing economies**, based on the **export of crops and minerals** to North America and Europe.

85 PER CENT of land in Brazil was owned by one per cent of the population in 1910.

THE MEXICAN REVOLUTION
Mexico's popular uprising of 1910, preceded and influenced the revolutions in Russia **≪300–01** and Eastern Europe. **Porfirio Diaz's** military regime was overthrown in 1911, but widespread conflict continued as Mexican soldiers, workers, and peasants joined in a **struggle for civil rights and agricultural reform**. Although briefly calmed by the Constitutional Congress of Mexico in 1917, violence flared again in the 1920s.

DEPRESSION AND INDUSTRIALIZATION
The **world economic crisis** triggered by the market crash of 1929, and the ensuing Great Depression **≪306–07**, devastated Latin America's export market, and **created shortages** in imported manufactured goods. The political response was to create economies that could provide for their own populations without reliance on foreign markets. The 1930s saw **rapid industrialization** and urban growth.

SOCIAL UNREST
In trends similar to those that occurred in Europe during the 19th century **≪266–67**, the growth in Latin America's **urban workforce** led to a rise in **political activism** and **calls for social and political change**.

The Arsenal
This 1928 mural by Mexican artist Diego Rivera shows his wife, the painter Frida Kahlo, handing arms to workers. Rivera and Kahlo belonged to the Mexican communist party. The fall of Diaz's regime (see above) in Mexico set a precedent that popular uprising could succeed.

In 1930, economic problems led the Brazilian military to install Getulio Vargas as provisional president. Although it operated as a dictatorship – a government ruled by one person with absolute power and no recognized opposition, or restriction from the country's law – his government permitted liberal measures such as social and welfare reforms. For several years, Vargas followed a modernization programme but, alarmed at the growth of communist support in the 1930s, he began to model the state along fascist lines (see pp.386–87), proclaiming an *"Estado Novo"* ("New Order"). Hitler's Germany became a major customer for Brazilian goods, and Vargas supported the Axis powers (Germany, Italy, and Japan) at the start of World War II.

In 1941, Vargas changed his allegiance to the Allies (Britain, the US, the USSR, and France). This caused the military to force Vargas from office in 1945. He was democratically re-elected in 1951, but committed suicide in 1954, after the army demanded his resignation.

Peron's "Third Way"
In Argentina, a populist government came to power in 1946 led by Juan Peron. "Peronism" was a contradictory mixture of progressive social values and authoritarian rule that Peron called the "Third Way". He transformed manufacturing in Argentina, launching an iron and steel industry, and ship and car production. Radical change came as women were given the vote, and corporations were nationalized. At the height of his popularity, Peron and his second wife Eva, known as "Evita", commanded huge mass support. Comparisons have been made with fascist regimes, and although he never pursued mass violence, he did crush any opposition to his rule. Argentina also provided a safe haven for Nazi war criminals after World War II.

Cuba breaks with America
In Cuba, the military regime of Fulgencio Batista was overthrown after a long struggle with revolutionaries. Having trained in Mexico, Fidel Castro landed on Cuba in 1956 with an army of political exiles including Che Guevara (see RIGHT). A guerrilla war ensued, in which small groups of armed rebels carried out repeated attacks to wear down the enemy, before the rebels seized power in 1959. Castro swiftly ended US dominance of Cuba's economy. Taking aid from the USSR, he implemented radical reforms including a Soviet-style agricultural policy (see pp.304–05). The 1962 Cuban Missile Crisis (see pp.328–29) further damaged US–Cuban relations. The US continues to impose an economic embargo on Cuba, but the Castro regime survives, under Fidel's brother, Raul.

Pinochet ends Chile's democracy
In 1970 an increased desire for extreme political change, or radicalism, brought socialist Salvador Allende to the Chilean presidency. Concerns were raised in the US when Allende established diplomatic relations with communist regimes in Cuba, China, North Korea, and North Vietnam. He attempted to restructure Chile's unstable economy, but was soon threatened by a variety of political opponents. Keen to influence the next regime, the US backed General Augusto Pinochet's military coup against Allende in 1973. When attackers entered the presidential palace, Allende was found dead from a gunshot wound.

Castro's camp
This photograph, taken around 1957, shows the bearded revolutionary leader Fidel Castro with commanders of his rebel army at a secret camp in Cuba. The rebels were poorly armed, but Castro's guerilla tactics won the conflict.

REVOLUTIONARY (1928–1967)

ERNESTO "CHE" GUEVARA

Che Guevara was born in Argentina in 1928. As a young man he travelled extensively in Latin America, and became convinced that only revolution would solve the problems of poverty and social inequality that marked the continent. A visit to President Guzman's populist regime in Guatemala in 1953, confirmed Che's enthusiasm for radical political solutions and, in 1956, he joined Fidel Castro's rebel army. In 1965, Che left Cuba with the intention of sparking revolutions in other countries. He was captured by the CIA – the US secret service – in Bolivia in 1967, and executed by the Bolivian army.

AFTER »

After authoritarian, often military-backed regimes in the 1960s and 1970s, many Latin American nations became more democratic.

COUNTER-REVOLUTION
In the 1970s, revolutionary and socialist ideals of previous decades were swept aside. **Military regimes 360–61 »** were established in many countries including Uruguay and Argentina.

ANTI-AMERICANISM
Left-wing presidents such as Venezuela's **Hugo Chávez** (1999–2013) **360 »** and Bolivia's **Evo Morales** (from 2006) increasingly spoke out against US policy in Latin America.

BEFORE

The Manchu Qing dynasty declined throughout the 19th century, as China increasingly fell under European influence. A period of chaos and rule by regional warlords followed its collapse.

OVERTHROW OF THE MANCHU EMPIRE
In 1905, the political revolutionary, **Sun Zhongshan** (Sun Yat-sen), founded the Revolutionary Alliance with the aim of **driving out the Manchus** and establishing a republican government. **Nationalist soldiers seized Wuchang** on 10 October 1911, and within weeks south China's provinces had broken away from the empire. When the Manchus asked the commander of the Northern Army, **Yuan Shikai**, for support, he **encouraged the emperor to abdicate**, and in March 1912 he became president of the republic. In January 1916 he accepted an invitation to **become emperor**, but shortly afterwards he gave up the position and died.

THE NATIONALIST PARTY
In 1912 the Revolutionary Alliance, led by Sun Zhongshan, became the **Nationalist Party**. Yuan Shikai expelled Nationalist Party members from parliament and they moved south to Guangzhou. There Sun Zhongshan, with help from the Soviet Union, **reorganized the party**. After the death of Sun Zhongshan in 1925, the party's leadership passed gradually to **Jiang Jieshi** (Chiang Kaishek).

WARLORDS FILL THE VOID
From 1916, China had no effective central government and was controlled by **regional warlords**. They included: **Zhang Xun**, the "pigtailed general", who briefly restored Puyi, the Manchu emperor; **Feng Yuxiang**, the "Christian General", who banned his troops from gambling; and **Yan Xishan**, the "Model Governor" of Shanxi, who supported educational reform.

THE MAY FOURTH MOVEMENT
On 4 May 1919, it was announced at the Paris Peace Conference **≪ 299**, that former German colonies in China were to be given to Japan, and major **demonstrations erupted**. The incident gave its name to the radical May Fourth Movement, which **attacked Confucianism ≪ 85**, called for a "literary revolution", and welcomed a **wave of new ideas**.

CHINESE COMMUNIST PARTY (CCP)
Founded by revolutionaries who had been involved in the May Fourth Movement, the first congress of the CCP was held in July 1921, and was attended by a young Mao Zedong (see right).

> **"Communism** is a hammer which we use to **crush the enemy."**
>
> MAO ZEDONG, 1950

毛主席革命路线胜

China's Long March

After the fall of the Manchu dynasty in 1911, China experienced a long period of political turmoil. The Nationalists reunified the country, but were frustrated by the 1937 Japanese invasion. The Communists came to power in 1949, and over the next 25 years attempted a revolutionary transformation of society.

In 1923, the Chinese Communist Party formed an uneasy alliance with the Nationalist Party (see BEFORE), and in 1926 supported them in the Northern Expedition to reunify the country. But the alliance collapsed in April 1927, when the Nationalist leader, Jiang Jieshi, ordered hundreds of Communists in Shanghai to be killed.

The Communist leaders fled to the countryside to plan insurrections. Mao Zedong (see right) led a revolt called the Autumn Harvest Uprising, and after defeat by the Nationalists, retreated to the southern province of Jiangxi. There, Mao formulated a new revolutionary strategy combining the formation of the Red Army – the military arm of the Communists – with land reform, and a promise to emancipate China's women.

The Nanjing decade
Jiang Jieshi's defeat of the Communists strengthened the position of the Nationalist Party, and in 1928 it effectively took control of the country, establishing its capital at Nanjing and reunifying China. Over the next decade, it reformed the currency, and established modern banks. New schools and colleges were opened, and railways and roads were improved.

Great endurance
Crossing 18 mountain ranges and 24 major rivers, the Long March lasted 368 days and cost thousands of lives.

The Long March
In October 1934, the Communists abandoned their Jiangxi base, broke through a Nationalist blockade, and began the "Long March" to shake off their enemies. A trek of around 10,000km (6,200 miles), it took

"Long live the victory of Chairman Mao's Revolution"
In a typical piece of propaganda, this celebration of the leadership of Mao Zedong, produced for the 50th anniversary of the creation of the Chinese Communist Party, shows him surrounded by adoring supporters.

perpetrated a massacre of around 300,000 men, women, and children that became known as the Rape of Nanjing. The Nationalist government relocated 1,600km (1,000 miles) up the Yangzi River, while the Communists operated behind Japanese lines.

Civil war and communist victory

With the Japanese attack on Pearl Harbor in 1941 (see pp.324–25), the Sino–Japanese hostilities became absorbed in the wider conflict of World War II, and Japan was ultimately defeated by the Allies. By July 1946, another civil war in China had broken out. While the Nationalist government was being seriously damaged by galloping inflation, the Communists were gaining rural support with revolutionary land reform in favour of the peasants. Manchuria fell to the Communists, and when, in January 1949, around 300,000 Nationalists surrendered, Mao's troops marched triumphantly into Beijing. On 1 October 1949 the communist People's Republic of China (PRC) was established. Jiang Jieshi and two million of his supporters fled to the island of Taiwan where they established the rival Republic of China.

Consolidation

The People's Republic then occupied all territory claimed by China, including Tibet. Mao negotiated the Sino-Soviet Treaty of Alliance and Mutual Assistance and, in 1950, when the Korean War broke out (see pp.328–29) China intervened on the side of North Korea. In China, the First Five Year

Mao's "little red book"
"Father is close, mother is close but neither is as close as Chairman Mao." 900 million copies of *Quotations from Chairman Mao* were printed.

Plan, launched in 1953 with Soviet assistance, achieved spectacular increases in industrial output. Reforms banned arranged marriages, and the subjugation of women. Farming was collectivized, so peasants handed over their land to agricultural producers' co-operatives.

The radical years

In 1958, Mao Zedong introduced the radical policy known as the Great Leap Forward. Industrial and agricultural co-operatives were amalgamated into communes – with collective kitchens and crèches – and industrial targets were raised.
At first it seemed as if spectacular increases of output had been achieved, but later evidence showed that these policies had caused disastrous famines and the death of millions of people. In 1966, the Cultural Revolution was launched, with the aim of cleansing the country of "bourgeois" influences. Children were recruited as Red Guards and to rekindle the spirit of revolution, were encouraged to report their schoolteachers and relatives if they failed to display sufficient communist fervour. Brandishing their "little red books" (see above) the Red Guards attacked the Four Olds: old ideas, old culture, old customs, and old habits.

CHINESE COMMUNIST LEADER (1893–1976)

MAO ZEDONG

The son of a rich peasant, Mao moved to Beijing from Hunan province at the time of the May Fourth Movement (see BEFORE), where he first encountered communist ideas. He joined the Chinese Communist Party at its inception in 1921, taking control in 1935 after proving his leadership during the Long March. As head of the country from 1949 until his death in 1976, Mao's attempts to implement his radical ideas led to disastrous famines. However, "Mao Zedong Thought" had far-reaching effects, and after his death the Party declared that it would remain "a guide to action for a long time to come".

AFTER ≫

China's Cultural Revolution saw millions "re-educated" through forced labour, and thousands executed. The terror did not end until the arrest of the Gang of Four in 1976.

GANG OF FOUR
Mao's wife **Jiang Qing**, party chief **Zhang Chunqiao**, critic **Yao Wenyuan**, and **Wang Hongwen**, a factory worker, expected to succeed Mao after his death. Instead, they were **arrested**, and found guilty of **plotting to seize power**.

THE FOUR MODERNIZATIONS
In 1978, Premier **Deng Xiaoping** announced the modernization of agriculture, industry, science, and defence, to make China a **great economic power** by the early 21st century 396–97 ≫.

TIANANMEN SQUARE
When **pro-democracy** students demonstrated in Tiananmen Square, Beijing, Premier **Li Peng** instructed the army to act. On 4 June 1989, troops opened fire on the protestors, killing 400–800.

TIANANMEN SQUARE PROTESTER DEFIES TANKS

---

more than 80,000 soldiers and workers northwest through harsh terrain, fighting the Nationalists all the way. By the time they established headquarters at Yan'an in October 1935, only about 8,000 of the orginal marchers had survived, and Mao had taken command of the Communist Party.

War with Japan

Japanese encroachment on Chinese territory had begun in 1931 with the seizure of Manchuria. In 1937, Japanese forces invaded China and

---

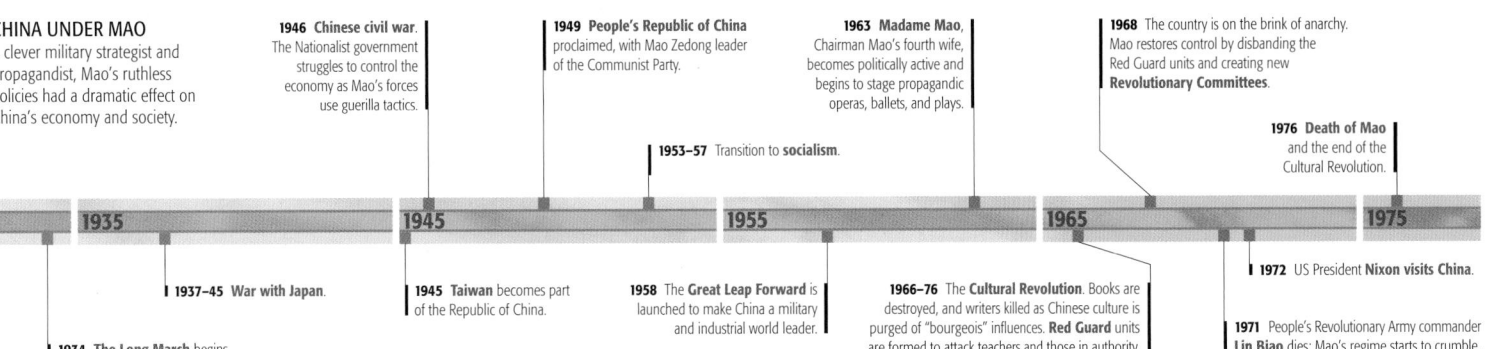

CHINA UNDER MAO
A clever military strategist and propagandist, Mao's ruthless policies had a dramatic effect on China's economy and society.

1946 Chinese civil war. The Nationalist government struggles to control the economy as Mao's forces use guerilla tactics.

1949 People's Republic of China proclaimed, with Mao Zedong leader of the Communist Party.

1963 Madame Mao, Chairman Mao's fourth wife, becomes politically active and begins to stage propagandic operas, ballets, and plays.

1968 The country is on the brink of anarchy. Mao restores control by disbanding the Red Guard units and creating new **Revolutionary Committees**.

1953–57 Transition to **socialism**.

1976 Death of Mao and the end of the Cultural Revolution.

1935 | 1945 | 1955 | 1965 | 1975

1937–45 War with Japan.

1945 Taiwan becomes part of the Republic of China.

1958 The Great Leap Forward is launched to make China a military and industrial world leader.

1966–76 The **Cultural Revolution**. Books are destroyed, and writers killed as Chinese culture is purged of "bourgeois" influences. **Red Guard** units are formed to attack teachers and those in authority.

1972 US President **Nixon visits China**.

1934 The Long March begins.

1971 People's Revolutionary Army commander **Lin Biao** dies; Mao's regime starts to crumble.

Berlin Wall

The peace of a Sunday morning in 1961 was shattered as Berliners woke up to the sounds of military vehicles unloading coils of barbed wire and concrete posts in the streets. In central Potsdamer Platz, men used pneumatic drills to break up the cobblestones and set up concrete pillars. These disturbing scenes were the first signs of a physical division of Berlin.

In February 1945, the leaders of the USA, USSR, and Britain met in Yalta (now in Ukraine but once part of the Soviet Union) to plan Europe's future after the defeat of Nazi Germany. They agreed to partition Germany and its capital, Berlin, into four zones of occupation divided between their three countries and France. Berlin lay deep inside the Soviet zone, but access between the western zones of the city and the three western zones of Germany was guaranteed along specified land and air links.

The agreement fell apart as the Cold War (see pp.328–29) gained pace in 1946–47. The election of an anti-communist mayor for Berlin in early 1948 and the planned creation of a federal state with a common currency in the western zones of Germany annoyed the Soviets. On 24 June 1948, they blocked traffic from entering the city from the west. The British and Americans responded with a massive airlift of supplies to sustain West Berlin until an agreement with the Soviets was reached in May 1949.

For the next 12 years, Berlin remained the uneasy epicentre of the Cold War. The western half became linked with West Germany, while the eastern half became the capital of communist East Germany, both created in 1949. Economic disparities between west and east led thousands of East Germans and Berliners – almost 200,000 in 1960 alone – to cross the open frontier between east and west in search of a better life.

In 1961 the East German government decided to act. Crossing points between East and West Berlin were sealed off with barbed wire and concrete posts. In places, this barrier ran down the middle of streets to avoid touching West Berlin's soil. It even bisected a cemetery. The border between East and West Germany was sealed. Russian tanks waited outside the city, while the Americans sent 1,500 troops to reassure West Berlin.

Over the next 19 years, the wall was strengthened with reinforced concrete blocks 3.6m (12ft) high and set back from the original fence to create a heavily armed "no-man's land" in between. The wall became the symbol of a divided world, but ultimately symbolized the futility of such confrontation. Its fall on 9 November 1989 ended the Cold War.

A city divided
Many families were split up when the wall was built. This photo, taken in 1962, shows a young woman standing precariously at the top of the western side of the wall to speak to her mother in East Berlin. About 5,000 people escaped from the east through gaps in the wall.

"You cannot be **held in slavery** for ever."

WILLY BRANDT, MAYOR OF WEST BERLIN, BROADCAST, AUGUST 1961

« BEFORE

Advances in science and mass production techniques transformed the way people lived after World War II.

POST WAR

In the late 1940s and early 1950s the world was reeling from the effects of World War II **«** 314–27, but by the mid-1950s the mood was changing. The US experienced **economic growth**, as did Germany, France, and Italy. In Britain, food rationing, which had been in place since 1940, ended in 1954. Employment rose throughout Europe, and with it came the beginnings of a **consumer boom**.

90 PER CENT of all Americans owned a TV set by 1960

1 IN 3 families in the UK owned a car in 1959

NEVER HAD IT SO GOOD

In 1957 the British Prime Minister Harold Macmillan said, "most of our people have never had it so good", a sentiment that echoed around the developed world. People bought **luxuries and labour saving devices**, developments in communication began to change the way people lived, and television took off as a mass medium.

ROCK 'N' ROLL

In 1955 Bill Haley and the Comets released the song *Rock Around The Clock*, unleashing a new musical style – Rock 'n' Roll. It was **music for a new generation** –

ELVIS PRESLEY

teenagers – and shocked older, more conservative people. The greatest and most controversial star of the new genre was Elvis Presley.

BIRTH OF "POP"

Pop is **short for popular**, and in the 1950s it spawned Pop Art, which British artist Richard Hamilton called "**glamorous** and big business!"

Black Panthers March
An African-American civil rights group founded in 1966, the Black Panther Party marched for "land, bread, housing, education, clothing, justice and peace". It became an icon of the counterculture revolutions of the 1960s.

The Sixties

The 1960s witnessed the rise of new forms of entertainment and a new political and social agenda. The changing attitudes on youth, gender, class, place, and race challenged the established order.

A t the end of World War II in 1945, soldiers returned home and started the families they had put on hold for four years. This led to an unusually steep rise in the population curve known as the "Baby Boom". In the United States alone some 70 million "baby-boomers" became teenagers and young adults during the 1960s.

As the decade opened it was a time of youthful optimism where anything seemed possible. And for the first time, the phrase "generation gap" was used. Where previously young people had aped their elders, new music such as rock 'n' roll empowered the younger generation, and adults were often left dumbfounded by what they considered the strange behaviour of the youth.

Swinging sixties
In an age of increased middle class affluence, the population had greater employment opportunities and a new buying power. In response to this, music and fashion became mass-market industries and were quick to cater to the demands of the youth market. The growing popularity of television helped spread popular culture around the globe, so trends could take off rapidly. Programmes such as *Top of the Pops* in the UK and the *Ed Sullivan Show* in the US made the 1960s swing to the beat of pop music. In 1962 The Beatles emerged from Liverpool's Cavern Club. Their first album, *Please Please Me* became famous around the globe within a year. They grew immensely popular, sparking such intense devotion in their fans that it became known as "Beatlemania". At one time during the 1960s they had the top five records on the US Billboard Hot 100 list, and The Beatles remain the best-selling pop band of all time.

Music groups provided the inspiration for fashion, from neat mod styles and blue jeans, to Elvis jumpsuits and the ethnic clothing of singers such as Joan

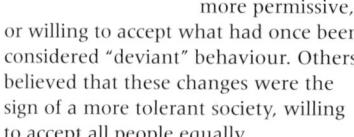

The Beatles
The Beatles' 8th album, *Sgt. Pepper's Lonely Hearts Club Band* was released in 1967, and is often voted the most influential album of all time.

Baez. This fashion revolution burst onto the high streets, led by designers like Mary Quant. Hems went up, then down. Adults found it hard to tell boys from girls. Both dressed in T-shirts and jeans; boys grew long hair; girls copied the model Twiggy by cutting theirs in a short "gamine" style. The unisex look had arrived. Boutiques sprang up to sell the new fashions, which were colourful, cheap, and informal. French New Wave cinema blossomed and also influenced style.

Permissive society?
Politics became more radical in the 1960s. There were many who felt that some laws were outdated and belonged to a bygone era. In 1966 the UK abolished the death penalty, and in the US support for the death penalty was at an all time low. Gay rights came to the fore, and in the UK in 1967 new laws were passed that allowed adult homosexuals to behave as they wished in private. Abortion became legal in the UK, and legal in some states in America. Not everyone welcomed these changes. Some insisted it would make society more permissive, or willing to accept what had once been considered "deviant" behaviour. Others believed that these changes were the sign of a more tolerant society, willing to accept all people equally.

In 1963 Betty Friedan published *The Feminine Mystique*, re-igniting the movement for women's rights. Friedan and journalist Gloria Steinem challenged remaining areas of sexual inequality, giving birth to a wave of radical feminism known as the Women's Liberation movement. More

Isle of Wight festival
Three music festivals were held on the Isle of Wight, situated off the British south coast, at the end of the 1960s. The 1969 festival, shown here, was attended by 150,000 people. In 1970 it became the largest ever music festival, with over 600,000 people in attendance.

THE CONTRACEPTIVE PILL

Before the development of "the Pill" women all over the world used a variety of different birth control methods, which were often ineffective and sometimes dangerous. American nurse Margaret Sanger was a lifelong advocate of birth control and underwrote the research necessary to create the first human birth control pill, described as the most significant medical advance of the 20th century. Between 1962–69 the number of users worldwide rose from approximately 50,000 to one million.

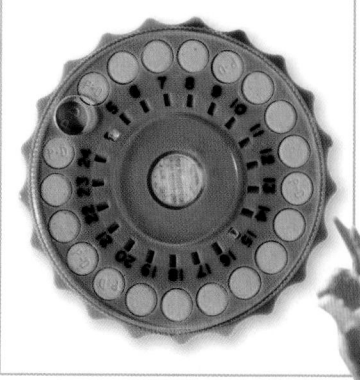

women went out to work, challenging conventional ideas of women as housewives and homemakers. Above all, the emergence of the contraceptive pill (see left) liberated women, offering them a reliable method of birth control for the first time.

Turn on, tune in, drop out

Known as the "Summer of Love", 1967 was the height of the hippie movement. Hippies embraced rock music, mystic religions, sexual freedom, and many experimented with drugs such as marijuana and LSD (lysergic acid diethylamide), a drug that was claimed to open the mind to previously uncharted areas. In June 1967, Monterey, California, held the first open-air mass pop festival, which was attended by over 200,000 people. Its potent combination of youth culture and pop music is seen as the apex of all that

The New Wave

A Bout de Souffle (*Breathless*), 1960, directed by Jean-Luc Godard, is one of the best-known films of French New Wave cinema.

the 1960s stood for. However, the optimism of the decade soon started to unravel, influenced by the assassinations in America of Senator Robert Kennedy and Martin Luther King (see pp.354–55) in 1968. Around the world students protested at the increased involvement of US troops in the Vietnam War (see pp.352–53). The US saw race riots in the inner cities, and the civil rights movement shifted from a non-violent position when elements of it were taken over by radical extremists.

In France, the student revolt of May 1968 in Paris linked up with a general strike of 10 million workers, who called for the overthrow of Charles de Gaulle's government.

The end of the decade was marked by two important

rock festivals held in 1969 – Woodstock in New York and the Altamont Free Concert in California. At Woodstock 450,000 people attended the three-day festival, gathering in the spirit of love and sharing, but at Altamont, a black fan was stabbed to death by a gang of white Hells Angels.

> "The thing **the sixties** did was to show us the possibilities and the responsibility that we all had. It wasn't the answer. It just **gave us a glimpse of the possibility**."
>
> JOHN LENNON, LAST RADIO INTERVIEW, 8 DECEMBER 1980

The 1970s saw an abrupt end to the idealism that characterized the 1960s.

1970s
In 1973 the world experienced an oil crisis **362–63 »**, which affected the economies of developed nations. In Britain there was a **downturn in economic fortunes** and unemployment was on the increase.

PUNK
The commercialism of pop music was soon challenged in the 1970s by Punk music. An **anti-establishment** and **rebellious** movement, it was epitomized by bands such as The Ramones in the US and the Sex Pistols in the UK.

SEX PISTOLS

GLOBAL POP
In the 1980s America's MTV was launched, and pop artists became global stars. In 1985 the Live Aid concert was watched by **1.5 billion viewers** across 100 countries.

‹‹ BEFORE

America's anti-communist foreign policy clashed with Vietnamese nationalists who wished to unite their country under communist rule.

LIBERTY LOANS

The American public's support for its armed services dates back to World War I, when **people bought billions of dollars of Liberty Loans** to finance the war effort. There was similar mass support for American troops during World War II and the Cold War **‹‹ 328–29**, of which Vietnam was part.

US POSTER FOR LIBERTY LOANS

TRUMAN'S POLICY

The US had fought alongside the communist USSR in World War II **‹‹ 314–27**, but relations between the two broke down as the Cold War began. In 1947, faced with a possible communist threat to Greece and Turkey, President Truman pledged **"American support for free peoples** who are resisting attempted subjugation by armed minorities or by outside pressures." Known as **the Truman Doctrine**, this guided US foreign policy throughout the Vietnam War.

COLONIAL VIETNAM

In 1941 **Ho Chi Minh**, a Vietnamese nationalist and communist, **created the Viet Minh** to fight Japanese occupation. He declared the country independent after Japan's defeat in World War II in 1945 **‹‹ 324–25**. When the French resumed their colonial control **‹‹ 334–35**, a bitter war began that ended in French defeat in 1954. The **Geneva Accords** of 1954 **divided Vietnam** temporarily into a communist north and a pro-American south.

The Vietnam War

The Vietnam War was the longest and bloodiest of the many conflicts of the Cold War. The American army was technologically superior, but was defeated by the far more effective tactics of the Vietnamese nationalist and communist army wishing to unite their country and free it from foreign control.

The division of Vietnam in 1954 (see BEFORE) did not bring peace to the country. The US wished to prevent the spread of communism throughout Southeast Asia, believing that one country after another would fall to communist regimes (the so-called "Domino Effect") and was prepared to use military action to prevent this. The Geneva Accords had stipulated that joint elections should take place in 1956 to decide the future of a reunified Vietnam – these elections never took place. In 1955 US president Dwight D Eisenhower helped the anti-communist Ngo Dinh Diem to take power in a corrupt election in the south, and sent hundreds of military advisors to support the new government.

North Vietnam did not accept the partition of their country and launched attacks on South Vietnam. Anti-Diem South Vietnamese – labelled Viet Cong "Vietnamese Communist" by Diem,

although many were nationalists – took up arms to fight Diem's government, led by the National Liberation Front, an alliance of political groups based in North Vietnam.

Eisenhower's support for South Vietnam increased under his successor, John F Kennedy. By the end of 1963, South Vietnam had received $500 million in US aid. In August 1964 the USS *Maddox* was conducting electronic surveillance of the North Vietnamese

coast in the Gulf of Tonkin. The ship was fired on by two torpedo boats challenging its presence in North Vietnamese waters. It fired back, sinking one boat. On 7 August the US Congress passed a resolution approving retaliatory raids against North Vietnamese naval bases and

Viet Cong
Viet Cong fighters lacked the sophisticated weaponry and kit of the US military, but they had the advantage of local knowledge and support.

Protests at home
US protests against the war were supported not just by traditional pacifists but also by a much larger constituency of peace campaigners, including civil rights campaigner Dr Martin Luther King. The war divided US society as no event had done so that century.

The effect of the Vietnam War was felt for many years to come but Vietnam is now a peaceful and prosperous nation.

CASUALTIES OF WAR
One million Vietnamese troops on both sides **lost their lives** in the war, along with **4 million** Vietnamese civilians, and **58,000** US troops. More than 153,000 US troops were seriously wounded; **the total number of Vietnamese casualties is unknown**.

UNIFICATION
The Paris Peace Accord held until renewed fighting broke out in January 1975. A final **communist offensive captured Saigon** on 30 April and reunified the country in 1976 as the Socialist Republic of Vietnam. Thousands fearing for their lives under the new government fled Vietnam in boats, many drowning before they could reach safety in neighbouring countries. More than **1 million refugees** from the conflict eventually **settled in the US**.

VETERANS
More than 660 US servicemen were taken prisoner during the war; 591 of these were repatriated under the peace accord. However, over **1,600 men are still missing in action**. Veterans' associations in the US became a vocal force in modern US politics.

MODERN VIETNAM
In 1986 the Vietnamese government relaxed its previous hard-line communist economic policies in favour of a more liberal policy of *doi moi* ("renovation") and began to **welcome foreign investment and tourism**. In 1995 Vietnam joined the Southeast Asian economic group, ASEAN. War damage was immense due to heavy US bombing, and the country continues to receive overseas aid for development.

"We are **determined to fight** for **independence**, national unity, democracy and **peace**."

HO CHI MINH, NORTH VIETNAMESE LEADER, 8 MAY 1954

Wounded in action
The sight of young American troops wounded in action appeared on US television news night after night and did as much to turn American opinion against the war as any political debate.

Civilian casualties
Many Vietnamese civilians were caught up in the war: US bombing raids to hit the Viet Cong only served to alienate those it claimed to support.

US troop deployment
The first US marines arrived in South Vietnam in March 1965. By July that year, more than 50,000 were in the country, as well as increasing numbers of US airmen and sailors. Numbers escalated to a peak of 543,500 troops in April 1969. In addition, 320,000 South Koreans, 47,000 Australians, and contingents from the Philippines, Thailand, and New Zealand fought alongside the Americans. The Viet Cong and North Vietnamese troops received military aid and financial support from communist China and USSR, although no ground troops were committed. However, they did have the advantage of fighting on home soil, often with the active support of the local people.

The American plan in Vietnam was to attack North Vietnam from the air in order to stop it aiding the Viet Cong. Operation "Rolling Thunder" targeted bridges, roads, railways, airfields, oil refineries and authorized Kennedy's successor, Lyndon B Johnson "to take all necessary steps, including the use of armed forces" to defend South Vietnam. Without a formal declaration of war, the US had committed itself to military conflict in Vietnam.

factories, fuel depots, and military installations, but failed to achieve its objectives. North Vietnam had a formidable air defence system, and kept supplies flowing to the south along the Ho Chi Minh Trail, a 20,000-km (12,500-mile) network of tracks and paved roads through the jungles of North Vietnam and neighbouring Laos and Cambodia. The trail was well defended by anti-aircraft batteries and hidden from observation by the jungle through which it passed. By 1970, 18,000 tonnes of supplies flowed down the trail each month.

The US tried to deny the Viet Cong jungle cover by spraying Agent Orange, a chemical deployed to defoliate the jungle. It also used napalm, an incendiary liquid that burned everything it touched. Such tactics deprived local farmers of their crops and therefore their livelihood and

Hand-made Viet Cong machine gun
The USSR and China supplied North Vietnam with most of its weapons, but its fighters also made their own arms – such as this machine gun – as well as using weaponry captured from the US.

further alienated the US-backed South Vietnamese government from the people.

US withdrawal
The Vietnam War was opposed by increasing numbers of Americans who did not see why their troops were fighting a war with no just cause. The first major anti-war demonstrations took place in 1965, and grew in strength as more and more young men were drafted, or forced into military service. Television brought the reality of the war into American homes on a daily basis. The last five years of the war were bloody and painful for both sides. The US started peace talks in Paris in August 1969 in order to find an orderly way out of the conflict. The talks continued until a peace accord was signed on 27 January 1973. US troops left South Vietnam to the Vietnamese 60 days later.

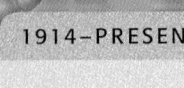

CIVIL RIGHTS LEADER Born 1929 Died 1968

Martin Luther King

"Our lives begin to end **the day we become silent** about things that matter.**"**

MARTIN LUTHER KING

artin Luther King Jr was born into a family commited to the struggle for civil rights (see pp.356–57). Both his father and his grandfather were preachers who had spoken out against the denial of rights black people were subjected to in the US. As a student, he became familiar with the ideas of non-violent protest of Mohandas Gandhi (see pp.330–31). What King knew of Gandhi chimed with his Christian faith; he once said, "I went to Gandhi through Jesus." King came to believe that by suffering violence without responding in kind, campaigners might build up an

irresistible moral force for change. King was recently married and newly established as a Baptist pastor in Montgomery, Alabama, when the Montgomery Bus Boycott, protesting against segregation on the city transport system, propelled him onto the national stage. King did not start the

A gift for eloquence
Martin Luther King's personal courage, eloquence as a public speaker, and unswerving dedication to non-violence made a vital contribution to the progress achieved by the civil rights movement in the USA in the 1950s and 1960s.

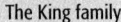

The King family
Martin Luther and Coretta Scott King had two sons and two daughters between 1955 and 1963. All four of the King children grew up to follow in their parents' footsteps, becoming civil rights activists.

Dexter Avenue Baptist Church
It was during his time as pastor of Dexter Avenue Baptist Church in Montgomery, Alabama, from 1954–1960, that Martin Luther King became an acknowledged leader of the civil rights movement. His predecessor as pastor, Vernon Johns, had also been a tireless campaigner against racial discrimination.

boycott in December 1955 and only reluctantly agreed to lead the campaign. He nearly pulled out when his home was bombed, but said he "heard the voice of Jesus saying still to fight on". When the boycott was shown on national TV, King's speeches and great dignity had an immediate impact.

In 1957 the Southern Christian Leadership Conference (SCLC) was formed to build on the

success of the Montgomery Bus Boycott. King became the leader of the SCLC, which was a more radical alternative to the long-established National Association for the Advancement of Colored People (NAACP). While unswerving in his commitment to non-violence, King was prepared to pursue civil disobedience energetically, breaking laws he considered unjust and provoking confrontation with racist authorities and the police. He did not then, or later, control the civil rights movement, which was a popular mass protest to which many individuals and groups made their diverse contributions. But King's charismatic example both inspired activists to engage in civil disobedience and attracted the support of white liberals for the movement.

Relentless campaigning

In the first half of the 1960s, King's influence was at its peak. He linked local direct action against segregation and for black voter registration in the southern states of the US to pressure at a national level for civil rights legislation. Many traditional black community and religious leaders felt King was too radical, for example, in backing the campaign of sit-ins at segregated lunch counters and other public facilities by the Student Nonviolent Coordinating Committee (SNCC) in 1960. President John F Kennedy and his brother, Robert "Bobby" Kennedy, repeatedly urged him to moderate his position. But in 1963 King raised the campaign to a high pitch of intensity, encouraging confrontation between protesters and police in Birmingham, Alabama – confrontations that resulted in police violence that shocked world opinion – and mounting a "March on Washington" by around 250,000 demonstrators.

Running for US president
King had planned to run in the 1968 elections with anti-Vietnam War campaigner Dr Benjamin Spock.

Outlawing discrimination

The passage of the Civil Rights Act in 1964, making many forms of discrimination illegal, and the Voting Rights Act the following year were the culmination of King's campaigning efforts. Awarded the Nobel Peace Prize, he stood at the height of his world fame. But at the same time his support among African-Americans was wavering. King's integrationist views – he wanted all races to have equal rights in a desegregated society – had always been rejected by black separatists. Many young African-Americans also began to turn away from non-violence, asserting the right to use force in self-defence. Young activists launched the aggressive slogan "Black Power", while King appeared hesitant and indecisive.

From 1965 onwards King grappled with causes and with his conscience. His attempt to establish contact with African-Americans in the ghettos of Chicago in 1966 was only partially successful. His outspoken opposition to America's involvement in the Vietnam

War offended many African-Americans, who were proud of their sons' service in an integrated army. His shift away from rights and race to poverty was seen as controversially "socialist", in an American context.

Assassination in Memphis

The hatred provoked by King's views had always made him a target. He was under covert surveillance by the

"I have a dream…"
King salutes the crowd in front of the Lincoln Memorial during the "March on Washington" on 28 August 1963. This was the occasion for King's "I have a dream…" speech, arguably his most inspired and inspiring flight of oratory.

Federal Bureau of Investigation (FBI), whose head, J Edgar Hoover, alleged King was a communist and was trying to use evidence of his alleged sexual promiscuity to blackmail him. On 4 April 1968 King was shot dead on a balcony of a motel in Memphis, Tennessee. A petty criminal, James Earl Ray, was convicted of the killing, though his guilt has been contested. King's death sparked rioting and arson in cities across the US: an ironic memorial to a man of non-violence. His place in the pantheon of American heroes is now secure.

Homage to King
A poster advertising an event in honour of King by a French anti-racism group, held in Paris on 9 April 1968, three days after his death.

MARTIN LUTHER KING ASSASSINE
HOMMAGE
MARDI 9 AVRIL 1968, A 20 H. 30
AU CIRQUE D'HIVER

"We, as a people, will get to the Promised Land."

MARTIN LUTHER KING JR, SPEECH IN MEMPHIS, TENNESSEE, 3 APRIL 1968

US CIVIL RIGHTS CAMPAIGNER (1913–2005)

ROSA PARKS

Born Rosa McCauley, Rosa Parks was an active campaigner against sexism and racism from the 1930s. Her refusal to give up her seat to a white man on a segregated bus and her subsequent arrest in Montgomery, Alabama, on 1 December 1955 ignited the civil rights movement and the Montgomery Bus Boycott. Rosa Parks grew famous, but she was forced out of her job in a department store and left Alabama for Detroit, Michigan. She later became especially active in aiding black youths. In 1996, Parks was named the "Mother of the Modern Day Civil Rights Movement" by the US Congress.

TIMELINE

- **15 January 1929** Martin Luther King Jr is born in Atlanta, Georgia, son of a Baptist pastor; the name entered on his birth certificate is Michael.

- **1948** Graduates from Morehouse College in Atlanta with a degree in sociology.

- **1951** Graduates from Crozer Theological Seminary in Chester, Pennsylvania, with a degree in divinity.

- **18 June 1953** Marries Coretta Scott.

- **September 1954** Becomes pastor of Dexter Avenue Baptist Church, Montgomery, Alabama.

- **5 June 1955** Receives a Ph.D in theology from Boston University.

- **December 1955** As head of the Montgomery Improvement Association, King becomes spokesman for the year-long Montgomery Bus Boycott protesting against segregation.

- **30 January 1956** A bomb explodes at King's home in Montgomery.

- **13 November 1956** The Supreme Court rules bus segregation illegal.

- **11 January 1957** King is elected head of the civil rights organization that will become the Southern Christian Leadership Conference.

- **20 September 1958** Stabbed by a woman during a book-signing in Blumstein's department store in Harlem, New York City.

- **1959** Resigns as pastor at Dexter to focus on civil rights work; returns to Atlanta, Georgia.

- **October 1960** King is imprisoned for participating in a sit-in protest in Atlanta, Georgia; presidential candidate John F Kennedy contrives his release.

- **1961** Attorney-General Robert Kennedy asks the FBI to put King under surveillance.

- **16 April 1963** Imprisoned during civil rights protests in Birmingham, Alabama, King writes his "Letter from Birmingham Jail", affirming the need to defy unjust laws.

- **28 August 1963** During the March on Washington for Jobs and Freedom, King delivers his "I have a dream…" speech from the steps of the Lincoln Memorial.

- **2 July 1964** Witnesses the signing of the Civil Rights Act, outlawing discrimination.

- **10 December 1964** At the age of 35 King becomes the youngest male recipient of the Nobel Peace Prize.

WINS NOBEL PRIZE 1964

- **7–25 March 1965** King's leadership is rejected by younger activists.

- **4 August 1965** Voting Rights Act is passed.

- **22 January 1966** Moves into a tenement in a black ghetto in Chicago to draw attention to the issue of black urban poverty.

- **4 April 1967** Denounces the Vietnam War and describes the United States as "the greatest purveyor of violence in the world today".

- **4 April 1968** King is assassinated at the Lorraine Motel in Memphis.

« BEFORE

The existence of social hierarchies often disadvantage vulnerable groups, such as the poor. The idea that everyone should have equal rights arose in the 18th century.

POLITICAL RIGHTS

The world's oldest written constitution for an independent state is the **US Constitution** of 1787 **« 232–33**, which set out the duties of government and its responsibilities towards its citizens. In 1789, the French Revolutionary Assembly issued the **Declaration of the Rights of Man « 237**. It stated that "all men are created equal" and defined various democratic principles, such as equality before the law and freedom from arbitrary arrest. Women, however, were excluded. In 1791 the US Bill of Rights guaranteed rights, such as **freedom of speech**, but it did not apply to black or American Indians.

PHILOSOPHICAL RIGHTS

Individual social reformers and philosophers were also important in the growth of human rights. The political thinker Tom Paine helped to draft the American Constitution and wrote *The Rights of Man* (1791–92) in support of the French Revolution **« 236–37**. English philosopher John Stuart Mill defended the freedom of the individual against state control.

JOHN STUART MILL, PROPONENT OF SOCIAL REFORM AND HUMAN RIGHTS

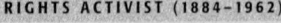

RIGHTS ACTIVIST (1884–1962)

ELEANOR ROOSEVELT

Eleanor Roosevelt, wife of US President Roosevelt, is often called America's most significant First Lady. She was active in the League of Women Voters and the Women's Trade Union League. After the President's death, she was elected chair of the UN Human Rights Commission and played a key role in drafting the "Declaration of Universal Human Rights" (1948). She hoped it would be a "Magna Carta of all men everywhere", the word "men" applying to both sexes.

THE
SUFFRAGETTE

A SACRED STRUGGLE

THE
SUFFRAGETTE

THE
SUFFRAGETTE
EDITED BY CHRISTABEL PANKHURST.
No. 2.   OCTOBER 25, 1912.   Price 1d.
AN
ANTI-SHOCK
BY
JAMES BARR

Civil Rights

The demand for civil and human rights has been a major feature of political and social movements worldwide since the early 20th century. Among the many causes that have been fought for are the right of women to vote and equal rights for ethnic minorities.

Human rights are built on the idea that all people should enjoy minimum standards in many areas of life, including the right to liberty, freedom of expression and conscience, to be treated equally before the law, and not to be tortured or subjected to degrading treatment. In 1948 these ideals were published by the General Assembly of the United Nations in the "Univeral Declaration of Human Rights". Other United Nation Conventions (agreements among member countries) have followed, including the elimination of racial discrimination (1969), outlawing torture (1987), and the rights of the child (1989).

By contrast, civil rights are written into the laws or constitution of a country to protect its citizens. They relate only to citizens in that country. Most democracies, including the United States, Canada, France, and Germany, have civil rights written into their constitutions, although this does not necessarily mean that in practice all people are treated equally. Nor do countries have to be full democracies to proclaim civil rights. In 1936, the Soviet Union proclaimed a new constitution outlining civil rights, but they only existed on paper and were never implemented.

The right to vote

A fundamental civil right is the right to full citizenship, but women and ethnic minorities have often had to fight hard to obtain it. In the early

Against the vote

Opponents of womens' fight to vote used any methods to attack the suffragettes. Posters lampooned them as harridans, who should be forcibly shackled and gagged.

Hunger strike medal of honour

In July 1909, Majorie Wallace Dunlop became the first suffragette to go on hunger strike. Many others followed her lead. In retaliation the British government introduced the brutal process of force-feeding. Women who braved the experience wore hunger-strike medals.

Selling The Suffragette

Women had to overcome many barriers to achieve their right to vote. In 1912 the Women's Social and Political Union (WSPU) launched its own newspaper, *The Suffragette*. Hundreds of long-skirted women sold the paper in public, challenging social convention and risking public hostility.

> ## "Civil liberties victories never stay won, but must be fought for over and over again."
>
> IRA GLASSER, EXECUTIVE DIRECTOR OF THE AMERICAN CIVIL LIBERTIES UNION, 1978–2001

20th century, in both Britain and the US, the demand for the vote for women became a major issue.

In Britain the campaign began in 1867 when parliament proposed to extend suffrage (the right to vote) to a wider range of men but still exclude women. For the next 50 years a growing tide of protests, demonstrations, and petitions made this one of the most divisive issues in modern British politics. In 1903, the militant Women's Social and Political Union (WPSU) was formed by Emmeline Pankhurst. Frustrated by the failure to achieve the vote by peaceful means, suffragettes, as these women became known, took direct action, including invading the Houses of Parliament. Many were imprisoned. The campaign finally achieved success in 1918 when women aged 30 and over obtained the vote. Equal voting rights with men were granted in 1928.

A similar but more peaceful campaign began in the US in the 1840s. The first state to grant women the vote was Wyoming in 1869; nationally women won the vote in 1920. In the end, in both countries, women got the vote as a direct acknowledgment of their crucial role in securing victory in World War I. However, voting alone did not confer equal citizenship. Discrimination in other areas continued and from about 1970 a second women's rights movement fought for and succeeded in changing the law to ensure equality at work and elsewhere. This campaign showed that changes in the law mean little unless economic inequalities are also addressed. Even if they have the vote, women worldwide still experience discrimination as do other minorities.

African-American and black rights

One of the best-known civil rights campaigns of modern times was waged in the US. During the 1950s and early 1960s, black Americans led by Martin Luther King (pp.432–33), fought for the end of segregation – whereby black people were discriminated against in many areas such as education and transport – and full civil rights. Years of civil disobedience resulted in a series of important legal changes that ended segregation in many areas and removed literacy tests preventing black Americans from voting.

In South Africa too a bitter struggle began against apartheid after 1948. This government-enforced policy of segregation denied black Africans the vote and many other rights (see pp.376–77). When apartheid ended after 1991 and South Africa held its first fully democratic elections in 1994, the sight of thousands of black voters queuing to exercise their new right to vote reaffirmed the importance of a basic civil right many of us now take for granted.

AFTER »

Human rights remain a key issue, with many at risk or being eroded worldwide.

CHALLENGES TO CIVIL LIBERTIES

Civil liberties, such as the right to privacy, may be suspended during wartime. After the 9/11 attacks on New York **390–91 »** and the start of the "war on terror", countries such as Britain and the US passed

SURVEILLANCE CAMERAS

anti-terrorist laws that allow authorities to intercept electronic data, and to detain suspected terrorists for longer without charge. Some people think these laws **threaten hard-won civil rights**; others think they are justified to prevent terrorism.

CIVIL RIGHTS AROUND THE WORLD

Since the 1960s many minority groups have struggled to put an end to discrimination. During the 1990s Britain and America introduced **disability acts**. Gay rights activists have struggled for years to achieve full citizenship. Denmark recognized same-sex **civil unions** in 1989. The Netherlands was the first country to take the further step

CIVIL PARTNERSHIP CEREMONY

of legalizing same-sex marriage in 2001, and it was followed by countries in Europe, Africa, North and South America, and Australasia.

1893 The year that New Zealand became the first country to grant women equal voting rights.

1902 The year that Australia granted equal voting rights to women.

Marching for rights

April 1968, National Guard troops – bayonets fixed – watch as African-American sanitation workers march peacefully in Memphis, Tennessee. This contrasts with a similar demonstration the day before, when a black teenager was killed by the police.

BEFORE ≪

Ireland, a mainly Catholic country, had a fraught relationship with its Protestant neighbour, Britain, for many centuries.

THE BRITISH IN IRELAND

After victory in the English Civil War, **Oliver Cromwell** ≪ **204–05** invaded and conquered the whole of Ireland, opening it up to colonization by English and Scottish Protestants. In 1782 Ireland received an independent parliament, but after revolts in 1798 this was abolished. Britain and Ireland were united in 1801.

THE EASTER RISING

Anger erupted in April 1916 in a rebellion known as the Easter Rising. Militant Irish Republicans seized several key locations in Dublin and issued the **Proclamation of the Republic**, declaring Ireland to be an independent state. After six days of fighting the British suppressed the uprising and executed its leaders, which generated sympathy for the Republican cause and awakened nationalist sentiment.

MICHAL COLLINS

IRISH FREE STATE

In 1921 Michael Collins, a Republican leader, was sent to London to negotiate a treaty with the British. Ireland was to be self-governing but kept within the British Empire. Six counties in the region of Ulster (Northern Ireland) remained part of the UK. In 1922 Collins founded the **Irish Free State** (later, the Irish Republic). A year of civil war followed, as many Republicans rejected partition.

THE NORTH

In the largely Protestant north, nationalists, in favour of a united Ireland, were seen as a threat. This led to preferential treatment of Protestant Unionists in jobs and housing. Despite brief campaigns by the paramilitary **Irish Republican Army** (IRA), formed in the 1920s, the province was stable. However, in 1966 Unionists formed the Ulster Volunteer Force (UVF) in response to the Republican threat and the violence escalated.

In September 1968, the Northern Ireland Civil Rights Association (NICRA), a mainly Catholic organization, announced a march was to take place in the city of Derry on 5 October 1968 to demand an end to discrimination against Irish Catholics. The Protestant Apprentice Boys of Derry announced they would also march at that time. NICRA were banned from marching by the British Government but decided to proceed. Armed with batons, the Royal Ulster Constabulary (RUC) charged at the marchers, and images of the violence shocked the world. Northern Irish Students formed a radical civil rights group called the People's Democracy (PD) based on socialist principles (see pp.266–67). Inspired by Martin Luther King (see pp.354–55), about 40 members of the PD marched from Belfast to Derry on 1 January 1969 to highlight social injustices in Northern Ireland. The march was attacked by Unionists with iron bars and stones. These events precipitated a split in the

SECTARIANISM Division of a society into religious factions, such as Protestant and Catholic, in which strong identification with the values within each faction leads to exclusion of those with different values.

IRA (see BEFORE): the Official IRA, and the Provisional IRA. Determined to use force to reunite Ireland, the Provisional IRA launched an armed attack against British rule.

Peaceful protest

The Provisional IRA became closely involved in civilian demonstrations and riots against the British. The Unionist UVF began to use violence to "protect the Protestant community" from the Provisional IRA and launched offensives against Catholics and the Irish Republic (see BEFORE). The British Government responded by implementing Operation "Demetrius" in Northern Ireland on 9 August 1971. This introduced internment, which allowed the British army and RUC to arrest and imprison

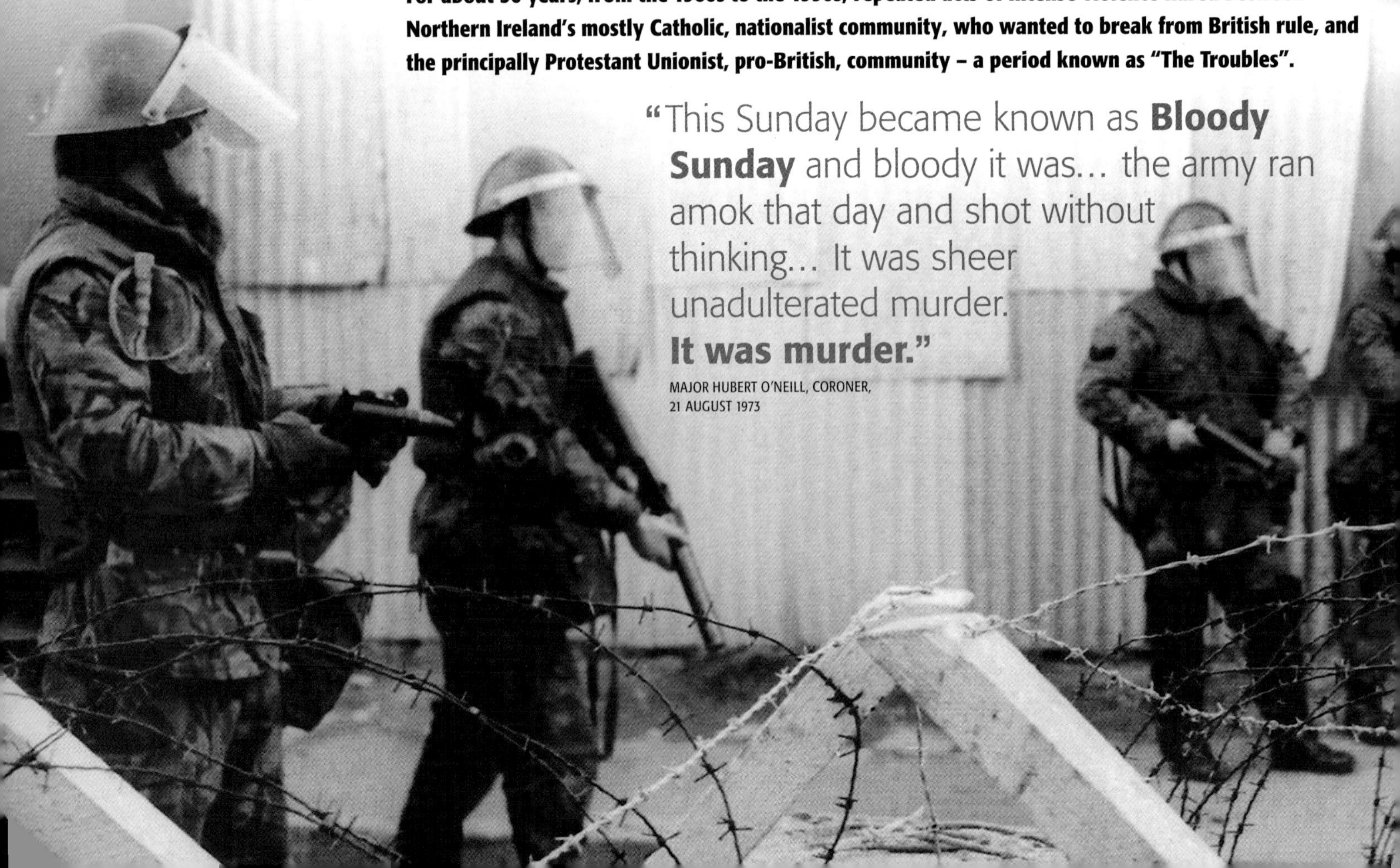

Confrontation

Civil rights protesters vent their frustrations at British soldiers dressed in riot gear, across a barricade in Derry on Bloody Sunday. The soldiers were armed with guns containing rubber bullets. Tensions came to a head when stones were thrown at the soldiers. Rubber bullets were switched for live ammunition, leaving 13 dead.

The Troubles

For about 30 years, from the 1960s to the 1990s, repeated acts of intense violence flared between Northern Ireland's mostly Catholic, nationalist community, who wanted to break from British rule, and the principally Protestant Unionist, pro-British, community – a period known as "The Troubles".

"This Sunday became known as **Bloody Sunday** and bloody it was… the army ran amok that day and shot without thinking… It was sheer unadulterated murder. **It was murder.**"

MAJOR HUBERT O'NEILL, CORONER,
21 AUGUST 1973

without trial those accused of being members of illegal paramilitary groups.

On Sunday 30 January 1972 NICRA organized a march in the city of Derry against the internment policy, in which 10–20,000 people took part. They were prevented from entering the city by the British army, so most moved to "Free Derry Corner" to attend a rally. Some young men threw stones at soldiers and members of the army moved to arrest them. Reports of an IRA sniper

Marking territory

The Republican mural on the left commemorates the Easter Rising; the Unionist mural on the right shows the paramilitary group, the Ulster Freedom Fighters. Both murals were in Northern Ireland's capital, Belfast.

were allegedly passed to the British command and the order to switch from rubber bullets to live rounds was given. Within 30 minutes soldiers shot dead 13 unarmed men and injured a further 14, many of whom were trying to flee.

IRA bombing
This shows the aftermath of one of the Guildford bombs in 1974. The Horse and Groom pub was packed with young soldiers, many back from duty in Northern Ireland. Four men, known as the "Guildford Four" were later arrested and wrongly convicted of the act.

Armed campaign

The events of "Bloody Sunday" caused revulsion worldwide. In Ireland the killings increased support for the IRA, especially among disaffected young people. It marked a major turning point in the fortunes of Northern Ireland. In March 1972, British Prime Minister Edward Heath suspended the Northern Ireland Parliament formed in 1920 at Stormont in east Belfast. He imposed direct rule from London and established the Northern Ireland Office to govern the province. Fresh rioting began and the IRA stepped up its armed campaign.

The Provisional IRA took its fight to force the British out of Northern Ireland to the mainland. On 5 October 1974 the IRA planted bombs in two pubs popular with army personnel in Guildford, killing 5 and injuring 65. On 21 November 1974 the IRA bombed two more pubs in Birmingham, killing 21 and injuring 182. In response, the British Government introduced the Prevention of Terrorism Act, allowing suspects to be held without charge for up to seven days. Most suspects were sent to the Maze prison, at Long Kesh in County Antrim. In the late 1970s several Republican prisoners began a bitter struggle for status as political prisoners. This culminated in the hunger strikes of 1981, in which ten inmates refused food and died of starvation in the prison hospital.

Support for the political wing of the IRA, Sinn Féin, soared, and the IRA adopted an "Armalite and ballot box" strategy. Small groups on the mainland targeted politicians, shopping areas, and financial districts to keep the British under pressure, while Sinn Féin made gains in elections. The level of violence gradually declined by the 1990s as both sides searched for a political solution to almost thirty years of conflict.

AFTER

After bombing campaigns on mainland Britain, both political leaders and paramilitary groups moved towards peace.

GOOD FRIDAY AGREEMENT

Changes in leadership in Britain, Dublin, and in Ulster Unionism led to the "Good Friday Agreement" in 1998. It recognized Northern Ireland's

STORMONT

right to exist, while acknowledging the nationalist desire for a united Ireland. Voters elected a new **Northern Ireland Assembly** (NIA) to form a parliament at Stormont.

IRA DISBANDS

The NIA was suspended when the Provisional IRA delayed the decommission of its weapons. On 15 August 1998 an IRA bomb killed 29 people in County Tyrone. On **28 July 2005** the IRA ceased its armed campaign, but dissident Republicans who rejected the peace settlement have continued to endorse acts of violence.

A NEW ERA

In March 2007, the leaders of Sinn Féin and the Ulster Unionists agreed to **share power at Stormont**, and on 8 May 2007 the Assembly was restored. In 2011 the **official visit to Ireland by Queen Elizabeth II** – the first by a British monarch since independence – cemented the new relationship between the UK and Ireland, and was reciprocated in 2014 when the Irish President, Michael D Higgins, made the first official visit to Britain by an Irish head of state.

Dictatorship and Democracy

In the latter part of the 20th century, Latin American countries veered between nationalist, authoritarian, revolutionary, and civilian regimes. Democracy and some stability have gradually been restored to some nations, but, while the region's economy has improved overall, inequality and poverty remain major challenges.

C hile's military coup, led by General Augusto Pinochet in 1973 was the first of several in 1970s Latin America (see pp.344–45). From 1976, Argentina was ruled by a succession of military figures, including General Leopardo Galtieri, who was among a number of Latin American leaders given training at the School of the Americas, a US army facility in Panama. Both the Pinochet and Galtieri regimes were characterized by the suppression of opposition – thousands of dissidents were tortured or disappeared without trace.

The corrupt Somoza dynasty, which ruled in Nicaragua from 1936, faced growing opposition in the early 1970s from the International Socialist

Sandinista group FSLN. Sandinista rebels were supported by the Catholic Church, and much of the Nicaraguan population. In 1979, Anastasio Somoza was overthrown by popular revolution, and a *junta* (council) of National Reconstruction dominated by the FSLN took over the country.

In 1970s El Salvador, the elitist government of Arturo Molina was resented by a population living in abject poverty. Violence between right-wing paramilitary units known as "death squads" and left-wing revolutionary groups escalated into civil war in 1979. Fearing a communist takeover, the US funded the El Salvadoran military. Fighting and human rights abuses continued throughout the 1980s until

mounting foreign debt, and Argentina slid into recession. The economy finally began to stabilize in 2005.

In the 1980s, General Pinochet's regime in Chile introduced some liberalizing measures as the state moved towards a free-market economy.

> **DISSIDENT** An individual who disagrees, protests, or acts against established opinion, policy, or government.

Greater freedoms of speech led inevitably to calls for democracy, which was restored in 1989. Chile experienced impressive growth in the 1990s and is one of the more robust post-dictatorship economies.

BEFORE

Latin America has been shaped by the interests and intervention of foreign powers, first by Europe, and later, the United States.

THE GREAT DEPRESSION
Economic depression in Europe and North America in the 1930s had a **catastrophic effect** on Latin American economies, most of which were **dependent on exports** of raw materials. The plight of the poor in many countries led to a growth of revolutionary movements **≪422–23**.

INDUSTRIALIZATION
During the economic crisis of the 1930s, many governments in Latin America **nationalized resources** previously controlled by **foreign interests**, and began industrialization programmes **≪422–23**.

GENERAL PINOCHET

THE COLD WAR
Rivalry between the Soviet Union and US after World War II **≪406–07** even extended to Latin America. The US supported the **Pinochet coup** in Chile, and the overthrow of left-wing regimes, while the Soviet Union backed **communist Cuba**. The 1962 Cuban Missile Crisis intensified this competition. The Soviet Union supported Cuba through America's economic embargo, and the US gave funding and military support to keep their **chosen regimes** in power.

"Sometimes **democracy** must be **bathed in blood**."

GENERAL AUGUSTO PINOCHET, ATTRIBUTED

in 1992, 12 years of violence ended with the El Salvador Peace Accords.

The return of democracy
In the 1980s and 1990s, the political tide turned again in Latin America; dictatorships were overthrown and democracy restored.

Democracy returned to Argentina in 1983. After a period of spiralling inflation President Carlos Menem introduced wide-ranging reforms in the 1990s, privatizing state assets and imposing a fixed exchange rate. However, Menem and his successor Fernando de la Rúa failed to address

The Mexico–US Border
The order for a fence, 1,126 km (700 miles) long, to separate the two countries was given by US President George W Bush in 2006 to prevent the flow of illegal immigrants into America.

The oil-rich state of Venezuela had regained democratic rule in 1958, but the gap between rich and poor caused discontent. In 1998, President Hugo Chávez (see right) was elected, vowing to bring greater equality. He launched "Plan Bolivar 2000", which introduced social and welfare reforms and halted the privatization of state assets. Oil profits helped ensure success for Chávez and growth in the economy.

US intervention
Frequently referred to as "America's Backyard", Latin America has often seen US interference. In 1983 the US invaded the island nation of Grenada after reports that an airport there was secretly intended for Soviet use, and even after the end of the Cold War (see pp.328–29) US troops invaded Panama in 1989, and removed General Noriega's government due in part to alleged drug trafficking.

Some Latin American nations have tried to avoid US economic domination. In 2007, the "Bank of the South" was formed by Hugo Chávez to finance regional infrastructure projects and social programmes.

AFTER

In the 21st century, a more politically stable Latin America is increasing its economic ambitions, and many of its leaders are calling for greater regional integration.

MIGRATION NORTH
Poverty in Latin America leads many people to migrate north in **search of a better life**. The American Census shows that migration patterns have shifted radically since World War II, when most immigrants were European. Today most of the US's legal migrants are from Latin America, and many more enter illegally. A large proportion of the US's estimated 12 million illegal immigrants crossed at the **Mexican border**.

GREATER POLITICAL STABILITY
Despite the problems in the region, in 2012–14 **democratic presidential elections** took place in 14 countries. Traditional authoritarianism is no longer tolerated by the peoples of Latin America.

Protests against Pinochet
Chileans take to the streets with pictures of those who went missing during Pinochet's military rule when more than 3,000 were arrested and murdered by the authorities. In 2001, relatives were finally given access to records and learnt the fate of "the disappeared".

VENEZUELAN PRESIDENT (1954–2013)

HUGO CHÁVEZ

Elected president of Venezuela in 1998, Hugo Chávez introduced the "Bolivarian Revolution", a brand of democratic socialism prioritizing social reform. An admirer of Fidel Castro, he was briefly removed from office in 2002 by the Venezuelan army, but returned to power by a popular uprising. His radical foreign policy criticized America, and called for improved trade and international aid. However, a 2007 referendum rejected his plans for wholesale constitutional reform.

« BEFORE

In 1948 the state of Israel was created from land belonging to Arab state of Palestine. The oil-rich Arab nations refused to accept Israel's legitimacy and began a series of military reprisals to regain the land.

SIX-DAY WAR

In 1967 Egypt closed the Gulf of Aqaba to Israel. In the ensuing Six-Day War, **Israel defeated Egypt, Syria, and Jordan,** and seized land later known as the Occupied Territories.

ISRAELI TANK IN SYRIA

UNREST IN THE MIDDLE EAST

The territorial losses and humiliation of the Six-Day War **intensified Arab resentment** towards both the Israelis and the Western governments that supported them.

FORMATION OF OAPEC

The Organization of Arab Petroleum Exporting Countries was **founded in 1968**. Its members, initially Kuwait, Libya, and Saudi Arabia, were all developing nations seeking to assert their rights in a market dominated by foreign-owned multi-national oil companies. As oil reserves in other parts of the world dwindled, **OAPEC became increasingly powerful**, and by 1973 OAPEC had expanded to include **10 Arab states.**

The Oil Crisis

By the 1970s, rising industrial and domestic consumption of fuel created a growing dependence on imports of foreign oil for the industrialized Western powers. Oil was the fuel of the global economy and most of the world's oil reserves were concentrated in the Middle East.

In October 1973 Egypt and Syria, backed by Iraq, Jordan, and Saudi Arabia invaded Israel on the holy Jewish holiday of Yom Kippur. The three-week Yom Kippur War represents a watershed in Middle Eastern history. With the element of surprise on their side and the advantage of improved arms, Arab troops fared better than in any previous Arab–Israeli conflict, regaining some of the territory lost during the Six-Day War (see BEFORE).

Oil supply cut

The Yom Kippur War also saw OAPEC flex its political muscle for the first time. Ten days into the war OAPEC leaders, King Faisal of Saudi Arabia and Egyptian President Anwar Sadat,

announced an embargo on shipments of crude oil to all Western nations that were providing supplies or aid to Israel. The embargo lasted six months – from October 1973 until March 1974. Its aim was to force Israel's allies to pressure her into giving up the occupied territories (see BEFORE).

The embargo targeted Israel's key ally, the US, but did not apply to all European nations. The Netherlands, who sent arms to Israel and allowed the Americans to use Dutch airfields for supply runs, faced a complete embargo. Supplies to the UK and France, who had embargoed arms and supplies to both Arabs and Israelis, were not cut off. However, the economic impact of restricting the flow of crude oil to the world market caused

Yom Kippur war
The Israeli army attack Syrian positions in the Golan Heights on 12 October 1973. Six days earlier the Syrians had invaded Israel, but they were quickly driven back beyond their own border.

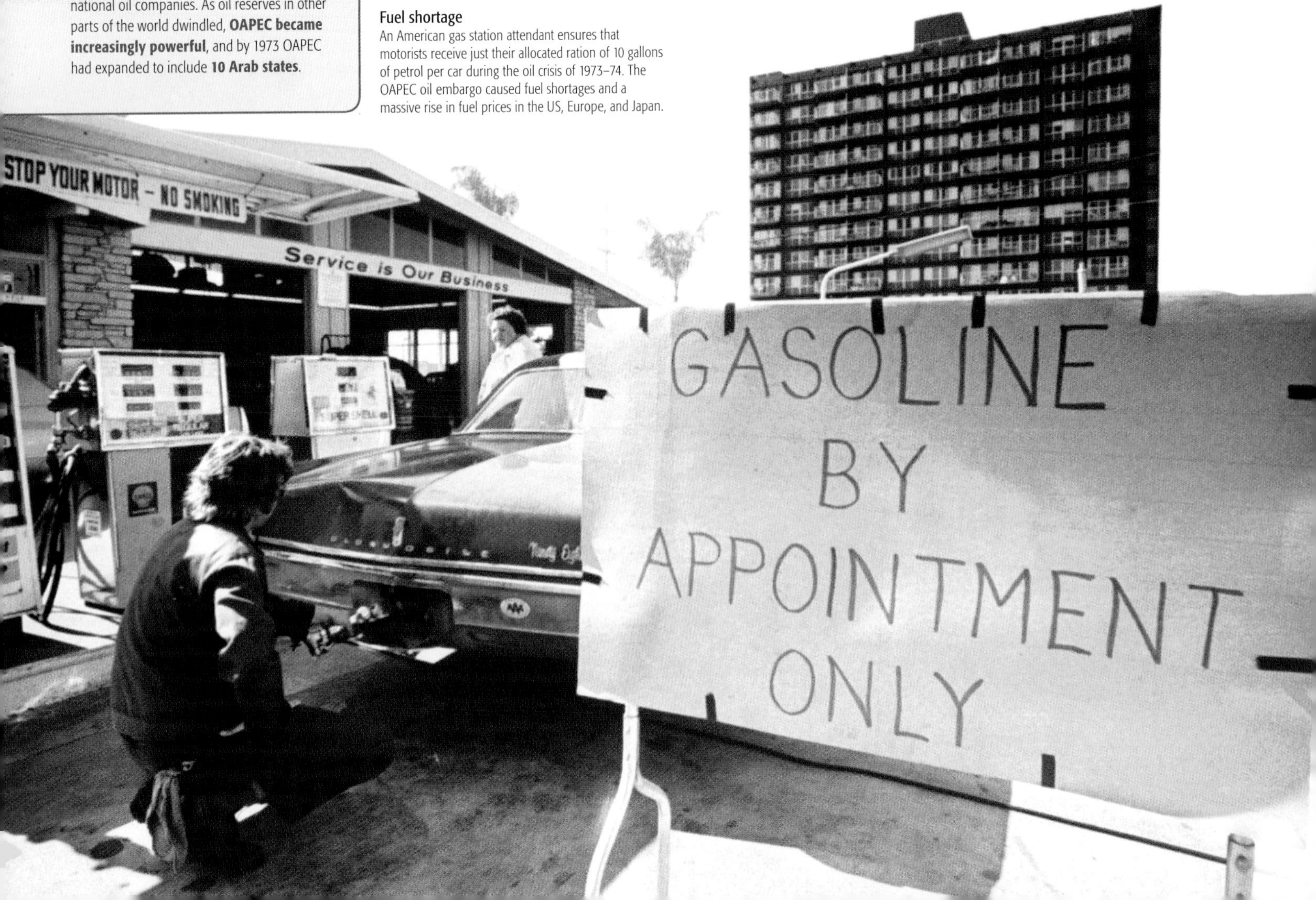

oil prices to treble. Even if countries were not embargoed from receiving oil, many could not afford to buy it in anything like the same quantities. Without fuel to power production,

Fuel shortage
An American gas station attendant ensures that motorists receive just their allocated ration of 10 gallons of petrol per car during the oil crisis of 1973–74. The OAPEC oil embargo caused fuel shortages and a massive rise in fuel prices in the US, Europe, and Japan.

STOP YOUR MOTOR – NO SMOKING

Service is Our Business

GASOLINE BY APPOINTMENT ONLY

5 PER CENT the annual rise in oil usage in the early 1970s.

98 PER CENT the drop in oil imports to the US from OAPEC.

400 PER CENT the rise in the price of oil between 1973–74.

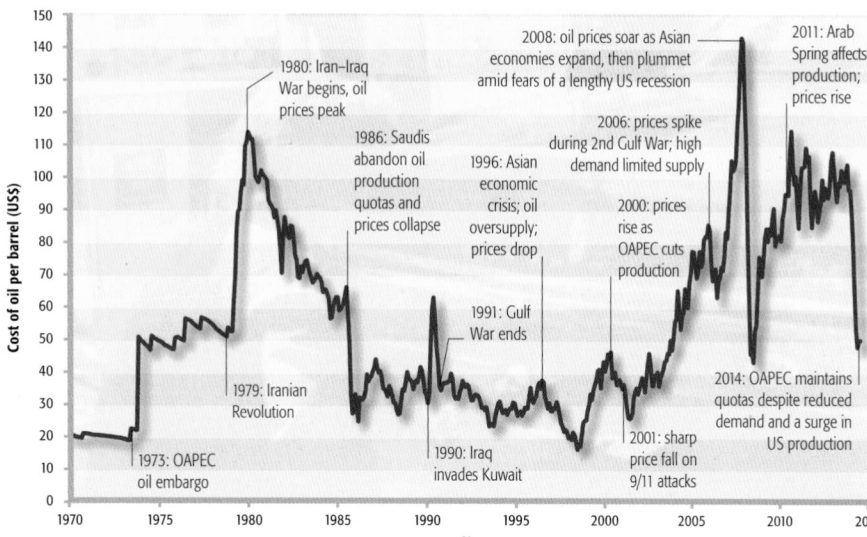

The politics of oil
This graph shows the rise and fall in oil prices from 1970 and its relationship to specific events. As oil supplies dwindled in other parts of the world, the value of oil reserves in the Middle East increased. Oil underpins industrial and domestic energy production, which means any political instability in the region has repercussions elsewhere. Increased demand from Asia, and fluctuations in developing Asian economies has also affected the price of oil and other commodities.

industrial output slowed dramatically, inflation spiralled, and the world slipped into economic recession. It became all too clear that the economic boom experienced by Western nations in the post-war years had been entirely dependent on their ability to dictate low fixed-rate prices to the oil-supplying nations.

Energy crisis

When the embargo hit the US, inflation rose to over 10 per cent, interest rates rocketed, and an enormous trade deficit developed. Schools and businesses adopted policies of regular closures to save on heating oil, while homeowners were called upon to turn down their heating thermostats. Unemployment rates, a growing issue since the start of the 1970s, continued to rise as industries were forced to lay off workers. The price of petrol for domestic consumption quadrupled during the embargo period, and up to 20 per cent of US gas stations were without fuel during the crisis. In an economy where 85 per cent of the workforce drove to their place of work, people began to queue for hours at a time to refuel their cars. At US President Nixon's request, petrol was rationed to a maximum of 10 gallons per customer.

Price rises in crude oil had a huge impact in Europe, especially in the UK, which imported over 80 per cent of its oil from the Middle East. Before the crisis struck, Edward Heath's Conservative government was already struggling with rising inflation and trade union unrest. In May 1973, 1.6 million workers went on strike to protest against the introduction of pay restraints. As the year progressed, relations between workers and government steadily worsened. In November 1973, a ban on over-time by electricity and coal workers exacerbated the British fuel shortage.

Heath's government was forced to announce a State of Emergency, limiting industrial and commercial users of electricity to a total of 5 days fuel supply per fortnight. When coal miners went on all-out strike in early 1974, the government introduced a compulsory "three-day week", to save on both energy consumption and the wage bill. The crisis ended with a settlement for the National Union of Mine Workers, which cost the country £113 million and increased the

Coping with a "Car Free" Sunday
During the oil crisis, an enterprising German hotel proprietor (above) circumvents the nationwide vehicle ban on Sundays by reverting to horse power. "The Big Freeze" is the cover story of the 3 December 1973 issue of *Time* magazine (right). Three months into the oil crisis, the article suggests it will be a cold holiday season for Americans.

national wage bill by 30 per cent. With full-time coal production re-established, Britain returned to a 5-day working week in March 1974, but restrictions on the use of electricity were retained for several months.

Coping with the crisis

A range of conservation measures were introduced by governments to cope with the oil crisis. Many lowered speed limits to 80kmph (50mph), which reduced oil consumption. In the US, the consumption of oil dropped by 20 per cent, as the public made efforts to conserve both oil and money by switching to other more affordable forms of energy, such as coal, or solar and wind power. America also extended Daylight Savings Time and, like Germany, developed a policy of "Car-free" Sundays. In Britain, the public became used to living and working by candlelight during a long winter of phased energy-conserving power cuts. Other restrictions included ending television broadcasts by 10.30pm, turning-off streetlights at midnight, and cancelling football matches played under floodlights. Civic Christmas lights were allowed to remain switched on by special government dispensation.

OAPEC's embargo inflicted serious damage on the global economy and left the leaders of many of the industrialized nations determined to reduce their reliance on Middle Eastern oil. Many began to fund research into alternative energy sources such as wind, tidal, and solar energy. In the US, President Nixon approved the building of a Trans–Alaskan oil pipeline, designed to supply 2,000,000 barrels of oil a day to the American market. Big automobile manufacturers began to consider smaller, more economic alternatives to the large "gas guzzling" cars of the 1950s and 1960s. Japan, in particular, pursued reforms in its energy policy to avoid a similar future crisis, developing its nuclear energy capacity and pioneering some of the world's most successful energy-efficient cars. Unlike other industrialized nations, Japan revived quickly after the crisis. This turnaround in economic fortune is generally credited to the Japanese government's investing in such industries as electronics (see pp.380–81) that are not dependent on oil.

AFTER

Since 1973, America has pursued policies to protect itself from a repeat of the oil crisis.

MIDDLE EAST PEACE PROCESS
The oil embargo radically changed the OAPEC nations' **power and standing in world politics**. Western nations were forced to give Arab objections to the existence of Israel a fair hearing. Throughout his term in office, President Jimmy Carter pursued **a peaceful resolution to Arab–Israeli conflict**. In 1979 a bilateral peace treaty between Israel and Egypt was a first step along this difficult diplomatic road **≪ 337**. However, US intervention in the Middle East was not confined to peace making. In the 1980s the US worked hard to gain interests in oil reserves by supporting regimes, such as that of **Saddam Hussein 392–93 ≫**, against Iran, but instability in Iraq after the 2003 invasion has challenged America's influence over the region's oil.

US ENERGY POLICY
The 1978 National Energy Act promoted the use of **renewable energy** and introduced higher taxes on fuel-inefficient vehicles. This led to the development of hybrid cars that run partly on electric motors. The US has also sought to exploit onshore **reserves of natural shale gas** with the development of hydraulic fracturing, or **fracking**. The policy is controversial due to concerns about the impact of fracking on the environment and public health, but proponents argue that shale gas can provide North America with **energy security** for almost 100 years – encouraging countries like the UK, Poland, and China to explore the viability of their own shale gas reserves.

‹‹ BEFORE

A desire to return to a purer, more traditional form of Islam (the Muslim faith), grew amongst Muslims tired of westernizing influences on their way of life.

DEOBANDI ISLAMIC MOVEMENT
Al Imam Muhammad Qasim Nanotvi established the **Deoband Madrassa** (religious school) in British-ruled India in 1866. The school taught **Sharia law** (see right) and aimed to **purify Islam** of "un-Islamic" practices, particularly the influences of British colonial culture. After the partition of India **‹‹ 332–33** in 1947, the Deoband Madrassa closed, and new madrassas in Pakistan were opened.

COLONIAL RULE

THE MUSLIM BROTHERHOOD
Founded by **Hasan al-Banna** in Egypt in 1928, the Muslim Brotherhood agitated for the introduction of Sharia law. The Brothers' leader bemoaned the sickness of the *Ummah*, or larger Muslim community, and gave the Brothers *jihadia* (**military training**) to help the "struggle in the way of God" against them. The Brotherhood's activities led to their being **outlawed in Egypt**. Saudi Arabia gave refuge to Brotherhood exiles.

The Iranian Revolution

The growth of nationalism in the aftermath of World War I was accompanied by the rise of "Islamism" in some Middle Eastern nations. The Islamist movement aimed to overthrow secular, pro-Western governments and establish Islamic states governed by Sharia law.

Many citizens of the Middle East resented the post-World War I settlements, which gave Britain and France mandates to administer their nations. Leaders of Middle Eastern countries were chosen for their willingness to collaborate with the foreign powers, and many were corrupt. Ordinary people were given few, if any, democratic rights. While Britain did provide constitutions and elected assemblies, her advisers ensured that British interests were served in any governmental decisions.

In World War I, Persia was divided between Russia and Britain, but the Russians withdrew after the Bolshevik revolution of 1917 (see pp. 300–01), leaving Britain sole rights to exploit Persian oil. In the early 1920s, the British identified Reza Khan, a senior figure in the Persian military, as a leader who could maintain the Anglo–Persian status quo. With British backing, Khan led an armed campaign to crush political opposition, declaring himself Shah of Persia in 1925.

Modernization and secularization
A fierce believer in Westernization, the Shah modernized the infrastructure of the country, which was renamed Iran in 1935. He abandoned Islamic education in favour of a more secular

Lavish lifestyle
Mohammad Reza Shah – shown here with his daughter, Princess Shahnaz, in 1957 – had an opulent lifestyle, while the majority of his people lived in abject poverty. Cold War tensions and the need for Iranian oil led Western powers to ignore the Shah's misrule.

curriculum, discarded much of Sharia law, and discouraged Iranians from obeying the call to prayer or from making pilgrimages. The result was ever-greater social division. While the upper classes became more secular and Western in their outlook, the masses – who were forced to pay heavy taxes to fund the Shah's reforms – remained impoverished and deeply religious.

World War II and after

Reza Shah offered support to the Nazis in World War II, hoping that Germany would help Iran to rid itself of British influence. The Shah's Nazi sympathies threatened Allied access to Iranian oil, so when Germany invaded Russia in

Protest against the Shah
The corrupt and brutal regime of Mohammed Reza Shah produced waves of demonstration during 1978. Protesters thronged the streets clutching pictures of the exiled religious cleric Ayatollah Khomeini. In December, the Shah abandoned his attempts to hold onto power and fled Iran, leaving the way open for Khomeini to return.

Iran hostage crisis
Student militants burn a US flag on the roof of the US embassy in Tehran during the 1979 hostage crisis when embassy staff were held hostage by protestors.

1941, British and Russian troops invaded Iran. Reza Shah was deposed and replaced by his son, Mohammed Reza. Resentment of Western interference deepened.

In the post-war years, students spearheaded a backlash against secularism and corruption. In 1951, political unrest forced the Shah to loosen his grip on power and appoint Mohammad Mossadegh as Prime Minister. Mossadegh soon nationalized the assets of the Anglo–Iranian Oil Company. With the Cold War at its height (see pp.328–29), fears of growing Soviet influence in the Middle East led Britain and the US to block sales of Iranian oil. Iran's economy descended into crisis.

In 1953, Western intelligence services supported a military coup, which restored absolute power to Mohammad Reza Shah. The Shah's rule became increasingly dictatorial. While his security police ran a terror campaign against dissenters and many of the rural poor were suffering from malnutrition, the Shah led a lavish life on oil revenues, which grew from an annual $285 million in 1960 to $18,523 million by the mid-1970s.

Islamic revolution
In Iran's mosques, the teachings of an exiled ayatollah (high-ranking Muslim cleric) were gaining ground. Ayatollah Ruhollah Khomeini had been exiled in 1964 for calling the Shah a "puppet" of the West. His teachings called for an end to the Shah's reign, insisting that only clerics should rule, since they are the true representatives of God.

Triumphant return
After 14 years in exile, Ayatollah Ruhollah Khomeini arrived in Tehran to an ecstatic reception. Khomeini rapidly set about creating a clerical state under Sharia Law.

By 1978, Khomeini had widespread support. Pro-Khomeini demonstrations were brutally suppressed, but unrest still spread from city to city as clerics, nationalists, and moderates united in a struggle for change. Although martial law was imposed, many troops refused to shoot at protestors. In December, the US tried to persuade the Shah to liberalize his regime, but revolution was now inevitable. The Shah and his family fled on 16 January 1979.

Khomeini returned to Iran on 1 February 1979. After initial fighting between political factions, a popular referendum voted for the creation of an Islamic republic. A new constitution named Khomeini as Iran's supreme leader, clergy were appointed to run state institutions, and Sharia law was introduced.

The Iran Hostage Crisis
On 22 October 1979, President Carter allowed the Shah to enter America for cancer treatment. Outraged Iranian students, who wanted the Shah to face trial in Iran, invaded the US embassy

in Tehran, taking 63 hostages. The Shah died in July 1980, but Khomeini refused to release the hostages and held 52 Americans captive for 444 days. The crisis finally ended with the signing of the Algiers Accord in January 1981.

Khomeini's defiance of America was a key factor in Western governments' support for Saddam Hussein's invasion of Iran in 1980, and their willingness to provide him with weapons during the Iran–Iraq war (see p.392). By the time Khomeini died in June 1989, Iran was a well-established Islamic state.

THE MANY FORMS OF ISLAM
The Islamic faith has several denominations, and smaller groups within each of them. Khomeini and his successor, Ali Khamenei, represent **Shia Islam**, based on allegiance to imam Ali ibn Abi Talib as Muhammad's successor. Shias make up about 12 per cent of the Islamic community. The vast majority of Muslims are **Sunnis**, acknowledging as Muhammad's successors the four caliphs, beginning with Abu Bakr Siddique. A reformist **Salafi or Wahhabist Islam**, committed to an austere interpretation of Islamic law, has influenced **Islamic State 393 ⟫** and its demands for **strict adherence to the Qur'an**. All forms of Islamic fundamentalism look back to a "purer" version of the religion.

IRAN AFTER KHOMEINI
Khomeini's successor as Iran's Supreme Leader, **Ali Khamenei**, has maintained a **strong clerical influence** on Iranian politics, and in 2005 his supporter **Mahmoud Ahmadinejad** was elected president. There remain tensions between conservative politicians and the clergy about the extent to which Islam should dominate the system. Iran has become a **regional power**, with interests in the fate of Shias in Iraq and Syria. Fears that Iran has developed nuclear weapons have involved regular warnings from the United Nations, including sanctions. Iran insists **nuclear research** is aimed at energy supply rather than weapons, and Khamenei has published a *fatwa* stating that nuclear weapons are incompatible with Islam. Relations between Iran and the West have continued to be volatile as Iran seeks to play a larger international role.

> " In Islam, the legislative **power and competence** to establish laws belong exclusively to God. "
>
> AYATOLLAH RUHOLLAH KHOMEINI

« BEFORE

Afghanistan is ethnically diverse, with a rugged geography. Dogged by clan and tribal issues, it has repeatedly been invaded.

A LANDLOCKED COUNTRY

Afghanistan lies at the **heart of Asia**, nestled between Iran in the west and Pakistan in the south and east. Its northern borders touch former Soviet countries such as Uzbekistan.

STABILITY AND UNREST

Between 1933–73, Afghanistan was stable under King Sahir Shah. In 1973, **a bloodless coup** saw his brother-in-law, Sardar Daoud Khan (below), seize control of the country. He was murdered in 1978 when the communist **People's Democratic Party of Afghanistan (PDPA)** launched the Great Saur Revolution.

PRIME MINISTER SARDAR DAOUD KHAN

COMMUNIST TAKEOVER

Supported by the USSR, the PDPA applied Marxist -style reforms **« 264–65**, such as state control of agriculture. In 1978, a treaty was signed allowing the use of Soviet troops if requested by Afghanistan.

When the People's Democratic Party of Afghanistan (PDPA) took power in 1978 (see BEFORE), conflict broke out immediately. After several days of internal power struggles, a party leader and Marxist scholar, Noor Mohammed Tureki, became President. There were primarily two Marxist groups: Tureki's Khalq Party and the Parcham Party. To establish a communist government in Afghanistan, the parties agreed to split power, but a few months later Tureki killed and jailed many Parchamis and pressed ahead with a rapid programme of communist reform, including secularism, equal rights for women, and land redistribution. Within months insurrection broke out all over the country. In March 1979, a resistance group declared a *jihad*, or "holy war", against the godless regime in Kabul. In the same month more than 100 Soviet citizens were killed in Herat, western Afghanistan. In September 1979,

1 MILLION Afghans died in the war.

5 MILLION Afghans became refugees in nearby countries.

52 THOUSAND Soviet soldiers were killed or wounded.

Kalashnikov AK47
The CIA, the US foreign intelligence agency, funnelled extensive aid to the Mujahideen via Pakistan, including hundreds of thousands of AK47s. Made in the USSR, they were cheap, reliable, and easily available.

Tureki tried to assassinate his prime minister, Hafizulla Amin. Amin had Tureki arrested, and took control of the government. He later announced that Tureki was dead.

American involvement

The Americans had been keeping a careful eye on the new Soviet-backed regime. In the 1950s and 1960s, four US presidents faced the significant task of defending American interests in the Middle East and South Asia, particularly the vast reservoirs of oil and natural gas in and around the Persian Gulf and the Arabian Peninsula. With the onset of the Cold War in 1946 (pp.328–29), America perceived the Soviet Union to be their main threat. This perception was to

continue for the next half century. America sought advice from politicians in anti-communist Muslim and Arab states, such as Pakistan and Saudi Arabia. This was the start of a curious relationship between the US and Islam.

Fighting back
From machine gun nests like this one above the Jagdalak Valley, insurgents attack Soviet forces, who were vulnerable in the mountainous terrain.

War in Afghanistan

When Soviet armed forces invaded neighbouring Afghanistan in December 1979, they were supremely confident of seizing immediate control. However, the Russian troops found themselves bogged down in a ten-year war that proved to be a disaster for both countries. The war hastened the break up of the Soviet Union, and plunged Afghanistan into a state of lawlessness.

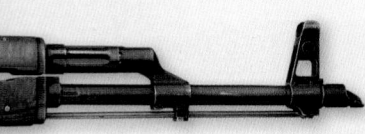

With the PDPA in power, US President Jimmy Carter and National Security Advisor Zbigniew Brzezinski authorized the covert funding and training of anti-government forces. Military and intelligence services, backed with Saudi Arabian finance and Pakistani logistical support, trained, equipped, and paid volunteers, the Mujahideen (Persian for "warriors"), who opposed the Marxists.

The Soviet presence in Afghanistan was increasing. Citing the 1978 Treaty of Friendship, allowing Soviet military

Soviet withdrawal
In May 1988, Afghanistan, Pakistan, the USSR, and the US signed agreements to end foreign intervention in Afghanistan, and the USSR began withdrawing its forces.

intervention if requested (see BEFORE), the Soviets stormed into Kabul on 24 December 1979. Up to 150,000 Soviet troops assisted by 100,000 pro-communist Afghan troops met with Mujahideen resistance. Despite Russia's superior weapons, the rebels frequently eluded them in the hostile terrain.

Stalemate
The international response ranged from stern warnings to a boycott of the 1980 Moscow Olympics. The conflict settled into a stalemate, with Soviet and government forces controlling the urban areas, while the rebels operated freely in the mountains. As the war progressed, the rebels improved their tactics and began using imported and captured weapons. Their leaders favoured sabotage, such as blowing up government office buildings. On

4 September 1985, insurgents shot down a domestic plane as it took off from Kandahar airport, killing 52 people.

In February 1988, under increasing international pressure, Soviet President Gorbachev announced the withdrawal of troops, a task completed a year later.

The war left Afghanistan with severe political, economic, and ecological problems. Many had died or fled the country, and economic production was curtailed. The guerrilla forces that had triumphed were unable to unite, and Afghanistan was divided between regional warlords. These divisions set the stage for the rise of the Afghan Taliban later in the decade.

> ## "We now have the opportunity of giving to **the USSR its Vietnam War**."
> ZBIGNIEW BRZEZINSKI, U.S. NATIONAL SECURITY ADVISER, 18 JANUARY 1978

AFTER »

Following Soviet withdrawal from Afghanistan in 1989, the United States and its allies did little to rebuild the country, leaving a dangerous leadership vacuum.

THE WARLORDS
Mujahideen factions gained power, but regional conflicts led to the rise of local warlords until in 1996 a **militant Islamic fundamentalist movement**, the Taliban, seized control of the state.

RISE OF THE TALIBAN
Led by **Mullah Omar** and initially supported by the anti-communist United States, the Taliban took control of Kabul and declared an Islamic state, insisting on strict adherence to **Islamic Sharia Law**, including an end to female education and employment. Islamic militants from outside Afghanistan, including Osama bin Laden's al-Qaeda, were given sanctuary and training. After the **9/11 attacks 390–91 »**, the US and Britain launched a bombing campaign in support of anti-Taliban forces, who overturned the Taliban regime by the end of the year.

THE WAR CONTINUES
In December 2001, the different Afghan opposition groups agreed to create a **democratic government**, and in 2004, with US support, Hamid Karzai was elected president. The Taliban retreated to the south of the country and into northern Pakistan, and have kept up a **continuous insurgency** against the Afghan army and NATO forces ever since. Although NATO forces withdrew in December 2014, the Taliban had not been eradicated. Links

with radical Islamic fundamentalism in Syria and Iraq have fuelled a new insurgency led by **Islamic State 393 »** committed, like the Taliban, to eradicating western influence and the imposition of strict Islamic laws.

HAMID KARZAI

ДОЛОЙ ЛЕНИНИЗМ

Perestroika

When Mikhail Gorbachev became leader of the Soviet Union in 1985, he acknowledged faults within the communist system and set out a new plan for political reform – *Perestroika*. He aimed to renew the Soviet Union, but *Perestroika* resulted in changes that altered the country beyond recognition.

G orbachev was a child of communism, the first leader of the USSR to have been born after the revolution (see pp.300–01). He did not question Lenin's view that communism could only be achieved through disciplined, central organization, but aimed to address failings elsewhere in the Soviet system. Through *Perestroika* (restructuring) he attempted to streamline the Soviet Communist Party (CPSU). Gorbachev also recognized that state repression of those who criticized the CPSU had created problems in Soviet society. He pledged a new openness – *Glasnost* –

in political affairs; exiled intellectuals were allowed to return and political debate was encouraged.

At first, *Glasnost* and *Perestroika* were met with general excitement, although there was resistance from those who resented reforms aimed at reducing their power and privilege. By the end of 1986, however, with the economic situation worsening, Gorbachev's talk of progress began to sound like an empty promise. His economic reforms were too cautious. He introduced limited rights for private enterprise, but most production remained under control of the state where restructuring

failed to stimulate growth. By 1987, *Perestroika* had led to longer food queues and food shortages.

Glasnost had enabled all Soviet citizens to express their dissatisfaction with both the CPSU and the Soviet system. In 1988, Gorbachev began to face internal resistance as nationalist movements in Kazakhstan, Armenia, Azerbaijan, and the Baltic States (Estonia, Latvia, and Lithuania) demanded independence from the centralized Soviet government.

In 1989, hoping that the Soviet people would accept a new "humane communism", Gorbachev allowed

BEFORE

The Soviet Union was economically stagnant and corrupt during the 1960s and 1970s.

THE ERA OF STAGNATION

In 1964, **Leonid Brezhnev** succeeded **Nikita Khrushchev** as leader of the USSR and stayed in office until 1982. Under his leadership the **economy stagnated,** and slow growth was experienced in some sectors. There were **perennial shortages** of manufactured goods and food, and reduced consumer options caused frustration among the people.

LEONID BREZHNEV

DOUBLE STANDARDS IN THE SYSTEM

Although all Soviet citizens were officially equal, in reality, **the system was corruptible**; bribes secured better jobs or housing and **senior communist party officials** had access to **privileges** unattainable by ordinary people.

Down with Lenin
Gorbachev's decision to allow criticism of the communist system resulted in demands for an end to repressive one-party government. Protesters called for multi-party elections and democracy.

"Upon the sucess of *Perestroika* depends the **future of peace**."

MIKHAIL GORBACHEV, 1987

PRESIDENT OF THE USSR (1931–)

MIKHAIL GORBACHEV

Mikhail Gorbachev was born in Stavropol in southwestern Russia. He became active in politics at an early age and became leader of the Soviet Union in 1985. Gorbachev transformed Soviet relations with the Western world, and is widely credited with reversing the Arms Race and ending the Cold War (see pp.328–29). He attempted to solve Soviet economic and political problems through programs of domestic reform. After the collapse of the Soviet Union in 1991, he made several failed attempts to return to the political stage in Russia. He was awarded the Nobel Peace Prize in 1990.

openly contested elections for some members of the Congress of People's Deputies (Soviet Parliament). However, he soon faced demands for greater concessions from a newly elected people's deputy, Boris Yeltsin.

Gorbachev and Yeltsin

Yeltsin had become popular in the Soviet Union because of his open criticism of Gorbachev and *Perestroika*. In 1990, he was elected President of the Russian Federation, the largest Soviet republic. He used this position to attack Gorbachev and the CPSU, insisting that the party should no longer dominate government. His resignation from the party in July 1990 was a public challenge. Next to Yeltsin, Gorbachev looked suddenly weak and old-fashioned.

Throughout 1990, Gorbachev struggled to hold the Soviet Union together, sending troops into

Azerbaijan to suppress inter-ethnic fighting, and opposing independence in the Baltic States. On 19 August 1991, a committee of CPSU hardliners staged a coup, arresting Gorbachev and his advisors. They declared a state of emergency and announced their intention to re-establish old-style Soviet rule. Yeltsin rushed to the White House (the Russian Parliament building), and called on the people to come and protect their parliament. Support for Yeltsin ended the coup. Gorbachev was reinstated as president after four days, but Yeltsin was the true hero of the hour and Gorbachev's prestige was irreversibly damaged.

In September 1991, the Congress of People's Deputies granted independence to all Soviet republics, dissolving the USSR. With no union to rule over, Gorbachev had effectively been made redundant. He resigned his post in December 1991.

The former USSR in 1991
After the USSR's collapse, the vast nation split into 15 separate states, the largest of which was the Russian Federation. These established independent governments and many agreed economic co-operation as members of the Commonwealth of Independent States (CIS).

KEY
⬚ Territory controlled by USSR from 1945
⬛ Russian Federation from 1991
⊙ Commonwealth of Independent States, 1991

The collapse of communism in Russia created economic instability and demands for independence in Chechnya.

YELTSIN IN POWER
With the collapse of communism, Boris Yeltsin introduced a **market economy**. As inflation soared, the country plunged into **recession**, suffering more material hardship than under communism or *Perestroika*. In 1993 the Congress of People's Deputies tried to impeach Yeltsin, but he survived in office until he resigned in 1999, a **deeply unpopular figure**.

BORIS YELTSIN

WAR IN CHECHNYA
After 1991, the Russian Federation faced demands for **independence** from its southern province of Chechnya. In 1994, Yeltsin sent troops into Grozny, the capital, to crush the rebels. The war lasted until 1996 with **serious casualties** on both sides. Unrest continued after Russia's withdrawl, and a second war broke out in 1999. The Russian military operation ended in 2009, but **terrorist activity** continues to affect the political stability of the North Caucasus region.

FIGHTING IN CHECHNYA

Raising the Iron Curtain

Following the defeat of Nazi Germany, tension between the superpowers split Europe into a communist "East" and a capitalist "West". Gorbachev's repeal of the "Brezhnev Doctrine" opened the floodgates for popular demands for reform leading to the dismantling of the Iron Curtain across Eastern Europe.

A new Hungary
Citizens wave pro-democracy banners as the Republic of Hungary is proclaimed on 23 October 1989 – the anniversary of the 1956 Hungarian Uprising against the Soviet Union.

It was the former British Prime Minister Winston Churchill (see pp.392–93) who likened the division of East and West in 1946 to "an iron curtain descended across the Continent". Inhabitants of Eastern Europe were prohibited from crossing into the West and most people knew little about the way of life on the other side. The first indications that the curtain might rise came in 1985 when Mikhail Gorbachev was appointed General Secretary of the Soviet Communist Party. Gorbachev proposed to set Russia on a new course (see pp.368–69), but his vision required a transformation in East–West relations.

BEFORE

As the Cold War intensified the Soviet Union acted to increase its control of political policy in the satellite Eastern Bloc states.

EUROPE DIVIDED
After World War II, **new national boundaries were created and countries divided** as the victorious Allies agreed the future shape of Europe. Stalin ensured that the Soviet Union incorporated eastern Poland and the Baltic States. **Germany and its capital, Berlin, were divided** into Eastern and Western sectors **《 348–49**.

COMMUNISM IN EASTERN EUROPE
By 1949 communist regimes had been established in Albania, Romania, Hungary, Bulgaria, Czechoslovakia, Poland, and East Germany. Although nominally independent, these nations were **dominated by the Soviet Union.** Collectively known as the **Eastern Bloc**, these Soviet satellite states were required to **mirror Soviet political structures** and to join the Soviet military alliance, the **Warsaw Pact**.

SOVIET IMPERIALISM
The Soviet Union did not tolerate rebellion or divergence from its party line. In 1953 Soviet troops suppressed riots and a general strike in East Germany and when, in 1956, discontent with the Hungarian communist government led to nationwide revolt, the uprising was crushed with massive military force. In 1968, during a period known as the **"Prague Spring"**, Czechoslovakia introduced liberalizing measures. Forces from the Warsaw Pact invaded and re-established communist party discipline.

In 1983, US President Ronald Reagan's decision to fund a space-based missile defence system, known as Star Wars, suggested a continuing escalation of the arms race (the competitive stockpiling of more and more powerful weapons), but in 1986 Gorbachev stunned the international community with a call to eliminate all nuclear weapons by the year 2000. This move led to the Intermediate-Range Nuclear Forces (INF) Treaty in 1987 – a first step towards dismantling the superpowers' massive nuclear arsenals.

Gorbachev's role in reversing the arms race won him worldwide acclaim. In 1988 he went on to push through his most radical reform of Soviet foreign policy: the abandonment of the "Brezhnev Doctrine", which prohibited Eastern Bloc (see BEFORE) and other satellite countries from reforming their political systems. This doctrine had led to military intervention in Czechoslovakia in 1968 and Afghanistan in 1979 (see pp.366–67).

Casting off communism
With the threat of Soviet interference removed, communist governments found it difficult to keep control.

Romanian revolution
People shelter behind army tanks in Bucharest during Eastern Europe's most violent transition to democracy. More than 1,000 Romanians were killed in clashes between demonstrators and security forces.

Turbulent times
A revolutionary holds a Romanian flag, the communist symbol defiantly torn from its centre, and looks down on Palace Square in Bucharest, days before the overthrow of Ceaușescu's regime in December 1989.

A wave of popular protest developed within the Eastern Bloc countries calling for an end to communist rule. By 1989 East Germany was faced with a rapidly depleting workforce as thousands of citizens decamped to West Germany via Hungary and Czechoslovakia. In November the government agreed to open its borders with West Germany and citizens poured across the border to greet their former countrymen. In 1990 politicans on both sides agreed to the reunification of Germany.

Solidarity wins out
In Poland, popular desire for change led to the emergence of the Solidarity Trade Union Movement in the early 1980s. The movement demanded workers rights and the freedom to practise Catholicism – banned

DECISIVE MOMENT

FALL OF THE BERLIN WALL

The Berlin Wall was the most famous physical manifestation of the Iron Curtain. The "anti-Fascist Protective Rampart" was built by the East German government in 1961 to prevent skilled workers crossing into West Berlin. For 30 years movement between West and East was highly restricted; it is claimed that as many as 200 people were shot by East German guards as they tried to escape to the West. In the 1970s and 1980s, graffiti artists covered the wall's west side with paintings and slogans protesting at the division of Berlin. On 9 November 1989, when the abandonment of border controls was announced, thousands of celebrating Berliners converged on the wall, and in the days that followed, began dismantling it with their own hands.

> " People have passed through a very dark tunnel at the end of which **there was a light...** "

VACLEV HAVEL, CZECH PRESIDENT, 1990

under the communist regime. The communist government attempted to repress Solidarity, but, by 1989, were forced to accept more open elections. Solidarity was elected as Poland's largest governing party by a huge majority, and its founder, Lech Walesa, served as president from 1990–95.

Democracy spreads

1989 also saw the "Velvet Revolution" in Czechoslovakia when mass protests secured the overthrow of the communist government. Alexander Dubček, hero of the Prague Spring (see BEFORE), was brought back from political isolation to serve in a new federal parliament. Hungary and Bulgaria also made peaceful transitions to democracy in the early 1990s. The Hungarian communist government tried offering reforms while maintaining a one-party system, but popular pressure led to the declaration of the Third Hungarian Republic and the promise of multi-party elections. Both Hungary and Bulgaria became parliamentary democracies in 1990.

Violent overthrow

Romania's communist leader, Nicolae Ceaușescu, ran a particularly repressive and ruthless regime. His overthrow in 1989 was the only instance of violent revolution in this period. Ceaușescu was arrested and subsequently shot by the army. His successor was Ion Iliescu, a former member of the communist regime and a dominant political figure in Romania since the revolution. He developed a brand of democratic socialism retaining some policies from the communist era.

The last Eastern Bloc state to adopt parliamentary democracy was Albania, in 1992. Charges of corruption and economic mismanagement followed, as well as problems with organized crime, but by 2014 the government's commitment to reform secured Candidate Country status for Albania from the European Union.

The transition to democracy triggered nationalist conflicts and economic hardship.

WAR IN YUGOSLAVIA

In 1992, waves of nationalist sentiment led to the violent dismemberment of the communist Federation of Yugoslavia **372–73**».

NATO IN EASTERN EUROPE

NATO 397» **has expanded** since the fall of communism to include most former Warsaw Pact countries. Consultations on international security have been held between NATO and non-member states, including Russia.

THE ORANGE REVOLUTION

Thousands **took to the streets of Kiev**, Ukraine, to protest at the disputed election in 2004. This forced a re-run that brought pro-EU leader Viktor Yushchenko to power, but five years later the Orange coalition had collapsed and Yushchenko was defeated in the 2009 presidential elections by Viktor Yanukovych, his opponent from 2004.

CAMPING OUT IN KIEV

A SECOND UKRAINIAN REVOLUTION

Ukraine has been the site of **persistent tension** since the Orange Revolution. Following his victory in 2009, Yanukovych's pro-Russian stance became unpopular and he was overthrown in a second popular rebellion in 2014. The crisis prompted Russia to **annex the Crimean peninsula** in the face of worldwide protest. The result has been a **civil war** in eastern Ukraine, fought between Russian separatists and the Ukrainian armed forces. The violence continued into 2015, amid growing fears that Russia seeks to reverse the independence settlement arrived at on the **dissolution of the USSR in 1991 «368–69**.

CZECH WRITER AND STATESMAN (1936–2011)

VACLAV HAVEL

Born into a wealthy and cultured family, Havel's "bourgeois" roots meant that he was not entitled to a university education. In the 1960s Havel's first plays were produced on stage, but his work became increasingly subversive and he was imprisoned for dissent. Havel was elected President of Czechoslovakia after the Velvet Revolution. Profoundly convinced that a politician should follow his individual conscience, his decisions as president were often controversial. Havel resigned in 1992, but was re-elected in 1993 and remained in office until 2003.

War in Yugoslavia

In 1991, Yugoslavia was torn apart by a dramatic and violent civil war, which ended with its break up. The world witnessed some of the worst atrocities committed since World War II, NATO faced its gravest challenge concerning a sovereign nation, and Bosnia was transformed into a killing field.

« BEFORE

Yugoslavia did not exist until after the end of World War I. Unification came about as Serbs called for a "land of the south slavs".

BIRTH OF A NATION
The Kingdom of Yugoslavia was formed out of the ashes of the **Austro–Hungarian Empire** in 1918 **« 296–97**. It included the formerly independent kingdoms of Serbia and Montenegro as well as the formerly Austro–Hungarian territories of Croatia, Slovenia, and Bosnia-Herzegovina.

JOSIP TITO'S DICTATORSHIP
Yugoslavia was invaded by Nazi Germany in World War II **« 392–405**. But the Germans faced **fierce resistance** from Yugoslav **communist partisans** – a resistance force under **Josip Tito**. Thanks to their ruthless tactics, and a flow of Russian, British, and American aid, Tito's partisans emerged at the end of the war as masters of the country.

In 1946, Tito reorganized the state into **six socialist republics**: Serbia, Croatia, Slovenia, Montenegro, Macedonia, and Bosnia-Herzegovina. There were also two semi-autonomous regions within Serbia: Kosovo and Vojvodina. Until his death in 1980, Tito ruled Yugoslavia as a **one-party dictatorship.**

JOSIP TITO

DISINTEGRATION OF YUGOSLAVIA
For the rest of the 1980s, Yugoslavia was ruled by a committee composed of the presidents of the six republics and two regions. The country slipped into **economic crisis**, and **national and ethnic rivalries** between the republics intensified.

By the end of the 1980s, Communism was in a state of collapse across Europe **« 370–71**. In 1990 the republics held multi-party elections, which further inflamed the ethnic tensions.

The collapse of communism in Europe in the 1980s encouraged the growth of nationalism in all the Yugoslav republics (see BEFORE). In 1990, in the first multi-party elections held in Yugoslavia after the end of the communist era, both Slovenia and Croatia elected nationalist governments and national groups demanded independence throughout Yugoslavia. In Serbia, however, Slobodan Milosevic opposed these calls. As president of the largest of the Yugoslav republics, Milosevic was determined to maintain the unity of greater Yugoslavia, with Serbia as the dominant power.

RATNI ZLOCINAC WAR CRIMINAL

For and against
A Bosnian poster calls the Bosnian Serb leader Karadzic a war criminal (left), but a protester demands Serbian leader Milosevic's release from jail, in 2001 (above).

Initial conflicts
Serbia's political posturing soon turned into violence. In 1989, Milosevic began a crackdown on the politically assertive Albanian Muslim majority in Kosovo, a semi-independent region in southern Serbia. In 1991, when the republic of Slovenia declared its independence from Yugoslavia, the Serb-dominated Yugoslav army intervened to prevent it seceding. In this instance the Yugoslav army was badly prepared and had to withdraw, but when the Croatian republic also claimed independence, the Yugoslav army under Milosevic launched a full-scale offensive. The city of Vukovar in eastern Croatia was destroyed, and Serbs began mass executions of Croat men. International response was limited. The US officially recognized Slovenia and Croatia's independence, but did not intervene in the conflict. In late 1992, the United Nations (see right) brokered a ceasefire between the Serbs and the Croats.

War in Bosnia
Bosnia was the most ethnically diverse of the six Yugoslav republics, with 43 per cent of the population Bosnian Muslim, 31 per cent Serbian, and 17 per cent Croatian. This ethnic mix proved extremely divisive: Bosnian Muslims and Croats favoured independence, but Bosnian Serbs were keen to remain as a part of the wider Yugoslavia. In 1992, following a referendum that was boycotted by the Bosnian Serbs, Bosnia declared itself independent from Yugoslavia.

Milosevic's Serbian forces responded by attacking the non-Serb population of Bosnia, and Bosnian Serbs laid siege to the capital Sarajevo. Many Bosnian Muslims were imprisoned in harsh Serb-run prison camps and Muslim women raped. The international media began to use the term "ethnic cleansing" to describe the systematic expulsion and killing of ethnic and religious groups as practised by the Serbs in Bosnia.

The siege of Sarajevo
Under siege from Bosnian Serbs, the mainly Bosnian Muslim civilians of Sarajevo struggled for survival. Water, medicine, and food were in short supply. The threat from snipers was constant and venturing into the streets perilous. A ceasefire was declared in late 1995, although the seige was not officially lifted until February 1996.

> **"Our time... has shown us that man's capacity for evil knows no limits."**
> KOFI ANNAN, UNITED NATIONS SECRETARY GENERAL, 1997

DEMISE OF YUGOSLAVIA
From the initial calls for independence in 1991 to the peace accord in 1995 Yugoslavia was scene of many bloody battles and human rights violations.

January 1992 Macedonia declares independence.

April 1992 Bosnia and **Herzegovina** declare independence.

August 1993 Shocking **photographs** emerge of emaciated Muslims held in Bosnian Serb **prison camps**.

April–May 1993 UN Security Council declares six "**Safe Areas**" for Bosnian Muslims.

February 1994 Mortar explodes in a Sarajevo market; 68 killed and nearly 200 wounded, prompting international calls for military intervention against Serbs.

December 1995 Bosnia, Serbia, and Croatia sign the **Dayton Peace Accord** to end the war in Bosnia.

August–September 1995 US leads **NATO bombing campaign** in response to the horrors of Srebrenica, targeting Serbian military positions.

1991

June 1991 Slovenia and **Croatia** declare **independence** from Yugoslavia.

July 1991 Milosevic's **Serbian forces invade Croatia**; the city of Vukovar is bombarded and reduced to rubble.

1992

April 1992 Open warfare begins as Bosnian Serbs commence four year long **siege of Sarajevo**.

1993

1993–1995 Lack of military intervention by international community allows Serbs in Bosnia to commit **genocide** against Bosnian Muslims.

1994

February 1994 NATO jets **shoot down four Serb aircraft** for violating UN no-fly zone.

1995

July 1995 Serbs under command of General Ratko Mladic kill 8,000 men and boys in **Srebrenica** in a policy of "ethnic cleansing".

July 1995 Radovan Karadzic and Ratko Mladic are **indicted for war crimes.**

The 1995 Dayton Peace Accord provided only a brief respite from troubles in the area.

AFTERMATH

The Dayton Peace Accord ruled that Bosnia would be **split** into the **Bosnian Serb Republic** and the **Muslim–Croat Federation**. Radovan Karadzic and Ratko Mladic were both indicted for **war crimes**. Karadzic was captured in 2008 to face trial at The Hague, but Mladic remains at large.

KOSOVO

Hundreds of people were injured in ethnic violence in Kosovo following the **Kosovo War** (1996–99). A nervous peace now exists in the region.

WAR CRIMES

Slobodan Milosevic lost the Serbian presidential election in 2000. He refused to accept the result, but was **forced out of office** by strikes and massive protests. He was handed over to a **UN war crimes tribunal** in The Hague, in the Netherlands, and put on trial for **crimes against humanity and genocide**. He spent five years in prison and died of a heart attack shortly before the trial was concluded.

SERBIA-MONTENEGRO

In February 2003, what remained of Yugoslavia was replaced with by loose federation called **Serbia and Montenegro**. On 3 June 2006 Montenegro formally declared its independence.

IDEAS

UNITED NATIONS

The name "United Nations" was first used in World War II when 26 nations pledged to continue fighting against the Axis Powers: Germany, Italy, and latterly Japan. Based in New York, the United Nations officially came into existence on 24 October 1945, when its charter was ratified by China, France, the Soviet Union, the UK, and the US. The charter gives the UN Security Council the power to take collective action in maintaining international peace and security. Although soldiers deployed by the UN share a uniform, they remain members of their respective armed forces. In July 1998 in Rome, the 120 Member States of the UN adopted a treaty to establish a permanent international criminal court.

Although the international community imposed economic sanctions on Serbia, UN troops in Bosnia were prohibited from using military force. Throughout 1993, confident that the UN would not take military action, Serbs continued to commit atrocities. Over a million people were driven from their homes by Serb forces under Radovan Karadzic, president of the Bosnian Serb Republic.

UN intervention

In 1994, a marketplace in Sarajevo was struck by a Serb mortar shell, killing 68 people. Scenes of the carnage were relayed around the globe, intensifying calls for intervention. The US issued an ultimatum through the North Atlantic Treaty Organization (NATO) demanding that the Serbs withdraw their arms from Sarajevo. The Serbs complied and a NATO-imposed ceasefire was declared.

Diplomatic efforts, however, did not stop Serbs from attacking Muslim towns in Bosnia, many of which had been declared "Safe Havens" by the UN. In

Kosovo
NATO peacekeeping troops clamber through an abandoned house in Kosovo. Forces were sent in following the 1999 war between the Serbian government and Kosovan Albanians fighting for independence from Serbia.

one "Safe Haven" at Srebrenica, UN peacekeeping forces watched helplessly as Serbs under General Ratko Mladic slaughtered an estimated 8,000 men and boys – the worst mass murder in Europe since the end of World War II. Serb forces also took hundreds of UN troops hostage and used them as human shields, chained to military targets.

In August 1995, NATO war planes began a fierce air campaign against Serb troops throughout Bosnia, and Slobodan

Milosevic, the Serb leader, finally agreed to peace talks. Three weeks later the Dayton Peace Accord was declared.

This was not the end of the wars in Yugoslavia, however. Fighting between ethnic Albanian minorities and the Serbian and Macedonian governments carried on. In Kosovo, this led to a new NATO bombing campaign in 1999. Eventually, Serb forces withdrew from Kosovo and in 2006 the province formally declared its independence.

« **BEFORE**

World War II left millions in Europe experiencing renewed hardship as governments faced the task of rebuilding their shattered nations. From 1947, US financial aid helped economic recovery.

POST-WAR REPARATIONS

In the aftermath of World War II, European governments **struggled to provide basic necessities** for their populations. Initially Allied nations demanded reparation (compensation) payments from Germany, in the form of coal and other natural resources. German machinery plants and factories were dismantled and transported to Britain, France, and the Soviet Union. France wanted to ensure that Germany could never re-arm again and took administrative control of key industrial regions. Germany faced two years of widespread hunger.

REBUILDING DRESDEN

THE MARSHALL PLAN

In 1947, US Secretary of State, **General George Marshall** introduced a plan to address **"the dislocation of the entire fabric of the European economy"** by proposing massive, long-term financial aid. Concerned that Communist revolutions in Eastern Europe would soon spread to West Germany and beyond, the ban on German industrial reconstruction was partially withdrawn. Over the next five years, the US poured billions of dollars into rebuilding Western Europe.

GEORGE MARSHALL

Symbol of unity
Twelve gold stars on the blue background of the European flag represent Europe as a whole and the equality of all nations within the union.

United Europe

After two devastating global conflicts, Europe had experienced more suffering than it could bear. In the decades following 1945, Europeans became inspired by a new vision of a united continent, where combined economic and political purpose would make wars between their nations unthinkable.

From 1945, Europeans began to demand reform in domestic government policies; welfare provision, such as free healthcare – an accepted ideal in Sweden – became a key feature of legislative changes across much of the continent. Widespread calls for a different approach to foreign relations led to some truly radical changes in political thinking, particularly in Germany and France. Konrad Adenauer, the chancellor of West Germany, skillfully pursued policies of reconciliation with Germany's European neighbours. In 1950, he sanctioned French political strategist Jean Monnet's proposal to integrate the French and German coal and steel industries, ensuring that neither country could re-arm without the support of the other. Monnet's strategy, known as the "Schuman Plan" led to the founding of the European Coal and Steel Community (ECSC) in 1951, which pooled the coal and steel resources of France, Germany, Italy, Belgium, Luxembourg, and the Netherlands. Economic co-operation between these six nations was extended in 1957 with the formation of the European Economic Community (EEC), or Common Market. The EEC allowed free movement of goods, services, and labour between member states and developed mutually beneficial joint agricultural, welfare, and foreign trade policies.

Britain and the EEC

Britain rejected the opportunity of becoming an EEC founder member. However, the economic growth of the six nations soon outstripped that of the UK and, in 1961, Prime Minister Harold Macmillan began negotiations to join. Throughout the 1960s, Britain and the EEC argued the terms of British membership. Britain finally joined in 1973 when the OAPEC oil crisis (see pp.362–63), had precipitated a period of stagflation – a combination of spiralling inflation, a slowdown in productivity, and rising unemployment. By the end of the decade the newly elected British Prime Minister, Margaret Thatcher, was calling for reductions in EEC controls and a return to a free-market economy.

European Union

Continental Europe took a different view, strengthening their economic co-operation. In 1986, the "Single European Act", created by French President François Mitterrand and the German Chancellor Helmut Kohl, established a single European market. In 1992, the Maastricht Treaty renamed the EEC the European Union (EU) and increased its powers. By 2014 an expanded EU had 28 member states, representing 506 million people with a combined GDP of US$18.4 trillion. The EU has also built on policies of reconciliation and nations have worked together to achieve unprecedented peace and unity in Europe.

European Union
German Chancellor Helmut Kohl and French President Francois Mitterand after French approval of the Maastricht Treaty in September 1992 moved both men closer to achieving their vision of a united Europe.

VOTING IN THE COUNCIL OF THE EU

Government ministers from each member state vote on legislation, budget, and economic policy. Decisions are agreed by a "qualified majority" vote comprising 55 per cent of eligible countries representing at least 65 per cent of the total EU population. The relative populations of the 28 member states in 2014 are listed below.

Austria	1.68%	Italy	12.05%
Belgium	2.21%	Latvia	0.39%
Bulgaria	1.43%	Lithuania	0.58%
Croatia	0.84%	Luxembourg	0.11%
Cyprus	0.17%	Malta	0.08%
Czech Rep.	2.05%	Netherlands	3.37%
Denmark	1.11%	Poland	7.49%
Estonia	0.26%	Portugal	2.06%
Finland	1.07%	Romania	3.93%
France	13.02%	Slovakia	1.06%
Germany	15.91%	Slovenia	0.41%
Greece	2.17%	Spain	9.17%
Hungary	1.95%	Sweden	1.90%
Ireland	0.91%	UK	12.63%

> "We **never want to wage war again** against each other… That is the most important reason for a **United Europe**."
>
> FORMER GERMAN CHANCELLOR HELMUT KOHL, 1 MAY 2004

BRITISH PRIME MINISTER (1925–2013)

MARGARET THATCHER

Margaret Thatcher served as Prime Minister of Britain from 1979–90. Her administration followed a disastrous period of recession in Britain and Thatcher was elected on the promise of tough measures to improve economic performance. Her attitude to the European Union was famously confrontational, but she signed up for the Single European Act (see above), which formally established the single European market and closer European political co-operation. Always a controversial figure, Thatcher once declared: "There is no such thing as society". She is remembered by many for bringing radical social and economic change to Britain, but many disliked her for her role in selling off state assets and weakening trade unions.

KEY
- EEC members, January 1981
- Joined January 1986
- Admitted October 1990
- Joined January 1995
- Joined May 2004
- Joined January 2007
- Joined July 2013
- Other countries applying for membership

Germany
- **Joined** 18 April 1951
- **Key industry** Car manufacture

Sweden
- **Joined** 1 January 1995
- **Key industry** Forestry

EU governments can be torn between the needs of the union and national interests.

MIGRATION AND RACE RELATIONS
EU membership allows workers to move freely across the borders of most member states. This has led to a large influx of migrant workers from poorer EU states into richer ones, **creating racial tensions** and demands for restrictions from **right-wing political elements** in Britain, France, Germany, and other member nations.

FINANCIAL UNION
Many countries joined **the Euro** (the single currency) in 2002, but some EU states have chosen to maintain their own currencies, partly to protect their own trade interests outside Europe, but also as a symbol of **national sovereignty**.

EUROS

Great Britain
- **Joined** 1 January 1973
- **Key industry** Finance

Hungary
- **Joined** 1 May 2004 (festivities above)
- **Key industry** Transport equipment

ICELAND

Faeroe Islands

IRELAND

UNITED KINGDOM

NETHERLANDS

DENMARK

NORWAY

SWEDEN

FINLAND

ESTONIA

LATVIA

LITHUANIA

RUSSIAN FEDERATION

RUSSIAN FEDERATION

BELARUS

POLAND

BELGIUM

GERMANY

LUXEMBOURG

LIECHTENSTEIN

CZECH REPUBLIC

SLOVAKIA

UKRAINE

Bay of Biscay

FRANCE

SWITZERLAND

AUSTRIA

HUNGARY

MOLDOVA

SLOVENIA

CROATIA

ROMANIA

ANDORRA

SAN MARINO

BOSNIA AND HERZEGOVINA

SERBIA

MONACO

PORTUGAL

SPAIN

Corsica

ITALY

MONT.

KOSOVO (disputed)

BULGARIA

Black Sea

GEORGIA

ARMENIA

Balearic Islands

Sardinia

ALBANIA

MACEDONIA

GIBRALTAR

Sicily

GREECE

TURKEY

MALTA

Crete

CYPRUS

IRAQ

SYRIA

0   500 km
0   500 miles

N

Countries of the EU
The European Union has continued to expand since its origins in 1945. This map shows states that have joined since 1981. Supported by the umbrella of economic unity, newer member states with developing economies hope to emulate the economic growth of the established nations. European industry is successful in areas from agriculture and tourism to finance and fashion.

Portugal
- **Joined** 1 January 1986
- **Key industry** Cork

Spain
- **Joined** 1 January 1986
- **Key industry** Tourism

France
- **Joined** 18 April 1951
- **Key industry** Agriculture

Italy
- **Joined** 18 April 1951
- **Key industry** Fashion

APARTHEID PASS LAWS

Racial segregation in South Africa dates back to 1797, when the British in Cape Colony used internal passports to restrict the native population. From 1952–1986 black South Africans over 16 were forced to carry "pass books" which not only included personal details such as fingerprints, but also notes about their conduct from their (white) employer.

> "Never, never and **never again** shall it be that this beautiful land will again experience **the oppression of one by another…**"
>
> NELSON MANDELA, INAUGURAL ADDRESS, 9 MAY 1994

r Hendrik Verwoerd, Prime Minister of South Africa between 1958–66, created a system of apartheid (see right), which embodied his "white supremacist" belief that not all races were equal. His views echoed Adolf Hitler's philosophy of the Aryan master race (see pp.322–23). The extreme inequalities created in South African society under apartheid raised voices of protest not only among Blacks, "Coloureds", and sections of South Africa's white population, but also internationally.

The struggle

In 1960, 69 people died and 180 were injured when police turned their guns on a non-violent demonstration organized by the anti-apartheid group, the Pan Africanist Congress (PAC). This massacre in the township of Sharpeville triggered a shift to more militant tactics among activists. In 1961, Nelson Mandela became leader of the military wing of the African National Congress (ANC) political party, beginning a campaign of sabotage targeting government installations. Mandela and other members of the ANC were arrested in 1962 and subsequently sentenced to life imprisonment. At his trial Mandela spoke of freedom, democracy, and equality for all South Africans. His long imprisonment became a subject of growing international condemnation.

The "Homeland System", introduced in the 1960s, aimed to complete the implementation of apartheid by creating independent homelands where Blacks were forced to live. These areas were impoverished rural areas with no real capacity to function as separate states. The relocation of Blacks to the homelands

13 PER CENT of the country was divided into 10 homelands.

80 PER CENT of the population lived in these homelands.

meant that they were no longer South African and worked in the country as foreign migrants without citizen's rights.

Steve Biko

This 1977 cover of *Drum*, a South African magazine for black issues and culture, features anti-apartheid activist Steve Biko. Biko died as a result of beatings sustained in police custody in 1977.

Apartheid and Beyond

Apartheid was a brutal system that imposed the will of a minority on the majority of the South African population. When it ended in the 1990s, there followed an extraordinary attempt to come to terms with the past, as South Africans of all races co-operated in a process known as "Truth and Reconciliation".

« BEFORE

South Africa's ruling powers maintained a divided population for much of 20th century.

THE PRE-APARTHEID ERA

Between 1910–1948 the South African Government pursued measures to deprive Blacks and "Coloureds" (those of mixed racial origins) of the right to vote or to own land. Acts such as the **Native Urban Areas Act** of 1923 resulted in "surplus" Blacks being removed from cities, creating many "Whites-only" areas.

THE NATIONAL PARTY

In 1948 the uncompromisingly **racist National Party** rose to power in South Africa and adopted a policy of "apartheid"

(see above), a legal system that completely segregated the political, social, and cultural lives of white and black South Africans.

APARTHEID LAW

Early apartheid measures included "blood laws"; such as the Immorality Act and Population Registration Act (1950), which banned intermarriage and sexual relations between races. Public transport and amenities were divided into **separate areas for Whites and Blacks** and segregation of the education system and employment ensured that Blacks had no prospects other than menial low-paid work.

WHITES COLOUREDS
BLANKES KLEURLINGE

OFFICIAL SEGREGATION

APARTHEID A policy of segregation and discrimination against the non-white population of South Africa. The term is from the Afrikaans for "separateness".

As the 1970s and 1980s progressed violence escalated, including violence between rival Black factions such as the ANC and the Inkatha Freedom Party. All dissent was suppressed by a police force and military who habitually committed atrocities, including torture. In 1986 the international community imposed economic sanctions on South Africa in an attempt to force an end to apartheid but, even with the majority of Whites now opposed to the system, the government still failed to respond with significant reform.

A new beginning

It took a new administration to open the way for change. President FW De Klerk was elected in 1989 and lifted bans on the ANC and other opposition groups. On 11 February 1990, Nelson Mandela was released. Mandela and De Klerk achieved the transition of South Africa to democratic majority rule under difficult circumstances. They faced different views from tribal and political factions within the black community and opposition to change from some Whites. Their solution was

to adopt a unified approach and in 1994 Nelson Mandela was elected President of South Africa, becoming head of the Government of National Unity in which minority parties, including vice-president De Klerk's National Party, were represented.

The new government recognized that if unity was to be achieved between its divided communities it must take action. The anti-apartheid campaigner Archbishop Desmond Tutu was appointed head of the Truth and Reconciliation Commission (TRC), which was an historic attempt to address the violence and human rights abuses of the apartheid era. Over a three year period the commission heard the testimonies of both the victims and the perpetrators of crimes. Although never intended as an instrument of punishment, the TRC

Act of defiance
Archbishop Desmond Tutu addresses a gathering of the Defiance Campaign against Unjust Laws in Cape Town, in 1988. Many "defiers" were imprisoned for peaceful protest.

ANC logo
On the flag, black represents those who fought for freedom; green, the land reclaimed from oppressors; and gold, South Africa's natural wealth. The shield and spear represent the early years of struggle, and the wheel is a symbol of unity.

bore witness to the suffering of victims and could grant perpetrators amnesty from possible prosecution. In 1998 the TRC published its findings. Atrocities committed by all sections of society were condemned, including the actions of the black vigilante group Mandela United Football Club, led by Nelson Mandela's former wife, Winnie.

The extraordinary ambition of the TRC was to heal the wounds of a brutal past by acknowledging their truth. South African willingness to engage in this process won the nation worldwide respect. In his response to the commission's findings, Nelson Mandela called on people to "celebrate and strengthen what we have done as a nation as we leave our terrible past behind us forever."

The apartheid system has disappeared, but its effects are still felt in South Africa.

LEGACIES IN SOUTH AFRICA
The majority of the poor are black and the bulk of property remains in white ownership. The government led by **Thabo Mbeki** (1999–2008) introduced various measures to create greater equality.

THABO MBEKI

ROLE IN AFRICA
South Africa's foreign policy now aims to **promote the economic, political, and cultural regeneration of Africa**, through the New Partnership for African Development (NEPAD). South Africa has also played an active role in seeking an end to crises in Burundi and the Democratic Republic of Congo.

AIDS
One of the major challenges facing South Africa is an **HIV/AIDS epidemic 388–89 ≫**. In 2011, around 17 per cent of the South African population were believed to be living with HIV.

AIDS AWARENESS RIBBON

Freedom day
On 27 April 1994, millions of South Africans queued to exercise their newly won right to vote in the first free election held after apartheid. A government of National Unity was elected.

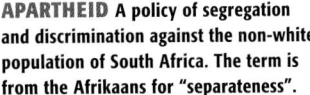

CIVIL RIGHTS LEADER Born 1918 Died 2013

Nelson Mandela

"Let there be **justice for all**… Let **freedom** reign!"

NELSON MANDELA, 10 MAY 1994

Nelson Mandela was born in a remote village in Eastern Cape, South Africa. He was a member of the Madiba clan, who were the ruling family of the Xhosa-speaking Thembu people. A bright boy, he took advantage of the educational opportunities open to Blacks in

mass movement against apartheid (see pp.376–77), the extreme form of racial oppression introduced by the South African government in 1948. From 1952 onwards, Mandela was subjected to a series of legal restrictions and arrests as confrontation between the ANC and the authorities intensified. Mandela was always absolute in his demand for full equal rights for Black Africans, but flexible on the means to achieve this. Like many others in the

Release Nelson Mandela
and all political prisoners of South Africa and Namibia!

Anti-Apartheid Movement 13 Mandela St London NW1 0DW 01-387 7966

The Free Nelson Mandela Campaign
Initiated by Oliver Tambo in 1980, the campaign acquired an international following and made Mandela a household name.

South Africa. He studied at the University of Fort Hare at Eastern Cape, but was expelled in 1940 for participating in a student protest. He then left for Johannesburg and settled in Alexandra, where he became involved in politics along with Walter Sisulu, an activist with the African National Congress (ANC). His other key comrade was Oliver Tambo, whom he met at the university.

Mandela and the ANC

The ANC had long been campaigning against the denial of Black rights, but in the mid-1940s it was an ineffective organization. It was Mandela and his comrades who turned the ANC into a

President Mandela
As South Africa's first black president, Mandela oversaw its transition from a white racist state to a multiracial democracy. His colourful Madiba shirts became a symbol of the "Rainbow Nation".

LONG WALK to FREEDOM

Life story
Mandela's memoir written while he was a prisoner at Robben Island continues to inspire millions today. The original draft of the book was painstakingly hidden from the prison authorities in tin containers that were buried in a vegetable patch.

Mandela's march to freedom
The release of Mandela in February 1990 was a turning point in South African history. He left the prison hand in hand with his wife Winnie, beaming and punching the air in a victory salute.

TIMELINE

- **18 July 1918** Born in the village of Mveso, South Africa; given the birth name Rolihlahla.

- **c.1925** Attends a Methodist mission school, where he is given the name Nelson.

- **1936–1940** Pursues European-style education until expelled from the University of Fort Hare.

- **1941** Moves to Johannesburg; meets African National Congress (ANC) activist Walter Sisulu.

- **1944** Becomes a founder-member of the ANC Youth League; marries Evelyn Mase.

- **1952** Given a suspended prison sentence for his part in the Defiance Campaign against apartheid.

- **1953** Opens the first black law firm in South Africa with comrade Oliver Tambo.

- **1956** Arrested with ANC leaders and charged with treason; the trial lasts until a not-guilty verdict is passed in 1961.

- **1958** Divorces his first wife, and marries Winnie Madikizela.

- **1960** Imprisoned for five months during the State of Emergency following the Sharpeville Massacre of black protestors.

- **1961** Helps found Umkhonto We Sizwe (Spear of the Nation), as an armed wing of the banned ANC.

- **1962** Sentenced to five years in prison.

- **1963** Returns to court as one of the accused in the Rivonia Trial, charged with sabotage.

- **1964** On 20 April, Mandela makes famous courtroom speech before being sentenced to life imprisonment on 12 June.

- **1964–82** Imprisoned at Robben Island.

- **1980** UN Security Council calls for his release after worldwide Free Mandela campaign.

- **1990** Released unconditionally, he begins seeking a negotiated path to majority rule.

- **1992** Separates from Winnie Mandela.

- **1993** Awarded the Nobel Peace Prize jointly with South African President FW De Klerk.

- **1994** Participates in South Africa's first fully democratic elections and is elected president by the National Assembly on 10 May.

1950s, he was influenced by communist ideology and regarded violence as an acceptable means to overthrow apartheid. The ruthless suppression of a peaceful protest, and the banning of the ANC in 1960 convinced Mandela to launch an armed campaign. He helped found Umkhonto we Sizwe (Spear of the Nation), the military wing of the ANC that carried out its first bombings in 1961. He travelled with false papers and visited independent African countries in search of finance, weapons, and military training. On his return, Mandela was arrested in August 1962. It was the subsequent Rivonia Trial that made him world famous. He was charged with planning a guerrilla war and acts of sabotage. Despite censorship, his impassioned speech about his political beliefs at this trial was publicized across the world to great acclaim.

Prisoner at Robben Island
Sentenced to life imprisonment with hard labour, Mandela spent 18 years at Robben Island. Later, in the 1980s he was transferred to other prisons where conditions were better. Although cut off from the increasingly active popular resistance to apartheid in South Africa, Mandela remained a symbolic figure of the struggle and an international campaign for his release kept his name in the headlines. In 1985, in an attempt to end riots, the apartheid government proposed releasing Mandela on condition that he renounce violence. Mandela refused to accept the terms. Still, the idea that he might in some way hold the key to resolving South Africa's political impasse had been launched, and Mandela engaged in sporadic talks with white politicians.

Democracy in South Africa
In 1989, FW De Klerk was elected President of South Africa and Mandela's unconditional release came the following February. He remained absolute in his demand for full democratic rights for Blacks and majority rule, but he was moderate, seeking a peaceful transition to a democratic South Africa. He also imposed himself upon the ANC, and his moral authority and goodwill convinced a majority of the Whites that he could be trusted. Separating from his wife Winnie Mandela due to the extreme violence she had incited during his imprisonment, Mandela used every means to persuade Black Africans to rely on the ballot box as the path to freedom.

Mandela's election as president after the ANC victory in 1994 was the summation of his life's work. In power, he worked for peace and reconciliation, establishing South Africa as a multiracial democracy. Although he was criticized for not doing enough to redress the balance of wealth between Blacks and Whites and for failing to stamp out corruption in the ANC, he was a benevolent and reassuring figurehead during a difficult period of transition. He stepped down as president after a single term, but continued for some years to intervene in international affairs and promote charitable causes. His last public appearance was at the football World Cup finals held in South Africa in 2010. Mandela died in December 2013 at the age of 95. After his death, more than 100,000 mourners filed past his body as it lay in state and his funeral was attended by leaders from across the globe.

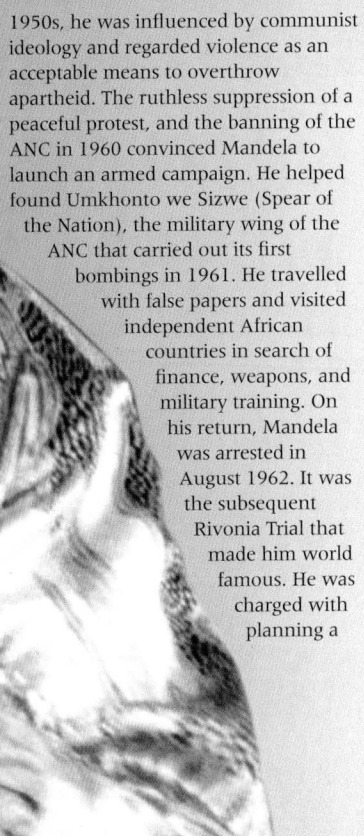

Prayers for Mandela
Hundreds of well-wishers took to the streets outside the hospital where Mandela was being treated in 2013. They lit candles and sang songs of prayer all night long for a leader who had earned the love and respect of his countrymen.

RUGBY WORLD CUP FINAL

- **1995** As a symbolic gesture of friendship, he presents the Rugby World Cup trophy to Afrikaner Springbok captain.

- **1996** Sets up the Truth and Reconciliation Commission to examine crimes of the apartheid era.

- **1998** Marries third wife, Graça Machel.

- **2013** Dies after prolonged lung infection at the age of 95.

Car manufacture
This is a highly automated production line at the Hyundai car plant in South Korea. Founded in 1947, the hugely successful Hyundai Group is a South Korean conglomerate, which has pioneered robotic engineering techniques in car production.

Tiger Economies

After World War II, Japan made economic reforms, establishing itself as one of the world's richest nations. Similar economic transformations occurred in South Korea, Taiwan, Hong Kong, and Singapore, who are known collectively as the "tiger economies" or "Asian tigers".

BEFORE

Japan's drive for growth led to the invasion of China and involvement in World War II.

THE MODERNIZATION OF JAPAN
Japan's **Meiji Restoration ‹‹ 286–87** triggered economic and social change in late 19th-century Japan. Increased trade with the West led to an era of rapid industrialization.

CONFLICT WITH CHINA
During the **Great Depression ‹‹ 306–07** loss of foreign capital and raw material imports badly affected Japanese industry. The acquisition of territories on the Asian mainland came to be seen as essential for economic survival. In 1931, Japan occupied the Chinese province of Manchuria. In 1937, a clash between Chinese and Japanese troops escalated into a renewed Sino–Japanese War.

JAPANESE TROOPS 1931

JAPAN IN WORLD WAR II
In 1941, Japan began extending its empire in East Asia and the Pacific. After bombing **Pearl Harbor ‹‹ 324–25** the Japanese invaded Indonesia, Burma, and other territories held by Europeans.

Worsening post-war relations between the Allies and the Soviet Union (see pp.328–29) combined with the rise of communist movements in territories including Vietnam, Korea, and Malaya (see pp.334–35), led many in the West to fear communist takeover in Asia and the Pacific. These fears increased when ongoing civil conflict in China ended with the founding of Mao Zedong's Communist People's Republic in 1949 (see pp.346–47). The new anxieties of the Cold War era led the US to provide economic support to non-communist governments in the region.

The rise of Japan

After World War II, Allied forces led by US General MacArthur occupied Japan for six years. MacArthur worked with Japanese Prime Minister Shigeru Yoshida to develop a blueprint for the future of Japan, drafting a new democratic constitution and reforming political and legal structures. Japan was banned from maintaining armed forces of its own; all energy was focused on rebuilding its economic potential. After the outbreak of the Korean War in 1950 (see pp.328–29), large US orders for Japanese-manufactured

Japanese Yen
The Yen is the currency of Japan. First introduced by the Meiji government in 1870, the modern Japanese Yen has a stable reputation and is widely chosen alongside the US dollar for foreign exchange reserves.

arms boosted the economy. Although the US occupation was a time of economic privation for many Japanese, much of the country's later prosperity was based on the access granted to the American market, an arrangement that continued after occupation ended in 1952. From the mid-1950s, Japan's economy entered a period of rapid growth. Having established the heavy industries – coal, steel, and energy production – the government began to support the development of shipbuilding and car manufacture. Through the 1960s industrial emphasis shifted to specialist high-tech production of cameras and videos; and electronic devices using new microchip technology, including computers. Global companies such as Sony, Toyota, and Nissan emerged.

In spite of setbacks during the 1973 Oil Crisis (see pp.362–63) and a period of recession in the 1990s, from 1978

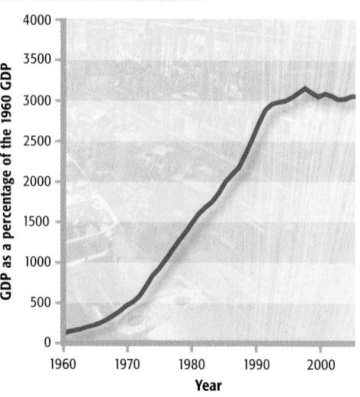

Japanese growth
This graph shows the astonishing growth in Japan's economy from 1960 to the mid-1990s by charting the gross domestic product (GDP) – the sum of the market value of all the goods produced within the country.

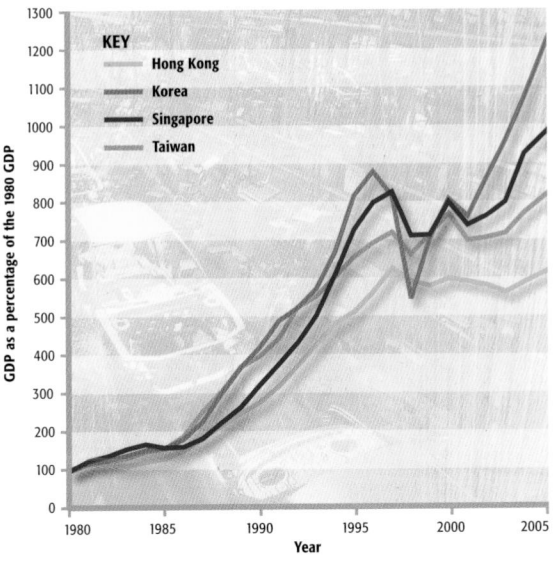

Rise of the early tiger economies

The first four tiger economies grew rapidly from the 1980s but suffered a drop after the Asian financial crisis of the late 1990s, as shown by the GDP growth charted left. All made a quick recovery, particularly Korea.

Within a few years the markets rallied and fears of a long recession faded.

The economic rise of South Korea began with an emphasis on light industry and shifted towards car manufacture and consumer electronics in the 1970s. The Asian financial crisis caused the collapse of South Korea's major car manufacturer KIA Motors, but assistance from the International Monetary Fund (IMF) and market-orientated reforms restored stability. In 2007, South Korea was ranked as the world's ninth largest economy, but it has since moved down into 14th place, and questions remain about the country's long-term prospects. An increasingly educated labour force is rising up against the regime's repressive labour laws. Commentators suggest that liberalizing reforms are needed to ensure continued growth.

In the 1950s, Taiwan, an island off the Chinese mainland, was a largely agricultural economy. From 1962, economic reforms encouraged industrial development, attracting foreign investment. Taiwan received support from the US, which was keen to bolster the regime against the threat of Communist China. Initially most of Taiwan's output was from industries such as textiles, but in the 1980s, focus shifted to high-tech products. Today Taiwan's economy dominates global computer production.

After gaining independence from Britain in 1965, Singapore's government adopted an export-orientated policy framework, to encourage foreign investment. The strategy resulted in growth of 8 per cent per annum between 1960–97. A skilled workforce and efficient infra-structure has attracted investment from over 7,000 multinational corporations, who account for over two-thirds of manufacturing output and direct export sales. Fields of production include electronics and pharmaceuticals.

Hong Kong was a British colony from 1842–1997. After 1950, the territory followed a similar pattern of industrialization, going on to become a market leader in toys and electronic equipment. Since 2005, the growing confidence of the Hong Kong stock exchange has been cementing its status as a financial hub in Southeast Asia.

By the late 20th century, the Four Tigers were nearing fully developed economic status. Investment in education had created skilled, educated

BULLET TRAIN

The Japanese *Shinkansen* or Bullet Train was one of the earliest high-speed trains. Services started in 1964, running at speeds of up to 210km/h (131mph). Operated by Japan Railways, the trains run between most major Japanese cities, achieving speeds of up to 300km/h (186mph). Current research is aimed at reducing the noise of the trains, which create a loud boom on entering tunnels.

until 2010 (when it was overtaken by China) Japan's economy ranked second only to that of the USA. This miraculous transformation was the result of efficient government control of finance. Industries were systematically targeted for development, government loans made available to fledgling companies, and competition from foreign imports was restricted. For many years post-war, economic growth was an absolute priority and expenditure in other areas, such as housing, was severely restricted. However, successive governments did prioritize education and Japan's skilled workforce have contributed to the success and technical excellence of Japanese products.

Asian tigers

Since the 1960s, South Korea, Taiwan, Singapore, and Hong Kong achieved economic growth of such speed that it earned them the nickname "tiger". The Asian tigers are among the only former European colonies to have closed their income gap with established industrialized nations. A range of measures, including the creation of government banks, subsidized credit for industry, and incentives for foreign investors, fostered export-driven markets, where the marriage of foreign technology with cheap labour produced goods at reduced cost. The tiger economies' dependence on exports makes them reliant on the behaviour of the economies they supply. In 1997, the Asian financial crisis occurred when foreign investors withdrew funds from Thailand. The crisis deepened when investors panicked, thinking that if one country's economy was failing then others must be affected, and rushed to dump Asian assets. Within months the crisis spread across the entire region.

Singapore harbour

Cranes and cargo ships line Singapore City's bustling industrial waterfront. In the background stand the towers of the city's business district.

workforces who required better wages and working conditions, and investors began to turn to other Asian countries – Thailand, Malaysia, and Indonesia – in search of continued profits. During the 1990s, strong export-dependent economies evolved in these nations, securing foreign investment. Thailand and Indonesia were badly affected by the 1997 financial crisis. Since then, both governments have pursued "dual track" economic measures, which prioritize the domestic development, as well as export-orientated production. At present, the new tigers all show rapid growth, and Malaysia seeks to emulate the original tigers by improving education and focusing the economy towards higher-technology production.

Towering success

A symbol of Malaysia's economic miracle, the Petronas Towers in Kuala Lumpur were designed by the architect Cesar Pelli and built in 1995–98. They are among the world's tallest buildings.

AFTER

The term "tiger" is adopted by other nations with rapid economic growth, but the impact of such growth on workers raises concerns.

LOW-WAGE WORKERS

Asian tiger governments have been accused of running their economies in the **sole interests of investors**, resulting in **low pay for workers**. A World Bank report noted that they were "less responsive than other developing economy governments" to having **a minimum wage**.

ASEAN

Founded in 1967 with five members, the **Association of South East Asian Nations** has grown to encompass almost all of Southeast Asia, increasingly adopting policies to produce a single market in the region. **Rapid economic growth**, particularly in Malaysia, Thailand, and Singapore, has allowed enormous strides in development.

scientific discovery has always pushed back the frontiers of knowledge and solved pressing human problems, but technological progress also raises serious ethical dilemmas – from the morality of genetic technology, to questions of regulation, such as censorship of the internet, or the ecological damage generated by industrialization. Scientific inventions have often generated changes undreamt of by their makers. Albert Einstein (see pp.338–39), the brilliant physicist who formulated the Theory of Relativity, saw his discovery used to create the atomic bomb. He later remarked, "It has become appallingly obvious

> "Almost everything that **distinguishes the modern world** from earlier centuries is attributable to **science.**"
>
> BERTRAND RUSSELL, BRITISH PHILOSOPHER, "A HISTORY OF WESTERN PHILOSOPHY", 1945

that our technology has exceeded our humanity."

Aerospace

Space travel is perhaps the greatest symbol of technological progress in the modern age. The race between the two opposing Cold War (see pp.328–29) superpowers, the US and the Soviet Union, for supremacy in space

gathered pace in the late 1950s and ended when Soviet astronaut Yuri Gagarin successfully orbited the Earth in 1961. The next goal was to put a man on the Moon. This was achieved in 1969 when the US Apollo 11 spacecraft landed on the Moon, and millions across the world watched astronauts Neil Armstrong and Buzz Aldrin step on to the lunar surface. In 1975, the superpowers adopted a policy of co-operation and simultaneously launched manned spacecraft into space, a mission known as the Apollo–Soyuz Test Project.

Volkswagen Beetle
"The Beetle" was first produced in Germany in 1938 as Adolf Hitler's affordable "people's car". Production of the classic VW Beetle peaked at 1.3 million in 1971 and ceased in 2003. It remains an icon of twentieth-century design.

NUCLEAR FISSION

Nuclear fission occurs when the nucleus of an atom splits into two or more smaller nuclei. It is used in the production of nuclear power and weapons. Scientists Otto Hahn and Fritz Strassman discovered the process during research carried out in 1938–39. In 1942, a team led by Enrico Fermi created the first controlled self-sustaining nuclear chain reaction. With World War II raging, governments funded scientists to develop an atomic bomb. In the US, physicist Robert Oppenheimer led the Manhattan Project, which built the bombs used on Japan (see p.327).

Uses for smart alloys are being investigated by the aircraft industry, seeking ways to improve aircraft manoeuvrability, and by the medical profession, for example by incorporating flexible traits into the metal plates and pins that are used to support broken limbs while they heal.

Progress in the understanding of natural polymers (compounds made up of simple repeating molecular units), led to the development of manmade polymers which are used in plastic-based materials such as Perspex, polythene, and many modern textile fabrics. Commercial production of Nylon, the first fibre to be made completely from petrochemicals (substances derived from petroleum), began in 1939. Nylon was the first of a new breed of manufactured

Modern Technology

Technological advances continue to transform daily life. Today we can understand the workings of the universe down to its tiniest particles and change the nature of living organisms. We live longer and travel further and faster than the most optimistic of inventors would have predicted in earlier centuries.

BEFORE

Scientific discoveries have at times caused controversy, but advances in radio, computing, and new materials in the 19th century made future breakthroughs possible.

BAKELITE TELEPHONE

SCIENCE AND ETHICS

Throughout history, the scientist's quest for understanding has led many into serious trouble. In 1633, the Catholic Inquisition tried **Galileo** << **208–09** for heresy for suggesting that the Earth moves around the Sun. **Charles Darwin's theories of evolution** << **270–71** challenged "creationist" views that God created the world, triggering a huge debate << **272–73**.

COMPUTERS

In 1801, **Joseph Jacquard** invented a power loom, which could base its weave on patterns read from punched wooden cards. **Charles Babbage** << **274** built on this concept in the 1830s, to create the **difference calculator,** which could store and calculate numbers. In 1890,

Herman Hollerith used punchcard techniques in the Hollerith Desk, a prototype computer.

SYNTHETIC MATERIALS

Many materials used in modern technology were invented in the 19th century – including parkesine – the first manmade plastic, in 1855, and cellulose triacetate – the earliest synthetic fibre – in 1869, a forerunner of rayon, nylon, and polyester. In 1907 Leo Baekeland created the first plastic made from synthetic materials and named it Bakelite.

TRANSATLANTIC RADIO

In 1901, **Guglielmo Marconi** << **274–75,** inventor of the radio-telegraph system, made the first Transatlantic radio transmission, across a distance of 3,400km (2,100 miles).

MARCONI

Subsequent collaborations have included the European Space Station, Mir, and the International Space Station, which draws on the scientific and technological resources of 16 nations.

New materials

Most modern manufactured items are made from materials specially developed to be durable, portable, and efficient. The production of so-called "smart materials" has had a big impact in recent times. Smart materials have the capacity to alter their properties when external conditions change. They include, smart alloys or "shape memory alloys", metals that "remember" their own geometry and can return to their original shape after being distorted.

First views of the moon
An American boy watches as the first televised pictures of the Moon's surface are beamed back to earth in March 1965. The Ranger 9 unmanned probe showed viewers unprecedented images of the lunar terrain.

fibres, which include polyester, Lycra, and Kevlar. In 1986, microfibres further revolutionized fabric technology, producing materials made from minute filaments that are as »

Apollo rocket
At 9:32 am on 16 July 1969 a plume of flame signals lift-off of the Apollo 11 Saturn V space vehicle. US astronauts Neil Armstrong, Michael Collins, and Buzz Aldrin leave the Kennedy Space Centre, heading for the Moon.

tough and resilient as other synthetics but much thinner and lighter. The lightness and durability of microfibres was first used in suits for astronauts, but is now found in sportswear. This trend for "high end" technology to filter down into everyday life is common. The polymer Teflon – discovered accidentally during a refrigeration experiment – is used to coat bullets, but also forms the surface of a non-stick frying pan.

Technology in everyday life

Breakthrough inventions of the 20th and early 21st centuries have entered everyday usage as a result of mass production techniques. The invention of household machines has led to an increase in leisure time in developed countries and the very concept of progress has become synonymous with the ready availability of new technology. The development of the microchip has

had a huge impact on the way we communicate since being pioneered by Jack Kilby and Robert Noyce in the 1950s (see p.409). Miniaturized technology combined with the advent of the internet has provided access to global instant communication.

> "The only way to discover the **limits of the possible** is to venture a little past them into the **impossible.**"
>
> ARTHUR C CLARKE, WRITER, 1962

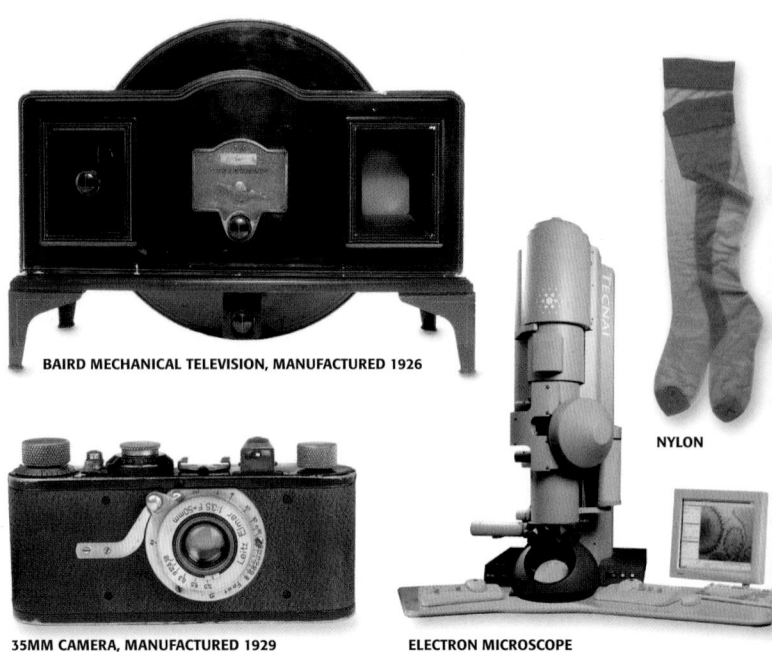

BAIRD MECHANICAL TELEVISION, MANUFACTURED 1926

35MM CAMERA, MANUFACTURED 1929

ELECTRON MICROSCOPE

NYLON

INVENTIONS

New technologies invented during the last 100 years have changed the world for ever.

1925 John Logie Baird creates the **first mechanical television**, successfully transmitting pictures in his London attic.

1930 Frank Whittle submits his plans for a turbo-jet aircraft engine, to the RAF.

1934 Percy Shaw invents **catseyes**, a safety device used in road construction.

1935 Wallace Carrothers and DuPont Labs invent **Nylon**; the first truly **manmade fibre**.

1945 The **atomic bomb** is invented by scientists working at the US Manhattan Project.

1948 The **vinyl LP** is introduced. Records used to be made from glass or shellac. Vinyl improved durability and sound quality.

1954 Chaplin, Fuller, and Parson invent the first **solar panels** using photovoltaic cells to convert the sun's energy into electrical energy.

1920

1920 The **electric food mixer** is produced by the Hobart Corporation providing a smaller version of industrial mixers for use in the home.

1930

1927 The first **photoflash bulb** is invented by Paul Vierkotter, allowing photographers to take pictures without natural light.

1931 Max Knott and Ernst Ruska invent the first **electron microscope**. It uses electrons to create a magnified image.

1934 Joseph Begun invents the first **tape recorder**, capable of storing and playing back sound.

1940

1940s Carbon fibre is developed in a British laboratory. It is light durable and extremely versatile. Modern applications include, engineering products, as well as motor sport, sailing, and cycling equipment.

1950

1953 The **portable transistor radio** is invented by Texas Instruments.

1959 Jack Kilby and Robert Noyce invent the **microchip**.

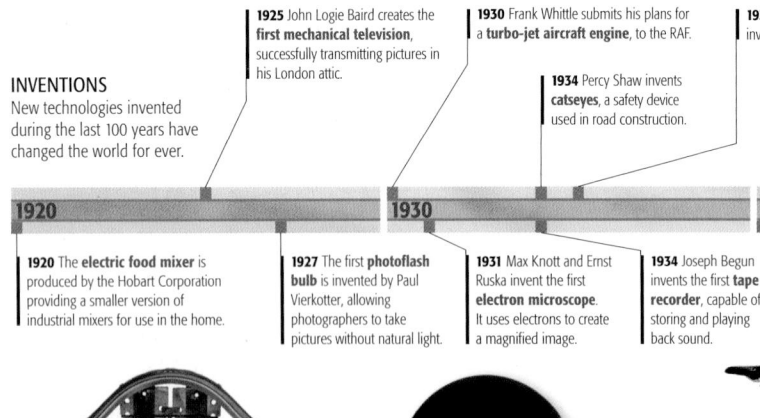

ELECTRIC TOASTER, MANUFACTURED 1920

VINYL RECORD

CATSEYES

CARBONFIBRE BIKE

ELECTRIC FOOD MIXER, MANUFACTURED 1950s

JET ENGINE

ENGINEER (1907–96)

FRANK WHITTLE

Frank Whittle joined the British Royal Air Force as an aircraft apprentice, at the age of 17. During his training he wrote a thesis proposing that piston aircraft engines be replaced by turbines. In 1936, Whittle set up the company Power Jets Ltd and developed these ideas, creating the "Gloster Whittle", the first jet engine aircraft to fly in the UK. He worked with engineering manufacturers, such as Rolls Royce, and then became a research professor at the US Naval Academy.

AUDIO TAPE PLAYER, MANUFACTURED 1950

HUBBLE SPACE TELESCOPE

Scientists continue to dream of pushing back the realms of possibility in the 21st century.

SPACE EXPLORATION

The **space elevator** is a proposed structure that would consist of a cable anchored to the Earth's surface and attached to a counterweight in space. Theoretically, vehicles could climb the cable and escape the planet's gravity without the use of rocket propulsion. Scientists are also pioneering the use of robots, such as the **Mars Exploration Rover**, to explore nearby planets.

MOVING MATTER

Scientists are also developing the process of **quantum tunnelling** in the hope of achieving matter transportation.

MARS EXPLORER

ADDING MACHINE, MANUFACTURED 1950s

PORTABLE TRANSISTOR RADIO

DVD

1969 Concorde flies for the first time. The commercial supersonic airliner commenced service in 1976 and set many speed records including the circumnavigation of the world in 31 hours, 27 minutes, and 49 seconds.

1977 The Commodore PET (personal electronic transactor) was one of the first home computers to be launched.

1983 First **mobile phones** go on sale. "Smartphones", like the BlackBerry and iPhone, later evolved, providing computerlike functions, including email access.

1990 Hubble Space Telescope is launched. It has confirmed theories about the birth of planets and produced images of galaxies at various stages of development.

1995 The **DVD** (digitally versatile disc) is used for data storage, including high-quality sound and moving images.

2001 Apple produce **the iPod**, a portable digital audio player. iPods have developed technical capability to incorporate video and mobile phone technology. Technology is further developed with Apple's iPhone in 2007 and the iPad in 2010.

2012 3D printers become available to a wider market; they can print almost anything, from prototype designs to medical parts.

1960	1970	1980	1990	2000	2010

1967 The first **handheld electronic calculator** provided features of earlier adding machines in a smaller and more portable form.

1980 Philips develops fluorescent energy-saving light bulbs. Low-Watt bulbs use up to 80 per cent less energy and last up to 10 times as long as traditional light bulbs.

1983 British inventor James Dyson builds a prototype **cyclone-action vacuum cleaner**, with no dust bag.

1991 Kodak produces the **Digital Camera System** having developed solid-state image sensors, which converted light into digital pictures, in the 1970s.

2001 First **AbioCor artificial heart** implant. The self-contained "organ" has no external wires or tubes: the internal battery is charged by transcutaneous energy transmission.

2003 Toyota launches a **hybrid electric car** in Japan.

COMPUTER MEMORY BOARD

COMMODORE PET PERSONAL COMPUTER

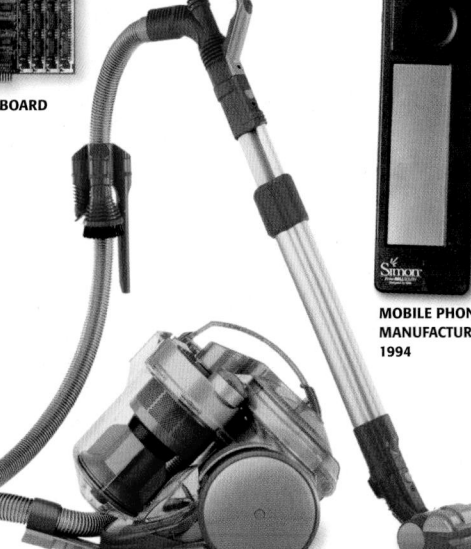

MOBILE PHONE, MANUFACTURED 1994

DYSON VACCUUM CLEANER

MakerBot Replicator 2

3D PRINTER

DIGITAL CAMERA, MANUFACTURED 1991

BRITISH AIRWAYS

CONCORDE

« BEFORE

Developments in new agricultural techniques – such as the introduction of farm machinery, pesticides, and fertilizers – revolutionized food production in the 19th and early 20th centuries.

THE ADVENT OF MECHANIZATION

By the middle of the 19th century steam engines were driving **farm machinery**. At the end of the 19th century the development of oil-powered **traction engines** led to a revolution in agricultural methods, allowing greater areas to be

TRACTOR STATION, 1930

farmed by fewer workers. In the Soviet Union, tractor stations rented machines to nearby **collectivized** farms – small peasant holdings that were joined together into vast co-operative farms under Stalin. The policy transformed agricultural production in the USSR « **218–19**.

FERTILIZERS AND PESTICIDES

Decline of the natural fertility of the soil was already a major concern in the mid-19th century « **290–91**. Both Europe and America had begun to depend on imports of **guano** (dried excrement of fish-eating birds) from South America. Guano improves crop yields by adding nitrogen and phosphorus to soil. The use of **pesticides** also increased during this period, with the discovery of pyrethrum oil and derris, both natural insecticides extracted from plants. Compounds of heavy metals, including copper and arsenic, were used to combat plant diseases.

Feeding the World

In the 1960s a "Green Revolution" in biotechnology boosted agricultural productivity. The efforts of agriculturalists and scientists resulted in improved fertilization and pest controls and the development of specially bred strains of high-yield, disease-resistant crops.

The founding of the United Nations' Food and Agriculture Organization (FAO) in 1945 signalled an international desire to create change in the postwar era through a sharing of knowledge and resources to improve crop performance and eliminate hunger. The FAO focused special attention on rural areas in developing nations as this is where the majority of the poor and hungry were, and still are, located.

New methods

In the 1940s the biochemist Norman Borlaug (see right) initiated an experimental programme to assist

America's breadbasket

Resembling a work of modern art, green crops cover what was once short grass prairie in Kansas, US. The crops are fed from underground water reserves and by circular sprinklers, which cause the round growth pattern.

poor Mexican farmers in increasing their wheat production. Borlaug concentrated on plant breeding. Over a 20-year period he developed a strain of high-yield dwarf wheat that was resistant to a variety of diseases and pests. Borlaug's wheat was cultivated in India and Pakistan with spectacular results. In 1960 the International Rice Research Institute was established in the Philippines to improve the production of rice, the staple diet of much of the world's population. The institute's work has helped rice farmers increase production by an average of 2.5 per cent each year since 1965. These transformations in agriculture became known as the Green Revolution. Research continues to develop a range of rice species or "cultivars" to suit the needs of different

> **INDIA AND PAKISTAN almost doubled their wheat production between 1965–70.**

regions including New Rice for Africa (NERICA) – a strain of rice suited to Africa's dry ecosystems.

In the 1960s the insecticide DDT was the first of a range of new organic chemical insecticides that were widely used for their capacity to control multiple species of pests with a single treatment. These chemicals were put to use in Third World countries. However, in 1962 the American biologist Rachel Carson catalogued the environmental impact of spraying DDT and said it may cause cancer. It was eventually banned worldwide. New methods, such as intensive irrigation, were introduced to maximize productivity on poor farming land.

However, the new agricultural methods have generated further problems. Pesticides, especially earlier,

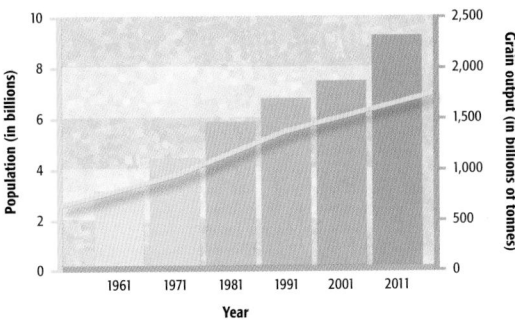

Rising demand
Despite fears that population growth would exceed our capacity to produce food, advances in farming methods have increased the productivity of the land. This graph charts world population against global grain output.

KEY
Population
Grain

Delivering aid
Drought-stricken Niger, in northwest Africa, faced widespread famine in 2005. Thousands of children died before foreign aid was received.

NORMAN BORLAUG

A key figure in the Green Revolution, Norman Borlaug was born into a farming family in Iowa, US. Borlaug studied forestry and microbiology before researching crop species and developing a new brand of high-yield wheat (see left). His goal was to feed the hungry people of the world. His ground-breaking work brought him many honours, including the Nobel Peace Prize in 1970.

cruder forms, killed not only the targeted pests but also other insects and organisms that previously acted as natural inhibitors of the pest population. Pests develop resistance to chemical treatments and the same is true of plant diseases. It is not uncommon for new plant varieties to become redundant in the space of three to four years, which is the time it takes for diseases and insects to adapt and destroy the crop. One serious effect of this problem is that the poorest farmers of the developing world are spending a large percentage of their income on new chemicals as they struggle to combat pest and disease resistance.

Food supply

The distribution of food aid to poorer countries came into practise to combat food shortages after World War II. The Indian famine of 1944 and China's great famine of 1959–61, where 30 million starved to death, triggered an international undertaking to establish secure and sustainable forms of food supply. Nations producing a food surplus pledged to maintain food supplies in the event of widespread crop failure. The US, the European Union (see pp.374–75), Canada, Japan, and Australia have

Rice research
Seedlings for "Golden Rice" a new rice species, modified to contain extra vitamin A, are grown in test tubes at an International Rice Research Institute laboratory.

been the biggest suppliers of food aid, but worldwide demand has often outstripped the ability to supply it.

Food production has matched the growth in worldwide population, but hunger and malnutrition remain a problem in some areas. This is especially the case in Africa where many people still live in fear of hunger and starvation, and an estimated 200 million people suffer from malnutrition. The governments of many African countries are dependent on food aid. In 2003 climate conditions led to crop failure and famine in southern Africa and in 2006 droughts created crises in Ethiopia, Kenya, and Somalia – stark evidence that the inequalities that the Green Revolution sought to erase persist.

Rising oil prices and a switch to growing biofuels led to big rises in basic food prices from 2007, provoking the "tortilla riots" in Mexico in 2007 and violent protests in many African countries in 2008.

While poorer regions are still dependent on one or two crops for survival, in the developed world an abundance and variety of food are available. Increased incomes have enabled an expanding middle class to adopt high-protein diets, and in the richest nations health risks associated with obesity are a growing problem. Many Western governments have felt compelled to introduce healthier eating initiatives to encourage the consumption of a balanced diet. Concerns have also been raised about the health risks created by chemical residues found in, or added to, produce. This has led to an increased demand for organic food, produced without the use of chemicals or artificial additives.

AFTER

Genetic modification is one of the newest methods of creating stronger crops.

GENETIC MODIFICATION
GMOs are organisms whose genetic material has been modified by adding extra material to generate new and useful **inherited traits**. Developed in the 1990s, the technique was applied to various crops, principally maize and soya beans, but also tomatoes, wheat, and many others, in the hope of **GM FRUIT** **creating crops with better pest resistance**, disease resistance, shelf life and taste. Concerns have arisen about the effects on **biodiversity** (the variety of species in a given ecosystem) that planting genetically-modified crops could have.

Food consumption
Although total food production has kept pace with the global rise in population (see above), the situation differs from country to country. Poorer nations have far less food available to their growing populations than more developed countries. This is reflected in the daily average calorific consumption (energy consumed from food) per person, as shown in this graph.

KEY
USA
Germany
Brazil
India
Vietnam
Somalia

« BEFORE

Scientific discoveries and improved sanitation in the 19th century laid the foundations for the medical revolution of the 20th.

SANITATION

In British cities c.1830, **infant mortality** was about 50 per cent – half of all children born died before 5 years of age. Most deaths were caused by water contaminated with swewage. In the second half of the 19th century, proper sewers were built and water was piped into cities. By 1914, infant mortality was less than 10 per cent.

1890S DISINFECTANT ADVERTISEMENT

HOSPITAL HYGIENE

In the 1840s, the Hungarian physician **Ignaz Philipp Semmelweis** noticed that cases of puerperal ("childbed") fever, which killed thousands of mothers after giving birth, were reduced if nurses and doctors washed their hands between handling corpses and treating patients. His discovery led to better hospital hygiene. Carbolic acid was used to sterilize surgical equipment and wounds from the 1860s.

BACTERIA AND DISEASE

In the 1870s and 1880s, the German physician Robert Koch isolated the different bacteria that cause tuberculosis, cholera, and anthrax, enabling more effective **vaccines « 257** to be developed.

VITAMINS

In the early 1900s, scientists investigating the link between **diet and health** identified key nutrients in food. In 1912, **Cashmir Funk** named them "vitamines"; "vita" meaning life, and "amine" from compounds isolated in his experiments.

BRITISH SCIENTIST (1881–1955)

ALEXANDER FLEMING

Born in Scotland, the pharmacologist and biologist Alexander Fleming made huge contributions to the fields of bacteriology, immunology, and chemotherapy. He is famous for isolating the antibiotic substance penicillin from the fungus *Penicillium notatum*. He shared the 1945 Nobel Prize for medicine with Ernst Chain and Howard Florey.

Protecting the troops
Sailors in the British Royal Navy receive inoculations against cholera before deployment overseas during World War I.

World Health

The past century has produced astonishing advances in health and medicine. Some infectious illnesses have been eradicated, but there are still many killer diseases at large, especially in the developing world.

In the early 20th century, Dr Sara Josephine Baker pioneered educating women in the slums of New York City in the basic hygiene and dietary care of their children. Baker's health education programme significantly reduced infant mortality rates, and by the 1950s most industrialized countries had adopted similar measures.

Health education, better sanitation, and rising living standards in industrialized countries resulted in steady, if unspectacular, improvements in public health. However, some developments were more dramatic. In 1928, Alexander Fleming (see left) found that a rare strain of mould inhibited the growth of bacteria. This discovery enabled him to develop penicillin, an infection-fighting "antibiotic" drug. Mass production of penicillin began in 1945. By the 1950s, antibiotics were providing effective treatments for many diseases, including syphilis, gangrene, and tuberculosis (TB).

In the late 20th century, vaccination programmes, funded by governments and the World Health Organization (WHO), further reduced mortality

Changing attitudes
A 1950s advert (left) shows Hollywood star and future US president Ronald Reagan promoting cigarettes. Two decades later, a French cancer charity (right) warns of the health risks of smoking to pregnant women and their babies.

rates. In 1980, the WHO announced the global elimination of smallpox. Polio is also close to being eradicated; in fact, the general trend for most infectious diseases is downward.

Furthermore, chemotherapy has made huge strides in the fight against cancer, and heart and organ transplants are now commonplace. Perhaps most amazingly, invitrofertilization (IVF) allows childless couples to have a family.

Rich and poor

Unfortunately, achievements in medicine and health care are not always passed on to the poor. The Diphtheria, Tetanus, Whooping cough (DTP) vaccine, available in the 1940s, all but eradicated these diseases in developed nations, but in Africa, India, and East Asia under 50 per cent of children are covered by DTP programmes. WHO statistics show the child mortality rate in the poorest countries to be 2.5 times higher than in developed nations.

The greatest killers in the developing world are water-borne illnesses such as typhoid, cholera, dysentery, and even diarrhoea. Nearly 40,000 people die each day from drinking water contaminated by sewage. Providing sanitation and clean drinking water is a major challenge for the governments of developing countries. Respiratory diseases such as bronchitis, emphysema, pneumonia, and lung cancer also take a heavy toll. They are often linked to the inhalation of smoke from indoor cooking fires. A simple solution is to provide a smoke hood and a chimney, rather than an open fire, but the first priority is education. Public health efforts in rich countries are increasingly focused on excessive consumption of food, alcohol, and tobacco. Incidence of

Global trends in HIV infection
Around 35 million people are infected with the HIV virus that causes AIDS; nearly two-thirds of them live in sub-Saharan Africa. In 2013 over 2 million new cases were recorded. Cocktails of antiretroviral drugs have improved the health and life expectancy of people with HIV.

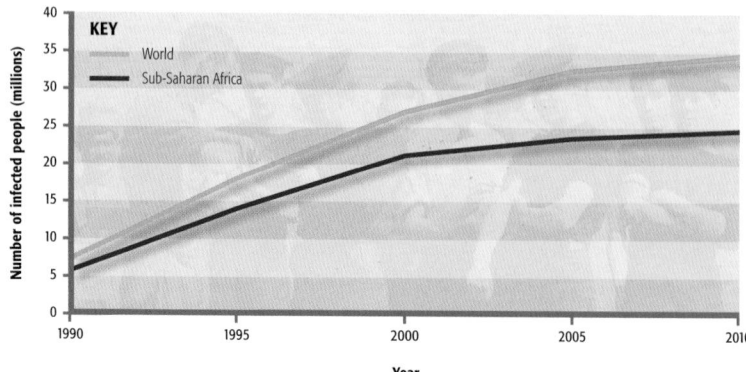

Number of infected people (millions)

KEY
World
Sub-Saharan Africa

40
35
30
25
20
15
10
5
0

1990   1995   2000   2005   2010

Year

DISCOVERY

HUMAN GENOME

Genetics is the science of genes and heredity. Inside living cells are chromosomes. These carry genes – "instructions" that determine every aspect of an organism. Chromosomes are long molecules of deoxyribonucleic acid, or DNA. In 2000, scientists announced that they had worked out the structure of the human genome, the sequence of thousands of individual nucleic acids that make up a DNA molecule. Armed with this knowledge, doctors hope to use gene therapy to treat hereditary diseases (genetic disorders).

CHROMOSOMES OF A HUMAN MALE

Flu pandemic

In Seattle, US, policemen wear protective masks during the outbreak of "Spanish Flu" in 1918. This was the most devastating pandemic in modern history.

obesity, diabetes, heart disease, and some cancers are seriously stretching healthcare systems.

Disease pandemics

Pandemics – epidemics that occur on a global scale – also threaten the world's population. Just after World War I, a pandemic of "Spanish flu" (influenza) killed up to 50 million people – more than the war itself. AIDS (Acquired Immunodeficiency Syndrome), first identified in 1981, has claimed some 30 million lives. The rise in international travel has helped contagious diseases to spread across the world: in 2002–03 the Severe Acute Respiratory Syndrome (SARS) spread from Hong Kong to 37 countries within weeks, infecting over 8,000 and killing 774. Viruses such as "avian flu" (H5N1), "swine flu" (H1N1), and Ebola – which in 2014 killed 10,000 and decimated communities in three West African countries – have also been a cause of global concern.

Fears of future pandemics have also been fuelled by the fact that the effects of antibiotics on disease have begun to weaken as bacteria develop immunity to drugs. "Superbugs", such as MRSA, are emerging with resistance to even the most powerful antibiotics.

9 Deaths per minute are related to inhaling cooking-fire smoke.

25 MILLION children worldwide have been orphaned by AIDS.

79 MILLION US citizens are clinically obese.

AFTER

Whether it is anticipating new pandemics or battling existing diseases, there are many challenges facing 21st-century medicine.

NEW DRUGS, NEW VACCINES
The rise of **antibiotic-resistant "superbugs"** means that new drugs and treatments will be needed to combat bacterial infection. There is some experimental use of **bacteriophages**, which are viruses that attack bacteria. Other priorities include developing **vaccines against HIV/AIDS** and **malaria**. Malaria kills over 1 million people per year, and in some regions the malaria parasite that causes the disease is growing increasingly resistant to current drug treatments.

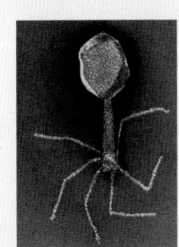

BACTERIOPHAGE

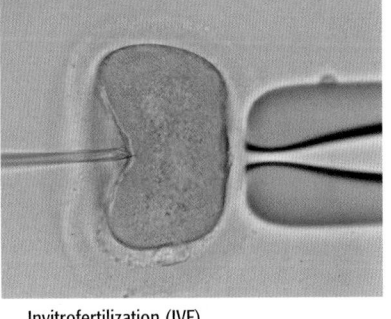

Invitrofertilization (IVF)

The first stage of the IVF artificial insemination process involves injecting sperm into an egg cell (shown above). The fertilized egg is then implanted into a woman's uterus so that a normal pregnancy process can occur.

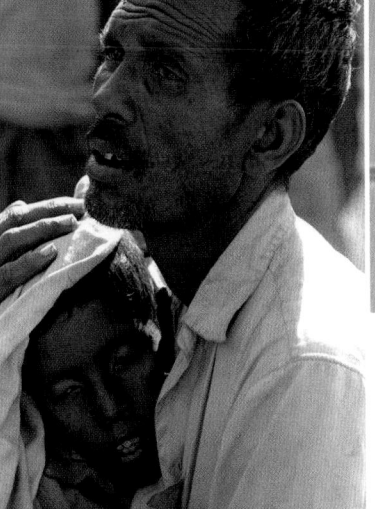

Cholera in Bangladesh

A father cradles his dying son during the 1971 cholera outbreak in Bangladesh. Lack of sanitation and access to clean drinking water led to the deaths of 6,500 people.

ADVANCES IN MEDICINE

Since the 1920s, tremendous advances have been made in medicine and surgery as scientists, researchers, and doctors seek solutions to world health problems.

1932 In Germany, Josef Klarer makes the first **sulfa drugs** (synthetic antibiotics).

1950 In the UK, Richard Doll publishes evidence that **smoking causes lung cancer**.

1960 The world's first internal **"pacemaker"**, a battery-powered device that stimulates and regulates the **human heartbeat**, is successfully implanted.

1967 South African heart surgeon Dr Christiaan Barnard performs the world's first **human heart transplant** in South Africa.

1978 Louise Brown, the **first IVF child**, is born in the UK.

1990s Highly Active Anti-Retroviral Therapy (**HAART**), using a "cocktail" of drugs, makes huge strides in suppressing **HIV/AIDS** in infected people.

1998 French surgeons perform the first successful **hand transplant**.

2000 After a decade of international effort, scientists announce that they have mapped the **human genome** – the sequence of nucleic acids in molecules of human **DNA**.

2010 Spinal injury patient first to receive treatment derived from **human embryonic stem cells**.

1920	1930	1940	1950	1960	1970	1980	1990	2000	2010

1922 Canadian doctors pioneer **insulin treatment for diabetes**.

1928 Alexander Fleming isolates **penicillin**, the first **antibiotic agent**.

1954 The first successful **kidney transplant** is carried out by Joseph Murray in Boston, US.

1960 The female oral **contraceptive pill** becomes available in the US.

1973 In the UK, Godfrey Hounsfield and Allan Cormack develop the **CAT or CT scan**, which produces X-ray **cross-sections of the body**.

1987 The first successful **lung transplant** is carried out by Joel Cooper in Baltimore, US.

1990 Gene therapy successfully treats SCID, a rare genetic disorder of the immune system.

2005 Surgeons in France carry out the first partial **face transplant**. In 2010 the first full face transplant is completed in Spain.

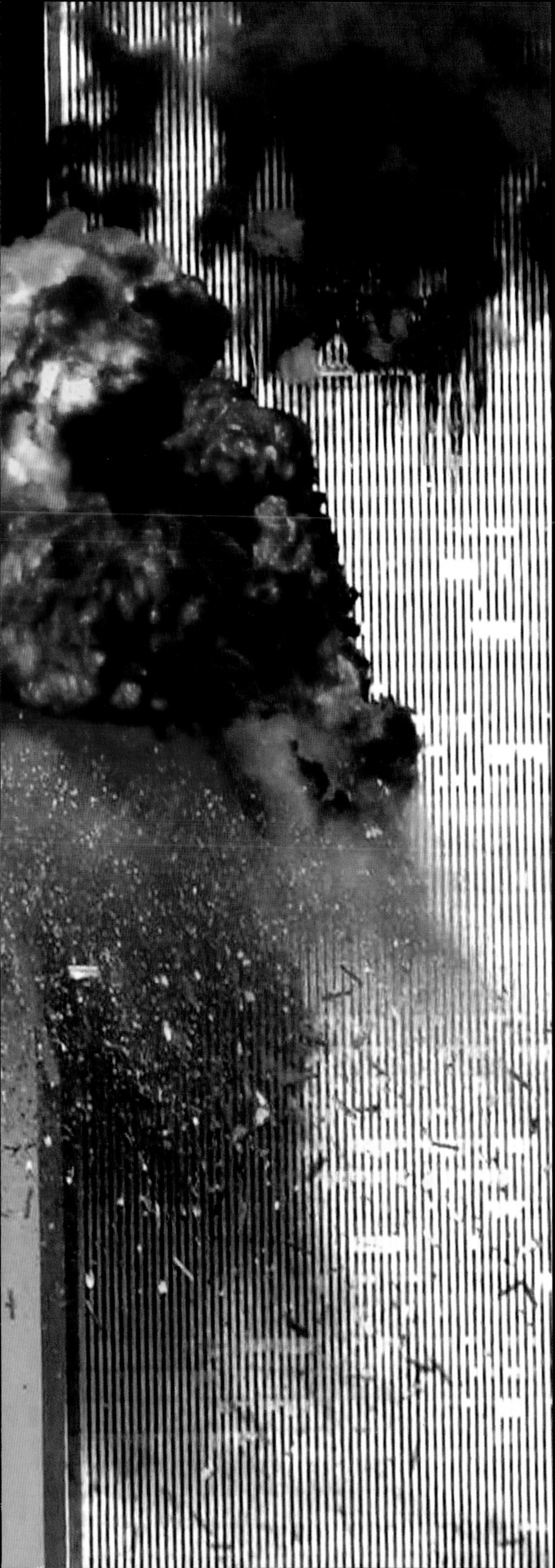

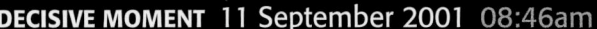

9/11

On 11 September 2001, 19 Islamic extremists launched attacks on the World Trade Center in New York and the Pentagon in Washington DC, killing thousands. This strike by members of the Al-Qaeda terrorist network on symbols of Western power shocked the world. It lead to an American declaration of "War on Terror" to end international terrorism.

At 8:46am local time, American Airlines Flight 11 crashed into the north tower of the World Trade Center, killing the 92 people on board – and killing or trapping a further 1,366 people at or above the point of impact. News teams rushed to the scene. Initial reports described the crash as a terrible accident but when, just 16 minutes later, news cameras witnessed United Airlines Flight 175 crashing into the centre's south tower, it was clear that America was under attack.

The hijackers, who were mainly Saudi-Arabian nationals, had taken over the California-bound flights soon after take-off from east coast airports. They used knives, mace, and the threat of bombs to subdue crews and passengers, then directed the fuel-laden jets towards their targets.

In the north tower, all routes down were cut off. People trapped inside made desperate calls to loved ones, begging for help or simply saying farewell. Around the world, millions watched the awful sight of people hurling themselves from the burning building. In the south tower one staircase was undamaged. Just 18 of the 600 people trapped in the building walked to safety before the tower collapsed. At 10:28am, the north tower also fell.

Flight controllers became aware that two more planes had been hijacked but were unable to locate them before 9:37am when American Airlines Flight 77 crashed into the Pentagon, headquarters of the US Department of Defense, killing a further 189 people. At 10:03am, United Airlines Flight 93 crashed into a field near Shanksville, Pennsylvannia, killing all those on board. Mobile phone records and evidence from black box recorders reveal that passengers, alerted to the fate of other hijacked planes by phone calls, planned to charge the cockpit and attack their hijackers. Although the passengers could not break into the cockpit, they did succeed in diverting the hijackers from their intended target, almost certainly the Capitol Building or White House in Washington DC. During the final minutes of the Flight 93 recordings the hijackers can be heard deciding to abort their mission and crash the plane. As the plane hurtles towards the ground, the terrorists are praying fervently.

New York terror attacks
The World Trade Center, great symbol of American wealth and power, moments after hijackers crashed their planes into its twin towers.

> **"** Today, our fellow citizens, **our way of life,** our very freedom came under attack.**"**
> PRESIDENT GEORGE W BUSH ADDRESSING THE NATION, 11 SEPTEMBER 2001

BEFORE ◀◀

The British mandate, which put Iraq under British administration, lasted from 1919–32. The mandate was awarded to Britain under the terms of the Covenant of the League of Nations following World War I.

THE BRITISH MANDATE

Britain's controlling interest in the Iraqi oil business **◀◀ 336** caused deep resentment among Iraqi nationalists, but Britain ensured that their oil concession continued post-mandate. During World War II the British prime minister, Winston Churchill, ordered troops into Iraq to safeguard Britain's oil supplies.

> **THE ARAB LEAGUE was founded by Egypt, Syria, Iraq, Lebanon, Jordan, Saudi Arabia, and Yemen in 1945 to serve the interests of Arab states. In 1950 its members signed a Defence and Economic Co-operation Treaty.**

SUEZ CRISIS

In 1956, the Egyptian president, **Gamel Abdel Nasser**, wrested control of the **Suez Canal** away from the French and British **◀◀ 334–35**. This encouraged Arab nationalists across the Middle East to push for independence. In 1961, Iraq nationalized the oil concession areas, ending foreign interests in the industry.

IRAN–IRAQ WAR

This conflict was triggered by a territorial dispute over the Shatt-al-Arab waterway between the two rival states. Iran's revolutionary leader,

IRAN–IRAQ WAR

Ayatollah Khomeini ◀◀ 364–65, was unpopular with both oil-rich Arab states and Western leaders, who he denounced, sanctioning the seizure of the US embassy in Tehran by militants in 1979. Saudi Arabia, the US, and others sold weapons to the Iraqi leader **Saddam Hussein** (see right), who waged chemical warfare against Iranian forces.

American carrier in the Suez Canal
The Suez Canal allows transportation between Europe and Asia without the need to circumnavigate Africa and is of great strategic significance. In the image above, a US aircraft carrier is covered by a gunner in an anti-submarine helicopter as it proceeds up the canal.

The Gulf Wars

Conflict erupted in the Persian Gulf in 1990 when the United Nations moved to oust Iraqi troops from neighbouring Kuwait. A military operation led by US forces put an end to the occupation, but concerns about the Iraqi leader Saddam Hussein led America and Britain to enter a second war in the Gulf in 2003.

On 2 August 1990 Saddam Hussein (see right) invaded the oil-rich gulf state of Kuwait. The United Nation's Security Council demanded an immediate unconditional withdrawal, but Saddam, a brutal dictator who had recently appointed himself Iraq's "President for Life", ignored the UN and announced that Kuwait had become a part of Iraq. The US acted to avert the crisis with a show of strength, sending troops to the gulf region. Many UN nations, including Britain and members of the Arab League (see BEFORE) followed suit. Saddam responded by placing captured foreign nationals of "hostile countries" at key strategic sites in Kuwait in the hope of deterring air attacks.

The First Gulf War

In late autumn a UN ultimatum effectively authorized the use of force if Saddam did not withdraw from Kuwait by 15 January 1991. He refused to comply. The First Gulf War began on 17 January when the US and coalition forces launched Operation "Desert Storm", attacking Iraq and Kuwait from the air. Saddam's response was to launch Scud missile attacks on the Israeli capital, Tel Aviv. As allied forces entered Kuwait, Iraq fired missiles on Saudi Arabia, but ultimately was no match for the fierce onslaught of Desert Storm. In February, after five weeks of war, US forces took Kuwait City and US President George Bush Snr announced a cessation of hostilities.

Saddam Hussein showed no sign of being humbled by his defeat. As Iraqi troops withdrew they placed land mines around Kuwaiti oil wells before setting the wells alight. It was an act of pure defiance. The Kuwait oil fires burned for several months, causing massive environmental damage.

After the conflicts Saddam was faced with uprisings in the southern Shi'a region of Iraq and in the Kurdish north. These revolts were speedily crushed. The extent of Saddam's brutality towards his own citizens was revealed years later when mass graves were uncovered. In the aftermath of the war the UN agreed that Saddam could remain in power, but economic

sanctions would remain in place until Iraq destroyed both its stockpile and manufacturing ability of weapons of mass destruction (WMD) – nuclear, chemical, and biological weapons. Over the succeeding years UN weapons inspectors visited Iraq to check this disarmament process. Saddam frequently obstructed the inspections, moving and concealing weapons, and in 1998 ordered the inspectors out of Iraq. The US and UK retaliated launching Operation "Desert Fox", a bombing campaign aimed at destroying Iraq's weapons.

The horrific terrorist attacks on New York in 2001 (see pp.390–91) led to a decisive shift in US tolerance of Saddam's defiant behaviour. In his 2002 State of the Union address, US President George W Bush declared, "I will not wait on events while danger gathers": the US was now prepared to make pre-emptive strikes against its enemies to combat any further potential terrorist attacks. Bush instructed the Pentagon, the US department of defence, to develop plans for war on Iraq. The US was supported in its plans for "War on Terror" by the British government, but there was grave concern among other world leaders about the legality of America's intentions. Arguments focused on whether Iraq

Outdated weapons
Coalition forces in the 2003 Iraq War had state-of-the-art equipment; but Iraqi soldiers had outdated Soviet-made arms such as this RPG-7V grenade-launcher.

actually still possessed WMD. George W Bush insisted that they did and he was supported in this view by the British prime minister, Tony Blair. In September 2002, Blair released a dossier detailing the goverment's assessment of Iraq's military capability. It claimed that Saddam had the capacity to deploy chemical and biological weapons within 45 minutes. The reliability of the dossier was soon called into question when it was revealed to be based in part on research written 12 years earlier, but President Bush continued to put pressure on the UN to sanction war against Iraq.

LEADER OF IRAQ (1937–2006)

SADDAM HUSSEIN

Saddam Hussein was born to a poor family in rural Iraq. In 1957 he joined the Ba'ath Party and a year later became involved in an unsuccessful plot to assassinate Iraq's then leader, General Quassim. By 1972 Saddam had a major role in government. He became Iraq's leader and gradually took absolute power, using torture, violence, and coercion to subdue the population. He was captured by US troops after the fall of Baghdad and tried and executed for war crimes.

A second conflict

With events escalating towards conflict, the UN sent weapons inspectors back into Iraq in an attempt to discover the truth about Saddam's military capacity.

Despite the chief weapons inspector's appeal for more time to verify the facts, and some of the largest popular protests in America and Europe since the Vietnam War (see pp.352–53), US patience had run out. On 17 March the UN was informed that the diplomatic process was over and on 20 March the US-led coalition attacked Iraq. The progress of the Second Gulf War, or Iraq War, was rapid and by

American helicopters in Kuwait
US gunship helicopters in the burning oil fields of Kuwait. The "scorched earth" policy was ordered by defeated Iraqi leader, Saddam Hussein.

"Highway of Death"
The road leading north out of Kuwait City was heavily bombed in coalition attacks on retreating Iraqi forces. It is lined with the remains of destroyed cars and trucks.

9 April the coalition forces took the Iraqi capital, Baghdad. Fully expecting that the war would soon be over, the US appointed a governing council to supervise the creation of a new Iraqi government. However, in many ways, the Iraq War was only just beginning.

Continuing violence

The fall of Saddam Hussein created national chaos as fighting erupted between different religious and ethnic Iraqi factions. In July 2003 George W Bush reported that his forces faced a "low-intensity" war. A brutal and bloody conflict ensued involving suicide bombings and guerrilla-style tactics. The US officially returned sovereignty to Iraq in 2004 and Iraq subsequently elected a government, but thousands of Iraqi civilians, police, allied soldiers, and political insurgents (rebels) died after the fall of Baghdad.

A fight for power

The ongoing violence in Iraq was not only directed against foreign troops and officials trying to cope with insurgency and organize a democratic political system, but increasingly became a fight for power between rival religious, political, and ethnic groups, such as the Kurds. The confusion in the aftermath of Saddam's defeat allowed terrorist groups to organize and recruit in Iraq, including al-Qaeda, which carried out the 9/11 attacks in New York and continues to operate in the region.

Under the military occupation a new constitution was drawn up and ratified by popular vote in October 2005. Iraqi jurisdiction was gradually restored and in 2009 the government took over responsibility for the entire territory. In December 2011 the last US troops left Iraq. Friction remained between Iraq's Sunni minority and the Shi'a dominated government of Nouri al-Maliki, which marginalized Sunni influence in the new state apparatus. The instability has led to widespread deprivation for much of the Iraqi population and numerous deaths from suicide attacks and political murders. In 2013 an estimated 8,000 civilians died in the firing line between different factions.

The rise of the movement for an Islamic State of Iraq and the Levant (ISIS, or ISIL) presented a new threat (see AFTER), as the Syrian civil war gave militant Muslims access to arms and equipment that could be used to promote a fundamental Islam by force. The Iraqi army and security forces faced widespread violence, and in 2014 US advisers and equipment were once again sent to Iraq, alongside support from other states in the Middle East that felt threatened by the rise of the militant Islamic movement. The failure of the Iraqi army to hold back the ISIS invasion brought about al-Maliki's resignation and the appointment of Muhhamad al-Ghabban. The renewed, often brutal fighting opened a new dimension in Iraq's troubled history since the Gulf Wars.

Dictator's downfall
When US Marines entered the centre of Baghdad, signalling Iraqi defeat, Saddam Hussein's statue outside the Palestine Hotel was pulled down by crowds celebrating the ousting of the brutal dictator.

The Gulf Wars helped to polarize the Islamic world and encouraged the rise of militant groups seeking to challenge Western intervention and reject Western values.

ISLAMIC MILITANCY

The crisis in Iraq helped to promote anti-Western Islamic violence, prompting what George W Bush termed a "War on Terror". Since the 9/11 attacks in the United States, **violence has occurred worldwide**, with bombings in London, Madrid, Moscow, Delhi, Mumbai, Paris, and other major cities. Some of the violence stems from other conflicts in Kashmir, Chechnya, or Afghanistan, but the mainly young militants are motivated by hostility to state power and secularism, and a desire to return to a fundamental form of Islam.

ISLAMIC STATE

The militant movement that emerged in 2013 calling itself **Islamic State of Iraq and the Levant** is a successor to Islamic State of Iraq, which was founded in 2006 in cooperation with al-Qaeda. Heavily armed men and women undertook a major offensive in predominantly Kurdish areas of northern Iraq, capturing Mosul and other towns, imposing a **basic Islamic law** and killing those regarded as enemies of their form of fundamental Islam. In June 2014 the name was changed to Islamic State, claiming to represent all Muslims worldwide. Hundreds of volunteers attracted by the idea of fighting for Islam have been recruited for the new cause, which has once again destabilized post-war Iraq.

Globalization

A phenomenon of the modern world, globalization often refers to the rise of multinational corporations that wield extraordinary economic power. Global consumption of increasingly uniform products has led to concern that the cultural differences of nations will be eroded.

BEFORE

The disastrous effects of protectionist economic policies in the Great Depression Era led to changes in economic thinking.

THE IMF AND GATT AGREEMENTS
In 1944, representatives of 45 nations met at Bretton Woods, US, and established the **International Monetary Fund (IMF)** to increase world trade through co-operation between nations. In 1947, the first General Agreement on Tariffs and Trade (GATT treaty) influenced over US$10 billion worth of trade between its members.

G6
In 1975, France, Italy, Japan, Germany, Britain, and the US formed the **Group of Six** – a forum for international trade policy discussions. Known as **G8** after Canada and Russia joined, they represent 65 per cent of the global economy.

Times Square
Animated neon and LED signs shimmer on the streets of New York, advertising global brands 24 hours a day. Some companies pay millions of dollars for an annual lease on a space in Times Square and tens of millions more to create an attention-grabbing advertisement.

> "Under the impact of globalization... **everyday life** is becoming opened up from the **hold of tradition.**"
>
> ANTHONY GIDDENS, SOCIOLOGIST, 1999

Distant production
In this toy factory in Guanyao, China, female workers assemble Barbie products. The Barbie doll was created by Mattel in the US in 1959 and is now produced and sold all over the world.

I n his book *The Gutenberg Galaxy*, published in 1962, communications theorist Marshall McLuhan predicted that the world would soon become recreated as a "global village". Today as US manufacturers make products in Southeast Asia for the European market and customer enquiries in Britain are dealt with through call centres in India, McLuhan's prophesy of an interdependent world seems truly visionary. The globalization of economies has allowed business to market products internationally, forming many global partnerships and alliances.

The global system

During the 20th century, national governments tended to provide "infrastructure" services, such as transport systems, and energy supplies. By the 1980s, economists agreed that under-investment in these services had led to low productivity and poor service; state control of the infrastructure hampered economic growth. From the 1980s, governments began to liberalize their economies, privatizing state assets, and encouraging "open" competitive markets. These reforms contributed to major global economic change. The tonnage of goods traded worldwide is currently estimated to be 16 times greater than in 1950. The rapidly developing Chinese economy is often cited as an example of the benefits of globalization. Since China turned its back, economically at least, on the communist system and opened up her markets to international trade and investment, it is estimated that there has been a seven-fold increase in income per head.

The growth in global trade is due in part to international trade agreements, another major factor being the impact of technological advances. The advent of the internet and digital communications systems has added new dimensions to the world's economic infrastructure. International trade can be conducted quickly and efficiently and companies are expanding their operations across the globe.

Global product
Apple launched its iPhone 6 in 10 countries and sold 10 million in its first weekend. Within two months, it was available in a further 60 countries. Apple has a revenue comparable to the GDP of an ecomony the size of New Zealand.

Multinational growth

The rise of multinational corporations, is a major feature of globalization. Many have annual turnovers larger than the value of the economies of many small countries.

A feature of the products and services provided by multinationals is that they offer customers an identical experience. This is particularly true of branded food companies, for example McDonalds, Coca-Cola, and Starbucks, and manufacturers of sports equipment, such as Nike and Reebok. The presence of these companies' logos, or "brands", promises the same product whether we purchase it in Melbourne, Mumbai, or Moscow. This corporate branding of goods has been hugely successful. Worldwide, the possession of "designer labelled" goods is seen as a mark of success, a marketing triumph that has generated phenomenal profits for multinationals. However, the uniformity of experience provided by such companies has resulted in complaints as local, regional, and even national cultural distinctions are being devalued and lost.

Many of those opposed to mutinational industry also complain that their wealth gives them the power to influence the economic and political decisions of governments, particularly in the area of trade restrictions. Some companies have been guilty of exploiting cheap labour to produce items that are then sold at a profit to Western consumers.

Whatever their opinion of the globalization of the world economy, commentators are united in the view that the world has been transformed by its impact. The consequences of these rapid and massive changes are only just beginning to be understood.

IDEA

ANTI-GLOBALIZATION

On 30 November 1999, riot police in Seattle, USA, used pepper spray and tear gas to disperse anti-globalization protestors at a World Trade Organization conference. Since the 1990s, the number of staged protests against global trade agreements has increased. Protestors are concerned that in order for governments and multinational companies to make a profit, there is a requirement that poor countries must remain the impoverished suppliers of raw materials and cheap labour.

AFTER

Globalization has helped to create a sense of global responsibility, with both governments and multinational businesses doing more to fight poverty and conserve the environment.

BATTLING POVERTY
For many people the **inequalities between** the lives of **rich and poor are no longer acceptable** and multinational companies and governments are increasingly facing demands to address world poverty. Campaigns, such as **"Make Poverty History"**, promote issues including trade justice for poorer nations and the cancellation of debts of developing nations.

THE GLOBAL ENVIRONMENT
The continuing rise in temperatures worldwide has put the issue of **global warming** at the centre of the political agenda **398–99 »**. Changes to the Earth's climate are directly linked to higher levels of carbon dioxide in the atmosphere created by human activity. International agreements to reduce greenhouse gas emissions, such as the **Kyoto Protocol**, enforced since 2005, and the Copenhagen Accord of 2010, have led to the promotion of cleaner manufacturing practices. In 2014 the United States and China agreed a new reduction of their carbon gas emissions.

‹‹ BEFORE

Until the late 1970s, China's communist leaders rejected a free market economy (in which production is controlled by the laws of supply and demand rather than the state) as against their socialist principles.

CHINA'S ECONOMY UNDER MAO
Under China's first communist leader, Mao Zedong **‹‹ 346–47** free enterprise was banned and peasants could not own their own land.

1 BILLION The size of China's population in 1982. It was about 540 million when the Communists took power in 1949.

LOW OUTPUT
When Mao died in 1976, China had roughly the same economic output as Canada, a country with a much smaller population of 23 million.

DENG XIAOPING
A member of the Chinese Communist Party from the 1920s, **Deng Xiaoping** (1904–97) took part in the Long March and the foundation of the **Chinese People's Republic ‹‹ 346–47**. By 1957 he was secretary-general of the Party, but during the Cultural Revolution he was subjected to public humiliation and sent to work in a factory. He later triumphed in the power struggle after Mao's death to lead the Communist Party and masterminded the **growth of China's economy** in the 1980s.

DENG XIAOPING

City of the future
Shanghai is the third most populous city in the world, after Tokyo and Delhi. It boasts the twisting Shanghai Tower (the world's second tallest building); the Oriental Pearl TV Tower with its 11 spheres; and the first commercial maglev railway.

W ithin three years of Mao Zedong's death in 1976, China's communist government began to turn away from the economic policies based on collective ownership and centralized planning that had previously been believed essential to any communist system. Deng Xiaoping advocated economic growth as the supreme goal – to be achieved at any cost.

Special ecomonic zones
A raft of measures in 1979 put the country on its new path. Four Special Economic Zones (SEZs) were established at the southern Chinese ports of Zhuhai, Shantou, and Xiamen, and foreign firms were invited to invest capital on favourable terms. Western capitalist businesses were given the opportunity to exploit cheap Chinese labour, while in return China gained foreign exchange with which to buy imported goods and was given access to new technology from the West. At the same time, in the countryside, where 80 per cent of the population lived, families were encouraged to cultivate their own land for profit.

When challenged by those who objected to capitalist free market economics, Deng defended his new policies as a practical path to prosperity: "It does not matter whether a cat is black or white," he stated, "as long as it catches mice it is a good cat." Many non-Chinese observers believed that economic freedom would be

Superpower China

By embracing the free market, from the 1980s China achieved extraordinarily rapid economic growth and underwent a major social transformation. But politically the country remained under the strictly authoritarian rule of the Communist Party.

linked to political freedom. But in 1989, when communist regimes were toppling in Europe (see pp.370–71), pro-democracy activists in China had their demands for reform brutally rejected. The 1989 massacre of demonstrators by the army in Beijing's Tiananmen Square (see p.347) was an unequivocal statement of the Chinese Communist Party's firm intention of keeping its authoritarian grip on society.

Despite this political stance, there was no turning back from the economic reforms. Although proceeding by stages and strictly supervised by the state, the transition to a free market economy gathered pace through the 1990s. So thorough was the transformation

> " Poverty is not socialism. **To be rich is glorious.**"
> DENG XIAOPING, 1979

that in 1997 China was able to absorb the British colony of Hong Kong, one of the major centres of global capitalism, without noticeably affecting the territory's business community. The success of the new policies in creating economic growth was huge – between 1979 and 2002 China's real Gross Domestic Product grew at 9.3 per cent per year, the fastest growth rate of any major country.

By the beginning of the new millennium a considerable part of the Chinese population had become part of a modern consumer society. It was said that under Mao people had wanted the "Four Musts" – a bicycle, radio, a watch, and sewing machine; but by the 1990s they aspired to the "Eight Bigs"– a colour TV, fridge, stereo, camera, motorbike, suite of furniture, washing machine, and an electric fan. By 2005 China had overtaken the United States in sales of televisions and mobile phones.

Gap between rich and poor

The transition to a free market caused massive social disruption. Corruption was rife and a wide gulf opened up between the winners and losers in the new economy. While successful Chinese businessmen drove around in Mercedes, millions of people in rural areas were

subsisting on less than US$1 a day and pay for factory workers was pitifully low. Some 150 million Chinese peasants were displaced from the land, roaming the country in search of work. Many migrated to China's cities; others abroad, making China one of the world's major sources of illegal migrant workers. Urban unemployment also soared as the government struggled to reduce the vast workforce relying on state employment. By the first decade of the 21st century, jobs in the state sector were disappearing at a rate of around 10 million a year.

Into the future

Deng Xiaoping died in 1997, the last Chinese leader of the heroic generation of the Long March. His successor, Jiang Zemin, reaffirmed communist rule, asserting that the Party had always represented the interests of the Chinese people.

Yet the regime was threatened by the desire of educated, well-off dissidents for Western-style freedoms and by the mass discontent of workers suffering from poverty and insecurity. The government's trump card was its assertion of national pride. Prestige events – such as the launch of China's first piloted space flight in 2004 and the staging of the Olympic Games in Beijing in 2008 – and an increasingly assertive foreign policy, appealed to most Chinese, who looked forward to their country being recognized as a major world power in the century ahead.

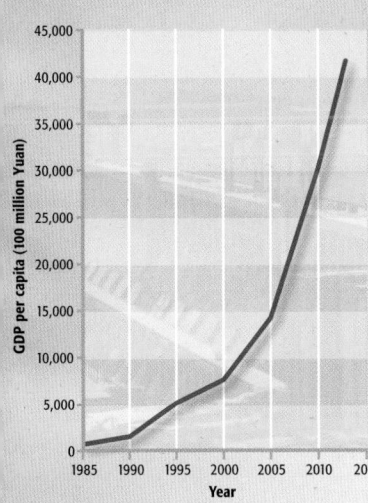

China's GDP takes a giant leap
China's level of economic output rose in the 1980s, and took off spectacularly in the 1990s as the pace of economic reform quickened. There were fears the economy might "overheat", causing high inflation.

If growth rates continue as they are, China will become the world's largest economy, overtaking the United States in about 2030.

HARMING THE PLANET
Rapid economic growth in China has been accompanied by severe **environmental damage**.

POPULATION GROWTH
China's **"one-child"** policy has recently been loosened. However, China's population is expected to stabilize at 1.5 billion by 2050.

CHINESE MOONSHOT
A manned Chinese moon landing is projected for 2020 at the latest.

The Three Gorges Dam
Spanning the Yangtze River, the world's most powerful hydroelectric dam provides energy and improves flood control. Its social costs, however, included relocating a million people.

Tourism in China
In 2005, the number of foreign tourists (excluding overseas Chinese) visiting China was 20 million. By 2020 it may be the world's most popular destination.

2008 Beijing Olympics
China enthusiastically embraced the opportunity to showcase its great achievements. "One World, One Dream", was the Games' motto.

Global Recession

The collapse of the US housing market in 2007 triggered an unprecedented financial crisis, which crippled the world's major economies and almost brought down the global financial system.

A t the turn of the century, the world's economy, particularly in the West, seemed relatively stable. Material wealth had increased, interest rates were low, and employment opportunities were on the rise.

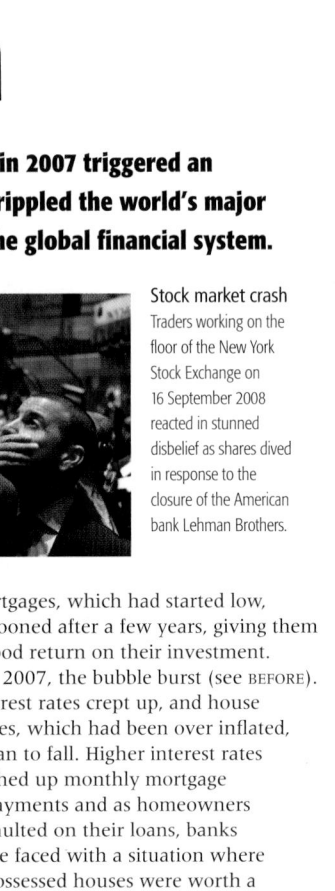

Stock market crash
Traders working on the floor of the New York Stock Exchange on 16 September 2008 reacted in stunned disbelief as shares dived in response to the closure of the American bank Lehman Brothers.

Bankers, notably in the US, began to offer mortgages to customers without checking their ability to repay the loans. These mortgages, called "subprime" mortgages, were attractive to borrowers who had a poor credit history. Getting a loan was easy, and people could buy their own homes. These loans were equally attractive to lenders because house prices were rising and interest rates against these mortgages, which had started low, ballooned after a few years, giving them a good return on their investment.

In 2007, the bubble burst (see BEFORE). Interest rates crept up, and house prices, which had been over inflated, began to fall. Higher interest rates pushed up monthly mortgage repayments and as homeowners defaulted on their loans, banks were faced with a situation where repossessed houses were worth a lot less than the amount originally loaned out by the bank.

Credit crunch

Trillions of dollars worth of investments in subprime mortgages were now potentially worthless, and bankers realized that they might never get their money back. On 9 August 2007, the French bank BNP Paribas announced that it was at risk from the subprime mortgage market and stopped investors from withdrawing money from some of its funds. A wave of fear engulfed the global banking industry. As banks stopped lending money to each other or to clients, funds were unavailable for day-to-day business or for long-term investments.

Northern Rock, a British bank, had borrowed large sums of money to fund mortgages for its customers. They had to pay off their debt by reselling these mortgages, but because demand for them had fallen, it faced a liquidity crisis – an acute shortage of ready cash. On 14 September 2007, it was forced to seek an emergency loan from the British government. Panic spread amongst its customers, prompting borrowers to withdraw their savings quickly. This, referred to as a "run" on a bank, was the first on a British bank for more than a century.

BEFORE

Economic bubbles, which have occurred for centuries, happen when trade in a particular commodity or business sector **gives it a vastly inflated value. When traders realize the value is inflated, the bubble bursts and prices plummet.**

TULIP MANIA

In the Netherlands, Tulip mania (1634–37) is generally regarded as the **first recorded economic bubble** in history. Tulip bulbs were seen as a luxury, and when demand for them outstripped supply their worth inflated. When prices crashed, it had widespread consequences for the Dutch economy.

MORE BUBBLES

The **Stock Market crash** of 1929 **《 306–07**, the **Oil Crisis** of the 1970s **《 362–63**, and the **Dotcom bubble** in the late 1990s were further examples of a bubble bursting.

Madrid protests
Over 30,000 young protestors camped out in the central Puerta del Sol Square, Madrid on 22 May 2011, angry at Spain's economic policies aimed at reversing the recession. Similar protests sprang up in other European cities.

Banks collapse
Employees of Christie's auction house carry in the Lehman Brothers sign, that hung above the bank's European headquarters in London, to be sold. The downfall of the financial giant was the defining moment of the credit crunch.

G20 Crisis meet
Leaders of the world's largest economies, the G20, met in London on 2 April 2009. It was the second time they had gathered together in an attempt to boost the global economy.

too late for some others, such as Goldman Sachs and JP Morgan Chase who had to wrap up their investment banking arms.

The global nature of the crisis meant that whole national economies were affected. People spent less and there was a drop in world trade. The economy of the 16 countries sharing the Euro currency (the Eurozone) declined. Ireland became the first European country to slip into a recession (a period of economic decline). On 30 September 2008, Ireland's government promised to underwrite the entire Irish banking system. Iceland's government was forced to resign after its three biggest banks collapsed between 7–8 October 2008, and the country essentially became bankrupt.

The leaders of the newly formed G20, a forum of the world's largest economies, met in Washington, DC, US, on 14 November 2008 to find a solution. They set out a detailed plan for financial reform, including a reduction in interest rates and a global stimulus package of $5 trillion, designed to boost economies by increasing government spending and reducing tax.

Widespread riots
Greece, which had borrowed large amounts of money, admitted it was deeply in debt and had to be bailed out by wealthier European countries. The Greek government unveiled an austerity plan aimed at reducing its

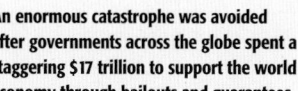

10 THOUSAND suicides as a result of the financial crisis

19.2 TRILLION lost in net worth by American households in 2012 as a result of the financial crisis, according to the US treasury

budget deficit by almost 10 per cent by 2012. Unlike a stimulus package, which pumped money into an economy, these austerity measures froze public-sector wages, applied rigid spending cuts, and increased taxes. They were controversial and protests swept across Greece.

Austerity policies were introduced in many European countries. Portugal, Spain, and Italy were under immense pressure to lower their debt and strengthen their economies. Lithuania

experienced severe recession, sparking riots and violent clashes with the police.

Household and business debt remained high, bankers were reluctant to lend, and many people lost their livelihoods. Even though a combination of stimulus packages and austerity measures were used worldwide in a desperate attempt to halt the crisis, the effects of the crash continue to ripple through the global economy.

AFTER ≫

An enormous catastrophe was avoided after governments across the globe spent a staggering $17 trillion to support the world economy through bailouts and guarantees.

RECESSION ENDS
In the summer of 2009, **manufacturing output started growing** again in the US. This was cause to celebrate as it suggested that the **economy** was now on the **upturn**. **Employment levels grew**, yet recovery for the US could only be regarded as moderate. About **8 million Americans had lost their jobs** during the global recession, and almost **4 million homes were repossessed** between January 2007 and December 2011.

IMPACT
Of the larger world economies, only **Australia emerged unscathed**. **China** and **Brazil** bounced back and **made a good recovery**. There was optimism in India, but Russia was hit hard. In **Europe**, the situation remained **unstable**. Austerity measures provoked **huge civil unrest** and many **governments were forced out**. As the global economic crisis devastated lives and livelihoods, the **impact on ordinary people was profound**.

Shares around the world began to plummet. The giant US mortgage lenders Fannie Mae and Freddie Mac, who had guaranteed thousands of subprime mortgages, were bailed out by the US government on 7 September 2008. The government seized control and guaranteed $100 billion to each to prevent their bankruptcies.

More governments intervene
Lehman Brothers, a Wall Street bank, was also involved in the subprime mortgage market. When it filed for bankruptcy on 15 September 2008,

the crisis came to a head, and there was worldwide financial panic. It was generally assumed that the governments would step in to rescue any bank that got into difficulties, although no one had expected that such a situation would ever arise. The unthinkable had become a reality.

Western governments pumped billions into their own banks to stop them from collapsing. Many were saved just in time; in Britain, several banks were bailed out, including the Royal Bank of Scotland and Halifax Bank of Scotland. However, it was

> "What we know about the **global financial crisis** is that we **don't know very much**."

PROFESSOR PAUL SAMUELSON, AMERICAN ECONOMIST

Dynamic Populations

More than half the people of the world currently live in urban areas. With global urban population numbers rising by 180,000 each day, it is predicted that by 2050 two-thirds of the world's population will be city dwellers.

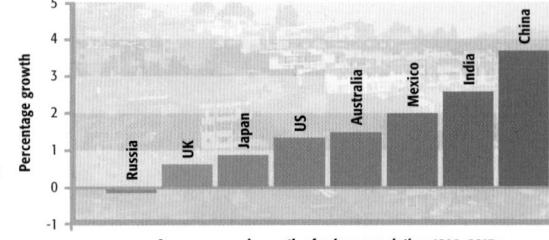

Average annual growth of urban population 1990–2013

Urbanization became a worldwide phenomenon in the 20th century as the populations of less economically developed nations in South America, Asia, and Africa followed the Western trend for urban migration.

Urbanization is not constrained by national boundaries. Many migrants move countries in search of a better life, generally moving from developing countries to the developed world.

Growing concerns

People continue to be drawn to cities by the promise of economic and social opportunity. Cities are political, cultural, and commercial centres where much of a nation's essential work is done. However, expanding urban population numbers place heavy demands on the infrastructures of modern cities where poverty often exists side by side with great affluence. Lack of accommodation has contributed to more people living on the streets and there is serious concern about the spread of infectious diseases, including tuberculosis and HIV/AIDS (see pp.368–69) among the poor and homeless.

Crime is another problem in most of the world's major cities. There is particular concern about violent crime among urban youth. Issues of poverty and social exclusion are thought to have contributed to growing youth violence and the use of firearms has led to the creation of "zones of lawlessness" in certain cities.

Cities in developing countries are currently expanding at the fastest rate. Here many migrants flee war or rural poverty, to find themselves living in slums without hope of work, adequate shelter, sanitation, or clean water supplies. In sub-Saharan Africa 60 per cent of the urban population are slum-dwellers.

KEY
- City population in 1950 (millions)
- City population in 1975 (millions)
- City population in 2000 (millions)

Shifting city populations
The recorded rises in urban population numbers since 1950 reflect differing rates of industrialization across the globe. Urban explosion in Latin America, India, Asia, and China can be seen in the leap in population numbers since 1975.

Urban growth
Comparative urban population numbers since 1990 show that European and Japanese urban population growth has slowed. Urbanization continues to increase in the US, Australia, and Mexico, and rates in India and China are rising at a dramatic rate.

BEFORE

During the Industrial Revolution there was a rapid mass migration of people from rural to urban areas across Europe and the US.

URBANIZATION

In 1800 one in four British people lived in cities, but by 1900 it was three in four. This process of migration, known as urbanization, occurred across Europe and North America during the Industrial Revolution **≪ 226–27**. The sudden concentration of large numbers of people in cities and towns **≪ 252–53** created crowded and unsanitary conditions. The Western world gradually addressed these social problems, developing infrastructures that could provide the necessary support for their industrial workforces. Because opportunity for advancement was located in the city, urban populations continued to grow.

ARRIVING IN NEW YORK

San Francisco's Chinatown was a ghetto established by Chinese immigrants in the city's downtown area in the 1850s. It was once an impoverished area shunned by non-Chinese, but today it is a vibrant, thriving tourist destination.

Mexico City, the capital of Mexico, has over 8 million inhabitants, the poorest of whom live in slums, or barrios. The shacks are built with whatever materials come to hand and are notoriously unsafe and vulnerable to landslides.

Masses of military personnel such as these Brazilian troops were deployed around the world during World War II. This movement led to more marriages between peoples of different nationalities. After the war ended, many "war brides" emigrated to their husbands' home countries.

NORTH AMERICA · New York · ATLANTIC OCEAN · Mexico city · PACIFIC OCEAN · SOUTH AMERICA · São Paulo

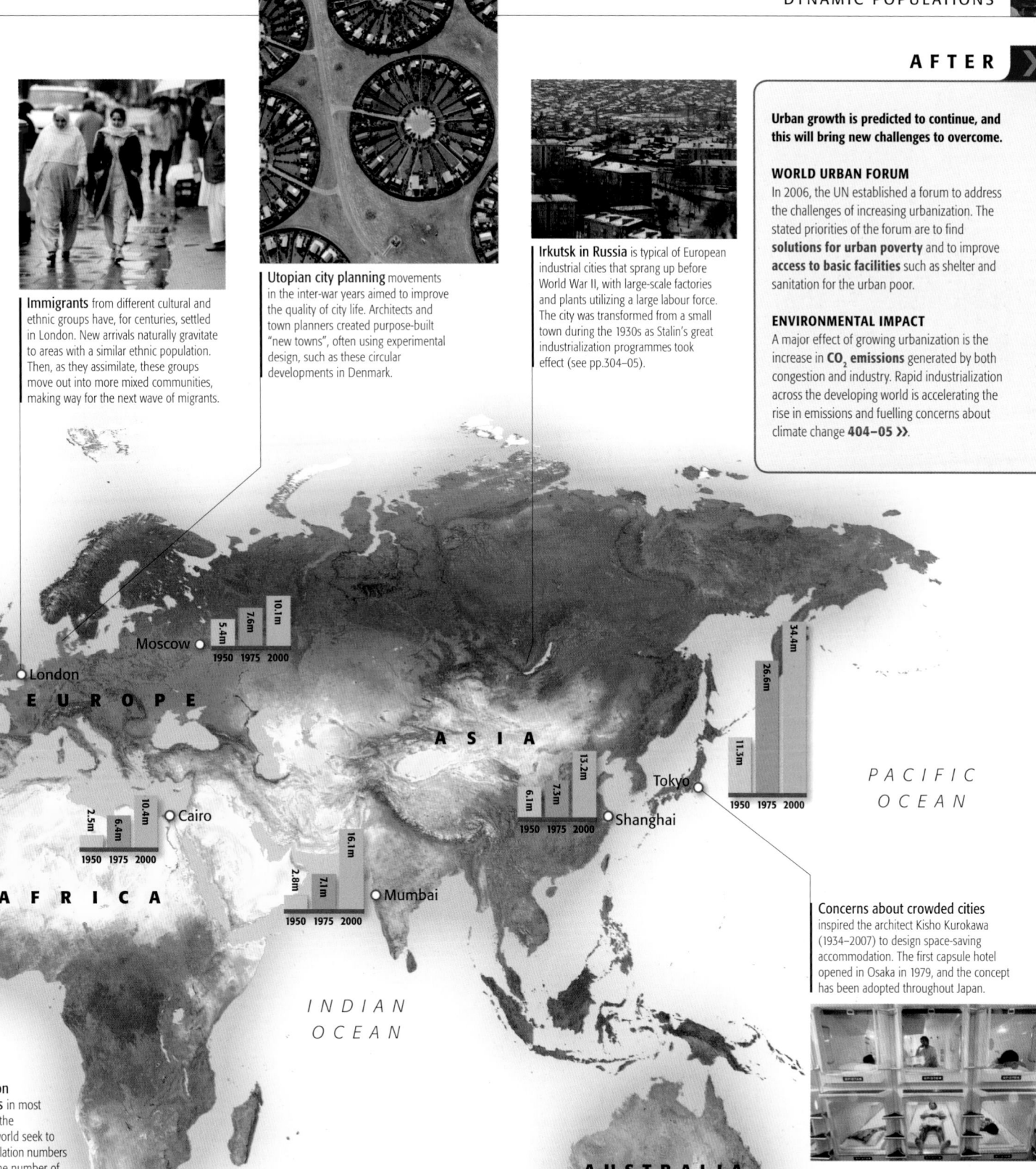

Urban growth is predicted to continue, and this will bring new challenges to overcome.

WORLD URBAN FORUM
In 2006, the UN established a forum to address the challenges of increasing urbanization. The stated priorities of the forum are to find **solutions for urban poverty** and to improve **access to basic facilities** such as shelter and sanitation for the urban poor.

ENVIRONMENTAL IMPACT
A major effect of growing urbanization is the increase in CO_2 **emissions** generated by both congestion and industry. Rapid industrialization across the developing world is accelerating the rise in emissions and fuelling concerns about climate change **404–05 »**.

Immigrants from different cultural and ethnic groups have, for centuries, settled in London. New arrivals naturally gravitate to areas with a similar ethnic population. Then, as they assimilate, these groups move out into more mixed communities, making way for the next wave of migrants.

Utopian city planning movements in the inter-war years aimed to improve the quality of city life. Architects and town planners created purpose-built "new towns", often using experimental design, such as these circular developments in Denmark.

Irkutsk in Russia is typical of European industrial cities that sprang up before World War II, with large-scale factories and plants utilizing a large labour force. The city was transformed from a small town during the 1930s as Stalin's great industrialization programmes took effect (see pp.304–05).

Concerns about crowded cities inspired the architect Kisho Kurokawa (1934–2007) to design space-saving accommodation. The first capsule hotel opened in Osaka in 1979, and the concept has been adopted throughout Japan.

Immigration regulations in most countries of the developed world seek to control population numbers by limiting the number of people officially allowed to enter. Economic migrants, who are often fleeing terrible poverty, sometimes take huge risks to circumvent these rules.

Large numbers of Europeans relocated to Australia after World War II, and in the 1970s the numbers of Asian migrants increased. It remains a popular destination today, particularly for workers seeking improved climate and lifestyles.

Moscow — 5.4m 7.6m 10.1m / 1950 1975 2000
London — 7.5m 8.2m / 1975 2000
EUROPE
ASIA
Cairo — 2.5m 6.4m 10.4m / 1950 1975 2000
AFRICA
Mumbai — 2.8m 7.1m 16.1m / 1950 1975 2000
Shanghai — 6.1m 7.3m 13.2m / 1950 1975 2000
Tokyo — 11.3m 26.6m 34.4m / 1950 1975 2000
PACIFIC OCEAN
INDIAN OCEAN
AUSTRALIA
Melbourne — 1.3m 2.9m 4m / 1950 1975 2000

In the 20th century, a new industrial era began in many countries, heralding an age of plenty and a new culture of consumerism.

RAPID CHANGE

In 1900, just 10,000 motor cars were produced per year worldwide, but by 1960, this figure had risen to 100 million. The global population also increased from under 1.5 billion in 1900 to more than 3 billion in 1960. **World energy consumption quadrupled** in the same period, with most of the excess requirement being met through the burning of oil, coal, and natural gas. By the 1960s materials for building and manufacturing were being extracted from the Earth at more than four times the rate in 1900 and factories were becoming more polluting.

STEEL FACTORY, GERMANY 1955

WRITER AND BIOLOGIST (1907–64)

RACHEL CARSON

American biologist Rachel Carson was passionate about nature conservation and made an immense contribution through her work on the ecology of aquatic habitats. She met huge resistance from powerful forces within the chemical industry after the publication of her book *Silent Spring* – the title alludes to the drastic reduction in songbird populations caused by the use of pesticides.

Green Technology

Industrialization, consumerism, and a growing global population require enormous amounts of energy and resources that have put pressure on the Earth's natural systems. Green technology is designed to reduce that pressure, enabling us to live more sustainably.

R apid industrialization along with new synthetic chemicals and materials developed in the 20th century caused unprecedented air, water, and land pollution. However, until the 1960s, few were concerned about these issues. Many historians trace the beginning of the modern environmental movement to the publication of *Silent Spring* by American biologist Rachel Carson in 1962 (see box). In her book, Carson uncovered the effects of the insecticide dichlorodiphenyltrichloroethane (DDT), which had decimated populations of animals other than the insects it aimed to control, and is said to cause cancer in humans.

Widening concerns

The environmental movement expanded during the 1970s as politicians and the general population alike became aware of other negative effects of the modern way of life. By the 1980s, scientists studying the global climate warned of the terrible consequences of global warming – the rise in the Earth's surface temperature mostly caused by massive deforestation and the carbon dioxide (CO_2) released into the atmosphere as a result of burning fossil fuels. These grave concerns led to a worldwide drive to adopt more sustainable lifestyles. Many countries drew up legislation aimed at reducing pollution and introducing new cleaner technologies and greener industrial processes. Campaigns encouraged individuals to be more

Solar power plant
The Ivanpah Solar Electric Generating System in the Mojave Desert, USA, generates enough electricity to power 140,000 homes.

Hundreds of reflectors focus sunlight onto boiler towers.

Water in the towers changes to superheated steam, which turns turbines to generate electricity.

Germany is Renewable!
A demonstration against nuclear power in Germany, which intends to eliminate the use of nuclear power by 2022 and to rely increasingly on renewable energy supplies.

Sustainable development
Beddington Zero Energy Development (BedZED), in the UK, takes sustainable living to a new level using energy generated on site and recycling rainwater. Even the buildings are largely made from recycled materials.

energy efficient, too – turning off lights and heating when they were not needed, for example, and improving insulation in roofs and walls to reduce the amount of energy required to keep warm. Compact fluorescent and LED (light-emitting diode) lamps – which used only around 25 per cent of the energy needed by conventional incandescent lamps to produce the same amount of light – became the norm. Recycling of materials also became more widespread, reducing the pressure on natural resources.

New generation

At the same time, utility companies increased efforts to generate electricity from renewable energy sources, such as wind, sun, and biofuels. Some renewable energy sources do not produce CO_2, while biofuels such as wood chips are considered "carbon neutral" because when burned they produce only as much CO_2 as they absorbed when they were alive. Reducing reliance on fossil fuels was slow at first, and much of the

development of renewable energy systems has taken place since the end of the 1990s. The amount of electricity generated worldwide from wind power increased from just 6 gigawatts in the mid-1990s to more than 400 gigawatts in 2015. Another low-carbon way of generating electricity is through nuclear power, but it is not without its problems – in particular, the risk of major accidents releasing radioactive substances into the environment, and the challenges of dealing with the radioactive waste.

20 PER CENT **onboard efficiency of a petrol-powered vehicle**

80 PER CENT **onboard efficiency of an electric vehicle**

Greener Transport

Renewable energy sources have so far played a very small role in the transport sector: in 2014, 95 per cent of vehicles were still powered by petrol and diesel engines. However, some progress has been made in making transport more efficient. Electric vehicles, in which the wheels are turned by an electric motor powered

by an onboard battery, produce no CO_2. Although the electricity used to charge the batteries is mainly generated by fossil fuels, these vehicles are on the whole much more efficient than conventional vehicles – and their "hybrid" cousins have petrol or diesel engines to recharge their batteries.

Research into electric and hybrid vehicles focuses largely on improving battery technology to increase the range of electric vehicles.

Hydrogen fuel is another promising option. Hydrogen may be burned directly in an engine, producing only water as a waste product, or the hydrogen may be used in a fuel cell, producing electricity to power a motor. The hydrogen is produced from water, in a process known as electrolysis, which requires an input of energy, but where this energy is generated from renewable sources, this too is carbon neutral. Other developments in green technology include carbon sequestration: this is another carbon-neutral process in which the CO_2 produced by burning fossil fuels is absorbed as it is produced.

Efficient hybrids
Hybrid electrical vehicles use a petrol or diesel engine to charge the battery, making them more efficient than conventional vehicles.

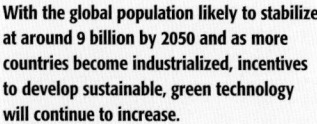
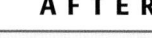

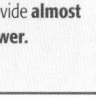

AFTER

With the global population likely to stabilize at around 9 billion by 2050 and as more countries become industrialized, incentives to develop sustainable, green technology will continue to increase.

GREEN INITIATIVES

The manufacturing process will become greener, with greater use of **biodegradable materials** and more recycling of waste – as a "cradle-to-cradle" approach becomes commonplace. In many countries, builders are being encouraged to go green. Electric and hydrogen-powered vehicles are set to gain popularity.

GREEN GENERATION

Research is making solar cells (photovoltaics) more efficient and cheaper, and solar panels installed on buildings and perhaps even on roadways will **reduce the need for large coal-, gas- and oil-fired power stations**. New ventures, such as solar farms in deserts, high-altitude wind farms, and tidal barrages, may begin to tip the balance in favour of renewable energy, and **hydrogen could become a "universal energy currency"**, powering homes and vehicles. A long-term hope is that **nuclear fusion**, a form of nuclear power that has fewer problems than nuclear fission used currently, may provide **almost limitless, greenhouse-gas-free power**.

‹‹ BEFORE

Since the end of the last ice age, natural factors and human actions have had an impact on the Earth's climate.

NATURAL CLIMATE CHANGES
The last ice age ended between 10,000–15,000 years ago, and since then the **world has been getting warmer**. Researchers have suggested a range of natural causes for this warming, including variations in the Earth's orbit, fluctuations in the Sun's output, and volcanic activity.

CONGESTED ROADS

INDUSTRIAL EFFECTS
Since the Industrial Revolution ‹‹ 226–27, the average global temperature has risen more quickly. Increased burning of fossil fuels, such as oil and coal, has led to **higher levels of carbon dioxide (CO_2)** in the Earth's atmosphere, and so increased the "Greenhouse Effect".

THE GREENHOUSE EFFECT
In 1824, French mathematician and physicist **Joseph Fourier** observed that the Earth's surface and atmosphere are warmed because the **Sun's heat is absorbed by naturally occurring "greenhouse" gases**, including methane (CH_4) and carbon dioxide (CO_2).

Since the Industrial Revolution (see pp.226–27), average global temperatures have risen by about 0.8°C (1.4°F). This warming has accelerated in the last four decades. The 21st century has seen 13 of the 14 warmest years on record.

The current situation
In 2007, the Intergovernmental Panel on Climate Change (IPCC) published a report in which it projected probable rises in temperature of between 1.8–4°C (3.2–7°F) by the end of the 21st century. The panel declared themselves confident that the "net

84 PER CENT of Antarctic glaciers have retreated since 1950.

34 PER CENT reduction in Arctic summer sea-ice since 1979.

10 PER CENT shrinkage in global snow and ice cover since 1960.

effect of human activity since 1750 has been one of warming". The IPCC was set up by the World Meteorological Organization (WMO) and the United Nations Environment Programme (UNEP) to investigate climate change. Its conclusion that humans have caused climate change is based on the fact that the atmospheric concentration of carbon dioxide (CO_2) has increased by 31 per cent since the pre-industrial era, intensifying the Greenhouse Effect (see BEFORE).

Increased CO_2 emissions are a direct result of industrialization. Coal-burning power stations generate CO_2 – as do air, sea, and road traffic; each of the 232 million cars in the US produces more than five tonnes of CO_2 every year.

Plants and trees naturally counteract emissions, by incorporating CO_2 into their tissues, and by releasing oxygen into the atmosphere, but 13 million hectares (32 million acres) of the

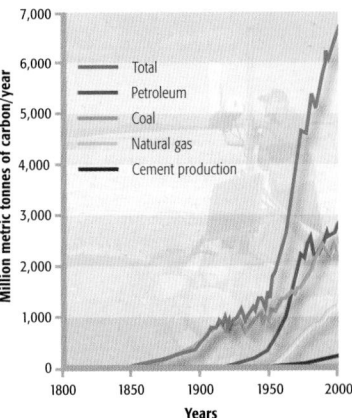

Carbon emissions
The graph shows the amount of carbon released yearly into the air by burning fossil fuels (coal, oil, and natural gas). The burning of fossil fuels has grown in parallel with increases in motorized transport and energy-hungry industrial activities, such as cement production. Annual carbon emissions reached 10 billion tonnes in 2014.

Climate Change

The Earth's atmosphere has a natural capacity to warm the planet. Without this heat, the planet could not sustain life, but the world is steadily getting warmer. Many experts believe human activity is to blame, calling for urgent action to prevent a global crisis and protect the planet for future generations.

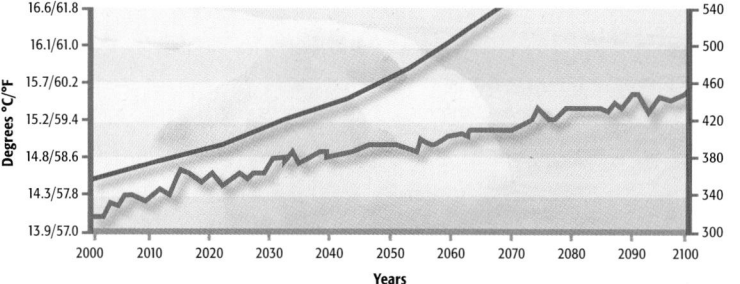

17.6 TONNES of CO_2 produced per person, per year in the US.

7.9 TONNES of CO_2 produced per person, per year in the UK.

1.7 TONNES of CO_2 produced per person, per year in India.

world's forests are lost each year to industrial logging; so less and less carbon is being neutralized.

The oceans also absorb CO_2 and contain the largest store of the gas on Earth, but warming of the oceans reduces the sea's capacity to absorb carbon dioxide from the atmosphere. There has been widespread retreat of glaciers in non-polar regions, and a

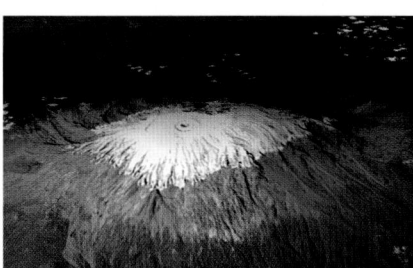

The Shining Mountain
According to some scientists, Mount Kilimanjaro's ice fields could be gone by the year 2020. The ice on the mountain's summit has dwindled by 82 per cent over the past century, which is particularly remarkable given that it has survived previous climate shifts – including a severe 300-year-long drought 4,000 years ago. These images show the peak in February 1993 (top) and February 2000 (right).

decrease in global snow and ice cover since the late 1960s. Sea levels are rising, and may rise a further 25–40cm (10–16in) by 2100.

Experts also believe climate change is responsible for changes in rainfall patterns, which have created severe water shortages in many regions of the world – tens of millions have suffered from drought in Africa since the 1980s. Climate change probably contributes to the increased intensity of heatwaves and tropical storms, although no direct causal link has been established with such extreme weather events as Hurricane Katrina, which devastated the US city of New Orleans in 2006.

The implications
The IPCC and many other organizations predict dire consequences for the world, and especially for the poorest nations, if CO_2 emissions continue to rise. Increasing sea-levels could displace

Lengthy fast
An adult female polar bear hauls out of the Arctic waters. The progressively earlier break-up of sea-ice shortens the vital spring hunting season for female polar bears. As a result, weight loss is affecting their ability to reproduce, and the survival of their cubs.

tens of millions of people from low-lying areas such as the Ganges and Nile deltas.

Many animal species are in danger of extinction. The World Conservation Union (WCU) considers 688 African fish, bird, and mammal species to be under threat, and 201 of these are classed as "critically endangered". The reduction of Arctic summer sea-ice is jeopardizing the survival of some species, including polar bears. The IPCC suggests that the summer sea-ice will disappear entirely in the second half of the 21st century.
The message from environmental lobby groups worldwide is that governments must act, and act now, to reduce CO_2 emissions. Industrialized countries are promoting personal carbon-offset schemes in which people are encouraged to plant trees to offset their "carbon footprints". However, given the amount of trees needed to offset the carbon emissions of just one car per year and the fact that large

portions of the world's forests are disappearing, the fear is that climate change may now be progressing so rapidly that humans will soon be unable to stop it.

The scientific debate
The factors that affect climate are complex, and the scientific community is not universally persuaded that human beings are – or have been – a major cause of climate change. Natural climate variability is certainly a factor, but most scientists believe that the Earth is undergoing significant warming as a direct result of human activities – and that this trend of global warming is set to continue.

13 MILLION hectares of forest lost each year.

240 TREES needed to absorb the CO_2 emitted by one car each year.

27 PER CENT of the world's coral reefs now destroyed.

"Future generations may well have occasion to ask themselves, 'What were our parents thinking?'" AL GORE, FROM "AN INCONVENIENT TRUTH", 2006

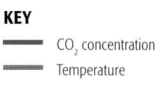

KEY
— CO_2 concentration
— Temperature

21st century warming
Current projections for global warming predict temperature rises of between 1.8–4°C (3.2–7°F) and a steady rise in atmospheric concentrations of CO_2. The increased levels of this gas in the atmosphere heighten the greenhouse effect, pushing temperatures upwards.

AFTER »

The race is on to cut greenhouse gases and to find alternatives to replace fossil fuels.

ALTERNATIVE POWER SOURCES
Since the 1950s some countries have been developing **nuclear power**, which produces few carbon emissions. However, the risk of accidents, as highlighted by the crisis at Fukushima, Japan (2011), has led some countries, including Germany, to close down their nuclear power industries. Other "clean" options include **wind, solar, tidal, wave, and hydroelectric power** « 402–03. Each of these has its environmental drawbacks, and engineers have struggled to make most of these power sources economically viable.

WIND TURBINES

AGREEING TARGETS IN EMISSION CUTS
The **Kyoto Protocol** was an agreement by 192 countries in 1997 to **reduce greenhouse gas emissions** to target amounts by 2012. The US famously failed to ratify the agreement, but it came into effect in 2008. When Kyoto's first phase expired in 2012, global emissions had reduced by 6 per cent, compared to baseline figures from 1990, but this is explained mainly by the contraction of heavy industry in the former Soviet Union and Eastern Europe in the 1990s.

NEW COMMITMENTS?
The **UN** holds a **Climate Change Conference** every year and searches for a successor to the Kyoto Protocol. A key stumbling block is the imbalance between **developed nations**, which emit more greenhouse gases, and **developing states** that are more at risk from the impacts of climate change. Despite this, some developed countries refuse to commit to reductions that are not imposed equally on the developing world.

HOW WE KNOW
MEASURING CLIMATE CHANGE
Scientists monitor glaciers in the Arctic and Antarctica to determine the current changes occurring in the polar regions. However, in order to assess climate change, they must form a picture of past climates. Clues to past climatic conditions are hidden in rocks and trees, but the most revealing indicators of the historical climate are preserved in ice. Scientists studying glaciers are able to analyse air bubbles trapped in the ice and determine the levels of gases in the atmosphere at the time the ice was formed, giving them information on how the atmosphere has changed over the centuries.

« BEFORE

Internet and Social Media

The internet, particularly, the World Wide Web, has offered many new ways for individuals, groups, and businesses to communicate. The rise of social media in the 21st century has made millions of people into producers as well as consumers of information.

Until the late 20th century, the "one-way traffic" of information disseminated by newspaper publishers and radio and TV broadcasters allowed media groups to be tremendously influential.

SPREADING INFORMATION

Printing technology swept through Europe in the 16th century « **192–93**; from the 18th century, **newspapers and journals** grew in popularity worldwide. In the 1920s radio was launched, and the late 1930s saw the dawn of the **television age**.

NEWSPAPERS FROM ITALY

The basis of most modern communications, the internet is an "inter-network": a network of computer networks. Launched in 1969 by the US Advanced Research Projects Agency (ARPA), it evolved from ARPANET, the first extensive wide area network. The idea behind ARPANET was to enable ARPA researchers at different sites to exchange data and software easily. ARPANET grew, although it was then available only to academic and military organizations. In the 1980s, connections were made to networks outside the US. Even in these early years of the internet, users could exchange information "socially" using e-mail and bulletin board systems – computers that could hold up-to-date information as well as messages.

World Wide Web

In 1989, British computer scientist Tim Berners-Lee adapted an existing technology, "hypertext", to link pieces of information in a document on one computer to a document on another machine via the internet (see p.409). The result was a "web" of information, with the documents being stored on and delivered by computers called "web servers". By 2000, over 300 million people were connecting to the internet and accessing websites, or sets of web pages. As internet access became widespread, so did websites that people could contribute to. Known as weblogs, or "blogs", these personal or business websites allowed people to post updates or pieces of information. The ability to share and comment on these posts are crucial social aspects of blogs. The first blogs went online in 1994, and they became the first truly social medium on the internet. Social media eventually became a common term describing any online channel or application enabling users to exchange ideas and data.

Internet traffic

These interconnected threads show internet routing paths from an ISP network. Networks that contact each other may take many routes. If there is a failure in one route, the information can take a different path to reach its target.

I was there: the rise of the selfie
The ability to upload photographs from portable devices has made self portraits, or "selfies", popular. This photograph taken at the 2014 Oscars became the most shared selfie of all time within days.

In 1994, informative websites known as Wikis were created and edited jointly by a large number of people. The best known Wiki is the collaborative encyclopedia Wikipedia that was created in 2001; by 2007, it was among the 10 most visited websites worldwide. As speeds and ease of access improved, people were increasingly able to share different kinds of content, such as photos and videos. In 2004, the video sharing website YouTube was founded and soon became one of the biggest social media sites.

Web 2.0

The internet, particularly the World Wide Web, had become an interactive tool used to contribute and exchange information and media, rather than simply consume it. Some people began referring to this social version of the Web as Web 2.0. The Web now had communal features such as forums – sites dedicated to particular topics and enabling online communities to post and reply to messages, forming conversations called threads. While forum threads could take days, weeks, or months to build up, instant messaging and chat rooms offered immediate communication in real time. Websites featuring all these social aspects, and through which users could connect to online "friends", became popular from the late 1990s. Important early friend-based social media sites included Tripod (1995) and TheGlobe (1995). Facebook (see box) became the largest social networking site, with over a billion users in 2012, ahead of China's biggest social media site, QZone, founded in 2005.

Since the early 2000s, the popularity of smartphones and tablets has made it easier to consume and produce social media content, such as the "selfie", from almost anywhere at any time. Microblogging – posting short comments to an audience of followers – rapidly became common from 2007. Twitter, a major microblogging service, coined the term "tweet" for these messages. Public figures from pop stars to world leaders soon saw tweets as an essential way of reaching the public. In 2007, US president Barack Obama even announced the imminent end of the war in Iraq by tweet.

MARK ZUCKERBERG

American computer genius Mark Zuckerberg founded Facebook while he was a student at Harvard University, US. He had been writing computer software since middle school and launched the TheFacebook, as the site was first called, from his dorm room in 2004. Since 2013, Zuckerberg has been the chairman and chief executive of Facebook Incorporated and is among the 100 wealthiest people in the world, his personal wealth valued at tens of billions of US dollars.

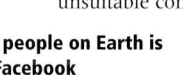

1 IN 9 people on Earth is on Facebook

5 HOURS of video uploaded on YouTube every 3 seconds

With the rise of participation in social media has come fears of invasions of privacy and online bullying, as well as efforts to protect children from unsuitable content or from online sexual predators. Social media have also become a potent force in advertising and in grass-roots politics, where they enable sharing of information and organization of meetings and protests. Social media services such as Twitter and Facebook played a major role in social uprisings that were sparked in Tunisia in 2010, leading up to the Arab Spring.

AFTER

Faster, easier, and cheaper access to online content will enable the use of the internet to make enormous changes in society.

ALL THINGS ARE CONNECTED

The **role of social media** in generating **public interest** in socially relevant causes, as was seen during the anti-capitalist protest, **Occupy Wall Street**, is an example of its **immense potential.** Internet access is becoming almost universal with devices as varied as heart monitors and refrigerators getting connected. This is likely to lead to an **"internet of things"**, which will probably lead to a world of increased convenience, but also to **issues of privacy and "information overload".**

OCCUPY WALL STREET, 2011

Shrinking World

Our experience of the world has been radically altered by modern technology. A journey that once took weeks by land or sea can now be flown in a matter of hours and messages are transmitted across the world at the click of a mouse, giving us the impression that the world is becoming smaller.

‹‹ BEFORE

Developments in communication and transport in the 19th and early 20th centuries wrought new social, political, and economic ties between people living thousands of kilometres apart.

BETTER COMMUNICATION NETWORKS
British engineers **George Stephenson and Isambard Kingdom Brunel** contributed to the development of efficient rail transport systems, making travel across countries and continents faster and more affordable. Improvements to the size and speed of ocean-going ships increased the transport of freight around the world, while the success of wire-based telephone and telegraph systems allowed **instant communication** across physical space for the first time.

THE BIRTH OF TOURISM
Until the late 19th century, **tourism**, or recreational travel, **was the preserve of the better off**, but many more people were taking holidays by the 1900s. Companies such as Thomas Cook & Son, the first travel agent, began to organize **package tours**, including a "round the world trip".

 ince World War I advances in technology have transformed global communications and transport systems allowing both economic and personal connections to flourish on a worldwide scale. Without these technological developments many features of modern life including the phenomena of globalization (see pp.394–95) and global tourism would not have occurred.

Revolutionizing travel
The 20th century boom in travel was largely due to advances in the design of the internal combustion engine, which still powers most motor vehicles, ships, airplanes, and helicopters. The Ford Motor Company (see right) began to mass-produce combustion engines in 1906, pioneering "assembly lines"

Transatlantic liners
Cunard Cruise Liners represented the height of luxurious travel for tourists crossing between Europe and the US during the inter-war years, when the company slogan, "getting there is half the fun" was a household phrase.

to speed up production. Motor manufacturing is now a multi-billion dollar industry: in 2010 more than 1 billion motor vehicles were in use worldwide, and with the growth of car ownership in countries such as China and Brazil statistics predict that this figure will more than double by 2030.

As motor vehicles improved so too did road networks. The first "high-speed" intersection-free road, the *Automobil-Verkehrs- und Übungsstraße* (AVUS), was constructed in Berlin in 1912. Soon multi-lane highways – such as Route 66, which runs from Chicago to Los Angeles in the US – shortened

Passenger jets
Lining up on the runway at Gatwick Airport near London UK, a passenger jet takes off every few minutes while others land nearby. Over a million people pass through the airport every year.

journey times, allowing the transport of people and goods over longer distances. In recent years, high-speed rail links have seen major investment. A world speed record was set when the French *train à grande vitesse* (TGV) reached speeds of 575km/h (357mph). These trains can halve average journey times, reducing a 500km- (315 mile-) trip from Paris to Stuttgart to 3¾ hours.

Advances in maritime engineering have produced faster, larger ships that are able to transport millions of tonnes of cargo around the world. Improved refrigeration techniques allow perishable foodstuffs to be carried by both sea and air, making products that were once a luxury readily available.

The development of cheaper and quicker modes of travel has brought previously inaccessible parts of the world within reach of ordinary people. In the century following the Wright brother's first powered flight in 1903, aeronautical science has revolutionized aircraft design, with wide-bodied, high performance jet airliners that carry millions of passengers every year.

Going places
Tourism is one of the world's fastest growing industries, driven by higher levels of disposable income in some societies, as well as developments in technology and transport. Taking holidays became the norm in the developed world in the early 20th century as terms of employment began to include paid leave. At first people holidayed in domestic locations, but from the 1950s, mass tourism, particularly to European destinations, became more common. Longhaul travel between continents remained expensive until the 1980s

INDUSTRIALIST (1863–1947)
HENRY FORD

Henry Ford founded the Ford Motor Company in 1903. From 1909, he began mass production of the Model T Ford, using assembly line methods and wage incentives. Soon the company was producing a complete car in 1 hour and 33 minutes and its price fell from $1,000 to $360. Ford became the world's leading car manufacturer. He opposed World War I and sponsored an international conference to try and negotiate an armistice. In the 1930s, he was violently opposed to unions and was the last car manufacturer to recognize union workers in his factories.

Satellite communications
A Western journalist transmits a report by satellite phone from the hills of Northern Afghanistan. Portable satellite communications devices can provide news of events from around the world as they occur.

when improved airline passenger capacity and shortened journey times led to an increase in longhaul traffic.

> " ... people's lives change so fast, that a person is **born into one kind of world** [and] **grows up in another**...""
>
> MARGARET MEAD, US ANTHROPOLOGIST

This upward trend has continued with growing numbers of people travelling between continents for their vacations.

In recent years, tourism has become more specialized. With the growth in "niche markets" catering for special interests such as extreme sports, the market has both grown and fragmented. Destinations, such as the Galapagos Islands (see pp.270–71), that were once the preserve of intrepid explorers are now tourist hotspots. Nowhere is inaccessible – even Mount Everest, the summit of which was only reached for the first time by Edmund Hilary and Tenzing Norgay in 1953, has become a tourist destination.

Instant communication
The technological revolution gathered pace from the late 1950s with the invention of the microchip (see pp.384–85). This transformed the modern world. Microtechnology has touched most fields of manufacturing and engineering, from weapons design to medical robotics. The impact on human communications has been huge. Microchips provide the "brains" for computers, tablets, and cellular phones allowing instant global communication and the storage of vast amounts of information. Data that previously filled libraries can now be stored on one tiny chip. The creation of the internet(see right) allowed this information to be shared among computer users worldwide.

It is often said that we are now living in a new era, that the 21st century will be the "Communications Age", an age centred on the sharing of information

The seemingly insatiable public appetite for travel to exotic locations shows no sign of fading in the 21st century. Not content with gaining access to the remotest corners of the Earth, there is now a new demand for holidays that are literally out of this world.

SPACE TOURISM
British entrepreneur Richard Branson has poured millions of dollars into the Virgin Spaceship to take passengers into space. Wealthy individuals and corporations are already booking "**personal spaceflights**" with the Russian Space Agency. Tourists undergo rigorous physical training and medical tests before they are passed fit to travel. Seven civillians holidayed on the International Space Station between 2001 and 2009, paying $20–40 million for the privilege. The first tourist, Californian financier Dennis Tito, described his eight-day voyage as "a trip to paradise".

between individuals, businesses, and nations. In the past, geographical distance impeded communication but technological advances have broken down these barriers (see p.395). The Communications Age offers the chance

3 BILLION people worldwide regularly access the internet.

for skills and knowledge to be shared across the world. After more than a century in which international conflicts have wrought so much carnage, some have begun to promote a new ideal for this age: that of the global citizen.

INVENTION
THE WORLD WIDE WEB

British physicist Tim Berners-Lee invented the World Wide Web in the late 1980s and early 1990s. Lee developed the concept of "hypertext" in order to share research with fellow scientists across a single computer network. His original ideas led to the popularization of the internet (see pp.406–07), as the technology was used to build websites that could be accessed from computers anywhere in the world. Berners-Lee heads the World Wide Web consortium, which concentrates on improving internet technology and accessibility.

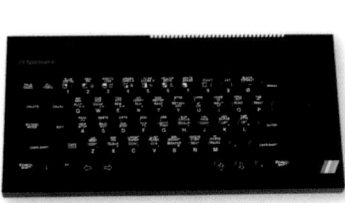

Personal computers
The Sinclair ZX Spectrum was one of the first personal computers. It was designed for use with an ordinary TV set, and its low price made home computing a reality for many – an essential precursor to internet connectivity.

Mobile communication
The development of smartphones and mobile devices such as tablets made it possible to keep up with national and international events – and those in our own social networks – at almost any time and place.

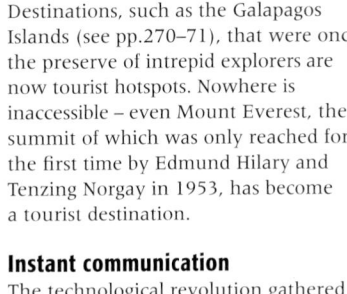

Global Positioning System (GPS)
Originally developed for the US military during the cold war, GPS technology uses signals transmitted by global navigation satellites to pinpoint the receiver's location – to within about 15m (50ft) – anywhere on the planet.

Index

Acknowledgments

Dorling Kindersley would like to thank the following people for their help in the preparation of this book: Richard Beatty and Sarah Levete for proof reading; John Breen, Michael Brett, Amy-Sue Bix, Howard Hotson, Rosamond McKitterick, and Chris Scarre for advice on content; Joanna Chisholm, Tarda Davison-Aitkins, Julie Ferris, Ben Hoare, Margaret Hynes, Neil Lockley, and Debra Wolter for editorial assistance; Smiljka Surla for design assistance; Laragh Kedwell for DTP support; Claire Morrey, Christine Pascall, and Joanne Grey at English Heritage for access to Dover Castle; Adam Howard at Invisiblecities Ltd for artworks (model by Andy Kay); Ailsa Heritage for advice on maps.

Dorling Kindersley would also like to thank the following people for their help in the preparation of updates to the book: consultant Philip Parker; Ferdie McDonald and Manisha Majithia for editorial; Gadi Farfour and Steve Woosnam-Savage for design; Dawn Bates for proofreading; John Searcy for Americanization.

PICTURE CREDITS

The publisher would like to thank the following for their kind permission to reproduce their photographs: Romaine Werblow at DK Images, Sonia

Harder at AKG Images, Everyone at The Art Archive, Jenny Page at The Bridgeman Art Library and Nejla Burnazoglu.

(**Key:** a-above; b-below/bottom; c-center; f-far; l-left; r-right; t-top)

Abbreviations:
AKG akg-images **Alamy** - Alamy Images;
AA&A - Ancient Art & Architecture Collection;
AA - The Art Archive; **BAL** - The Bridgeman Art Library; **BM** - The Trustees of the British Museum; **DK** - DK Images; **Getty** - Getty Images; **LoC** - Library Of Congress, Washington, D.C.; **NHM** - The Natural History Museum, London; **S&S** - Science & Society Picture Library; **WFA** - Werner Forman Archive.

2-3 Alamy: Visual Arts Library (London). **4-5 Getty:** National Geographic / Richard T. Nowitz. **6 akg-images:** Erich Lessing (c). Tribaleye Images / J. Marshall (bl). **123RF.com:** Luca Mason / lkpro (br). **WFA:** Egyptian Museum, Cairo (tl). **WFA:** Private Collection (cr). **7 Alamy:** Classic Image (c); IML Image Group Ltd (bl). **BAL:** Edinburgh University Library, Scotland, With kind permission of the University of Edinburgh (br). **S&S:** National Railway Museum (tr). **8 Alamy:** ArkReligion.com (bl). **BAL:** Musée du Louvre, Paris (br). **Corbis:** Bettmann (c). **9 Corbis:** (bl). **Getty Images:** Andy Brandl (br). **10 WFA:** Egyptian Museum, Cairo. **12 DK:** The Science Museum, London (tr, bc). **Rex Features:** Sipa Press

(cla). **WFA:** Egyptian Museum, Cairo (clb). **13 AKG:** Erich Lessing (tl). **AA:** Musée Condé Chantilly / Dagli Orti (br). **S&S:** (cr). **The Wellcome Institute Library, London:** (bl). **14 AKG:** (bl). **AA&A:** (cl). **BAL:** Private Collection, Photo © Heini Schneebeli (tl). **DK:** The British Museum, London (tc). **15 AKG:** Erich Lessing (bl). **Alamy:** Visual Arts Library (London) (crb). **AA:** Musée du Louvre, Paris / Dagli Orti (cra). **DK:** The British Museum, London (bl). **16 AKG:** Erich Lessing (c). **AA:** Dagli Orti (cra). **Corbis:** Sandro Vannini (cla). **DK:** The British Museum, London (bl). **17 Alamy:** Tor Eigeland (cra). **AA:** Musée du Louvre, Paris / Dagli Orti (cl). **Corbis:** Brooklyn Museum (crb). **DK:** The British Museum, London (bl). **Getty:** The Image Bank / Michael John O'Neill (tl). **18 AKG:** Gérard Degeorge (tr). **AA:** National Museum, Karachi / Dagli Orti (cl). **BAL:** Ashmoleon Museum, University of Oxford (crb). **DK:** Courtesy of The National Museum, New Delhi (c). **19 Getty:** Robert Harding World Imagery / Ursula Gahwiler. **20 Corbis:** Asian Art & Archaeology, Inc. (cl). **20-21 DK:** The British Museum, London (c). **21 DK:** Courtesy of The British Library, London (cr, bc); Courtesy of the University Museum of Archaeology and Anthropology, Cambridge (c).
National Geographic Image Collection: O. Louis Mazzatenta (tr). **22 DK:** The British Museum, London (bl). **Photo Scala, Florence:** The Metropolitan Museum of Art, New York / Art Resource

(br). **The Schøyen Collection, Oslo and London:** MS 4631 (tl). **23 Alamy:** Visual Arts Library (London) (tr). **AA:** Egyptian Museum Turin / Dagli Orti (tl). **Corbis:** Gianni Dagli Orti (crb, cb). **DK:** The British Museum, London (c); Courtesy of the London College of Printing (br). **24 AA:** Egyptian Museum Turin / Dagli Orti (ca). **Corbis:** Gianni Dagli Orti (cl). **Jürgen Liepe:** Egyptian Museum, Cairo (crb). **25 AA:** Egyptian Museum, Cairo / Dagli Orti (cra); Tribaleye Images / J. Marshall (l). **BAL:** Musée du Louvre, Paris, Peter Willi (br). **26 Alamy:** The Print Collector (c). **AA:** Musée du Louvre, Paris / Dagli Orti (bc). **Corbis:** Zefa / Paul C. Pet (l). **27 AA:** Dagli Orti (tc). **Corbis:** Roger Wood (crb). **Getty:** The Bridgeman Art Library (bc). **AA:** Musée du Louvre, Paris / Dagli Orti (cl). **DK:** The British Museum, London (tl, cr). **29 AA:** Egyptian Museum, Cairo / Dagli Orti (br). **DK:** The British Museum, London (tl, tr, bl). **30 Deutsches Archäologisches Institut:** (cla). **30-31 Getty:** Robert Harding World Imagery / Gavin Hellier (b). **31 Alamy:** ImageState (cra). **AA:** Private Collection / Dagli Orti (br). **Corbis:** Michael S. Yamashita (cla). **Panos Pictures:** Georg Gerster (cl). **32 AA:** Xalapa Museum Veracruz, Mexico / Dagli Orti (bl). **Corbis:** Danny Lehman (c); Reuters / Sengo Perez (cla). **33 AA:** National Anthropological Museum, Mexico / Dagli Orti (bl). **John W. Rick:** (tc). **34 Alamy:** Wolfgang Kaehler (tr); Visual Arts Library (London) (bl). **BAL:**

Ashmolean Museum, University of Oxford (br). **Corbis:** The Art Archive (cl); Christie's Images (cla). **35 Alamy:** Ian Dagnall (cb); Helene Rogers (bl). **AA:** Dagli Orti (cr). **36 AKG:** Erich Lessing (tl). **Photo Scala, Florence:** The Metropolitan Museum of Art, New York / Art Resource (cl). **WFA:** (r); E. Strouhal (bl). **37 Alamy:** Visual Arts Library (London) (br). **AA&A:** (cra). **Corbis:** Yann Arthus-Bertrand (cb). **38 AKG:** Erich Lessing (tl, bc, bl). **Corbis:** Gianni Dagli Orti (br). **39 AKG:** Erich Lessing (c). **AA:** The British Museum, London / Dagli Orti (tl). **40 Alamy:** Ken Welsh (tc). **Corbis:** Werner Forman Archive (cl). **New Carlsberg Glyptotek, Copenhagen:** Ole Haupt (cr). **Photo Scala, Florence:** The Metropolitan Museum of Art, New York / Art Resource (bl). **41 Alamy:** Visual Arts Library (London) (cr). **BM:** (tl). **Corbis:** Gianni Dagli Orti (c). **DK:** The British Museum, London (tr). **Réunion des Musées Nationaux Agence Photographique:** Hervé Lewandowski (tc). **42 akg-images:** Erich Lessing. **44 AA:** Archaeological Museum, Florence / Dagli Orti (tr); Musée Rolin Autun / Dagli Orti (tl). **BAL:** Iraq Museum, Baghdad (bl). **Corbis:** Francis G. Mayer (bc/left); Roger Wood (bc/right). **Getty:** De Agostini Picture Library (tc). **WFA:** Theresa McCullough Collection, London (br). **45 AA:** Real biblioteca de lo Escorial / Dagli Orti (cr). **BAL:** The British Museum, London (cra). **Still Pictures:** Transit (bl). **46 AA:** Archaeological Museum, Istanbul / Dagli Orti (tl). **Panos Pictures:** Insight / Marcus Rose (b). **47 AA:** Musée du Louvre, Paris / Dagli Orti (bl). **BM:** (c). **Corbis:** Bettmann (br). **WFA:** Archaeological Museum, Teheran (cl). **48 AKG:** Orsi Battaglini (bl); Electa (tl). **Alamy:** Andrew Holt (tr). **DK:** Archaeological Receipts Fund (TAP) (br); D'Ephorate of Prehistoric and Classical Antiquities. Archaeological Receipts Fund (bc). **49 AA:** Museo Nazionale Palazzo Altemps, Rome / Dagli Orti (tc). **50 Alamy:** Peter Horree. **51 AKG:** (bc). **Alamy:** Mary Evans Picture Library (c). **Corbis:** Bettmann (cra); John Heseltine (tl). **52 Corbis:** Werner Forman Archive (clb). **Getty:** Robert Harding World Imagery / Lee Frost (t). **53 AA:** Musée Guimet, Paris / Dagli Orti (tr). **Corbis:** Archivo Iconografico, S.A. (br). **Wikipedia, The Free Encyclopedia:** (cl). **54 AKG:** (crb). **AA:** Agora Museum, Athens / Dagli Orti (cl, clb). **Corbis:** Gianni Dagli Orti (bl). **DK:** The British Museum, London (cla). **55 Panos Pictures:** Georg Gerster. **56 Alamy:** The Print Collector (br). **AA:** Archaeological Museum, Aleppo / Dagli Orti (bl); Bardo Museum, Tunis / Dagli Orti (ca). **57 AKG:** (br). **AA:** The British Library, London (tr); National Archaeological Museum, Athens (bl). **Corbis:** Archivo Iconografico, S.A. (tl). **58 The British Library, London:** (bc). **Corbis:** Araldo de Luca (tr). **DK:** The British Museum, London (cla). **WFA:** Dr. E. Strouhal (bl). 59 **AKG:** The British Library, London (tr). **The Wellcome Institute Library, London:** (br). **60 AA:** Museo Capitolino, Rome / Dagli Orti (br). **DK:** The British Museum, London (cl, cla). **WFA:** (bl). **60-61 AA:** Musée du Louvre, Paris / Dagli Orti (c). **61 Alamy:** Mary Evans Picture Library (crb). **DK:** The British Museum, London (clb). **62 AA&A:** PRISMA (c). **BAL:** Bibliothèque Nationale, Paris, Archives Charmet (bl). **63 AKG:** (cr). **Alamy:** CuboImages srl (c); Hideo Kurihara (tc). **AA:** Galleria d'Arte Moderna, Rome / Dagli Orti (bc). **The British Library, London:** (cla). **64 Alamy:** Art Kowalsky (bl); David Robertson (cl); Visual Arts Library (London) (tl); Ken Welsh (clb). **BM:** (tr). **Corbis:** Zefa / José Fusta Raga (br). **WFA:** Museo Archeologico Nazionale, Naples (bc). **65 Alamy:** Robert Harding Picture Library (br). **Getty:** Photographer's Choice / Michael Dunning (cb). **Panos Pictures:** Georg Gerster (tl). **66 AKG:** (bl). **Alamy:** Ace Stock Limited (br). **DK:** The British Museum, London (tc). **67 Alamy:** Brian Hoffman (ca); Martin Jenkinson (tl). **AA:** Archaeological Museum, Naples / Dagli Orti (b/Bracelet); Musée du Louvre, Paris / Dagli Orti (br); Museo della Civilta Romana, Rome / Dagli Orti (cr). **DK:** The British Museum, London (Spoon, b/Ladle, b/Grooming Kit, b/Coins). **68 AA:** Archaeological Museum, Châtillon-sur-Seine / Dagli Orti (clb). **DK:** The British Museum, London (crb, br). **Panos Pictures:** Georg Gerster (tr). **69 DK:** Courtesy of the Ermine Street Guard. **70 AA:** National Archaeological Museum, Athens / Dagli Orti (bl). **Corbis:** Araldo de Luca (r). **DK:** The British Museum, London (cl). **71 Alamy:** Ken Welsh (br). **BAL:** Villa Farnesina, Rome (cr). **DK:** The British Museum, London (tc). **72 AKG:** Erich Lessing (bl). **BAL:** Musée de la Vieille Charite, Marseille / Giraudon (tl). **Stéphane Compoint:** (cra). **Corbis:** Alinari Archives (crb). **73 AA:** Museo Prenestino, Palestrina / Dagli Orti. **74 Alamy:** North Wind Picture Archives (bc). **AA:** (r). **BM:** (clb). **75 AKG:** (br); Hilbich (tc). **AA:** Musée du Louvre, Paris / Dagli Orti (cr, bc). **BAL:** Musée du Louvre, Paris / Giraudon / Lauros (cl). **76 Alamy:** Visual Arts Library (London) (crb). **AA&A:** (cb). **AA:** Archaeological Museum, Teheran / Dagli Orti (clb). **BM:** (cla). **Corbis:** Pierre Colombel (tl). 77 BAL. **78 AKG:** Jean-Louis Nou (bc). **Alamy:** IML Image Group Ltd (tr); Sherab (br). **79 Alamy:** Bildarchiv Monheim GmbH (br); World Religions Photo Library (ca). **BAL:** National Museum of India, New Delhi (crb). **Corbis:** Charles & Josette Lenars (tr). **80 Corbis:** Keren Su. **81 AA&A:** (tr). **AA:** The British Library, London (bc). **Corbis:** Bettmann (br). **DK:** The British Museum, London (cla). 82 **BAL:** Bibliothèque Nationale, Paris (tr). **DK:** The British Museum, London (bl); The British Library, London (br). **83 AKG:** (bc). **AA:** Jan Vinchon Numismatist, Paris / Dagli Orti (cra). **84 Alamy:** Visual Arts Library (London) (cla, clb). **BAL:** Vatican Museums and Galleries, Vatican City (r). **85 AA:** Archaeological Museum, Naples / Dagli Orti (bl); Museo Civico, San Gimignano / Dagli Orti (br). **BAL:** Musée d'Archeologie et d'Histoire, Lausanne (crb); Museo Archeologico Nazionale, Naples (cla). **Corbis:** Archivo Iconografico, S.A. (cr). **86 AKG:** (bl). **AA&A:** (br). **AA:** Archaeological Museum, Bagdad / Dagli Orti (tr). **BM:** (cla). **87 AA:** Bodleian Library, Oxford (cra). **Getty:** Robert Harding World Imagery / Neale Clark (tl). **88 AKG:** Erich Lessing (cl). **Alamy:** Mary Evans Picture Library (bl). **Corbis:** Araldo de Luca (tc). **88-89 AKG:** (bc). **89 AKG:** Erich Lessing (cla). **BAL:** Boltin Picture Library (tr). **BM:** (tc). **90 Alamy:** Visual Arts Library (London) (bl). **Panos Pictures:** Georg Gerster (tl). **WFA:** Hermitage Museum, St. Petersburg (tr). **90-91 Corbis:** Michael Setboun (b). **91 AKG:** Mark De Fraeye (cla). **BM:** (tr). **Corbis:** Burstein Collection (tc). **92 BAL:** Bildarchiv Steffens (bl). **Panos Pictures:** Georg Gerster (cra). **WFA:** David Bernstein Fine Art, New York (tl); Museum für Völkerkunde, Berlin (c, crb). **93 Corbis:** Bettmann. **94 AKG:** Andrea Baguzzi (r); Erich Lessing (bl). **95 AKG:** (bl); Erich Lessing (cl). **BM:** (br). **WFA:** The British Museum, London (ca). **96 AA:** Museo Civico, Orvieto (tl). **Getty:** AFP / Menahem Kahana (b). **97 Alamy:** Visual Arts Library (London) (cr). **98 Alamy:** The Print Collector (br). **AA:** Musée Guimet, Paris / Dagli Orti (bl). **Corbis:** Nathan Benn (tc). **DK:** The British Museum, London (tl, tr). **99 Alamy:** Steve Allen Travel Photography (tl). **Corbis:** JAI / Michele Falzone (fbr); Patrick Ward (ca). **Getty:** National Geographic / Martin Gray (cra); Riser / China Tourism Press (bl); Taxi / Gavin Hellier (br). **Panos Pictures:** Dominic Harcourt-Webster (fbl). **100-101 AKG. 102 Alamy:** Visual Arts Library (London) (tr). **AA:** Gioviana Archives, Florence / Dagli Orti (bl). **BM:** (cla). **102-103 AKG:** Erich Lessing (bc). **103 DK:** The British Museum, London (br). **104 WFA:** Private Collection. **106 Alamy:** Gus (bc); Visual Arts Library (London) (tl, ca). **AA:** Rheinische Landesmuseum, Trier / Dagli Orti (clb). 107 **AKG:** The British Library, London (tl). **Alamy:** Visual Arts Library (London) (bl). **AA:** The Bodleian Library, Oxford (br). **BAL:** S. Ambrogio, Florence (tr). **108 BAL:** Musée Guimet, Paris / Archives Charmet (bl). **DK:** Judith Miller / Ancient Art (tl). **WFA:** (br). **109 Corbis:** Christie's Images (clb). **DK:** The British Library, London (br); Judith Miller / Sloans & Kenyon (cra). **Terra Galleria Photography:** Quang-Tuan Luong (tl). **110 AA:** Musée Guimet, Paris / Dagli Orti (clb). **Dennis Cox / ChinaStock:** Sun Kerang (crb). **110-111 AA:** National Palace Museum, Taiwan (t). **111 AKG:** (crb). **BAL:** Private Collection / Archives Charmet (bl). **112 BAL:** Bibliothèque Nationale, Paris (clb); The British Museum, London (bl); Private Collection (r). **113 AKG:** (bc). **Alamy:** Visual Arts Library (London) (br). **AA:** Biblioteca Nazionale Marciana, Venice / Harper Collins Publishers (tl). **DK:** Courtesy of the University Museum of Archaeology and Anthropology, Cambridge (c). **114 DK:** Judith Miller / Sloan's (bc). **WFA:** Private Collection, London (clb). **114-115 Still Pictures:** UNEP (t). **115 Alamy:** View Stock (bl). **Getty:** AFP / Goh Chai Hin (c). **116 AA&A:** (bl). **AA:** Private Collection, Paris / Dagli Orti (cra). **Corbis:** Sakamoto Photo Research Laboratory (cla). **WFA:** Burke Collection, New York (br). **117 AA:** (tr). **DK:** Board of Trustees of the Royal Armouries (l). **118 King Sejong the Great Memorial Society:** (tr, br). **119 Corbis:** Christie's Images (c). **Getty:** AFP / Kim Jae-Hwan (bl). **King Sejong the Great Memorial Society:** (cr, br). **120 Alamy:** Visual Arts Library (London) (tl). **Panos Pictures:** Georg Gerster (clb). **WFA:** (cra). **120-121 Kenny Grant:** (b). **121 AKG:** Erich Lessing (cb). **Alamy:** Ken Welsh (cra). **122 AA:** Museum of Islamic Art, Cairo (bc). **DK:** Courtesy of the Pitt Rivers Museum, University of Oxford (cla). **123 Corbis:** Richard T. Nowitz (tr). **DK:** Courtesy of the National Maritime Museum, London (crb). **Wikipedia, The Free Encyclopedia:** Bilkent University / Department of History (bc). **124 AKG:** (cl). **AA:** The British Library, London (br). **125 Alamy:** Lebrecht Music and Arts Photo Library (tl); Nicholas Pitt (cra); Andrew Watson (cl). **AA:** Turkish and Islamic Art Museum, Istanbul / Dagli Orti (bc). **Getty:** Lonely Planet Images / Richard l'Anson (c). **Magnum Photos:** Abbas (crb). **Wikipedia, The Free Encyclopedia:** (tc). **126 AA:** Musée Guimet, Paris / Dagli Orti (cla). **Corbis:** Charles & Josette Lenars (cra). **127 Alamy:** Trip (c). **BAL:** Bonhams, London (tl). **Corbis:** Macduff Everton (b). **128 AKG:** Robert Aberman (br). **BAL:** Heini Schneebeli (cra). **Corbis:** Cordaiy Photo Library Ltd / Colin Hoskins (clb). **Still Pictures:** Frans Lemmens (cla). **WFA:** Robert Aberman (bl, crb). **129 AKG:** Erich Lessing (bl). **Corbis:** Christie's Images (crb); Sandro Vannini (cra). **WFA:** The British Museum, London (tl). **130 Alamy:** Images&Stories (tr). **AA:** Bibliothèque Nationale, Paris (bl). **WFA:** (cla). **131 Alamy:** Iain Masterton (br); World Religions Photo Library (tl). **Corbis:** Michael S. Yamashita (tr). **132 Corbis:** Reuters / Kin Cheung (crb). **Science Photo Library:** Dr. Gary Gaugler (bc). **Wikipedia, The Free Encyclopedia:** Royal Ontario Museum, Toronto (cl). **133 AKG. 134 BAL:** Archives du Ministère des Affaires Étrangères, Paris / Archives Charmet (br). **Getty:** Imagno (c). **135 Alamy:** John Goulter (br); Visual Arts Library (London) (tl). **National Archives and Records Administration, USA:** (tr). **136 DK:** By kind permission of the Trustees of The Wallace Collection, London (tc). **137 Alamy:** Mary Evans Picture Library (tl). **BAL:** Chetham's Library, Manchester (cr). **DK:** By kind permission of the Trustees of The Wallace Collection, London (bc). **138-139 Wikipedia, The Free Encyclopedia. 140 Alamy:** Visual Arts Library (London) (cl). **BAL:** Santa Maria Novella, Florence (br). **Corbis:** Michel Setbourn (c). **141 Alamy:** Visual Arts Library (London) (tr). **Corbis:** Jan Butchofsky-Houser (br). **142 Alamy:** Jim Lane (br); Visual Arts Library (London) (tl). **AA:** The British Library, London (c). **143 Alamy:** Classic Image (cra). **144 AA:** Dagli Orti (br). **Corbis:** Paul H. Kuiper (tr). **WFA:** Cathedral Treasury, Limburg (c). **145 AKG:** Erich Lessing (cr, bl). **146 DK:** (c); The British Museum, London (cl). **147 Alamy:** Mary Evans Picture Library (tr). **AA:** Biblioteca Capitolare, Padua / Dagli Orti (tl). **BAL:** Centre Historique des Archives Nationales, Paris / Lauros / Giraudon (bl). **148 Alamy:** Visual Arts Library (London) (tl). **DK:** Danish National Museum (br/Spear); Courtesy of The Museum of London (br/Sword); Courtesy of the Universitets Oldsaksamling, Oslo (cl). **The Fitzwilliam Museum, Cambridge:** Department of Coins and Medals (bc). **149 Corbis:** Ted Spiegel (c). **DK:** The British Museum, London (cr); Courtesy of the Statens Historiska Museum, Stockholm (tl, cl, tc); Courtesy of the Universitetets kulturhistoriske Museer / Vikingskipshuset / Frits Solvang (b). **150-151 BAL:** Edinburgh University Library, Scotland, With kind permission of the University of Edinburgh. **152 Alamy:** Vehbi Koca (c). **AA:** Turkish and Islamic Art Museum, Istanbul / Dagli Orti (cl). **153 Alamy:** Visual Arts Library (London) (bl). **AA&A:** (br). **BM:** (bc). **Corbis:** The Art Archive (t). **154 Alamy:** Peter Horree (ca). **AA:** Dagli Orti (cl, cb). **Corbis:** Archivo Iconografico, S.A. (bl). **155 AKG:** The British Library, London (l); Electa (tr). **BAL:** Hermitage, St. Petersburg (br). **Corbis:** Zefa / José Fusta Raga (c). **156 Alamy:** AA World Travel Library (bc). **AA:** National Anthropological Museum, Mexico / Dagli Orti (br). **WFA:** The British Museum, London (cra, cl). **157 AA. 158 Corbis:** Nathan Benn (bc); Werner Forman Archive (tc). **159 Alamy:** Robert Fried (t). **Still Pictures:** Jim Wark (bl). **160 BM:** (ca). **DK:** International Sailing Craft Association, Lowestoft (cr). **NHM:** (cl). **160-161 Getty:** Altrendo Images (b).

161 BM: (tr). **National Maritime Museum, London:** (tc). **162 Alamy:** Classic Image. **164 AA:** Marine Museum, Lisbon / Dagli Orti (bc). **Corbis:** Gordon R. Gainer (cl). **165 DK:** Courtesy of the National Maritime Museum, London (cr). **166 AKG:** (r). **AA:** Museo Colonial Antigua, Guatemala / Dagli Orti (bl). **BAL:** Fitzwilliam Museum, University of Cambridge (cl). **167 AA:** Academia BB AA S Fernando, Madrid / Dagli Orti (tl); Museo del Prado, Madrid (ca); Museo Navale, Pegli / Dagli Orti (cr). **The Bridgeman Art Library:** Prado, Madrid, Spain (bc). **168-169 AKG. 170 AA:** Museo Ciudad, Mexico / Dagli Orti (cl); Private Collection / Ellen Tweedy (cr). **Corbis:** Sygma / Lorpress / J.C. Kanny (clb). **171 Alamy:** Humberto Olarte Cupas (bl); The Print Collector (cra). **DK:** Courtesy of the Charlestown Shipwreck and Heritage Centre, Cornwall (br); Courtesy of the University Museum of Archaeology and Anthropology, Cambridge (tc). **WFA:** N.J. Saunders (clb). **172 AKG:** (cr). **LoC:** The Foundation Press, Inc., Cleveland, Ohio (tc). **172-173 Alamy:** Mike Hill (b). **173 Alamy:** Edward Parker (tl). **BAL:** Private Collection (c). **DK:** Courtesy of the National Maritime Museum, London (cra). **174 Alamy:** Visual Arts Library (London) (br). **Getty:** Time & Life Pictures / Mansell (t). **175 Alamy:** Eye Ubiquitous (bc); V&A Images (cl). **BAL:** Museo de America, Madrid / Giraudon (tr). **Corbis:** Arte & Immagini srl (cra). **176 Alamy:** North Wind Picture Archives (bl). **AA:** Terry Engell Gallery / Eileen Tweedy (t). **Corbis:** The Mariners' Museum (bc). **177 Alamy:** Swerve (bl, bc). **The British Library, London:** (tr). **BM:** (c). **Corbis:** Photo Images / Lee Snider (cr). **178 BM:** (cr). **DK:** Courtesy of the Musée de Saint-Malo (tr). **Getty:** Hulton Archive (tc). **National Maritime Museum, London:** (bl). **178-179 Corbis:** Stapleton Collection (b). **179 Alamy:** Mary Evans Picture Library (tl). **180 The British Library, London:** (tc). **181 DK:** The British Museum, London (crb); Judith Miller / Wallis and Wallis (c/ Jade, c/Porcelain); Courtesy of the National Maritime Museum, London (l). **Réunion des Musées Nationaux Agence Photographique:** Thierry Ollivier (cra). **182 Corbis:** Christie's Images (b). **183 AKG:** VISIOARS (tr). **BAL:** Leeds Museums and Art Galleries (City Museum, br). **Corbis:** Werner Forman (bl). **DK:** The British Museum, London (fbr); Courtesy of the Pitt Rivers Museum, University of Oxford (tl). **WFA:** Noh Theatre Collection, Kongo School, Kyoto (bc). **184 Corbis:** Angelo Hornak (cl). **185 Alamy:** Tibor Bognar (tr). **BAL:** Private Collection, Dinodia (cr). **186 Alamy:** Images&Stories (cla). **Corbis:** Werner Forman (bc). **DK:** By kind permission of the Trustees of the Wallace Collection (c, clb). **187 Alamy:** ArkReligion.com (l). **AA:** Turkish and Islamic Art Museum, Istanbul / Dagli Orti (cr). **Wikipedia, The Free Encyclopedia:** (br). **188-189 AKG:** Cameraphoto. **190 AKG:** Rabatti - Dominqie (bc). **Alamy:** Lebrecht Music and Arts Photo Library (c). **AA:** Duomo, Florence / Dagli Orti (tr). **BAL:** Bibliothèque Nationale, Paris (bl). **Corbis:** Sandro Vannini (cr). **191 Alamy:** Visual Arts Library (London) (br). **AA:** Galleria degli Uffizi, Florence / Dagli Orti (cl). **Corbis:** Jim Zuckerman (bl). **192 Corbis:** Archivo Iconografico, S.A. (bl); By kind permission of the Trustees of the National Gallery, London (tr). **193 Alamy:** INTERFOTO Pressebildagentur (cr). **AA:** Bibliothèque des Arts Décoratifs, Paris / Dagli Orti (tr). **BAL:** The British Museum, London (c). **Corbis:** Archivo Iconografico, S.A. (tl). **DK:** Courtesy of the Saint Bride Printing Library, London (bc). **194 Corbis:** Alinari Archives (b/Signature); Bettmann (r); Dennis Marsico (cl); Ted Spiegel (clb). **195 Alamy:** imagebroker (c); INTERFOTO Pressebildagentur (cr); Visual Arts Library (London) (b). **196 AKG:** (tl). **Alamy:** Anatoly Pronin (cl); Visual Arts Library (London) (bl). **196-197 DK:** Courtesy of The British Library, London (c). **197 Corbis:** Summerfield Press (cr). **198 AKG:** (r). **Corbis:** Archivo Iconografico, S.A. (bl). **199 BAL:** Bibliothèque Nationale, Paris / Lauros / Giraudon (cl); Church of St. Ignatius, Rome / Alinari (tr). **200 Alamy:** The Print Collector (r). **BAL:** Walker Art Gallery, National Museums, Liverpool (clb). **Corbis:** Francis G. Mayer (bl). **201 AA:** National Maritime Museum, London / Harper Collins Publishers (tl); Eileen Tweedy (crb). **BAL:** Ashmolean Museum, University of Oxford (bc). **Corbis:** Bettmann (ca); Baldwin H. Ward & Kathryn C. Ward (bl). **202 AKG:** Erich Lessing (cl). **Corbis:** (tl). **DK:** By kind permission of the Trustees of The Wallace Collection, London (cr). **203 Alamy:** Visual Arts Library (London) (t). **BAL:** Archives du Ministère des Affaires Étrangères, Paris / Archives Charmet (br). **204 Alamy:** David Stares (cl). **BAL:** The British Library, London (r). **205 Alamy:** Glenn Harper (cr). **BAL:** Private Collection / Bonhams, London (bc); Houses of Parliament, Westminster, London (tr). **DK:** English Civil War Society (english-civil-war-society.org) (tc). **206 Corbis:** Stefano Bianchetti (bc); Massimo Listri (cl). **DK:** Courtesy of the National Maritime Museum, London (r); The Science Museum, London (tl). **207 Alamy:** The Print Collector (tr). **Corbis:** Bettmann (tc). **DK:** Courtesy of The Science Museum, London (tl). **Photo Scala, Florence:** Biblioteca Nazionale, Florence (cr). **208-209 Corbis:** Bettmann. **210 AA:** National Gallery of Scotland (cla). **Corbis:** Archivo Iconografico, S.A. (bc); Michel Setboun (clb). **210-211 BAL:** Bibliothèque Nationale, Paris (c/1); Musée de la Ville de Paris, Musée Carnavalet, Paris / Lauros / Giraudon (c/2); Stapleton Collection (c/3). **211 Alamy:** INTERFOTO Pressebildagentur (bc). **Corbis:** Bob Krist (cr). **212 AKG:** Nimatallah (tc). **Alamy:** The Print Collector (bc). **212-213 National Maritime Museum, London:** (b). **213 DK:** Scottish United Services Museum, Edinburgh Castle / National Museums of Scotland (t, c). **214 BAL:** The British Museum, London (br). **Corbis:** Bettmann (ca). **DK:** The British Museum, London (clb). **215 Alamy:** Andrew Holt (br). **BM:** (c). **DK:** The British Museum, London (tr). **Getty:** Hulton Archive (tl). **216 AA:** Galleria degli Uffizi, Florence / Dagli Orti (r). **BAL:** Bibliothèque Nationale, Paris / Archives Charmet (bc). **217 AKG:** (bc). **Alamy:** Visual Arts Library (London) (tl, tc). **AA:** Musée de Tessé, Le Mans / Dagli Orti (cra); Dagli Orti (c). **218 DK:** Wilberforce House, Hull Museums (bl). **218-219 BAL:** Private Collection / Michael Graham-Stewart (c). **219 BAL:** Peter Newark American Pictures (cr). **Corbis:** Bojan Brecelj (br). **DK:** Wilberforce House, Hull Museums (tc). **220 National Maritime Museum, London:** (tc). **220-221 Corbis:** Historical Picture Archive (b). **221 Getty:** Iconica / John W. Banagan (crb). **WFA:** Auckland Institute and Museum, Auckland (clb). **222 S&S:** National Railway Museum. **224 BAL:** Peter Newark American Pictures (tr). **Corbis:** Yann Arthus-Bertrand (cla). **S&S:** Royal Photographic Society (b). **225 Alamy:** Mary Evans Picture Library (tc); The Print Collector (br). **Getty:** Riser / Fernando Bueno (cra). **S&S:** The Science Museum, London (cla, bl). **226 Corbis:** Minnesota Historical Society (tr). **S&S:** Science Museum Pictorial (clb). **227 AA:** Private Collection / Marc Charmet (cra). **Corbis:** (tl). **DK:** Courtesy of The Science Museum, London (bc). **Getty:** Topical Press Agency (c). **228 Corbis:** Hulton-Deutsch Collection (tl). **Getty:** General Photographic Agency (clb); Topical Press Agency (cr); Roger Viollet / Boyer (cla). **229 Corbis:** Charles E. Rotkin (br). **Getty:** Hulton Archive / Alex Inglis (tl); London Stereoscopic Company (tc). **230 AA:** Museum der Stadt, Wien / Dagli Orti (tl). **230-231 AKG:** (b). **231 AA:** Musée des Beaux Arts, Nantes / Dagli Orti (ca). **Getty:** Hulton Archive (cra). **232 Alamy:** Danita Delimont (bc); North Wind Picture Archives (cla). **Wikipedia, The Free Encyclopedia:** (tr). **233 BAL:** Capitol Collection, Washington, D.C. (b); Collection of the New-York Historical Society (tc). **DK:** Confederate Memorial Hall, New Orleans (tr). **234-235 Alamy:** Visual Arts Library (London). **236 Alamy:** Visual Arts Library (London) (cl, b). **237 Alamy:** Visual Arts Library (London) (cla). **AA:** (bc). **Magnum Photos:** Bruno Barbey (crb). **238 BAL:** Archives du Ministère des Affaires Étrangères, Paris / Archives Charmet (clb); Private Collection / Agnew's, London (r). **Corbis:** Hulton-Deutsch Collection (bc). **239 AKG:** VISIOARS (cla). **Alamy:** North Wind Picture Archives (ca); The Print Collector (bc). **BAL:** Bibliothèque des Arts Décoratifs, Paris / Archives Charmet (tc). **Corbis:** Elio Ciol (cr/Above). **DK:** The British Museum, London (cr/Below). **240 AKG:** Laurent Lecat (tl). **BAL:** Musée de la Marine, Paris / J.P. Zenobel (b). **241 AKG:** (crb). **Alamy:** The Print Collector (bc). **242 Corbis:** (cla, bl); Bettmann (br). **DK:** Courtesy of the American Museum of Natural History (tc). **243 BAL:** Peter Newark American Pictures (tl). **Corbis:** Bettmann (tr). **LoC:** Underwood & Underwood (cr). **National Archives and Records Administration, USA:** (bc). **244 AA:** Culver Pictures (ca). **LoC:** (bl). **244-245 LoC:** Timothy H. O'Sullivan (b). **245 Corbis:** Smithsonian Institution (cl). **DK:** Confederate Memorial Hall, New Orleans (c). **LoC:** (cra). **246 AA:** Culver Pictures (bl). **BAL:** Peter Newark American Pictures (cl). **Corbis:** Bettmann (cb). **LoC:** Alexander Gardner (tr). **247 BAL:** Collection of the New-York Historical Society (bc). **Corbis:** (cr); Profiles in History (tc). **DK:** Rough Guides / Angus Osborn (cb). **LoC:** Alexander Gardner (tl). **248 BAL:** Private Collection / Index (br). **Corbis:** (t). **249 Alamy:** Marco Regalia (tl). **AA:** Museo Historico Nacional, Buenos Aires / Dagli Orti (tr). **Corbis:** Bettmann (cr). **250 Alamy:** The Print Collector (tr); Visual Arts Library (London) (tc). **National Maritime Museum, London:** (c). **250-251 Getty:** Hulton Archive (b). **251 Alamy:** Mary Evans Picture Library (crb). **BAL:** Royal Geographical Society, London (tl/Map). **DK:** Royal Geographical Society, London (tl/Pith Helmet). **NASA:** (cra). **252-253 Corbis:** (b). **254 The Art Institute Of Chicago:** Ryerson & Burnham Libraries (tl). **Corbis:** Austrian Archives (tr). **Getty:** Central Press (bc); Hulton Archive (cr, bl); Hulton Archive / Thomas Annan (tc). **255 Alamy:** Peter Treanor (cr). **Magnum Photos:** Stuart Franklin (tr). **National Archives and Records Administration, USA:** (tc). **256 AKG:** (cla). **Corbis:** Bettmann (b). **S&S:** The Science Museum, London (tr). **257 Corbis:** Hulton-Deutsch Collection (cra). **DK:** The Science Museum, London (bc). **The Wellcome Institute Library, London:** (tc). **258 Alamy:** Mary Evans Picture Library (bc). **BAL:** Musée du Louvre, Paris / Peter Willi (cl). **258-259 BAL:** Musée du Louvre, Paris (c). **259 AKG:** (cr). **260 Alamy:** Mary Evans Picture Library (br). **BAL:** Archives du Ministère des Affaires Étrangères, Paris / Archives Charmet (cl). **LoC:** (ca). **262 Corbis:** Hulton-Deutsch Collection. **263 Getty:** Imagno (clb). **iStockphoto.com:** Lance Bellers (crb). **Kansallisarkisto, National Archives of Finland:** Reko Etelävuori (cra). **LoC:** Frances Benjamin Johnston (tc). **264 AKG:** (bc). **AA:** Karl Marx Museum, Trier (r). **Getty Images:** AFP(clb). **265 AKG:** (cl, bc, cra). **Alamy:** The Print Collector (tl). **Corbis:** Bettmann (tc). **266 Alamy:** Bill Bachman (cl). **BAL:** Bibliothèque des Arts Décoratifs, Paris / Archives Charmet (cr); The Science Museum, London (bc). **Getty:** MPI (bl). **267 BAL:** Private Collection / Archives Charmet (l, br). **Getty:** Hulton Archive (cr). **268 Alamy:** Visual Arts Libary, London (br). **AA:** The British Museum, London (clb). **Corbis:** Christie's Images (c). **269 AKG:** (tl). **Alamy:** Patrick Ashby (tr); Lebrecht Music and Arts Photo Library (bl). **Corbis:** Christie's Images (bc). **270 Alamy:** Visual Arts Library (London) (tl). **NHM:** (bl, c, r). **271 Alamy:** Mary Evans Picture Libray (bl); Popperfoto (cr). **BAL:** The British Library, London (cl). **DK:** Judith Miller / Gardiner Houlgate (br). **272 Alamy:** Mary Evans Picture Library (tr); North Wind Picture Archives (tl). **Corbis:** Jim Zuckerman (br). **DK:** Courtesy of the National Maritime Museum, London (clb). **273 Alamy:** Mary Evans Picture Library (tl); Phototake Inc. (tr). **Getty:** Lambert (bc). **S&S:** The Science Museum, London (cra). **274 BAL:** The British Museum, London (cl). **DK:** Museum of Artillery, The Rotunda, Woolwich, London (b/ Gatling Gun); Courtesy of The Science Museum, London (b/Bell Telephone, b/ Can Opener, b/Gramophone). **S&S:** The Science Museum, London (b/Tin Can). **275 DK:** Courtesy of the National Motor Museum, Beaulieu (Benz Velo); Courtesy of the Robert Opie Collection, The Museum of Advertising and Packaging, Gloucester (Brownie Camera); Courtesy of the Phoenix Mueum of History, Arizona / Alan Keohane (Cash Register); Courtesy of The Science Museum, London (Leclanché Cell, Diving Helmet); Courtesy of The Shuttleworth Collection, Bedfordshire (Wright Flyer). **LoC:** (Edison). **S&S:** The Science Museum, London (Filament Bulb, Typewriter). **276 DK:** Judith Miller / Wallis and Wallis (bc). **277 AKG:** (bl). **278 Alamy:** Mary Evans Picture Library (bl). **AA:** (r). **BAL:** Ashmolean Museum, University of Oxford (clb). **279 Alamy:** Alan King (crb). **BAL:** Cotehele House, Cornwall (ca); Private Collection (tl). **DK:** Courtesy of the Royal Green Jackets Museum, Winchester (cl). **Getty:** Hulton Archive (bl). **280 AA:** Travelsite / Global (bc). **BAL:** National Gallery of Victoria, Melbourne / Gilbee Bequest (tl); National Library of Australia, Canberra (bl). **281 AA:** Eileen Tweedy (tr). **Corbis:** Bettmann (br); North Carolina Museum of Art (c). **282 AA:** Private Collection (bl). **BAL:** The British Library, London (cla). **DK:** Courtesy of the National Railway Museum, New Delhi (cb). **283 AKG:** François Guénet (bl).

Corbis: Hulton-Deutsch Collection (tl); Sygma / Jean Pierre Amet (bc). **284 Corbis:** Hulton-Deutsch Collection (ca). **Getty:** Hulton Archive (b). **National Maritime Museum, London:** (tr). **285 Corbis:** Leonard de Selva (bc); Hulton-Deutsch Collection (crb). **The National Archives:** (t). **286 Corbis:** Bettmann (b); Sakamoto Photo Research Laboratory (cla). **287 Corbis:** Asian Art & Archaeology, Inc. (tl, br); **Getty images** (cr). **288 Corbis:** Bettmann (bl). **DK:** Courtesy of the Ashmolean Museum, Oxford (cla). **Getty:** Imagno (tc). **289 Alamy:** Mary Evans Picture Library (tl). **Corbis:** (cr). **Getty:** General Photographic Agency (bc). **290 AA:** John Meek (bl). **DK:** Courtesy of the Royal Geographic Society, London (tl). **Wikipedia, The Free Encyclopedia:** (tr). **291 Alamy:** Popperfoto (cra). **BAL:** Private Collection / Archives Charmet (tl). **Getty:** Pascal Sebah (cb). **Inkartha Freedom Party (www.ifp.org.za):** (br). **292 Corbis:** Bettmann. **294-295 Corbis:** Rykoff Collection. **296 AA:** The British Library, London (cla). **296-297 AA:** Imperial War Museum, London (b). **297 Getty:** Hulton Archive (tr). **298 AA:** Imperial War Museum, London. **299 Alamy:** David J. Green (crb). **AA:** Museum of the City of New York (c). **300 AA:** (tr). **Corbis:** Swim Ink 2, LLC (bl). **301 Alamy:** The Print Collector (bl). **Corbis:** Bettmann (c). **DK:** Courtesy of the Imperial War Museum, London (cr); Courtesy of the H. Keith Melton Collection (br); Courtesy of the Museum of the Revolution, Moscow (tc). **Getty:** Hulton Archive (tr). **302 Alamy:** Popperfoto (cl, tr). **303 Alamy:** The Print Collector (bc). **BAL:** Private Collection / Archives Charmet (crb). **Corbis:** (cl). **DK:** Courtesy of the Museum of the Revolution, Moscow / Andy Crawford (cr). **David King Collection:** (tc, cla). **304 Alamy:** Visual Arts Library (London) (cla). **Getty:** Time Life Pictures / Margaret Bourke-White (b). **305 Alamy:** Mary Evans Picture Library (bl). **AA:** Culver Pictures (tr). **BAL:** Private Collection (crb). **Corbis:** Bettmann (cl). **DK:** Courtesy of the Museum of the Revolution, Moscow (tl). **306 AKG:** (cl). **Corbis:** Bettmann (c). **307 DK:** Rough Guides / Greg Ward (br). **Getty:** MPI / Dorothea Lange (tl). **308 AA:** John Meek (bl); Dagli Orti (crb). **Getty:** Pierre Petit (cla). **308-309 Corbis:** Bettmann (tc). **309 Alamy:** Mary Evans Picture Library (clb). **AA:** Private Collection / Marc Charmet (tr). **Corbis:** Hulton-Deutsch Collection (br). **310 Corbis:** Archivo Iconografico, S.A. (tl). **Magnum Photos:** Robert Capa © 2001 By Cornell Capa (bl, crb). **311 AKG:** (c). **AA:** Private Collection / Marc Charmet (ftl); Reina Sofia Museum, Madrid, Guernica, 1937 by Pablo Picasso (1881-1973). Oil on Canvas. 351 x 782 cm © Succession Picasso / DACS (tr). **BAL:** Private Collection (crb). **Corbis:** (tl); Hulton-Deutsch Collection (bl). **312 AKG:** (r). **Alamy:** Mary Evans Picture Library (bl). **BAL:** Private Collection (cl); Private Collection / Archives Charmet (c). **313 AKG:** Ullstein Bild (cl). **Alamy:** Popperfoto (bc). **AA:** John Meek (tc). **Corbis:** Leonard de Selva (crb). **314 AA:** Imperial War Museum, London (tr). **BAL:** Peter Newark Historical Pictures (bl). **Getty:** Hulton Archive (cla). **315 Alamy:** Lebrecht Music and Arts Photo Library (c). **BAL:** Peter Newark Military Pictures (br). **Corbis:** Hulton-Deutsch Collection (tl). **316-317 Magnum Photos:** Soviet Group / Georgi Zelma. **318 AKG:** (tl). **Corbis:** (cl); Bettmann (b). **319 AKG:** (cra). **320-321 Magnum Photos:** Robert Capa © 2001 By Cornell Capa. **322 AKG:** Ullstein Bild (cl). **Alamy:** Mary Evans Picture Library (c). **Corbis:** Bettmann (tr). **DK:** Courtesy of the Imperial War Museum, London (cr). **322-323 Corbis:** Reuters / Auschwitz Museum (b). **323 AKG:** (c, clb). **Corbis:** Bettmann (cl). **Getty:** AFP / Simon Christophe (cr). **324 Corbis:** David J. & Janice L. Frent Collection (crb). **Getty:** Keystone (cra). **325 Alamy:** David South (cr). **Corbis:** Bettmann (tl, br); Hulton-Deutsch Collection (bc). **326-327 Corbis:** Peace Memorial Museum / EPA. **328 AA:** Eileen Tweedy (cr). **Corbis:** (cl); Bettmann (b). **David King Collection:** (tl). **329 Magnum Photos:** Rene Burri (c). **NATO Media Library:** (cra). **330 Alamy:** Popperfoto (clb, r). **DK:** Courtesy of The British Library, London (bl). **331 Alamy:** The Print Collector (c). **Corbis:** Bettmann (tl, cra); Ted Streshinsky (bc). **DK:** Courtesy of the John Frost Historical Archive (br). **332-333 Corbis:** Bettmann (b). **333 Getty:** AFP (cl); Keystone (ca). **334 Alamy:** Popperfoto (cr). **Corbis:** Hulton-Deutsch Collection (bc). **335 Magnum Photos:** Henri Cartier-Bresson (clb); Nicolas Tikhomiroff (t). **PA Photos:** AP Photo / Olivier Asselin (br). **336 Getty:** GPO (cla). **Magnum Photos:** Robert Capa © 2001 by Cornell Capa (ca). **337 AKG:** Bildarchiv Pisarek (c). **Getty:** Hulton Archive (cla); Liaison / Stephen Ferry (br); Time Life Pictures / John Phillips (tc). **Magnum Photos:** Robert Capa © 2001 By Cornell Capa (bl). **338 Alamy:** The Print Collector (bl). **Corbis:** Bettmann (tr). **Wikipedia, The Free Encyclopedia:** (bc). **339 Corbis:** Bettmann (cra, cl). **Getty:** Time Life Pictures (cb). **NASA:** W. Couch (University of New South Wales) , R. Ellis (Cambridge University) (tc). **340 The Advertising Archives:** (tr, cra, crb). **Corbis:** (cl). **341 Corbis:** James Leynse (br); Genevieve Naylor (cl). **Getty:** Lambert (t); Time Life Pictures / Hank Walker (bc). **Magnum Photos:** Dennis Stock (cr). **342-343 Corbis:** Bettmann. **344 Alamy:** Danita Delimont. **345 Alamy:** Popperfoto (tr). **Corbis:** Bettmann (bc). **Magnum Photos:** Rene Burri (cr). **346 BAL:** Private Collection (br). **Corbis:** (cla). **Imagine China:** (tr). **347 Alamy:** AA World Travel Library (c). **Corbis:** Bettmann (tr, crb). **348-349 Corbis:** Bettmann. **350 Alamy:** Pictorial Press Ltd (c). **Corbis:** Bettmann (bl). **Getty:** Frank Driggs Collection (cl). **S&S:** The Science Museum, London (cra). **351 Alamy:** Pictorial Press Ltd (cra). **The Kobal Collection:** SNC (tl). **Magnum Photos:** David Hurn (b). **352 Getty:** Time Life Pictures / Larry Burrows (tr). **LoC:** L.A. Shafer (cla). **Magnum Photos:** Bruno Barbey (br). **353 AA:** US Naval Museum, Washington D.C. (bc). **Getty:** Hulton Archive (ca); Hulton Archive / Three Lions (tc). **354 Corbis:** Raymond Gehman (bc); Flip Schulke (clb). **Magnum Photos:** Bob Adelman (tr). **355 Alamy:** Popperfoto (br); The Print Collector (crb). **Corbis:** Bettmann (tc); David J. & Janice L. Frent Collection (cl); Reuters / William Philpott (bc). **356 Alamy:** Popperfoto (r); The Print Collector (cl). **Corbis:** Hulton-Deutsch Collection (bl). **357 Alamy:** Roger Bamber (cr); Mary Evans Picture Library (ca). **AA:** London Museum / Eileen Tweedy (bl). **Corbis:** Bettmann (br). **iStockphoto.com:** Philipp Baer (tr). **358 Getty:** Hulton Archive (tc). **Magnum Photos:** Gilles Peress (b). **359 Alamy:** Joe Fox (tc); Tim Graham (bc); TNT Magazine (tr). **Getty:** Evening Standard / Maurice Hibberd (cl). **360 Corbis:** Karen Kasmauski (bc). **Getty:** AFP / Cris Bouroncle (bl); AFP / Pedro Rey (br). **361 Corbis:** Michael Freeman. **362 Corbis:** Bettmann (cra); Vittoriano Rastelli (tl). **Getty:** Time Life Pictures / Ted Thai (b). **363 AKG:** (cl). **Getty:** Time Life Pictures / Time Inc. (cb). **364 Alamy:** Popperfoto (cra). **BAL:** Private Collection / Archives Charmet (cl). **Corbis:** Bettmann (b). **365 Corbis:** Bettmann (tc); Michel Setboun (cb). **366 PA Photos:** AP Photo (cl). **366-367 Corbis:** Reuters (b). **367 Corbis:** Reuters / Jean-Marc Loos (br). **Getty:** Liaison / Robert Nickelsberg (tc). **368 Getty:** Keystone (bl); Time Life Pictures / Igor Gavilov (t). **369 Corbis:** Sygma / Patrick Chauvel (cr); Peter Turnley (cl, tr). **370 Corbis:** Reuters / Charles Platiau (cb); Sygma / Bernard Bisson (tr); Peter Turnley (br). **371 Getty:** AFP / Pascal George (br); Reportage / Tom Stoddart (tl). **Magnum Photos:** Thomas Dworzak (cr). **372 Corbis:** Reuters / Ivan Milutinovic (ca); Reuters / Zika Milutinovic (cl). **Magnum Photos:** Abbas (c). **373 Corbis:** Chris Rainier (tl). **Getty:** AFP / Dimitar Dilkoff (cr). **Rex Features:** Action Press (br); Andrew Testa (cb). **374 Alamy:** Peter Jordan (br); Alex Segre (bl). **Getty:** AFP / Joel Robine (c); Hulton Archive / Keystone Features / Fred Ramage (cla); Time Life Pictures / Francis Miller (clb). **375 Alamy:** Imagebroker (fbr); Nature Picture Library (bl). **Corbis:** Charles O'Rear (fbl). **Getty:** AFP / Ben Stansall (cla); AFP / Attila Kisbenedek (cr); Aurora / Jose Azel (tr); Photographer's Choice / Werner Dieterich (br). **376 Getty Images:** Selwyn Tait / Contributor (cla). **African Pictures:** Baileys African History Archive (tc). **Magnum Photos:** Ian Berry (bc). **377 African National Congress:** (tc). **African Pictures:** iAfrica Photos / Eric Miller (c). **Alamy:** ImageState (cr). **Getty:** AFP / Alexander Joe (cra). **Magnum Photos:** Ian Berry (b). **378 Corbis:** Reuters / Radu Sigheti (cl). **378-379 Corbis:** STR / Reuters. **379 Corbis:** Dai Kurokawa / epa (bc); Ulli Michel / Reuters (tl). **Getty Images:** Jean-Pierre Muller (crb). Little,Brown Book Group: (tc). **380 Corbis:** Hulton-Deutsch Collection (bl). **Getty Images:** AFP (cr). **Rex Features:** Sipa Press (t). **381 Alamy:** Maximilian Weinzierl (c). **Corbis:** Craig Lovell (cra). **Getty:** Science Faction / Louie Psihoyos (bl). **382 Alamy:** Popperfoto (bl). **Corbis:** Bettmann (crb). **DK:** Judith Miller / Luna (clb). **Getty:** Aurora / Peter Essick (cr). **382 NASA. 384 Alamy:** Popperfoto (Whittle). **DK:** Courtesy of Glasgow Museum (TV); Courtesy of The Science Museum, London (Tape Recorder, Cats Eye). **385 Corbis:** James Leynse (crb). **Getty Images**: Rob Stothard (cb). Used with permission from Kodak: (br). **Alamy:** Mark Boulton (Lightbulb); Hugh Threlfall (DVD). **Courtesy of Apple. Apple and the Apple logo are trademarks of Apple Computer Inc., registered in the US and other countries:** (iPod). **Courtesy of Canon (UK) Ltd:** (Camera). **Corbis:** Roger Ressmeyer (Solar Energy). **DK:** Courtesy of the Design Museum, London (Food Mixer); Courtesy of Dyson (Dyson); Courtesy of the Imperial War Museum, Duxford (Concorde); Courtesy of The Science Museum, London (Transistor Radio, Memory Board). **NASA:** (Mars Rover). **Research In Motion Limited:** (Blackberry). **S&S:** The Science Museum, London (Computer). **386 AA:** Culver Pictures (cl). **NASA:** GSFC / METI / ERSDAC / JAROS, and U.S. / Japan ASTER Science Team (b). **387 Corbis:** Sygma / Micheline Pelletier (cra). **Getty:** AFP / Issouf Sanogo (tc). **Panos Pictures:** Chris Stowers (c). **Still Pictures:** Leonard Lessin (br). **388 Alamy:** Popperfoto (bl). **BAL:** Peter Newark American Pictures (cl); Private Collection / Archives Charmet (cr). **Corbis:** Bettmann (tc). **The Wellcome Institute Library, London:** (cla). **389 Alamy:** Popperfoto (clb). **AA:** Culver Pictures (tl). **Science Photo Library:** CNRI (tr); Eye of Science (crb). **Still Pictures:** Jochen Tack (cb). **388-391 Getty:** Spencer Platt. **392 Corbis:** Sygma (cr). **Getty:** USAF (bl). **Magnum Photos:** Jean Gaumy (clb). **393 Corbis:** In Visu / Christophe Calais (c); Peter Turnley (tl). **Magnum Photos:** Abbas (b). **394 Corbis:** Lester Lefkowitz. **395 Courtesy of Apple. Apple and the Apple logo are trademarks of Apple Computer Inc., registered in the US and other countries:** (c). **Corbis:** Reuters / Andy Clark (cr). **Rex Features:** Emma Sklar (bl). **396 Corbis:** Wally McNamee (cl). **396-397 Getty Images:** Andy Brandl. **397 Corbis:** Xiaoyang Liu (cr). **Getty:** National Geographic / Todd Gipstein (clb); Guang Niu (cla). **398 Bridgeman Images:** Netherlands / Holland: The 'Semper Augustus' tulip, unknown artist, early 17th century / Pictures From History (clb). **Getty Images:** Spencer Platt (cla). **Rex Features:** Sipa Press (bc). **398-399 Getty Images:** Eric Feferberg (tr). **Rex Features:** Nils Jorgensen (t). **400 Corbis:** Bettmann (bl); Hulton-Deutsch Collection (bc). **Getty:** FPG / Keystone (c). **Still Pictures:** UNEP / Monica Terrazas Glavan (cb). **401 Alamy:** Andrew Fox (tl). **AA:** Eileen Tweedy (bc). **Corbis:** Gideon Mendel (tr); Tom Nebbia (tc); Roger Ressmeyer (br). **Getty:** AFP / Desiree Martin (bl). **402 Corbis:** Bettmann (cl). **Getty Images:** Stock Montage (bl). **402-403 Corbis:** Chris Sattlberger / Blend Images. **403 Dreamstime.com:** Sillein1 (tl). **Getty Images:** View Pictures (tr). **404 Corbis:** Derek Trask (cla). **FLPA:** Minden Pictures / Flip Nicklin (b). **405 Alamy:** Nick Cobbing (bc); Jesper Jensen (cr). **NASA:** Jim Williams, GSFC Scientific Visualization Studio, and the Landsat 7 Science Team (cl). **406-407** Chris Harrison. **407 Corbis:** Robert Galbraith / Reuters (cra); Ramin Talaie (br). **Getty Images:** Handout (tc). **408 Alamy:** Roger Bamber (t). **Corbis:** Stapleton Collection (bc). **409 © CERN Geneva:** (fbr). **Corbis:** Reuters / Samsung Electronics (bc). **DK:** Judith Miller / Hugo Lee-Jones (fbl). **Courtesy of Garmin (Europe) Ltd:** (br). **Getty:** (tc); Scott Peterson (c).

All other images © Dorling Kindersley
For further information see:
www.dkimages.com